# THE DICTIONARY OF CLASSICAL HEBREW

Volume III

ט—ז

# The Dictionary of Classical Hebrew


David J.A. Clines
*Editor*

Philip R. Davies    J. Cheryl Exum    John W. Rogerson
*Consulting Editors*




Volume III

ז—ט


John Elwolde
*Executive Editor*

Frank Gosling, David Stec,
with
Kate Dove Davis, Wilfred G.E. Watson
*Research Associates*



Published under the auspices of
The Society for Old Testament Study

and with the support of
The University of Sheffield

# The Dictionary of Classical Hebrew

David J.A. Clines
*Editor*

## Volume III

ט—ז

John Elwolde
*Executive Editor*

Sheffield
Sheffield Academic Press

1996

Published by Sheffield Academic Press Ltd
The Mansion House, Kingfield Road, Sheffield
England

Typeset by the Hebrew Dictionary Project
University of Sheffield
and
Printed on acid-free paper in Great Britain
by Bookcraft
Midsomer Norton, Somerset

British Library Cataloguing in Publication Data

Dictionary of Classical Hebrew. – Vol. 3: Zayin–Teth
I. Clines, David J. A.
492.43

ISBN 1 85075 634 1

# CONTENTS

# PREFACE

This third volume of the Dictionary is being sent, camera-ready, to the printer just fifteen months after Volume 2. For the rapid progress on the work, thanks are due both to the researchers who have been preparing it and to the institutions that have given their financial support to the work.

In this third phase of the research, it is the Editor's pleasant duty to record his thanks for the excellent work of John Elwolde as Executive Editor, of David Stec and of Frank Gosling as full-time Research Associates, and of Kate Dove Davis and Wilfred Watson as part-time Research Associates. Anne Lee and Rosemarie Kossov, students in the Department of Biblical Studies, also made valuable contributions.

The work of this volume was shared in this way: Frank Gosling and David Stec wrote the entries for all verbs and common nouns in Zayin and for most of the words in Ḥeth. Frank Gosling was responsible for drafting the majority of words occurring more than fifty times and David Stec for most of the less common ones. David Stec also compiled a detailed index of the Dead Sea Scrolls for this volume and updated the Qumran and inscriptions indices. David Stec wrote the entries for Ṭeth-Mem and Frank Gosling those from Ṭeth-Nun to the end of Ṭeth.

Kate Dove Davis drafted all the personal and place name entries for Zayin and many of those for Ḥeth. She also arranged the acquisition of bibliographic items and input most of the bibliographic entries. Wilfred Watson read the items listed in the Bibliography and drafted the entries for previously unregistered words such as newly proposed homonyms.

John Elwolde, in addition to his role as Executive Editor, wrote the adjective and particle entries for Zayin, all the articles for Ṭeth up to the end of Ṭeth-Lamedh, and some for Ḥeth. David Clines edited and proofread the entire volume.

It should be recorded that the whole of this volume, as of the previous two volumes, has not only been composed, but also typeset, by the researchers involved in the project. The accuracy, consistency and attractiveness of the text is due to the vigilance and skill of the researchers as they have followed detailed and rigorous rules for the composition of their articles.

Thanks are due to those who have funded the work of this volume. The work of one Research Associate was supported in part by a grant from the Research Fund of the University of Sheffield and in part by a major grant from the British Academy. The Department of Biblical Studies has also made from its own funds a significant contribution to the work of the Dictionary. The principal source of funding, as for the previous volume, has been Sheffield Academic Press, the publisher of the Dictionary, which has pledged very considerable resources to sustaining this work of scholarship.

Among those who have kindly contributed to the work on this volume of the Dictionary have been: Marilyn J. Lundberg, who provided a list of Psalms variants in 11QPs[a], David Talshir who made many corrections to the Hebrew of the volume, and Wilfred Lambert and John Rogerson who checked, respectively, the Akkadian and the Arabic transliterations in the Bibliography. As with the previous volume, Graham Davies made available a further printout of Hebrew epigraphic texts supplementary to his *Ancient Hebrew Inscriptions*.

Volume 4, containing Yodh, Kaph and Lamedh, is scheduled for publication in the middle of 1998. All those involved in the work of the Dictionary are grateful to the very large number of subscribers who are making the project viable.

DJAC
Sheffield
September 30, 1996

# INTRODUCTION

Readers are referred to the Introductions in Volume 1 and Volume 2 for details of the principles and procedures of this Dictionary. No substantive changes have been made in this volume, but there are a few minor points on which our practice has changed since Volume 2.

1. *Bibliography*
Readers of the Dictionary will be aware that the Bibliography is intended as a resource for journal articles and monographs on the philology and semantics of Classical Hebrew words. An asterisk at the beginning of an article means that the existence of the word depends on the literature cited in the Bibliography. An asterisk at the end of an article refers the reader to further literature on the semantics of the word or to an argument for a new or specialized sense of the word. In this volume, an asterisk has also been inserted at a particular point in an article to which the literature cited is particularly pertinent.

2. *Sources*
For the Qumran texts, since the publication of new manuscripts continues, we have printed afresh, in the section called The Sources, a complete list of all the Qumran texts we have considered for this volume, noting the edition we have used. Beside each Qumran text there appear the page numbers of the translation by Florentino García Martínez, *The Dead Sea Scrolls Translated: The Qumran Texts in English* (tr. Wilfred G.E. Watson; Leiden: E.J. Brill, 1994).

For the epigraphic material, we present a list of additions to the texts contained in *Ancient Hebrew Inscriptions: Corpus and Concordance*, by Graham I. Davies (Cambridge: Cambridge University Press, 1991). Most of these additions have been published since the completion of that volume. Many of them will be incorporated by Graham Davies in a future supplementary publication, but of course those that are later than c. 200 BCE will not, since his corpus does not extend beyond that date.

3. *Exhaustive Treatment*
In this volume every word beginning with Zayin, Ḥeth and Ṭeth has been treated exhaustively. That is to say, for every word this Dictionary cites every place it occurs in classical Hebrew, and every occurrence has been analysed according to the principles of the Dictionary.

4. *Numbers of Occurrences*
In this volume, and in subsequent volumes, we are noting the number of occurrences of each verb in each of its voices or *binyanim*. In Volumes 1 and 2, the number of occurrences in each of the four corpora of classical Hebrew surveyed for the volume were noted for each word; but now the reader will be able to see at a glance the comparative usage of the qal and the piel, for example, of a particular verb.

## THE SOURCES

a. *Qumran and Related Texts*

The following list replaces those published in Volume 1, pp. 35-45, and in Volume 2, pp. 15-31. In this volume we have chosen either the editio princeps or another scholarly edition as the base text. What follows is a complete list of all the Qumran texts reviewed for this volume, with a notation of the edition we have used. Beside each Qumran text there appears the page numbers of the translation by Florentino García Martínez, *The Dead Sea Scrolls Translated: The Qumran Texts in English* (tr. Wilfred G.E. Watson; Leiden: E.J. Brill, 1994). The second list of Qumran references published in Volume 1 (pp. 45-51), which correlates the sigla used in the Dictionary with the cave numbers, has not been reprinted, since it is still serviceable as it stands.

### QUMRAN AND RELATED NON-BIBLICAL TEXTS IN CAVE AND NUMBER ORDER

In this list there appears, in the five columns, the following:

(1) The number by which the texts are known (in the case of four major Qumran texts from Cave 1, no number is assigned, and the text is known simply by its siglum; such cases are listed first).

(2) The generally agreed siglum or abbreviation of name by which the text is usually referred to; in the few cases where the siglum used in the Dictionary differs from that in current use, this Dictionary's siglum is given first.

(3) The name of the text that prevails in current scholarship (occasionally two names are in current use, in which case they are separated by an oblique line); if no name seems to have been agreed, some indication of the nature of the work is given in lower-case letters (e.g. 'sapiential', 'liturgical').

(4) A reference to the edition of the text that has been the standard for this Dictionary.

(5) A reference to the page numbers of the translation of the text by Florentino García Martínez, *The Dead Sea Scrolls Translated: The Qumran Texts in English* (tr. Wilfred G.E. Watson; Leiden: E.J. Brill, 1994); but occasionally the reference is to another translation.

The following table attempts to be a complete list of known non-biblical Hebrew texts, published and unpublished, from Qumran (from related sites, on the other hand, only those texts that have been published are included). As far as we can tell, all published texts—that is, texts that have been printed in transcription, with or without translation and technical notes—have been read for the Dictionary and incorporated in it. For all the texts used in the Dictionary there is an entry in the fourth column, which notes the primary edition we have followed. When further texts are published, their data will be included in future volumes of the Dictionary.

| No. | Siglum | Name / Description | Edition | Translation |
|---|---|---|---|---|
| **Cave 1** | | | | |
| | 1QH | Hymns / Hodayot | Licht | 317-61 |
| | 1QM | War Scroll | Yadin | 95-115 |
| | 1QpHab | Habakkuk Pesher | Horgan, 1-9 | 197-202 |
| | 1QS | Community Rule / Manual of Discipline | Charlesworth I, 6-51 | 3-19 |
| 1Q14 | 1QpMic | Micah Pesher | DJD, I, 77-80 | 193-94 |
| 1Q15 | 1QpZeph | Zephaniah Pesher | DJD, I, 80 | 202 |
| 1Q16 | 1QpPs | Psalms Pesher | DJD, I, 81-82 | 206 |
| 1Q17 | 1QJub[a] | Jubilees | DJD, I, 82-83 | 245 |
| 1Q18 | 1QJub[b] | Jubilees | DJD, I, 83-84 | 245 |
| 1Q19 | 1QNoah | Noah | DJD, I, 84-86 | 263 |
| 1Q19b | 1QNoah | Noah | DJD, I, 152 | 263 |
| 1Q22 | 1QDM | Dibre Mosheh / Words of Moses | DJD, I, 91-97 | 276-77 |
| 1Q25 | | prophecy | DJD, I, 100-101 | |
| 1Q26 | | sapiential | DJD, I, 101-102 | |
| 1Q27 | 1QMyst | prophecy | DJD, I, 102-107 | 399-400 |
| 1Q28a | 1QSa | Community Rule | Charlesworth, I, 110-17 | 126-28 |
| 1Q28b | 1QSb | Community Rule | Charlesworth, I, 122-31 | 432-33 |
| 1Q29 | | Three Tongues of Fire | DJD, I, 130-32 | 277-78 |
| 1Q30 | | liturgical | DJD, I, 132-33 | 438 |
| 1Q31 | | liturgical | DJD, I, 133-34 | 438 |
| 1Q33 | 1QM | War Scroll | Yadin, 353 | 113-15 |
| 1Q34 | 1QLitPr | Festival Prayers | DJD, I, 152-55 | 411 |
| 1Q35 | 1QH[b] | Hymns/Hodayoth | DJD, I, 136-38 | 317-61 |
| 1Q36 | | hymns | DJD, I, 138-41 | |
| 1Q37–40 | | hymns | DJD, I, 141-43 | 438 |
| 1Q41–62 | | unidentified | DJD, I, 144-47 | |
| 1Q69 | | unidentified | DJD, I, 148 | |

**Cave 2**

| | | | | |
|---|---|---|---|---|
| 2Q19 | 2QJub[a] | Jubilees | DJD, III, 77-78 | 244 |
| 2Q20 | 2QJub[b] | Jubilees | DJD, III, 78-79 | 245 |
| 2Q21 | 2QapMoses | Apocryphon of Moses | DJD, III, 79-81 | 281 |
| 2Q22 | 2QapDavid | Apocryphon of David | DJD, III, 81-82 | 224 |
| 2Q23 | 2QapProph | prophecy | DJD, III, 82-84 | |
| 2Q25 | | halakhah | DJD, III, 90 | 86 |
| 2Q27–33 | | unidentified | DJD, III, 91-93 | |

**Cave 3**

| | | | | |
|---|---|---|---|---|
| 3Q4 | 3QpIsa | Isaiah Pesher | DJD, III, 95-96 | 185 |
| 3Q5 | 3QJub | Jubilees | DJD, III, 96-98 | 244 |
| 3Q6 | 3QHymn | hymnic | DJD, III, 98 | 401 |
| 3Q7 | 3QTJud | Testament of Judah | DJD, III, 99 | 265 |
| 3Q8 | | Angel of Peace | DJD, III, 100 | |
| 3Q9 | | sectarian | DJD, III, 100-101 | |
| 3Q10-11 | | unidentified | DJD, III, 101-102 | |
| 3Q15 | 3QTr | Copper Scroll | DJD, III, 284-302 | 461-63 |

**Cave 4**

| | | | | |
|---|---|---|---|---|
| 4Q158 | 4QBibPar | Biblical Paraphrase | DJD, V, 1-6 | 219-22 |
| 4Q159 | 4QOrd[a] | Ordinances | Charlesworth, I, 150-57 | 86-87 |
| 4Q160 | 4QVisSam | Visions of Samuel | DJD, V, 9-11 | 284 |
| 4Q161 | 4QpIsa[a] | Isaiah Pesher | DJD, V, 11-15 | 185-86 |
| 4Q162 | 4QpIsa[b] | Isaiah Pesher | DJD, V, 15-17 | 186-87 |
| 4Q163 | 4QpIsa[c] | Isaiah Pesher | DJD, V, 17-27 | 187-90 |
| 4Q164 | 4QpIsa[d] | Isaiah Pesher | DJD, V, 27-28 | 190-91 |
| 4Q165 | 4QpIsa[e] | Isaiah Pesher | DJD, V, 28-30 | 191 |
| 4Q166 | 4QpHos[a] | Hosea Pesher | DJD, V, 31-32 | 191-92 |
| 4Q167 | 4QpHos[b] | Hosea Pesher | DJD, V, 32-36 | 192-93 |
| 4Q168 | 4QpMic | Micah Pesher | DJD, V, 36 | 194-95 |
| 4Q169 | 4QpNah | Nahum Pesher | DJD, V, 37-42 | 195-97 |
| 4Q170 | 4QpZeph | Zephaniah Pesher | DJD, V, 42 | 203 |
| 4Q171 | 4QpPs[a] | Psalms Pesher | DJD, V, 42-50 | 203-206 |
| 4Q172 | 4QpUnid | unidentified pesher | DJD, V, 50-51 | |
| 4Q173 | 4QpPs[b] | Psalms Pesher | DJD, V, 51-53 | 206-207 |
| 4Q174 | 4QMidrEschat[a] | eschatological | Steudel, 23-29 | 136-37 |
| 4Q175 | 4QTestim | Testimonia | DJD, V, 57-60 | 137-38 |
| 4Q176 | 4QTanḥ | Consolations | DJD, V, 60-67 | 208-209 |
| 4Q176.19-21 | 4QJub[f] | Jubilees | Kister, *RQ* 12 (1987) | 244 |
| 4Q177 | 4QMidrEschat[b] | eschatological | Steudel, 71-76 | 209-11 |
| 4Q178 | | unidentified | DJD, V, 74-75 | |

| | | | | |
|---|---|---|---|---|
| 4Q179 | 4QapLam[a] | Lamentation on Jerusalem | DJD, V, 75-77 | 401-402 |
| 4Q180 | 4QAges | Pesher on the Periods | DJD, V, 77-79 | 211-12 |
| 4Q181 | | Ages of Creation | DJD, V, 79-80 | 212-13 |
| 4Q182 | 4QCat | Catena | DJD, V, 80-81 | 213 |
| 4Q183 | | historical | DJD, V, 81-82 | 213 |
| 4Q184 | 4QWiles | Wiles of the Wicked Woman | DJD, V, 82-85 | 379-80 |
| 4Q185 | | Eulogy on Wisdom | DJD, V, 85-87 | 380-82 |
| 4Q186 | 4QCrypt | horoscopes | DJD, V, 88-91 | 456 |
| 4Q200 | 4QTob | Tobit | cf. Milik, *RB* 73 (1966) | 297-99 |
| 4Q215 | 4QTNaph | Testament of Naphtali | Nebe, *ZAW* (1994) | 270-71 |
| 4Q216 | 4QJub[a] | Jubilees[a] | VanderKam–Milik, *JBL* 110 (1991) | 238-40 |
| 4Q217 | 4QJub[b] | Jubilees[b] | | |
| 4Q218 | 4QJub[c] | Jubilees[c] | VanderKam–Milik, *Textus* 17 (1994) | |
| 4Q219 | 4QJub[d] | Jubilees[d] | VanderKam–Milik, *Bib* 73 (1992) | 242-43 |
| 4Q220 | 4QJube | Jubilees[e] | VanderKam–Milik, *Textus* 17 (1994) | 242 |
| 4Q221 | 4QJub[f] | Jubilees[f] | cf. VanderKam, *Madrid*, 645 | 243-44 |
| 4Q222 | 4QJub[g] | Jubilees[g] | VanderKam–Milik, *New Qumran*, 105-14 | |
| 4Q223–224 | 4QJub[h] | Jubilees[h] | | |
| 4Q225 | 4QpsJub[a] | | WA, II, 204-6 | |
| 4Q226 | 4QpsJub[b] | | WA, II, 207-10 | |
| 4Q227 | 4QpsJub[c] | Pseudo-Jubilees | EW, 96-97 | 245 |
| 4Q228 | | work citing Jubilees | | |
| 4Q229 | | pseudepigraphon (Mishnaic) | | |
| 4Q230 | | Catalogue of Spirits[a] | | |
| 4Q231 | | Catalogue of Spirits[b] | | |
| 4Q232 | | New Jerusalem (?) | | |
| 4Q233 | | place names | | |
| 4Q234 | | exercise on Genesis 27 | | |
| 4Q237 | | psalter | | |
| 4Q239 | | pesher on the true Israel | | |
| 4Q240 | | commentary on Canticles (?) | | |
| 4Q241 | | fragments citing Lamentations | | |
| 4Q247 | | pesher on Apocalypse of Weeks | Milik, *Enoch*, 256 | |
| 4Q248 | | Acts of a Greek King | | |
| 4Q249 | 4QMSM | Midrash Sepher Mosheh | Milik, *JJS* 23 (1972) | |
| 4Q250 | | text on verso of MSM | | |
| 4Q251 | | Halakhah/A Pleasing Fragrance | Baumgarten, *JJS* 27 (1976), 36-38 | 87-88 |
| 4Q252 | 4QpGen[a] | Patriarchal Blessings/ | WA, II, 212-15 | 212-15 |

| | | | | |
|---|---|---|---|---|
| | | Genesis Florilegium | | |
| 4Q253 | 4QpGen$^{b}$ | Patriarchal Blessings/commentary on Malachi? | Brooke, *JSS* 40 (1995) 230-38 | 215 |
| 4Q254 | 4QpGen$^{c}$ | Patriarchal Blessings | WA, II, 218-22; Brooke, *Proceedings* | 215-16 |
| 4Q254a | | Genesis Florilegium | Brooke, *Proceedings* | 216 |
| 4Q255 | 4QS$^{a}$ | Community Rule | Charlesworth, I, 58 | 20 |
| 4Q256 | 4QS$^{b}$ | Community Rule (previously 4QS) | Charlesworth, I, 60-67 | 21, frag 5 |
| 4Q257 | 4QS$^{c}$ | Community Rule | Charlesworth, I, 68-71 | 21-22 1.2, 1.3 |
| 4Q258 | 4QS$^{d}$ | Community Rule (previously 4QS) | Charlesworth, I, 72-83 | 22, frag 1.1 |
| 4Q259 | 4QS$^{e}$ | Community Rule | Charlesworth, I, 84-89; WA, I, 96-101 | 26-29 |
| 4Q260 | 4QS$^{f}$ | Community Rule | Charlesworth, I, 90-93 | 29-30 |
| 4Q261 | 4QS$^{g}$ | Community Rule | Charlesworth, I, 94-97 | 30-31 |
| 4Q262 | 4QS$^{h}$ | Community Rule | Charlesworth, I, 98-99 | 31 |
| 4Q263 | 4QS$^{i}$ | Community Rule | Charlesworth, I, 100-101 | 31 |
| 4Q264 | 4QS$^{j}$ | Community Rule | Charlesworth, I, 102-103 | 31-32 |
| 4Q265 | 4QSD | Community Rule + Damascus Document | Baumgarten (1994), 3-4, Milik, *Ten Years*, 96 | 72 |
| 4Q266 | 4QD$^{a}$ | Damascus Document $^{a}$ | WA, I, 3-22 | 48-57 |
| 4Q267 | 4QD$^{b}$ | Damascus Document$^{b}$ | WA, I, 28-35 | 60-62 |
| 4Q268 | 4QD$^{c}$ | Damascus Document$^{c}$ | WA, I, 1-2 | 47-48 |
| 4Q269 | 4QD$^{d}$ | Damascus Document$^{d}$ | WA, I, 48-53 | 67-69 |
| 4Q270 | 4QD$^{e}$ | Damascus Document$^{e}$ | WA, I, 36-47 | 62-67 |
| 4Q271 | 4QD$^{f}$ | Damascus Document$^{f}$ | WA, I, 23-27 | 57-60 |
| 4Q272 | 4QD$^{g}$ | Damascus Document$^{g}$ | WA, I, 54-56 | 69-70 |
| 4Q273 | 4QD$^{h}$ | Damascus Document$^{h}$ | WA, I, 57-59 | 70 |
| 4Q274 | 4QTohA | Purities | EW, 207-208 | 88-89 |
| 4Q275 | 4QTohB | Purities | cf. Milik, *JJS* 23 (1972) | 89, 434 |
| 4Q276 | 4QTohB$^{a}$ | Laws of the Red Heifer | EW, 211 | 89 |
| 4Q277 | 4QTohB$^{b}$ | Laws of the Red Heifer | EW, 211 | 89-90 |
| 4Q278 | 4QTohC? | | | 90 |
| 4Q279 | 4QTohD$^{a}$? | Laws | | 90 |
| 4Q280 | 4QTohD | Curses against Melkiresha | Milik, *JJS* 23 (1972) | 434 |
| 4Q281–282 | | 4QTohE$^{a}$? | | |
| 4Q283 | 4QTohF? | | | |
| 4Q284 | 4QNid | Rule of the Menstruants | | |
| 4Q284a | | Leqet | | |
| 4Q285 | | Destruction of the Kittim / Messianic Leader | WA, II, 223-7 | 123-24 |
| 4Q286 | 4QBer$^{a}$ | The Chariots of Glory | EW, 226-28 | 434-35 |

| | | | | |
|---|---|---|---|---|
| 4Q287 | 4QBer[b] | The Chariots of Glory | Milik, *JJS* 23 (1972) | 435-36 |
| 4Q288 | 4QBer[c] | | | |
| 4Q289 | 4QBer[d] | | | |
| 4Q290 | 4QBer[e] | | | |
| 4Q291–293 | | prayers | | |
| 4Q294–297 | | rules and prayers | | |
| 4Q298 | | Admonitions to the Sons of Dawn | EW, 164-65 | 382 |
| 4Q299 | 4QMyst[a] | = 1Q27 | WA, II, 1-28 | 400 |
| 4Q300 | 4QMyst[b] | = 1Q27 | Schiffman, *RQ* 16 (1993) 203-23 | 400-401 |
| 4Q301 | 4QMyst[c] | = 1Q27 | WA, II, 35-37 | 401 |
| 4Q302 | | Praise of God | WA, II, 228-31 | |
| 4Q302a | | Parable of the Tree | WA, II, 228-31 | |
| 4Q303 | | Meditation on Creation A[a] | WA, II, 232 | |
| 4Q304 | | Meditation on Creation A[b] | | |
| 4Q305 | | Meditation on Creation B | | |
| 4Q306 | | Men of People who Err | | |
| 4Q307 | | sapiential | | |
| 4Q308 | | sapiential | | |
| 4Q311 | | unidentified | | |
| 4Q312 | | Hebrew text in cursive Phoenician | | |
| 4Q313 | | unidentified cryptic script | | |
| 4Q316 | | unidentified | | |
| 4Q317 | | Phases of Moon (cryptic script) | Milik, *Enoch*, 68-69 | 451 |
| 4Q319 | 4QOtot | Heavenly Concordances | EW, 130-31 | 27-29 |
| 4Q320 | 4QMish A | Priestly Courses II | WA, I, 60-67 | 452-54 |
| 4Q321 | 4QMish B[a] | Priestly Courses I | WA, I, 68-73 | 454-55 |
| 4Q321a | 4QMish B[b] | Priestly Courses I | WA, I, 74-76 | |
| 4Q322 | 4QMish C[a] | Priestly Courses III | WA, I, 77-78 | |
| 4Q323 | 4QMish C[b] | Priestly Courses III | WA, I, 79-81 | EW, 119 |
| 4Q324 | 4QMish C[c] | Priestly Courses III | WA, I, 81-82 | EW, 119 |
| 4Q324a | 4QMish C[d] | Priestly Courses III | WA, I, 82-84 | EW, 119 |
| 4Q324b | 4QMish C[e] | Priestly Courses III | WA, I, 84-85 | EW, 119 |
| 4Q324c | 4QMish C[f] | | | |
| 4Q325 | 4QMish D | Priestly Courses IV | WA, I, 86-87 | EW, 127 |
| 4Q326 | 4QMish E[a] | | WA, I, 88 | |
| 4Q327 | 4QMish E[b] | | WA, I, 89-91 | 455 |
| 4Q328 | 4QMish F[a] | | WA, I, 92 | |
| 4Q329 | 4QMish F[b] | | WA, I, 93-95 | |
| 4Q329a | 4QMish G | | WA, I, 94 | |
| 4Q330 | 4QMish H | | WA, I, 95 | |
| 4Q331 | | Historical Work[a] | | |
| 4Q332 | | Historical Work[b] | | |

| | | | | |
|---|---|---|---|---|
| 4Q333 | | Historical Work[c] | | |
| 4Q334 | 4QOrdo | Ordo | | |
| 4Q335–336 | | astronomical | | |
| 4Q337 | | calendar | | |
| 4Q338 | | genealogical | | |
| 4Q339 | | list of false prophets | | |
| 4Q340 | | list of Nethinim | | |
| 4Q341 | | list of proper names | Naveh, *IEJ* 36 (1986) | |
| 4Q344 | | debt acknowledgment | | |
| 4Q348 | | act regarding ownership | | |
| 4Q349 | | sale of property | | |
| 4Q356 | | account of money | | |
| 4Q360 | | exercise / Therapeia | | |
| 4Q362 | | cryptic script | | |
| 4Q363 | | cryptic script | | |
| 4Q363a | | cryptic script | | |
| 4Q364 | 4QPentPar[a] | Pentateuchal Paraphrase | White, *Madrid*, 217-28 | 222-24 |
| 4Q365 | 4QPentPar[b] | Pentateuchal Paraphrase | White, *Madrid*, 217-28 | 222-24 |
| 4Q365a | | Temple Scroll? | | |
| 4Q366 | 4QPentPar[c] | Pentateuchal Paraphrase | | |
| 4Q367 | 4QPentPar[d] | Pentateuchal Paraphrase | | |
| 4Q368 | | Pentateuch Apocryphon | | |
| 4Q369 | | Prayer of Enosh? | | |
| 4Q370 | | Flood Apocryphon | Newsom, *RQ* 13 (1988) | 224-25 |
| 4Q371 | 4QApocJos[a] | Joseph Apocryphon | Schuller, *Madrid*, 529-30* | |
| 4Q372 | 4QApocJos[b] | Joseph Apocryphon | Schuller, *Madrid*, 528-29 | 225-26 |
| 4Q373 | 4QApocJos[c] | Joseph Apocryphon | Schuller, *Madrid*, 515-27 | 226 |
| 4Q374 | 4QApocMos A | Moses Apocryphon A | Newsom, *Forty Years*, 40-52 | 278 |
| 4Q375 | 4QApocMos B | Moses Apocryphon B | Strugnell, JSPS, VIII, 221-34 | 278 |
| 4Q376 | | Three Tongues of Fire | Strugnell, JSPS, VIII, 234-45 | 279 |
| 4Q377 | 4QApocMos C | Moses Apocryphon C | | |
| 4Q378 | 4QPsJos[a] | Psalms of Joshua | Newsom, *JJS* 39 (1988) 56-65 | 282 |
| 4Q379 | 4QPsJos[b] | Psalms of Joshua | Newsom, *JJS* 39 (1988) 65-73 | 283 |
| 4Q380 | 4QapPs[a] | Non-Canonical Psalms A | Schuller, *Non-Canonical*, 241-65 | 311-12 |
| 4Q381 | 4QapPs[b] | Non-Canonical Psalms B | | |
| 4Q382 | | Kings Paraphrase | | |
| 4Q383 | 4QApocJer A | Jeremiah Apocryphon A | | |
| 4Q384 | 4QApocJer B | Jeremiah Apocryphon B | | |
| 4Q385 | 4QpsEzek[a] | Pseudo-Ezekiel | EW, 57-58, 60 | |
| | | | Dimant, *Madrid*, 405-48 | 286 |
| 4Q385a | 4QpsMos[a] | Pseudo-Moses | Dimant, *Madrid*, 405-48 | |
| 4Q385b | 4QApocJer C | Jeremiah Apocryphon C | Dimant, *New Qumran*, 11-30 | 285 |
| 4Q386–389 | 4QpsEzek[b] | Second Ezekiel, etc. | EW, 60-62 | 287 |

| | | | | |
|---|---|---|---|---|
| 4Q390 | 4QpsMos[e] | Pseudo-Moses Apocalypse / Angels of Mastemoth | Dimant, *Madrid*, 405-47 | 280-81 |
| 4Q391 | 4QpsEzek[g] | Pseudo-Ezekiel | | |
| 4Q392 | | liturgical | WA, II, 38-39 | 438 |
| 4Q393 | | liturgical | Falk, *JJS* 45 (1994), 187-90 | |
| 4Q394-99 | 4QMMT | Halakah / Letter on Works | DJD, X, 44-63 | 77-85 |
| 4Q400 | 4QShirShabb[a] | Songs of the Sabbath Sacrifice | Newsom, *Songs*, 85-123 | 419-20 |
| 4Q401 | 4QShirShabb[b] | Songs of the Sabbath Sacrifice | Newsom, *Songs*, 125-46 | 420 |
| 4Q402 | 4QShirShabb[c] | Songs of the Sabbath Sacrifice | Newsom, *Songs*, 147-66 | 420-21 |
| 4Q403 | 4QShirShabb[d] | Songs of the Sabbath Sacrifice | Newsom, *Songs*, 185-247 | 421-24 |
| 4Q404 | 4QShirShabb[e] | Songs of the Sabbath Sacrifice | Newsom, *Songs*, 249-55 | 424-25 |
| 4Q405 | 4QShirShabb[f] | Songs of the Sabbath Sacrifice | Newsom, *Songs*, 257-354 | 426-30 |
| 4Q406 | 4QShirShabb[g] | Songs of the Sabbath Sacrifice | Newsom, *Songs*, 255-57 | |
| 4Q407 | 4QShirShabb[h] | Songs of the Sabbath Sacrifice | Newsom, *Songs*, 259-60 | |
| 4Q408 | | sapiential | WA, II, 240-43 | |
| 4Q409 | | liturgical | Qimron, *JQR* 80 (1990) | 402 |
| 4Q410 | | sapiential | WA, II, 40 | |
| 4Q411 | | sapiential | WA, II, 244 | |
| 4Q412 | | sapiential | WA, II, 41-2 | |
| 4Q413 | | sapiential | WA, II, 43 | 382-83 |
| 4Q414 | | Baptismal Hymn | EW, 231-32 | 439 |
| 4Q415 | | Sapiential Work A[d] | WA, II, 44-53 | |
| 4Q416 | | Sapiential Work A[b]/ The Children of Salvation | WA, II, 54-62 | 383-85 |
| 4Q417 | | Sapiential Work A[c] | WA, II, 63-76 | 385-87 |
| 4Q418 | | Sapiential Work A[a]/ The Children of Salvation | WA, II, 77-154 | 388-93 |
| 4Q419 | | Sapiential Work B | WA, II, 155-58 | 393 |
| 4Q420 | | Ways of Righteousness[a] | WA, II, 159-60 | |
| 4Q421 | | Ways of Righteousness[b] | WA, II, 161-65 | |
| 4Q422 | | Treatise on Genesis and Exodus | Elgvin, *DSD* 1 (1994) Tov, *DSD* 1 (1994) | |
| 4Q423 | | Sapiential Work A[e] | WA, II, 166-73 | |
| 4Q423a | | Sapiential Work E | WA, II, 166 | |
| 4Q424 | | sapiential / The Sons of Righteousness | WA, II, 174-76 | 393-94 |
| 4Q425 | | Sapiential Work C | WA, II, 177-79 | |
| 4Q426 | | sapiential | WA, II, 180-84 | |
| 4Q427 | 4QHod[a] | Hymns | Schuller, *JBL* 112 (1993) | 362-66 |
| 4Q428 | 4QHod[b] | Hymns | WA, II, 262-74 | 367 |
| 4Q429 | 4QHod[c] | Hymns | WA, II, 275-78 | 367-69 |
| 4Q430 | 4QHod[d] | Hymns | WA, II, 279 | 369 |
| 4Q431 | 4QHod[e] | Hymns | WA, II, 280 | 369 |

| | | | | |
|---|---|---|---|---|
| 4Q432 | 4QHod[f] | Hymns | WA, II, 281-84 | |
| 4Q433 | | hymnic | | |
| 4Q434 | 4QBark[a] | Barki Naphshi[a] | EW, 238-39 | 436 |
| 4Q434a | | Grace after Meals | Weinfeld, *JBL* 111 (1992) | 439 |
| 4Q435 | 4QBark[b] | Barki Naphshi[b] | | |
| 4Q436 | 4QBark[c] | Barki Naphshi[c] | EW, 238-39 | 437 |
| 4Q437 | 4QBark[d] | Barki Naphshi[d] | | |
| 4Q438 | 4QBark[e] | Barki Naphshi[e] | | |
| 4Q439 | | similar to Barki Naphshi | | |
| 4Q440 | | hymnic | | |
| 4Q441–444 | | prayers | | |
| 4Q445–447 | | poetic | | |
| 4Q448 | | Paean for King Jonathan Apocryphal Psalms | Eshel–Yardeni, *IEJ* 42 | EW 273 |
| 4Q449–457 | | prayers | | |
| 4Q458 | | The Tree of Evil | EW, 47-49 | 228 |
| 4Q459–460 | | pseudepigraphic | | |
| 4Q461 | | narrative | | |
| 4Q462 | | Second Exodus / The Era of Light is Coming | Smith, *RQ* 15 (1991) 57 | 226-27 |
| 4Q463 | | sapiential | Steudel, 54-56 | |
| 4Q464 | | Exposition on the Patriarchs | Stone–Eshel, *Muséon* 105 | |
| 4Q464a | | unidentified | Stone–Eshel, *Muséon* 105 | |
| 4Q464b | | unidentified | Stone–Eshel, *Muséon* 105 | |
| 4Q464–465 | | unidentified | | |
| 4Q466–469 | | apocryphon | | |
| 4Q470 | | Zedekiah fragment | WA, II, 292-93 | |
| 4Q471 | 4QM[h] | The Servants of Darkness | Eshel, *Madrid*, 611-20, WA II 294-96 | 124-25 |
| 4Q471a | | polemical | WA, II, 294 | 125 fr. 2 |
| 4Q472 | | sapiential | | |
| 4Q473 | | The Two Ways | | |
| 4Q474–475 | | sapiential | | |
| 4Q476 | | sapiential | WA, II, 297-98 | |
| 4Q477 | | Decrees of Sect /He Loved His Bodily Emissions | Eshel, *JJS* 45 (1994) | 90-91 |
| 4Q479–481a-f | | unidentified | | |
| 4Q482 | | Jubilees? | DJD, VII, 1-2 | |
| 4Q483 | | Jubilees? | DJD, VII, 2 | |
| 4Q484 | 4QTJud | Testament of Judah | DJD, VII, 3 | |
| 4Q485 | 4QProph | prophetic or sapiential | DJD, VII, 4 | |
| 4Q486 | 4QSap[a] | sapiential | DJD, VII, 4-5 | |
| 4Q487 | 4QSap[b] | sapiential | DJD, VII, 5-10 | |

| | | | | |
|---|---|---|---|---|
| 4Q491 | 4QM[a] | War Scroll | DJD, VII, 12-44 | 115-19 |
| 4Q492 | 4QM[b] | War Scroll | DJD, VII, 45-49 | 120 |
| 4Q493 | 4QM[c] | War Scroll | DJD, VII, 49-53 | 120-21 |
| 4Q494 | 4QM[d] | War Scroll | DJD, VII, 53-54 | 121 |
| 4Q495 | 4QM[e] | War Scroll | DJD, VII, 54-56 | 121 |
| 4Q496 | 4QM[f] | War Scroll | DJD, VII, 57-68 | 121-23 |
| 4Q497 | 4QM[g(?)] | War Scroll | DJD, VII, 69-72 | |
| 4Q498 | 4QHymSap | hymnic or sapiential | DJD, VII, 73-74 | |
| 4Q499 | 4QHymPr | hymnic or prayers | DJD, VII, 74-79 | |
| 4Q500 | 4QBen | Song of the Vineyard | DJD, VII, 78-79 | 402 |
| 4Q501 | 4QapLam[b] | Lamentation | DJD, VII, 79-80 | 403 |
| 4Q502 | 4QRitMar | Ritual of Marriage | DJD, VII, 81-105 | 440-41 |
| 4Q503 | 4QPrQuot | Daily Prayers | DJD, VII, 105-36 | 407-10 |
| 4Q504 | 4QDibHam[a] | Words of the Luminaries | DJD, VII, 137-68 | 414-17 |
| 4Q505 | 4QDibHam[b] | Words of the Luminaries | DJD, VII, 168-70 | 418 |
| 4Q506 | 4QDibHam[c] | Words of the Luminaries | DJD, VII, 170-75 | 418 |
| 4Q507 | 4QPrFêtes[a] | Festival Prayers | DJD, VII, 175-77 | 411-12 |
| 4Q508 | 4QPrFêtes[b] | Festival Prayers | DJD, VII, 177-84 | 412 |
| 4Q509 | 4QPrFêtes[c] | Festival Prayers | DJD, VII, 184-215 | 412-13 |
| 4Q510 | 4QShir[a] | Songs of the Sage | DJD, VII, 215-19 | 371 |
| 4Q511 | 4QShir[b] | Songs of the Sage | DJD, VII, 219-62 | 371-76 |
| 4Q512 | 4QRitPur | Ritual of Purification | DJD, VII, 262-86 | 441-42 |
| 4Q513 | 4QOrd[b] | Ordinances | Charlesworth, I, 158-75 | 91 |
| 4Q514 | 4QOrd[c] | Ordinances | Charlesworth, I, 178-79 | 91-92 |
| 4Q515–520 | | unidentified fragments | DJD, VII, 299-312 | |
| 4Q521 | | Messiah of Heaven and Earth | Puech, *RQ* 15 (1992) | 394-95 |
| 4Q522 | | Joshua Apocryphon | EW, 90-91; Puech, *RB* 99 (1992), 677-78 | 227-28 |
| 4Q523 | | Hebrew fragment B | | |
| 4Q524 | | halakic | | |
| 4Q525 | | Beatitudes / The Demons of Death | WA, II, 185-203 | 395 |
| 4Q526 | | Hebrew fragment C | | |
| 4Q527 | | Hebrew fragment D | | |
| 4Q528 | | Hebrew fragment E | | |
| 4QAcademyFr | | Academy Fragments | | |

**Cave 5**

| | | | | |
|---|---|---|---|---|
| 5Q9 | | toponyms | DJD, III, 179-80 | |
| 5Q10 | 5QapMal | Malachi Pesher? | DJD, III, 180 | 203 |
| 5Q11 | 5QS | Community Rule | Charlesworth, I, 106-107 | 32 |
| 5Q12 | 5QD | Damascus Document | DJD, III, 181 | 70-71 |

| | | | | |
|---|---|---|---|---|
| 5Q13 | 5QRègle | Damascus Document + Rule | Charlesworth, I, 134-43 | 73 |
| 5Q14 | | curses | DJD, III, 183-84 | 403 |
| 5Q16–24 | | unclassified | DJD, III, 193-96 | |
| 5Q16 | | unclassified | DJD, III, 193-94 | |
| 5Q17 | | unclassified | DJD, III, 194 | |
| 5Q18 | | unclassified | DJD, III, 195 | |
| 5Q19 | | unclassified | DJD, III, 195 | |
| 5Q20 | | unclassified | DJD, III, 195 | |
| 5Q21 | | unclassified | DJD, III, 195 | |
| 5Q22 | | unclassified | DJD, III, 196 | |
| 5Q23 | | unclassified | DJD, III, 196 | |
| 5Q24 | | unclassified | DJD, III, 196 | |
| 5Q25 | | unclassified | DJD, III, 196-97 | |
| **Cave 6** | | | | |
| 6Q9 | 4QapSam/Kings | Samuel–Kings apocryphon | DJD, III, 119-23 | 284 |
| 6Q10 | 6QProph | prophetic | DJD, III, 123-25 | |
| 6Q11 | 6QAllegory | Song of the Vine | DJD, III, 125-26 | 403 |
| 6Q12 | 6QapProph | prophetic | DJD, III, 126 | |
| 6Q13 | 6QPriestProph | priestly prophecy | DJD, III, 126-27 | |
| 6Q15 | 6QD | Damascus Document | DJD, III, 128-31 | 71 |
| 6Q16 | 6QBen | blessings | DJD, III, 131-32 | 437 |
| 6Q17 | 6QCal | calendar | DJD, III, 132-33 | |
| 6Q18 | 6QHym | hymnic | DJD, III, 133-36 | 403 |
| 6Q20 | 6QDeut(?) | Deuteronomy-related? | DJD, III, 136-37 | 228 |
| 6Q21 | 6QfrProph | unidentified | DJD, III, 137 | |
| 6Q22 | | unidentified | DJD, III, 137 | |
| 6Q24–25 | | unidentified | DJD, III, 138 | |
| 6Q26 | | account or contract | DJD, III, 139 | |
| 6Q27–31 | | unclassified | DJD, III, 139-41 | |
| 6QX1–2 | | unclassified | | |
| **Cave 8** | | | | |
| 8Q3 | 8QPhyl | phylactery | DJD, III, 149-57 | |
| 8Q5 | 8QHymn | hymnic | DJD, III, 161-63 | 404 |
| **Cave 9** | | | | |
| 9Q | | unclassified | DJD, III | |
| **Cave 10** | | | | |
| 10Q | | ostracon? | DJD, III | |

**Cave 11**

| | | | | |
|---|---|---|---|---|
| 11Q5 | 11QPs[a] | | DJD, IV, 39-49 | 304-10 |
| 11Q11 | 11QapPs[a] | Apocryphal Psalms | Puech, *RQ* 14 (1990) | 376 |
| 11Q12 | 11QJub | Jubilees | van der Woude, *Fs Kuhn* | |
| | | | Milik, *Biblica* 54 (1973) | 241-42 |
| 11Q13 | 11QMelch | Melchizedek | van der Woude, *OTS* 14 (1965); | |
| | | | Puech, *RQ* 12 (1987) | 139-40 |
| 11Q14 | 11QBer | Benedictions (= 4Q285) | van der Woude, *Bibel und Qumran* | 124 |
| 11Q15 | 11QHod[a] | Hymns | cf. van der Ploeg, *RQ* 12 (1985) 11 | 404 |
| 11Q16 | 11QHod[b] | Hymns | cf. van der Ploeg, *RQ* 12 (1985) 11 | |
| 11Q17 | 11QShirShabb | Songs of the Sabbath Sacrifice | Newsom, *Songs*, 361-87 | 430-31 |
| 11Q19–20 | 11QT | Temple Scroll | Yadin, *Temple Scroll* | 154-79 |
| 11QT[b] | | Temple Scroll | García Martínez, 363-91 | 179-84 |
| 11Q21–23 | | unidentified | | |

**Masada**

| | | | |
|---|---|---|---|
| | MasShirShabb | Songs of the Sabbath Sacrifice | Newsom, *Songs*, 167-84 |

**Murabba'at**

| | | | | |
|---|---|---|---|---|
| Mur 6 | | hymnic | DJD, II, 86 | |
| Mur 7 | | contract | DJD, II, 86 | |
| Mur 22 | | deed of sale of land | DJD, II, 118-19 | |
| Mur 24 | | farming contracts | DJD, II, 122-34 | |
| Mur 29 | | deed of sale | DJD, II, 140-44 | |
| Mur 30 | | deed of sale | DJD, II, 144-48 | |
| Mur 42 | MurEpBeth-Mashiko | letter of administrators | DJD, II, 155-59 | Pardee, 124 |
| Mur 43 | MurEpBarC[a] | letter of Shimon b. Kosibah | DJD, II, 159-61 | Pardee, 130 |
| Mur 44 | MurEpBarC[b] | letter of Shimon b. Kosibah | DJD, II, 161-63 | Pardee, 132 |
| Mur 45 | | letter | DJD, II, 163-64 | Pardee, 34 |
| Mur 46 | MurEpJonathan | letter of Jonathan | DJD, II, 164-66 | Pardee, 136 |
| Mur 47 | | letter | DJD, II, 166-67 | Pardee, 137 |
| Mur 48 | | letter | DJD, II, 167-68 | Pardee, 138 |

**Naḥal Ḥever**

| | | | |
|---|---|---|---|
| 5/6 ḤevBA 44 | contract | AHL, 406 | Yadin, *Bar-Kokhba*, 176 |
| 5/6 ḤevBA fr. 1–2 | contract | AHL, 406 | Yadin, *Bar-Kokhba*, 176-77 |
| 5/6 ḤevBA 45 | contract | AHL, 407 | Yadin, *Bar-Kokhba*, 178 |
| 5/6 ḤevBA 45 fr. 1–2 | | AHL, 407 | Yadin, *Bar-Kokhba*, 178 |
| 5/6 ḤevBA 46 | contract | AHL, 410 | Yadin, *Bar-Kokhba*, 180 |

| | | |
|---|---|---|
| 5/6 ḤevEp 1 | letter | AHL, 420 |
| 5/6 ḤevEp 5 | letter | AHL, 421 |
| 5/6 ḤevEp 12 | letter | AHL, 422 |
| 5/6 ḤevEp 12 fr. | letter | AHL, 422 |

*Bibliography*

AHL, *see Materials for the Dictionary*

Allegro, John M. , *Qumrân Cave 4. I (4Q158–4Q186)* (Discoveries in the Judaean Desert of Jordan, 5; Oxford: Clarendon Press, 1968)

Baillet, M., *Qumrân Grotte 4 (4Q482–4Q520)* (Discoveries in the Judaean Desert, 7; Oxford: Clarendon Press, 1982)

—, J.T. Milik and R. de Vaux, *Les 'petites grottes' de Qumrân* (Discoveries in the Judaean Desert of Jordan, 3; Oxford: Clarendon Press, 1962)

Barthélemy, D. and J.T. Milik, *Qumran Cave I* (Discoveries in the Judaean Desert, 1; Oxford: Clarendon Press, 1955)

Baumgarten, Joseph, 'The Disqualifications of Priests in 4Q Fragments of the "Damascus Document", a Specimen of the Recovery of pre-Rabbinic Halakha', in *The Madrid Congress: Proceedings of the International Congress on the Dead Sea Scrolls, Madrid, 18–21 March 1991* (ed. J. Trebolle Barrera and L. Vegas Montaner; Studies on the Texts of the Desert of Judah, 11; Madrid: Universidad Complutense and Leiden: E.J. Brill, 1992), pp. 503-13

—'4QHalakah[a] 5, the Law of Hadash, and the Pentecontad Calendar', *Journal of Jewish Studies* 27 (1976), pp. 36-46

—'The 4Q Zadokite Fragments on Skin Disease', *Journal of Jewish Studies* 41 (1990), pp. 153-65

—'Purification after Childbirth and the Sacred Garden in 4Q465 and Jubilees', in *New Qumran Texts and Studies* (ed. George J. Brooke; Studies on the Texts of the Desert of Judah, 15; Leiden: E.J. Brill, 1994), pp. 3-10

Benoit, P., J.T. Milik and R. de Vaux, *Les grottes de Murabba'ât* (Discoveries in the Judaean Desert, 2; Oxford: Clarendon Press, 1961)

Brooke, George J., '4Q254 Fragments 1 and 4, and 4Q254a: Some Preliminary Comments', in *Proceedings of the Eleventh Congress of Jewish Studies* (Division A; Jerusalem: World Union of Jewish Studies, 1994), pp. 185–92

—'4Q253: A Preliminary Edition', *Journal of Semitic Studies* 40 (1995), pp. 227-39

Burrows, M. (ed.), *The Dead Sea Scrolls of St. Mark's Monastery*, 2 vols. (New Haven: American Schools of Oriental Research, 1951)

Charlesworth, James H. (ed.), *The Dead Sea Scrolls: Hebrew, Aramaic, and Greek Texts with English Translations* (Tübingen: J.C.B. Mohr [Paul Siebeck] and Louisville: Westminster John Knox Press, 1994)

Dimant, Devorah, 'New Light from Qumran on the Jewish Pseudepigrapha—4Q*390*', in *The Madrid Congress: Proceedings of the International Congress on the Dead Sea Scrolls, Madrid, 18–*

*21 March 1991* (ed. J. Trebolle Barrera and L. Vegas Montaner; Studies on the Texts of the Desert of Judah, 11; Madrid: Universidad Complutense and Leiden: E.J. Brill, 1992), pp. 405-48

—and John Strugnell, 'The Merkabah Vision in *Second Ezekiel* (*4Q385* 4)', *Revue de Qumran* 14 (1990), pp. 331-48

—'An Apocryphon of Jeremiah from Cave 4 (4Q385$^{b}$ = 4Q285 16)', in *New Qumran Texts and Studies: Proceedings of the First Meeting of the International Organization for Qumran Studies, Paris, 1992* (ed. George J. Brooke with Florentino García Martínez; Studies on the Texts of the Desert of Judah, 15; Leiden: E.J. Brill, 1994), pp. 11-30

DJD, I, *see* Barthélemy, D. and J.T. Milik

DJD, II, *see* Benoit, P., J.T. Milik and R. de Vaux

DJD, III, *see* Baillet, M., J.T. Milik and R. de Vaux

DJD, IV, *see* Sanders, J.A.

DJD, V, *see* Allegro, J.M.

DJD, VI, *see* Vaux, R. de and J.T. Milik

DJD, VII, *see* Baillet, M.

DJD, X, *see* Qimron, Elisha and John Strugnell

Eisenman, Robert H. and Michael Wise, *The Dead Sea Scrolls Uncovered* (Shaftesbury, Dorset: Element, 1992)

Elgvin, Torleif, 'The Genesis Section of 4Q422 (4QParaGenExod)', *Dead Sea Discoveries* 1 (1994), pp. 180-96

Eshel, Esther, '4Q477: The Rebukes by the Overseer', *Journal of Jewish Studies* 45 (1994), pp. 111-22

Eshel, Esther and Hanan, '*4Q471* Fragment 1 and *Ma'amadot* in the War Scroll', in *The Madrid Congress: Proceedings of the International Congress on the Dead Sea Scrolls, Madrid, 18–21 March 1991* (ed. J. Trebolle Barrera and L. Vegas Montaner; Studies on the Texts of the Desert of Judah, 11; Madrid: Universidad Complutense and Leiden: E.J. Brill, 1992), pp. 612-20

Eshel, Esther and Menahem Kister, 'A Polemical Qumran Fragment', *Journal of Jewish Studies* 43 (1992), pp. 277-81

Eshel, Esther and Hanan, and Ada Yardeni, 'A Qumran Composition Containing Part of Ps 154 and a Prayer for the Welfare of King Jonathan and his Kingdom', *IEJ* 42 (1992), pp. 199-229

EW, *see* Eisenman and Wise

Falk, Daniel, '4Q393: A Communal Confession', *Journal of Jewish Studies* 45 (1994), pp. 184-207

Fitzmyer, Joseph A., SJ, *The Dead Sea Scrolls. Major Publications and Tools for Study* (revised edition; SBL Resources for Biblical Study, 20; Atlanta: Scholars Press, 1990)

García Martínez, Florentino, 'Lista de mss procedentes de Qumran', *Henoch* 11 (1989), pp. 149-232

—*Textos de Qumrán. Introducción y edición* (Madrid: Editorial Trotta, 1992); *The Dead Sea Scrolls Translated: The Qumran Texts in English* (tr. Wilfred G.E. Watson; Leiden: E.J. Brill, 1994).

—'*11QTemple$^{b}$*. A Preliminary Publication', in *The Madrid Congress: Proceedings of the International Congress on the Dead Sea Scrolls, Madrid, 18–21 March 1991* (ed. J. Trebolle

Barrera and L. Vegas Montaner; Studies on the Texts of the Desert of Judah, 11; Madrid: Universidad Complutense and Leiden: E.J. Brill, 1992), pp. 363-91

Horgan, Maurya P., *Pesharim: Qumran Interpretations of Biblical Books* (The Catholic Biblical Quarterly Monograph Series, 8; Washington, DC: The Catholic Biblical Association of America, 1979)

Kister, M., 'Newly Identified Fragments of the Book of Jubilees: Jub. 23:21-23, 30-31', *Revue de Qumran* 12 (1985–87), pp. 529-36

Licht, J., *The Thanksgiving Scroll* (Jerusalem, 1965) [Hebrew]

*Materials for the Dictionary. Series I. 200 B.C.E.—300 C.E.* (The Academy of the Hebrew Language—The Historical Dictionary of the Hebrew Language; Jerusalem, 1988)

Milik, J.T., *Ten Years of Discovery in the Wilderness of Judaea* (trans. J. Strugnell; London: SCM Press, 1959)

—'Le travail d'édition des manuscrits du désert de Juda', *Supplements to Vetus Testamentum* 4 (1957), pp. 17-26

—'Notes d'épigraphie et de topographie palestiniennes', *Revue Biblique* 67 (1960), pp. 354-67, 550-91

—'Fragment d'une source du Psautier (4Q Ps 89) et fragments des Jubilés, du Document de Damas, d'un phylactère dans la grotte 4 de Qumrân', *Revue Biblique* 73 (1966), pp. 94-106

—'A propos de 11QJub', *Biblica* 54 (1973), pp. 77-79

—*The Books of Enoch: Aramaic Fragments of Qumran Cave 4* (Oxford: Clarendon Press, 1976)

—'*Milkî-ṣedeq* et *Milkî-reša'* dans les anciens écrits juifs et chrétiens', *Journal of Jewish Studies* 23 (1972), pp. 95-144

—'Numérotation des feuilles des rouleaux dans le scriptorium de Qumrân', *Semitica* 27 (1977), pp. 75-81

Naveh, Joseph, 'A Medical Document or a Writing Exercise? The So-called 4Q Therapeia', *Israel Exploration Journal* 36 (1986), pp. 52-55

Nebe, G.W., 'Qumranica I: Zu unveröffentlichten Handschriften aus Höhle 4 von Qumran', *Zeitschrift für die alttestamentliche Wissenschaft* 106 (1994), pp. 307-22

Newsom, Carol, *Songs of the Sabbath Sacrifice: A Critical Edition* (Harvard Semitic Studies, 27; Atlanta: Scholars Press, 1985)

—'The "Psalms of Joshua" from Qumran Cave 4', *Journal of Jewish Studies* 39 (1988), pp. 56-73

—'*4Q370*: An Admonition Based on the Flood', *Revue de Qumran* 13 (1988), pp. 23-41

—'4Q374: A Discourse on the Exodus/Conquest Tradition', in *The Dead Sea Scrolls: Forty Years of Research* (ed. Devorah Dimant and Uriel Rappaport; Leiden: E.J. Brill; Jerusalem: Magnes Press and Yad Izhak Ben-Zvi, 1992), pp. 40-52

Pardee, Dennis, *Handbook of Ancient Hebrew Letters: A Study Edition* (SBL Sources for Biblical Study, 15; Chico, CA: Scholars Press, 1982)

Ploeg, J. van der, 'Les manuscrits de la grotte XI de Qumran', *Revue de Qumran* 12 (1985), pp. 3-15

Puech, Emile, '*11QPsAp*[a]: Un rituel d'exorcismes. Essai de reconstruction', *Revue de Qumran* 14 (1990), pp. 377-408

—'4Q apocalypse messianique (4Q521)', *Revue de Qumran* 15 (1992), pp. 475-519

—'La pierre de Sion et l'autel des holocaustes d'après un manuscrit hébreu de la grotte 4',

*Revue Biblique* 99 (1992), pp. 676-96

Qimron, Elisha, 'Times for Praising God: A Fragment of a Scroll from Qumran (4Q409)', *Jewish Quarterly Review* 80 (1990), pp. 341-47

—and John Strugnell, 'An Unpublished Halakhic Letter from Qumran', in *Biblical Archaeology Today: Proceedings of the International Congress on Biblical Archaeology, Jerusalem, April 1984* (Jerusalem: Israel Exploration Society, 1985), pp. 400-407

—and John Strugnell, *Qumran Cave 4/V: Miqṣat Ma'aśe ha-Torah* (Discoveries in the Judaean Desert, 10; Oxford: Clarendon Press, 1994)

Sanders, J.A., *The Psalms Scroll of Qumrân Cave 11* (Discoveries in the Judaean Desert of Jordan, 4; Oxford: Clarendon Press, 1965)

Schiffman, L.H., '4Qmysteries[b], A Preliminary Edition', *Revue de Qumran* 16 (1993), pp. 203-223.

Schuller, Eileen, *Non-Canonical Psalms from Qumran: A Pseudepigraphic Collection* (Harvard Semitic Studies, 28; Atlanta: Scholars Press, 1986)

—'*4Q372* 1: A Text about Joseph', *Revue de Qumran* 14 (1990), pp. 349-76

—'A Preliminary Study of 4Q*373* and Some Related (?) Fragments', in *The Madrid Congress: Proceedings of the International Congress on the Dead Sea Scrolls, Madrid, 18–21 March 1991* (ed. J. Trebolle Barrera and L. Vegas Montaner; Studies on the Texts of the Desert of Judah, 11; Madrid: Universidad Complutense and Leiden: E.J. Brill, 1992), pp. 515-30

—'A Hymn from a Cave Four *Hodayot* Manuscript: 4Q*427* 7 i+ii', *Journal of Biblical Literature* 112 (1993), pp. 605-28

Smith, M., '*4Q462* (Narrative) Fragment 1: A Preliminary Edition', *Revue de Qumran* 15 (1991), pp. 55-77

Steudel, Annette, *Der Midrash zur Eschatologie aus der Qumrangemeinde (4QMidrEschat[b])* (Leiden: E.J. Brill, 1994)

Stone, M.E. and E. Eshel, 'An Exposition on the Patriarchs (4Q464) and Two Other Documents (4Q464[a] and 4Q464[b])', *Le Muséon* 105 (1992), pp. 243-64

Strugnell, John, 'Moses-Pseudepigrapha at Qumran: 4Q375, 4Q376, and Similar Works', in *Archaeology and History in the Dead Sea Scrolls: The New York University Conference in Memory of Yigael Yadin* (ed. Lawrence H. Schiffman; Journal for the Study of the Pseudepigrapha Supplement Series, 8; JSOT/ASOR Monographs, 2; Sheffield: JSOT Press, 1990), pp. 221-56

— and Devorah Dimant, '4Q Second Ezekiel', *Revue de Qumran* 13 (1988), pp. 45-58

Sukenik, E.L., *The Dead Sea Scrolls of the Hebrew University* (Jerusalem: The Magnes Press, 1955)

Tov, Emanuel, 'The Unpublished Qumran Texts from Caves 4 and 11', *Biblical Archaeologist* 55 (1992), pp. 94-104

—'The Exodus Section of 4Q422', *Dead Sea Discoveries* 1 (1994) , pp. 197-209

—(ed.), *The Dead Sea Scrolls on Microfiche: A Comprehensive Facsimile Edition of the Texts from the Judean Desert. Companion Volume* (Leiden: E.J. Brill and IDC, 1993)

VanderKam, J.C., 'The Jubilees Fragments from Qumran Cave 4', in *The Madrid Congress: Proceedings of the International Congress on the Dead Sea Scrolls, Madrid, 18–21 March 1991* (ed. J. Trebolle Barrera and L. Vegas Montaner; Studies on the Texts of the Desert of Judah, 11;

Madrid: Universidad Complutense and Leiden: E.J. Brill, 1992), pp. 635-48
—and J.T. Milik, 'The First *Jubilees* Manuscript from Qumran Cave 4: A Preliminary Publication', *Journal of Biblical Literature* 110 (1991), pp. 243-70
—and J.T. Milik, 'A Preliminary Publication of a Jubilees Manuscript from Qumran Cave 4: 4QJub$^{d}$ (4Q219)', *Biblica* 73 (1992), pp. 62-83
—and J.T. Milik, '4QJubilees$^{g}$ (4Q222)', in *New Qumran Texts and Studies: Proceedings of the First Meeting of the International Organization for Qumran Studies, Paris, 1992* (ed. George J. Brooke with Florentino García Martínez; Studies on the Texts of the Desert of Judah, 15; Leiden: E.J. Brill, 1994), pp. 105-14
—and J.T. Milik, '4QJub$^{c}$ (4Q218) and 4QJub$^{e}$ (4Q220): A Preliminary Edition', *Textus* 17 (1994), pp. 43-58
Vaux, R. de and J.T. Milik, *Qumrân Grotte 4:* I. *Archéologie.* II. *Tefillin, Mezuzot et Targums (4Q128–4Q157)* (Discoveries in the Judaean Desert, 6; Oxford: Clarendon Press, 1977)
Vermes, G., 'Preliminary Remarks on Unpublished Fragments of the Community Rule from Qumran Cave 4', *Journal of Jewish Studies* 42 (1991), pp. 250-55
—'The Oxford Forum for Qumran Research—Seminar on the Rule of War from Cave 4 (4Q285)', *Journal of Jewish Studies* 43 (1992), pp. 85-90
WA, *see* Wacholder and Abegg
Wacholder, Ben Zion and Martin G. Abegg, *A Preliminary Edition of the Unpublished Dead Sea Scrolls: The Hebrew and Aramaic Texts from Cave Four*, Fascicles 1, 2 (Washington, DC: Biblical Archaeology Society, 1991, 1992)
Weinfeld, Moshe, 'Grace after Meals in Qumran', *Journal of Biblical Literature* 111 (1992), pp. 427-40
White, Sidnie A., '4Q*364* & *365*: A Preliminary Report', in *The Madrid Congress: Proceedings of the International Congress on the Dead Sea Scrolls, Madrid, 18–21 March 1991* (ed. J. Trebolle Barrera and L. Vegas Montaner; Studies on the Texts of the Desert of Judah, 11; Madrid: Universidad Complutense and Leiden: E.J. Brill, 1992), pp. 217-28
Woude, Adam van der, 'Melchisedek als himmlisch Erlösergestalt in den neugefundenen eschatologischen Midraschim aus Qumran Höhle XI', *Oudtestamentische Studiën* 14 (1965), pp. 354-73
—'Ein neuer Segensspruch aus Qumran (11QBer)', in *Bibel und Qumran: Beiträge zur Erforschung der Beziehungen zwischen Bibel- und Qumranwissenschaft: Hans Bardtke zum 22.8.1966* (ed. S. Wagner; Berlin: Evangelische Haupt-Bibelgesellschaft, 1968)
—'Fragmente des Buches Jubiläen aus Qumran Höhle XI (11QJub)', in *Tradition und Glaube: Das frühe Christentum in seiner Umwelt: Festgabe für Karl Georg Kuhn zum 65. Geburtstag* (ed. J. Jeremias *et al.*; Göttingen: Vandenhoeck & Ruprecht, 1971), pp. 140-46
Yadin, Yigael, *The Scroll of the War of the Sons of Light against the Sons of Darkness* (Oxford: Oxford University Press, 1962)
—(ed.) *The Temple Scroll* (3 vols.; Jerusalem: Israel Exploration Society, 1983)
—*Bar-Kokhba: The Rediscovery of the Legendary Hero of the Last Jewish Revolt against Imperial Rome* (London: Weidenfeld and Nicolson, 1971)
* publication in part

b. *Inscriptions*

The following list is supplementary to that published in Volume 1, pp. 55-66, and replaces the list published in Volume 2, pp. 31-35. The numbers (e.g. 100.902) in the left-hand column are those that will designate these inscriptions in the future Supplement to *Ancient Hebrew Inscriptions: Corpus and Concordance*, by Graham I. Davies (Cambridge: Cambridge University Press, 1991), which has been used as the standard edition of the Hebrew inscriptions.

Arrowhead 1
T.C. Mitchell, 'Another Palestinian Inscribed Arrowhead', in *Palestine in the Bronze and Iron Ages. Papers in Honour of Olga Tufnell* (ed. J.N. Tubb; London: Institute of Archaeology, 1985), pp. 136-53

Arrowhead 2 (11th cent.)
F.M. Cross, 'An Inscribed Arrowhead of the Eleventh Century BCE in the Bible Lands Museum in Jerusalem', *EI* 23 (1992), pp. 21*-26*

Arrowhead 3 (11th cent.)
F.M. Cross, 'An Inscribed Arrowhead of the Eleventh Century BCE in the Bible Lands Museum in Jerusalem', *EI* 23 (1992), pp. 21*-26*

Bar Kokhba IOU (2nd cent. CE)
M. Broshi and E. Qimron, 'I.O.U. Note from the Time of the Bar Kokhba Revolt', *EI* 20 (1989), pp. 256-61 [Heb.]; P. Segal, 'The Hebrew IOU Note from the Time of the Bar Kokhba Period', *Tarb* 60 (1990), pp. 113-18 [Heb.]

100.901 Bulla 901 (7th cent.)
N. Avigad, 'Two Hebrew "Fiscal" Bullae', *IEJ* 40 (1990), pp. 262-65

100.902 Bulla 902 (7th cent.)
N. Avigad, 'Two Hebrew "Fiscal" Bullae', *IEJ* 40 (1990), pp. 265-66

100.904 Bulla 904 (Jerusalem, 7th/6th cent.)
G. Barkay, 'A Bulla of Ishmael, the King's Son', *BASOR* 290–91 (1993), pp. 109-14

100.922 Bulla 922 (7th/6th cent.)
R. Deutsch and M. Heltzer, *Forty New Ancient West Semitic Inscriptions* (Tel Aviv, 1994), pp. 37-38

100.923 Bulla 923 (7th/6th cent.)
Deutsch and Heltzer, *Forty New Inscriptions*, pp. 38-39

100.924 Bulla 924
Deutsch and Heltzer, *Forty New Inscriptions*, pp. 39-40

100.925 Bulla 925 (7th cent.)
Deutsch and Heltzer, *Forty New Inscriptions*, pp. 42-43

100.926 Bulla 926 (7th/6th cent.)
Deutsch and Heltzer, *Forty New Inscriptions*, pp. 43-44

100.927 Bulla 927
Deutsch and Heltzer, *Forty New Inscriptions*, p. 44

100.928 Bulla 928 (7th/6th cent.)
Deutsch and Heltzer, *Forty New Inscriptions*, p. 44

100.929 Bulla 929 (7th cent.)
Deutsch and Heltzer, *Forty New Inscriptions*, p. 45

100.930 Bulla 930 (7th/6th cent.)
Deutsch and Heltzer, *Forty New*

*Inscriptions*, p. 46

100.931 Bulla 931 (7th cent.)
Deutsch and Heltzer, *Forty New Inscriptions*, p. 47

Bulla a1 (Samaria, 4th cent.)
Y. Meshorer and S. Qedar, *The Coinage of Samaria in the Fourth Century BCE* (Jerusalem, 1991)

4.124 City of David inscr. 1 (8th cent.)
Y. Shiloh, 'The Material Culture of Judah and Jerusalem in Iron Age II: Origins and Influences', *OLA* 19 (1985), p. 144; Y. Nadelman, *IEJ* 40 (1990), p. 39

4.126 City of David inscr. 2
Y. Shiloh, 'South Arabian Inscriptions from the City of David, Jerusalem', *PEQ* 119 (1987), pp. 11-12; Y. Nadelman, *IEJ* 40 (1990), p. 41

City of David ostraca 1-2 (4th/3rd cent.)
J. Naveh, *On Sherd and Papyrus* (Jerusalem, 1992) [Heb.]

Coins
Ya'aqob Meshorer, *Jewish Coins of the Second Temple Period* (Tel Aviv: Am Hassepher, 1967)

99.002 Decanter inscr. (7th cent.)
R. Deutsch and M. Heltzer, *Forty New Ancient West Semitic Inscriptions* (Tel Aviv, 1994), pp. 23-24

Er-Ram ossuary inscr.
Joseph A. Fitzmyer and Daniel J. Harrington, *A Manual of Palestinian Aramaic Texts (Second Century B.C.–Second Century A.D.)* (Biblica et Orientalia, 34; Rome: Biblical Institute Press, 1978), p. 182, no. 144

108.010 'Gerah' weight
D. Diringer, 'The Hebrew Weights Found at Lachish', *PEQ* 74 (1942), p. 97; R. Kletter, 'The Inscribed Weights of the Kingdom of Judah', *Tel Aviv* 18 (1991), pp. 122, 151

Ḥorvat Ma'on ostr.
D. Amit and Z. Ilan, 'The Ancient Synagogue at Ma'on in Judah', *Qadmoniot* 23 (1990), pp. 115-25 [Heb.]

37.006 Ḥorvat 'Uza bowl inscr. (Beit-Arieh) (7th cent.)
I. Beit-Arieh, 'A Literary Ostracon from Ḥorvat 'Uza', *Tel Aviv* 20 (1993), pp. 55-63

37.007 Ḥorvat 'Uza bowl inscr. (Cross) (7th cent.)
I. Beit-Arieh, 'A Literary Ostracon from Ḥorvat 'Uza', *Tel Aviv* 20 (1993), pp. 64-65

37.004 Ḥorvat 'Uza jar inscr. 1 (7th–6th cent.)
I. Beit-Arieh, 'An Inscribed Jar from Ḥorvat 'Uza', *EI* 24 (1993), pp. 34-40 [Heb.]

37.005 Ḥorvat 'Uza jar inscr. 2 (7th–6th cent.)
as 37.004

100.919 Jar stamp 1
R. Deutsch and M. Heltzer, *Forty New Ancient West Semitic Inscriptions* (Tel Aviv, 1994), pp. 31-33

100.920 Jar stamp 2 (8th cent.)
R. Deutsch and M. Heltzer, *Forty New Ancient West Semitic Inscriptions* (Tel Aviv, 1994), pp. 33-34

100.943 Jar Stamp 3 (T. Beit Mirsim?, 8th cent.)
G. Barkay, 'A Collection of Jar handles with Seal Impressions from Judah', *EI* 23 (1992), p. 116, no. 16

100.944 Jar Stamp 4 (T. Beit Mirsim?, 8th cent.)
Barkay, 'Collection', p. 116, no. 17

100.945 Jar Stamp 5 (T. Beit Mirsim?, 8th cent.)
Barkay, 'Collection', p. 116, no. 18

100.946 Jar Stamp 6 (T. Beit Mirsim?, 8th cent.)
Barkay, 'Collection', p. 116, no. 19

100.947 Jar Stamp 7 (T. Beit Mirsim?, 8th cent.)
Barkay, 'Collection', p. 116, no. 20

100.948 Jar Stamp 8(T. Beit Mirsim?, 8th cent.)
Barkay, 'Collection', p. 117, no. 21

100.949 Jar Stamp 9 (T. Beit Mirsim?, 8th cent.)

Barkay, 'Collection', p. 117, no. 22
100.950 Jar Stamp 10 (T. Beit Mirsim?, 8th cent.)
Barkay, 'Collection', p. 117, no. 23
100.951 Jar Stamp 11 (T. Beit Mirsim?, 8th cent.)
Barkay, 'Collection', p. 117, no. 24
100.952 Jar Stamp 12 (T. Beit Mirsim?, 8th cent.)
Barkay, 'Collection', p. 117, no. 25
100.953 Jar Stamp 13 (T. Beit Mirsim?, 8th cent.)
Barkay, 'Collection', p. 118, no. 26
100.954 Jar Stamp 14 (T. Beit Mirsim?, 8th cent.)
Barkay, 'Collection', p. 118, no. 27
100.955 Jar Stamp 15 (T. Beit Mirsim?, 8th cent.)
Barkay, 'Collection', p. 118, no. 28
100.956 Jar Stamp 16 (T. Beit Mirsim?, 8th cent.)
Barkay, 'Collection', p. 119, no. 32
100.957 Jar Stamp 17 (T. Batash, 8th cent.)
Z. Ilan, 'Eretz Hemdah', *Tel-Aviv* 1978, pp. 188-90; cf. Barkay, 'Collection', pp. 126-27, no. 34
100.958 Jar Stamp 18 (Lachish, 8th cent.)
A.S. Ackerman and S.L. Braunstein, *Israel in Antiquity* (New York, 1982), p. 71, no. 56; cf. Barkay, 'Collection', p. 127, no. 39
100.959 Jar Stamp 19 (T. eṣ-Ṣafi, 8th cent.)
M. Israel, 'A Hebrew Sealing on a Jar Handle from Kfar Menahem', in *Mitmol wehayom, peraqim biyediat haaretz* (ed. I. Roth; Merhavia, 1958), pp. 64-66; Israel, 'Survey and Research on the region of Kfar Menahem', *Teva vaAretz* 5 (1963), p. 4; Barkay, 'Collection', p. 127, no. 39
100.964 Jar Stamp 20 (Lachish, 8th cent.)
G. Barkay, 'The King of Babylonia or a Judaean Official?', *IEJ* 45 (1995), p. 45
Jerusalem ossuary inscr. 1-3 (1st cent. CE)
T. Ilan, 'New Ossuary Inscriptions from Jerusalem', in *Scripta Classica Israelica* 11 (1991–1992), pp. 149-59
Jerusalem ossuary inscr. 4 (1st cent. CE)
A. Kloner and H. Stark, 'A Burial Cave on Mount Scopus, Jerusalem', *Bulletin of the Anglo-Israel Archaeological Society* 11 (1991–92), pp. 7-17; 'A Burial Cave on Mt Scopus', *Atiqot* 20 (1991), pp. 27*-30* [Heb.]
Jerusalem ossuary inscr. 5
V. Sussman, 'A Burial Cave on Mount Scopus', *Atiqot* 21 (1992), pp. 89-96
Jerusalem ossuary inscr. 6
Joseph A. Fitzmyer and Daniel J. Harrington, *A Manual of Palestinian Aramaic Texts (Second Century B.C.–Second Century A.D.)* (Biblica et Orientalia, 34; Rome: Biblical Institute Press, 1978), p. 182, no. 145
Jerusalem storage jar
Fitzmyer and Harrington, *Palestinian Aramaic Texts*, p. 168, no. 66
25.006 Kh. el-Qom tomb inscr. 4
R. Deutsch and M. Heltzer, *Forty New Ancient West Semitic Inscriptions* (Tel Aviv, 1994), pp. 27-29
48.001 Kh. Rosh Zayit jar inscr. (10th cent.)
Z. Gal, 'Khirbet Roš Zayit—Biblical Cabul: A Historical-Geographical Case', *BA* 53 (1990), p. 95
1.033 Lachish cooking-pot inscr.
D. Ussishkin, *Tel Aviv* 10 (1983), p. 133; Y. Nadelman, *IEJ* 40 (1990), p. 38
Masada coin (number as in Meshorer)
Y. Meshorer, 'The Coins of Masada', in *Masada I. The Y. Yadin Excavations 1963–5. Final Reports* (Jerusalem, 1989), pp. 69-132, pls. 61-81
Masada ostr.
Y. Yadin and J. Naveh, 'The Aramaic and Hebrew Ostraca and Jar Inscriptions', in *Masada I. The Y. Yadin Excavations 1963–5. Final Reports* (Jerusalem, 1989), pp. 1-68, pls. 1-60
50.001-3 Mt Gerizim inscr. 1-3
Y. Magen, 'Mount Gerizim—A

Temple-City', *Qadmoniot* 23 (1990), pp. 70-96 [Heb.]

31.003 Ramat Raḥel inscr. (8th cent.)
Y. Aharoni, *Ramat Raḥel* II (1961–1962) (Rome, 1964), p. 60; Y. Nadelman, *IEJ* 40 (1990), p. 38

Samaria Coins (4th cent.)
Y. Meshorer and S. Qedar, *The Coinage of Samaria in the Fourth Century BCE* (Jerusalem, 1991)

100.903 Seal 903 (Dan, 9th/8th cent.)
A. Biran, 'A Mace-Head and the Office of Amadiyo at Dan', *Qadmoniot* 21 (1988), pp. 11-17 (16) [Heb.]

100.905 Seal 905 (7th cent.)
J. Elayi, 'Inscriptions nord-ouest sémitiques inédites', *Sem* 38 (1990), pp. 101-102

100.906 Seal 906 (8th cent.)
A. Lemaire, 'Sept nouveaux sceaux nord-ouest sémitiques inscrits', *Sem* 41/42 (1991–92), pp. 63-69

100.907 Seal 907 (8th cent.)
Lemaire, *Sem* 41/42 (1991–92), pp. 69-71

100.908 Seal 908 (7th cent.)
Lemaire, *Sem* 41/42 (1991–92), pp. 71-72

100.909 Seal 909 (7th/6th cent.)
Lemaire, *Sem* 41/42 (1991–92), pp. 72-74

100.910 Seal 910 (7th cent.)
Lemaire, *Sem* 41/42 (1991–92), pp. 74-76

100.911 Seal 911 (8th cent.)
Lemaire, *Sem* 41/42 (1991–92), pp. 76-77

100.912 Seal 912 (8th cent.)
A. Lemaire, 'Cinq nouveaux sceaux inscrits ouest-sémitiques', *SEL* 7 (1990), pp. 97-101

100.913 Seal 913 (7th/6th cent.)
Lemaire, *SEL* 7 (1990), pp. 101-103

100.914 Seal 914
W.E. Aufrecht, 'Three Inscribed Seals', *EI* 23 (1992), p. 1*

100.915 Seal 915 (Beth-Shemesh, 7th cent.)
V.S. Mähner, 'Ein Namen- und Bildsiegel aus *'Ēn Šems'*, *ZDPV* 108 (1992), pp. 68-81

100.916 Seal 916
N. Avigad, *Burnt Archive*, p. 45, no. 56; *ZDPV* 108 (1992), p. 72

100.917 Seal 917
*Bulletin of the Museum of Fine Arts of Boston* 68 (1970), p. 202, no. 353

100.918 Seal 918 (8th cent.)
A. Lemaire, 'Trois sceaux inscrits inédits avec lion rugissant', *Sem* 39 (1991), pp. 13-16

100.921 Seal 921
R. Deutsch and M. Heltzer, *Forty New Ancient West Semitic Inscriptions* (Tel Aviv, 1994), pp. 35-36

100.932 Seal 932 (7th cent.)
Deutsch and Heltzer, *Forty New Inscriptions*, pp. 49-51

100.933 Seal 933 (7th cent.)
Deutsch and Heltzer, *Forty New Inscriptions*, pp. 51-53

100.934 Seal 934 (7th cent.)
Deutsch and Heltzer, *Forty New Inscriptions*, pp. 54-55

100.935 Seal 935 (9th cent.)
Deutsch and Heltzer, *Forty New Inscriptions*, pp. 55-56

100.936 Seal 936 (8th cent.)
Deutsch and Heltzer, *Forty New Inscriptions*, pp. 56-58

100.937 Seal 937 (7th cent.)
Deutsch and Heltzer, *Forty New Inscriptions*, pp. 58-59

100.938 Seal 938 (7th cent.)
Deutsch and Heltzer, *Forty New Inscriptions*, pp. 60-61

100.939 Seal 939

G. Barkay, 'A Bulla of Ishmael, the King's Son', *BASOR* 290-1 (1993), p. 111, no. 1

100.940 Seal 940
N. Avigad, 'The Seals of Neriahu the King's Son', in *Exile and Diaspora (Studies in the History of the Jewish People Presented to Prof. H. Beinart* (ed. A. Mirsky, A. Grossman and Y. Kaplan; Jerusalem, 1988), pp. 41-42

100.941 Seal 941
G. Barkay, 'A Bulla of Ishmael, the King's Son', *BASOR* 290-1 (1993), p. 111, no. 13

100.942 Seal 942
G. Barkay, 'A Bulla of Ishmael, the King's Son', *BASOR* 290-1 (1993), p. 111, no. 16

100.962 Seal 962 (8th cent.)
A. Lemaire, 'Name of Israel's Last King Surfaces in a Private Collection', *Biblical Archaeology Review* 21/6 (1995), pp. 48-52

100.963 Seal 963 (8th cent.)
L.A. Wolfe and F. Sternberg, *Objects with Semitic Inscriptions 1100 B.C.–A.D. 700*; cf. A. Lemaire, *BAR* 21/6 (1995), pp. 51-52.

Seal a1
Josette Elayi, 'Name of Deuteronomy's Author Found on Seal Ring', *BAR* 13 (1987), pp. 54-56

Seals b1-13 (T. Beit Mirsim?, 8th cent.)
G. Barkay, 'A Group of Stamped Jar Handles from Judah', *EI* 23 (1992), pp. 113-28 [Heb.]

T. Batash inscr.
G.L. Kelm and A. Mazar, 'Tel Batash (Timnah) Excavations: Third Preliminary Report, 1984–89', in *Preliminary Reports of ASOR-Sponsored Excavations 1982–89* (ed. W.E. Rast; BASOR Supplements, 27; 1991), p. 56

18.006 T. Beit Mirsim bowl inscr. (8th cent.)
G. Barkay, 'A Bowl with the Hebrew Inscription *qdš*', *IEJ* 40 (1990), pp. 124-29

46.001 T. Haror jar inscr. (7th/6th cent.)
E. Oren *et al.*, 'Tel Haror after Six Seasons', *Qadmoniot* 24 (1991), pp. 16-18

47.001 Veered Eyrieḥo inscr. (7th cent.)
Y. Nadelman, '"Chiselled" Inscriptions and Markings on Pottery Vessels from the Iron Age II (Discussion and Catalogue)', *IEJ* 40 (1990), p. 37

108.049 Weight 49 (8th/7th cent.)
R. Deutsch and M. Heltzer, *Forty New Ancient West Semitic Inscriptions* (Tel Aviv, 1994), p. 65

108.050 Weight 50 (8th/7th cent.)
Deutsch and Heltzer, *Forty New Inscriptions*, pp. 66-67

Weight a1
A. Kloner, 'Ḥorvat Aim, Weight from the Time of Bar Kokhba', *Excavations and Surveys in Israel* 6 (1987–88), p. 1

Weight a2
A. Kloner, 'A Lead Plaque Weight of the Bar-Kokhba Administration', *Qadmoniot* 21 (1988), pp. 44-48 [Heb.], *EI* 20 (1989), pp. 345-51 [Heb.], *IEJ* 40 (1990), pp. 58-67

106.020 Yehud Stamp (x2) (Kh. Nisya, 5th/4th cent.)
B.G. Wood and D.P. Livingston, 'Notes and News - Khirbet Nisya, 1993', *IEJ* 44 (1994), pp. 144-45 and fig. 4

# WORDS BEGINNING WITH ZAYIN, ḤETH AND ṬETH IN ORDER OF FREQUENCY

In these tables are listed all the words beginning with Zayin, Ḥeth, and Ṭeth, in descending order of their frequency of occurrence in the corpus of classical Hebrew. Including proper names, there are 224 words beginning with Zayin, 797 with Ḥeth, and 113 with Ṭeth, 1134 in all. Words that are conjectured, and for which therefore no occurrence statistics are noted in the Dictionary, are of course absent from this list. Words for which the lemma form is reconstructed (for example, when only plural forms are attested and the presumed singular form is therefore shown within square brackets) are included, without their square brackets.

In the first column, a number ranks the words in order of frequency. Following the Hebrew word itself, and (in the case of homonyms) a roman numeral to distinguish one word from another spelled alike, five columns of figures follow. They record in turn the number of occurrences of the word in the four corpora of texts that comprise classical Hebrew—the Masoretic text of the Hebrew Bible (MT), Ben Sira (Si), the Dead Sea Scrolls (Qumran and related texts) (Q) and the Hebrew inscriptions (Inscr)—and the total number of occurrences. It is this total that determines a word's position in the table. In the next column the part of speech is noted, and a simple gloss follows, to identify the word in question.

# ז

| Rank | Lemma | | MT | Si | Q | Inscr | Total | Type | Gloss |
|---|---|---|---|---|---|---|---|---|---|
| 1 | זֶה | | 1173 | 21 | 193 | 13 | 1400 | pron | *this* |
| 2 | זֹאת | | 600 | 4 | 67 | 4 | 675 | pron | *this* |
| 3 | זָהָב | I | 387 | 10 | 40 | 2 | 439 | nm | *gold* |
| 4 | זכר | I | 231 | 20 | 44 | 1 | 296 | vb | *remember* |
| 5 | זֶ֫רַע | | 229 | 15 | 49 | 2 | 295 | nm | *seed* |
| 6 | זָקֵן | I | 186 | 2 | 30 | | 218 | adj | *old* |
| 7 | זֶ֫בַח | I | 162 | 1 | 26 | | 189 | nm | *sacrifice* |
| 8 | זבח | | 134 | | 29 | | 163 | vb | *sacrifice* |
| 9 | זור | I | 77 | 13 | 11 | | 101 | vb | *be strange* |
| 10 | זְרוֹעַ | | 91 | 1 | 5 | 2 | 99 | nm & f | *arm* |
| 11 | זָכָר | | 80 | 2 | 10 | | 92 | adj | *male* |
| 12 | זעק | | 73 | | 11 | | 84 | vb | *cry out* |
| 13 | זנה | I | 60 | 2 | 5 | | 67 | vb | *prostitute oneself* |
| 14 | זרע | | 56 | 2 | 5 | | 63 | vb | *sow* |
| 15 | זמר | I | 45 | | 13 | | 58 | vb | *sing (praise)* |
| 16 | זִכָּרוֹן | | 24 | 2 | 29 | | 55 | nm | *memorial* |
| 17 | זוב | | 40 | 2 | 10 | | 52 | vb | *flow* |
| 18 | זְכַרְיָה | | 41 | | 5 | 5 | 51 | prnm | *Zechariah* |
| 19 | זְבוּלֻן | | 45 | | 3 | | 48 | prnm | *Zebulun* |
| 20 | זרה | I | 40 | 2 | 5 | | 47 | vb | *scatter* |
| 21 | זַ֫יִת | | 38 | 1 | 4 | | 43 | nm | *olive* |
| 22 | זֵ֫כֶר | I | 23 | 10 | 8 | | 41 | nm | *remembrance* |
| 23 | זִמָּה | I | 29 | 2 | 10 | | 41 | nf | *wickedness, plan* |
| 24 | זרק | I | 35 | | 5 | | 40 | vb | *scatter* |
| 25 | זָדוֹן | | 11 | 11 | 9 | | 31 | nm | *presumptuousness* |
| 26 | זוּלַת | | 16 | 2 | 11 | | 29 | prep | *apart from* |
| 27 | זעם | | 12 | 3 | 11 | | 26 | vb | *be indignant* |
| 28 | זַ֫עַם | | 22 | 2 | 2 | | 26 | nm | *indignation* |
| 29 | זהר | I | 21 | 2 | 2 | | 25 | vb | *warn* |

## *Words Beginning with Zayin*

| Rank | Lemma | | MT | Si | Q | Inscr | Total | Type | Gloss |
|---|---|---|---|---|---|---|---|---|---|
| 30 | זמם | | 13 | 1 | 11 | | 25 | vb | *plan* |
| 31 | זְנוּת | | 9 | 2 | 12 | | 23 | nf | *prostitution* |
| 32 | זנח | I | 19 | 1 | 3 | | 23 | vb | *reject* |
| 33 | זַכּוּר | | 10 | | | 12 | 22 | prnm | *Zaccur* |
| 34 | זְעָקָה | | 20 | | 2 | | 22 | nf | *cry* |
| 35 | זקן | | 20 | 1 | 1 | | 22 | vb | *be old* |
| 36 | זָקָן | | 19 | | 3 | | 22 | nm & f | *beard* |
| 37 | זֶ֫רַח | II | 21 | | | 1 | 22 | prnm | *Zerah* |
| 38 | זֵד | | 15 | 4 | 2 | | 21 | adj | *presumptuous* |
| 39 | זוֹב | | 13 | | 8 | | 21 | nm | *discharge* |
| 40 | זְרֻבָּבֶל | | 21 | | | | 21 | prnm | *Zerubbabel* |
| 41 | זרח | | 18 | | 1 | 1 | 20 | vb | *arise* |
| 42 | זוּ | | 14 | | 3 | | 17 | part | *which* |
| 43 | זיד | | 10 | 2 | 3 | | 15 | vb | *be presumptuous* |
| 44 | זִיף | I | 9 | | | 5 | 14 | pln | *Ziph* |
| 45 | זִמְרִי | I | 14 | | | | 14 | prnm | *Zimri* |
| 46 | זֶ֫רֶם | | 9 | | 5 | | 14 | nm | *downpour* |
| 47 | זְבֻל | I | 5 | | 8 | | 13 | n[m] | *dwelling place* |
| 48 | זוע | I | 3 | 3 | 7 | | 13 | vb | *tremble* |
| 49 | זכה | | 8 | | 5 | | 13 | vb | *be pure* |
| 50 | זִכְרִי | | 12 | | | 1 | 13 | prnm | *Zichri* |
| 51 | זָנָב | | 11 | | 2 | | 13 | nm | *tail* |
| 52 | זְנוּנִים | | 12 | | 1 | | 13 | nm | *prostitution* |
| 53 | זקק | | 7 | | 6 | | 13 | vb | *refine* |
| 54 | זֶ֫בַח | II | 12 | | | | 12 | prnm | *Zebah* |
| 55 | זֹה | | 11 | 1 | | | 12 | pron | *this (one)* |
| 56 | זַךְ | | 11 | | 1 | | 12 | adj | *pure* |
| 57 | זְמָן | | 4 | 2 | 5 | | 11 | nm | *(set) time* |
| 58 | זִמְרָה | I | 7 | | 4 | | 11 | nf | *song* |
| 59 | זֵר | | 10 | 1 | | | 11 | nm | *border* |
| 60 | זְאֵב | I | 7 | 2 | 1 | | 10 | nm | *wolf* |
| 61 | זְבַדְיָה | | 9 | | | 1 | 10 | prnm | *Zebadiah* |
| 62 | זִלְפָּה | I | 7 | | 2 | | 9 | prnf | *Zilpah* |
| 63 | זָמִיר | I | 7 | | 2 | | 9 | nm | *song* |
| 64 | זַעֲוָה | | 6 | | 3 | | 9 | nf | *trembling* |

| Rank | Lemma | | MT | Si | Q | Inscr | Total | Type | Gloss |
|---|---|---|---|---|---|---|---|---|---|
| 65 | זַ֫עַף | | 6 | | 3 | | 9 | nm | *anger* |
| 66 | זָבָד | | 8 | | | | 8 | prnm | *Zabad* |
| 67 | זֵק | I | 4 | | 4 | | 8 | n[m] | *fetter* |
| 68 | זֶ֫רֶת | | 7 | | 1 | | 8 | nf | *span* |
| 69 | זַבְדִּי | | 7 | | | | 7 | prnm | *Zabdi* |
| 70 | זכר | III | 7 | | | | 7 | vb | *boast* |
| 71 | זְאֵב | II | 6 | | | | 6 | prnm | *Zeeb* |
| 72 | זְבֻל | III | 6 | | | | 6 | prnm | *Zebul* |
| 73 | זְוָעָה | | 6 | | | | 6 | nf | *trembling* |
| 74 | זור | IV | 5 | | 1 | | 6 | vb | *depart* |
| 75 | זְכוּר | | 4 | | 2 | | 6 | nm | *male* |
| 76 | זכך | | 4 | | 2 | | 6 | vb | *be pure* |
| 77 | זַלְעָפָה | | 3 | 1 | 2 | | 6 | nf | *raging* |
| 78 | זִקְנָה | | 6 | | | | 6 | nf | *old age* |
| 79 | זַרְחִי | | 6 | | | | 6 | gent | *Zerahite* |
| 80 | זְרַחְיָה | | 5 | | | 1 | 6 | prnm | *Zerahiah* |
| 81 | זוֹ | | 4 | | | 1 | 5 | pron | *this* |
| 82 | זלל | II | 4 | 1 | | | 5 | vb | *be gluttonous* |
| 83 | זְמוֹרָה | I | 5 | | | | 5 | nf | *branch* |
| 84 | זַן | | 3 | 2 | | | 5 | n[m] | *kind* |
| 85 | זָנוֹחַ | | 5 | | | | 5 | pln | *Zanoah* |
| 86 | זַעֲטוּט | | | | 5 | | 5 | nm | *lad* |
| 87 | זְעֵיר | I | 5 | | | | 5 | n[m] | *a little* |
| 88 | זעף | I | 5 | | | | 5 | vb | *be angry* |
| 89 | זֶ֫פֶת | | 3 | 1 | 1 | | 5 | nf | *pitch* |
| 90 | זקף | | 2 | | 3 | | 5 | vb | *raise* |
| 91 | זָהִיר | | | 4 | | | 4 | adj | *cautious* |
| 92 | זֹ֫הַר | | 2 | | 2 | | 4 | nm | *brightness* |
| 93 | זחל | I | 2 | | 2 | | 4 | vb | *crawl* |
| 94 | זִיו | II | 2 | | 2 | | 4 | nm | *splendour* |
| 95 | זִיקָה | | 2 | 1 | 1 | | 4 | nf | *flaming arrow* |
| 96 | זַכַּי | 4 | | | | | 4 | prnm | *Zaccai* |
| 97 | זמר | II | 3 | | 1 | | 4 | vb | *prune* |
| 98 | זֵק | II | 1 | 1 | 2 | | 4 | n[m] | *flaming arrow* |
| 99 | זְקֻנִים | | 4 | | | | 4 | n[m] | *old age* |

## Words Beginning with Zayin

| Rank | Lemma | | MT | Si | Q | Inscr | Total | Type | Gloss |
|---|---|---|---|---|---|---|---|---|---|
| 100 | זֶ֫רֶד | | 4 | | | | 4 | pln | *Zered* |
| 101 | זֶ֫רֶק | | | | 4 | | 4 | nm | *javelin* |
| 102 | זֶ֫רֶשׁ | | 4 | | | | 4 | prnf | *Zeresh* |
| 103 | זַתּוּא | | 4 | | | | 4 | prnm | *Zattu* |
| 104 | זֶ֫בֶד | | 1 | 2 | | | 3 | nm | *gift* |
| 105 | זְבוּלֹנִי | | 3 | | | | 3 | gent | *Zebulunite* |
| 106 | זהר | II | 1 | 2 | | | 3 | vb | *be bright* |
| 107 | זוּז | | | | 3 | | 3 | nm | *zuz* |
| 108 | זוֹנוּת | | | | 3 | | 3 | nf | *fornication* |
| 109 | זור | II | 3 | | | | 3 | vb | *squeeze, flow* |
| 110 | זִיזָא | | 3 | | | | 3 | prnm | *Ziza* |
| 111 | זִיפִי | | 3 | | | | 3 | gent | *Ziphite* |
| 112 | זלל | I | 2 | | 1 | | 3 | vb | *be worthless* |
| 113 | זִמָּה | II | 3 | | | | 3 | prnm | *Zimmah* |
| 114 | זמן | | 3 | | | | 3 | vb | *set time* |
| 115 | זֶ֫מֶר | I | | | 3 | | 3 | n[m] | *song (of praise)* |
| 116 | זִמְרָה | III | 3 | | | | 3 | nf | *refuge* |
| 117 | זִמְרָה | IV | 3 | | | | 3 | n[f] | *warrior* |
| 118 | זָרָא | | 1 | 2 | | | 3 | n[f] | *abhorrence* |
| 119 | זרם | I | 2 | | 1 | | 3 | vb | *pour* |
| 120 | זבד | | 1 | 1 | | | 2 | vb | *endow* |
| 121 | זַבְדִּיאֵל | | 2 | | | | 2 | prnm | *Zabdiel* |
| 122 | זְבוּב | | 2 | | | | 2 | nm | *fly* |
| 123 | זָבוּד | | 2 | | | | 2 | prnm | *Zabud* |
| 124 | זַבַּי | | 2 | | | | 2 | prnm | *Zabbai* |
| 125 | זִו | I | 2 | | | | 2 | prnm | *Ziv* |
| 126 | זוֹחֵת | | 2 | | | | 2 | prnm | *Zoheth* |
| 127 | זָוִית | | 2 | | | | 2 | nf | *corner* |
| 128 | זור | III | 1 | 1 | | | 2 | vb | *be abhorrent* |
| 129 | זחח | | 2 | | | | 2 | vb | *displace* |
| 130 | זֵידָה | | | | 2 | | 2 | nf | *presumptuousness* |
| 131 | זִיז | I | 2 | | | | 2 | nm | *moving thing* |
| 132 | זִיז | II | 1 | | 1 | | 2 | n[m] | *teat* |
| 133 | זלל | III | 2 | | | | 2 | vb | *quake* |
| 134 | זָמִיר | II | 1 | | | 1 | 2 | nm | *pruning* |

| Rank | Lemma | | MT | Si | Q | Inscr | Total | Type | Gloss |
|---|---|---|---|---|---|---|---|---|---|
| 135 | זִמְרָן | | 2 | | | | 2 | prnm | *Zimran* |
| 136 | זנב | | 2 | | | | 2 | vb | *cut off rear* |
| 137 | זנח | II | 1 | | 1 | | 2 | vb | *stink* |
| 138 | זעה | | 1 | | 1 | | 2 | vb | *bark* |
| 139 | זַעֲוָן | | 2 | | | | 2 | prnm | *Zaavan* |
| 140 | זעף | II | 2 | | | | 2 | vb | *be thin* |
| 141 | זָעֵף | | 2 | | | | 2 | adj | *angry, upset* |
| 142 | זרה | II | 2 | | | | 2 | vb | *measure* |
| 143 | זֵרוּעַ | | 2 | | | | 2 | n[m] | *sowing* |
| 144 | זִרְמָה | | 2 | | | | 2 | nf | *ejaculate* |
| 145 | זֵרֹעַ | | 1 | | 1 | | 2 | n[m] | *vegetable* |
| 146 | זֵרְעֹן | | 2 | | | | 2 | n[m] | *vegetable* |
| 147 | זֵתָם | | 2 | | | | 2 | prnm | *Zetham* |
| 148 | זְבוּדָה | | 1 | | | | 1 | prnf | *Zebuddah* |
| 149 | זְבִידָה | | 1 | | | | 1 | prnf | *Zebidah* |
| 150 | זְבִינָא | | 1 | | | | 1 | prnm | *Zebina* |
| 151 | זְבִינוּת | | | | 1 | | 1 | nf | *purchase* |
| 152 | זבל | I | 1 | | | | 1 | vb | *exalt* |
| 153 | זְבֻל | II | 1 | | | | 1 | n[m] | *dais* |
| 154 | זָג | | 1 | | | | 1 | nm | *skin, seed, tip* |
| 155 | זְדָה | | | | | 1 | 1 | nf | *fissure* |
| 156 | זָהָב | II | 1 | | | | 1 | n[m] | *spice, incense* |
| 157 | זְהִירָה | | | 1 | | | 1 | nf | *brightness* |
| 158 | זהם | | 1 | | | | 1 | vb | *abhor* |
| 159 | זַהַם | | 1 | | | | 1 | prnm | *Zaham* |
| 160 | זוג | | | | 1 | | 1 | vb | *be joined* |
| 161 | זוּזִי | | 1 | | | | 1 | gent | *Zuzite* |
| 162 | זוח | I | | 1 | | | 1 | vb | *move* |
| 163 | זוח | II | | 1 | | | 1 | vb | *be high* |
| 164 | זוֹחֵלְזָלַף | | | | 1 | | 1 | prnm | *Zohelzalaph* |
| 165 | זול | I | 1 | | | | 1 | vb | *be lavish* |
| 166 | זון | | 1 | | | | 1 | vb | *feed* |
| 167 | זוע | II | 1 | | | | 1 | vb | *stand aside* |
| 168 | זוּרֶה | | 1 | | | | 1 | n[f] | *rotten egg* |
| 169 | זָזָא | | 1 | | | | 1 | prnm | *Zaza* |

## *Words Beginning with Zayin*

| Rank | Lemma | | MT | Si | Q | Inscr | Total | Type | Gloss |
|---|---|---|---|---|---|---|---|---|---|
| 170 | זַחַט | | | | | 1 | 1 | prnm | *Zahat* |
| 171 | זחל | II | 1 | | | | 1 | vb | *fear* |
| 172 | זֵידוֹן | | 1 | | | | 1 | adj | *seething* |
| 173 | זִיזָה | | 1 | | | | 1 | prnm | *Zizah* |
| 174 | זִימְיָא | | | | 1 | | 1 | nf | *penalty* |
| 175 | זִינָא | | 1 | | | | 1 | prnm | *Zina* |
| 176 | זִיעַ | I | | | 1 | | 1 | n[m] | *trembling* |
| 177 | זִיעַ | II | 1 | | | | 1 | prnm | *Zia* |
| 178 | זִיף | II | 1 | | | | 1 | prnm | *Ziph* |
| 179 | זִיפָה | | 1 | | | | 1 | prn | *Ziphah* |
| 180 | זֵיתָן | | 1 | | | | 1 | prnm | *Zethan* |
| 181 | זַכָּא | | | | | 1 | 1 | prn | *Zacca* |
| 182 | זְכוֹכִית | | 1 | | | | 1 | nf | *glass* |
| 183 | זָכוּר | | 1 | | | | 1 | adj | *mindful* |
| 184 | זכר | II | 1 | | | | 1 | vb | *be strong* |
| 185 | זֶכֶר | II | 1 | | | | 1 | prnm | *Zecher* |
| 186 | זְכָרִיאֵל | | | | 1 | | 1 | prn | *Zechariel* |
| 187 | זֻלּוּת | | 1 | | | | 1 | nf | *worthlessness* |
| 188 | זַלְזַל | | 1 | | | | 1 | n[m] | *shoot* |
| 189 | זִלְפָּה | II | | | 1 | | 1 | pln | *Zilpah* |
| 190 | זִמָּה | III | 1 | | | | 1 | nf | *cord* |
| 191 | זְמוֹרָה | II | 1 | | | | 1 | nf | *stench* |
| 192 | זְמוֹרָה | III | 1 | | | | 1 | nf | *band of toughs* |
| 193 | זְמוֹרָה | IV | 1 | | | | 1 | n[f] | *warrior* |
| 194 | זַמְזֻמִּי | | 1 | | | | 1 | gent | *Zamzummite* |
| 195 | זָמִיר | III | 1 | | | | 1 | n[m] | *guardian* |
| 196 | זְמִירָה | | 1 | | | | 1 | prnm | *Zemirah* |
| 197 | זָמָם | | 1 | | | | 1 | n[m] | *plan* |
| 198 | זֶמֶר | II | 1 | | | | 1 | n[m] | *mountain sheep* |
| 199 | זִמְרָה | II | 1 | | | | 1 | nf | *choice produce* |
| 200 | זִמְרִי | II | 1 | | | | 1 | gent | *Zimrite* |
| 201 | זְמַרְיָה | | | | | 1 | 1 | prnm | *Zemariah* |
| 202 | זנה | II | 1 | | | | 1 | vb | *be angry* |
| 203 | זנזח | | | | 1 | | 1 | vb | *reject* |
| 204 | זְנִי | | | | 1 | | 1 | n[m] | *disgrace* |

| Rank | Lemma | | MT | Si | Q | Inscr | Total | Type | Gloss |
|---|---|---|---|---|---|---|---|---|---|
| 205 | זנק | | 1 | | | | 1 | vb | *leap* |
| 206 | זֵעָה | | 1 | | | | 1 | nf | *sweat* |
| 207 | זָעִיר | | | 1 | | | 1 | adj | *little* |
| 208 | זעך | | 1 | | | | 1 | vb | *extinguish* |
| 209 | זְעָמָה | | | | 1 | | 1 | nf | *curse* |
| 210 | זִפְרֹן | | 1 | | | | 1 | pln | *Ziphron* |
| 211 | זָקֵן | II | | | | 1 | 1 | prn | *Zaken* |
| 212 | זֹקֶן | | 1 | | | | 1 | n[m] | *old age* |
| 213 | זרב | | 1 | | | | 1 | vb | *scorch* |
| 214 | זֶרֶב | | | | 1 | | 1 | n[m] | *gutter* |
| 215 | זָרוּת | | 1 | | | | 1 | nf | *strangeness* |
| 216 | זרז | | | 1 | | | 1 | vb | *be strong* |
| 217 | זַרְזִיף | | 1 | | | | 1 | n[m] | *sprinkling* |
| 218 | זַרְזִיר | | 1 | | | | 1 | adj | *strong, girded* |
| 219 | זֶרַח | I | 1 | | | | 1 | nm | *shining* |
| 220 | זרם | II | 1 | | | | 1 | vb | *destroy* |
| 221 | זרק | II | 1 | | | | 1 | vb | *creep up* |
| 222 | זרר | I | 1 | | | | 1 | vb | *sneeze* |
| 223 | זרר | II | 1 | | | | 1 | vb | *squeeze, flow* |
| 224 | זֵתַר | | 1 | | | | 1 | prnm | *Zethar* |

## ח

| Rank | Lemma | | MT | Si | Q | Inscr | Total | Type | Gloss |
|---|---|---|---|---|---|---|---|---|---|
| 1 | חֶרֶב | | 411 | 2 | 55 | | 468 | nf | *sword* |
| 2 | חזק | I | 293 | 13 | 91 | | 397 | vb | *be strong* |
| 3 | חָמֵשׁ | | 344 | | 34 | 2 | 380 | nm & f | *five* |
| 4 | חֹדֶשׁ | I | 281 | 2 | 87 | 8 | 378 | nm | *month* |
| 5 | חֶסֶד | I | 246 | 26 | 104 | 1 | 377 | nm | *loyalty* |
| 6 | חַטָּאת | I | 291 | 5 | 52 | | 348 | nf | *sin* |
| 7 | חַי | I | 249 | 16 | 52 | 2 | 319 | adj | *living* |
| 8 | חַיִל | | 267 | 11 | 32 | 1 | 311 | nm | *power* |

## *Words Beginning with Ḥeth*

| Rank | Lemma | MT | Si | Q | Inscr | Total | Type | Gloss |
|---|---|---|---|---|---|---|---|---|
| 9 | חיה I | 282 | 2 | 19 | | 303 | vb | *live* |
| 10 | חֹק | 129 | 19 | 107 | | 255 | nm | *statute* |
| 11 | חטא | 238 | 5 | 7 | | 250 | vb | *sin* |
| 12 | חַיִּים I | 147 | 39 | 57 | 2 | 245 | nmpl | *life* |
| 13 | חָכְמָה | 153 | 25 | 44 | | 222 | nf | *wisdom* |
| 14 | חָצֵר | 190 | | 19 | | 209 | nm & f | *court* |
| 15 | חֲמִשִּׁים | 165 | | 30 | | 195 | nm & f | *fifty* |
| 16 | חוּץ I | 164 | | 24 | | 188 | n[m] | *outside* |
| 17 | חשׁב | 123 | 10 | 55 | | 188 | vb | *think* |
| 18 | חָכָם | 138 | 20 | 14 | | 172 | adj | *wise* |
| 19 | חנה I | 143 | 3 | 7 | | 153 | vb | *encamp* |
| 20 | חֵמָה I | 125 | 2 | 23 | | 150 | nf | *anger* |
| 21 | חוֹמָה | 133 | | 11 | | 144 | nf | *wall* |
| 22 | חֹשֶׁךְ | 80 | 2 | 57 | | 139 | nm | *darkness* |
| 23 | חֲצִי | 126 | | 9 | 3 | 138 | nm | *half* |
| 24 | חִזְקִיָּהוּ | 125 | 2 | 3 | 4 | 134 | prnm | *Hezekiah* |
| 25 | חָלָל I | 91 | 1 | 41 | | 133 | nm | *slain one* |
| 26 | חַיָּה I | 96 | 3 | 23 | | 122 | nf | *beast* |
| 27 | חֻקָּה | 100 | | 19 | | 119 | nf | *statute* |
| 28 | חֵלֶב I | 91 | 2 | 20 | | 113 | nm | *fat* |
| 29 | חרה I | 96 | 4 | 13 | | 113 | vb | *burn* |
| 30 | חנן I | 78 | 4 | 26 | 1 | 109 | vb | *be gracious* |
| 31 | חפץ I | 86 | 7 | 12 | | 105 | vb | *desire* |
| 32 | חֲמוֹר I | 96 | 1 | 5 | 1 | 103 | nm & f | *ass* |
| 33 | חלל I | 79 | 3 | 17 | | 99 | vb | *profane* |
| 34 | חֶרְפָּה I | 73 | 9 | 13 | | 95 | nf | *reproach* |
| 35 | חַג | 62 | 1 | 26 | | 89 | nm | *festival* |
| 36 | חֵפֶץ I | 40 | 8 | 39 | | 87 | nm | *desire* |
| 37 | חָמָס | 60 | 10 | 15 | | 85 | nm | *violence* |
| 38 | חֵן I | 69 | 11 | 3 | | 83 | nm | *favour* |
| 39 | חָדָשׁ | 53 | 3 | 26 | | 82 | adj | *new* |
| 40 | חֲצוֹצְרָה | 29 | 1 | 51 | | 81 | nf | *trumpet* |
| 41 | חֵלֶק I | 66 | 6 | 7 | | 79 | nm | *portion* |
| 42 | חלק I | 56 | 10 | 9 | | 75 | vb | *divide* |
| 43 | חָרוֹן | 41 | 2 | 32 | | 75 | nm | *burning* |

| Rank | Lemma | | MT | Si | Q | Inscr | Total | Type | Gloss |
|---|---|---|---|---|---|---|---|---|---|
| 44 | חֲלוֹם | | 65 | 2 | 5 | | 72 | nm | *dream* |
| 45 | חזה | I | 59 | 6 | 4 | | 69 | vb | *see* |
| 46 | חֶבְרוֹן | I | 63 | | | 5 | 68 | pln | *Hebron* |
| 47 | חָזָק | I | 57 | 3 | 7 | | 67 | adj | *strong* |
| 48 | חֲמִישִׁי | | 34 | | 33 | | 67 | adj | *fifth* |
| 49 | חדל | I | 59 | 3 | 4 | | 66 | vb | *cease* |
| 50 | חלל | II | 54 | | 12 | | 66 | vb | *begin* |
| 51 | חלה | I | 59 | | 5 | | 64 | vb | *be weak* |
| 52 | חֲנַנְיָה | | 28 | | 3 | 33 | 64 | prn | *Hananiah* |
| 53 | חרם | I | 51 | 1 | 9 | | 61 | vb | *destroy* |
| 54 | חתת | I | 57 | | 3 | | 60 | vb | *be shattered* |
| 55 | חֵץ | | 53 | 1 | 5 | | 59 | nm | *arrow* |
| 56 | חֶ֫דֶר | | 38 | 1 | 15 | 2 | 56 | nm | *chamber* |
| 57 | חֲנִית | | 47 | 1 | 7 | | 55 | nf | *spear* |
| 58 | חרשׁ | II | 47 | 5 | 3 | | 55 | vb | *be silent* |
| 59 | חֶ֫בֶל | I | 51 | | 3 | | 54 | mn | *rope, territory, band* |
| 60 | חיל | I | 46 | 3 | 3 | | 52 | vb | *be in pain* |
| 61 | חמל | | 41 | 4 | 7 | | 52 | vb | *spare* |
| 62 | חבר | I | 31 | 10 | 9 | | 50 | vb | *join* |
| 63 | חִלְקִיָּ֫הוּ | | 34 | | | 16 | 50 | prnm | *Hilkiah* |
| 64 | חָלָב | | 44 | 2 | 3 | | 49 | nm | *milk* |
| 65 | חפר | I | 22 | | 27 | | 49 | vb | *search* |
| 66 | חִתִּי | | 48 | | 1 | | 49 | gent | *Hittite* |
| 67 | חָזוֹן | I | 35 | 2 | 11 | | 48 | nm | *vision* |
| 68 | חִטָּה | | 30 | | 13 | 5 | 48 | nf | *wheat* |
| 69 | חֵטְא | | 33 | 5 | 8 | | 46 | nm | *sin* |
| 70 | חֵיק | | 38 | 1 | 7 | | 46 | nm | *fold* |
| 71 | חכם | | 28 | 15 | 3 | | 46 | vb | *be wise* |
| 72 | חגר | | 44 | | 1 | | 45 | vb | *gird* |
| 73 | חָרְבָּה | | 41 | 1 | 3 | | 45 | nf | *waste* |
| 74 | חרף | I | 39 | 3 | 2 | 1 | 45 | vb | *reproach* |
| 75 | חרב | I | 37 | 1 | 6 | | 44 | vb | *be dry, desolate* |
| 76 | חָרָשׁ | | 37 | 1 | 6 | | 44 | nm | *artisan* |
| 77 | חקר | I | 27 | 8 | 8 | | 43 | vb | *search* |
| 78 | חבא | | 34 | | 8 | | 42 | vb | *hide* |

# *Words Beginning with Ḥeth*

| Rank | Lemma | | MT | Si | Q | Inscr | Total | Type | Gloss |
|---|---|---|---|---|---|---|---|---|---|
| 79 | חסה | | 37 | 2 | 3 | | 42 | vb | *seek refuge* |
| 80 | חָסִיד | | 32 | 1 | 9 | | 42 | adj | *loyal* |
| 81 | חתם | | 28 | | 12 | 2 | 42 | vb | *seal* |
| 82 | חרד | I | 39 | | 2 | | 41 | vb | *tremble* |
| 83 | חקק | | 19 | 1 | 19 | | 39 | vb | *engrave* |
| 84 | חֵ֫רֶם | I | 29 | 2 | 7 | | 38 | nm | *devoted object* |
| 85 | חֶשְׁבּוֹן | II | 38 | | | | 38 | pln | *Heshbon* |
| 86 | חלף | I | 28 | 5 | 4 | | 37 | vb | *pass* |
| 87 | חִנָּם | | 32 | 1 | 4 | | 37 | adv | *for nothing* |
| 88 | חסר | | 25 | 6 | 6 | | 37 | vb | *lack* |
| 89 | חבשׁ | | 33 | | 3 | | 36 | vb | *bind* |
| 90 | חֲמָת | | 36 | | | | 36 | pln | *Hamath* |
| 91 | חַלּוֹן | | 31 | 1 | 2 | | 34 | nm | *window* |
| 92 | חרשׁ | I | 27 | 4 | 3 | | 34 | vb | *plough* |
| 93 | חִירָם | | 33 | | | | 33 | prnm | *Hiram* |
| 94 | חמד | | 21 | 3 | 8 | | 32 | vb | *desire* |
| 95 | חָסֵר | | 16 | 9 | 6 | 1 | 32 | adj | *lacking* |
| 96 | חִיצוֹן | | 25 | | 5 | 1 | 31 | adj | *outer* |
| 97 | חלם | I | 26 | | 5 | | 31 | vb | *dream* |
| 98 | חֹ֫מֶר | I | 17 | 1 | 13 | | 31 | nm | *clay* |
| 99 | חצב | I | 25 | 1 | 1 | 4 | 31 | vb | *hew* |
| 100 | חשׂך | I | 28 | 2 | 1 | | 31 | vb | *withhold* |
| 101 | חֳלִי | | 24 | 3 | 3 | | 30 | nm | *sickness* |
| 102 | חֹ֫שֶׁן | | 25 | 2 | 2 | | 29 | nm | *breastpiece* |
| 103 | חוס | | 25 | | 2 | | 27 | vb | *pity* |
| 104 | חושׁ | I | 19 | 2 | 6 | | 27 | vb | *hasten* |
| 105 | חלץ | I | 23 | | 4 | | 27 | vb | *loosen* |
| 106 | חִוִּי | | 25 | | 1 | | 26 | gent | *Hivvite* |
| 107 | חול | I | 23 | 2 | 1 | | 26 | nm | *sand* |
| 108 | חמם | | 26 | | | | 26 | vb | *be warm* |
| 109 | חפשׂ | I | 23 | | 2 | | 25 | vb | *search* |
| 110 | חֵ֫קֶר | | 12 | 2 | 11 | | 25 | nm | *searching* |
| 111 | חִידָה | | 17 | 2 | 5 | | 24 | nf | *riddle* |
| 112 | חָלָק | I | 10 | | 14 | | 24 | adj | *smooth* |
| 113 | חֶלְקָה | I | 23 | | 1 | | 24 | nf | *plot of land* |

| Rank | Lemma | | MT | Si | Q | Inscr | Total | Type | Gloss |
|---|---|---|---|---|---|---|---|---|---|
| 114 | חֶ֫בֶר | I | 3 | | 6 | 14 | 23 | n[m] | *company* |
| 115 | חדשׁ | I | 10 | 2 | 11 | | 23 | vb | *renew* |
| 116 | חֲזָאֵל | | 23 | | | | 23 | prn | *Hazael* |
| 117 | חלה | V | 20 | 2 | 1 | | 23 | vb | *be alone* |
| 118 | חלץ | II | 21 | | 2 | | 23 | vb | *equip (for war)* |
| 119 | חָנָן | | 12 | | | 11 | 23 | prnm | *Hanan* |
| 120 | חוֹתָם | I | 14 | 4 | 2 | 2 | 22 | nm | *seal* |
| 121 | חֵךְ | I | 18 | 3 | 1 | | 22 | nm | *palate* |
| 122 | חֶמְדָּה | | 17 | 1 | 4 | | 22 | nf | *desire* |
| 123 | חרץ | | 11 | | 11 | | 22 | vb | *decide* |
| 124 | חכה | | 14 | | 7 | | 21 | vb | *wait* |
| 125 | חָלִ֫ילָה | | 21 | | | | 21 | interj | *may it not be* |
| 126 | חֶ֫רֶשׂ | | 17 | | 4 | | 21 | nm | *pot* |
| 127 | חֹתֵן | | 21 | | | | 21 | nm | *father-in-law* |
| 128 | חֹזֶה | I | 16 | 1 | 3 | | 20 | nm | *seer* |
| 129 | חַטָּא | | 19 | | 1 | | 20 | nm & adj | *sinner, sinful* |
| 130 | חֹ֫רֶב | I | 16 | 4 | | | 20 | nm | *dryness, desolation* |
| 131 | חשׁה | | 16 | 2 | 2 | | 20 | vb | *be silent* |
| 132 | חָתָן | | 20 | | | | 20 | nm | *bridegroom* |
| 133 | חגג | | 16 | | 3 | | 19 | vb | *celebrate festival* |
| 134 | חַגַּי | | 11 | | | 8 | 19 | prnm | *Haggai* |
| 135 | חלה | II | 16 | 2 | 1 | | 19 | vb | *entreat* |
| 136 | חֲנוֹךְ | I | 16 | 1 | 2 | | 19 | prnm | *Enoch, Hanoch* |
| 137 | חָצִיר | I | 18 | 1 | | | 19 | nm | *grass* |
| 138 | חַלָּה | | 14 | | 4 | | 18 | nf | *cake* |
| 139 | חַנָּה | | 13 | | 3 | 2 | 18 | prnf | *Hannah* |
| 140 | חפר | II | 17 | 1 | | | 18 | vb | *be ashamed* |
| 141 | חֹרֵב | | 17 | 1 | | | 18 | pln | *Horeb* |
| 142 | חשׁך | | 17 | | 1 | | 18 | vb | *be dark* |
| 143 | חֵבֶל | | 9 | | 8 | | 17 | nm | *labour pains* |
| 144 | חָזֶה | I | 13 | | 4 | | 17 | nm | *breast* |
| 145 | חָנֵף | I | 13 | 3 | 1 | | 17 | adj | *profane* |
| 146 | חָפְשִׁי | | 17 | | | | 17 | adj | *free* |
| 147 | חָרָן | I | 10 | | 7 | | 17 | pln | *Haran* |
| 148 | חֲלִיפָה | I | 12 | 1 | 3 | | 16 | nf | *change* |

## *Words Beginning with Ḥeth*

| Rank | Lemma | | MT | Si | Q | Inscr | Total | Type | Gloss |
|---|---|---|---|---|---|---|---|---|---|
| 149 | חצה | I | 14 | | 2 | | 16 | vb | *divide* |
| 150 | חָצוֹר | I | 16 | | | | 16 | pln | *Hazor* |
| 151 | חֶצְרוֹן | I | 16 | | | | 16 | prnm | *Hezron* |
| 152 | חבל | II | 11 | 1 | 3 | | 15 | vb | *act corruptly* |
| 153 | חָבֵר | | 12 | 3 | | | 15 | nm | *companion* |
| 154 | חָם | I | 12 | | 3 | | 15 | prnm | *Ham* |
| 155 | חַנּוּן | | 13 | | 2 | | 15 | adj | *gracious* |
| 156 | חָרִם | | 11 | | 4 | | 15 | prnm | *Harim* |
| 157 | חֲשַׁבְיָה | | 15 | | | | 15 | prnm | *Hashabiah* |
| 158 | חבק | | 13 | 1 | | | 14 | vb | *embrace* |
| 159 | חוּר | I | 14 | | | | 14 | prn | *Hur* |
| 160 | חוּשַׁי | | 14 | | | | 14 | prnm | *Hushai* |
| 161 | חֵזִיר | | 2 | | 11 | 1 | 14 | prnm | *Hezir* |
| 162 | חַיָּה | II | 12 | 1 | 1 | | 14 | nf | *life* |
| 163 | חֹם | | 6 | 1 | 6 | 1 | 14 | nm | *heat* |
| 164 | חָמֵץ | | 11 | | 3 | | 14 | adj | *leavened* |
| 165 | חֹמֶר | II | 12 | | | 2 | 14 | nm | *homer* |
| 166 | חֹר | I | 13 | 1 | | | 14 | nm | *noble* |
| 167 | חֶרְמוֹן | | 14 | | | | 14 | pln | *Hermon* |
| 168 | חרת | | 1 | 1 | 12 | | 14 | vb | *engrave* |
| 169 | חשק | | 11 | 2 | 1 | | 14 | vb | *desire* |
| 170 | חֵת | | 14 | | | | 14 | prnm | *Heth* |
| 171 | חבל | I | 13 | | | | 13 | vb | *take in pledge* |
| 172 | חֶלֶץ | | 5 | | | 8 | 13 | prnm | *Helez* |
| 173 | חֲמוֹר | II | 13 | | | | 13 | prnm | *Hamor* |
| 174 | חֲמִישִׁית | | 11 | | 2 | | 13 | nf | *fifth* |
| 175 | חֲנָנִי | | 12 | | | 1 | 13 | prnm | *Hanani* |
| 176 | חשׂף | I | 11 | 2 | | | 13 | vb | *make bare* |
| 177 | חֵל | | 9 | | 3 | | 12 | nm | *rampart* |
| 178 | חלק | II | 10 | | 2 | | 12 | vb | *be smooth* |
| 179 | חפה | | 12 | | | | 12 | vb | *cover* |
| 180 | חפז | | 9 | | 3 | | 12 | vb | *hurry* |
| 181 | חַרְטֹם | | 11 | | 1 | | 12 | nm | *magician* |
| 182 | חֵרֶם | II | 9 | | 3 | | 12 | nm | *net* |
| 183 | חֵרֵשׁ | | 9 | | 3 | | 12 | adj | *deaf* |

| Rank | Lemma | | MT | Si | Q | Inscr | Total | Type | Gloss |
|---|---|---|---|---|---|---|---|---|---|
| 184 | חֶבֶר | III | 11 | | | | 11 | prnm | *Heber* |
| 185 | חַד | I | 4 | | 7 | | 11 | adj | *sharp* |
| 186 | חוֹחַ | I | 11 | | | | 11 | nm | *thorn, hook* |
| 187 | חֹזֶק | | 5 | 2 | 4 | | 11 | nm | *strength* |
| 188 | חָלִיל | | 6 | 1 | 4 | | 11 | nm | *flute* |
| 189 | חֶמְאָה | | 11 | | | | 11 | nf | *curd* |
| 190 | חֲמֻדוֹת | | 9 | 1 | 1 | | 11 | nfpl | *preciousness* |
| 191 | חָמוֹת | | 11 | | | | 11 | nf | *mother-in-law* |
| 192 | חָנוּן | | 11 | | | | 11 | prnm | *Hanun* |
| 193 | חנף | I | 11 | | | | 11 | vb | *be polluted* |
| 194 | חָרֵב | | 10 | | 1 | | 11 | adj | *dry, desolate* |
| 195 | חתן | | 11 | | | | 11 | vb | *marry* |
| 196 | חַטָּאָה | | 2 | | 8 | | 10 | nf | *sin* |
| 197 | חכר | I | | | 10 | | 10 | vb | *rent* |
| 198 | חֲלָצַיִם | | 10 | | | | 10 | n[f]du | *loins* |
| 199 | חמס | I | 8 | 1 | 1 | | 10 | vb | *be violent* |
| 200 | חֻפָּה | II | 1 | | 9 | | 10 | prnm | *Huppah* |
| 201 | חֲצֵרוֹת | | 6 | | | 4 | 10 | pln | *Hazeroth* |
| 202 | חָרָבָה | | 8 | | 2 | | 10 | nf | *dry land* |
| 203 | חרר | | 10 | | | | 10 | vb | *burn* |
| 204 | חֶשְׁבּוֹן | I | 3 | 5 | 2 | | 10 | nm | *reckoning* |
| 205 | חוה | I | 6 | 2 | 1 | | 9 | vb | *declare* |
| 206 | חוּט | | 7 | | 2 | | 9 | nm | *thread* |
| 207 | חול | I | 8 | | 1 | | 9 | vb | *whirl* |
| 208 | חִזָּיוֹן | | 9 | | | | 9 | nm | *vision* |
| 209 | חטב | | 9 | | | | 9 | vb | *cut* |
| 210 | חֹל | | 7 | | 2 | | 9 | n[m] | *profaneness* |
| 211 | חֲרָדָה | I | 9 | | | | 9 | nf | *trembling* |
| 212 | חָרְמָה | | 9 | | | | 9 | pln | *Hormah* |
| 213 | חֵשֶׁב | | 8 | | 1 | | 9 | nm | *girdle* |
| 214 | חֶבֶר | II | 6 | | 2 | | 8 | nm | *noise, spell* |
| 215 | חֶבְרוֹן | II | 8 | | | | 8 | prnm | *Hebron* |
| 216 | חַטָּאָה | | 8 | | | | 8 | nf | *sin* |
| 217 | חֵלְכָה | | 3 | | 5 | | 8 | adj | *wretched wicked* |
| 218 | חלל | III | 8 | | | | 8 | vb | *be pierced* |

## *Words Beginning with Ḥeth*

| Rank | Lemma | | MT | Si | Q | Inscr | Total | Type | Gloss |
|---|---|---|---|---|---|---|---|---|---|
| 219 | חֶמֶד | | 6 | | 2 | | 8 | n[m] | *desire* |
| 220 | חַמָּן | | 8 | | | | 8 | nm | *incense altar* |
| 221 | חֹמֶץ | | 6 | | 1 | 1 | 8 | nm | *vinegar* |
| 222 | חֲנֻכָּה | | 8 | | | | 8 | nf | *dedication* |
| 223 | חֹסֶר | | 3 | 3 | 2 | | 8 | n[m] | *lack* |
| 224 | חֵפֶר | II | 7 | | | 1 | 8 | prnm | *Hepher* |
| 225 | חָרוּץ | I | 6 | 2 | | | 8 | nm | *gold* |
| 226 | חֹרֶף | I | 6 | | 2 | | 8 | nm | *winter* |
| 227 | חרק | I | 5 | | 3 | | 8 | vb | *gnash* |
| 228 | חָשׁוּק | | 8 | | | | 8 | nm | *band* |
| 229 | חִתִּית | | 8 | | | | 8 | nf | *terror* |
| 230 | חתר | | 8 | | | | 8 | vb | *dig* |
| 231 | חבה | | 5 | | 2 | | 7 | vb | *hide* |
| 232 | חַבּוּרָה | | 7 | | | | 7 | nf | *blow* |
| 233 | חֶבֶל | II | 2 | | 5 | | 7 | nm | *destruction* |
| 234 | חָגָב | I | 5 | | 2 | | 7 | nm | *locust* |
| 235 | חדד | | 6 | | 1 | | 7 | vb | *be sharp* |
| 236 | חַוָּה | I | 7 | | | | 7 | nf | *tent village* |
| 237 | חוֹף | | 7 | | | | 7 | n[m] | *shore* |
| 238 | חֲזִיר | | 7 | | | | 7 | nm | *swine* |
| 239 | חָח | | 7 | | | | 7 | nm | *hook* |
| 240 | חַלָּמִישׁ | | 5 | | 2 | | 7 | nm | *flint* |
| 241 | חַמָּה | | 6 | 1 | | | 7 | nf | *heat, sun* |
| 242 | חָסִיל | | 6 | | 1 | | 7 | nm | *locust* |
| 243 | חֹסֶן | | 5 | | 2 | | 7 | nm | *wealth* |
| 244 | חֹר | II | 7 | | | | 7 | n[m] | *hole* |
| 245 | חֹרִי | II | 7 | | | | 7 | gent | *Horite* |
| 246 | חֳרִי | | 6 | | 1 | | 7 | nm | *heat* |
| 247 | חבט | I | 5 | 1 | | | 6 | vb | *beat (out)* |
| 248 | חבר | II | 3 | 1 | 2 | | 6 | vb | *mutter* |
| 249 | חֶבְרוֹנִי | | 6 | | | | 6 | gent | *Hebronite* |
| 250 | חַגִּית | | 5 | | | 1 | 6 | prnf | *Haggith* |
| 251 | חוב | | 1 | 1 | 4 | | 6 | vb | *be guilty* |
| 252 | חַטּוּשׁ | | 5 | | | 1 | 6 | prnm | *Hattush* |
| 253 | חיל | II | 5 | | 1 | | 6 | vb | *wait* |

| Rank | Lemma | | MT | Si | Q | Inscr | Total | Type | Gloss |
|---|---|---|---|---|---|---|---|---|---|
| 254 | חִיל | | 6 | | | | 6 | nm | *pain, birth* |
| 255 | חַלְחָלָה | | 4 | | 2 | | 6 | nf | *anguish* |
| 256 | חלם | II | 2 | 2 | 2 | | 6 | vb | *be healthy* |
| 257 | חֵ֫לֶק | II | 2 | | | 4 | 6 | prnm | *Helek* |
| 258 | חֲסִידָה | | 6 | | | | 6 | nf | *stork* |
| 259 | חֹ֫פֶן | | 6 | | | | 6 | nm | *hollow of hand* |
| 260 | חצצר | | 6 | | | | 6 | vb | *sound trumpet* |
| 261 | חָרֵד | | 6 | | | | 6 | adj | *trembling* |
| 262 | חֲשֵׁכָה | | 6 | | | | 6 | nf | *darkness* |
| 263 | חבב | I | 1 | 2 | 2 | | 5 | vb | *love* |
| 264 | חֹבֵל | | 5 | | | | 5 | nm | *sailor* |
| 265 | חָגָב | II | 1 | | | 4 | 5 | prnm | *Hagab* |
| 266 | חֲגוֹרָה | | 5 | | | | 5 | nf | *belt* |
| 267 | חוּג | | 3 | 1 | 1 | | 5 | n[m] | *circle* |
| 268 | חֲוִילָה | II | 5 | | | | 5 | pln | *Havilah* |
| 269 | חָזוּת | I | 4 | 1 | | | 5 | nf | *vision* |
| 270 | חֲזִיז | I | 3 | 2 | | | 5 | n[m] | *thunderstorm* |
| 271 | חֶזְקָה | | 4 | | 1 | | 5 | nf | *strength* |
| 272 | חָזְקָה | | 5 | | | | 5 | nf | *strength* |
| 273 | חָכְמוֹת | | 4 | 1 | | | 5 | nf | *wisdom* |
| 274 | חֶלְאָה | I | 5 | | | | 5 | nf | *rust* |
| 275 | חֶ֫לֶד | | 5 | | | | 5 | n[m] | *duration, world* |
| 276 | חלה | IV | 5 | | | | 5 | vb | *be anxious* |
| 277 | חֵלֹן | | 5 | | | | 5 | prnm | *Helon* |
| 278 | חֶלֶצְיָ֫הוּ | | | | | 5 | 5 | prnm | *Heleziah* |
| 279 | חָם | III | 4 | 1 | | | 5 | nm | *father-in-law* |
| 280 | חמר | I | 4 | 1 | | | 5 | vb | *foam* |
| 281 | חמשׁ | | 5 | | | | 5 | vb | *be five* |
| 282 | חָנִין | | | | 4 | 1 | 5 | prnm | *Hanin* |
| 283 | חנך | | 5 | | | | 5 | vb | *dedicate, train* |
| 284 | חָפְנִי | | 5 | | | | 5 | prnm | *Hophni* |
| 285 | חקה | | 4 | | 1 | | 5 | vb | *carve* |
| 286 | חרד | III | 5 | | | | 5 | vb | *separate* |
| 287 | חָרוּץ | VI | 5 | | | | 5 | adj | *diligent* |
| 288 | חַשּׁוּב | | 5 | | | | 5 | prnm | *Hasshub* |

## *Words Beginning with Ḥeth*

| Rank | Lemma | | MT | Si | Q | Inscr | Total | Type | Gloss |
|---|---|---|---|---|---|---|---|---|---|
| 289 | חָשֻׁם | | 5 | | | | 5 | prnm | *Hashum* |
| 290 | חֻשָׁתִי | | 5 | | | | 5 | gent | *Hushathite* |
| 291 | חתה | I | 4 | | 1 | | 5 | vb | *take* |
| 292 | חֹבֶרֶת | | 4 | | | | 4 | nf | *series* |
| 293 | חָגְלָה | I | 4 | | | | 4 | prnf | *Hoglah* |
| 294 | חדה | II | 4 | | | | 4 | vb | *see* |
| 295 | חָדֵל | | 4 | | | | 4 | adj | *ceasing* |
| 296 | חוד | | 4 | | | | 4 | vb | *propound a riddle* |
| 297 | חֲוִילָה | I | 4 | | | | 4 | prnm | *Havilah* |
| 298 | חוּם | | 4 | | | | 4 | adj | *brown* |
| 299 | חוֹנִי | | | | 4 | | 4 | prnm | *Honi* |
| 300 | חזה | II | 4 | | | | 4 | vb | *be opposite* |
| 301 | חטף | | 4 | | | | 4 | vb | *seize* |
| 302 | חֹטֶר | | 2 | 1 | 1 | | 4 | nm | *shoot* |
| 303 | חיל | IV | 3 | 1 | | | 4 | vb | *take heed* |
| 304 | חַיִץ | | 1 | | 3 | | 4 | nm | *wall* |
| 305 | חִירָה | II | 3 | | 1 | | 4 | nf | *court* |
| 306 | חֶלְדַּי | | 2 | | | 2 | 4 | prnm | *Heldai* |
| 307 | חָלָל | II | 4 | | | | 4 | adj | *profane* |
| 308 | חֲלַקְלַקּוֹת | I | 4 | | | | 4 | nfpl | *smoothness* |
| 309 | חַם | | 2 | | 2 | | 4 | adj | *hot* |
| 310 | חָם | II | 4 | | | | 4 | pln | *Ham* |
| 311 | חמץ | I | 4 | | | | 4 | vb | *be sour* |
| 312 | חֶמֶר | | 2 | 2 | | | 4 | n[m] | *wine* |
| 313 | חֹמֶשׁ | II | 4 | | | | 4 | n[m] | *abdomen* |
| 314 | חֵנָדָד | | 4 | | | | 4 | prnm | *Henadad* |
| 315 | חֲנַמְאֵל | | 4 | | | | 4 | prnm | *Hanamel* |
| 316 | חֲנַנְאֵל | I | 4 | | | | 4 | pln | *Hananel* |
| 317 | חנף | III | 4 | | | | 4 | vb | *be outraged* |
| 318 | חֶסֶד | II | 2 | 1 | 1 | | 4 | nm | *shame* |
| 319 | חֹסָה | I | 4 | | | | 4 | prnm | *Hosah* |
| 320 | חסם | | 2 | 1 | 1 | | 4 | vb | *stop up* |
| 321 | חֻפָּה | I | 3 | 1 | | | 4 | nf | *shelter* |
| 322 | חֵצִי | I | 4 | | | | 4 | nm | *arrow* |
| 323 | חֲצַר עֵינוֹן | | 4 | | | | 4 | pln | *Hazar-enon* |

| Rank | Lemma | | MT | Si | Q | Inscr | Total | Type | Gloss |
|---|---|---|---|---|---|---|---|---|---|
| 324 | חֲצַר שׁוּעָל | | 4 | | | | 4 | pln | *Hazar-shual* |
| 325 | חרב | II | 4 | | | | 4 | vb | *destroy* |
| 326 | חָרוּל | | 3 | | 1 | | 4 | nm | *nettles, thistles* |
| 327 | חֹרוֹנַ֫יִם | | 4 | | | | 4 | pln | *Horonaim* |
| 328 | חָרוּץ | II | 4 | | | | 4 | nm | *threshing sledge* |
| 329 | חֹ֫רֶשׁ | II | 4 | | | | 4 | pln | *Horesh* |
| 330 | חֲרֹ֫שֶׁת | | 4 | | | | 4 | nf | *carving* |
| 331 | חֻשָׁם | | 4 | | | | 4 | prnm | *Husham* |
| 332 | חֵ֫שֶׁק | | 4 | | | | 4 | nm | *desire* |
| 333 | חתף | | 1 | 1 | 2 | | 4 | vb | *snatch away* |
| 334 | חָבוֹר | | 3 | | | | 3 | pln | *Habor* |
| 335 | חבל | III | 3 | | | | 3 | vb | *be pregnant with* |
| 336 | חֲבֹל | | 3 | | | | 3 | nm | *pledge* |
| 337 | חֲבַקּוּק | | 2 | | 1 | | 3 | prnm | *Habakkuk* |
| 338 | חָגוּ | | 3 | | | | 3 | nm | *cleft* |
| 339 | חֲגוֹר | | 3 | | | | 3 | n[m] | *belt* |
| 340 | חָגְלָה | II | | | | 3 | 3 | pln | *Hoglah* |
| 341 | חדה | I | 3 | | | | 3 | vb | *rejoice* |
| 342 | חֶדְוָה | | 3 | | | | 3 | nf | *joy* |
| 343 | חָדִיד | | 3 | | | | 3 | pln | *Hadid* |
| 344 | חדל | II | 3 | | | | 3 | vb | *be fat* |
| 345 | חוּל ׳ | | 2 | | 1 | | 3 | prnm | *Hul* |
| 346 | חוּר | II | 2 | | 1 | | 3 | n[m] | *white* |
| 347 | חָזֶה | II | 3 | | | | 3 | adj | *prominent* |
| 348 | חִטָּא | | | | 3 | | 3 | prnm | *Hitta* |
| 349 | חַיָּה | III | 3 | | | | 3 | nf | *troop* |
| 350 | חַכָּה | | 3 | | | | 3 | nf | *fish-hook* |
| 351 | חֲכִילָה | | 3 | | | | 3 | pln | *Hachilah* |
| 352 | חָכִיר | | | | 3 | | 3 | n[m] | *rent* |
| 353 | חֲלַח | | 3 | | | | 3 | pln | *Halah* |
| 354 | חֹלֹן | | 3 | | | | 3 | pln | *Holon* |
| 355 | חלף | II | 2 | 1 | | | 3 | vb | *pierce through* |
| 356 | חֵ֫לֶק | III | | | | 3 | 3 | pln | *Helek* |
| 357 | חֲמוּטַל | | 3 | | | | 3 | prnf | *Hamutal* |
| 358 | חָמוּל | | 3 | | | | 3 | prnm | *Hamul* |

# *Words Beginning with Ḥeth*

| Rank | Lemma | | MT | Si | Q | Inscr | Total | Type | Gloss |
|---|---|---|---|---|---|---|---|---|---|
| 359 | חֲמִיטַל | | 3 | | | | 3 | prnf | *Hamital* |
| 360 | חֵמָר | | 3 | | | | 3 | n[m] | *bitumen* |
| 361 | חֹמֶשׁ | I | 1 | | 2 | | 3 | n[m] | *fifth* |
| 362 | חֵמֶת | | 3 | | | | 3 | n[m] | *skin (bottle)* |
| 363 | חנט | I | 3 | | | | 3 | vb | *embalm* |
| 364 | חֲנִינָה | | 1 | | 2 | | 3 | nf | *grace, favour* |
| 365 | חנק | | 2 | | 1 | | 3 | vb | *strangle* |
| 366 | חֲסַדְיָה | | 1 | | | 2 | 3 | prnm | *Hasadiah* |
| 367 | חִפָּזוֹן | | 3 | | | | 3 | nm | *haste* |
| 368 | חֻפִּים | | 3 | | | | 3 | prnm | *Huppim* |
| 369 | חֲצוֹת | | 3 | | | | 3 | nf | *middle* |
| 370 | חָצִיר | II | 3 | | | | 3 | n[m] | *reed* |
| 371 | חֹצֶן | I | 3 | | | | 3 | nm | *fold* |
| 372 | חצץ | | 3 | | | | 3 | vb | *divide* |
| 373 | חֲצַר סוּסָה | | 2 | | | 1 | 3 | pln | *Hazar-susa* |
| 374 | חֶרֶא | | 3 | | | | 3 | n[m] | *dung* |
| 375 | חַרְחוּר | I | 1 | 1 | 1 | | 3 | nm | *burning* |
| 376 | חֶרֶט | | 2 | | 1 | | 3 | nm | *stylus* |
| 377 | חֹרִי | I | 3 | | | | 3 | prnm | *Hori* |
| 378 | חָרִישׁ | | 3 | | | | 3 | nm | *ploughing* |
| 379 | חַרְצֻבָּה | | 2 | | 1 | | 3 | nf | *fetter* |
| 380 | חֹרֶשׁ | I | 3 | | | | 3 | nm | *wood* |
| 381 | חֲרֹשֶׁת הַגּוֹיִם | | 3 | | | | 3 | pln | *Harosheth-ha-goiim* |
| 382 | חִשָּׁבוֹן | | 2 | | 1 | | 3 | nm | *device* |
| 383 | חַשְׁמַל | | 3 | | | | 3 | nm | *amber* |
| 384 | חתה | II | 3 | | | | 3 | vb | *kindle* |
| 385 | חֶתֶף | | 1 | 2 | | | 3 | nm | *robber* |
| 386 | חֹבָב | | 2 | | | | 2 | prnm | *Hobab* |
| 387 | חֲבַיָּה | | 2 | | | | 2 | prnm | *Habaiah* |
| 388 | חבל | IV | 1 | 1 | | | 2 | vb | *bind* |
| 389 | חֹבְלִים | | 2 | | | | 2 | n[m] | *union* |
| 390 | חֲבַצֶּלֶת | | 2 | | | | 2 | nf | *asphodel* |
| 391 | חִבֻּק | | 2 | | | | 2 | n[m] | *folding* |
| 392 | חֲבֶרֶת | | 1 | | 1 | | 2 | nf | *companion* |
| 393 | חֲגָבָה | | 2 | | | | 2 | prnm | *Hagabah* |

| Rank | Lemma | | MT | Si | Q | Inscr | Total | Type | Gloss |
|---|---|---|---|---|---|---|---|---|---|
| 394 | חַגִּי | I | 2 | | | | 2 | prnm | *Haggi* |
| 395 | חֲדַד | | 2 | | | | 2 | prnm | *Hadad* |
| 396 | חַדּוּד | | 1 | | 1 | | 2 | adj | *sharp* |
| 397 | חֶדֶל | | 2 | | | | 2 | n[m] | *world, duration* |
| 398 | חֵדֶק | | 2 | | | | 2 | n[m] | *brier* |
| 399 | חִדֶּקֶל | | 2 | | | | 2 | pln | *Tigris* |
| 400 | חדר | I | 1 | 1 | | | 2 | vb | *surround* |
| 401 | חֲדַר | | 2 | | | | 2 | prnm | *Hadar* |
| 402 | חַוָּה | II | 2 | | | | 2 | prnf | *Eve* |
| 403 | חוֹטֶא | | 2 | | | | 2 | n[m] | *sin* |
| 404 | חוּקֹק | | 2 | | | | 2 | pln | *Hukok* |
| 405 | חור | I | 1 | | 1 | | 2 | vb | *be white* |
| 406 | חור | III | 1 | | 1 | | 2 | vb | *turn* |
| 407 | חַוְרָן | | 2 | | | | 2 | pln | *Hauran* |
| 408 | חוש | II | 2 | | | | 2 | vb | *feel* |
| 409 | חוּשִׁים | I | 2 | | | | 2 | prnf | *Hushim* |
| 410 | חוּשִׁים | II | 2 | | | | 2 | prnm | *Hushim* |
| 411 | חוֹתָם | II | 2 | | | | 2 | prnm | *Hotham* |
| 412 | חַטָּאת | III | 2 | | | | 2 | nf | *step* |
| 413 | חֲטִיטָא | | 2 | | | | 2 | prnm | *Hatita* |
| 414 | חַטִּיל | | 2 | | | | 2 | prnm | *Hattil* |
| 415 | חֲטִיפָא | | 2 | | | | 2 | prnm | *Hatipha* |
| 416 | חַי | II | 2 | | | | 2 | n[m] | *kinsfolk* |
| 417 | חַיָּב | | | 1 | | 1 | 2 | adj | *guilty* |
| 418 | חיל | III | 2 | | | | 2 | vb | *endure* |
| 419 | חֵילָא | | | | | 2 | 2 | prnm | *Hela* |
| 420 | חֵילָם | | 2 | | | | 2 | pln | *Helam* |
| 421 | חַיִּם | | | | | 2 | 2 | prn[m] | *Haim* |
| 422 | חִירָה | I | 2 | | | | 2 | prnm | *Hirah* |
| 423 | חֲכַלְיָה | | 2 | | | | 2 | prnm | *Hacaliah* |
| 424 | חַכְמוֹנִי | I | 2 | | | | 2 | prnm | *Hachmoni* |
| 425 | חלא | I | 2 | | | | 2 | vb | *be diseased* |
| 426 | חֶלְאָה | II | 2 | | | | 2 | prnf | *Helah* |
| 427 | חֵלֶד | | 2 | | | | 2 | prnm | *Heled* |
| 428 | חֹלֶד | | 1 | | 1 | | 2 | n[m] | *weasel* |

## *Words Beginning with Ḥeth*

| Rank | Lemma | | MT | Si | Q | Inscr | Total | Type | Gloss |
|---|---|---|---|---|---|---|---|---|---|
| 429 | חֻלְדָּה | | 2 | | | | 2 | prnf | *Huldah* |
| 430 | חֲלִי | I | 2 | | | | 2 | nm | *ornament* |
| 431 | חֲלִיפָא | | | | 2 | | 2 | prnm | *Halipha* |
| 432 | חֲלִיצָה | | 2 | | | | 2 | nf | *spoil* |
| 433 | חלל | IV | 2 | | | | 2 | vb | *play the flute* |
| 434 | חֵלֶף | I | 2 | | | | 2 | prep | *in return for* |
| 435 | חלק | III | 2 | | | | 2 | vb | *destroy* |
| 436 | חָלָק | II | 2 | | | | 2 | pln | *Halak* |
| 437 | חֲלֻקָּה | | 1 | | 1 | | 2 | nf | *division* |
| 438 | חֶלְקָה | II | 2 | | | | 2 | nf | *smoothness* |
| 439 | חֶלְקַת | | 2 | | | | 2 | pln | *Helkath* |
| 440 | חלשׁ | I | 2 | | | | 2 | vb | *defeat* |
| 441 | חֶמְדָּן | | 2 | | | | 2 | prnm | *Hemdan* |
| 442 | חַמּוּאֵל | | 2 | | | | 2 | prnm | *Hammuel* |
| 443 | חַמּוֹן | | 2 | | | | 2 | pln | *Hammon* |
| 444 | חָמוֹץ | | 1 | | 1 | | 2 | nm | *oppressor* |
| 445 | חֲמוֹר | III | 2 | | | | 2 | n[m] | *heap* |
| 446 | חֹמֶט | | 1 | | 1 | | 2 | n[m] | *lizard* |
| 447 | חָמָל | | | | | 2 | 2 | prnm | *Hamal* |
| 448 | חֶמְלָה | | 2 | | | | 2 | nf | *compassion* |
| 449 | חַמֹּן | | | | | 2 | 2 | prnm | *Hammon* |
| 450 | חמק | | 2 | | | | 2 | vb | *turn* |
| 451 | חֹמֶר | III | 2 | | | | 2 | n[m] | *foaming* |
| 452 | חֹמֶר | IV | 2 | | | | 2 | n[m] | *heap* |
| 453 | חֲמָתִי | | 2 | | | | 2 | gent | *Hamathite* |
| 454 | חָנְיָא | | | | | 2 | 2 | prnm | *Honia* |
| 455 | חַנִּיאֵל | | 2 | | | | 2 | prnm | *Hanniel* |
| 456 | חֲנִינָא | | | | 2 | | 2 | prnm | *Hanina* |
| 457 | חֲנָמַל | | 1 | | 1 | | 2 | n[m] | *frost* |
| 458 | חָנֵס | | 1 | | 1 | | 2 | pln | *Hanes* |
| 459 | חֹנֶף | | 1 | | 1 | | 2 | n[m] | *profaneness* |
| 460 | חֲנֻפָּה | | 1 | | 1 | | 2 | nf | *impiousness* |
| 461 | חסד | I | 2 | | | | 2 | vb | *be loyal* |
| 462 | חָסֹן | I | 2 | | | | 2 | adj | *strong* |
| 463 | חֶסֶר | | 2 | | | | 2 | nm | *want* |

| Rank | Lemma | | MT | Si | Q | Inscr | Total | Type | Gloss |
|---|---|---|---|---|---|---|---|---|---|
| 464 | חֶפְצִי־בָהּ | | 2 | | | | 2 | prnf | *Hephzi-bah* |
| 465 | חֵ֫פֶר | I | 2 | | | | 2 | pln | *Hepher* |
| 466 | חפשׂ | II | 2 | | | | 2 | vb | *throw* |
| 467 | חפשׁ | | 1 | 1 | | | 2 | vb | *be free* |
| 468 | חָפְשׁוּת | | 2 | | | | 2 | nf | *freedom* |
| 470 | חֵ֫צִי | II | | | | 2 | 2 | prnm | *Hezi* |
| 471 | חָצָץ | | 2 | | | | 2 | nm | *gravel* |
| 472 | חַצְצוֹן תָּמָר | | 2 | | | | 2 | pln | *Hazazon-tamar* |
| 473 | חֶצְרוֹ | | 2 | | | | 2 | prnm | *Hezro* |
| 474 | חֶצְרוֹנִי | | 2 | | | | 2 | gent | *Hezronite* |
| 475 | חֲצַרְמָוֶת | | 2 | | | | 2 | prnm | *Hazarmaveth* |
| 476 | חֲקוּפָא | | 2 | | | | 2 | prnm | *Hakupha* |
| 477 | חֹר | | 2 | | | | 2 | n[m] | *hole* |
| 478 | חַרְבוֹנָא | | 2 | | | | 2 | prnm | *Harbona* |
| 479 | חָרְבָּן | | | | 2 | | 2 | n[m] | *desolation* |
| 480 | חַרְגֹּל | | 1 | | 1 | | 2 | n[m] | *locust* |
| 481 | חרד | II | 2 | | | | 2 | vb | *be angry* |
| 482 | חֲרָדָה | V | 2 | | | | 2 | pln | *Haradah* |
| 483 | חֹר הַגִּדְגָּד | | 2 | | | | 2 | pln | *Hor-hagidgad* |
| 484 | חֲרוּב | | | | 2 | | 2 | n[m] | *carob* |
| 485 | חַרְחוּר | II | 2 | | | | 2 | prnm | *Harhur* |
| 486 | חָרִיט | | 2 | | | | 2 | nm | *purse* |
| 487 | חָרִיף | | 2 | | | | 2 | prnm | *Hariph* |
| 488 | חָרִיץ | I | 2 | | | | 2 | nm | *pick axe* |
| 489 | חֲרִישִׁי | | 1 | | 1 | | 2 | adj | *sultry* |
| 490 | חרם | II | 2 | | | | 2 | vb | *split* |
| 491 | חֶרְמֵשׁ | | 2 | | | | 2 | n[m] | *sickle* |
| 492 | חָרָן | II | 2 | | | | 2 | prnm | *Haran* |
| 493 | חֶ֫רֶס | I | 2 | | | | 2 | nm | *sun* |
| 494 | חרף | II | 1 | 1 | | | 2 | vb | *spend winter* |
| 495 | חרף | III | 1 | | 1 | | 2 | vb | *designate* |
| 496 | חָרֵף | | 1 | | | 1 | 2 | prnm | *Hareph* |
| 497 | חַרְשָׁא | | 2 | | | | 2 | prnm | *Harsha* |
| 498 | חֶ֫רֶת | II | | | 2 | | 2 | nf | *ink* |
| 499 | חֲשׂוּפָא | | 2 | | | | 2 | prnm | *Hasupha* |

# *Words Beginning with Ḥeth*

| Rank | Lemma | | MT | Si | Q | Inscr | Total | Type | Gloss |
|---|---|---|---|---|---|---|---|---|---|
| 500 | חשׁף | II | 2 | | | | 2 | vb | *scoop up* |
| 501 | חֲשַׁבְנְיָה | | 2 | | | | 2 | prnm | *Hashabniah* |
| 502 | חַשְׁמֹנָה | | 2 | | | | 2 | pln | *Hashmonah* |
| 503 | חֲשַׁשׁ | | 2 | | | | 2 | nm | *dried grass* |
| 504 | חַת | I | 2 | | | | 2 | nm | *terror* |
| 505 | חַת | II | 2 | | | | 2 | adj | *shattered* |
| 506 | חֲתִים | | 2 | | | | 2 | n[m] | *signet ring* |
| 507 | חתך | | 1 | | 1 | | 2 | vb | *determine* |
| 508 | חתל | | 2 | | | | 2 | vb | *wrap* |
| 509 | חֶתְלוֹן | | 2 | | | | 2 | pln | *Hethlon* |
| 510 | חֹב | | 1 | | | | 1 | n[m] | *fold* |
| 511 | חֻבָּא | | | | | 1 | 1 | prnm | *Hubba* |
| 512 | חבב | II | 1 | | | | 1 | vb | *be pure* |
| 513 | חֻבָּה | | 1 | | | | 1 | prnm | *Hubbah* |
| 514 | חָבוּר | | 1 | | | | 1 | n[m] | *community* |
| 515 | חִבּוּר | | | | 1 | | 1 | n[m] | *community* |
| 516 | חבט | II | | 1 | | | 1 | vb | *pour* |
| 517 | חָבִיב | | | | 1 | | 1 | adj | *beloved* |
| 518 | חֶבְיוֹן | | 1 | | | | 1 | n[m] | *hiding* |
| 519 | חִבֵּל | | 1 | | | | 1 | n[m] | *mast* |
| 520 | חַבְלָה | | | 1 | | | 1 | nf | *rope* |
| 521 | חֲבֹלָה | | 1 | | | | 1 | nf | *pledge* |
| 522 | חַבָּלִי | | | | | 1 | 1 | prn | *Habbali* |
| 523 | חֲבַצִּנְיָה | | 1 | | | | 1 | prnm | *Habazziniah* |
| 524 | חבר | III | 1 | | | | 1 | vb | *be brilliant* |
| 525 | חבר | IV | 1 | | | | 1 | vb | *be high* |
| 526 | חַבָּר | | 1 | | | | 1 | nm | *partner* |
| 527 | חֲבַרְבּוּרָה | | 1 | | | | 1 | nf | *spot* |
| 528 | חֶבְרָה | | 1 | | | | 1 | nf | *company* |
| 529 | חֶבְרִי | | 1 | | | | 1 | gent | *Heberite* |
| 530 | חֲבִתִּים | | 1 | | | | 1 | n[m]pl | *flat cakes* |
| 531 | חָגָּא | | 1 | | | | 1 | n[f] | *terror* |
| 532 | חָגוֹר | | 1 | | | | 1 | adj | *belted* |
| 533 | חַגִּי | II | 1 | | | | 1 | gent | *Haggite* |
| 534 | חַגִּיָּה | | 1 | | | | 1 | prnm | *Haggiah* |

| Rank | Lemma | | MT | Si | Q | Inscr | Total | Type | Gloss |
|---|---|---|---|---|---|---|---|---|---|
| 535 | חִגֵּר | | | | 1 | | 1 | adj | *limping* |
| 536 | חַד | II | 1 | | | | 1 | adj | *one* |
| 537 | חֲדִיתָא | | | | 1 | | 1 | pln | *Haditha* |
| 538 | חַדְלַי | | 1 | | | | 1 | prnm | *Hadlai* |
| 539 | חדר | II | | 1 | | | 1 | vb | *remain* |
| 540 | חַדְרָךְ | | 1 | | | | 1 | pln | *Hadrach* |
| 541 | חֹדֶשׁ | II | 1 | | | | 1 | prnf | *Hodesh* |
| 542 | חֲדָשָׁה | | 1 | | | | 1 | pln | *Hadashah* |
| 543 | חוֹב | | 1 | | | | 1 | n[m] | *debt* |
| 544 | חוֹבָה | I | 1 | | | | 1 | pln | *Hobah* |
| 545 | חוֹבָה | II | | | 1 | | 1 | nf | *condemnation* |
| 546 | חוג | | 1 | | | | 1 | vb | *draw as a circle* |
| 547 | חִוָּהְיָהוּ | | | | | 1 | 1 | prnm | *Hivvahiah* |
| 548 | חוֹזַי | | 1 | | | | 1 | prnm | *Hozai* |
| 549 | חוֹחַ | II | 1 | | | | 1 | n[m] | *hole* |
| 550 | חוט | | 1 | | | | 1 | vb | *weigh out* |
| 551 | חוֹט | | | | 1 | | 1 | n[m] | *incisor* |
| 552 | חֲוִיל | | 1 | | | | 1 | prnm | *Havil* |
| 553 | חול | II | 1 | | | | 1 | vb | *be weak* |
| 554 | חוֹל | II | 1 | | | | 1 | n[m] | *phoenix* |
| 555 | חוֹנָן | | | | | 1 | 1 | prnm | *Honan* |
| 556 | חוּפָם | | 1 | | | | 1 | prnm | *Hupham* |
| 557 | חוּפָמִי | | 1 | | | | 1 | gent | *Huphamite* |
| 558 | חוץ | | 1 | | | | 1 | vb | *be strong* |
| 559 | חוּץ | II | 1 | | | | 1 | prnm | *Huz* |
| 560 | חוּץ | III | 1 | | | | 1 | adv | *loudly* |
| 561 | חוק | | 1 | | | | 1 | vb | *gather* |
| 562 | חוּק | | | 1 | | | 1 | n[m] | *circle* |
| 563 | חור | II | 1 | | | | 1 | vb | *be feeble* |
| 564 | חוֹרוֹן | | | | 1 | | 1 | pln | *Horon* |
| 565 | חוֹרַי | | 1 | | | | 1 | n[m] | *white stuff* |
| 566 | חוּרַי | | 1 | | | | 1 | prnm | *Hurai* |
| 567 | חוּרִי | | 1 | | | | 1 | prnm | *Huri* |
| 568 | חוֹרֶץ | | | | | 1 | 1 | prnm | *Horaz* |
| 569 | חוֹשׁ | III | 1 | | | | 1 | vb | *be anxious* |

# *Words Beginning with Ḥeth*

| Rank | Lemma | | MT | Si | Q | Inscr | Total | Type | Gloss |
|---|---|---|---|---|---|---|---|---|---|
| 570 | חושׁ | IV | 1 | | | | 1 | vb | *be sated* |
| 571 | חושׁ | V | | | 1 | | 1 | vb | *cease* |
| 572 | חוּשָׁה | | 1 | | | | 1 | prnm | *Hushah* |
| 573 | חזה | III | 1 | | | | 1 | vb | *be vile* |
| 574 | חֹזֶה | II | 1 | | | | 1 | n[m] | *agreement* |
| 575 | חֲזוֹ | | 1 | | | | 1 | prnm | *Hazo* |
| 576 | חָזוֹן | II | 1 | | | | 1 | nm | *pact* |
| 577 | חָזוֹן | III | 1 | | | | 1 | n[m] | *magistrate* |
| 578 | חָזָה | | 1 | | | | 1 | nf | *vision* |
| 579 | חָזוּת | II | 1 | | | | 1 | nf | *agreement* |
| 580 | חֲזִיאֵל | | 1 | | | | 1 | prnm | *Haziel* |
| 581 | חֲזָיָה | | 1 | | | | 1 | prnm | *Hazaiah* |
| 582 | חֶזְיוֹן | | 1 | | | | 1 | prnm | *Hezion* |
| 583 | חֲזִיז | II | 1 | | | | 1 | n[m] | *dream* |
| 584 | חזק | II | 1 | | | | 1 | vb | *outwit* |
| 585 | חָזָק | II | | | | 1 | 1 | prn[m] | *Hazak* |
| 586 | חֵ֫זֶק | | 1 | | | | 1 | n[m] | *strength* |
| 587 | חִזְקִי | | 1 | | | | 1 | prnm | *Hizki* |
| 588 | חזר | | | 1 | | | 1 | vb | *turn around* |
| 589 | חֶטְאָה | | 1 | | | | 1 | nf | *sin* |
| 590 | חַטָּאת | II | 1 | | | | 1 | nf | *penury* |
| 591 | חֲטֻבוֹת | | 1 | | | | 1 | nfpl | *multicoloured cloth* |
| 592 | חטם | | 1 | | | | 1 | vb | *restrain* |
| 593 | חטר | | 1 | | | | 1 | vb | *cut* |
| 594 | חִיאֵל | | 1 | | | | 1 | prnm | *Hiel* |
| 595 | חִיד | | | | 1 | | 1 | n[m] | *community* |
| 596 | חַיָּה | IV | 1 | | | | 1 | nf | *dwelling place* |
| 597 | חָיֶה | | 1 | | | | 1 | adj | *lively* |
| 598 | חַיּוּת | I | 1 | | | | 1 | nf | *living* |
| 599 | חַיּוּת | II | 1 | | | | 1 | nf | *shame* |
| 600 | חִילָה | | 1 | | | | 1 | nf | *pain, anguish* |
| 601 | חִילֵז | | 1 | | | | 1 | pln | *Hilez* |
| 602 | חֵילֵךְ | | 1 | | | | 1 | pln | *Helech* |
| 603 | חִילֵן | | 1 | | | | 1 | pln | *Hilen* |
| 604 | חין | | 1 | | | | 1 | vb | *die* |

| Rank | Lemma | | MT | Si | Q | Inscr | Total | Type | Gloss |
|---|---|---|---|---|---|---|---|---|---|
| 605 | חִין | | 1 | | | | 1 | n[m] | *gracefulness* |
| 606 | חִיר | | | | 1 | | 1 | n[m] | *den* |
| 607 | חִישׁ | | 1 | | | | 1 | adv | *quickly* |
| 608 | חֵךְ | II | 1 | | | | 1 | n[m] | *disposition* |
| 609 | חֲכוֹר | | | | 1 | | 1 | n[m] | *rent* |
| 610 | חֲכִירוּת | | | | | 1 | 1 | nf | *rent* |
| 611 | חֶכֶל | | | | | 1 | 1 | prnm | *Hechel* |
| 612 | חַכְלִילוּת | | 1 | | | | 1 | nf | *dullness* |
| 613 | חַכְלִילִי | | 1 | | | | 1 | adj | *dull* |
| 614 | חכר | II | 1 | | | | 1 | vb | *oppress* |
| 615 | חלא | II | | 1 | | | 1 | vb | *be rusty* |
| 616 | חֶלֶא | | | | | 1 | 1 | prn[m] | *Hele* |
| 617 | חֵלֶב | II | 1 | | | | 1 | prnm | *Heleb* |
| 618 | חֶלְבָּה | | 1 | | | | 1 | pln | *Helbah* |
| 619 | חֶלְבּוֹן | | 1 | | | | 1 | pln | *Helbon* |
| 620 | חֶלְבְּנָה | | 1 | | | | 1 | nf | *galbanum* |
| 621 | חֲלוֹף | | 1 | | | | 1 | nm | *passing away* |
| 622 | חֲלוּשָׁה | | 1 | | | | 1 | nf | *defeat* |
| 623 | חַלְחוּל | | 1 | | | | 1 | pln | *Halhul* |
| 624 | חלט | | 1 | | | | 1 | vb | *accept* |
| 625 | חֲלִי | II | 1 | | | | 1 | pln | *Hali* |
| 626 | חֶלְיָה | | 1 | | | | 1 | nf | *jewellery* |
| 627 | חֶלְיָה | | | | 1 | | 1 | nf | *sediment* |
| 628 | חַלְיוֹ | | | | | 1 | 1 | prn[m] | *Hallio* |
| 629 | חלל | V | 1 | | | | 1 | vb | *tremble* |
| 630 | חֵלֶם | | 1 | | | | 1 | prnm | *Helem* |
| 631 | חֲלָמָה | | | | 1 | | 1 | nf | *seamed robe* |
| 632 | חַלָּמוּת | | 1 | | | | 1 | nf | *mallow* |
| 633 | חלף | III | 1 | | | | 1 | vb | *grow* |
| 634 | חֵלֶף | II | 1 | | | | 1 | pln | *Heleph* |
| 635 | חֲלַפְתָּא | | | | | 1 | 1 | prnm | *Halaphta* |
| 636 | חלק | IV | 1 | | | | 1 | vb | *surround* |
| 637 | חלק | V | 1 | | | | 1 | vb | *strip* |
| 638 | חלק | VI | 1 | | | | 1 | vb | *create* |
| 639 | חלק | VII | 1 | | | | 1 | vb | *flee* |

## *Words Beginning with Ḥeth*

| Rank | Lemma | | MT | Si | Q | Inscr | Total | Type | Gloss |
|---|---|---|---|---|---|---|---|---|---|
| 640 | חָלָק | III | | 1 | | | 1 | n[m] | *creature* |
| 641 | חַלֶּק | | 1 | | | | 1 | adj | *smooth* |
| 642 | חֵ֫לֶק | IV | 1 | | | | 1 | n[m] | *smoothness* |
| 643 | חִלְקָא | | | | | 1 | 1 | prn[m] | *Hilka* |
| 644 | חֲלָקוֹת | | 1 | | | | 1 | nf | *perdition* |
| 645 | חֶלְקַי | | 1 | | | | 1 | prnm | *Helkai* |
| 646 | חֶלְקִי | I | 1 | | | | 1 | gent | *Helekite* |
| 647 | חֶלְקִי | II | 1 | | | | 1 | prnm | *Helki* |
| 648 | חֲלַקְלַקּוֹת | II | 1 | | | | 1 | nfpl | *darkness* |
| 649 | חֶלְקַת הַצֻּרִים | | 1 | | | | 1 | pln | *Helkath-hazzurim* |
| 650 | חלשׁ | II | 1 | | | | 1 | vb | *be weak* |
| 651 | חַלָּשׁ | | 1 | | | | 1 | adj | *weak* |
| 652 | חֶמְדָּא | | | | | 1 | 1 | prnm | *Hemda* |
| 653 | חמה | I | | 1 | | | 1 | vb | *see* |
| 654 | חֵמָה | II | 1 | | | | 1 | nf | *family* |
| 655 | חָמוּלִי | | 1 | | | | 1 | gent | *Hamulite* |
| 656 | חָמוּץ | | 1 | | | | 1 | adj | *bright red* |
| 657 | חַמּוּק | | 1 | | | | 1 | nm | *curve* |
| 658 | חֻמְטָה | | 1 | | | | 1 | pln | *Humtah* |
| 659 | חֲמִיאֹהֶל | | | | | 1 | 1 | prnf | *Hamiohel* |
| 660 | חָמִיד | | | 1 | | | 1 | n[m] | *unreliable guide* |
| 661 | חֲמִיעֲדָן | | | | | 1 | 1 | prnf | *Hamiadan* |
| 662 | חָמִיץ | | 1 | | | | 1 | n[m] | *sorrel* |
| 663 | חמס | II | 1 | | | | 1 | vb | *devise* |
| 664 | חמס | III | 1 | | | | 1 | vb | *make bare* |
| 665 | חמץ | II | 1 | | | | 1 | vb | *oppress* |
| 666 | חמר | II | 1 | | | | 1 | vb | *cover with bitumen* |
| 667 | חמר | III | 1 | | | | 1 | vb | *be red* |
| 668 | חַמְרָן | | 1 | | | | 1 | prnm | *Hamran* |
| 669 | חַמַּת | I | 1 | | | | 1 | prnm | *Hammath* |
| 670 | חַמַּת | II | 1 | | | | 1 | pln | *Hammath* |
| 671 | חַמֹּת דֹּאר | | 1 | | | | 1 | pln | *Hammoth-dor* |
| 672 | חֲמָת צוֹבָה | | 1 | | | | 1 | pln | *Hamath-zobah* |
| 673 | חֵן | II | 1 | | | | 1 | prnm | *Hen* |
| 674 | חַנָּא | | | | | 1 | 1 | prn[m] | *Hanna* |

| Rank | Lemma | | MT | Si | Q | Inscr | Total | Type | Gloss |
|---|---|---|---|---|---|---|---|---|---|
| 675 | חַנִּאָב | | | | | 1 | 1 | prn[m] | *Hanniab* |
| 676 | חנג | | | 1 | | | 1 | vb | *dance* |
| 677 | חנה | II | 1 | | | | 1 | vb | *have compassion* |
| 678 | חֲנוֹךְ | II | 1 | | | | 1 | pln | *Enoch* |
| 679 | חֲנוּת | | 1 | | | | 1 | nf | *vault* |
| 680 | חנט | II | 1 | | | | 1 | vb | *ripen* |
| 681 | חֲנֻטִים | | 1 | | | | 1 | n[m]pl | *embalming* |
| 682 | חַנִּיָּהוּ | | | | | 1 | 1 | prnm | *Hanniah* |
| 683 | חָנִיךְ | | 1 | | | | 1 | nm | *retainer* |
| 684 | חֲנֹכִי | | 1 | | | | 1 | gent | *Hanochite* |
| 685 | חַנִּמֶּלֶךְ | | | | | 1 | 1 | prn[m] | *Hannimelech* |
| 686 | חנן | II | 1 | | | | 1 | vb | *be loathsome* |
| 687 | חֲנַנְאֵל | II | | | | 1 | 1 | prnm | *Hananel* |
| 688 | חֲנָנָה | | | | | 1 | 1 | prnf | *Hananah* |
| 689 | חָנֵף | II | 1 | | | | 1 | adj | *haughty* |
| 690 | חַנָּתֹן | | 1 | | | | 1 | pln | *Hannathon* |
| 691 | חסד | II | 1 | | | | 1 | vb | *be ashamed* |
| 692 | חַסְדָּא | | | | | 1 | 1 | prn[m] | *Hasda* |
| 693 | חֹסָה | II | 1 | | | | 1 | pln | *Hosah* |
| 694 | חָסוּת | | 1 | | | | 1 | nf | *refuge* |
| 695 | חָסִין | | 1 | | | | 1 | adj | *strong* |
| 696 | חסל | | 1 | | | | 1 | vb | *consume* |
| 697 | חסן | | 1 | | | | 1 | vb | *be strong* |
| 698 | חסף | | 1 | | | | 1 | vb | *be scaly* |
| 699 | חַסְרָה | | 1 | | | | 1 | prnm | *Hasrah* |
| 700 | חֶסְרוֹן | | 1 | | | | 1 | nm | *deficiency* |
| 701 | חַף | I | 1 | | | | 1 | adj | *pure* |
| 702 | חפא | | 1 | | | | 1 | vb | *hide* |
| 703 | חפף | | 1 | | | | 1 | vb | *shelter* |
| 704 | חֲפַפְיוֹ | | | | | 1 | 1 | prn[m] | *Haphahiah* |
| 705 | חפץ | I | 1 | | | | 1 | vb | *stretch out* |
| 706 | חֶפְרִי | | 1 | | | | 1 | gent | *Hepherite* |
| 707 | חֲפָרַיִם | | 1 | | | | 1 | pln | *Hapharaim* |
| 708 | חָפְרַע | | 1 | | | | 1 | prnm | *Hophra* |
| 709 | חֲפַרְפָּרָה | | 1 | | | | 1 | nf | *mole* |

## Words Beginning with Ḥeth

| Rank | Lemma | | MT | Si | Q | Inscr | Total | Type | Gloss |
|---|---|---|---|---|---|---|---|---|---|
| 710 | חֵ֫פֶשׂ | | 1 | | | | 1 | nm | *plot* |
| 711 | חֹ֫פֶשׁ | | 1 | | | | 1 | nm | *woven material* |
| 712 | חֹ֫פֶשׁ | I | | 1 | | | 1 | nm | *freedom* |
| 713 | חֹ֫פֶשׁ | II | 1 | | | | 1 | n[m] | *prison* |
| 714 | חֻפְשָׁה | | 1 | | | | 1 | nf | *freedom* |
| 715 | חצב | I | 1 | | | | 1 | vb | *rake* |
| 716 | חֲצָד | | | | 1 | | 1 | nm | *date* |
| 717 | חצה | I | 1 | | | | 1 | vb | *reach to* |
| 718 | חָצוֹר חֲדַתָּה | | 1 | | | | 1 | pln | *Hazor-hadattah* |
| 719 | חָצִיר | II | 1 | | | | 1 | n[m] | *leek* |
| 720 | חֹ֫צֶן | I | 1 | | | | 1 | n[m] | *war-horses* |
| 721 | חָצָף | | | 1 | | | 1 | adj | *impudent* |
| 722 | חֲצַר אַדָּר | | 1 | | | | 1 | pln | *Hazar-addar* |
| 723 | חֲצַר אֲסָם | | | | | 1 | 1 | pln | *Hazar-asam* |
| 724 | חֲצַר גַּדָּה | | 1 | | | | 1 | pln | *Hazar-gaddah* |
| 725 | חָצֵר הַתִּיכוֹן | | 1 | | | | 1 | pln | *Hazar-hatticon* |
| 726 | חֶצְרוֹן | II | 1 | | | | 1 | pln | *Hezron* |
| 727 | חֶצְרַי | | 1 | | | | 1 | prnm | *Hezrai* |
| 728 | חקר | II | 1 | | | | 1 | vb | *despise* |
| 729 | חִקָּר | | | | 1 | | 1 | pln | *Hikkar* |
| 730 | חֲרָא | | | | 1 | | 1 | adv | *afterwards* |
| 731 | חֶרְבָּה | | 1 | | | | 1 | nf | *deceit* |
| 732 | חֲרָבוֹן | | 1 | | | | 1 | nm | *dry heat* |
| 733 | חרג | | 1 | | | | 1 | vb | *come fearfully* |
| 734 | חרד | IV | 1 | | | | 1 | vb | *weave* |
| 735 | חֲרֹד | | 1 | | | | 1 | pln | *Harod* |
| 736 | חֲרָדָה | II | 1 | | | | 1 | nf | *anger* |
| 737 | חֲרָדָה | III | 1 | | | | 1 | nf | *lodging* |
| 738 | חֲרָדָה | IV | 1 | | | | 1 | nf | *loincloth* |
| 739 | חֲרֹדִי | | 1 | | | | 1 | gent | *Harodite* |
| 740 | חרה | II | 1 | | | | 1 | vb | *dwindle away* |
| 741 | חַרְהֲיָה | | 1 | | | | 1 | prnm | *Harhaiah* |
| 742 | חָרוּז | | 1 | | | | 1 | nm | *necklace* |
| 743 | חֲרוּמַף | | 1 | | | | 1 | prnm | *Harumaph* |
| 744 | חֲרוּפִי | | 1 | | | | 1 | gent | *Haruphite* |

| Rank | Lemma | | MT | Si | Q | Inscr | Total | Type | Gloss |
|---|---|---|---|---|---|---|---|---|---|
| 745 | חָרוּץ | III | 1 | | | | 1 | nm | *channel* |
| 746 | חָרוּץ | IV | 1 | | | | 1 | prnm | *Haruz* |
| 747 | חָרוּץ | V | 1 | | | | 1 | adj | *mutilated* |
| 748 | חָרוּץ | VII | 1 | | | | 1 | adj | *sickly* |
| 749 | חַרְחַס | | 1 | | | | 1 | prnm | *Harhas* |
| 750 | חֹרִי | III | 1 | | | | 1 | n[m] | *white bread* |
| 751 | חֲרִיבָה | | | | 1 | | 1 | nf | *ruin* |
| 752 | חֹרֵיבָּה | | | | 1 | | 1 | pln | *Horebbah* |
| 753 | חָרִיץ | II | | | 1 | | 1 | n[m] | *channel* |
| 754 | חָרִיץ | III | 1 | | | | 1 | nm | *slice* |
| 755 | חָרִיץ | IV | | 1 | | | 1 | n[m] | *gold* |
| 756 | חרך | | 1 | | | | 1 | vb | *roast* |
| 757 | חָרָךְ | | 1 | | | | 1 | nm | *lattice* |
| 758 | חֳרֵם | | 1 | | | | 1 | pln | *Horem* |
| 759 | חַרְנֶפֶר | | 1 | | | | 1 | prnm | *Harnepher* |
| 760 | חֶרֶס | II | 1 | | | | 1 | nm | *itch* |
| 761 | חֶרֶס | III | 1 | | | | 1 | pln | *Heres* |
| 762 | חַרְסִית | | 1 | | | | 1 | nf | *potsherd* |
| 763 | חֶרֶף | | | | 1 | | 1 | nm | *catapult* |
| 764 | חֹרֶף | II | 1 | | | | 1 | n[m] | *youth* |
| 765 | חֶרְפָּה | II | 1 | | | | 1 | nf | *knife* |
| 766 | חַרְצָן | | 1 | | | | 1 | nm | *sour grape* |
| 767 | חָרָר | | | | 1 | | 1 | n[m] | *dispute* |
| 768 | חָרֵר | | 1 | | | | 1 | nm | *parched places* |
| 769 | חרשׁ | | | 1 | | | 1 | vb | *provoke* |
| 770 | חֶרֶשׁ | I | 1 | | | | 1 | nm | *sorcery* |
| 771 | חֶרֶשׁ | II | 1 | | | | 1 | adv | *secretly* |
| 772 | חֶרֶשׁ | III | 1 | | | | 1 | prnm | *Heresh* |
| 773 | חֶרֶת | I | 1 | | | | 1 | pln | *Hereth* |
| 774 | חָשִׂיף | | 1 | | | | 1 | nm | *little flock* |
| 775 | חשׂך | II | 1 | | | | 1 | vb | *be continuous* |
| 776 | חַשְׁבַּדָּנָה | | 1 | | | | 1 | prnm | *Hashbadana* |
| 777 | חֲשֻׁבָה | | 1 | | | | 1 | prnm | *Hashubah* |
| 778 | חֲשַׁבְנָה | | 1 | | | | 1 | prnm | *Hashabnah* |
| 779 | חִשּׁוּק | | 1 | | | | 1 | nm | *spoke* |

| | | | | | | | | | |
|---|---|---|---|---|---|---|---|---|---|
| 780 | חִשּׁוּר | | 1 | | | | 1 | nm | *hub* |
| 781 | חָשֹׁךְ | | 1 | | | | 1 | adj | *obscure* |
| 782 | חשל | | 1 | | | | 1 | vb | *be feeble* |
| 783 | חֶשְׁמוֹן | | 1 | | | | 1 | pln | *Heshmon* |
| 784 | חַשְׁמַן | | 1 | | | | 1 | nm | *envoy* |
| 785 | חַשְׁרָה | | 1 | | | | 1 | nf | *sieve* |
| 786 | חִתָּה | | 1 | | | | 1 | nf | *terror* |
| 787 | חִתּוּל | | 1 | | | | 1 | nm | *bandage* |
| 788 | חַתְחַת | | 1 | | | | 1 | nm | *terror* |
| 789 | חֲתִימָה | | | | 1 | | 1 | nf | *seal* |
| 790 | חֲתֻלָּה | | 1 | | | | 1 | nf | *swaddling-band* |
| 791 | חֹתֶמֶת | | 1 | | | | 1 | nf | *signet ring* |
| 792 | חֹתֶנֶת | | 1 | | | | 1 | nf | *mother-in-law* |
| 793 | חֲתֻנָּה | | 1 | | | | 1 | nf | *wedding* |
| 794 | חַתֻּס | | | | | 1 | 1 | prnm | *Hattus* |
| 795 | חתת | II | 1 | | | | 1 | vb | *be dry* |
| 796 | חֲתַת | I | 1 | | | | 1 | n[m] | *terror* |
| 797 | חֲתַת | II | 1 | | | | 1 | prnm | *Hathath* |

# ט

| | | | | | | | | | |
|---|---|---|---|---|---|---|---|---|---|
| 1 | טוֹב | I | 262 | 30 | 32 | 2 | 326 | adj | *good* |
| 2 | טמא | | 162 | | 57 | | 219 | vb | *be impure* |
| 3 | טוֹב | II | 141 | 11 | 29 | 3 | 184 | n[m] | *good* |
| 4 | טהר | | 94 | 1 | 65 | | 160 | vb | *be pure* |
| 5 | טָהוֹר | | 95 | | 48 | | 143 | adj | *pure* |
| 6 | טָמֵא | | 87 | | 45 | | 132 | adj | *impure* |
| 7 | טוב | | 113 | 6 | | | 119 | vb | *be good* |
| 8 | טוֹבָה | I | 66 | 23 | 2 | | 91 | nf | *good* |
| 9 | טֶרֶם | | 56 | 5 | 25 | 1 | 87 | conj | *before* |
| 10 | טֻמְאָה | | 36 | | 47 | | 83 | nf | *impurity* |

| Rank | Lemma | | MT | Si | Q | Inscr | Total | Type | Gloss |
|---|---|---|---|---|---|---|---|---|---|
| 11 | טוּב | I | 32 | 12 | 35 | | 79 | nm | *good* |
| 12 | טָהֳרָה | | 13 | 1 | 48 | | 62 | nf | *purity* |
| 13 | טַבַּעַת | | 49 | | 2 | | 51 | nf | *ring* |
| 14 | טַף | | 42 | | 6 | | 48 | nm | *children* |
| 15 | טמן | | 31 | 3 | 3 | | 37 | vb | *conceal* |
| 16 | טַל | | 31 | 1 | 4 | | 36 | nm | *dew* |
| 17 | טַבָּח | | 32 | | 1 | | 33 | nm | *butcher* |
| 18 | טֶרֶף | | 22 | 1 | 10 | | 33 | nm | *prey* |
| 19 | טרף | | 25 | | 5 | | 30 | vb | *tear* |
| 20 | טוּר | I | 26 | | 1 | | 27 | nm | *row* |
| 21 | טוֹבִיָּה | | 18 | | | 4 | 22 | prnm | *Tobiah* |
| 22 | טֹהַר | | 3 | 1 | 16 | | 20 | n[m] | *purity* |
| 23 | טבל | | 16 | | 2 | | 18 | vb | *immerse* |
| 24 | טִיט | | 13 | | 5 | | 18 | nm | *mud* |
| 25 | טול | | 14 | | 2 | | 16 | vb | *throw* |
| 26 | טַעַם | | 13 | 3 | | | 16 | nm | *taste* |
| 27 | טבח | | 11 | | 4 | | 15 | vb | *slaughter* |
| 28 | טוח | | 11 | | 4 | | 15 | vb | *cover* |
| 29 | טעם | | 11 | 2 | | | 13 | vb | *taste* |
| 30 | טֶבַח | I | 12 | | | | 12 | nm | *slaughter* |
| 31 | טבע | | 10 | | 2 | | 12 | vb | *sink* |
| 32 | טֶפַח | | 9 | | 2 | | 11 | nm | *handbreadth* |
| 33 | טרד | | 2 | 2 | 6 | | 10 | vb | *continue* |
| 34 | טְרֵפָה | | 9 | | 1 | | 10 | nf | *savaged beast* |
| 35 | טחן | | 8 | | | | 8 | vb | *grind* |
| 36 | טְחֹר | | 8 | | | | 8 | nm | *haemorrhoid* |
| 37 | טלא | | 8 | | | | 8 | vb | *patch* |
| 38 | טִירָה | | 7 | | | | 7 | nf | *row* |
| 39 | טֶנֶא | | 4 | 1 | 2 | | 7 | nm | *basket* |
| 40 | טוֹב | VI | 6 | | | | 6 | nm | *rain* |
| 41 | טַלְמוֹן | | 5 | | | | 5 | prnm | *Talmon* |
| 42 | טוֹב | III | 4 | | | | 4 | pln | *Tob* |
| 43 | טפל | | 3 | 1 | | | 4 | vb | *cover* |
| 44 | טִבְחָה | | 3 | | | | 3 | nf | *slaughter* |
| 45 | טֹבְשָׁלֹם | | | | | 3 | 3 | prnm | *Tob-shalom* |

## *Words Beginning with Ṭeth*

| Rank | Lemma | | MT | Si | Q | Inscr | Total | Type | Gloss |
|---|---|---|---|---|---|---|---|---|---|
| 46 | טוֹטֶפֶת | | 3 | | | | 3 | nf | *symbol* |
| 47 | טָלֶה | | 3 | | | | 3 | nm | *lamb* |
| 48 | טָמָא | | | | 3 | | 3 | n[m] | *impurity* |
| 49 | טעה | | 1 | | 2 | | 3 | vb | *stray* |
| 50 | טֹ֫רַח | | 2 | | 1 | | 3 | nm | *burden* |
| 51 | טָרָף | | 2 | | 1 | | 3 | adj | *fresh* |
| 52 | טָבְאֵל | | 1 | | | 1 | 2 | prnm | *Tabeel* |
| 53 | טַבּוּר | | 2 | | | | 2 | n[m] | *navel, centre* |
| 54 | טַבָּעוֹת | | 2 | | | | 2 | prnm | *Tabbaoth* |
| 55 | טוֹב | IV | 2 | | | | 2 | n[m] | *word* |
| 56 | טוֹב | V | 2 | | | | 2 | n[m] | *perfume* |
| 57 | טוה | | 2 | | | | 2 | vb | *spin* |
| 58 | טַוָּה | | 2 | | | | 2 | nf | *cloth* |
| 59 | טֻחוֹת | I | 2 | | | | 2 | nf | *innards* |
| 60 | טמם | | 1 | 1 | | | 2 | vb | *stop up* |
| 61 | טִפְסָר | | 2 | | | | 2 | nm | *scribe* |
| 62 | טָרִי | | 2 | | | | 2 | adj | *fresh* |
| 63 | טאטא | I | 1 | | | | 1 | vb | *sweep (away)* |
| 64 | טאטא | II | | | 1 | | 1 | vb | *be muddy* |
| 65 | טָבְאַל | | 1 | | | | 1 | prnm | *Tabal* |
| 66 | טבב | | 1 | | | | 1 | vb | *speak* |
| 67 | טְבוּל | | 1 | | | | 1 | n[m] | *turban* |
| 68 | טֶ֫בַח | II | 1 | | | | 1 | prn[m] | *Tebah* |
| 69 | טַבָּחָה | | 1 | | | | 1 | nf | *cook* |
| 70 | טִבְחַת | | 1 | | | | 1 | pln | *Tibhath* |
| 71 | טְבִילָה | | | | 1 | | 1 | nf | *immersion* |
| 72 | טְבַלְיָ֫הוּ | | 1 | | | | 1 | prnm | *Tebaliah* |
| 73 | טַבְרִמֹּן | | 1 | | | | 1 | prnm | *Tabrimmon* |
| 74 | טַבָּת | | 1 | | | | 1 | pln | *Tabbath* |
| 75 | טֵבֵת | | 1 | | | | 1 | prn[m] | *Tebeth* |
| 76 | טְהָר | | 1 | | | | 1 | n[m] | *purity* |
| 77 | טוּב | II | 1 | | | | 1 | n[m] | *word* |
| 78 | טוֹב אֲדֹנִיָּה | | 1 | | | | 1 | prnm | *Tob-adonijah* |
| 79 | טוֹבָה | II | 1 | | | | 1 | nf | *word* |
| 80 | טוּר | II | | | 1 | | 1 | n[m] | *rock* |

| Rank | Lemma | | MT | Si | Q | Inscr | Total | Type | Gloss |
|---|---|---|---|---|---|---|---|---|---|
| 81 | טושׁ | | 1 | | | | 1 | vb | *rush* |
| 82 | טושׂ | | | | 1 | | 1 | vb | *cover* |
| 83 | טחה | | 1 | | | | 1 | vb | *throw* |
| 84 | טְחוֹן | | 1 | | | | 1 | nm | *millstone* |
| 85 | טֻחוֹת | II | 1 | | | | 1 | nf | *darkness* |
| 86 | טֻחוֹת | III | 1 | | | | 1 | nf | *ibis* |
| 87 | טחח | | 1 | | | | 1 | vb | *be covered* |
| 88 | טַחֲנָה | | 1 | | | | 1 | nf | *mill* |
| 89 | טִיב | | | 1 | | | 1 | nm | *character* |
| 90 | טִיחַ | | 1 | | | | 1 | nm | *plaster* |
| 91 | טֵיף | | | | 1 | | 1 | n[m] | *a little* |
| 92 | טִיף | | | | 1 | | 1 | n[m] | *stand* |
| 93 | טִיר | | | | 1 | | 1 | nm | *wall* |
| 94 | טְלָאִים | | 1 | | | | 1 | pln | *Telaim* |
| 95 | טַלְטֵלָה | | 1 | | | | 1 | nf | *hurling* |
| 96 | טלל | I | 1 | | | | 1 | vb | *cover* |
| 97 | טלל | II | | | 1 | | 1 | vb | *fall* |
| 98 | טֶ֫לֶם | I | 1 | | | | 1 | prnm | *Telem* |
| 99 | טֶ֫לֶם | II | 1 | | | | 1 | pln | *Telem* |
| 100 | טָמְאָה | | 1 | | | | 1 | nf | *impurity* |
| 101 | טמה | | 1 | | | | 1 | vb | *be impure* |
| 102 | טנף | | 1 | | | | 1 | vb | *to defile* |
| 103 | טען | I | 1 | | | | 1 | vb | *pierce* |
| 104 | טען | II | 1 | | | | 1 | vb | *load* |
| 105 | טפח | I | 1 | | | | 1 | vb | *be broad* |
| 106 | טפח | II | 1 | | | | 1 | vb | *be pregnant* |
| 107 | טִפֻּחִים | | 1 | | | | 1 | n[m] | *birth* |
| 108 | טפף | | 1 | | | | 1 | vb | *walk carefully* |
| 109 | טִפֵּשׁ | | | 1 | | | 1 | adj | *foolish* |
| 110 | טפשׁ | | 1 | | | | 1 | vb | *be fat* |
| 111 | טָפַת | | 1 | | | | 1 | prnm | *Taphath* |
| 112 | טֶ֫קַח | | | | | 1 | 1 | prn | *Tekah* |
| 113 | טרח | | 1 | | | | 1 | vb | *be weary* |

# ABBREVIATIONS AND SIGNS

TEXTS

Gn Ex Lv Nm Dt Jos Jg 1 S 2 S 1 K 2 K Is Jr Ezk Ho Jl Am Ob Jon Mc Na Hb Zp Hg Zc Ml Ps Jb Pr Ru Ca Ec Lm Est Dn Ezr Ne 1 C 2 C

Si $Si_{(M)}$ (Sirach from Masada)

SIGNS

+ = the following is used in association with the preceding

:: = the following is used in contrast or opposition to the preceding

|| = the following is used in parallel to the preceding, or, the following text is parallel to the preceding

§ = section

† = not all these occurrences are listed in this article

* (at the beginning of an article) = see the Bibliography for discussion of the existence of this word

* (at the end of an article) = see the Bibliography for further semantic studies

⇒ = the following are related words

ABBREVIATIONS

abs. = absolute
add. = additional (inscription)
adj. = adjective
adv. = adverb
AHL = Academy of the Hebrew Language
Akk. = Akkadian
alw. = always
anat. = anatomical
app. = apposition
appar. = apparently
Arab. = Arabic
Aram. = Aramaic
architect. = architectural
assoc. = associated, association
BCE = before the Common Era
BHS = *Biblia hebraica stuttgartensia*
CE = Common Era
cent. = century
coll. = miscellaneous collocations
conj. = conjunction
corrupt. = corruption
cpl = common plural
cs = common singular
cstr. = construct
del. = delete
der. = derivands, derivatives, i.e. morphologically related forms
descr. = describing, description
design. = designation, designating
du. = dual
em., *see* if em., or em.
emph. = emphatic
encl. = enclitic
erased = erased reading
esp. = especially
Eth. = Ethiopic
EW = Eisenman & Wise
f., fem. = feminine

fpl = feminine plural
fr. = fragment
freq. = frequently
fs = feminine singular
gent. = gentilic
Gnz = Genizah fragment, manuscript
graf. = graffito
Heb. = Hebrew
hi. = hiphil
HN = Horbury & Noy
ho. = hophal
hothp. = hothpael
htp. = hithpael
htpal = hithpalel
htpalp. = hithpalpel
htpo. = hithpoel
htpol. = hithpolal, hithpolel
I = inscription
ident. = to be identified
if em. = the foregoing results from an emendation
impf. = imperfect
impv. = imperative
inf. = infinitive
ins. = insert
inscr. = inscription
intens. = intensive
interj. = interjection
intrans. = intransitive
interrog. = interrogative
Kh. = Khirbet
Kt = ketiv
L = Codex Leningradensis B19 A, text of *BHS*
lit. = literally
m., masc. = masculine
mg = marginal, sublinear, supralinear reading
MH = Mishnaic Hebrew
mod. = modern
mpl = masculine plural
ms = manuscript; (in morphology) masculine singular
n. = noun
ni. = niphal
nom. cl. = noun clause
ntp. = nithpael
obj. = object
oft. = often
or em. = the foregoing will not be the case if the following emendation is accepted
orig. = originally
OSA = Old South Arabic
ost. = ostracon
part. = particle
pass. = passive
perh. = perhaps
pf. = perfect
Phoen. = Phoenician
pi. = piel
pilp. = pilpel
pl., plur. = plural
pl.n. = place name
po. = poel, poal,
pol. = polal, polel
prep. = preposition
pr.n. = personal name
prob. = probably
pron. = pronoun
pronom. = pronominal
ptc. = participle
pu. = pual
pulp. = pulpal
Q = Qumran
Qr = qere
ref. = reference
Seb = Sebir (supposed reading)
sf. = suffix
sg. = singular
Si = Ben Sira
sim. = similar, similarly
sing. = singular
specif. = specifially
subj. = subject
Sup = supplementary text(s)

syn. = synonym
Syr. = Syriac
T. = Tel, Tell
t = times
TiqSof = tiqqun soferim
trans. = transitive
Ug. = Ugaritic
usu. = usually
var. = variant
vb. = verb
W. = Wadi
WA = Wacholder & Abegg
Y. = Yhwh

OTHER ABBREVIATIONS

Other abbreviations will be found in The Sources and in the Bibliography

# ז

**זְאֵב** I 7.2.1 n.m. **wolf**—Q זב; cstr. זְאֵב; pl. זְאֵבִים; cstr. זְאֵבֵי—<SUBJ> טרף *tear* Gn 49$_{27}$ Ezk 22$_{27}$, אכל *eat* Gn 49$_{27}$, רעה *graze* with lamb Is 65$_{25}$ (|| אַרְיֵה *lion*, + נָחָשׁ *serpent*), חלק pi. *divide* spoil Gn 49$_{27}$, ארב *wait in ambush* Si 11$_{30}$ (+ עוֹף *bird*, כֶּלֶב *dog*), גור *sojourn* with lamb Is 11$_6$ (|| נָמֵר *leopard*), שׁדד *destroy* Jr 5$_6$ (|| אַרְיֵה *lion*, נָמֵר), עזב *abandon* Zp 3$_3$ (if em. זְאֵבֵי עֶרֶב לֹא גָרְמוּ *wolves of the evening [that] set aside nothing* to זְאֵבִים לֹא עָזְבוּ גֶרֶם *wolves [that] do not leave a bone*), גרם *set aside* Zp 3$_3$ (or em.), חבר pu. *be allied* with lamb Si 13$_{17}$. <NOM CL> בִּנְיָמִין זְאֵב *Benjamin is a wolf* Gn 49$_{27}$, שֹׁפְטֶיהָ זְאֵבֵי עֶרֶב *her judges are wolves of the evening* Zp 3$_3$ (or em.; || אֲרִי *lion*). <CSTR> זְאֵב עֲרָבוֹת *wolf of [the] steppe* Jr 5$_6$ (or em. עֶרֶב *of [the] evening* or עַד־בַּיִת *until [they reach their] house*), זְאֵבֵי עֶרֶב *wolves of the evening* Hb 1$_8$=1Qp Hab 3$_7$ (|| נָמֵר *leopard*) Zp 3$_3$ (or em.). <PREP> כְּ *as* Ezk 22$_{27}$ Si 11$_{30}$; מִן of comparison, *(more) than*, + חדד *be sharp* Hb 1$_8$=1QpHab 3$_7$. <SYN> נָמֵר *leopard*, אַרְיֵה *lion*.*

⇒ זְאֵב *Zeeb*.

**זְאֵב** II 6 pr.n.m. **Zeeb**, Midianite prince killed by Ephraimite supporters of Gideon, alw. assoc. with Oreb, <OBJ> נתן *give* Jg 8$_3$, לכד *capture* Jg 7$_{25}$, הרג *kill* Jg 7$_{25}$. <CSTR> יֶקֶב־זְאֵב *winepress of Zeeb* Jg 7$_{25}$, רֹאשׁ ... זְאֵב *head of ... Zeeb* Jg 7$_{25}$. <APP> שַׂר *prince* Jg 7$_{25}$ 8$_3$. <PREP> כְּ *as* Ps 83$_{12}$.

⇒ זְאֵב *wolf*.

**זֹאת** 600.4.67.4 demonst. pronoun sing. f. and adj. **this**—Kt זאתה (Jr 26$_6$), Q זות, זאות, זואת).

**1. as predicative adjective or pronoun,** *this (one)*
- **Subjects,** p. 70b
- **Nominal Clauses**
  - **a.** common noun as complement, p. 71a
  - **b.** proper noun as complement, p. 71b
  - **c.** pronoun as complement, p. 71b
  - **d.** adjective as complement, p. 71b
  - **e.** preposition as complement, p. 71b
  - **f.** undetermined noun as complement, p. 71b
  - **g.** miscellaneous constructions, p. 71b
- **Objects,** p. 71b
- **Constructs,** p. 72a
- **Prepositions,** p. 72a
- **Collocations,** p. 73a

**2. as attributive adjective,** *this*
- **a.** הַזֹּאת following determined noun, p. 73a
- **b.** זֹאת (not הַזֹּאת) following suffixed noun, p. 73b
- **c.** זֹאת following undetermined noun, p. 73b
- **d.** זֹאת preceding undetermined or proper noun, p. 74a
- **e.** זֹאת preceding determined noun, p. 74a

**3. as adverb,** *thus*, p. 74a

**1. as predicative adjective or pronoun, this (one),** also **such (a one)** (e.g. Is 23$_7$), oft. with neuter or indeterminate reference, esp. in מַה־זֹּאת *what is this?* (except at Ex 13$_{14}$, alw. followed by עשׂה *do* in asyndetic relative clause: *what is this that have you done?*, *what have you done?*, etc.); also **the other (one)** (e.g. 1 K 3$_{26}$); perh. in ref. to space, **in this place, here**, or time, **at that time, then** (e.g. Lv 26$_{44}$ [or em.; see Cstr.] Is 28$_{12}$ Jr 31$_{26}$ Zc 5$_7$ Jb 42$_{16}$).

<SUBJ> היה *be* Lv 14$_2$ 16$_{34}$ 17$_7$ Nm 34$_{12}$ Jos 4$_6$ Jg 21$_3$ 1 S 25$_{31}$ 1 K 11$_{11}$ Is 50$_{11}$ Ezk 21$_{32}$ (or em. גַּם־זֹאת לֹא הָיָה *this too was not* to אוֹי לָהּ כָּזֹאת תִּהְיֶה *alas for her; she will be like this* or גַּם־זֹאת לֹא זֹאת *this too is not this*, i.e. will not remain the same)* Jl 1$_2$ Zc 14$_{12.19}$ Ml 1$_9$ Ps 118$_{23}$ 119$_{56}$ Jb 21$_2$ 2 C 1$_{11}$ 1QH 14$_{27}$, קטן *be little* 2 S 7$_{19}$||1 C 17$_{17}$, קלל ni. *be slight* 2 K 3$_{18}$, ידע ho. *be made known* Is 12$_{5(Qr)}$ (Kt pu. appar. in same sense), כתב ni. *be written* Ps 102$_{19}$, קרא ni. *be called* Gn 2$_{23}$, לקח pu. *be taken* Gn 2$_{23}$, נתן ni. *be given* Gn 29$_{27}$, קטר pu. *be perfumed* (or

em. מְקֻטֶּרֶת *perfumed* to מִקְטֹרֶת *of the incense of*), בוא *come*, i.e. befall Ps 44$_{18}$, יצא *go out* Is 28$_{29}$, עלה *go up* Ca 3$_{6}$ 8$_{5}$ perh. 4Q418 167$_{3}$, מצא *find*, i.e. befall Jg 6$_{13}$, perh. פגע *strike*, i.e. befall 1QH fr. 4$_{16}$, שׁקף *overhang*, i.e. look down Ca 6$_{10}$, רפק htp. *lean* Ca 8$_{5}$.

<NOM CL> **a.** common noun as complement, אִשָּׁה *woman* Gn 12$_{12}$ 2 S 11$_{3}$ 2 K 8$_{5}$, בַּת *daughter* 2 S 11$_{3}$, אָמָה *female servant* Gn 21$_{10.10}$, חַיָּה *animal* Lv 11$_{2}$, בְּהֵמָה *beast* Dt 14$_{4}$.

אֶרֶץ *land* Nm 34$_{2.13}$ Dt 34$_{4}$ Jos 13$_{2}$, מַיִם *water* Is 54$_{9}$ (or em. כִּי־מֵי *for the waters of* Noah are this to כְּמֵי *as the waters of*; =4QTanḥ 8$_{10}$ כימי *as the days of*) Ezk 48$_{29}$, נַחֲלָה *inheritance* Jos 13$_{23.28}$ 15$_{20}$ 18$_{20.28}$ 19$_{8.16.23.31.39.48}$ Is 54$_{17}$, מְנוּחָה *(place of) rest* Is 28$_{12}$ Mc 2$_{10}$ Ps 132$_{14}$, מַרְגֵּעָה *(place of) rest* Is 28$_{12}$, מוֹשָׁב *dwelling place* 1 C 4$_{33}$, עִיר *city* Zp 2$_{15}$ Lm 2$_{15}$, עַלִּיזָה *joyful (city)* Is 23$_{7}$, פֵּאָה *corner* Jos 18$_{14}$ Ezk 47$_{20}$, בְּאֵר *well* Gn 21$_{30}$, נְקָבָה *excavation* Siloam tunnel inscr.$_{1}$ ([זאת]; others [תמת] *was complete* [from תמם] or הנה *behold*), קְבֻרָה *grave* Silwan royal steward tomb inscr. 1$_{1}$ ([קברת]) 2$_{1}$ ([זאת]).

חֶרֶב *sword* Jg 7$_{14}$ (אֵין זֹאת בִּלְתִּי אִם־חֶרֶב גִּדְעוֹן *this is nothing other than the sword of Gideon*), אֵיפָה *ephah* Zc 5$_{5}$ (if em. מָה הַיּוֹצֵאת הַזֹּאת *what is this that is coming out?* to מָה הָאֵיפָה הַזֹּאת *what is this ephah?*) 5$_{6}$, perh. עֶצֶם *bone* Gn 2$_{23}$ (see below on פַּעַם), יָד *hand* Is 14$_{26}$=4QpIsa$^{c}$ 8$_{5}$ Ps 109$_{27}$, עַיִן *eye* Zc 5$_{7}$ (or em. עָוֹן *wickedness* and/or del. זאת).

עֵצָה *counsel* Is 14$_{26}$=4QpIsa$^{c}$ 8$_{4}$ ([זוא]ת העצה]), בְּרָכָה *blessing* Dt 33$_{1}$, אָלָה *curse* Zc 5$_{3}$, אוֹת *sign* Gn 9$_{12.17}$ Jr 44$_{29}$, בְּרִית *covenant* Gn 17$_{10}$ Is 59$_{21}$ Jr 31$_{33}$, תְּעוּדָה *testimony* 4QJub$^{a}$ 2$_{24}$, תּוֹרָה *law* Lv 6$_{2.7.18}$ 7$_{1.11.37}$ 11$_{46}$ 12$_{7}$ 13$_{59}$ 14$_{32.54.57}$ 15$_{3.32}$ Nm 5$_{29}$ 6$_{13.21}$ 19$_{14}$ Dt 4$_{44}$ 2 S 7$_{19}$ (or em. זאת to ראה hi. *show*) Ezk 43$_{12.12}$ 4QJub$^{a}$ 2$_{24}$ 11QT 57$_{1}$, חֻקָּה *statute* Ex 12$_{43}$ Nm 19$_{2}$ 31$_{21}$, מִצְוָה *commandment* Dt 6$_{1}$ 11$_{22}$.

פְּעוּלָה *deed* Ps 109$_{20}$, תְּעוּדָה *(established) practice* Ru 4$_{12}$, עֲבוֹדָה *service* Nm 4$_{4.24.28.33}$, מִשְׁמֶרֶת *observance* Nm 4$_{31}$.

עֹלָה *burnt offering* Nm 28$_{14}$=11QT 14$_{7}$ ([זאות עולת]), חֲנֻכָּה *dedication (sacrifice)* Nm 7$_{84.88}$, תְּרוּמָה *contribution* Ex 25$_{3}$ Ezk 45$_{13}$, מִשְׁחָה *ointment*, i.e. consecrated portion Lv 7$_{35.35}$.

קוֹמָה *height* Ca 7$_{8}$ (unless זֹאת קוֹמָתֵךְ = *this height of yours*, as §2e), צְדָקָה *righteousness* Is 54$_{17}$, נֶחָמָה *consolation* Ps 119$_{50}$, רָעָה *evil* 2 K 6$_{33}$ (unless זֹאת הָרָעָה = *this evil* is from Y., as §2e) Jr 4$_{18}$ Arad ost. 40$_{14}$ ([וז]את]), עָוֹן *wickedness* Zc 5$_{7}$ (if em. עַיִן *eye*), רִשְׁעָה *wickedness* Zc 5$_{8}$, מַגֵּפָה *plague* Zc 14$_{15}$.

**b.** proper noun as complement, Jezebel 2 K 19$_{31}$, Naomi Ru 1$_{19}$, Jerusalem Ezk 5$_{5}$ (unless זֹאת יְרוּשָׁלַםִ = *this Jerusalem*, as §2d).

**c.** pronoun as complement, מָה *what?* Gn 3$_{13}$ 12$_{18}$ 26$_{10}$ 29$_{25}$ 42$_{28}$ Ex 13$_{14}$ 14$_{5.11}$ Jg 2$_{2}$ Jon 1$_{10}$, מִי *who?* Ca 3$_{6}$ 6$_{10}$ 8$_{5}$,* זאת *this* Ezk 21$_{31}$ (זֹאת לֹא־זֹאת *this is not this*, i.e. this will not remain as it is) 21$_{32}$ (if em.; see Subj.); זאת אֲשֶׁר *this is what/the one that* Gn 49$_{28}$ Nm 8$_{24}$.

**d.** adjective as complement, רַע *evil* 2 S 19$_{8}$.

**e.** preposition as complement, לְ *to* or *concerning* Dt 33$_{7}$, *(belonging) to* Zp 2$_{10}$, *as* 11QPs$^{a}$ 17$_{17}$, בְּ *on account of* Mc 1$_{5}$=1QpMic 1$_{5}$=8$_{2}$ (1$_{5}$ [זא]ת ... [בפשע] *on account of the sin of* Jacob ... was all *this*; 8$_{2}$ [זאת]), כְּ *as* the days/waters of Noah Is 54$_{9}$ (if em. כִּי־מֵי *for the waters of* to כְּמֵי *as the waters of*) 4QTanḥ 8$_{10}$, עַל *(incumbent) upon* 2 C 2$_{3}$, עִם *with* Jb 10$_{13}$, אַחַר *after* 4QM$^{a}$ 13$_{7}$.

**f.** undetermined noun as complement, אִשָּׁה *woman*, זאת אִשָּׁה אַחַת *there was one woman* Zc 5$_{7}$ (unless *this one woman*, as §2d; or em. הִנֵּה *behold*, a woman).

**g.** miscellaneous constructions, אֵין זאת *there is not this*, appar. it is not so 1 S 20$_{2}$ Am 2$_{11}$ (הַאַף אֵין־זֹאת *is it not indeed so?*); see also Jg 7$_{14}$ in §1a.

<OBJ> עשׂה *do* Gn 3$_{13.14}$ 12$_{18}$ 20$_{5.6}$ 26$_{10}$ 29$_{25}$ 42$_{18.28}$ 43$_{11}$ 44$_{17}$ 45$_{17.19}$ Ex 14$_{5.11}$ Lv 26$_{16}$ Nm 14$_{35}$ 16$_{6}$ Jos 9$_{20}$ 22$_{24}$ Jg 2$_{2}$ 15$_{6}$ 2 S 12$_{5}$ 23$_{17}$||1 C 11$_{19}$ Is 9$_{6}$ 37$_{32}$ 41$_{20}$ 56$_{2}$ Jr 2$_{17}$ Ezk 23$_{38}$ Am 4$_{12}$ 9$_{12}$ Jon 1$_{10}$ Ml 2$_{13}$ Ps 7$_{4}$ (or em. גֵּאוּת *pride*, i.e. act proudly) Jb 12$_{9}$ Pr 6$_{3}$ 2 C 25$_{16}$ Si 15$_{1}$ GnzPs 3$_{6}$, פעל *do* Dt 32$_{27}$ Si 19$_{1}$, כלה pi. *complete* 2 C 31$_{1}$.

נתן *give* Gn 29$_{27(Sam)}$, גמל *repay* Dt 32$_{6}$, בקשׁ pi. *seek* Is 1$_{12}$ 1 C 21$_{3}$, מצא *find* Gn 37$_{32}$, שׁלח *send* 2 S 13$_{17}$, שׁוב hi. *take back* Lm 3$_{21}$ 2 C 27$_{5}$, שׁמר *keep* 1 C 29$_{18}$, טהר pi. *purify* 11QT 45$_{11}$, פתח *open* Silwan royal steward tomb inscr. 1$_{3}$, נקף pi. *strike off*, perh. flay Jb 19$_{26}$ (unless, as §3, זאת = *like this, thus*; or ins. כְּ they will be struck off/come around *like* this; or em. זְקָפַנִי אִתּוֹ *he has raised me up with himself* or נִזְקַף אִתִּי testimony *was vindicated in my presence*).

ראה *see* GnzPs 2$_{13}$ 1QH 18$_{18}$, שׁמע *hear* Is 47$_8$ 48$_{1.16}$ 51$_{21}$ Jr 5$_{21}$ Ho 5$_1$ Jl 1$_2$ Am 8$_4$ Mc 3$_9$ Ps 49$_2$ Jb 34$_{16}$, hi. *announce* Is 45$_{21}$ 48$_{20}$, אזן hi. *hear* Is 42$_{23}$ Jb 37$_{14}$, זכר *remember* Is 46$_8$ Ps 74$_{18}$ Ne 13$_{22}$ (but see Coll.), ידע *know* Gn 41$_{39}$ 1 S 20$_3$ Ps 73$_{16}$ Jb 20$_4$, בין *understand* Jr 9$_{11}$ Ps 50$_{22}$ 92$_7$, שׂכל hi. *consider* Dt 32$_{29}$, חשׁב *reckon* Jb 35$_2$ Si 16$_{23}$, חקר *investigate* Ps 44$_{22}$ Jb 5$_{27}$, יעץ *advise* Is 23$_8$, אמר *say* 1 K 3$_{22.23.23.26}$, דבר pi. *speak* Gn 49$_{28}$, נגד hi. *tell* Is 43$_9$ Jr 5$_{20}$, קרא *call* Jl 4$_9$, כתב *write* Ex 17$_{14}$ (+ זִכָּרוֹן as *a memorial*).

**<CSTR>** שְׁבֻעַ זֹאת *this one's week* Gn 29$_{27.28}$, כָּל־זֹאת *all this* Gn 41$_{39}$ Dt 32$_{27.29}$ (if ins. כָּל־) Jg 6$_{13}$ 1 S 22$_{15}$ 2 S 14$_{19}$ Is 5$_{25}$=4QpIsa$^b$ 2$_9$=4QpIsa$^c$ 4.1$_{18}$ ([כול זאת]) Is 9$_{11.16.20}$ 10$_4$ Jr 3$_{10}$ Ho 7$_{10}$ Mc 1$_5$=1QpMic 1$_5$=8$_2$ (1$_5$ כול זא[ת]; 8$_2$ [כול זאת]) Ps 44$_{18}$ 78$_{32}$ Jb 1$_{22}$ 2$_{10}$ Ne 10$_1$ 2 C 21$_{18}$ 31$_1$ 35$_{20}$ Si 48$_{15}$ 4QDibHam$^a$ 1.5$_6$.

**<PREP>** לְ of direction, *to(wards)*, + שׂית *place* heart, i.e. pay attention to Ex 7$_{23}$; קרא לְ *name* Is 30$_7$, of cause, *on account of*, + חרד *quake* Jb 37$_1$, ברא *create* 1QLitPr 3.1$_7$.

בְּ of accompaniment, *in, with*, + בוא *come* Lv 16$_3$, specif. on (this [condition]), + אות ni. *agree* Gn 34$_{15.22}$, כרת *cut*, i.e. make covenant 1 S 11$_2$, despite (this), nevertheless Lv 26$_{44}$ (if ins. בְּ; וְאַף־גַּם־זֹאת appar. *but even then*), + שׂבע *be satisfied* Ezk 16$_{29}$, שׁמע *hear* Lv 26$_{27}$, מאס *reject* 4QDibHam$^a$ 1.5$_6$, געל *abhor* 4QDibHam$^a$ 1.5$_6$, בקשׁ pi. *seek* Ho 7$_{10}$, שׁוב *go back* Is 5$_{25}$=9$_{11}$=$_{16}$=$_{20}$=10$_4$=4QpIsa$^b$ 2$_9$=4QpIsa$^c$ 4.1$_{18}$ ([בכול זאת]) Jr 3$_{10}$ Ho 7$_{10}$ Si 48$_{15}$, חטא *sin* Ps 78$_{32}$ Jb 1$_{22}$ 2$_{10}$, חדל *cease* from sinning Si 48$_{15}$.

בְּ of instrument, *by (means of), through*, + בחן *test* Ml 3$_{10}$, ni. *be tested* Gn 42$_{15}$, כפר pu. *be covered* Is 27$_9$, ידע *know* Gn 42$_{33}$ Ex 7$_{17}$ Nm 16$_{28}$ Jos 3$_{10}$, מצא *find* 4Q521 2.2$_4$; appar. partitive, *some of, any of*, + ידע *know* 1 S 22$_{15}$; of cause, *on account of*, + היה *be* 1 C 27$_{24}$, הלל htp. *boast* Jr 9$_{23}$, ידע *know* Ps 41$_{12}$, כרת *cut*, i.e. make covenant Ne 10$_1$, כתב *write* Ne 10$_1$; *in (connection with)* 2 S 14$_{19}$; בטח בְּ *trust in* Ps 27$_3$, בין בְּ hi. *understand* or *explain* 4Q302 2.2$_2$.

כְּ *as* 2 S 14$_{13}$ 1 K 7$_{37}$ Est 4$_{14}$ Ezr 9$_{13}$ 1 C 29$_{14}$ 2 C 31$_{20}$ 32$_{15}$ 4QM$^a$ 17$_8$ ([כזו]את) Lachish ost. 5$_5$ (כזא[ת]; others הזא[ת] *this* garment, as §2a) 6$_{10}$, + היה *be* 1 S 4$_7$ Jr 2$_{10}$ Ezk 21$_{32}$ (if em.; see Subj.) 2 C 30$_{6(mss)}$, ni. *occur* Jg 19$_{30}$, ראה ni. *be seen* Jg 19$_{30}$, נקף ni. *be struck off* Jb 19$_{26}$ (if em. pi.; see Obj.).

כְּ *something like* Is 66$_8$, + נתן *give* Ezr 7$_{27}$, perh. בשׂר pi. *announce* 1QH 4$_{29}$ (מי בשר כזאת perh. *who has announced anything like this?* or *who, being flesh, is like this?*); כָּ/כְּזֹאת *as this*, i.e. accordingly, as follows, + עשׂה *do* Jg 15$_7$, שׁלח *send* Gn 45$_{23}$, דבר pi. *speak* Jg 8$_8$ 2 C 34$_{22}$, שׁמע hi. *announce* Jg 13$_{23}$; כָּזֹאת וְכָזֹאת *like this and like this*, i.e. accordingly, as follows, + עשׂה *do* Jos 7$_{20}$, אמר *say* 2 K 9$_{12}$, דבר pi. *speak* 2 K 5$_4$, יעץ *advise* 2 S 17$_{15.15}$.

מִן of comparison, *(more) than*, + קלל ni. *be held in low esteem* 2 S 6$_{22}$.

עַל *concerning, on account of* Ezr 10$_2$ (but perh. עַל = *despite*) 2 C 19$_2$ 29$_9$, + שׁמם *be appalled* Jr 2$_{12}$ Jb 17$_8$, סכל ni. *be foolish* 2 C 16$_9$, זעף *be angry* 2 C 16$_{10}$ (if em. בְּזַעַף *in anger* to זָעַף *he was angry*), זכה *be pure*, i.e. justified, or pi. *make pure*, i.e. acquit Jr 11$_{15}$ (if em. אָז תַּעֲלֹזִי *will you then exult?* to הֲתִזְכִּי/הַאֲזַכֶּה עַל־זֹאת *will you be justified/shall I acquit concerning*, or *despite, this?*), רגז *quake* Am 8$_8$, חגר *gird oneself* Jr 4$_8$, ספד *mourn* Jr 4$_8$ Mc 1$_8$, אבל *mourn* Jr 4$_{28}$, צום *fast* Ezr 8$_{23}$, קדר *be dark* Jr 4$_{28}$, ילל hi. *wail* Jr 4$_8$ Mc 1$_8$, נחם ni. *repent* Am 7$_{3.6}$, זכר *remember* Ne 13$_{14}$, פלל htp. *pray* Ps 32$_6$ 2 C 32$_{20}$, בקשׁ pi. *seek* Ezr 8$_{23}$, דבר pi. *speak* 1QH 12$_{32}$, עמד *stand* Ezr 9$_{15}$ 10$_{15}$, לחם ni. *fight* 2 C 20$_{17}$ (unless עַל = *at* this [time]); *at* this (time), + קיץ hi. *awake* Jr 31$_{26}$, ראה *see* Jr 31$_{26}$ (or em. רוה *be saturated*, i.e. refreshed).

עַד *unto*, i.e. up to this time, + עצר *detain*, i.e. retain one's strength 4QVisSam 3.2$_1$; appar. *beside, in comparison with*, + חשׁב ni. *be reckoned* 1QH 18$_{27}$.

אַחֲרֵי *after*, + חיה *live* Jb 42$_{16}$, אמר *say* Ezr 9$_{10}$, נגף *strike* 2 C 21$_{18}$, טהר pi. *purify* 11QT 45$_{11}$, עלה *go up* 2 C 35$_{20}$.

אַחַר *after* 4QM$^a$ 13$_7$.

תַּחַת *in place of*, i.e. on account of, + מות ho. *be put to death* 2 S 19$_{22}$ (mss qal *die*).

בַּעֲבוּר *on account of*, + עמד hi. *establish* Ex 9$_{16}$.

לְמַעַן *on account of*, + ענה pi. *humiliate* 1 K 11$_{39}$.

# זאת

<COLL> עוֹד זֹאת גִּדְּפוּ אוֹתִי *(in) this (way) too they reviled me* Ezk $20_{27}$, עוֹד זֹאת אִדָּרֵשׁ *(in) this (way) too, I let myself be inquired of* Ezk $36_{37}$, הֶן־זֹאת לֹא־צָדַקְתָּ *behold, (in) this (matter), you are not right* Jb $33_{12}$, perh. גַּם־זֹאת זָכְרָה־לִּי *(in) this (matter) too, remember me* Ne $13_{22}$ (unless *remember this too on my behalf*).

**2.** as attributive adjective, **this.**

**a.** הַזֹּאת following determined noun, אִשָּׁה *woman* Dt $22_{14}$=11QT $65_{8}$ 1 S $2_{20}$ 2 S $3_{17.18.19}$ 2 K $6_{28}$, נַעֲרָה *girl* Ru $2_{5}$ $4_{12}$, יַלְדָּה *girl* Gn $34_{4}$, ארר pass. ptc. *accursed one* 2 K $9_{34}$, שׁוּנַמִּית *Shunamite woman* 2 K $4_{12.36}$, נֶפֶשׁ *soul* Jr $38_{16}$ (Kt Or זֶה *this*), עֵדָה *congregation* Nm $14_{27.35}$ $16_{21}$ $17_{10}$, שְׁאֵרִית *remnant* Jr $42_{2}$, מִשְׁפָּחָה *family* Jr $8_{3}$ Mc $2_{3}$.

אֶרֶץ *land* Gn $12_{7}$ $15_{7.18}$ $24_{5.7}$ $26_{3}$ $31_{13}$ $48_{4}$ $50_{24}$ Ex $32_{13}$ Nm $14_{3.8.14}$ $32_{5.22}$ Dt $3_{12.18}$ $4_{22.22}$ $9_{4}$ $9_{6}$ $26_{9}$ $29_{23}$ Jos $1_{13}$ $11_{16}$ $13_{7}$ $17_{12}$ Jg $1_{27}$ $2_{2}$ 1 K $9_{8}$ 2 K $18_{25}$‖2 C $7_{21}$ Is $36_{10.10}$ Jr $13_{13}$ $14_{15}$ $16_{3}$ $16_{6.13}$ $22_{12}$ $24_{6.8}$ $25_{9.11}$ $26_{20}$ $32_{15.22.41.43}$ $36_{29}$ $37_{19}$ $42_{10.13}$ Ezk $47_{14.21}$ 2 C $20_{7}$ $30_{9}$ 4QBibPar $3_{2}$.

אֲדָמָה *land* Gn $28_{15}$ Jos $23_{13}$ $23_{15}$ 1 K $14_{15}$,* חֶלְקָה *plot (of land)* 2 K $9_{26}$, מַכְשֵׁלָה *ruin* Is $3_{6}$, אֶבֶן *stone* Gn $28_{22}$ Jos $24_{27}$, מַצֵּבָה *pillar* Gn $31_{52}$, חוֹמָה *wall* Ne $5_{16}$ (unless זאת modifies מְלָאכָה *work*, i.e. this work of the wall), דֶּרֶךְ *way* 11QT $56_{18}$, פִּנָּה *corner* 11QT $41_{02}$ ([הפנה הזואת]) $41_{2}$ ([הפנה]) $41_{7}$ $44_{16}$ $45_{03}$ ([הפנה הזואת]), חָצֵר *court* 11QT $39_{4}$ (לחצר) $39_{11}$ (ל[ח]צר) $40_{4}$ (ה[חצ]ר), מְסִבָּה *staircase* 11QT $31_{8}$.

אֵשׁ *fire* Dt $5_{25}$ $18_{16}$=11QT $61_{04}$ ([האש ... הזואת]), שֶׁמֶשׁ *sun* 2 S $12_{11}$, גֶּפֶן *vine* Ezk $17_{7}$, לְבֹנָה *frankincense* 11QT $8_{10}$ ([ה]לבונה), מְגִלָּה *scroll* Jr $36_{29}$ Ezk $3_{1.2.3}$, אִגֶּרֶת *letter* Est $9_{26.29}$, מִנְחָה *tribute* Gn $43_{15}$, תְּרוּמָה *contribution* Ezk $45_{16}$, עוֹלָה *burnt offering* 11QT $24_{10}$ $25_{8}$ ([העולה ה]זואת), שִׂמְלָה *garment* Lachish ost. $5_{5}$ ([ה]שמל[ה/א הזא[ת]; others [ה]ספ[רם כזא[ת you have sent *letters like this*, as §1, Prep.), perh. כּוֹס *cup* Jr $25_{15}$ (if em. כּוֹס הַיַּיִן הַחֵמָה הַזֹּאת *the cup of wine—this anger* to כּוֹס יֵין הַחֶמֶר הַזֹּאת *this cup of unmixed wine* or *the cup of this unmixed wine*).

עִיר *city* Gn $19_{20}$ Jos $6_{26}$=4QTestim$_{22}$=4QPsJos$^{b}$ $22.2_{8}$ (הע[י]ר) Jg $19_{11}$ 1 S $9_{6}$ 2 K $18_{30}$‖Is $36_{15}$ 2 K $19_{32.33.34}$‖Is $37_{33.34.35}$ 2 K $20_{6}$‖Is $38_{6}$ 2 K $23_{27}$ Jr $17_{24.25}$ $19_{8.11.11}$ $19_{15}$ $20_{5}$ $21_{4.6.7.9.10}$ $22_{8.8}$ $26_{6(Qr)}$ (Kt appar. זֹאתָה) $26_{9.11.12.15.20}$ $27_{17.19}$ $29_{16}$ $32_{3.28.29.29.31.36}$ $33_{4.5}$ $34_{2.22}$ $37_{8.10}$ $38_{2.3.4.17.18.23}$ $39_{16}$ Ezk $11_{2.6}$ Ne $13_{18}$ 2 C $6_{34}$ 4QTestim$_{26}$=4QPsJos$^{b}$ $22.2_{12}$ (Testim [העיר הזות]; PsJos [העיר ה]זאת) 4QpGen$^{a}$ $1.3_{3}$.

עֵת *time* Jos $11_{6}$ Est $4_{14}$ 1QS $9_{20}$, פַּעַם *occasion* Ex $8_{28}$ $9_{14}$ 2 S $17_{7}$ Jr $10_{18}$ $16_{21}$,* שָׁנָה *year* Lv $25_{13}$=11QMelch$_{1}$ ([הזואת]) 1QDM $3_{4}$ ([בש]נה הזא[ת]) $3_{7}$ ([בשנה הזאת]), appar. (!) לַיְלָה *night* 1QJub$^{a}$ $27_{19}$ ([בלילה הזאת]), שָׁבוּעָה *week* 1QJub$^{a}$ $27_{19}$ ([בשבועה הזאת]).

בְּרִית *covenant* Dt $5_{3}$ $29_{8.13}$ 2 K $23_{3}$ Jr $11_{2.3.6.8}$ 1QS $2_{12.13.16}$, תְּעוּדָה *testimony* 4QJub$^{a}$ $1_{8}$, תּוֹרָה *law* Nm $5_{30}$ Dt $1_{5}$ $4_{8}$ $17_{18}$=11QT $56_{21}$ Dt $17_{19}$ $27_{3.8.26.58}$ $28_{61}$ (סֵפֶר הַתּוֹרָה הַזֹּאת *the book of this law*; Sam, mss זֶה *this* book of the law) $29_{28}$ $31_{9.11.12}$ $32_{46}$ 11QT $50_{7.17}$ $59_{10}$, מִצְוָה *commandment* Dt $6_{25}$ $11_{22}$=1QDM $3_{4}$ ([המצוה הזאת]) Dt $15_{5}$ $19_{9}$ $30_{11}$ Ml $2_{1.4}$ 4QJub$^{d}$ $21_{15}$ ([המצוה הזאת]), חֻקָּה *statute* Ex $13_{10}$, שִׁירָה *song* Ex $15_{1}$ Nm $21_{17}$ Dt $31_{19.19.21.22.24.30}$ $32_{44}$ 2 S $22_{1}$‖Ps $18_{1}$, קִינָה *lament* 2 S $1_{17}$, בְּרָכָה *blessing* 1 S $25_{27}$, אָלָה *curse* Dt $29_{13.18}$, תְּפִלָּה *prayer* 2 S $7_{27}$ 1 K $8_{54}$, תְּחִנָּה *plea* 1 K $8_{54}$ (כָּל־הַתְּפִלָּה וְהַתְּחִנָּה הַזֹּאת *all this prayer and plea*), מַרְאָה *vision* Dn $10_{8}$, תְּרוּעָה *shout* 1 S $4_{6}$, עֵצָה *counsel* 11QMelch$_{15}$ ([ע]צ[ה]).

תְּשׁוּעָה *salvation* Jg $15_{18}$, יְשׁוּעָה *salvation* 1 S $14_{45}$, גְּמוּלָה *recompense* 2 S $19_{37}$, טוֹבָה *goodness* 2 S $2_{6}$ $7_{28}$‖1 C $17_{26}$, גְּדוּלָּה *greatness* 2 S $7_{21}$‖1 C $17_{19}$, מִדָּה *measure* Ezk $45_{3}$ 4QTohA $1.1_{2}$ 11QT $36_{5}$ ([כמדה הזואת]) $40_{8.15.15}$ $41_{02}$ ([כמדה הזואת]) $41_{04}$ ([כמדה הזואת]), עֲבוֹדָה *service* Ex $12_{25.26}$ $13_{5}$, מְלָאכָה *work* Ne $5_{16}$ (unless זאת modifies חוֹמָה *wall*, i.e. the work of this wall) $6_{16}$.

תּוֹעֵבָה *abomination* Dt $13_{15}$=11QT $55_{6}$ Dt $17_{4}$=11QT $55_{20}$ Dt $32_{35}$ Jr $44_{4}$, נְבָלָה *folly* Jg $19_{23.24}$ 2 S $13_{12}$, רָעָה *evil* Gn $39_{9}$ Jg $20_{3.12}$ 1 S $6_{9}$ $12_{20}$ 2 S $13_{16}$ 1 K $9_{9}$‖2 C $7_{22}$ Jr $16_{10}$ $32_{23.42}$ $40_{2}$ $44_{23}$ Ezk $6_{10}$ Jon $1_{7.8}$ Jb $2_{11}$ Dn $9_{13}$ Ne $13_{18.27}$, חַטָּאת *sin* 1 S $14_{38}$, perh. חֵמָה *anger* Jr $25_{15}$ (or em. חֶמֶר *[unmixed] wine*; see above on כּוֹס *cup*), צָרָה *distress* Gn $42_{21}$, מַכָּה *plague* 11QapPs$^{a}$ fr. $A_{8}$ ([המכה]) 11QapPs$^{a}$ $2_{11}$ ([המכה ... הזוא[ת]) $3_{14}$ ([המ]כה ... [הזואת]), חֲרָדָה *trembling* 2 K $4_{13}$.

**b.** זאת (not הַזֹּאת) following suffixed noun, שְׁבוּעָה *oath* Gn $24_{8}$, אַשְׁמָה *guilt* 2 C $24_{18}$.

**c.** זאת following undetermined noun, גֶּפֶן *vine* Ps $80_{15}$ (or em. גֶּפֶן זֹאת : וְכַנָּה *this vine; and a stock* to גֶּפֶן זוֹ תְכִינֶהָ *a vine that you establish*), perh. תְּעָלָה *conduit* 11QT$^{b}$ $10_{3}$.

**d.** זאת preceding undetermined or proper noun, זאת יְרוּשָׁלַםִ *this Jerusalem* Ezk 5$_5$ (unless *this is Jerusalem*, as §1, Nom. Cl., §b), זאת אִשָּׁה אַחַת *this one woman* Zc 5$_7$ (unless *there was a woman*, as §1, Nom. Cl., §f).

**e.** זאת preceding determined noun, פַּעַם *occasion* Gn 2$_{23}$,* רָעָה *evil* 2 K 6$_{33}$, קוֹמָה *height* Ca 7$_8$; but in all three perh. זאת = *this is* the occasion, the evil from Y., your stature, as §1, Nom Cl., §a).

**3.** as adverb, **thus,** נִקְּפוּ זאת perh. *they will strike off,* perh. flay, *thus* Jb 19$_{26}$ (or ins. כְּ strike off *like* this; or em.; see §1, Obj.).

Also 1QDM 3$_7$ (הז[את]) 4QpIsa$^c$ 11.1$_5$ 4QpIsa$^c$ 35 (זוא[ת]) 4Q418 167$_3$ 4QPrFêtes$^c$ 183$_8$ 4Q525 38$_2$ (הזו[ת]) perh. 4QCrypt 2.1$_{10}$ 4Q458 2.1$_6$.*

**זבד** 1.1 vb. **endow—Qal** 1.1 Pf. זְבָדַנִי; impv. Si זבדה—**endow (with)** (Gn 30$_{25}$), **give** in marriage (Si 7$_{25[C]}$), <SUBJ> אֱלֹהִים *God* Gn 30$_{20}$, בֵּן *son* Si 7$_{25(C)}$. <OBJ> (1) beneficiary of endowment: Leah Gn 30$_{20}$, appar. בַּת *daughter* Si 7$_{25(C)}$; (2) object given in endowment: זֵבֶד *endowment* Gn 30$_{20}$. <PREP> אֶל *to*, + גֶּבֶר *man* Si 7$_{25(C)}$ (ג[בר]).

→ זֵבֶד *gift*, זָבָד *Zabad*, זַבְדִּי *Zabdi*, זַבְדִּיאֵל *Zabdiel*, זְבַדְיָה *Zebadiah*, זָבוּד *Zabud*, זְבוּדָּה *Zebuddah*, זְבִידָה *Zebidah*, אֶלְזָבָד *Elzabad*, יְהוֹזָבָד *Jehozabad*, עַמִּיזָבָד *Ammizabad*.

**זָבָד** 8 pr.n.m. **Zabad, 1.** son of Nathan and father of Ephlal, descendant of Judah, <SUBJ> ילד hi. *beget* 1 C 2$_{37}$. <OBJ> ילד hi. *beget* 1 C 2$_{36}$.

**2.** son of Tahath and father of Shuthelah, descendant of Ephraim, <NOM CL> בְּנֵי אֶפְרַיִם ... זָבָד *the sons of Ephraim were ... Zabad* 1 C 7$_{21}$. <APP> בֵּן *son* 1 C 7$_{21}$.

**3.** one of David's warriors, son of Ahlai, <NOM CL> גִּבּוֹרֵי הַחֲיָלִים ... זָבָד *the mighty ones of valour were ... Zabad* 1 C 11$_{41}$. <APP> בֶּן *son* 1 C 11$_{41}$.

**4.** conspirator against Joash, son of Shimeath, appar. ident. with Jozacar at ||2 K 12$_{22}$. <SUBJ> קשׁר htp. *conspire* 2 C 24$_{26}$ (mss Jozacar). <APP> בֶּן *son* 2 C 24$_{26}$.

**5.** Israelite husband of foreign wife, descendant of Zattu, <NOM CL> מִבְּנֵי זַתּוּא ... זָבָד *of the sons of Zattu were ... Zabad* Ezr 10$_{27}$.

**6.** Israelite husband of foreign wife, descendant of Hashum, <NOM CL> מִבְּנֵי חָשֻׁם ... זָבָד *of the sons of Hashum were ... Zabad* Ezr 10$_{33}$ (or em. Zacar).

**7.** Israelite husband of foreign wife, descendant of Nebo, <NOM CL> מִבְּנֵי נְבוֹ ... זָבָד *of the sons of Nebo were ... Zabad* Ezr 10$_{43}$ (ms Zecher).

→ זבד *endow*.

**זֵבֶד** 1.2 n.m. **gift**—<OBJ> זבד *endow* Gn 30$_{20}$. <CSTR> מטעמי זבד *delicacies of*, i.e. given as, *a gift* Si 36$_{24(Bmg, C)}$ 40$_{29(Bmg)}$. <ADJ> טוֹב *good* Gn 30$_{20}$.

→ זבד *endow*.

**זַבְדִּי** 7 pr.n.m. **Zabdi, 1.** son of Zerah, grandson of Judah, father of Carmi, and grandfather of Achan, appar. ident. with Zimri at 1 C 2$_6$, <SUBJ> לכד ni. *be captured* Jos 7$_{17}$ (or em. Zimri). <NOM CL> בְּנֵי זֶרַח זַבְדִּי וְאֵיתָן *the sons of Zerah were Zabdi and Ethan* 1 C 2$_6$ (if em. Zimri). <CSTR> בֶּן־זַבְדִּי *son of Zabdi* Jos 7$_{1.18}$ (or em. Zimri in both). <APP> בֶּן *son* Jos 7$_{1.18}$.

**2.** son of Shimei/Shema, descendant of Benjamin, <NOM CL> זִכְרִי וְזַבְדִּי ... : בְּנֵי שִׁמְעִי *Zichri and Zabdi ... were the sons of Shimei* 1 C 8$_{19}$.

**3.** son of Shashak, descendant of Benjamin, <NOM CL> זַבְדִּי וְחָנָן ... : בְּנֵי שָׁשָׁק *Zabdi and Hanan ... were the sons of Shashak* 1 C 8$_{23}$ (if em. Zichri).

**4.** Shiphmite officer of David, <NOM CL> עַל שֶׁבַּכְּרָמִים לְאֹצְרוֹת הַיַּיִן זַבְדִּי *over that which is in the vineyards for the stores of wine was Zabdi* 1 C 27$_{27}$ (or em. עַל אֹצְרוֹת *over the stores of*). <APP> שִׁפְמִי *Shiphmite* 1 C 27$_{27}$.

**5.** Levite, son of Asaph and father of Micha, appar. ident. with Zichri at ||1 C 9$_{15}$. <CSTR> בֶּן־זַבְדִּי *son of Zabdi* Ne 11$_{17}$||1 C 9$_{15(mss)}$. <APP> בֶּן *son* Ne 11$_{17}$||1 C 9$_{15(mss)}$.

→ זבד *endow*.

**זַבְדִּיאֵל** 2 pr.n.m. **Zabdiel, 1.** priest, son of Haggedolim (unless הַגְּדוֹלִים = son of *the great ones*; or em. הַגָּדוֹל son of *Haggadol*), <NOM CL> פָּקִיד עֲלֵיהֶם זַבְדִּיאֵל *Zabdiel was an official over them* Ne 11$_{14}$. <APP> בֶּן *son* Ne 11$_{14}$.

**2.** father of Jashobeam (or em. Ishbaal), perh. ident.

with Hachmoni at 1 C $11_{11}$, <CSTR> בֶּן־זַבְדִּיאֵל *son of Zabdiel* 1 C $27_{2}$.
⇒ זבד *endow* + אֵל *God.*

**זְבַדְיָה** 9.0.0.1 pr.n.m. **Zebadiah**—זְבַדְיָהוּ, I זבדיו—**1.** son of Michael, descendant of Shephatiah, and leader of returning exiles, <NOM CL> מִבְּנֵי שְׁפַטְיָה זְבַדְיָה *of the sons of Shephatiah was Zebadiah* Ezr $8_{8}$. <APP> בֵּן *son* Ezr $8_{8}$. <PREP> עִם *with* Ezr $8_{8}$.

**2.** priest, husband of foreign wife, and descendant of Immer, <NOM CL> מִבְּנֵי אִמֵּר חֲנָנִי וּזְבַדְיָה *of the sons of Immer were Hanani and Zebadiah* Ezr $10_{20}$ (mss Zechariah).

**3.** son of Beriah, descendant of Benjamin, <NOM CL> זְבַדְיָה וַעֲרָד ... : ... בְּנֵי בְרִיעָה *Zebadiah and Arad ... were sons of Beriah* 1 C $8_{15}$.

**4.** son of Elpaal, descendant of Benjamin, <NOM CL> זְבַדְיָה וּמְשֻׁלָּם ... : ... בְּנֵי אֶלְפָּעַל *Zebadiah and Meshullam ... were sons of Elpaal* 1 C $8_{17}$.

**5.** son of Jeroham, brother of Joelah (or em. Jalah), and one of David's warriors, <APP> בֵּן *son* 1 C $12_{8}$.

**6.** one of David's officers, son of Asahel, and nephew of Joab, <NOM CL> זְבַדְיָה ... אַחֲרָיו *Zebadiah ... was after him* 1 C $27_{7}$. <APP> בֵּן *son* 1 C $27_{7}$.

**7.** third son of Meshelemiah, Korahite gatekeeper, <NOM CL> זְבַדְיָהוּ הַשְּׁלִישִׁי *Zebadiah was the third (son)* 1 C $26_{2}$ (mss Zechariah).

**8.** Levitical teacher at time of Jehoshaphat, <NOM CL> עִמָּהֶם ... נְתַנְיָהוּ וּזְבַדְיָהוּ *with them were ... Nethaniah and Zebadiah* 2 C $17_{8}$ (mss Zechariah). <APP> לֵוִי *Levite* 2 C $17_{8}$.

**9.** royal arbitrator of secular disputes at time of Jehoshaphat, <NOM CL> עֲלֵיכֶם ... זְבַדְיָהוּ *over you ... is Zebadiah* 2 C $19_{11}$ (mss Zechariah). <APP> בֵּן *son* of Ishmael 2 C $19_{11}$, נָגִיד *prince* 2 C $19_{11}$.

**10.** father of Manassite official at time of David, <CSTR> בֶּן־זְבַדְיָהוּ Iddo *son of Zebadiah* 1 C $27_{21}$ (if em. Zechariah).

**11.** <PREP> לְ of possession, *of, (belonging) to* Stamp/Coin 15 (5th/4th cent.; לזבדיו; others עזבק *Azbuk* or יהעזר *Joezer*).
⇒ זבד *endow* + יְ *Y.*

**זְבַדְיָהוּ**, see זְבַדְיָה *Zebadiah.*

**[זְבַדְיוֹ]**, see זְבַדְיָה *Zebadiah.*

**זְבוּב** 2 n.m. **fly**—pl. cstr. זְבוּבֵי—<SUBJ> באשׁ hi. *stink* or *cause* oil *to stink* Ec $10_{1}$, נבע hi. *cause to ferment* Ec $10_{1}$ (or del. יַבִּיעַ *causes to ferment* or em. גְּבִיעַ causes *cup* to stink), מות *die* Ec $10_{1}$ (if em.; see Cstr.). <NOM CL> זְבוּב אֲשֶׁר בִּקְצֵה יְאֹרֵי מִצְרַיִם *the fly that is at the end of the streams of Egypt* Is $7_{18}$ (|| דְּבוֹרָה *bee*). <CSTR> זְבוּבֵי מָוֶת *flies of death*, perh. dead flies or deadly flies Ec $10_{1}$ (or em. זְבוּב מֵת *dead fly*). <PREP> לְ of direction, *to, for,* + שׁרק *whistle* Is $7_{18}$. <SYN> דְּבוֹרָה *bee.*

**זָבוּד** 2 pr.n.m. **Zabud, 1.** officer of Solomon and son of Nathan the priest, <NOM CL> זָבוּד ... רֵעֶה הַמֶּלֶךְ *Zabud ... was the friend of the king* 1 K $4_{5}$ (mss Zaccur). <APP> בֵּן *son* 1 K $4_{5}$.

**2.** leader of returning exiles and son of Bigvai, <NOM CL> מִבְּנֵי בִגְוַי עוּתַי וזבוד *of the sons of Bigvai were Uthai and Zabud* Ezr $8_{14(Kt)}$ (Qr Zaccur; or em. בֶּן Uthai, *son of* Zabud/Zaccur). <PREP> עִם *with* Ezr $8_{14(Kt)}$.
⇒ זבד *endow.*

**זְבוּדָּה** 1 pr.n.f. **Zebuddah,** daughter of Pedaiah of Rumah and mother of Jehoiakim, <NOM CL> שֵׁם אִמּוֹ זְבוּדָּה *the name of his mother was Zebuddah* 2 K $23_{36(Qr)}$ (Kt appar. Zebidah). <APP> בַּת *daughter* 2 K $23_{36(Qr)}$.
⇒ זבד *endow.*

**[זְבוּל]**, see זְבֻל I *dwelling place,* II *dais.*

**[זְבוּלוֹן]**, see זְבוּלֻן *Zebulun.*

**זְבוּלֻן** 45.0.3 pr.n.m. **Zebulun**—זְבֻלוּן (14 times), Q זבולון—**1.** sixth son of Jacob and Leah and father of Sered, Elon, and Jahleel, <NOM CL> בְּנֵי לֵאָה ... יִשָּׂשכָר וּזְבוּלֻן *the sons of Leah were ... Issachar and Zebulun* Gn $35_{23}$. <OBJ> קרא *call,* i.e. name Gn $30_{20}$. <CSTR> בְּנֵי זְבוּלֻן *sons of Zebulun* Gn $46_{14}$. <COLL> יִשָּׂשכָר וּזְבוּלֻן Gn

3523 Ex 13(Sam) 1 C 21(mss) (זְבֻלוּן).

**2.** usu. tribe descended from preceding, with its assoc. territory, <SUBJ> שׁכן *dwell* at sea shore Gn 4913 (or em. שׁכן to זבל *dwell*), יצא *go out* Dt 3318, עמד *stand* Dt 2713, ירשׁ hi. *(dis)possess* Canaanites Jg 130, שׂמח *rejoice* Dt 3318. <NOM CL> זְבֻלוּן עַם *Zebulun is a people* Jg 518, עַל גְּבוּל יִשָּׂשכָר ... זְבוּלֻן *on the border of Issachar ... was Zebulun* Ezk 4826, זבולון ... לים *Zebulun ... is to the west* 11QT 3913. <OBJ> זעק hi. *summon* to battle at Kedesh Jg 410. <CSTR> בְּנֵי זְבוּלֻן *sons of Zebulun* Nm 130 27 724 1016 2626 3425 Jos 1910.16 Jg 46 (זְבֻלוּן) 11QT 4501 ([בני זבולון]), מַטֵּה *tribe of* Nm 131 27 1310 Jos 217.34||1 C 648.62, משפחת זבולן *families of Zebulun* Nm 2627(Sam) (MT Zebulunites), גְּבוּל זְבוּלֻן *border of Zebulun* Ezk 4827, אֶרֶץ *land of* Jg 1212 Is 823 (אַרְצָה זְבֻלוּן *to the land of Zebulun*; 1QIsaa ארץ זבולון), שָׂרֵי זְבֻלוּן *princes of Zebulun* Ps 6828, שַׁעַר זְבוּלֻן *gate of Zebulun* or *Zebulun Gate* Ezk 4833 11QT 414 ([שער זבולון]) 415 4501.01 (both [שער זבולון]), עולת זבולון *burnt offering of Zebulun* 11QT 2415. <PREP> לְ of possession, *of, (belonging) to* Nm 19 1 C 2719; *concerning*, + אמר *say* Dt 3318; בְּ of place, *in(to), through*, + שׁלח *send* messengers Jg 635; *against*, + פגע *strike*, i.e. touch (of border) Jos 1927.34; מִן of direction, *from*, + ירד *go down* Jg 514; of possession, *of, (belonging) to* 1 C 1234; partitive, *(some) of, from among* 2 C 3011.18; עַד *unto* 1 C 1241, + עבר *pass* 2 C 3010 (or em. זְבֻלוּן *unto Zebulun* to גְּבֻל דָּן *border of Dan*); בְּקֶרֶב *among*, + ישׁב *dwell* Jg 130.

→ זְבוּלֹנִי *Zebulunite.*

**זְבוּלֹנִי** 3 gent. **Zebulunite,** descendant of Zebulun or inhabitant of territory allotted to tribe of Zebulun. **1.** as collective sing. noun, **Zebulunites,** <CSTR> מִשְׁפַּחַת הַזְּבוּלֹנִי *families of the Zebulunite(s)* Nm 2627 (Sam. of Zebulun).

**2.** as sing. noun, a particular **Zebulunite,** <APP> אֵילוֹן הַזְּבוּלֹנִי *Elon the Zebulunite* Jg 1211.12(mss) (L אֵלוֹן).

→ זְבוּלֻן *Zebulun.*

**זבח** 134.0.29 vb. **sacrifice—Qal** 112.0.25 Pf. זָבַח, זָבַחְתִּי, זָבְחוּ, זְבַחְתֶּם; impf. 2ms תִּזְבַּח (תִּזְבָּחֶנּוּ), אֶזְבַּח (אֶזְבְּחָה), יִזְבְּחוּ, 2mpl תִּזְבְּחוּ (תִּזְבָּחוּ, תִּזְבָּחֻהוּ, Q תזבחוהו), (יִזְבָּחוּ), נִזְבַּח (נִזְבְּחָה); + waw וְזָבַח, וְזָבַחְתָּ (Q וזבחתה), וַיִּזְבָּחֻנוּ, וַיִּזְבַּח; 2fs וַתִּזְבָּחִים, 3fs וַתִּזְבָּחֵהוּ, וַיִּזְבָּחֵהוּ; impv. זְבַח, זִבְחוּ; ptc. זֹבֵחַ (זוֹבֵחַ), זֹבְחִים (Q זובחים), זֹבְחֵי (Q זובחי); inf. זְבֹחַ (זְבֹחַ, זָבְחוֹ)—usu. **offer in sacrifice, slaughter for sacrifice** (perh. at Ps 5014.23 **offer** thanksgiving); also **slaughter** beast for non-sacrificial eating (e.g. Dt 1215.21 1 S 2824), **kill** human beings, perh. as sacrifice (1 K 132 2 K 2320 perh. Ho 132).

<SUBJ> Y. Ezk 3917.19, Aaron Ex 53 821.22.22.23.24, perh. Absalom 2 S 1512, Adonijah 1 K 19.19.25, Ahab 2 C 182, Ahaz 2 C 2823.23, Balak Nm 2240, David 2 S 613 1 C 2128, Elisha 1 K 1921, Elkanah 1 S 13.4.21, Jacob/Israel Gn 3154 461, Jonah Jon 210, Josiah 1 K 132 2 K 2320, Manasseh 2 C 3316, Moses Ex 318 53 821.22.22.23.24 Lv 2229.29, Samuel 1 S 108 (|| עלה hi. *raise*, i.e. offer sacrifice) 162.5, Solomon 1 K 863||2 C 75 1 K 863.

Benjamin 2 C 1511, Ephraim Ho 813 perh. 132, Issachar Dt 3319, Israel 1 K 862 2 K 1735.36 (both || שׁחה htpal. *bow down*) Ml 18 Ps 5014, Israelite(s) Ex 2318 Lv 2229.29 Dt 1215 (+ אכל *eat*) 1221 1521 162.4.5.6 171 277 (+ אכל) 4QJuba 111 ([ויזבחו]) 11QT 177.7 4716.16 524.5.6.10.13.15.18 533 ([וז]ב[חת]ה) 5310, Jerusalem Ezk 1620, Jeshurun Dt 3217, Judah 2 C 1511, Jews Ne 334, Kittim 1QpHab 64, Zebulun Dt 3319.

עַם *people* Ex 58 84.25 328 (|| שׁחה htpal. *bow down*) 1 S 1115 1515.21 1 K 862(ms)||2 C 74 Is 653 Ps 5014 2 C 3317, קָהָל *assembly* 1 C 2921 (|| עלה hi. *raise*, i.e. offer sacrifice), עֵדָה *congregation* Lv 195.5, בַּיִת *house(hold)* 1 S 121, זֶרַע *seed*, i.e. offspring Is 577.

מֶלֶךְ *king* 1 K 34 862||2 C 74, סֶרֶן Philistine *lord* Jg 1623, כֹּהֵן *priest* 11QT 3711, perh. לֵוִי *Levite* 1 C 1526, זָקֵן *elder* Ex 318 Lv 94(Sam), אִישׁ *man* 1 S 13 (+ שׁחה htpal. *bow down*) 121 213.15.19 615 (|| עלה hi. *raise*, i.e. offer sacrifice) Jon 116 (|| נדר *vow*), אִשָּׁה *woman* 1 S 2824, אָב *father* Ezk 2028 Ps 10637, Israelite father Ex 1315, בֵּן *son* 1 K 132 Is 577 Ps 46, specif. son of Israel Ex 517 2024 Lv 94 (Sam זָקֵן *elder*) 175.5.7 195(Gnz, mss).5(Gnz, mss) Jos 831 Jg 25, נַעַר *lad* Ex 245 (|| עלה hi.).

גֵּר *sojourner* 2 C 1511, גּוֹי *gentile* CD 129 4QMMT B8 ([זובחים]) 11QT 5120, צַר *adversary* Ezr 42, יֹשֵׁב *inhabitant* Ex 3415=11QT 213 ([יושב ... ו]זבחו), רֹעֶה *shepherd* Ezk 343 (or em. רַע *evil one*), נֹכֵל *cheat* Ml 114 (|| נדר

*vow)*, אֱוִיל *fool* Ps 107$_{22}$, נתן ptc. *one who gives* heart 2 C 11$_{16}$, psalmist Ps 27$_{6}$ 54$_{8}$ 116$_{17}$; subj. not specified, Ex 22$_{19}$ Dt 18$_{3}$ Is 66$_{3}$ (|| שׁחט *slaughter*, + נכה hi. *strike*, ערף *behead*) Zc 14$_{21}$ Ps 50$_{23}$ Ec 9$_{2.2}$ (לַזֹּבֵחַ וְלַאֲשֶׁר אֵינֶנּוּ זֹבֵחַ *to one who sacrifices and to one who does not sacrifice*) Ne 12$_{43}$ 2 C 34$_{4}$ 4QpMos$^{e}$ 2.2$_{10}$ 4QMMT B$_{11}$ ([זב]חם) 4QMMT B$_{36}$ ([אין לזבוח] *one is not to sacrifice*) 11QT 47$_{7.11.14}$ 52$_{20}$ 60$_{7}$.

<OBJ> זֶבַח *sacrifice* Gn 31$_{54}$ 46$_{1}$ Ex 24$_{5}$ Lv 17$_{5.5.7}$ 19$_{5.5}$ 22$_{29.29(Sam, mss)}$ Dt 18$_{3}$ 33$_{19}$ Jg 16$_{23}$ 1 S 1$_{21}$ 2$_{13.19}$ 6$_{15}$ 10$_{8}$ 11$_{15}$ 2 S 15$_{12}$ 1 K 8$_{62.63}$||2 C 7$_{4.5}$ 1 K 8$_{63}$ Is 57$_{7}$ Ezk 20$_{28}$ 39$_{17.19}$ Ho 8$_{13}$ Jon 1$_{16}$ Ps 4$_{6}$ 27$_{6}$ 107$_{22}$ 116$_{17}$ Ne 12$_{43}$ 1 C 29$_{21}$ 2 C 33$_{16}$ 4QJub$^{e}$ 21$_{7}$ (ת]ז[בח) 21$_{7}$ (ת]ז[בחנו) 11QT 37$_{11}$ 47$_{14}$ 60$_{7}$, עֹלָה *burnt offering* Ex 20$_{24}$ 4QJub$^{e}$ 21$_{7.7}$, שֶׁלֶם *peace offering* Ex 20$_{24}$ Dt 27$_{7}$ Jos 8$_{31}$, פֶּסַח *passover* Dt 16$_{2.5.6}$, תּוֹדָה *thanksgiving (offering)* Ps 50$_{14.23}$.

בְּהֵמָה *beast* CD 12$_{9}$ 11QT 47$_{7}$, פַּר *bull* 1 C 15$_{26}$, בָּקָר *cattle* Ex 20$_{24}$ Nm 22$_{40}$ Dt 16$_{2}$ 1 S 15$_{15.21}$ 1 K 1$_{9}$ 8$_{63}$ 2 C 18$_{2}$, צֶמֶד *yoke (of cattle)* 1 K 19$_{21}$, מְרִיא *fatling* 2 S 6$_{13}$ 1 K 1$_{9.19.25}$, בָּרִיא *fatling* Ezk 34$_{3}$, שׁוֹר *ox* Lv 9$_{4}$ Dt 17$_{1}$ 2 S 6$_{13}$ 1 K 1$_{19.25}$ 4QPrFêtes$^{b}$ 15 ([שו]ר) 11QT 52$_{4.5.6.13.15}$, שָׂעִיר *goat* Lv 9$_{4}$, עֵז *goat* 11QT 52$_{13.15}$, כֶּבֶשׂ *lamb* Lv 9$_{4}$, שֶׂה *sheep* Dt 17$_{1}$ Is 66$_{3}$ 11QT 52$_{4.5.6.13.15}$, צֹאן *flock* Ex 20$_{24}$ Nm 22$_{40}$ Dt 16$_{2}$ 1 S 15$_{15.21}$ 1 K 1$_{9.19.25}$ 8$_{63}$ 2 C 18$_{2}$, אַיִל *ram* Lv 9$_{4}$ 1 C 15$_{26}$, עֵגֶל *calf* Lv 9$_{4}$ 1 S 28$_{24}$, עוֹף *bird* CD 12$_{9}$, שׁחת ho. ptc. *flawed (beast)* Ml 1$_{14}$, עִוֵּר *blind (beast)* Ml 1$_{8}$.

חֵלֶב *fat* 4QMMT B$_{11}$ ([זב]חם), בָּשָׂר *flesh* Dt 16$_{4}$ Ho 8$_{13}$ 4QMMT B$_{11}$ 11QT 47$_{16.16}$, דָּם *blood* Ex 23$_{18}$, תּוֹעֵבָה *abomination* Ex 8$_{22.22}$.

אֵם *mother* of beast 4QMMT B$_{36}$ ([לזבוח]), וָלָד *foetus* of beast 4QMMT B$_{36}$ ([לזבוח]), בְּכוֹר *firstborn* of cattle Dt 15$_{21}$=11QT 52$_{10}$, פֶּטֶר *firstborn* Ex 13$_{15}$, רֵאשִׁית *first*, i.e. best of booty 1 S 15$_{21}$, בֵּן *son* of beast Lv 9$_{4}$ 11QT 52$_{6}$, of human being Ezk 16$_{20}$ Ps 106$_{37}$ 4QJub$^{a}$ 1$_{11}$, בַּת *daughter* of human being Ezk 16$_{20}$ Ps 106$_{37}$, כֹּהֵן *priest* 1 K 13$_{2}$ 2 K 23$_{20}$, perh. אָדָם *human being* Ho 13$_{2}$ (זֹבְחֵי אָדָם *sacrificers of human beings*; or em. זֹבְחִים *sacrificing* human beings or זָבְחוּ *they sacrificed* human beings or זִבְחוּ to them they say, *sacrifice*; human beings).

<PREP> לְ of direction, *(offer in sacrifice) to*, + י׳ Y. Ex 3$_{18}$ 5$_{3.17}$ 8$_{4.22.23.24.25}$ 13$_{15}$ 24$_{5}$ Lv 17$_{5}$ 19$_{5}$ 22$_{29}$ Dt 15$_{21}$ 16$_{2}$ 17$_{1}$ Jg 2$_{5}$ 1 S 1$_{3.21}$ 6$_{15}$ 15$_{15.21}$ 16$_{2.5}$ 1 K 8$_{63}$ 2 K 17$_{36}$ Jon 1$_{16}$ 2$_{10}$ Ps 54$_{8}$ 116$_{17}$ 1 C 29$_{21}$ 2 C 11$_{16}$ 15$_{11}$ 33$_{17}$ 11QT 52$_{10}$, אֱלֹהִים *God* Gn 46$_{1}$ Ex 3$_{18}$ 5$_{3.8}$ 8$_{21.22.23.24}$ Dt 15$_{21}$ 16$_{2}$ 17$_{1}$ 1 S 15$_{15.21}$ Jon 2$_{10}$ Ps 50$_{14}$ Ezr 4$_{2(Qr)}$ Ne 3$_{34}$ (if em. לָהֶם *to them* to לֵאלֹהִים *to God*) 2 C 11$_{16}$ 33$_{17}$, non-Israelite *gods* Ex 22$_{19}$ 34$_{15}$ Jg 16$_{23}$ 2 K 17$_{35}$ 2 C 28$_{23.23}$ 11QT 2$_{13}$ ([ו]זבחו ל[אלוהיהמה]), אֲשֵׁרָה *Asherah* 2 C 34$_{4}$, דָּגוֹן *Dagon* Jg 16$_{23}$, פֶּסֶל *image* 2 C 34$_{4}$, מַסֵּכָה *image* 2 C 34$_{4}$, צֶלֶם *image* Ezk 16$_{20}$, עֵגֶל image of *calf* Ex 32$_{8}$, שָׂעִיר *demon* Lv 17$_{7}$, שֵׁד *demon* Dt 32$_{17}$ Ps 106$_{37}$ 4QJub$^{a}$ 1.2$_{11}$, אוֹת *sign*, i.e. standard 1QpHab 6$_{4}$, מַעֲשֶׂה *work* 4QJub$^{a}$ 1.2$_{11}$.

לְ of benefit, *to, for*, + עַם *people* 2 C 18$_{2}$, Jehoshaphat 2 C 18$_{2}$, צִפּוֹר *bird* Ezk 39$_{17.19}$, חַיָּה *beast* Ezk 39$_{17.19}$; *at, in*, + בֹּקֶר *morning* Dt 16$_{4}$, *in accordance with*, + רָצוֹן *desire* Lv 19$_{5}$ 22$_{29}$ 4QJub$^{e}$ 21$_{7}$ (ת]ז[בחנו); לָרֹב *in abundance* 1 K 1$_{19.25}$.

בְּ of place/time, *in, on, at, among, during* 4QpMos$^{e}$ 2.2$_{10}$, + Gilgal 1 S 15$_{21}$, Shiloh 1 S 1$_{3}$, מָקוֹם *place* Ex 20$_{24}$ Dt 16$_{2}$, אֶרֶץ *land* Ex 8$_{21}$, מִדְבָּר *steppe* Ex 8$_{24}$, הַר *mountain* Gn 31$_{54}$, בָּמָה *high place* 2 C 33$_{17}$, גַּנָּה *garden* Isa 65$_{3}$, אֹהֶל *tent* Ps 27$_{6}$, שַׁעַר *gate* Dt 16$_{5}$, יוֹם *day* Dt 16$_{4}$ 1 S 6$_{15}$ Ne 12$_{43}$ 2 C 15$_{11}$ 4QMMT B$_{36}$ ([לזבוח]) 11QT 52$_{6}$, עֶרֶב *evening* Dt 16$_{4.6}$, מוֹעֵד *appointed time* 11QT 17$_{7}$ ([במועדו]); of accompaniment, *with*, + קוֹל *voice* Jon 2$_{10}$, נְדָבָה *free will (offering)* Ps 54$_{8}$; *in accordance with*, + אַוָּה *desire* Dt 12$_{15}$.

כְּ *in accordance with*, + בְּרָכָה *blessing* Dt 12$_{15}$; *at the time of*, + בוא inf. *coming*, i.e. setting, of sun Dt 16$_{6}$.

מִן of direction, *from*, + יוֹם *day* Ezr 4$_{2}$; partitive, *(some) of, (any) of, from among*, + בָּקָר *cattle* Dt 12$_{21}$ =11QT 53$_{3}$ ([וז]ב[חת]ה), צֹאן *flock* Dt 12$_{21}$=11QT 53$_{3}$.

אֶל *at*, + מָקוֹם *place* Dt 16$_{6}$; עַל *upon*, + מִזְבֵּחַ *altar* Ex 20$_{24}$ 1 K 13$_{2}$ 2 K 23$_{20}$ 2 C 33$_{16}$, חָמֵץ *leavened food* Ex 23$_{18}$ (perh. עַל = *in addition to, with*); עִם *at*, + אֶבֶן *stone* 1 K 1$_{9}$.

בְּתוֹךְ *among*, + מִקְדָּשׁ *sanctuary* 11QT 52$_{15}$; לִפְנֵי *before (the time of)*, + מִנְחָה *cereal offering* 11QT 17$_{7}$, *in the presence of* Y. Lv 9$_{4}$ 1 S 11$_{15}$ 1 K 8$_{62}$||2 C 7$_{4}$ 11QT 53$_{10}$; לְעֵינֵי *in the presence of* Egyptians Ex 8$_{22}$; עַל־פְּנֵי *upon (the surface of), in*, + שָׂדֶה *field* Lv 17$_{5}$.

<SYN> עלה hi. *raise,* i.e. offer sacrifice, שׁחה htpal. *bow down,* נדר *vow,* שׁחט *slaughter.*

**Pi.** 22.0.2 Pf. זִבֵּחַ, זִבְּחוּ (זִבְּחוּ); impf. יְזַבֵּחַ, אֲזַבֵּחַ, יְזַבְּחוּ; + waw וַיְזַבַּח; ptc. מְזַבֵּחַ, מְזַבְּחִים, מְזַבְּחוֹת; inf. זַבֵּחַ—as Qal, usu. **sacrifice, offer in sacrifice,** appar. also **capture for sacrifice** by means of net (Hb 1$_{16}$).

<SUBJ> Ahaz 2 K 16$_4$||2 C 28$_4$ (|| קטר pi. *burn incense*), Amon 2 C 33$_{22}$, Jeroboam 1 K 12$_{32}$, Solomon 1 K 3$_3$ (|| קטר hi. *burn incense*) 8$_5$||2 C 5$_6$, Israel Ho 11$_2$ (|| קטר pi.), appar. Ephraim Ho 12$_{12}$, appar. Chaldaeans Hb 1$_{16}$=1QpHab 5$_{14}$=6$_2$ (5$_{14}$ [יזב]ח; || קטר pi.), עַם *people* 1 K 3$_2$ 22$_{44}$ 2 K 12$_4$ 14$_4$ 15$_{4.35}$ Ho 4$_{13}$ (all six || קטר pi.) 4$_{14}$ (+ פרד ni. *separate oneself* [if em. pi.]), עֵדָה *congregation* 1 K 8$_5$||2 C 5$_6$, מֶלֶךְ *king* 1 K 8$_5$||2 C 5$_6$, לֵוִי *Levite* 2 C 30$_{22}$ (|| ידה htp. *give thanks* or *confess*), אָב *father* Ps 106$_{38}$, בֵּן *son* of Jesse 4Q522 8.2$_7$ ([מ]זובח), אִשָּׁה *woman* 1 K 11$_8$ (|| קטר hi.).

<OBJ> זֶבַח *sacrifice* 2 C 30$_{22}$, בָּקָר *cattle* 1 K 8$_5$||2 C 5$_6$, שׁוֹר *ox* Ho 12$_{12}$ (or em. שְׁוָרִים *oxen* to לַשֵּׁדִים *to the demons*), צֹאן *flock* 1 K 8$_5$||2 C 5$_6$, בֵּן *son* Ps 106$_{38}$, בַּת *daughter* Ps 106$_{38}$.

<PREP> לְ of direction, *(offer in sacrifice) to,* + י׳ *Y.* 2 C 30$_{22}$, אֱלֹהִים *God* 2 C 30$_{22}$, non-Israelite *gods* 1 K 11$_8$, בַּעַל *lord,* i.e. non-Israelite god Ho 11$_2$, פֶּסֶל *image* 2 C 33$_{22}$, עָצָב *image* Ps 106$_{38}$, שֵׁד *demon* Ho 12$_{12}$ (if em.), עֵגֶל *calf* 1 K 12$_{32}$; of instrument, *by (means of), with,* + חֵרֶם *net* Hb 1$_{16}$=1QpHab 5$_{14}$=6$_2$; בְּ of place, *in, on, at, among,* + Gilgal Ho 12$_{12}$, בָּמָה *high place* 1 K 3$_{2.3}$ 22$_{44}$ 2 K 12$_4$ 14$_4$ 15$_{4.35}$ 16$_4$||2 C 28$_4$; עַל *upon,* + גִּבְעָה *hill* 2 K 16$_4$||2 C 28$_4$, רֹאשׁ *head,* i.e. top, of mountain Ho 4$_{13}$, סֶלַע *rock* 4Q522 8.2$_7$ ([מ]זובח); עִם *with,* + קְדֵשָׁה *sacred female* Ho 4$_{14}$; תַּחַת *under,* + עֵץ *tree* 2 K 16$_4$||2 C 28$_4$.

<SYN> קטר pi./hi. *burn incense,* ידה htp. *give thanks* or *confess.*

Also 4QOrd$^b$ 12$_4$.*

→ זֶבַח *sacrifice,* מִזְבֵּחַ *altar.*

**זֶבַח** I 162.1.26 n.m. **sacrifice**—זֶבַח; cstr. זֶבַח; sf. זִבְחוֹ, זְבָחַי, זִבְחֵיכֶם, זְבָחֵינוּ, זְבָחֶיךָ, זִבְחֲכֶם; pl. זְבָחִים; cstr. זִבְחֵי; sf. זִבְחֵיהֶם (זְבָחֵימוֹ, זִבְחוֹתָם)—religious offerings in general, oft. defined by assoc. term (זֶבַח־פֶּסַח *sacrifice of passover,* זֶבַח תּוֹדָה *sacrifice of thanksgiving,* etc.), usu. as offered to Y., but also to non-Israelite gods (e.g. Ex 34$_{15}$ Nm 25$_2$ Dt 32$_{38}$ Is 57$_7$). **1. sacrifice,** as object sacrificed (e.g. Ex 34$_{25}$ Lv 3$_1$ Dt 12$_{11}$ Is 43$_{24}$). **2.** less commonly, **sacrifice,** as act or ceremony of sacrificing (e.g. 1 S 9$_{12}$ 16$_3$ 20$_{29}$ Is 34$_6$ Jr 46$_{10}$).

<SUBJ> היה *be* complete Lv 22$_{21}$, ערב *be pleasing* Jr 6$_{20}$ Ho 9$_4$ (mss ערך *array* sacrifices), htp. *be mixed* 11QT 37$_{11}$, אכל ni. *be eaten* Lv 7$_{16}$ 19$_6$, לין *pass night,* i.e. be left overnight Ex 34$_{25}$.

<NOM CL> זֶבַח־פֶּסַח הוּא *it is a sacrifice of passover* Ex 12$_{27}$, אִם־נֶדֶר אוֹ נְדָבָה זֶבַח קָרְבָּנוֹ *if a vow or voluntary offering is the sacrifice of his offering* Lv 7$_{16}$, אִם־זֶבַח שְׁלָמִים קָרְבָּנוֹ *if a sacrifice of peace offerings is his offering* Lv 3$_1$, זִבְחֵי אֱלֹהִים רוּחַ נִשְׁבָּרָה לֵב־נִשְׁבָּר וְנִדְכֶּה *the sacrifices of God are a broken spirit, a broken and crushed heart* Ps 51$_{19}$ (or em. זִבְחִי *my sacrifice,* O God, is), זֶבַח רְשָׁעִים תּוֹעֲבַת י׳ *the sacrifice of the wicked is an abomination to Y.* Pr 15$_8$, sim. Pr 21$_{27}$=CD 11$_{20}$, זֶבַח מִשְׁפָּחָה לָנוּ *a sacrifice of (the) family is to us,* i.e. we have a family sacrifice 1 S 20$_{29}$, זֶבַח גָּדוֹל לִי *a great sacrifice is to me,* i.e. I have a great sacrifice 2 K 10$_{19}$, זֶבַח לַי׳ בְּבָצְרָה *a sacrifice for Y. is in Bozrah* Is 34$_6$, זִבְחֵיהֶם לְרָצוֹן *their sacrifices are for pleasure,* i.e. acceptable Is 56$_7$, זֶבַח לַאדֹנָי י׳ צְבָאוֹת *a sacrifice is to the Lord Y. of hosts* Jr 46$_{10}$, זֶבַח הַשְּׁלָמִים אֲשֶׁר לַי׳ *the sacrifice of peace offerings that is to Y.* Lv 7$_{20}$, sim. Lv 9$_{18}$ (לָעָם *to the people*), זִבְחֵי שְׁלָמִים עָלָי *sacrifices of peace are (incumbent) upon me* Pr 7$_{14}$, זֶבַח הַיּוֹם לָעָם בַּבָּמָה *a sacrifice is today for the people at the high place* 1 S 9$_{12}$, זֶבַח הַיָּמִים שָׁם *the sacrifice of the days,* i.e. the yearly sacrifice, *is there* 1 S 20$_6$, אֵין זֶבַח *there is no sacrifice* Ho 3$_4$.

<OBJ> זבח *sacrifice* Gn 31$_{54}$ 46$_1$ Ex 24$_5$ Lv 17$_{5.5.7}$ 19$_{5.5}$ 22$_{29.29(Sam, mss)}$ Dt 18$_3$ 33$_{19}$ Jg 16$_{23}$ 1 S 1$_{21}$ 2$_{13.19}$ 6$_{15}$ 10$_8$ 11$_{15}$ 2 S 15$_{12}$ 1 K 8$_{62.63}$||2 C 7$_{4.5}$ 1 K 8$_{63}$ Is 57$_7$ Ezk 20$_{28}$ 39$_{17.19}$ Ho 8$_{13}$ Jon 1$_{16}$ Ps 4$_6$ 27$_6$ 107$_{22}$ 116$_{17}$ Ne 12$_{43}$ 1 C 29$_{21}$ 2 C 30$_{22}$ (pi.) 33$_{16}$ 4QJub$^e$ 21$_7$ ([ז]ב[ח]) 11QT 37$_{11}$ 47$_{14}$ 60$_7$, קרב hi. *bring forward,* i.e. offer Lv 7$_{11.16.29}$ 22$_{21}$ 23$_{37}$, עלה hi. *raise,* i.e. offer Lv 17$_8$ 1 C 29$_{21}$, עשׂה *do,* i.e. offer, prepare Ex 10$_{25}$ Nm 6$_{17}$ 15$_{3.8}$ Jos 22$_{23}$ 1 K 12$_{27}$ 2 K 5$_{17}$ 10$_{24}$ Jr 33$_{18}$ 11QT 52$_{15}$, נגשׁ hi. *bring forward,* i.e. offer Am 5$_{25}$, עבד *serve (with),* i.e. offer Is 19$_{21}$, שׁחט *slaughter* Ezk 40$_{42}$ 44$_{11}$, ערך *array* Ho 9$_{4(mss)}$, בוא hi.

*bring* Lv 17$_{5}$ Dt 12$_{6.11}$ Jr 17$_{26}$ Am 4$_{4}$ 2 C 29$_{31.31}$, לקח *take* Ex 18$_{12}$, נתן *give* Ex 10$_{25}$ Ec 4$_{17}$ Si 7$_{31}$ ([ת]ן ... [זבח]י), כון hi. *prepare* Zp 1$_{7}$, בשל pi. *boil* Ezk 46$_{24}$ 4QMMT B$_{5}$ ([זבח]) 11QT 37$_{14}$, אכל *eat* Ps 106$_{28}$ 11QT 63$_{15}$ (subj. Israelites in both) 2 C 7$_{1}$ (subj. fire), כבד pi. *honour (with)* Is 43$_{23}$, חפץ *desire* Ho 6$_{6}$ Ps 40$_{7}$ 51$_{18.21}$, ברך pi. *bless* 1 S 9$_{13}$, צוה pi. *command* 1 S 2$_{29}$, שׁבת hi. *cause to cease* Dn 9$_{27}$.

<CSTR> זֶבַח י׳ *sacrifice of Y.* Zp 1$_{8}$, זִבְחֵי אֱלֹהִים *sacrifices of God* Ps 51$_{19}$ (or em. זִבְחִי *my sacrifice*, O God), זִבְחֵי אֱלֹהֵיהֶן *sacrifices of their gods* Nm 25$_{2}$, זבחי קדושים *sacrifices of holy ones* 11QShirShab 8$_{2}$, זִבְחֵי מֵתִים *sacrifices of*, i.e. offered to, *the dead* Ps 106$_{28}$.

זֶבַח שְׁלָמִים *sacrifice of peace offerings* Lv 3$_{1.6}$ 19$_{5}$ 22$_{21}$ 23$_{19}$ Nm 6$_{17}$ 11QT 52$_{15}$ 63$_{15}$,* הַשְּׁלָמִים *of the peace offerings* Lv 3$_{3.9}$ 4$_{10.26.31.35}$ 7$_{11.20.21.37}$ 9$_{18}$ Nm 6$_{18}$ 7$_{17+12t}$ 1 K 8$_{63}$ 4QJub$^{de}$ 21$_{8}$ 4QMMT B$_{9}$ ([זבח] השל[מים]), שְׁלָמָיו *of his peace offerings* Lv 7$_{18.29.29}$, זִבְחֵי שְׁלָמִים *sacrifices of peace offerings* Lv 17$_{5}$ Jos 22$_{23}$ 1 S 10$_{8}$ Pr 7$_{14}$ 2 C 30$_{22}$ 33$_{16}$, שַׁלְמֵי *of peace offerings of* Lv 10$_{14}$ 11QT 37$_{5}$, שַׁלְמֵיכֶם *of your peace offerings* Lv 7$_{32}$ Nm 10$_{10}$, שַׁלְמֵיהֶם *of their peace offerings* Lv 7$_{34}$ 11QT 37$_{11}$ (שלמיהמה).

[זבח החטאת] *the sacrifice of sin offering* 4QMMT B$_{5}$, זֶבַח הַיָּמִים *sacrifice of days*, i.e. the yearly sacrifice* 1 S 1$_{21}$ 2$_{19}$ 20$_{6}$, זֶבַח־פֶּסַח *sacrifice of passover* Ex 12$_{27}$, זֶבַח חַג הַפָּסַח *sacrifice of the pilgrimage of passover* Ex 34$_{25}$, זֶבַח תּוֹדָה *sacrifice of thanksgiving* Lv 22$_{29}$ (זֶבַח־) Ps 116$_{17}$, הַתּוֹדָה *of thanksgiving* Lv 7$_{12}$, תּוֹדַת שְׁלָמָיו *of thanksgiving of his peace offerings*, i.e. his thanksgiving sacrifice of peace offerings Lv 7$_{13.15}$, זִבְחֵי תוֹדָה *sacrifices of thanksgiving* Ps 107$_{22}$, זִבְחֵי תְרוּעָה *sacrifices of*, perh. accompanied by, *a shout* Ps 27$_{6}$, הַבְהָבַי *of my gifts* Ho 8$_{13}$ (or em. זֶבַח *offering of* and/or הַבְהַב offering[s] of *passion* or זְבָחִים אָהֵבוּ *they loved sacrifices*), זֶבַח קָרְבָּנוֹ *sacrifice of his offering* Lv 7$_{16}$, הַבָּקָר *of cattle* 2 C 7$_{5}$.

זבח הגוים *sacrifice of the gentiles* 4QMMT B$_{8}$, זבחי הכוהנים *sacrifices of the priests* 11QT 37$_{12}$, זֶבַח מִשְׁפָּחָה *sacrifice of*, i.e. attended by, *family* 1 S 20$_{29}$, זֶבַח רְשָׁעִים *sacrifice of wicked ones* Pr 15$_{8}$ 21$_{27}$=CD 11$_{20}$.

זִבְחֵי־רִיב *sacrifices (consumed in a spirit) of contention* Pr 17$_{1}$, זִבְחֵי־צֶדֶק *sacrifices of righteousness* Dt 33$_{19}$ Ps 4$_{6}$ 51$_{21}$ Si 7$_{31}$ ([זבח]י צדק), זבח הצד[ק] *the sacrifice of righteousness* 4QMidrEschat$^{a}$ 2$_{1}$.

[מנחת זבח] *grain offering of sacrifice of* 4QMMT B$_{9}$, דַּם־זֶבַח *blood of sacrifice* 2 K 16$_{15}$, זִבְחִי *of my sacrifice* Ex 23$_{18}$ 34$_{25}$, זְבָחֶיךָ *of your sacrifices* Dt 12$_{27}$, דם זבחם *blood of their sacrifice* 4QD$^{d}$ 10$_{3}$, בְּשַׂר זֶבַח *flesh of sacrifice of* Lv 7$_{15.18.21}$ (both בְּשַׂר־), הַזֶּבַח *of the sacrifice* Lv 7$_{17}$, בשר זבחיהם *flesh of their sacrifices* 4QMMT B$_{7}$, עורות זבחי *skins of offerings of* 11QT 47$_{13}$, מרק זבחם *broth of their sacrifice* 4QMMT B$_{8}$, בְּקַר זֶבַח *cattle of the sacrifice of* Nm 7$_{88}$, שׁוֹר *ox of* Lv 4$_{10}$, חלבי זבח *fat parts of sacrifice* 1QS 9$_{4}$ (=4QS$^{d}$ 3.1$_{5}$ זבחים), חֵלֶב זֶבַח *fat of the sacrifice of* Lv 4$_{26}$ 4QJub$^{de}$ 21$_{8}$, זְבָחֶיךָ *of your sacrifices* Is 43$_{24}$, זְבָחֵימוֹ *of their sacrifices* Dt 32$_{38}$, עַל־דִּבְרֵי עוֹלָה וָזָבַח *according to words of*, i.e. concerning, *burnt offering and sacrifice* Jr 7$_{22}$, בֵּית זָבַח *house of sacrifice* 2 C 7$_{12}$, תּוֹרַת זֶבַח *law of sacrifice of* Lv 7$_{11}$, יוֹם *day of* Zp 1$_{8}$, זִבְחֲכֶם *of your sacrifice* Lv 19$_{6}$, רֹב־זִבְחֵיכֶם *abundance of your sacrifices* Is 1$_{11}$, כל הזבחים *all the sacrifices* 4Q421 13$_{2}$.

<APP> בָּקָר *cattle* 1 K 8$_{63}$, שׁוֹר *ox* Lv 9$_{18}$, בֵּן *son* of cow Nm 15$_{8}$, אַיִל *ram* Lv 9$_{18}$ Nm 6$_{17}$, צֹאן *flock* 1 K 8$_{63}$, אִשֶּׁה *fire offering* Lv 23$_{37}$ Nm 15$_{3}$, חֵלֶק *portion* Si 7$_{31}$ ([ח]לקם ... [זבח]י), זֶבַח Ezk 39$_{17}$, perh. בָּשָׂר *flesh* Ho 8$_{13}$, זְבָחִים שְׁלָמִים *sacrifices (consisting of) peace offerings* Ex 24$_{5}$ 1 S 11$_{15}$.

<ADJ> גָּדוֹל *great* Jg 16$_{23}$ 2 K 10$_{19}$ Ezk 39$_{17}$ Ne 12$_{43}$.

<PREP> לְ of direction, *to*, + קרא *call (to come)* Nm 25$_{2}$ 1 S 16$_{5}$; of benefit, *to, for* (but sometimes perh. לְ = *as*), Lv 3$_{6}$ Nm 7$_{17+11t}$ 11QShirShab 8$_{2}$, + עשׂה *do*, i.e. prepare lambs Lv 23$_{19}$, libation Nm 15$_{5}$, *make* altar Jos 22$_{28}$, pass. *be made* (of places) 11QT 37$_{10}$ (לז[בח]יהמה) 37$_{11}$, בנה *build* altar Jos 22$_{26.29}$, קרב hi. *bring forward*, i.e. offer 11QT 20$_{1}$; *in respect of* Lv 7$_{37}$ (+ תּוֹרָה *law*).

בְּ of place, *in, at*, + היה *be* Lv 22$_{21}$, בוא *come* to 1 S 16$_{5}$, קרא *call*, i.e. invite to 1 S 16$_{3}$; of instrument, *by (means of), with*, + עבד *serve* Jos 22$_{27}$, כפר htp. *be expiated* 1 S 3$_{14}$; of accompaniment, *with*, + ערב htp. *be mixed* 11QT 37$_{12}$; *against*, + בעט *kick* 1 S 2$_{29}$ (unless בעט בְּ = *trample on*); חפץ בְּ *desire* 1 S 15$_{22}$.

מִן of direction, *from*, + סור ho. *be removed* Lv 4$_{35}$; perh. partitive, *some of, any of, from among*, + היה *be* Ex 29$_{28}$, בוא hi. *bring* Lv 7$_{29}$, קרב hi. *offer* Lv 3$_{3.9}$, נתן *give* Lv 7$_{32}$ 10$_{14}$, לקח *take* Lv 7$_{34}$, אכל *eat* Ex 34$_{15}$ Lv 7$_{20}$

11QT 2$_{14}$ ([זבחיהמה]), שׁתה *drink* Ezk 39$_{19}$; of instrument, *by (means of)*, or of cause, *on account of, through*, + בושׁ *be ashamed* Ho 4$_{19}$ (or em. מִזְבֵּחַ *altar*); of comparison, *(more) than* 1 S 15$_{22}$, + בחר ni. *be chosen* Pr 21$_{3}$.

עַל *at, to*, + אסף ni. *be gathered* Ezk 39$_{17}$, קבץ ni. *be gathered* Ezk 39$_{17}$, בוא *come* Ezk 39$_{17}$, יצב htp. *position oneself* 1QM 2$_5$; *over*, + תקע *sound* trumpets Nm 10$_{10}$; *(in addition) to, with*, + יסף *add* Jr 7$_{21}$, קרב hi. *offer* Lv 7$_{12.13}$; *by (means of), through*, + כרת *cut*, i.e. make covenant Ps 50$_5$; *on account of*, + יכח hi. *reprove* Ps 50$_8$, חשׁב *reckon* 4QMMT B$_8$ ([חושבים]), *concerning* 4QMMT B$_5$ ([ועל זבח]); בטח עַל *trust in* Si 32$_{15}$.

מֵעַל *from (upon)*, + סור ho. *be removed* Lv 4$_{31}$.

תַּחַת *under* Nm 6$_{18}$ (+ אֵשׁ *fire* that is under sacrifice).

<COLL> בַּיִת מָלֵא זִבְחֵי־רִיב *a house full of sacrifices of contention* Pr 17$_1$, עֹלָה אוֹ־זֶבַח *burnt offering or sacrifice* Lv 17$_8$ (זֶבַח) Nm 15$_{3.8}$ (זֶבַח).

זֶבַח || עֹלָה *burnt offering* Ex 10$_{25}$ 18$_{12}$ 24$_5$ Lv 7$_{37}$ 17$_8$ 23$_{37}$ Nm 7$_{17+11t}$ 10$_{10}$ 15$_{3.5}$ (+) 15$_8$ Dt 12$_{6.11.27}$ (+) Jos 22$_{23.26.27.28.29}$ 1 S 6$_{15}$ 15$_{22}$ 10$_8$ 2 K 5$_{17}$ 10$_{24}$ 16$_{15}$ Is 34$_6$ 43$_{23}$ (+) Jr 6$_{20}$ 7$_{22}$ 17$_{26}$ 33$_{18}$ Ezk 40$_{42}$ 44$_{11}$ Ho 6$_6$ Ps 40$_7$ 50$_8$ (both +) 1 C 29$_{21}$ 2 C 7$_1$ 1QS 9$_4$ 1QM 2$_5$.

זֶבַח || מִנְחָה *cereal offering* Lv 7$_{37}$ 23$_{37}$ Jos 22$_{23.29}$ 1 S 2$_{29}$ 3$_{14}$ Is 19$_{21}$ 43$_{23}$ (+) Jr 17$_{26}$ 33$_{18}$ Am 5$_{25}$ Ps 40$_7$ 51$_{18.21}$ (both +) Dn 9$_{27}$.

זֶבַח || חַטָּאת *sin offering* Lv 7$_{37}$ 23$_{19}$ Nm 7$_{17+11t}$ 11QT 37$_{14}$, חֲטָאָה *sin offering* Ps 40$_7$ (+).

זֶבַח || נֶדֶר *vow (offering)* Dt 12$_{6.11}$ (+) 1 S 1$_{21}$ Is 19$_{21}$ Jon 1$_{16}$ Pr 7$_{14}$ (+).

זֶבַח || תּוֹדָה *thanksgiving (offering)* Jr 17$_{26}$ 2 C 29$_{31.31}$ 33$_{16}$.

זֶבַח || תְּרוּמָה *heave offering* Dt 12$_6$ Si 7$_{31}$ (י[זבח]).

זֶבַח || שֶׁלֶם *peace offering* Jos 22$_{27}$, אָשָׁם *guilt offering* Lv 7$_{37}$, נֶסֶךְ *libation* Lv 23$_{37}$, נָסִיךְ *libation* Dt 32$_{38}$, נְדָבָה *freewill offering* Dt 12$_6$, מִלֻּא *installation (offering)* Lv 7$_{37}$ (+), כָּלִיל *whole (offering)* Ps 51$_{21}$ (+).

זֶבַח || מַעֲשֵׂר *tithe* Dt 12$_{6.11}$, בְּכוֹר *firstborn* Dt 12$_6$, תְּפִלָּה *prayer* Pr 15$_8$, טֶבַח *slaughter* Is 34$_6$, מַצֵּבָה *pillar* Ho 3$_4$, אֵפֹד *ephod* Ho 3$_4$ (+), תְּרָפִים *teraphim* Ho 3$_4$ (+), לְבוֹנָה *frankincense* Is 43$_{23}$ (+) Jr 17$_{26}$, חַג *pilgrimage* Ex 23$_{18}$ 34$_{25}$ (+).

זֶבַח || מֶלֶךְ *king* Ho 3$_4$, שַׂר *prince* Ho 3$_4$.

זֶבַח :: חֶסֶד *loyalty* Ho 6$_6$, דַּעַת *knowledge* Ho 6$_6$.

<SYN> עֹלָה *burnt offering*, מִנְחָה *cereal offering*, חַטָּאת *sin offering*, נֶדֶר *vow (offering)*, תּוֹדָה *thanksgiving (offering)*, תְּרוּמָה *heave offering*, שֶׁלֶם *peace offering*, אָשָׁם *guilt offering*, נְדָבָה *freewill offering*, נֶסֶךְ *libation* Lv 23$_{37}$, נָסִיךְ *libation*, לְבוֹנָה *frankincense*, מַעֲשֵׂר *tithe*, בְּכוֹר *firstborn*, תְּפִלָּה *prayer*, טֶבַח *slaughter*, מַצֵּבָה *pillar*, חַג *pilgrimage*, מֶלֶךְ *king*, שַׂר *prince*.

<ANT> חֶסֶד *loyalty*, דַּעַת *knowledge*.

Also 4QMish A 2.2$_2$ 4QShirShab$^f$ 94$_2$ 4QOrd$^c$ 2$_3$.*

⇒ זבח *sacrifice*.

**זֶבַח** II 12 pr.n.m. **Zebah,** king of Midian killed by Gideon, alw. assoc. with Zalmunna, <SUBJ> נוס *flee* Jg 8$_{12}$, הרג *kill* Jg 8$_{18}$, חיה hi. *keep alive* Jg 8$_{18}$, אמר *say* Jg 8$_{18.21}$. <NOM CL> זֶבַח ... בַּקַּרְקֹר *Zebah ... was in Karkor* Jg 8$_{10}$. <OBJ> נתן *give* Jg 8$_7$, רדף *pursue* Jg 8$_5$, לכד *capture* Jg 8$_{12}$, הרג *kill* Jg 8$_{18.18.21}$, חרף pi. *reproach (concerning)* Jg 8$_{15}$. <CSTR> כַּף זֶבַח *hand of Zebah* Jg 8$_{6.15}$. <APP> מֶלֶךְ *king* Jg 8$_{5.12}$. <PREP> בְּ *against*, + פגע *strike* Jg 8$_{21}$; כְּ *as* Ps 83$_{12}$ (or del. כְּזֶבַח); אֶל *to*, + אמר *say* Jg 8$_{18}$; עִם *with* Jg 8$_{10}$; אַחֲרֵי *after*, + רדף *pursue* Jg 8$_{12}$. <COLL> הִנֵּה זֶבַח *behold, Zebah* Jg 8$_{15}$.

**זַבַּי** 2 pr.n.m. **Zabbai, 1.** Israelite husband of foreign wife, descendant of Bebai, <NOM CL> מִבְּנֵי בֵּבָי ... זַבַּי *of the sons of Bebai were ... Zabbai* Ezr 10$_{28}$ (mss Zaccai). **2.** Levite, father of one who helped repair walls of Jerusalem, בֶּן־זבי Baruch *son of Zabbai* Ne 3$_{20(Kt)}$ (Qr Zaccai).

**[זַבִּי]** pr.n.m. **Zabbi,** Israelite and ancestor of returning exiles, <CSTR> בְּנֵי זַבִּי *sons of Zabbi* Ezr 2$_9$||Ne 7$_{14}$ (if em. זַכַּי *Zaccai*).

**[זְבִידָה]** 1 pr.n.f. **Zebidah,** daughter of Pedaiah of Rumah and mother of Jehoiakim, <NOM CL> שֵׁם אִמּוֹ זבידה *the name of his mother was Zebidah* 2 K 23$_{36(Kt)}$ (Qr Zebuddah). <APP> בַּת *daughter* 2 K 23$_{36(Kt)}$.

⇒ זבד *endow*.

**זְבִינָא** 1 pr.n.m. **Zebina,** Israelite husband of foreign wife, descendant of Nebo, <NOM CL> מִבְּנֵי נְבוֹ ... זְבִינָא *of the sons of Nebo were ... Zebina* Ezr 10$_{43}$.

[זְבִינוּת] 0.0.1 n.f. **purchase**—Q זבנות—<PREP> מִן of instrument, *by (means of)* MurEpBeth-Mashiko4 (שהי שלו מזבנות *that it is his by purchase*).

זבל I 1 vb. **exalt—Qal** 1 Impf. יִזְבְּלֵנִי—**exalt, honour,** <SUBJ> אִישׁ *husband* Gn 30$_{20}$. <OBJ> Leah Gn 30$_{20}$. <COLL> with adverb, הַפַּעַם *this time* Gn 30$_{20}$.*

[זבל] II vb. **dwell,** <SUBJ> Zebulun Gn 49$_{13}$ (if em. שׁכן *dwell*). <PREP> לְ *at,* + חוֹף *shore* Gn 49$_{13}$ (if em.).
→ זְבֻל *dwelling place.*

[זבל] III vb. **rule—Qal, rule (over),** <SUBJ> גָּלוּת *diaspora* Ob20 (if em. גָּלֻת הַחֵל־הַזֶּה לִבְנֵי יִשְׂרָאֵל אֲשֶׁר *the diaspora of this fortress of the sons of Israel, which* to גָּלֻת בְּנֵי יִשְׂרָאֵל אֲשֶׁר בַּחֲלַח יִזְבְּלוּ *the diaspora of the sons of Israel who are in Halah will rule*). <OBJ> כְּנַעֲנִי *Canaanite* Ob20 (if em.).

זְבֻל I 5.0.8 n.[m.] **dwelling place**—Q זבול; cstr. זְבֻל (Q זבול); + ה- of direction זְבֻלָה—alw. in ref. to abode of deities or demons, <SUBJ> המה *make a noise* 1QH 3$_{34}$. <NOM CL> שְׁאוֹל זְבוּל לָמוֹ *Sheol is their dwelling place* Ps 49$_{15}$ (if em. שְׁאוֹל מִזְּבֻל לוֹ perh. *Sheol is without its dwelling place*; or em. מִזְּבֻל to מִזְּבוּל/מִזְּבֻל/מְזֻבָּל *dwelling place*). <CSTR> זְבֻל קָדְשְׁךָ וְתִפְאַרְתֶּךָ *abode of your holiness and your glory* Is 63$_{15}$, זבול קודש *dwelling place of holiness* 1QS 10$_{3}$ (+ מָעוֹן *dwelling place*) 4Q408 1$_{5}$ ([קודש]), קודשכה *of your holiness* 1QM 12$_{1}$, קודשו *of his holiness* 1QH 3$_{34}$, כבודכה *of your glory* 1QM 12$_{2}$ (+ מָעוֹן), רום רומים *of the height of heights* 4QShirShabbd 1.1$_{41}$; מלאכי זב[ול] *angels of the dwelling place* 4QShirShabbf 81$_{2}$, בֵּית זְבֻל *house of,* i.e. fit for, *a (divine) dwelling place* 1 K 8$_{13}$‖2 C 6$_{2}$ (+ מָכוֹן *place*), כול ז[בולי] *all the dwelling places of* 11QShirShabb 1$_{7}$. <PREP> לְ of possession, *of, (belonging) to* 4QShirShabbd 1.1$_{41}$ (עמודי משא לזבול רום רומים *pillars of lifting of the dwelling place of the height of heights*), perh. 11QShirShabb 1$_{7}$ ([לכול ז]בולי); בְּ of place, *in* 1QM 12$_{1.2}$, + עמד *stand* Hb 3$_{11}$ (if em.; see below); מִן of direction, *from,* + נבט hi. *look* Is 63$_{15}$, יפע hi. *shine out* 1QS 10$_{3}$ 4Q408 1$_{5}$; perh. privative, *without,* Ps 49$_{15}$ (שְׁאוֹל מִזְּבֻל לוֹ *Sheol is without its dwelling place;* or em.; see Nom. Cl.); with ה- of direction, *at, in,* שֶׁמֶשׁ יָרֵחַ עָמַד זְבֻלָה *sun (and) moon (each) stood in its dwelling place* Hb 3$_{11}$ (or em. זְבֻלֹה *its dais*; or ins. בְּ *in* the dwelling place, and join שֶׁמֶשׁ to preceding verse). Also 4Q 298 2$_{1}$ 3$_{3}$.*
→ זבל *dwell.*

*[זְבֻל] II 1 n.[m.] **dais,** <COLL> יָרֵחַ עָמַד זְבֻלֹה *(the) moon stood (on) his dais* Hb 3$_{11}$ (if em. זְבֻלָה *in [its] dwelling place*).

זְבֻל III 6 pr.n.m. **Zebul,** governor of Shechem at time of Gideon, <SUBJ> שׁלח *send* Jg 9$_{30}$, גרשׁ pi. *expel* Jg 9$_{41}$, שׁמע *hear* Jg 9$_{30}$, אמר *say* Jg 9$_{36.38}$, עבד *serve* Jg 9$_{28}$ (if em. עִבְדוּ *serve,* to עָבְדוּ *they served*). <NOM CL> הֲלֹא ... זְבֻל פְּקִידוֹ *is not ... Zebul his officer?* Jg 9$_{28}$ (or, if em. זְבֻל פְּקִידוֹ עבד, has not *Zebul, his officer,* served?). <APP> שַׂר *prince* Jg 9$_{30}$, פָּקִיד *officer* Jg 9$_{30}$ (if em.). <PREP> אֶל *to,* + אמר *say* Jg 9$_{36}$.

זְבֻלוּן, see זְבוּלֻן *Zebulun.*

זָג 1 n.m. perh. **skin** or **seed** of grape, or **tip** of vine shoot, prohibited as food for Nazirite, <PREP> עַד *unto,* מֵחַרְצַנִּים וְעַד־זָג *from the seeds and unto the skin* Nm 6$_{4}$.

זֵד 15.4.2 adj. **presumptuous**—pl. זֵדִים (Q זידים); sf. Q זדיך—**1. presumptuous, arrogant, impudent,** used attributively of אִישׁ *man* Jr 43$_{2}$ (or del. זֵד).

**2.** as noun, **presumptuous, arrogant, impudent one,** perh. presumptuous deed or thought, i.e. **sin** (Ps 19$_{14}$), <SUBJ> היה *be* chaff Ml 3$_{19}$ (+ עֹשֵׂה רִשְׁעָה *evil-doer*), בושׁ *be ashamed* Ps 119$_{78}$, ארר pass. *be cursed* Ps 119$_{21}$ (unless אֲרוּרִים הַשֹּׁגִים *cursed are those who stray* is separate clause), שׁגה *stray* from commandments Ps 119$_{21}$, קבל hi. *encounter* Si 12$_{5}$, קום *arise* Ps 54$_{5(mss)}$=86$_{14}$ (L זָר *stranger;* + עָרִיץ *tyrannical*), שׂים *place* God Ps 86$_{14}$ (or del.), משׁל *rule* Ps 19$_{14}$ (or em. זָר *stranger*), ידע *know* wisdom 11QPsa 18$_{13}$ (‖ רָשָׁע *evil*), ליץ hi. *deride* Ps

$119_{51}$, עות pi. *bend*, i.e. subvert Ps $119_{78}$, לקח *take*, i.e. apprehend commandment Si $35_{18}$, טפל *smear* with lies Ps $119_{69}$, עשק *oppress* Ps $119_{122}$, עשׂה *do*, i.e. act presumptuously Pr $21_{24}$ (but see Adj.), כרה *dig* pit Ps $119_{85}$. <OBJ> אשׁר pi. *pronounce blessed* Ml $3_{15}$ (+ עֹשֵׂה רִשְׁעָה), גער *rebuke* Ps $119_{21}$ (mss זָר *stranger*; ms גּוֹי *nation*), להט pi. *burn* Ml $3_{19}$.

<CSTR> גְּאוֹן זֵדִים *pride of the presumptuous* Is $13_{11}$ (‖ עָרִיץ *tyrannical*) $25_{5}$ (if em. שְׁאוֹן זָרִים *uproar of strangers*), שְׁאוֹן *uproar of* Is $25_{5}$ (if em. זָר; or em. גְּאוֹן *pride of* the presumptuous), אַרְמוֹן *fortress of* Is $25_{2(mss)}$ (L זָר), המון זדיך *tumult of your presumptuous ones* 1QIsa[a] $29_{5}$ (MT זָר), מלחמות זדים *battles of*, i.e. against, *presumptuous ones* 1QH $6_{35}$, ריב זדים *striving of the presumptuous* Si $11_{9(C)}$, רב זדים perh. *multitude of the presumptuous* Si $11_{9(A)}$, כָּל־זֵדִים *all presumptuous ones* Ml $3_{19}$ 11QPs[a] $18_{13}$ (כול זדים).

<ADJ> יָהִיר *proud* Pr $21_{24}$ (זֵד יָהִיר לֵץ שְׁמוֹ *a proud presumptuous one—scoffer is his name*, unless *presumptuous [and] proud scoffer is his name*, i.e. זֵד attributive of לֵץ *scoffer*, as §1). <PREP> לְ of direction, *to*, + נתן *give* Si $12_{5.5}$, perh. of benefit, *to, for*, + עזב *abandon* root and branch Ml $3_{19}$ (or em. ni. *be abandoned*); מִן of direction, *(away) from*, + חשׂך *withhold*, i.e. keep away from Ps $19_{14}$ (or em. זָר *stranger*); לְנֶגֶד *before*, + שׂים *place* God Ps $86_{14}$ (or del.). <COLL> גר וזד נכרי ורש תפראתם יןרא]ת י' *sojourner and presumptuous one, alien and pauper—their glory is the fear of Y.* Si $10_{22(A)}$ (C זָר *stranger*; Cmg ביראת *in the fear of*), זד ולץ *a presumptuous one and a scornful one* Si $35_{18}$.

<SYN> §2 עָרִיץ *tyrannical*, רָשָׁע *evil*.*

⇒ זיד *be presumptuous*.

[זָדָה] 0.0.0.1 n.f. **fissure,** unless **overlap, contact, narrowing, turbulence, resonance, echo, heat, excitement,*** <SUBJ> היה *be* Siloam tunnel inscr.3 (כי הית זדה בצר מימן ו[עד שמא]ל perh. *for there was a fissure in the rock from right to left*).

זָדוֹן 11.11.9 n.m. **presumptuousness**—Q perh. זודן (1QH fr. $45_{5}$); cstr. זְדוֹן; sf. זְדֹנְךָ—**presumptuousness, arrogance, impudence,** perh. also presumptuous person (e.g. Jr $50_{31.32}$ Si $13_{24}$ $32_{23}$).

<SUBJ> בוא *come* Pr $11_{2}$ (‖ קָלוֹן *shame*, + צְנוּעַ *decorous one*), נפל *fall* Jr $50_{32}$, פרח *flower* Ezk $7_{10}$ (‖ מַטֶּה *rod* [or em. מֻטֶּה *perversity*]), צלח hi. *prosper* Si $9_{12}$ (unless זדון מצליח = *the presumptuousness of one who succeeds*), נאה pilel *befit* Si $10_{18}$ (+ עזות אף *strength of anger*), ערב htp. *be mixed* with joy Pr $14_{10}$ (if em. זָר *stranger* to זָדוֹן), נשׂא hi. *deceive* Jr $49_{16}$=Ob3, כשׁל *stumble* Jr $50_{32}$.

<OBJ> ידע *know* 1 S $17_{28}$ (+ רֹעַ *evil*), שׁבת hi. *cause to cease* Si $7_{6}$, בוא hi. *bring* 4Q Wiles $1_{16}$ (זד[ו]ן), קום hi. *raise* Jr $50_{32}$.

<CSTR> זְדוֹן לִבֶּךָ *presumptuousness of your heart* Jr $49_{16}$=Ob3 (לִבְּךָ), לבם *of their heart* Si $16_{10}$, לבבם *of their heart* 4QShir[b] $43_{8}$, מעשׂי *of deeds of* abomination 1QS $4_{10}$, אשמתם *of their wickedness* 4QpNah 3.$3_{4}$; עֶבְרַת זָדוֹן *overflowing of presumptuousness* Pr $21_{24}$, מקוה *reservoir of* Si $10_{13}$, שׁבט *sceptre of* Si $32_{23(B)}$ (Bmg שבטי *sceptres of*; ‖ רֶשַׁע *wickedness*), קנאת זדון *zeal of presumptuousness of* abominable deeds 1QS $4_{10}$, איש זודן *man of presumptuousness* 1QH fr. $45_{5}$ (+ מַעַל *treachery*), אנשי זדון *men of presumptuousness* Si $15_{7}$ (‖ שָׁוְא *vanity*), אשׁת *woman of* Si $12_{14}$, אחרית *posterity of* Si $16_{3(B).3}$.

<APP> appar. תִּפְלֶצֶת *horror* Jr $49_{16}$ (‖Ob3 lacks תִּפְלֶצֶת).

<PREP> לְ of possession, *of, (belonging) to* Jr $50_{32}$, *against*, + גור *attack* 1QH fr. $3_{15}$ (+ עַוְלָה *injustice*, רְמִיָּה *deceit*); בְּ of accompaniment, *with, in (a state of)* Si $9_{12}$, + דבר pi. *speak* Dt $18_{22}$= 11QT $61_{4}$, עשׂה *do* Dt $17_{12}$=11QT $56_{8}$ (+ לְבִלְתִּי שְׁמֹעַ *so as not to obey*), נתן *give* strife Pr $13_{10}$, אסף ni. *be gathered* Si $16_{10}$; כְּ *according to* 4QShir[b] $43_{8}$; אֶל *against* Jr $50_{31}$ (הִנְנִי אֵלֶיךָ זָדוֹן *behold, I am against you, O presumptuous one*); עַל *on account of*, + כאר pi. perh. *abhor* 4QpNah 3.$3_{4}$; עַל פִּי *according to* Si $13_{24}$ (רע העוני על פי זדון *poverty is evil according to a presumptuous one*). Also 5Q16 $2_{2}$.

<SYN> שָׁוְא *vanity*, רֶשַׁע *wickedness*, קָלוֹן *shame*.*

⇒ זיד *be presumptuous*.

זֶה 1173.21.193.13 demonst. pronoun sing. (sometimes pl.) m. (rarely f.) and adj. **this**—Q זו, I perh. זָ; זֶה־שְּׁמִי Ex $3_{15}$, זֶה־מִזְבֵּחַ 1 C $22_{1}$.

# זֶה

**1. as predicative adjective or pronoun,** *this (one)*
**Subjects,** p. 83a
**Nominal Clauses**
**a.** common noun as complement, p. 83b
**b.** proper noun as complement, p. 84b
**c.** pronoun as complement, p. 84b
**d.** adjective as complement, p. 84b
**e.** preposition as complement, p. 84b
**f.** undetermined noun as complement, p. 85a
**Objects,** p. 85a
**Constructs,** p. 85a
**Prepositions,** p. 85a
**Collocations,** p. 86a
**2. as combined relative pronoun with antecedent,** *that which*, p. 86a
**3. as relative pronoun,** *that, which*, p. 86b
**4.** perh. *one that is of, possessor of, lord of*, p. 86b
**5. as attributive adjective,** *this*
**a.** הַזֶּה following determined noun, p. 86b
**b.** זֶה (not הַזֶּה) following suffixed noun, p. 88a
**c.** הַזֶּה/זֶה following undetermined or proper noun, p. 88a
**d.** זֶה preceding undetermined noun, p. 88b
**e.** זֶה preceding determined noun, p. 88b
**f.** זֶה following particle, p. 88b
**6.** אֵי־זֶה *whither?, in which direction?*, p. 89a
**7.** אֵי־זֶה *what?, which?*, p. 89a
**8.** אֵי־מִזֶּה *whence?*, p. 89a
**9.** אֵי־מִזֶּה *from which?*, p.89a
**10.** לָמָּה־זֶּה *why?*, p. 89a
**11.** מַה־זֶּה *why?, what?, how?*, p. 89b
**12.** מִזֶּה ... וּמִזֶּה *over here ... and over there*, p. 89b

**1.** as predicative adjective or pronoun, **this (one), such (a one),** esp. in Ec (where זֶה occurs 37 times, always as pronoun, never as adj.) with neuter or indeterminate reference ('what I have been talking about, the foregoing', etc.), also, esp. when preceded by preposition, in ref. to space, **this place, here** (Gn $37_{17}$ $38_{21.22}$ $42_{15}$ $48_{9}$ etc.); sometimes perh. as simple pronoun, **it** (e.g. Si $16_{11}$).

<SUBJ> היה *be* Ex $10_{7}$ $30_{31}$ Nm $18_{9}$ $34_{6.7.9}$ $35_{5}$ Dt $18_{3}$ Jos $15_{4}$ 1 S $8_{11}$ Mc $5_{4}$ (unless וְהָיָה זֶה שָׁלוֹם = *and* Assyria *will be the lord of peace,* as §4) Ec $2_{10}$ 4QJub[a] $2_{24}$ ([וינתן לזה להיות] *and it was given to this to be*) 11QT $18_{8}$ $35_{13}$ Siloam tunnel inscr.$_{1}$, שׁוה *be equal* Est $5_{13}$, שׁנה *be different* Si $42_{24(B)}$ (כולם שונים זה מזה *all of them were different, this one from that one;* or em. שנים זה לעמת זה all of them were *pairs, this one was in correspondence with that one*), בדל ho. *be separated* 11QT $35_{11.13}$ $46_{17}$, עשׂה ni. *be made* 4QJub[a] $2_{23}$, ילד pu. *be born* Ps $87_{4.6}$, כבד ni. *be honoured* 1QSa $1_{18}$ ([זה]), ברך pass. *be blessed* 4QJub[a] $2_{23.23}$ ([זה ברוך ... וזה ברוך]) $2_{24}$ (וינתן לזה] [להיות ... ברוכים *and it was given to this to be ... blessed*), נבל *wither* Si $14_{18}$, מות *die* Jb $21_{23.25}$ perh. Ec $3_{19.19}$ (see Cstr.), הלך *go* Jg $7_{4.4}$, בוא *come* 1 K $14_{13}$ Jb $1_{16.17.18}$ 1QpHab $4_{12}$ (ה[ז]) 11QT $45_{5}$, יצא *go out* Gn $38_{28}$ 11QT $45_{5}$, עבר *pass* 1QS $2_{20.21}$, קרב *approach* Ex $14_{20}$, נגשׁ *approach* Jr $30_{21}$, שׁלח *send* 1 K $20_{7}$ 2 K 5, שׂים *place* perh. 1QpHab $4_{9.13}$ (see זוּ, §2), חלף *exchange* Si $42_{25}$, בקשׁ pi. *seek* 1 K $20_{7}$, נחם pi. *console* Gn $5_{29}$, רצה htp. *ingratiate oneself* 1 S $29_{4}$, כשׁר *prosper* Ec $11_{6.6}$, ירשׁ *inherit* Gn $15_{4}$, ישׁע hi. *save* 1 S $10_{27}$, עצר *restrain* 1 S $9_{17}$, נגע *touch* Is $6_{7}$, חטא hi. *miss (target)* Jg $20_{16}$, אמר *say* 1 K $22_{20.20}$‖2 C $18_{19.19}$ Is $44_{5}$, דבר pi. *speak* Jb $1_{16.17.18}$, בשׂר pi. *announce* 2 S $18_{26}$, קרא *call* Is $6_{3}$ $44_{5}$, כתב *write* Is $44_{5}$, ילד *give birth* Pr $23_{22}$ (unless זֶה יְלָדֶךָ = your father, *who gave birth to you*, as §3).

<NOM CL> a. common noun (usu. sing. but sometimes pl. with sing. ref.) as complement, אֵל *God* Ex $15_{2}$, אֱלֹהִים *God* Is $25_{9}$ (unless אֱלֹהֵינוּ זֶה = *our God, whom* we have awaited, as §3) perh. Ps $48_{15}$ (if זֶה אֱלֹהִים is obj. of ספר pi. in v. 14, 'that you might recount ... that this is our God') Ne $9_{18}$.

אָדָם *human being* Ec $12_{13}$ (כִּי־זֶה כָּל־הָאָדָם perh. *for this is the entire duty of a human being* or *for this applies to everyone*), אִישׁ *man* 2 S $18_{27}$ Is $14_{16}$, בֵּן *son* Gn $35_{17}$ 1 K $3_{23}$ 2 K $8_{5}$, בְּכוֹר *firstborn* Gn $48_{18}$, אָח *brother* Gn $43_{29}$, דּוֹד *beloved* Ca $5_{16}$, רֵעַ *companion* Ca $5_{16}$, עַם *people* Jg $9_{38}$ Is $23_{13}$ Jr $52_{28}$, גּוֹי *nation* Jr $7_{28}$, דּוֹר *generation* Ps $24_{6}$, מוֹשָׁב *session* CD $13_{20}$.

קָרְבָּן *offering* Lv $6_{13}$ Nm $7_{17.23.29.35.41.47.53.59.65.71.77.83}$, אִשֶּׁה *fire offering* Nm $28_{3}$, תְּרוּמָה *contribution* Nm $18_{11}$, חֵלֶק *portion* Is $17_{14}$ Jb $20_{29}$ $27_{13}$ Si $41_{4(B)}$, מְנָת *portion* Jr

13$_{25}$, גּוֹרָל *lot* Is 17$_{14}$ Jr 13$_{25}$, מַתַּת *gift* Ec 5$_{18(Gnz)}$ (זֶה מַתַּת אֱלֹהִים הִיא *this is a gift of God*; L זֹה), פְּרִי *fruit* Nm 13$_{27}$ Is 27$_{9}$ (or del. כָּל־פְּרִי *all the fruit*, or em. to לְכַפֵּר this is *to cover* the removal of sin), לֶחֶם *bread* Jos 9$_{12}$ (זֶה לַחְמֵנוּ *this is our bread*, unless *this bread of ours*, as §5e), דָּם *blood* 2 K 3$_{23}$, נֶפֶשׁ *soul* Bene Ḥezir tomb inscr. (Frey 1394), יָמִין *right hand* perh. 4QMyst$^{b}$ 8$_{1(WA)}$ ([ו]זה ימינו; Schiffman [מ]חזה ימינו *the vision of our days*), בְּהֵמָה *beast* 4QCrypt 1.2$_{9}$, שָׁלָל *booty* 1 S 30$_{20}$, טָמֵא *impure one* Lv 11$_{29}$, אוּד *firebrand* Zc 3$_{2}$, סֵפֶר *book* Gn 5$_{1}$ 1QM 1$_{1}$ (זו[ה] [ספר]), פַּרְשֶׁגֶן *copy* of text Ezr 7$_{11}$, חֶשְׁבּוֹן *reckoning* 4Q 254a 1$_{2}$.

יוֹם *day* Jg 4$_{14}$ Ps 118$_{24}$ Lm 2$_{16}$, אֶחָד *one*, i.e. first, day 4QMishC$^{c}$ 1$_{2}$ ([זה אח]ד) 1$_{5}$ ([זה א]חד) 4QMishC$^{d}$ 1.2$_{3}$ 2$_{5}$ 3$_{2}$ (both [זה אחד]), מָקוֹם *place* Ezk 46$_{20}$ Jb 18$_{21}$, דֶּרֶךְ *way* 2 K 6$_{19}$ Is 30$_{21}$=4QpIsa$^{c}$ 23.2$_{18}$ ([וזה הדרך]) Jr 22$_{21}$ Ps 49$_{14}$, גְּבוּל *border* Jos 15$_{12}$ 18$_{19}$ Ezk 47$_{15}$, יָם *sea* Ps 104$_{25}$ (11QPs$^{a}$ lacks זֶה), הַר *mountain* perh. Ps 75$_{9}$ (unless הַר־צִיּוֹן זֶה = *this Mount Zion*, as §5c), מַחֲנֶה *camp* Gn 32$_{3}$, בַּיִת *house* 1 C 22$_{1}$ (זֶה הוּא בֵּית י׳ *this is the house of Y.*), גַּב *mound* Ezk 43$_{13}$ (or em. גֹּבַהּ *height*), שַׁעַר *gate* Ps 118$_{20}$=4QpPs$^{b}$ 5$_{4}$ ([זה]), שֻׁלְחָן *table* Ezk 41$_{22}$, מִזְבֵּחַ *altar* 1 C 22$_{1}$ (if em. זֶה־מִזְבֵּחַ to זֶה־הַמִּזְבֵּחַ), קֶבֶר *grave* Bene Ḥezir tomb inscr. (Frey 1394; זה קבר והנפש שלאלעזר *this is the tomb and the soul of Eleazar*), עָפָר *dust* Mur 24 2$_{12}$ ([העפר] שהזה *the dust that is this*, i.e. the aforementioned land) 3$_{9}$ (העפר שהזה).

דָּבָר *word, thing, matter* Ex 14$_{12}$ 16$_{16.32}$ 29$_{1}$ 35$_{4}$ Lv 8$_{5}$ 9$_{6}$ 17$_{2}$ Nm 30$_{2}$ 36$_{6}$ Dt 15$_{2}$ 19$_{4}$ Jos 5$_{4}$ Jg 20$_{9}$ 21$_{11}$ 1 K 9$_{15}$ 11$_{27}$ 2 K 11$_{5}$||2 C 23$_{4}$ 2 K 19$_{21}$||Is 37$_{22}$ Is 16$_{13}$ Jr 38$_{21}$ Jon 4$_{2}$ Zc 4$_{6}$ 11QMelch$_{2}$ ([וזה ד]בר),* עִנְיָן *matter* Ec 4$_{8}$ (unless זֶה הֶבֶל וְעִנְיַן רָע הוּא = *this was vanity and it was a bad matter*; Gnz, mss עִנְיָן), פֵּרוּשׁ *explanation* CD 14$_{17.18}$ 4QD$^{a}$ 18.5$_{18}$ (הזה פרוש *this is the exact statement of* the ordinances) 4QD$^{b}$ 8$_{3}$ 4QD$^{d}$ 11.2$_{3}$ ([פר]וש) 4QD$^{f}$ 1.1$_{5}$ ([פרו]ש), מַעֲשֶׂה *deed* Nm 8$_{4}$ 1 K 7$_{28}$, אוֹת *sign* Ex 3$_{12}$ 1 S 2$_{34}$ 14$_{10}$ 2 K 19$_{29}$||Is 37$_{30}$ 2 K 20$_{9}$ 1QMyst 1.1$_{5}$ 4Qps Ezek$^{b}$ 4$_{5.13}$, מִשְׁפָּט *judgment* 4QD$^{a}$ 9.1$_{13}$, סֶרֶךְ *order* CD 12$_{22}$ 13$_{7}$ 14$_{12}$ ([וזה]) 1QS 5$_{1}$ 6$_{8}$ 1QSa 1$_{1.6(mg)}$ 4QAges 1$_{4}$ 4QD$^{a}$ 6.2$_{14}$ 4QD$^{f}$ 1.2$_{12}$ ([וזה סרך]) 4QM$^{a}$ 1$_{6}$, מוֹפֵת *wonder* 1 K 13$_{3}$, פִּתְרוֹן *solution* Gn 40$_{12.18}$.

הָחֵל hi. inf. *beginning* Gn 11$_{6}$, מוֹלֶד *time of birth* 4QCrypt 1.2$_{8}$ (זה הואה), אַחֲרִית *end* 4QMMT C$_{21}$ (זה הוא), קֵץ *end* Si 41$_{4(M)}$, קֹדֶשׁ *holiness*, i.e. holy of holies Ezk 41$_{4}$, חֶסֶד *loyalty* Gn 20$_{13}$ 2 S 16$_{17}$, זֵכֶר *remembrance* Ex 3$_{15}$, חֵפֶץ *desire* GnzPs 3$_{2}$, קוֹל *voice* 1 S 24$_{17}$ 26$_{17}$, שֵׁם *name* Ex 3$_{15}$ Jr 23$_{6}$, מַרְאֶה *appearance* Ezk 1$_{5}$, רַעְיוֹן *striving* Ec 1$_{17}$ (זֶה הוּא רַעְיוֹן) 4$_{16}$, רְעוּת *striving* Ec 2$_{26}$ 4$_{4}$ 6$_{9}$, הֶבֶל *vanity* Ec 2$_{15.19.21.23}$ (זֶה הֶבֶל הוּא) 2$_{26}$ 4$_{4.8.16}$ 5$_{9}$ 6$_{2.9}$ 7$_{6}$ (or del. גַּם־זֶה הָבֶל *this too is vanity*) 8$_{10.14}$, רָעָה *evil* Ec 2$_{21}$, רֹעַ *evil* Ne 2$_{2}$ (אֵין זֶה כִּי־אִם רֹעַ לֵב *this is nothing but evil of heart*), חֳלִי *illness* Jr 10$_{19}$ Ec 6$_{2}$ (unless זֶה הֶבֶל וָחֳלִי רָע הוּא = *this was vanity and it was a bad illness*), אֵבֶל *mourning* Gn 50$_{11}$.

b. proper noun as complement, Y. Is 25$_{9}$, Leviathan Ps 104$_{26}$ (unless לִוְיָתָן זֶה = *this Leviathan*, as §5c, or *Leviathan, who*, as §3), David 1 S 21$_{12}$ 29$_{3.5}$, Halah Ob$_{20}$ (if em. הַחֵל הַזֶּה *this force/rampart* to חֲלַח זֶה *this is Halah*).

c. pronoun as complement, אַתָּה *you* Gn 27$_{21.24}$ 2 S 2$_{20}$ 1 K 18$_{7.17}$, הוּא *he* Ex 22$_{8}$ 1 S 16$_{12}$ 4QBibPar 10$_{11(mg)}$, מָה *what?* Ex 4$_{2}$ (Qr מַה זֶּה; Kt appar. מַזֶּה; + מַטֶּה *rod*) Est 4$_{5}$ Si 39$_{34}$; מִי *who?* Est 7$_{5}$ (מִי הוּא זֶה) Si 13$_{23}$ 34$_{9.10}$ (both מי הוא זה); for מִי(־)זֶה at Is 63$_{1.1}$ Jr 30$_{21}$ 46$_{7}$ Zc 5$_{3.3}$ (if em.) Lm 3$_{37}$ Jb 38$_{2}$ 42$_{3}$, see §2; זֶה אֲשֶׁר *this is what/the one that* Gn 6$_{15}$ 44$_{5}$ Ex 29$_{38}$ Dt 14$_{12}$ Jr 33$_{16}$ 1QLitPr 3.1$_{7}$ ([אש]ר) 11QMelch$_{2}$ ([הזה אשר כתוב] *this is what is written*) 11QT 13$_{10}$.

d. adjective as complement, חָדָשׁ *new* (unless רְאֵה־זֶה חָדָשׁ הוּא = *see that which is new* or *see this; it is new*), רִאשׁוֹן *first* 11QJub 4$_{17}$ ([ריאשו]ן, without article), קָדֹשׁ *holy* 4QJub$^{a}$ 2$_{23.23}$ ([וזה ... קדש וזה ...] קדש) 2$_{24}$ ([ויתנן לזה להיות ... קדשים] *and it was given to this to be ... holy*), רַע *evil* Ec 9$_{3}$ Si 39$_{21.34}$.

e. preposition as complement, לְ *for* what purpose? Si 39$_{21}$ (זה למה זה *this, what is this for?*), perh. *after* 1QS 10$_{4.7}$ 4Q416 1$_{9}$, בְּ boast *about* valley Jr 49$_{4}$ (if em. בָּעֲמָקִים זָב עִמְקֵךְ you boast *about the valleys, your valley flows* to בָּעֲמָקִים זֶה בְעִמְקֵךְ *in the valleys, that is, in your valley*), appar. *at* the base of 4QpsEzek$^{a}$ 4$_{8}$, מִן *from among* Ex 2$_{6}$, עַל *concerning* Est 4$_{5}$ Ne 2$_{4}$ (עַל־מַה־זֶּה אַתָּה מְבַקֵּשׁ appar. *concerning what is this [that] you are seeking?*), לְעֻמַּת *in correspondence with* Si 36$_{15}$ 42$_{24(M)}$ (if ins. זֶה), נֹכַח *opposite* 11QT 33$_{10}$.

f. undetermined noun as complement, מִזְבֵּחַ *altar* 1 C 22$_{1}$ (or em. זֶה־הַמִּזְבֵּחַ to זֶה־מִזְבֵּחַ *this is the altar*), צוֹם *fast* Is 58$_{6}$ (1QIsa$^{a}$ הַצּוֹם), תְּמַהּ *wonder* Si 16$_{11}$ (תמה זה אם ינקה *it would be a wonder if he were to go unpunished*, unless תְּמַהּ *wonder [at]* this), קֶדֶם *ancient time* perh. 4QMyst$^{b}$ 8$_{2(WA)}$ (Schiffman מה *what?*), סֶרֶךְ *order* CD 10$_{4}$ 1QSa 1$_{6}$ (mg הסרך).

<OBJ> נתן *give* Gn 29$_{33}$ Ex 30$_{13}$ 2 K 4$_{43}$ Ec 9$_{1}$, לקח *take* Gn 44$_{29}$, שׂים *place* 1 K 22$_{27}$‖2 C 18$_{26}$, בוא hi. *bring* 1 S 21$_{16}$, רום hi. *raise* Ps 75$_{8}$, שׁפל hi. *make low* Ps 75$_{8}$, מצא *find* Ec 7$_{27.29}$ (unless רְאֵה[־]זֶה מָצָאתִי = *see what I have found* or *see this, I have found*), אכל *eat* Lv 11$_{4.9}$‖Dt 14$_{7.9}$ Lv 11$_{21}$.

קרא *read aloud* Is 29$_{11}$=4QpIsa$^{c}$ 15$_{3}$ ([קרא ... זה]) Is 29$_{12}$, ידע *know* Ps 56$_{10}$ (unless זֶה = *that which* I knew) Pr 24$_{12}$, בור *explain* Ec 9$_{1.1}$ (or em. ראה *see*, תור *spy out*, or ברר *cleanse*, i.e. examine), ראה *see* Ec 1$_{10}$ (unless רְאֵה־זֶה חָדָשׁ הוּא = *see that which is new* or *see, this is new*) 8$_{9}$ 9$_{1}$ (if em. בור *examine*) 7$_{27.29}$ (unless in both רְאֵה[־]זֶה מָצָאתִי = *see what I have found*, as §2, or *see, this I have found*), חזה *behold* Jb 15$_{17}$=Si 42$_{15(B)}$ (unless וְזֶה־חָזִיתִי = *and that which I beheld*, as §2), חטא *sin (in respect of)* 1QIsa$^{a}$ 42$_{24}$ (MT י׳ זוּ חָטָאנוּ לוֹ *Y., against whom we sinned*), תמה *wonder (at)* Si 16$_{11}$ (unless תמה זה אם ינקה = *it would be a wonder* [תְּמַהּ] *if he were to go unpunished*).

<CSTR> [זה בעקר ז[ה *perh. this was at the root*, i.e. base, *of this* 4QpsEzek$^{a}$ 4$_{8}$, perh. כֶּסֶף מְחִיר זֶה *silver (to the value) of the price of this (vineyard)* 1 K 21$_{2}$ (unless *this silver of the price*, as §5c), מוֹת זֶה *the death of this one* Ec 3$_{19.19}$ (unless in both *this one dies*), כָּל־זֶה *all this*, specif. all of them, all these Jg 20$_{16.17}$ Est 5$_{13}$, all this time 11QT 59$_{4}$ (כול זה), appar. all the foregoing statements 4QD$^{e}$ 11.2$_{14}$ ([כול ה[זה; =4QD$^{a}$ 18.5$_{20}$ הכו[ל הזה]) appar. *this totality*, as §5a).

<PREP> לְ of direction, *to*, + נתן ni. *be given* 4QJub$^{a}$ 2$_{24}$ ([וינתן לזה]); of possession, *of, (belonging) to* 1 S 25$_{21}$ Ec 6$_{5}$ (4QQoh$^{a}$ perh. נוחות לְ *it is better for* this one than for this one); appar. of agent, *by*, + כבד ni. *be honoured* 1QSa 1$_{18}$ (others [על] זה in same sense or *over*, i.e. more than, *this*), perh. *after* 1QS 10$_{4.7}$ 4Q416 1$_{9}$.

בְּ of place/time, *in, at, during* 1 S 9$_{11}$ 21$_{10}$, + היה *be* Gn 38$_{21.22}$ Ne 13$_{6}$ 11QT 59$_{4}$, תפשׂ ni. *be seized* CD 4$_{18.19}$, בוא *come* Est 2$_{13}$ (unless בְּ of accompaniment, *with, in a state of*), ישׁב *sit* Ex 24$_{14}$ Nm 22$_{19}$ 2 S 11$_{12}$, נצב ni. *stand* 1 S 1$_{26}$, שׁכב *lie down* Kh. el-Qom tomb inscr. 4$_{2}$, נתן *give* Gn 48$_{9}$, בנה *build* Nm 23$_{1.29}$, עשׂה *do* Jg 18$_{3}$ Ec 7$_{14}$, שׁחט *slaughter* 1 S 14$_{34}$ (+ שָׁם *there*); of instrument, *by means of, through*, + שׁתה *drink* Gn 44$_{5}$ (unless בְּ = *from*), כבד pi. *honour* 4Q418 81$_{4}$; בחר בְּ *choose* 1 S 16$_{8.9}$; אחז בְּ *hold (onto)* Ec 7$_{18}$.

כְּ *as* Gn 41$_{38}$ (כָּזֶה אִישׁ *a man like this*) Jr 5$_{9.29}$ 9$_{8}$ (all three גּוֹי אֲשֶׁר־כָּזֶה *a nation that is like this*) Si 45$_{13}$ (Segal כָּכָה *thus*), + היה *be* Is 56$_{12}$ 58$_{5}$; כָּזֹה וְכָזֶה *like this and like this*, i.e. *accordingly, thus*, + עשׂה *do* Jg 18$_{4}$, אכל *eat* 2 S 11$_{25}$, דבר pi. *speak* 1 K 14$_{5}$.

מִן of direction, *from* 11QT 10$_{11}$ (מל[מ]עלה מזה *upwards from here*), + בדל ho. *be separated* 11QT 35$_{11.13}$ 46$_{17}$, הלך *go* 1 K 17$_{3}$, יצא *go out* Gn 42$_{15}$, hi. *take out* Ex 13$_{3}$, נסע *set out* Gn 37$_{17}$, מושׁ *depart* Jg 6$_{18}$, מהר pi. *be in haste* Dt 9$_{12}$, עבר *pass* Ru 2$_{8}$, עלה *go up* Ex 33$_{1}$ CD 4$_{18}$, hi. *raise* Gn 50$_{25}$ Ex 13$_{19}$ 33$_{15}$, נשׂא *raise* Jos 4$_{3}$, שׁלח pi. *send away* Ex 11$_{1}$, נוח hi. *make rest*, i.e. relax, hand Ec 7$_{18}$, גרשׁ pi. *expel* Ex 11$_{1}$, לקח *take* Jr 38$_{10}$ Lachish ost. 3$_{18}$ (unless מזה = take *provisions*; others מיה perh. take *provisions* or take *from his hand*), נצל ni. *be rescued* CD 4$_{18}$, נגר hi. *pour* wine Ps 75$_{9}$ (or em. אֶל pour wine *into*), פוק hi. *provide* food Ps 144$_{13}$ (if em. זַן *kind*).

מִן partitive, *(some) of, (any) of, from among* 1QM 5$_{7}$ 1QS$^{e}$ 1.5$_{17}$ 1.6$_{5.13}$ (מ[ז]ה) 1.6$_{19}$ ([מזה]) 1.7$_{8.17}$ 4QOtot 1$_{17}$ 2$_{5.13}$ (מ[ז]ה) 2$_{19}$ ([מזה]) 3$_{8.17}$ (but perh. מִן = *after* in all thirteen), + היה *be* Ezk 45$_{2}$; of instrument, *by (means of), through*, + ידע *know* 1QMyst$^{a}$ 1.1$_{8}$; of comparison, *(more) than* Ec 6$_{5}$ Si 39$_{21.34(mg)}$, + נתן *give* 2 C 25$_{9}$, שׁנה *be different* from Si 42$_{24(B)}$ Si 42$_{24(B)}$ (or em.; see Subj.), מֵאֵת *from*, + יצא *go out* Jr 2$_{37}$.

אֶל *(in)to*, + קרב *approach* Ex 14$_{20}$, קרא *call* Is 6$_{3}$, נבט hi. *look* Is 66$_{2}$, נגר hi. *pour* wine Ps 75$_{9}$ (if em. מִן pour wine *from*), פוק hi. *provide* food Ps 144$_{13}$ (if em. זַן *kind*).

עַל *towards*, + פקח *open (eyes)*, i.e. look at Jb 14$_{3}$; *concerning*, + היה *be* Lm 5$_{17}$, שׁאל *ask* Ec 7$_{10}$; *on account of*, + עשׂה ni. *be done* Est 6$_{3}$, בחר pu. *be chosen* Jb 36$_{21}$ (if em. qal *choose*), *with*, + חלף *exchange* goodness Si 42$_{25}$, בחר עַל *choose* Jb 36$_{21}$ (or em.).

עִם *with*, + עשׂה ni. *be made* 4QJub$^a$ 2$_{23}$, specif. *despite*, + בקשׁ pi. *seek* Ne 5$_{18}$; אַחַר *after*, + בוא *come* 1QpHab 4$_{12}$, עבר *pass* 1QS 2$_{20.21}$, שׁלח *send* 2 C 32$_9$; לִפְנֵי *before* this (time), + נתן pass. *be given* Ne 13$_4$; לְעֻמַּת *in correspondence with* Si 36$_{15(Segal)}$ ([זה] זה לעומת *this was in correspondence with this*) 42$_{24(M)}$, + עשׂה *do* Ec 7$_{14}$; נֹכַח *opposite* 11QT 33$_{10}$; לְפִי *in accordance with* or *at the command of* 4Q415 9$_{11}$; without prep. or ה- of direction, + עלה *go up* Nm 13$_{17}$.

<COLL> כִּי־זֶה *because (of) this*, i.e. therefore, followed by verbal sentence Si 34$_{13}$ (+ עַל־כֵּן *therefore* 34$_{14}$), זֶה לְבַדּוֹ *this one alone* 1 K 14$_{13}$, גַּם־זֶה *this one too* Gn 35$_{17}$ 2 S 18$_{26}$ Ec 1$_{17}$ 2$_{15.19.21.23.26}$ 4$_{4.8.16}$ 5$_9$ 6$_9$ 7$_6$ 8$_{10.14}$, זה למה זה *(as for) this, what is this for?* Si 39$_{21}$, זֶה הוּא *this is* Ec 1$_{17}$ Est 7$_5$ 1 C 22$_1$ 4QMMT C$_{21}$ 4QCrypt 1.2$_8$ (הואה).

**2.** as combined relative pronoun with antecedent, **that which, what, the one(s) that, (s)he who(m),** etc., הוא זה שמרו אמ[ריו] *he is the one whose words they kept* 4QapPs$^a$ 1.2$_2$, בַּעֲבוּר זֶה י׳ עָשָׂה *on account of that which Y. did* Ex 13$_8$, זֶה־אָהַבְתִּי נֶהְפְּכוּ־בִי *those whom I loved have turned against me* Jb 19$_{19}$, perh. וְזֶה־חָזִיתִי וַאֲסַפֵּרָה *and that which I beheld I shall recount* Jb 15$_{17}$=Si 42$_{15(B)}$ (unless *and this I beheld, and I shall recount [it]*), רְאֵה־זֶה חָדָשׁ הוּא *see that which is new* Ec 1$_{10}$ (unless *see this; it is new* or *see, this is new*), רְאֵה זֶה מָצָאתִי *see what I have found* Ec 7$_{27.29}$ (רְאֵה־זֶה; unless *see, this I have found* or *see this, I have found*), בְּיוֹם אֶקְרָא זֶה־יָדַעְתִּי כִּי אֱלֹהִים לִי perh. *on the day when I cry out what I (already) knew, that God is for me* Ps 56$_{10}$ (unless אֶקְרָא זֶה־יָדַעְתִּי *I cry out; this I know…*), וישם זה כוחו לאלוהו *and he turns that which is his strength into his god* 1QpHab 4$_{9.13}$ ([וישם]; unless *and he turns this strength of his*, as §5e, *into his god*; =Hb 1$_{11}$ זוּ *that which*); esp. מִי(־)זֶה *who is the one that* + pf. or impf. of עלה *go up* Jr 46$_7$, ערב *pledge* Jr 30$_{21}$ (מִי הוּא־זֶה), אמר *say* Lm 3$_{37}$, אבד *die* 11QPs$^a$ 22$_9$, מלט ni. *escape* 11QPs$^a$ 22$_9$, נקה ni. *be held innocent* Zc 5$_{3.3}$ (if em. מִזֶּה ... מִזֶּה *on this side ... on that side* [§12]); perh. also מִי(־)זֶה + ptc. of בוא *come* Is 63$_1$ (or em. בָּא who is this *coming?* to הַבָּא who is this *that comes?*), חמץ pass. *be reddened* Is 63$_1$, הדר pass. *be adorned* Is 63$_1$, צעה *stoop* Is 63$_1$ (or em. צעד *march*), חשׁך hi. *obscure* Jb 38$_2$, עלם hi. *obscure* Jb 42$_3$ (unless in all the foregoing מִי־זֶה = *who is this?*, as nom. cl., followed by asyndetic relative clause, *who is this, who goes up*, etc., or by participial expression, *who is this, coming*, etc.).*

**3.** as relative pronoun, **that, which,** מְקוֹם זֶה יָסַדְתָּ *place (of) that you founded* Ps 104$_8$ (mss lack זֶה), בְּרִיתִי וְעֵדֹתִי זֶה אֲלַמְּדֵם *my covenant and my testimony, which I shall teach them* Ps 132$_{12(Gnz, ms, 11QPs^a)}$ (L זוֹ in same sense; or em. עֵדֹתַי *my testimonies* or עֵדוּתִי *my testimony*; =11QPs$^a$ 6$_4$ (עדוותי) perh. לִוְיָתָן זֶה־יָצַרְתָּ *Leviathan, whom you formed* Ps 104$_{26}$ (unless *this Leviathan [whom] you formed*, as §5c), הַר־צִיּוֹן זֶה שָׁכַנְתָּ בּוֹ *Mount Zion, where you dwelt* Ps 74$_2$ (unless *this Mount Zion, in which you dwelt*, as §5c, or *this is Mount Zion, in which you dwelt*, as §1), הַר־זֶה קָנְתָה יְמִינוֹ *a mountain that his right hand had acquired* Ps 78$_{54}$, הִנֵּה אֱלֹהֵינוּ זֶה קִוִּינוּ לוֹ *behold, our God, whom we have awaited* Is 25$_9$ (unless *behold, this is our God; we have waited for him*; + זֶה י׳ קִוִּינוּ לוֹ *this is Y.; we have waited for him*), אָבִיךָ זֶה יְלָדֶךָ *your father, who gave birth to you* (unless *your father; this*, i.e. he, *gave birth to you*) Pr 23$_{22}$, perh. בת ז *this is (the) house* Hazor inscr. 3.*

**4. one that is of, possessor of, lord of,** י׳ זֶה סִינַי *Y., the lord of Sinai* Jg 5$_5$ (+ י׳ אֱלֹהֵי יִשְׂרָאֵל *Y., the God of Israel*), sim. Ps 68$_9$ (mss lack זֶה סִינַי), וְהָיָה זֶה שָׁלוֹם *and* Assyria *will be the lord of peace* Mc 5$_4$ (unless *and this will be peace*, as §1), זֶה עָנִי *the possessor of poverty*, i.e. the poor person Ps 34$_7$ (if em. זֶה עָנִי *this poor one*, as §5d).*

**5.** as attributive adjective, usu. **this,** also **such and such, a certain** (e.g. 1 S 17$_{12}$ 2 K 4$_{16.17}$), and, followed by numeral plus noun (§5d), **these.**

**a.** הַזֶּה following determined noun (usu. sing. but sometimes pl. with sing. ref.), אֱלֹהִים *God* 1 S 6$_{20}$, אִישׁ *man* Gn 24$_{58}$ 26$_{11}$ Jg 19$_{23.24}$ 1 S 17$_{12.25}$ 25$_{25}$ 1 K 20$_{39}$ Jr 22$_{28.30}$ 26$_{11.16}$ 38$_{4.4}$ Jon 1$_{14}$ Ne 1$_{11}$ 8QHymn 1$_2$ 11QT 65$_{11}$, בֵּן *son* 2 K 6$_{32}$ (unless בֶּן־הַמְרַצֵּחַ הַזֶּה = *a son of this murderer*), יֶלֶד *child* Ex 2$_9$ 1 K 17$_{21}$, נַעַר *lad* 1 S 1$_{27}$, שׁגע pu. ptc. *one who is mad* 2 K 9$_{11}$, אָדוֹן *lord* Dn 10$_{17}$ (אֲדֹנִי זֶה *this lord of mine*), נָשִׂיא *prince* Ezk 12$_{10}$ (if del. מַשָּׂא *burden*), עֶבֶד *servant* Dn 10$_{17}$, סֹכֵן *steward* Is 22$_{15}$, יֹצֵר *potter* Jr 18$_6$, פְּלִשְׁתִּי *Philistine* 1 S 17$_{26.32.33.36.37}$, אֲרַמִּי *Aramaean* 2 K 5$_{20}$.

# זֶה

עַם *people* Ex 3$_{21}$ 5$_{22.23}$ 17$_{4}$ 18$_{18.23}$ 32$_{9.21.31}$ 33$_{12}$ Nm 11$_{11.12.13.14}$ 14$_{11.13.14.15.16.19.19}$ 21$_{2}$ 22$_{6.17}$ 24$_{14}$ 32$_{15}$ Dt 3$_{28}$ 5$_{28}$=4QTestim$_{2}$ Dt 9$_{13.27}$ 31$_{7.16}$ Jos 1$_{2.6}$ 7$_{7}$ Jg 9$_{29}$ 20$_{16}$ 2 S 16$_{18}$ 1 K 3$_{9}$ 5$_{21}$ 12$_{6.7.9}$‖2 C 10$_{6.7.9}$ 12$_{10.27.27}$ 14$_{2}$ 18$_{37}$ Is 6$_{10}$ 8$_{6.11}$=4QMidrEschat[a] 3$_{16}$ Is 8$_{12}$ Is 6$_{9}$ 9$_{15}$ 28$_{11.14}$ 29$_{13.14}$ Jr 4$_{10.11}$ 5$_{14.23}$ 6$_{19.21}$ 7$_{16.33}$ 8$_{5}$ 9$_{14}$ 11$_{14}$ 13$_{10}$ 14$_{10.11}$ 15$_{1.20}$ 16$_{5.10}$ 19$_{11}$ 21$_{8}$ 23$_{32.33}$ 27$_{16}$ 28$_{15}$ 29$_{32}$ 32$_{42}$ 33$_{24}$ 35$_{16}$ 36$_{7}$ 37$_{18}$ 38$_{4}$ Mc 2$_{11}$ Hg 1$_{2}$ 2$_{14}$ Zc 8$_{6}$ 8$_{11.12}$ Ne 5$_{18.19}$ 2 C 1$_{10}$ 4QPsJos[a] 3.2$_{10}$ ([העם הזה]).

גּוֹי *nation* Ex 33$_{13}$ Jg 2$_{20}$ 2 K 6$_{18}$ Hg 2$_{14}$, קָהָל *assembly* Ex 16$_{3}$ Nm 20$_{12}$ 1 S 17$_{47}$, הָמוֹן *multitude* 1 K 20$_{13.28}$ 1 C 29$_{16}$ 2 C 14$_{10}$ 20$_{12.15}$ 31$_{10}$, דּוֹר *generation* Gn 7$_{1}$ Dt 1$_{35}$, גְּדוּד *troop* 1 S 30$_{8.15.15}$.

גְּדִי *kid* Gn 38$_{23}$, עֵגֶל *calf* Ex 32$_{24}$, כֶּלֶב *dog* 2 S 16$_{9}$, אַיִל *ram* 11QT 18$_{2}$.

יוֹם *day* Gn 7$_{11.13.23.26}$ 26$_{33}$ 32$_{33}$ 39$_{11}$ 47$_{26}$ 48$_{15}$ 50$_{20}$ Ex 10$_{6}$ 12$_{14.17.17.41.51}$ 13$_{3}$ 19$_{1}$ Lv 8$_{34}$ 16$_{30}$ 23$_{14.21.28.29.30}$ Nm 22$_{30}$ Dt 2$_{22.25.30}$ 3$_{14}$ 4$_{20.38}$ 5$_{24}$ 6$_{24}$ 8$_{18}$ 10$_{8.15}$ 11$_{4}$ 26$_{16}$ 27$_{9}$ 29$_{3.27}$ 32$_{48}$ 34$_{6}$ Jos 3$_{7}$ 4$_{9}$ 5$_{9.11}$ 6$_{25}$ 7$_{25.26.26}$ 8$_{28.29}$ 9$_{27}$ 10$_{27}$ 13$_{13}$ 14$_{14}$ 15$_{63}$ 16$_{10}$ 22$_{3.17.22}$ 23$_{8.9}$ Jg 1$_{21.26}$ 6$_{24}$ 9$_{19}$ 10$_{4.15}$ 12$_{3}$ 15$_{19}$ 18$_{12}$ 19$_{30}$ 1 S 5$_{5}$ 6$_{18}$ 8$_{8}$ 11$_{13}$ 12$_{2.5}$ 14$_{45}$ 17$_{10.46.46}$ 22$_{8.13}$ 24$_{11.20}$ 25$_{32.33}$ 26$_{21.24}$ 27$_{6}$ 28$_{18}$ 29$_{3.6.8}$ 30$_{25}$ 2 S 3$_{38}$ 4$_{3.8}$ 6$_{8}$‖1 C 13$_{11}$ 2 S 7$_{6}$‖1 C 17$_{5}$ 2 S 16$_{12}$ 18$_{18.20}$ 1 K 1$_{30}$ 2$_{26}$ 3$_{6}$ 8$_{8}$‖2 C 5$_{9}$ 1 K 8$_{24}$‖2 C 6$_{15}$ 1 K 8$_{61}$ 9$_{13.21}$‖2 C 8$_{8}$ 1 K 10$_{12}$ 12$_{19}$‖2 C 10$_{19}$ 2 K 2$_{22}$ 7$_{9}$ 8$_{22}$‖2 C 21$_{10}$ 2 K 14$_{7}$ 16$_{6}$ 17$_{23.34.41}$ 19$_{3}$ 20$_{17}$ 21$_{15}$ Is 37$_{3}$ 39$_{6}$ Jr 1$_{10}$ 3$_{25}$ 7$_{25}$ 11$_{5.7}$ 25$_{3.18}$ 32$_{20.20.31}$ 35$_{14}$ 36$_{2}$ 44$_{2.6.10.22.23}$ Ezk 2$_{3}$ 20$_{29}$ 24$_{2.2}$ 40$_{1}$ Hg 2$_{15.18.19}$ Est 1$_{18}$ 3$_{14}$ 8$_{13}$ Dn 9$_{7.15}$ Ezr 9$_{7.7.15}$ Ne 9$_{10.32}$ 1 C 4$_{41.43}$ 5$_{26}$ 28$_{7}$ 1QM 15$_{12}$ 1QDM 2$_{1}$ ([היו]ם) 2$_{6}$ ([היום]) 3$_{9}$ 4QJub[c] 22$_{7}$ (הז[ה]) 4QBibPar 1$_{9.13}$ (ה[יום הזה]) 4QJub[a] 2$_{4}$ ([ביום הזה]) 4Q392 2$_{3}$ 4QM[a] 11.2$_{16}$ 4QRitMar 2$_{7}$ 22$_{4}$ ([היום]) 4QPrQuot 1$_{2}$ (הי[ו]ם) 70$_{4}$ 4QDibHam[a] 1.6$_{4}$ 11 QT 17$_{3}$ 18$_{3}$ 19$_{7}$ (היו[ם הזה]) 19$_{15}$ 21$_{3}$ ([ביום הזה]) 21$_{8}$ ([ביו]ם הזה) 21$_{9}$ (בי[ום הזה]) 22$_{13.15}$ 25$_{9.10.12}$ 27$_{5.8}$ 5/6 ḤevBA 44$_{2}$.*

לַיְלָה *night* Ex 12$_{8.12.42}$ 4QPrQuot 76$_{3}$, חֹדֶשׁ *month* Ex 12$_{2.3.6}$ 13$_{5}$ Lv 23$_{6.27.34}$ Nm 9$_{3}$ 28$_{17}$ 29$_{7}$ Ne 9$_{1}$ 4QJub[a] 1$_{1}$ ([לחודש ה]זה) 11QT 17$_{10}$ 25$_{10}$ 27$_{10}$, עֵת *time* Lachish ost. 6$_{2}$, מוֹעֵד *appointed time* Gn 17$_{21}$ 2 K 4$_{16.17}$ 1QLitPr 1$_{3}$ ([במוע]ד הזה]), פַּעַם *occasion* (fem.) Jg 16$_{28}$ (or em. הַזֶּה to יי *Y.*), פֶּסַח *passover* 2 K 23$_{22.23}$‖2 C 35$_{19}$, יוֹבֵל *jubilee* 4QJub[d] 21$_{1}$ (ל[יובל הזה]) 4QpsJub[b] 1$_{6}$.

מָקוֹם *place* Gn 19$_{13.14}$ 20$_{11}$ 28$_{16.17}$ Nm 20$_{5}$ Dt 1$_{31}$ 9$_{7}$ 11$_{5}$ 26$_{9}$ 29$_{6}$ 1 S 12$_{8}$ 1 K 8$_{29.30.35}$‖2 C 6$_{20.21.26}$ 1 K 13$_{8.16}$ 2 K 6$_{9}$ 18$_{25}$ 22$_{16.17.19.20}$‖2 C 34$_{24.25.27.28}$ Jr 7$_{3.6.7.20}$ 14$_{13}$ 16$_{2.3}$ 16$_{9}$ 19$_{3.4.6.7.12}$ 22$_{3.11}$ 24$_{5}$ 27$_{22}$ 28$_{3.3.4.6}$ 29$_{10}$ 32$_{37}$ 33$_{10.12}$ 40$_{2}$ 42$_{18}$ 44$_{29}$ 51$_{62}$ Hg 2$_{9}$ Zp 1$_{4}$ 2 C 6$_{40}$ 7$_{12.15}$ 1QJub[a] 27$_{20}$ ([הזה]) Mur 22 1$_{11}$ ([המ]קום ה[זה]) Kfar Alma inscr. Kfar Baram inscr.*

מִדְבָּר *steppe* Ex 16$_{3}$ Nm 14$_{2.29.32.35}$ 20$_{4}$ Dt 2$_{7}$ Jos 1$_{4}$ (מֵהַמִּדְבָּר וְהַלְּבָנוֹן הַזֶּה *from this steppe and Lebanon*), הַר *mountain* Nm 27$_{12}$ Dt 1$_{6}$ 2$_{3}$ 3$_{25}$ 32$_{49}$ Jos 14$_{12}$ Is 25$_{6.7.10}$ 4QJub[a] 1$_{5}$ ([בהר הזה]) 11QT 51$_{7}$,* נַחַל *valley* 2 K 3$_{16}$, אִי *island* Is 20$_{6}$, גַּל *heap* Gn 31$_{48.51.52.52.52}$, סֶלַע *rock* 4Q522 8.2$_{7}$ (הס[לע הזה]), בּוֹר *pit* Gn 37$_{22}$, דֶּרֶךְ *way* Gn 28$_{20}$ Dt 17$_{16}$, סֶלַע *rock* Nm 20$_{10}$.

מַחֲנֶה *camp* Gn 33$_{8}$, מָעוֹז *stronghold* Jg 6$_{26}$, בַּיִת *house* Gn 39$_{9}$ 40$_{14}$ 1 K 6$_{12}$ 8$_{27.29.31.33.38.42.43}$‖2 C 6$_{18.20.22.24.29.32.33}$ 1 K 9$_{3.8.8}$‖2 C 7$_{16.21.21}$ 2 K 21$_{7}$‖2 C 33$_{7}$ Jr 7$_{10.11}$ 22$_{5}$ 26$_{6.9.12}$ Hg 1$_{4}$ 2$_{3.7.9}$ Zc 4$_{9}$ 2 C 7$_{20}$ 20$_{9.9}$ 11QT 31$_{6}$ (הב[ית הזה]) 11QT 32$_{9}$ 33$_{11}$.

מִגְדָּל *tower* Jg 8$_{9}$, אוּלָם *porch* 1 K 7$_{8}$, שַׁעַר *gate* Ezk 44$_{2}$ 11QT 31$_{7}$ 38$_{9}$ ([ה]שער), חֶדֶר *chamber* Kh. el-Qom tomb inscr. 1$_{3}$, מִזְבֵּחַ *altar* 2 K 18$_{22}$‖Is 36$_{7}$, שְׁקוֹף *lintel* Kfar Baram inscr.

דָּם *blood* Dt 21$_{7}$=11QT 63$_{6}$, לֵבָב *heart* 4QBibPar 6$_{5}$ (=Dt 5$_{29}$ לבבם זה *this heart of theirs*), אָדֹם *brown (stew)* Gn 25$_{30}$, דְּבַשׁ *honey* 1 S 14$_{29}$, קָלִי *grain* 1 S 17$_{17}$, לֶחֶם *bread* 1 S 17$_{17}$ 11QT 8$_{13}$ ([ה]ל[ח]ם), חוּט *thread* Jos 2$_{18}$, מַטֶּה *rod* Ex 4$_{17}$, פַּךְ *flask* 2 K 9$_{1}$ (unless פַּךְ הַשֶּׁמֶן חַזֶּה = *a flask of this oil*), שֶׁמֶן *oil* Arad ost. 13$_{2}$ ([הש]מן) 11QT 21$_{16}$ ([השמן הזה]) 22$_{03}$ 22$_{05}$ perh. 2 K 9$_{1}$, יַיִן *wine* 11QT 19$_{15}$ (הזה erased), נֶסֶךְ *drink offering* 11QT 20$_{02}$, קָנֶה *reed* 2 K 18$_{21}$‖Is 36$_{6}$, סַעַר *whirlwind* Jon 1$_{12}$, כָּבוֹד *glory*, i.e. wealth Gn 31$_{1}$, חַיִל *valour*, i.e. wealth Dt 8$_{17}$, *force* perh. Ob$_{20}$ (unless חֵל = *rampart*; or em. הַחֵל הַזֶּה *this force/rampart* to חֲלַח זֶה *this is Halah*).

דָּבָר *word, thing, matter* Gn 18$_{25}$ 19$_{21}$ 20$_{10}$ 21$_{26}$ 22$_{16}$ 24$_{9}$ 30$_{31}$ 32$_{20}$ 34$_{14}$ 44$_{7}$ Ex 1$_{18}$ 2$_{15}$ 9$_{5.6}$ 12$_{24}$ 18$_{14.23}$ 33$_{4.17}$ Nm 32$_{20}$ Dt 1$_{32}$ 3$_{26}$ 4$_{32}$ 13$_{12}$=11QT 55$_{1}$ ([הרע הזה]) Dt 15$_{10.15}$ 17$_{5}$ 19$_{20}$=11QT 61$_{11}$ Dt 22$_{20.26}$=11QT 66$_{7}$ Dt 24$_{18.22}$ 32$_{47}$ Jos 9$_{24}$ 14$_{10}$ Jg 6$_{29.29}$ 8$_{1.3}$ 11$_{37}$ 1 S 9$_{21}$ 12$_{16}$ 17$_{27.30}$ 18$_{8}$ 20$_{2}$ 24$_{7}$ 26$_{16}$ 28$_{18}$ 28$_{10}$ 30$_{24}$ 2 S 2$_{6}$ 11$_{11.25}$ 12$_{6.12.14.21}$ 13$_{20}$ 14$_{3.13.15.20.21}$ 15$_{6}$ 17$_{6}$ 19$_{43}$ 24$_{3}$ 1 K 1$_{27}$ 2$_{23}$

$3_{10.11}$ $11_{10}$ $12_{24}$||2 C $11_{4}$ 1 K $12_{30}$ $13_{33.34}$ $20_{9.12.24}$ 2 K $5_{18}$ $6_{11}$ $7_{2.19}$ $8_{13}$ $17_{12}$ Is $8_{20}$ $24_{3}$ $30_{12}$ $38_{7}$ Jr $5_{14}$ $7_{2.23}$ $13_{12}$ $14_{17}$ $22_{1.4}$ $23_{38}$ $26_{1}$ $27_{1}$ $28_{7}$ $31_{23}$ $36_{1}$ $40_{3(Qr)}$ (Kt lacks article before noun) $40_{16}$ Am $3_{1}$ $4_{1}$ $5_{1}$ Dn $1_{14}$ $10_{11}$ Ezr $9_{3}$ $10_{5}$ $10_{13.14}$ Ne $2_{19}$ $5_{12.13.13}$ $6_{4.4.5}$ $13_{17}$ 1 C $21_{7.8}$ 4QMMT $B_{12}$ $11QMelch_{6}$ 11QT $55_{19}$ Arad ost. $6_{12}$ (הד[ב]ר).*

מָשָׁל *proverb* Is $14_{4}$ Ezk $12_{22.23}$ $18_{2.3}$, מַשָּׂא *burden* Ne $5_{10}$, specif. *pronouncement* 2 K $9_{25}$ Is $14_{28}$=4QpIsa[c] $8_{11}$ ([המשא הזה]) Ezk $12_{10}$ (or del. מַשָּׂא, thus הַנָּשִׂיא הַזֶּה *this prince*), שְׁבוּעָה *oath* (fem.) Jos $2_{17}$ (mss lack זֶה; mss זֹאת *this* [fem.]; or em. זוֹ *this* [fem.]), מִשְׁפָּט *judgment, ordinance* Ex $21_{31}$ Jos $6_{15}$ CD $8_{19(A)}$=$19_{32(B)}$ $20_{8}$ $12_{22}$ 1QS $8_{19}$ 4QD[a] 9.$1_{3}$ 17.$2_{2}$ ([זה]) 4Q376 1.$3_{1}$ $4QM^{c}_{12}$ ([כמש]פט הזה]) 11QT $15_{3}$ $29_{4}$ $50_{7}$, חֹק *statute* 1QSa $2_{21}$, סֶרֶךְ *order* 1QM $7_{16}$ ([הס]רך הזה]) $8_{14}$ $16_{2}$ 4QM[a] $1_{19}$ ([הזה]) $4QM^{c}_{9}$, שִׁיר *song* Is $26_{1}$, מַעֲשֶׂה *deed* Gn $44_{15}$ 1 K $7_{8}$, מֶכֶר *sale* Mur 22 $1_{12}$ 30 $1_{4.7}$ $2_{16.17.22.24.28}$.

סֵפֶר *book* Dt $28_{58}$ $29_{19.20.26}$ $30_{10}$ $31_{26}$ Jos $1_{8}$ 2 K $5_{6}$ $10_{2}$ $22_{13.13}$||2 C $34_{21}$ 2 K $23_{3}$||2 C $34_{31}$ 2 K $23_{21}$ Jr $25_{13}$ $29_{29}$ $32_{14.14}$ (or del. הַזֶּה) $51_{63}$ Nimrud ivory inscr. $1_{3}$ ([הספר הזה]), כְּתָב *writing* 3QTr $12_{11}$.

חֲלוֹם *dream* Gn $37_{6.10}$, מַרְאֶה *vision* Ex $3_{3}$, חָזוֹן *vision* 1 C $17_{15}$, חִזָּיוֹן *vision* 2 S $7_{17}$, אוֹת *sign* Ex $8_{19}$, סֶמֶל *image* Ezk $8_{5}$, קוֹל *voice* 1 S $4_{14}$ $15_{14}$, שֵׁם *name* Dt $28_{58}$.

חֶסֶד *loyalty* 2 S $2_{5}$ 1 K $3_{6}$, בִּטָּחוֹן *confidence* 2 K $18_{19}$||Is $36_{4}$, אַף *anger* Dt $29_{23}$, מַעַל *sin* Jos $22_{16.31}$ Ezr $9_{2}$, עָוֹן *wickedness* Is $22_{14}$ $30_{13}$, מָוֶת *death* Ex $10_{17}$, כֹּל *all* 4QD[a] 18.$5_{20}$ ([הכו]ל הזה]) appar. *this totality*; =4QD[e] 11.$2_{14}$ ([כול ה[זה]) *all this*, as §1, Cstr.).

הָמָן *Haman* Est $7_{6}$ (הָמָן הָרָע הַזֶּה *this evil Haman*), יַרְדֵּן *Jordan* Gn $32_{11}$ Dt $4_{6}$ $31_{2}$ Jos $1_{2.11}$ $4_{22}$, לְבָנוֹן *Lebanon* Jos $1_{4}$ (מֵהַמִּדְבָּר וְהַלְּבָנוֹן הַזֶּה *from this steppe and Lebanon*).

**b.** זֶה (not הַזֶּה) following suffixed noun, לֵבָב *heart* Dt $5_{29}$=$4QTestim_{3}$ (זה in mg; =4QBibPar 65 הלבב הזה *this heart*), בֵּן *son* Dt $21_{20}$=11QT $64_{3}$, דָּבָר *word* Jos $2_{14.20}$, כֹּחַ *strength* Jg $6_{14}$, חֳלִי *illness* 2 K $1_{2}$ $8_{8.9}$ (if em. in all three חֳלִי זֶה *this illness*, as §5c, to חָלְיִי זֶה *this illness of mine*).

**c.** הַזֶּה/זֶה following undetermined or proper noun, חֳלִי *illness* 2 K $1_{2}$ $8_{8.9}$ (or em.; see §5b), perh. כֶּסֶף *silver* 1 K $21_{2}$ (but see §1, Cstr.), יוֹם *day* 11QT $21_{12}$ (מיום הזה *from this day*), שַׁעַר *gate* 11QT $39_{15}$ (משער הזה *from this gate*; erased reading in mg שמעון appar. the gate of *Simeon* for הזה); עם זה יצרתי *I formed this people* 1QIsa[a] $43_{21}$ (unless §2, as MT עַם־זוּ *a people whom* I formed), הַר־זֶה *this mountain* Ps $78_{54}$ (unless *this is a mountain* or *a mountain that*), הַר־צִיּוֹן זֶה appar. *this Mount Zion* Ps $74_{2}$ (unless *this is Mount Zion* or *Mount Zion, which*), לִוְיָתָן זֶה *this Leviathan* Ps $104_{26}$ (unless *this is Leviathan* or *Leviathan, who*), דוסתס *Dositheus* Mur 30 $2_{2}$ 6 (דוסתס זה *this Dositheus*), perh. [מ]שא ז שלם *this burden he repaid* Hazor ost. 11 (others ]שא ז של[ [Phoenician] or שא זי ל[ [Aramaic]).

**d.** זֶה preceding undetermined noun, זֶה פַּעֲמַיִם *these two times* Gn $27_{36}$ $43_{10}$ (זֶה פַעֲמָיִם), זֶה עֶשֶׂר פְּעָמִים *these ten times* Nm $14_{22}$ Jb $19_{3}$, sim. Nm $24_{10}$ Jg $16_{15}$, זֶה שָׁלֹשׁ רְגָלִים *these three times* Nm $22_{28.32}$ (שָׁלוֹשׁ) $22_{33}$, זֶה שְׁנָתַיִם *these two years* Gn $45_{6}$, זֶה עֶשְׂרִים שָׁנָה *these twenty years* Gn $31_{38.41}$ (זֶה־לִּי עֶשְׂרִים שָׁנָה *these twenty years of mine*), sim. Dt $2_{7}$ $8_{2.4}$ Jos $14_{10}$ Jr $25_{3}$ Zc $1_{12}$ $7_{5}$ 1QDM $2_{5}$ ([זה] ארבעים [שנה] *these forty years*), זֶה כַּמֶּה שָׁנִים *these several years* Zc $7_{3}$, זֶה יָמִים רַבִּים *these many days* Jos $22_{3}$ 2 S $14_{2}$, זֶה יָמִים אוֹ־זֶה שָׁנִים *these days or these years* 1 S $29_{3}$, זה ימם *these days*, i.e. a few days ago Meṣad Ḥashavyahu ost. $1_{9}$, זֶה שְׁלוֹשִׁים יוֹם *these thirty days* Est $4_{11}$, מִי־זֶה רֹעֶה *who is this*, i.e. the, *shepherd* who will stand before me? Jr $49_{19}$=$50_{44}$, זֶה עָנִי *this poor one* Ps $34_{7}$ (or em. זֶה עֳנִי *the possessor of poverty*, i.e. the poor person, as §4), זֶה אֱלֹהִים appar. *this God* Ps $48_{15}$ (but perh. *this is our God*).*

**e.** זֶה preceding determined noun, esp. in form מִי זֶה *who is this* king, man, etc.? (Ps $24_{8}$ $25_{12}$) or מִי הוּא זֶה in same sense (Ps $24_{10}$), אִישׁ *man* Ex $32_{1.23}$ (both זֶה מֹשֶׁה הָאִישׁ *this man Moses*) Ps $25_{12}$, נַעַר *lad* 1 S $17_{55}$, עֶלֶם *lad* 1 S $17_{56}$, מֶלֶךְ *king* Ps $24_{8.10}$, יוֹם *day* 1 K $14_{14}$ (or em. בַּיּוֹם הַהוּא *on that day*), בַּיִת *house* Ezr $3_{12}$ (or del. זֶה הַבַּיִת *this house*), אַחֲרוֹן *last one* Jr $50_{17}$, ישב inf. *sitting* Ru $2_{7}$ (זֶה שִׁבְתָּהּ הַבַּיִת מְעָט *this sitting of hers at home was little*; or em.; see §5f), לֶחֶם *bread* Jos $9_{12}$ (זֶה לַחְמֵנוּ *this bread of ours* unless *this is our bread*, as §1), כֹּחַ *strength* 1QpHab $4_{9.13}$ (זה כוחו *this strength of his*, or, *that which was his strength*, as §2); but perh. in all these cases, זֶה is not an adj. but pronoun (as §1) in apposition to a following noun, e.g. זֶה הַנַּעַר *this one, the lad* (1 S $17_{55}$).

**f.** זֶה following particle, עַתָּה זֶה *right now*, + pf. of ידע

*know* 1 K $17_{24}$ (mss lack זֶה), בוא *come* 2 K $5_{22}$ (mss lack זֶה); עַד עַתָּה זֶה *unto just now;* her sitting at home was little Ru $2_7$ (if em. עַתָּה זֶה unto *now, this* sitting; see §5e); הִנֵּה־זֶה *there he is, there it was,* etc. + ptc. of בוא *come* Is $21_9$ Ca $2_8$, עמד *stand* Ca $2_9$, נגע *touch* 1 K $19_5$; הִנֵּה־זֶה הָיָה appar. *here it is,* the sin of Sodom, your sister—arrogance Ezk $16_{49}$.

**6.** אֵי־זֶה **whither?, in which direction?, a.** with verb, אֵי־זֶה עָבַר רוּחַ־י׳ מֵאִתִּי *in which direction did the spirit of Y. pass from me?* 1 K $22_{24}$ (ms and ||2 C $18_{23}$ אֵי זֶה הַדֶּרֶךְ *where is the way?*). **b.** in nom. cl., **where is?,** with (pro)noun, בַּיִת *house* 1 S $9_{18}$ (+ נגד hi. *tell* me) Is $66_1$, מָקוֹם *place* $66_1$ Jb $28_{12.20}$ (both אֵי זֶה; + מֵאַיִן *whence?*) $38_{19}$, דֶּרֶךְ *way* 1 K $13_{12}$ 2 C $18_{23}$||1 K $22_{24(ms)}$ (2 C אֵי זֶה) 2 K $3_8$ Jr $6_{16}$ Jb $38_{19.24}$, תְּהִלָּה *praise* 4QD$^{c}$ $1_2$, סֵפֶר *book* Is $50_1$ (אֵי זֶה), סֹפֵר *scribe* 4QD$^{c}$ $1_2$, הוּא *he* Est $7_5$ (+ מִי *who?*).

**7.** אֵי־זֶה **what?, which?, a.** with verb, אֵינְךָ יוֹדֵעַ אֵי זֶה יִכְשַׁר הֲזֶה אוֹ־זֶה *you do not know which will prosper—this one or this one* Ec $11_{6(L)}$. **b.** in nom. cl., עַד אֲשֶׁר־אֶרְאֶה אֵי־זֶה טוֹב *until I might see what is good* Ec $2_3$. **c.** בְּאֵיזֶה **by which?,** באיזה ד[רך תבקשנו] *by which way will you seek him?* Si $30_{40(Segal)}$.

**8.** אֵי־מִזֶּה **whence?, a.** with verb, בוא *come* Gn $16_8$ (+ אָנָה *whither*) 2 S $1_3$ Jb $2_2$ (both אֵי מִזֶּה). **b.** in nom. cl., with pronoun, אַתָּה *you* 1 S $30_{13}$ (+ לְמִי *to whom?*) 2 S $1_{13}$ (both אֵי מִזֶּה), הוּא *he* Jg $13_6$ (+ שׁאל *ask*), הֵמָּה *they* 1 S $25_{11}$ (אֵי מִזֶּה; + ידע *know*).

**9.** אֵי־מִזֶּה **from which?,** אֵי־מִזֶּה עִיר אַתָּה *from which town are you?* 2 S $15_2$, אֵי־מִזֶּה עַם אָתָּה *from which people are you?* Jon $1_8$ (+ זֹאת *this*).

**10.** לָמָּה(־)זֶּה **why?, a.** followed by pf. of יצא *go out* Nm $11_{20}$, ירד *go down* 1 S $17_{28}$, עזב *abandon* Ex $2_{20}$, שׁלח pi. *send away* Ex $5_{22}$ 2 S $3_{24}$, עלה hi. *raise* Ex $17_3$, צחק *laugh* Gn $18_{13}$. **b.** followed by impf. of בוא *come* Jr $6_{20}$ (or em. hi.), hi. *bring* 1 S $20_8$ Jr $6_{20}$ (if em.), נפל *fall* Si $37_8$, שׁאל *ask* Gn $32_{30}$ Jg $13_{18}$, מצא *find* grace Gn $33_{15}$, יגע *toil* Jb $9_{29}$, הבל *be vain* Jb $27_{12}$. **c.** in nom. cl., with pronoun, אָנֹכִי *I,* i.e. what is my reason for being? Gn $25_{22}$. **d.** followed by ptc. of נכר ni. *disguise oneself* 1 K $14_6$, רוץ *run* 2 S $18_{22}$, עבר *pass* Nm $14_{41}$, רדף *pursue* 1 S $26_{18}$, נפל *fall* Jos $7_{10}$, צום *fast* 2 S $12_{23}$. **e.** followed by nom. cl., Gn $25_{32}$ Am $5_{18}$ Pr $17_{16}$.

**11.** מַה־זֶּה usu. **why?** (Jg $18_{24}$ 1 K $21_5$ 2 K $1_5$), perh. also **what?** (1 S $10_{11}$), **how?** (Gn $27_{20}$), **a.** followed by pf. of היה *be* 1 S $10_{11}$, שׁוב *go back* 2 K $1_5$, מהר pi. *be in haste* Gn $27_{20}$. **b.** followed by impf. of אמר *say* Jg $18_{24}$. **c.** followed by nom. cl., מַה־זֶּה רוּחֲךָ סָרָה וְאֵינְךָ אֹכֵל לָחֶם *why is your spirit stubborn and you do not eat bread?* 1 K $21_5$.

**12.** מִזֶּה ... וּמִזֶּה **over here ... and over there, on this side ... and on that side,** מִזֶּה אֶחָד וּמִזֶּה אֶחָד *by this (hand) was one and by this (hand) was one* Ex $17_{12}$, sim. Ex $25_{19}$||$37_8$ $26_{13.13}$ $32_{15}$ $38_{15}$ Nm $22_{24}$ Jos $8_{22.33}$ 1 S $14_4$ $17_3$ $23_{26}$ 2 S $2_{13}$ 1 K $10_{19.20}$||2 C $9_{18.19}$ Ezk $45_7$ $47_{7.12}$ $48_{21}$ 1QM $5_{8.12}$ $6_7$ 4QM$^{c}$ ([מזה ו]מזה) 11QT $7_{11}$ ([מזה ומז]ה), sim. Zc $5_3$ (or em. מִי זֶה ... מִי זֶה *who is the one who ... who is the one who,* as §2).*

Also 4Q415 $9_{10}$ (זה מז[ה]) 4QD$^{d}$ $7_2$ 4QD$^{e}$ $6_6$ 4QApoc Mos B $1.2_9$ 4QPrQuot $60_2$ 4QPrFêtes$^{c}$ 286 6QHymn $11_1$ 8QHymn $1_3$ perh. 4QMishC$^{a}$ $2_2$ $3_3$.*

**זֹה** 11.1 demonst. pronoun sing. f. **this (one),** at Ec $2_{24}$ $7_{23}$ with neuter or indeterminate reference ('what I have been talking about', 'the foregoing', etc.), <SUBJ> עשׂה *do* Ec $2_2$. <NOM CL> with complement עִיר *city* 2 K $6_{19}$ (|| זֶה *this*), לִשְׁכָּה *chamber* Ezk $40_{45}$, מַתַּת *gift* Ec $5_{18}$ (זֹה מַתַּת אֱלֹהִים הִיא *this is a gift of God;* Gnz זו *this,* זֶה *this*), רָעָה *evil* Ec $5_{15}$. <OBJ> ראה *see* Ec $2_{24}$ $9_{13}$, נסה pi. *test* Ec $7_{23}$, עשׂה *do* Si $35_{23}$. <PREP> כְּ *as,* כָּזֹה וְכָזֶה *like this and like this,* i.e. accordingly, thus, + עשׂה *do* Jg $18_4$, אכל *eat* 2 S $11_{25}$, דבר pi. *speak* 1 K $14_5$. <CSTR> כָּל־זֹה *all this* Ec $7_{23}$. <COLL> גַּם־זֹה *this one too* Ec $2_{24}$ $5_{15}$ $9_{13}$. <SYN> זֶה *this.**

**זָהָב** I 387.10.40.2 n.m. **gold**—cstr. זְהַב (Gn $2_{12}$ וּזְהַב); sf. זְהָבִי, זְהָבְךָ (זְהָבֶךְ), זְהָבוֹ, זְהָבָם—**gold,** in ref. to gold ore (e.g. Gn $2_{11.12}$ Pr $17_3$ Jb $28_1$), to gold as wealth, as spoil, etc.; used in jewellery (e.g. Gn $24_{22}$ Ex $32_{2.3}$ Jg $8_{24.26}$) and in construction of cult objects (e.g. Ex $26_{37}$ $32_3$ Jg $8_{27}$), etc.; also appar. **object made of gold** (1 C $29_{2.5}$).

<SUBJ> היה *be* Ex $28_8$ $38_{24}$ Nm $31_{52}$ Ezk $7_{19}$ 11QT $3_{12}$ (מ[נ]קיותיו יהיו זהב *its bowls will be gold*), יתר ni. *remain* 1 K $15_{18}$, מצא ni. *be found* 2 K $12_{19}$ $16_8$ perh. $14_{14}$, רבה

*be great* Dt 8$_{13}$, יכל *be able* to save Ezk 7$_{19}$ Zp 1$_{18}$, אסף pu. *be gathered* Zc 14$_{14}$, עשׂה pass. *be made*, i.e. prepared Ex 38$_{24}$, שׁחט pass. *be beaten*, i.e. alloyed 1 K 10$_{16.17}$||2 C 9$_{15.16}$, פזז ho. *be refined* 1 K 10$_{18}$ (מוּפָז *refined*; mss מֵאוּפָז *from Uphaz*; ||2 C 9$_{17}$ טָהוֹר *pure*), זקק pu. *be refined* 1 C 28$_{18}$, סגר pass. *be closed*, appar. in ref. to old or select gold 1 K 6$_{20.21}$ 7$_{49.50}$ 10$_{21}$||2 C 9$_{20}$ 2 C 4$_{20.22}$, טהר *be pure* Nm 31$_{22}$, שׁקל ni. *be weighed* Ezr 8$_{33}$, ערך *be comparable* Jb 28$_{17}$, עמם ho. *be dark* Lm 4$_{1}$, בוא *come* Nm 31$_{22}$, ho. *be brought* Jr 10$_{9}$, אתה *come* Jb 37$_{22}$ (or em. זֹהַר *brightness*), עמד hi. *establish* Si 40$_{25}$(B Segal) ([יעמידו]), מלא *fill* Ezk 28$_{13}$ (if em.; see Nom. Cl.), פחז hi. *make arrogant* Si 8$_{2}$ (+ הוֹן *wealth*).

<NOM CL> הַזָּהָב נְדָבָה *the gold is a freewill offering* Ezr 8$_{28}$, הַזָּהָב זְהַב פַּרְוָיִם *the gold was gold of Parvaim* 2 C 3$_{6}$, וָוֵיהֶם זָהָב *their hooks are gold* Ex 26$_{32.37}$ 36$_{36}$, דַּלְתֵי הַבַּיִת ... זָהָב *the doors of the house ... were gold* 2 C 4$_{22}$, מַחְתֹּתֶיהָ זָהָב *its pans are gold* Ex 25$_{38}$, כֻּלָּהּ ... זָהָב *all of it* (the candlestick) *was ... gold* Ex 37$_{22}$, כֹּל כְּלֵי מַשְׁקֵה הַמֶּלֶךְ שְׁלֹמֹה זָהָב *all the drinking vessels of King Solomon were gold* 1 K 10$_{21}$||2 C 9$_{20}$, sim. 1 K 10$_{21}$||2 C 9$_{20}$, כֹּל כֶּסֶף וְזָהָב ... קֹדֶשׁ הוּא *all silver and gold is ... sacred* Jos 6$_{19}$, עֲצַבֵּיהֶם כֶּסֶף וְזָהָב *their images are silver and gold* Ps 115$_{4}$, זְהָב מְלֶאכֶת תֻּפֶּיךָ *gold was the work of your tambourines* Ezk 28$_{13}$ (if athnach moved; or em. זָהָב מָלֵא בֵּית־נְכֹתֶיךָ *gold fills the house of your riches*), וְאֶת־הַמַּחְתּוֹת ... וְאֶת־הַמִּזְרָקוֹת אֲשֶׁר זָהָב זָהָב *and the firepans and the basins ... that were of gold, gold*, i.e. made entirely of gold 2 K 25$_{15}$||Jr 52$_{19}$.

הוּא ... זָהָב *it was ... gold* Ex 39$_{5}$.

זֲהַב הָאָרֶץ הַהִוא טוֹב *the gold of that land is good* Gn 2$_{12}$(Qr).

זְהָבְךָ לִי־הוּא *your gold is mine* 1 K 20$_{3}$, לִי הַזָּהָב *the gold is mine* Hg 2$_{8}$, זָהָב לָהֶם *they have gold* Jb 3$_{15}$, זָהָב לוֹ *it has gold* Jb 28$_{6}$, לְמִי זָהָב *to whom is gold?* Ex 32$_{24}$, יֶשׁ־לִי ... זָהָב *there is to me ... gold* 1 C 29$_{3}$ (or em. שֶׁלִּי in *my* house was gold), אֵין־לָנוּ כֶּסֶף וְזָהָב *we do not have silver or gold* 2 S 21$_{4}$(Qr).

שָׁם הַזָּהָב *there is gold* Gn 2$_{11}$, אין [פ]ה כסף וזהב *there is no silver and gold here* Silwan royal steward tomb inscr. 1$_{1}$, יֵשׁ זָהָב *there is gold* Pr 20$_{15}$.

<OBJ> בוא hi. *bring* Ex 35$_{5}$ Nm 31$_{54}$ 1 K 7$_{51}$||2 C 5$_{1}$ 1 K 9$_{28}$ 15$_{15}$||2 C 15$_{18}$ Is 60$_{9.17}$ 2 C 9$_{10.14}$ 4QDibHam[a] 1.4$_{10}$ 4Q522 8.2$_{5}$ ([יב]יא), יצא hi. *take out* 2 C 16$_{2}$, שׁלח *send* 2 K 12$_{19}$ 2 C 16$_{3}$ perh. 1 K 15$_{18}$, עבר hi. *transfer* Nm 31$_{22}$, שׂים *place* Jb 31$_{24}$, עלה hi. *raise* 2 K 12$_{19}$, נשׂא *raise* 1 K 10$_{2}$||2 C 9$_{1}$ 1 K 10$_{11.22}$||2 C 9$_{21}$ 2 K 7$_{8}$ Is 60$_{6}$ Ezk 38$_{13}$, רום hi. *raise*, i.e. contribute Nm 31$_{52}$, נתן *give* Gn 24$_{35}$ Nm 22$_{18}$ 24$_{13}$ Jos 6$_{24}$ 1 K 7$_{51}$||2 C 5$_{1}$ 1 K 15$_{18}$ 20$_{5}$ 2 K 23$_{35}$ Ezk 27$_{22}$ Ezr 2$_{69}$||Ne 7$_{69}$ Ne 7$_{70.71}$ 1 C 29$_{7}$ 2 C 1$_{15}$, לקח *take* Ex 28$_{5}$ Nm 31$_{51.54}$ Dt 7$_{25}$ 1 K 9$_{28}$ 15$_{18}$ 2 K 12$_{19}$ 14$_{14}$ 16$_{8}$ Jl 4$_{5}$ Zc 6$_{11}$.

ריק hi. *pour* Zc 4$_{12}$ (or em. יִצְהָר *new oil*), זול *pour* Is 46$_{6}$, רדד hi. *beat out* 1 K 6$_{32}$, בחן *test* Zc 13$_{9}$=4QTanḥ 15$_{4}$ ([זהב]), זקק *refine* Jb 28$_{1}$, נגשׂ *fine, exact* 2 K 23$_{35}$ (or del. זָהָב), שׁקל *weigh* Ezr 8$_{25.26}$, כון hi. *establish* 1 C 22$_{14}$ 29$_{2}$, בזז *plunder* Na 2$_{10}$, כנס *gather* Ec 2$_{8}$, קנה *acquire* Si 51$_{28}$, ראה *see* Dt 29$_{16}$, hi. *show* 2 K 20$_{13}$||Is 39$_{2}$, חמד *desire* Dt 7$_{25}$=11QT 2$_{8}$.

רבה hi. *increase* Dt 17$_{17}$ 11QT 56$_{17}$ 56$_{19}$, צבר *amass* Si 47$_{18}$, עשׂה *make*, i.e. amass Ezk 28$_{4}$ Ho 2$_{10}$=4QpHos[a] 2$_{2}$, *make (of)* Ex 25$_{18.29}$||37$_{7.16}$ 26$_{29}$||36$_{34}$ 28$_{6}$||39$_{2}$ 28$_{13.15.22.36}$||39$_{15.30}$ 37$_{17.23}$ 39$_{8}$ 1 K 7$_{48.49.49.50.50}$ Ho 8$_{4}$ Ca 3$_{10}$ 2 C 4$_{20.21.22.22}$ 11QT 3$_{8}$ 9$_{1}$ ([ועשיתה ... זהב]), מלא pi. *fill (with)* 1QM 12$_{11}$=19$_{5}$ ([זהב]), צפה pi. *overlay (with)* Ex 25$_{11.13.24.28}$||37$_{2.4.11.15}$ 26$_{29.29.37}$||36$_{34.34.38}$ 30$_{3.5}$||37$_{26.28}$ 36$_{36}$ 1 K 6$_{20.21.21.22.22.28.30.32.35}$ 10$_{18}$||2 C 9$_{17}$ 2 C 3$_{4.10}$ 11QT 4$_{14}$ ([צ]ף [זה]ב) 8$_{6}$ ([וצפיתה ... זהב]) 31$_{8}$, חפה pi. *cover* 2 C 3$_{5.7.8.9}$, עדה *decorate oneself (with)* Jr 4$_{30}$ (if del. עֲדִי־ decorate oneself with *decoration of* gold) Ezk 16$_{13}$.

<CSTR> זֲהַב הָאָרֶץ *gold of the land* Gn 2$_{12}$, זְהַב שְׁבָא *gold of Sheba* Ps 72$_{15}$, אוֹפִיר *of Ophir* 1 C 29$_{4}$ Si 7$_{18}$ T. Qasile ost. 2$_{1}$ (אפר), פַּרְוָיִם *of Parvaim* 2 C 3$_{6}$, הַתְּנוּפָה *of the wave offering* Ex 38$_{24}$, הַתְּרוּמָה *of the contribution* Nm 31$_{52}$, הַכַּפּוֹת *of the pans* Nm 7$_{86}$.

חללי זהב *ones slain (through love) of gold* Si 34$_{6}$(Bmg), אֱלֹהֵי זָהָב *gods of gold* Ex 20$_{23}$ 32$_{31}$, אֱלִילֵי זְהָבוֹ *his images of gold* Is 2$_{20}$ 31$_{7}$, אֲפֻדַּת מַסֵּכַת זְהָבֶךָ *ephod of your image(s) of gold* Is 30$_{22}$, דְּמוּת זָהָב *image of gold* Ezr 8$_{27}$ (if em.; see Prep, כְּ).

עשתות זהב *ingots of gold* 3QTr 1$_{6}$ 2$_{4}$, כִּכַּר זָהָב *talent of gold* 2 S 12$_{30}$||1 C 20$_{2}$ (1 C כִּכַּר־) 1 K 9$_{14}$ 10$_{10}$||2 C 9$_{9}$ 1 K 10$_{14}$ 2 K 18$_{14}$ 23$_{33}$ 2 C 8$_{18}$ 36$_{3}$, כִּכְּרֵי *talents of* 2 K 5$_{5}$ (כִּכְּרֵי־ ... זָהָב) 1 C 29$_{4}$ 2 C 9$_{13}$ GnzPs 2$_{25}$, שִׁקְלֵי *shekels of* 1 C $21_{25}$, לָשׁוֹן *tongue*, i.e. bar, *of* Jos $7_{21.24}$ (הַזָּהָב), מְנֹרַת *lampstand of* Ex $25_{31}$ (מְנֹרַת) Zc $4_2$ 2 C $13_{11}$ (הַזָּהָב), מְנֹרוֹת הַזָּהָב *the lampstands of gold* 1 C $28_{15}$ 2 C $4_7$, נֵרוֹת הַזָּהָב *the lamps of gold* Zc $4_{12}$ (if em. הַזָּהָב pouring from them *gold* to אֶת־הַיִּצְהָר לְנֵרוֹת הַזָּהָב pouring from them *the new oil for the lamps of gold*), פַּעֲמֹן זָהָב *bell of gold* Ex $28_{34.34}$, פַּעֲמֹנֵי *bells of* Ex $28_{33}$∥$39_{25}$, כְּלֵי *vessels of* Gn $24_{53}$ Ex $3_{22}$ $11_2$ $12_{35}$ $35_{22}$ Nm $31_{50}$ (כְּלִי) 1 S $6_8$ (כְּלֵי הַזָּהָב; mss כָּל־ *all* the gold) $6_{15}$ (כְּלִי) 2 S $8_{10}$∥1 C $18_{10}$ (2 S כְּלֵי־) 1 K $10_{25}$∥2 C $9_{24}$ 2 K $12_{14}$ $24_{13}$ (הַזָּהָב) Est $1_7$ 1 C $28_{14}$ (if ins. כְּלֵי) 2 C $24_{14}$ Si $50_9$ 3QTr $3_2$ (כלי כסף וזהב) $12_6$.

מָגִנֵּי הַזָּהָב *the shields of gold* 2 S $8_7$∥1 C $18_7$, שִׁלְטֵי הַזָּהָב *the shields of gold* 1 K $14_{26}$∥2 C $12_9$, כַּפּוֹת זָהָב *pans of gold* Nm $7_{84.86}$, גֻּלַּת הַזָּהָב *the bowl of gold* Ec $12_6$, כְּפוֹרֵי זָהָב *bowls of gold* Ezr $1_{10}$ $8_{27}$ (כְּפֹרֵי) 1 C $28_{17}$ (הַזָּהָב), מזרק הזהב *the bowl of gold* 11QT $26_6$, מִזְרְקֵי זָהָב *bowls of gold* 2 C $4_8$, אֲגַרְטְלֵי *baskets of* Ezr $1_9$, כיס זהב *bag of gold* Si $35_5$, כּוֹס־זָהָב *cup of gold* Jr $51_7$, גְּלִילֵי *rods of* Ca $5_{14}$, עֲטֶרֶת *crown of* Est $8_{15}$, רְבִד הַזָּהָב *the necklace of gold* Gn $41_{42}$ (Sam זָהָב) Si $35_5$ (רביד זהב), שַׁרְשְׁרֹת זָהָב *chains of gold* Ex $28_{14}$, רַתּוּקוֹת *chains of* 1 K $6_{21(Qr)}$, צַנְתְּרוֹת הַזָּהָב *the pipes of gold* Zc $4_{12}$, עֲבֹתֹת הַזָּהָב *the cords of gold* Ex $28_{24}$∥$39_{17(Sam)}$.

טַבְּעֹת זָהָב *rings of gold* Ex $25_{12.26}$∥$37_{3.13}$ $28_{23.26.27}$∥$39_{16.19.20}$ (Ex 28 טַבְּעוֹת) $30_4$∥$37_{27}$, נֶזֶם זָהָב *(nose) ring of gold* Gn $24_{22}$ Jb $42_{11}$ Pr $11_{22}$ $25_{12}$, נִזְמֵי הַזָּהָב *the (nose) rings of gold* Ex $32_{2.3}$ Jg $8_{24}$ (נֶזֶם זָהָב) $8_{26}$, קַרְסֵי זָהָב *hooks of gold* Ex $26_6$∥$36_{13}$, מִשְׁבְּצוֹת *settings of* Ex $28_{11}$∥$39_6$ $28_{13}$ (both מִשְׁבְּצֹת) $39_{13.16}$ (מִשְׁבְּצֹת) Ps $45_{14}$, זֵר *moulding of* Ex $25_{11.24}$∥$37_{2.11}$ $25_{25}$∥$37_{12}$ (זֵר־) $30_3$∥$37_{26}$, שבולת זהב *ear of gold* 1QM $5_{10.12}$, עֲדִי זָהָב *decoration of gold* 2 S $1_{24}$ Jr $4_{30}$ (or del. עֲדִי־) Si $6_{30}$ (if em. עלי *yokes of*), עלי זהב appar. *yokes of gold* Si $6_{30}$ (or em.), תּוֹרֵי זָהָב perh. *pendants of gold* Ca $1_{11}$.

פַּחֵי הַזָּהָב *the leaves of gold* Ex $39_3$, ניב זהב *fruit of gold* Si $35_{5(B)}$ (Bmg נוב זיר appar. *fruit [that is to say] crown*), שַׁרְבִיט הַזָּהָב *the sceptre of gold* Est $4_{11}$ $5_2$ $8_4$, צִיץ הַזָּהָב *the flower of gold* Lv $8_9$, פרוכת זהב *veil of gold* 11QT $7_{13}$, כַּפֹּרֶת זָהָב *cover of gold* Ex $25_{17}$∥$37_6$, מִזְבַּח הַזָּהָב *the altar of gold* Ex $39_{38}$ $40_{5.26}$ Nm $4_{11}$ 1 K $7_{48}$∥2 C $4_{19}$, תְּנוּפַת זָהָב *wave offering of gold* Ex $35_{22}$, שֹׁחַד ... זָהָב *present of ... gold* 1 K $15_{19}$, טְחֹרֵי זָהָב *tumours of gold* 1 S $6_{4(Qr).17}$ (הַזָּהָב), עפלי זָהָב *tumours of gold* 1 S $6_{4(Kt).17(mss)}$ (עָפְלֵי הַזָּהָב), עַכְבְּרֵי זָהָב *mice of gold* 1 S $6_{4.11.18}$ (both הַזָּהָב), עֶגְלֵי *calves of* 1 K $12_{28}$ 2 K $10_{29}$ (הַזָּהָב) 2 C $13_8$, תַּפּוּחֵי *apples of* Pr $25_{11}$ (or em. פִּתּוּחֵי *engravings of*), מִטּוֹת *couches of* Est $1_6$, מִכְמַנֵּי הַזָּהָב *the stores of gold* Dn $11_{43}$.

מִשְׁקַל ... הַזָּהָב *weight of ... the gold* 1 K $10_{14}$∥2 C $9_{13}$ Ezr $8_{30}$, מִכְלוֹת זָהָב *perfection(s) of gold* 2 C $4_{21}$, אַלְפֵי זָהָב *thousands (of pieces) of gold* Ps $119_{72}$, כָּל־הַזָּהָב *all the gold* Ex $38_{24}$ 1 K $15_{18}$ (כָּל־ ... הַזָּהָב) 2 K $12_{19}$ $14_{14}$∥2 C $25_{24}$, כֹּל ... זָהָב *all ... gold* Ex $38_{24(Sam)}$ Jos $6_{19}$, כָּל־זְהַב *all gold of* Nm $7_{86}$ $31_{52}$.

<APP> אֱלֹהִים *gods* 11QT $59_4$, תְּרוּמָה *contribution* Ex $35_5$ Ezr $8_{25}$, קֹדֶשׁ *holiness*, i.e. holy thing 1 K $7_{51}$ (mss, ∥2 C $5_1$ add וְ *and* gold) $15_{15}$∥2 C $15_{18}$, מִנְחָה *offering* 4QDibHam[a] $1.4_{10}$, בֶּגֶד *garment* Si $45_{10}$, סְגֻלָּה *personal property* 1 C $29_3$, כִּכָּר *talent* Ex $25_{39}$∥$37_{24}$ 1 K $9_{28}$ Ezr $8_{26}$ 1 C $22_{14}$ $29_7$ 3QTr $7_{16}$ $8_7$ (ככ) $10_{11}$ $12_1$ (ככ) 11QT $9_{12}$ ([זהב]), מָנֶה *mina* 1 K $10_{17}$, דַּרְכְּמֹן *daric* Ezr $2_{69}$∥Ne $7_{69}$ Ne $7_{70.71}$ 1 C $29_7$, מְלֹא *fullness* Nm $22_{18}$ $24_{13}$, חַיִל *wealth* Zc $14_{14}$, מַעֲשֶׂה *deed*, i.e. product Jr $10_9$ Ps $115_4$ 1QM $5_5$ 11QT $59_4$, מִשְׁקָל *weight* 1 C $28_{14}$ (if em. לַזָּהָב weight *of gold* to זָהָב *weight [in] gold*) $28_{16}$ (or em. בְּמִשְׁקָל *by weight*), מִקְשָׁה *hammered work* Ex $25_{36}$∥$37_{22}$ Nm $8_4$, אֶבֶן precious *stone* Ezk $28_{13}$ (or em.; see Nom. Cl.), צִנָּה *shield* 1 K $10_{16}$∥2 C $9_{15}$, מָגֵן *shield* 1 K $10_{17}$∥2 C $9_{16}$, כְּלִי *vessel* Dn $11_8$, perh. כַּף *pan* Nm $7_{14+11t}$, נֵר *lamp* 1 C $28_{15}$, מֶרְכָּבָה *chariot* 1 C $28_{18}$, כְּרוּב *cherub* 1 C $28_{18}$, גִּלּוּל *idol* Dt $29_{16}$, שִׁקּוּץ *abomination* Dt $29_{16}$, עָצָב *idol* Ps $115_4$∥$135_{15}$, דָּבָר *word* Nm $31_{22}$.

<ADJ> טָהוֹר *pure* Ex $25_{11+7t}$ $28_{14.22.36}$ $30_3$ $37_{2+8t}$ $39_{15.25.30}$ 1 C $28_{17}$ 2 C $3_{4.5(mss).8(mss)}$ $9_{17}$ 1QM $5_{10.12}$ 11QT $3_8$ (טהו[ר]) $3_{9.12}$ $5_{11}$ $6_9$ $8_6$ $9_{1.12}$ $13_4$ (all six [זהב טהור]) $36_{11}$ $41_{17}$, טוֹב *good* 2 C $3_{5.8}$ (mss טָהוֹר in both), רַב *great* 1 K $10_2$.

<PREP> לְ of benefit, *to, for* Pr $17_3$ $27_{21}$, + עשׂה *make* treasuries 2 C $32_{27}$, כון hi. *establish* 1 C $29_2$, נתן *give* 1 C $29_5$; of possession, *belonging to, of* Jb $28_1$ 1 C $22_{16}$ $28_{14.14}$ (לַזָּהָב בְּמִשְׁקָל לַזָּהָב) plan *of*, or perh. *concerning, gold, according to the weight belonging to gold*; or em. לְכָל־כְּלֵי הַזָּהָב בְּמִשְׁקָל זָהָב *of all the vessels of gold, according to*

*weight [in] gold); for, in order to obtain,* + הלך *go* 1 K 22$_{48}$, שׁלח *send* 1 K 20$_{7}$; *(made) of* Ezr 1$_{11}$; *(consisting) of,* + נתן *give* presents 2 C 21$_{3}$.

בְּ of instrument, *by (means of), with,* + עשׂה *make* Ex 31$_{4}$||35$_{32}$ 2 C 2$_{6.13}$, רקע pi. *overlay* Is 40$_{19}$, יפה pi. *adorn* Jr 10$_{4}$ (or em. צפה pi. *overlay*), לקח ni. *be taken* 4Q525 3.3$_{2}$, אחז ho. *be held* 2 C 9$_{18}$ (if move בַּזָּהָב), כבד pi. *honour* Dn 11$_{38}$, נשׂא pi. *help* 1 K 9$_{11}$ Ezr 1$_{4}$, חזק pi. *strengthen* Ezr 1$_{6}$; of accompaniment, *in, with,* + יצא hi. *take out* Ps 105$_{37}$, שׁוב *go back* Jos 22$_{8}$ (+ מִקְנֶה *livestock,* כֶּסֶף *silver,* נְחֹשֶׁת *bronze,* בַּרְזֶל *iron*); *(made) of* 2 C 9$_{18}$ 1QM 5$_{8.14}$ perh. 4QD$^{b}$ 8$_{4}$ ([בזהב]) 4Q525 3.3$_{7}$; *in respect of,* + כבד *be rich* Gn 13$_{2}$; *(in exchange) for,* + מור hi. *exchange* Si 7$_{18}$; חפץ בְּ *desire* Is 13$_{17}$.

כְּ *as* Ml 3$_{3}$ Ezr 8$_{27}$ (or em. חֲמוּדֹת כַּזָּהָב *precious things, as gold* to דְּמוּת זָהָב *image of gold*) 1QH 5$_{16}$ ([ז]הב), + יצא *go out* Jb 23$_{10}$.

מִן of comparison, *more (than)* Pr 22$_{1}$, + אהב *love* Ps 119$_{127}$, חמד ni. *be desired* Ps 19$_{11}$; partitive, *(any) of, (some) of, from among* 1 C 29$_{4}$ 4QD$^{e}$ 7$_{20}$, + נתן *give* Ps 72$_{15}$, לקח *take* 11QT 2$_{8}$; *(made) of,* + לקח *take* Ezk 16$_{17}$.

עִם *with,* + קדשׁ hi. *sanctify* 2 S 8$_{11}$||1 C 18$_{11}$, בוא hi. *bring* Dn 11$_{8}$.

אֵת appar. plan *of, concerning* 1 C 28$_{16}$.

<COLL> זָהָב *gold* followed by (and oft. || to) כֶּסֶף *silver* Ex 25$_{3}$ 26$_{32}$ 31$_{4}$ 35$_{5.32}$ 36$_{36}$ Nm 31$_{22}$ Jos 7$_{21}$ 1 K 10$_{21.22}$||2 C 9$_{20.21}$ 2 K 12$_{14}$ 14$_{14}$||2 C 25$_{24}$ 2 K 23$_{35}$ 25$_{15}$ Is 40$_{19}$ 46$_{6}$ 60$_{17}$ Jr 52$_{19}$ Ezk 7$_{19}$ 16$_{13.17}$ 28$_{4}$ Hb 2$_{19}$ Zc 14$_{14}$ Ml 3$_{3}$ Ps 119$_{72}$ Jb 3$_{15}$ Pr 25$_{11}$ Ca 1$_{11}$ Est 1$_{6}$ Dn 11$_{38.43}$ Ezr 1$_{9.10.11}$ 2$_{69}$||Ne 7$_{70}$ Ne 7$_{71}$ 1 C 18$_{10}$ 22$_{14.16}$ 28$_{14.15.16.17}$ 29$_{2.3.4.5.7}$ 2 C 2$_{6.13}$ 9$_{14}$ 24$_{14}$ Si 40$_{25(B)}$ 47$_{18}$ 1QM 5$_{5}$ 4QD$^{b}$ 8$_{4}$ ([בזהב ו]בכס[ף]).

זָהָב *gold* preceded by (and oft. || to) כֶּסֶף *silver* Gn 13$_{2}$ 24$_{35.53}$ 44$_{8}$ Ex 3$_{22}$ 11$_{2}$ 12$_{35}$ 20$_{23}$ Nm 7$_{84}$ 22$_{18}$ 24$_{13}$ Dt 7$_{25}$ 8$_{13}$ 17$_{17}$ 29$_{16}$ Jos 6$_{19.24}$ 7$_{21.24}$ 22$_{8}$ 2 S 8$_{10.11}$||1 C 18$_{11}$ 21$_{4}$ 1 K 7$_{51}$||2 C 5$_{1}$ 1 K 10$_{25}$||2 C 9$_{24}$ 1 K 15$_{15.18.19}$||2 C 16$_{2.3}$ 1 K 20$_{3.5.7}$ 2 K 5$_{5}$ 7$_{8}$ 12$_{14}$ 16$_{8}$ 18$_{14}$ 20$_{13}$ 23$_{33.35}$||2 C 36$_{3}$ Is 2$_{7.20}$ 13$_{17}$ 30$_{22}$ 31$_{7}$ 39$_{2}$ 60$_{9}$ Jr 10$_{4.9}$ Ezk 7$_{19}$ 38$_{13}$ Ho 2$_{10}$ 8$_{4}$ Jl 4$_{5}$ Na 2$_{10}$ Zp 1$_{18}$ Hg 2$_{8}$ Zc 6$_{11}$ 13$_{9}$ Ml 3$_{3}$ Ps 105$_{37}$ 115$_{4}$ 135$_{15}$ Jb 28$_{1}$ Pr 17$_{3}$ 22$_{1}$ 27$_{21}$ Ca 3$_{10}$ Ec 2$_{8}$ 12$_{6}$ Est 1$_{6}$ Dn 11$_{8}$ Ezr 1$_{4.6}$ 8$_{25.26.28.30.33}$ 2 C 1$_{15}$ 15$_{8}$ 21$_{3}$ 24$_{14}$ 32$_{27}$ 1QM 12$_{11(mg)}$=19$_{5}$ ([כסף וזהב]) 3QTr 3$_{2}$ 12$_{6}$ 4QDibHam$^{a}$ 1.4$_{10}$ 11QT 3$_{5}$ 59$_{4}$.

זָהָב + כְּלִי *vessel* Gn 24$_{53}$ Ex 3$_{22}$ 11$_{2}$ 12$_{35}$ 25$_{39}$ 35$_{22}$ 37$_{16.24}$ Nm 31$_{50.51}$ Jos 6$_{19.24}$ 1 S 6$_{8.15}$ 2 S 8$_{10}$||1 C 18$_{10}$ 1 K 7$_{48}$||2 C 4$_{19}$ 1 K 7$_{51}$||2 C 5$_{1}$ 1 K 10$_{21.25}$||2 C 9$_{24}$ 1 K 15$_{15}$||2 C 15$_{18}$ 2 K 12$_{14}$ 14$_{14}$ 20$_{13}$ 24$_{13}$ Is 39$_{2}$ Ezk 16$_{17}$ Na 2$_{10}$ Jb 28$_{17}$ Pr 20$_{15}$ Est 1$_{7.7}$ Dn 11$_{8}$ Ezr 1$_{6.10.11}$ Ezr 8$_{25.26.27.28.30.33}$ 1 C 28$_{14}$ 2 C 9$_{20}$ 24$_{14.14}$ 25$_{24}$ 32$_{27}$.

זָהָב + נְחֹשֶׁת *bronze* Ex 25$_{3}$ 26$_{37}$ 31$_{4}$ 35$_{5.32}$ 36$_{38}$ Nm 31$_{22}$ Jos 6$_{19.24}$ 22$_{8}$ 2 S 8$_{10}$||1 C 18$_{10}$ Is 60$_{17}$ (::) Ezr 8$_{27}$ 1 C 22$_{14.16}$ 29$_{2.7}$ 2 C 2$_{6.13}$.

זָהָב + בַּרְזֶל *iron* Nm 31$_{22}$ Jos 6$_{19.24}$ 22$_{8}$ Is 60$_{17}$ 1 C 22$_{14.16}$ 29$_{2.7}$ 2 C 2$_{6.13}$, עֹפֶרֶת *lead* Nm 31$_{22}$ Jb 28$_{6}$, בְּדִיל *tin* Nm 31$_{22}$, זְכוֹכִית *glass* Jb 28$_{17}$.

זָהָב + כֶּתֶם *gold* Jb 31$_{24}$ Pr 25$_{12}$ Lm 4$_{1}$ (all three ||), פַּז *(fine) gold* Nm 4$_{11}$ Ps 19$_{11}$ (||) 119$_{127}$ Jb 28$_{17}$ (||), הוֹן *wealth* Si 8$_{2}$, נֶכֶס *wealth* Jos 22$_{8}$.

זָהָב + צֹאן *flock* Gn 24$_{35}$ Dt 8$_{13}$ (||) Jos 7$_{24}$, בָּקָר *cattle* Gn 24$_{35}$ Dt 8$_{13}$ 2 C 13$_{11}$, מִקְנֶה *livestock* Gn 13$_{2}$ Jos 22$_{8}$ (||) Ezk 38$_{13}$, גָּמָל *camel* Gn 24$_{22.35}$ 1 K 10$_{2}$ Is 60$_{6}$ 2 C 9$_{1}$, סוּס *horse* 1 K 10$_{25}$||2 C 9$_{24}$ Is 2$_{7}$ (||) 11QT 56$_{17}$, חֲמוֹר *ass* Gn 24$_{35}$ Jos 7$_{24}$

זָהָב + עֶבֶד *servant* Gn 24$_{53}$ 2 C 8$_{18}$, שִׁפְחָה *female servant* Gn 24$_{35}$.

וַתִּמָּלֵא אַרְצוֹ ... זָהָב *and his land was filled ... (with) gold* Is 2$_{7}$, הוּא תָּפוּשׂ זָהָב *it is seized (of),* i.e. overlaid with, *gold* Hb 2$_{19}$=1QpHab 12$_{16}$ ([הוא תפוש זהב]), מְצֻפִּים זָהָב *overlaid (with) gold* Ex 26$_{32}$ 11QT 5$_{11}$ (מצופה [זהב]) 13$_{4}$ ([מצופות זהב]) 32$_{10}$ (מצופות) 36$_{11}$ (מצופה) 36$_{11}$ 39$_{3}$ (מצופו[ת ז]הב) 41$_{16}$ (מצופים) 41$_{17}$ (מצופות) 11QT$^{b}$ 11$_{1}$ (מצופות), רבים היו חבולי זהב *many were bound of,* i.e. by/to, *gold* Si 34$_{6(B)}$ (Bmg חללי *ones slain [through love] of* gold), מְשֻׁבָּצִים זָהָב perh. *being set in gold* Ex 28$_{20}$ (Sam מְשֻׁבָּצוֹת in same sense).

עֲשָׂרָה זָהָב *ten (units of) gold* Gn 24$_{22}$ perh. Nm 7$_{14+11t}$, חֲמִשִּׁים זָהָב *fifty (units of) gold* 2 C 3$_{9}$, אֶלֶף וּשְׁבַע־מֵאוֹת זָהָב *one thousand and seven hundred (units of) gold* Jg 8$_{26}$, שְׁלֹשׁ מֵאוֹת זָהָב *three hundred (units of) gold* 2 C 9$_{16}$, שֵׁשׁ(־)מֵאוֹת זָהָב *six hundred (units of) gold* 1 K 10$_{16}$|| 2 C 9$_{15}$.

Also 3QTr 11$_{1}$.

<SYN> כֶּסֶף *silver,* כֶּתֶם *gold,* פַּז *(fine) gold,* צֹאן *flock,* מִקְנֶה *livestock,* סוּס *horse.* <ANT> נְחֹשֶׁת *bronze.**

***זָהָב** II 1 n.[m.] **spice** or **incense**—<OBJ> נשׂא *raise* Is 60$_{6}$ (|| לְבוֹנָה *frankincense*). <SYN> לְבוֹנָה *frankincense.*

**זָהִיר** 0.4 adj. **cautious**—Si זָהִיר—**1.** as predicative adjective, **cautious, prudent,** alw. preceded by היה *be* cautious, Si 13$_{13}$ (+ ואל תהלך *and do not walk* with violent people; + שׁמר ni. *guard oneself*) 35$_{22(E)}$ (B שׁמר ni., זהר ni. *be warned*) 42$_{8}$ (+ באמת *truly*; + צָנוּעַ *decorous*). **2.** without היה *be* preceding, as interjection, **beware,** משוכן זָרִיו זָהִיר דרכיך appar. *beware, in respect of your conduct, of one who accommodates a stranger* Si 11$_{34}$ (or ins. בְּ *in respect of* before דרכיך and/or em. משוכן to משכן beware the *dwelling place of* a stranger, and/or זָרִיו to זָר *guilty one* or זָרִיו זָהִיר to זָר הִזָּהֵר *be warned* concerning one who accommodates/the dwelling place of *a stranger*).
⇒ זהר *warn.*

**[זְהִירָה]** 0.1 n.f. **brightness**—sf. Si זהירתו—<PREP> מִן of material, *with,* + רצף pi. *pave* firmament Si 43$_{8(B)}$.
⇒ זהר *be bright.*

**זהל**, see זחל *crawl.*

**זהם** 1 vb. **abhor**—**Pi.** 1 + waw וְזִהֲמַתּוּ—**abhor,** <SUBJ> חַיָּה *life* Jb 33$_{20}$, נֶפֶשׁ *soul* Jb 6$_{7}$ (if em. הֵמָּה כִּדְוֵי *they are as the sickness of* to זָהֲמָה כְדֵי my soul *abhors as often as* I eat) 33$_{20}$. <OBJ> לֶחֶם *bread* Jb 33$_{20}$ (וְזִהֲמַתּוּ חַיָּתוֹ לָחֶם *and his life abhors it, bread*; or em. וְזָהֲמָה *and* his life *abhors* bread), מַאֲכָל *food* Jb 33$_{20}$.

**[זַהַם]** 1 pr.n.m. **Zaham**—זָהַם—son of Rehoboam and Mahalath or Abihail, <OBJ> ילד *give birth (to)* 2 C 11$_{19}$. <APP> בֵּן *son* 2 C 11$_{19}$.

**זהר I** 21.2.2 vb. **warn**—**Ni.** 8.2.1 Pf. נִזְהַר; impv. הִזָּהֵר; ptc. נִזְהָר; inf. הִזָּהֵר—**be warned, be careful,** <SUBJ> בֵּן *son* Ec 12$_{12}$ Si 11$_{34}$ (if em. משוכן זָרִיו זָהִיר appar. *beware of one who accommodates a stranger* to משוכן זָר הִזָּהֵר *be careful concerning one who accommodates a stranger*) 35$_{22(Bmg)}$ (B שׁמר ni. *guard oneself,* E היה זָהִיר *be cautious*) 35$_{22(B)}$ (|| שׁמר ni.) 4QMMT B$_{12(A, B)}$ ([בני]; Amg hi. *warn*) B$_{48}$ ([בני ישראל ... להזהר]), מֶלֶךְ *king* Ec 4$_{13}$, עֶבֶד *servant* Ps 19$_{12}$, עַם *people* Ezk 33$_{6}$, שׁמע ptc. *one who hears* Ezk 33$_{4.5.5}$ (or em. hi. *warn*), סֻמָּה *blind one* 4QMMT B$_{50}$ ([להזהר]). <PREP> בְּ of instrument, *by (means of),* + מִשְׁפָּט *ordinance* Ps 19$_{12}$; *concerning, in respect of,* + אַחֲרִית *end* Si 35$_{22(Bmg)}$, אֹרַח *way* Si 35$_{22(B)}$, דֶּרֶךְ *way* Si 11$_{34}$ (if em. זָהִיר [see Subj.] and ins. בְּ [see Coll.]), דָּבָר *word* 4QMMT B$_{12}$; מִן *concerning in respect of,* + תַּעֲרֹבֶת *mixture* of persons, i.e. illegal marriage 4QMMT B$_{48}$ (להזהר מכול ת]ערובת]) B$_{50}$ (להזהר מכל] [תערובת), שׁכן ptc. appar. *one who accommodates* Si 11$_{34}$ (if em. זָהִיר [see Subj.]; or em. מִשְׁכַּן be careful [of] *the dwelling place of* a stranger). <COLL> with adverb, עוֹד *again* Ec 4$_{13}$, הִזָּהֵר דרכיך *take care in respect of your ways* Si 11$_{34}$ (if em.; see Subj.; or ins. בְּ *in respect of* your ways); להזהר ... בשל שלוא י]היו מסיא[י]ם *to take care ... that they will not cause* the people *to bear* punishment 4QMMT B$_{12(A, B)}$ (Amg appar. hi. *warn*). <SYN> שׁמר ni. *guard oneself.*

**Hi.** 13.0.2 Pf. הִזְהַרְתָּ (הִזְהַרְתּוֹ); impf. יַזְהִרוּ; + waw וְהִזְהַרְתָּ (וְהִזְהַרְתָּה), וְהִזְהִיר (וְהִזְהִירוֹ [Kt והזהירה]), וְהִזְהַרְתֶּם (Q והזהרתמה); inf. הַזְהִיר—**instruct, teach, warn, give warning,** <SUBJ> Moses Ex 18$_{20}$ (+ ידע hi. *make known*) Lv 15$_{31(Sam)}$ perh. 11QT 51$_{5}$, Aaron Lv 15$_{31(Sam)}$ (MT נזר hi. *keep separate*) perh. 11QT 51$_{5}$, אִישׁ *man* 2 K 6$_{10}$, בֵּן *son* of priest 4QMMT B$_{12(Amg)}$ ([בני]; A, B ni. *be warned*), of man, i.e. Ezekiel Ezk 3$_{17.18.18.19.20.21}$ 33$_{7.8.9}$, כֹּהֵן *priest* 2 C 19$_{10}$, לֵוִי *Levite* 2 C 19$_{10}$, ראשׁ *head* of ancestral house 2 C 19$_{10}$, צֹפֶה *guard* Ezk 33$_{3}$, שׁמע ptc. *one who hears* Ezk 33$_{5}$ (if em. ni. *be warned*); subj. not specified, Jr 4$_{16}$ (if em. הַזְכִּירוּ לַגּוֹיִם הִנֵּה *announce to the nations, behold* to הַזְהִירוּ לְבִנְיָמִין *warn Benjamin*). <OBJ> (1) recipient of instruction or warning: בֵּן *son* of Israel Lv 15$_{31(Sam)}$, אָח *brother* 2 C 19$_{10}$, מֶלֶךְ *king* 2 K 6$_{10}$, עַם *people* Ex 18$_{20}$ Ezk 33$_{3}$, בַּיִת *house* of Israel Ezk 3$_{17}$ 33$_{7}$, רָשָׁע *wicked one* Ezk 3$_{18.18.19}$ 33$_{8.9}$, צַדִּיק *righteous one* Ezk 3$_{20.21}$; (2) contents of instruction: חֹק *statute* Ex 18$_{20}$, תּוֹרָה *law* Ex 18$_{20}$. <PREP> לְ introducing object, or of direction, give warning *to,* + בִּנְיָמִין *Benjamin* Jr 4$_{16}$ (if em.; see Subj.); מִן of direction, give warning *from,* + ״ *Y.* Ezk 3$_{17}$ 33$_{7}$; *concerning,* + דֶּרֶךְ *way* Ezk 3$_{18}$ 33$_{8.9}$, טֻמְאָה *uncleanness* Lv 15$_{31(Sam)}$ 11QT 51$_{5}$.

<COLL> followed by לְבִלְתִּי *in order not* and inf. of חטא *sin* Ezk $3_{21}$; להזהיר ... בשל שלוא ]יהיו[ מסיא[ י]ם *to warn ... so that they will not cause* the people *to bear* punishment 4QMMT $B_{12(Amg)}$ (A, B ni. *be warned*).*

⇒ זָהִיר *careful*.

**זהר II** $_{1.2}$ vb. **be bright—Qal** $_{0.1}$ Ptc. Si זהרת—intrans. **shine,** <SUBJ> שֶׁמֶשׁ *sun* Si $42_{16(M)}$. <PREP> עַל *upon*, + כֹּל *everything* Si $42_{16(M)}$.

**Hi.** $_{1.1}$ Impf. יַזְהִרוּ; ptc. Si מזהיר—intrans. **shine,** <SUBJ> שׂכל hi. ptc. *wise one* Dn $12_3$, אוֹר *light* Si $43_{9(B)}$. <PREP> בְּ of place, *in*, + מָרוֹם *height* Si $43_{9(B)}$; כְּ *as*, + זֹהַר *brightness* Dn $12_3$.*

⇒ זֹהַר *brightness*, זְהִירָה *brightness*.

**זֹהַר** $_{2.0.2}$ n.m. **brightness**—cstr. זֹהַר (Q זוהר); pl. cstr. Q זהרי—**brightness, brilliance, splendour,** <SUBJ> אתה *come* Jb $37_{22}$ (if em. זָהָב *gold*). <CSTR> זֹהַר הָרָקִיעַ *brightness of the firmament* Dn $12_3$, זהרי הוד *brilliance of splendour* 4QBer[a] $1_3$, [זו]הר רוקמת perh. *splendour of embroidery of* spirits 4QBer[b] $1_4$, זוהר טהורים *brightness of pure ones* 4QShirShabb[d] $1.1_{42(erased)}$ (new text טוהר *purity of*); מַרְאֵה־זֹהַר *appearance of brightness* Ezk $8_2$ (‖ חַשְׁמַל *amber*), מק[ום ז]והר *place of brightness* 4QBer[a] $1_4$. <PREP> כְּ *as*, + זהר hi. *shine* Dn $12_3$.

Also 4QMyst[c] $4_4$ perh. 4Q425 $4.2_6$.

<SYN> חַשְׁמַל *amber*.*

⇒ זהר *be bright*.

**זִו I** $_2$ pr.n.m. **Ziv**, second month of pre-exilic calendar, falling within April and May, and corresponding to Babylonian month of Iyyar, <CSTR> חֹדֶשׁ זִו *month of Ziv* 1 K $6_1$, יֶרַח זִו *month of Ziv* 1 K $6_{37}$.

**זִו II**, see זִיו II *splendour*.

**זוֹ** $_{4.0.0.1}$ demonst. pronoun sing. f. and adj. **this**—I זוא—**1.** as adjective, **this,** following determined fem. noun, שְׁבוּעָה *oath* Jos $2_{17}$ (if em. זֶה *this* [masc.]; mss lack זֶה; mss זֹאת *this* [fem.]). **2.** as pronoun, **this (one),** <NOM CL> with complement לַעַג *mockery* Ho $7_{16}$ (or em. וְזָל *and* their mockery *will cease* [from זול II]), מַתַּת *gift* Ec $5_{18(Gnz)}$ (זוֹ מַתַּת אֱלֹהִים הִיא *this is a gift of God*; L זֹה, Gnz זֶה in same sense), אֲרוֹן *ark*, i.e. coffin Beth Shearim tomb inscr. 22. **3.** as relative pronoun, **that, which,** בְּרִיתִי וְעֵדֹתִי זוֹ אֲלַמְּדֵם *my covenant and my testimony, which I shall teach them* Ps $132_{12}$ (11QPs[a] $6_4$, Gnz, ms זֶה in same sense; or em. עֵדֹתַי *my testimonies*), גֶּפֶן זוֹ תְּכִינֶהָ *a vine, which you have established* Ps $80_{15}$ (if em. גֶּפֶן זֹאת : וְכַנָּה *this vine; and a stock*).*

**זוּ** $_{14.0.3}$ part. of relation, **which, that, who(m), 1.** as relative pronoun, **a.** with indefinite antecedent as object (including adverbial accusative) of verb following זוּ, עַם־זוּ גָּאָלְתָּ *a people that you redeemed* Ex $15_{13}$, עַם־זוּ קָנִיתָ *a people that you acquired* Ex $15_{16}$=4QPent Par[b] $6_1$, עַם־זוּ יָצַרְתִּי *a people that I formed* Is $43_{21}$ (1QIsa[a] זה I formed *this* people, as זֶה, §5c), רֶשֶׁת־זוּ טָמָנוּ *the net that they had hidden* Ps $9_{16}$=4QapPs[b] $31_1$ (עם זו טמ[נו]) Ps $31_5$ (זוּ טָמְנוּ), מְזִמּוֹת זוּ חָשָׁבוּ *devices that they had considered* Ps $10_2$, שְׁתַּיִם־זוּ שָׁמָעְתִּי *two things that I heard* Ps $62_{12}$ (mss שָׁמָעְנוּ *we have heard*), דֶּרֶךְ־זוּ אֵלֵךְ *a way that I am to go* Ps $143_8$, בְּאֹרַח־זוּ אֲהַלֵּךְ *in a way that I am to go* Ps $142_4$, בְּדֶרֶךְ זוּ תֵלֵךְ *in a way that you are to go* Ps $32_8$.

**b.** with antecedent as subj. of verb following זוּ, רְשָׁעִים זוּ שַׁדּוּנִי *evil ones who have devastated me* Ps $17_9$, עוּזָּה אֱלֹהִים זוּ פָּעַלְתָּ *be strong, O God, who acted* for us Ps $68_{29}$ (or em. הָאֱלֹהִים עֻזְּךָ as the strength *of God is your strength*, which you exercised for us).

**c.** with definite antecedent as subject of nom. cl. predicate, הַדּוֹר זוּ לְעוֹלָם appar. *the generation that is for ever* Ps $12_8$ (unless זוּ is adj., guard us for ever from *this generation*; or em. זוּ לְעוֹלָם *that is for ever* to זוֹלֵל וְעָוֶל *worthless and wicked* generation).

**d.** with definite antecedent in non-subject/object relationship with זוּ, י׳ זוּ חָטָאנוּ לוֹ *Y., against whom we sinned* Is $42_{24}$ (1QIsa[a] זֶה appar. *this* we did wrong against him, as זֶה, §1, Obj.), ארץ זו הגברת [בה] *a land in which you prevailed* 4QapPs[b] $44_2$ (or del. [בה], *a land that you made mighty*, as §1a).

**2.** as combined relative pronoun and antecedent, **that which,** וְאָשֵׁם זוּ כֹחוֹ לֵאלֹהוֹ *and he incurs guilt; that which is his strength (belongs) to his god* Hb $1_{11}$ (or em. לֵאלֹהָיו to לֵאלֹהוֹ *to his god[s]* and/or וְאָשֵׁם זוּ to וְיָשֵׂם

*and he places*, i.e. attributes, his strength to his god, or וְיָשֶׂם זוֹ *and he places*, i.e. turns, *that which is* his strength into his god; =1QpHab 4.13 וישם זה כוחו לאלוהו *and he turns that which is his strength into his god* or *and this one turns his strength into his god*).

Also 4QShirShabbd 1.142(erased) (זו is appar. beginning of זֹהַר *brilliance*).*

**זוּב** 40.2.10 vb. **flow—Qal** 40.1.9 Pf. זָב; impf. יָזוּב, 3fs תָּזוּב, יָזוּבוּ; + waw וַיָּזֻבוּ (וַיָּזוּבוּ); ptc. זָב, זָבָה, זָבַת, Q זבים—**1. flow, run, a.** of promised land flowing with milk and honey (alw. אֶרֶץ זָבַת חָלָב וּדְבָשׁ *a land flowing with milk and honey* or sim.), <SUBJ> אֶרֶץ *land* Ex 38.17 135 333 Lv 2024 Nm 1327 148 1613.14 Dt 63 119 269.15 273 Jos 56 Jr 115 3222 Ezk 206.15 Si 468 4QJuba 17 (ארץ זבת חלב ודב[ש]) 4QPsJosa 116, אֲדָמָה *land* Dt 3120, נַחֲלָה *inheritance* Si 468.

**b.** appar. of lush valley of Ammon, <SUBJ> עֵמֶק *valley* Jr 494 (or em. בְּעֲמָקִים זָב עִמְקֵךְ you boast *in the valleys, your valley flows* to בְּעִמְקֵךְ you boast *in your valley*, or בְּעֲמָקִים זֶה בְעִמְקֵךְ *in the valleys, that is, in your valley*, or understand עִמְקֵךְ as *your wealth*; see §3).

**2. flow, gush,** of water from rock (Is 4821 Ps 7820 10541) or spring (Jr 1814 [if em.]) or of discharge from woman (Lv 1525), <SUBJ> מַיִם *water* Is 4821 (+ נזל hi. *cause to flow*) Jr 1814 (if em. זור *be strange*) Ps 7820 (|| שׁטף *overflow*) 10541 (|| הלך *go*, i.e. flow), זוֹב *discharge* Lv 1525.

**3. pine away,** because of hunger, <SUBJ> חָלָל *battle victim* Lm 49, perh. עֵמֶק *wealth* Jr 494 (see §1b). <COLL> שֶׁהֵם יָזוּבוּ מְדֻקָּרִים תְּנוּבֹת שָׂדָי appar. *who pine away, stabbed, for (lack of) fruits of the field* Lm 49 (or em. שֶׁהֵם יַדּוּ בִּמְקוֹר דָּמָם מֵתוּ בְחִישׁ *whose source of blood they shot at so that they died swiftly*).

**4a. discharge, have discharge,** of woman, in ref. to menstruation (Lv 1519 perh. 4QDg 1.29 4QTohA 1.14) or to non-menstrual bleeding (Lv 1525 4QTohA 1.16), of man, appar. in ref. to venereal disease (Lv 152.3 4QDa 9.114), of man or woman (Lv 1533), <SUBJ> אִישׁ *man* Lv 152, אִשָּׁה *woman* Lv 1519.25 4QTohA 1.16 (ז[ב]ה); subj. not specified, Lv 1533 4QDa 9.114 4QDg 1.29 4Q TohA 1.14. <OBJ> זוֹב *discharge* Lv 1533 4QDa 9.114, דָּם *blood* 4QDg 1.29 4QTohA 1.14.6 (ז[ב]ה). <PREP> לְ *of*, i.e. lasting for, + יוֹם *day* 4QTohA 1.14.6 (ז[ב]ה); מִן of direction, *from*, + בָּשָׂר *flesh* Lv 152; עַל *upon*, i.e. beyond, + נִדָּה *impurity*, i.e. menstrual period Lv 1525.

**4b.** ptc. as noun, **one who has a discharge,** <SUBJ> בוא *come* 11QT 4618 (|| צרע pu. *be leprous*; + אִישׁ *man*), טהר *be clean* Lv 1513 4QRitPur 7.111 ([ז]ב), כרת ni. *be cut off* 2 S 329 (|| צרע pu., + חזק hi. *hold* spindle, נפל *fall* by sword, חָסֵר *lacking* bread), שׁכב *lie down* Lv 154, ישׁב *sit* Lv 154.6 4QTohA 1.14 ([י]שב), עשׂה *do* 4QRitPur 7.111 ([י]עשה הזב), נגע *touch* Lv 1511.12 4QTohA 1.14, רכב *ride* Lv 159, ירק *spit* Lv 158. <NOM CL> הוּא צָרוּעַ אוֹ זָב *he is a leper or one suffering a discharge* Lv 224. <OBJ> שׁלח pi. *send away* Nm 52 (|| צרע pass. *be leprous*, + טָמֵא *unclean*). <CSTR> תּוֹרַת הַזָּב *law of the one with a discharge* Lv 1532 (+ אֲשֶׁר תֵּצֵא מִמֶּנּוּ שִׁכְבַת־זֶרַע *one from whom semen goes out*), בְּשַׂר הַזָּב *flesh of the one with a discharge* Lv 157, כָּל־זָב *everyone with a discharge* Nm 52. <PREP> לְ of benefit, *to, for*, + עשׂה *make*, i.e. prepare cities 11QT 4815 (+ נגע pu. *be struck* with leprosy, etc., אִשָּׁה menstruous *woman*); בְּ *against*, + נגע *strike*, i.e. touch 4QToh A 1.14.7 ([י]גע בזבה).

<SYN> §2 שׁטף *overflow*, הלך *go*, i.e. flow; §4b צרע pass./pu. *be leprous*.

Also 11QTb 174 ([ז]בים).

**Hi.** 0.1.1 Pf. Q הזיב; impv. Si הזיב—**cause to flow,** <SUBJ> Y. 1QIsaa 4821 (MT נזל hi. *cause to flow*; + זוב [qal] *flow*), בֵּן *son* Si 3816. <OBJ> מַיִם *water* 1QIsaa 4821, דִּמְעָה *tears* Si 3816. <PREP> לְ of benefit, *to, for*, + Israel 1QIsaa 4821; מִן of direction, *from*, + צוּר *rock* 1QIsaa 4821; עַל *concerning*, + מֵת *dead one* Si 3816.

⇒ זוֹב *discharge*.

**זוֹב** 13.0.8 n.m. **discharge**—cstr. זוֹב (Sam זָב); sf. זוֹבוֹ, זוֹבָהּ (זָבָהּ)—from man, appar. in ref. to venereal disease (Lv 152.3.3.3.13.15 4QDa 9.114 4QDe 9.212 4QTohA 1.18 4Q TohBb 111 4QRitPur 10.101 11QT 4515), from woman, in ref. to menstrual and other bleeding (Lv 1519.25.25.26. 28.30 CD 57 4QTohA 1.18); from man or woman (Lv 1533).

<SUBJ> היה *be* Lv 1519 (+ דָּם *blood*) 4QDa 9.114 ([ז]וב יה[יה]), זוב *flow* Lv 1525. <NOM CL> זוֹבוֹ טָמֵא הוּא

*his discharge is unclean* Lv 15$_{2}$. <OBJ> ריר *flow*, i.e. discharge Lv 15$_{3}$, זוֹב *flow*, i.e. discharge Lv 15$_{33}$ 4QD$^{a}$ 9.1$_{14}$, נגע hi. *touch* 4QTohA 1.1$_{8}$ (unless זוֹב is subj.). <CSTR> זוֹב דָּמָהּ *discharge of her blood* Lv 15$_{25}$, טֻמְאָתָהּ *of her uncleanness* Lv 15$_{25.30}$, טמאתו *of his uncleanness* 4QRitPur 10.10$_{1}$, זֹב בְּשָׂרוֹ *discharge of his flesh* Lv 15$_{3(Sam)}$; דם זובה *blood of her discharge* CD 5$_{7}$, יְמֵי זוֹב *days of the discharge of* Lv 15$_{3(Sam)}$ (זֹב) 15$_{25}$, יְמֵי זוֹבָהּ *days of her discharge* Lv 15$_{26}$. <ADJ> טָמֵא *unclean* 4QD$^{e}$ 9.2$_{12}$ ([טמ]א). <PREP> בְּ of cause, *on account of*, + היה *be* (of impurity) Lv 15$_{3}$; of agent, *by*, + נגע pu. *be stricken* 4QD$^{e}$ 9.2$_{12}$; *against*, + נגע *strike*, i.e. touch 4QTohB$^{b}$ 1$_{12}$ ([בז]ובו); כְּ *as*, + חשב ni. *be reckoned* 4QTohA 1.1$_{8}$; מִן privative, *without*, i.e. so as not to suffer from, + חתם hi. *seal oneself*, i.e. be cured of Lv 15$_{3.3(Sam)}$, טהר *be clean* Lv 15$_{13.28}$ 4QRitPur 7.11$_{2}$ ([מז]ובו), htp. *clean oneself* 11QT 45$_{15}$; of cause, *on account of*, + כפר pi. *atone* Lv 15$_{15.30}$.

Also 4QTohB$^{b}$ 1$_{11}$.

⇒ זוב *flow*.

**זוג** 0.0.1 vb. **be joined—Htp.** 0.0.1 Pf. Q הזדוגא—appar. **be held together,** <SUBJ> אֶבֶן *stone* 3QTr 10$_{9}$. <PREP> בְּ of instrument, *by (means of), with,* + perh. עֲזָה *support* 3QTr 10$_{9}$.

**זוד**, see זיד *be presumptuous.*

**[זוּז]** 0.0.3 n.[m.] **zuz**—Q זוז; pl. Q זוזין—silver coin worth a quarter of a shekel (tetradrachma), half a half-shekel (didrachma), and six oboli (meah), abbreviated to ז on weight from Lachish (Weight 13), <NOM CL> [מ]חצית [השקל מעה שתים ]עשרה זו[זים שנים] *the half-shekel is (worth) twelve oboli, (that is) two zuzim* 4QOrd$^{b}$ 1$_{3}$, זוזין מאה וששין שהם סלעים ארבעין *a hundred and sixty zuzim, which are (worth) forty tetradrachmas* 5/6Ḥev BA 46. <APP> מְעָה *grain*, i.e. obolus 4QOrd$^{b}$ 1$_{3}$, סֶלַע *rib*, i.e. tetradrachma Mur 30 2$_{21}$, כֶּסֶף *silver* Mur 22 1$_{1}$ ([זוזין]) 1$_{4}$ Mur 30 2$_{21}$ 5/6ḤevBA 46. <ADJ> טובין [זוזין] *good zuzim* Mur 22 1$_{1}$ ([זוזין]). <PREP> בְּ *in exchange for* Mur 22 1$_{4}$, + מכר *sell* Mur 30 2$_{21}$. <COLL> זו[זים שנים] *two zuzim* 4QOrd$^{b}$ 1$_{3}$, ש[מו]נים ושמונה זוז *eighty-eight zuzim* Mur 30 2$_{21}$, זוזין מאה וששין *a hundred and sixty zuzim* 5/6ḤevBA 46, 50 [זוזין] *fifty zuzim* Mur 22 1$_{1}$, זוז 40 *forty zuzim* Mur 22 1$_{4}$.

**[זוּזִי]** 1 gent. **Zuzite**—pl. זוּזִים—as noun, ancient inhabitants of Canaan defeated by Chedorlaomer, appar. ident. with the Zamzummim (and, therefore, also with the Rephaim) at Dt 2$_{20}$, <OBJ> נכה hi. *strike* Gn 14$_{5}$.

**זוח I** 0.1 vb. **move—Qal** 0.1 Impf. 2ms Si תזוח—**be moved, depart,** <SUBJ> בֵּן *son* Si 8$_{11}$. <PREP> מִפְּנֵי *from (before)*, + לֵץ *scoffer* Si 8$_{11}$ (or em. בִּפְנֵי *on account of*, with זוח II *be proud*).

**זוח II** 0.1 vb. **be high—Qal** 0.1 Impf. 2ms Si תזוח—**be proud,** <SUBJ> בֵּן *son* Si 8$_{11}$. <PREP> בִּפְנֵי *on account of*, + לֵץ *scoffer* Si 8$_{11}$ (if em. מִפְּנֵי *from before*, with זוח I *be moved*).

**[זוֹחֵלְזָלָף]** 0.0.1 perh. pr.n.m. **Zohelzalaph,** appar. invented as sequence within writing exercise, 4Q341$_{8}$.

**זוֹחֵת** 2 pr.n.m. **Zoheth, 1.** son of Ishi, descendant of Judah. **2.** son or brother of preceding.

<NOM CL> בְּנֵי יִשְׁעִי זוֹחֵת וּבֶן־זוֹחֵת *the sons*, perh. descendants, *of Ishi were Zoheth and the son of Zoheth* 1 C 4$_{20}$ (unless בֶּן־זוֹחֵת = *Ben-zoheth*, as pr.n.m.; or em. וּבְנֵי־זוֹחֵת *and the sons of Zoheth were*, with names of sons lacking).

**[זָוִית]** 2 n.f. **corner**—pl. זָוִיּת; cstr. זָוִיּוֹת—**corner, cornerstone,** <SUBJ> חטב pu. *be cut* Ps 144$_{12}$ (+ נָטִיעַ *plant*). <CSTR> זָוִיּוֹת מִזְבֵּחַ *corners of the altar* Zc 9$_{15}$. <APP> מִזְרָק *bowl* Zc 9$_{15}$ (or del. זָוִית or מִזְרָק). <PREP> כְּ *as* Ps 144$_{12}$, + מלא *be full* Zc 9$_{15}$ (or del.).

**זול I** 1 vb. **be lavish—Qal** 1 Ptc. זָלִים—**spend,** <OBJ> זָהָב *gold* Is 46$_{6}$ (or em. hi. [מְ]זִלִּים in same sense; + שקל *weigh*, i.e. pay). <PREP> מִן of direction, *from*, + כִּיס *purse* Is 46$_{6}$.

**[זול] II** vb. **cease,** <SUBJ> לַעַג *mockery* Ho 7$_{16}$ (if em.

זוֹ לַעְגָּם *this is their mockery* to וְזָל לַעְגָּם *and their mockery will cease)*. <PREP> בְּ of place, *in*, + אֶרֶץ *land* Ho 7₁₆ (if em.).

**[זוּלָה]**, see זוּלַת *apart from.*

**זוּלַת** 16.2.11 prep. **apart from**—זוּלַת (2 K 24₁₄ 1QS 9₂₄ 4Q416 2.3₈), זוּלָתִי; sf. זוּלָתִי, זוּלָתְךָ (זוּלָתֵךְ, Q זולתכה), Q זוּלָתָהּ, זולתו, Q זולתם—followed by noun (or suffix in ref. to noun), Y. 2 S 7₂₂‖1 C 17₂₀ (+ כְּ *as*) Is 26₁₃ 45₅.₂₁ 64₃ Ho 13₄ Si 33₅ 1QH 7₃₂ 10₉ (+ עִם *with*, לְנֶגֶד *corresponding to*) 1QS 11₁₈ 4QDibHamᵃ 1.5₉, Caleb Dt 1₃₆, appar. Michael 4QMᵃ 11.1₁₃, Hazor Jos 11₁₃ לֹא שְׂרָפָם יִשְׂרָאֵל זוּלָתִי אֶת־חָצוֹר לְבַדָּהּ שָׂרַף יְהוֹשֻׁעַ) *Israel did not burn them, apart from Hazor alone, [which] Joshua burned;* unless זוּלָתִי is here used as adverb introducing new sentence, *only* Hazor, it alone, Joshua burned), אֱלֹהִים *God* Is 26₁₃ Ps 18₃₂ (‖2 S 22₃₂ בִּלְעֲדֵי *apart from;* ms כְּ *as*), בֵּן *son* Dt 1₃₆, גֹּאֵל *redeemer* Ru 4₄, פֵּאָה *corner*, i.e. chief of Y.'s adversaries Si 33₁₂, שֵׁבֶט *tribe* of Judah 1 K 12₂₀ (+ לְבַדּוֹ *it alone*), דַּלָּה *poor people* 2 K 24₁₄, אֲנַחְנוּ *we*, i.e. two prostitutes 1 K 3₁₈ (אֵין־זָר אִתָּנוּ בַּבַּיִת זוּלָתִי שְׁתַּיִם־אֲנַחְנוּ בַּבָּיִת *no stranger was with us in the house apart from the two of us in the house;* unless זוּלָתִי is here used as adverb introducing new sentence, *only* the two of us were in the house; or del. first בַּבַּיִת), חֶרֶב *sword* 1 S 21₁₀, קוֹל *voice* Dt 4₁₂, מְחֻקְקָה *statute* CD 6₁₀, נַחֲלָה *inheritance* 4Q416 2.3₈, appar. תְּעוּדָה *statute* 1QH 12₁₀, רָצוֹן *desire* 1QS 9₂₄.

With לֹא *not* and verb (negation and verb follow זוּלַת at Is 26₁₃ [if em.] Ho 13₄ CD 6₁₀ 1QH 12₁₀ 1QS 9₂₄), היה *be* 1 K 12₂₀ 1QH 12₁₀.₁₀, שׁאר ni. *remain* 2 K 24₁₄, בעל *be lord* Is 26₁₃ (or ins. בַּל־נֵדַע *we do not know* as negation and verb assoc. with זוּלַת), נשׂג *overtake*, i.e. attain to CD 6₁₀, ראה *see* Dt 1₃₆ 4₁₂ (obj. קוֹל *voice*) Is 64₃, חפץ *desire* 1QS 9₂₄, אוה htp. *desire* 4Q416 2.3₈ (אַל *do not* desire), ידע *know* Is 26₁₃ (if em.) Ho 13₄, שׂרף *burn* Jos 11₁₃; following verb introduced by מִי *who?*, רום pol. *be exalted* 4QMᵃ 11.1₁₃; in nom. cl. introduced by אַיִן *there is not*, 1 S 21₁₀ 2 S 7₂₂‖1 C 17₂₀ 1 K 3₁₈ Is 45₅.₂₁ (‖ בִּלְעֲדֵי *apart from*) Ru 4₄ Si 33₅.₁₂ 1QH 7₃₂ 10₉ 1QS 11₁₈ 4QDibHamᵃ 1.5₉; in nom. cl. introduced by מִי *who* is a rock?, Ps 18₃₂ (‖2 S 22₃₂ בִּלְעֲדֵי *apart from;* ms כְּ *as*); אשר ימשיל בה זולתכה *(if there is) one who rules over her other than you* 4Q416 2.4₆.

Also 4QMystᵇ 2.2₅ 4Q417 7₂ ([זול]ת).

<SYN> בִּלְעֲדֵי *apart from.*

**זון** 1 vb. **feed—Qal, feed,** <SUBJ> Y. Jb 36₃₁ (if em. דין *judge*). <OBJ> עַם *people* Jb 36₃₁ (if em.). <PREP> בְּ of instrument, *by (means of), with*, + appar. נֶטֶף *drop (of water)* Jb 36₃₁ (if em.).

**Ho.** 1 Kt Occ מוזנים—**be well fed,** <SUBJ> סוּס *horse* Jr 5₈₍Kt Occ₎ (Qr מְיֻזָּנִים, i.e. יזן pu. *be weighty [with testicles];* + שׁכה hi. *be well endowed [with testicles];* ms שׁמם hi. *ravage;* or em. אשׁך hi. in same sense as שׁכה hi. or משׁך *drag*).

⇒ מָזוֹן *food.*

**[זוֹנוּת]** 0.0.3 n.f. **fornication**—Q זונות—perh. with ref. to illegal marriages, <SUBJ> עשׂה ni. *be done* 4QMMT B₇₅. <CSTR> דרכי זונות *ways of fornication* CD 8₅₍A₎ (unless זוֹנוֹת *harlots;* =9₁₇₍B₎ זנות, i.e. זְנוּת *fornication*). <PREP> מִן privative, *without*, i.e. so as not to indulge in, + נזר hi. *be a Nazirite*, i.e. abstaining one CD 7₁ (unless pl. ptc. of זנה *prostitute oneself*); עַל *concerning* 4QMMT B₇₅.

⇒ זנה *prostitute oneself.*

**זוע I** 3.3.7 vb. **tremble—Qal** 2.2.2 Pf. זָע; impf. 3fs Si תזוע, יָזֻעוּ—**tremble,** or, of eye, **flicker,** <SUBJ> Elisha Si 48₁₂, Mordecai Est 5₉ (+ קום *arise*), שֹׁמֵר *keeper* of house Ec 12₃ (+ עות htp. *be bent*, בטל *cease*, חשׁך *be dark*), עַיִן *eye* Si 34₁₃₍B₎ (Bmg hi. *drip* tears; + דמע *weep*), רוּחַ *spirit* 1QS 7₁₈ 4QDᵉ 11.1₉ ([רוחו]), חוֹמָה *wall* 1QH 5₃₇ ([תזוע]). <PREP> מִן of direction, *from*, + יְסוֹד *foundation*, i.e. authority 1QS 7₁₈; of cause, *on account of*, + Haman Est 5₉, כֹּל *everything* Si 48₁₂ (+ מימיו *in his days*); מִפְּנֵי *on account of*, + דָּבָר *word* Si 34₁₃₍B₎.

**Pilp.** 1.0.1 Ptc. מְזַעְזְעֶיךָ (unless זעה pilp. *bark at*)—**terrify,** <OBJ> גֶּבֶר *man* Hb 2₇=1QpHab 8₁₄ (‖ נשׁך *bite* [Q נשׁה *be a creditor*]).

**Hi.** 0.2 Impf. 3fs Si תזיע; ptc. Si מזיע—**1.** appar. **flicker** (Si 34₁₃₍Bmg₎; B qal in same sense). **2. shed** tears (Si 34₁₃₍Bmg₎; B דמע *weep;* Bmg [second reading] נסע hi.

*move* tears). **3.** appar. **be greedy** (Si 37$_{30[Bmg, D]}$; or em. זיד hi. *boil*, i.e. cook food; B רבה hi. *increase*).

<SUBJ> עַיִן *eye* Si 34$_{13(Bmg).13(Bmg)}$; subj. not specified, Si 37$_{30(Bmg, D)}$. <OBJ> דִּמְעָה *tears* Si 34$_{13(Bmg)}$. <PREP> מִן of direction, *from*, + פָּנִים *face* Si 34$_{13(Bmg)}$; מִפְּנֵי *on account of*, + דָּבָר *word* Si 34$_{13(Bmg)}$.

**Htpalp.** 0.0.4 Impf. Q יזד עזרע (1QS 11$_{4}$), יזדעזעו, 3fs תתזעזע—**be shaken,** <SUBJ> חוֹמָה *wall* 1QH 6$_{27}$ ([חומת]) 7$_{9}$, כָּפִיס *crossbeam* 1QH 6$_{36}$ ([יזדעזעו]), יְסוֹד *foundation* 1QS 8$_{8}$ (+ חוש hi. *fall apart*), דֶּרֶךְ *way* 1QS 11$_{4}$.

⇒ זְוָעָה *trembling*, זַעֲוָה *trembling*, זִיעַ *trembling*.

* **זוע II** 1 vb. **stand aside—Qal** 1 Pf. זָע—**stand aside,** <SUBJ> Mordecai Est 5$_{9}$ (|| קום *arise*). <SYN> קום *arise*.

**זְוָעָה** 6 n.f. **trembling**—Qr זַעֲוָה—**trembling, cause of trembling,** i.e. something terrible, <SUBJ> היה *be* Is 28$_{19}$ (וְהָיָה רַק־זְוָעָה הָבִין שְׁמוּעָה *and to understand the report will be*, i.e. result in, *nothing but trembling*). <PREP> לְ, *as*, + היה *be* Dt 28$_{25(mss, Sam)}$ (L זַעֲוָה in same sense), נתן *give*, i.e. make into Jr 15$_{4(Kt)}$ 24$_{9(Kt)}$ (+ רָעָה *evil*, חֶרְפָּה *reproach*, מָשָׁל *proverb*, שְׁנִינָה *taunt*, קְלָלָה *curse*) 29$_{18(Kt)}$ (+ אָלָה *curse*, חֶרְפָּה, שַׁמָּה *desolation*, שְׁרֵקָה *hissing*) 34$_{17(Kt)}$ Ezk 23$_{46(Kt Or)}$ (|| בַּז *spoil*) 2 C 29$_{8(Kt)}$ (|| שַׁמָּה, שְׁרֵקָה; in all six Qr זַעֲוָה). <COLL> זְוָעָה לְכֹל מַמְלְכוֹת הָאָרֶץ *a cause of trembling for all the kingdoms of the earth* Dt 28$_{25(mss, Sam)}$ Jr 15$_{4(Kt)}$ 24$_{9(Kt)}$ 29$_{18(Kt)}$ 34$_{17(Kt)}$. <SYN> שַׁמָּה *desolation*, שְׁרֵקָה *hissing*, בַּז *spoil*. ⇒ זוע *tremble*.

[זוֹעָן], see זַעֲוָן *Zaavan*.

**זור I** 77.13.11 vb. **be strange—Qal** 74.11.10 Pf. זָרָה, זָרוּ (זֹרוּ); ptc. זָר (Si זריו), זָרִים (זָרָיִךְ), זָרוֹת—**1. be strange** (Is 28$_{21}$), **be estranged** (Ps 58$_{4}$), **depart** (Jb 19$_{13}$ [unless זור IV *depart*]) **desist** (Ps 78$_{30}$ [unless זור IV *depart*]), <SUBJ> Israel Ps 78$_{30}$, Jacob Ps 78$_{30}$, רָשָׁע *wicked one* Ps 58$_{4}$ (or em. ni. *depart*; || תעה *stray*), ידע ptc. *one who knows, acquaintance* Jb 19$_{13}$ (|| רחק hi. *distance oneself*), רוּחַ *spirit* Jb 19$_{17}$ (unless זור III *be abhorrent*; || חנן *be abhorrent*), מַעֲשֶׂה *deed* Is 28$_{21}$ (+ נָכְרִי *foreign*).

<PREP> לְ of direction, *to*, + אִשָּׁה *wife* Jb 19$_{17}$.

מִן of direction, time, *from*, + Job Jb 19$_{13}$, רֶחֶם *womb* Ps 58$_{4}$, תַּאֲוָה *desire* Ps 78$_{30}$.

**2.** participle (זָר) as adjective,* **foreign** (and hence, sometimes, **forbidden**), used attributively of אִישׁ *man* Lv 22$_{12}$ Nm 17$_{5}$ Dt 25$_{5}$, אִשָּׁה *woman* Pr 2$_{16}$ 7$_{5}$ (both + נָכְרִיָּה *foreign woman*) Si 9$_{3}$ (+ זוֹנָה *prostitute*), אֵל *god* Ps 44$_{21}$ 81$_{10}$ (+ נֵכָר *foreignness*), אֱלֹהִים *gods* Dt 32$_{16}$ (if ins. אֱלֹהִים), בֵּן *son* Ho 5$_{7}$, אֵשׁ *fire* Lv 10$_{1}$ Nm 3$_{4}$ 26$_{61}$, קְטֹרֶת *incense* Ex 30$_{9}$, מַיִם *water* 2 K 19$_{24}$||1QIsa$^{a}$ 37$_{25}$ (2 K 19$_{24[ms]}$||Is 37$_{25}$ lack זָרִים) Jr 18$_{14}$ (or em. מַיִם זָרִים קָרִים *foreign* [or *flowing* (i.e. II)] *cold waters* to מִמִּצְרַיִם מְקֹרִים *springs from Egypt*, or מֵימֵי קֶדֶם קָרִים *cold waters of antiquity*, or מַיִם זָבִים מְקֹרִים *gushing waters*, flowing *springs*).

**3.** participle as noun,* **stranger, strange one, foreigner,** in ref. to **a non-Israelite,** oft. as enemy,* Is 1$_{7.7}$ (or em. זָרִים *strangers* to סְדֹם *Sodom*) 25$_{2}$ (mss זֵד *presumptuous*) 25$_{5}$* (or em. זֵד; + עָרִיץ *ruthless*) 29$_{5}$ (1QIsa$^{a}$ זֵד; || עָרִיץ) 61$_{5}$ (+ נֵכָר *foreignness*) Jr 5$_{19}$ 30$_{8}$ 51$_{2}$ (or em. זֹרֶה *winnower*) 51$_{51}$ Ezk 7$_{21}$* (+ רָשָׁע *wicked*) 11$_{9}$* 28$_{10}$* 30$_{12}$* (+ רַע *evil*) 31$_{12}$ Ho 7$_{9}$ 8$_{7}$=4QpHos$^{b}$ 11$_{7}$ (or em. זָרִים *strangers* to קָדִים *east wind*) Jl 4$_{17}$ Ob$_{11}$ (+ נָכְרִי *foreign*) Ps 54$_{5}$* (ms זֵד; + עָרִיץ) Jb 15$_{19}$ Ezk 28$_{7}$* Lm 5$_{2}$ Si 10$_{22(B)}$ (A זֵד; || נָכְרִי, גֵּר *sojourner*, רָשׁ *poor one*) 37$_{5}$ (+ עָרִיץ) 39$_{24}$ GnzPs 1$_{5}$ 1QH 6$_{27}$ 8$_{12}$ ([זור]) 4QMidrEschat$^{a}$ 3$_{5}$ 4QapLam$^{b}$ $_{1}$ perh. 5QRègle 2$_{3}$.

**b.** more generally, an **unfamiliar, unrelated person,** 1 K 3$_{18}$ Ezk 16$_{32}$ (or em. אֶת־זָרִים to אֶתְנַנִּים *fees*, or אֶתְנַנִּים מֵאֵת זָרִים *fees from strangers*) Jb 19$_{15}$ (+ נָכְרִי) 19$_{27}$ Ps 109$_{11}$ (+ נֹשֶׁה *creditor*) Pr 5$_{10}$ (+ נָכְרִי) 5$_{17}$ 6$_{1}$ (|| רֵעַ *companion*) 11$_{15}$ 14$_{10}$ (or em. זֵד *presumptuous* or זָדוֹן *presumptuousness*) 20$_{16}$ (+ נָכְרִי) 27$_{2}$ (|| נָכְרִי; :: פֶּה *[one's own] mouth*, i.e. oneself, שָׂפָה *lip* in same sense) 27$_{13}$ (+ נָכְרִי) Si 8$_{18}$ 11$_{34}$ (זריו) 14$_{4}$ (+ אַחֵר *another*) 40$_{29}$ 45$_{18}$ 4Q418 87$_{7}$ 4QShir$^{b}$ 18.2$_{10}$ 11QPs$^{a}$ 18$_{16}$ ([זר]ים).

**c. lay Israelite,** i.e. one who is not a priest or Levite or member of a priestly family, Ex 29$_{33}$ 30$_{33}$ Lv 22$_{10}$ (+ תּוֹשָׁב *sojourner*, שָׂכִיר *hired labourer*) 22$_{13}$ Nm 1$_{51}$ 3$_{10.38}$ 17$_{5}$ 18$_{4.7}$.

**d. foreign woman,** perh. **a woman to whom one is not married,** Pr 5$_{3.20}$ (+ נָכְרִי *foreign*) 22$_{14}$ (mss זָרוֹת

strangeness for זָרוֹת *prohibited women*) $23_{27}$ (if em. זֹנָה *prostitute*; + נָכְרִי) Si $41_{20(M)}$.

**e. alien god,** Dt $32_{16}$ (or ins. אֱלֹהִים foreign *gods*, as §2) Is $17_{10}$ $43_{12}$ Jr $2_{25}$ $3_{13}$.

**f. strange thing,** Ho $8_{12}$ Pr $23_{33}$ (|| תַּהְפֻּכָה *perversity*) Si $41_{19(B)}$ (זר; Bmg, M יד *[sleight of] hand*).

<SUBJ> היה *be* Jr $51_2$ (or em.), מות ho. *be killed* Nm $1_{51}$ $3_{10.38}$ $18_7$, בוא *come* Jr $51_{51}$ 1QH $6_{27}$ $8_{12}$ ([יבוא]) 5QRègle $26_3$, קרב *approach* Nm $1_{51}$ $3_{10.38}$ $17_5$ $18_{4.7}$, עבר *pass* Jl $4_{17}$ Jb $15_{19}$, קום *arise* Ps $54_5$, ירד hi. *take down* Ezk $28_7$, נטש *abandon* Ezk $31_{12}$, עמד *stand* Is $61_5$, זרה *scatter* Jr $51_2$ (or em.), ערב htp. *be mixed* Pr $14_{10}$, כרת *cut* Ezk $31_{12}$, עבד *serve* Jr $30_8$, רעה *tend (beasts)* Is $61_5$, שמם hi. *devastate* 4QMidrEschat$^{a}$ $3_5$, בקק po. *devastate* Jr $51_2$ (or em.), חלל pi. *defile* Ezk $28_7$, ריק hi. *empty*, i.e. draw sword Ezk $28_7$, שבה *take captive* Ob$_{11}$, בזז *plunder* Ps $109_{11}$, ראה *see* Jb $19_{27}$, הלל pi. *praise* Pr $27_2$, אכל *eat* Ex $29_{33}$ Lv $22_{10.13}$ Is $1_7$ Ho $7_9$, שתה *drink* 1QH $8_{12}$, בלע *swallow* Ho $8_7$=4QpHos$^{b}$ $11_7$ (or em.), שבע *be satisfied* Pr $5_{10}$, בוע htpalp. *enjoy* Si $14_4$, חרה *be inflamed* Si $45_{18}$, קנא pi. *be jealous* Si $45_{18}$.

<NOM CL> שׁוּחָה עֲמֻקָּה זָרָה *a foreign woman is a deep pit* Pr $23_{27}$ (if em.), אֵין־זָר אִתָּנוּ *there was no stranger with us* 1 K $3_{18}$, אֵין בָּכֶם זָר *there is no stranger among you* Is $43_{12}$.

<OBJ> ראה *see* Pr $23_{33}$, בוא hi. *bring* Ezk $28_7$, שלח pi. *send away* Jr $51_2$ (or em.), לקח *take* Ezk $16_{32}$ (or em.), אהב *love* Jr $2_{25}$, עבד *serve* Jr $5_{19}$, ערב *guarantee* Pr $11_{15}$ $20_{16}$ $27_{13}$ perh. 4Q418 $87_7$, perh. שכן *accommodate* Si $11_{34}$.

<CSTR> בני זרים *sons of strangers* GnzPs $1_5$, שְׁאוֹן זָרִים *uproar of strangers* Is $25_5$ (or em.), הֲמוֹן זָרַיִךְ *abundance of your strangers* Is $29_5$, אַרְמוֹן זָרִים *fortress of strangers* Is $25_2$, מַהְפֵּכַת זָרִים *overthrow of strangers* Is $1_7$ (or em.), שלחן זר *table of a stranger* Si $40_{29}$, זְמֹרַת זָר *branch of a stranger* Is $17_{10}$, שִׂפְתֵי זָרָה *lips of a foreign woman* Pr $5_3$, פִּי זָרוֹת *mouth of foreign women* Pr $22_{14}$ (or em.), יַד זָרִים *hand of strangers* (see also Prep.) Ezk $7_{21}$ (הַזָּרִים) $11_9$, כָּל־זָר *every stranger* Lv $22_{10.13}$ 4Q426 $1.1_{10}$ (כול).

<APP> עָרִיץ *ruthless one* Ezk $28_7$ $31_{12}$.

<PREP> לְ of direction, *to*, + נתן *give* 4QapLam$^{b}$$_1$, פזר pi. *scatter* Jr $3_{13}$, הפך ni. *be overturned*, i.e. given Lm $5_2$; of benefit, *to, for*, + תקע *strike* hand, i.e. act as guarantor Pr $6_1$, סלל htpo. *be blocked* Si $39_{24}$; of possession, *of, (belonging) to* Pr $5_{17}$; *as*, + חשב *reckon* Jb $19_{15}$.

בְּ of instrument, *by (means of)*, + קנא hi. *make jealous* Dt $32_{16}$ (if em.); of cause, *on account of*, + שׁגה *stray* Pr $5_{20}$.

כְּ *as*, + חשב ni. *be reckoned* Ho $8_{12}$.

אֶל *to*, i.e. at, + בין htpol. *look* Si $41_{20(M)}$.

עַל *upon*, + נתן *give*, i.e. place oil Ex $30_{33}$; *(because) of*, + בושׁ *be ashamed* Si $41_{19(B)}$ ([ע]ל).

מֵאֵת *from*, + לקח *take* Ezk $16_{32}$ (if em.; see Obj.).

עִם *with*, + לחם ni. *fight* Si $37_{5(B)}$, נחל *inherit* Si $37_{5(Bmg)}$.

לִפְנֵי *in the presence of*, + עשׂה *do* Si $8_{18}$.

אַחֲרֵי *after*, + הלך *go* Jr $2_{25}$.

בְּיַד *by (the hand/power of)*, + מות *die* Ezk $28_{10}$, שׁמם hi. *devastate* Ezk $30_{12}$.

מִיַּד *from (the hand/power of)*, + גאל *redeem* 11QPs$^{a}$ $18_{16}$.

<COLL> גר זר נכרי ורש תפארתם יראת י׳ *(as for) the sojourner, the stranger, the alien and the pauper, their glory is the fear of Y.* Si $10_{22(B)}$ (Bmg ביראת *in the fear of* Y.).

<SYN> §1 רחק hi. *distance oneself*, חנן *be abhorrent*; §3a עָרִיץ *ruthless one*, נָכְרִי *foreign(er)*, גֵּר *sojourner*, רָשׁ *poor one*; §3b רֵעַ *companion*, נָכְרִי *foreign(er)*; §3f תַּהְפֻּכָה *perversity*. <ANT> §3b פֶּה *mouth*, i.e. oneself, שָׂפָה *lip*, i.e. oneself.

Also Si $45_{13}$ perh. 4QOrd$^{a}$ $2_2$.

**Ni.** 2.0.1 Pf. נָזֹרוּ (Q נזורו)—**become estranged, depart** (perh. זור IV]) <SUBJ> עַם *people* Is $1_4$ (or del. זור ni.; + עזב *abandon*, נאץ pi. *despise*), גּוֹי *nation* Is $1_4$, בַּיִת *house* of Israel Ezk $14_5$ (+ שׁוב *go back*), בֵּן *son* Is $1_4$, זֶרַע *seed* Is $1_4$, רָשָׁע *wicked one* Ps $58_4$ (if em. qal [§1]), אֲשֶׁר *one who* 1QH $4_{19}$. <PREP> בְּ of instrument, *by (means of)*, + גִּלּוּל *idol* Ezk $14_5$; מִן of direction, *from*, + בְּרִית *covenant* 1QH $4_{19}$, רֶחֶם from (the time of) the *womb* Ps $58_4$ (if em.); מֵעַל *from (upon)*, + י׳ *Y.* Ezk $14_5$. <COLL> with adverb, אָחוֹר *backwards* Is $1_4$.

**Ho.** 1.1 Ptc. מוּזָר—participle as noun, **stranger,** <SUBJ> היה *be* Ps $69_9$ (+ נָכְרִי *foreign*) Si $4_{30(A)}$ (unless זור III ho. ptc. *abhorrent*; + ירא htp. *be fearsome*; במלאכתך *in your work*; B מתפחז בעבודתך *arrogant in*

*your service).**
⇒ זָרוּת *strangeness.*

**זור II** 3 vb. **squeeze, flow—Qal** 3 Impf. 3fs תְּזוּרֶהָ; + waw וַיָּזַר; ptc. זוּרֶה (Q האזורה)—**1. squeeze, crush,** <SUBJ> Gideon Jg 6$_{38}$ (+ מצה *wring*), רֶגֶל *foot* Jb 39$_{15}$ (|| דושׁ *trample*). <OBJ> גִּזָּה *fleece* Jg 6$_{38}$, בֵּיצָה *egg* Jb 39$_{15}$.

**2.** pass. ptc. as noun, **crushed one,** in ref. to crushed egg (unless זוּרֶה *rotten egg*), <SUBJ> בקע ni. *be hatched* Is 59$_{5}$ (הַזּוּרֶה תִּבָּקַע אֶפְעֶה *the crushed one is hatched out as a viper;* or em. הַזּוּרָה [i.e. fem.]; 1QIsa[a] האזורה).

**3. flow (with),** <SUBJ> שָׂפָה *lip* Pr 15$_{7}$ (if em. יְזָרוּ *they will scatter* [i.e. זרה pi.] to יָזֻרוּ *they will flow;* + דַּעַת flow with *knowledge*), מַיִם *water* Jr 18$_{14}$ (unless זור I *be strange*).*

<SYN> §1 דושׁ *trample.*

**זור III** 1.1 vb. **be abhorrent—Qal** 1 Pf. זָרָה—<SUBJ> רוּחַ *spirit* Jb 19$_{17}$ (unless זור I *be strange;* or em. רֵיחַ *smell;* || חנן *be abhorrent*), רֵיחַ *smell* Jb 19$_{17}$ (if em. רוּחִי to רֵיחִי). <PREP> זור לְ *be abhorrent to,* + אִשָּׁה *woman* Jb 19$_{17}$.*

<SYN> חנן *be abhorrent.*

**Hi. make abhorrent,** <SUBJ> עַם *people* Is 30$_{22}$ (if em. תְּזָרֵם *you will scatter them* to תְּזִירֵם *you will make them loathsome*). <OBJ> פֶּסֶל *idol* Is 30$_{22}$ (if em.), אֵפֹד *ephod* of idol Is 30$_{22}$ (if em.). <PREP> כְּ *as (though it were),* + דָּוָה perh. *garment stained by menstruation* Is 30$_{22}$ (or em. כְּמוֹ *as* to כְּמֵי *as the waters of* a menstruating woman [דָּוָה]).

**Ho.** 0.1 Ptc. Si מוזר—participle as adjective, **abhorrent,** used predicatively with היה *be* Si 4$_{30(A)}$ (unless זור I ho. ptc. *stranger;* + ירא htp. *be fearsome;* במלאכתך *in your work;* B מתפחז בעבודתך *arrogant in your service*).*

⇒ זָרָא *abhorrence,* זוּרֶה *rotten egg.*

**זור IV** 5.0.1 vb. **depart—Qal** 3 Pf. זָרוּ (זֹרוּ)—**depart** (unless זור I *be strange*), <SUBJ> Israel Ps 78$_{30}$ (or del. Israel), Jacob Ps 78$_{30}$, רָשָׁע *wicked one* Ps 58$_{4}$ (or em. ni. *depart;* || תעה *stray*), ידע ptc. *one who knows* Jb 19$_{13}$ (|| רחק hi. *distance oneself*), אֱנוֹשׁ *human being* Ps 90$_{5}$ (if em. זְרַמְתָּם שֵׁנָה *you overwhelmed them,* they are [as] *sleep* to בְּזוּרָם מִשֵּׁנָה *in their departing from sleep*), בֵּן *son* of human beings Ps 90$_{5}$ (if em.), שֵׁנָה *sleep* Ps 90$_{5}$ (if em. זְרַמְתָּם שֵׁנָה to בְּזוּר מֵהֶם שֵׁנָה *when sleep departs from them*). <PREP> מִן of direction, time, *from,* + Job Jb 19$_{13}$, רֶחֶם *womb* Ps 58$_{4}$, תַּאֲוָה *desire* Ps 78$_{30}$, שֵׁנָה *sleep* Ps 90$_{5}$ (if em.), אֱנוֹשׁ *human being* Ps 90$_{5}$ (if em.), בֵּן *son* of human beings Ps 90$_{5}$ (if em.).

**Ni.** 2.0.1 Pf. נָזֹרוּ (Q נזורו)—**depart** (unless זור I *be estranged*), <SUBJ> עַם *people* Is 1$_{4}$ (or del. זור ni.; + עזב *abandon,* נאץ pi. *despise*), גּוֹי *nation* Is 1$_{4}$, בַּיִת *house* of Israel Ezk 14$_{5}$ (+ שׁוב *go back*), בֵּן *son* Is 1$_{4}$, זֶרַע *seed* Is 1$_{4}$, רָשָׁע *wicked one* Ps 58$_{4}$ (if em. qal [§1]), אֲשֶׁר *one who* 1QH 4$_{19}$. <PREP> בְּ of instrument, *by (means of),* + גִּלּוּל *idol* Ezk 14$_{5}$; מִן of direction, *from,* + בְּרִית *covenant* 1QH 4$_{19}$, רֶחֶם from (the time of) the *womb* Ps 58$_{4}$ (if em.); מֵעַל *from (upon),* + ״ Y. Ezk 14$_{5}$. <COLL> with adverb, אָחוֹר *backwards* Is 1$_{4}$.*

**זוּרֶה** 1 n.[f.] **rotten egg** (unless זור II pass. ptc. *crushed one*), <SUBJ> בקע ni. *be hatched* Is 59$_{5}$ (הַזּוּרֶה תִּבָּקַע אֶפְעֶה *the rotten egg is hatched out as a viper*).

⇒ זור *be abhorrent.*

**זָזָא** 1 pr.n.m. **Zaza,** son of Jonathan, descendant of Judah, <NOM CL> בְּנֵי יוֹנָתָן פֶּלֶת וְזָזָא *the sons of Jonathan were Peleth and Zaza* 1 C 2$_{33}$.

**זחח** 2 vb. **displace—Ni.** 2 Impf. יִזַּח—**be detached,** <SUBJ> חֹשֶׁן *breastpiece* Ex 28$_{28}$||39$_{21}$. <PREP> מֵעַל *from (upon),* + אֵפֹד *ephod* Ex 28$_{28}$||39$_{21}$.

**[זַחַט]** 0.0.0.1 perh. pr.n.m. **Zahat,** or part of alphabetic sequence, Kadesh Barnea ost. 1.

**זחל I** 2.0.2 vb. **crawl—Qal** 2.0.2 Ptc. זֹחֲלֵי (Sam זהלי; Q זוחלי)—ptc. as noun, **crawling thing,** in ref. to snakes, <CSTR> זֹחֲלֵי עָפָר *crawling things of the dust* Dt 32$_{24}$ (Sam mss זהלי; + בְּהֵמָה *beast*) 1QH 5$_{27}$ (+ תַּנִּין *snake,* פֶּתֶן *viper*), אֶרֶץ *of the earth* Mc 7$_{17}$=1QpMic 23 ([ארץ]; + נָחָשׁ *snake* ); חֲמַת זֹחֲלֵי *venom of crawling things of* Dt 32$_{24}$. <PREP> כְּ *as,* + לחך *lick* dust Mc 7$_{17}$, ירה hi. *throw* 1QH 5$_{27}$.

**זחל II** 1 vb. **fear—Qal** 1 Pf. זָחַלְתִּי—**fear,** <SUBJ> Elihu Jb $32_{6}$ (|| ירא *fear*), בֵּן *son* Jb $32_{6}$, בּוּזִי *Buzite* Jb $32_{6}$. <PREP> זחל מִן *be afraid of*, + חוה pi. inf. *declaration*, i.e. declaring Jb $32_{6}$.* <SYN> ירא *fear*.*

**זְחֶלֶת**, see אֶבֶן, *stone*, §5b.

**זיד** 10.2.3 vb. **be presumptuous—Qal** 2 Pf. זָדוּ, זָדָה—**be presumptuous, be arrogant, be impudent,** <SUBJ> Egypt and Pharaoh Ex $18_{11}$, Babylon Jr $50_{29}$, בֵּן *son* Si $7_{14}$ (if em. סוד *converse*). <PREP> בְּ of place, *in*, + עֵצָה *assembly* Si $7_{14}$ (if em.); אֶל *towards, against*, + Y. Jr $50_{29}$; עַל *against*, + Israel Ex $18_{11}$. <COLL> בַּדָּבָר אֲשֶׁר זָדוּ *in the matter (in) which they were presumptuous* Ex $18_{11}$.

**Hi.** 7.2.3 Pf. Q הזיד, הֵזִידוּ; impf. יָזִיד (יָזִד), 2ms Si תזיד, יְזִידוּן (Q יזידו), תָּזִדוּ; + waw וַיָּזֶד; ptc. Si מזיד—**1.** as Qal, **be presumptuous,** etc., **display presumptuousness,** <SUBJ> אִישׁ *man* Ex $21_{14}$ perh. 4QpPs^a $3.4_{15}$, אָב *father* Ne $9_{16}$ (+ קשׁה hi. *make hard*, i.e. stiffen, neck), בֵּן *son* Dt $1_{43(mss)}$ Ne $9_{29}$ (+ לֹא שׁמע *not hear*) Si $37_{29(D)}$ (B זרע *sow*, Bmg זרה *scatter*; + חנג htp. *luxuriate*), נָבִיא *prophet* Dt $18_{20}$=11QT $61_{07}$ ([הנביא ... יזיד]; + לְדַבֵּר דָּבָר בִּשְׁמִי *so as to speak a word in my name*), עֶבֶד *servant* Ne $9_{10}$, עַם *people* Dt $17_{13}$=11QT $56_{11}$ (+ שׁמע *hear*, ירא *fear*) Ne $9_{10}$, Israel Dt $1_{43}$ (+ מרה hi. *rebel*) Ne $9_{29}$, Pharaoh Ne $9_{10}$; subj. not specified, Si $3_{16(A)}$ (C גדף pi. *revile*; + כעס hi. *anger*).

<PREP> בְּ of place, *in*, + יִשְׂרָאֵל *Israel* 11 QT $56_{11}$; of accompaniment, *with*, + יָד high *hand* 4QpPs^a $3.4_{15}$; אֶל *to*, i.e. in respect of, + תַּעֲנוּג *delicacy* Si $37_{29(D)}$; עַל *against*, + אָב *father* Ne $9_{10}$, רֵעַ *companion* Ex $21_{14}$ (+ לְהָרְגוֹ בְעָרְמָה *so as to kill him with guile*). <COLL> with adverb, עוֹד *again* Dt $17_{13}$=11QT $56_{11}$.

**2. boil, seethe,** <SUBJ> Jacob Gn $25_{29}$, subj. not specified, Si $37_{30(Bmg, D)}$ (if em. זוע hi. appar. *be greedy*; B רבה hi. *increase*). <OBJ> נָזִיד *stew* Gn $25_{29}$.

Also 4QShir^b $68_{4}$.*

⇒ זֵד *presumptuous*, זָדוֹן *presumptuousness*, זֵידָה *presumptuousness*, זֵידוֹן *seething*, נָזִיד *pottage*.

**[זֵידָה]** 0.0.2 n.f. **presumptuousness**—Q זידה; pl. Q זידות—<CSTR> מחשבת זידה *thought(s) of presumptuousness* 1Q29 $13_{4}$, רוח זידות *spirit of presumptuousness* 1Q29 $14_{1}$.

⇒ זיד *be presumptuous*.

**[זֵידוֹן]** 1 adj. **seething**—pl. זֵידוֹנִים—used attributively of מַיִם *water(s)* Ps $124_{5}$.

⇒ זיד *be presumptuous*.

**[זִיו]** I, see זו I *Ziv*.

**זִיו II** 2.0.2 n.m. **splendour**—sf. Q זוך, Q זיוה—**splendour, brightness,** <SUBJ> רעה *graze* Ps $80_{14(mss)}$ (L זִיז *moving things*). <NOM CL> זִיו שָׂדַי עִמָּדִי *the splendour of the field is with me* Ps $50_{11(mss)}$ (L זִיז *moving things*). <CSTR> זִיו שָׂדַי *the splendour of the field* Ps $50_{11(mss)}$ $80_{14(mss)}$, כבוד זוך *glory of your splendour* 1QNoah $13_{1}$. <PREP> שׁנה בְּ htp. *be changed into* 4Q$462_{16}$.

**זִיז I** 2 n.m. **moving thing**—cstr. זִיז—used collectively, perh. in ref. to particular insect, e.g. **locust,*** <SUBJ> רעה *graze* Ps $80_{14}$ (mss זִיו *splendour*). <NOM CL> זִיז שָׂדַי עִמָּדִי *the moving things of the field are with me* Ps $50_{11}$ (mss זִיו). <CSTR> זִיז שָׂדַי *moving things of the field* Ps $50_{11}$ (+ עוֹף *bird*) $80_{14}$ (+ חֲזִיר *pig*).

**זִיז II** 1.0.1 n.[m.] **teat**—cstr. זִיז—<OBJ> ינק *suck* 11QPs^a $22_{4}$. <CSTR> זִיז כְּבוֹדָהּ *teat of her glory* Is $66_{11}$ (|| שֹׁד *breast*) 11QPs^a $22_{4}$. <PREP> ענג מִן htp. *luxuriate in* Is $66_{11}$. <SYN> שֹׁד *breast*.*

**זִיזָא** 3 pr.n.m. **Ziza, 1.** son of Shiphi, descendant of Simeon, <APP> בֵּן *son* 1 C $4_{37}$.

**2.** son of Rehoboam and Maacah, <OBJ> ילד *give birth (to)* 2 C $11_{20}$.

**3.** second son of Shimei, Levite, appar. ident. with Zizah at 1 C $23_{11}$, <NOM CL> בְּנֵי שִׁמְעִי יַחַת זִיזָא *the sons of Shimei were Jahath (and) Ziza* 1 C $23_{10(ms)}$ (L זִינָא *Zina*).

**זִיזָה** 1 pr.n.m. **Zizah,** second son of Shimei, Levite, <SUBJ> היה *be* second child 1 C $23_{11}$.

**[זִימְיָא]** 0.0.1 n.f. **penalty**—Q זימו—<PREP> לְ *as*, + אבד *die* by sword Mur 45$_{7}$ ([לזימו[ן ואין פליט] *as a penalty, and there was no survivor*).

**זִינָא** 1 pr.n.m. **Zina,** appar. ident. with Zizah at 1 C 23$_{11}$, <NOM CL> בְּנֵי שִׁמְעִי יַחַת זִינָא *the sons of Shimei were Jahath (and) Zina* 1 C 23$_{10}$ (ms זִיזָא *Ziza*).

**[זִיעַ]** I 0.0.1 n.[m.] **trembling**—Q זיע—<OBJ> הפך *overturn*, i.e. turn trembling into confidence GnzPs 4$_{2}$ (+ דְּוָיָה *grief*, רְתֵת *shaking*).

**זִיעַ** II 1 pr.n.m. **Zia,** son of Abihail, and descendant of Gad, <NOM CL> אֲחֵיהֶם ... יַעְכָּן וְזִיעַ *their brothers were ... Jacan and Zia* 1 C 5$_{13}$.

**זִיף**, see שׁוּף *glare*.*

**זִיף** I 9.0.0.5 pl.n. **Ziph**—I זף; + ה- זִיפָה—**1.** town in hill country of Judah, appar. founded by Mesha (1 C 2$_{42}$), and fortified by Rehoboam (2 C 11$_{8}$), perh. T. Zīf 6 km SSE of Hebron, <NOM CL> בָּהָר ... זִיף *in the mountain(s) were ... Ziph* Jos 15$_{55}$. <OBJ> בנה *build* 2 C 11$_{8}$. <CSTR> אֲבִי־זִיף *(founding) father of Ziph* 1 C 2$_{42}$, מלך זיף *king of Ziph* Royal stamp 6 7 (זף) 8 9, מִדְבַּר־זִיף *steppe of Ziph* 1 S 23$_{14.15}$ 26$_{2.2}$. <PREP> with ה- of direction, *to(wards)*, + הלך *go* 1 S 23$_{24}$.

**2.** town of Judah in Negeb, <SUBJ> היה *be* Jos 15$_{24}$. <APP> עִיר *city* Jos 15$_{24}$. <PREP> לְ of direction, *to*, + שלח *send* Arad ost. 17$_{5}$ (לזף; others להם *to them*).

**3.** Royal Stamp 10 (זף; 8th cent.).

Also Kenyon inscr. 1098 ]לזפ[.*

⇒ זִיפִי *Ziphite.*

**זִיף** II 1 pr.n.m. **Ziph,** son of Jehallelel, descendant of Judah, <NOM CL> בְּנֵי יְהַלֶּלְאֵל זִיף וְזִיפָה *the sons of Jehallelel were Ziph and Ziphah* 1 C 4$_{16}$.

**זִיפָה** 1 pr.n. **Ziphah,** son or daughter of Jehallelel, descendant of Judah, <NOM CL> בְּנֵי יְהַלֶּלְאֵל זִיף וְזִיפָה *the sons of Jehallelel were Ziph and Ziphah* 1 C 4$_{16}$.

**[זִיפִי]** 3 gent. **Ziphite**—pl. זִ(י)פִים—as noun, inhabitants of Ziph, <SUBJ> ברך *be blessed* 1 S 23$_{19}$, הלך *go* 23$_{19.19}$, בוא *come* 26$_{1}$ Ps 54$_{2}$, עלה *go up* 1 S 23$_{19}$, קום *arise* 23$_{19}$, שׁוב *go back* 23$_{19}$, סגר hi. *deliver* to Saul 23$_{19}$, חמל *pity* 23$_{19}$, כון hi. *prepare* 23$_{19}$ (mss בין hi. *understand*), ראה *see* 23$_{19.19}$, ידע *know* 23$_{19.19}$, אמר *say* 23$_{19}$=Ps 54$_{2}$ 1 S 26$_{1}$. <PREP> לְ of possession, *of, (belonging) to* 1 S 23$_{19}$; עִם *with*, + סתר htp. *conceal oneself* 1 S 23$_{19}$=Ps 54$_{2}$ 1 S 26$_{1}$ (if ins. עִם); אֵת *with*, + הלך *go* 1 S 23$_{19}$.

⇒ זִיף *Ziph* (pl.n.).

**[זִיקָה]** 2.1.1 n.f. **flaming arrow**—pl. זִיקוֹת—**flaming arrow, firebrand, lightning flash,** <OBJ> אזר pi. *gird oneself* Is 50$_{11}$ (unless em. אור hi. *kindle*; + אֵשׁ *fire*), בער pi. *kindle* Is 50$_{11}$ CD 5$_{13}$, נצח pi. *make brilliant* Si 43$_{17(B, M)}$ (Bmg זיקים *flaming arrows*, i.e. pl. of זִק; Bmg יְקוּם *existence*; + בָּרָד *hail* [M]; + בָּרָק *lightning* [B]). <CSTR> זיקות משפט *flaming arrows of judgment* Si 43$_{17(M)}$, זיקות קורי עכביש *firebrands of spiders' webs* CD 5$_{13}$. <PREP> בְּ perh. of instrument, *by (means of)* (light from), + הלך *go* Is 50$_{11}$ (+ אוּר אֶשְׁכֶם *light of your fire*).

**זַיִת** 38.1.4 n.m. **olive**—(appar. f. at Jg 9$_{9[mss]}$) זָיִת; cstr. זֵית; sf. זֵיתְךָ (זֵיתֶךָ); pl. זֵיתִים; sf. זֵיתֵיהֶם, זֵיתֵיכֶם—usu. **olive tree** or, esp. in pl., **olive grove** (Ex 23$_{11}$ Dt 6$_{11}$ Jos 24$_{13}$ 1 S 8$_{14}$ 2 K 5$_{26}$ Ne 5$_{11}$ 9$_{25}$); also **olive,** i.e. fruit of olive tree (e.g. Ex 27$_{20}$ 30$_{24}$ Lv 24$_{2}$ Mc 6$_{15}$ 11QT 22$_{15}$).

<SUBJ> היה *be* Dt 28$_{40}$, נשׁל *be detached* Dt 28$_{40}$, מלך *rule* Jg 9$_{8}$ (+ תְּאֵנָה *fig*, גֶּפֶן *vine*, אָטָד *bramble*), אמר *say* Jg 9$_{9}$ (+ תְּאֵנָה, גֶּפֶן, אָטָד), כחשׁ pi. *deceive*, i.e. fail to yield Hb 3$_{17}$ (if em. מַעֲשֶׂה the *produce of* olive deceives to מַעֲשֶׂהוּ/מַעֲשֶׂה [the] olive deceives [its] produce, i.e. fails to produce; + שְׂדֵמָה *field*, תְּאֵנָה, גֶּפֶן *grape*, צֹאן *sheep*, בָּקָר *cattle*), מלא *be full* of fruit Si 50$_{10}$ (+ עֵץ שֶׁמֶן *tree of oil*, i.e. wild olive).

<NOM CL> שְׁנַיִם זֵיתִים עָלֶיהָ *two olive trees were by it* Zc 4$_{3}$, מַה־שְּׁנֵי הַזֵּיתִים הָאֵלֶּה *what are these two olive trees?* Zc 4$_{11(L)}$, הַזֵּיתִים וְהַשִּׁקְמִים אֲשֶׁר בַּשְּׁפֵלָה *the olives and the sycamore trees that were in the Shephelah* 1 C 27$_{28}$.

<OBJ> נטע *plant* Dt 6$_{11}$ (+ בּוֹר *cistern*, בַּיִת *house*) Jos 24$_{13}$ (both || כֶּרֶם *vineyard*) 1QDM 2$_{3}$ [וזיתים] אשר [לוא נטעתה] (*and olive groves which you did not plant*),

חבט beat Dt 24$_{20}$, דרך tread Mc 6$_{15}$=1QpMic 17$_{2}$ ([תדרך] [זית]; || תִּירוֹשׁ new wine), נתן give Dt 6$_{11}$ 1QDM 2$_{3}$ ([לתת] ... [וזיתים]), ירשׁ possess Ne 9$_{25}$ (|| כֶּרֶם vineyard, + עֵץ מַאֲכָל tree of fruit, בַּיִת, בּוֹר), לקח take 1 S 8$_{14}$ (|| כֶּרֶם, שָׂדֶה field) 2 K 5$_{26}$ (|| כֶּרֶם, + כֶּסֶף money, בֶּגֶד garment, בָּקָר cattle, צֹאן flock, עֶבֶד slave, שִׁפְחָה female slave), שׁוב hi. take back Ne 5$_{11}$ (|| כֶּרֶם, שָׂדֶה, בַּיִת, + כֶּסֶף, דָּגָן grain, תִּירוֹשׁ, יִצְהָר fresh oil), אכל eat Jos 24$_{13}$ Am 4$_{9}$ (|| תְּאֵנָה fig, + כֶּרֶם, גַּן garden), קרא call name Jr 11$_{16}$.

<CSTR> זֵית שֶׁמֶן olive(s) of oil Dt 8$_{8}$ (+ חִטָּה wheat, שְׂעֹרָה barley, גֶּפֶן vine, רִמּוֹן pomegranate, דְּבַשׁ honey) 4QPsJos$^{a}$ 11$_{6}$ ([זית שמן]), יִצְהָר of fresh oil 2 K 18$_{32}$ (or del. זַיִת; + דָּגָן grain, תִּירוֹשׁ new wine, לֶחֶם bread, כֶּרֶם vineyard, דְּבַשׁ); עֵץ הַזַּיִת tree of the olive Hg 2$_{19}$ (+ גֶּפֶן, תְּאֵנָה fig, רִמּוֹן), [עץ זית] wood (consisting) of olive 4QJub$^{d}$ 21$_{12}$, עֲלֵה־זַיִת leaf of olive tree Gn 8$_{11}$=4QpGen$^{a}$ 1.1$_{16}$ (עלי), עֲלֵי leaves of Ne 8$_{15}$ (|| הֲדַס myrtle, תָּמָר palm, + עֵץ שֶׁמֶן tree of oil, i.e. wild olive, עֵץ עָבֹת leafy tree), שְׁתִלֵי זֵיתִים cuttings of olive trees Ps 128$_{3}$ (+ גֶּפֶן), שִׁבֳּלֵי הַזֵּיתִים twigs of the olive trees Zc 4$_{12}$, שֶׁמֶן זַיִת oil of olive Ex 27$_{20}$ 30$_{24}$ Lv 24$_{2}$, מַעֲשֶׂה produce of Hb 3$_{17}$ (or em.; see Subj.), נֹקֶף beating of Is 17$_{6}$ 24$_{13}$ 4QD$^{e}$ 6$_{15}$ ([נ]קוף הזית), כֶּרֶם זָיִת vineyard of olive(s) Jg 15$_{5}$ (or em.; see Prep.; + קָמָה standing grain, גָּדִישׁ shock), הַר הַזֵּיתִים the mountain of olives, i.e. Mount of Olives Zc 14$_{4.4}$, אֶרֶץ זֵית land of olives of Dt 8$_{8}$ 2 K 18$_{32}$ (or del. זית) 4QPsJos$^{a}$ 11$_{6}$ ([ארץ] [זית]), מַעֲלֵה הַזֵּיתִים the ascent of olives, i.e. ascent of Mount of Olives 2 S 15$_{30}$, שְׁנֵי הַזֵּיתִים the two olive trees Zc 4$_{11}$.

<ADJ> טוֹב good 1 S 8$_{14}$, רַעֲנָן luxuriant Jr 11$_{16}$ Ps 52$_{10}$ Si 50$_{10}$, אֵלֶּה these Zc 4$_{11}$, כָּתִית beaten Ex 27$_{20}$ Lv 24$_{2}$.

<APP> perh. מֶכֶר sale Mur 30 2$_{18}$ (+ תְּאֵנָה fig).

<PREP> לְ of direction, to, + אמר say Jg 9$_{8}$; of benefit, to, for, + עשׂה do Ex 23$_{11}$ (|| כֶּרֶם vineyard); כְּ as Ps 52$_{10}$ Si 50$_{10}$, + היה be Ho 14$_{7}$ (+ לְבָנוֹן Lebanon), שׁלך hi. cast blossom Jb 15$_{33}$ (|| גֶּפֶן vine); מִן of instrument, by (means of), with, + סוך anoint oneself; perh. partitive, (some) of, + אכל eat 11QT 22$_{15}$ (+ שֶׁמֶן oil); עַל over, i.e. in charge of 1 C 27$_{28}$; עַד unto, + בער hi. burn Jg 15$_{5}$ (if ins. עַד).

<COLL> שְׁנַיִם זֵיתִים two olive trees Zc 4$_{3}$.

Also 4Q393 3.2$_{9}$.*

<SYN> כֶּרֶם vineyard, גֶּפֶן vine, שָׂדֶה field, תְּאֵנָה fig, תִּירוֹשׁ new wine, הֲדַס myrtle, תָּמָר palm, בַּיִת house.

**זֵיתָן** 1 pr.n.m. **Zethan,** son of Bilhan, descendant of Benjamin, <NOM CL> בְּנֵי בִלְהָן יְעוּשׁ ... וְזֵיתָן the sons of Bilhan were Jeush ... and Zethan 1 C 7$_{10(Qr)}$.

**זַךְ** 11.0.1 adj. **pure**—זָךְ; f. זַכָּה—**1.** used attributively, alw. in ref. to unadulterated substances, of לְבֹנָה frankincense Ex 30$_{34}$=4QBibPar 13$_{3}$ ([ל]בונה) Lv 24$_{7}$=11QT 8$_{10}$ ([לבונה זכה]), שֶׁמֶן olive oil Ex 27$_{20}$||Lv 24$_{2}$ (+ כָּתִית beaten).

**2.** used predicatively, in ref. to righteous person, <NOM CL> זַךְ אֲנִי בְּלִי פָשַׁע I am pure, without sin Jb 33$_{9}$ (|| חַף pure), אִם זַךְ ... אַתָּה if you are ... pure Jb 8$_{6}$ (|| יָשָׁר upright), אִם־זַךְ ... פָּעֳלוֹ if his behaviour ... is pure Pr 20$_{11}$ (|| יָשָׁר; or em. יָשָׁר to רָשָׁע wicked or זָר crooked and/or פָּעֳלוֹ to דַּרְכּוֹ his way), וְזַךְ יָשָׁר פָּעֳלוֹ appar. as for the pure, his activity is upright Pr 21$_{8}$, זַךְ לִקְחִי my understanding is pure Jb 11$_{4}$ (|| בַּר pure), תְּפִלָּתִי זַכָּה my prayer is pure Jb 16$_{17}$, כָּל־דַּרְכֵי־אִישׁ זַךְ בְּעֵינָיו all the ways of a man are pure in his own eyes Pr 16$_{2}$.

<SYN> §2 יָשָׁר upright, בַּר pure, חַף pure.

⇒ זכך be pure.

**[זַכָּא]** 0.0.0.1 pr.n. **Zacca,** appar. son of Chisse (כסא), Seal 107 (Beth Shemesh, 8th cent.).

**זכה** 8.0.5 vb. **be pure**—**Qal** 4.0.2 Impf. יִזְכֶּה, 2ms תִּזְכֶּה, אֶזְכֶּה—**be** morally **pure, be worthy, be justified,** <SUBJ> ׳י Y. Mc 6$_{11}$ (or em. pi. acquit), אֱלֹהִים God Ps 51$_{6}$ (|| צדק be righteous), יְדִיד beloved, i.e. Judah and Jerusalem Jr 11$_{15}$ (if em. אָז תַּעֲלֹזִי will you then exult? to הֲתִזְכִּי עַל־זֹאת will you be justified concerning this?), אֱנוֹשׁ human being Jb 15$_{14}$ (|| צדק), ילד pass. ptc. one who is born Jb 25$_{4}$ (|| צדק), מִי who? 1QH fr. 4$_{10}$; subj. not specified, GnzPs 4$_{25}$ 1QH 9$_{15}$ ([י]זכה). <PREP> בְּ of accompaniment, with, in (the presence of), + מֹאזְנַיִם scales of wickedness Mc 6$_{11}$ (or em. pi.), כִּיס bag of deceitful weights Mc 6$_{11}$ (or em.); in respect of, + שׁפט inf. judging Ps 51$_{6}$ (or em. ni. being judged), מִשְׁפָּט judgment 1QH fr. 4$_{10}$, רִיב struggle 1QH 9$_{15}$ ([י]זכה ב[ריבכה]), קֹדֶשׁ holiness GnzPs 4$_{25}$; עַל despite, + זֹאת this Jr 11$_{15}$ (if em.). <SYN>

צדק *be righteous.*

**Pi.** 3 Pf. זִכִּיתִי; impf. יְזַכֶּה—**purify, declare pure, acquit,** <SUBJ> Y. Is $53_{10}$ (if em.; see Prep.) Jr $11_{15}$ (if em. אָז תַּעֲלֹזִי *will you then exult?* to הַאֲזַכֶּה/הָאֲזַכֶּה עַל־זֹאת *shall I acquit [it] concerning this?*) Mc $6_{11}$ (if em. qal), נַעַר *lad* Ps $119_9$, worshipper Ps $73_{13}$ (|| רחץ *wash* hands), מִי *who?* Pr $20_9$ (+ טהר *be clean*). <OBJ> עֶבֶד *servant* of Y. Is $53_{10}$ (if em.; see Prep.), יָדִיד *beloved*, i.e. Judah and Jerusalem Jr $11_{15}$, לֵבָב *heart* Ps $73_{13}$, לֵב *heart* Pr $20_9$, אֹרַח *way* Ps $119_9$ (or em.; see Qal Subj.; + לִשְׁמֹר כִּדְבָרֶךָ *keeping [it] according to your word*), עִיר *city* Mc $6_{11}$ (if em.; see Subj.). <PREP> בְּ of accompaniment, *with, in (the presence of)*, + מֹאזְנַיִם *scales* of wickedness Mc $6_{11}$ (if em. qal), כִּיס *bag* of deceitful weights Mc $6_{11}$ (if em.); of instrument, *by (means of), with*, + מָה *what?* Ps $119_9$ (or em. qal); מִן privative, *without*, i.e. so as not to suffer from, + חֳלִי *illness* Is $53_{10}$ (if em. דַּכְּאוֹ הֶחֱלִי *to crush him, he made him ill* to זַכְּאוֹ מֵחֳלִי *to cleanse him from illness*); עַל *concerning*, + זֹאת *this* Jr $11_{15}$ (if em.). <COLL> with adverb, רִיק *in vain* Ps $73_{13}$. <SYN> רחץ *wash.*

**Htp.** 1.0.3 Impf. Q יזכה, Q יזכו; impv. הִזַּכּוּ—**purify oneself, clean oneself, be purified, be cleaned,** <SUBJ> קָצִין *ruler* of Sodom Is $1_{16}$ (+ רחץ *wash*, סור hi. *remove* evil), עַם *people* of Gomorrah Is $1_{16}$, מאס ptc. *one who refuses* to enter covenant 1QS $3_4$ (|| טהר htp. *clean oneself*, קדשׁ htp. *sanctify oneself*), מַעֲשֶׂה *deed* 1QS $8_{18}$; subj. not specified, 5QRègle $4_2$. <PREP> בְּ of instrument, *by*, + כִּפֻּרִים *atonement* 1QS $3_4$ 5QRègle $4_2$ (בכפור[ים]); מִן privative, *without*, i.e. so as not to suffer, + עָוֶל *unrighteousness* 1QS $8_{18}$ (+ להלך בתמים דרך *by walking in perfection [of] way*). <SYN> טהר htp. *clean oneself*, קדשׁ htp. *sanctify oneself.**

[זָכֶה] adj. **pure,** as noun, **unblemished beast,** suitable for sacrifice, <NOM CL> יֵשׁ בְּעֶדְרוֹ זָכֶה *there is a pure one in his flock* Ml $1_{14}$ (if em. זָכָר *male* or perh. *ram*).

זְכוֹכִית 1 n.f. **glass,** <SUBJ> ערך *be comparable* to wisdom Jb $28_{17}$ (|| זָהָב *gold*). <SYN> זָהָב *gold.*

⇒ זכך *be pure.*

זָכוּר 1 adj. **mindful** (or זכר pass. ptc. as adj.), used predicatively of הוּא *he* (Y.) Ps $103_{14}$ (הוּא ... זָכוּר כִּי *he ... is mindful that*).

זַכּוּר 10.0.0.12 pr.n.m. **Zaccur**—I זכר (§§10–22) perh. זֶכֶר *Zecher*—**1.** son of Bigvai, leader of exiles returning with Ezra, <NOM CL> מִבְּנֵי בִגְוַי עוּתַי וזבוד *of the sons of Bigvai were Uthai and Zaccur* Ezr $8_{14(Qr)}$ (Kt Zabud; or em. בֶּן־ Uthai, *son of* Zabud/Zaccur). <PREP> עִם *with* Ezr $8_{14(Qr)}$. **2.** son of Imri, one who helped repair walls of Jerusalem, <SUBJ> בנה *build* Ne $3_2$. <APP> בֵּן *son* Ne $3_2$. **3.** Levite and co-signatory of Nehemiah's pledge, <NOM CL> אֲחֵיהֶם ... זַכּוּר *their brothers were ... Zaccur* Ne $10_{13}$. **4.** Simeonite, son of Mishma, <NOM CL> בְּנֵי מִשְׁמָע ... זַכּוּר *the sons of Mishma were ... Zaccur* 1 C $4_{26}$. <APP> בֵּן *son* 1 C $4_{26}$. **5.** Levite, son of Jaaziah, descendant of Merari, <NOM CL> לְיַעֲזִיָּהוּ בְנוֹ ... וְזַכּוּר *(the sons) of Jaaziah were Beno ... and Zaccur* 1 C $24_{27}$. **6.** temple musician, descendant of Asaph, <NOM CL> לִבְנֵי אָסָף זַכּוּר וְיוֹסֵף *of the sons of Asaph were Zaccur and Joseph* 1 C $25_2$, הַשְּׁלִשִׁי זַכּוּר *the third (lot) was (for) Zaccur* 1 C $25_{10}$. <APP> בֵּן *son* 1 C $25_2$. **7.** perh. ident. with preceding, priest, son of Asaph and father of Micaiah, <CSTR> בֶּן־זַכּוּר *son of Zaccur* Ne $12_{35}$. <APP> בֵּן *son* Ne $12_{35}$ (or del.). **8.** Reubenite, father of Shammua, <CSTR> בֶּן־זַכּוּר *son of Zaccur* Nm $13_4$. **9.** son of Mattaniah and father of Hanan, <CSTR> בֶּן־זַכּוּר *son of Zaccur* Ne $13_{13}$. <APP> בֵּן *son* Ne $13_{13}$.

**10.** son of Neriah, <APP> בֵּן *son* Seal 550 551 ([לז]כר; both T. Beit Mirsim?, 7th/6th cent.). <PREP> לְ of possession, *of, (belonging) to* Seal 550 551. **11.** father of Tobshalom, <CSTR> בן זכר *son of Zaccur* Seal 804 828 (both City of David, 7th/6th cent.). **12.** father of Amadiah, <CSTR> בן זכר *son of Zaccur* Ḥorvat ʿUza ost. $1_2$. **13.** son of Shelemiah, <APP> בֵּן *son* Seal 929 ([ל]זכר; 7th cent.). <PREP> לְ of possession, *of, (belonging) to,* Seal 929 ([ל]זכר; 7th cent.). **14.** appar. son of Hoshea, Seal 46 (8th cent.). **15.** appar. son of Ezer, Seal 47 (7th cent.). **16.** appar. father of Jehoasah, Seal 171 (7th cent.). **17.** appar. father of Chilcheliah, Seal 329 (7th–6th cent.). **18.** appar. recipient of goods at Samaria, Samaria ost. $31_3$. **19.** Kh. el-Mashash ost. $1543.1_1$. **20.** Arad ost. $38_7$

(כר[ז]). **21.** Arad ost. $48_3$ (כר[ז]). **22.** Arad ost. $67_5$.
→ זכר *remember.*

**[זָכוּר]** 4.0.2 n.m. **male**—sf. זְכוּרְךָ, זְכוּרָהּ, Q זכורם—used collectively, <SUBJ> ירא ni. *appear* Ex $23_{17}$||$34_{23}$||Dt $16_{16}$, כרת ni. *be cut off* CD $3_7$. <OBJ> נכה hi. *strike* Dt $20_{13}$=11QT $62_9$. <CSTR> כָּל־זְכוּרְךָ *all your males* Ex $23_{17}$||$34_{23}$||Dt $16_{16}$, כָּל־זְכוּרָהּ *all its males* Dt $20_{13}$.*

**זַכַּי** 4 pr.n.m. **Zaccai**—זַכָּי—**1.** ancestor of postexilic Judaean family, <CSTR> בְּנֵי זַכָּי *sons of Zaccai* Ezr $2_9$||Ne $7_{14}$ (or em. זַבִּי *Zabbi*). **2.** Levite, father of Baruch, <CSTR> בֶּן־זַכַּי *son of Zaccai* Ne $3_{20(Qr)}$ (Kt Zabbai). **3.** Israelite husband of foreign wife, descendant of Bebai, <NOM CL> מִבְּנֵי בֵּבָי ... זַכַּי *of the sons of Bebai were ... Zaccai* Ezr $10_{28(mss)}$ (L Zabbai).

**זכך** 4.0.2 vb. **be pure**—**Qal** 3.0.1 Pf. זַכּוּ; inf. Q זכו—**be pure, be clean,** <SUBJ> אִישׁ *man* CD $10_3$ (=4QDa $17.3_2$ ho. *be purified*), נָזִיר *prince* Lm $4_7$ (|| צחח *be pure*), שָׁמַיִם *heaven* Jb $15_{15}$ (+ זכה *be pure*, צדק *be righteous*), כּוֹכָב *star* Jb $25_5$ (|| אהל [mss הלל] hi. *shine*, + זכה, צדק). <PREP> בְּעֵינֵי *in the eyes*, i.e. estimation, *of*, + אֵל *God* Jb $15_{15}$ $25_5$; מִן of comparison, *(more) than*, + שֶׁלֶג *snow* Lm $4_7$. <COLL> עד זכו לשוב *until he is pure (enough) to return* CD $10_3$.

<SYN> צחח *be white*, אהל hi. *be light*.

**Hi.** 1.0.1 Pf. הֲזִכּוֹתִי, Q הזכו—**clean, purify,** <SUBJ> אִישׁ *man* 1QS $9_9$, Job Jb $9_{30}$ (|| רחץ htp. *wash oneself*). <OBJ> כַּף *hand* Jb $9_{30}$, דֶּרֶךְ *way* 1QS $9_9$ (+ להבדל מעול וללכת בתמים דרך *to be separate from unrighteousness and walking in perfection [of] way*). <PREP> בְּ of instrument, *by (means of), with*, + בֹּר *soap* Jb $9_{30}$. <SYN> רחץ htp. *wash oneself*.

**Ho. be purified,** <SUBJ> אִישׁ *man* 4QDa $17.3_2$ ([איש] ... הו]זכו]; =CD $10_3$ qal). <COLL> [ע]ד ה[ו]זכו ל]שוב *until he is purified so as to return* 4QDa $17.3_2$.

→ זַךְ *pure*, זְכוֹכִית *glass*, זַכַּי *Zaccai*.

**זכר I** 231.20.44.1 vb. **remember**—**Qal** 171.17.34.1 Pf. זָכַר (זָכָר, זָכְרָנוּ), זָכְרָה, Q זכרת (זכרתה), זָכַרְתָּם, זְכַרְתַּנִי, זכרתי), זָכַרְתִּי (זָכָרְתִּי, זְכַרְתִּיךְ), Kt זכרתי, זָכַרְתְּ (זָכְרְתְּ), זָכְרוּ, זְכַרְנוּ, זְכַרְתֶּם.

Impf. יִזְכֹּר (יִזְכּוֹר, יִזְכָּר־), 3fs תִּזְכֹּר, 2ms תִּזְכֹּר (תִּזְכּוֹר), Si תזכרהו, תִּזְכְּרֵנוּ, תִּזְכְּרֵנִי, תִּזְכָּר־, אֶזְכֹּר (אֶזְכּוֹר), תִּזְכְּרִי, אֶזְכְּרֵנוּ, אֶזְכְּרֵכִי, אֶזְכָּרְךָ, אֶזְכְּרָה, אֶזְכָּר־, יִזְכְּרוּ (יִזְכְּרוּנִי), Si יזכרוה, Q יזכרוכה, יִזְכְּרוּךָ, 2mpl תִּזְכְּרוּ.

+ waw וְזָכַרְתָּ (Q וזכרתה, וּזְכַרְתַּנִי), וְזָכַרְתְּ, וְזָכַרְתִּי, וְאֶזְכֹּר, 2ms Q ותזכור, וַיִּזְכְּרֶהָ, וַיִּזְכֹּר, וּזְכַרְתֶּם, וְזָכְרוּ, וַיִּזְכְּרוּ; impv. זְכֹר (זְכוֹר), זְכָר־, Q זכורנא [1QIsa $39_3$; MT זְכָר־נָא], זָכְרָה, Q זכורה, זָכְרֵנִי, Q זכורני), זִכְרוּ (זְכֹרוּ); ptc. זֹכֵר, זָכוּר, זֹכְרֵי; inf. זָכֹר (זָכוֹר), זְכֹר (Q זוכרי, זכרו, זָכְרֵנוּ)—**1. remember, call to mind; be mindful of, consider** (e.g. Ps $22_{28}$ Ec $5_{19}$); **mention** (e.g. Jr $3_{16}$ $20_9$ CD $15_2$); perh. **give an order** or **muster** (Na $2_6$).*

<SUBJ> יי *Y.* Ex $6_5$ $32_{13}$ Lv $26_{42.42.42.45}$ Dt $9_{27}$ Jg $16_{28}$ (+ חזק pi. *strengthen*) 1 S $1_{11.19}$ 2 K $20_3$||Is $38_3$ Is $43_{25}$ $63_{11}$ $64_8$ Jr $2_2$ $14_{10.21}$ $15_{15}$ $18_{20}$ $31_{20.34}$ $44_{21}$ (+ עלה עַל לֵב *go up into heart*, i.e. be remembered) Ezk $16_{60}$ Ho $7_2$ $8_{13}$ $9_9$ (or del.) Hb $3_2$ (or del.) Ps $8_5$ $20_4$ $25_{6.7.7}$ $83_6$ $89_{48}$ (or em. אֲדֹנָי *Adonai*) $89_{51(mss)}$ $98_3$ $105_8$||1 C $16_{15}$ (if em. זִכְרוּ *remember*, O worshippers) Ps $79_8$ $105_{42}$ $106_{4.45}$ (+ נחם ni. *repent*) $111_5$ $115_{12}$ (+ ברך pi. *bless*) $119_{49}$ $132_1$ $136_{23}$ $137_7$ Lm $2_{1(mss)}$ $5_1$ (+ ראה *see*, נבט hi. *look*) Ne $1_8$ 2 C $6_{42}$ GnzPs $4_9$ 4QapPsa $1.1_9$ (זכ[ר]) 11QPsa $24_{10}$ perh. 4Q 416 $2.3_2$ 4QapLamb$_{1.2}$ 4Q462$_{3.19}$.

אֲדֹנָי *Adonai* Jg $16_{28}$ Ezk $16_{60}$ (or del. אֲדֹנָי) Ps $89_{48}$ (if em.; see at end of Obj.) $89_{51}$ Lm $2_1$ 1QLitPr $1_6$ (זכו[ר] [א]דוני) $3.2_5$ 4QDibHama $1.2_{11}$ $1.5_9$ $3.2_5$ $4_6$=4QDib Hamc $131_{12}$ 4QDibHama $5.2_3$=4QDibHamc $124_3$ 4QDib Hama $6_6$ (ז]כור[) $8_1$ (זכו]ר אדו[נ]י[) 4QPrFêtesa $3_3$ (זכ]ור [אדוני) 4QPrFêtesb $2_2$ $3_4$ 4QPrFêtesc $131.2_5$ זכורה (א]דו[ני).

אֵל *God* Jb $14_{13}$ CD $1_4$ $6_2$ GnzPs $4_{13}$ 4Q370 $1_7$ 4Q463 $1_1$, אֵל עֶלְיוֹן *God Most High* Ps $78_{39}$, אֱלוֹהַּ *God* Jb $10_9$, אֱלֹהִים *God* Gn $8_1$ $9_{15.16}$ $19_{29}$ $30_{22}$ Ex $2_{24}$ (both + שׁמע *hear*) $6_5$ Ps $74_{2.18.22}$ $78_{39}$ $88_6$ Ne $1_8$ $5_{19}$ $6_{14}$ $13_{14.22.29.31}$, דרשׁ ptc. *one seeking*, i.e. requiting, blood, i.e. God Ps $9_{13}$, מִי *who?*, i.e. God Si $16_{17}$.

בַּיִת *house* of Jacob Is $46_8$ (+ אשׁשׁ htpo. *make firm* or *experience grief*) $46_9$, of Israel Ezk $20_{43}$ $36_{31}$, שְׁאֵרִית *remnant* of house of Israel Is $46_{8.9}$, יֶתֶר *remnant* of people Ne $4_8$, עַם *people* Ex $13_3$ Dt $32_7$ Mc $6_5$, Israel Is $17_{10}$ $43_{18}$ $44_{21}$ Ml $3_{22}$, Israelite(s) Ex $20_8$ (Sam שׁמר *keep*) Dt $5_{15}$

$7_{18}$ $8_{2.18}$ $9_{7}$ $15_{15}$ $16_{3.12}$ $24_{9.18.22}$ $25_{17}$.

Ephraim Zc $10_{9}$, Jacob Is $43_{18}$ $44_{21}$, Reubenites, Gadites, and Manassites Jos $1_{13}$, Jerusalem Ezk $16_{22(Qr).43(Qr).61.63}$ Lm $1_{7.9}$, Zion 11QPs$^{a}$ $22_{6}$, Babylon Is $47_{7}$ (+ שִׂים עַל־לֵב *place upon heart*, i.e. pay attention), Tyre Am $1_{9}$, אֶפֶס *end* of earth Ps $22_{28}$ (+ שׁוּב *go back*).

Abraham 4QJub$^{d}$ $21_{2}$ ([אברהם ... זכרתי]), Ahasuerus Est $2_{1}$, Ben Sira Si $42_{15}$ $51_{8.11}$, Bidkar 2 K $9_{25}$, David 1 S $25_{31}$ 2 S $14_{11}$ $19_{20}$, Eliphaz Jb $7_{7}$, Jehu 2 K $9_{25(ms)}$, Jeremiah Jr $20_{9}$, Job Jb $4_{7}$ $11_{16}$ $21_{6}$ (+ בהל ni. *be terrified*) $36_{24}$ $40_{32}$, Joash 2 C $24_{22}$, Jonah Jon $2_{8}$, Joseph Gn $42_{9}$, Oholibah Ezk $23_{19.27}$.

מֶלֶךְ *king* 2 S $14_{11}$ Est $2_{1}$ 2 C $24_{22}$, אָדוֹן *lord* 1 S $25_{31}$ 2 S $14_{11(mss)}$ $19_{20}$ Lachish ost. $2_{4}$, בַּעַל *lord* Jg $9_{2}$, סָגָן *prefect* Ne $4_{8}$, חֹר *noble* Ne $4_{8}$, שַׂר *prince*, i.e. chief cup bearer Gn $40_{14.23}$.

אָדָם *human being* Ec $5_{19}$ $9_{15}$ $11_{8}$, אִישׁ *man* Jr $23_{36}$ (or em. hi. *mention*) Si $15_{8}$, גֶּבֶר *man*, i.e. mourner Lm $3_{19}$ (or em. זֵכֶר *memory*; see Obj.) $3_{20}$, אָב *father*, i.e. ancestor Ps $78_{35.42}$ $106_{7}$ Ne $9_{17}$, זֶרַע *seed*, i.e. offspring Is $57_{11}$ (+ שִׂים עַל־לֵב *place upon heart*, i.e. pay attention), אָחוֹת *sister* Ezk $23_{19}$, בָּחוּר *youth* Ec $12_{1}$.

בֵּן *son* Is $57_{11}$ Jr $3_{16}$ (+ עלה עַל־לֵב *go up to heart*, i.e. come to mind) $17_{2}$ (or em. כִּזְכֹר בְּנֵיהֶם *when their children remember* to לְזִכָּרוֹן בָּהֶם *as a memorial among them*) Si $7_{11.16.36}$ $8_{5.7}$ $9_{12}$ $14_{12}$ $34_{13}$ (mg ידע *know*) $38_{20}$ (mg נכר hi. *recognize*) $38_{21.22}$ $41_{3}$, specif. son of Israel Nm $11_{5}$ $15_{39.40}$ (both + עשׂה *do*, i.e. fulfil commandment) Jg $8_{34}$.

פֶּה *mouth* of wicked one Ps $109_{16}$, עֲקָרָה *barren woman* Is $54_{4}$=4QTanḥ $8_{6}$ ([תזכרי]), אבד ptc. *one who is dying* Pr $31_{7}$, מַר *one who is bitter* Pr $31_{7}$, שׂישׂ ptc. *one who rejoices* Is $64_{4}$ (or del. שׂישׂ ptc.), עשׂה ptc. *one who does*, i.e. practises, righteousness Is $64_{4}$, פָּלִיט *fugitive* Jr $51_{50}$ (פָּלֵיט) Ezk $6_{9}$, מַעֲרָכָה *(member of) battle-line* 1QM $17_{2}$, member of Qumran community CD $15_{2}$, worshipper Ps $42_{5}$ (or em. hi. *offer as token offering*) $42_{7}$ $63_{7}$ $77_{4.7.12(Qr).12}$ (Kt hi. *proclaim*) $105_{5.8(mss)}$‖1 C $16_{12.15}$ Ps $119_{52.55}$ $137_{1.6}$ $143_{5}$ GnzPs $4_{9}$ 1QH $4_{34.35}$ $5_{2}$ ([זוכרי]) 4QapPs$^{b}$ $33_{11}$ 11QPs$^{a}$ $19_{12}$; subj. not specified, Na $2_{6}$ (or em. ni. *be remembered*) Ps $6_{6}$ (if em. זֵכֶר *remembrance*) $103_{18}$ 4Q370 $2_{7}$ 4QMMT $C_{23.25}$ 4Q525 $14.2_{16}$.

**<OBJ>** ׳׳ Y. Dt $8_{18}$ Jg $8_{34}$ 2 S $14_{11}$ Is $57_{11}$ $64_{4}$ (or em. בִּדְרָכֶיךָ יִזְכְּרוּךָ *they will remember you in your ways* to וּדְרָכֶיךָ יִזְכֹּרוּ *and your ways they will remember*) Jr $20_{9}$ $51_{50}$ Ezk $6_{9}$ Jon $2_{8}$ Zc $10_{9}$ Ps $6_{6}$ (if em. זֵכֶר *remembrance*) $42_{7(ms)}$ $143_{5}$ (if em. יוֹם *day*) Si $51_{8}$ 4QapPs$^{b}$ $33_{11}$ 4Q525 $14.2_{16}$.

אֲדֹנָי *Adonai* Is $57_{11}$ Ne $4_{8}$, אֱלֹהִים *God* Jg $8_{34}$ 2 S $14_{11}$ Is $44_{21}$ (if em. אֵלֶּה *these*) Is $57_{11}$ Ps $42_{7}$ $63_{7}$ $77_{4}$ 4QJub$^{d}$ $21_{2}$ (זכרתי ... את א[לוהינו]), בּוֹרֵא *creator* Ec $12_{1}$ (or em. בּוֹר *pit*, i.e. grave), חָכְמָה *wisdom* Si $15_{8}$.

Egypt Ezk $23_{27}$, Israel 4Q$462_{19(erased)}$ (ישׂרא), Ephraim Jr $31_{20}$, Zion Ps $137_{1}$, Jerusalem Ps $137_{6}$ 4Q$462_{19}$, עַם *people* Is $63_{11}$ (or del. עַם), בַּיִת *house* of Aaron, Israel Ps $115_{12}$, עֵדָה *congregation* Ps $74_{2}$.

Abraham Gn $19_{29}$, David 4QMMT $C_{25}$, Hannah 1 S $1_{11.19}$, appar. Jehu and Bidkar 2 K $9_{25}$, Jeremiah Jr $15_{15}$, Job Jb $14_{13}$, Joseph Gn $40_{14.23}$, Moses Is $63_{11}$ (or del. מֹשֶׁה *Moses*), Noah Gn $8_{1}$, Rachel Gn $30_{22}$, Samson Jg $16_{28}$, Vashti Est $2_{1}$.

אַדִּיר *majestic one* Na $2_{6}$ (or em. ni. *be remembered*), מֶלֶךְ *king* 4QMMT $C_{23}$, אֱנוֹשׁ *human being* Ps $8_{5}$, אִישׁ poor *man* Ec $9_{15}$, אִשָּׁה *woman* 1 S $1_{19}$, בֵּן *son* Si $16_{17}$ 4QapLam$^{b}$$_{2}$, עֶבֶד *servant* Ex $32_{13}$ Is $63_{11(mss)}$ Lachish ost. $2_{4}$ (ע[בדה]), אָמָה *female servant* 1 S $1_{11}$ $25_{31}$, עָנִי *poor one* Ps $9_{13(Kt)}$ (Qr עָנָו in same sense) GnzPs $4_{9}$, דַּל *poor one* GnzPs $4_{9}$, worshipper Ps $106_{4}$ 11QPs$^{a}$ $24_{10}$, מֵת *dead one* Si $38_{21}$, חָלָל *pierced one* Ps $88_{6}$.

חַיָּה *beast* Gn $8_{1}$, בְּהֵמָה *beast* Gn $8_{1}$, דָּגָה *fish* Nm $11_{5}$, קִשֻּׁאָה *cucumber* Nm $11_{5}$, אֲבַטִּיחַ *melon* Nm $11_{5}$, חָצִיר *leek* Nm $11_{5}$, בָּצָל *onion* Nm $11_{5}$, שׁוּם *garlic* Nm $11_{5}$.

אֶרֶץ *land* Lv $26_{42}$, צוּר *rock* Is $17_{10}$, דֶּרֶךְ *way* Dt $8_{2}$ Is $64_{4}$ (if em. בִּדְרָכֶיךָ יִזְכְּרוּךָ *they will remember you in your ways* to וּדְרָכֶיךָ יִזְכֹּרוּ *and your ways they will remember*) Ezk $16_{61}$ $20_{43}$ $36_{31}$, הֲדֹם *footstool* Lm $2_{1}$, יָד *hand* of Y. Ps $78_{42}$.

קְטֹרֶת *incense* Jr $44_{21}$, מִנְחָה *cereal offering* Ps $20_{4}$, תּוֹעֵבָה *abomination* Ezk $16_{22}$ (or del. תּוֹעֵבָה), תַּזְנוּת *fornication* Ezk $16_{22}$, מִזְבֵּחַ *altar* Jr $17_{2}$, אֲשֵׁרָה *Asherah* Jr $17_{2}$ (or em. כִּזְכֹר בְּנֵיהֶם *when their children remember* ... their Asherahs to לְזִכָּרוֹן בָּהֶם *as a memory among them; ...* their Asherahs).

בְּרִית *covenant* Gn $9_{15.16}$ Ex $2_{24}$ $6_{5}$ Lv $26_{42.42.42.45}$ perh. Jr $14_{21}$ Ezk $16_{60}$ Am $1_{9}$ Ps $105_{8}$‖1 C $16_{15}$ $106_{45}$ $111_{5}$ CD

1$_{4}$ 6$_{2}$ GnzPs 4$_{13}$ 1QPrLit 3.2$_{5}$ 4Q370 1$_{7}$ 4QDibHam$^{a}$ 1.5$_{9}$, תּוֹרָה *law* Ml 3$_{22}$ CD 15$_{2}$, מִצְוָה *commandment* Nm 15$_{39.40}$, חֹק *statute*, i.e. appointed lot Si 38$_{22}$, פִּקּוּד *precept* Ps 103$_{18}$, מִשְׁפָּט *judgment* Ps 105$_{5}$||1 C 16$_{12}$ Ps 119$_{52}$ 1QM 17$_{2}$, דָּבָר *word* Jos 1$_{13}$ Ps 105$_{8}$||1 C 16$_{15}$ Ps 105$_{42}$ 119$_{49}$ Ne 1$_{8}$ 4Q463 1$_{1}$, שֵׁם *name* Ps 119$_{55}$, מַשָּׂא *burden* of Y. Jr 23$_{36}$ (or em. hi. *mention*), חֲלוֹם *dream* Gn 42$_{9}$, נְגִינָה *music* Ps 77$_{7}$ (or שָׁנָה *year*, if אֶזְכְּרָה belongs to previous verse).

יוֹם *day* Ex 13$_{3}$ 20$_{8}$ (Sam שמר *keep*) Dt 16$_{3}$ 32$_{7}$ Is 63$_{11}$ Ezk 16$_{22.43}$ 23$_{19}$ Ps 78$_{42}$ 89$_{48}$ (if em.; see below) 137$_{7}$ 143$_{5}$ (or em. 'י *Y.*) Ec 5$_{19}$ 11$_{8}$.

רִאשׁוֹן *former (event)* Is 43$_{18}$ 46$_{9}$, אַחֲרִית *end* Is 47$_{7}$ Lm 1$_{9}$ Si 7$_{36}$ 38$_{20}$ (mg נכר hi. *recognize*), עֲלִילָה *deed* Ezk 20$_{43}$, מַעֲלָל *deed* Ezk 36$_{31}$ Ps 77$_{12(Qr)}$, מַעֲשֶׂה *deed* Si 42$_{15}$, נִפְלָא *wonder* Ps 105$_{5}$||1 C 16$_{12}$ Ne 9$_{17}$ 4Q185 1.1$_{14}$ 4Q370 2$_{7}$ 4QDibHam$^{a}$ 1.2$_{11}$, פֶּלֶא *wonder* Ps 77$_{12}$ (or em. אַדִּיר your wonder is *majestic*), מוֹפֵת *wonder* Ps 105$_{5}$||1 C 16$_{12}$ 4Q185 1.1$_{14}$.

רֹב *abundance* of loyalty, forgiveness Ps 106$_{7}$ 1QH 5$_{2}$ ([זוכרי רוב]), הָמוֹן *abundance* of mercies 1QH 5$_{2}$, גְּבוּרָה *might* GnzPs 4$_{9}$, עֹז *strength* GnzPs 4$_{9}$ 11QPs$^{a}$ 19$_{12}$, כֹּחַ *strength* 1QH 4$_{35}$, עמד inf. *standing* Jr 18$_{20}$, אֱמוּנָה *faithfulness* Ps 98$_{3}$, חֶסֶד *loyalty* Jr 2$_{2}$ Ps 25$_{6}$ 98$_{3}$ 2 C 24$_{22}$ Si 51$_{8}$ 11QPs$^{a}$ 22$_{6}$, רַחַם *compassion* Ps 25$_{6}$ Si 51$_{8}$, רחם pi. inf. *compassion* Hb 3$_{2}$, אַהֲבָה *love* Jr 2$_{2}$, מַחְמָד *desire*, i.e. desirable thing Lm 1$_{7}$.

חֶרְפָּה *reproach* Is 54$_{4}$=4QTanḥ 8$_{6}$ ([ח]רפת ... [תזכרי]) Ps 74$_{22}$ 89$_{51}$, עָמָל *toil* Pr 31$_{7}$ appar. Jb 11$_{16}$, עֳנִי *affliction* Lm 3$_{19}$ (or em. זֵכֶר the *memory* of my affliction), ענה pu. inf. *affliction* Ps 132$_{1}$ (or em. עֲנָוָה *humility*), עֶבְרוֹן *anger* Si 7$_{16}$, אָנָּה *distress* Ps 89$_{48}$ (if em.; see below), מִלְחָמָה *war* Jb 40$_{32}$, מָרוּד *homelessness* Lm 3$_{19}$ (or em. זֵכֶר *memory*), רָעָה *evil* Ho 7$_{2}$, חַטָּאת *sin* Is 43$_{25}$ Ps 25$_{7}$, עָוֹן *iniquity* Is 64$_{8}$ Jr 14$_{10}$ Ho 8$_{13}$ 9$_{9}$ Ps 79$_{8}$ 4QDibHam$^{a}$ 4$_{6}$, אַשְׁמָה *guilt* 1QH 4$_{34}$, פֶּשַׁע *sin* Ps 25$_{7}$ (or del. פשע).

זאת *this* Is 46$_{8}$ Ps 74$_{18}$ Ne 13$_{22}$, אֵלֶּה *these* Is 44$_{21}$ (or em. אֱלֹהַיִךְ *your God*) Ps 42$_{5}$ (or em. hi. *offer as token offering*), אֲשֶׁר *that which* Dt 7$_{18}$ 24$_{9}$ 25$_{17}$ Est 2$_{1.1}$ Ne 5$_{19}$, i.e. how (I walked, etc.) Dt 9$_{7}$ 2 S 19$_{20}$ 2 K 20$_{3}$||Is 38$_{3}$, מָה *what?*, i.e. that which Ps 89$_{48}$ (זְכָר־אֲנִי מֶה־חָלֶד perh. *remember what my duration is*; or em. אֲדֹנָי *O, my Lord* or מֶה־חָדֵל אָנִי *how lacking I am* or אֲנִי יְמֵי־הַחָלֶד *my distress, the days of my duration*) Mc 6$_{5}$ Lm 5$_{1}$.

<PREP> לְ of benefit, *to, for, in the favour of, against*, + worshipper Ps 25$_{7}$ 4QDibHam$^{a}$ 4$_{6}$, Israel(ites) Lv 26$_{45}$ Ps 79$_{8}$, יְהוּדִי *Judaean* Ne 13$_{29}$, אָב *father* Ps 106$_{45}$, בֵּן *son* of Edom Ps 137$_{7}$, Jerusalem Jr 2$_{2}$, David Ps 132$_{1}$, Nehemiah Ne 13$_{14.22}$, Sanballat Ne 6$_{14}$, Tobiah Ne 6$_{14}$, טוֹבָה *goodness* Ne 5$_{19}$ 13$_{31}$.

לְ introducing object or *concerning*, + worshipper Ps 25$_{7}$ 136$_{23}$, Abraham Ex 32$_{13}$ Dt 9$_{27}$, Isaac Ex 32$_{13}$ Dt 9$_{27}$, Jacob Ex 32$_{13(Sam)}$ (MT Israel) Dt 9$_{27}$, Nehemiah Ne 5$_{19}$ 13$_{31}$, עֶבֶד *servant* Dt 9$_{27}$, חֶסֶד *loyalty* 2 C 6$_{42}$, חַטָּאת *sin* Jr 31$_{34}$.

לְעוֹלָם *for ever* Ps 105$_{8}$||1 C 16$_{15}$ Ps 111$_{5}$, לָעַד *for ever* Is 64$_{8}$, לָנֶצַח *for ever* GnzPs 4$_{13}$.

בְּ of place/time, *at, in, on, among, during*, + מֶרְחָק *distant (land)* Zc 10$_{9}$, מָרוֹם *height* Si 16$_{17}$, גּוֹי *nation* Ezk 6$_{9}$, perh. מָקוֹם *place* 4QapPs$^{b}$ 33$_{11}$ ([מקו]ם), מָוֶת *death* Ps 6$_{6}$ (if em. זֵכֶר *remembrance*) 4QMidrEschat$^{b}$ 11$_{11}$ ([דברכה]), לַיְלָה *night* Ps 77$_{7}$ (unless זכר moved to previous verse) 119$_{55}$, יוֹם *day* Ec 12$_{1}$ Lm 2$_{1}$, כֹּל *every* day 4QJub$^{d}$ 21$_{2}$; perh. of instrument, *by (means of), through*, + תְּפִלָּה *prayer* Si 51$_{8}$; of accompaniment, *with, in (a state of)*, + רֹגֶז *anger* Hb 3$_{2}$, רָצוֹן *pleasure* Ps 106$_{4}$ (but perh. בְּ = *in accordance with*) 4QapPs$^{a}$ 1.1$_{9}$ ([זכ]רו), רַחֲמִים *compassion* GnzPs 4$_{9.13}$, עטף htp. inf. *faintness* Jon 2$_{8}$, מַעֲשֶׂה *deed* Si 7$_{36}$; perh. *despite*, + שֵׁפֶל *lowliness* Ps 136$_{23}$; זכר בְּ appar. *make mention of*, + אֲרוֹן *ark* Jr 3$_{16}$ (mss עוֹד *again* for בְּ)

כְּ *in accordance with*, + חֶסֶד *loyalty* Ps 25$_{7}$, מַעֲשֶׂה *deed* Ne 6$_{14}$.

מִן of direction, *from*, + אֶרֶץ *land* Ps 42$_{7}$, קֶדֶם *antiquity* Ps 77$_{12}$ (or em. אֶזְכְּרָה *I shall remember* to אַדִּיר your wonder is *majestic*), רָחוֹק *distant (place)* Jr 51$_{50}$.

עַל *on, upon*, + יָצוּעַ *bed* Ps 63$_{7}$; *concerning*, + זאת *this* Ne 13$_{14}$, גֹּאַל *defilement* Ne 13$_{29}$.

עִם *with*, i.e. by means of, + לֵבָב *heart* Ps 77$_{7}$ (unless אֶזְכְּרָה *I remember* or עִם־לְבָבִי *with my heart* belongs to previous verse), + מַעַל *unfaithfulness* 1QH 4$_{34}$, הָמוֹן *abundance* of mercies 1QH 4$_{35}$.

<COLL> וְזָכַרְתָּ כִּי־עֶבֶד הָיִיתָ *and you shall remember that you were a slave* Dt 5$_{15}$ 15$_{15}$ 16$_{12}$ 24$_{18.22}$, וּזְכַרְתֶּם

כִּי־עַצְמְכֶם וּבְשַׂרְכֶם אָנִי *and you will remember that I am your bone and your flesh* Jg $9_2$, וַיִּזְכְּרוּ כִּי־אֱלֹהִים צוּרָם *and they remembered that God was their rock* Ps $78_{35}$, וַיִּזְכֹּר כִּי־בָשָׂר הֵמָּה *and he remembered that they were flesh* Ps $78_{39}$, זְכֹר כִּי־רוּחַ חַיָּי *remember that my life is a breath* Jb $7_7$, זְכָר־נָא כִּי־כַחֹמֶר עֲשִׂיתָנִי *remember, pray, that you made me like clay* Jb $10_9$, זְכֹר כִּי־תַשְׂגִּיא פָעֳלוֹ *remember that you are to extol his work* Jb $36_{24}$.

זכר כי יש מרים ומשפיל *remember that there is one who makes high and makes low* Si $7_{11}$, זכר כי כלנו חייבים *remember that we are all guilty* Si $8_5$, זכר כי עת מות לא ינקה *remember that it will not go unpunished at the time of death* Si $9_{12}$, זכור כי לא בשאול תענוג *remember that there is no delight in Sheol* Si $14_{12}$, זכור כי רעה עין רעה *remember that an evil eye is an evil thing* Si $34_{13}$ (mg ידע *know*), ז[כו]ר כי ראשנים ואחרנים עמך *remember that former ones and latter ones are with you* Si $41_{3(B)}$ (M זכר קדמון ואחרון עמך in similar sense), זכר כלנו נאספים *remember (that) we are all to be gathered* Si $8_7$.

זכור כיא [אנחנו עצור]י עמכה *remember that we are (the) prohibited ones of your people* 4QapLam[b] 1, וזכור כי ראש אתה *and remember that you are (the) head* 4Q416 $2.3_2$.

לֹא זָכַר עֲשׂוֹת חָסֶד *he did not remember to perform (deeds of) loyalty* Ps $109_{16}$, זֹכְרֵי פִקֻּדָיו לַעֲשׂוֹתָם *those who remember his precepts to do them* Ps $103_{18}$, זְכָר־נָא מִי ... אָבָד *remember, pray: who ... has died?* Jb $4_7$.

זכר with adverb, עוֹד *again, still* Jr $3_{16(mss)}$ $31_{20.34}$ Ezk $23_{27}$ Ps $88_6$ Pr $31_7$, תָּמִיד *always* 4QJub[d] $21_2$ ([זכרתי] [תמי]ד), עַתָּה *now* Ho $8_{13}$; with inf. abs. used as adverb, הַרְבֵּה *greatly* Ec $5_{19}$.

זָכֹר אֶזְכְּרֶנּוּ *I shall indeed remember him* Jr $31_{20}$, sim. Dt $7_{18}$ Lm $3_{20}$.

זכר || הגה *meditate* Ps $63_7$ $143_5$, שׂיח *consider* Ps $77_4$ $143_5$, בין *understand* Dt $32_7$, htpol. *consider* Is $43_{18}$ 4QMMT $C_{23}$, שׂכל hi. *consider* Ps $106_7$, דשׁן pi. *regard as fat*, i.e. acceptable Ps $20_4$ (or em. דרשׁ *seek*), שׁמר *keep* Ps $103_{18}$, פקד *visit* (sometimes specif. *punish*) Jr $3_{16}$ $14_{10}$ $15_{15}$ Ho $8_{13}$ $9_9$ (or del.) Ps $8_5$ $106_4$ 4QapPs[a] $1.1_9$ ([זכ]רו).

זכר :: שׁכח *forget* Gn $40_{23}$ Dt $9_7$ 1 S $1_{11}$ Is $17_{10}$ $54_4$=4QTanḥ $8_6$ Ps $9_{13}$ $137_6$ Jb $11_{16}$, סלח *forgive* Jr $31_{34}$.

**2.** passive participle as adj., **mindful**, used predicatively of הוּא *he* (Y.) Ps $103_{14}$ (הוּא ... זָכוּר כִּי *he ... is mindful that*).

<SYN> §1 הגה *meditate*, שׂיח *consider*, בין *understand*, htpol. *consider*, שׂכל hi. *consider*, שׁמר *keep*, פקד *visit*.

<ANT> §1 שׁכח *forget*, סלח *forgive*.

**Ni.** 20.1.3 Impf. 3ms יִזָּכֵר, 3fs תִּזָּכֵר (תִּזָּכֶר), 2fs תִּזָּכְרִי, 3mpl יִזָּכְרוּ, 3fpl תִּזָּכַרְנָה (תִּזָּכַרְןָ); + waw L וְנִזְכַּרְתֶּם (mss וְנִזְכַּרְתֶּם, Q ונזכרתמה); ptc. נִזְכָּרִים; inf. הִזָּכֶרְכֶם—**be mentioned, be remembered,** <SUBJ> בַּעַל *lord*, i.e. Baal Ho $2_{19}$, אַדִּיר *majestic one* Na $2_6$ (if em. qal), עָצָב *idol* Zc $13_2$, appar. בֵּן *son* of Ammon Ezk $21_{37}$ $25_{10}$ (or Moab, if repeated בְּנֵי־עַמּוֹן *sons of Ammon* deleted), Israel(ite) Nm $10_9$=1QM $10_7$ Ezk $21_{29}$, רָשָׁע *wicked one* 4QapPs[b] $50_3$, wicked Jb $24_{20}$, זוֹנָה *prostitute* Is $23_{16}$, פֶּטֶר *firstborn* Ex $34_{19}$, מִקְנֶה *livestock* Ex $34_{19}$ (Sam mss זכר hi. you are to *mention*; or em. זָכָר *male* livestock), רָאמוֹת *coral* or *pearls* Jb $28_{18}$, גָּבִישׁ *crystal* Jb $28_{18}$, יוֹם *day* Est $9_{28}$ (|| עשׂה ni. *be done*, i.e. re-enacted), רִאשׁוֹן *first (event)* Is $65_{17}$ (+ עלה עַל־לֵב *go up upon the heart*, i.e. be considered), שֵׁם *name* Jr $11_{19}$ Na $2_6$ (if em. לֹא־יִזָּרַע מִשְּׁמְךָ עוֹד *of your name, no longer will it be sown*, i.e. you will have no more descendants, to לֹא־יִזָּכֵר עוֹד שְׁמֶךָ *no longer will your name be remembered*) Ps $83_5$, צְדָקָה *righteousness* Ezk $3_{20}$ $18_{24}$ $33_{13}$ Si $3_{15}$ (:: שׁכח ni. *be forgotten*), פֶּשַׁע *sin* Ezk $18_{22}$ 11QPs[a] $24_{11}$, עָוֹן *iniquity* Ps $109_{14}$, חַטָּאת *sin* Ezk $33_{16}$.

<PREP> לְ of benefit, *to, for, in the favour of, against*, + worshipper 11QPs[a] $24_{11}$, בֵּן *son* Si $3_{15}$, רָשָׁע *wicked one* Ezk $18_{22}$ $33_{16}$ (ms lacks לוֹ *for him*); בְּ of place, *at, among*, or of agent, *by*, + גּוֹי *nation* Ezk $25_{10}$ (or em. עַם *people*), דּוֹר *generation* Est $9_{28}$; בְּשֵׁם mention *by name* Ho $2_{19}$; אֶל *to*, i.e. by, Y. Ps $109_{14}$; לִפְנֵי *before* or *by* 4QapPs[b] $50_3$, + Y. Nm $10_9$=1QM $10_7$. <COLL> זכר ni. with adverb, עוֹד *again, still* Jr $11_{19}$ Ho $2_{19}$ Zc $13_2$ Ps $83_5$ (or del. עוֹד) Jb $24_{20}$. <SYN> עשׂה ni. *be done*, i.e. re-enacted. <ANT> שׁכח ni. *be forgotten*.*

**Hi.** 40.2.6 Pf. הִזְכִּיר; impf. יַזְכִּיר, Q תזכיר, אַזְכִּיר (אַזְכִּירָה) נַזְכִּיר, תַּזְכִּירוּ, יַזְכִּירוּ, 2mpl (אזכירך Q, אַזְכִּירָה); + waw וְהִזְכַּרְתַּנִי, impv. הַזְכִּירוּ, הַזְכִּירֵנִי; ptc. מַזְכִּיר, מַזְכִּרִים, מַזְכֶּרֶת; inf. הַזְכִּיר (הַזְכִּירוֹ)—**1. cause to remember, cause to be remembered, cause to mention, cause to be mentioned,** esp. of name of deity,

**mention** (e.g. Gn 40$_{14}$ Si 49$_{9}$), specif. **invoke** (e.g. Ps 20$_{8}$ 1 C 16$_{4}$ 4QDibHam$^{a}$ 1.3$_{4}$), **announce, proclaim** (e.g. Is 12$_{4}$ Jr 4$_{16}$).

<SUBJ> ״ *Y.* Ex 20$_{24}$ (or em. יַזְכִּיר *he will cause to be mentioned* to תַּזְכִּיר *you*, i.e. son of Israel, *will mention*) Is 49$_{1}$ appar. Ps 87$_{4}$, David Ps 38$_{1}$, Elijah 1 K 17$_{18}$, Ezekiel Si 49$_{9}$.

לֵוִי *Levite* 1 C 16$_{4}$ (מִן־הַלְוִיִּם *some of the Levites*), Israel(ite) Ex 23$_{13}$ (+ שׁמע ni. *be heard*) Jos 23$_{7}$ (+ שׁבע hi. *adjure*) Is 12$_{4}$ 26$_{13}$ 43$_{26}$ Ezk 21$_{29}$, worshipper Is 63$_{7}$ Ps 20$_{8}$ (unless זכר II hi. *display strength*; or em. גבר hi. *display strength*) 45$_{18}$ (or em. אַזְכִּירָה *I shall proclaim* to יַזְכִּירוּ *they will proclaim*) 71$_{16}$ 77$_{12(Kt)}$ (Qr qal *remember*) 87$_{4}$ 4QDibHam$^{a}$ 1.3$_{4}$ ([הז]כרנו) 11QPs$^{a}$ 22$_{1.12}$, אִישׁ *man* 1 K 17$_{18}$ Jr 23$_{36}$ (if em. qal), בַּיִת *house* of Israel Ezk 29$_{16}$.

בֵּן *son* 2 S 18$_{18}$ Ps 45$_{18}$ (if em.) Si 50$_{16}$, specif. son of Israel Ex 20$_{24}$ (if em.), נגד hi. ptc. *one who declares* Jr 4$_{16}$ (or em. זכר hi. to נגד hi. *declare* or זהר hi. *warn*; || שׁמע hi. *announce*), שׁמע hi. ptc. *one who announces* Jr 4$_{16}$, בשׂר pi. ptc. *one who announces* 1 S 4$_{18}$, שׁמר ptc. *sentry* Is 62$_{6}$, מֶלֶךְ *king* of Babylon Ezk 21$_{28}$, שַׂר *prince*, i.e. chief cup bearer Gn 40$_{14}$ 41$_{9}$ (+ הַיּוֹם *today*), mourner Am 6$_{10}$, מִנְחָה *cereal offering* Nm 5$_{15}$, אֲשֶׁר *one who* 1QS 6$_{27}$ ([א]שר), one who escapes war 4QJub$^{f}$ 23$_{21}$ ([יזכירו]), כֹּל *anyone* Is 19$_{17}$; subj. not specified, Ca 1$_{4}$ (or em. שׁכר *be drunk*) 4Q477 1$_{2}$.

<OBJ> ״ *Y.* Is 43$_{26}$ 62$_{6}$, Rahab and Babylon Ps 87$_{4}$, Zion 11QPs$^{a}$ 22$_{1.12}$, Job Si 49$_{9}$, Joseph Gn 40$_{14}$, נָבִיא *prophet* Si 49$_{9}$ (נ[ב]יא), חֵטְא *sin* Gn 41$_{9}$, עָוֹן *iniquity* Nm 5$_{15}$ 1 K 17$_{18}$ Ezk 21$_{28.29}$ 29$_{16}$, נַעֲוָיָה *offence* 4Q477 1$_{2}$, מַעֲלָל *deed* Ps 77$_{12(Kt)}$, מַשָּׂא *burden* Jr 23$_{36}$ (if em. qal), שֵׁם *name* Ex 20$_{24}$ 23$_{13}$ 2 S 18$_{18}$ Is 26$_{13}$ 49$_{1}$ Ps 45$_{18}$, דָּבָר *word* 1QS 6$_{27}$, תְּהִלָּה *praise* Is 63$_{7}$, דּוֹד *love* Ca 1$_{4}$ (or em. דּוֹד to דַּד *breast* and/or זכר hi. to שׁכר *be drunk*), חֶסֶד *loyalty* Is 63$_{7}$, צְדָקָה *righteousness* Ps 71$_{16}$, אֲרוֹן *ark* 1 S 4$_{18}$, אֲדָמָה *land* of Judah Is 19$_{17}$, הֵנָּה *these (things)* Jr 4$_{16}$ (if em. הִנֵּה *behold*).

<PREP> לְ of direction, announce *to*, + גּוֹי *nation* Jr 4$_{16}$ (or em. נגד hi. *declare* or זהר hi. *warn*); of benefit, *to, for*, + בְּרָכָה *blessing* 11QPs$^{a}$ 22$_{1.12}$; *as*, + ידע ptc. *one who knows* Y. Ps 87$_{4}$.

בְּ of place/time, *at, in, during*, + מָקוֹם *place* Ex 20$_{24}$, דּוֹר *generation* Ps 45$_{18}$; appar. of instrument, *by (means of), through*, + Y. Is 26$_{13}$ (or em. לְבַד־בְּךָ *only through you* to לְבַדְּךָ *only you*); introducing object, שֵׁם *name* Jos 23$_{7}$ Am 6$_{10}$ Ps 20$_{8}$ (unless זכר II hi. *display strength*; or em. גבר hi. *display strength*) 4QJub$^{f}$ 23$_{21}$ 4QDibHam$^{a}$ 1.3$_{4}$; בְּשֵׁם mention *by name* 1QS 6$_{27}$.

מִן of direction, *from*, + מֵעֶה *innard(s)* Is 49$_{1}$; of comparison, *more (than)*, + יַיִן *wine* Ca 1$_{4}$.

אֶל mention *to*, + פַּרְעֹה *Pharaoh* Gn 40$_{14}$, כֹּל *all*, i.e. anyone Is 19$_{17}$.

לִפְנֵי *before*, + עֶלְיוֹן *Most High* Si 50$_{16}$.

<COLL> הַזְכִּירוּ כִּי נִשְׂגָּב שְׁמוֹ *announce that his name is exalted* Is 12$_{4}$.

**2.** participle (מַזְכִּיר) as noun, **recorder,** royal functionary, <SUBJ> בוא *come* 2 K 18$_{37}$||Is 36$_{22}$ 2 C 34$_{8}$, יצא *go out* 2 K 18$_{18}$||Is 36$_{3}$, *take out* money 2 C 34$_{8}$, שׁוב *go back* 2 C 34$_{8(Qr)}$, נתן *give* money 2 C 34$_{8}$ (or em. נתך *pour* money) 34$_{8.8}$ (||2 K 22$_{6}$ lacks verb), נגד hi. *declare* 2 K 18$_{37}$||Is 36$_{22}$, חזק pi. *strengthen*, i.e. repair temple 2 C 34$_{8}$. <NOM CL> וִיהוֹשָׁפָט בֶּן־אֲחִילוּד מַזְכִּיר/הַמַּזְכִּיר *and Jehoshaphat son of Ahilud was recorder/the recorder* 2 S 8$_{16}$||20$_{24}$||1 C 18$_{15}$ 1 K 4$_{3}$ (|| סֹפֵר *scribe*). <OBJ> שׁלח *send* 2 C 34$_{8}$. <APP> יוֹאָח בֶּן־אָסָף הַמַּזְכִּיר *Joah, son of Asaph, the recorder* 2 K 18$_{18.37}$||Is 36$_{3.22}$ (both || סֹפֵר *scribe*), יוֹאָח בֶּן־יוֹאָחָז הַמַּזְכִּיר *Joah, son of Jehoahaz, the recorder* 2 C 34$_{8}$ (|| סֹפֵר).

**3. offer (as) token offering** (אַזְכָּרָה), <SUBJ> worshipper Ps 42$_{5}$ (if em. אֶזְכְּרָה *I will remember* to אַזְכִּיר *I will offer as a token offering*); subj. not specified, Is 66$_{3}$. <OBJ> לְבֹנָה *frankincense* Is 66$_{3}$, אֵלֶּה *these (things)* Ps 42$_{5}$ (if em.; see Subj.). <COLL> לְדָוִד לְהַזְכִּיר (a psalm) *of David, for offering the token offering* Ps 38$_{1}$ 70$_{1}$.

<SYN> §2 סֹפֵר *scribe*.

Also 4Q415 9$_{8}$ 4Q418 200$_{3}$ (hi.) 4QM$^{a}$ 19$_{3}$ (זכר perh. זֵכֶר *remembrance*) 4QRitMar 120$_{2}$ (זכו[ר]) 4QPrFêtes$^{c}$ 12.3$_{5}$ (זכ[ור]) 25$_{1}$ (זכ[ור]) 5Q19 2$_{1}$ (תזכ[ר]).*

⇒ זִכָּרוֹן *memorial*, אַזְכָּרָה *token offering*, זֵכֶר I *remembrance*, II *Zecher*, זַכּוּר *Zaccur*, זְכַרְיָה *Zechariah*, זְכָרִיאֵל *Zechariel*, זִכְרִי *Zichri*.

* **זכר II** $_{1}$ **be strong—Hi.** $_{1}$ Impf. נַזְכִּיר—**1. display strength,** <PREP> בְּ appar. of instrument, *by (means of),*

*through*, + שֵׁם *name* of Y. Ps $20_8$ (unless זכר I hi. *invoke*; or em. גבר hi. *be mighty*). **2. cause male to be born,** <SUBJ> Y. Is $66_9$ (if em. ילד hi. *cause to give birth*; + שׁבר hi. *bring into labour*).

*זכר **III** $_7$ vb. **boast—Qal** $_2$ Impf. יִזְכֹּר, יִזְכְּרוּ—<SUBJ> בֵּן *son* Jr $3_{16}$, <OBJ> אַדִּיר *majestic one* Na $2_6$. <PREP> בְּ *about, concerning*, + אֲרוֹן *ark* Jr $3_{16}$.

**Ni.** $_1$ Impf. יִזָּכְרוּ—<SUBJ> בַּעַל *lord*, i.e. Baal Ho $2_{19}$. <PREP> בְּ *about, concerning*, + שֵׁם *name* Ho $2_{19}$.

**Hi.** $_4$ Impf. יַזְכִּירוּ, נַזְכִּיר, 2mpl תַּזְכִּירוּ; inf. הַזְכִּיר—**boast,** <SUBJ> Israelite Jos $23_7$ (+ שׁבע hi. *adjure*), worshipper Ps $20_8$, בַּיִת *house* of Jacob Is $48_1$ (|| שׁבע hi.). <PREP> בְּ *about, concerning*, + שֵׁם *name* Jos $23_7$ Is $48_1$ Am $6_{10}$ Ps $20_8$. <SYN> שׁבע hi. *adjure*.

זָכָר $_{80.2.10}$ adj. **male**—pl. זְכָרִים—**1.** used attributively of סוּס *horse* 1QM $6_{11}$, שֶׂה *sheep* Ex $12_5$, שָׂעִיר *goat* Lv $4_{23}$, עָרֵל *uncircumcised one* Gn $17_{14}$, בְּכוֹר *firstborn* Nm $3_{40.43}$, בֵּן *son* Jos $17_2$ Jr $20_{15}$.

**2.** used predicatively or as noun (sometimes collective), of human beings (Gn $1_{27}$ $17_{10.12}$ $34_{15.22.24.25}$ Ex $12_{48}$ $13_{12}$ Lv $6_{11.22}$ $7_6$ $12_{2.7}$ $15_{33}$ $27_{3.5.6.7}$ Nm $5_3$ $18_{10}$ $31_{7.17.17.18.35}$ Jos $5_4$ Jg $21_{11.12}$ 1 K $11_{15.16}$ Is $66_7$ Jr $30_6$ Ezr $8_{3+11t.}$ Si $36_{26}$ $42_{12}$ CD $4_{21}$ $5_9$ 1QSa $1_{10}$ 4QSD $7.2_{14}$ 4QDa $9.2_5$ 4QTohA $1.1_7$ 6QD $5_3$), beasts (Gn $6_{19}$ $7_{3.9.16}$ Ex $13_{12}$), esp. sacrificial beasts (Ex $13_{15}$ Lv $1_{3.10}$ $3_{1.6}$ $22_{19}$ Dt $15_{19}$=11QT $52_8$ Ml $1_{14}$ 11QT $60_2$), gods (Dt $4_{16}$ perh. Ezk $16_{17}$).

<SUBJ> היה *be* Gn $6_{19}$ Nm $26_{62}$, מול ni. *be circumcised* Gn $17_{10.12}$ $34_{15.22.24}$ Ex $12_{48}$, יחשׂ htp. *be genealogically enrolled* Ezr $8_{3+11t}$, פקד hotp. *be mustered* Nm $26_{62}$, אכל *eat* Lv $6_{11.22}$ $7_6$ Nm $18_{10}$, ילד *give birth* Jr $30_6$ (+ גֶּבֶר *man*), עשׂה *do* Ex $12_{48}$, בוא *come* Gn $7_{9.16}$, קרב *approach* Ex $12_{48}$, מות *die* Lv $20_{13}$ Jos $5_4$.

<NOM CL> אִם־זָכָר *if it is a male* Lv $3_1$ $27_7$ 4QTohA $1.1_7$, לִי ... הַזָּכָר *to me ... is the male* Ex $34_{19}$ (if em. תִּזָּכֵר appar. *it shall be remembered*), הַזְּכָרִים לי׳ *the males are*, i.e. belong to, *Y.* Ex $13_{12}$ (or ins. קדשׁ hi. *consecrate* males to Y.), לִרְצֹנְכֶם ... זָכָר *for your acceptance ... is (required) a male* Lv $22_{19}$, כָּל־זָכָר לְגֻלְגְּלֹתָם *all males will be (counted) according to their skulls* Nm $1_{2.20(Sam)}$, פְּקֻדָיו ... כָּל־זָכָר *his mustered ones ... were all males* Nm $1_{22}$, כָּל־זָכָר ... שְׁנַיִם וְעֶשְׂרִים אֶלֶף *all (the) males ... were two hundred and twenty thousand* Nm $3_{39}$, יֵשׁ בְּעֶדְרוֹ זָכָר *there is a male in his flock* Ml $1_{14}$ (or em. זַכָּה *pure one*), וְעִמּוֹ מָאתַיִם הַזְּכָרִים *and with him two hundred were*, i.e. numbered, *the males* Ezr $8_4$, sim. $8_5$ (300) $8_6$ (50) $8_7$ (70) $8_8$ (80) $8_9$ (218) $8_{10}$ (160) $8_{11}$ (28) $8_{12}$ (110) $8_{13}$ (60) $8_{14}$ (70).

<OBJ> ברא *create* human beings as Gn $1_{27}$ $5_2$ CD $4_{21}$, עשׂה *make* human beings as 4QJuba $2_{14}$ ([עשה]), ילד *give birth (to)* Lv $12_2$ 4QSD $7.2_{14}$ ([ילדה זכר]) 4QDa $9.2_5$, מלט hi. *be delivered (of), give birth (to)* Is $66_7$, חיה hi. *keep alive* Gn $6_{19(Sam)}$, פקד *count* Nm $3_{15}$, קבל pi. *receive*, i.e. accept in marriage Si $36_{26}$, לקח *take* Gn $7_3$ $17_{23}$, קדשׁ hi. *consecrate* Ex $13_{12}$ (if ins. קדשׁ hi.) Dt $15_{19}$=11QT $52_8$, קרב hi. *bring near* in sacrifice Lv $1_{3.10}$ $3_6$, נכה hi. *strike* 1 K $11_{15}$, הרג *kill* Gn $34_{25}$ Nm $31_{7.17}$, כרת hi. *cut off* 1 K $11_{16}$, חרם hi. *put to ban* Jg $21_{11}$.

<CSTR> צַלְמֵי זָכָר *images of a male* Ezk $16_{17}$, תַּבְנִית זָכָר *image of a male* Dt $4_{16}$, מִשְׁכַּב זָכָר *lying down of*, i.e. intercourse with, *a male* Nm $31_{17.18.35}$ Jg $21_{11.12}$ 1QSa $1_{10}$ (משכבי זכר), כָּל־פֶּטֶר רֶחֶם הַזְּכָרִים *any that first breaches the womb of*, i.e. from among, *the males* Ex $13_{15}$, כָּל־זָכָר *every male* Gn $17_{10.12.23}$ $34_{15.22.24.25}$ Ex $12_{48}$ Lv $6_{11.22}$ $7_6$ Nm $1_{2.20.22}$ $3_{15.22.28.34}$ (all three + מִסְפַּר *number of* every male) $3_{39}$ $18_{10}$ $26_{62}$ $31_{7.17}$ Jg $21_{11}$ 1 K $11_{15.16}$ 2 C $31_{19}$ Si $36_{26}$ (כ[ל] [ז]כר) $42_{12}$.

<APP> אִישׁ *man* Jos $5_4$, עַם *people* Jos $5_4$, בֵּן *son* Gn $17_{12}$, יָלִיד *one who is born* Gn $17_{12.23}$, פקד pass. ptc. *one who is mustered* Nm $3_{39}$ $26_{62}$, מִקְנָה *purchase* Gn $17_{12.23}$, קָרְבָּן *offering* Lv $3_6$ $4_{23}$, יצא ptc. *one who goes out* Gn $34_{24}$, שְׁנַיִם *two* Gn $7_9$.

<ADJ> תָּמִים *perfect* (unless noun *perfect one*, in app. to זָכָר) Ex $12_5$ Lv $1_{3.10}$ $4_{23}$ $22_{19}$.

<PREP> לְ of direction, *to*, + נתן *give* 2 C $31_{19}$ Si $42_{12(B)}$, ni. *be given* Nm $26_{62}$; *concerning*, + כתב pass. *be written* CD $5_9$; appar. *among*, + יחשׂ htp. *be genealogically enrolled* Ezr $8_3$, זוב *flow*, i.e. have discharge Lv $15_{33}$; introducing object, + ילד *give birth* Lv $12_7$; בין לְ hi. *explain to* Si $42_{12(M)}$; מִן partitive, *from among*, + שׁלח pi. *send away* Nm $5_3$; אֵת *with*, + שׁכב *lie down* Lv $18_{22}$ $20_{13}$; עִם *with*, + שׁכב *lie down* 6QD $5_3$ ([ישכב ... עם]).

<COLL> זָכָר :: נְקֵבָה *female* Gn $1_{27}$ $5_{2}$ $6_{19}$ $7_{3.9.16}$ Lv $3_{1.6}$ $12_{7}$ $15_{33}$ $27_{3.5.6.7}$ Nm $5_{3}$ Dt $4_{16}$ CD $4_{21}$ 4QJub$^{a}$ $2_{14}$ (נק[בה]) 4QTohA $1.1_{7}$, זָכָר + אִשָּׁה *woman* Jg $21_{11}$ Lv $18_{22}$ $20_{13}$ Si $36_{26}$ $42_{12}$.

וְהָיָה עֶרְכְּךָ הַזָּכָר *and your valuation shall be (of) the male* Lv $27_{3.5.6}$.

<ANT> נְקֵבָה *female.**

⇒ זָכוּר *male.*

**זֵכֶר** I $_{23.10.8}$ n.m. **remembrance**—cstr. זֵכֶר; sf. זִכְרִי, זִכְרְךָ (זִכְרֶךָ, Q זכרכה), זִכְרוֹ, זִכְרָם—**(act of) remembrance; memory** (i.e. what is remembered about someone or something), **memorial,** of remembrance, etc. of Y. Ex $3_{15}$ (∥ שֵׁם *name*) Is $26_{8}$ (∥ שֵׁם) Ps $6_{6}$ $30_{5}$ $97_{12}$ $102_{13}$ $135_{13}$ (∥ שֵׁם) $145_{7}$ Ho $12_{6}$ Ps $111_{4}$ GnzPs $4_{10}$ 1QM $13_{8}$ 11QPs$^{a}$ $22_{2}$, of human beings Dt $32_{26}$ Jr $17_{2}$ (if em.; see Prep.) Ho $14_{8}$ Ps $109_{15}$ Si $10_{17}$ 4QJub$^{df}$ $21_{22}$ (∥ שֵׁם) 4Q416 $2.3_{7}$, specif. of evil persons Ps $9_{7}$ $34_{17}$ Jb $18_{17}$ (+ שֵׁם) Si $47_{23}$, specif. of good persons Ps $112_{6}$ Pr $10_{7}$ (+ שֵׁם) Si $44_{9.13(B)}$ $46_{11}$, specif. of Amalek Ex $17_{14}$ Dt $25_{19}$ 4QpGen$^{a}$ $1.4_{2}$, Josiah Si $49_{1}$, Moses Si $45_{1}$, Nehemiah Si $49_{13}$, of the dead Is $26_{14}$ Ec $9_{5}$ Si $38_{20.23}$, of death Si $41_{1(M)}$, of affliction Lm $3_{19}$ (if em.; see Nom. Cl.), of days of Purim Est $9_{28}$.

<SUBJ> היה *be* Si $46_{11}$ $47_{23}$ 1QM $13_{8}$, עמד *stand,* i.e. continue Si $44_{13(B)}$ (M זֶרַע *seed*), אדר ni. *be majestic* Si $49_{13}$, ברך pass. *be blessed* 11QPs$^{a}$ $22_{2}$, מתק hi. *be sweet* Si $49_{1}$, נחל *inherit* 4Q416 $2.3_{7}$ (+ אַחֲרִית *posterity*), אבד *die* Ps $9_{7}$ (or em. pi. *destroy* remembrance) Jb $18_{17}$ 4QJub$^{df}$ $21_{22}$, כרת ni. *be cut off* Ps $109_{15(mss)}$, שׁכח ni. *be forgotten* Ec $9_{5}$, סוף *be ended* Est $9_{28}$, שׁבת *cease* Si $10_{17}$ $38_{23}$.

<NOM CL> זֶה זִכְרִי *this is my memorial* Ex $3_{15}$, י׳ זִכְרוֹ *Y. is his memorial* Ho $12_{6}$, זֵכֶר־עָנְיִי וּמְרוּדִי לַעֲנָה וָרֹאשׁ *the memory of my affliction and homelessness is wormwood and gall* Lm $3_{19}$ (if em. זְכָר־ *remember*), זִכְרוֹ כְּיֵין לְבָנוֹן *his memorial is as the wine of Lebanon* Ho $14_{8}$, אֵין בַּמָּוֶת זִכְרֶךָ *there is no remembrance of you in death* Ps $6_{6}$ (or em. זֹכְרֶיךָ *those who remember you*), זִכְרְךָ לְדֹר וָדֹר *your reputation is from generation to generation* Ps $102_{13}$ (mss כִּסְאֲךָ *your throne*) $135_{13}$, זֵכֶר צַדִּיק לִבְרָכָה *the memory of the righteous is for a blessing* Pr $10_{7}$, אין לו זכר *there is no memory of him* Si $44_{9}$, זכרו לטובה *his memory is for good* Si $45_{1}$, [מה מר ז]כרך *how bitter is the memory of you* Si $41_{1(M\ [Yadin])}$.

<OBJ> עשׂה *do,* i.e. make reputation Ps $111_{4}$, נבע hi. *pour out,* i.e. declare Ps $145_{7}$ (+ צְדָקָה *righteousness*), ברך pi. *bless* GnzPs $4_{10}$, פרע *let go* Si $38_{20}$, מחה *wipe out* Ex $17_{14}$ Dt $25_{19}$ 4QpGen$^{a}$ $1.4_{2}$, שׁבת hi. *cause to cease* Dt $32_{26}$, אבד pi. *destroy* Is $26_{14}$ (1QIsa$^{a}$ אסר pi. perh. *forbid*) Ps $9_{7}$ (if em.; see Subj.), כרת hi. *cut off* Ps $34_{17}$ $109_{15}$.

<CSTR> זֵכֶר קָדְשׁוֹ *name of his holiness,* i.e. his holy name Ps $30_{5}$ $97_{12}$, זכר קדושים *remembrance of holy ones* 4QMyst$^{a}$ $70_{3}$ (unless זכר *remember*), [היות]כה *of your being* 1QM $13_{8}$, זֵכֶר רַב־טוּבְךָ *remembrance of the greatness of your goodness* Ps $145_{7}$ (or em. רָב־ *of the abundance of*), צַדִּיק *of the righteous* Pr $10_{7}$, עֲמָלֵק *of Amalek* Ex $17_{14}$ Dt $25_{19}$ 4QpGen$^{a}$ $1.4_{2}$, עוֹלָם *of eternity* Ps $112_{6}$, עָנְיִי וּמְרוּדִי *of my affliction and homelessness* Lm $3_{19}$ (if em.; see Nom. Cl.); תבנית זכר *pattern of memorial* 4QMyst$^{c}$ $2_{5}$, כָּל־זֵכֶר *all remembrance* Is $26_{14}$.

<PREP> לְ of direction, *to(wards),* לְזִכְרְךָ תַּאֲוַת־נָפֶשׁ *a soul's desire is towards the remembrance of you* Is $26_{8}$ (1QIsa$^{a}$ תורה towards your *law*); *as* 4QMyst$^{a}$ $70_{3}$, + היה *be* Ps $112_{6}$, כתב pass. *be written* Jr $17_{2}$ (if em. כִּזְכֹּר בְּנֵיהֶם: *when their sons remember* to : לְזֵכֶר בָּהֶם *as a memorial against them*); introducing object, + ידה hi. *give thanks* Ps $30_{5}$ $97_{12}$.

<SYN> שֵׁם *name.**

⇒ זכר *remember.*

**[זֵכֶר]** II $_{1}$ pr.n.m. **Zecher**—זֶכֶר—Benjaminite, son of Jeiel and Maacah, appar. ident. with Zechariah at 1 C $9_{37}$, <NOM CL> בְּנוֹ הַבְּכוֹר עַבְדּוֹן ... וָזָכֶר *his firstborn son was Abdon ... then Zecher* 1 C $8_{31}$.

⇒ זכר *remember.*

**זִכָּרוֹן** $_{24.2.29}$ n.m. **memorial**—זִכְרוֹן, זִכָּרֹן (Ec $1_{11}$ $2_{16}$); cstr. זִכְרוֹן; sf. זִכְרוֹנֵךְ; pl. זִכְרֹנוֹת; sf. זִכְרֹנֵיכֶם—**1.** usu. **memorial,** in ref. to written records (Ex $17_{14}$ Jr $17_{2}$ [if em.; see Prep.] Mal $3_{16}$ Ne $2_{20}$ Est $6_{1}$ CD $20_{19}$ 1QH $1_{24}$ 4Q417 $2.1_{14.15.16}$ 4QpGen$^{b}$ $4.1_{2}$), stones in Jordan (Jos $4_{7}$), stones of ephod (Ex $28_{12}$∥$39_{7}$ $28_{29}$ Si $45_{11}$), crowns

(Zc 6$_{14}$), gold (Nm 31$_{54}$), silver (Ex 30$_{16}$), plating on altar (Nm 17$_{5}$), trumpets (Nm 10$_{10}$), days of remembrance (Ex 12$_{14}$ Lv 23$_{24}$=11QT 25$_{3}$ 11QT 27$_{5.9}$), symbol (Is 57$_{8}$). **2. (act of) remembering** (Ec 1$_{11.11}$ 2$_{16}$). **3. (act of) reminding** (Jb 13$_{12}$).

<SUBJ> היה *be* Lv 23$_{24}$=11QT 25$_{3}$ ([יהיה]) Ec 1$_{11}$.

<NOM CL> זִכְרֹנֵיכֶם מִשְׁלֵי־אֵפֶר *your reminders are proverbs of ashes* Jb 13$_{12}$, לָכֶם אֵין־חֵלֶק וּצְדָקָה וְזִכָּרוֹן בִּירוּשָׁלִָם *you have no portion or right or memorial,* i.e. documented authority, *in Jerusalem* Ne 2$_{20}$, אֵין זִכְרוֹן לָרִאשֹׁנִים *there is no remembrance of former (things)* Ec 1$_{11}$, sim. 2$_{16}$ (לֶחָכָם *of the sage*).

<OBJ> בוא hi. *bring* Nm 31$_{54}$, שׂים *place* on door Is 57$_{8}$, עשׂה *make* 4QOrd$^{b}$ 3$_{3}$, רקע pi. *beat* Nm 17$_{5}$, כתב *write* Ex 17$_{14}$ 1QM 3$_{7}$.

<CSTR> זִכְרוֹן תְּרוּעָה *memorial of,* i.e. marked by, *(trumpet) blast* Lv 23$_{24}$=11QT 25$_{3}$, זכרון ניחו[ח] *memorial of soothing* 4QRitPur 29.7$_{10}$, נקם *of vengeance* 1QM 3$_{7}$, [הע]ת *of the time* 4Q417 2.1$_{14}$; אַבְנֵי זִכָּרֹן *stones of remembrance* Ex 28$_{12}$||39$_{7}$ (זִכָּרוֹן), מִנְחַת זִכָּרוֹן *cereal offering of remembrance* Nm 5$_{15.18}$ (הַזִּכָּרוֹן), יום הזכרון *the day of memorial* 4QS$^{e}$ 8$_{4}$ ([יום הזכר]ון) 4QMishA 4.3$_{6}$ 4.4$_{2}$ ([הזכ]רון) 4.4$_{11}$ ([יום הזכרון]) 4.5$_{5.14}$ 4.6$_{9}$ (both יום] [הזכרון) 4QMishB$^{a}$ 2.2$_{2.6}$ (י[ום]) 2.3$_{1}$ ([י]ום [הזכרון]) 2.3$_{5}$ ([יום הזכרו]ן) 2.3$_{9}$ ([י]ום [הזכרון]) 2.4$_{4}$ ([יום הזכרון]) 4Q MMT A 2$_{16}$ 4Q409 1.1$_{5}$ (both זכרון) 11QT 11$_{13}$ ([יום [הזכרון), סֵפֶר זִכָּרוֹן *book of remembrance* Ml 3$_{16}$ CD 20$_{19}$ 4Q417 2.1$_{15.16}$ 4QpGen$^{b}$ 4.1$_{2}$ ([זכרון]), סֵפֶר הַזִּכְרֹנוֹת *the book of remembrances* Est 6$_{1}$ (+ דִּבְרֵי הַיָּמִים *events of the days,* i.e. chronicles), חרת זכרון *ink of remembrance* 1QH 1$_{24}$, חצוצרות הזכרון *trumpets of the memorial* 1QM 7$_{12}$ 16$_{3}$ 18$_{4}$ ([חצוצר]ות) 4QM$^{c}$ 2.

<APP> שַׁבָּתוֹן *sabbath observance* Lv 23$_{24}$=11QT 25$_{3}$ perh. 11QT$^{b}$ 10$_{5}$, מִקְרָא *convocation* Lv 23$_{24}$=11QT 25$_{3}$ perh. 11QT$^{b}$ 10$_{5}$, זָהָב *gold* Nm 31$_{54}$.

<ADJ> זֹאת *this* Ex 17$_{14}$.

<PREP> לְ *as* Si 45$_{11}$ 1QS 10$_{5}$ (+ אוֹת *sign*) 4QMyst$^{a}$ 75$_{7}$ 4Q448 2$_{8}$ 4QPrFêtes$^{b}$ 32$_{3}$ ([לזכרו]ן) 11QPs$^{a}$ 17$_{17}$ (||Ps 145$_{21}$ lacks זִכָּרוֹן) 11QT 10$_{5}$ 19$_{9}$ 39$_{9}$, + היה *be* Ex 12$_{14}$ 13$_{9}$ (|| אוֹת *sign*) 30$_{16}$ Nm 10$_{10}$ Jos 4$_{7}$ Zc 6$_{14}$ 11QT 27$_{5}$, שׁמע hi. *cause to hear* voice Si 45$_{9}$, קדשׁ pi. *consecrate* 11QT 27$_{9}$, נשׂא *raise,* i.e. wear Ex 28$_{12.29}$, כתב pass. *be written* Jr 17$_{2}$ (if em. כִּזְכֹּר בְּנֵיהֶם *when their sons remember* to לְזִכָּרוֹן בָּהֶם: *as a memorial against them*); בְּ perh. *in comparison with,* + בין hi. *understand* deeds 4Q417 2.1$_{14}$.

<COLL> זִכָּרוֹן לִבְנֵי יִשְׂרָאֵל *a memorial to the sons of Israel* Ex 28$_{12}$||39$_{7}$ Nm 17$_{5}$ 31$_{54}$ Jos 4$_{7}$, זִכָּרוֹן לִפְנֵי י׳ אֱלֹהֵיכֶם *a memorial before Y. your God* Ex 28$_{29}$ Nm 10$_{10}$, זִכָּרוֹן בֵּין עֵינֶיךָ *a memorial between your eyes* Ex 13$_{9}$.

<SYN> אוֹת *sign.**

⇒ זכר *remember.*

**זִכְרִי** 12.0.0.1 pr.n.m. **Zichri, 1.** Levite, son of Izhar, and grandson of Kohath, <NOM CL> בְּנֵי יִצְהָר קֹרַח וָנֶפֶג וְזִכְרִי *the sons of Izhar were Korah and Nepheg and Zichri* Ex 6$_{21}$. **2.** head of priestly family at time of Joiakim, <NOM CL> לַאֲבִיָּה זִכְרִי *(belonging) to Abijah was Zichri* Ne 12$_{17}$. **3.** Benjaminite, son of Shimei/Shema, <NOM CL> זִכְרִי וְזַבְדִּי ... בְּנֵי שִׁמְעִי: *Zichri and Zabdi ... were the sons of Shimei* 1 C 8$_{19}$. **4.** Benjaminite, son of Shashak, <NOM CL> זִכְרִי וְחָנָן ... בְּנֵי שָׁשָׁק: *Zichri and Hanan ... were the sons of Shashak* 1 C 8$_{23}$ (or em. זַבְדִּי *Zabdi*). **5.** Benjaminite, son of Jeroham (or em. Jeremoth), <NOM CL> אֵלִיָּה וְזִכְרִי בְּנֵי יְרֹחָם *Elijah and Zichri were the sons of Jeroham* 1 C 8$_{27}$. **6.** treasury official at time of David, <NOM CL> זִכְרִי בְנוֹ *Zichri was his* (Eliezer's) *son* 1 C 26$_{25}$. **7.** Ephraimite warrior at time of Ahaz and Pekah, <SUBJ> הרג *kill* 2 C 28$_{7}$. <APP> גִּבּוֹר *mighty one* 2 C 28$_{7}$. **8.** Benjaminite, father of Joel, <CSTR> בֶּן־זִכְרִי *son of Zichri* Ne 11$_{9}$. **9.** Levite, son of Asaph and father of Micha, appar. ident. with Zabdi at ||Ne 11$_{17}$, <CSTR> בֶּן־זִכְרִי *son of Zichri* 1 C 9$_{15}$ (mss זַבְדִּי *Zabdi*). <APP> בֵּן *son* 1 C 9$_{15}$. **10.** Reubenite, father of military commander (נָגִיד) at time of David, <CSTR> בֶּן־זִכְרִי Eliezer *son of Zichri* 1 C 27$_{16}$. **11.** Judahite, father of military leader (שַׂר אֶלֶף *captain of a thousand*) at time of Jehoshaphat, <CSTR> בֶּן־זִכְרִי Amasiah *son of Zichri* 2 C 17$_{16}$. **12.** father of military commander (שַׂר מֵאָה *captain of a hundred*) at time of Athaliah, <CSTR> בֶּן־זִכְרִי Elishaphat *son of Zichri* 2 C 23$_{1}$. **13.** father of Igal, <CSTR> בן זכרי *son of Zichri* Seal 309 (6th/5th cent.).

⇒ זכר *remember.*

**[זְכַרְיָאֵל]** 0.0.1 pr.n. **Zechariel,** name in writing

exercise, 4Q341$_9$.
⇒ זכר *remember*.

**זְכַרְיָה** 41.0.5.5 pr.n.m. **Zechariah**—זְכַרְיָהוּ, I זכריו—**1.** prophet, son of Berechiah, Zc $1_{1.7}$ $7_{1.8}$ CD $19_7$ 4QpIsa$^c$ $8_8$ 4QMidrEschat$^b$ $9_2$, <SUBJ> אמר *say* Zc $1_1$ (+ 23t in Zc), ראה *see* $1_7$ (+ 11t in Zc), לקח *take* $1_7$, נשׂא *raise* $1_7$, ידע *know* $1_7$, רעה *tend (beasts)* $7_8$, ענה *reply* $1_7$, קרא *call* $1_7$, בוא *come* $1_7$, שׁוב *go back* $1_7$, שׁלך hi. *throw* $7_8$, גדע *hew* $7_8$, עשׂה *do* $1_7$, שׁמע *hear* $1_7$, שׂים *place* $1_7$, כחד hi. *efface* $7_8$, פרר hi. *break* $7_8$, כרת *cut*, i.e. make covenant $7_8$, יקר *be precious* $7_8$. <OBJ> ראה hi. *show* Zc $1_7$, שׁמר *watch* $7_8$, עור hi. *rouse* $1_7$, בחל *abhor* $7_8$. <CSTR> ספר זכריה *book of Zechariah* 4QpIsa$^c$ $8_8$ 4QMidrEschat$^b$ $9_2$ ([זכריה]). <APP> בֵּן *son* Zc $1_{1.7}$, נָבִיא *prophet* Zc $1_{1.7}$ CD $19_7$ 4QMidrEschat$^b$ $9_2$. <PREP> בְּ *to, with*, + דבר pi. *speak* Zc $1_7$; אֶל *to*, + היה *be* Zc $1_1$, אמר *say* Zc $1_7$, דבר pi. *speak* Zc $1_7$, שׁלח *send* Zc $1_7$; אֵת *with, to*, + זעק *cry out* Zc $1_7$; בְּיַד speak *through* CD $19_7$.

**2.** king of Israel, son and successor of Jeroboam, <SUBJ> מלך *rule* 2 K $14_{29}$ $15_8$ (זְכַרְיָהוּ), עשׂה *do* 2 K $15_8$, סור *depart* 2 K $15_8$. <OBJ> נכה hi. *strike* 2 K $15_8$, מות hi. *kill* 2 K $15_8$. <CSTR> דִּבְרֵי זְכַרְיָה *words (in respect) of Zechariah* 2 K $15_{11}$. <APP> בֵּן *son* 2 K $14_{29}$ $15_8$. <PREP> עַל *against*, + קשׁר *plot* 2 K $15_8$; תַּחַת *instead of*, + מלך *rule* 2 K $15_8$.

**3.** father of Abi(jah) the mother of Hezekiah, <CSTR> בַּת־זְכַרְיָה *daughter of Zechariah* 2 K $18_2$ 2 C $29_1$ (זְכַרְיָהוּ).

**4.** son of Jehoshaphat and brother of Jehoram, <APP> בֵּן *son* 2 C $21_2$, אָח *brother* 2 C $21_2$.

**5.** son of Jehoiada the priest, murdered after prophesying against Judah, <SUBJ> מות *die* 2 C $24_{20}$, עמד *stand* 2 C $24_{20}$, אמר *say* 2 C $24_{20.20}$. <OBJ> לבשׁ *clothe*, i.e. take possession of 2 C $24_{20}$, רגם *stone* 2 C $24_{20}$, הרג *kill* 2 C $24_{20}$. <APP> בֵּן *son* 2 C $24_{20}$. <PREP> עַל *against*, + קשׁר *plot* 2 C $24_{20}$.

**6.** priest and trumpet player in procession of ark to Jerusalem in time of David, <SUBJ> חצר pi. *sound (trumpet)* 1 C $15_{24(Qr)}$. <APP> כֹּהֵן *priest* 1 C $15_{24}$.

**7.** priest, son of Pashhur, and father of Amzi, <CSTR> בֶּן־זְכַרְיָה *son of Zechariah* Ne $11_{12}$. <APP> בֵּן *son* Ne $11_{12}$.

**8.** priest and family head at time of Joiakim, <NOM CL> לְעִדּוֹא זְכַרְיָה *(belonging) to Iddo was Zechariah* Ne $12_{16(Qr)}$ (Kt appar. Adaia).

**9.** priest of Dor, <APP> כֹּהֵן *priest* Seal 323. <PREP> לְ of possession, *of, (belonging) to* Seal 323 (לז]כריו]).

**10.** Asaph's deputy as senior levitical musician at time of David, <NOM CL> עִמָּהֶם ... זְכַרְיָהוּ *with them were ... Zechariah* 1 C $15_{18}$, זְכַרְיָה וַעֲזִיאֵל ... בִּנְבָלִים *Zechariah and Aziel ... were on harps* 1 C $15_{20}$, מִשְׁנֵהוּ זְכַרְיָה *second to him was Zechariah* 1 C $16_5$. <APP> אָח *brother* 1 C $15_{18}$, perh. שֹׁעֵר *gatekeeper* 1 C $15_{18}$.

**11.** Levite, descendant of Asaph at time of Hezekiah, <SUBJ> בוא *come* 2 C $29_{13}$, קום *arise* 2 C $29_{13}$, אסף *gather* brothers 2 C $29_{13}$, קדשׁ htp. *sanctify oneself* 2 C $29_{13}$, טהר pi. *cleanse* temple 2 C $29_{13}$. <NOM CL> מִן־בְּנֵי אָסָף זְכַרְיָהוּ וּמַתַּנְיָהוּ *of the sons of Asaph were Zechariah and Mattaniah* 2 C $29_{13}$.

**12.** Levite at time of David, <SUBJ> נפל hi. *cause to fall*, i.e. cast lots 1 C $24_{25}$. <NOM CL> לִבְנֵי יִשִּׁיָּה זְכַרְיָהוּ *of the sons of Isshiah was Zechariah* 1 C $24_{25}$.

**13.** Levite, son of Benaiah, and father of Jahaziel, <CSTR> בֶּן־זְכַרְיָהוּ *son of Zechariah* 2 C $20_{14}$. <APP> בֵּן *son* 2 C $20_{14}$.

**14.** Asaphite, temple musician, son of Jonathan, <SUBJ> הלך *go* Ne $12_{35}$ (unless וּמִבְּנֵי הַכֹּהֲנִים בַּחֲצֹצְרוֹת *and of the sons of the priests with trumpets* belongs with v. 34), עמד *stand* Ne $12_{41}$. <APP> כֹּהֵן *priest* Ne $12_{41}$, בֵּן *son* Ne $12_{35}$. <PREP> לִפְנֵי *before* Ne $12_{35}$.

**15.** gatekeeper at tent of meeting at time of David and son of Meshelemiah (or em. Meshullam at 1 C $9_{21}$), <SUBJ> יעץ *advise* 1 C $26_{14}$. <NOM CL> זְכַרְיָה ... שֹׁעֵר *Zechariah ... was gatekeeper* 1 C $9_{21}$, זְכַרְיָהוּ הַבְּכוֹר *Zechariah was the firstborn* 1 C $26_2$. <APP> בֵּן *son* 1 C $9_{21}$ $26_{14}$. <PREP> לְ of benefit, *to, for*, + נפל hi. *cause to fall*, i.e. cast lots 1 C $26_{14}$ (if ins. לְ).

**16.** Merarite, son of Hosah and gatekeeper at time of David, <NOM CL> זְכַרְיָהוּ הָרְבִעִי *Zechariah was the fourth* 1 C $26_{11}$.

**17.** Kohathite overseer of repairs to temple at time of Josiah, <SUBJ> פקד ho. *be appointed* 2 C $34_{12}$, נצח pi. *supervise* 2 C $34_{12}$.

**18.** official sent by Jehoshaphat to teach the law in

Judah, <SUBJ> למד pi. *teach* 2 C 17$_{7.7.7}$, סבב *go around* 2 C 17$_{7}$. <APP> שַׂר *prince* 2 C 17$_{7}$. <PREP> לְ introducing object, + שׁלח *send* 2 C 17$_{7}$; עִם *with* 2 C 17$_{7.7.7}$.

**19.** teacher of Uzziah, <SUBJ> בין hi. *(cause to) understand* 2 C 26$_{5}$. <CSTR> יְמֵי זְכַרְיָהוּ *days of Zechariah* 2 C 26$_{5}$.

**20.** official of Josiah, <SUBJ> נתן *give* 2 C 35$_{8}$ (זְכַרְיָהוּ). <APP> נָגִיד *prince* 2 C 35$_{8}$.

**21.** envoy from Ezra, <SUBJ> בוא hi. *bring* Ezr 8$_{16}$, דבר pi. *speak* Ezr 8$_{16}$. <OBJ> צוה pi. *command* Ezr 8$_{16}$. <APP> רֹאשׁ *head* Ezr 8$_{16}$ (or em. אִישׁ *man*). <PREP> שׁלח לְ appar. *send for* Ezr 8$_{16}$.

**22.** family head of exiles returning with Ezra, descendant of Parosh, <NOM CL> מִבְּנֵי פַרְעֹשׁ זְכַרְיָה *of the sons of Parosh was Zechariah* Ezr 8$_{3}$. <PREP> עִם *together with*, + יחשׂ htp. *be genealogically enrolled* Ezr 8$_{3}$.

**23.** family head of exiles returning with Ezra, descendant of Bebai, <NOM CL> מִבְּנֵי בֵבַי זְכַרְיָה *of the sons of Bebai was Zechariah* Ezr 8$_{11}$. <APP> בֵּן *son* Ezr 8$_{11}$. <PREP> עִם *with* Ezr 8$_{11}$.

**24.** Israelite husband of foreign wife, descendant of Elam, <NOM CL> מִבְּנֵי עֵילָם ... זְכַרְיָה *of the sons of Elam were ... Zechariah* Ezr 10$_{26}$.

**25.** Benjaminite, son of Jeiel and Maacah, appar. ident. with Zecher at 1 C 8$_{31}$, <NOM CL> בְּנוֹ הַבְּכוֹר עַבְדּוֹן ... וּזְכַרְיָה *his firstborn son was Abdon ... then Zechariah* 1 C 9$_{37}$.

**26.** Judahite, son of Amariah, father of Uzziah, <CSTR> בֶּן־זְכַרְיָה *son of Zechariah* Ne 11$_{4}$. <APP> בֵּן *son* Ne 11$_{4}$.

**27.** Judahite, son of Shilohite father (or em. בֶּן־הַשִּׁלֹנִי *son of the Shilonite* to מִן־הַשֵּׁלָנִי *of the Shelanite*), ancestor of Maaseiah, family head in postexilic Jerusalem, <CSTR> בֶּן־זְכַרְיָה *son of Zechariah* Ne 11$_{5}$. <APP> בֵּן *son* Ne 11$_{5}$ (or em.).

**28.** contemporary of Isaiah, son of Jeberechiah, <OBJ> עוד hi. *call as witness* Is 8$_{2}$ (זְכַרְיָהוּ; + Uriah the priest). <APP> בֵּן *son* Is 8$_{2}$.

**29.** Judaean leader at time of Ezra, <SUBJ> עמד *stand* Ne 8$_{4}$.

**30.** Gileadite, father of Iddo, military commander (נָגִיד) at time of David, <CSTR> בֶּן־זְכַרְיָהוּ Iddo *son of Zechariah* 1 C 27$_{21}$.

**31.** Reubenite family head, 1 C 5$_{7}$ (זְכַרְיָהוּ).

**32.** father of purchaser named in deed of sale, <CSTR> אלעזר בר זכריה *Eleazar son of Zechariah* Mur 29 1$_{2}$ (אל[עזר]) 2$_{12}$.

**33.** father of witness to sale, <CSTR> שמעון בר זכריה *Simeon son of Zechariah* Mur 29 2$_{10}$.

**34.** father of Shema, <CSTR> בן זכריו *son of Zechariah* Seal 167 (c. 700).

**35.** perh. son of Jair, <PREP> לְ of possession, *of, (belonging) to* Weight 54 (לזכרהו; 7th cent.).

**36.** Seal 882 (T. Dan, 8th cent.).

**37.** Kh. el-Meshash ost. 1682.2$_{3}$.

⇒ זכר *remember.*

**זְכַרְיָהוּ**, see זְכַרְיָה *Zechariah.*

**[זְכַרְיוֹ]**, see זְכַרְיָה *Zechariah.*

**[זַלָּא]** pr.n. **Zalla,** Nimrud ivory inscr. 3 (others צלא *Zalla*).

**זְלוּת** 1 n.f. **worthlessness**—ms זֻלֻּת; pl. ms זְלוּת—<SUBJ> רום *be exalted* Ps 12$_{9}$ (or em. הֲזִלּוֹתָ *you despise,* i.e. זלל hi.; or em. כְּרֻם זְלוּת *when worthlessness is exalted* to כְּרִמָּה זַלּוֹתָ *you regard as worthless as a worm,* i.e. זלל qal).*

⇒ זלל *be worthless.*

**[זַלְזַל]** 1 n.[m.] **shoot**—pl. זַלְזַלִּים—of shoot, tendril of plant, tree, <OBJ> כרת *cut* with knives Is 18$_{5}$ (|| נְטִישָׁה *branch*). <SYN> נְטִישָׁה *branch.*

**זלל I** 2.0.1 vb. **be worthless—Qal** 1.0.1 Ptc. זוֹלֵל, זוֹלְלָה—

**1. despise, regard as worthless,** <SUBJ> Y. Ps 12$_{9}$ (if em. כְּרֻם זְלוּת *when worthlessness is exalted* to כְּרִמָּה זַלּוֹתָ *you regard as worthless as a worm*). <PREP> לְ introducing object, + בֵּן *son* Ps 12$_{9}$ (if em.); כְּ *as (though)*, + רִמָּה *worm* Ps 12$_{9}$ (if em.).

**2.** participle as adj., **worthless. a.** used attributively of דּוֹר *generation* Ps 12$_{8}$ (if em. זוּ לְעוֹלָם appar. *generation that is for ever* or *this generation* to זוֹלֵל וְעָוֶל *worth* *less and wicked* generation). **b.** used predicatively, with היה *be* (of Jerusalem) Lm $1_{11}$.

**3.** participle as noun, **worthlessness,** <PREP> מִן of place, *from*, + יצא hi. *take out* Jr $15_{19}$ (:: יָקָר *precious [thing]*).

<ANT> §3 יָקָר *precious.*

**Hi.** 1 Pf. הִזִּילוּהָ—as Qal, **despise, regard as worthless,** <SUBJ> Y. Ps $12_9$ (if em. זֻלּוּת *worthlessness* to הֲזִלּוֹתָ *you regard as worthless*), Israel Jr $2_{36}$ (if em. תֵּזְלִי *you go* to תָּזִלִּי *you regard as a light matter;* + לְשַׁנּוֹת אֶת־דַּרְכֵּךְ *to change your way*), כבד pi. ptc. *one who honours* Lm $1_8$. <OBJ> Jerusalem Lm $1_8$. <PREP> לְ introducing object, + בֵּן *son* Ps $12_9$ (if em.). <COLL> with adverb מְאֹד *very* Jr $2_{36}$ (if em.; see Subj.).*

⇒ זֻלּוּת *worthlessness.*

**זלל II** 4.1 **be gluttonous—Qal** 4.1 Ptc. זוֹלֵל, זוֹלְלִים, זוֹלְלֵי—participle as noun, **glutton,** <SUBJ> היה *be* Si $18_{33}$ (|| סֹבֵא *drunkard*), ירשׁ ni. *be dispossessed* Pr $23_{21}$ (|| סֹבֵא). <NOM CL> בְּנֵנוּ זֶה ... זוֹלֵל *this son of ours is ... a glutton* Dt $21_{20}$=11QT $64_5$ (|| סֹבֵא *imbiber*). <OBJ> רעה *associate (with)* Pr $28_7$. <CSTR> זֹלְלֵי בָשָׂר *gluttons of*, i.e. for, *flesh* Pr $23_{20}$ (|| סֹבְאֵי). <PREP> בְּ of place, *among*, + היה *be* Pr $23_{20}$.

**Hi. be a glutton,** <SUBJ> Israel Jr $2_{36}$ (if em. תֵּזְלִי *you go* to תָּזִלִּי *you are a glutton;* + לְשַׁנּוֹת אֶת־דַּרְכֵּךְ *for changing your way*). <COLL> with adverb מְאֹד *very* Jr $2_{36}$ (if em.; see Subj.).

<SYN> §4 סֹבֵא *drunkard.*

**זלל III** 2 vb. **quake—Ni.** 2 Pf. נָזֹלּוּ—**quake,** <SUBJ> הַר *mountain* Jg $5_5$ (if em. נזל *flow*) Is $63_{19}$ (or em. נזל) $64_2$ (or del.). <PREP> מִפְּנֵי *from before*, + Y. Jg $5_5$ (if em.) Is $63_{19}$ (or em.) $64_2$ (or del.).*

**זַלְעָפָה** 3.1.2 n.f. **raging**—pl. זַלְעָפוֹת; cstr. זַלְעֲפוֹת—<SUBJ> אחז *seize* Ps $119_{53}$ 1QH $5_{30}$ ([אחזוני]; + חֵבֶל *pain*) 4QapLam$^b$6. <CSTR> זַלְעֲפוֹת רָעָב *ragings of famine* Lm $5_{10}$, זלעפות צפון *ragings of north (wind)* Si $43_{17(B)}$ (Bmg, M עִלְעוֹל *whirlwind;* + סוּפָה *storm wind*, סְעָרָה *tempest*); רוּחַ זִלְעָפוֹת *wind of ragings* Ps $11_6$ (+ פַּח *trap* [or em. פֶּחָם *coal*], אֵשׁ *fire*, גָּפְרִית *brimstone*). <PREP> מִפְּנֵי *on account of*, + כמר ni. *be hot* Lm $5_{10}$.*

**זִלְפָּה I** 7.0.2 pr.n.f. **Zilpah,** sister of Bilhah, daughter of Hannah, female servant first of Laban and then of Leah, secondary wife of Jacob and natural mother of Gad and Asher, <SUBJ> ילד *give birth* Gn $30_{10.12}$ $46_{18}$. <OBJ> ילד *give birth (to)* 4QTNaph $1.1_3$ ([ותלד]), נתן *give* Gn $29_{24}$ $30_9$ $46_{18}$, specif. give name 4QTNaph $1.1_3$, לקח *take* Gn $30_9$. <CSTR> בְּנֵי זִלְפָּה *sons of Zilpah* Gn $35_{26}$ $37_2$ $46_{18}$. <APP> שִׁפְחָה *female servant* Gn $29_{24}$ $30_{9.10.12}$ $35_{26}$, אִשָּׁה *woman* $37_2$, בַּת *daughter* 4QTNaph $1.1_3$ ([בת]).

**זִלְפָּה II** 0.0.1 pl.n. **Zilpah,** <COLL> זלפה בשם העיר אשר נשבה אל[יה] he gave her the name *Zilpah, after the name of the city to which he had been carried captive* 4QTNaph $1.1_3$.

**זִלֶּת**, see זִלּוּת *worthlessness.*

**זִמָּה I** 29.2.10 n.f. **wickedness; plan**—cstr. זִמַּת; sf. זִמָּתֵךְ, זִמַּתְכֶנָה; pl. זִמּוֹת; cstr. Q זמות; sf. זִמֹּתַי—**1. wickedness,** e.g. Ho $6_9$=4QpHos$^b$ $10_1$ Pr $10_{23}$ $21_{27}$, specif. in ref. to fornication or incest (e.g. Lv $18_{17}$ Jg $20_6$ Jr $13_{27}$ Ezk $16_{27}$ $23_{21}$ Jb $31_{11}$ CD $8_{7[A]}$=$19_{19[B]}$ 11QT $66_{15}$). **2. plan, planning, device,** with evil intent (except Jb $17_{11}$), e.g. Is $32_7$ Ps $26_{10}$ $119_{150}$ Pr $24_9$ 1QH $4_{13}$ $5_6$.

<SUBJ> היה *be* Lv $20_{14}$, נתק ni. *be wrenched out* Jb $17_{11}$ (unless זְמָה III *cord;* or em. זִמֹּתַי *my plans* are wrenched up to זִמַּתִּי appar. *I planned* my days that have passed; the desires of my heart are torn up), גלה ni. *be revealed* Ezk $23_{29}$ (or del. וְ *and* your wickedness, and transfer noun to following verse; + תַּזְנוּת *fornication*, עֶרְוָה *nakedness*), עשׂה *do* Ezk $23_{29}$ (if em.).

<NOM CL> זִמָּה הִיא *it is wickedness* Lv $18_{17(Qr)}$ $20_{14(Qr)}$ 11QT $66_{15}$, הִיא זִמָּה *it is wickedness* Jb $31_{11(Qr)}$ (+ עָוֹן *iniquity*), בִּידֵיהֶם זִמָּה *in their hands is wickedness* Ps $26_{10}$ (+ שֹׁחַד *bribe*), זִמַּת אִוֶּלֶת חַטָּאת *planning of folly is a sin* Pr $24_9$ (or em. אֱוִיל *fool*), בְּטֻמְאָתֵךְ זִמָּה *in your uncleanness is wickedness* Ezk $24_{13}$ (or em. טְמֵאַת הַזִּמָּה *O unclean one of wickedness*).

<OBJ> נשׂא *raise*, i.e. suffer punishment for Ezk $16_{58}$

(|| תּוֹעֵבָה *abomination*) $23_{35}$ (|| תַּזְנוּת *fornication*), חשׁב *reckon* 1QH $4_{13}$, appar. בחר *choose* 4Q525 $21_{4}$, עשׂה *do* Jg $20_{6}$ (or del. זִמָּה; + נְבָלָה *folly*) Ezk $16_{43}$ (+ תּוֹעֵבָה) $22_{9}$ $23_{44}$ (if em.; see Cstr.) Ho $6_{9}$=4QpHos$^{b}$ $10_{1}$ ([עשׂו]) Pr $10_{23}$ (:: חָכְמָה *wisdom*) 4QMidrEschat$^{b}$ $11_{2}$ ([עו]שי זמה]), נתן *give* Ezk $23_{49}$, נבע hi. *pour out* Si $10_{13}$, ראה *see* Jr $13_{27}$ (+ נִאֻף *adultery*, מִצְהָלָה *neighing*), פקד *visit*, i.e. seek Ezk $23_{21}$, רדף *pursue* Ps $119_{150}$ (רֹדְפֵי זִמָּה *pursuers of wickedness*), מצא *find* Pr $17_{3}$ (if em. זַמֹּתִי *I have planned* to זַמֹּתִי or זִמֹּתַי *my wickedness*, as part of first half-verse), שׁבת hi. *cause to cease* Ezk $23_{27}$ (+ זְנוּת *fornication*) $23_{48}$, יעץ *counsel* Is $32_{7}$=4QpIsa$^{e}$ $6_{5}$=4QMidrEschat$^{b}$ $8_{6}$ ([ז]מות).

<CSTR> זִמַּת זְנוּתֵךְ *wickedness of your prostitution* Jr $13_{27}$, זִמַּת אִוֶּלֶת *planning of folly* Pr $24_{9}$ (or em. אֱוִיל *of a fool*; ms אֱוִילִים *fools*), זִמַּת נְעוּרָיִךְ *wickedness of your youth* Ezk $23_{21}$, זמות בליעל *devices of Belial* 1QH $4_{13}$ $5_{26}$ ([זמות ב]ליעל), יצרי *of my desire* 1QH $5_{6}$; אִשֹּׁת הַזִּמָּה *the women of wickedness* Ezk $23_{44}$ (or em. לַעֲשׂוֹת זִמָּה *to do wickedness*), טְמֵאָה *unclean one of* Ezk $24_{13}$ (if em.; see Nom. Cl.), שפתי זמה *lips of wickedness* Si $51_{5}$ (+ שֶׁקֶר *falsehood*, מִרְמָה *deceit*), [מ]חשבת *thought of* 4QD$^{g}$ 1.$2_{4}$, עון *iniquity of* 4QOrd$^{b}$ $11_{3}$.

<APP> דֶּרֶךְ *way* Ezk $16_{27}$ (or del. זִמָּה), perh. שִׁקּוּץ *abomination* Jr $13_{27}$.

<PREP> לְ of benefit, *for (the purpose of)*, + נגשׁ *approach* CD $8_{7(A)}$=$19_{19(B)}$; בְּ of instrument, *by (means of), through*, + טמא pi. *defile* Ezk $22_{11}$; of accompaniment, *with, in (a state of)*, + בוא hi. *bring* sacrifice Pr $21_{27}$, עזב *abandon* worshipper 1QH $5_{6}$, פתח *open* tongue 1QH $5_{26}$ ([בזמות]); כְּ *in accordance with*, + עשׂה *do* Ezk $23_{48}$; שׁמר מִן *keep from* Pr $5_{2}$ (if em. מְזִמּוֹת *plans* to מִזִּמּוֹת *from wickednesses*), כלם מִן ni. *be ashamed of* Ezk $16_{27}$ (or del. זִמָּה).

<COLL> קָרְבוּ רֹדְפֵי זִמָּה *those who pursue me wickedly have drawn near* or *(with) wickedness* Ps $119_{150}$(mss) (L רֹדְפֵי זִמָּה *pursuers of wickedness*), מָלְאָה הָאָרֶץ זִמָּה *the land was full of wickedness* Lv $19_{29}$.

<SYN> תּוֹעֵבָה *abomination*, תַּזְנוּת *fornication*.

<ANT> חָכְמָה *wisdom*.*

⇒ זמם *plan*.

**זִמָּה II** 3 pr.n.m. **Zimmah, 1.** ancestor of levitical singer at time of David, son of Jahath, father of Joah, and descendant of Gershom, <NOM CL> perh. זִמָּה בְנוֹ *Zimmah was his son* 1 C $6_{5}$. <CSTR> בֶּן־זִמָּה *son of Zimmah* 2 C $29_{12}$. **2.** Levite, son of Shimei, father of Ethan, and descendant of Gershom, <CSTR> בֶּן־זִמָּה *son of Zimmah* 1 C $6_{27}$. <APP> בֵּן *son* 1 C $6_{27}$.

* **[זִמָּה] III** 1 n.f. **cord**—sf. זִמֹּתַי—(unless זִמָּה I *plan*), <SUBJ> נתק ni. *be wrenched out* Jb $17_{11}$. <APP> מוֹרָשֵׁי לְבָבִי perh. *strings of my heart* Jb $17_{11}$.

**זְמוֹרָה I** 5 n.f. **branch**—cstr. זְמֹרַת; pl. sf. זְמֹרֵיהֶם—assoc. with non-Israelite cult (Is $17_{10}$ Ezk $8_{17}$ [in latter passage perh. specif. **vine branch**, unless זְמוֹרָה II *stench* or III *band of toughs*]), <OBJ> כרת *cut* Nm $13_{23}$ (+ אֶשְׁכּוֹל *cluster*), זרע *sow* Is $17_{10}$ (+ נֶטַע *plant*), שׁלח *send* Ezk $8_{17}$ (הִנָּם שֹׁלְחִים אֶת־הַזְּמוֹרָה אֶל־אַפָּם *behold they send*, i.e. place, *the branch to their nose*; TiqSof אַפִּי *my nose*), שׁחת pi. *destroy* Na $2_{3}$ (unless זְמוֹרָה IV *warrior*; or em. זַיִת *olive grove*). <CSTR> זְמֹרַת זָר *shoot of a stranger* Is $17_{10}$; עֵץ הַזְּמוֹרָה *wood of a branch* Ezk $15_{2}$ (if em. עֵץ; or del. הַזְּמוֹרָה). <APP> עֵץ *wood* Ezk $15_{2}$ (or em.). <PREP> מִן of comparison, *(more) than*, + היה *be* better Ezk $15_{2}$ (or em.).*

⇒ זמר *prune*.

**זְמוֹרָה II** 1 n.f. **stench** (unless זְמוֹרָה I *branch* or III *band of toughs*), <OBJ> שׁלח *send* Ezk $8_{17}$ (הִנָּם שֹׁלְחִים אֶת־הַזְּמוֹרָה אֶל־אַפָּם *behold they send the stench to their nose*; TiqSof אַפִּי *my nose*).

***זְמוֹרָה III** 1 n.f. **band of toughs** (unless זְמוֹרָה I *branch* or II *stench*), <OBJ> שׁלח *send* Ezk $8_{17}$ (+ אֶל־אַפָּם *in the execution of their anger*).

* **[זְמוֹרָה] IV** 1 n.[f.] **warrior**—pl. sf. זְמֹרֵיהֶם—<OBJ> שׁחת pi. *destroy* Na $2_{3}$ (unless זְמוֹרָה I *branch*).

**[זַמְזֻמִּי]** 1 gent. **Zamzummite**—pl. זַמְזֻמִּים—as noun, name used by Ammonites for Rephaim, appar. ident. with the Zuzim at Gn $14_{5}$, <OBJ> קרא *call* Dt $2_{20}$.

**זָמִיר I** $_{7.0.2}$ n.m. **song**—cstr. זְמִיר; pl. זְמִרוֹת (Q זמירות); cstr. זְמִרֹת—**song, singing,** <SUBJ> היה *be* Ps 119$_{54}$ (+ חֹק *statute*), ענה *be low* Is 25$_{5}$ (or em. ni. *be made low*). <OBJ> שׁמע *hear* Is 24$_{16}$, נתן *give* Jb 35$_{10}$. <CSTR> זְמִיר עָרִיצִים *song of the ruthless* Is 25$_{5}$ (+ שָׁאוֹן *noise* of aliens), זְמִרוֹת יִשְׂרָאֵל *songs of Israel* 2 S 23$_{1}$, זמירו[ו]ת קודשו *songs of his holiness* MasShirShabb 2$_{22}$; עֵת הַזָּמִיר *time of singing* Ca 2$_{12}$ (or זָמִיר II *pruning*), נְעִים זְמִרוֹת *pleasant one of the songs of* Israel 2 S 23$_{1}$, תהלי זמירו[ו]ת *psalms of songs of* MasShirShabb 2$_{22}$. <PREP> בְּ of accompaniment, *with*, + רוע hi. *shout* Ps 95$_{2}$ (|| תּוֹדָה *thanksgiving*), קדם pi. *precede* GnzPs 2$_{15}$ (|| תּוֹדָה, הוֹדָאָה *thanksgiving song*, שִׁירָה *song*).

<SYN> תּוֹדָה *thanksgiving*, הוֹדָאָ *thanksgiving song*, שִׁירָה *song*.*

⇒ זמר pi. *sing*.

**זָמִיר II** $_{1.0.0.1}$ n.m. **pruning**—I זמר—<CSTR> עֵת הַזָּמִיר *time of pruning* Ca 2$_{12}$ (or זָמִיר I *song*), ירחו זמר *months of pruning* Gezer calendar$_{6}$.*

⇒ זמר *prune*.

* **[זָמִיר] III** $_{1}$ n.[m.] **guardian**—pl. cstr. זְמִרוֹת—<CSTR> נְעִים זְמִרוֹת יִשְׂרָאֵל *the beloved of the guardian of Israel* 2 S 23$_{1}$.

**זְמִירָה** $_{1}$ pr.n.m. **Zemirah** (or em. זְמַרְיָה *Zemariah*), son of Becher and grandson of Benjamin, <SUBJ> יחשׂ htp. *be genealogically enrolled* 1 C 7$_{8}$. <NOM CL> בְּנֵי בֶכֶר זְמִירָה וְיוֹעָשׁ *the sons of Becher were Zemirah and Joash* 1 C 7$_{8}$.

**[זִמְכִי]** pl.n. **Zimchi,** as coded form of עֵילָם *Elam* (if em. זִמְרִי *Zimrite*), <CSTR> מַלְכֵי זִמְכִי *kings of Zimchi* Jr 25$_{25}$ (if em.).

**זמם** $_{13.1.11}$ vb. **plan—Qal** $_{13.1.11}$ Pf. זָמַם (זָמָם), זָמְמָה, זַמּוֹתָ, זָמַמְתִּי (זַמֹּתִי, Si זמותי), זָמָמוּ; impf. Q יזום, Q אזום, יָזְמוּ (Q יזומו); ptc. זֹמֵם (Q זוממ); inf. Q זום (זַמֹּתִי, Q זוממ)—**1. plan, intend, determine, devise, plot (evil),** appar. **make plans for** field (Pr 31$_{16}$), <SUBJ> Y. Jr 4$_{28}$ (+ דבר pi. *speak*, נחם ni. *repent*, שׁוב *go back*) Jr 51$_{12}$ (+ עשׂה *do*, דבר pi.) Zc 1$_{6}$ 8$_{14}$ (+ נחם ni.) 8$_{15}$ Lm 2$_{17}$ MasShirShabb 1$_{6}$, Ben Sira 11QPs$^{a}$Si 51$_{18}$ (B חשׁב *reckon*), perh. Ithiel and Ucal Pr 30$_{32}$, Job Jb 17$_{11}$ (if em. זַמֹּתַי *my plans* are wrenched out to זַמֹּתַי appar. *I planned* my days that have passed; the desires of my heart are wrenched out), עַם *people* Gn 11$_{6}$, עֵד *witness* Dt 19$_{19}$=11QT 61$_{10}$, כֹּהֵן *priest* 1QpHab 12$_{6}$, אִשָּׁה *woman* Pr 31$_{16}$ (+ לקח *buy*), psalmist Ps 17$_{3}$ (זַמֹּתִי בַּל־יַעֲבָר־פִּי appar. *I have determined that my mouth shall not transgress*; or em. זִמָּתִי or זַמֹּתַי *my wickedness*, as part of first half-verse) 1QH 10$_{5}$, רָשָׁע *wicked one* Ps 37$_{12}$=4QpPs$^{a}$ 1.2$_{12}$ (+ חרק *gnash* teeth), חֶלְכָּה *wretch* 1QH 4$_{26}$, גֵּאֶה *proud one* Ps 140$_{9}$ (if em.; see Obj.), עָרִיץ *ruthless one* 4QpPs$^{a}$ 1.2$_{14}$, רַב pl. *many* Ps 31$_{14}$ (+ יסד ni. *take counsel*), ליץ hi. ptc. *interpreter* of lies 1QH 4$_{10}$, חֹזֶה *seer* of deceit 1QH 4$_{10}$, קום hi. ptc. *one who raises* wickedness 4QTohD$_{6}$ ([מ]קימי) 4QBer$^{a}$ 3.2$_{11}$ ([ל]זום), enemy 1QH 6$_{22}$ (ל[זו]ם) 9$_{20}$ 4QapPs$^{b}$ 45$_{2}$ (+ רבה hi. *increase* sin).

<OBJ> שָׂדֶה *field* Pr 31$_{16}$, מַאֲוַי *desire* Ps 140$_{9}$ (if em. מַאֲוַיֵּי רָשָׁע זְמָמוֹ *desires of the wicked one, his plan* to מַאֲוַיֵּי רֶשַׁע זָמָמוּ *desires of wickedness they have planned*), מַחֲשָׁבָה *thought* of evil 1QH 6$_{22}$ (ל[זו]ם), בְּלִיַּעַל *worthlessness* 1QH 4$_{10}$, יוֹם *day* Jb 17$_{11}$ (if em.; see Subj.), אֲשֶׁר *that which* Lm 2$_{17}$ (עָשָׂה י׳ אֲשֶׁר זָמָם *Y. has done that which he purposed*), מַה *what?* 1QH 10$_{5}$ MasShirShabb 1$_{6}$.

<PREP> לְ *against*, + צַדִּיק *righteous one* Ps 37$_{12}$=4QpPs$^{a}$ 1.2$_{12}$, יעד ni. ptc. *one who meets* for covenant 1QH 4$_{26}$, worshipper 1QH 9$_{20}$; בְּ of time, *in*, + יוֹם *day* Zc 8$_{15}$; עַל *against*, + worshipper 1QH 4$_{10}$ 4QapPs$^{b}$ 45$_{2}$, בְּרִית *covenant* 4QTohD$_{6}$ 4QBer$^{a}$ 3.2$_{11}$ ([ל]זום על ברית).

<COLL> with inf. of עשׂה *do* Gn 11$_{6}$ Dt 19$_{19}$=11QT 61$_{10}$ Zc 1$_{6}$, רעע hi. *do evil* Zc 8$_{14}$, יטב hi. *do good* Zc 8$_{15}$, לקח *take* life Ps 31$_{14}$, כלה pi. *destroy* 1QpHab 12$_{6}$ 4QpPs$^{a}$ 1.2$_{14}$.*

⇒ זָמָם *plan*, זִמָּה *plan*, מְזִמָּה *plan*.

**[זָמָם]** $_{1}$ n.[m.] **plan**—sf. זְמָמוֹ—<OBJ> פוק hi. *produce*, i.e. realize Ps 140$_{9}$ (+ מַאֲוַי *desire* of wicked one; or em. זָמָמוּ *they have planned*).*

⇒ זמם *plan*.

**זמן** $_{3}$ vb. **set time—Pu.** $_{3}$ Ptc. מְזֻמָּנִים, מְזֻמָּנוֹת—**be set,**

<SUBJ> עֵת *time* Ezr 10$_{14}$ Ne 10$_{35}$ 13$_{31}$.

→ זְמָן *(appointed) time.*

**זְמָן** 4.2.5 n.m. **(set) time**—cstr. Q זמן, זמון; sf. זְמַנָּם; pl. cstr. Si זמני; sf. זְמַנֵּיהֶם—<SUBJ> שלם *be complete* 5/6ḤevBA 45 fr. 2 5/6ḤevBA 46. <OBJ> נתן *give*, i.e. set Ne 2$_{6}$. <NOM CL> לַכֹּל זְמָן *for everything there is a time* Ec 3$_{1}$ (+ עֵת *time*), בם מועד וזמני חוק *by means of them are the set feast(s) and set times of statute* Si 43$_{7(B)}$ (or em. חג set times of *feast*; Bmg, M וממנו *and from it* for וזמני). <CSTR> [ז]מן צוקה *time of distress* Si 32$_{26}$ (|| עֵת *time*), זמן הגנות *time of the gardens* of En-gedi 5/6ḤevBA 45 fr. 2, זמן הפרות *of the fruit* of En-gedi 5/6ḤevBA 46, זמני חוק *times of statute*, i.e. prescribed times Si 43$_{7(B)}$ (or em. חג *feast*); סוף הזמן *the end of time* 5/6ḤevBA 45 fr. 2. <ADJ> הַלָּז *that* 5/6ḤevBA 45 fr. 2. <PREP> בְּ of place/time, *at, in, during* Si 32$_{26}$ (ב[ז]מן) 4QApocJosa 3$_{4}$ (בזמון), + קום pi. *establish* Est 9$_{31}$, עשׂה *do*, i.e. keep Est 9$_{27}$ (if. em.); כְּ *in accordance with*, + עשׂה *do*, i.e. keep Est 9$_{27}$ (+ כְּתָב *writing*; or em. בְּ *at*); עַד *until* 5/6ḤevBA 45 fr. 2. <SYN> עֵת *time*.*

→ זמן *set time.*

**זמר I** 45.0.13 vb. **sing (praise)**—**Pi.** Impf. אֲזַמֵּר, יְזַמֶּרְךָ, יְזַמְּרוּ, (אזמרכה Q), אֲזַמְּרֶךָּ, אֲזַמֶּרְךָּ, אֲזַמֵּרָה, אֲזַמְּרָה (אזמרה), נְזַמְּרָה, (ויזמרו); + waw Q וזמר; impv. זַמְּרוּ (זַמֵּרוּ); inf. זַמֵּר (זַמְּרָה)—**sing (praise), praise,** sometimes with musical instruments (see בְּ, under Prep.).

<SUBJ> אֶרֶץ *earth* Ps 66$_{2.2}$ (if em. שִׂים *place*) 66$_{4.4}$ 98$_{4.5}$, מַמְלָכָה *kingdom* Ps 68$_{33}$, עַם *people* Ps 47$_{7.7.7.7}$ (lacking in mss) 47$_{8}$, Deborah and Barak Jg 5$_{3}$ (or del.), בֵּן *son* of Zion Ps 149$_{3}$, יֹשֵׁב *inhabitant* of Zion Ps 9$_{12}$, נָשִׂיא *prince* 4QShirShabbd 1.1$_{7}$, חָסִיד *pious one* Ps 30$_{5}$, צַדִּיק *righteous one* Ps 33$_{2}$, יָדִיד *beloved one* 4QHoda 7.1$_{13}$, worshipper 2 S 22$_{50}$||Ps 18$_{50}$ Ps 7$_{18}$ 9$_{3}$ 21$_{14}$ 27$_{6}$ 57$_{8.10}$||108$_{2.4}$ 59$_{18}$ (or em. שׁמר *keep*) 61$_{9}$ 68$_{5}$ 71$_{22.23}$ (or del.) 75$_{10}$ 92$_{2}$ 101$_{1}$ (or em. אֶשְׁמְרָה *I will keep watch*) 104$_{33}$ 105$_{2}$||1 C 16$_{9}$ Ps 138$_{1}$=11QPsa 21$_{2}$ Ps 144$_{9}$ 146$_{2}$ 147$_{1.7}$ GnzPs 3$_{23}$ 1QH 11$_{5.23}$ 1QS 10$_{9}$ 4QapPsb 31$_{1}$ 4QMa 11.1$_{20}$ (ו[זמרוה]), עֶבֶד *servant* of Y. Ps 135$_{3}$, אֵל *god* 4QShirShabba 2$_{4}$ ([יזמרו]) 4QShirShabbd 1.1$_{39}$, קָדוֹשׁ *holy one* 4QShirShabba 2$_{4}$ ([יזמרו]), רוּחַ *spirit* 4QShirShabbd 1.1$_{41}$ ([רוחי] ... [זמ]רו), כָּבוֹד *glory* Ps 30$_{13}$ (or em. כָּבֵד *liver*).

<OBJ> (1) object of praise: יי *Y.* Is 12$_{5}$ Ps 30$_{13}$ 57$_{10(mss)}$ ||108$_{4}$ (L אֲדֹנָי *Adonai*) 66$_{4}$ 68$_{33}$ (אֲדֹנָי) 138$_{1(mss)}$=11QPsa 21$_{2}$, אֱלֹהִים *God* Ps 47$_{7}$ 147$_{1}$ 4QShirShabbd 1.1$_{41}$ (זמ[רו] [אלו]הים) 4QMa 11.1$_{20}$ (ו[זמרוה]), גְּבוּרָה *might* Ps 21$_{14}$, כָּבוֹד *glory* Ps 66$_{2.2}$ (if em. שִׂים *place*), שֵׁם *name* Ps 7$_{18}$ 9$_{3}$ 61$_{9}$ 66$_{4}$ 68$_{5}$; (2) song as object: מַשְׂכִּיל *maskil* Ps 47$_{8}$; (3) without obj., Ps 47$_{7.7}$ 57$_{8}$ 98$_{4}$ 108$_{2}$

<PREP> לְ *to*, + Y. Jg 5$_{3}$ Ps 9$_{12}$ 27$_{6}$ 30$_{5}$ 33$_{2}$ 68$_{33(mss)}$ (אֲדֹנָי *Adonai*) 98$_{5}$ 101$_{1}$ 105$_{2}$||1 C 16$_{9}$ Ps 149$_{3}$ GnzPs 3$_{23}$ 4QapPsb 31$_{1}$ (לי[הוה]), אֱלֹהִים *God* Ps 47$_{7(mss)}$ 66$_{4}$ 75$_{10}$ 104$_{33}$ 144$_{9}$ 146$_{2}$ 147$_{1(ms).7}$ 4QShirShabbd 1.1$_{39}$, קָדוֹשׁ *holy one* Ps 71$_{22.23}$ (or del. זמר), מֶלֶךְ *king* Ps 47$_{7}$ 4QShirShabbd 1.1$_{7}$, שֵׁם *name* 2 S 22$_{50}$||Ps 18$_{50}$ Ps 68$_{5(mss)}$ 92$_{2}$ 135$_{3}$; לָעַד *for ever* Ps 61$_{9}$.

בְּ of place, *in, at, among*, + לְאֹם *people* Ps 57$_{10(mss)}$ ||108$_{4(mss)}$ (both בִּלְאֻמִּים; L בַּל־אֻמִּים appar. *not peoples*), מָרוֹם *height* 4QShirShabba 2$_{4}$ ([יזמרו]); of instrument, *by (means of)*, or of accompaniment, *with*, + כִּנּוֹר *lyre* Ps 71$_{22}$ 98$_{5.5}$ (mss lack בְּכִנּוֹר) 147$_{7}$ 149$_{3}$ 1QH 11$_{23}$, נֵבֶל *harp* Ps 33$_{2}$ 144$_{9}$ 1QH 11$_{23}$, תֹּף *tambourine* Ps 149$_{3}$ 1QH 11$_{23}$ (ו[תוף]), חָלִיל *pipe* 1QH 11$_{23}$, קוֹל *voice* Ps 98$_{5}$, דָּבָר *word* 4QShirShabbd 1.1$_{7}$ (ב[שבעה ד]ברי *with seven words of* song), דַּעַת *knowledge* 1QS 10$_{9}$, מְנָת *portion of* spirit 4QShirShabbd 1.1$_{39}$; *concerning*, + חֶסֶד *loyalty* 1QH 11$_{5}$; בְּעוֹדִי *in my continuance*, i.e. as long as I live Ps 104$_{33}$ 146$_{2}$.

אֶל *to*, + עֹז *strength*, Ps 59$_{18}$.

נֶגֶד *before*, + אֱלֹהִים *gods* Ps 138$_{1}$=11QPsa 21$_{2}$.

לְפִי *in accordance with* 4QShirShabba 2$_{4}$ לפי כול ([בינתם יזמרו] *in accordance with all their understanding they sing*).

<COLL> אזמרה ... לאין השבת *I shall sing ... without ceasing* 1QH 11$_{23}$, [ו]זמר ... שבעה *and he will sing praise ... seven times* 4QShirShabbd 1.1$_{7}$.

זמר || הלל pi. *praise* Ps 146$_{2}$ 4QHodb 15$_{1}$, ידה hi. *give thanks* or praise Ps 33$_{2}$ 57$_{10}$||108$_{4}$, פצח *break out* (in song) Ps 98$_{4}$, רנן pi. *exult* Ps 98$_{4}$, שׁיר *sing* Ps 21$_{14}$ 27$_{6}$ 33$_{2}$ 68$_{33}$ 104$_{33}$ 105$_{2}$||1 C 16$_{9}$ Ps 108$_{2}$ GnzPs 3$_{23}$, שחה htpal. *worship* Ps 66$_{4}$.

זמר + חלל pi. *praise* Ps 135$_{3}$ 147$_{1}$ 149$_{3}$, ידה hi. *give thanks* or *praise* 2 S 22$_{50}$||Ps 18$_{50}$ Is 12$_{5}$ Ps 7$_{18}$ 30$_{5.13}$ 71$_{22}$ 92$_{2}$ 105$_{2}$||1 C 16$_{9}$ 138$_{1}$, שׂים *place*, i.e. give praise Ps 66$_{2}$, שׂיח *meditate* Ps 105$_{2}$||1 C 16$_{9}$ GnzPs 3$_{23}$ 1QH 11$_{5}$, נגד hi. *declare* Ps 9$_{12}$ 75$_{10}$ (or em. נגד hi. to גיל *rejoice* or גדל pi. *magnify*), רוע hi. *shout* Ps 66$_{2}$ 98$_{4}$, עלץ *exult* Ps 9$_{3}$, רנן pi. *exult* Ps 33$_{2}$ 71$_{23}$ (or del. זמר) 4QHod$^{b}$ 15$_{1}$, גיל *rejoice* Ps 75$_{10}$ (if em.) 149$_{3}$, שׂמח *rejoice* Ps 9$_{3}$, שׁיר *sing* Jg 5$_{3}$ Ps 57$_{8}$ 68$_{5}$ 101$_{1}$ 144$_{9}$ 4QHod$^{a}$ 7.1$_{13}$, ענה *sing* Ps 147$_{1}$.

זמר :: דמם *be silent* Ps 30$_{13}$.

Also 4QShirShabb$^{b}_{?}$ 25 4QHod$^{b}$ 15$_{1}$.

<SYN> שׁיר *sing*, רנן pi. *exult*, הלל pi. *praise*, ידה hi. *give thanks* or *praise*, פצח *break out* (in song), שׁחה htpal. *worship*.

<ANT> דמם *be silent*.*

→ זֶמֶר *song (of praise)*, זָמִיר *song*, זִמְרָה *song*, מִזְמוֹר *melody*.

**זמר** II $_{3.0.1}$ vb. **prune—Qal** $_{2.0.1}$ Impf. Q יזמור, 2ms תִּזְמֹר—<SUBJ> בֵּן *son* of Israel Lv 25$_{3}$ (+ שֵׁשׁ שָׁנִים *[for] six years*; + אסף *gather*) 25$_{4}$ (both || זרע *sow*), אִישׁ *man* 1QDM 3$_{2}$ ([אי]שׁ). <OBJ> כֶּרֶם *vineyard* Lv 25$_{3.4}$ 1QDM 3$_{2}$ ([כרם]). <SYN> זרע *sow*.

**Ni.** $_{1}$ Impf. יִזָּמֵר—**be pruned,** <SUBJ> כֶּרֶם *vineyard* Is 5$_{6}$ (|| עדר ni. *be hoed*). <SYN> עדר ni. *be hoed*.

→ זָמִיר II *pruning*, זְמוֹרָה I *branch*, זִמְרָה II *choice products*, מַזְמֵרָה *pruning-knife*.

**[זָמָר]**, see בַּעַל־זָמָר *Baal-zamar*.

**[זֶמֶר]** I $_{0.0.3}$ n.[m.] **song (of praise)**—cstr Q זמר; pl. זמרי—<CSTR> זמר עוז *song of strength* 4QShirShabb$^{d}$ 1.1$_{6}$, [זמרי] נפ[לא] *songs of a wonderful one* 4QShir Shabb$^{d}$ 1.1$_{6}$ (=MasShirShabb 2$_{17}$ [זמרי נפלאותיה] *songs of its wonders*, i.e. its wonderful songs), זמ[רי פלא] *songs of wonder* 4QShirShabb$^{d}$ 1.1$_{7}$ (=MasShirShabb 2$_{18}$ [זמרי] פלא]); תהלת [זמר] *psalm (consisting) of song (of praise)* 4QShirShabb$^{d}$ 1.1$_{6}$ (=4QShirShabb$^{e}$ 1$_{1}$ [תהל]ת זמר; =MasShirShabb 2$_{16}$ [תה]לת זמר), [ד]ברי זמ[רי] *words of songs of* 4QShir Shabb$^{d}$ 1.1$_{8}$. <COLL> שׁ[בעה זמרי] *seven songs of* 4QShirShabb$^{d}$ 1.1$_{6}$.

Also 4QShirShabb$^{f}$ 83$_{2}$.

→ זמר *sing*.

**[זֶמֶר]** II $_{1}$ n.[m.] perh. **mountain sheep**—זֶמֶר—fit for consumption, <OBJ> אכל *eat* Dt 14$_{5}$.

**[זְמֹרָה]**, see זְמוֹרָה I *branch*.

**זִמְרָה** I $_{7.0.4}$ n.f. **song**—זִמְרָת; sf. mss, Q, Sam זִמְרָתִי; cstr. זִמְרַת; sf. Q זמרתה; pl. Q זמרות—**song, melody,** <SUBJ> שׁמע ni. *be heard* 11QPs$^{a}$ 18$_{11}$ (|| קוֹל *voice*). <NOM CL> עָזִּי וְזִמְרָת יָהּ *Y. is my strength and (my) song* (unless זִמְרָה III *refuge*) Ex 15$_{2}$ (mss, Sam זִמְרָתִי *my refuge*) Is 12$_{2}$ (mss, 1QIsa$^{a}$ זִמְרָתִי) Ps 118$_{14}$ (ms זִמְרָתִי; or in all three em. סִתְרָתִי *my hiding place* and/or del. 'י; all three + יְשׁוּעָה *salvation*). <OBJ> שׁמע *hear* Am 5$_{23}$, נשׂא *raise* Ps 81$_{3}$ (+ תֹּף *tambourine*, כִּנּוֹר *lyre*, נֵבֶל *harp*). <CSTR> זִמְרַת נְבָלֶיךָ *melody of your harps* Am 5$_{23}$ (or em. נִבְלֵיכֶם *of your* [pl.] *harps*; + הֲמוֹן שִׁרֶיךָ *noise of your songs*), זמרת עו[ז] *song of might* 4QShirShabb$^{f}$ 67$_{1}$, זמרות פלא *songs of wonder* 4QShirShabb$^{d}$ 1.1$_{40}$, קודשו *of his holiness*, i.e. his holy songs 4QShirShabb$^{a}$ 3.2$_{1}$; קוֹל זִמְרָה *sound of melody* Is 51$_{3}$ (+ תּוֹדָה *thanksgiving*, שִׂמְחָה *gladness*, שָׂשׂוֹן *joy*) Ps 98$_{5}$ (+ כִּנּוֹר *lyre*). <PREP> לְ *as*, *for*, 4QShirShabb$^{d}$ 1.1$_{40}$. <SYN> קוֹל *voice*, עֹז *strength*.*

→ זמר *sing*.

**[זִמְרָה]** II $_{1}$ n.f. **choice produce**—cstr. זִמְרַת—<CSTR> זִמְרַת הָאָרֶץ *choice produce of the land* Gn 43$_{11}$. <PREP> מִן partitive, *(some) of*, + לקח *take* Gn 43$_{11}$.

→ זמר *prune*.

**[זִמְרָה]** III $_{3}$ n.f. **refuge**—זִמְרָת; sf. mss, Q, Sam זִמְרָתִי—(unless זִמְרָה I *song* or IV *warrior*), <NOM CL> עָזִּי וְזִמְרָת יָהּ *Y. is my strength and (my) refuge* Ex 15$_{2}$ (mss, Sam זִמְרָתִי *my refuge*) Is 12$_{2}$ (mss, 1QIsa$^{a}$ זִמְרָתִי) Ps 118$_{14}$ (ms זִמְרָתִי; or in all three em. סִתְרָתִי *my hiding place* and/or del. 'י; all three + יְשׁוּעָה *salvation*). <SYN> עֹז *strength*.

* **[זִמְרָה]** IV $_{3}$ n.[f.] **warrior**—זִמְרָת; sf. mss, Q, Sam זִמְרָתִי—(unless זִמְרָה I *song* or III *refuge*), <NOM CL> עָזִּי וְזִמְרָת יָהּ *Y. is my protector and warrior* Ex 15$_{2}$ Is 12$_{2}$ Ps 118$_{14}$. <SYN> עֹז *protector*.

**[זִמְרוֹן]**, see זִמְרָן *Zimran.*

**זִמְרִי I** 14 pr.n.m. **Zimri, 1.** army commander, murderer of King Elah and his family and usurper of throne of Israel, <SUBJ> הלך *go* 1 K 16$_{18}$, בוא *come* 16$_{10.18}$, ישׁב *sit* 16$_{11}$, נכה hi. *strike* 16$_{10.11.15}$, מות *die* 16$_{18}$, hi. *kill* 16$_{10}$, הרג *kill* 2 K 9$_{31}$, שׁמד hi. *destroy* 16$_{12}$, שׁאר hi. *leave* male survivor 16$_{11}$, קשׁר *plot* 16$_{9.16}$, שׂרף *burn* 16$_{18}$, מלך *rule* 16$_{10.11.15}$, ראה *see* 16$_{18}$, חטא *sin* 16$_{18}$, hi. *cause to sin* 16$_{18}$, עשׂה *do* evil 16$_{18.18}$. <CSTR> דִּבְרֵי זִמְרִי *words (in respect) of Zimri* 1 K 16$_{20}$. <APP> עֶבֶד *servant* 1 K 16$_{9}$, שַׂר *prince* 1 K 16$_{9}$.

**2.** son of Salu, descendant of Simeon, executed with his Midianite lover Cozbi by Phinehas son of Eleazar, <NOM CL> שֵׁם אִישׁ יִשְׂרָאֵל ... זִמְרִי *the name of the man of Israel ... was Zimri* Nm 25$_{14}$. <APP> בֵּן *son* Nm 25$_{14}$.

**3.** son of Zerah and grandson of Judah, appar. ident. with Zabdi at Jos 7$_{1.17.18}$, <SUBJ> לכד ni. *be captured* Jos 7$_{17}$ (if em. זַבְדִּי *Zabdi*). <NOM CL> בְּנֵי זֶרַח זִמְרִי וְאֵיתָן *the sons of Zerah were Zimri and Ethan* 1 C 2$_{6}$ (or em. זַבְדִּי *Zabdi*). <CSTR> בֶּן־זַבְדִּי *son of Zabdi* Jos 7$_{1.18}$ (if em. זַבְדִּי *Zabdi* in both). <APP> בֵּן *son* Jos 7$_{1.18}$ (if em.)

**4.** descendant of Saul, son of Jehoaddah/Jarah (mss Jadah; or em. Jehoiada), and father of Moza. <SUBJ> ילד hi. *beget* 1 C 8$_{36}$=9$_{42}$. <OBJ> ילד hi. *beget* 1 C 8$_{36}$=9$_{42}$.*

**זִמְרִי II** 1 gent. **Zimrite,** as collective noun, **Zimrites,** perh. in ref. to descendants of Zimran (or em. זִמְכִּי *Zimchi* as coded form of pl.n. עֵילָם *Elam*), <CSTR> מַלְכֵי זִמְרִי *kings of (the) Zimrite(s)* Jr 25$_{25}$.

**[זְמַרְיָה]** 0.0.0.1 pr.n.m. **Zemariah**—I זמריהו—**1.** (if em. Zemirah), son of Becher and grandson of Benjamin, <SUBJ> יחשׂ htp. *be genealogically enrolled* 1 C 7$_{8}$. <NOM CL> בְּנֵי בֶכֶר זְמַרְיָה וְיוֹעָשׁ *the sons of Becher were Zemariah and Joash* 1 C 7$_{8}$ (if em.). **2.** appar. father of Jarim (ירם), Seal 54 (Egypt, 7th cent.).

**[זְמַרְיָהוּ]**, see זְמַרְיָה *Zemariah.*

**זִמְרָן** 2 pr.n.m. **Zimran**—Sam זמרון—son of Abraham and Keturah, <NOM CL> בְּנֵי קְטוּרָה ... זִמְרָן וְיָקְשָׁן *the sons of Keturah ... were Zimran and Jokshan* 1 C 1$_{32}$ (if em.). <OBJ> ילד *give birth (to)* Gn 25$_{2}$||1 C 1$_{32}$ (or nom. cl., if del. ילד; Sam Zimron).

**זַן** 3.2 n.[m.] **kind**—pl. זְנִים; cstr. Si זני—**kind, sort,** <SUBJ> רקח pu. *be mixed as ointment* 2 C 16$_{14}$ (or em. וּזְנִים מְרֻקָּחִים *and kinds mixed as perfume* to וּזְנֵי מְרֻקָּחִים *and kinds of perfume*; + בֹּשֶׂם *spice*). <OBJ> מלא pi. *fill with* 2 C 16$_{14}$, בחר *choose* Si 37$_{28}$, נגד hi. *declare* Si 49$_{8}$. <CSTR> זְנֵי מְרֻקָּחִים *(various) kinds of perfume* 2 C 16$_{14}$ (if em.), זני מרכבה *kinds of chariot* Si 49$_{8}$; כל זן *all kinds (of food)* Si 37$_{28}$. <PREP> מִזַּן אֶל־זַן *from kind to kind,* i.e. all kinds (of food), + פוק hi. *provide* Ps 144$_{13}$ (or em. מָזוֹן עַל־מָזוֹן *provision upon provision* or מִזֶּה אֶל־זֶה *from here to here*).

<SYN> בֹּשֶׂם *spice.*

**זנב** 2 vb. **cut off rear—Pi.** 2 + waw וַיְזַנֵּב ;וְזִנַּבְתֶּם—**cut off rear, attack from behind,** perh. **massacre rearguard** or **cut off retreat,*** <SUBJ> Amalek Dt 25$_{18}$ (+ קרה *meet*), בֵּן *son* of Israel Jos 10$_{19}$ (+ רדף *pursue*). <OBJ> אֹיֵב *enemy*, i.e. Amalekites Jos 10$_{19}$, חשׁל ni. ptc. *shattered one* Dt 25$_{18}$. <PREP> בְּ of place, *in, among,* or *from,* + Israel Dt 25$_{18}$.

⇒ זָנָב *tail.*

**זָנָב** 11.0.2 n.m. **tail**—sf. זְנָבוֹ; pl. זְנָבוֹת; cstr. זַנְבוֹת—of snake (Ex 4$_{4}$), fox (Jg 15$_{4.4.4}$), hippopotamus (Jb 40$_{17}$); in ref. to stump of firebrand (Is 7$_{4}$), people of low status (Is 9$_{13.14}$=4QpIsa$^{c}$ 4.1$_{6}$ Is 19$_{15}$), Israel as subservient (Dt 28$_{13.44}$), king ruled by enemies (11QT 59$_{21}$), <SUBJ> עשׂה *do* Is 19$_{15}$ (|| אַגְמוֹן *rush*, :: ראשׁ *head*). <NOM CL> נָבִיא ... הוּא הַזָּנָב *the prophet ... is the tail* Is 9$_{14}$=4QpIsa$^{c}$ 4.1$_{6}$ (or del. הוּא הַזָּנָב; :: ראשׁ). <OBJ> כרת hi. *cut off* Is 9$_{13}$ (|| אַגְמוֹן *rush*, :: ראשׁ), חפץ *bend* Jb 40$_{17}$, פנה *turn* Jg 15$_{4}$ (וַיַּפֶן זָנָב אֶל־זָנָב *and he turned them* [foxes] *tail to tail*). <CSTR> שְׁנֵי זַנְבוֹת הָאוּדִים *two tails,* i.e. stumps, *of firebrands* Is 7$_{4}$, שְׁנֵי הַזְּנָבוֹת *the two tails* Jg 15$_{4}$. <PREP> לְ *as,* + היה *be* Dt 28$_{44}$ (:: ראשׁ *head*), נתן *give*, i.e. make into Dt 28$_{13}$ 11QT 59$_{21}$ (both :: ראשׁ); בְּ אחז *grasp* Ex 4$_{4}$; מִן of cause, *on account of,* + רכך *be weak* Is 7$_{4}$; אֶל *to,* + פנה

*turn* (intrans.) Jg 15$_{4}$; בֵּין *between*, + שִׂים *place* torch Jg 15$_{4}$. <SYN> אַגְמוֹן *rush*. <ANT> רֹאשׁ *head*.
⇒ זנב *have tail*.

**זנה** I $_{60.2.5}$ vb. **prostitute oneself—Qal** $_{51.2.5}$ Pf. זָנְתָה (Q זנת), זָנִית, זָנִית, זָנוּ; impf. Kt יזנה, 3fs תִּזְנֶה, תִּזְנִי, Qr יִזְנוּ, 3fpl תִּזְנֶינָה; + waw וְזָנָה, וְזָנְתָה, וְזָנוּ, 3fs וַתִּזְנֶה (וַתִּזְנִי־), 2fs וַתִּזְנִי (וַתִּזְנִים), וַיִּזְנוּ, 3fpl וַתִּזְנֶינָה (וַתִּזֶן); ptc. זוֹנָה (זֹנָה), זוֹנָה (זֹנָה), זֹנִים, זוֹנוֹת (זֹנוֹת); inf. זָנֹה, זְנוֹת (זְנֹת), זְנוּתֵךְ (זְנֻתֵךְ)—**1a.** of a woman **be** or **act as a prostitute,** for hire perh. Gn 38$_{24}$ Lv 21$_{9}$ Jr 2$_{20}$ Ho 2$_{7}$ 3$_{3}$ Am 7$_{17}$ (see also §4 זֹנָה *prostitute*).

**1b.** of countries and cities as women, **act as a prostitute,** Tyre Is 23$_{17}$, land Lv 19$_{29}$ Ho 1$_{2}$, Israel Jr 3$_{1.6}$, Judah Jr 3$_{8}$ (|| נאף pi. *commit adultery*), Oholah (= Samaria) Ezk 23$_{5}$, Oholibah (= Jerusalem) Ezk 16$_{15.16.17.26.28.28}$ 23$_{19.30}$, Oholah and Oholibah Ezk 23$_{3.43}$ (if em. לַבָּלָה נִאוּפִים עַתָּה יִזְנוּ תַזְנוּתֶהָ וָהִיא [Qr] perh. *now they will commit fornication with the woman worn out by adultery too* to הֲלֹא כָאֵלֶּה נִאֲפוּ וּמַעֲשֵׂי זוֹנָה תַעֲשֶׂינָה *have they not like these committed adultery and practised the deeds of a prostitute?*).

**1c. fornicate,** perh. Gn 38$_{24}$ Dt 22$_{21}$ Jg 19$_{2}$ (unless זנה II *be angry*) Is 57$_{3}$ (|| נאף pi. *commit adultery*) Ho 4$_{13.14}$ (both || נאף pi.).

**2.** of men, **fornicate,** Nm 25$_{1}$ Ezk 23$_{43}$ (unless em.; see §1b); specif. of improper sexual act with one's wife, 4QD$^{e}$ 11.1$_{13}$ (unless לזנות is לִזְנוּת *for harlotry*).

**3a.** of Israel generally, usu. זנה אַחֲרֵי **whore after,** i.e. seek for illicit sex, in ref. to worship of foreign gods (Ex 34$_{15.16}$=11QT 2$_{13.14}$ Lv 20$_{5.5}$ [Molech] Dt 31$_{16}$ Jg 2$_{17}$ 8$_{33}$ [Baalim] 1 C 5$_{25}$ 1QpHab 5$_{7}$), of demons (שָׂעִיר, Lv 17$_{7}$), of abominations (שִׁקּוּץ, Ezk 20$_{30}$), of ephod (Jg 8$_{27}$), or to association with necromancers (Lv 20$_{6}$) or other nations (Ezk 23$_{30}$), or to fulfilment of one's desires (Nm 15$_{39}$) or deeds (Ps 106$_{39}$, with בְּ).

**3b.** of women specifically, Ex 34$_{16}$ 4QMMT B$_{9}$.

**3c.** of heart and eyes, Ezk 6$_{9}$ 11QT 59$_{14}$.

<SUBJ> Israel Jg 8$_{27}$ Jr 3$_{6}$ Ho 4$_{15}$ 9$_{1}$, בַּיִת *house* of Israel Ezk 20$_{30}$, Ephraim Ho 6$_{10}$ (if em. זְנוּת *harlotry* to זָנִיתָ *you prostituted yourself*) Judah Jr 3$_{8}$ (+ נאף pi. *commit adultery*), Tyre Is 23$_{17}$, עַם *people* Nm 25$_{1}$ (+ חלל hi. *begin*) Dt 31$_{16}$ Ho 4$_{12}$ 1QpHab 5$_{7}$, Jerusalem Jr 2$_{20}$ 3$_{1}$ Ezk 16$_{15.16.17.26.28.28}$, Oholah Ezk 23$_{5}$, Oholibah Ezk 23$_{19.30}$, Tamar Gn 38$_{24}$, אָב *father*, i.e. ancestor Ps 106$_{39}$ (|| טמא *be unclean*), אֵם *mother* Ho 2$_{7}$ (|| בושׁ *be ashamed*), אִישׁ *man* Lv 20$_{5}$, אִשָּׁה *woman* Ezk 23$_{3.3}$ (or del. זנה) Ho 3$_{3}$ (+ היה לְ *be to* a man) Am 7$_{17}$, פִּילֶגֶשׁ *secondary wife* Jg 19$_{2}$ (unless זנה II *be angry*; or em. זנח *reject* or זעף *be angry*), בֵּן *son* of Israel Lv 17$_{7}$ Nm 15$_{39}$ Jg 2$_{17}$ 8$_{33}$, of tribe of Manasseh 1 C 5$_{25}$ (+ מעל *act unfaithfully*), בַּת *daughter* Ex 34$_{16}$=11QT 2$_{14}$ ([וזנו בנותיכה]) Lv 21$_{9}$ (+ חלל ni. *defile oneself*) Ho 4$_{13.14}$ (both || נאף pi. *commit adultery*), כַּלָּה *daughter-in-law* Gn 38$_{24}$, אָחוֹת *sister* Jr 3$_{8}$ (+ נאף pi.) Ezk 23$_{19}$, נַעֲרָה *girl* Dt 22$_{21}$ (Sam hi. *prostitute*), נֶפֶשׁ *soul* Lv 20$_{6}$, לֵב *heart* Ezk 6$_{9}$ 11QT 59$_{14}$, עַיִן *eye* Ezk 6$_{9}$ 11QT 59$_{14}$, Molech worshipper Lv 20$_{5.5}$, יֹשֵׁב *inhabitant* Ex 34$_{15}$=11QT 2$_{13}$ ([יושב ... וזנו]), אֶרֶץ *land* Lv 19$_{29}$ Ho 1$_{2}$, מִי שֶׁ *one who* 4QMMT B$_{9}$ (מי שזנת *one who prostituted herself*); subj. not specified, Is 57$_{3}$ (or em. וַתִּזְנֶה *and she prostituted herself* to וְזֹנָה *and a prostitute*) perh. Ezk 23$_{43}$ (or em.; see §2 Cstr.) Ps 73$_{27}$ perh. 4QD$^{e}$ 11.1$_{13}$ (unless לזנות is לִזְנוּת *for harlotry*).

<OBJ> רֵעַ *companion* Jr 3$_{1}$, בֵּן *son* Ezk 16$_{28}$ (unless em. וַתִּזְנִים *and you acted as a prostitute with them* to וַתִּזְנִי *and you acted as a prostitute*).

<PREP> לְ appar. *with*, + אִשָּׁה *woman* 4QD$^{e}$ 11.1$_{13}$ (unless לזנות is לִזְנוּת *for harlotry*).

בְּ of place/time, *in, at, during*, + Egypt Ezk 23$_{3}$, אֶרֶץ *land* Ezk 23$_{19}$, עִיר *city* Am 7$_{17}$, נְעוּר *youth* Ezk 23$_{3}$, קֵץ *time* 1QpHab 5$_{7}$; *with*, + צֶלֶם *image* Ezk 16$_{17}$, מַעֲלָל *deed* Ps 106$_{39}$.

מִן of direction, *from*, i.e. by deserting, + Y. Ps 73$_{27}$, מִצְוָה *commandment* 11QT 59$_{14}$.

אֶל *with* 4QMMT B$_{9}$, + בֵּן *son* Ezk 16$_{26.28}$, בַּת *daughter* Nm 25$_{1}$ (mss אֵת *with*), שָׁכֵן *neighbour* Ezk 16$_{26}$.

עַל *upon*, + בָּמָה *high place* Ezk 16$_{16}$; *on account of*, + שֵׁם *name* Ezk 16$_{15}$; *against*, + אִישׁ *man* Jg 19$_{2}$ (unless זנה II *be angry*; or em. זנח *reject* or זעף *be angry*).

מֵעַל *from (upon)*, + אֱלֹהִים *God* Ho 9$_{1}$.

אֵת *with*, + בַּת *daughter* Nm 25$_{1(mss)}$ (L אֶל *with*), מַמְלָכָה *kingdom* Is 23$_{17}$.

אחר *after*, i.e. with + עַיִן *eye*, i.e. what is seen 1QpHab 5$_{7}$.

אַחֲרֵי *after*, i.e. with + אֱלֹהִים *gods* Ex $34_{15}$=11QT $2_{13}$ ([וזנו] אחרי אל[והיהמה]]); + זבח לְ *sacrifice to*) $34_{16}$=11QT $2_{14}$ ([וזנו אחרי אלוהיהנ]ה]) Dt $31_{16}$ Jg $2_{17}$ (+ שׁחה לְ htpal. *bow down to*) 1 C $5_{25}$, בְּעָלִים *Baalim* Jg $8_{33}$, מֹלֶךְ *Molech* Lv $20_5$, שָׂעִיר *demon* Lv $17_7$, גִּלּוּל *idol* Ezk $6_9$, שִׁקּוּץ *abomination* Ezk $20_{30}$, אֵפוֹד *ephod* Jg $8_{27}$, גּוֹי *nation* Ezk $23_{30}$, אוֹב *ghost* Lv $20_6$ (+ פנה אֶל *turn to*), יִדְּעֹנִי *soothsayer* Lv $20_6$, לֵבָב *(desire of) heart* Nm $15_{39}$, עַיִן *(desire of) eye(s)* Nm $15_{39}$; *following the example of*, + אִישׁ *man* Lv $20_5$.

מֵאַחֲרֵי *from (after)*, + י׳ *Y.* Ho $1_2$.

תַּחַת *underneath*, i.e. *from*, + י׳ *Y.* Ezk $23_5$, אֱלֹהִים *God* Ho $4_{12}$ (מִתַּחַת).

<COLL> לִזְנוֹת בֵּית אָבִיהָ *by committing fornication in the house of her father* Dt $22_{21}$, אַתְּ צֹעָה זֹנָה *you lay sprawled as a prostitute* Jr $2_{20}$, יִזְנוּ תַזְנוּתֶהָ *they commit fornication with her* Ezk $23_{43}$(Qr) (or em.; see §2 Cstr.); with adverb, שָׁם *there* Jg $8_{27}$ Jr $3_6$ Ho $6_{10}$ (if em. זְנוּת *fornication*), בִּלְתִּי *not* Ezk $16_{28}$ (וַתִּזְנִי ... מִבִּלְתִּי שָׂבְעָתֵךְ *and you prostituted yourself ... without satisfaction*).

**4.** ptc. as noun (alw. fem.) זֹנָה, **prostitute, harlot,** (often אִשָּׁה זוֹנָה *a woman, a prostitute*),* of a city (Is $1_{21}$), <SUBJ> חיה *live* Jos $6_{17}$, ישׁב *dwell* Jos $6_{25}$, בוא *come* 1 K $3_{16}$, סבב *go around* Is $23_{16}$, שׁכח ni. *be forgotten* Is $23_{16}$, זכר ni. *be remembered* Is $23_{16}$, שׁמע *hear* Ezk $16_{35}$, לקח *take* Is $23_{16}$, יטב hi. *make good* melody Is $23_{16}$, רבה hi. *increase* song Is $23_{16}$, יצא hi. *take out*, i.e. utter 4QWiles $1_1$ (זונ[ה]), רחץ *wash* 1 K $22_{38}$, חבא hi. *hide* Jos $6_{25}$, שׁחר pi. *seek* 4QWiles $1_1$ (זונ[ה]), קלס pi. *deride* fee Ezk $16_{31}$ (or em. לקט pi. *collect*).

<NOM CL> שׁוּחָה עֲמֻקָּה זוֹנָה *a prostitute is a deep pit* Pr $23_{27}$ (or em. זָרָה *foreign woman*).

<OBJ> ראה *see* Jg $16_1$, חיה hi. *keep alive* Jos $6_{25}$, רעה *associate (with)* Pr $29_3$, לקח *take* Lv $21_{7.14}$(Sam) (‖ אַלְמָנָה *widow*, גרשׁ pass. ptc. fem. *divorced woman*; both ‖ חָלָל *profaned one*).

<CSTR> בֶּן־ ... זוֹנָה *son of ... a prostitute* Jg $11_1$, ... זֶרַע *seed of ...* Is $57_3$ (זֹנָה; if em. וַתִּזְנֶה *and she prostituted herself*), ... מֵצַח *forehead of ...* Jr $3_3$ (or em.; see App.), (...) בֵּית *house of (...)* Jos $2_1$ $6_{22}$ Jr $5_7$, שִׁית *garment of* Pr $7_{10}$, אֶתְנַן *fee of* Dt $23_{19}$ (+ כֶּלֶב *dog*, perh. sodomite) Mc $1_{7.7}$, ... בַּעַד *price of ...* Pr $6_{26}$ (if em.; see Prep.), זְנוּנֵי *fornication(s) of* Na $3_4$=4QpNah 3.$2_7$, ... מַעֲשֵׂה *deed of ...* Ezk $16_{30}$, מַעֲשֵׂי *deeds of* Ezk $23_{43}$ (if em. לַבָּלָה נִאוּפִים עַתָּה יִזְנוּ תַזְנוּתֶהָ וָהִיא [Qr] perh. *now they will commit fornication with the woman worn out by adultery too* to הֲלֹא כָאֵלֶּה נִאֲפוּ וּמַעֲשֵׂי זוֹנָה תַעֲשֶׂינָה *have they not like these committed adultery and practised the deeds of a prostitute?*), שִׁירַת הַזּוֹנָה *song of the prostitute* Is $23_{15}$, כָּל־זֹנוֹת *all prostitutes* Ezk $16_{33}$.

<APP> Rahab Jos $6_{25}$, אִשָּׁה *woman* Lv $21_7$ Jos $2_1$* $6_{22}$ Jg $11_1$ $16_1$ 1 K $3_{16}$ Jr $3_3$ (or em. אִשָּׁה זוֹנָה to נְחֹשֶׁה *bronze*) Ezk $16_{30}$ $23_{44}$ Pr $6_{26}$ (or del. אִשָּׁה),* טוֹב *good one* Na $3_4$=4QpNah 3.$2_7$, בַּעֲלָה *lady* Na $3_4$=4QpNah 3.$2_7$, חָלָל *profaned one* Lv $21_{14}$.

<ADJ> שַׁלֶּטֶת *domineering* Ezk $16_{30}$.

<PREP> לְ of direction, *to*, + נתן *give* Ezk $16_{33}$ Si $9_6$; *as*, + היה *be* Is $1_{21}$, חשׁב *reckon* Gn $38_{15}$.

בְּ of price, *(in exchange) for*, + נתן *give* Jl $4_3$ (‖ יַיִן *wine*).

כְּ *as* Gn $34_{31}$, + היה *be* Ezk $16_{31}$.

מִן privative, *without*, i.e. so as not to be, + שׁבת hi. *cause to cease* Ezk $16_{41}$ (וְהִשְׁבַּתִּיךְ מִזּוֹנָה appar. *and I will cause you to cease from [being] a prostitute*).

אֶל *to*, + בוא *come* for sex Jg $16_1$ Ezk $23_{44}$.

עִם *with*, + פרד pi. *depart* Ho $4_{14}$ (or em. ni. in sim. sense), סוד htp. *converse* Si $9_3$ (+ אִשָּׁה *woman*), טמא pi. *defile* seed 4QMMT $B_{82}$.

בְּעַד *on account of* Pr $6_{26}$ (בְּעַד־אִשָּׁה זוֹנָה עַד־כִּכַּר לָחֶם perh. *to a crust of bread is*, i.e. one descends to a crust of bread, *on account of a woman, a prostitute*, or em. בְּעַד אִשָּׁה *on account of a woman* to בְּעַד or to בְּקֶשָׁה a prostitute *seeks* even a crust, or em. בְּעַד to בַּעַד *the price of* a prostitute is).

<COLL> זֹנָה *prostitute* + אֶתְנַן *hire* Dt $23_{19}$ Is $23_{17}$ Ezk $16_{31.41}$ Mc $1_7$, + נֵדֶה *gift* Ezk $16_{33}$ (cf. Ho $1_2$), + שִׁירָה *song* Is $23_{15}$, שִׁיר *song* Is $23_{16}$.

<SYN> §1 נאף pi. *commit adultery*, טמא *be unclean*, בושׁ *be ashamed*; §3 אַלְמָנָה *widow*, גרשׁ pass. ptc. fem. *divorced woman*, חָלָל *profaned one*, יַיִן *wine*.

**Pu.** 1 Pf. זוּנָּה—appar. **be prostituted**, i.e. accompany for purpose of prostitution, <PREP> אַחֲרֵי *after*, אַחֲרַיִךְ לֹא זוּנָּה *no one prostituted himself (by going) after you* (Jerusalem) Ezk $16_{34}$.

**Hi.** 8 Pf. הִזְנוּ ,הִזְנֵית; + waw וְהִזְנוּ ;וַיֶּזֶן, 2ms וַתַּזְנֶה; inf.

(הַזְּנוֹתָהּ) הַזְּנוֹת, הַזֹּנֶה—**1.** as qal, **prostitute oneself, commit fornication,** <SUBJ> עַם *people* Ho 4$_{10}$ (mss qal; :: פרץ *break through,* i.e. increase, || אכל *eat*), Ephraim Ho 4$_{18}$ (+ אהב *love*) 5$_{3}$ (+ טמא ni. *be defiled*), כֹּהֵן *priest* Ho 4$_{10}$. <COLL> הַזְנֵה הִזְנוּ *they continuously fornicated* Ho 4$_{18}$.

**2. prostitute, lead into prostitution** (including religious infidelity), <SUBJ> Judah 2 C 21$_{13}$, Israelite Lv 19$_{29}$ (+ חלל pi. *defile*), בַּיִת *house* of Ahab 2 C 21$_{13}$, Jehoram 2 C 21$_{11}$ (|| נדח hi. *lead astray*) 21$_{13.13}$, בַּת *daughter* Ex 34$_{16}$=11QT 2$_{15}$ ([בנותיכה ... וה]זנו), נַעֲרָה *young woman* Dt 22$_{21(Sam)}$. <OBJ> בַּת *daughter* Lv 19$_{29}$, בֵּן *son* Ex 34$_{16}$=11QT 2$_{15}$ ([ה]זנו את בניכה), בַּיִת *house* of father Dt 22$_{21(Sam)}$, יֹשֵׁב *inhabitant* 2 C 21$_{11.13}$. <PREP> אַחֲרֵי *after,* + אֱלֹהִים *gods* Ex 34$_{16}$=11QT 2$_{15}$ ([וה]זנו ... אחרי אלוהיהמה).

<SYN> §1 אכל *eat;* §2 נדח hi. *lead astray.*

<ANT> פרץ *break through,* i.e. increase.*

→ זְנוּת *prostitution,* זוֹנוּת *prostitution,* זְנוּנִים *prostitution,* תַּזְנוּת *prostitution.*

**זנה II** 1 vb. **be angry—Qal** + waw 3fs וַתִּזְנֶה—**be angry,** or **abhor.***

<SUBJ> פִּילֶגֶשׁ *secondary wife* Jg 19$_{2}$ (unless זנה I *prostitute oneself;* or em. זנח *reject* or זעף *be angry*). <PREP> עַל *against, for,* + אִישׁ *husband* Jg 19$_{2}$.

**זָנוֹחַ** 5 pl.n. **Zanoah**—זָנֹחַ—**1.** town in lowland of Judah appar. founded by Jekuthiel, perh. Kh. Zanū' 23 km WSW of Jerusalem, <NOM CL> בַּשְּׁפֵלָה אֶשְׁתָּאוֹל ... : וְזָנוֹחַ *in the lowland were Eshtaol ... and Zanoah* Jos 15$_{34}$. <CSTR> אֲבִי זָנוֹחַ *(founding) father of Zanoah* 1 C 4$_{18}$, יֹשְׁבֵי *inhabitants of* Ne 3$_{13}$. <APP> עִיר *city* Jos 15$_{34}$. <PREP> perh. בְּ of place, *in, at,* + ישׁב *dwell* Ne 11$_{30}$ (זָנֹחַ).

**2.** town in hill country of Judah, <NOM CL> בָּהָר שָׁמִיר ... וְזָנוֹחַ *in the mountain(s) were Shamir ... and Zanoah* Jos 15$_{56}$ (or rd. זָנוֹחַ־הַקַּיִן *Zanoah-Kain,* joining with 15$_{57}$, perh. Kajin, 30 km SSW of Jerusalem). <APP> עִיר *city* Jos 15$_{56}$.

**[זָנוֹחַ־קַיִן]**, see זָנוֹחַ *Zanoah,* §2.

**זְנוּנִים** 12.0.1 n.m. **prostitution**—cstr. זְנוּנֵי; sf. זְנוּנַיִךְ, זְנוּנֶיהָ—**prostitution, fornication,** also in ref. to religious infidelity (2 K 9$_{22}$ Ezk 23$_{11.29}$ Ho 2$_{4.6}$ 4$_{12}$ 5$_{4}$), <NOM CL> שָׁם זְנוּנִים לְאֶפְרַיִם *the fornication of Ephraim is there* Ho 6$_{10}$ (if em. זְנוּת *prostitution*). <OBJ> סור hi. *remove* Ho 2$_{4}$ (|| נַאֲפוּף *adultery*), שׁמר *keep* Ho 4$_{11}$ (if em. זְנוּת וְיַיִן *fornication and wine* to זְנוּנִים *fornication,* and join with 4$_{10}$). <CSTR> זְנוּנֵי אִיזֶבֶל אִמְּךָ *fornication of Jezebel, your mother* 2 K 9$_{22}$ (+ כֶּשֶׁף *sorcery*), אֲחוֹתָהּ *of her sister* Ezk 23$_{11}$, זוֹנָה *of the prostitute* Na 3$_{4}$=4QpNah 3.2$_{7}$; אֵשֶׁת זְנוּנִים *wife of prostitution* Ho 1$_{2}$,* יַלְדֵי *children of* Ho 1$_{2}$, בְּנֵי *sons of* Ho 2$_{6}$, רוּחַ *spirit of* Ho 4$_{12}$ 5$_{4}$, עֶרְוַת זְנוּנַיִךְ *nakedness of your prostitution* Ezk 23$_{29}$ (+ תַּזְנוּת *prostitution,* זִמָּה *wickedness*), רֹב זְנוּנֵי *abundance of fornication of* Na 3$_{4}$=4QpNah 3.2$_{7}$ (רוב; + כֶּשֶׁף *sorcery*). <PREP> לְ of instrument, *by (means of), through,* + הרה *conceive* Gn 38$_{24}$; בְּ of instrument, *by (means of), through,* + מכר *sell* Na 3$_{4}$ (or em. כמר *minister [to];* =4QpNah 3.2$_{7}$ זְנוּת *prostitution;* || כֶּשֶׁף *sorcery*); מִן of comparison, *(more) than,* + שׁחת hi. *corrupt* Ezk 23$_{11}$ (+ עֲגָבָה *lustfulness*); עַד *unto* 2 K 9$_{22}$ (mss עִם *with;* or em. עַד to עֹד *still*); עִם *with* 2 K 9$_{22(mss)}$ (L עַד *unto*). <SYN> נַאֲפוּף *adultery,* כֶּשֶׁף *sorcery.**

→ זנה *prostitute oneself.*

**זְנוּת** 9.2.12 n.f. **prostitution**—sf. זְנוּתֵךְ, זְנוּתָהּ, זְנוּתָם, זְנוּתַיִךְ, זְנוּתֵיכֶם—**prostitution, fornication,** also in ref. to religious infidelity (Nm 14$_{33}$ Jr 3$_{2.9}$ 13$_{27}$ Ezk 23$_{27}$ 43$_{7.9}$ Ho 6$_{10}$); at Qumran appar. in ref. to illicit marriage or improper sexual acts (e.g. CD 4$_{17.20}$ 4QD$^{e}$ 11.1$_{13}$),* <SUBJ> appar. לקח *take* Ho 4$_{11}$ (+ יַיִן *wine,* תִּירוֹשׁ *new wine;* or em. זְנוּת וְיַיִן *fornication and wine* to זְנוּנִים *fornication*). <NOM CL> שָׁם זְנוּת לְאֶפְרַיִם *the fornication of Ephraim is there* Ho 6$_{10}$=4QpHos$^{b}$ 10$_{1}$ ([שם זנות לאפרים]; or em. זְנוּנִים *fornication,* or זָנִית *you committed fornication*), הראשונה היא הזנות *the first (net of Belial) is fornication* CD 4$_{17}$ (+ הוֹן *wealth,* טמא pi. inf. *defiling* of sanctuary).

<OBJ> נשׂא *raise,* i.e. suffer punishment for Nm 14$_{33}$ (or em. תְּלֻנָּה *murmuring*), שׁבת hi. *cause to cease* Ezk 23$_{27}$ (mss תַּזְנוּתֵךְ/תַּזְנוּתַיִךְ *your fornication[s];* + זְנוּתֵךְ מֵאֶרֶץ מִצְרַיִם *your prostitution from,* i.e. which you learned in, *the land of Egypt;* + זִמָּה *wickedness*), רחק pi.

*distance* Ezk 43$_9$ (|| פֶּגֶר *corpse*). <CSTR> עיני זנות *eyes of fornication* CD 2$_{16}$ (עיני) 1QS 1$_6$ (+ לב אשמה *heart of guilt*), רוח *spirit of* 1QS 4$_{10}$, דרכי *ways of* CD 19$_{17(B)}$ (= 8$_{5[A]}$ זוֹנוּת *fornication*), עוון הזנות perh. *iniquity of fornication* 4QpsJub$^a$ 1$_1$, קֹל זְנוּתָהּ *easiness of her fornication* Jr 3$_9$, זִמַּת זְנוּתֵךְ *wickedness of your fornication* Jr 13$_{27}$ (+ נְאֻף *adultery*, מִצְהָלָה *neighing*), כול הזנות *all the fornication* 4QOrd$^b$ 2.2$_2$.

<PREP> לְ of benefit, *to, for* 4QOrd$^b$ 2.2$_2$, + קרב *approach* 4QD$^e$ 11.1$_{13}$ (יקר[ב]; but perh. לזנות *to prostitute himself*, i.e. inf. of זנה); בְּ of instrument, *by (means of), through*, + חנף hi. *pollute* Jr 3$_2$ (|| רָעָה *evil*), טמא pi. *defile* Ezk 43$_7$ (|| פֶּגֶר *corpse*, + בָּמָה *high place*), מכר pi. *sell* 4QpNah 3.2$_7$ (=Na 3$_4$ זְנוּנִים *prostitution*), תפש ni. *be caught* CD 4$_{20}$; of accompaniment, *with, in (a state of)*, + נטל *take* counsel Si 42$_{8(B)}$, שׁאל *ask* counsel Si 42$_{8(Bmg)}$; ענה בְּ *be occupied with* Si 42$_{8(Bmg\ M)}$; אֶל *(because) of*, + בושׁ *be ashamed* Si 41$_{17(B)}$ (Bmg, M פַּחַז *wantonness*; || כַּחַשׁ *lying*); בִּגְלַל *on account of*; + אבד *be destroyed* 4QMMT C$_5$ ([בגלל]; || חָמָס *violence*).

<SYN> רָעָה *evil*, כַּחַשׁ *lying*, חָמָס *violence*, פֶּגֶר *corpse*. Also 4QOrd$^b$ 2.2$_5$.*

→ זנה *prostitute oneself*.

**זנוח** 0.0.1 vb. **reject—Pi.** Impf. 2ms Q תזונוח—**reject,** <SUBJ> Y. 4QapPs$^b$ 46$_6$ (or em. תזנוח *you will reject* to תזניח, from זנח I or II hi., *you will reject* or *you will declare foul*). <OBJ> שׂנא pass. ptc. *hated one* 4QapPs$^b$ 46$_6$ (שׂנא[ים]). <PREP> כְּ *as (though it were)*, + נִדָּה *impurity* 4QapPs$^b$ 46$_6$.

**זנח I** 19.1.3 vb. **reject—Qal** 16.1 Pf. זָנַח, זָנַ֫חְתָּ, (זְנַחְתָּ֫נִי), זְנַחְתָּ֫נוּ), זְנַחְתִּים; impf. 2ms תִּזְנַח, 3fs Si. תזנח—**reject,** or perh. **be angry,*** <SUBJ> Y. Zc 10$_6$ Ps 43$_2$ 44$_{10}$ (|| כלם hi. *shame*, :: יצא בְּצָבָא *go out with army*) 44$_{24}$ (ms שכח *forget*) 60$_3$ (|| פרץ *break out [against]*, + אנף *be angry*) 60$_{12}$=108$_{12}$ (:: יצא בְּצָבָא *go out with army*) 74$_1$ (+ יֶעְשַׁן אַפְּךָ *your anger smokes*) 77$_8$ (:: רצה *desire*) 88$_{15}$ (+ תַּסְתִּיר פָּנֶיךָ *you hide your face*) 89$_{39}$ (|| מאס *reject*, + עבר htp. *be angry*, נאר pi. *reject*) Lm 2$_7$ (|| נאר pi.) appar. 3$_{17}$ (or em. ni. *be rejected*) 3$_{31}$, Israel Ho 8$_3$, פִּילֶגֶשׁ *secondary wife* Jg 19$_2$ (if em. זנה I *prostitute oneself* or II *be angry*), appar. עֵגֶל *calf* Ho 8$_5$ (or em. זָנַח *he has rejected* to זָנַחְתִּי *I* (Y.) *have rejected*, or זְנַח *reject*, with Samaria as subj.; + חָרָה אַפִּי *my anger burned*), גְּעָרָה *rebuke* Si 43$_{13(Bmg)}$ (B, M נצח pi. *make bright*).

<OBJ> Israel Zc 10$_6$ Ps 43$_2$ Ps 44$_{10(mss)}$ (זְנַחְתָּנוּ *you have rejected us*; L זָנַחְתָּ *you have rejected*) 60$_{3.12}$=108$_{12}$, נֶפֶשׁ *soul* Ps 88$_{15}$ Lm 3$_{17}$, יְקוּם *existence* Si 43$_{13(Bmg)}$, עֵגֶל *calf* Ho 8$_5$ (if em.; see Subj.), מִזְבֵּחַ *altar* Lm 2$_7$, טוֹב *good* Ho 8$_3$. <PREP> מִן privative, *(so as to be) without*, + שָׁלוֹם *peace* Lm 3$_{17}$ (וַתִּזְנַח מִשָּׁלוֹם נַפְשִׁי *and you have rejected my soul [so that it is] without peace*; or em. ni.); עַל introducing object, + אִישׁ *man* Jg 19$_2$ (if em. זנה I *prostitute oneself* or II *be angry*). <COLL> with interrogative, לָמָה *why?* Ps 43$_2$ 74$_1$ 88$_{15}$; with adverb, לָנֶצַח *for ever* Ps 44$_{24}$ 74$_1$, לְעוֹלָם *for ever* Lm 3$_{31}$, לְעוֹלָמִים *for ever* Ps 77$_8$. <SYN> כלם hi. *shame*, פרץ *break out (against)*, מאס *reject*, נאר pi. *reject*. <ANT> רצה *desire*, יצא בְּצָבָא *go out with army*.

**Ni. be rejected,** <SUBJ> נֶפֶשׁ *soul* Lm 3$_{17}$ (if em. qal). <PREP> מִן privative, *(so as to be) without*, + שָׁלוֹם *peace* Lm 3$_{17}$ (if em. qal).

**Hi.** 3.0.3 Pf. הִזְנִיחַ (הִזְנִיחָם), Q הזנחתה (Q הזנחתני); impf. יַזְנִיחֲךָ—**reject, exclude,** <SUBJ> Y. 1 C 28$_9$ (+ עזב *abandon*) 1QH 9$_{7.11}$ (|| גער *rebuke*, עזב) 4QapPs$^b$ 46$_6$ (if em. תזנוח pi. *reject*), Ahaz 2 C 29$_{19}$, Jeroboam 2 C 11$_{14}$, בֵּן *son* 2 C 11$_{14}$, מֶלֶךְ *king* 2 C 29$_{19}$. <OBJ> Solomon 1 C 28$_9$, לֵוִי *Levite* 2 C 11$_{14}$, worshipper 1QH 9$_7$, שׂנא pass. ptc. *hated one* 4QapPs$^b$ 46$_6$ (שׂנא[ים]; if em.), כְּלִי *vessel* 2 C 29$_{19}$, שָׁלוֹם *peace* 1QH 9$_{11}$. <PREP> בְּ of place/time, *in, during*, + מַלְכוּת *reign* 2 C 29$_{19}$; of accompaniment, *with, in (a state of)*, + מַעַל *faithlessness* 2 C 29$_{19}$, חֶסֶד *loyalty* 1QH 9$_7$; כְּ *as (though they were)*, + נִדָּה *impurity* 4QapPs$^b$ 46$_6$ (if em.); מִן privative, *without*, i.e. so as not to be, + כהן pi. *ministering (as priest)* 2 C 11$_{14}$ (... הִזְנִיחָם מִכַּהֵן לַי׳ *he rejected them ... from serving as priests to Y.*). <COLL> with adverb, לָעַד *for ever* 1 C 28$_9$. <SYN> גער *rebuke*, עזב *abandon*.*

**זנח II** 1.0.1 vb. **stink—Hi.** 1.0.1 + waw וְהֶאֶזְנִיחוּ (1QIsa$^a$ והזניחו)—**1. stink, be foul,** <SUBJ> נָהָר *river* Is 19$_6$ (+ דלל *be diminished*, חרב *be dry*).

**2. declare foul,** <SUBJ> Y. 4QapPs$^b$ 46$_6$ (if תזנוח is error for תזניח). <OBJ> שׂנא pass. ptc. *hated one* 4QapPs[b] $46_6$ ([שנאי]ם; if תזנוח is error for תזניח). <PREP> כְּ *as (though they were)*, + נִדָּה *impurity* 4QapPs[b] $46_6$ (if em.).

**זָנַח**, see זָנוֹחַ *Zanoah*.

**[זְנִי]** 0.0.1 n.[m.] perh. **disgrace,** <PREP> בְּ *(in exchange) for*, + מור ho. *be exchanged* (appar. of wealth) 4Q418 $8_{11}$.

**זנק** 1 vb. **leap—Pi.** 1 Impf. יְזַנֵּק—**leap,** <SUBJ> גּוּר *lion's cub* Dt $33_{22}$. <PREP> מִן of direction, *from*, + בָּשָׁן *Bashan* Dt $33_{22}$.

**זעה** 1.0.1 vb. **bark—Pilp.** 1.0.1 Ptc. מְזַעְזְעֶיךָ (unless זוע pilp. *terrify*)—**bark at,** <OBJ> גֶּבֶר *man* Hb $2_7$=1QpHab $8_{14}$ (|| נשׁך *bite*). <SYN> נשׁך *bite*.*

**[זֵעָה]** 1 n.f. **sweat**—cstr. זֵעַת—<CSTR> זֵעַת אַפֶּיךָ *sweat of your face* Gn $3_{19}$. <PREP> בְּ of instrument, *by (means of)*, + אכל *(obtain food to) eat* Gn $3_{19}$.

**זַעֲוָה** 6.0.3 n.f. (object of) **trembling**—cstr. Q זעות—**trembling, cause of trembling,** i.e. something terrible, <CSTR> זעות נצח *terror of eternity* 1QS $4_{12}$ (|| חֶרְפָּה *reproach*, + כְּלִמָּה *insult*). <PREP> לְ *as* 1QS $4_{12}$, + היה *be* Dt $28_{25}$ (mss, Sam זְוָעָה *horror*), נתן *give*, i.e. make into Jr $15_{4(Qr)}$ $24_{9(Qr)}$ (+ רָעָה *evil* [or del.], מָשָׁל ,חֶרְפָּה *proverb*, שְׁנִינָה *taunt*, קְלָלָה *curse*) $29_{18(Qr)}$ (+ אָלָה ,חֶרְפָּה *curse*, שַׁמָּה *desolation*, שְׁרֵקָה *hissing*) $34_{17(Qr)}$ Ezk $23_{46}$ (mss, KtOr זַעֲוָה *trembling*; || בַּז *spoil*) 2 C $29_{8(Qr)}$ (|| שַׁמָּה, שְׁרֵקָה; Kt in all six זַעֲוָה) 1QS $2_6$ 4QTohD$_3$ ([יתנכה]). <COLL> זַעֲוָה לְכֹל מַמְלְכוֹת הָאָרֶץ *a cause of trembling to all the kingdoms of the earth* Dt $28_{25}$ (mss, Sam זְוָעָה) Jr $15_{4(Qr)}$ $24_{9(Qr)}$ $29_{18(Qr)}$ $34_{17(Qr)}$ (Kt in all four זַעֲוָה). <SYN> שַׁמָּה *desolation*, שְׁרֵקָה *hissing*, בַּז *spoil*, חֶרְפָּה *reproach*, כְּלִמָּה *insult*.

⇒ זוע *tremble*.

**זַעֲוָן** 2 pr.n.m. **Zaavan,** son of Ezer and grandson of Seir the Horite, <NOM CL> בְּנֵי־אֵצֶר ... זַעֲוָן *the sons of Ezer were ... Zaavan* 1 C $1_{42}$ (||Gn $36_{27}$ אֵלֶּה בְּנֵי־אֵצֶר ... וְזַעֲוָן *these were the sons of Ezer: ... Zaavan* [Sam. appar. זוֹעָן *Zoan*]).

**[זַעֲטוּט]** 0.0.5 n.m. **lad**—Q זעטוט—<SUBJ> בוא *come* 1QM $7_3$. <APP> נער זעטוט *a lad (who is) a young man* 1QM $7_3$ 4QM[a] $1_6$ (both + אִשָּׁה *woman*) 4QD[a] $17.1_8$ (+ פִּסֵּחַ ,*lame one* חִגֵּר *limping one*, חֵרֵשׁ *deaf and dumb one*). Also 4QRitMar $28_4$ ([ז]עטוטי[ם]) 311 (זע[טוטים]).

**[זְעִיר]** 0.1 adj. **little**—pl. Si זעירים (appar. זְעִירִים; or זְעֵירִים, i.e. זְעֵיר II)—used as noun, **little one, inferior,** <CSTR> יד זעירים be given into *the hand/power of inferiors* Si $11_6$ (+ כבד ni. ptc. *honoured one*).

**זְעֵיר I** 5 n.[m.] **a little,** <COLL> זְעֵיר שָׁם זְעֵיר שָׁם *a little here, a little there* Is $28_{10.13}$ (unless זְעֵיר III *servant*; both + קַו *line*, צַו *precept*); used adverbially, *(for) a little (time)*, כַּתַּר־לִי זְעֵיר *wait for me a little* Jb $36_2$.

**זְעֵיר II**, see זְעִיר *little*.

***זְעֵיר III** 5 n.[m.] **servant,** <COLL> זְעֵיר שָׁם זְעֵיר שָׁם *servant, listen; servant, listen* Is $28_{10.13}$ (i.e. שָׁם = שְׁמַע *listen*; unless זְעֵיר שָׁם = *a little here*).

**זעך** 1 vb. **extinguish—Ni.** 1 Pf. נִזְעָכוּ—**be extinguished,** <SUBJ> יוֹם *day* Jb $17_1$ (mss דעך ni. *be extingushed*; or em. עזב ni. *be abandoned*; + חבל pu. *be broken*).

**זעם** 12.3.11 vb. **be indignant—Qal** 11.1.11 Pf. זָעַם (Q זעמני), זְעַמְתָּה; impf. יִזְעָמוּהוּ ,אֶזְעֹם; + waw וְזָעַם, Q וזעמו; impv. זָעֲמָה; ptc. זֹעֵם (Si זועם), pass. Q זעום (cstr. זְעוּם), זְעוּמָה, Q זעומים—**1. be indignant, show indignation (against)** (but distinction from §2 not alw. clear), <SUBJ> Y. Is $66_{14}$ (or em. זַעְמוֹ *his indignation*) Na $1_6$ (if em. לִפְנֵי זַעְמוֹ *before his indignation* to זֹעֵם הוּא *he is indignant*) Zc $1_{12}$ (+ זֶה שִׁבְעִים שָׁנָה *[for] these seventy years*) Ml $1_4$ Ps $7_{12}$ 4Q525 $22_{10}$ (אל[והים] *God*), מֶלֶךְ *king* Dn $11_{30}$. <OBJ> אֹיֵב *enemy* Is $66_{14}$ (or em.; see Subj.), עַם *people* Ml $1_4$. <PREP> בְּ of place/time, *during*, + יוֹם *day* Ps $7_{12}$; עַל *against*, + בְּרִית *covenant* Dn $11_{30}$; עַד *unto*, + עוֹלָם *eternity* Ml $1_4$.

**2. curse, denounce,*** <SUBJ> Y. Nm $23_8$ Balaam Nm

23$_7$ (|| ארר *curse*) 23$_8$ (|| קבב *curse*), בֵּן *son* Si 3$_{16(C)}$ (A כעס hi. *provoke to anger*; + גדף pi. *revile*), אָח *brother* 1QM 13$_1$ (:: ברך pi. *bless*), כֹּהֵן *priest* 1QM 13$_1$ ([כו]הנים), לֵוִי *Levite* 1QM 13$_1$, זָקֵן *elder* 1QM 13$_1$, עֵצָה *council* 4QBer$^a$ 3.2$_1$ ([יזעמו]ן), לְאֹם *people* Pr 24$_{24}$ (|| קבב). <OBJ> יִשְׂרָאֵל *Israel* Nm 23$_7$, one cursed by Y. 23$_8$ (מָה אֶזְעֹם לֹא זָעַם י׳ *how shall I curse one whom Y. has not cursed?*; Sam mss זְעָמוֹ *cursed him*), אֹמֵר *speaker* Pr 24$_{24}$, בְּלִיַּעַל *Belial* 1QM 13$_1$ 4QBer$^a$ 3.2$_1$, רוּחַ *spirit* 1QM 13$_1$, גּוֹרָל *lot* of Belial 4QBer$^a$ 3.2$_1$. <COLL> with adverb, שָׁם *there* 1QM 13$_1$.

**3a.** passive (alw. ptc.), **be accursed,** <SUBJ> אֵיפָה short *ephah* Mc 6$_{10}$, אִישׁ *man* of Belial's lot 1QS 2$_7$ (|| ארר pass. *be cursed*), בֵּן *son* of Belial 4QBer$^a$ 3.2$_5$, בְּלִיַּעַל *Belial* 1QM 13$_4$ (|| ארר pass.) 13$_5$ 4QBer$^a$ 3.2$_3$ (|| ארר pass.), רוּחַ *spirit* 1QM 13$_5$ 4QBer$^a$ 3.2$_4$ ([רו]חי) 3.2$_8$ ([רו]ח ... [ז]עום), מַלְאָךְ *angel* 4QBer$^a$ 3.2$_8$ ([מלא]ך ... [ז]עום); subj. not specified, 4QTohD$_5$ (+ ארר pass.). <PREP> בְּ of place, *in*, + אֲפֵלָה *darkness* 1QS 2$_7$; of cause, *on account of*, + מִשְׂרָה *rule* 1QM 13$_4$ 4QBer$^a$ 3.2$_{3.8}$ ([במשרת] ... [ז]עום), מֶמְשָׁלָה *dominion* 4QBer$^a$ 3.2$_8$ ([ז]עום במ[ממש]ל[ת]), עֲבֹדָה *work* 1QM 13$_5$, מַחֲשָׁבָה *plan* 4QBer$^a$ 3.2$_4$, עָוֹן *iniquity* 4QBer$^a$ 3.2$_5$; לְאֵין *without*, + פְּלֵיטָה *remnant* 4QTohD$_5$.

**b.** passive participle as noun, **cursed one,** <SUBJ> נפל *fall* Pr 22$_{14}$. <CSTR> זְעוּם י׳ *cursed one of Y.*, i.e. one cursed by Y. Pr 22$_{14}$.

Also 4Q525 21$_9$ (unless זַעַם *indignation*).

<SYN> §2 ארר *curse*, קבב *curse*; §3a ארר pass. *be cursed*.

<ANT> §2 ברך pi. *bless*.

**Ni.** $_1$ Ptc. נִזְעָמִים—**be made indignant,** <SUBJ> פָּנִים *face* Pr 25$_{23}$.

**Hi.** $_{0.2}$ Impf. Si. יזעים; ptc. Si מזעים—appar. **make indignant, cause to curse,** <SUBJ> Y. Si 43$_{16(B)}$ (M נוף hi. *wave*; + חרף pi. *reproach*), appar. יִסּוּר *torture* Si 40$_{29}$ (Bmg) (יסור מזעים *torture [which] makes indignant* (B, M מיעים, i.e. מֵעֶה pl. *innards*). <OBJ> הַר *mountain* Si 43$_{16(B)}$. <PREP> בְּ of accompaniment, *with, in (a state of)*, + כֹּחַ *strength* Si 43$_{16(B)}$.*

⇒ זַעַם *indignation*, זְעָמָה *curse*.

**זַעַם** $_{22.2.2}$ n.m. **indignation**—זָעַם; cstr. זַעַם; sf. זַעְמִי, זַעַמְךָ (זַעְמֶךָ), זַעְמוֹ—usu. **indignation;** perh. **cursing** or **stammering** (Ho 7$_{16}$). <SUBJ> יצא *go out* Si 5$_7$ (+ נָקָם *vengeance*), כלה *be finished* Is 10$_{25}$=4QpIsa$^a$ 2$_8$ ([זעם]; || אַף *anger*) Dn 11$_{36}$, עבר *pass* Is 26$_{20}$, ירשׁ hi. *dispossess* nations Si 39$_{23}$. <NOM CL> מַטֵּה־הוּא בְיָדָם זַעְמִי perh. *my indignation is a staff in their hand* Is 10$_5$ (+ אַף *anger*; or em. מַטֵּה זַעְמִי he is *the staff of my indignation* in their hand), זַעְמוֹ אֶת־אֹיְבָיו *his indignation is with*, i.e. against, *his enemies* Is 66$_{14}$ (if em. זָעַם *he is indignant*).

<OBJ> מלא *be full of* Is 30$_{27}$, pi. *fill with* Jr 15$_{17}$, שׁפך *pour* Ezk 21$_{36}$ 22$_{31}$ (both + עֶבְרָה *anger*) Zp 3$_8$ (+ חֲרוֹן אַף *heat of anger*) Ps 69$_{25}$ (+ חֲרוֹן אַף), שׁלח pi. *send away* Ps 78$_{49}$ (|| עֶבְרָה, צָרָה *distress*; + חֲרוֹן אַף), כול hi. *contain* Jr 10$_{10}$. <CSTR> זַעַם לְשׁוֹנָם *cursing of their tongue* Ho 7$_{16}$, זעם שונאי *indignation of those who hate* your people 4QVis Sam 3.2$_4$, זַעַם־אַפּוֹ *indignation of his anger* Lm 2$_6$; יוֹם זַעַם *day of indignation* Ezk 22$_{24}$, אַחֲרִית הַזָּעַם *end of the indignation* Dn 8$_{19}$, כְּלֵי זַעְמוֹ *weapons of his indignation* Is 13$_5$ Jr 50$_{25}$, מַטֵּה זַעְמִי *staff of my indignation* Is 10$_5$ (if em.; see Nom. Cl.). <APP> מַטֶּה *staff* Is 10$_5$ (or em.).

<PREP> בְּ of accompaniment, *with, in (a state of)*, + צעד *march* Hb 3$_{12}$ (|| אַף *anger*), נאץ *spurn* Lm 2$_6$, גבר hi. *be mighty* 4QVisSam 3.2$_4$, perh. שׁבת *cease* 4QHod$^e$ 1$_2$; מִן of cause, *on account of*, + נפל *fall* Ho 7$_{16}$; לִפְנֵי *before*, + עמד *stand* Na 1$_6$=4QpNah 1$_{10}$ ([זעמו]); or em. לִפְנֵי זַעְמוֹ *before his indignation* to זַעְמוֹ לְפָנָיו *his indignation is before him* or זֹעֵם הוּא *he is indignant*; + חֲרוֹן אַף *heat of anger*); מִפְּנֵי *on account of* Ps 38$_4$ (+ חַטָּאת *sin*), + אכל *eat* ashes Ps 102$_{11}$ (|| קֶצֶף *anger*), מסך *mix* tears with drink Ps 102$_{11}$. <COLL> עֶבְרָה וָזַעַם וְצָרָה *anger and indignation and distress* Ps 78$_{49}$, שְׂפָתָיו מָלְאוּ זַעַם *his lips are full of indignation* Is 30$_{27}$. <SYN> אַף *anger*, קֶצֶף *anger*, ע�ֶבְרָה *anger*, צָרָה *distress*.*

⇒ זעם *be indignant*.

**[זְעָמָה]** $_{0.0.1}$ n.f. **curse**—Q זעמה—<PREP> לְ *for, as*, [ישא פני אפו] לכה לזעמה *may he* (Y.) *lift up his angry face to you for a curse* 4QToh D$_4$.

⇒ זעם *be indignant*.

**זעף** I $_5$ vb. **be angry**—**Qal** $_3$ Impf. יִזְעַף; + waw וַיִּזְעַף;

inf. זַעְפּוֹ—**be angry, enraged** (at Gn $40_6$ Dn $1_{10}$ perh. זעף II *be thin*), <SUBJ> Uzziah 2 C $26_{19.19}$ (unless בְּזַעְפּוֹ *in his anger*, from זַעַף), Daniel, Hananiah, Mishael, Azariah Dn $1_{10}$, שַׂר *chief* butler and baker Gn $40_6$, פִּילֶגֶשׁ *secondary wife* Jg $19_2$ (if em. זנה I *prostitute oneself* or II *abhor*), לֵב *heart* Pr $19_3$. <PREP> מִן of comparison, *than*, + יֶלֶד *child* Dn $1_{10}$; עַל *against, with*, + י׳ *Y.* Pr $19_3$, אִישׁ *man* Jg $19_2$ (if em.); עִם *with, against*, + כֹּהֵן *priest* 2 C $26_{19}$.*

→ זַעַף *anger*, זָעֵף *angry*.

**זעף II** 2 vb. **be thin**—**Qal** 2 Ptc. זֹעֲפִים—**be thin** or **be wretched-looking** (but perh. זעף I *be angry*, i.e. out of humour, vexed) <SUBJ> Daniel, Hananiah, Mishael, Azariah Dn $1_{10}$, שַׂר *chief* butler and baker Gn $40_6$. <PREP> מִן of comparison, *than*, + יֶלֶד *child* Dn $1_{10}$.*

**זַעַף** 6.0.3 n.m. **anger**—cstr. זַעַף; sf. זַעְפּוֹ—**anger, raging,** of Y. (Is $30_{30}$ $7_9$ 4QShir[b] $35_1$), Asa (2 C $16_{10}$), king (Pr $19_{12}$), Israelites (2 C $28_9$), Kittim (1QpHab $3_{12}$), sea (Jon $1_{15}$ 1QH $6_{23}$), perh. wind (1QH $7_4$), <NOM CL> נַהַם כַּכְּפִיר זַעַף מֶלֶךְ *the raging of a king is a growling like (that of) the lion* Pr $19_{12}$, זַעַף בָּעָם *anger was among the people* 2 C $16_{10}$ (if em.; see Prep.). <OBJ> נשׂא *bear*, i.e. suffer as punishment Mc $7_9$. <CSTR> זַעַף י׳ *anger of Y.* Mc $7_9$, מֶלֶךְ *of a king* Pr $19_{12}$, ימים *of the seas* 1QH $6_{23}$ (unless זעפו is inf. of זעף *be angry*), חרישית *of bitter wind* 1QH $7_4$ (unless זעפו is inf. of זעף *be angry*), אַף *of anger* Is $30_{30}$ (|| לַהַב *flame* of fire, + נֶפֶץ *cloudburst*, זֶרֶם *storm*, אֶבֶן hail *stone*), אפים *of anger* 1QpHab $3_{12}$ (|| חָרוֹן *heat*, + חֵמָה *rage*), אפי *of anger of* God 4QShir[b] $35_1$ ([לזע]ף). <PREP> לְ *for, as* 4QShir[b] $35_1$ ([זע]ף); בְּ of accompaniment, *with, in (a state of)* 2 C $16_{10}$ (בְּזַעַף עִמּוֹ appar. *he was in (a state of) anger with him*; or em. זַעַף בָּעָם *anger was among the people*) 1QH $6_{23}$ $7_4$, + ראה hi. *show* arm Is $30_{30}$, הרג *kill* 2 C $28_9$, דבר pi. *speak* 1QpHab $3_{12}$ ([ב]חרן אף וזעף *with heat of anger and rage*); עמד מִן *stand*, i.e. cease, *from* Jon $1_{15}$ (unless זעפו is inf. of זעף *be angry*). <SYN> חָרוֹן *wrath*, לַהַב *flame*.*

→ זעף *be angry*.

**זָעֵף** 2 adj. **angry, upset,** as predicate of הלך *go* 1 K $20_{43}$ (|| סַר *resentful*), בוא *come* 1 K $21_4$ (|| סַר). <SYN> סַר *resentful*.*

→ זעף *be enraged*.

**זעק** 73.0.11 vb. **cry out**—**Qal** 58.0.10 Pf. זָעֲקָה, זָעַקְתִּי, זָעֲקוּ; impf. יִזְעַק, 3fs תִּזְעַק (תִּזְעָק), 2ms תִּזְעַק, אֶזְעַק (אֶזְעָק, Q אזעקה), יִזְעֲקוּ (יִזְעָקוּ), נִזְעַק; + waw וַיִּזְעַק; וּזְעַקְתֶּם, וְזָעֲקוּ, 3fs וַתִּזְעַק, וָאֶזְעַק, וַיִּזְעֲקוּ (וַיִּזְעָקוּ, וַיִּזְעָקוּךָ); impv. זְעַק, זַעֲקִי, זַעֲקוּ (Qr זְעָקוּ); inf. זְעֹק (זַעֲקֵךְ, Q זועקכה, זַעֲקֵךְ)—usu. intrans. **cry, cry out (for help),** rarely trans. **summon (for help)** (Jg $6_{34.35}$ [if em. in both] $12_2$ [or em.] Ne $9_{28}$).

<SUBJ> י׳ *Y.* Jr $48_{31}$ (+ ילל hi. *wail*), עַם *people* Is $30_{19}$=4QpIsa[c] $23.2_{16}$ 2 C $20_9$ perh. 4Q$462_{12}$, בַּיִת *house* of Israel Jr $11_{11}$, of Judah Jr $11_{11}$, זֶרַע *seed*, i.e. offspring Is $57_{13}$ Jr $30_{15}$ 2 C $20_9$, בֵּן *son* Is $57_{13}$, specif. son of Israel Ex $2_{23}$ Jg $3_{9.15}$ $6_{6.7}$ $10_{10.14}$, of Reuben 1 C $5_{20}$, of human being, i.e. Ezekiel Ezk $21_{17}$ (|| ילל hi.), Israel Ho $8_2$ 2 C $20_9$, Israelites 11QT $59_6$ (|| קרא *call*), Ephraim Ho $7_{14}$ (+ ילל hi. *wail*) $8_2$, Reubenites, Gadites and Manassites 1 C $5_{20}$, Ekronites 1 S $5_{10}$, Heshbon Is $15_4$, Elealeh Is $15_4$, עִיר *city* Is $14_{31}$ (|| ילל hi.) Jr $11_{12}$, Babylon Jr $50_{46}$ (if em. זְעָקָה *outcry* to זַעֲקָהּ *its crying out*), perh. Moab Jr $48_{20}$ (|| ילל hi.).

Ezekiel Ezk $9_8$ $11_{13}$, Gideon Jg $6_{34.35}$ (if em. ni. *be called* in both), Habakkuk Hb $1_2$=1QpHab $1_4$ ([אזעק]; || שׁוע pi. *cry out*), Hezekiah 2 C $32_{20}$, Isaiah 2 C $32_{20}$, Jephthah Jg $12_2$, Jehoshaphat 1 K $22_{32}$||2 C $18_{31}$, Jeremiah Jr $20_8$ (+ קרא *call*), Jeshua and other Levites Ne $9_4$, Mephibosheth 2 S $19_{29}$, Mordecai Est $4_1$, Moses 4Q PentPar[b] $6.2_{10}$, Samuel 1 S $7_{8.9}$ $15_{11}$, Tamar 2 S $13_{19}$.

אִישׁ *man* Jon $1_5$, אִשָּׁה *woman* 1 S $28_{12}$, נַעֲרָה *girl* 11QT $66_{2.7}$ (=Dt $22_{24.27}$ צעק *cry*), אָדָם *human being* Jr $47_2$ (|| ילל hi. *wail*), אָב *father* 1 S $12_{8.10}$ Ps $22_6$ Ne $9_{28}$, מֶלֶךְ *king* 2 S $19_5$, קָצִין *ruler* Mc $3_4$, ראשׁ *head* Mc $3_4$, הָרָה *pregnant (woman)* Is $26_{17}$, מַלָּח *sailor* Ezk $27_{30}$ (+ שׁמע בְּקוֹל hi. *make voice heard*) Jon $1_5$, חֹבֵל *sailor* Ezk $27_{30}$, יֹשֵׁב *inhabitant* Is $30_{19}$ (if em. יֵשֵׁב *he will dwell* to יֹשֵׁב) Jr $11_{12}$, רֹעֶה *shepherd* Jr $25_{34}$ (|| ילל hi. *wail*, + פלשׁ htp. *roll in dust*), כֹּהֵן *priest* Jl $1_{14}$, שׁרת pi. ptc. *minister* Jl $1_{14}$, לֵוִי *Levite* Ne $9_4$, worshipper Ps $142_2$ (|| חנן htp. *intercede*) $142_6$ Lm $3_8$ (|| שׁוע pi. *cry out*) 11QPs[a] $24_{14}$, גאל pass. ptc.

*redeemed one* Ps 107$_{13.19}$, לֵב *heart* Is 15$_{5}$=4QpIsa$^{e}$ 4$_{1}$ ([לבי ... יזעק]), אֶבֶן *stone* Hb 2$_{11}$=1QpHab 9$_{15}$ (+ ענה *answer*), אֲדָמָה *earth* Jb 31$_{38}$ (+ בכה *weep*); subj. not specified, 1QpHab 1$_{4}$ (יז[עקו ... אזעק]).

<OBJ> Y. Ne 9$_{28}$, Abiezer Jg 6$_{34}$ (if em. ni. *be called*), Manasseh Jg 6$_{35}$ (if em. ni.), אִישׁ *man* of Ephraim Jg 12$_{2}$ (or em. אֶתְכֶם summon *you* to אֲלֵיכֶם cry out *to you*).

<PREP> לְ of direction, *to*, + Y. Ho 8$_{2}$ 1 C 5$_{20}$, מִי *who?* 11QPs$^{a}$ 24$_{14}$; *concerning*, or of cause, *on account of*, + Moab Is 15$_{5}$=4QpIsa$^{e}$ 4$_{1}$ ([למועב יזעק]) Jr 48$_{31}$.

בְּ of place, *in*, + עִיר *city* 11QT 66$_{2}$ ([זעק[ה]), מִלְחָמָה *battle* 1 C 5$_{20}$; of instrument, *by (means of), with*, + קוֹל *voice* 1 S 28$_{12}$ 2 S 19$_{5(mss)}$ Ne 9$_{4}$, לֵב *heart* Ho 7$_{14}$; of accompaniment, *with, in (a state of)*, + חֵבֶל *pain* Is 26$_{17}$, צַר *distress* Ps 107$_{13.19}$ 4QapPs$^{a}$ 2$_{4}$ ([יזעקו]).

מִן of direction, *from*, + קִיר *wall* Hb 2$_{11}$=1QpHab 9$_{15}$; of cause, *on account of*, + צָרָה *distress* 2 C 20$_{9}$.

אֶל *to* 4Q462$_{12}$, + ׳י Y. Jg 3$_{9.15}$ 6$_{6.7}$ 10$_{10}$ 1 S 7$_{8.9}$ 12$_{8.10}$ 15$_{11}$ Jr 11$_{11}$ Ho 7$_{14}$ Jl 1$_{14}$ Mc 3$_{4}$ Hb 1$_{2}$=1QpHab 1$_{4}$ ([אזעק אליכה]) Ps 107$_{13.19}$ 142$_{2.6}$ Ne 9$_{4}$ 2 C 20$_{9}$ 4QPent Par$^{b}$ 6.2$_{10}$ 4QapPs$^{a}$ 2$_{4}$ ([ויזעקו אל]), אֱלֹהִים *God* Ps 22$_{6}$, *gods* Jg 10$_{14}$ Jr 11$_{12}$ Jon 1$_{5}$, מֶלֶךְ *king* 2 S 19$_{29}$, אִישׁ *man* of Ephraim Jg 12$_{2}$ (if em.; see Obj.).

עַל *on account of, concerning*, + שֶׁבֶר *breach*, i.e. injury Jr 30$_{15}$; *against*, + Job Jb 31$_{38}$, אִישׁ *man* 1QpHab 1$_{4}$ ([יז]עקו על [אנשי]).

עַל אֹדוֹת *on account of*, + Midianite Jg 6$_{7}$.

אַחֲרֵי *(to follow) after*, + Gideon Jg 6$_{34.35}$ (if em. ni. in both).

בְּעַד *on behalf of*, + Israel 1 S 7$_{9}$.

מִלִּפְנֵי *(from) before*, i.e. because of, + מֶלֶךְ *king* 1 S 8$_{18}$.

<COLL> וַיִּזְעַק הַמֶּלֶךְ קוֹל גָּדוֹל *and the king cried out with a loud voice* 2 S 19$_{5}$ (mss בְּ *with* voice), sim. Ezk 11$_{13}$, קוֹלִי אֶל־י׳ אֶזְעָק *with my voice I cry out to Y.* Ps 142$_{2}$, וְיִזְעֲקוּ מָרָה *and they cry out bitterly* Ezk 27$_{30}$, וַיִּזְעַק זְעָקָה גְדֹלָה וּמָרָה *and he cried out with a great and bitter cry* Est 4$_{1}$, וַיִּזְעֲקוּ הַשָּׁמָיִם *and they cried out to heaven* 2 C 32$_{20}$, מַה־יֶּשׁ־לִי עוֹד צְדָקָה וְלִזְעֹק עוֹד *what further right have I to cry out* 2 S 19$_{29}$, וַיִּזְעַק ... כָּל־הַלָּיְלָה *and he cried ... all the night* 1 S 15$_{11}$, וַתֵּלֶךְ הָלוֹךְ וְזָעָקָה *and she went, crying out as she went* 2 S 13$_{19}$.

זעק with אמר *say* introducing direct speech, Jg 10$_{10}$ 1 S 5$_{10}$ 12$_{10(Qr)}$ 28$_{12}$ Ezk 9$_{8}$ 11$_{13}$ Ps 142$_{6}$, זעק followed directly by direct speech, Ho 8$_{2}$ Hb 1$_{2}$=1QpHab 1$_{4}$ ([אזעק]).

<SYN> קרא *call*, שׁוע pi. *cry out*, חנן htp. *intercede*, ילל hi. *wail*.

Also perh. 4QPrFêtes$^{c}$ 28$_{3}$ (unless זעקת *cry of*, from זְעָקָה *cry*) 4Q518 31$_{2}$.

**Ni.** $_{6}$ Pf. נִזְעֲקוּ, נִזְעֲקְתָּ; + waw וַיִּזָּעֵק, וַיִּזָּעֲקוּ—**be called (together), be assembled,** <SUBJ> עַם *people* Jos 8$_{16}$ 1 S 14$_{20}$, Abiezer Jg 6$_{34}$ (or em. qal), Manasseh Jg 6$_{35}$ (or em. qal), Micah Jg 18$_{23}$, Saul 1 S 14$_{20}$, אִישׁ *man* Jg 18$_{22}$. <PREP> אַחֲרֵי *after*, + Gideon Jg 6$_{34.35}$ (or em. qal in both).

**Hi.** $_{7.0.1}$ Impf. יַזְעִיקוּ; + waw וַיַּזְעֵק; impv. הַזְעֶק־; ptc. Q מזעיקים; inf. הַזְעִיק—**1.** transitive, **cry out to, call together, summon,** esp. for military service, <SUBJ> Y. Zc 10$_{9}$ (if em. וְאֶזְרָעֵם *and I shall sow them* to וְאַזְעִקֵם *and I shall cry out to them*), Amasa 2 S 20$_{4}$ (+ שְׁלֹשֶׁת יָמִים *[within] three days*) 20$_{5}$, Barak Jg 4$_{10}$, Sisera Jg 4$_{13}$. <OBJ> עַם *people* Jg 4$_{13}$, Israel Zc 10$_{9}$ (if em.), Judah 2 S 20$_{5}$, Naphtali Jg 4$_{10}$, Zebulun Jg 4$_{10}$, Zechariah Zc 6$_{8}$, אִישׁ *man* of Judah 2 S 20$_{4}$, מַלְאָךְ *messenger* Zc 6$_{8}$ (+ דבר pi. *speak*), רֶכֶב *chariot* Jg 4$_{13}$. <PREP> לְ of direction, *to*, + מֶלֶךְ *king* 2 S 20$_{4}$; בְּ of place, *among*, + עַם *people* Zc 10$_{9}$ (if em.; see Subj.; or del. בָּעַמִּים); with ה- of direction, *(to come) to(wards)*, + קֶדֶשׁ *Kedesh* Jg 4$_{10}$.

**2.** intransitive, **cry out (for help); make proclamation** (Jon 3$_{7}$), <SUBJ> מֶלֶךְ *king* of Nineveh Jon 3$_{7}$, Israelites 11QT 59$_{6}$ (‖ אנח htp. *groan*), oppressors Jb 35$_{9}$ (‖ שׁוע pi. *cry out*). <PREP> בְּ of place, *in*, + ארץ *land* 11QT 59$_{6}$; מִן of cause, *because of*, + רֹב *abundance* of oppressions Jb 35$_{9}$; מִפְּנֵי *on account of*, + עֹל *yoke* 11QT 59$_{6}$. <COLL> זעק followed by אמר *say* to introduce direct speech, Jon 3$_{7}$.

<SYN> §2 שׁוע pi. *cry for help*, אנח htp. *groan*.*

⇒ זְעָקָה *cry*.

**זְעָקָה** $_{20.0.2}$ n.f. **cry**—cstr. זַעֲקַת; sf. זַעֲקָתִי, זַעֲקָתָם—usu. **cry** of distress or for help; also **outcry, clamour** (Gn 18$_{20}$), <SUBJ> שׁמע ni. *be heard* Jr 18$_{22}$ 50$_{46}$ (or em. זַעֲקָהּ *its cry*, from זַעַק *cry*), נקף hi. *go around* Is 15$_{8}$ (+ יְלָלָה *howling*).

<NOM CL> זַעֲקַת חֶשְׁבּוֹן עַד־אֶלְעָלֵה *the cry of Heshbon is as far as Elealeh* Jr 48$_{34}$ (if em. מִזַּעֲקַת *on account of the cry of*), זַעֲקַת סְדֹם וַעֲמֹרָה כִּי־רָבָּה *because the outcry of Sodom and Gomorrah is indeed great* Gn 18$_{20}$ (Sam צְעָקָה *cry*), perh. זְעָקָה מִבָּבֶל *a cry is from Babylon* Jr 51$_{54}$ (but see Cstr.).

<OBJ> עור pilp. *rouse*, i.e. raise Is 15$_{5}$=4QpIsa$^{e}$ 4$_{2}$ ([זעקת ... יעערו]); unless em. יְעֹרֵרוּ *they rouse* to יְעוֹרֵרוּ poel or יָעִירוּ hi. *rouse*, or יָרִעוּ *they raise*, i.e. רוע polel), שׁמע *hear* Jr 20$_{16}$ (|| תְּרוּעָה *shout*) Ne 5$_{6}$ (+ דָּבָר *word*) 9$_{9}$, hi. *proclaim* Jr 48$_{4}$, זעק *cry* Est 4$_{1}$.

<CSTR> זַעֲקַת חֶשְׁבּוֹן *cry of Heshbon* Jr 48$_{34}$, זַעֲקַת סְדֹם וַעֲמֹרָה *cry of Sodom and Gomorrah* Gn 18$_{20}$ (Sam צעקת *cry of*), זַעֲקַת חֹבְלָיִךְ *cry of your sailors* Ezk 27$_{28}$, זַעֲקַת־דָּל *cry of a poor one* Pr 21$_{13}$, זַעֲקַת מוֹשֵׁל *cry of a ruler* Ec 9$_{17}$, זַעֲקַת־שֶׁבֶר *cry of destruction* Is 15$_{5}$=4QpIsa$^{e}$ 4$_{2}$ ([זעקת שבר]); קוֹל זְעָקָה *sound of a cry* Is 65$_{19}$ (+ בְּכִי *weeping*) Jr 51$_{54}$ (unless קוֹל is interjection, *hark!*; + שֶׁבֶר *destruction*), קוֹל זַעֲקַת *sound of cry of* Ezk 27$_{28}$, דִּבְרֵי הַצֹּמוֹת וְזַעֲקָתָם *matters of the fasts and their cry*, i.e. lamentings Est 9$_{31}$.

<ADJ> גָּדוֹל *great* Est 4$_{1}$, מַר *bitter* Est 4$_{1}$.

<PREP> לְ of benefit, *to, for*, + היה *be* (of place) Jb 16$_{18}$; מִן privative, *without*, i.e. so as not to hear, + אטם *shut* ear Pr 21$_{13}$; of comparison, *(more) than*, + שׁמע ni. *be heard* Ec 9$_{17}$, perh. of cause, *on account of*, + נתן *give*, i.e. utter Jr 48$_{34}$ (or del. מִן).

<COLL> וַיִּזְעַק זְעָקָה גְדֹלָה וּמָרָה *and he cried out with a great and bitter cry* Est 4$_{1}$.

<SYN> תְּרוּעָה *shout*.

Also 4QPrFêtes$^{c}$ 28$_{3}$ (unless זעקת is from זעק *cry out*) 4Q471$^{a}$ 1$_{7}$.*

→ זעק *cry*.

[זִף], see זִיף I *Ziph*.

[זִפִי], see זִיפִי *Ziphite*.

זִפְרֹן 1 pl.n. **Ziphron**—+ ה- of direction זִפְרֹנָה—on northern border of Israel, perh. Za'ferān, 35 km NE of Tripoli, <PREP> with ה- of direction, *to(wards)*, + יצא *go out* (of border) Nm 34$_{9}$.

* [זפת] **be black—Shaphel, make as black as pitch,** <SUBJ> שֶׁמֶשׁ *sun* Ca 1$_{6}$ (if em. שֶׁזְּפָתְנִי *looked at me* to שֶׁזִּפְּתַנִי *made me black as pitch*) <OBJ> female lover Ca 1$_{6}$ (if em.).

זֶפֶת 3.1.1 n.f. **pitch**—זָפֶת—<SUBJ> בער *burn* Is 34$_{9}$, דבק *adhere* Si 13$_{1}$. <CSTR> נחלי זפת *streams of pitch* 1QH 3$_{31}$. <PREP> לְ *as, into*, + היה *be* Is 34$_{9}$, הפך ni. *be turned* Is 34$_{9}$ (|| גָּפְרִית *brimstone*); + בְּ of material, *with*, + חמר *cover (with bitumen)* Ex 2$_{3}$ (|| חֵמָר *bitumen*); *against*, + נגע *strike*, i.e. touch Si 13$_{1}$. <SYN> חֵמָר *bitumen*, גָּפְרִית *brimstone*.

[זֵק] I 4.0.4 n.[m.] **fetter**—pl. זִקִּים; cstr. Q זקי—<SUBJ> שׁבר pu. *be broken* 1QH 5$_{37}$ (זקים ללוא ישבורו *fetters which shall not be broken*; || עֲבֹת *cord*; + חוֹמָה *wall*). <CSTR> זקי מכשול *fetters of stumbling* 1QH 8$_{35}$, משפט *of judgment* 1QH 8$_{37}$. <PREP> בְּ of place, *in*, i.e. wearing, + עבר *pass* Is 45$_{14}$ (or rd. בַּזִּקִּים), הלך *go* Is 45$_{14}$ (if rd. בַּזִּקִּים); of instrument, *by (means of), with*, + אסר *bind* Ps 149$_{8}$ (|| כֶּבֶל *fetter*), pass. *be bound* Jb 36$_{8}$ (|| חֶבֶל *cord*), רתח pu. *be bound* Na 3$_{10}$=4QpNah 3.4$_{3}$, נתק pu. *be wrenched out* 1QH 8$_{35}$ (נו[תקו]); of cause, *on account of* 1QH 8$_{37}$. <SYN> כֶּבֶל *fetter*, חֶבֶל *cord*, עֲבֹת *cord*.

→ אָזֵק *manacle*.

[זֵק] II 1.1.2 n.[m.] **flaming arrow**—pl. זִקִּים (Si זיקים); cstr. Q זיקי—**flaming arrow, firebrand, lightning flash,** perh. **meteor,** <SUBJ> perh. היה *be* 1QH 1$_{12}$ (|| בָּרָק *lightning*), נפל hi. *cause to fall* 1QM 6$_{3}$. <OBJ> נצח pi. *make brilliant* Si 43$_{17(Bmg)}$ (B, M זיקות *flaming arrows*; Bmg יְקוּם *existence*), ירה hi. *throw* Pr 26$_{18}$ (|| חֵץ *arrow*, מָוֶת *death*), כתב *write* 1QM 6$_{3}$. <CSTR> זיקי דם *flaming arrows of blood* 1QM 6$_{3}$. <SYN> חֵץ *arrow*, מָוֶת *death*.

זקן 20.1.1 vb. **be old—Qal** 18.0.1 Pf. זָקֵן, זָקְנָה, זָקַנְתִּי, זָקַנְתָּ; + waw וַיִּזְקַן—**be old, grow old** (זָקֵן *was old* sometimes difficult to distinguish from זָקֵן *old*), <SUBJ> Abraham Gn 24$_{1}$ (|| בוא בַּיָּמִים *come into days*, i.e. be advanced in years) 4QJub$^{d}$ 21$_{1}$ (זק[נתי]), David 1 K 1$_{1}$ (|| בוא בַּיָּמִים) 1 C 23$_{1}$ (|| שׂבע יָמִים *be satisfied with days*), Isaac Gn 27$_{1}$ (+ וַתִּכְהֶיןָ עֵינָיו מֵרְאֹת *and his eyes became too dim to see*)

$27_2$ (+ לֹא יָדַעְתִּי מוֹתִי *I do not know [the time of] my death*), Jehoiada 2 C $24_{15}$ (|| שׂבע יָמִים, מות *die*), Jesse 1 S $17_{12}$, Joshua Jos $13_{1.1}$ $23_{1.2}$ (all four || בוא בַּיָּמִים), Naomi Ru $1_{12}$, Samuel 1 S $8_{1.5}$ $12_2$ (|| שׂיב *be grey-haired*), Sarah Gn $18_{13}$, אֵם *mother* Pr $23_{22}$, מֶלֶךְ *king* 1 K $1_1$, worshipper Ps $37_{25}$=4QpPs$^a$ $1.3_{17}$ (:: היה נַעַר *be a youth*).

<PREP> מִן of comparison, *(more) than*, + היה inf. *being* Ru $1_{12}$ (זָקַנְתִּי מִהְיוֹת לְאִישׁ *I am too old to belong to a man*, i.e. be married). <SYN> בוא בַּיָּמִים *come into days*, i.e. be advanced in years, שׂבע יָמִים *be satisfied (with) days*, שׂיב *be grey-haired*, מות *die*. <ANT> היה נַעַר *be a youth*.

**Hi.** 2.1 Impf. יַזְקִין, 3fs Si תזקין—**1. grow old,** <SUBJ> נַעַר *youth* Pr $22_6$, שֹׁרֶשׁ *root* Jb $14_8$ (|| מות *die*), humans Si $8_6$ (if em. נמנה מזקנים appar. *we are reckoned to be of the elders* to ממנו מזקינים *some of us will grow old*). <PREP> בְּ of place, *in*, + אֶרֶץ *earth* Jb $14_8$.

**2. make old,** <SUBJ> דְּאָגָה *anxiety* Si $30_{24}$. <PREP> בְּ of time, *in*, + עֵת *time* Si $30_{24}$ (בלא עת *without [appointed] time*, i.e. prematurely).

<SYN> §1 מות *die*.

⇒ זָקֵן *old*, זֹקֶן *old age*, זִקְנָה *old age*, זְקֻנִים *old age*.

**זָקָן** 19.0.3 n.m. (sometimes f.) **beard**—cstr. זְקַן; sf. זְקָנִי, זְקָנְךָ, זְקָנוֹ, זְקַנְכֶם, זְקָנָם—**beard,** sometimes perh. **chin*** (e.g. Lv $13_{29.30}$ 1 S $21_{14}$ Ps $133_2$ 4QD$^a$ $9.1_{5.6}$), usu. of man; also of animal (1 S $17_{35}$), <SUBJ> צמח pi. *grow* 2 S $10_5$||1 C $19_5$, גרע pass. *be diminished*, i.e. shorn Is $15_2$ (+ ראשׁ *head*) Jr $48_{37}$ (mss גדע pass. *be hewn*; + ראשׁ). <OBJ> גלח pi. *shave* Lv $14_9$ (|| ראשׁ *head*, גַּב *(eye)brow*, שֵׂעָר *hair*) 2 S $10_4$, ספה *sweep away* Is $7_{20}$ (+ ראשׁ, שֵׂעָר).

<CSTR> זְקַן אַהֲרֹן *beard of Aaron* Ps $133_2$ (+ פֶּה *mouth*, i.e. collar), עֲמָשָׂא *of Amasa* 2 S $20_9$; פְּאַת זְקָנֶךָ *corner of your beard* Lv $19_{27}$ (|| ראשׁ *head*), זְקָנָם *of their beard* Lv $21_5$ (+ ראשׁ, בָּשָׂר *flesh*), שְׂעַר ... זְקָנִי *hair ... of my beard* Ezr $9_3$ (|| ראשׁ), צָרַעַת ... הַזָּקָן *leprosy of ... the beard* Lv $13_{30}$ (|| ראשׁ *head*), נתק ... הזקן *scab ... of the beard* 4QD$^a$ $9.1_5$ (|| ראשׁ), מְגֻלְּחֵי זָקָן *those shaved of beard* Jr $41_5$ (|| בֶּגֶד *garment*), חֲצִי זְקָנָם *half their beard* 2 S $10_4$, כָּל־זָקָן *every beard* Is $15_2$ Jr $48_{37}$. <APP> שֵׂעָר *hair* Lv $14_9$, זָקָן *beard* Ps $133_2$.

<PREP> בְּ of place, *in* Lv $13_{29}$ (|| ראשׁ *head*), בוא *come* 4QD$^a$ $9.1_6$ (|| ראשׁ); introducing object, + אחז *grasp* 2 S $20_9$, חזק hi. *grasp* 1 S $17_{35}$; אֶל *to*, + ירד hi. *cause* spittle *to go down* 1 S $21_{14}$ (mss עַל *upon*); עַל *upon, over*, + ירד *go down* Ps $133_2$ (|| ראשׁ *head*), hi. *cause* spittle *to go down* 1 S $21_{14(mss)}$ (L אֶל *to*), עבר hi. *cause to pass* Ezk $5_1$ (|| ראשׁ).

Also 4QCrypt $2.1_1$. <SYN> ראשׁ *head*, גַּב *(eye)brow*, שֵׂעָר *hair*, בֶּגֶד *garment*.

**זָקֵן I** 186.2.30 adj. **old**—cstr. זְקַן; pl. זְקֵנִים (I זקנם); cstr. זִקְנֵי; sf. זְקֵנַי, זְקֵנֶיךָ, זְקֵנָיו, זְקֵנֶיהָ, זְקֵנֵינוּ (זְקִינֵינוּ), זִקְנֵיכֶם, זְקֵנוֹת.

**1.** as attributive adj., **old, elderly,** used of אִישׁ *man* Jg $19_{16.17.20.22}$ 1 S $28_{14}$ (or em. זֹקֵף *startling*) 1QSa $2_7$, אָב *father* Gn $43_{27}$ $44_{20}$, מֶלֶךְ *king* Ec $4_{13}$ (+ כְּסִיל *foolish*; חָכָם *wise*, מִסְכֵּן *poor*), נָבִיא *prophet* 1 K $13_{11.25.29}$, כֹּהֵן *priest* Ezr $3_{12}$, לֵוִי *Levite* Ezr $3_{12}$, ראשׁ *head* of father's house Ezr $3_{12}$ (mss ins. וְ *and* elders, as §2b).

**2.** as predicative adj. or noun, **a. old (one), elderly (one)** (זָקֵן *old* sometimes difficult to distinguish from זָקֵן *he was old*), <SUBJ> היה *be* 1 S $2_{31.32}$ 1 K $12_6$||2 C $10_6$, שׁבת *cease* Lm $5_{14}$ (:: בָּחוּר *youth*), הדר ni. *be honoured* Lm $5_{12}$ (if em.; see Cstr.), לכד ni. *be captured* Jr $6_{11}$ (+ מְלֵא *full* of days, אִישׁ *man*, אִשָּׁה *woman*), עמד *stand* 1 K $12_6$||2 C $10_6$, שׁכב *lie down* Lm $2_{21}$ (:: נַעַר *lad*), גוע *expire* Gn $25_8$ (+ בְּשֵׂיבָה טוֹבָה *in a good old age*) $35_{29}$ CD $14_{14}$ (יגו[ע]; =4QD$^a$ $18.3_8$ יכרע who *bows down*), מות *die* Gn $25_8$ $35_{29}$ Jb $42_{17}$, אסף ni. *be gathered* to ancestors Gn $25_8$ $35_{29}$, ישׁב *dwell* Zc $8_{4.4}$, מלא pi. *fill* Is $65_{20}$ (+ עוּל *suckling*), בין *understand* Jb $32_9$ (+ רַב *great one*), הלל pi. *praise* Ps $148_{12}$ (:: נַעַר, + בְּתוּלָה *young woman*), חלם *dream* Jl $3_1$ (:: בָּחוּר *youth*, + בֵּן *son*, בַּת *daughter*), שׂמח *rejoice* Jr $31_{13}$ (:: בָּחוּר, + בְּתוּלָה), משׁל *rule* Gn $24_2$.

<NOM CL> אַבְרָהָם וְשָׂרָה זְקֵנִים *Abraham and Sarah were old* Gn $18_{11}$ (+ בוא בַּיָּמִים *come into days*, i.e. become old), בַּרְזִלַּי זָקֵן מְאֹד *Barzillai was very old* 2 S $19_{33}$, עֵלִי זָקֵן מְאֹד *Eli was very old* 1 S $2_{22}$, הַמֶּלֶךְ זָקֵן מְאֹד *the king was very old* 1 K $1_{15}$, אֲדֹנִי זָקֵן *my lord is old* Gn $18_{12}$, אָבִינוּ זָקֵן *our father is old* Gn $19_{31}$, זָקֵן הָאִישׁ *the man was old* 1 S $4_{18}$ (+ כָּבֵד *heavy*), sim. 1 S $17_{12}$ (+ בוא בַאֲנָשִׁים *come among men*, perh. be recognized as mature), אִישָׁהּ זָקֵן *her husband is old* 2 K $4_{14}$, זְקֵנִים־הֵמָּה מִמֶּנּוּ *they were older than he* Jb $32_4$.

<OBJ> חנן *pity*, i.e. be gracious to 4QapPsb 79$_{2}$, נפץ pi. *smash* Jr 51$_{22}$ (:: נַעַר *lad*, + בָּחוּר *youth*, בְּתוּלָה *young woman*, אִישׁ *man*, אִשָּׁה *woman*), הרג *kill* Ezk 9$_{6}$ (:: בָּחוּר, + בְּתוּלָה, אִשָּׁה, טַף *child*), קבר *bury* Gn 25$_{8}$ 35$_{29}$, אבד pi. *destroy* 1QpHab 6$_{11}$ (+ נַעַר, אָשִׁישׁ *adult*, אִשָּׁה, טַף), נהג *lead away* Is 20$_{4}$ (:: נַעַר).

<CSTR> זְקַן בֵּיתוֹ *old one*, i.e. oldest (slave), *of his house(hold)* Gn 24$_{2}$; פְּנֵי זָקֵן appar. *face*, i.e. presence, *of an old man* Lv 19$_{32}$ (|| שֵׂיבָה *grey-hair[ed]*) Lm 5$_{12}$ (זְקֵנִים; or del. פְּנֵי, leaving זָקֵן as subj. of הדר ni. *be honoured*; + שַׂר *prince*), עֲטֶרֶת זְקֵנִים *crown of old ones* Pr 17$_{6}$ (:: בֵּן *son*), הֲדַר זְקֵנִים *splendour of old men* Pr 20$_{29}$ (:: בָּחוּר *youth*), סוד זקני[ם] זקנו[ת] *council of old men [and] old women* 4QRitMar 24$_{4}$, יגון זקנינו *grief of our aged* 4QPr Fêtesc 16.4$_{4}$, עֲצַת הַזְּקֵנִים *counsel of the aged* 1 K 12$_{8.13}$|| 2 C 10$_{8.13}$ (both :: יֶלֶד *child*).

<APP> Abraham Gn 25$_{8}$, Isaac Gn 35$_{29}$, Job Jb 42$_{17}$, עֶבֶד *servant* Gn 24$_{2}$, שְׁבִי *captive* Is 20$_{4}$, גָּלוּת *exiles* Is 20$_{4}$, שְׂבַע יָמִים *one satisfied*, i.e. full, *of days* Gn 25$_{8}$ (if em. וְשָׂבֵעַ *and full*) 35$_{29}$ Jb 42$_{17}$ 2QJuba 23$_{8}$, רַב pl. *many* 1QpHab 6$_{11}$.

<PREP> לְ of direction, *to*, + נתן *give* CD 14$_{14}$, of possession, *of, (belonging) to* Dt 28$_{50}$ (:: נַעַר *lad*) 4QJubf 23$_{23}$ ([לזקן]; both + נשׂא *raise* face of aged, i.e. show them pity); בְּ of accompaniment, *with*, + הלך *go* Ex 10$_{9}$ (:: נַעַר *lad*); *against*, + רהב *storm* Is 3$_{5}$ (:: נַעַר); מִן partitive, *(some) of, from among*, + מנה ni. *be counted (as)* Si 8$_{6}$; of comparison, *(more) than*, + בין htpol. *understand* Ps 119$_{100}$; עַל *upon*, + כבד hi. *make heavy* Is 47$_{6}$; חמל עַל *pity* 2 C 36$_{17}$ (or em. יֹנֵק *suckling child*; || יָשֵׁשׁ *mature one*, :: בָּחוּר *youth*, בְּתוּלָה *young woman*); בְּתוֹךְ *among* 4QRit Mar 24$_{6}$ ([ב]תוך זק[נים]); עִם *with* 4QRitMar 110$_{1}$; אֵת *with*, + יעץ ni. *take counsel* 1 K 12$_{6}$||2 C 10$_{6}$; עַד *unto*, מִנַּעַר וְעַד־זָקֵן *from lad (and) unto old one*, i.e. both young and old Gn 19$_{4}$ Jos 6$_{21}$ (+ אִישׁ *man*, אִשָּׁה *woman*, שׁוֹר *ox*, שֶׂה *sheep*, חֲמוֹר *ass*) Est 3$_{13}$ (+ טַף *child*, אִשָּׁה).

<COLL> [ויתם את ימי חייו] זקן *and he ended the days of his life as an old man* 2QJuba 23$_{8}$, זְקֵנִים וּזְקֵנוֹת *old men and old women* Zc 8$_{4}$ 4QRitMar 19$_{2}$ (וזק[נות]) 24$_{4}$ (זקני[ם] זקנו[נ]ת); זָקֵן מִן *older than* Jb 32$_{4}$ (זְקֵנִים־הֵמָּה מִמֶּנּוּ לְיָמִים *they were older than he in respect of days*).

**2b.** specif. as noun, **elder,*** i.e. leading member of community (sometimes difficult to distinguish from §2a).

<SUBJ> היה *be* Ezk 27$_{9}$ (|| חָכָם *wise one*) 1 C 15$_{25}$ (+ שַׂר *prince*) 11QT 42$_{13}$ (+ שַׂר, נָשִׂיא *prince*, ראשׁ *head*), כסה pu. *be covered* 1 C 21$_{16}$, htp. *cover oneself* 2 K 19$_{2}$||Is 37$_{2}$, דמם *be silent* Lm 2$_{10}$, גוע *expire* Lm 1$_{19}$ (|| כֹּהֵן *priest*), מות *die* CD 5$_{4}$.

הלך *go* Nm 16$_{25}$ 22$_{7.7}$ Jg 11$_{5}$ 1 C 15$_{25}$ (+ שַׂר *prince*), בוא *come* Ex 3$_{18}$ 18$_{12}$ Nm 22$_{7}$ 1 S 8$_{4}$ 2 S 5$_{3}$||1 C 11$_{3}$ 1 K 8$_{3}$ 2 C 5$_{4}$, יצא *go out* Dt 21$_{2}$ (|| שֹׁפֵט *judge*), שׁוב *go back* Jg 11$_{8}$ 1QM 19$_{11}$ ([ושבו] ... [זקני]), hi. *bring back* Lm 1$_{19}$, נגשׁ *approach* 1QM 19$_{11}$ ([זקני]), קרב *approach* Dt 5$_{23}$ (+ ראשׁ *head*), קרא *meet* 1 S 16$_{4}$, עלה *go up* Gn 50$_{7.7}$ Jos 8$_{10}$ 11QT 42$_{13}$, hi. *raise* Jos 7$_{6}$ Lm 2$_{10}$ 1 C 15$_{25}$ 2 C 5$_{2}$, קום *arise* 2 S 12$_{17}$, hi. *raise* 2 S 12$_{17}$, עמד *stand* Jos 8$_{33}$ (+ שֹׁטֵר *officer*, שֹׁפֵט) 1QM 18$_{6}$ ([זקני]), נצב ni. *stand* Dt 29$_{9}$ (+ ראשׁ, שֹׁטֵר, שֵׁבֶט *tribe*), נפל *fall* Jos 7$_{6}$ 1 C 21$_{16}$, ירד hi. *take down* Dt 21$_{4}$=11QT 63$_{1}$ ([והורידו זקני]), שׁכב *lie down* Kh. el-Qom tomb inscr. 4$_{2}$, ישׁב *sit, dwell* Ex 24$_{14}$ 1 K 21$_{11}$ (|| חֹר *noble*) 2 K 6$_{32}$ Ezk 8$_{1}$ Lm 2$_{10}$ 1QS 6$_{8}$ (+ כֹּהֵן *priest*) 11QT 42$_{13}$, שׁלח *send* Dt 19$_{12}$ 1 S 11$_{3}$ 2 K 10$_{5}$ (|| אֹמֵן *guardian*), אסף *gather* trans. Jos 20$_{4}$, perh. intrans. Jl 1$_{14}$, ni. *be gathered* Nm 11$_{30}$, קבץ htp. *be gathered* 1 S 8$_{4}$, בקשׁ pi. *seek* Lm 1$_{19}$, נתן *give*, i.e. place Dt 19$_{12}$ 11QT 16$_{02}$ ([ונתנו]), לקח *take* Dt 19$_{12}$ 21$_{3}$ 22$_{18}$=11QT 65$_{13}$ Jg 11$_{5}$ 1 S 4$_{3}$ 11QT 16$_{02}$, שׁפך *pour* 11QT 16$_{02}$, סמך *rest* hands on Lv 4$_{15}$ 11QT 15$_{18}$, ארך hi. *prolong* days Jos 24$_{31}$ Jg 2$_{7}$.

עשׂה *do* Jg 21$_{16}$ Ezk 8$_{12}$ 1 K 21$_{11}$, עבד *serve* CD 5$_{4}$, חזק hi. *strengthen* Ezk 27$_{9}$, רחץ *wash* Dt 21$_{6}$=11QT 63$_{4}$, חגר *gird oneself* Lm 2$_{10}$, יסר pi. *discipline* Dt 22$_{18}$=11QT 65$_{13}$, ענשׁ *fine* Dt 22$_{18}$=11QT 65$_{13}$.

אמר *say* Dt 21$_{6}$=11QT 63$_{4}$ Dt 32$_{7}$ (|| אָב *father*) Jos 9$_{11}$ (+ יֹשֵׁב *inhabitant*) Jg 11$_{5.8.10}$ 21$_{16}$ 1 S 4$_{3}$ 8$_{4}$ 11$_{3}$ 1 K 20$_{8}$ (|| עַם *people*) Ezk 8$_{12}$ Ru 4$_{11}$ (+ עַם) 1QM 18$_{6}$ ([זקני]), דבר pi. *speak* Nm 22$_{7}$ Dt 25$_{8}$, ענה *answer* Dt 21$_{6}$=11QT 63$_{4}$ 1QM 18$_{6}$ ([זקני]), קרא *call* Dt 25$_{8}$, ברך pi. *bless* 1QM 13$_{1}$ (+ כֹּהֵן, לֵוִי *Levite*) 18$_{6}$ 1QM 19$_{11}$ ([וברכו] ... [זקני]), צוה pi. *command* Dt 27$_{1}$, הלל pi. *praise* 1QM 19$_{11}$ ([זקני] ... [ה]ללו), ידע *know* Jos 24$_{31}$, ראה *see* Jg 2$_{7}$ Ezr 3$_{12(mss)}$, שׁמע *hear* Jl 1$_{2}$ (+ יֹשֵׁב *inhabitant*), חרד *quake* 1 S 16$_{4}$, בכה *weep* Ezr 3$_{12(mss)}$.

<NOM CL> זָקֵן ... הוּא הָרֹאשׁ *an elder is the head* Is 9$_{14}$

(|| נְשׂוּא־פָנִים *one lifted of face*, i.e. honoured one, + נָבִיא *prophet*), הֵם זִקְנֵי הָעָם *they are elders of the people* Nm $11_{16}$ (|| שֹׁטֵר *officer*).

<OBJ> חנן *pity*, i.e. be gracious to Lm $4_{16}$ (|| כֹּהֵן *priest*), ישׁע hi. *save* 1 S $4_3$ $11_3$, שׁלח *send* 2 K $19_2$||Is $37_2$, אסף *gather* Ex $3_{16}$ $4_{29}$ 2 K $23_1$||2 C $34_{29}$ Jl $1_{14}$ (unless זָקֵן subj.), קבץ *gather* Jl $2_{16}$ (|| עַם *people*, קָהָל *congregation*, + עוֹלֵל *child*, יֹנֵק *suckling child*), קהל hi. *summon* Dt $31_{28}$ (mss lack זָקֵן; + שֹׁטֵר *officer*) 2 C $5_2$ (+ רֹאשׁ *head*, נָשִׂיא *prince*), לקח *take* Nm $1_{16}$ Jg $8_{16}$, סור hi. *remove* Is $3_2$ (|| שֹׁפֵט *judge*, נָבִיא *prophet*, קֹסֵם *diviner*, + גִּבּוֹר *mighty one*, אִישׁ מִלְחָמָה *man of war*), נגף *strike* 1 S $4_3$, יעץ *counsel* 2 S $17_{15}$, שׁאל *ask* Dt $32_7$, כתב *write*, i.e. register Jg $8_{14}$ (|| שַׂר *prince*), חכם pi. *instruct* Ps $105_{22}$ (+ שַׂר).

<CSTR> זִקְנֵי הָאָרֶץ *elders of the land* 1 K $20_7$ (or em. הַזְּקֵנִים *the elders*) Jr $26_{17}$, אֶרֶץ *of the land of* Gn $50_7$ Pr $31_{23}$ (אָרֶץ), יִשְׂרָאֵל *of Israel* Ex $3_{16.18}$ $12_{21}$ $17_{5.6}$ $18_{12}$ $19_7$ (Gnz) $24_{1.9}$ Lv $9_1$ (or del.) Nm $11_{16.24(mss).30}$ $16_{25}$ Dt $27_1$ $31_9$ Jos $7_6$ $8_{10}$ $24_1$ (+ רֹאשׁ *head*, שֹׁטֵר *officer*, שֹׁפֵט *judge*) 1 S $4_3$ $8_4$ 2 S $3_{17}$ $5_3$||1 C $11_3$ 2 S $17_4$ (ms lacks זִקְנֵי) $17_{15}$ 1 K $8_3$ Ezk $14_1$ $20_{1.3}$ 1 C $15_{25}$ 2 C $5_{2.4}$, יְהוּדָה *of Judah* 1 S $30_{26}$ 2 S $19_{12}$ 2 K $23_1$||2 C $34_{29}$ Ezk $8_1$, גְּבַל *of Gebal* Ezk $27_9$, גִּלְעָד *of Gilead* Jg $11_{5.7.8.9.10.11}$, יָבֵישׁ *of Jabesh* 1 S $11_3$, מִדְיָן *of Midian* Nm $22_{4.7}$, מוֹאָב *of Moab* Nm $22_7$, הָעָם *of the people* Ex $19_7$ Nm $11_{16.24}$ Jr $19_1$, עַמִּי *of my people* 1 S $15_{30}$ Ru $4_4$, עַמּוֹ *of his people* Is $3_{14}$ (+ שַׂר *prince*), הָעֵדָה *of the congregation* Lv $4_{15}$ Jg $21_{16}$ 11QT $42_{13}$, שִׁבְטֵיכֶם *of your tribes* Dt $31_{28}$ (mss lack זִקְנֵי or rd. רָאשֵׁי *heads of*), הַכֹּהֲנִים *of the priests* 2 K $19_2$||Is $37_2$ Jr $19_1$ (or del. זִקְנֵי) 11QT $15_{18}$ ([הכוהנים]) $16_{02}$ (הכוהנים), הָעִיר *of the city* Dt $21_{3.4}$=11QT $63_1$ ([זקני]) Dt $21_6$=11QT $63_4$ Dt $22_{15.17.18}$= 11QT $65_{13.13}$ Jos $20_4$ Jg $8_{16}$ 1 S $16_4$ Ru $4_2$ Ezr $10_{14}$ (עִיר וָעִיר *of every city*), עִירוֹ *of his city* Dt $19_{12}$ $21_{19.20}$= 11QT $64_{4.4}$ (Sam אַנְשֵׁי *men of* at Dt $21_{20}$) Dt $25_8$, הסרך *of the rule* 1QM $13_1$ $18_6$ ([זקני]), בֵּיתוֹ *of his house* Gn $50_7$ 2 S $12_{17}$, בֵּית *of house of* Israel Ezk $8_{11.12}$, בְּנֵי *of sons of* Israel Ex $3_{16(Sam)}$ $4_{29}$, בַּת *of daughter of* Zion Lm $2_{10}$, הַגּוֹלָה *of the diaspora* Jr $29_1$.

מוֹשַׁב זְקֵנִים *assembly of elders* Ps $107_{32}$ (|| עַם *people*), טַעַם זְקֵנִים *discretion of elders* Jb $12_{20}$, עֲצַת ... הַזְּקֵנִים *counsel of ... the elders* Ezr $10_8$ (|| שַׂר *prince*), יְמֵי הַזְּקֵנִים *days of the elders* Jos $24_{31}$ Jg $2_7$, יֶתֶר זִקְנֵי *remnant of elders of* Jr $29_1$ (+ כֹּהֵן *priest*, נָבִיא *prophet*, עַם *people*), כָּל־הַזְּקֵנִים *all the elders* 1 K $20_7$ (if em. כָּל־זִקְנֵי *all the elders of*) $20_8$, כָּל־זִקְנֵי *all the elders of* Gn $50_7$ (כֹּל) Ex $4_{29}$ $12_{21}$ $18_{12}$ (כֹּל; Sam מִזִּקְנֵי *some of the elders of*) Dt $21_6$=11QT $63_4$ (Dt כֹּל; 11QT כול) Dt $31_{9.28}$ (mss רָאשֵׁי *heads of*) 1 S $8_4$ (כֹּל) 2 S $5_3$||1 C $11_3$ 2 S $17_4$ (mss lack כָּל־; ms lacks זִקְנֵי) 1 K $8_3$ (כֹּל) $20_7$ (or em. כָּל־הַזְּקֵנִים) 2 K $23_1$ 2 C $5_{2(mss).4}$ (כֹּל) 1QM $13_1$ (כול) $19_{11}$ ([כול זקני]).

<APP> יִשְׂרָאֵל *Israel* Jos $23_2$, שַׂר *prince* 2 K $10_1$, אִישׁ *man* Nm $11_{25}$ Dt $29_9$ 1 K $21_{11}$, רֵעַ *friend* 1 S $30_{26}$, כֹּל *everyone* Dt $29_9$.

<PREP> לְ of direction, *to*, + שׁלח pi. *send away* 1 S $30_{26}$, אמר *say* Jg $11_7$, קרא *call* Ex $12_{21}$ $19_7$ Lv $9_1$ (or del.) Jos $23_2$ (|| רֹאשׁ *head*, שֹׁפֵט *judge*, שֹׁטֵר *officer*) $24_1$ 1 K $20_7$, ספר pi. *recount* CD $9_4$; of possession, *of, (belonging) to*, + היה *be* Jg $11_8$; of benefit, *to, for*, + רפה hi. *loosen*, i.e. give respite 1 S $11_3$, עשׂה ni. *be made* 11QT $42_{13}$.

מִן of direction, *from*, + אבד *perish* (of law) Ezk $7_{26}$ (|| כֹּהֵן *priest*); partitive, *(some) of, from among* Jr $26_{17}$ Ezr $3_{12(mss)}$, + בוא *come* Ex $18_{12(Sam)}$ Ezk $14_1$ $20_1$, עלה *go up* Ex $24_{1.9}$, עמד *stand* Ezk $8_{11}$, אסף *gather* Nm $11_{16.24}$, לקח *take* Ex $17_5$ Jr $19_1$ (if em. וּמִזִּקְנֵי *and some of the elders of* to וְלָקַחְתָּ אִתְּךָ מִזִּקְנֵי *and you shall take with you some of the elders of*) $19_1$ (if em.; or del. זִקְנֵי) Ru $4_2$; אִישׁ/אֲנָשִׁים מִזִּקְנֵי *man/men of the elders of* Nm $11_{16.24}$ Jr $26_{17}$ Ezk $8_{11}$ $14_1$ $20_1$ Ru $4_2$.

אֶל *to*, + עלה *go up* Dt $25_7$, יצא hi. *take out* Dt $21_{19}$=11QT $64_4$ Dt $22_{15}$=11QT $65_{10}$, שׁוב *go back* Ex $24_{14}$, שׁלח *send* 1 K $21_8$ (|| חֹר *noble*) 2 K $10_1$ (|| שַׂר *prince*, אֹמֵן *guardian*), נתן *give* Dt $31_9$, אמר *say* Ex $3_{16}$ $24_{14}$ Nm $22_4$ Dt $21_{20}$=11QT $64_4$ (Sam אִישׁ *man* for זָקֵן) Dt $22_{16}$=11QT $65_{11}$ Jos $23_2$ Jg $11_{7(mss).9}$ 2 K $6_{32}$, דבר pi. *speak* 2 S $19_{12}$ Ezk $20_{3(mss)}$.

עַל *upon*, + נתן *give*, i.e. place, spirit Nm $11_{25}$; אֵת *with*, + דבר pi. *speak* Ezk $20_3$; עִם *with*, + היה *be* 2 S $3_{17}$, בוא *come* Is $3_{14}$ 4QApocMos B 1.17 (|| שֹׁפֵט *judge*), הלך *go* Jg $11_{8.11}$, ישׁב *sit* Pr $31_{23}$; בֵּין *between* elders and Jephthah, + שׁמע *hear*, i.e. act as witness Jg $11_{10}$, *among* elders, + קום pol. *raise oneself* Si $35_9$ (+ שַׂר *prince*).

לִפְנֵי *in the presence of*, + פרשׂ *spread* garment Dt $22_{17}$= 11QT $65_{13}$; לְעֵינֵי *in the presence of*, + נגשׁ ni. *approach* Dt $25_9$, עשׂה *do* Ex $17_6$; בְּעֵינֵי *in the presence of*, + ישׁר *be upright*, i.e. seem fitting 2 S $17_4$ (ms lacks זָקֵן), בְּאָזְנֵי *in the hearing of*, + דבר pi. *speak* Jos $20_4$; נֶגֶד *in the presence of* Is $24_{23}$, + כבד ni. *be honoured* Is $24_{23}$ (if em. כָּבוֹד *glory*), pi. *honour* 1 S $15_{30}$, קנה *purchase* Ru $4_4$.

Also 4QpIsa^c^ 4.1$_5$ 4QToh B $3_1$ 4QRitMar $19_{2.2}$ ([זקנ]נות) $57_2$ $107_1$ ([זקנ]ים).

<SYN> §2a יָשֵׁשׁ *mature*, שֵׂיבָה *grey-hair(ed)*; §2b שֹׁטֵר *officer*, שַׂר *prince*, חֹר *noble*, שֹׁפֵט *judge*, ראשׁ *head*, אָמֵן *guardian*, אָב *father*, כֹּהֵן *priest*, נָבִיא *prophet*, קֹסֵם *diviner*, חָכָם *wise one*, נְשׂוּא־פָנִים *one lifted of face*, i.e. honoured one, עַם *people*, קָהָל *congregation*.

<ANT> §2a בָּחוּר *youth*, נַעַר *lad*, יֶלֶד *child*, בְּתוּלָה *young woman*, בֵּן *son*.*

⇒ זקן *be old*.

**[זָקֵן] II** 0.0.0.1 pr.n. **Zaken,** appar. son of Ahaziah, <PREP> לְ of possession, *of, (belonging) to*, Seal 342 (8th–6th cent.).

**זֹקֶן** 1 n.[m.] **old age,** <PREP> מִן of cause, *on account of*, + כבד *be heavy*, i.e. dim (of eyes) Gn $48_{10}$.*

⇒ זקן *be old*.

**זִקְנָה** 6 n.f. **old age**—cstr. זִקְנַת; sf. זִקְנָתָהּ, זִקְנָתוֹ—<CSTR> זִקְנַת שְׁלֹמֹה *old age of Solomon* 1 K $11_4$, אֵם *of a mother* Pr $30_{17}$ (if em.; see Prep.); עֵת זִקְנָה *time of old age* Ps $71_9$ (+ כִּכְלוֹת כֹּחִי *when my strength is spent*), זִקְנַת *of old age of* Solomon 1 K $11_4$, זִקְנָתוֹ *of his old age* 1 K $15_{23}$. <PREP> לְ introducing object, + לעג *mock* Pr $30_{17}$ (if em. לִיקֲהַת *the obedience of* to לְזִקְנַת *the old age of*); עַד *until* Is $46_4$ (|| שֵׂיבָה *grey hair*, i.e. old age), + עזב *abandon* Ps $71_{18}$ (|| שֵׂיבָה); אַחֲרֵי *after (reaching)*, + ילד *give birth* Gn $24_{36}$. <SYN> שֵׂיבָה *grey hair*, i.e. old age.*

⇒ זקן *be old*.

**זְקֻנִים** 4 n.[m.] **old age**—sf. זְקֻנָיו—<CSTR> יֶלֶד זְקֻנִים *child of old age* Gn $44_{20}$, בֶּן־זְקֻנָיו *son of his old age* Gn $37_3$. <PREP> לְ of benefit, *for*, or *during*, + ילד *give birth* Gn $21_{2.7}$.

⇒ זקן *be old*.

**זקף** 2.0.3 vb. **raise—Qal** 2.0.3 Impf. Q יזקף, Q [erased] יזקפו; ptc. זֹקֵף (זוֹקֵף)—**1. raise** another, Ps $145_{14}$ (|| סמך *uphold*) $146_8$ (|| פקח *open [eyes]*, אהב *love*, שׁמר *keep*, + עדד po. *relieve*) 4QapLam^b^$_4$ ([זו]קף) 4Q521 2.2$_8$ (|| נתר hi. *release*, פקח). **2.** appar. **raise oneself, stand erect** (unless ni.), 1QS $7_{11}$ 4QpsEzek^a^ $2_{10}$ (+ כפף *bow down* intrans.).

<SUBJ> Y. Ps $145_{14}$ $146_8$ 4Q521 2.2$_8$, perh. רַב pl. *many* 1QS $7_{11}$, perh. עֵץ *tree* 4QpsEzek^a^ $2_{10}$; subj. not specified, 4QapLam^b^$_4$ ([זו]קף). <OBJ> כפף pass. ptc. *one bowed down* Ps $146_8$ 4QapLam^b^$_4$ (כפופים ואין זו[קף] *those bowed down, and there is no one who raises [them] up*) 4Q521 2.2$_8$ ([כפ]ופים). <PREP> לְ introducing object, + כפף pass. ptc. *one bowed down* Ps $145_{14}$.

<SYN> §1 סמך *uphold*, פקח *open (eyes)*, נתר hi. *release*, אהב *love*, שׁמר *keep*.

***[זָקֵף]** adj. **startling,** used attributively of אִישׁ *man* 1 S $28_{14}$ (if em. זָקֵן *old*).

**זקק** 7.0.6 vb. **refine—Qal** 2 Impf. יָזֹקּוּ—**refine, distil,** <SUBJ> metal-workers Jb $28_1$, appar. נָטָף *drop* of water Jb $36_{27}$ (or em. יָזֹקּוּ *they refine* to יָזֹק *he* [Y.] *refines*). <OBJ> זָהָב *gold* Jb $28_1$ (מָקוֹם לַזָּהָב יָזֹקּוּ *a place for gold [which] they refine*), מָטָר *rain* Jb $36_{27}$. <PREP> לְ perh. *into*, + אֵד *stream* or *mist* Jb $36_{27}$.

**Pi.** 1.0.2 Impf. Q יזקק, Q תזקקם; + waw וְזִקַּק—**refine, purify,** <SUBJ> Y. 1QH $6_5$ ([ותזקקני]) $6_8$ (+ טהר htp. *clean oneself*) 1QS $4_{20}$ (+ ברר pi. *purify*), מַלְאָךְ *messenger* Ml $3_3$ (+ טהר pi. *clean*, צרף pi. *refine*). <OBJ> בֵּן *son* of Levi Ml $3_3$, worshipper 1QH $6_5$ ([ותזקקני]), מִחְיָה *community* 1QH $6_8$, שְׁאֵרִית *remnant* 1QH $6_8$. <PREP> לְ of benefit, *to*, *for*, + Y. 1QS $4_{20}$; כְּ *as (though it were)*, + זָהָב *gold* Ml $3_3$, כֶּסֶף *silver* Ml $3_3$; מִן privative, *without*, i.e. so as to remove, + עָוֺן *iniquity* 1QH $6_5$ ([ותזקקני מעוון]); partitive, *(some) of*, *from among*, + בֵּן *son* 1QS $4_{20}$.

**Pu.** 4.0.4 Ptc. מְזֻקָּק (Q מזוקק), מְזֻקָּקִים, Q מזוקקי—**be refined, be purified,** in ref. to refining of metals (1 C $28_{18}$ $29_4$ Ps $12_7$ 1QH $5_{16}$), clearing of wine by settling of lees (Is $25_6$), perh. cleansing of person from sin (1QH $14_3$ 4QShir^b^ $35_2$), <SUBJ> ענה pass. ptc. *afflicted one* perh. 1QH $14_3$, זָהָב *gold* 1 C $28_{18}$, כֶּסֶף *silver* Ps $12_7$ (+ צרף pass. *be refined*) 1 C $29_4$ 1QH $5_{16}$ (+ טהר pi. *purify*)

4QMidrEschat$^{b}$ $9_{1}$ (ק[מזק]), שֶׁמֶר *lees* Is $25_{6}$ (|| מחה pu. *be full of marrow*); subj. not specified, 4QShir$^{b}$ $35_{2}$. <PREP> בְּ of place, *in*, + כּוּר *oven* 1QH $5_{16}$. <COLL> + שִׁבְעָתַיִם *seven times* Ps $12_{7}$ 4QMidrEschat$^{b}$ $9_{1}$ (ק[מזק]) 4QShir$^{b}$ $35_{2}$ (מזוקקי *those purified [of]* seven times). <SYN> מחה pu. *be full of marrow*.

Also 4QMidrEschat$^{b}$ $9_{11}$ ([מזוקק]ים).

**[זֵר]** 10.1 n.m. **border**—cstr. זֵר (Si זיר); sf. זֵרוֹ—**1. border,** around ark (Ex $25_{11}$||$37_{2}$), table (Ex $25_{24.25}$||$37_{11.12}$ 11QT $8_{6}$), altar (Ex $30_{3.4}$||$37_{26.27}$). **2.** appar. **setting** in item of jewellery (Si $35_{5[Bmg]}$). <OBJ> עשׂה *make* Ex $25_{11.24.25}$|| $37_{2.11.12}$ $30_{3}$||$37_{26}$ 11QT $8_{6}$ ([זר]). <CSTR> זֵר זָהָב *border of gold* Ex $25_{11.24.25}$||$37_{2.11.12}$ $30_{3}$||$37_{26}$ Si $35_{5(Bmg)}$ (זיר; B ניב *fruit*). <PREP> מִתַּחַת לְ *underneath*, + עשׂה *make* Ex $30_{4}$|| $37_{27}$; עַל *upon* Si $35_{5(Bmg)}$ (כומז אודם על זיר זהב *ornament of ruby upon a setting of gold*).

**זָרָא** 1.2 n.[f.] **abhorrence**—Sam, Si זרה—**abhorrence, nausea; something disgusting,** <PREP> לְ *as, (in)to*, + היה *be* Nm $11_{20}$ (וְהָיָה לָכֶם לְזָרָא *and it* [flesh] *shall be to you as something disgusting*), הפך *be turned* Si $39_{27(Bmg, M)}$ (נהפ[כו]; B רָעָה into *evil*); אֶל *to*, + נגע hi. *reach* Si $37_{30(B)}$ (+ חֳלִי *sickness*); עַל of cause, *on account of*, + גוע *expire* Si $37_{30(D)}$.

⇒ זור *be abhorrent.*

**זרב** 1 vb. **scorch—Pu.** 1 Impf. יְזֹרְבוּ—**be scorched, be dried up,** or perh. **be in spate,*** <SUBJ> נַחַל *wadi* Jb $6_{17}$ (|| חמם *be hot*, קדר *be dark*, + דעך ni. *be dried up*, צמת ni. *disappear*). <SYN> חמם *be hot*, קדר *be dark*.

**[זֶרֶב]** 0.0.1 n.[m.] **gutter**—Q זרב (perh. זָרָב)—perh. **gutter** or **ossuary** or **lining,** <PREP> בְּ of place 3QTr $1_{7}$ (Allegro) (Milik יָרֵךְ *side*) $5_{5(Allegro)}$ ([בזר[ב; Milik מזרו[ה] *east*), + חפר *dig* (unless pass. *be dug*, i.e. buried) 3QTr $9_{8}$.*

**זְרֻבָּבֶל** 21 pr.n.m. **Zerubbabel,** leading figure in return from Babylonian exile, governor of Judah, son of Shealtiel (or, as 1 C $3_{19}$, of Pedaiah), father of Meshullam, Hananiah and Shelomith (1 C $3_{19}$), and grandson of Jehoiakim (1 C $3_{19}$), perh. ident. with Sheshbazzar at Ezr $1_{8.11}$.

<SUBJ> בוא *come* Ezr $3_{8}$ Hg $1_{14}$, קום *arise* Ezr $3_{2}$, בנה *build* Ezr $3_{2}$ $4_{3.3}$, עמד hi. *establish* Ezr $3_{8}$, כון hi. *establish* Ezr $3_{2}$, עלה hi. *raise*, i.e. offer, sacrifice Ezr $3_{2}$, שׁמע *hear* Hg $1_{12}$, ירא *fear* Hg $2_{4}$, אמר *say* Ezr $4_{3}$, חזק *be strong* Hg $2_{4}$, עשׂה *do* Hg $1_{14}$ $2_{4}$ Ezr $3_{2}$, חלל hi. *begin* Ezr $3_{2.8}$. <NOM CL> בְּנֵי פְדָיָה זְרֻבָּבֶל וְשִׁמְעִי *the sons of Pedaiah were Zerubbabel and Shimei* 1 C $3_{19}$. <OBJ> לקח *take* Hg $2_{23}$, שׂים *place* Hg $2_{23}$, צוה pi. *command* Ezr $4_{3}$.

<CSTR> רוּחַ זְרֻבָּבֶל *spirit of Zerubbabel* Hg $1_{14}$, יַד *hand of* Zc $4_{10}$, בֶּן *son of* 1 C $3_{19}$ (Seb בְּנֵי *sons of*), יְדֵי *hands of* Zc $4_{9}$, יְמֵי *days of* Ne $12_{47}$. <APP> בֶּן *son* Hg $1_{1.12.14}$ $2_{2.23}$ (or del. בֶּן) Ezr $3_{2.8}$ Ne $12_{1}$, פֶּחָה *governor* Hg $1_{1.14}$ $2_{2.21}$, עֶבֶד *servant* Hg $2_{23}$. <PREP> לְ of direction, *to*, + אמר *say* Ezr $4_{2}$; *(incumbent) upon* Ezr $4_{3}$; בְּ of place, *among* Zerubbabel and others, + שׁאר ni. *remain*; בחר בְּ *choose* Hg $2_{23}$; אֶל *(in)to* Zc $4_{6}$, + היה *be* Hg $1_{1}$, נגשׁ *approach* Ezr $4_{2}$, אמר *say* Hg $2_{2.21}$; עִם *with*, + בוא *come* Ezr $2_{2}$||Ne $7_{7}$, עלה *come up* Ne $12_{1}$, בנה *build* Ezr $4_{2}$; אֵת *with* Hg $2_{4}$, + כרת *cut* word, i.e. promise to Hg $2_{4}$; עַל *upon* Ezr $3_{2}$; לִפְנֵי *before* Zc $4_{7}$; בְּתוֹךְ *among*, + עמד *stand* Hg $2_{4}$. <COLL> זְרֻבָּבֶל *O Zerubbabel* Hg $2_{4.23}$.

**זֶרֶד** 4 pl.n. **Zered**—זֶרֶד—wadi near Moab, perh. Sēl el-Qurāḥī and W. el-Ḥesā SE of the Dead Sea, <CSTR> נַחַל זֶרֶד *valley (of) Zered* Nm $21_{12.13(Sam)}$ Dt $2_{13.13}$ $2_{14}$ (זָרֶד).

**זרה I** 40.2.5 vb. **scatter—Qal** 9.2.1 Impf. Q יזרה, 2ms תִּזְרֶה (Si תזר, תִּזְרֵם), Si תזרו; + waw וָאֱזָרֵם, וַיִּזֶר; impv. זְרֵה; ptc. זֹרֶה (Si, Q זורה); inf. זְרוֹת—**1. scatter** dust of golden calf Ex $32_{20}$, fire Nm $17_{2}$, hair Ezk $5_{2}$, idols Is $30_{22}$, Israelites Ezk $5_{12(Or)}$. **2. winnow,** Is $30_{24}$ $41_{16}$ Jr $4_{11}$ (+ ברר hi. *clean* or *separate*) $15_{7}$ Ru $3_{2}$ Si $5_{9}$ 4Q424 $3_{4}$. **3.** appar. **vomit,** Si $37_{29(Bmg)}$.

<SUBJ> Y. Jr $15_{7}$ Ezk $5_{12(Or)}$ (L pi. *scatter*), עַם *people* Is $30_{22}$ (or em. זור hi. *make abhorrent*), Boaz Ru $3_{2}$, Eleazar Nm $17_{2}$, Moses Ex $32_{20}$, מַת *man* Is $41_{16}$, בֶּן *son* Nm $17_{2}$ Si $5_{9}$ $37_{29(Bmg)}$, specif. son of man, i.e. Ezekiel Ezk $5_{2}$, יֹשֵׁב *inhabitant* Is $30_{22}$ (if em. יֵשֵׁב *he dwells* to יֹשֵׁב), כֹּהֵן *priest* Nm $17_{2}$, farmer Is $30_{24}$ (or em. זֹרֶה *one scatters* to

זֹרָה pu. *it has been scattered*), תּוֹלֵעָה *worm*, i.e. Jacob Is 41$_{16}$, רוּחַ *wind* Jr 4$_{11}$; subj. not specified, Jr 51$_{2}$ (if em. pi. *scatter*) 4Q424 3$_{4}$.

<OBJ> עַם *people* Jr 15$_{7}$, Babylon Jr 51$_{2}$ (if em.), פָּסִיל *idol* Is 30$_{22}$ (or em.; see Subj.), אֵפֹד *ephod* of idol Is 30$_{22}$ (if em.; see Subj.), הַר *mountain* Is 41$_{16}$, גִּבְעָה *hill* Is 41$_{16}$, גֹּרֶן *threshing floor* Ru 3$_{2}$, אֵשׁ *fire* Nm 17$_{2}$, בְּלִיל *fodder* Is 30$_{24}$ (or em.), שְׁלִשִׁית *third (of hair)* Ezk 5$_{2.12(Or)}$, dust of golden calf Ex 32$_{20}$.

<PREP> לְ of direction, *to*, + רוּחַ *wind* Ezk 5$_{2.12(Or)}$ Si 5$_{9}$ 4Q424 3$_{4}$; בְּ of place, *in, at*, + שַׁעַר *gate* Jr 15$_{7}$; of instrument, *by (means of), with*, + רַחַת *winnowing shovel* Is 30$_{24}$, מִזְרֶה *winnowing fork* Is 30$_{24}$ Jr 15$_{7}$; כְּ *as* Is 30$_{22}$ (or em. זור hi. *make abhorrent*); אֶל *on account of*, + תַּעֲנוּג *delicacy* Si 37$_{29(Bmg)}$; עַל־פְּנֵי *upon the face of*, + מַיִם *waters* Ex 32$_{20}$.

<COLL> + הָלְאָה *yonder* Nm 17$_{2}$, הַלַּיְלָה *tonight* Ru 3$_{2}$.

**Ni.** 2 + waw וַיִּזָּרוּ; inf. הִזָּרוֹתֵיכֶם—**be scattered,** <SUBJ> הַר *mountain* of Israel Ezk 6$_{8}$ (or del.), בַּיִת *house* of Israel Ezk 36$_{19}$ (+ פוץ hi. *scatter*). <PREP> בְּ of place, *in, among*, + אֶרֶץ *land* Ezk 6$_{8}$ 36$_{19}$.

**Pi.** 25.0.4 Pf. זֵרִיתָ (Q זריתה, זֵרִיתָנוּ), זֵרוּ; impf. אֱזָרֶה, יְזָרוּ; + waw וָאֱזָרֵם, וְזֵרִיתִי (וְזֵרִיתִי), וְזֵרִיתִיךְ, וְזֵרִיתִים, (וְזֵרְתִּים, וְזֵרִיתֶם), וְזֵרוּהָ; ptc. מְזָרֶה, מְזָרִים, מְזָרֶה; inf. זָרוֹת (זָרוֹתָם, זָרוֹתָהּ)—**1. scatter, disperse, spread,** <SUBJ> Y. Lv 26$_{33}$ 1 K 14$_{15}$ Jr 31$_{10}$ (:: קבץ pi. *gather*) 49$_{32.36}$ Ezk 5$_{10.12}$ (Or יִזְרֶה, i.e. qal) 6$_{5}$ 12$_{14.15}$ 20$_{23}$ 22$_{15}$ 29$_{12}$ 30$_{23.26}$ (all six ‖ פוץ hi. *scatter*) Zc 10$_{9}$ (if em. זרע *sow*) Ml 2$_{3}$ Ps 44$_{12}$ 106$_{27}$ (+ נפל hi. *cause to fall*) GnzPs 1$_{5}$ (+ טהר pi. *clean*) perh. 6QapProph$_{4}$, זָר *stranger* Jr 51$_{2}$ (or em. זָרִים *strangers* to זֹרִים *winnowers*; + בקק po. *devastate*), שָׂפָה *lip* Pr 15$_{7}$ (or em. יְזָרוּ *they will scatter* to יוֹרוּ *they will teach*, from ירה hi., or יָזֹרוּ *they will flow*, from זרר, or יָזֻרוּ *they will flow*, from זור II), קֶרֶן *horn* Zc 2$_{2.4.4}$; subj. not specified, 1QH fr. 6$_{3}$ (unless מְזָרִים *north winds*) 9$_{11}$.

<OBJ> Israel 1 K 14$_{15}$ Jr 31$_{10}$ Zc 2$_{2}$, Judah Zc 2$_{2.4.4}$, Ephraim Zc 10$_{9}$ (if em.), Babylon Jr 51$_{2}$, Egypt Ezk 29$_{12}$ 30$_{23.26}$, Elam Jr 49$_{36}$, עִיר *city* Ezk 22$_{15}$, Jerusalem Zc 2$_{2}$, שְׁאֵרִית *remnant* Ezk 5$_{10}$, אֲגַף *troop* Ezk 12$_{14.15}$, בֵּן *son* Ezk 20$_{23}$ GnzPs 1$_{5}$, specif. son of Israel Lv 26$_{33}$ perh. 6QapProph$_{4}$ ([לזורות]ם), זֶרַע *seed*, i.e. offspring Ps 106$_{27}$, רָשָׁע *wicked one* Pr 20$_{26}$, worshipper Ps 44$_{12}$, קָצוּץ pass. ptc. *one* whose hair is *cut* to the corner Jr 49$_{32}$, עֹזֵר *helper* Ezk 12$_{14}$ (if em. עֵזֶר *help*), עֶצֶם *bone* Ezk 6$_{5}$, עֵזֶר *help* Ezk 12$_{14}$ (or em. עֶזְרֹה *his help* to עֹזְרָיו *his helpers*) 12$_{15}$, דַּעַת *knowledge* Pr 15$_{7}$, פֶּרֶשׁ *dung* Ml 2$_{3}$, שְׁלִשִׁית *third (of hair)* Ezk 5$_{12}$, כֹּל *everyone* Ezk 12$_{14.15}$.

<PREP> לְ of direction, *to*, + רוּחַ *wind* Jr 49$_{32.36}$ Ezk 5$_{10.12}$ 12$_{14}$; מֵעֵבֶר לְ *beyond*, + נָהָר *river* 1 K 14$_{15}$; בְּ of place, *in, at, among*, + גּוֹי *nation* Lv 26$_{33}$ Ps 44$_{12}$, עַם *people* Zc 10$_{9}$ (if em.; see Subj.; or del. בְּעַמִּים), אֶרֶץ *land* Ezk 12$_{15}$ 20$_{23}$ 22$_{15}$ 29$_{12}$ 30$_{23.26}$ Ps 106$_{27}$ 6QapProph$_{4}$ ([לזורות]ם בארצות); מִן of direction, *from*, + עַם *people* GnzPs 1$_{5}$; עַל־פְּנֵי *upon (the face of)*, + כֹּהֵן *priest* Ml 2$_{3}$; סָבִיב *around*, + מִזְבֵּחַ *altar* Ezk 6$_{5}$ (סְבִיבוֹת).

**2.** pl. ptc. (מְזָרִים) as noun, **scatterers,** appar. in ref. to **north wind(s),** Jb 37$_{9}$ perh. 1QH fr. 6$_{3}$ 9$_{11}$, <PREP> מִן of direction, *from*, + בוא *come* Jb 37$_{9}$ (+ חֶדֶר *chamber*).

**3. winnow, sift** (unless זרה II *measure*), <SUBJ> Y. Ps 139$_{3}$ (+ סכן hi. *be familiar with*), מֶלֶךְ *king* Pr 20$_{8.26}$. <OBJ> אֹרַח *way* Ps 139$_{3}$, רבע inf. *lying down* Ps 139$_{3}$, רַע *evil* Pr 20$_{8}$. <PREP> בְּ of instrument, *by (means of), with*, + עַיִן *eye* Pr 20$_{8}$.

<SYN> §1 פוץ hi. *scatter*. <ANT> קבץ pi. *gather*.

**Pu.** 2 Impf. יְזֹרֶה; ptc. מְזֹרָה—**be scattered, be sprinkled, be strewn,*** <SUBJ> גָּפְרִית *brimstone* Jb 18$_{15}$, רֶשֶׁת *net* Pr 1$_{17}$ (or em. מְזֻרָה *spread out* [i.e. pass. ptc. of מזר *spread*], בְּלִיל *fodder* Is 30$_{24}$ (if em. qal). <PREP> בְּ of instrument, *by (means of), with*, + רַחַת *winnowing shovel* Is 30$_{24}$ (if em. qal), מִזְרֶה *winnowing fork* Is 30$_{24}$ (if em. qal); עַל *upon*, + נָוֶה *dwelling place* Jb 18$_{15}$; בְּעֵינֵי *in the presence of*, + בַּעַל *lord* of wing, i.e. bird Pr 1$_{17}$ (or em.). <COLL> with adverb, חִנָּם *in vain* Pr 1$_{17}$.

⇒ מִזְרֶה *winnowing fork*.

**זרה II** 2 vb. **measure—Pi** 2 Pf. זֵרִיתָ—**measure, discern** (unless זרה I *winnow*), <SUBJ> Y. Ps 139$_{3}$ (+ סכן hi. *be familiar with*), מֶלֶךְ *king* Pr 20$_{8.26}$. <OBJ> אֹרַח *way* Ps 139$_{3}$, רבע inf. *lying down* Ps 139$_{3}$. <PREP> בְּ of instrument, *by (means of), with*, + עַיִן *eye* Pr 20$_{8}$.

⇒ זֶרֶת *span*.

**[זָרָה]**, see זָרָא *abhor*; זור I *be strange*, §§2–3.

**זֵרוּעַ** $_2$ n.[m.] **sowing**—sf. זֵרוּעֶיהָ—**sowing, thing sown,** <OBJ> צמח hi. *cause to grow* Is $61_{11}$ (|| צֶמַח *shoot*). <CSTR> זֶרַע זֵרוּעַ *seed of,* i.e. for, *sowing* Lv $11_{37}$. <SYN> צֶמַח *shoot.*

→ זרע *sow.*

**זְרוֹעַ** $_{91.1.5.2}$ n.f. (sometimes m.) **arm**—זְרֹעַ; cstr. זְרוֹעַ (זְרֹעַ); sf. זְרוֹעִי (זְרֹעִי), זְרוֹעֲךָ (זְרֹעֲךָ, זְרֹעֶךָ, זְרוֹעֵךְ), זְרוֹעוֹ (זְרֹעוֹ), זְרוֹעָם (זְרֹעָם); pl. זְרֹעִים, זְרוֹעוֹת (זְרֹעוֹת, זְרֹעֹת); cstr. זְרֹעֵי; sf. זְרֹעַי (זְרֹעֹתַי, זְרוֹעֹתַי), זְרֹעָיו, זרעתיכה I (זְרוֹעוֹתָיו), זְרֹעֹתָיו, זְרוֹעֹתָיו, Sam זרועתו, זְרוֹעֹתֶיהָ, זְרֹעֹתֵיכֶם, זְרוֹעֹתָם—**arm,** perh. specif. **forearm** (2 S $1_{10}$); **shoulder** (2 K $9_{24}$); **wrist** (Gn $49_{24}$); **leg, shoulder** of animal (Nm $6_{19}$ Dt $18_3$); arm of God (e.g. Ex $15_{16}$ Dt $4_{34}$ $5_{15}$ 1 K $8_{42}$Is $51_9$ Ps $89_{14}$=4QapPs[b] $15_5$), assoc. with physical power (e.g. Is $33_2$ Ezk $30_{22.24}$ Jr $17_5$ $48_{25}$ Jb $22_8$ $38_{15}$* Ps $71_{18}$ 1QH $8_{33}$ Ḥorvat ‘Uza bowl inscr.$_{11}$); perh. **army** (e.g. Ezk $17_9$ Dn $11_{6.6.15.22.31}$).

<SUBJ> היה *be* Is $33_2$ (or em. עֶזְרָה *help;* + יְשׁוּעָה *salvation*) Ps $83_9$, יבשׁ *be dry* Zc $11_{17}$ (+ עַיִן right *eye*), לבשׁ *be dressed* Is $51_9$, חשׂף pass. *be stripped* Ezk $4_7$ (+ פָּנִים *face*), גלה ni. *be revealed* Is $53_1$, פזז *be agile* Gn $49_{24}$ (or em. וַיָּפֹזּוּ זְרֹעֵי יָדָיו *the wrists of his hands were agile* to וַיִּפָּזְרוּ גִּידֵי זְרֹעָיו *and the sinews of his arms were dispersed,* i.e. weakened), שׁטף ni. *be swept away* Dn $11_{22}$.

נטה pass. *be extended* Ex $6_6$ (+ שֶׁפֶט *judgment*) Dt $4_{34}$ (|| יָד *hand,* + מַסָּה *testing,* אוֹת *sign,* מוֹפֵת *wonder,* מִלְחָמָה *war,* מוֹרָא *fear*) $5_{15}$ (|| יָד) $7_{19}$ (|| יָד *hand,* + מַסָּה, אוֹת, מוֹפֵת) $9_{29}$ (|| כֹּחַ *strength*) $11_2$ (|| יָד, גֹּדֶל *greatness,* + אוֹת, מַעֲשֶׂה *deed*) $26_8$ (|| יָד, + מוֹרָא, אוֹת, מוֹפֵת) 1 K $8_{42}$||2 C $6_{32}$ (|| יָד, שֵׁם *name*) 2 K $17_{36}$ Jr $27_5$ $32_{17}$ (all three || כֹּחַ) Ezk $20_{33.34}$ (both || יָד, חֵמָה *anger*) Ps $136_{12}$ (=11QPs[a] $15_{14}$ אֶזְרוֹעַ *arm;* || יָד).*

דכא pu. *be crushed* Jb $22_9$ (or em. pi. *crush* arm), שׁבר ni. *be broken* Jr $48_{25}$ (|| קֶרֶן *horn*) Ps $37_{17}$ Jb $38_{15}$ 1QH $7_2$ (זרו[ע]) $8_{33}$ (+ יָד, מֹתֶן *hip,* בָּשָׂר *flesh,* בֶּרֶךְ *knee*).

רום *be high* Jb $38_{15}$, עמד *stand* Dn $11_6$ (or em. זֶרַע *seed*) $11_{15.31}$, נפל *fall* Ezk $30_{25}$, סור hi. *remove* Dn $11_{31}$, ירד *go down* Ezk $31_{17}$ (or em. זֶרַע *seed,* עֹזֵר *helper,* or גוע *expire*), ישׁב *dwell* Ezk $31_{17}$ (or em.).

ישׁע hi. *save* Is $59_{16}$ (+ צְדָקָה *righteousness*) $63_5$ (+ חֵמָה *anger*) Ps $44_{4.4}$ (|| יָמִין *right hand,* + אוֹר *light* of face) $98_1$ (+ יָמִין), משׁל *rule* Is $40_{10}$, שׁפט *judge* Is $51_5$, אמץ pi. *strengthen* Ps $89_{22}$ (+ יָד), חזק pi. *strengthen* GnzPs $1_{25}$ (+ יָמִין).

נתן *give,* i.e. place Dn $11_{31}$, קצר *reap* Is $17_5$, חלל pi. *profane* Dn $11_{31}$, נחת pi. *press,* i.e. bend bow 2 S $22_{35}$||Ps $18_{35}$ (or em. שׁית *place* or נתן *give,* i.e. make arms into bow, or נוח hi. *cause to rest,* i.e. place, bow in arms [also ins. בְּ *in*] or נַחַת *pressing,* i.e. bending of bow, with זְרוֹעַ as obj. of למד pi. *teach* arms to bend bow; + יָד *hand*).

<NOM CL> זְרוֹעַ לֹא־עֹז *an arm (that) is,* i.e. has, *no strength* Jb $26_2$, זְרֹעוֹ כַּשְׂדִּים perh. *his arm is (against) the Chaldaeans* Is $48_{14}$ (or em. זֶרַע *seed* of the Chaldaeans), זְרֹעֹתָיו ... כְּעֵין נְחֹשֶׁת *his arms ... were as the appearance of bronze* Dn $10_6$ (|| מַרְגְּלֹה *foot*), לְךָ זְרוֹעַ *you have an arm* Ps $89_{14}$=4QapPs[b] $15_5$ (+ יָד *hand,* יָמִין *right hand*), עִמּוֹ זְרוֹעַ בָּשָׂר *with him is an arm of flesh* 2 C $32_8$ (+ ״ Y.), מִתַּחַת זְרֹעֹת עוֹלָם *below are arms of eternity* Dt $33_{27}$ (Sam mss זרועתו appar. below are *his arms* eternally; or em. מִתַּחְתּוֹ *below him* are), וְאִם־זְרוֹעַ כָּאֵל לָךְ *or is there an arm like (that of) God to you?* Jb $40_9$.

<OBJ> לקח *take* Nm $6_{19}$, נתן *give* Dt $18_3$ (+ לְחִי *cheek,* קֵבָה *stomach*), *give,* i.e. turn into bow 2 S $22_{35}$||Ps $18_{35}$ (if em.; see Subj.), שׂים *place,* i.e. cause flesh to be Jr $17_5$, שׁית *place,* i.e. turn into bow 2 S $22_{35}$||Ps $18_{35}$ (if em.; see Subj.), הלך hi. *lead* Is $63_{12}$ (+ יָמִין *right hand*), כון hi. *establish* Ezk $4_7$, חזק pi. *strengthen* Ezk $30_{24}$ (+ יָד *hand*) $30_{25}$ (hi.) Ho $7_{15}$, אמץ pi. *strengthen* Pr $31_{17}$ (+ מָתְנַיִם *loins*) Si $33_{7(B)}$ (|| יָד, יָמִין) Arad ost. $88_2$, סמך *support* GnzPs $1_{16}$, למד pi. *teach* 2 S $22_{35}$||Ps $18_{35}$ (if em.; see Subj.), יסר pi. *discipline* Ho $7_{15}$ (or del. יסר pi.), ישׁע hi. *save* Jb $26_2$, טרף *tear* Dt $33_{20}$=4QMidrEschat[a] $2_3$ ([טרף] [זרוע;+ קָדְקֹד *pate*), גדע *hew* 1 S $2_{31.31}$, שׁבר *break* Ezk $30_{21.22.24}$ Ps $10_{15}$, מחץ *shatter* Ḥorvat ‘Uza bowl inscr.$_{11}$, דכא pi. *crush* Jb $22_9$ (if em. pu. *be crushed*), ראה *see* Dt $11_2$, חשׂף *strip* Is $52_{10}$, שׁמע *hear (of)* 1 K $8_{42}$||2 C $6_{32}$ (if ins. שׁמע), נגד hi. *declare* Ps $71_{18}$ (+ גְּבוּרָה *might*), גער *rebuke* Ml $2_3$ (if em. זֶרַע *seed*).

<CSTR> זְרוֹעַ ״ *arm of Y.* Is $51_9$, פַּרְעֹה *of Pharaoh* Ezk $30_{21}$, זְרֹעוֹת פַּרְעֹה *arms of Pharaoh* Ezk $30_{24.25}$, מֶלֶךְ *of king of* Babylon Ezk $30_{24.25}$, זְרוֹעַ רַבִּים *arm of great ones* Jb $35_9$ (+ עֲשׁוּקִים *oppression*), רָשָׁע *of the wicked* Ps $10_{15}$, זְרוֹעוֹת רְשָׁעִים *arms of the wicked* Ps $37_{17}$, יְתֹמִים *of*

*orphans* Jb $22_{9}$ (זְרֹעוֹת), עוֹלָם *of eternity* Dt $33_{27}$ (Sam mss זרועתו appar. below are *his arms* eternally), זְרוֹעַ תִּפְאַרְתּוֹ *arm of his glory* Is $63_{12}$, כֹּחוֹ *of his strength* Is $44_{12}$ (+ מַקֶּבֶת *hammer*), עֻזּוֹ *of his strength* Is $62_{8}$ (+ יָמִין *right hand*), עֻזְּךָ *of your strength* Ps $89_{11}$=4QapPs$^{b}$ $15_{5}$ ([זרע עוזך]) 4QapPs$^{b}$ $86_{3}$, קָדְשׁוֹ *of his holiness* Ps $98_{1}$ Is $52_{10}$ $62_{8}$ (Gnz), בֵּית *of the house of* your father 1 S $2_{31}$ (זְרֹעַ), בָּשָׂר *of flesh* 2 C $32_{8}$, זְרֹעֵי יָדָיו *arms of his hands* Gn $49_{24}$ (or em. גִּידֵי זְרֹעָיו *sinews of his arms*), זְרֹעוֹת הַנֶּגֶב *arms*, i.e. armies, *of the south* Dn $11_{15}$, הַשֶּׁטֶף *of the flood* Dn $11_{22}$ (or em. הִשָּׁטֹף armies will *indeed be washed away*).

אִישׁ זְרוֹעַ *man of arm*, i.e. powerful man Jb $22_{8}$, גְּדֹל זְרוֹעֲךָ perh. *great one of your arm* Ex $15_{16}$, גֹּדֶל זְרוֹעֲךָ *greatness of your arm* Ex $15_{16}$ (if em. גֹּדֶל) Ps $79_{11}$, כֹּחַ הַזְּרוֹעַ *strength of the arm*, i.e. perh. army Dn $11_{6}$ (or del. הַזְּרוֹעַ), בְּשַׂר־זְרֹעוֹ *flesh of his arm* Is $9_{19}$ (or em. זַרְעוֹ *of his seed*, i.e. offspring, or רֵעוֹ *of his companion*), גִּידֵי זְרֹעָיו *sinews of his arms* Gn $49_{24}$ (if em.), [גידי ז]רועי *sinews of my arm* 1QH $8_{35}$, נַחַת זְרוֹעוֹ *descent of his arm* Is $30_{30}$.

<APP> perh. מוּסָר *discipline* Dt $11_{2}$.

<ADJ> חָזָק *strong* Jr $21_{5}$, גָּדוֹל *great* Ezk $17_{9}$ (or del.), בָּשֵׁל *boiled* Nm $6_{19}$.

<PREP> לְ appar. *in accordance with* strength Ezk $22_{6}$ (or em. זֶרַע on behalf of *seed*).

בְּ of place, *in(to)*, + נוח hi. *cause to rest*, i.e. place 2 S $22_{35}$||Ps $18_{35}$ (if em.; see Subj.); of instrument, *by (means of)*, *with* Ezk $17_{9}$ (or del.; || עַם *people*) 4QapPs$^{b}$ $86_{3}$, + קבץ pi. *gather* Is $40_{11}$ (but perh. בְּ of place, gather *into* arm) Ezk $20_{34}$, לקח *take* Dt $4_{34}$, עלה hi. *take up* 2 K $17_{36}$, יצא hi. *take out* Dt $5_{15}$ $9_{29}$ $26_{8}$ Ps $136_{12}$, פזר pi. *scatter* Ps $89_{11}$=4QapPs$^{b}$ $15_{5}$ ([בזרע ... פזרת]), לחם ni. *fight* Jr $21_{5}$ (|| יָד *hand*, + אַף *anger*, חֵמָה *anger*, קֶצֶף *anger*), שׁבע ni. *swear* Is $62_{8}$, מלך *rule* Ezk $20_{33}$, גאל *redeem* Ex $6_{6}$ Ps $77_{16}$, פעל *make* idol Is $44_{12}$, עשׂה *make* creation Jr $27_{5}$ $32_{17}$; בְּיָד חֲזָקָה וּבִזְרוֹעַ נְטוּיָה (and vars.) *with mighty hand and outstretched arm* Dt $4_{34}$ $5_{15}$ $7_{19}$ $9_{29}$ (if ins. יָד חֲזָקָה *mighty hand*) $11_{2}$ $26_{8}$ 1 K $8_{42}$||2 C $6_{32}$ Ezk $20_{33.34}$ Ps $136_{12}$, בְּיָד נְטוּיָה וּבִזְרוֹעַ חֲזָקָה *with outstretched hand and mighty arm* Jr $21_{5}$, בְּכֹחַ גָּדוֹל וּבִזְרוֹעַ נְטוּיָה (and vars.) *with great strength and outstretched arm* Dt $9_{29}$ 2 K $17_{36}$ Jr $27_{5}$ $32_{17}$.

כְּ *as* 1QH $7_{2}$ ([כזרו]ע).

מִן of cause, *on account of*, + שׁוע pi. *cry out* Jb $35_{9}$.

אֶל *to*, i.e. for, + יחל pi. *wait* Is $51_{5}$.

מֵעַל *from (upon)*, + נתק pi. *wrench out* ropes Jg $16_{12}$, קרע *tear* pads Ezk $13_{20}$.

עַל *upon* Jg $15_{14}$ 2 S $1_{10}$ Zc $11_{17}$ (+ עַיִן right *eye*) Ca $8_{6}$ (|| לֵב *heart*), + לקח *take* Ho $11_{3}$.

בֵּין *between* shoulders, i.e. in the back, + נכה hi. *strike* 2 K $9_{24}$.

לְמַעַן *on account of*, + בוא *come* 2 C $6_{32}$ (or ins. שׁמע in order to *hear* of your arm).

<COLL> הַזְּרֹעַ הַנְּטוּיָה אֲשֶׁר הוֹצִאֲךָ י׳ *the outstretched arm (with) which Y. brought you out* Dt $7_{19}$, זְרוֹעַ עִם גְּבוּרָה *an arm (endowed) with might* Ps $89_{14}$=4QapPs$^{b}$ $15_{5}$ ([גבורה]).

<SYN> יָד *hand*, יָמִין *right hand*, מַרְגְּלָה *foot*, לֵב *heart*, כֹּחַ *strength*, גֹּדֶל *greatness*, מוֹרָא *fear*, שֵׁם *name*, חֵמָה *anger*, קֶרֶן *horn*, עַם *people*.*

⇒ אֶזְרוֹעַ *arm*.

**זָרוּת** 1 n.f. **strangeness**, perh. in ref. to prostitution, <CSTR> פִּי זָרוּת *mouth of strangeness* Pr $22_{14(mss)}$ (L זָרוֹת *strange women*, i.e. adulteresses, etc.).

⇒ זור *be strange*.

**זרז** 0.1 vb. **be strong—Pi.** 0.1 Impv. or inf. Si זריז—**strengthen,** <SUBJ> אֱלֹהִים *God* Si $33_{7(Bmg)}$. <OBJ> יָמִין *right hand* Si $33_{7(Bmg)}$ (האריך יד וזריז ימים *lengthen [your] hand and strengthen [your] right hand*; B האדר יד ואמץ זרוע וימין *make/making glorious [your] hand and strengthen/strengthening [your] arm and right hand* [Segal האריר perh. *cursing*]).

**[זַרְזִיף]** 1 n.[m.] **sprinkling**—cstr. זַרְזִיף—<CSTR> זַרְזִיף אָרֶץ *a sprinkling of the earth* Ps $72_{6}$ (or em. יַזְרִיפוּ or זַרְזִפוּ *[that] sprinkle*, i.e. זרף hi. or pilp.). <APP> רְבִיב *shower* Ps $72_{6}$. <PREP> כְּ *as*, + ירד *go down* Ps $72_{6}$.*

**[זַרְזִיר]** 1 appar. adj. **strong, girded**—cstr. זַרְזִיר—used as noun, <CSTR> זַרְזִיר מָתְנַיִם *one strong/girded of loins*, perh. in ref. to greyhound or cockerel Pr $30_{31}$ (or em. מָתְנַיִם to מִתְנַשֵּׂא *exalted*, i.e. strutting, with זַרְזִיר as noun, *cockerel*; + תַּיִשׁ *goat*).

**זרח** 18.0.1.1 vb. **arise—Qal** 18.0.1.1 Pf. זָרַח (זָרָח), זָרְחָה; impf. יִזְרַח (יִזְרָח), 3fs תִּזְרַח; + waw וַיִּזְרַח ,וְזָרַח ,וְזָרְחָה; ptc. זוֹרֵחַ; inf. זְרֹחַ—**1. appear, emerge, arise, (start to) shine,** usu. of sun, light, deity; also of leprosy (2 C 26$_{19}$) and hair (Ho 7$_{9}$ [if em.]), <SUBJ> Y. Dt 33$_{2}$ (+ יפע hi. *shine*, בוא *come*, אתה *come*) Is 60$_{2}$ (|| ראה ni. *be seen*), perh. אֵל *God* Kuntillet ʿAjrud add. inscr. 3$_{1}$, כָּבוֹד *glory* of Y. Is 60$_{1}$ (+ בוא), שֶׁמֶשׁ *sun* Gn 32$_{32}$ Ex 22$_{2}$=4QBibPar 10$_{5}$ Jg 9$_{33}$ 2 S 23$_{4}$ 2 K 3$_{22}$ Jon 4$_{8}$ Na 3$_{17}$ Ml 3$_{20}$ Ps 104$_{22}$ (or em. hi. *cause to rise*) Ec 1$_{5}$ (|| בוא *come*, i.e. set [of sun], + שׁאף *pant*, i.e. hasten) 1$_{5}$ (or del.) Si 26$_{16}$ (זור[ח]ת) 42$_{16(B)}$ (זור[ח]ת; M זהרת *shining*) 4QJub$^{a}$ 2$_{12}$ ([ויזרח השמש]) 11QapPs$^{a}$4$_{10}$ ([יזרח]), חֶרֶס *sun* Jb 9$_{7}$, כּוֹכָב *star* Nm 24$_{17}$ (if em. דרך *tread*), אוֹר *light* Is 58$_{10}$ (+ אֲפֵלָתְךָ כַּצָּהֳרָיִם *your darkness will be as the noon*) Ps 97$_{11(ms)}$ (זָרַח; L זָרֻעַ *is sown*) 112$_{4}$ Pr 13$_{9}$ (if em. שׂמח *rejoice*), צָרַעַת *leprosy* 2 C 26$_{19}$, שֵׂיבָה *grey hairs* Ho 7$_{9}$ (if em. זרק I *be profuse* or II *creep up*).

<PREP> לְ appar. arise *over*, shine *upon*, appear *to*, + Jacob Gn 32$_{32}$, בֵּן *son* of Israel Dt 33$_{2}$, ירא ptc. *one who fears* name of Y. Ml 3$_{20}$, יָשָׁר *upright one* Ps 112$_{4}$, צַדִּיק *righteous one* Ps 97$_{11(ms)}$; of benefit, *for*, + מַרְפֵּה *healing* 4QJub$^{a}$ 2$_{12}$ ([ויזרח ... ל]מרפה); בְּ of place, *in*, + חֹשֶׁךְ *darkness* Is 58$_{10}$ Ps 112$_{4}$, מָרוֹם *height* Si 26$_{16}$ ([זור[ח]ת), מֵצַח *forehead* 2 C 26$_{19}$, Ephraim Ho 7$_{9}$ (if em. זרק I *be profuse* or II *creep up*); כְּ *as*, + אוֹר *light* of morning 2 S 23$_{4}$; מִן of direction, *from*, + שֵׂעִיר *Seir* Dt 33$_{2}$, יַעֲקֹב *Jacob* Nm 24$_{17}$ (if em. דרך *tread*); עַל *upon*, + גַּנָּב *thief* Ex 22$_{2}$=4QBibPar 10$_{5}$, Zion Is 60$_{1.2}$, צַדִּיק *righteous one* 11QapPs$^{a}$ 4$_{10}$ ([יזרח]), all living things 4QJub$^{a}$ 2$_{12}$ ([ויזרח ... ]עליהם), מַיִם *water* 2 K 3$_{22}$, כֹּל *all* 4QJub$^{a}$ 2$_{12}$ ([ויזרח ... ]ועל כל); לִפְנֵי *before*, + כֹּהֵן *priest* 2 C 26$_{19}$.

<COLL> with adverb, שָׁם *there* Ec 1$_{5}$ (or del.).

<SYN> ראה ni. *be seen*, בוא *come*, i.e. set (of sun).

**Hi. cause (sun) to rise,** <SUBJ> Y. Ps 104$_{22}$ (if em. תִּזְרַח the sun *rises* to תַּזְרִיחַ *you cause to rise*). <OBJ> שֶׁמֶשׁ *sun* Ps 104$_{22}$ (if em.).*

→ זֶרַח I *shining*, II *Zerah*, זַרְחִי *Zerahite*, זְרַחְיָה *Zerahiah*, מִזְרָח *east*.

**[זֶרַח] I** 1 n.m. **shining**—sf. זַרְחֵךְ—<OBJ> ראה *see* Is 53$_{10}$ (if em. זֶרַע *seed*). <CSTR> נֹגַהּ זַרְחֵךְ *brightness of your shining* Is 60$_{3}$ (+ אוֹר *light*).

→ זרח *arise*.

**זֶרַח II** 21.0.0.1 pr.n.m. **Zerah**—זָרַח—son of Judah and Tamar and twin brother of Perez, <NOM CL> בְּנֵי יְהוּדָה עֵר ... וָזָרַח *the sons of Judah were Er ... and Zerah* Gn 46$_{12}$. <OBJ> ילד *give birth (to)* 1 C 2$_{4}$. <CSTR> בֶּן־זֶרַח *son of Zerah* Jos 7$_{1.18.24}$ 22$_{20}$, בְּנֵי זֶרַח *the sons of Zerah* Ne 11$_{24}$ (בְּנֵי־) 1 C 2$_{6}$ 9$_{6}$ (בְּנֵי־). <PREP> לְ of possession, *of (belonging) to* Nm 26$_{20}$. <COLL> וַיִּקְרָא שְׁמוֹ זָרַח *and he called his name Zerah* Gn 38$_{30}$ (Sam, mss וַתִּקְרָא *and she called*).

**2.** son of Reuel, and grandson of Esau, <NOM CL> בְּנֵי רְעוּאֵל נַחַת זֶרַח *the sons of Reuel were Nahath (and) Zerah* 1 C 1$_{37}$. <APP> אַלּוּף *chief* Gn 36$_{17}$. <COLL> אֵלֶּה בְּנֵי רְעוּאֵל נַחַת וָזֶרַח *these are the sons of Reuel: Nahath and Zerah* Gn 36$_{13}$, sim. 36$_{17}$.

**3.** father of Jobab king of Edom, <CSTR> בֶּן־זֶרַח *son of Zerah* Gn 36$_{33}$||1 C 1$_{44}$.

**4.** son of Simeon, appar. ident. with Zohar at Gn 46$_{10}$ Ex 6$_{15}$, <NOM CL> בְּנֵי שִׁמְעוֹן ... זֶרַח *the sons of Simeon were ... Zerah* 1 C 4$_{24}$. <PREP> לְ of possession, *of, (belonging) to* Nm 26$_{13}$.

**5.** Levite, son of Iddo/Adaiah, father of Jeatherai/Ethni, and descendant of Gershom, <NOM CL> זֶרַח בְּנוֹ *Zerah was his son* 1 C 6$_{6}$. <CSTR> בֶּן־זֶרַח *son of Zerah* 1 C 6$_{26}$. <APP> בֵּן *son* 1 C 6$_{26}$.

**6.** Cushite leader who confronted Asa in battle, <SUBJ> בוא *come* 2 C 14$_{8}$, יצא *go out* 2 C 14$_{8}$. <APP> כּוּשִׁי *Cushite* 2 C 14$_{8}$. <PREP> לִפְנֵי *before*, + יצא *go out* 2 C 14$_{8}$.

**7.** appar. father of Hananiah, Seal 562 (T. Beit Mirsim?, 7th/6th cent.).

→ זרח *arise*.

**זַרְחִי** 6 gent. **Zerahite,** as collective noun, **Zerahites, 1.** usu. in ref. to descendants of Zerah son of Judah. **2.** in ref. to descendants of Zerah son of Simeon, Nm 26$_{13}$. <CSTR> מִשְׁפַּחַת הַזַּרְחִי *family of the Zerahite(s)* Nm 26$_{13.20}$ Jos 7$_{17.17}$. <PREP> לְ of possession, *of, (belonging) to* 1 C 27$_{11.13}$.

→ זרח *arise*.

**זַרַחְיָה** $5.0.0.1$ pr.n.m. **Zerahiah**—I זרחיו—**1.** Levite, son of Uzzi, father of Meraioth, and ancestor of Ezra, <SUBJ> ילד hi. *beget* 1 C $5_{32}$. <NOM CL> זַרַחְיָה בְנוֹ *Zerahiah was his son* 1 C $6_{36}$. <OBJ> ילד hi. *beget* 1 C $5_{32}$. <CSTR> בֶּן־זְרַחְיָה *son of Zerahiah* Ezr $7_4$. <APP> בֵּן *son* Ezr $7_4$. **2.** member of the family of Pahath-moab and father of Elioenai, <CSTR> בֶּן־זְרַחְיָה *son of Zerahiah* Ezr $8_4$. **3.** perh. inhabitant of Rabbath Bene-Ammon, <APP> זרחיו הרבת perh. *Zerahiah the Rabbathite* Seal 301 (9th cent.), <PREP> לְ of possession, *of, (belonging) to* Seal 301.

→ זרח *arise.*

**זרם I** $2.0.1$ vb. **pour**—**Qal** $_1$ זְרַמְתָּם—**overwhelm,** <SUBJ> Y. Ps $90_5$ (or em. זְרַמְתָּם שֵׁנָה יִהְיוּ *you overwhelmed them, they are [as] sleep* to זְרַעְתָּם שָׁנָה שָׁנָה יִהְיוּ *you sow them each year; they are* in the morning; unless זרם II *destroy;* + חלף *pass*), נָהָר *river* 1QH $6_{17}$ ([נהר יזרום]). <OBJ> אֱנוֹשׁ *human being* Ps $90_5$, בֵּן *son* of *human being* Ps $90_5$. <PREP> עַל *throughout,* + תֵּבֵל *world* 1QH $6_{17}$ ([יזרום]); לְאֵין *without,* + אֶפֶס *end* 1QH $6_{17}$ ([יזרום]).

**Po.** $1.0.1$ Pf. זֹרְמוּ—**pour** rain, **be squeezed, be wrung out,** <SUBJ> עָב *cloud* Mur 88 Hb $3_{10}$ (זרמו מים עבות *the clouds poured out water,* or *were wrung out;* MT זֶרֶם מַיִם עָבָר *the downpour of water passed on*) Ps $77_{18}$ (+ נתן קוֹל *give voice,* i.e. thunder, הלך htp. *go about,* i.e. flash [of lightning]). <OBJ> מַיִם *water* Mur 88 Hb $3_{10}$ Ps $77_{18}$.*

→ זֶרֶם *downpour,* זִרְמָה *ejaculate.*

**זרם II** $_1$ vb. **destroy**—**Qal** זְרַמְתָּם—**destroy, put an end to, stop,** <SUBJ> Y. Ps $90_5$ (or em. זְרַמְתָּם שֵׁנָה יִהְיוּ *you destroyed them, they are [as] sleep* to זְרַעְתָּם שָׁנָה שָׁנָה יִהְיוּ *you sow them each year; they are,* or בְּזוֹרְם מִשֵּׁנָה *in their departing from sleep,* they are, or בְּזוּר מֵהֶם שֵׁנָה *when sleep departs from them* they are; unless זרם I *overwhelm;* + חלף *pass away*). <OBJ> אֱנוֹשׁ *human being* Ps $90_5$, בֵּן *son* of *human being* Ps $90_5$.

**זֶרֶם** $9.0.5$ n.m. **downpour**—זֶרֶם; cstr. זֶרֶם—**downpour, rainstorm,** <SUBJ> עבר *pass* Hb $3_{10}$ (זֶרֶם מַיִם עָבָר *the downpour of water passed on;* Mur 88 appar. זרמו מים עבות *the clouds poured out water*), שׁקה hi. *give to drink* 1QM $12_9$ (+ עָנָן *cloud,* עָב *cloud* of dew) $19_2$. <NOM CL> [נפץ ו]זרם כלי מלחמה המה *cloudburst and downpour are weapons of war* 4QpIsa^c $25_3$. <CSTR> זֶרֶם בָּרָד *downpour of hail* Is $28_2$ (|| שַׂעַר *whirlwind*), זרם רביבים *downpour of showers* 1QM $12_9$ $19_2$, זֶרֶם מַיִם *downpour of water(s)* Is $28_2$ Hb $3_{10}$, הָרִים *of,* i.e. from, *mountains* Jb $24_8$, קִיר *of,* appar. against, *a wall* Is $25_4$ (or em. קֹר *coldness;* :: חֹרֶב *heat*); נפץ זרם *cloudburst of a downpour* 1QH $2_{27}$, סֵתֶר זֶרֶם *shelter of,* i.e. from, *a downpour* Is $32_2$ (or ins. מִן shelter *from;* || רוּחַ *wind*). <PREP> בְּ of instrument, *by (means of), through,* + ראה hi. *show* majesty Is $30_{30}$ (|| נֶפֶץ *cloudburst,* + אֶבֶן hail *stone,* זַעַף *raging,* לַהַב *flame* of fire); כְּ *as* Is $25_4$ $28_{2.2}$ 1QM $12_9$ $19_2$; מִן *(offering protection) from,* מִסְתּוֹר מִזֶּרֶם *shelter from a downpour* Is $4_6$ (|| מָטָר *rain,* + חֹרֶב *heat*), סֵתֶר מִזֶּרֶם *shelter from a downpour* Is $32_2$ (if em. סֵתֶר זֶרֶם *shelter of a downpour*), מַחְסֶה מִזֶּרֶם *shelter from the downpour* Is $25_4$; of cause, *on account of,* + רטב *be drenched* Jb $24_8$; מִפְּנֵי *(from) before,* + נתר ni. *be released* 4Q424 $1_4$. <COLL> נֶפֶץ וָזֶרֶם *cloudburst and downpour* Is $30_{30}$ 4QpIsa^c $25_3$ ([נפץ ו]זרם). <SYN> שַׂעַר *whirlwind,* מָטָר *rain,* נֶפֶץ *cloudburst,* רוּחַ *wind.* <ANT> חֹרֶב *heat.*

→ זרם *pour.*

**[זִרְמָה]** $_2$ n.f. **ejaculate**—cstr. זִרְמַת; sf. זִרְמָתָם—<NOM CL> זִרְמַת סוּסִים זִרְמָתָם *their ejaculate is the ejaculate of horses* Ezk $23_{20}$ (|| בָּשָׂר *flesh,* i.e. penis). <CSTR> זִרְמַת סוּסִים *ejaculate of horses* Ezk $23_{20}$. <SYN> בָּשָׂר *flesh,* i.e. penis.

→ זרם *pour.*

**זרע** $56.2.5$ vb. **sow**—**Qal** $46.1.4$ Pf. זָרַע, זְרַעְתִּיהָ, זָרְעוּ, זְרַעְתֶּם; impf. יִזְרַע, 3fs תִּזְרָעֶנּוּ, 2ms תִּזְרַע (תִּזְרֶע), אֶזְרָעָה, וַיִּזְרַע; נִזְרַע, (תִּזְרָעוּ) תִּזְרְעוּ, יִזְרְעוּ, (אֶזְרָעֵם) + waw וָאֶזְרָעֶהָ; וַיִּזְרְעוּ, (וַיִּזְרָעֶהָ); impv. זְרַע, זִרְעוּ; ptc. זֹרֵעַ (זוֹרֵעַ), זֹרְעִים, זֹרְעֵי, (זורעים Q), pass. זָרוּעַ, זְרוּעָה; inf. זְרֹעַ (זרוע Q)—**1a.** active, usu. **sow,** also **bear (seed)** (Gn $1_{29.29}$), <SUBJ> Y. Jr $31_{27}$ Ho $2_{25}$ Zc $8_{12}$ (if em. זֶרַע *seed* of peace to אֶזְרָעָה *I shall sow*) $10_9$ (or em. זעק hi. *summon* or זרה pi. *scatter*) Ps $90_5$ (if em. זְרַמְתָּם שֵׁנָה *you sweep them away;* they are [as] *sleep* to זְרַעְתָּם שָׁנָה שָׁנָה *you sow them each year,* appar. מַטֶּה *tribe* Mc $6_{15}$=1QpMic $17_2$ ([תזרע];

:: קצר *reap*, + דרך *tread* olives), Israel Dt 11$_{10}$ Jg 6$_{3}$ Is 17$_{10}$ Ho 8$_{7}$=4QpHos$^{b}$ 11$_{6}$ (+ קצר), Ephraim, Judah, and Jacob Ho 10$_{12}$ (+ קצר, ניר *till*), עַם *people* Gn 47$_{23}$ Is 30$_{23}$ 32$_{20}$ Hg 1$_{6}$ (:: בוא hi. *bring*), עֵדָה *congregation* Lv 19$_{19}$ (Gnz, mss lack עֵדָה, leaving בֵּן *son* of Israel as subj.; + רבע hi. *mate*), Jerusalem Jr 4$_{3}$ (mss יֹשֵׁב *inhabitant* of Jerusalem; ‖ ניר), Abimelech Jg 9$_{45}$, Eliezer, son of Samuel 5/6ḤevBA 45 fr. 2 (+ כנס *gather*), Hezekiah 2 K 19$_{29}$‖Is 37$_{30}$ (+ קצר, נטע *plant*, אכל *eat*), Isaac Gn 26$_{12}$, Job Jb 31$_{8}$ (+ אכל).

Israelite Ex 23$_{10}$ (+ שֵׁשׁ שָׁנִים *[for] six years* you will sow; + אסף *gather*) 23$_{16}$ Dt 22$_{9.9}$ 4QMMT B$_{78}$, אִישׁ *man* 1QDM3$_{2}$ ([אי]ש ... [יז]רע), specif. man of Judah Jr 4$_{3}$, בֵּן *son* Si 37$_{29(B)}$ (Bmg זרה תזורו/תזור *scatter*, D זיד hi. *display presumptuousness*), specif. son of Israel Lv 19$_{19}$ (Gnz, mss) 25$_{3}$ (+ שֵׁשׁ שָׁנִים; ‖ זמר II *prune*, + אסף) 25$_{4}$ (‖ זמר II) 25$_{11}$ (+ קצר *reap*, בצר *harvest grapes*) 25$_{20}$ (‖ אסף) 25$_{22}$ 26$_{16}$ (both + אכל), of house of Rechabites Jr 35$_{7}$ (‖ נטע *plant*, בנה *build*), רֹעֶה *shepherd* Jr 12$_{13}$ (:: קצר), שמר ptc. *one who keeps*, i.e. watches wind Ec 11$_{4}$ (‖ קצר), חרשׁ *ploughman* Is 28$_{24}$ (or del. זרע), רָעֵב *hungry one* Ps 107$_{37}$ (‖ נטע), tearful one Ps 126$_{5}$ (:: קצר), wicked one Jb 4$_{8}$ (+ קצר) 22$_{8}$ (+ קצר), righteous one Pr 11$_{18}$ (or em. זֹרֵעַ צְדָקָה *sowing righteousness* to זֶרַע צַדִּיקִים *offspring of the righteous*) 11$_{21}$ (if em. זֶרַע צַדִּיקִים to זֹרֵעַ צְדָקָה), addressee of proverb Ec 11$_{6}$, עֵץ *tree* Gn 1$_{29}$, עֵשֶׂב *plant* Gn 1$_{29}$; subj. not specified, 4Q418 103.2$_{8}$.

**<OBJ>** (1) ground, etc. that is sown: אֶרֶץ *land* Ex 23$_{10}$, אֲדָמָה *earth* Gn 47$_{23}$ Is 30$_{23}$, כֶּרֶם *vineyard* Dt 22$_{9}$ 4QMMT B$_{78}$ ([כ]רמו), שָׂדֶה *field* Lv 19$_{19}$ 25$_{3.4}$ Ps 107$_{37}$ 1QDM 3$_{2}$ ([שדהו לו]א יז[רע] *he shall not sow his field*) 4QMMT B$_{78}$, עִיר *city* Jg 9$_{45}$, בַּיִת *house* Jr 31$_{27.27}$ Zc 10$_{9}$ (or em. זעק hi. *summon* or זרה pi. *scatter*).

(2) seed, etc. that is sown: זֶרַע *seed* Gn 1$_{29.29}$ Lv 26$_{16}$ Dt 11$_{10}$ 22$_{9}$ Is 30$_{23}$ Jr 31$_{27.27}$ 35$_{7}$ Ec 11$_{6}$, חִטָּה *wheat* Jr 12$_{13}$, זְמוֹרָה *branch* Is 17$_{10}$, כִּלְאַיִם *two kinds (of seed)* Lv 19$_{19}$ Dt 22$_{9}$ 4QMMT B$_{78}$ ([כלאים]) 4Q418 103.2$_{8}$, מֶלַח *salt* Jg 9$_{45}$, רוּחַ *wind* Ho 8$_{7}$=4QpHos$^{b}$ 11$_{6}$, שָׁלוֹם *peace* Zc 8$_{12}$ (if em. זֶרַע *seed* of peace), צְדָקָה *righteousness* Pr 11$_{18}$ (or em. זֹרֵעַ צְדָקָה *sowing righteousness* to זֶרַע צַדִּיקִים *offspring of the righteous*) 11$_{21}$ (if em. זֶרַע צַדִּיקִים to זֹרֵעַ צְדָקָה), עַוְלָה *wickedness* Pr 22$_{8}$, עָמָל *trouble* Jb 4$_{8}$, רבה hi. inf. *to increase*, i.e. much Hg 1$_{6}$, אֲשֶׁר *that which you sow* Ex 23$_{16}$, אֵם *mother* Ho 2$_{25}$ (or em. וּזְרַעְתִּיהָ *and I shall sow her* to וּזְרַעְתִּיהוּ *and I shall sow him* [perh. Lo-ammi]).

(3) time of sowing: שָׁנָה eighth *year* Lv 25$_{22}$.

**<PREP>** לְ of benefit, *to, for*, + Y. Ho 2$_{25}$, Ephraim, Judah, and Jacob Ho 10$_{12}$, רִיק *vanity* Lv 26$_{16}$, appar. תַּעֲנוּג *delicacy* Si 37$_{29(B)}$ (אל תזרע ל; Bmg אל תזר על *do not scatter for*; D אל תזד אל appar. *do not display presumptuousness*); introducing object, + צְדָקָה *righteousness* Ho 10$_{12}$.

בְּ of place/time, *in, at, among*, + עַם *people* Zc 10$_{9}$ (or del. בָּעַמִּים *among the peoples*), אֶרֶץ *land* Gn 26$_{12}$ Ho 2$_{25}$, שָׂדֶה *field* Ex 23$_{16}$, שָׁנָה *year* 2 K 19$_{29}$‖Is 37$_{30}$, בֹּקֶר *morning* Ec 11$_{6}$; of accompaniment, *with, in (a state of)*, + דִּמְעָה *tear(s)*, i.e. weeping Ps 126$_{5}$.

אֶל *among*, + קוֹץ *thorn* Jr 4$_{3}$.

עַל *beside*, + מַיִם *water* Is 32$_{20}$.

**1b.** ptc. as noun, **sower, <OBJ>** כרת *cut*, i.e. remove Jr 50$_{16}$ (or em. hi. *cut off* and/or זֶרַע *seed*). **<PREP>** לְ of direction, *to*, + נתן *give* Is 55$_{10}$ (‖ אכל *eat*).

**1c.** passive, **be sown, <SUBJ>** אֶרֶץ *land* Jr 2$_{2}$ (or del.), אוֹר *light* Ps 97$_{11}$ (ms זרח *arise*). **<PREP>** לְ of benefit, *to, for*, + צַדִּיק *righteous one* Ps 97$_{11}$.

**<SYN>** §1a קצר *reap*, ניר *till*, זמר *prune*, אסף *gather*, נטע *plant*, בנה *build*; §1b אכל *eat*. **<ANT>** §1a קצר *reap*, בוא hi. *bring*.

**Ni.** 6.0.1 Impf. יִזָּרַע (יִזָּרֵעַ), 3fs תִּזָּרַע; + waw וְנִזְרְעָה, וְנִזְרַעְתֶּם—**be sown,** of seed (Lv 11$_{37}$ Nm 5$_{28[Sam\ mss]}$), including name/posterity (Na 1$_{14}$), of ground (Dt 21$_{4}$ 29$_{22}$ Ezk 36$_{9}$), or of woman (Nm 5$_{28}$), **<SUBJ>** אִשָּׁה *woman* Lv 12$_{2(Sam)}$ (+ ילד *give birth*) Nm 5$_{28}$ (+ זֶרַע *[with] seed*; mss, Sam have זֶרַע as subj.), אֶרֶץ *land* Dt 29$_{22}$ (Sam hi. *produce seed*), הַר *mountain* of Israel Ezk 36$_{9}$ (‖ עבד ni. *be served*, i.e. tilled), נַחַל *valley* Dt 21$_{4}$=11QT 63$_{2}$ (+ עבד ni.), זֶרַע *seed* Lv 11$_{37}$ Nm 5$_{28(Sam\ mss)}$; subj. not specified, Na 1$_{14}$ (לֹא־יִזָּרַע מִשִּׁמְךָ עוֹד *of your name, no longer will it be sown*, i.e. you will have no more descendants; or em. לֹא־יִזָּכֵר עוֹד שִׁמְךָ *no longer will your name be remembered*). **<CSTR>** זֶרַע זֵרוּעַ *seed of*, i.e. for, *sowing* Lv 11$_{37}$. **<PREP>** מִן partitive, *(some) of, (any) of*, + שֵׁם *name* Na 1$_{14}$ (or em.; see Subj.).

<SYN> עבד ni. *be served*, i.e. tilled.

**Pu.** 1 Pf. זֹרָעוּ—**be sown,** <SUBJ> רֹזֵן *prince* Is 40$_{24}$ (|| נטע ni. *be planted,* שׁרשׁ poel *take root*), שֹׁפֵט *judge* Is 40$_{24}$. <SYN> נטע ni. *be planted,* שׁרשׁ poel *take root.*

**Hi.** 3.1 Impf. 3fs תַּזְרִיעַ; ptc. מַזְרִיעַ—**produce seed; conceive** (Lv 12$_{2}$ Si 42$_{10[M]}$ 4QD$^{a}$ 9.2$_{5}$), <SUBJ> אִשָּׁה *woman* Lv 12$_{2}$ (Sam ni. *be sown;* + ילד *give birth*) 4QD$^{a}$ 9.2$_{5}$ (תזרי[ע]), בַּת *daughter* Si 42$_{10(M)}$ (Bmg פחז *be wanton*), עֵשֶׂב *plant* Gn 1$_{11.12}$ (unless in both דֶּשֶׁא עֵשֶׂב = *grass of plant*, i.e. with דֶּשֶׁא *grass* as subj.), אֶרֶץ *land* Dt 29$_{22(Sam)}$ (|| צמח hi. *cause to grow*), זֶרַע *seed* 4QJub$^{a}$ 2$_{7}$ ([זרע מזריע]). <OBJ> זֶרַע *seed* Gn 1$_{11.12}$. <PREP> לְ *according to,* + מִין *kind* Gn 1$_{12}$; בְּ appar. *in accordance with,* + זֶרַע *seed* 4QJub$^{a}$ 2$_{7}$ ([מזריע בזרעו]). <SYN> צמח hi. *cause to grow.**

→ זֶרַע *seed,* זֵרוּעַ *sowing,* זֵרֻעַ *vegetable,* זֵרְעֹן *vegetable,* יִזְרְעֶאל *Jezreel,* יִזְרְעֵאלִי *Jezreelite,* מִזְרָע *place of sowing.*

[זֵרֹעַ] 1.0.1 n.[m.] **vegetable**—pl. זֵרֹעִים—<OBJ> נתן *give* 1QDan$^{a}$ 1$_{16}$ (MT זֵרְעֹן *vegetable;* + יַיִן *wine,* פַּתְבַּג *delicacy*). <PREP> מִן partitive, *(some) of,* + נתן *give* Dn 1$_{12}$ (mss זֵרְעֹן; + מַיִם *water*).

→ זרע *sow.*

זֶרַע 229.15.49.2 n.m. **seed**—זָרַע; cstr. זֶרַע (זְרַע); sf. זַרְעִי, זַרְעֲךָ (זרעכה Q ,זַרְעֵךְ) זַרְעֵךְ, זַרְעוֹ, זַרְעָהּ, זַרְעֲכֶם, זַרְעָם (זרעמה Q); pl. sf. זַרְעֵיכֶם—**1. seed,** for sowing (e.g. Gn 47$_{19.23}$ Lv 26$_{16}$ Nm 24$_{7}$ Dt 28$_{38}$ Is 55$_{10}$). **2.** human seed, i.e. **semen** (e.g. Lv 15$_{16.17.32}$ Nm 5$_{28}$ Jr 31$_{27}$ 4QTohA 2.1$_{4}$). **3.** produce of seed, **grain** (Nm 20$_{5}$), **offspring,** rarely of animals (Gn 7$_{3}$ Jr 31$_{27}$), usu. of human beings (e.g. Gn 12$_{17}$ Ex 32$_{13.13}$ 33$_{1}$ Jos 24$_{3}$). **4.** perh. **seed time** (Gn 8$_{22}$ Lv 26$_{5}$ 1QS 10$_{7}$ Gezer calendar$_{1}$).

<SUBJ> (sometimes with sing. noun and plur. verb) היה *be* Gn 15$_{5.13}$ (+ גֵּר be a *sojourner*) 28$_{14}$ (+ כְּ *as* dust) 38$_{9}$ 48$_{19}$ (+ מְלֹא be *fullness* of nations) Is 48$_{19}$ (+ כְּ *as* sand; + צֶאֱצָא *offspring*) Jr 31$_{36}$ 35$_{9}$ (or em. וְשָׂדֶה וָזֶרַע *and field and seed* to וּשְׂדֵה־זֶרַע *and field of seed*) Ps 89$_{37}$ (+ לְעוֹלָם *for ever;* + כִּסֵּא *throne*) 112$_{2}$ (+ גִּבּוֹר *mighty;* or em. גְּבִיר *lord*) 1 C 17$_{11}$ (+ מַלְכוּת *kingdom*) 1QH 17$_{14}$ (+ לִפְנֵי *before* Y.) 4QJub$^{g}$ 25$_{12}$ ([יהי זרעו]) 4QpsJub$^{a}$ 2.1$_{7}$ 4Q464 3.2$_{3}$ ([גר יהיה זרעך] *your offspring will be a sojourner*) 4QapLam$^{b}$$_{7}$ (+ מִן *from* [sons of] covenant), חיה *live* Dt 30$_{19}$, שׁבת *cease* Gn 8$_{22}$ Jr 31$_{36}$, שׁאר ni. *remain* 4QpsEzek$^{b}$ 3.2$_{4}$.

זרע ni. *be sown* Lv 11$_{37}$ Nm 5$_{28(Sam\ mss)}$, hi. *produce seed* 4QJub$^{a}$ 2$_{7}$ ([זרע מזריע]), פרה *be fruitful* 1QS 4$_{7}$, צדק *be righteous* Is 45$_{25}$, ברך pu. *be blessed* GnzPs 4$_{24}$, כבד ni. *be honoured* Si 10$_{19(A)}$, pi. *honour* Ps 22$_{24}$, קלה ni. *be dishonoured* Si 10$_{19(B).19(A,\ B)}$, מנה ni. *be counted* Gn 13$_{16}$, ספר ni. *be counted* Gn 16$_{10}$, קרא ni. *be called* Gn 21$_{12}$ Is 14$_{20}$, ערב htp. *be mixed* Ezr 9$_{2}$, כון ni. *be established* Ps 102$_{29}$ (|| בֵּן *son*) Jb 21$_{8}$, בדל ni. *be separated* Ne 9$_{2}$, קדשׁ *be holy,* i.e. be forfeit Dt 22$_{9}$ (or em. htp. in same sense; Sam hi. *forfeit* seed) 4Q418 103.2$_{8}$ ([יקד[שׁ]; + מְלֵאָה *fullness*), מלט ni. *be delivered* Pr 11$_{21}$ (or em. זֶרַע צַדִּיקִים *seed of righteous ones* to זֹרֵעַ צְדָקָה *one who sows righteousness*), משׁל *rule* 11QT 59$_{15}$, טול ho. *be thrown down* Jr 22$_{28}$ (or del. זֶרַע), שׁלך ho. *be thrown down* Jr 22$_{28}$ (or del. זֶרַע), כרת ni. *be cut off* Ps 37$_{28}$=4QpPs$^{a}$ 3.4$_{1}$ ([נכרת]), שׁדד pu. *be devastated* Jr 49$_{10}$ (+ אָח *brother* [or em. אֵין *not*], שָׁכֵן *neighbour*).

הלך htp. *go* CD 12$_{22}$, בוא *come* Gn 46$_{6}$, יצא *go out* 2 S 7$_{12}$ (+ מַמְלָכָה *kingdom*), שׁוב *go back* Jb 39$_{12(Kt)}$, מושׁ hi. *depart* 4Q415 2.1$_{5}$, עמד *stand* Is 66$_{22}$ (|| שֵׁם *name*) Ne 9$_{2}$ Si 44$_{12.13(M)}$ (B זֵכֶר *remembrance;* + כָּבוֹד *glory*), יצב htp. *stand* 11QapPs$^{a}$ 2$_{6}$ ([זר[ע] ... התי[צבו]), נתן *give,* i.e. yield, fruit Zc 8$_{12}$ (or em.; see Cstr.), עשׂה *do,* i.e. produce, ephah of grain Is 5$_{10}$, שׁמר *keep* covenant Gn 17$_{9}$, עבד *serve* Ps 22$_{31}$ (or em. זֶרַע יַעַבְדֶנּוּ *seed will serve him* to זְרֹעוֹ וְכַבְּדוּן ... *his arm now, glorify;* or del.), ירשׁ *possess* Gn 22$_{17}$ 24$_{60}$ (both + שַׁעַר possess *gate* of enemy) Nm 14$_{24(Sam)}$ (MT hi. *possess*) Is 54$_{3}$ Ps 25$_{13}$ (+ נֶפֶשׁ *soul*) Si 46$_{9}$, נחל *inherit* Ex 32$_{13}$ Ps 69$_{37}$, ישׁב hi. *settle* cities Is 54$_{3}$, בקשׁ pi. *seek* bread Ps 37$_{25}$=4QpPs$^{a}$ 1.3$_{18}$, הלל htp. *boast* Is 45$_{25}$, ידה htp. *confess* sins Ne 9$_{2}$, ידע *know* Jr 22$_{28}$ (or del. זֶרַע) Si 46$_{10}$, ni. *be known* Is 61$_{9}$ (|| צֶאֱצָא *offspring*), בין hi. *understand* 1QLitPr 3.2$_{3}$, גור *fear* Ps 22$_{24}$, עבר *transgress* Si 10$_{19}$.

<NOM CL> זַרְעֲךָ הוּא *he is your offspring* Gn 21$_{13}$, הֲלוֹא־אַתֶּם ... זֶרַע שָׁקֶר *are you not ... offspring of deceit?* Is 57$_{4}$ (|| יֶלֶד *child*), זרע נכבד מה זרע לאנוש *what is honoured seed? Human seed* Si 10$_{19(A)}$ (B נקלה *dishonoured*), כֻּלֹּה זֶרַע אֱמֶת *all of it was a seed of reliability* Jr 2$_{21}$

(Qr mss כֻּלּוֹ), זֶרַע בְּרוּכֵי י׳ הֵמָּה *they are the offspring of the blessed ones of Y.* Is $65_{23}$, זֶרַע קֹדֶשׁ מַצַּבְתָּהּ *seed of holiness is its stump* Is $6_{13}$ (or del.), רַב זַרְעֶךָ *great is your offspring* Jb $5_{25}$, הַזֶּרַע שָׁלוֹם *the seed is peace* Zc $8_{12}$ (if em.; see Cstr.), זַרְעָהּ שָׁלוֹם *her seed is peace* Zc $8_{12}$ (if em.).

זַרְעוֹ לִבְרָכָה *his offspring is as a blessing* Ps $37_{26}$=4QpPs$^{a}$ $1.3_{18}$ (זר[עו]); or em. זִכְרוֹ *his memory*), זַרְעוֹ בְּמַיִם רַבִּים *his seed is on many waters* Nm $24_7$ (unless זֶרַע subj. of נזל *flow* into waters; or em. זְרֹעוֹ בְּעַמִּים *his arm is against* many *peoples*), בְּמַיִם רַבִּים זֶרַע שִׁחֹר *on many waters was the seed*, i.e. people, *of Shihor* Is $23_3$ (or rd. זֶרַע שִׁחֹר קְצִיר יְאוֹר תְּבוּאָתָהּ *the seed of Shihor, the harvest of the Nile, is its produce*; or em. קְצִירוֹ תְּבוּאָתה the seed of Shihor *is his harvest, his produce*), אֲשֶׁר זַרְעוֹ־בוֹ fruit, *the seed of which is in it* Gn $1_{11.12}$.*

זרעה אין בה *its* (f.) *seed is not in it* 4QD$^{a}$ $12_6$, הֵא־לָכֶם זֶרַע *behold, for you there is seed* Gn $47_{23}$, זֶרַע אֵין לָהּ *she does not have seed* Lv $22_{13}$, הַעוֹד הַזֶּרַע בַּמְּגוּרָה *is the seed still in the store?* Hg $2_{19}$ (or em. הַזֶּרַע *the seed* to מִגְרַע *lack* or ins. נִגְרַע is the seed *diminished?*).

<OBJ> בוא hi. *bring* Gn $46_7$ Is $43_5$=4QTanḥ $4_2$ (אב[י]א [זרעך]) Jr $23_8$ (or del. זֶרַע), יצא hi. *take out* Is $65_9$, specif. produce Dt $28_{38}$, שׁוב hi. *take back* Jb $39_{12(Qr)}$, עלה hi. *take up* Jr $23_8$ (or del. עלה and/or זֶרַע), קום hi. *raise*, i.e. establish Gn $38_8$ 2 S $7_{12}$||1 C $17_{11}$ 4QMidrEschat$^{a}$ $3_{10}$, נשׂג hi. *overtake* Lv $26_5$, נתן *give* Gn $15_3$ $38_9$ $47_{19}$ 1 S $1_{11}$ Is $55_{10}$ (|| לֶחֶם *bread*) Ru $4_{12}$, שׂים *place* Gn $13_{16}$ $32_{13}$ 1 S $2_{20}$ (4QSam$^{a}$ שׁלם pi. *repay*) Ps $89_{30}$ (+ כִּסֵּא *throne*) 4QJub$^{g}$ $25_{12}$ ([זרע]), שׁית *place* Gn $4_{25}$, כון hi. *establish* Ps $89_5$, עמד hi. *establish* 4Q419 $1_5$ ([להעמיד]), נדח hi. *scatter* Jr $23_8$ (or del. זֶרַע), נפל hi. *cause to fall* Ps $106_{27}$ (or em. פוץ hi. *scatter*), שׁלך hi. *throw* Jr $7_{15}$.

אסף *gather* Jb $39_{12}$ (if em. זַרְעֲךָ וְגָרְנְךָ he will take back *your seed, and* he will gather *your threshing floor* to וְזַרְעֲךָ גָרְנָה *and your seed* he will gather *onto the threshing floor*), משׁך *drag*, i.e. sow Am $9_{13}$ (or em. בְּמֹשֵׁךְ הַזָּרַע strike *against*, i.e. meet, *one who drags seed* to בְּמֹשֵׁךְ *against the one who drags* or בְּזֹרֵעַ *against the one who sows*) Ps $126_6$ (if em. מֶשֶׁךְ־הַזָּרַע *the trail*, or perh. *pouch, of seed* to מֹשֵׁךְ *dragging*).

זרע *sow* Lv $26_{16}$ Dt $11_{10}$ $22_9$ Is $30_{23}$ Jr $31_{27.27}$ $35_7$ (|| כֶּרֶם *vineyard*) Ec $11_6$, specif. bear (seed) Gn $1_{29.29}$, hi. *produce (seed)* Gn $1_{11.12}$, פרח hi. *cause to bud* Is $17_{11}$, רבה hi. *increase* Gn $16_{10}$ $22_{17}$ $26_{4.24}$ Ex $32_{13}$ Jos $24_3$ Jr $33_{22}$, חיה pi. *keep alive* Gn $7_3$ $19_{32.34}$, ישׁע hi. *save* Jr $30_{10}$=$46_{27}$, עזר *help* 11QapPs$^{a}$ $2_6$ ([לעזור] ... זר[ע]).

ראה *see* Is $53_{10}$ (or em. זָרַח *shining*), hi. *show* Jacob Gn $48_{11}$, בקשׁ pi. *seek* Ml $2_{15}$, נגד hi. *declare* Ezr $2_{59}$||Ne $7_{61}$, עשׂר *tithe* 1 S $8_{15}$ (|| כֶּרֶם *vineyard*), קדשׁ pi. *sanctify* 1QSb $3_4$, hi. *sanctify*, i.e. forfeit Dt $22_{9(Sam)}$, ברך pi. *bless* 4QJub$^{d}$ $21_{25}$ (ל[ברך את זרעכה]) *to bless your offspring*), חלל pi. *profane* Lv $21_{15}$ 4QpsMos$^{e}$ $2.1_{10}$ (יחלל[ו] א[ת זר[ע]ם *they will profane their offspring*), טמא pi. *defile* 4QMMT $B_{81.82}$ ([זרע]ם), גער *rebuke* Ml $2_3$ (or em. גדע *hew* and זְרוֹעַ *arm*), מאס *reject* Jr $33_{26}$, כרת hi. *cut off* 1 S $24_{22}$ Jr $50_{16}$ (if em. qal *cut* and זוֹרֵעַ *sower*) 4QJub$^{f}$ $21_3$ ([ויכריתכה]) 4QJub$^{d}$ $21_{22}$ ([זרעכה]) 11QT $59_{15}$, ענה pi. *afflict* 1 K $11_{39}$, אכל *eat*, perh. destroy Lv $26_{16}$, אבד pi. *destroy* 2 K $11_1$||2 C $22_{10(mss)}$ (L דבר pi. *destroy* or *expel*) Ps $21_{11}$ (|| פְּרִי *fruit*).

<CSTR> זֶרַע אֱלֹהִים *seed*, i.e. people, *of God* Ml $2_{15}$, זֶרַע שִׁחֹר *offspring of Shihor* Is $23_3$, זֶרַע אַבְרָהָם *offspring of Abraham* Is $41_8$=4QTanḥ $1.1_{10}$ ([זרע אבר[הם]) Jr $33_{26}$ Ps $105_6$||1 C $16_{13(mss)}$ 2 C $20_7$ 4Q302 $1_7$, אַהֲרֹן *of Aaron* Lv $21_{21}$ $22_4$ Nm $17_5$ 4Q419 $1_5$ (אהרון), דָּוִד *of David* 1 K $11_{39}$ Jr $33_{22.26}$, יִשְׂחָק *of Isaac* Jr $33_{26}$, יַעֲקֹב *of Jacob* Is $45_{19}$ Jr $33_{26.26}$ Ps $22_{24}$ Si $46_{10}$ 4QJub$^{a}$ $2_{20}$ 4QDibHam$^{a}$ $1.5_7$ (both יעקוב), צָדוֹק *of Zadok* Ezk $43_{19}$.

זֶרַע יִשְׂרָאֵל *offspring/people of Israel* 2 K $17_{20}$ Is $45_{25}$ Jr $23_8$ (if del. בֵּית offspring of *house of* Israel [or del. זֶרַע]) $31_{36.37}$ Ezk $44_{22(mss)}$ Ps $22_{24}$ Ne $9_2$ Ps $105_{6(mss)}$||1 C $16_{13}$ CD $12_{22}$ 4QD$^{a}$ $18.2_{11}$ ([ז]רע י[שראל]) 4QDibHam$^{a}$ $1.3_{19}$, זֶרַע אֶפְרָיִם *offspring of Ephraim* Jr $7_{15}$, זֶרַע הַיְּהוּדִים *offspring of the Jews* Est $6_{13}$, זֶרַע מָדָי *offspring of (the) Medes* Dn $9_1$.

זֶרַע מַמְלָכָה *offspring of (the) kingdom*, i.e. (of) royal descent 2 K $11_1$||2 C $22_{10}$, זֶרַע הַמְּלוּכָה *offspring of (the) kingship*, i.e. (of) royal descent 1 K $11_{14}$ (if em. הַמֶּלֶךְ *of the king*)* 2 K $25_{25}$||Jr $41_1$ Ezk $17_{13}$ Dn $1_3$.

זֶרַע בֵּית *offspring of house of* Jr $23_8$ (or del. זֶרַע בֵּית or em. בֵּית to בְּנֵי *sons of*) Ezk $20_5$ $44_{22}$ (mss lack בֵּית), זֶרַע זַרְעֲךָ *offspring of your offspring* Is $59_{21}$, זֶרַע בְּרוּכֵי י׳ *offspring of the blessed ones of Y.* Is $65_{23}$, זֶרַע צַדִּיקִים *off-*

spring of the righteous Pr $11_{18}$ (if em. זֹרֵעַ צְדָקָה *sowing righteousness*) $11_{21}$ (or em. זֹרֵעַ צְדָקָה), זרע הקד[ושי]ם *offspring of holy ones* 11QapPs$^a$ $4_6$ (+ אָדָם *human being*), זֶרַע רְשָׁעִים *offspring of the wicked* Ps $37_{28}$=4QpPs$^a$ $3.4_1$ ([ר]שעים]) 4Q426 $1.1_2$, זֶרַע מְרֵעִים *offspring of evildoers* Is 14 $14_{20}$, זֶרַע מְנָאֵף וַתִּזְנֶה *offspring of an adulterer and her who prostitutes herself* Is $57_3$ (or em. זֶרַע מְנָאֶפֶת וְזֹנָה *offspring of an adulteress and a prostitute*), זֶרַע שָׁקֶר *offspring of deceit* Is $57_4$, זרע ברכה *offspring of blessing* 4QRitMar $19_2$.

זֶרַע אָדָם *seed of human being(s)* Jr $31_{27}$ 1QLitPr $3.2_3$ ([האד]ם]), זֶרַע אֲנָשִׁים *seed of men*, perh. male offspring 1 S $1_{11}$, זֶרַע בְּהֵמָה *seed of beast(s)* Jr $31_{27}$, זֶרַע אֱמֶת *seed of reliability* Jr $2_{21}$, זֶרַע זֵרוּעַ *seed of sowing* Lv $11_{37}$, זֶרַע קֹדֶשׁ *seed of holiness* Is $6_{13}$ (or del.) Ezr $9_2$ (הַקֹּדֶשׁ), *offspring of holiness* 4QMMT $B_{75}$ ([זרע]) $B_{81}$ ([הקודש]) 11QapPs$^a$ $2_6$ ([זר]ע הקודש]), זֶרַע הַשָּׁלוֹם *the seed of peace* Zc $8_{12}$ (or em. זרע *sow* peace or הַזֶּרַע שָׁלוֹם *the seed is peace* or זַרְעָהּ שָׁלוֹם *her seed is peace*).

זֶרַע הָאָרֶץ *seed of the land* Lv $27_{30}$ Ezk $17_5$, זֶרַע הַשָּׂדֶה *seed of the field* Gn $47_{24}$, זרע חטים *seed of wheat(s)* Mur $30.1_2$ $30.2_{14}$ ([זר]ע]), זֶרַע גַּד *seed of coriander* Ex $16_{31}$ Nm $11_7$ (זֶרַע־), זֶרַע חֹמֶר *seed of*, i.e. measuring, *homer (of)* Lv $27_{16}$ Is $5_{10}$.

מְקוֹם זֶרַע *place of grain* Nm $20_5$ (‖ תְּאֵנָה *fig*, גֶּפֶן *vine*, רִמּוֹן *pomegranate*), שְׂדֵה־זֶרַע *field of seed* Jr $35_9$ (if em. שָׂדֶה וָזֶרַע *field and seed*) Ezk $17_5$ (זָרַע), מוצא זרע *going out*, i.e. growth, *of seed* Si $37_{11}$(Bmg, D) (Bmg מצא; B מוציא רע *one who brings out evil*), בית זרע *house*, i.e. capacity, *of seed of* Mur $30.1_2$ $30.2_{14}$ ([בית זר[ע]).

שִׁכְבַת־זֶרַע *lying down of seed*, i.e. ejaculate Lv $15_{16.17.18}$ (all three זֶרַע) $15_{32}$ $19_{20}$ $22_4$ (זָרַע) Nm $5_{13}$ 4QD$^g$ $1.2_9$ ([שכ]בת זרע]) 4QTohA $1.1_8$ ([ש]כבת הזרע]) 4QTohA 2.14 11QT $45_{11}$.

תְּבוּאַת זַרְעֶךָ *produce of your seed* Dt $14_{22}$, מְטַר זַרְעֲךָ *rain of*, i.e. for, *your seed* Is $30_{23}$, מַכּוֹת זַרְעֶךָ *plagues of your seed* Dt $28_{59}$, מֶשֶׁךְ־הַזָּרַע *the trail*, or perh. *pouch*, *of seed* Ps $126_6$ (or em. מֹשֵׁךְ *dragging*, i.e. sowing).

מועד זרע *season of sowing* 1QS $10_7$ (+ דֶּשֶׁא *grass*, קָצִיר *harvest*, קַיִץ *summer*), [מועדי זרע] *seasons of sowing* 4Q PrFêtes$^c$ $3.1_5$, ירחו זרע *months of sowing* Gezer calendar$_1$.

[בן]ני זרע] *sons of offspring of* holiness 4QMMT $B_{75}$, רֹאשׁ זַרְעוֹ *head of his offspring* 1 K $2_{33}$, לְבַב זַרְעֶךָ *heart of your offspring* Dt $30_6$, פִּי זֶרַע *mouth of offspring of* Is $59_{21}$, פִּי זַרְעֲךָ *mouth of your offspring* Is $59_{21}$, פִּי זַרְעוֹ *mouth of his offspring* Dt $31_{19}$, [שאר זר]עכה] *remnant of your offspring* 4QJub$^d$ $21_{25}$.

כָּל־זֶרַע *all seed of* Lv $11_{37.38}$ (if ins. כָּל־), *all offspring/people of* 2 K $11_1$‖2 C $22_{10}$ 2 K $17_{20}$ Is $45_{25}$ Jr $23_8$ (if ins. כָּל־) $31_{37}$ (or del. כָּל־) Ps $22_{24.24}$ Si $46_{10}$ 4QD$^a$ $18.2_{11}$ ([כו]ל [ז]רע]) 11QapPs$^a$ $2_6$ ([כול זר[ע]), כָּל־זַרְעוֹ *all his offspring/people* Gn $46_{6.7}$ Est $10_3$ Si $45_{25}$, כול זרעכה *all your offspring* 1QSb $3_2$, כָּל־זַרְעֲכֶם *all your offspring* Lv $22_3$ (mss lack כָּל־).

<APP> Jacob 4QJub$^g$ $25_{12}$ ([יע]וב ... זרע]), אָח *brother* Jr $7_{15}$, גֶּפֶן *vine* Zc $8_{12}$ (or em.; see Cstr.), סְאָה *seah* 1 K $18_{32}$, מְלֵאָה *fullness* Dt $22_9$, בֵּן *son* 4QJub$^g$ $25_{12}$ ([בן ... ] זרע]).

<ADJ> רַב *great* Dt $28_{38}$, אַחֵר *another* Gn $4_{25}$, קָדוֹשׁ *holy* 4QJub$^g$ $25_{12}$ ([זרע קדוש]).

<PREP> לְ of direction, *to*, + נתן *give* Gn $12_7$ $13_{15}$ $15_{18}$ $17_8$ $24_7$ $26_{3.4}$ $28_{4.13}$ $35_{12}$ $48_4$ Ex $32_{13}$ $33_1$ Dt $1_8$ $11_9$ $34_4$ Ne $9_8$ 2 C $20_7$ 4QJub$^a$ $1_7$ ([לזרע]כם אתנה]) 4QD$^a$ $18.5_{11}$, ni. *be given* 4QpGen$^a$ $1.5_4$, נשׂא *raise* hand, i.e. swear oath Ezk $20_5$, אמר *say* Is $45_{19}$, דבר *speak* Est $10_3$; of possession, *of*, *(belonging) to* (sometimes לְ of benefit) Gn $17_{19}$ Ex $28_{43}$ Nm $18_{19}$ Si $45_{21.25}$ 4QpPs$^a$ $1.3_2$ 11QT $21_{05}$ perh. 4QMidrEschat$^b$ $10_{13}$ 4QD$^a$ $18.2_{11}$ ([לכו]ל [ז]רע]), + היה *be* Gn $17_7$ Ex $30_{21}$ Nm $25_{13}$ 1 K $2_{33}$ Si $45_{15.24}$; of benefit, *to, for*, + עשׂה *do* 2 S $22_{51}$‖Ps $18_{51}$, appar. נתן *give* lying down, i.e. have sex with, for the benefit of seed/offspring Lv $18_{20}$, קום hi. *fulfil* 1QM $13_7$, כרת ni. *be cut off*, i.e. abrogated Si $50_{24}$; *as*, + היה *be* Gn $47_{24}$.

בְּ of place, *in*, *among*, + היה *be* Dt $28_{46}$; of agent/instrument, *by (means of)*, + ברך ni. *be blessed* Gn $28_{14}$ (or del.), pi. *bless* Si $44_{21}$, htp. *bless oneself* Gn $22_{18}$=$26_4$; *in accordance with*, + זרע hi. *produce (seed)* 4QJub$^a$ $2_7$ ([מזריע בזרעו]); דבק בְּ *cling to* 2 K $5_{27}$, בחר בְּ *choose* Dt $4_{37}$ $10_{15}$ 4QJub$^a$ $2_{20}$ 4Q419 $1_5$ 4QDibHam$^a$ $5.2_1$ ([ותבחר]), מאס בְּ *reject* 2 K $17_{20}$ Jr $31_{37}$ 4QDibHam$^a$ $1.5_7$.

כְּ *as* Ex $16_{31}$ Nm $11_7$ GnzPs $4_{24}$.

מִן partitive, *(some) of*, *(any) of*, *from among* (some

times) Gn 17$_{12}$ Lv 21$_{17.21}$ 22$_4$ 27$_{30}$ Nm 17$_5$ 1 K 11$_{14}$ 2 K 25$_{25}$||Jr 41$_1$ Ezk 43$_{19}$ 44$_{22}$ Est 6$_{13}$ Dn 1$_{3(mss)}$ 9$_1$, + לקח *take* Jr 33$_{26}$ Ezk 17$_{5.13}$, בוא hi. *bring* Dn 1$_3$, קרב *approach* Lv 22$_3$, נתן *give* to Molech Lv 18$_{21}$ 20$_{2.3.4}$, צלח *prosper* Jr 22$_{30}$, ארר pass. *be cursed* 11QapPs$^a$ 4$_6$ ([ארור]).

מִן perh. of direction, *from*, + סוף *cease*, i.e. be removed Est 9$_{28}$; of instrument, *by (means of)*, + היה *be* Ru 4$_{12}$; *in respect of*, + נתן *give* vengeance 2 S 4$_8$; מלא מן pi. *fill* face of world *with* CD 2$_{12}$.

אֶל *over*, + לקח *take* those who rule Jr 33$_{26}$.

עַל *upon*, + נתן *give*, i.e. appoint 4Q522 8.2$_{11}$ ([וזרעו]), ho. *be given*, i.e. be placed Lv 11$_{38}$, נפל *fall* Lv 11$_{37}$, יצק *pour* Is 44$_3$ (|| צֶאֱצָא *offspring*); *(incumbent) upon*, + קום pi. *confirm (as)* Est 9$_{27}$ (Gnz נֶפֶשׁ *soul*) 9$_{31}$, קבל pi. *accept (as)* Est 9$_{27(Qr)}$ (Gnz נֶפֶשׁ); *against*, + פקד *visit* in punishment Jr 29$_{32}$ 36$_{31}$ (+ עֶבֶד *servant*).

אֵת *with*, + קום hi. *raise*, i.e. establish covenant Gn 9$_9$.

עִם *with*, + אמן ni. *be established* Si 44$_{11(B)}$ (M appar. אִם *if*).

בֵּין *between*, + היה *be* 1 S 20$_{42}$ (+ זֶרַע between my offspring and your *offspring*), שׁית *place* Gn 3$_{15.15}$ (+ זֶרַע between your offspring and her *offspring*), קום hi. *raise*, i.e. establish covenant among me and you and your offspring Gn 17$_7$, שׁמר *keep* covenant among me and you and your offspring Gn 17$_{10}$.

לְפִי *according to*, + היה *be* Lv 27$_{16}$.

**<COLL>** זַרְעִי אַחֲרַי *my seed after me* 1 S 24$_{22}$, זַרְעֲךָ אַחֲרֶיךָ *your* (sg.) *seed after you* Gn 17$_{7.7.8.9.10}$ 35$_{12}$ 48$_4$ 2 S 7$_{12}$||1 C 17$_{11}$ 4QMidrEschat$^a$ 3$_{10}$, זַרְעוֹ אַחֲרָיו *his seed after him* Gn 17$_{19}$ Ex 28$_{43}$ Nm 25$_{13}$ Dt 4$_{37}$, זַרְעֲכֶם אַחֲרֵיכֶם *your* (pl.) *seed after you* Gn 9$_9$, זַרְעָם אַחֲרֵיהֶם *their seed after them* Dt 1$_8$ 4$_{37(Sam)}$ 10$_{15}$ 4QDibHam$^a$ 5.2$_1$, אַתָּה וְזַרְעֲךָ *you and your seed* Gn 17$_9$ Dt 30$_{19}$ (זַרְעֲךָ), הוּא וְזַרְעוֹ *he and his seed* Jr 22$_{28}$ (or del.), זרע לאנוש *seed of humanity* Si 10$_{19}$.

זֶרַע נִזְרְעָה *she has been sown*, i.e. impregnated, *with seed* Nm 5$_{28}$, זֶרַע וְקָצִיר *seed (time) and harvest* Gn 8$_{22}$, זרע למלך *seed for the king* Lachish ost. 5$_{10}$.

**<SYN>** צֶאֱצָא *offspring*, בֵּן *son*, יֶלֶד *child*, שֵׁם *name*, כֶּרֶם *vineyard*, לֶחֶם *bread*, פְּרִי *fruit*, תְּאֵנָה *fig*, גֶּפֶן *vine*, רִמּוֹן *pomegranate*.

Also (unless זרע *sow*) Si 41$_{6(B)}$ ([זר[עו) 4QMidrEschat$^a$ 6$_3$ 4QapPs$^b$ 55$_2$ 4Q415 2.1$_4$ 4Q420 3$_5$ 4QRitMar 14 29$_2$ 4QPrFêtes$^c$ 39$_1$ 107$_2$ 4QShir$^b$ 165$_1$.*

⇒ זרע *sow*.

**זְרֹעַ**, see זְרוֹעַ *arm*.

**[זֵרְעֹן]** 2 n.[m.] **vegetable**—זֵרְעֹנִים—**<OBJ>** נתן *give* Dn 1$_{16}$ (1QDan$^a$ זֵרֹעַ *vegetable*; + יַיִן *wine*, פַּתְבַּג *delicacy*). **<PREP>** מִן partitive, *(some) of*, + נתן *give* Dn 1$_{12(mss)}$ (L זֵרֹעַ).

⇒ זרע *sow*.

**[זרף]** vb. **be scattered—Hi., sprinkle, <SUBJ>** רָבִיב *shower* Ps 72$_6$ (if em. זַרְזִיף *sprinkling* to יַזְרִיפוּ showers *[that] sprinkle* the earth). **<OBJ>** אֶרֶץ *earth* Ps 72$_6$ (if em.).

**Pilp., sprinkle, <SUBJ>** רָבִיב *shower* Ps 72$_6$ (if em. זַרְזִיף *sprinkling* to זִרְזְפוּ showers *[that] sprinkle* the earth). **<OBJ>** אֶרֶץ *earth* Ps 72$_6$ (if em.).

**זרק I** 35.0.5 vb. **scatter—Qal** Pf. זָרַק, זָרְקָה, זָרְקוּ; impf. יִזְרֹק (Q יזורוק), 2ms תִּזְרֹק; + waw וְזָרַק (וּזְרָקוֹ), וְזָרַקְתָּ, וַיִּזְרְקוּ (וַיִּזְרְקֻהוּ) וַיִּזְרֹק ,וְזָרְקוּ ,וְזָרַקְתִּי; impv. זְרֹק; ptc. זֹרֵק, זֹרְקִים (Q זורקים); inf. זְרֹק—**1. scatter, sprinkle, toss, <SUBJ>** Y. Ezk 36$_{25}$, Aaron Nm 18$_{17}$ (+ קטר hi. *offer incense*), Josiah 2 C 34$_4$, Moses Ex 9$_{8.10}$ 24$_6$=4QBibPar 4$_5$ Ex 24$_8$ 29$_{16.20}$ Lv 8$_{19.24}$, Uriah 2 K 16$_{13.15}$, אִישׁ *man* Ezk 10$_2$, בֵּן *son* of Aaron Lv 1$_{5.11}$ 3$_{2.8.13}$ 9$_{12.18}$ 11QT 22$_5$ ([וזור[קו), כֹּהֵן *priest* Lv 1$_{5.11}$ 3$_{2.8}$ (if ins. (כֹּהֵן) 3$_{13(Sam)}$ Lv 7$_{2.14}$ 17$_6$ 2 K 16$_{15}$ Ezk 43$_{18}$ 2 C 29$_{22.22}$ 30$_{16}$ 35$_{11}$ 4QToh B$^b$ 1$_9$ ([הכו[הן ... [יז]רוק]) 11QT 16$_{17}$ 22$_5$ ([וזור[קו]) 23$_{13}$ 34$_8$ 52$_{21}$, מֶלֶךְ *king* (Ahaz) 2 K 16$_{13}$, חֹרֵשׁ *one who ploughs* Is 28$_{25}$ (|| פוץ hi. *scatter*), רֵעַ *companion* of Job Jb 2$_{12}$.

**<OBJ>** עָפָר *dust* Jb 2$_{12}$, פִּיחַ *soot* Ex 9$_{8.10}$, גַּחֶלֶת *coal* Ezk 10$_2$, כַּמֹּן *cummin* Is 28$_{25}$, דָּם *blood* Ex 24$_6$ (חֲצִי הַדָּם *half the blood*; =4QBibPar 4$_5$ חצ[י ה]דם) 24$_8$ 29$_{16.20}$ Lv 1$_{5.11}$ 3$_{2.8.13}$ 7$_{2.14}$ 8$_{19.24}$ 9$_{12.18}$ 17$_6$ Nm 18$_{17}$ 2 K 16$_{13.15}$ Ezk 43$_{18}$ 2 C 29$_{22.22}$ 30$_{16}$ 35$_{11}$ (if ins. (דָּם) 4QJub$^e$ 21$_7$ 11QT 16$_{17}$ 22$_5$ ([וזור[קו]) 23$_{13}$ 34$_8$ ([דם]) 52$_{21}$, מַיִם *water* Ezk 36$_{25}$ 4QTohB$^b$ 1$_9$ ([יז]רוק]), dust 2 C 34$_4$.

**<PREP>** מִן of direction, *from*, + יָד *hand* of Levites 2 C

30$_{16}$ 35$_{11}$; עַל *upon, against,* + עַם *people* Ex 24$_{8}$, טָמֵא *unclean one* perh. 4QTohB$^{b}$ 1$_{9}$ (ויז[רוק]), בַּיִת *house* of Israel Ezk 36$_{25}$, עִיר *city* Ezk 10$_{2}$, מִזְבֵּחַ *altar* Ex 24$_{6}$=4QBibPar 4$_{5}$ ([ה]מזבח) Ex 29$_{16.20}$ Lv 1$_{5.11}$ 3$_{2.8.13}$ 7$_{2}$ 8$_{19.24}$ 9$_{12.18}$ (all twelve + סָבִיב *round about*) 17$_{6}$ Nm 18$_{17}$ 2 K 16$_{13.15}$ Ezk 43$_{18}$ 4QJub$^{e}$ 21$_{7}$, פִּנָּה *corner* of altar 11QT 16$_{17}$ (עו[ל]; + סָבִיב), יְסוֹד *base* of altar 11QT 23$_{13}$ ([יסו]ד) 34$_{8}$ (both + סָבִיב) 52$_{21}$, רֹאשׁ *head* Jb 2$_{12}$; עַל־פְּנֵי *upon (face of),*+ קֶבֶר *grave* 2 C 34$_{4}$; לְעֵינֵי *in the presence of,* + פַּרְעֹה *Pharaoh* Ex 9$_{8}$; with ה- of direction, *to(wards),* + שָׁמַיִם *heaven* Ex 9$_{8.10}$ Jb 2$_{12}$, מִזְבֵּחַ *altar* 2 C 29$_{22.22}$.

**2.** perh. **be profuse** (unless זרק II *creep up*) <SUBJ> שֵׂיבָה *grey hair* Ho 7$_{9}$ (or em. pu. *be profuse* or זרח *arise*). <PREP> בְּ of place, *upon,* + Ephraim Ho 7$_{9}$ (or em.).

<SYN> §1 פוץ hi. *scatter.*

**Pu.** 2 Pf. זֹרַק—**be sprinkled,** <SUBJ> מַיִם *water(s)* of impurity Nm 19$_{13.20}$, שֵׂיבָה *grey hair* Ho 7$_{9}$ (if em. qal). <PREP> בְּ of place, *upon,* + Ephraim Ho 7$_{9}$ (if em.); עַל *upon,* + נֹגֵעַ *one who touches* dead person Nm 19$_{13}$, אִישׁ unclean *man* Nm 19$_{20}$.*

⇒ מִזְרָק *bowl.*

**זרק II** 1 vb. **creep up—Qal** 1 Pf. זָרְקָה—(unless זרק I *be profuse*), <SUBJ> שֵׂיבָה *grey hair* Ho 7$_{9}$ (or em. זרח *arise*). <PREP> בְּ of place, *upon,* + Ephraim Ho 7$_{9}$ (or em.).*

**[זֶרֶק]** 0.0.4 n.m. appar. **javelin**—Q זרק; pl. cstr. Q זרקות—<OBJ> חזק hi. *hold* 1QM 6$_{15}$ ([ו]יחזיק), שלך hi. *throw* 1QM 6$_{2}$. <CSTR> זרקות מלחמה *javelins of war* 1QM 6$_{2.15}$; לוהב הזרק *the blade of the javelin* 1QM 6$_{2}$. <ADJ> הזרק השלישי *the third javelin* 1QM 6$_{3}$. <PREP> עַל *upon,* + כתב *write* 1QM 6$_{3}$. <COLL> שבעה זרקות *seven javelins* 1QM 6$_{2}$.*

⇒ זרק *scatter.*

**זרר I** 1 vb. **sneeze—Po.** 1 + waw וַיְזוֹרֵר—**sneeze,** <SUBJ> נַעַר *lad* 2 K 4$_{35}$ (+ פקח *open* eyes). <COLL> + adverbial phrase, עַד־שֶׁבַע פְּעָמִים *as much as seven times* 2 K 4$_{35}$.

**זרר II** 1 vb. **squeeze, flow—Qal pass.** 1 Pf. זֹרוּ (unless זור II qal pass.)—**1. be squeezed,** <SUBJ> פֶּצַע *bruise* Is 1$_{6}$ (‖ חבשׁ pu. *be bound;* + רכך pu. *be made soft* with oil), חַבּוּרָה *stripe* Is 1$_{6}$, מַכָּה *wound* Is 1$_{6}$.

**2. flow (with),** <SUBJ> שָׂפָה *lip* Pr 15$_{7}$ (if em. יְזָרוּ *they will scatter,* from זרה pi., to יָזֹרוּ *they will flow;* + דַּעַת flow with *knowledge*).

<SYN> חבשׁ pu. *be bound.*

**זֶרֶשׁ** 4 pr.n.f. **Zeresh,** wife of Haman, <SUBJ> אמר *say* Est 5$_{14}$ 6$_{13}$. <OBJ> בוא hi. *bring* Est 5$_{10}$. <APP> אִשָּׁה *wife* Est 5$_{10.14}$ 6$_{13.13}$. <PREP> לְ of direction, *(in)to,* + ספר pi. *recount* Est 6$_{13}$.*

**זֶרֶת** 7.0.1 n.f. **span**—זֶרֶת; sf. Q זרתו—**span, handbreadth,** equivalent to half a cubit, or about one foot, used in measuring Aaron's breastplate (Ex 28$_{16.16}$‖39$_{9.9}$), part of altar (Ezk 43$_{13}$), height of person (1 S 17$_{4}$); perh. **outstretched hand** (Is 40$_{12}$=4QpIsa$^{e}$ 1$_{4}$ 4QShir$^{b}$ 30$_{4}$), <NOM CL> זֶרֶת אָרְכּוֹ וְזֶרֶת רָחְבּוֹ *its length is a span and its breadth is a span* Ex 28$_{16.16}$‖39$_{9.9}$, גָּבְהוֹ שֵׁשׁ אַמּוֹת וָזָרֶת *his height was six cubits and a span* 1 S 17$_{4}$, גְּבוּלָהּ אֶל־שְׂפָתָהּ סָבִיב זֶרֶת הָאֶחָד appar. *its border to its rim round about was one span* Ezk 43$_{13}$ (or em. גְּבוּלֹה עַל־שְׂפָתֹת סָבִיב זֶרֶת אַחַת *its* [altar's] *border above the surrounding edges was one span*). <ADJ> זֶרֶת הָאֶחָד appar. *one span* Ezk 43$_{13}$ (or em. זֶרֶת אַחַת in same sense). <PREP> בְּ of instrument, *by means of, with,* + תכן pi. *measure* Is 40$_{12}$= 4QpIsa$^{e}$ 1$_{4}$ ([ב]זרת תכן; ‖ שֹׁעַל *palm [of hand]*), ni. *be measured* 4QShir$^{b}$ 30$_{4}$ ([י]תכנו; + שֹׁעַל). <SYN> שֹׁעַל *palm (of hand).**

**זַתּוּא** 4 pr.n.m. **Zattu,** family head, co-signatory with Nehemiah, <NOM CL> רָאשֵׁי הָעָם ... זַתּוּא *the heads of the people were ... Zattu* Ne 10$_{15}$. <CSTR> בְּנֵי זַתּוּא *sons of Zattu* Ezr 2$_{8}$ 10$_{27}$ Ne 7$_{13}$.

**זֵתָם** 2 pr.n.m. **Zetham,** Levite, son of Ladan and brother of Jehiel and Joel or descendant of Ladan, son of Jehieli and brother of Joel, <NOM CL> בְּנֵי לַעְדָּן ... יְחִיאֵל וְזֵתָם *the sons of Ladan were ... Jehiel and Zetham* 1 C 23$_{8}$, בְּנֵי יְחִיאֵלִי זֵתָם וְיוֹאֵל אָחִיו עַל־אֹצְרוֹת בֵּית י׳ *the sons of Jehieli, Zetham and Joel his brother, were in charge of the treasuries of the house of Y.* 1 C 26$_{22}$ (or em.

יוֹאֵל וְאֶחָיו the sons of Jehieli were Zetham and *Joel; and his brothers* were over the treasuries of the house of Y.). <APP> בֵּן *son* 1 C $26_{22}$ (or em.).

**זֵתַר** 1 pr.n.m. **Zethar,** eunuch at the court of Ahasuerus, <SUBJ> בוא hi. *bring* Est $1_{10}$, שׁרת pi. *minister* $1_{10}$. <APP> סָרִיס *eunuch* Est $1_{10}$.

# ח

[חֹאֵב] pr.n.[m.] **Hoeb,** <PREP> לְ of possession, *(belonging) to* Seal 48$_{2}$ (לחאב; others לחאה *to Hoah*; Beth-Shemesh, 7th cent.).

[חֹאָה] pr.n.[m.] **Hoah,** <PREP> לְ of possession, *(belonging) to* Seal 48$_{2}$ (לחאה; others חאב *Hoeb*; Beth-Shemesh, 7th cent.).

[חֹב] $_{1}$ n.[m.] **fold**—sf. חֻבִּי—**fold of garment,** <PREP> בְּ of place, *in* 1QH 16$_{13}$ ([בח[ובך), + טמן *hide* iniquity Jb 31$_{33}$ (or em. בַּחֲבִי *in secret*).

**חבא** $_{34.0.8}$ vb. **hide**—**Ni.** $_{16}$ Pf. נֶחְבָּא, נַחְבֵּאתָ, נֶחְבְּאוּ (נֶחְבָּאוּ), נַחְבֵּתֶם; impf. תֵּחָבֵא, יֵחָבְאוּ; + waw וָאֵחָבֵא; ptc. נֶחְבָּא, נֶחְבָּאִים; inf. נַהֲבֹה, הֵחָבֵא (הֵחָבֵה)—**be hidden, hide oneself,** <SUBJ> מֶלֶךְ *king* Jos 10$_{16.17.27}$, David 1 S 19$_{2}$ 2 S 17$_{9}$, Jacob Gn 31$_{27}$ (+ ברח *flee*), Job Jb 5$_{21}$, Jotham Jg 9$_{5}$, Saul 1 S 10$_{22}$, אָדָם *human being* Gn 3$_{10}$, אִישׁ *man* Jos 2$_{16}$ Dn 10$_{7}$, נַעַר *lad* Jb 29$_{8}$, קוֹל *voice* Jb 29$_{10}$; subj. not specified, Am 9$_{3}$ 2 C 18$_{24}$. <PREP> בְּ of place, *in, at, among,* + מְעָרָה *cave* Jos 10$_{16.17}$. <COLL> וְנַחְבֵּתֶם שָׁמָּה שְׁלֹשֶׁת יָמִים *and you shall hide yourselves yonder for three days* Jos 2$_{16}$.

**Pi.** $_{0.0.5}$ Pf. Q חבא, Q חבתה; + waw Q ותחבא—**hide,** <SUBJ> אֵל *God* 1QH 5$_{11}$ 9$_{24}$ 1QS 4$_{6}$, אֲדֹנָי *Lord* 1QH 5$_{25}$; subj. not specified, 4QpsEzek$^{a}$ 4$_{3}$. <OBJ> תּוֹרָה *law* 1QH 5$_{11}$, אֱמֶת *truth* 1QH 9$_{24}$, רָז *mystery* 1QH 5$_{25}$. <PREP> לְ of direction, *to,* + קֵץ *time* 1QH 9$_{24}$; introducing object, + אֱמֶת *truth* 1QS 4$_{6}$; בְּ of accompaniment, *in, with,* + worshipper 1QH 5$_{11.25}$.

Also perh. 5Q16 4$_{2}$.

**Pu.** $_{1.0.2}$ Pf. חֻבְּאוּ; ptc. Q מחובאים—**keep oneself hidden,** <SUBJ> עָנִי *poor one* Jb 24$_{4}$, עֵץ *tree* of life 1QH 8$_{6}$; subj. not specified, 1QH 8$_{18}$. <PREP> בְּתוֹךְ *among,* + עֵץ *tree* 1QH 8$_{6}$.

**Hi.** $_{6.0.1}$ Pf. הֶחְבִּיאָה (הֶחְבִּיאָנִי), הֶחְבְּאַתָה; + waw וַיַּחְבִּיאֵם, וַתַּחְבִּא, וָאַחְבִּא—**hide, keep hidden,** <SUBJ> י׳ Y. Is 49$_{2}$, Obadiah 1 K 18$_{4.13}$, Rahab Jos 6$_{17.25}$, אִשָּׁה *woman* 2 K 6$_{29}$; subj. not specified, 4QShir$^{b}$ 8$_{7}$. <OBJ> נָבִיא *prophet* 1 K 18$_{4}$, מַלְאָךְ *messenger* Jos 6$_{17.25}$, עֶבֶד *servant* Is 49$_{2}$, בֵּן *son* 2 K 6$_{29}$; obj. not specified, 4QShir$^{b}$ 8$_{7}$. <PREP> בְּ of place, *in, at, among,* + מְעָרָה *cave* 1 K 18$_{4}$, צֵל *shadow* of hand Is 49$_{2}$; מִן partitive, *some of,* + נָבִיא *prophet* 1 K 18$_{13}$. <COLL> וַיַּחְבִּיאֵם חֲמִשִּׁים *and he hid them by fifties* 1 K 18$_{4}$.

**Ho.** $_{1}$ Pf. הָחְבָּאוּ—**be kept hidden,** <SUBJ> עַם *people* Is 42$_{22}$. <PREP> בְּ of place, *in,* + בַּיִת *house* of confinement, i.e. prison Is 42$_{22}$.

**Htp.** $_{10}$ Pf. הִתְחַבְּאוּ; impf. יִתְחַבֵּא, יִתְחַבְּאוּ (יִתְהַבָּאוּ); ptc. מִתְחַבֵּא, מִתְחַבְּאִים—**keep oneself hidden,** <SUBJ> עַם *people* 1 S 13$_{6}$, Hebrew 1 S 14$_{11}$, אָדָם *human being* Gn 3$_{8}$, אִישׁ *man* of Israel 1 S 14$_{22}$, אִשָּׁה *woman* Gn 3$_{8}$, Ahaziah 2 C 22$_{9}$, David 1 S 23$_{23}$, Joash 2 K 11$_{3}$‖2 C 22$_{12}$, בֵּן *son* 1 C 21$_{20}$, מַיִם *water* Jb 38$_{30}$. <PREP> בְּ of place, *in, at, among,* + Samaria 2 C 22$_{9}$, הַר *mountain* 1 S 14$_{22}$, מְעָרָה *cave* 1 S 13$_{6}$, חוֹחַ *hollow* 1 S 13$_{6}$, סֶלַע *rock* 1 S 13$_{6}$, צְרִיחַ *cellar* 1 S 13$_{6}$, בּוֹר *cistern* 1 S 13$_{6}$; מִפְּנֵי *from (before),* + י׳ *Y.* Gn 3$_{8}$. <COLL> מִתְחַבֵּא שֵׁשׁ שָׁנִים *hidden for six years* 2 K 11$_{3}$‖2 C 22$_{12}$.*

→ חבה *hide*, חֶבְיוֹן *hiding*, מַחֲבֵא *hiding place*, מַחֲבֹא *hiding place*.

[חֻבָּא] $_{0.0.0.1}$ pr.n.m. **Hubba,** son of Mattan, <APP> בֵּן *son* Seal 552$_{1}$ (T. Beit Mirsim?, 7th/6th cent.). <PREP> לְ of possession, *(belonging) to* Seal 552$_{1}$ (T. Beit Mirsim?, 7th/6th cent.).

**חבב I** $_{1.2.2}$ vb. **love**—**Qal** $_{1}$ Ptc. חֹבֵב—<SUBJ> Y. Dt 33$_{3}$ (unless חֹבֵב *pure one* of the peoples [חבב II] or em. חֹבֵב *loving* to חִבֵּב pi. *he loved* or חָבֵב pass. or חָבֵב adj. *beloved of* the nations),* אָב *father* Dt 33$_{3(Sam\ mss)}$, appar. קָדוֹשׁ *holy one* Dt 33$_{3}$ (if em. חֹבְבֵי *those who love*). <OBJ> עַם *people* Dt 33$_{3}$. <PREP> כְּ *as (though it were),* + נֶפֶשׁ *soul,* i.e. self 4QHymSap 1.1$_{2}$ (ח[ו]בב).

**Pi.** $_{0.2.2}$ Pf. Q חבב; impv. Si חביב (Si חבב); inf. Q חבב—**love,** <SUBJ> Y. Dt 33$_3$ (if em. חֹבֵב to חָבַב), בֵּן *son* Si 7$_{21(A)}$ (C אהב *love*) 10$_{25(B)}$. <OBJ> עֶבֶד *servant* Si 7$_{21(A)}$ 10$_{25(B)}$, עַם *people* Dt 33$_3$ (if em.; see Subj.). <PREP> כְּ *as*, + נֶפֶשׁ *soul*, i.e. self Si 7$_{21(A)}$ 10$_{25(B)}$.

Also 4QRitMar 95$_1$ 96$_6$.

⇒ חֹבָב *Hobab*, חֻבָּה *Hubbah*, חָבִיב *beloved*.

*חבב II $_1$ vb. **be pure**—**Qal** $_1$ Ptc. חֹבֵב—ptc. as noun, **pure one** (unless חבב I *love*), perh. used collectively, <CSTR> חֹבֵב עַמִּים *the pure one[s] of the peoples* Dt 33$_3$ (|| קָדוֹשׁ *holy one*). <SYN> קָדוֹשׁ *holy one*.

**חֹבָב** $_2$ pr.n.m. **Hobab,** appar. father-in-law (or brother-in-law, if em.; see App.) of Moses, <SUBJ> היה *be* Nm 10$_{29}$, הלך *go* Nm 10$_{29.29.29.29}$, עזב *desert* Nm 10$_{29}$, נסע *set out* Nm 10$_{29}$, אמר *say* Nm 10$_{29}$, ידע *know* Nm 10$_{29}$. <CSTR> בְּנֵי חֹבָב *sons of Hobab* Jg 1$_{16}$ (if em. בְּנֵי קֵינִי *sons of [the] Kenite* to בְּנֵי חֹבָב הַקֵּינִי *sons of Hobab, the Kenite*) 4$_{11}$. <APP> בֵּן *son* or *descendant* of Reuel Nm 10$_{29}$, perh. מִדְיָנִי *Midianite* Nm 10$_{29}$, קֵינִי *Kenite* Jg 1$_{16}$ (if em.; see Cstr.), חֹתֵן *father-in-law* Nm 10$_{29}$ (unless em. חֹתֵן *father-in-law of* to חָתָן *brother-in-law of* Moses) Jg 1$_{16}$ 4$_{11}$ (unless em. חֹתֵן to חָתָן). <PREP> לְ of direction, *to*, + אמר *say* Nm 10$_{29}$; of benefit, *to, for*, + יטב hi. *be good* Nm 10$_{29.29}$.

**חבה** $_{5.0.2}$ vb. **hide**—**Qal** $_{1.0.2}$ Pf. 2ms Q חבתה (or חבא pi. *hide*); impv. חֲבִי—**1.** trans. **hide,** <SUBJ> Y. 1QH 5$_{11.25}$. <OBJ> תּוֹרָה *law* 1QH 5$_{11}$, רָז *mystery* 1QH 5$_{25}$. <PREP> בְּ of place, + psalmist 1QH 5$_{11}$ ([בן]) 5$_{25}$.

**2.** intrans. **hide (oneself),** <SUBJ> עַם *people* Is 26$_{20}$. <PREP> כְּ *as*, כִּמְעַט רֶגַע *as the smallness of a moment*, i.e. for a short time Is 26$_{20}$.

**Ni.** $_4$ + waw וְנֶחְבֵּתֶם, וְנֶחְבָּה (or חבא ni. *hide oneself*); inf. הֵחָבֵה (or חבא ni.)—**hide oneself,** <SUBJ> Esau Jr 49$_{10}$, Zedekiah 1 K 22$_{25}$ (Gnz, mss and ||2 C 18$_{24}$ לְהֵחָבֵא), אִישׁ *man* Jos 2$_{16}$, בֵּן *son* 1 K 22$_{25}$, אֲרָם *Arameans* 2 K 7$_{12}$ (Gnz, mss לְהֵחָבֵא), רגל pi. ptc. *spy* Jos 2$_{16}$. <PREP> בְּ of place, + שָׂדֶה *field* 2 K 7$_{12}$. <COLL> inf. of חבה preceded by verb, בוא *come* 1 K 22$_{25}$, יצא *go out* 2 K 7$_{12}$; חבה + adverb, שָׁמָּה *there* Jos 2$_{16}$, שְׁלֹשֶׁת יָמִים *(for) three days* Jos 2$_{16}$; וְנֶחְבָּה לֹא יוּכָל appar. *and he hides himself, he is not able* Jr 49$_{10}$ (or em. וְנַחְבֹּה *and* he is not able *to hide himself*).*

⇒ חבא *hide*.

**חֻבָּה** $_1$ pr.n.m. **Hubbah,** son of Shemer (ms Shomer), descendant of Asher, <NOM CL> בְּנֵי שֶׁמֶר ... וְחֻבָּה *the sons of Shemer were ... and Hubbah* 1 C 7$_{34(Qr)}$ (Kt יחבה *Jahbah*).

**חָבוֹר** $_3$ pl.n. **Habor,** river in Northern Mesopotamia, tributary of Euphrates, <APP> נְהַר גּוֹזָן *river of Gozan* 2 K 17$_6$ 18$_{11}$. <PREP> לְ of direction, *(in)to*, וַיְבִיאֵם לַחְלַח וְחָבוֹר *and he brought them to Halah and Habor* 1 C 5$_{26}$; בְּ of place, *(in)to*, + ישׁב hi. *cause to dwell* 2 K 17$_6$, נוח hi. *set down* 2 K 18$_{11}$.

**[חִבּוּר]** $_{0.0.1}$ n.[m.] **community**—cstr. Q חבור—**community, company,** <CSTR> חבור ישראל *company of Israel* CD 12$_8$.

⇒ חבר I *join*.

**חַבּוּרָה** $_7$ n.f. **blow**—sf. חֶבְרָתוֹ, חַבֻּרָתִי; pl. cstr. חַבֻּרוֹת; sf. חַבּוּרֹתָי—**blow, bruising, wound,** <SUBJ> זור *squeeze* Is 1$_6$ (|| פֶּצַע *wound*, מַכָּה *wound*), חבשׁ pu. *be bound* Is 1$_6$, רכך pu. *be made soft* Is 1$_6$, באשׁ hi. *stink* Ps 38$_6$, מקק ni. *fester* Ps 37$_6$. <NOM CL> מִכַּף־רֶגֶל וְעַד־רֹאשׁ ... חַבּוּרָה *from the sole of the foot to the head ... is bruising* Is 1$_6$, חַבֻּרוֹת פֶּצַע תַּמְרוּק בְּרָע *blows that cause wounds are a scouring for evil* Pr 20$_{30(Qr)}$ (|| מַכָּה *stroke*). <OBJ> נתן *give* Ex 21$_{25}$ (|| פֶּצַע *wound*, כְּוִיָּה *burn*). <CSTR> [ח]בורת אלהים *blows of God* 4Q185 1.1$_{14}$, חַבֻּרוֹת פֶּצַע *blows of wounds*, i.e. that cause wounds Pr 20$_{30}$. <PREP> לְ *(in exchange) for*, + הרג *kill* Gn 4$_{23}$ (|| פֶּצַע *wound*); בְּ of instrument, *by means of*, + רפא ni. *be healed* Is 53$_5$ (+ מוּסָר *chastisement*); מִן of cause, *on account of* + תמם *come to an end* 4Q185 1.1$_{14}$ ([ח]בורת); תַּחַת *(in exchange) for*, + נתן *give* Ex 21$_{25}$. <COLL> חַבּוּרָה תַּחַת חַבּוּרָה *blow for blow* Ex 21$_{25}$. <SYN> פֶּצַע *wound*, כְּוִיָּה *burn*, מַכָּה *stroke*.

**חבט** I $_{5.1}$ vb. **beat (out)**—**Qal** $_{4.1}$ Impf. יַחְבֹּט, 3fs Si

תחבט, 2ms תַּחְבֹּט; + waw 3fs וַתַּחְבֹּט; ptc. חֹבֵט—**beat, beat out,** <SUBJ> Y. Is $27_{12}$, Gideon Jg $6_{11}$, Ruth Ru $2_{17}$, Israelite Dt $24_{20}$, בֵּן *son* Jg $6_{11}$, אַלְמָנָה *widow* Si $32_{17(Bmg)}$ (unless חבט II *pour;* B רבה hi. *make great*). <OBJ> זַיִת *olive tree* Dt $24_{20}$, חִטָּה *wheat* Jg $6_{11}$, שִׁבֹּלֶת *ears of grain* Is $27_{12}$ (if em.; see Prep.), שִׂיחַ *complaint* Si $32_{17(Bmg)}$, אֲשֶׁר *that which* Ru $2_{17}$ (וַתַּחְבֹּט אֵת אֲשֶׁר־לִקֵּטָה *and she beat out that which she had gleaned*). <PREP> מִן of direction, *from,* + שִׁבֹּלֶת *stream* Is $27_{12}$ (unless em. מִשִּׁבֹּלֶת הַנָּהָר *from the stream of the river* to שִׁבֹּלֶת מֵהַנָּהָר *ears of grain from the river*).

**Ni.** 1 Impf. יֵחָבֶט—**be beaten out,** <SUBJ> קֶצַח *black cumin* Is $28_{27}$ (+ דוש ho. *be threshed*), כַּמֹּן *cumin* Is $28_{27}$. <PREP> בְּ of instrument, *with, by means of,* + מַטֶּה *staff* Is $28_{27}$, שֵׁבֶט *rod* Is $28_{27}$.

*חבט II 0.1 vb. **pour**—**Qal** 0.1 Impf. 3fs Si תחבט—**pour (out)** (unless חבט I *beat*), <SUBJ> אַלְמָנָה *widow* Si $32_{17}$ (Bmg) (B רבה hi. *make great*). <OBJ> שִׂיחַ *complaint* Si $32_{17(Bmg)}$.

[חֶבִי] n.[m.] **hiding, secret,** <PREP> טמן בְּ *hide in secret* Jb $31_{33}$ (if em. בְּחֻבִּי *in my bosom*, from חב).

[חָבִיב] 0.0.1 adj. **beloved,** used as noun, **beloved one,** <CSTR> עם החביב *people of the beloved one* 4Q462$_{11}$; חֹבֵב עַמִּים *one beloved of the nations* Dt $33_3$ (if em. חֹבֵב *loving* the nations).* <APP> Jacob 4Q462$_{11}$ (יעקוב).
→ חבב *love.*

חֲבַיָּה, see חֳבַיָּה *Habaiah.*

חֳבַיָּה 2 pr.n.m. **Habaiah**—mss חֲבַיָּה—ancestor of priestly family among exiles, <CSTR> בְּנֵי חֳבַיָּה *sons of Habaiah* Ezr $2_{61}$ Ne $7_{63}$.
→ חבה *hide* + יה *Y.*

[חֶבְיוֹן] 1 n.[m.] **hiding**—cstr. חֶבְיוֹן—**hiding** or perh. **veil,** in description of theophany, <NOM CL> שָׁם חֶבְיוֹן עֻזֹּה *there was the hiding of his power* Hb $3_4$ (or del.). <CSTR> חֶבְיוֹן עֻזֹּה *hiding of his power* Hb $3_4$.*
→ חבא *hide.*

חֲבִילָה, see חֲכִילָה *Hachilah.*

חבל I 13 vb. **take in pledge**—**Qal** 12 Pf. חָבַל; impf. יַחְבֹּל, 2ms תַּחְבֹּל (תַּחֲבֹל), יַחְבְּלוּ (יַחֲבֹלוּ); impv. חַבְלֵהוּ; ptc. חֹבֵל; ptc. pass. חֲבֻלִים; inf. abs חָבֹל—**1a. take in pledge, hold in pledge,** <SUBJ> Israelite Ex $22_{25}$ Dt $24_{6.6.17}$, בַּיִת *house* of Jacob Mc $2_{10}$ (if em. תְּחַבֵּל וְחֶבֶל *it destroys, and destruction* to חָבֹל תַּחְבְּלוּ *you take a pledge,* or תַּחְבְּלוּ *you take a pledge*), אִישׁ *man* Ezk $18_{16}$ (|| גזל *rob*); subj. not specified, Jb $24_3$ (unless חבל *bind*) $24_9$ (if em.; see §2 Prep.). <OBJ> שַׂלְמָה *garment* Ex $22_{25}$ (Sam שִׂמְלָה *garment*), בֶּגֶד *garment* Dt $24_{17}$, רֵחַיִם *millstone* Dt $24_6$, רֶכֶב *upper millstone* Dt $24_6$, נֶפֶשׁ *soul* Dt $24_6$, עוּל *infant* Jb $24_9$ (if em.; see §2 Prep.), שׁוֹר *ox* Jb $24_3$ (unless חבל *bind*), חֲבֹל *pledge* Ezk $18_{16}$ Mc $2_{10}$ (if em.; see Subj.). <PREP> בַּעֲבוּר *on account of,* + מְאוּמָה *something* Mc $2_{10}$ (if em.; see Subj., and em. טֻמְאָה *uncleanness* to מְעַט מְאוּמָה *something small*). <COLL> חָבֹל תַּחְבֹּל *you indeed take in pledge* Ex $22_{25}$.

**1b.** pass. **be taken in pledge,** <SUBJ> בֶּגֶד *garment* Am $2_8$.

**2. take a pledge from, impose (the giving of) a pledge,** <SUBJ> Job Jb $22_6$ (+ פשט hi. *strip*); subj. not specified, Jb $24_9$. <OBJ> אָח *brother* Jb $22_6$. <PREP> עַל *upon,* + עָנִי *poor one* Jb $24_9$ (unless emend עַל to עֻל *infant,* as obj. of חבל, i.e. §1). <COLL> חבל + adv. חִנָּם *for nothing* Jb $22_6$.

**3. hold liable for pledge given,** <SUBJ> subj. not specified, Pr $20_{16}$=$27_{13}$ ( + לקח *take* garment). <OBJ> obj. not specified, Pr $20_{16}$=$27_{13}$. <PREP> בְּעַד *on behalf of, for,* בְּעַד נָכְרִים חַבְלֵהוּ *hold him liable for (his) pledge given for foreigners* Pr $20_{16(Kt)}$ (Qr נָכְרִיָּה for *a foreign woman*)=$27_{13}$ (נָכְרִיָּה). <SYN> §1 גזל *rob.*

**Ni.** 1 Impf. יֵחָבֶל—**have a pledge taken,** i.e. become a debtor (unless חבל II), <SUBJ> בוז ptc. *one who despises* Pr $13_{13}$ (or em. יְחֻבָּל *he will be ruined,* from חבל II pu.; :: שׁלם pu. *be rewarded*). <ANT> שׁלם pu. *be rewarded.**
→ חֲבֹל *pledge,* חֲבֹלָה *pledge.*

חבל II 11.1.3 vb. **act corruptly**—**Qal** 3 Pf. חָבַלְנוּ; impf. אֶחְבֹּל; pass. ptc. Si חבולי; inf. חֲבֹל—**1. act corruptly,**

<SUBJ> Nehemiah Ne $1_7$ (:: שׁמר *keep* commandments), בַּיִת *house* Ne $1_7$; subj. not specified, Ps $140_6$ (if em. חֲבָלִים *cords* to חֹבְלִים *those who act corruptly*) Jb $34_{31}$. <COLL> חֲבֹל חָבַלְנוּ *we have acted very corruptly* Ne $1_7$ (unless em. חֲבֹל to חָבֹל, inf. abs.); חבל with adv. עוֹד *again* Jb $34_{31}$ (if em. בִּלְעֲדֵי *apart from* to : עוֹד).

**2.** pass. **be corrupted,** <SUBJ> רַבִּים *many* Si $34_{6(B)}$ (רבים היו חבולי זהב *many have been the ones corrupted of,* i.e. by, *gold*; Bmg חללי *slain ones*; unless *bound of,* i.e. to, *gold*, from חבל *bind*).

**Ni.** Impf. יֵחָבֵל—**ruin oneself** (unless חבל I), <SUBJ> בוז ptc. *one who despises* Pr $13_{13}$ (or em. יֵחָבֵל *he will be ruined*; :: שׁלם pu. *be rewarded*). <ANT> שׁלם pu. *be rewarded.*

**Pi.** $_{6.0.3}$ Pf. Q חבל; impf. 3fs תְּחַבֵּל, 2ms Q תחבל; + waw וְחִבֵּל; ptc. מְחַבְּלִים; inf. חַבֵּל—**ruin, destroy,** <SUBJ> Y. Is $13_5$ Ec $5_5$, כֵּלַי *knave* Is $32_7$=4QpIsa[e] $6_5$ ([כלי ... לחבל])=4QMidrEschat[b] $8_6$ ([לח]בל), מַשְׁחִית hi. ptc. *destroyer* Is $54_{16}$, יֶלֶד *boy* 6QAllegory$_5$, יַלְדָּה *girl* 6QAllegory$_5$ (חב[לה]), Israelite 4Q416 2.3$_6$, שׁוּעָל *fox* Ca $2_{15}$, כְּלִי *weapon* Is $13_5$, טֻמְאָה *uncleanness* Mc $2_{10}$= 4QMidrEschat[b] $8_{10}$ ([תחבל]; or em. תְּחַבְּלוּ חֶבֶל *you will be destroyed [with] a* grievous *destruction*, or em. תְּחַבֵּל וְחֶבֶל *it destroys, and destruction* to חֲבֹל תַּחְבְּלוּ *you take a pledge*, or תַּחְבְּלוּ *you take a pledge*), רוּחַ *spirit*, i.e. anger Jb $17_1$ (if em. חֻבְּלָה *it is broken* to חִבְּלָה *it has destroyed*); subj. not specified, Ps $140_6$ (if em. חֲבָלִים *cords* to מְחַבְּלִים *destroyers*).

<OBJ> עָנִי *poor one* Is $32_{7(Qr)}$ (Kt עָנָו *humble one*) =4QpIsa[e] $6_5$ ([לחבל ענוים])=4QMidrEschat[b] $8_6$ (לח]בל [ענוים]), רוּחַ *spirit* 4Q416 2.3$_6$, אֶרֶץ *earth* Is $13_5$, כֶּרֶם *vineyard* Ca $2_{15}$, מַעֲשֶׂה *work* Ec $5_5$, יוֹם *day* Jb $17_1$ (if em.; see Subj.). <PREP> בְּ of instrument, *by, with,* + אֹמֶר *word* Is $32_7$=4QpIsa[e] $6_5$ ([לחבל ... באמרי])=4QMidr Eschat[b] $8_6$ (לח]בל ... באמרי]); *because of* 4Q416 2.3$_6$.

Also 4QMidrEschat[b] $9_{12}$ perh. 6QHymn 19.

**Pu.** $_2$ Pf. חֻבְּלָה; + waw וְחֻבַּל—**be destroyed, be broken,** <SUBJ> בוז ptc. *one who despises* Pr $13_{13}$ (if em.; see Ni. Prep.), בַּיִת *house* of Jacob Mc $2_{10}$ (if em.; see Pi. Subj.), רוּחַ *spirit* Jb $17_1$ (or em.; see Pi. Subj.; + זעך ni. *be extinguished*), עֹל *yoke* Is $10_{27}$. <PREP> מֵעַל *from upon,* + צַוָּאר *neck* Is $10_{27}$; מִפְּנֵי *because of,* + שֶׁמֶן *fatness* Is $10_{27}$ (unless em. עֹל מִפְּנֵי־שָׁמֶן *a yoke because of fatness* to עָלָה מִפְּנֵי־רִמּוֹן *he has gone up from before Rimmon*).*

→ חֶבֶל *destruction.*

**חבל III** $_3$ vb. **be pregnant—Pi.** $_3$ Pf. חִבְּלָה (חִבְּלַתְךָ; mss חִבְּלָתֶךָ); impf. יְחַבֶּל־—trans., **be pregnant (with), be in labour (with), give birth (to),** <SUBJ> אֵם *mother* Ca $8_5$, ילד ptc. *one that gives birth* Ca $8_5$ (if em. יְלָדַתְךָ *she [who] gave you birth* to יֹלַדְתֶּךָ *the one* [f.] *who gave you birth*), רָשָׁע *wicked one* Ps $7_{15}$ (|| הרה *be pregnant,* ילד *give birth*). <OBJ> אָוֶן *iniquity* Ps $7_{15}$, male lover Ca $8_5$ (unless em. חִבְּלַתְךָ *she was in labour with you* [m.] to חִבְּלָתֶךָ *she was in labour with you* [female lover]). <COLL> with adverb שָׁמָּה *there* Ca $8_5$. <SYN> הרה *be pregnant,* ילד *give birth.*

→ חֵבֶל *labour pains.*

**חבל IV** $_{1.1}$ vb. **bind—Qal** $_{1.1}$ Impf. יַחְבְּלוּ; pass. ptc. Si חבולי—**1. bind,** <OBJ> שׁוֹר *ox* Jb $24_3$ (unless חבל I *take on pledge*). **2.** pass. **be bound,** רבים היו חבולי זהב *many have been the ones bound of,* i.e. to, *gold* Si $34_{6(B)}$ (Bmg חללי *slain ones*; unless *corrupted by gold*, from חבל II *act corruptly*).

→ חֶבֶל *rope,* חֲבָלָה *rope,* חִבֵּל *mast,* חֹבֵל *sailor,* חֹבְלִים *union,* תַּחְבֻּלָה *guidance.*

**[חַבָּל]** n.m. **wrongdoer,** <SUBJ> פרשׂ *spread* net Ps $140_6$ (if em. חֲבָלִים *ropes* to חַבָּלִים *wrongdoers*). <OBJ> חלק pi. *scatter* Jb $21_{17}$ (if em. חֲבָלִים *destruction* to חַבָּלִים *wrongdoers*).

→ חבל *act corruptly.*

**חֲבֹל** $_3$ n.[m.] **pledge,** i.e. item taken in pledge for debt, <OBJ> שׁוב hi. *return* Ezk $18_7$ (or em.; see Cstr.) $18_{12}$ $33_{15}$ (|| גְּזֵלָה *plunder*), חבל *take in pledge* Ezk $18_{16}$ (|| גְּזֵלָה) Mc $2_{10}$ (if em. תְּחַבֵּל וְחֶבֶל *it will destroy, and destruction* to חֲבֹל תַּחְבְּלוּ *you will take a pledge*). <CSTR> חֲבֹל הַחַיָּב *the pledge of the debtor* Ezk $18_7$ (if em. חֲבֹלָתוֹ חוֹב *his pledge [as to his] debt*). <SYN> גְּזֵלָה *plunder.**

→ חבל *take in pledge.*

**חֶ֫בֶל** 9.0.8 n.m. **labour pains**—pl. חֲבָלִים; cstr. חֶבְלֵי; sf. חֶבְלֵיהֶם, חֲבָלֶ֫יהָ, mss חֶבְלֵיהֶן—**1. labour pains,** <SUBJ> בוא *come* Is 66$_7$ Jr 22$_{23}$ Ho 13$_{13}$, אחז *seize* Is 13$_8$ (|| צִיר *pang*) Jr 13$_{21}$ 49$_{24}$ (|| צָרָה *distress*) 1QH 5$_{30}$ ([אחזוני]; + זַלְעָפָה *(hot) raging*, צִיר), מרץ ni. *be grievous* 1QH 3$_{8.12}$, חושׁ hi. *hasten* 1QH 3$_{11}$. <NOM CL> [חבלי מרץ] ... ליצר אשׁמה *labour pains of agony ... (shall be) to the inclination of guilt* 1QH 6$_{31}$. <OBJ> חלק pi. *apportion* perh. Jb 21$_{17}$ (but prob. חֲבָלִים *destruction*, from חֶבֶל, or em. חֹבְלִים *wrongdoers*). <CSTR> חֶבְלֵי יוֹלֵדָה *labour pains of one giving birth* Ho 13$_{13}$, שׁאול *of Sheol* 1QH 3$_9$, מרץ *of agony* 1QH 3$_{11}$ 6$_{31}$ ([חבלי מרץ]), כול מעשׂה *of every deed* 4QMyst$^a$ 2.2$_{15}$. <APP> חִיל *writhing* Jr 22$_{23}$. <PREP> לְ of possession, *(belonging) to* 1QH 3$_{12}$; בְּ of accompaniment, *with, in*, + זעק *cry out* Is 26$_{17}$, צרר hi. *be distressed* 1QH 3$_9$, גיח *burst out* 1QH 3$_9$; מִן of direction, *from* 1QH 9$_6$ (מחבלים למשׁברים *from labour pains to birth-throes*; || מַכְאוֹב *pain*).

**2. foetus,** <OBJ> שׁלח pi. *send*, i.e. give birth to Jb 39$_3$ (unless חֶבֶל *band*, i.e. herd; || יֶלֶד *child*).

<SYN> §1 צִיר *pang*, מַכְאוֹב *pain*, צָרָה *distress*; §2 יֶלֶד *child*.*

⇒ חבל *be pregnant*.

**חֶ֫בֶל** I 51.0.3 n.m. (f. at Zp 2$_6$) **rope, territory, band**—mss חֲבֶל; cstr. חֶבֶל; sf. חַבְלוֹ; pl. חֲבָלִים; cstr. חַבְלֵי (חֶבְלֵי); sf. חֲבָלָיו, חֲבָלַ֫יִךְ—**1. rope, cord,** sometimes specif. as **measuring line** (2 S 8$_{2.2.2}$ Am 7$_{17}$ Mc 2$_4$ [if em.] Zc 2$_5$ Ps 16$_6$ 78$_{55}$), <SUBJ> נתק ni. *be torn apart* Is 33$_{20}$ (+ יָתֵד *peg*) Ec 12$_6$ (if em. to נתק ni.), רתק ni. *be snapped* Ec 12$_{6(Qr)}$ (or em.), נטשׁ ni. *be left*, i.e. loosened Is 33$_{23}$ (or em. חֹבְלֶיהָ *its sailors*), רחק *be distant* ni. Ec 12$_{6(Kt)}$ (or em. נתק ni. or חרק ni. *be broken*), טמן pass. *be hidden* Jb 18$_{10}$ (+ מַלְכֹּדֶת *snare*), נפל *fall* Ps 16$_6$, אפף *surround* 2 S 22$_{5(mss)}$||Ps 18$_5$ (L מִשְׁבְּרֵי *breakers of*; or em. יִבְלֵי *streams of*; || נַחַל *torrent*) Ps 116$_3$ (|| מֵצַר *distress*, + צָרָה *distress*, יָגוֹן *grief*) 1QH 3$_{28}$, סבב *surround* 2 S 22$_6$||Ps 18$_6$ (|| מוֹקֵשׁ *snare*), עוד pi. *surround* Ps 119$_{61}$, עור pi. *bind* Ps 119$_{61}$ (mss), עות pi. *make crooked* Ps 119$_{61(mss)}$, חזק pi. *hold* mast Is 33$_{23}$ (or em.; see above), פרשׂ *spread* sail Is 33$_{23}$ (or em.; see above). <NOM CL> בְּיָדוֹ חֶבֶל *in his hand was a measuring line* Zc 2$_5$.

<OBJ> מדד pi. *measure* 2 S 8$_2$, נשׂא *carry* 2 S 17$_{13}$, שׂים *place* 1 K 20$_{31}$ (|| שַׂק *sack*), חגר *gird oneself with* 1 K 20$_{32}$ (|| שַׂק), שׁלך hi. *cast* Mc 2$_5$, פרשׂ *spread* Ps 140$_6$ (חֲבָלִים פָּרְשׂוּ רֶשֶׁת *they have spread cords as a net*, or *they have spread a net with cords*; or em. חֹבְלִים *ones who act corruptly*, or מְחַבְּלִים *destroyers*, or חֹבְלִים *wrongdoers*; + פַּח *trap*), טמן *hide* Ps 140$_6$ (if em. to חֲבָלִים). <CSTR> חֶבֶל מִדָּה *line of measuring* Zc 2$_5$, חַבְלֵי אָדָם *cords of humanity* Ho 11$_4$ (or em. אָדָם to אֱמֶת *of truth* or חֶסֶד *of loyalty*; || עֲבֹת *cord*), רְשָׁעִים *of wicked ones* Ps 119$_{61}$ (חֶבְלֵי), שְׁאוֹל *of Sheol* 2 S 22$_6$||Ps 18$_6$ (חֶבְלֵי), מָוֶת *of death* 2 S 22$_{5(mss)}$ (L מִשְׁבְּרֵי *breakers of*)||Ps 18$_5$ (or em.; see Subj.) Ps 116$_3$ (both חֶבְלֵי־) 1QH 3$_{28}$, הַשָּׁוְא *of vanity* Is 5$_{18}$ (or em. הַשָּׁוְא to הַשּׁוֹר *of the ox*; + עֲבֹת), עֹנִי *of affliction* Jb 36$_8$ (זִק *fetter*), חַטָּאתוֹ *of his sin* Pr 5$_{22}$, חֶבֶל הַכֶּסֶף *cord of silver* Ec 12$_6$ (|| גֻּלָּה *bowl*), חַבְלֵי־בוּץ *cords of byssus* Est 1$_6$; מְלֹא הַחֶבֶל *fullness of the line*, i.e. a full line 2 S 8$_2$, שְׁנֵי־חֲבָלִים *two lines* 2 S 8$_2$, כָּל־חֲבָלָיו *all his cords* Is 33$_{20}$.

<PREP> בְּ of instrument, *by, with*, + לכד ni. *be caught* Jb 36$_8$, אחז pass. *be held* Est 1$_6$, תמך ni. *be held* Pr 5$_{22}$, חבשׁ pass. *be bound* Ezk 27$_{24}$, ירד hi. *let down* Jos 2$_{15}$, עלה hi. *bring up* CD 11$_{17}$ (|| סולם *ladder*, כְּלִי *vessel*), שׁלח pi. *send*, i.e. let down Jr 38$_{6.11}$, משׁך *draw* Is 5$_{18}$ (or em. בְּחַבְלֵי to כְּחַבְלֵי *as [with] cords of*) Jr 38$_{13}$ Ho 11$_4$, שׁקע hi. *cause to sink* Jb 40$_{25}$ (+ חַכָּה *hook*), מדד ni. *be measured* Mc 2$_4$ (if em. יָמִיר *he will change* to יִמַּד בַּחֶבֶל *it will be measured with a line*), pi. *measure* 2 S 8$_{2.2}$, חלק pu. *be divided* Am 7$_{17}$, נפל hi. *cause to fall*, i.e. apportion Ps 78$_{55}$; כְּ *as [with]*, + משׁך *draw* Is 5$_{18}$ (if em.); מִתַּחַת לְ *underneath*, + שׂים *place* Jr 38$_{12}$.

**2. territory, region, (allotted) portion,** as measured out by cord, <SUBJ> היה *be* Zp 2$_6$ (+ נָוֶה *pasture*, גְּדֵרָה *wall*; or del. (חֶבֶל) Zp 2$_7$ (+ לְ *to* remnant of house of Judah), נפל *fall* Jos 17$_5$. <NOM CL> יַעֲקֹב חֶבֶל נַחֲלָתוֹ *Jacob is the allotted portion of his heritage* Dt 32$_9$ (or em. יַעֲקֹב חֶבֶל נַחֲלָתוֹ יִשְׂרָאֵל Y. is the portion *of Jacob, Israel is the allotted portion of his heritage*; + חֵלֶק *portion*), לוֹ חֶבֶל אַרְגֹּב אֲשֶׁר בַּבָּשָׁן *to him was the region of Argob which is in Bashan* 1 K 4$_{13}$. <OBJ> נתן *give* Dt 3$_{13}$ Jos 17$_{14}$ (|| גּוֹרָל *lot*), לקח *take* Dt 3$_{4.14}$.

<CSTR> חֶבֶל אַרְגֹּב *region of Argob* Dt 3$_4$ (Sam הָאַרְגֹּב) 3$_{13}$ (הָאַרְגֹּב) 3$_{14}$ (mss, Sam הָאַרְגֹּב; all three mss חֶבֶל)

1 K $4_{13}$, אַכְזִיבָה *of Achzib* Jos $19_{29}$ (or em.; see Prep.), בבל *of Babylon* 4QpIsa$^c$ 4.$2_4$, בְּנֵי *of sons of* Jos $19_9$, נַחֲלָתוֹ *of his heritage* Dt $32_9$, נַחֲלַתְכֶם *of your inheritance* Ps $105_{11}$||1 C $16_{18}$, הַיָּם *of the sea* Zp $2_{5.6}$ (or del. חֶבֶל חַיִּם) $2_7$ (if ins. הַיָּם) perh. 4Q418 148.$1_7$ (חלביים), חַבְלֵי־מְנַשֶּׁה *portions of Manasseh* Jos $17_5$; יֹשְׁבֵי חֶבֶל *inhabitants of the region of* Zp $2_5$, כָּל־חֶבֶל *all the region of* Dt $3_{4.13}$ (כֹּל) $3_{14}$ (mss חֶבֶל in all three). <APP> עִיר *city* Dt $3_4$ 1 K $4_{13}$, מַמְלָכָה *kingdom* Dt $3_{4.13}$, בָּשָׁן *Bashan* Dt $3_{13}$, נַחֲלָה *inheritance* Jos $17_{14}$. <ADJ> אֶחָד *one* Jos $17_{14}$. <PREP> מִן of direction, *from* Jos $19_{29}$ (or em. מֵחֶבֶל to מַחֲלֵב *Mahaleb* or מְחַלֵּב *Mehalleb*); partitive, *(some) of* Jos $19_9$; עַל *concerning* 4QpIsa$^c$ 4.$2_4$. <COLL> חֶבֶל + numeral עֶשֶׂר *ten* Jos $17_5$; יוֹסֵף חֲבָלִים perh. *Joseph (shall have) portions* Ezk $47_{13}$ (or em. חֲבָלַיִם *two portions*), אֶתֵּן אֶת־אֶרֶץ־כְּנָעַן חֶבֶל נַחֲלַתְכֶם *I will give the land of Canaan as the portion of your inheritance* Ps $105_{11}$||1 C $16_{18}$.

**3. band** of prophets (2 S $10_{5.10}$), perh. **herd** of goats and hinds (Jb $39_3$;* but prob. חֵבֶל *foetus*), <SUBJ> קרא *meet* 2 S $10_{10}$. <NOM CL> הִנֵּה חֶבֶל *behold, there was a* band of prophets 2 S $10_{10}$. <OBJ> פגע *meet* 1 S $10_5$, שׁלח pi. *send* perh. Jb $39_3$. <CSTR> חֶבֶל נְבִיאִים *band of prophets* 2 S $10_{5.10}$ (נְבָאִים).

<SYN> §1 עֲבֹת *cord*, מוֹקֵשׁ *snare*, שַׂק *sack*, סוּלָּם *ladder*, כְּלִי *vessel*, גֻּלָּה *bowl*, נַחַל *torrent*, מֵצַר *distress*; §2 גּוֹרָל *lot*.*

→ חבל *bind*.

**חֶבֶל** II 2.0.5 n.m. **destruction**—pl. חֲבָלִים—<SUBJ> מרץ ni. *be grievous* Mc $2_{10}$ (or em. תְּחַבֵּל וְחֶבֶל *it destroys, and destruction* to תַּחְבְּלוּ חֲבֹל *you take a pledge*, or תַּחְבְּלוּ *you take a pledge*; see also Coll.). <OBJ> חלק pi. *apportion* Jb $21_{17}$ (unless חֲבָלִים *labour pains*, from חֵבֶל, or em. חַבָּלִים *wrongdoers*), מטר hi. *rain* Jb $20_{23}$ (if em. בִּלְחוּמוֹ *on his flesh* to חֲבָלִים). <CSTR> מלאכי חבל *angels of destruction* CD $2_6$ 1QM $13_{12}$ 1QS $4_{12}$ 4QShir$^a$ $1_5$, רוחי *spirits of* 4QShir$^b$ $43_6$, רוחי [ח]בלו *spirits of his destruction*, i.e. his spirits of destruction 1QM $14_{10}$. <COLL> תְּחַבְּלוּ חֶבֶל *you will be destroyed [with] a* grievous *destruction* Mc $2_{10}$ (if em. תְּחַבֵּל וְחֶבֶל *it destroys, and destruction*; see also Subj.).

→ חבל *act corruptly*.

**[חֶבֶל]** III n.[m.] **mountain**, <CSTR> רֹאשׁ חֶבֶל *top of a mountain* Pr $23_{34}$ (if em. רֹאשׁ חִבֵּל *top of a mast/tackle*).*

**חִבֵּל** 1 n.[m.] **mast**,* or perh. **tackle, rigging**, <CSTR> רֹאשׁ חִבֵּל *top of a mast/tackle* Pr $23_{34}$ (or em. חִבֵּל to חֶבֶל *mountain*, or כְּשֹׁכֵב רֹאשׁ חִבֵּל *as one who lies on top of a mast* to כְּחֹבֵל בְּסַעַר גָּדוֹל *as a sailor in a great storm*, or כְּרֹכֵב בְּרַעַשׁ חֹבֵל *as one who sails in a storm, a sailor*, or כְּשֹׂכֵךְ רֹאשׁ חִבֵּל *as one who covers the top of a mast*).

→ חבל *bind*.

**חֹבֵל** 5 n.m. **sailor**—pl. cstr. חֹבְלֵי; sf. חֹבְלָיִךְ—**sailor, pilot**, used collectively at Jon $1_6$, <SUBJ> עמד *stand* Ezk $27_{29}$ (+ תֹּפְשֵׂי מָשׁוֹט *ones who handle the oar*), נפל *fall* Ezk $27_{27}$ (|| מַלָּח *mariner*, + חזק hi. ptc. *caulker*, ערב ptc. *merchant*), נטשׁ ni. *be left*, i.e. dispersed Is $33_{23}$ (if em. חֲבָלַיִךְ *your ropes* to חֹבְלֶיהָ *her sailors*), חזק pi. *strengthen* Is $33_{23}$ (if em.), פרשׂ *spread* Is $33_{23}$ (if em.). <NOM CL> הֵמָּה חֹבְלָיִךְ *they were your sailors* Ezk $27_8$, הוּא חֹבֵל *he is a sailor* Gn $49_{13}$ (if em. לְחוֹף *as a shore* to חֹבֵל).

<CSTR> חֹבְלֵי הַיָּם *sailors of the sea* Ezk $27_{29}$, חֹבֵל אֳנִיּוֹת *sailor of ships* Gn $49_{13}$ (if em.; see Nom. Cl.); רַב חֹבֵל *chief of sailors*, i.e. captain Jon $1_6$, זַעֲקַת חֹבְלָיִךְ *cry of your sailors* Ezk $27_{28}$, כֹּל חֹבְלֵי *all sailors of* Ezk $27_{29}$. <APP> מַלָּח *mariner* Ezk $27_{29}$, רכב ptc. *one who rides*, i.e. sails Pr $23_{34}$ (if em. כְּשֹׁכֵב רֹאשׁ חִבֵּל *as one who lies on top of a mast* to כְּרֹכֵב בְּרַעַשׁ חֹבֵל *as one who sails in a storm, a sailor*). <PREP> כְּ *as*, + היה *be* Pr $23_{34}$ (if em. כְּשֹׁכֵב רֹאשׁ חִבֵּל *as one who lies on top of a mast* to כְּחֹבֵל בְּסַעַר גָּדוֹל *as a sailor in a great storm*). <SYN> מַלָּח *mariner*.*

→ חבל *bind*.

**[חֲבָלָה]** 0.1 n.f. **rope**—sf. Si חבלתה—<SUBJ> היה *be* Si $6_{29}$ (+ בגדי כתם *garments of gold*; || רֶשֶׁת *net*). <SYN> רֶשֶׁת *net*.

→ חבל *bind*.

**[חֲבֹלָה]** 1 n.f. **pledge**—sf. חֲבֹלָתוֹ—<OBJ> שׁוב hi. *return* Ezk $18_7$. <COLL> חֲבֹלָתוֹ חוֹב *his pledge [as to his] debt* Ezk $18_7$ (or em. חֲבֹל הַחַיָּב *the pledge of the debtor*).*

→ חבל *take in pledge*.

[חַבָּלִי] 0.0.0.1 pr.n. **Habbali,** Seal 963 (8th cent.).

חֹבְלִים 2 n.[m.] **union,** as name given to a staff, <OBJ> גדע *break* Zc 11$_{14}$ (or vocalize חֲבָלִים or חֲבָלִים with same meaning). <APP> מַקֵּל *staff* Zc 11$_{14}$. <COLL> לְאַחַד קָרָאתִי חֹבְלִים *I called the one 'Union'* Zc 11$_{7}$ (or vocalize חֲבָלִים or חֲבָלִים *union*).*
→ חבל *bind.*

[חֲבַצֶּלֶת] 2 n.f. **asphodel**—חֲבַצֶּלֶת; cstr. חֲבַצֶּלֶת—**asphodel,** or perh. **meadow saffron** or **narcissus,** <NOM CL> אֲנִי חֲבַצֶּלֶת הַשָּׁרוֹן *I am an asphodel of Sharon* Ca 2$_{1}$. <CSTR> חֲבַצֶּלֶת הַשָּׁרוֹן *asphodel of Sharon* Ca 2$_{1}$. <APP> שׁוֹשַׁנַּת הָעֲמָקִים *lily of the valleys* Ca 2$_{1}$. <PREP> כְּ *as,* + פרח *flower* Is 35$_{1}$.*

חֲבַצִּנְיָה 1 pr.n.m. **Habazziniah,** father of Jeremiah, and grandfather of Jaazaniah the Rechabite, <CSTR> בֶּן־חֲבַצִּנְיָה *son of Habazziniah* Jr 35$_{3}$.

חבק 13.1 vb. **embrace—Qal** 2 Ptc. חֹבֵק, חֹבֶקֶת; inf. חֲבוֹק—**embrace** (2 K 4$_{16}$ Ec 3$_{5}$), **fold** hands in idleness (Ec 4$_{5}$), <SUBJ> אִשָּׁה *woman* 2 K 4$_{16}$, כְּסִיל *fool* Ec 4$_{5}$, יָד *hand* Ec 4$_{5}$. <OBJ> בֵּן *son* 2 K 4$_{16}$. <PREP> לְ of time, *at,* + מוֹעֵד *appointed time* 2 K 4$_{16}$; כְּ *at,* + עֵת *time* 2 K 4$_{16}$. <COLL> עֵת לַחֲבוֹק *a time to embrace* Ec 3$_{5}$.

**Pi.** 11.1 Pf. חִבְּקוּ; impf. Si יחבק, 3fs תְּחַבְּקֶנִּי, 2ms תְּחַבֵּק (תְּחַבְּקֶנָּה); + waw וַיְחַבֵּק (וַיְחַבֶּק־, וַיְחַבְּקֵהוּ); inf. חַבֵּק—**embrace,** <SUBJ> Esau Gn 33$_{4}$ (+ נפל עַל־צַוָּאר *fall upon neck,* נשׁק *kiss*), Israel (Jacob) Gn 48$_{10}$ (|| נשׁק), Laban Gn 29$_{13}$ (|| נשׁק), בֵּן *son* Pr 4$_{8}$ 5$_{20}$, אֶבְיוֹן *poor one* Jb 24$_{8}$, עָנִי *needy one* Jb 24$_{8}$, סָרִיס *eunuch* Si 30$_{20}$ (סירים appar. error for סריס), אמן pass. ptc. *one brought up* on purple, יָמִין *right hand* Ca 2$_{6}$ 8$_{3}$. <OBJ> Jacob Gn 33$_{4}$, נַעֲרָה *young woman* Si 30$_{20}$, female lover Ca 2$_{6}$ 8$_{3}$, חֵק *bosom* Pr 5$_{20}$, צוּר *rock* Jb 24$_{8}$, אַשְׁפֹּת *refuse heap* Ca 2$_{6}$ 8$_{3}$, חָכְמָה *wisdom* Pr 4$_{8}$, בִּינָה *understanding* Pr 4$_{8}$. <PREP> לְ introducing object, + Jacob Gn 29$_{13}$, בֵּן *son* Gn 48$_{10}$. <COLL> עֵת לִרְחֹק מֵחַבֵּק *a time to refrain from embracing* Ec 3$_{5}$; מִבְּלִי מַחְסֶה חִבְּקוּ צוּר *they embrace a rock* (as if it were a friend) *through lack of shelter* Jb 24$_{8}$. <SYN> נשׁק *kiss.* → חֵבֶק *folding.*

[חֵבֶק] 2 n.[m.] **folding**—cstr. חִבֻּק—**folding** of hands, <CSTR> מְעַט חִבֻּק יָדַיִם *a little folding of the hands* Pr 6$_{10}$ =24$_{33}$ (+ לִשְׁכָּב *to lie down*).
→ חבק *embrace.*

חֲבַקּוּק 2.0.1 pr.n.m. **Habakkuk,** prophet of Judah in time of Nebuchadrezzar, <SUBJ> שׁוב hi. *return,* i.e. answer Hb 2$_{1}$, עמד *stand* Hb 2$_{1}$, יצב htp. *station oneself* Hb 2$_{1}$, חזה *see* Hb 1$_{1}$=1QpHab 1$_{1}$ ([חבקוק]), נבט hi. *behold* Hb 1$_{3}$ (if em. תַּבִּיט *you show me* to אַבִּיט *I behold*), צפה pi. *watch* Hb 2$_{1}$, ידע hi. *make* person *know* 1QpHab 7$_{1}$, ירא *fear* Hb 3$_{2}$, שׁמע *hear* Hb 3$_{2}$, נבא *prophesy* 1QpHab 1$_{2}$ ([חבקוק]), שׁוע pi. *cry out* Hb 1$_{2}$=1QpHab 1$_{1}$ ([חבקוק]), זעק *cry out* Hb 1$_{2}$, עלז *exult* Hb 3$_{18}$, גיל *rejoice* Hb 3$_{18}$, רגז *quake* Hb 3$_{16}$, כתב *write* Hb 2$_{2}$ 1QpHab 7$_{1}$, באר pi. *clarify* Hb 2$_{2}$. <OBJ> ראה hi. *show* Hb 1$_{3}$, ענה *answer* Hb 2$_{2}$. <APP> נָבִיא *prophet* Hb 1$_{1}$=1QpHab 1$_{1}$ ([חבקוק]) Hb 3$_{1}$. <PREP> לְ of possession, *of, (belonging) to* Hb 3$_{1}$; בְּ *to, with,* + דבר pi. *speak* Hb 2$_{1}$; אֶל *to,* + דבר pi. *speak* 1QpHab 7$_{1}$; לְנֶגֶד *in front of* Hb 1$_{3}$.

חבר I 31.10.9 vb. **join—Qal** 13.4.3 Pf. חָבְרוּ; impf. יְחָבְרְךָ (Ps 94$_{20}$, unless pu.); ptc. חֹבֵר (חוֹבֵר), Q חוברת, חֹבְרוֹת (חֹבְרֹת); ptc. pass. cstr. חֲבוּר—**1a.** intrans. **join,** i.e. **be joined (together),** of two things joined together, <SUBJ> כָּנָף *wing* Ezk 1$_{9.11}$, יְרִיעָה *curtain* Ex 26$_{3.3}$ perh. 26$_{10}$||36$_{17}$ (but prob. חֹבֶרֶת is noun *series*), כָּתֵף *shoulder piece* Ex 28$_{7}$||39$_{4}$, שִׁבֹּלֶת figures of *ear of grain* 1QM 5$_{12}$, אוֹפַן *wheel* 4QpsEzek$^{a}$ 4$_{11}$. <PREP> בְּ of place, *in, on,* + כִּידוֹן *sword* 1QM 5$_{12}$; אֶל *to,* + אָחוֹת *sister* Ex 26$_{3.3}$ Ezk 1$_{9}$ (all three אִשָּׁה אֶל־אֲחֹתָהּ *a woman to her sister,* i.e. one to the other) 1$_{11}$ (if em. אִישׁ *a man,* i.e. one, to אִשָּׁה אֶל־אֲחֹתָהּ), אֶחָד *one* Ex 26$_{3(Sam).3(Sam)}$ (both אַחַת אֶל־אַחַת *one to one,* i.e. one to the other), אוֹפַן *wheel* 4QpsEzek$^{a}$ 4$_{11}$.

**1b. join (together), ally oneself (with), unite,** pass. **be joined (to), be allied (with),** <SUBJ> Ephraim Ho 4$_{17}$,* מֶלֶךְ *king* Ps 48$_{5}$ (if em. עָבְרוּ *they passed on* to חָבְרוּ *they allied themselves*), כִּסֵּא *throne* of destruction Ps 94$_{20}$, אֵלֶּה *these* Gn 14$_{3}$; subj. not specified, Si 12$_{14}$ 13$_{1}$ 42$_{3(B)}$ (Bmg, M שׁתף ptc. *partner*). <OBJ> Y. Ps 94$_{20}$.

<PREP> אֶל *to*, + אִשָּׁה *woman* Si 12$_{14}$, לֵיץ ptc. *scorner* Si 13$_{1}$, עָצָב *idol* Ho 4$_{17}$; *in*, + עֵמֶק *valley* Gn 14$_{3}$. <COLL> חבר + adverb, יַחְדָּו *together* Ps 48$_{5}$ (if em.; see Subj.).

**2. cast spell, charm** (perh. חבר II *be noisy*, i.e. mutter spells), <SUBJ> subj. not specified, Dt 18$_{11}$=11QT 60$_{18}$ (+ קסם *practise divination*, ענן po. *practise soothsaying*, נחשׁ pi. *practise divination*, כשׁף pi. *practise sorcery*, עבר hi. *make* child *pass* into fire, שׁאל *inquire* of ghost, דרשׁ *inquire* of dead) Ps 58$_{6}$ Si 12$_{13}$ 4QHod$^{c}$ 1.3$_{11}$ (חוב[ר]; =1QH 5$_{28}$ חבר appar. noun חֶבֶר *charm*). <OBJ> חֶבֶר *spell, charm* Dt 18$_{11}$=11QT 60$_{18}$ Ps 58$_{6}$. <COLL> מ[י] יוחן חובר נשוך *who has pity on one who charms (snakes and) has been bitten* Si 12$_{13}$.

**Ni.** 0.0.1 Impf. Q יחברו—**be joined together,** i.e. **be gathered,** <PREP> בְּ of place, *in*, + בַּיִת *house* perh. 4Q Shir$^{b}$ 8$_{11}$ ([ב]בתי כבודם יבחרו *in the houses of their glory they will be gathered*).

**Pi.** 9.1.1 Pf. חִבֵּר; + waw וְחִבַּרְתָּ ;וַיְחַבֵּר (וַיְחַבְּרֵהוּ); impv. Si חברה; inf. חַבֵּר—**1.** trans. **join (together), couple,** <SUBJ> Bezalel Ex 36$_{13.16.10.10.18}$ (+ היה אֶחָד *be one*), Moses Ex 26$_{6.9.11}$ (+ היה אֶחָד). <OBJ> יְרִיעָה *curtain* Ex 26$_{6.9}$||36$_{13.16}$ 36$_{10}$, אֹהֶל *tent* Ex 26$_{11}$||36$_{18}$, אִשָּׁה *woman*, i.e. (each) one Ex 26$_{6}$, אֶחָד *one* Ex 36$_{10.10.13}$. <PREP> בְּ of instrument, *by (means of), with*, + קֶרֶס *hook* Ex 26$_{6}$||36$_{13}$; אֶל *to*, + אָחוֹת *sister*, Ex 26$_{6}$ (אִשָּׁה אֶל־אֲחֹתָהּ *a woman to her sister*, i.e. one to the other), אֶחָד *one* Ex 36$_{10.10.13}$ (all three אַחַת אֶל־אֶחָת *one to one*, i.e. one to the other). <COLL> + adverb, לְבַד *separately*, i.e. by themselves Ex 26$_{9}$||36$_{16}$.

**2. join,** i.e. **make an ally of, bring into alliance (with),** <SUBJ> אֵל *God* 1QS 11$_{8}$, Jehoshaphat 2 C 20$_{36}$ (+ לַעֲשׂוֹת אֳנִיּוֹת *to make ships*), מֶלֶךְ *king* 2 C 20$_{36}$, worshipper 11QPs$^{a}$ 18$_{1}$ ([חברו]). <OBJ> Ahaziah 2 C 20$_{36}$, מֶלֶךְ *king* 2 C 20$_{36}$, נֶפֶשׁ *soul* 11QPs$^{a}$ 18$_{1}$ ([חברו]), סוֹד *assembly* 1QS 11$_{8}$. <PREP> לְ of direction, *to*, + טוֹב *good one* 11QPs$^{a}$ 18$_{1}$ ([חברו]), תָּמִים *pure one* 11QPs$^{a}$ 18$_{1}$ ([חברו]); *for (the purpose of)*, + עֵצָה *council* 1QS 11$_{8}$; עִם *with*, + Jehoshaphat 2 C 20$_{36}$, מֶלֶךְ *king* 2 C 20$_{36}$, בֵּן *son* of heaven 1QS 11$_{8}$.

**3. join in marriage,** <SUBJ> בֵּן *son* Si 7$_{25(A)}$ (C זבד *endow*). <OBJ> בַּת *daughter* Si 7$_{25(A)}$. <PREP> אֶל *to*, + בין ni. ptc. *intelligent one* Si 7$_{25(A)}$.

**Pu.** 4.2.1 Pf. חֻבַּר ,חֻבְּרָה; impf. Sam, Qr יְחֻבַּר (Si יחובר); + waw וְחֻבַּר; ptc. Q מחברת—**1. be joined (together), attached,** <SUBJ> יָד *hand* 4QpsEzek$^{a}$ 4$_{10}$ ([יד]), אֵפוֹד *ephod* Ex 28$_{7}$||39$_{4}$, עִיר *city* Ps 122$_{3}$ (or em.; see Prep.). <PREP> לְ with ref. to subj. of חבר, *for (itself)*, + עִיר *city* Ps 122$_{3}$ (or em. שֶׁחֻבְּרָה לָּהּ *that is joined together for itself* to שֶׁחֶבְרָתָהּ *whose company*, or em. שֶׁחֶבְרָה to שֶׁחֶבְרָה *whose community* is together [ms שחיברה]); מִן of direction, *from*, + גַּב *back* 4QpsEzek$^{a}$ 4$_{10}$. <COLL> + adverb, יַחְדָּו *together* Ps 122$_{3}$ (11QPs$^{a}$ לו *for itself* [m.] for לָהּ יַחְדָּו *for itself* [f.] *together*).

**2. be joined (to), be allied (with), be joined together** as allies, <SUBJ> אָדָם *human being* Si 13$_{16}$, כֹּהֵן *priest* Ho 6$_{9}$ (if em. חֶבֶר *company of* priests, to חִבְּרוּ *they are joined together*), מִי *who(ever)* Ec 9$_{4(Qr)}$, זְאֵב *wolf* Si 13$_{17}$. <PREP> אֶל *to*, + חַי *living one* Ec 9$_{4(Qr)}$, מִין *kind* Si 13$_{16}$, כֶּבֶשׂ *lamb* Si 13$_{17}$.

**Hi.** 1.0.1 Pf. Q החבירו; impf. אַחְבִּירָה—trans. **join (together)** (unless חבר II hi. *harangue* or III hi. *be brilliant* or IV hi. *heap up*), <SUBJ> Job Jb 16$_{4}$, worshipper 11QPs$^{a}$ 18$_{1}$. <OBJ> יַחַד *assembly* 11QPs$^{a}$ 18$_{1}$. <PREP> בְּ introducing object, + מִלָּה *word* Jb 16$_{4}$; עַל *against*, + friends of Job Jb 16$_{4}$.

**Htp.** 4.3.2 Pf. אֶתְחַבַּר, 2ms Si תתחבר; impf. יִתְחַבְּרוּ; inf. הִתְחַבֶּרְךָ (Q התחברכה, Q התחברו)—**join oneself (to), make an alliance (with),** <SUBJ> Jehoshaphat 2 C 20$_{35.37}$, בֵּן *son* Si 13$_{2}$, מֶלֶךְ *king* Dn 11$_{6}$ 2 C 20$_{35}$, עָשִׁיר *rich one* Si 13$_{2}$ (י[ת]חבר), פָּרוּר *pot* Si 13$_{2}$ (י[ת]חבר); subj. not specified, perh. Dn 11$_{23}$ (but prob. הִתְחַבְּרוּת is noun, *making an alliance*) 4Q416 2.3$_{21}$. <PREP> לְ *at*, + קֵץ *end* of years Dn 11$_{6}$; אֶל *to*, + מֶלֶךְ *king* perh. Dn 11$_{23}$ (but prob. הִתְחַבְּרוּת is noun, *making an alliance*), עָשִׁיר *rich one* Si 13$_{2}$, דַּל *poor one* Si 13$_{2}$ (י[ת]חבר), סִיר *pot* Si 13$_{2}$ (י[ת]חבר); עִם *with*, + Ahaziah 2 C 20$_{37}$. <COLL> + adverb, יַחַד *together* 4Q416 2.3$_{21}$, אַחֲרֵיכֵן *afterwards* 2 C 20$_{35}$.

Also 4QApocMosA 1$_{3}$.*

⇒ חִבּוּר *company*, חַבָּר *partner*, חָבֵר *companion*, חֶבֶר *company, spell*, חֶבְרָה *company, community*, חֲבֶרֶת *companion*, חֹבֶרֶת *series*.

* **חבר II** 3.1.2 vb. **mutter—Qal** 2.1.1 Ptc. חֹבֵר (חוֹבֵר)—

**mutter** incantation, charm (unless חבר I *join*, i.e. weave together spell), <OBJ> חֶבֶר *spell, charm* Dt 18$_{11}$ =11QT 60$_{18}$ (+ קסם *practise divination*, ענן po. *practise soothsaying*, נחשׁ pi. *practise divination*, כשׁף pi. *practise sorcery*, עבר hi. *make* child *pass* into fire, שׁאל *inquire* of ghost, דרשׁ *inquire* of dead) Ps 58$_{6}$. <COLL> מ[י] יוחן חובר נשוך *who has pity on one who charms (snakes and) has been bitten* Si 12$_{13}$. וְיוֹשִׁיעֻךְ חֹבְרֵי שָׁמַיִם *and mutterers of heavens*, i.e. those who cast spells, *will save you* Is 47$_{13(Qr)}$ (if em. הֹבְרֵי *worshippers of* heavens, as 1QIsa$^{a}$).* Also 4QHod$^{c}$ 1.3$_{11}$ (ר[חוב]; =1QH 5$_{28}$ חבר appar. noun חֶבֶר *charm*).

**Hi.** $_{1}$ Impf. אַחְבִּירָה—**harangue** (unless חבר I hi. *join together* or III *be brilliant* or IV hi. *heap up*), <SUBJ> Job Jb 16$_{4}$. <PREP> בְּ of instrument, *by (means of), with*, + מִלָּה *word* 16$_{4}$; עַל *against* Job's companions 16$_{4}$.

**חבר III** $_{1}$ vb. **be brilliant—Hi** $_{1}$ Impf. אַחְבִּירָה—**be brilliant** in words, <SUBJ> Job Jb 16$_{4}$ (unless חבר I hi. *join together* or II hi. *harangue* or IV hi. *heap up*). <PREP> בְּ of accompaniment, *with, in*, + מִלָּה *word* Jb 16$_{4}$; עַל *against*, + Job's companions Jb 16$_{4}$.

⇒ חֲבַרְבֻּרָה *spot.*

***חבר IV** $_{1}$ vb. **be high—Hi** $_{1}$ Impf. אַחְבִּירָה—**heap up** words, <SUBJ> Job Jb 16$_{4}$ (unless חבר I hi. *join* or II hi. *harangue* or III *be brilliant*). <PREP> בְּ introducing object, + מִלָּה *word* Jb 16$_{4}$; עַל *against*, + Job's companions Jb 16$_{4}$.

**[חַבָּר]** $_{1}$ n.m. **partner**—pl. חַבָּרִים—in trade, <SUBJ> כרה *trade* Jb 40$_{30}$, חצה *divide* Jb 40$_{30}$ (unless emend בֵּין *among* the merchants, to בְּנֵי *sons of* the merchants, as subj. of חצה).

⇒ חבר I *join.*

**חָבֵר** $_{12.3}$ n.m. **companion**—Si חביר; sf. חֲבֵרוֹ; pl. חֲבֵרִים; cstr. חַבְרֵי; sf. חֲבֵרֶיךָ (mss חֲבָרֶךָ), חֲבָרָיו—**companion, associate,** with ref. to allied tribe, **confederate** (Jg 20$_{11}$), <SUBJ> בושׁ *be ashamed* Is 44$_{11}$ (or em. חֲבָרָיו *his companies*, from חֶבֶר; 1QIsa$^{a}$ חוברי ו *ones joining him*, i.e. ptc. of חבר *join*), פחד *fear* Is 44$_{11}$, אסף *gather together* intrans. Jg 20$_{11}$, קבץ htp. *gather together* intrans. Is 44$_{11}$, עמד *stand* Is 44$_{11}$, קשׁב hi. *pay attention* Ca 8$_{13}$, חזק hi. *hold* shield Si 37$_{6(Bmg)}$.

<NOM CL> יֵשׁ ... חבר *there is ... a companion* Si 6$_{10}$, חָבֵר אָנִי *I am a companion* Ps 119$_{63}$, חָבֵר אַתָּה *you are a companion* 1 S 20$_{30}$ (if em. בֹּחֵר *you choose*), חָבֵר הוּא *he is a companion* Pr 28$_{24}$, שָׂרַיִךְ ... חַבְרֵי גַּנָּבִים *your princes are ... companions of thieves* Is 1$_{23}$, חֲבוּר עֲצַבִּים אֶפְרָיִם *Ephraim is an associate of idols* Ho 4$_{17}$ (if em. חָבוּר *is joined to*).

<OBJ> קום hi. *raise up* Ec 4$_{10}$, נגשׁ hi. *bring near* Jb 40$_{19}$ (if em. חַרְבּוֹ *his sword* to חֲבֵרָיו *his companions*), שׁכח *forget* Si 37$_{6(B, D)}$, עזב *forsake* Si 37$_{6(B, D)}$, כחשׁ pi. *deceive* Si 37$_{6(Bmg)}$. <CSTR> חבר שלחן *companion of*, i.e. at, *a table* Si 6$_{10}$, חַבְרֵי גַּנָּבִים *companions of thieves* Is 1$_{23}$; עֶדְרֵי חֲבֵרֶיךָ *flocks of your companions* Ca 1$_{7}$, עֵץ ... חֲבֵרָיו *stick of ... his associates* Ezk 37$_{19(Qr)}$, כָּל־חֲבֵרָיו *all his associates* Is 44$_{11}$ (or em.; see Subj.). <APP> אֹהֵב *friend* Si 6$_{10}$, אִישׁ *man* Jg 20$_{11}$, בֵּן *son* of Israel Ezk 37$_{16.16(ms)}$, בַּיִת *house* of Israel Ezk 37$_{16}$, שֵׁבֶט *tribe* Ezk 37$_{19}$. <PREP> לְ of possession, *(belonging) to* Ezk 37$_{16.16}$; מִן of comparison, *(more) than*, + משׁח *anoint* Ps 45$_{8}$; בושׁ מִן *be ashamed before* Si 41$_{18(B)}$ (ר[מחב]; M משותף *before a partner*); עַל *against*, + חרשׁ *devise* violence Si 7$_{12}$ (∥ רֵעַ *friend*, אָח *brother*).

<SYN> רֵעַ *friend*, אָח *brother*.*

⇒ חבר I *join.*

**חֶבֶר I** $_{3.0.6.14}$ n.[m.] **company**—חֶבֶר; cstr. חֶבֶר; sf. Q חברך; pl. חֲבָרִים—**company, association;** at Qumran and on coins, **community, council,** <SUBJ> היה *be* 4Q448 1$_{9}$. <NOM CL> חֶבְרָה יַחְדָּו *its company is together* Ps 122$_{3}$ (if em. שֶׁחֻבְּרָה לָּהּ *that is joined together for itself* to שֶׁחֶבְרָהּ *whose company*). <OBJ> עשׂה *make* CD 13$_{15}$.

<CSTR> חבר היהודים *community of the Jews* Coins 12 (חבר היה) 13 (חב יה) 14 17 (חבר [ה]י) Hyrcanus II Coins 18 (החבר היהדים) 18A (חבר הידי) 19 20 (החבר היהדים) 22 (חב היהו) 23 (החבר הידי) appar. 26 (ח) 28 29 (חבר היחד) 30 (all fourteen 1st cent.), חֶבֶר כֹּהֲנִים *company*, i.e. gang, *of priests* Ho 6$_{9}$=4QpIsa$^{c}$ 23. 2$_{14}$ ([חבר כהנים]; or em. חֻבְּרוּ *they are joined together*, i.e. חבר pu., or חֻבְּאוּ *they are hidden*, i.e. חבא pu.), אִישׁ גְּדוּדִים *of men of*

*troops* Ho 69 (if em. כְּחַכֵּי *as the lying in wait of* to כְּחֶבֶר *as a company of*), חֶבֶר צֹרְפִים *company*, i.e. guild, *of goldsmiths* Ne 38 (if em. חַרְהֲיָה *Harhaiah* to חֶבֶר); בֶּן חֶבֶר *son*, i.e. member, *of the company of* goldsmiths Ne 38 (if em.; see above), בֵּית חָבֶר *house of association*, i.e. shared house Pr 219 2524 (unless חֶבֶר II *noise*; or em. in both בַּיִת רָחָב *broad house*), i.e. house of the community 4QDa 18.310 (החבר), עבודת החבר *work of the community* CD 1416.

<PREP> לְ *to, for,* 4Q448 26 (ממלכה לחברך appar. *a kingdom for your community*); בְּ of place, *in*, + שׁתה *drink* 11QPsa 1811; כְּ *as*, Ho 69 (if em. חֶבֶר to כְּחֶבֶר). <COLL> חבר למקח ולממכר *a company for buying and selling* CD 1315, חבר בשמך *a community in your name* 4Q448 19.*

**חֶבֶר II** 6.0.2 n.m. **noise; spell**—חֶבֶר; pl. חֲבָרִים; sf. חֲבָרַיִךְ—**1. noise, tumult,** <CSTR> בֵּית חֶבֶר *house of noise*, i.e. noisy household Pr 219 2524 (unless חֶבֶר I *company*; or em. in both בַּיִת רָחָב *broad house*). **2. spell, incantation,** <NOM CL> אין חבר *there is no charming* 1QH 528. <OBJ> חבר I *join*, i.e. weave, or II *mutter* Dt 1811=11QT 6018 Ps 586. <CSTR> עָצְמַת חֲבָרַיִךְ *power of your spells* Is 479 (|| כֶּשֶׁף *sorcery*). <PREP> בְּ of place, *in*, + עמד *stand* Is 4712 (|| כֶּשֶׁף *sorcery*). <COLL> פתנים לאין חבר *vipers for whom there is no charming*, i.e. which cannot be charmed 1QH 528. <SYN> כֶּשֶׁף *sorcery*.*

→ חבר II *be noisy.*

**חֶבֶר III** 11 pr.n.m. **Heber**—חֶבֶר—**1.** descendant of Asher and son of Beriah, <SUBJ> ילד hi. *beget* 1 C 732. <NOM CL> בְּנֵי בְרִיעָה חֶבֶר וּמַלְכִּיאֵל *the sons of Beriah were Heber and Malchiel* Gn 4617||1 C 731. <PREP> לְ of possession, *of, (belonging) to* Nm 2645. **2.** son of Elpaal, descendant of Benjamin, <NOM CL> ... זְבַדְיָה ... וָחֶבֶר: ... בְּנֵי אֶלְפָּעַל *Zebadiah ... and Heber ... were sons of Elpaal* 1 C 817. **3.** son of Mered and father of Soco, <OBJ> ילד *give birth* 1 C 418. <APP> אָב *father* 1 C 418. **4.** Kenite husband of Jael, <SUBJ> פרד ni. *separate* Jg 411, נטה *stretch out*, i.e. pitch, tent Jg 411. <CSTR> אֵשֶׁת חֶבֶר *wife of Heber* Jg 417.21 524, בֵּית *house of* Jg 417. <APP> קֵינִי *Kenite* Jg 411.17.17 524.

→ חֶבְרִי *Heberite.*

**[חֲבַרְבֻּרָה]** 1 n.f. **spot**—pl. sf. חֲבַרְבֻּרֹתָיו—**spot, mark** on leopard, <OBJ> הפך *change* Jr 1323 (|| עוֹר *skin*). <SYN> עוֹר *skin*.*

→ חבר III *be brilliant.*

**חֶבְרָה** 1 n.f. **company, community,** <NOM CL> חֶבְרָה לָּהּ יַחְדָּו *there is to it a community together*, i.e. its community is together Ps 1223 (if em. שֶׁחֻבְּרָה *that is joined together* to שֶׁחֶבְרָה *whose community* is together [ms שחיברה]). <PREP> לְ *for (the purpose of)*, + ארח *go* Jb 348 (וְאָרַח לְחֶבְרָה עִם־פֹּעֲלֵי אָוֶן *and he goes for company with evildoers*).

→ חבר I *join.*

**חֶבְרוֹן I** 63.0.0.5 pl.n. **Hebron**—I חברן; with ה- of direction חֶבְרֹנָה, חֶבְרוֹנָה—city in Judah, 30 km SSW of Jerusalem, site of royal court for first seven years of reign of David, <SUBJ> היה *be* Jos 1414, בנה ni. *be built* Nm 1322. <NOM CL> קִרְיַת אַרְבַּע הִוא חֶבְרוֹן *Kiriath-arba, that is, Hebron* Gn 232 3527 (הָאַרְבַּע) Jos 1554 207, sim. Gn 2319 Jos 1513 2111. <OBJ> נתן *give* Jos 1413 2113 Jg 120 1 C 640.42, בנה *build* 2 C 1110. <APP> עִיר *city* Jos 2113 1 C 642. <CSTR> מֶלֶךְ חֶבְרוֹן *king of Hebron* Jos 103.5.23 1210 Royal Stamp 1 2 3 4 (all four חברן),* אֲבִי *father of* 1 C 242, שֵׁם *name of* Jos 1415 Jg 110, עֵמֶק *valley of* Gn 3714, עָרֵי *towns of* 2 S 23.

<PREP> לְ of benefit, *to, for*, + עשׂה *do* Jos 1039; בְּ of place, *in(to), at, upon* Gn 1318 1 S 3031 2 S 322 412, + היה *be* 2 S 211, ילד ni. *be born* 2 S 32 (Qr) (Kt ילד pu. *be born*) 1 C 31.4, pu. *be born* 2 S 35, הלך *go* 2 S 319.20(mss.) (MT חֶבְרוֹן), בוא hi. *bring* 48(mss.) (MT חֶבְרוֹן), ישׁב *dwell* Jg 110, מות *die* 2 S 41, קבר *bury* 2 S 332 412, מלך *rule* 2 S 55 1510 1 K 211||1 C 2927, כרת *cut*, i.e. make covenant 2 S 53||1 C 113, נדר *vow* 2 S 157, אור ni. *be light* 2 S 232; מִן of direction, *from*, + בוא *come* 2 S 513, כרת hi. *cut off* Jos 1121; עַד *unto*, + בוא *come* Nm 1322; עַל־פְּנֵי *in front of* Jg 163; with ה- of direction, *to(wards)*, + הלך *go* 2 S 159, בוא *come* 2 S 51.3||1 C 113 1224.39, עלה *go up* Jos 1036 2 S 21 (חֶבְרֹנָה), שׁוב *return* 2 S 327 (without ה-; Q חברונה),

קבץ ni. *assemble* 2 C $11_1$. Also Royal Stamp 5 (חברן).
⇒ חֶבְרוֹנִי *Hebronite.*

**חֶבְרוֹן** II 8 pr.n.m. **Hebron, 1.** son of Kohath, father of Eliel, Jeriah, Amariah, Jahaziel and Jekameam, <NOM CL> בְּנֵי קְהָת ... יִצְהָר וְחֶבְרוֹן *the sons of Kohath were … Izhar and Hebron* Ex $6_{18}$ Nm $3_{19}$ 1 C $5_{28}$ $6_3$ $23_{12}$. <CSTR> בְּנֵי חֶבְרוֹן *sons of Hebron* 1 C $15_9$ $23_{19}$ $24_{23(\text{mss}^{mg})}$. **2.** father of Korah, Tappuah, Rekem and Shema, <CSTR> בְּנֵי חֶבְרוֹן *sons of Hebron* 1 C $2_{43}$ (or del.).

**חֶבְרוֹנִי** 6 gent. **Hebronite**—חֶבְרֹנִי—as noun, of inhabitants of Hebron, <CSTR> מִשְׁפַּחַת הַחֶבְרֹנִי *family of the Hebronites* Nm $3_{27}$ $26_{58}$. <PREP> לְ of possession, *of, (belonging) to* 1 C $24_{23}$ (if em. וּבְנָי *and Benai* to לַחֶבְרֹנִי) $26_{23.30.31.31}$.
⇒ חֶבְרוֹן II *Hebron.*

**חֶבְרִי** 1 gent. **Heberite,** as collective noun, of descendants of Heber, <CSTR> מִשְׁפַּחַת הַחֶבְרִי *family of the Heberites* Nm $26_{45}$.
⇒ חֶבֶר *Heber.*

**[חֲבֶ֫רֶת]** 1.0.1 n.f. **companion**—sf. חֲבֶרְתְּךָ—in marriage, i.e. wife, <NOM CL> הִיא חֲבֶרְתְּךָ *she is your companion* Ml $2_{14}$ (+ אִשָּׁה *wife*).
Also perh. 4QRitMar 246 ([ ]חברתו).
⇒ חבר I *join.*

**[חֹ֫בֶרֶת]** 4 n.f. **series**—חֹבֶרֶת—**series** of curtains joined together, or perh. **place of joining** of curtains, <ADJ> שֵׁנִי *second* Ex $26_{10}$∥$36_{17}$ (unless ptc. חבר *join*). <PREP> בְּ of place, *in, on* Ex $26_4$ (or em. מִקָּצָה בַּחֹבֶרֶת *at the end in the series* to בִּקְצֵה הַמַּחְבָּרוֹת *at the end of the joining*) $26_{10}$ (both Sam בַּמַּחְבֶּרֶת *in the joining*). <COLL> הַיְרִיעָה הַחֹבֶרֶת הַשֵּׁנִית *the curtain (of) the second series* Ex $26_{10}$∥$36_{17}$ (unless ptc. חבר *join*).
⇒ חבר I *join.*

* **[חבשׁ]** vb. **seek**—**Qal, inquire,** <SUBJ> שׂנא ptc. *one who hates* justice Jb $34_{17}$ (if em. חבשׁ *bind,* i.e. govern). **Pi., seek,** <OBJ> מַבֶּךְ *source* of river Jb $28_{11}$ (if em. חבשׁ pi. *dam up*).
⇒ חפשׂ *seek.*

**חבשׁ** 33.0.3 vb. **bind**—**Qal** 29.0.3 Pf. חֲבַשְׁתֶּם; impf. יַחֲבוֹשׁ (יֶחְבַּשׁ, יַחְבְּשֵׁנוּ), אֶחֱבֹשׁ (אֶחְבְּשָׁה); + waw וְחָבַשְׁתָּ, וַיַּחֲבֹשׁ (וַיַּחֲבָשׁ־), וַתַּחֲבֹשׁ, וָאֶחְבָּשֵׁךְ, וַיַּחְבְּשׁוּ (וַיַּחֲבֹשׁוּ); impv. חֲבוֹשׁ (חֲבֹשׁ), חִבְשׁוּ; ptc. חֹבֵשׁ, pass. חָבוּשׁ, pl. חֲבוּשִׁים (חֲבֻשִׁים); inf. חֲבֹשׁ (חָבְשָׁה)—**bind, bind up** wound (e.g. Is $30_{26}$ $61_1$ Ezk $30_{21}$ Ho $6_1$), **saddle** ass (e.g. Gn $22_3$ Nm $22_{21}$ 2 S $17_{23}$ $19_{27}$), **tie around** cap, turban (e.g. Ex $29_9$ Lv $8_{13}$ Ezk $24_{17}$), **twist** rope (e.g. Ezk $27_{24}$), **fetter, imprison** (Jb $40_{13}$), perh. **govern** (Is $3_7$ Jb $34_{17}$).

<SUBJ> Abraham Gn $22_3$, Ahithophel 2 S $17_{23}$, Balaam Nm $22_1$, Mephibosheth 2 S $19_{27}$, Moses Ex $29_9$ Lv $8_{13}$, Shimei 1 K $2_{40}$, אֵם *mother* 2 K $4_{24}$, בֵּן *son* 1 K $13_{13.13.27}$, appar. אָח *brother* Is $3_7$, נָבִיא *prophet* 1 K $13_{23}$, שׂנא ptc. *one who hates* justice Jb $34_{17}$ (or em. יַחֲבוֹשׁ *he seeks*), חֲמוֹר *ass* Jg $19_{10}$ 2 S $16_1$.

<OBJ> חֲמוֹר *ass* Gn $22_3$ 2 S $17_{23}$ $19_{27}$ 1 K $2_{40}$ $13_{13.13.23.27}$, אָתוֹן *she-ass* Nm $22_{21}$ 2 K $4_{24}$, מִגְבָּעָה *headband* Ex $29_9$ Lv $8_{13}$.

<PREP> לְ of direction, *to,* + Aaron Ex $29_9$ Lv $8_{13}$, בֵּן *son* Ex $29_9$ Lv $8_{13}$; of benefit, *for,* + Mephibosheth 2 S $19_{27}$, נָבִיא *prophet* 1 K $13_{13.13.23.27}$.

**Pi.** 2 Pf. חִבֵּשׁ; ptc. מְחַבֵּשׁ—**bind, dam up,** <SUBJ> Y. Ps $147_3$ (+ רפא *heal*). <OBJ> עַצֶּבֶת *injury* Ps $147_3$, מֶבֶךְ *source* of river Jb $28_{11}$ (or em. חִבֵּשׂ *he sought*).

**Pu.** 2 Pf. חֻבָּשָׁה, חֻבָּשׁוּ—**be bound, be bandaged,** <SUBJ> פֶּצַע *bruise* Is $1_6$ (∥ זרר pass. *be squeezed;* + רכך pu. *be made soft* with oil), חַבּוּרָה *stripe* Is $1_6$, מַכָּה *wound* Is $1_6$, זְרוֹעַ *arm* Ezk $30_{21}$. <SYN> זרר pass. *be squeezed.**

**חֲבִתִּים** 1 n.[m.]pl. **flat cakes,** i.e. prob. as baked on מַחֲבַת *flat plate,* <CSTR> מַעֲשֵׂה הַחֲבִתִּים *work,* i.e. making, *of the flat cakes* 1 C $9_{31}$.

**חַג** 62.1.26 n.m. **festival**—cstr. חַג; sf. חַגִּי, חַגֵּךְ, חַגָּהּ, חַגֵּנוּ; pl. חַגִּים; sf. חַגֵּיךְ, חַגֵּיכֶם—**festival, feast,** in ref. to festivals of passover and unleavened bread (e.g. Ex $23_{15}$ $34_{18}$ Lv $23_6$ Dt $16_{16}$ 2 C $8_{13}$), booths (e.g. Lv $23_{34}$ Dt $16_{13}$ Zc $14_{16}$), etc.; **festival offering** (Ps $118_{27}$).

<SUBJ> היה *be* Ezk $45_{21}$, נקף *revolve yearly,* i.e. be cel-

ebrated in yearly cycle Is 29$_{1}$, קדשׁ htp. *celebrate as holy* Is 30$_{29}$.

<NOM CL> חַג לַי״ *there is a feast to Y.* Ex 13$_{6}$ 32$_{5}$, חַג־לַי״ בְּשִׁלוֹ *a feast to Y. is in Shiloh* Jg 21$_{19}$, חַג הַמַּצּוֹת לַי״ *there is the feast of unleavened bread to Y.* Lv 23$_{6}$, חַג הַסֻּכּוֹת ... לַי״ *there is the feast of booths ... to Y.* Lv 23$_{34}$, חַג־י״ לָנוּ *we have a feast of Y.* Ex 10$_{9}$, בַּחֲמִשָּׁה עָשָׂר יוֹם ... חָג *on the fifteenth day ... is a feast* Nm 28$_{17}$, וממנו חג *and from it* (the moon) *there is a feast* Si 43$_{7}$.

<OBJ> עשׂה *do*, i.e. institute 1 K 12$_{32.33}$, celebrate Ex 34$_{22}$ Dt 16$_{10.13}$ 1 K 8$_{65}$||2 C 7$_{8}$ Ezr 3$_{4}$ 6$_{22}$ Ne 8$_{18}$ 2 C 7$_{9}$ 30$_{13.21}$ 35$_{17}$ 4QJub$^{d}$ 22$_{1}$, שׁמר *keep* Ex 23$_{15.16.16}$ 34$_{18}$, חגג *celebrate* Lv 23$_{39}$ Nm 29$_{12}$ Na 2$_{1}$ Zc 14$_{16.18.19}$, אסר *bind* Ps 118$_{27}$, הפך *turn* Am 8$_{10}$, שׁבת hi. *cause to cease* Ho 2$_{13}$=4QpHos$^{a}$ 2$_{15}$ ([ח]גה), מאס *reject* Am 5$_{21}$, שׂנא *hate* Am 5$_{21}$.

<CSTR> חַג־י״ *feast of Y.* Ex 10$_{9}$ Lv 23$_{39}$ Jg 21$_{19}$ Ho 9$_{5}$, חַג הַפֶּסַח *feast of the passover* Ex 34$_{25}$ 11QT 11$_{10}$, מַצּוֹת *of unleavened bread* Ex 23$_{15}$ 34$_{18}$ Lv 23$_{6}$ Dt 16$_{16}$ Ezr 6$_{22}$ 2 C 8$_{13}$ 30$_{13.21}$ 35$_{17}$ (הַמַּצּוֹת) 4QMishE$^{a}$ 1$_{3}$ 11QT 11$_{10}$ (both המצות) 17$_{11}$.

חַג הַשָּׁבֻעוֹת *feast of weeks* Ex 34$_{22}$ (שָׁבֻעֹת) Dt 16$_{10}$ (שָׁבֻעוֹת) 16$_{16}$ Ezk 45$_{21}$ (שְׁבֻעוֹת) 2 C 8$_{13}$ 4QJub$^{d}$ 22$_{1}$ 4QS$^{e}$ 7$_{1}$ 4QMishA 4.3$_{5}$ 4.4$_{1.10}$ 4.5$_{4.13}$ 4QMishB$^{a}$ 2.2$_{1.5}$ 2.3$_{1.4.8}$ 2.4$_{3}$ (all twelve השבועים) 4QMMT A 1$_{16}$ (שבועות) 11QT 11$_{11}$ 19$_{9}$ (שבועות).

חַג הַסֻּכּוֹת *feast of booths* Lv 23$_{34}$ Dt 16$_{13}$ (הַסֻּכֹּת) 16$_{16}$ 31$_{10}$ Zc 14$_{16.18.19}$ Ezr 3$_{4}$ 2 C 8$_{13}$ 4QMishA 4.3$_{9}$ 4.4$_{4.13}$ 4.5$_{7}$ 4QMishB$^{a}$ 2.2$_{2.7}$ 2.3$_{2.5}$ (all three הסוכות) 2.3$_{9}$ 2.4$_{4}$ (הסוכות) 11QT 11$_{13}$ (הסוכות) 42$_{13.17}$ (both הסוכות), הַקָּצִיר *of the harvest* Ex 23$_{16}$, הָאָסִף *of the ingathering* Ex 23$_{16}$ 34$_{22}$ (הָאָסִיף), הבכורים *of the firstfruits* 11QT 11$_{11}$ 19$_{9}$ 43$_{6.7}$, כבוד *of glory* 4QPrQuot 33.11$_{23}$, חגי שמחה *feasts of joy* 4QPrQuot 1$_{13}$.

יְמֵי־הֶחָג *days of the feast* Ezk 45$_{23}$, יוֹם חַג *day of feast of* Ho 9$_{5}$, יוֹם חַגֵּנוּ *day of our feast* Ps 81$_{4}$, חֵלֶב־חַגִּי *fat of my festival*, i.e. festival sacrifice Ex 23$_{18}$, פֶּרֶשׁ חַגֵּיכֶם *refuse of your feasts* Ml 2$_{3}$.

<PREP> לְ of direction, *to* 4QPrQuot 1$_{13}$; בְּ of time, *in, on, during* 2 C 8$_{13.13.13}$ 4QPrQuot 33.11$_{23}$ 11QT 11$_{13}$, + היה *be* Ezk 45$_{17}$ 46$_{11}$, ראה ni. *appear* Dt 16$_{16.16.16}$, קהל ni. *assemble* 1 K 8$_{2}$||2 C 5$_{3}$, ישׁב *dwell* Ne 8$_{13}$, עשׂה *do*, i.e. celebrate Ezk 45$_{25}$, שׂמח *rejoice* Dt 16$_{14}$, קרא *read* law Dt 31$_{10}$; כְּ *as* 1 K 12$_{32}$; מִן of direction, *from* 1QSb 29$_{3}$, + אכל *eat* 11QT 43$_{6}$.

<COLL> וְחַגֹּתֶם אֹתוֹ חַג *and you will celebrate it as a feast* Ex 12$_{14}$ Lv 23$_{41}$.*

⇒ חגג *celebrate.*

**חָגָא** 1 n.[f.] **terror, (object of) dread,** <PREP> לְ introducing predicate, + היה *be* Is 19$_{17}$ (וְהָיְתָה אַדְמַת יְהוּדָה לְמִצְרַיִם לְחָגָּא *and the land of Judah will be a terror to Egypt*).*

**חָגָב** I 5.0.2 n.m. **locust**—pl. חֲגָבִים—**locust, grasshopper,** an edible species (Lv 11$_{22}$=11QT 48$_{4}$), <SUBJ> אכל *eat* 2 C 7$_{13}$, בוא *come* CD 12$_{14}$, סבל htp. *make oneself heavy* Ec 12$_{5}$ (mss סכל htp. *be foolish*). <OBJ> אכל *eat* Lv 11$_{22}$=11QT 48$_{4}$ (+ לְמִינֵהוּ *according to its kind*, || אַרְבֶּה *locust*, סָלְעָם *locust*, חַרְגֹּל *locust*). <CSTR> כל החגבים *all the locusts* CD 12$_{14}$ (+ במיניהם *in their kinds*). <PREP> כְּ *as* Is 40$_{22}$, + היה *be* Nm 13$_{33}$; עַל introducing object, + צוה pi. *command* 2 C 7$_{13}$. <SYN> אַרְבֶּה *locust*, סָלְעָם *locust*, חַרְגֹּל *locust*.

**חָגָב** II 1.0.0.4 pr.n.m. **Hagab, 1.** ancestor of Nethinim, temple servants, in time of Zerubbabel, <CSTR> בְּנֵי־חָגָב *sons of Hagab* Ezr 2$_{46}$. **2.** son of Jaazaniah, <APP> בֵּן *son* Lachish ost. 1$_{3}$. **3.** <CSTR> בן חגב *son of Hagab* Ḥorvat ʿUza ost. 3. **4.** son of Zephaniah, <APP> בֵּן *son* Seal 553$_{1}$ (T. Beit Mirsim?, 7th/6th cent.) Seal 554$_{1}$ (T. Beit Mirsim?, 7th/6th cent.). <PREP> לְ of possession, *(belonging) to* Seal 553$_{1}$ (T. Beit Mirsim?, 7th/6th cent.) 554$_{1}$ (T. Beit Mirsim?, 7th/6th cent.).

**חֲגָבָה** 2 pr.n.m. **Hagabah,** ancestor of Nethinim, temple servants, in time of Zerubbabel, <CSTR> בְּנֵי־חֲגָבָה *sons of Hagabah* Ezr 2$_{45}$||Ne 7$_{48}$.

**חגג** 16.0.3 vb. **celebrate festival—Qal** 16.0.3 Pf. Q חגו; impf. 2ms תָּחֹג, תָּחֹגּוּ (תְּחָגֻּהוּ), יָחוֹגּוּ (Q יחגו), Q נחגה; + waw וְחַגֹּתֶם; impv. חָגִּי; ptc. חוֹגֵג, חֹגְגִים; inf. חֹג—**1. celebrate, celebrate festival, keep** a certain day **as a festival,** <SUBJ> Israel Ex 12$_{14.14}$ 23$_{14}$ Lv 23$_{39.41.41}$ Nm 29$_{12}$

Dt 16$_{15}$ 11QT 28$_{02}$ ([וחגותתה]), Judah Na 2$_{1}$ (|| שׁלם pi. *pay* vows), עַם *people* Ex 5$_{1}$, גּוֹי *nation* Zc 14$_{16}$ (+ שׁחה htpal. *worship*) 14$_{18.19}$, הָמוֹן *multitude* Ps 42$_{5}$, perh. worshipper 4QDibHam$^{a}$ 5.2$_{4}$. <OBJ> יוֹם *day* Ex 12$_{14.14}$ appar. Lv 23$_{41}$ Nm 29$_{12(mss)}$, חַג *feast* Ex 12$_{14}$ Lv 23$_{39.41.41}$ Nm 29$_{12}$ Na 2$_{1}$ Zc 14$_{16.18.19}$ 11QT 28$_{02}$ ([וחגותתה חג]), גְּאֻלָּה *redemption* 4QDibHam$^{a}$ 5.2$_{4}$ (גאל[תנו]).

<PREP> לְ of benefit, *to, for,* + Y. Ex 5$_{1}$ 23$_{14}$ Lv 23$_{41}$ Nm 29$_{12}$ Dt 16$_{15}$ 11QT 28$_{02}$ ([וחגותתה ... לי]); בְּ of place, time, *in,* + מָקוֹם *place* Dt 16$_{15}$, מִדְבָּר *steppe* Ex 5$_{1}$, יוֹם *day* Lv 23$_{39}$, חֹדֶשׁ *month* Lv 23$_{41}$. <COLL> חֻקַּת עוֹלָם תְּחָגֻּהוּ *you shall keep the festival (as) an everlasting statute* Ex 12$_{14}$ Lv 23$_{41}$, חֻקֵּי עוֹלָם ... תָּחֹגּוּ אֹתוֹ *you shall keep it (the festival) ... (as) an everlasting statute* Lv 23$_{41}$, שָׁלֹשׁ רְגָלִים תָּחֹג לִי בַּשָּׁנָה *three times in the year you shall keep a festival to me* Ex 23$_{14}$, תָּחֹגּוּ ... שִׁבְעַת יָמִים, and vars. *you shall celebrate a festival ... for seven days* Lv 23$_{39.41}$ Nm 29$_{12}$ Dt 16$_{15}$ 11QT 28$_{02}$ ([וחגותתה ... שבעת ימים]).

**2. dance,** after victory (1 S 30$_{16}$), **reel, stagger,** of sailors in storm (Ps 107$_{27}$), perh. of Canaanites, through fear (4QApocMosA 2.2$_{9}$), <SUBJ> Amalekites 1 S 30$_{16}$ (|| אכל *eat,* שׁתה *drink*), perh. Canaanites 4Q ApocMosA 2.2$_{9}$ (+ מוג htpol. *melt,* נוע htpol. *totter*), ירד ptc. *one who goes down* to the sea Ps 107$_{27}$ (+ יָנוּעוּ כַּשִּׁכּוֹר *they staggered like a drunkard*). <PREP> לְ *at,* + קוֹל *sound* 4QApocMosA 2.2$_{9}$ ([לק]ול); *as,* + שִׁכּוֹר *drunkard* 4Q418 115$_{3}$; בְּ of cause, *on account of,* + שָׁלָל *spoil* 1 S 30$_{16}$.

<SYN> §1 שׁלם pi. *pay vows;* §2 אכל *eat,* שׁתה *drink.**

⇒ חַג *feast,* מְחִגָּה *cause of reeling.*

**[חָגוּ]** 3 n.m. **cleft**—pl. cstr. חַגְוֵי—**cleft, cranny** in rock, <CSTR> חַגְוֵי הַסֶּלַע *clefts of the rock* Jr 49$_{16}$||Ob$_{3}$ Ca 2$_{14}$. <APP> סֵתֶר *hiding place* Ca 2$_{14}$. <PREP> בְּ of place, *in* Ca 2$_{14}$ (יוֹנָתִי בְּחַגְוֵי הַסֶּלַע *my dove in the clefts of the rock*), + שׁכן *dwell* Jr 49$_{16}$||Ob$_{3}$.

**[חָגוֹר]** 1 adj. **belted**—pl. cstr. חֲגוֹרֵי—as noun, **belted one,** <CSTR> צַלְמֵי ... חֲגוֹרֵי אֵזוֹר *images of ones belted of,* i.e. by, *a belt* around their waist Ezk 23$_{15}$. <APP> כַּשְׂדִּי *Chaldaean* Ezk 23$_{15}$, חקק pass. ptc. *engraved one* Ezk 23$_{15}$, סרח pass. ptc. *one overhung* of, i.e. with respect to, turban Ezk 23$_{15}$.*

⇒ חגר *gird.*

**חֲגוֹר** 3 n.[m.] **belt**—cstr. חֲגוֹר; sf. חֲגֹרוֹ—**belt, girdle,** <NOM CL> עָלָיו חֲגוֹר *upon him was a belt* 2 S 20$_{8(Qr)}$ (or em.; see Cstr.). <OBJ> נתן *give* Pr 31$_{24}$ (+ סָדִין *linen wrapper*). <CSTR> חֲגוֹר חֶרֶב *a belt of,* i.e. with, *a sword* 2 S 20$_{8}$ (or em. חָגוּר *girded* with a sword, i.e. חגר pass.). <PREP> עַד *unto* 1 S 18$_{4}$ (|| קֶשֶׁת *bow,* חֶרֶב *sword,* + מַד *garment*). <SYN> קֶשֶׁת *bow,* חֶרֶב *sword.**

⇒ חגר *gird.*

**חֲגוֹרָה** 5 n.f. **belt**—חֲגֹרָה; sf. חֲגֹרָתוֹ; pl. חֲגֹרֹת—**belt; loincloth** (Gn 3$_{7}$), <NOM CL> חֲגֹרָתוֹ אֲשֶׁר בְּמָתְנָיו *his belt which was about his waist* 1K 2$_{5}$ (|| נַעַל *sandal*). <OBJ> חגר *gird* 2 K 3$_{21}$, נתן *give* 2 S 18$_{11}$ (+ כֶּסֶף *silver*), עשׂה *make* Gn 3$_{7}$. <PREP> בְּ of place, *in, on,* + נתן *give,* i.e. place, blood 1K 2$_{5}$; תַּחַת *instead of* Is 3$_{24}$ (:: נִקְפָּה *encircling rope*). <SYN> נַעַל *sandal.* <ANT> נִקְפָּה *encircling rope.**

⇒ חגר *gird.*

**[חֶגֶז]** pr.n.[m.] **Hegez,** Seal 2 (חגז; others חגי *Haggai,* or חפז *Hephez*).

**חַגַּי** 11.0.0.8 pr.n.m. **Haggai, 1.** prophet to Zerubbabel and Joshua in time of Darius, <SUBJ> אמר *say* Hg 1$_{13.13}$ 2$_{1.1.13.14.20.20}$, ענה *answer* Hg 2$_{14}$. <OBJ> שׁלח *send* Hg 1$_{12}$. <CSTR> יַד־חַגַּי *hand of Haggai* Hg 1$_{1.3}$ 2$_{1}$, דִּבְרֵי חַגַּי *words of Haggai* Hg 1$_{12}$. <APP> מַלְאָךְ *messenger* Hg 1$_{13}$, נָבִיא *prophet* Hg 1$_{1.3.12}$ 2$_{1.10}$. <PREP> אֶל *to,* + היה *be* Hg 2$_{1}$ (Mur 88; [ה]יה) 2$_{10.20}$.

**2.** Seal 2 (חגי; others חפז *Hephez,* or חגז *Hegez*). **3.** son of Shebaniah, Seal 20$_{1}$ (Jerusalem, c. 700). **4.** Seal 203$_{1}$ (Tel Aviv, 7th cent.). **5.** Seal 213$_{1}$ (Jerusalem, 7th cent.). **6.** Seal 355$_{2}$ (T. Zakariya/Gezer, 8th cent.). **7.** Seal 407$_{2}$ (7th cent.). **8.** son of Hodaviah, Seal 555$_{1}$ (T. Beit Mirsim?, 7th/6th cent.). **9.** father of Hoshea or Hosheam, Seal 774$_{2}$ (Jerusalem, 7th cent.). **10.** Seal 872$_{2}$ (7th/6th cent.).

<CSTR> [ב]ן חגי *son of Haggai* Seal 774$_{2}$ (Jerusalem, 7th cent.), נער חגי *servant of Haggai* Seal 407$_{2}$ (7th cent.).

<APP> בֵּן *son* Seal 20 (Jerusalem, c. 700) $203_1$ (Tel Aviv, 7th cent.) $555_1$ (T. Beit Mirsim?, 7th/6th cent.). <PREP> לְ of possession, *(belonging) to* Seal $20_1$ (Jerusalem, c. 700) $203_1$ (Tel Aviv, 7th cent.) $213_1$ (Jerusalem, 7th cent.) $555_1$ (ל[חגי]; T. Beit Mirsim?, 7th/6th cent.).

**חַגִּי** I 2 pr.n.m. **Haggi,** son of Gad, <NOM CL> בְּנֵי גָד ... חַגִּי *the sons of Gad were ... Haggi* Gn $46_{16}$. <PREP> לְ of possession, *of, (belonging) to,* Nm $26_{15}$.
→ חַגִּי *Haggite.*

**חַגִּי** II 1 gent. **Haggite,** as noun, of descendants of Haggi, <CSTR> מִשְׁפַּחַת הַחַגִּי *family of the Haggites* Nm $26_{15}$.
→ חַגִּי *Haggi.*

**חַגִּיָּה** 1 pr.n.m. **Haggiah,** Levite, descendant of Merari, son of Shimea and father of Asaiah, <NOM CL> בְּנֵי מְרָרִי ... חַגִּיָּה *the sons of Merari were ... Haggiah* 1 C $6_{15}$. <APP> בֵּן *son* 1 C $6_{15}$.

**חַגִּית** 5.0.0.1 pr.n.f. **Haggith**—I חגת—**1.** a wife of David and mother of Adonijah, 2 S $3_4$‖1 C $3_2$ 1 K $1_{5.11}$ $2_{13(mss.)}$ (L חַגֵּית *Haggeth*). **2.** mother of Temachel, Seal $347_2$ (8th–6th cent.).

<CSTR> בֶּן־חַגִּית *son of Haggith* 2 S $3_4$‖1 C $3_2$ 1 K $1_{5.11}$ $2_{13(mss)}$ (L חַגֵּית *Haggeth*) Seal $347_2$ (בן חגת; 8th–6th cent.).

**חָגְלָה** I 4 pr.n.f. **Hoglah,** descendant of Manasseh and daughter of Zelophehad, <SUBJ> היה *be* wife Nm $36_{11.11}$. <NOM CL> בְּנוֹת צְלָפְחָד ... חָגְלָה *the daughters of Zelophehad were ... Hoglah* Nm $26_{33}$, אֵלֶּה שְׁמוֹת בְּנֹתָיו מַחְלָה ... וְחָגְלָה *these are the names of his daughters: Mahlah ... and Hoglah* Nm $27_1$ Jos $17_3$. <APP> בַּת *daughter* Nm $36_{11}$.

**[חָגְלָה]** II 0.0.0.3 pl.n. **Hoglah,** appar. district east of Samaria and south of Noah, <PREP> מִן of direction, *from* Samaria ost. $45_1$ ([מחגל[ה) $46_1$ ([מ]חגלה]) $47_1$ ([מ]חגלה]). Also Samaria ost. 66 (חגל[ה]).
→ בֵּית חָגְלָה *Beth-hoglah.*

**חגר** 44.0.1 vb. **gird—Qal** 43.0.1 Pf. חָגְרוּ, חָגְרָה; impf. יַחְגֹּר (וַתַּחְגְּרוּ ,וְחָגַרְתָּ ,תַּחְגֹּרְנָה ,יַחְגְּרוּ ,תַּחְגֹּר ,(יַחְגְּרֶהָ; + waw וַתַּחְגְּרוּ ,וְחָגַרְתָּ; impv. חֲגֹרְנָה ,חִגְרוּ ,חִגְרִי ,(חֲגוֹרָה ,חֲגֹר) חֲגוֹר; ptc. חֹגֵר, pass. חָגוּר, f. cstr. חֲגֻרַת, pl. חֲגֻרִים (חֲגוּרִים)—**gird, gird oneself, gird someone with,** <SUBJ> אֱלֹהִים *God* Ps $76_{11}$, Israel Dt $1_{41}$, Judah Jr $4_8$, Moab Is $15_3$, Israelite(s) Ezk $7_{18}$, עַם *people* 2 S $3_{31}$, Jerusalem Jr $4_8$, Aaron Lv $16_4$, Ben-hadad 1 K $20_{32}$, David 1 S $17_{39}$ $25_{13}$, Ehud Jg $3_{16}$, Gehazi 2 K $4_{29}$, Joab 2 S $3_{31}$, Moses Ex $29_9$ Lv $8_{7.7.13}$.

אִישׁ *man* Dt $1_{41}$ 1 S $25_{13.13}$, אִשָּׁה *woman* Is $32_{11}$ Pr $31_{17}$, בֵּן *son* 2 S $22_{46}$ (‖Ps $18_{46}$ וְיַחְרְגוּ *and they came out trembling*) 2 K $9_1$ Ezk $44_{18}$, בַּת *daughter* Jr $6_{26}$ $49_3$, בְּתוּלָה *young woman* Jl $1_8$, כֹּהֵן *priest* Ezk $44_{18}$ Jl $1_{13}$ 1QM $7_9$, זָקֵן *elder* Lm $2_{10}$, גִּבּוֹר *mighty one* Ps $45_4$, עֶבֶד *servant* 1 K $20_{32}$, מַלָּח *seaman* Ezk $27_{31}$, רָשָׁע *wicked one* Ps $109_{19}$, soldier 2 K $3_{21}$, mourner Is $22_{12}$, גִּבְעָה *hill* Ps $65_{13}$.

Subj. not specified, 1 K $20_{11}$; subj. of pass., David 2 S $6_{14}$, Ishbi-benob 2 S $21_{16}$, Joab 2 S $20_8$, אִישׁ *man* Jg $18_{11.16}$, נַעַר *lad* 1 S $2_{18}$ (1QIsa[a] חוגר), הוּא *he* 2 S $21_{16}$, מָתְנַיִם *waist* Ex $12_{11}$ Dn $10_5$.

<OBJ> (1) person girded, Aaron Ex $29_9$ Lv $8_{7.7}$, בֵּן *son* Ex $29_9$ Lv $8_{13}$; (2) object girded on, כְּלִי *weapon* Dt $1_{41}$, חֶרֶב *sword* Jg $3_{16}$ 1 S $17_{39}$ $25_{13.13.13}$ Ps $45_4$, אַבְנֵט *girdle* Ex $29_9$, חֲגוֹרָה *girdle* 2 K $3_{21}$, מֵזַח *girdle* Ps $109_{19}$, שַׂק *sackcloth* 2 S $3_{31}$ 1 K $20_{32}$ Is $15_3$ $22_{12}$ Jr $4_8$ $6_{26}$ $49_3$ Ezk $7_{18}$ $27_{31}$ Jl $1_8$ Lm $2_{10}$; (3) part of body girded, מָתְנַיִם *waist* 2 K $4_{29}$ $9_1$ Pr $31_{17}$.

<PREP> בְּ *with,* + כֶּתֶם *gold* Dn $10_5$, אַבְנֵט *sash* Lv $8_{7.13}$ $16_4$ 1QM $7_9$, חֵשֶׁב *girdle* of ephod Lv $8_7$, יֶזַע *sweat* Ezk $44_{18}$, עוֹז *strength* Pr $31_{17}$; *on, upon,* + מָתְנַיִם *waist* 1 K $20_{32}$; מִן *in, at, among,* + מִסְגֶּרֶת *fortress* 2 S $22_{46}$; עַל *upon,* + חֲלָצַיִם *waist* Is $32_{11}$, יָרֵךְ *thigh* Ps $45_4$; מֵעַל לְ *from (upon) to,* + מַד *garment* 1 S $17_{39}$; מִתַּחַת לְ *from (underneath) to,* + מַד *garment* Jg $3_{16}$.

<COLL> וְחָגַרְתָּ אֹתָם אַבְנֵט *and you shall gird them with girdle(s)* Ex $29_9$, אִישׁ חָגוּר כְּלֵי מִלְחָמָה 600 *men girded with weapons of war* Jg $18_{11}$, sim. Jg $18_{16.17}$, נַעַר חָגוּר אֵפוֹד בָּד *a lad girded with an ephod of linen* 1 S $2_{18}$, דָּוִד חָגוּר אֵפוֹד בָּד *David was girded with an ephod of linen* 2 S $6_{14}$, יוֹאָב חָגוּר מִדּוֹ *Joab was girded with his garments* 2 S $20_8$.*

[חִגֵּר] 0.0.1 adj. **limping,** used as noun, **limping one,** in list of persons disqualified from entering the congregation, **<SUBJ>** בוא *enter* 4QD$^{a}$ 17.1$_{8}$ (‖ פִּסֵּחַ *lame,* חֵרֵשׁ *deaf*). **<SYN>** פִּסֵּחַ *lame,* חֵרֵשׁ *deaf.*

חֲגֹרָה, see חֲגוֹרָה *belt.*

[חַד] I 4.0.7 adj. **sharp**—חַדָּה—**sharp, shrill, 1.** used attributively of חֶרֶב *sword* Is 49$_{2}$ Ezk 5$_{1}$ Ps 57$_{5}$ 4QBark$^{c}$ 1$_{7}$, חֲנִית *spear* 1QH 5$_{10}$, קוֹל *sound* 1QM 8$_{9.12}$ 16$_{6}$ (all three קול חד טרוד *a shrill staccato sound*) 4QM$^{a}$ 11.2$_{21}$ ([קול חד טרוד]) 13$_{6}$ (קול חד טרוד) 4QM$^{c}$$_{6}$.

**2.** in nom. cl. used predicatively, חַדָּה כְּחֶרֶב פִּיּוֹת the end (אַחֲרִית) of a foreign woman is *sharp like a two-edged sword* Pr 5$_{4}$ (+ מַר *bitter*).

⇒ חדד *be sharp.*

חַד II 1 adj. **one,** used as noun, **one (person), <SUBJ>** דבר pi. *speak* Ezk 33$_{30}$. **<COLL>** חַד אֶת־אַחַד *one with another* Ezk 33$_{30}$ (+ אִישׁ אֶת־אָחִיו *a man with his brother*).

⇒ אֶחָד *one.*

[חֹד] n.[m.] **limit, <OBJ>** נטה *extend* Is 34$_{12}$ (if em. חֹרֶיהָ *her nobles* to חֲדֶיהָ *its limits* and join to preceding verse).*

[חַדָּא] pr.n.m. **Hadda, <CSTR>** בן חדא *son of Hadda* Frey 1285$_{3}$ (AHL יהודא *Judah*)

חדד 6.0.1 vb. **be sharp—Qal** 1.0.1 Pf. חַדּוּ—**be sharp,** i.e. **be quick, <SUBJ>** סוּס *horse* Hb 1$_{8}$=1QpHab 3$_{6}$ (‖ קלל *be quick*). **<PREP>** מִן of comparison, *(more) than,* + זְאֵב *wolf* Hb 1$_{8}$=1QpHab 3$_{6}$. **<SYN>** קלל *be swift.*

**Hi.** 2 Impf. יַחַד (יָחַד)—**sharpen, <SUBJ>** Y. Ezk 21$_{16}$ (if em.; see Ho. Subj.), אִישׁ *man* Pr 27$_{17}$ (יַחַד as if from חדה; perh. em. יָחַד), חָרָשׁ *smith* Is 44$_{12}$ (if ins. יָחֵד) Zc 2$_{4}$ (if em. לְהַחֲרִיד אֹתָם *to terrify them* to לְהָחֵד אִתִּים *to sharpen blades*), בַּרְזֶל *iron* Pr 27$_{17}$ (יָחַד as if from חדה; perh. em. יָחֵד, or em. יֻחַד *it is sharpened,* i.e. ho.). **<OBJ>** חֶרֶב *sword* Ezk 21$_{16}$ (if em.; see Ho. Subj.), אֵת *blade* Zc 2$_{4}$ (if em.; see Subj.), מַעֲצָד *axe* Is 44$_{12}$ (if em.; see Subj.), פָּנִים *face,* i.e. wits, of friend Pr 27$_{17}$. **<PREP>** בְּ introducing obj., + בַּרְזֶל *iron* Pr 27$_{17}$.

**Ho.** 3 Pf. הוּחַדָּה—**be sharpened, <SUBJ>** חֶרֶב *sword* Ezk 21$_{14}$ (+ מרט pass. *be polished*) 21$_{15}$ (+ לְמַעַן טְבֹחַ טֶבַח *in order to make a slaughter,* מרט pu. *be polished*) 21$_{16}$ (or em. הוּחַדָּה חֶרֶב *a sword has been sharpened* to הֵחֵד הַחֶרֶב *he has sharpened the sword;* ‖ מרט pu.), בַּרְזֶל *iron* Pr 27$_{17}$ (if em.; see Hi. Subj.). **<PREP>** בְּ of place, *on,* + בַּרְזֶל *iron* Pr 27$_{17}$ (if em.; see Hi. Subj.). **<SYN>** מרט pu. *be polished.*

**Htp. show oneself sharp, <SUBJ>** חֶרֶב *sword* Ezk 21$_{21}$ (if em. הִתְאַחֲדִי *do it all at once* to הִתְחַדִּי or הִתְחַדְּדִי *show yourself sharp*).

⇒ חַד I *sharp,* חַדּוּד *sharp.*

חֲדַד 2 pr.n.m. **Hadad,** son of Ishmael, **<SUBJ>** שׁכן *dwell* Gn 25$_{15}$. **<COLL>** אֵלֶּה שְׁמוֹת בְּנֵי יִשְׁמָעֵאל ... חֲדַד *these are the names of the sons of Ishmael ... Hadad* Gn 25$_{15}$, sim. 1 C 1$_{30}$ (in both, mss הֲדַר *Hadar*).

חדה I 3 vb. **rejoice—Qal** 2 Impf. יִחַדְּ; + waw וַיִּחַדְּ—**<SUBJ>** Jethro Ex 18$_{9}$, בָּחוּר *youth* Jr 31$_{13}$ (if em. יַחְדָּו *together* to יֶחֱדוּ *they will rejoice*), זָקֵן *old man* Jr 31$_{13}$ (if em.), לַיְלָה *night* Jb 3$_{6}$* (or em. יִחַדְּ to יֵחַד *let it not be united* with, i.e. יחד qal, or יֵחָד *let it* not *appear,* i.e. חדה II ni.), לֵבָב *heart* Ps 86$_{11}$ (if em. יַחֵד *unite* to יִחַדְּ *let it rejoice;* + לְיִרְאָה שְׁמֶךָ *to fear your name*). **<PREP>** בְּ of time, *among,* + יוֹם *day* Jb 3$_{6}$; עַל *on account of,* + טוֹבָה *good* Ex 18$_{9}$.

**Pi.** 1 Impf. 2ms תְּחַדֵּהוּ—**make joyful, <SUBJ>** Y. Ps 21$_{7}$ (or em. תְּרַוֵּהוּ *you saturate him,* i.e. רוה pi.). **<OBJ>** מֶלֶךְ *king* Ps 21$_{7}$ (or em.; see Subj.). **<PREP>** בְּ of accompaniment, *with, in,* + שִׂמְחָה *joy* Ps 21$_{7}$ (or em.; see Subj.).

⇒ חֶדְוָה *joy,* יַחְדִּיאֵל *Jahdiel,* יֶחְדְּיָהוּ *Jehdeiah.*

חדה II 4 vb. **see—Qal** 3 Impf. יַחַד (יָחַד)—**see, look (at),** unless adv. יַחַד *together,* **<SUBJ>** Y. Jb 34$_{29}$ (or em. יֶחֱזֶה *he sees,* from חזה), אִישׁ *man* Ps 49$_{11}$ (‖ ראה *see*), יצר ptc. *one who forms* Ps 33$_{15}$ (‖ בין htp. *understand*). **<OBJ>** לֵב *heart* Ps 33$_{15}$. **<PREP>** עַל look *at,* + אָדָם *human being* Jb 34$_{29}$, גּוֹי *nation* Jb 34$_{29}$. **<COLL>** יַחַד כְּסִיל וָבַעַר יֹאבֵדוּ *he sees (that) the fool and the brutish one perish* Ps 49$_{11}$.

<SYN> רָאָה *see*, בִּין htp. *understand*.

**Ni.** 1 Impf. 3fs תֵּחַד—**appear,** unless from יחד *be united*, <SUBJ> worshipper Ps 139$_{16}$ (if em. אֶחָד *one* to אֶחָדָה *I did not appear*), כָּבוֹד *glory* Gn 49$_6$ (Sam יֵחַר *let it not be hot*, i.e. angry, from חרה; or em. כָּבוֹד to כָּבֵד *liver*; || בוא *come*),* לַיְלָה *night* Jb 3$_6$ (if em. יִחַד *let it not rejoice* to יֵחַד *let it not appear*). <PREP> בְּ of place, time, *in*, + קָהָל *congregation* Gn 49$_6$, יוֹם *day* Ps 139$_{16}$ (if em.; see Subj.) Jb 3$_6$ (if em.; see Subj.). <SYN> בוא *come*.*

⇒ חזה *see*.

[חָדוּד] 1.0.1 adj. **sharp**—pl. cstr. חַדּוּדֵי—used as noun, **sharp one,** i.e. **splinter** of shard, of sharp scales of Leviathan (Jb 41$_{22}$), **ray** of sun (1QNoah 3$_5$), <NOM CL> תַּחְתָּיו חַדּוּדֵי חָרֶשׂ *beneath him are sharp (pieces) of potsherd* Jb 41$_{22}$ (+ חָרוּץ *threshing sledge*). <CSTR> חַדּוּדֵי חָרֶשׂ *sharp ones of potsherd*, i.e. the sharpest of potsherds Jb 41$_{22}$, חדודי השמש *sharp ones*, i.e. rays, *of the sun* 1QNoah 3$_5$. <PREP> כְּ *as* 1QNoah 3$_5$.

⇒ חדד *be sharp*.

חֶדְוָה 3 n.f. **joy**—cstr. חֶדְוַת—<SUBJ> אור hi. *cause to shine* Ec 8$_1$ (if em.; see Cstr.). <NOM CL> חֶדְוַת י׳ הִיא מָעֻזְּכֶם *the joy of Y. is your strength* Ne 8$_{10}$, חֶדְוָה בִּמְקֹמוֹ *joy is in his place* 1 C 16$_{27}$||Ps 96$_{6(mss)}$ (L תִּפְאֶרֶת בְּמִקְדָּשׁוֹ *beauty is in his sanctuary*; || עֹז *strength*, + הָדָר *honour*, הוֹד *splendour*). <CSTR> חֶדְוַת י׳ *joy of Y.* Ne 8$_{10}$, אָדָם *of a human being* Ec 8$_1$ (if em. חָכְמַת *wisdom of*). <SYN> עֹז *strength*.

⇒ חדה *rejoice*.

חָדִיד 3 pl.n. **Hadid,** town in territory of Benjamin, 35 km NW of Jerusalem, Ezr 2$_{33}$ Ne 7$_{37}$ 11$_{34}$, <CSTR> בְּנֵי ... חָדִיד *sons of Hadid* Ezr 2$_{33}$||Ne 7$_{37}$ (or em. אַנְשֵׁי *men of*).

[חֲדִיתָא] 0.0.1 pl.n. **Haditha,** in list of place names, 4Q522 1.1$_6$.

חדל I 59.3.4 vb. **cease**—**Qal** 56.3.4 Pf. חָדַל, חָדְלוּ (חָדֵלוּ), חָדַלְנוּ; impf. יֶחְדַּל (יֶחְדָּל), תֶּחְדַּל (תֶּחְדָּל), אֶחְדַּל, נֶחְדַּל, יֶחְדָּלוּן (יֶחְדָּלוּ), (אֶחְדְּלָה); + waw וַיֶּחְדְּלוּ; וְחָדַלְתָּ; impv. חֲדַל (חֲדָל), חִדְלוּ (חֲדָלוּ); inf. חֲדֹל—**cease, leave off, come to an end,** <SUBJ> י׳ *Y.* Am 7$_5$, אֲדֹנָי *Lord* Am 7$_5$, אֱלוֹהַּ *God* Jb 7$_{16}$ 10$_{20(Qr)}$, אָדָם *human being* Jb 14$_6$ (or em. חלד *live*), גּוֹי *nation* Ezk 2$_{5.7}$ (both + שׁמע *hear*), עַם *people* Si 48$_{15}$, Israelite(s) Ex 23$_5$ Dt 23$_{23}$ (+ נדר *vow*) Is 1$_{16}$ (+ רעע hi. *do evil*), בַּיִת *house* of Jacob Is 2$_{22}$.

Ahab 1 K 22$_{6.15}$||2 C 18$_{5.14}$, Baasha 1 K 15$_{21}$||2 C 16$_5$ (+ בנה *build*), Ishmael Jr 41$_8$ (+ מות hi. *put to death*), Jehoshaphat 1 K 22$_{15}$||2 C 18$_{14}$, Jeremiah Jr 40$_4$, Job Jb 16$_6$, Joseph Gn 41$_{49}$ (+ ספר *count*), Moses Ex 14$_{12}$, Naomi Ru 1$_{18}$ (+ דבר pi. *speak*), Phineas Jg 20$_{28}$, Samson Jg 15$_7$, Saul 1 S 12$_{23}$ (+ פלל htp. *pray*) 23$_{13}$ (+ יצא *go out*).

אִישׁ *man* Nm 9$_{13}$ Jr 44$_{18}$ (+ קטר pi. *burn incense*), אָב *father* 1 S 9$_5$, בֵּן *son* of human being, i.e. mortal Gn 11$_8$ (+ בנה *build*), *son* of Israel Ezk 2$_{5.7}$ (both + שׁמע *hear*), *son* of your people Ezk 3$_{11}$ (+ שׁמע *hear*), *son* Pr 19$_{27}$ (+ שׁמע *hear*).

מֶלֶךְ *king* 2 C 35$_{21}$, נָבִיא *prophet* 2 C 25$_{16.16}$, גִּבּוֹר *mighty one* Jr 51$_{30}$ (+ לחם ni. *fight*), גּוֹלָה *exile(s)* Ezk 3$_{11}$ (+ שׁמע *hear*), קָרוֹב *near one*, i.e. close relative Jb 19$_{14}$, מְיֻדָּע *relative* Jb 19$_{14}$, אֶבְיוֹן *poor one* Dt 15$_{11}$, עָנִי *poor one* Zc 11$_{12}$, רָעֵב *hungry one* 1 S 2$_5$, פְּרָזוֹן *country dweller* Jg 5$_{7.7}$,* חָדֵל *rejected one* Ezk 3$_{27}$, רָשָׁע *wicked one* Ps 36$_4$ (+ שׂכל hi. *act wisely*) Jb 3$_{17}$ 1QM 4$_3$.

אֹרְחָה *caravan* Jg 5$_6$, שָׁאוֹן *uproar* Is 24$_8$, מַבּוּל *flood* Si 44$_{17}$, בָּרָד *hail* Ex 9$_{29.33.34}$, קוֹל pl. *thunder* Ex 9$_{29.33.34}$, מָטָר *rain* Ex 9$_{33.34}$, יוֹנֶקֶת *shoot* Jb 14$_7$, פִּדְיוֹן *ransom* Ps 49$_9$ (or em. וְחָלַד *and he will live*), אֹרַח *manner* Gn 18$_{11}$, פֶּשַׁע *transgression* Pr 10$_{19}$; subj. not specified, Pr 23$_4$ Si 34$_{17}$ 1QS 5$_{17}$ 4QM$^h$ 6$_2$ 11QT 53$_{12}$.

<PREP> לְ of direction, *for*, + עוֹלָם *eternity* Ps 49$_9$; of benefit, *to, for* 1QS 5$_{17}$, + בַּיִת *house* of Jacob Is 2$_{22}$, מֶלֶךְ *king* 2 C 35$_{21}$, נָבִיא *prophet* 2 C 25$_{16}$; בְּ of place, *in, at, among*, + Israel Jg 5$_7$; of instrument, *by (means of)*, + בְּרִית *covenant* Si 44$_{17}$; מִן of direction, *from*, + אָדָם *human being* Is 2$_{22}$ 1QS 5$_{17}$, בֵּן *son* of Israel Ex 14$_{12}$, חַטָּאת *sin* Si 48$_{15}$; of cause, *because of*, + אָתוֹן *she-ass* 1 S 9$_5$; בַּעֲבוּר *on account of*, + מוּסָר *discipline* Si 34$_{17}$; מִקֶּרֶב *from (among)*, + אֶרֶץ *land* Dt 15$_{11}$.

<COLL> שָׁם רְשָׁעִים חָדְלוּ רֹגֶז *there the wicked have ceased from turmoil* Jb 3$_{17}$.

**Ho.** 3 Pf. הָחֳדַּלְתִּי—**be made to leave off,** <SUBJ> זַיִת *olive tree* Jg 9₉, תְּאֵנָה *fig tree* Jg 9₁₁, גֶּפֶן *vine* Jg 9₁₃. <OBJ> דֶּשֶׁן *fatness* Jg 9₉, מֹתֶק *sweetness* Jg 9₁₁, תִּירוֹשׁ *wine* Jg 9₁₃.*

→ חָדֵל *ceasing,* חֶדֶל *world, duration.*

**חדל II** 3 vb. **be fat—Qal** 3 Pf. חָדֵלּוּ; impv. חֲדַל (חָדֵל חָדֵל)—**1. be fat,** <SUBJ> רָעֵב *hungry one* 1 S 2₅* (:: שׂכר ni. *hire oneself out* for bread). **2. be successful,** <SUBJ> בֵּן *son* Pr 19₂₇ (+ לִשְׁמֹעַ מוּסָר *to hear instruction*) perh. 23₄. <PREP> מִן *on account of,* + בִּינָה *understanding* Pr 23₄. <ANT> §1 שׂכר ni. *hire oneself out.**

**חָדֵל** 4 adj. **ceasing**—cstr. חֲדַל—**1. transient,** used predicatively, מֶה־חָדֵל אָנִי *how transient I am* Ps 39₅ (+ מִדַּת יָמַי מַה־הִיא *the measure of my days, what is it?*), var. 89₄₈(mss). **2.** as noun, **one refusing** to hear, <SUBJ> חדל *cease,* i.e. refuse Ezk 3₂₇ (וְהֶחָדֵל יֶחְדָּל *let him who refuses [to hear] refuse;* + שׁמע ptc. *one who hears*). **3.** as noun, **one shunning,** or **one being shunned,** i.e. who shuns or is object of shunning, <CSTR> חֲדַל אִישִׁים *one shunning of,* i.e. who shuns or is shunned by, *men* Is 53₃ (+ בזה ni. *be despised).*

→ חדל *cease.*

**[חֶדֶל]** 2 n.[m.] **world; duration**—חֶדֶל—**1. world,** <CSTR> יוֹשְׁבֵי חָדֶל *inhabitants of the world* Is 38₁₁ (mss חָלֶד *world;* + אֶרֶץ הַחַיִּים *land of the living*).

**2. duration of life, lifespan,** <NOM CL> מֶה־חָדֶל *what is the duration of life* Ps 89₄₈(mss) (L חָלֶד *duration of life;* or em. אֲנִי מֶה־חָדֶל *I, what is the span of life* to מֶה־חָדֵל אָנִי *how I am coming to an end,* from חדל I, or אֲנִי מֶה־חָלֶד *I am not everlasting).*

→ חדל *cease.*

**[חַדְלַי]** 1 pr.n.m. **Hadlai**—חַדְלָי—father of Amasa, one of the chiefs of Ephraim, <CSTR> בֶּן־חַדְלָי *son of Hadlai* 2 C 28₁₂.

**[חַדָּן]** pr.n.m. **Haddan,** Al-Minya inscr. (HN 118; others יודן *Judan).*

**חֵדֶק** 2 n.[m.] **brier**—חֵדֶק—**brier,** perh. **nightshade** (*solanum coagulans*), <CSTR> מְשֻׂכַת חֵדֶק *hedge of brier* Pr 15₁₉. <PREP> כְּ *as* Mc 7₄ (+ מְסוּכָה *hedge*).

**חִדֶּקֶל** 2 pl.n. **Tigris, Hiddekel**—חִדֶּקֶל—river flowing to the east of Assyria, <NOM CL> שֵׁם הַנָּהָר הַשְּׁלִישִׁי חִדֶּקֶל *the name of the third river was Tigris* Gn 2₁₄, הַנָּהָר הַגָּדוֹל הוּא חִדָּקֶל *the great river, that is the Tigris* Dn 10₄.

**חדר I** 1.1 vb. **surround—Qal** 1.1 Impf. Si אחדר; ptc. חֹדֶרֶת—**surround, encircle,** perh. **enter, penetrate deeply,** <SUBJ> Ben Sira Si 51₁₉(B) (unless חדר II *keep oneself*), חֶרֶב *sword* Ezk 21₁₉ (mss הַחֹרֶדֶת *which trembles*), הוֹד *splendour* Si 50₁₁ (if em. ויהדר *and he* [Simon] *made glorious* to יחדר splendour *would surround*), stars Jb 9₉ (if em. חַדְרֵי *chambers of* to חֹדְרֵי *ones that encircle* the south). <OBJ> עֲזָרָה *court* of temple Si 50₁₁ (if em.; see Subj.). <PREP> לְ introducing object, + חָלָל *slain one* Ezk 21₁₉, חָכְמָה *wisdom* Si 51₁₉(B).

**חדר II** 0.1 vb. **remain—Qal** 0.1 Impf. Si אחדר—**remain, keep oneself,** <SUBJ> Ben Sira Si 51₁₉(B) (unless חדר I *penetrate deeply*). <PREP> לְ *for (the purpose of),* + חָכְמָה *wisdom* Si 51₁₉(B).

**חֲדַר** 2 pr.n.m. **Hadar,** son of Ishmael, <SUBJ> שׁכן *dwell* Gn 25₁₅. <COLL> אֵלֶּה שְׁמוֹת בְּנֵי יִשְׁמָעֵאל ... חֲדַר *these are the names of the sons of Ishmael ... Hadar* Gn 25₁₅(mss), sim. 1 C 1₃₀(mss) (in both, L הֲדַד *Hadad*).

**חֶדֶר** 38.1.15.2 n.m. **chamber**—חֶדֶר; + ה- of direction הַחַדְרָה (הֶחֱדְרָה); cstr. חֲדַר (חֶדֶר); sf. חֶדְרוֹ; pl. חֲדָרִים; cstr. חַדְרֵי; sf. Si חדרי, חֲדָרֶיךָ, חֲדָרָיו—**chamber, inner room,** in ref. to inner rooms or chambers, e.g. Gn 43₃₀ Dt 32₂₅ 1 K 20₃₀ 2 K 6₁₂ 11₂, to inner recesses of human body Pr 18₈, to burial place Silwan royal steward tomb inscr. 2₁, to chambers of Sheol Pr 7₂₇, to constellations of southern heaven Jb 9₉.

<SUBJ> מלא ni. *be filled* Pr 24₄, פתח pass. *be opened* Bar-Kochba deed of sale₂ (תחדר שפתוח *the room that is opened).*

<NOM CL> חדר בכתף הצר *the chamber that is in the slope of the mountain* Silwan royal steward tomb inscr. 2$_{1}$, חדריהמה ... כתחתונות *their rooms are ... as the lower (apartments)* 11QT 42$_{9}$, לבני יהודה ... חדריהמה *to the sons of Judah are ... their rooms* 11QT 44$_{8}$, sim. 11QT 44$_{10.12}$.

<OBJ> עשׂה *make* Jb 9$_{9}$ 11QT 42$_{5}$, לקח *take*, i.e. allot 11QT 44$_{3}$ ([חדריהמה]) 44$_{6}$, חפשׂ *search* Pr 20$_{27}$, מרק hi. *cleanse* Pr 20$_{30}$.

<CSTR> חַדְרֵי תֵמָן *chambers of the south*, i.e. constellations of the southern heaven Jb 9$_{9}$, שאול *of Sheol* 1QH 10$_{34}$, הבית *of the house* 1QNoah 3$_{5}$, מַשְׂכִּיתוֹ *of his imagery* or *imagination* Ezk 8$_{12}$, מַלְכֵיהֶם *of their kings* Ps 105$_{30}$, חַדְרֵי־בָטֶן *chambers of (the) belly*, i.e. innards of body Pr 18$_{8}$ 20$_{27.30}$ 26$_{22}$ 4Q185 1.3$_{12}$,* חֲדַר מִשְׁכָּבְךָ *chamber of your bed* Ex 7$_{28}$ 2 K 6$_{12}$ Ec 10$_{20(mss)}$, חַדְרֵי *chambers of* Ec 10$_{20}$, חֲדַר מִשְׁכָּבוֹ *chamber of his bed* 2 S 4$_{7}$, הַמִּטּוֹת *of the beds* 2 K 11$_{2}$||2 C 22$_{11}$, הַמְּקֵרָה *of the cooling* Jg 3$_{24}$, חַדְרֵי־מָוֶת *chambers of death* Pr 7$_{27}$.

תַּבְנִית ... חֲדָרָיו *plan of ... its chambers* 1 C 28$_{11}$, רוחב החדר *width of the room* 11QT 42$_{01}$ ([חדר]), כָּל־חַדְרֵי *all the chambers of* Pr 20$_{27}$ 4Q185 1.3$_{12}$.

<ADJ> זֶה *this* Kh. el-Qom inscr. 1$_{3}$.

<PREP> לְ of direction, *to* 4QapPs$^{b}$ 23$_{2}$; of benefit, *to, for*, + עשׂה *do* 11QT 42$_{3}$ ([חדריה]מה)).

בְּ of place, *in, at, among* 2 K 11$_{2}$ 11QHod$^{a}$3, + חפשׂ ni. *be searched out* 1QH 10$_{34}$, בוא *come* Ex 7$_{28}$ 1 K 20$_{30}$ 22$_{25}$||2 C 18$_{24}$ Is 26$_{20}$, hi. *bring* 2 K 9$_{2}$, שׁרץ *swarm* Ps 105$_{30}$, ישׁב *sit* Jg 16$_{9.12}$, שׁכב *lie* 2 S 4$_{7}$, חנה *encamp* Si 4$_{15}$, נתן *give*, i.e. place 2 C 22$_{11}$, עשׂה *do* Ezk 8$_{12}$, סכך hi. *cover* feet, i.e. relieve oneself Jg 3$_{24}$, דבר pi. *speak* 2 K 6$_{12}$, קלל pi. *curse* Ec 10$_{20}$.

מִן of direction, *from*, + בוא *come* Jb 39$_{9}$, יצא *go out* Jl 2$_{16}$, שׁכל pi. *bereave* Dt 32$_{25}$.

אֶל *to*, + בוא hi. *bring* Ca 3$_{4}$, ירד *go down* Pr 7$_{27}$.

הַחַדְרָה (with ה- of direction) *into, (the chamber of)*, + בוא *come* Gn 43$_{30}$ Jg 15$_{1}$ 2 S 13$_{10(mss)}$ 1 K 1$_{15}$, בוא hi. *bring* 2 S 13$_{10}$; חֶדֶר (without preposition or ה- of direction) *into, (the chamber of)*, + בוא *come* 1 K 20$_{30}$ 22$_{25}$||2 C 18$_{24}$, hi. *bring* 2 S 13$_{10}$ 2 K 9$_{2}$ Ca 1$_{4}$, ירד *go down* Pr 18$_{8}$ 26$_{22}$.

Also 4QMyst$^{a}$ 6.1$_{14}$ 4Q426 5$_{1}$ XḤev/Se 8$_{2}$.*

⇒ חדר *surround*.

**חֲדְרָךְ** $_{1}$ pl.n. **Hadrach,** place against which Zechariah delivered oracle, perh. Āfiṣ, 290 km NNE of Damascus, <CSTR> אֶרֶץ חַדְרָךְ *land of Hadrach* Zc 9$_{1}$ (unless em. בְּאֶרֶץ *against the land of* to בָּא צַר *the distress/enemy of* Hadrach *has come*).

**חדשׁ I** $_{10.2.11}$ vb. **renew—Pi.** $_{9.1.7}$ Pf. Q חדשתה; impf. Q יחדש, 2ms תְּחַדֵּשׁ, נְחַדֵּשׁ; + waw וַיְחַדֵּשׁ, וְחִדְּשׁוּ; impv. חַדֵּשׁ; inf. חַדֵּשׁ (Q חדשה)—**renew, repair,** perh. at Ps 51$_{12}$, **create, engender,*** <SUBJ> Y. Zp 3$_{17}$ (if em.; see Obj.) Ps 51$_{12}$ (+ ברא *create*) 104$_{30}$ (+ שׁלח pi. *send* spirit) Jb 10$_{17}$ (+ רבה hi. *increase*) Lm 5$_{21}$ (+ שׁוב hi. *bring back*) Si 33$_{6}$ (|| שׁנה pi. *change*) 1QSb 3$_{26}$ ([יח]דש) 5$_{21}$ 1QLitPr 3.2$_{6}$ perh. 4QPrQuot 1$_{2}$ (א[ל] ... חדש *God ... he has renewed*) 29.8$_{9}$ 33.11$_{2}$ (א[ל] ... חדש[תה] *God ... you have renewed*), Asa 2 C 15$_{8}$, Joash 2 C 24$_{4}$, Samuel 1 S 11$_{14}$, Israelites Is 61$_{4}$ (|| בנה *build*, קום po. *raise up*), עַם *people* 1 S 11$_{14}$, חֹצֵב *mason* 2 C 24$_{12}$, חָרָשׁ *carpenter* 2 C 24$_{12}$.

<OBJ> Zion Zp 3$_{17}$ (if em. יַחֲרִישׁ *he will be silent* to יְחַדֶּשְׁךָ *he will renew you*), רוּחַ *spirit* Ps 51$_{12}$, עֵד *witness* Jb 10$_{17}$, עִיר *city* Is 61$_{4}$, מְלוּכָה *kingdom* 1 S 11$_{14}$, שׁמם ptc. *desolate place* Is 61$_{4}$, פָּנִים *face* of ground Ps 104$_{30}$, בַּיִת *house* of Y. 2 C 24$_{4.12}$, מִזְבֵּחַ *altar* 2 C 15$_{8}$, יוֹם *day* Lm 5$_{21}$, אוֹת *sign* Si 33$_{6(B)}$, תְּמָה *wonder* Si 33$_{6(Bmg)}$, בְּרִית *covenant* 1QSb 3$_{26}$ ([יח]דש) 5$_{21}$ 1QLitPr 3.2$_{6}$, אַהֲבָה *love* Zp 3$_{17}$ (if em. יַחֲרִישׁ בְּאַהֲבָתוֹ *he will be silent in his love* to יְחַדֵּשׁ אַהֲבָתוֹ *he will renew his love*).

<PREP> לְ of benefit, *to, for* perh. 1QSb 5$_{5}$, + Y. 1QSb 5$_{21}$, עַם *people* 1QLitPr 3.2$_{6}$; בְּ of accompaniment, *with, in*, + אַהֲבָה *love* Zp 3$_{17}$ (if em. יַחֲרִישׁ *he will be silent* to יְחַדֶּשְׁךָ *he will renew you*), מַרְאָה *vision* 1QLitPr 3.2$_{6}$, דָּבָר *word* 1QLitPr 3.2$_{6}$, מַעֲשֶׂה *deed* 1QLitPr 3.2$_{6}$; of instrument, *by (means of), with*, + אוֹר *light* 4QPrQuot 33.11$_{2}$; כְּ *as*, + קֶדֶם *(in) ancient time* Lm 5$_{21}$; בְּקֶרֶב *within*, + worshipper Ps 51$_{12}$; נֶגֶד *against*, + Job Jb 10$_{17}$.

<COLL> + adverb, שָׁם *there* 1 S 11$_{14}$, הי[ו]ם הזה חדש *today he has renewed* 4QPrQuot 1$_{2}$.

Also 4QTNaph 2$_{2}$ ([לחד]ש) 3$_{1}$ perh. 4Q434$^{a}$2.

<SYN> בנה *build*, קום po. *raise up*, שׁנה pi. *change*.

**Hi. renew,** <SUBJ> Y. Zp 3$_{17}$ (if em. יַחֲרִישׁ *he will be* silent to יְחַדֵּשׁ *he will renew*). <PREP> בְּ introducing object, + אַהֲבָה *love* Zp 3$_{17}$ (if em.; see Subj.).

**Htp.** 1.1.4 Impf. 3fs תִּתְחַדֵּשׁ; ptc. Si מתחדש; inf. Q התחדש (Q התחדשם)—**renew oneself,** <SUBJ> נְעוּרִים *youth* Ps 103$_5$, תּוֹלַעַת *worm* 1QH 11$_{13}$, חֹדֶשׁ *new moon* Si 43$_8$ (+ שׁנה htp. *change oneself*), מָאוֹר *luminary* 1QS 10$_4$. <PREP> בְּ of time, *in*, + חֹדֶשׁ *month* Si 43$_{8(B)}$, כְּ *as*, + נֶשֶׁר *eagle* Ps 103$_5$; *according to*, + שֵׁם *name* Si 43$_{8(M, Yadin)}$ (מת[חדש]); עִם *with*, + נִהְיָה ni. ptc. *existence* 1QH 11$_{13}$, ידע ptc. *one who knows* 1QH 11$_{13}$.

Also 4Q415 2.1$_9$ 4Q418 236$_1$.

→ חָדָשׁ *new*, חֹדֶשׁ *month*.

* [חדשׁ] II vb. **attack—Pi.,** ptc. as noun **invader,** <SUBJ> אכל *eat* Ho 5$_7$ (if em. יֹאכְלֵם חֹדֶשׁ *the new moon will devour them* to יֹאכַל מְחַדֵּשׁ *an invader will consume*). <OBJ> חֵלֶק *portion* Ho 5$_7$ (if em.).

**חָדָשׁ** adj. 53.3.26 **new**—fem. חֲדָשָׁה; pl. masc. חֲדָשִׁים (L חֳדָשִׁים); fem. Q חדשות—**1.** used attributively of מֶלֶךְ *king* Ex 1$_8$, מִנְחָה *cereal offering* Lv 2$_{16}$ Nm 28$_{26}$ 4Q409 1.1$_2$ ([מ]נחה) 11QT 18$_{13}$ 19$_6$ ([מחנה חד]שה) 19$_{11}$, מֶגֶד *excellence*, i.e. choice produce Ca 7$_{14}$ (:: יָשָׁן *old*), חִטָּה *wheat* 4Q251 2$_5$, חָמֵץ *leaven* 11QT 18$_{14}$, יַיִן *wine* Si 9$_{10}$ (:: יָשָׁן) 11QT 11$_{12}$ ([יין חדש]) 19$_{14}$ 21$_{10}$ 11QT$^b$ 8.1$_{10}$, לֶחֶם *bread* 11QT$^b$ 5$_4$, שֶׁמֶן *oil* 11QT 21$_{14.15}$ 22$_{15}$ 43$_{10}$, שִׂמְלָה *mantle* 1 K 11$_{29.30}$, עֲבֹת *rope* Jg 15$_{13}$ 16$_{11.12}$, עֲגָלָה *cart* 1 S 6$_7$ 2 S 6$_3$||1 C 13$_7$ 2 S 6$_3$ (or del. חָדָשׁ), מוֹרַג *threshing board* Is 41$_{15}$ (or del. חָדָשׁ), אוֹב *wineskin* Jb 32$_{19}$, צְלֹחִית *dish* 2 K 2$_{20}$, חֶרֶב *sword* 2 S 21$_{16}$ (if ins. חֶרֶב), בַּיִת *house* Dt 20$_5$ 22$_8$ 11QT 65$_5$, שַׁעַר *gate* Jr 26$_{10}$ 36$_{10}$, אֶרֶץ *earth* Is 65$_{17}$ (:: רִאשׁוֹן *first*) 66$_{22}$, שָׁמַיִם *heavens* Is 65$_{17}$ 66$_{22}$, אֱלֹהִים *gods* Jg 5$_8$, אִשָּׁה *woman* Dt 24$_5$, אהב ptc. *lover* Si 9$_{10(mg)}$, שִׁיר *song* Is 42$_{10}$ Ps 33$_3$ 40$_4$ 96$_1$ 98$_1$ 144$_9$ 149$_1$, שֵׁם *name* Is 62$_2$, בְּרִית *covenant* Jr 31$_{31}$ CD 6$_{19}$ 8$_{21(A)}$=19$_{34(B)}$ 20$_{12}$ 1QpHab 2$_3$ ([ברית]), רוּחַ *spirit* Ezk 11$_{19}$ 18$_{31}$ 36$_{26}$ 4Q393 1$_5$, לֵב *heart* Ezk 11$_{19(mss)}$ (L אֶחָד *one*) 18$_{31}$ 36$_{26}$, עשׂה inf. *deed* 1QS 4$_{25}$ (עשות חדשה), appar. רַחַם *compassion* Lm 3$_{23}$ (if rd. לֹא־כָלוּ רַחֲמָיו חֲדָשִׁים לַבְּקָרִים *his new mercies do not cease each morning*; or ins. הֵם *they* are new, as §2).

**2.** used predicatively in nom. cl., with subj. נֹאד *wineskin* Jos 9$_{13}$, כָּבוֹד *honour* Jb 29$_{20}$, זֶה *this (event)* Ec 1$_{10}$, הֵם *they*, i.e. mercies Lm 3$_{23}$ (if ins. הֵם).

**3.** as noun, **(the) new, new (one), newcomer, novelty,** etc. (but sometimes perh. used adverbially, **anew**), of new grain and other produce (Lv 26$_{10}$ 4QD$^f$ 1.2$_{10.10}$), gods (Dt 32$_{17}$), friends (Si 9$_{10}$), coming events (Is 42$_9$ 48$_6$), unheard of deeds or events (Jr 31$_{22}$ Ec 1$_9$ 4QShir Shabb$^c$ 4$_{11}$), deeds (Is 43$_{19}$), new creation (1QH 13$_{12}$ 16$_{14}$).

<SUBJ> בוא *come* Dt 32$_{17}$ (:: רִאשׁוֹן *first*), צמח *sprout* Is 42$_9$ 43$_{19}$, ידע *know* Si 10$_9$ (ח[ד]ש), appar. דמם *be silent* Si 10$_{9(erased)}$ (ח[ד]ש). <OBJ> ידע *know* Is 43$_{19}$ 48$_6$ (|| נצר pass. ptc. *secret*), שׂער *know* Dt 32$_{17}$, נגד hi. *declare* Is 42$_9$, שׁמע hi. *announce* Is 42$_9$ 48$_6$, עשׂה *do* Is 43$_{19}$, ברא *create* Jr 31$_{22}$ 1QH 13$_{12}$ (+ קֶדֶם *antiquity*) 16$_{14}$ (ח[דש]ה תבר]א). <CSTR> מעשי חדשות *deeds of new (things)*, i.e. new deeds 4QShirShabb$^c$ 4$_{11}$, כָּל־חָדָשׁ *every new (thing)* Ca 1$_9$ (אֵין כָּל־חָדָשׁ תַּחַת הַשָּׁמֶשׁ *there is not anything new under the sun*). <APP> אֱלֹהִים *gods* Dt 32$_{17}$, שֵׁד *demon* Dt 32$_{17}$. <PREP> לְ of direction, *to*, + זבח *sacrifice* Dt 32$_{17}$; מִן partitive, *(any) of, from among*, + בוא hi. *bring* 4QD$^f$ 1.2$_{10}$ (מן חד[ש]) 1.2$_{10}$; מֵחָדָשׁ *from new*, i.e. anew, + ברא *create* 4QBer$^b$ 2$_4$; מִפְּנֵי *before*, i.e. in order to make room for, + יצא hi. *take out* old grain Lv 26$_{10}$. <COLL> חֲגוּר חֲדָשָׁה appar. *girded (with) new (armour)/a new (sword)* 2 S 21$_{16}$ (or ins. חֶרֶב *sword*, as §1). Also 6QDeut(?)$_6$ 11QT 37$_2$. <SYN> §3 נצר pass. ptc. *secret*. <ANT> §1 יָשָׁן *old*, §§1, 3 רִאשׁוֹן *first*.*

→ חדשׁ *be new*.

**חֹדֶשׁ** I 281.2.87.8 n.m. **month**—Q חודש; cstr. חֹדֶשׁ (Q חודש); sf. חָדְשׁוֹ, חָדְשָׁהּ; pl. חֳדָשִׁים (Q חודשים); cstr. חָדְשֵׁי; sf. חָדְשָׁיו, חָדְשֵׁיכֶם (חָדְשֵׁכֶם), Q חודשיהם—**month** (e.g. Gn 7$_{11}$ 8$_{4.14}$ Ex 12$_2$ 1 S 6$_1$ 1 K 4$_7$), esp. beginning of month, **new moon,** and assoc. feast (e.g. 1 S 20$_{5.24.27.34}$ 2 K 4$_{23}$ Ezk 46$_{1.6}$ Ho 2$_{13}$ Am 8$_5$ Ps 81$_4$); also appar. of **mating season** of female camel (Jr 2$_{24}$).

<SUBJ> היה *be* 1 S 20$_{24}$ 1 K 4$_7$ 5$_{28}$, הפך ni. *be overturned* Est 9$_{22}$, נגע *arrive* Ezr 3$_1$||Ne 7$_{72}$, עבר *pass* Am 8$_5$ Arad ost. 5$_{13}$, אכל *eat*, i.e. devour Ho 5$_7$ (or em. יֹאכְלֵם חֹדֶשׁ *the new moon shall devour them* to יֹאכַל הֶחָסִיל *the locust shall devour*, or יֹאכַל מַשְׁחִית *the destroyer shall*

devour, or יְאָכְלוּ מְחַרְשִׁית *they will be destroyed by the scorching wind*, or יֹאכַל מְחַדֵּשׁ *an invader will consume*, from חדשׁ II), חדשׁ htp. *renew oneself* Si 43$_{8}$.

<NOM CL> הַחֹדֶשׁ הַזֶּה ... רֹאשׁ חֳדָשִׁים *this month shall be ... a beginning of months* Ex 12$_{2}$, חֹדֶשׁ מָחָר *(the) new moon is tomorrow* 1 S 20$_{5}$, מָחָר חֹדֶשׁ *tomorrow is (the) new moon* 1 S 20$_{18}$, הוּא הַחֹדֶשׁ הַשֵּׁנִי *it is the second month* (and vars.) 1 K 6$_{1.38}$ (+ יֶרַח *month*) 1 K 8$_{2}$||2 C 5$_{3}$ (1 K + יֶרַח), הוּא־חֹדֶשׁ שְׁבָט *it is the month of Shebat* (and vars.) 1 K 6$_{1}$ (הַחֹדֶשׁ) Zc 1$_{7}$ Est 2$_{16}$ 3$_{7.7.13}$ 8$_{9.12}$ 9$_{1}$ Ezr 10$_{9}$ 2 C 5$_{3}$ (הַחֹדֶשׁ), הַיּוֹם לֹא־חֹדֶשׁ *today, (which) is not a new moon* 2 K 4$_{23}$ (|| שַׁבָּת *sabbath*).

<OBJ> יכל *be able (to endure)* Is 1$_{13}$ (|| שַׁבָּת *sabbath*; + קְרֹא מִקְרָא *calling of assembly*), שׂנא *hate* Is 1$_{14}$ (|| מוֹעֵד *appointed time*), שׁמר *keep*, i.e. observe Dt 16$_{1}$, שׁבת hi. *cause to cease* Ho 2$_{13}$=4QpHos$^{a}$ 2$_{15}$ (חו]דשה]; || מָשׂוֹשׂ *joy*, חַג *festival*, שַׁבָּת *sabbath*, מוֹעֵד), שׁכח *forget* 4QJub$^{a}$ 1$_{14}$ ([ושכ]חו חודש]), בדא *devise* 1 K 12$_{33}$, כתב *write* perh. 4QpsJub$^{c}$ 2$_{5}$ ([החוד[שים]).

<CSTR> חֹדֶשׁ הָאָבִיב *month of Abib* Ex 13$_{4}$ 23$_{15}$ 34$_{18.18}$ (בְּחֹדֶשׁ הָאָבִיב; Sam בּוֹ *in it*) Dt 16$_{1.1}$, אֲדָר *of Adar* Est 3$_{7.13}$ 8$_{12}$ 9$_{1.15.17.19.21}$, אייר *of Iyar* GnzPs 2$_{4}$ (חודש) 3$_{10}$ 4$_{16}$ (חודש), גמול *of Gamul* 4QMishF$^{b}$ 1$_{4}$ ([חו]דש גמול), כִּסְלֵו *of Chislev* Ne 1$_{1}$, נִיסָן *of Nisan* Est 3$_{7}$ Ne 2$_{1}$, שְׁבָט *of Shebat* Zc 1$_{7}$, סִיוָן *of Sivan* Est 8$_{9}$, טֵבֵת *of Tebeth* Est 2$_{16}$, זִו *of Ziv* 1 K 6$_{1}$, יָמִים *of days*, i.e. a whole month Gn 29$_{14}$ Nm 11$_{20.21}$ 11QT 63$_{13}$ (חודש), חָדְשֵׁי הַשָּׁנָה *months of the year* Ex 12$_{2}$ Nm 28$_{14}$ 1 C 27$_{1}$ 11QT 14$_{9}$ ([חודשי]), חדש קציר *month of harvest of* wheat 4QPsJos$^{b}$ 12$_{7}$.

רוש החודש *head*, i.e. beginning, *of the month* 4QMish D 1$_{3.6}$ 2$_{4}$ ([רו]ש) 4QMishE$^{a}$ 1$_{5}$ ([רוא]ש החודש]) 4QRitPur 33.4$_{3}$ ([ר]אש ח]ודש), רֹאשׁ חֳדָשִׁים *head*, i.e. beginning, *of months* Ex 12$_{2}$ 11QT 14$_{9}$ ([ראוש חודשי]ם]), ראשי חודשים *heads*, i.e. beginnings, *of months* 4QPrFêtes$^{b}$ 32$_{2}$ 11QPs$^{a}$ 27$_{8}$ (החודשים) 11QT 11$_{10}$ ([ראשי החודשים]), רָאשֵׁי חָדְשֵׁיכֶם *heads*, i.e. beginnings, *of your months* Nm 10$_{10}$ (+ מוֹעֵד *appointed feast*, יוֹם *day* of joy) 28$_{11}$ 11QT 14$_{02}$ ([ראשי חודשיכמה]) 14$_{7}$ ([רא]שי חודשיכמה), מָחֳרַת הַחֹדֶשׁ *morrow of the new moon* 1 S 20$_{27}$, בֶּן־חֹדֶשׁ *son of a month*, i.e. one month old Lv 27$_{6}$ Nm 3$_{15+6t}$ 18$_{16}$ 26$_{62}$, דגלי חודשים *battalions of the months* 4QBer$^{a}$ 1$_{9}$, יוֹם הַחֹדֶשׁ *day of the month* Ex 40$_{2}$ 1 S 20$_{34}$ Ezk 46$_{1}$ (|| שַׁבָּת *sabbath*) 46$_{6}$, ימי חודש *days of the month* 1QS 10$_{3}$, עֹלַת חֹדֶשׁ *burnt offering of (each) month* Nm 28$_{14}$ (Sam החדש) 29$_{6}$ (הַחֹדֶשׁ) Ne 10$_{34}$ עוֹלַת הַתָּמִיד ... הֶחֳדָשִׁים appar. *the burnt offering of continuity*, i.e. daily burnt offering, ... *[and] of months*) 11QT 14$_{7}$ ([עולת חודש]) 14$_{13}$ ([עו]ל[ת] [החודש]) 25$_{7}$ ([עו]לת החודש), מַחֲלֹקֶת הַחֹדֶשׁ *division of the month* 1 C 27$_{4}$, מִסְפַּר חֳדָשָׁיו *number of his months* Jb 14$_{5}$ 21$_{21}$, שְׁנֵי חֳדָשִׁים *two months* Jg 11$_{38}$, שְׁלֹשׁ *three* months Gn 38$_{24}$ (Sam שלשת), שֵׁשֶׁת *six* months 1 K 11$_{16}$, כל חודש *every month* CD 14$_{13}$, כֹּל חָדְשֵׁי *all the months of* 1 C 27$_{1}$.

<APP> מוֹעֵד *appointed time* Ex 23$_{15}$ 34$_{18}$.

<ADJ> זֶה *this* Ex 12$_{2.3.6}$ 13$_{5}$ Lv 23$_{6.27.34}$ Nm 9$_{3}$ 28$_{17}$ 29$_{7.12(mss)}$ Ne 9$_{1}$ 4QJub$^{a}$ 1$_{1}$ ([לחודש ה]זה) 11QT 17$_{10}$ 25$_{10}$ 27$_{10}$.

רִאשׁוֹן *first* Ex 40$_{2.17}$ Lv 23$_{5}$ Nm 9$_{1}$ 20$_{1}$ 28$_{16}$ 33$_{3.3}$ Jos 4$_{19}$ Est 3$_{7.12}$ Dn 10$_{4}$ Ezr 6$_{19}$ 7$_{9}$ 8$_{31}$ 10$_{17}$ 1 C 12$_{16}$ 27$_{2.3}$ 2 C 29$_{3.17.17}$ 35$_{1}$ 1QJub$^{a}$ 27$_{19}$ ([לחודש חראשון]) 4QpGen$^{a}$ 1.1$_{22}$ 4QMishA 1.1$_{4}$ 4QMishB$^{a}$ 2.1$_{8}$ (החוד[ש הראש]ון) 4QMishH 1.2$_{1}$ ([הר]אשון]) 2$_{2}$ ([בחודש הראשון]) 2$_{4}$ ([ב]חודש הראשו]ן]) 3$_{2}$ ([בחוד]ש הראש]ון]) 4QShir Shabb$^{a}$ 1.1$_{1}$ 3.2$_{8}$ ([להחודש הראישון]) 4QShirShabb$^{b}$ 1$_{1}$ ([לחודש הראישון]) 14$_{9}$ ([בח]ודש הראישון]) 11QT 11$_{10}$ ([ה]ראישון]) 17$_{6}$, שֵׁנִי *second* Gn 7$_{11}$=4QpGen$^{a}$ 1.1$_{4}$ Gn 8$_{14}$ Ex 16$_{1}$ Nm 1$_{1.18}$ 9$_{11}$ 10$_{11}$ 1 S 20$_{27.34}$ 1 K 6$_{1}$ Ezr 3$_{8}$ 1 C 27$_{4}$ 2 C 3$_{2}$ 30$_{2.13.15}$ 4QMishD 1$_{3}$ ([ה]שני) 4QShirShabb$^{d}$ 1.2$_{18}$ ([לחודש השני]) 6QCal$_{1}$ ([החדש ה]שני) MasShirShabb 1$_{8}$ ([השני]), שְׁלִישִׁי *third* Ex 19$_{1}$ Est 8$_{9}$ 1 C 27$_{5}$ 2 C 15$_{10}$ 31$_{7}$ 4QJub$^{a}$ 1$_{1}$ ([בחוד]ש השל]ישי]) 4QpGen$^{a}$ 1.1$_{6}$ 1.2$_{1}$ 4QD$^{a}$ 18.5$_{17}$ 4QMishD 1$_{6}$ 4QShirShabb$^{f}$ 20.2$_{6}$ ([לחודש] השלישי), רְבִיעִי *fourth* 2 K 25$_{4}$ (if ins.) Jr 39$_{2}$ (mss הַחֲמִישִׁי) 52$_{6}$ 1 C 27$_{7}$, חֲמִישִׁי *fifth* Nm 33$_{38}$ 2 K 25$_{8}$||Jr 52$_{12}$ Jr 1$_{3}$ 28$_{1}$ 39$_{2(mss)}$ Zc 7$_{3}$ Ezr 7$_{8.9}$ 1 C 27$_{8}$, שִׁשִּׁי *sixth* Hg 1$_{1}$ 1 C 27$_{9}$ 4QMishC$^{a}$ 1$_{1}$ ([בחודש הששי]) 1$_{3}$ ([הששי]) 4Q MishD 2$_{4}$, שְׁבִיעִי *seventh* Gn 8$_{4}$ Lv 16$_{29}$ 23$_{24.27.34.39.41}$ 25$_{9}$ Nm 29$_{1.7.12}$ 1 K 8$_{2}$ 2 K 25$_{25}$||Jr 41$_{1}$ Jr 28$_{17}$ Ezr 3$_{1}$||Ne 7$_{72}$ 3$_{6}$ Ne 8$_{2.14}$ 1 C 27$_{10}$ 2 C 5$_{3}$ 7$_{10}$ 31$_{7}$ 4QpGen$^{a}$ 1.1$_{8.10}$ 4QMishA 4.3$_{8}$ ([ב]חדש ה]שביעי) 4QMishC$^{d}$ 2$_{5}$ ([חוד]ש) 11QMelch$_{26}$ ([בח]וד]ש ה]שביעי]) 11QT 25$_{2}$ (בח]ודש השביעי]), שְׁמִינִי *eighth* 1 K 6$_{38}$ 12$_{32.33}$ Zc 1$_{1}$ 1 C 27$_{11}$, תְּשִׁיעִי *ninth* Jr 36$_{9.22}$ Zc 7$_{1}$ Ezr 10$_{9}$ (חֹדֶשׁ הַתְּשִׁיעִי) 1 C 27$_{12}$ 4QMishC$^{b}$ 1$_{4}$ ([הת]שיעי), עֲשִׂירִי *tenth* Gn 8$_{5}$ 2 K

$25_{1}$||Jr $52_{4}$ Jr $39_{1}$ Ezk $24_{1}$ Est $2_{16}$ Ezr $10_{16}$ 1 C $27_{13}$ 4QpGen[a] $1.1_{11}$ (ה[ע]שירי]) 4QMishC[d] $1.2_{3}$; see also Coll.

<PREP> לְ of direction, *to*, + נפל hi. *cause to fall*, i.e. cast lot Est $3_{7}$ (מֵחֹדֶשׁ לְחֹדֶשׁ cause lot to fall *from month to month*, i.e. for each month).

לְ of possession, *of, (belonging) to* (usu. in ref. to first, etc., day of month) Gn $7_{11}$ $8_{4.5.13.14}$ Ex $12_{2.3.6.18.18}$ $16_{1}$ $40_{2.17}$ Lv $16_{29}$ $23_{5+6t}$ $25_{9}$ Nm $1_{1.18}$ $9_{5}$ $28_{16.17}$ $29_{1.7.12}$ $33_{3.38}$ Dt $1_{3}$ Jos $4_{19}$ $5_{10}$ 1 K $12_{32}$ 2 K $25_{1.3.8.27}$||Jr $52_{4.6.12.31}$ Jr $39_{2}$ Ezk $1_{1.2}$ $8_{1}$ $20_{1}$ $24_{1}$ $26_{1}$ $29_{1.17}$ $30_{20}$ $31_{1}$ $32_{1.17}$ $33_{21}$ $40_{1}$ $45_{18.20(mss).21.25}$ Hg $1_{1.15}$ $2_{1.20}$ Zc $1_{7}$ $7_{1}$ Est $3_{13}$ $8_{12}$ $9_{15.17.19.21}$ Dn $10_{4}$ Ezr $3_{6}$ $6_{19}$ $7_{9.9}$ $8_{31}$ $10_{9(mss).16.17}$ Ne $8_{2}$ $9_{1}$ 2 C $7_{10}$ $29_{17.17}$ $30_{15}$ $35_{1}$ CD $14_{13}$ 1QJub[a] $27_{19}$ ([לחודש]) 1QDM $1_{2}$ (לחו[דש]) perh. $3_{8}$ $3_{10.10.11}$ (ל[חודש]) perh. $3_{11}$ 4QJub[a] $1_{1}$ ([לחודש]) 4QpGen[a] $1.1_{17.19}$ (לשנים עשר] החודש] *on the twelfth month*) $1.2_{1}$ 4Q254a $3_{1}$ 4QShirShabb[a] $1.1_{1}$ $3.2_{8}$ ([לההחודש]) 4QShirShabb[d] $1.1_{30}$ $1.2_{18}$ ([לחודש]) 4QShirShabb[f] $20.2_{6}$ ([לחודש]) 4QPrQuot $1_{6}$ ([לחודש]) $1_{18}$ ([לחו[דש]) $7.4_{6}$ ([ל]חודש]) $11.5_{2}$ $29.8_{2}$ ([לחודש]) $29.8_{12}$ ([לחו]דש]) $29.8_{22}$ $33.10_{6}$ (both [לחודש]) $33.10_{18}$ ([ל]חודש]) $33.11_{6}$ ([ל]חודש]) $33.11_{14.22}$ $37.12_{13.23}$ (all four [לחודש]) $42_{4}$ ([ל]חודש]) $48_{3}$ $51_{6.17}$ $64_{1}$ $72_{8}$ $76_{1}$ (all six [לחודש]) $215_{2}$ ([לח]ודש]) $215_{11}$ ([לחוד]ש]) 11QT $11_{10}$ ([לחודש]) $14_{9}$ $17_{10}$ $25_{3}$ ([לחודש]) $27_{10}$ MasShirShabb $1_{8}$ Arad ost. $7_{3.5.7}$ $8_{3.4}$ $17_{8}$ 32.

לְ *at* or *in accordance with* Nm $28_{14}$ 1 C $27_{2+11t}$ 2 C $2_{3}$ $31_{3}$ (both || שַׁבָּת *sabbath*, מוֹעֵד *appointed feast*) 4QMishA $1.1_{4}$ perh. 4QMishA $4.2_{11}$ perh. 4QapPs[b] $1_{8}$ ([לח]דש]; || יוֹם ,מוֹעֵד *day*) 11QT $14_{8}$, + יצב htp. *stand* 1QM $2_{4}$ (|| שַׁבָּת ,מוֹעֵד), ידע hi. *make known* Is $47_{13}$, בכר pi. *bear early fruit* Ezk $47_{12}$, עשׂה *do*, i.e. offer sacrifice Ezr $3_{5}$ (+ מוֹעֵד), עלה hi. *offer sacrifice* 1 C $23_{31}$ 2 C $8_{13}$ (both || שַׁבָּת ,מוֹעֵד), אכל *eat* Ex $23_{15}$ $34_{18}$; [אות] ... ל[חודשים] *a sign ... for months* 4QJub[a] $2_{9}$.

לְ *as* 11QT $14_{9}$ ([לחודשי]).

בְּ of time, *in, on*, i.e. (day) of, *at, during* Gn $7_{11}$ Ex $19_{1}$ Lv $23_{5}$ Nm $9_{3}$ $10_{11}$ $28_{14.16}$ 1 K $5_{28}$ $6_{1}$ Is $66_{23}$ (|| שַׁבָּת *sabbath*) Jr $1_{3}$ Ezk $45_{17}$ (|| שַׁבָּת ,חַג *festival*, מוֹעֵד *appointed time*, ) $45_{20}$ Ezr $10_{9}$ GnzPs $2_{4}$ 4QpGen[a] $1.1_{6.8.10.14.22}$ 4QBer[a] $2_{7}$ 4QMishA $1.2_{3}$ $1.3_{2}$ ([בשנים עשר החדש] *on the twelfth month*) $1.3_{13.14}$ 4QMishB[a] $1.1_{4.5}$ $1.2_{7}$ (בעש[תי] עשר החודש] *on the eleventh month*) $1.2_{8}$ $1.3_{6.7}$ $2.1_{6}$ ([בעשתי ע]שר החודש]) $2.1_{7}$ ([בשנים] עשר החודש]) 4QMishB[b] $1.2_{5}$ ([באחד עשר החודש] *on the eleventh month*) $1.2_{7}$ ([בשנים עש]ר החודש]) $3_{6}$ ([באחד עשר החודש]) $3_{8}$ 4QMishC[a] $1_{1}$ ([ב]חודש]) $1_{3}$ $2_{3}$ 4QMishC[b] $1_{4}$ 4QMishC[d] $1.2_{3}$ $2_{5}$ (ב[חוד]ש]) $3_{2}$ ([ב]חודש]) 4QMishE[b] $2.3_{10}$ 4QMishF[b] $1_{4}$ ([בחו]דש]) 4QMishH $1.2_{1}$ $2_{2}$ ([בחוד]ש]) $2_{4}$ ([בחוד]ש]) $3_{2}$ ([ב]חודש]) 4QapPs[b] $1_{8}$ ([בח]דש]; || מוֹעֵד *appointed time*, יוֹם *day*) 4QShirShabb[b] $1_{1}$ ([בחו]דש]) 4QShirShabb[f] $68_{2}$ ([בחודש]) $14_{7}$ ([בחודשו]) 11QT $25_{2}$ ([בח]ודש]) $25_{10}$, + היה *be* Ex $40_{17}$ Lv $23_{24}$ Nm $10_{11}$ $29_{1}$ Dt $1_{3}$ 2 K $25_{25}$||Jr $41_{1}$ 2 K $25_{27}$||Jr $52_{31}$ Jr $36_{9}$ $52_{4}$ Ezk $24_{1}$ $32_{1}$ Hg $1_{1}$ Zc $1_{1}$ Ne $1_{1}$ $2_{1}$ 4QJub[a] $1_{1}$ ([ויהי] ... [בחוד]ש]), יבשׁ *be dry* Gn $8_{14}$, קרא ni. *be called* Est $3_{12}$ $8_{9}$, חזק *be strong* Jr $52_{6}$, בקע ni. *break out* Gn $7_{11}$=4QpGen[a] $1.1_{4}$, ho. *be breached* Jr $39_{2}$, מות *die* Nm $33_{38}$ Jr $28_{17}$.

בוא *come* Ex $19_{1}$ Nm $20_{1}$ 2 K $25_{1.8}$||Jr $52_{4.12}$ Jr $39_{1}$ Ezr $7_{8}$ 1 C $27_{1}$, קבץ ni. *be gathered* 2 C $15_{10}$, קהל ni. *be assembled* 4QD[a] $18.5_{17}$, עלה hi. *offer sacrifice* 1 K $12_{33.33}$, עבר *cross* 1 C $12_{16}$ 4QPsJos[b] $12_{3}$ ([ע]ברו]), hi. *cause* trumpet *to pass*, i.e. make proclamation Lv $25_{9}$ 11QMelch$_{26}$ ([בחו]ד[ש]), נסע *set out* Nm $33_{3}$, יצא *go out* Ex $13_{4}$ $34_{18}$ 1 C $27_{1}$, hi. *take out* Dt $16_{1}$, לקח ni. *be taken* Est $2_{16}$, גלה *go into exile* Jr $1_{3}$, נפל hi. *cause to fall*, i.e. cast lot Est $3_{7}$, מצא *find* Jr $2_{24}$ (or em. חָדְשָׁהּ *her month* to עָנֹּתָהּ *her being humiliated*).

עשׂה *do* Nm $9_{11}$ 1 K $12_{32}$ 2 C $30_{2.13}$ 11QT $17_{6}$ ([ועש]ו]), חלל hi. *begin* Ezr $3_{8}$ 2 C $3_{2}$ $31_{7}$, ראה *see* GnzPs $2_{4}$ $3_{10}$ $4_{16}$, ישׁב *dwell* Jr $36_{22}$ Ne $8_{14}$, נוח *rest* Gn $8_{4}$, יסד *lay foundation* 2 C $31_{7}$, בנה *build* 2 C $3_{2}$, כלה pi. *complete* 2 C $31_{7}$, עבד *serve* Ex $13_{5}$, חגג *celebrate (festival)* Lv $23_{41}$, שׁחה htpal. *bow down* Ezk $46_{3}$ (|| שַׁבָּת *sabbath*), חדשׁ htp. *renew oneself* Si $43_{8(B)}$ (בחדשו *in its month*; Bmg, M כשמו *according to its name*).

ענה pi. *afflict* Lv $16_{29}$, פתח *open* door 2 C $29_{3}$, בכה *weep* Zc $7_{3}$, תקע *blow* trumpet Ps $81_{4}$ (+ כֶּסֶא *full moon*), אמר *say* Jr $28_{1}$, דבר pi. *speak* Nm $9_{1}$, קרא *call* 1QDM $1_{1}$ ([ויקרא] ... בחו]דש]).

מִן of direction, *from*, + נפל hi. *cause to fall*, i.e. cast lot Est $3_{7}$ (מֵחֹדֶשׁ לְחֹדֶשׁ cause lot to fall *from month to month*, i.e. for each month), חרשׁ hi. *be silent* 4QD[b] $10_{1}$

(החריש לו[ מחודש לחודש] *he has kept silent concerning him from month to month*), שׁטף *overflow* 4QPsJos[b] 12₇.

כְּמִן *about*, + היה *be* 1 S 10₂₇ (if em. כְּמַחֲרִישׁ *as one who kept silent* to כְּמֵחֹדֶשׁ *about a month later*; 4QSam[a] [corrected] כמו חדש *about a month*).

מִדֵּי *according to the sufficiency of*, i.e. as often/so long as there is, + היה *be* Is 66₂₃ (|| שַׁבָּת *sabbath*).

עַד *unto*, i.e. for the duration of, + אכל *eat* Nm 11₂₀; *until* 4QPsJos[b] 12₇, + חסר *be lacking* Gn 8₅=4QpGen[a] 1.1₁₁.

<COLL> שְׁנַיִם חֳדָשִׁים *two months* Jg 11₃₇.₃₈(mss).₃₉ 1 K 5₂₈, שְׁלֹשָׁה חֳדָשִׁים (and vars.) *three months* 2 S 6₁₁||1 C 13₁₄ 2 S 24₁₃||1 C 21₁₂ 2 K 23₃₁||2 C 36₂ 2 K 24₈||2 C 36₉ Am 4₇ 1QS 7₆.₉ 4QD[a] 18.4₄ ([חודשי]ם), אַרְבָּעָה חֳדָשִׁים *four months* Jg 19₂ 20₄₇ 1 S 27₇, שִׁשָּׁה חֳדָשִׁים (and vars.) *six months* 2 S 2₁₁ 5₅ 2 K 15₈ Est 2₁₂.₁₂ 1 C 3₄ 1QS 7₃.₄.₅.₈ (corrected to שנה אחת *one year*) 7₁₂.₁₈ 4QD[a] 18.4₃ ([שו]שה חודשים) 18.4₁₀ ([חודשים]), שִׁבְעָה חֳדָשִׁים *seven months* 1 S 6₁ Ezk 39₁₂.₁₄, תִּשְׁעָה חֳדָשִׁים *nine months* 2 S 24₈.

עַשְׁתֵּי־עָשָׂר חֹדֶשׁ (and vars.) *eleventh month* Dt 1₃ Zc 1₇ 1 C 27₁₄ 1QDM 1₁ ([חו]דש ע[שתי עש]ר) 4QpGen[a] 1.1₁₄ (עשתי עשר החודש) 1.1₁₇ (עש[תי עשר ]החודש) 4QMishA 1.3₁₃ 4QMishB[a] 1.1₄ 1.2₇ ([בעש]תי עשר החודש) 1.3₆ 4QMishB[a] 2.1₆ (בעשתי ע[שר]) 2.2₃.₇ (ע[שתי עשר]) 2.3₂ ([עשתי) 2.4₁ ([עש]ר [החודש]) 2.3₆ (עש[תי עשר החודש]) [עשר החודש) 2.4₅ (עש]ר ה[חודש), אחד עשר החודש *eleventh month* 4QMishB[b] 1.2₅ 3₆ (both אחד עשר] [החודש), שְׁנֵים עָשָׂר חֹדֶשׁ (and vars.) *twelfth month* 2 K 25₂₇||Jr 52₃₁ Est 2₁₂ 3₁₃ 8₁₂ 9₁ 1 C 27₁₅ (הַחֹדֶשׁ) 4QpGen[a] 1.1₁₉ (שנים עשר [החודש]) 4QMishA 1.2₃ 4QMishA 1.3₂ ([בשנים עשר החדש]) 1.3₁₄ 4QMishB[a] 1.1₅ 1.2₈ 1.3₇ 2.1₇ ([שנים] עש[ר]) 2.2₃.₈ (שני]ם עשר הח[וד]ש) 2.3₃ ([בשנים]) 2.3₆ 2.4₁ (both [שנים עשר החודש]) 4QMishB[b] 1.2₇ (עש]ר החודש]) 3₈, appar. 4QMishB[a] 2.4₆ ([שנים החודש]), שְׁנֵי־עָשָׂר חֹדֶשׁ *twelfth month* Ezk 32₁.

וַיֵּשֶׁב עִמּוֹ חֹדֶשׁ יָמִים *and he dwelt with him a month of days* Gn 29₁₄, וְאָכְלוּ חֹדֶשׁ יָמִים *and they shall eat for a month of days* Nm 11₂₁, ובכתה את אביה ואת אמה חודש ימים *and she shall bewail her father and her mother for a month of days* 11QT 63₁₃, שֵׁשֶׁת חֳדָשִׁים יָשַׁב־שָׁם *he dwelt there for six months* 1 K 11₁₆, וַיֵּשֶׁב ... שְׁלֹשָׁה חֳדָשִׁים *and the ark of God remained ... for three months* 1 C 13₁₄, שְׁלֹשָׁה חֳדָשִׁים מָלַךְ *he reigned for three months* 2 K 23₃₁ ||2 C 36₂ 2 K 24₈||2 C 36₉, שִׁשָּׁה חֳדָשִׁים ... מָלַךְ *he reigned ... for six months* 2 K 15₈, [והובדל] שלושה חודשי[ם] (and var.) *and he shall be separated for three months* 4QD[a] 18.4₄.₁₀ ([חודשים]), ונענש ששה חודשים (and var.) *and he shall be punished for six months* 1QS 7₃.₄.₅.₆.₈.₁₂.₁₈ 4QD[a] 18.4₃ (ונע[נ]ש ש[שה חודשים]), וּקְבָרוּם ... שִׁבְעָה חֳדָשִׁים *and they shall bury them ... for seven months* Ezk 39₁₂, הַבָּאָה וְהַיֹּצֵאת חֹדֶשׁ בְּחֹדֶשׁ *which came and went month by month* 1 C 27₁, וְכִלְכְּלוּ ... אִישׁ חָדְשׁוֹ *and they supplied ... each one his month*, i.e. his monthly allocation 1 K 5₇, אוֹ־יֹמַיִם אוֹ־חֹדֶשׁ אוֹ־יָמִים ... יַחֲנוּ *whether it was for a couple of days or a month or days ... they would encamp* Nm 9₂₂.

Also 4QBer[b] 1₇ 4QMishA 5₁ 4QMishC[b] 1₁ ([חודש]) 4QPrQuot 219₁ .

<SYN> שַׁבָּת *sabbath*, חַג *festival*, מוֹעֵד *appointed time/festival*, מָשׂוֹשׂ *joy*.*

⇒ חדש *make new*.

**חֹדֶשׁ II** ₁ pr.n.f. **Hodesh,** wife of Shaharaim and mother of Jobab, Zibia, Mesha, Malcam, Jeuz, Sachia and Mirmah, <APP> אִשָּׁה *woman* 1 C 8₉. <PREP> מִן of instrument, *by (means of)*, + ילד hi. *beget* 1 C 8₉.

**חֲדָשָׁה** ₁ pl.n. **Hadashah,** city in the lowland of Judah, <NOM CL> בַּשְּׁפֵלָה אֶשְׁתָּאוֹל ... וַחֲדָשָׁה *in the lowland were Eshtaol ... and Hadashah* Jos 15₃₇. <APP> עִיר *city* Jos 15₃₇.

**חָדְשִׁי**, see תַּחְתִּים חָדְשִׁי *Tahtim-hodshi.*

**חֲדַתָּה**, see חָצוֹר חֲדַתָּה *Hazor-hadattah.*

**חוב** ₁.₁.₄ vb. **be guilty—Qal** ₀.₀.₃ Pf. Q חבו; + waw Q וחב—**be guilty,** <SUBJ> David 1 S 22₂₂ (if em. סַבֹּתִי perh. *I have caused* to חַבְתִּי *I am guilty*), בוא ptc. *one who enters* covenant CD 3₁₀ (הבו; appar. error for חבו *they were guilty*). <PREP> בְּ *in (respect of)*, + נֶפֶשׁ *soul*, i.e. life 1 S 22₂₂; of accompaniment, *with, in*, + נַחֲלָה *inheritance* 4Q418 138₁; of instrument, *by (means of)*, or of cause, *on account of* CD 3₁₀ (הבו), + דָּם *blood* 4QD[a] 6.2₁₃.

**Pi.** 1.1.1 + waw Q וחיב, וְחִיַּבְתֶּם—**make guilty,** i.e. **endanger** (Dn $1_{10}$ Si $11_{18}$); **declare guilty,** perh. **declare impure** (4QTohB$^a$ $1_2$), <SUBJ> Daniel, Hananiah, Mishael, Azariah Dn $1_{10}$, miser Si $11_{18}$ ([יש] יחו[י]ב שכרו *there is one who endangers his reward,* unless שָׂכָר *reward* is subj., i.e. *there is one whom his reward makes guilty*). <OBJ> רֹאשׁ *head* Dn $1_{10}$, שָׂכָר *reward* Si $11_{18}$ (unless שָׂכָר is subj.), בֶּגֶד *garment* 4QTohB$^a$ $1_2$. <PREP> לְ *before,* + מֶלֶךְ *king* Dn $1_{10}$.
→ חוֹב *debt,* חוֹבָה *condemnation.*

חוֹב 1 n.[m.] **debt,** <COLL> חֲבֹלָתוֹ חוֹב יָשִׁיב *he returns his pledge [as to his] debt* Ezk $18_7$ (or em. חֲבֹל הַחַיָּב *the pledge of the debtor*).
→ חוב *be guilty.*

חוֹבָה I 1 pl.n. **Hobah,** appar. town (perh. ancient Ube, mod. Tell es-Salihiye, 15 km E of Damascus), <NOM CL> חוֹבָה אֲשֶׁר מִשְּׂמֹאל לְדַמָּשֶׂק *Hobah which is to the left* (perh. north) *of Damascus* Gn $14_{15}$. <PREP> עַד *unto,* + רדף *pursue* Gn $14_{15}$.

[חוֹבָה] II 0.0.1 n.f. **condemnation**—Q cstr. חובת—**condemnation,** or perh. **doom,** <CSTR> חובת הארץ *condemnation of the land* 4QpIsa$^b$ $2_1$. <PREP> לְ *concerning* 4QpIsa$^b$ $2_1$. <COLL> חובת הארץ מפני החרב והרעב *the condemnation of the land before the sword and the famine* 4QpIsa$^b$ $2_1$.
→ חוב *be guilty.*

חוג 1 vb. **draw a circle—Qal** 1 Pf. חָג—<SUBJ> Y. Jb $26_{10}$ (or em. חָקַק/חַק חוּג *he decreed a horizon*). <OBJ> חֹק *statute,* i.e. boundary Jb $26_{10}$. <PREP> עַל *upon,* + פָּנִים *face* of waters Jb $26_{10}$; עַד *unto,* + תַּכְלִית *end,* boundary of light and darkness Jb $26_{10}$.*
→ חוּג *circle,* מְחוּגָה *compass.*

חוּג 3.1.1 n.[m.] **circle**—cstr. חוּג—with ref. to **horizon** (Is $40_{22}$ Jb $26_{10}$ [if em.] Pr $8_{27}$ 1QM $10_{13}$), **vault** of heaven (Jb $22_{14}$ Si $43_{12}$), <OBJ> חקק *mark out* Jb $26_{10}$ (if em. חָק־חָג *he drew a circle* to חָקַק/חַק חוּג *he decreed a circle*) Pr $8_{27}$, נקף hi. *surround* Si $43_{12(M[Yadin])}$ ([הקיפה] חוג; B חוק, either חֹק *statute,* i.e. boundary, or חוּק *circle;* Bmg הוד *splendour*), הלך htp. *walk* upon Jb $22_{14}$, ברא *create* 1QM $10_{13}$. <CSTR> חוּג שָׁמַיִם *circle,* i.e. vault *of heaven* Jb $22_{14}$, חוּג הָאָרֶץ *circle of the earth,* appar. vault of heaven Is $40_{22}$, חוג ימים *circle of the seas* 1QM $10_{13}$. <PREP> עַל *upon, above,* + ישׁב *sit* Is $40_{22}$. <COLL> חוּג עַל־פְּנֵי תְהוֹם *a circle on the face of the deep* Pr $8_{27}$, sim. Jb $26_{10}$ (מַיִם on the face of *the waters;* if em.; see Subj.).*
→ חוג *draw a circle.*

חוד 4 vb. **propound a riddle—Qal** 4 Pf. חַדְתָּ; impf. אָחוּדָה; impv. חוּד (חוּדָה)—**propound a riddle, recite a mocking poem** (Hb $2_6$; if em.; see Subj.), <SUBJ> Samson Jg $14_{12.13.16}$, בֵּן *son* of man Ezk $17_2$ (|| משׁל *tell a parable*), אֵלֶּה *these* nations Hb $2_6$ (if em. חִידוֹת *riddles* to יָחוּדוּ *they will recite a mocking poem*). <OBJ> חִידָה *riddle* Jg $14_{12.13.16}$ Ezk $17_2$, מְלִיצָה *mocking poem* Hb $2_6$ (if em.; see Subj.). <PREP> לְ of direction, *to,* + מֵרֵעַ *friend* Jg $14_{12}$, בֵּן *son* of people Jg $14_{16}$; *against,* + גֶּבֶר arrogant *man* Hb $2_6$ (if em.; see Subj.). <SYN> משׁל *tell a parable.**
→ חִידָה *riddle.*

חוה I 6.2.1 vb. **declare—Pi.** 6.2 Impf. אֲחַוֶּה, יְחַוֶּה (אֲחַוְּךָ); + waw וַאֲחַוֶּךָּ; ptc. Si מחוה; inf. חַוֹּת—**declare (to), proclaim, inform,** <SUBJ> Y. Hb $3_2$ (if em. חַיֵּיהוּ *revive it* to חַוֵּהוּ *declare it* or יְחַוֵּהוּ *he will declare it*) Si $42_{19}$ (|| גלה pi. *reveal*), Ben Sira Si $16_{25}$ (+ בהצנע *with carefulness;* || נבע hi. *pour out* spirit), Elihu Jb $32_{6.10.17}$ (+ ענה *answer*) $36_2$, Eliphaz Jb $15_{17}$ (+ ספר pi. *tell*), לַיְלָה *night* Ps $19_3$ (|| נבע hi. *pour out* speech), Job Jb $13_{17}$ (if em. וְאַחֲוָתִי *and my declaration* to וַאֲחַוֶּה *and I shall declare*), worshipper Ps $52_{11}$ (if em. וַאֲקַוֶּה *and I will wait for* to וַאֲחַוֶּה *and I will proclaim*). <OBJ> Job Jb $15_{17}$ $36_2$, רֵעַ *friend* of Job Jb $32_6$, דֵּעַ *opinion* Jb $32_{6.10.17}$ Si $16_{25}$, דַּעַת *knowledge* Ps $19_3$, פֹּעַל *work* Hb $3_2$ (if em.; see Subj.), שֵׁם *name* Ps $52_{11}$ (if em.; see Subj.), חֲלִיפָה *change* Si $42_{19}$, היה ni. ptc. *what has been* Si $42_{19}$. <PREP> לְ of direction, *to,* + לַיְלָה *night* Ps $19_3$; בְּ of place, *in,* + אֹזֶן *ear* Jb $13_{17}$ (if em.; see Subj.), קֶרֶב *middle* of years Hb $3_2$ (if em.; see Subj.); נֶגֶד *before,* + חָסִיד *loyal one* Ps $52_{11}$ (if em.; see Subj.). Also perh. 1Q42 $1_2$. <SYN> נבע hi. *pour out,* גלה pi. *reveal.*
→ אַחֲוָה *declaration.*

**חוה** II,* see שׁחה, htpal. *bow down.*

[חַוָּה] I 7 n.f. **tent village**—pl. cstr. חַוֹּת; sf. חַוֹּתֵיהֶם (Sam חוותים)—**tent village,** esp. חַוֹּת יָאִיר *tent villages of Jair,* as pl.n. *Havvoth-jair,* in Argob region of Bashan, **army camp** (2 S 23$_{13}$ if em.; see Cstr.), <SUBJ> היה *be* Jos 13$_{30}$, חנה *encamp* 2 S 23$_{13}$ (if em.; see Cstr.). <NOM CL> לוֹ חַוֹּת יָאִיר ... אֲשֶׁר בַּגִּלְעָד *belonging to him were the tent villages of Jair ... which are in Gilead* 1 K 4$_{13}$.

<OBJ> לכד *capture* Nm 32$_{41}$, לקח *take* 1 C 2$_{23}$, קרא *call,* i.e. name Nm 32$_{41}$ Dt 3$_{14}$ Jg 10$_{4}$.

<CSTR> חַוֹּת יָאִיר *tent villages of Jair,* usu. as pl.n. *Havvoth-jair* Nm 32$_{41}$ Dt 3$_{14}$ Jos 13$_{30}$ Jg 10$_{4}$ 1 K 4$_{13}$ 2 K 15$_{25}$ (if em.; see Prep.) 1 C 2$_{23}$, חַוֹּת חָם *tent villages of Ham* Nm 32$_{41}$ (if em. חַוֹּתֵיהֶם *their tent villages*), חַוַּת פְּלִשְׁתִּים *camp of Philistines* 2 S 23$_{13}$ (if em. חַיַּת *band of*); כָּל־חַוֹּת *all the tent villages of* Jos 13$_{30}$.

<PREP> אֵת *with* appar. 2 K 15$_{25}$ (if em. וְאֶת־הָאַרְיֵה *and with Arieh* to חַוֹּת יָאִיר *Havvoth-jair*).

חַוָּה II 2 pr.n.f. **Eve,** wife of Adam, mother of Cain, Abel and Seth, <SUBJ> היה *be* Gn 3$_{20}$, הרה *conceive* Gn 4$_{1}$, ילד *give birth* Gn 4$_{1.1}$, קנה *acquire* Gn 4$_{1}$, יסף hi. *add,* i.e. do again Gn 4$_{1}$, אמר *say* Gn 4$_{1}$. <OBJ> קרא *call,* i.e. name Gn 3$_{20}$, ידע *know* Gn 4$_{1}$. <APP> אִשָּׁה *woman* Gn 4$_{1}$.*

[חִוָּהְיָהוּ] 0.0.0.1 pr.n.m. **Hivvahiah,** father of Asaiah, <CSTR> בן חוהיהו *son of Hohiah* Seal 365 (8th/7th cent.). ⇒ ׳י Y.

[חוֹזֶה], see חֹזֶה I *seer.*

[חוֹזַי] 1 pr.n.m. **Hozai**—חוֹזָי—keeper or writer of chronicle concerning deeds of Manasseh, <CSTR> דִּבְרֵי חוֹזָי *words of Hozai* 2 C 33$_{19}$ (or em. חוֹזָיו *of his seers;* ms חוזים *of the seers*).

חוֹחַ I 11 n.m. **thorn; hook**—pl. חוֹחִים (חֹחִים)—**1. thorn(s), brier(s), thistle(s),** <SUBJ> יצא *go out,* i.e. grow Jb 31$_{40}$ (|| בָּאְשָׁה *stinkweed*), עלה *go up* Pr 26$_{9}$, שׁלח *send* 2 K 14$_{9}$||2 C 25$_{18}$. <NOM CL> הַחוֹחַ אֲשֶׁר בַּלְּבָנוֹן *the thistle that was in Lebanon* 2 K 14$_{9}$||2 C 25$_{18}$, חוֹחַ בְּמִבְצָרֶיהָ *thorns shall be in its strongholds* Is 34$_{13}$ (|| קִמּוֹשׂ *nettle,* + סִיר *thorn*), חוֹחַ בְּאָהֳלֵיהֶם *thorns shall be in their tents* Ho 9$_{6}$ (+ קִמּוֹשׂ). <OBJ> רמס *trample* 2 K 14$_{9}$||2 C 25$_{18}$. <PREP> בְּ of place, *among,* + חבא htp. *hide* perh. 1 S 13$_{6}$ (but prob. חוֹחַ II *hole*); כְּ *as* Ps 58$_{10}$ (if em. חַי *alive*); בֵּין *among* Ca 2$_{2}$ (שׁוֹשַׁנָּה בֵּין הַחוֹחִים *a lily among the thorns*). <COLL> קִמּוֹשׂ וָחוֹחַ *nettles and briers* Is 34$_{13}$.

**2. hook,** <PREP> בְּ of instrument, *by (means of), with,* + נקב *pierce* Jb 40$_{26}$, לכד *capture* 2 C 33$_{11}$ (unless בַּחֹחִים *in holes,* i.e. חוֹחַ II; || נְחֻשֶׁת du. *fetters*).

<SYN> §1 בָּאְשָׁה *stinkweed,* קִמּוֹשׂ *nettle;* §2 נְחֻשֶׁת du. *fetters.*

חוֹחַ II 1 n.[m.] **hole**—pl. חֲוָחִים—**hole, crevice,** <PREP> בְּ of place, *among,* + חבא htp. *hide* 1 S 13$_{6}$ (unless חוֹחַ I *briers;* or em. בַּחוֹרִים *in holes;* || מְעָרָה *cave,* סֶלַע *rock,* צְרִיחַ *excavation,* בּוֹר *pit*), לכד *capture* perh. 2 C 33$_{11}$ (but prob. בַּחֹחִים *with hooks,* i.e. חוֹחַ I). <SYN> מְעָרָה *cave,* סֶלַע *rock,* צְרִיחַ *excavation,* בּוֹר *pit.*

[חוט] 1 vb. **weigh out**—Hi. 1 Impf. Sam[mss] אחיטנה—**weigh out, account for,** <SUBJ> Jacob Gn 31$_{39}$(Sam[mss]) (MT חטא pi. *bear the loss of*). <OBJ> טְרֵפָה *torn animal* Gn 31$_{39}$(Sam[mss]).

[חוֹט] 0.0.1 n.[m.] **incisor**—pl. Q חטן (perh. pl. of חֵט)—appar. in ref. to **tusk** of hippopotamus or elephant, <COLL> שתין חטן *two tusks* 3QTr 9$_{2}$(Wolters) (Milik חפור *dig* two [cubits]).

חוּט 7.0.2 n.m. **thread**—cstr. חוּט; pl. cstr. Q חוטי—**thread, cord,** <SUBJ> סבב *go around* 1 K 7$_{15}$ Jr 52$_{21}$, נתק ni. *be snapped* Ec 4$_{12}$, שׁלשׁ pu. *be in three parts* Ec 4$_{12}$ (הַחוּט הַמְשֻׁלָּשׁ *the three-ply cord*). <OBJ> perh. קצה pi. *cut off* 1QpHab 9$_{14}$ 10$_{2}$. <CSTR> חוּט הַשָּׁנִי *thread of scarlet* Jos 2$_{18}$ Ca 4$_{3}$ 11QT 49$_{3}$ (ח[וט שני]), חוּט שְׁתֵּים־עֶשְׂרֵה אַמָּה *thread of twelve cubits* 1 K 7$_{15}$ Jr 52$_{21}$, חוטי נפשכה *threads of your life* 1QpHab 9$_{14}$ (נפ[שכה]; =Hb 2$_{10}$ חוֹטֵא נַפְשֶׁךָ appar. *[you] endanger/forfeit your life,* from חטא *sin*) 10$_{2}$; תִּקְוַת חוּט *cord of thread* Jos 2$_{18}$. <ADJ> זֶה *this* Jos 2$_{18}$. <PREP> בְּ of instrument, *by (means of), with* 11QT 49$_{3}$

(בח[וט]); כְּ *as* Jg 16$_{12}$ Ca 4$_{3}$; מִן *from*, מִחוּט וְעַד שְׂרוֹךְ־נַעַל *from a thread to the thong of a sandal*, i.e. neither of them (would I take) Gn 14$_{23}$.

***חוֹטֶא** 2 n.[m.] **sin**—cstr. חוֹטֵא—<SUBJ> אבד pi. *destroy* Ec 9$_{18}$ (unless ptc. of חטא *sin*, used nominally, *sinner* destroys; or em. חֵטְא *sin*). <OBJ> יעץ *counsel* Hb 2$_{10}$ (‖ בֹּשֶׁת *shame*). <CSTR> חוֹטֵא נַפְשֶׁךָ *sin of your soul*, i.e. a sin against yourself Hb 2$_{10}$ (unless ptc. of חטא *sin*, used verbally, *endangering your life*).

**חִוִּי** 25.0.1 gent. **Hivite,** and as collective sing. noun, **Hivites,** ancient inhabitant(s) of Canaan. **1. Hivites,** <SUBJ> היה *be* Jg 3$_{3}$, הלך *go* Jos 9$_{7}$ (or em. Horite), בוא *come* Jos 9$_{7.7}$, יצא *go out* Jos 9$_{7}$ 11$_{3}$, קבץ htp. *gather together* Jos 9$_{1}$, ישׁב *dwell* Jos 9$_{7}$ Jg 3$_{3}$ (or em. Hittite), שׁלם hi. *make peace* Jos 11$_{19}$ (לֹא־הָיְתָה עִיר אֲשֶׁר הִשְׁלִימָה ... בִּלְתִּי הַחִוִּי *there was not a city that made peace ... except the Hivites*), לחם ni. *fight* Jos 9$_{1}$ 24$_{11}$, לקח *take* Jos 9$_{7}$, אמר *say* Jos 9$_{7.7.7}$, שׁמע *hear* Jos 9$_{1.7}$, ציד htp. *provision oneself* Jos 9$_{7}$, מכא pi. *fill* Jos 9$_{7}$. <NOM CL> הַחִוִּי תַּחַת חֶרְמוֹן *the Hivites (who) were under Hermon* Jos 11$_{3}$. <OBJ> ילד *give birth*, i.e. beget Gn 10$_{17}$ 1 C 1$_{15}$, גרשׁ *expel* Ex 34$_{11}$ 11QT 2$_{3}$ ([גורש] ... [החוי]), pi. *expel* Ex 23$_{28}$ 33$_{2}$, ירשׁ *dispossess* Jos 3$_{10}$, נשׁל *clear away* Dt 7$_{1}$, חרם hi. *exterminate* Dt 20$_{17}$=11QT 62$_{15}$, חיה pi. *let live* Jos 9$_{7}$, נתן *give* Jos 24$_{11}$. <CSTR> עָרֵי הַחִוִּי *cities of the Hivites* 2 S 24$_{7}$, אֶרֶץ ... הַחִוִּי *land of ... the Hivites* Ex 3$_{17}$ 13$_{5}$, מְקוֹם ... הַחִוִּי *place of ... the Hivites* Ex 3$_{8}$, קֶרֶב ... הַחִוִּי *midst of ... the Hivites* Jg 3$_{5}$. <APP> גּוֹי *nation* Dt 7$_{1}$, יֹשֵׁב *inhabitant* Jos 11$_{19}$, בָּהָר וּבַשְּׁפֵלָה וּבָעֲרָבָה וּבָאֲשֵׁדוֹת וּבַמִּדְבָּר וּבַנֶּגֶב ... הַחִוִּי *in the hill country, and in the lowland, and in the Arabah, and on the slopes, and in the steppe country and in the Negeb ... the (land of) the Hivites*, etc. Jos 12$_{8}$. <PREP> לְ *to*, + שׁבע ni. *swear* Jos 9$_{7}$; *with*, + כרת *cut*, i.e. make covenant Jos 9$_{7.7.7.7}$, עשׂה *make* peace Jos 9$_{7}$; בְּ of instrument, *by (means of)*, + נסה pi. *test* Jg 3$_{3}$; מִן partitive, *(from) among*, + יתר ni. *remain over* 1 K 9$_{20}$‖2 C 8$_{7}$; אֶל *to(wards)*, + בוא hi. *bring* Ex 23$_{23}$, שׁלח *send* Jos 11$_{3}$, אמר *say* Jos 9$_{7.7.7}$.

**2.** as sing. noun, an individual **Hivite,** <APP> חֲמוֹר הַחִוִּי *Hamor the Hivite* Gn 34$_{2}$, צִבְעוֹן *Zibeon* Gn 36$_{2}$ (or em. הַחֹרִי *the Horite*).

**[חָוִיל]** 1 pr.n.m. **Havil,** son of Aram and grandson of Shem, בני ארם ... חויל *the sons of Aram were ... Havil* Gn 10$_{23(Sam)}$ (MT חול *Hul*).

**חֲוִילָה I** 4 pr.n.m. **Havilah, 1.** son of Joktan, grandson of Eber and descendant of Shem, <OBJ> ילד *give birth*, i.e. beget Gn 10$_{29}$ 1 C 1$_{23}$. **2.** son of Cush, descendant of Ham, <NOM CL> בְּנֵי כוּשׁ סְבָא וַחֲוִילָה *the sons of Cush were Seba and Havilah* Gn 10$_{7}$ 1 C 1$_{9}$.

**חֲוִילָה II** 5 pl.n. **Havilah, 1.** territory perh. east of Egypt, <PREP> מִן of direction, *from*, + שׁכן *dwell* Gn 25$_{18}$, נכה hi. *strike* 1 S 15$_{7}$. **2.** land where river Pishon flowed, <CSTR> אֶרֶץ הַחֲוִילָה *land of Havilah* Gn 2$_{11}$ (Sam[mss] חֲוִילָה). **3.** hill in Judaean desert, appar. ident. with חֲכִילָה *Hachilah*, <CSTR> גִּבְעַת הַחֲוִילָה *hill of Havilah* 1 S 23$_{19(mss)}$ 26$_{1(mss)}$ (both L הַחֲכִילָה *Hachilah*, mss חֲבִילָה *Habilah*).

**חול I** 8.0.1 vb. **whirl—Qal** 5 Pf. חָלָה, חָלוּ; impf. יָחוּל, יָחִלוּ; inf. חוּל—**dance** (Jg 21$_{21}$), **whirl, move about** (Jr 23$_{19}$ 30$_{23}$ Ho 11$_{6}$ Lm 4$_{6}$ [unless חול II *be weak* or em. חָלוּ *they whirled* to חָלוּ (חלה) *they were weak*]), **fall** (2 S 3$_{29}$).

<SUBJ> בַּת *daughter* Jg 21$_{21}$, יָד *hand* Lm 4$_{6}$, סַעַר *tempest* Jr 23$_{19}$ 30$_{23}$, חֶרֶב *sword* Ho 11$_{6}$, דָּם *blood(guilt)* 2 S 3$_{29}$. <PREP> בְּ of accompaniment, *with, in*, + מָחוֹל *dance* Jg 21$_{21}$; *against*, + Sodom Lm 4$_{6}$, עִיר *city* Ho 11$_{6}$; עַל *upon*, + רֹאשׁ *head* 2 S 3$_{29}$ Jr 23$_{19}$ 30$_{23}$, בַּיִת *house* 2 S 3$_{29}$ (mss, 4QSam[a]) (L אֶל *to*).

**Pol.** 2.0.1 Ptc. מְחֹלְלוֹת (Q מחוללות)—**1. dance,** <SUBJ> עַם *people* 1 K 1$_{40}$ (if em. מְחַלְּלִים בַּחֲלִלִים *playing flutes* to מְחֹלְלִים בִּמְחֹלוֹת *dancing with dances*). <PREP> בְּ of accompaniment, *with* + מְחוֹלָה *dance* 1 K 1$_{40}$ (if em.; see Subj.).

**2.** ptc. used as noun, **dancer,** masc. Ps 87$_{7}$ (if em. חֹלְלִים *flautists*, from חלל IV, to מְחֹלְלִים *dancers*), fem. Jg 23$_{13}$ 1 S 18$_{6}$ (if em.; see Subj.) perh. 4Q285 5$_{5}$, <SUBJ> יצא *go out* 1 S 18$_{6}$ (if em. וְהַמְּחֹלוֹת *and the dances* to וּמְחֹלְלוֹת *and dancers*), קרא *meet* 1 S 18$_{6}$ (if em.). <OBJ>

גזל *snatch* Jg 23$_{13}$. <PREP> בְּ of place. *among* Ps 87$_{7(ms)}$ (if em.); כְּ *as* Ps 87$_7$ (if em.; + שׁיר ptc. *singer*); of accompaniment, *with* perh. 4Q285 5$_5$; מִן of direction, + נשׂא *take* Jg 23$_{13}$.

**Htpol.** 1 Ptc. מִתְחוֹלֵל—**whirl,** <SUBJ> סַעַר *tempest* Jr 23$_{19}$.*

→ מָחוֹל *dance,* מְחוֹלָה *dance.*

*חול II 1 vb. **be weak—Qal** Pf. חָלוּ—**be weak,** <SUBJ> יָד *hand* Lm 4$_6$ (unless חול I *writhe*; or em. חָלוּ, i.e. חלה *be weak*). <PREP> בְּ of instrument, *by (means of), through* Lm 4$_6$ (if em.).

חוֹל I 23.2.1 n.m. **sand**—cstr. חוֹל—<SUBJ> ספר ni. *be counted* Gn 32$_{13}$ Ho 2$_1$, מדד ni. *be measured* Jr 33$_{22}$ Ho 2$_1$. <NOM CL> חוֹל אֲשֶׁר עַל־שְׂפַת הַיָּם (and vars.) *the sand that is upon the seashore* Gn 22$_{17}$ Jos 11$_4$ Jg 7$_{12}$ 1 S 13$_5$ 2 S 17$_{11}$ 1 K 4$_{20}$ 5$_9$ 4QpsJub$^a$ 2.1$_6$ (כול corrected to החול). <OBJ> שׂים *place* as a border Jr 5$_{22}$.

<CSTR> חוֹל הַיָּם *sand of the sea* Gn 32$_{13}$ 41$_{49}$ Is 10$_{22}$=4QpIsa$^a$ 2$_2$ ([חול הים])=4QpIsa$^c$ 4.2$_{13}$ ([חול הים]) Jr 33$_{22}$ Ho 2$_1$, יַמִּים *of the seas* Jr 15$_8$ Ps 78$_{27}$ Jb 6$_3$; טְמוּנֵי חוֹל *hidden treasures of the sand* Dt 33$_{19}$, נֵטֶל הַחוֹל *weight of the sand* Pr 27$_3$.

<PREP> בְּ of place, *in*, + טמן *hide* Ex 2$_{12}$; כְּ *as* Gn 22$_{17}$ 32$_{13}$ 41$_{49}$ Jos 11$_4$ Jg 7$_{12}$ 1 S 13$_5$ 2 S 17$_{11}$ 1 K 4$_{20}$ 5$_9$ Hb 1$_9$=1QpHab 3$_{14}$ (כח[ול]) Ps 78$_{27}$ Jb 29$_{18}$ (unless חול II *phoenix*), + היה *be* Is 10$_{22}$=4QpIsa$^a$ 2$_2$ ([כחו]ל)=4QpIsa$^c$ 4.2$_{13}$ ([כחול]) Is 48$_{19}$ Ho 2$_1$; מִן of direction, *from* Si 40$_{13(B)}$ (Bmg, M חַיִל *wealth*); of comparison, *(more) than*, + רבה *be many* Ps 139$_{18}$, עצם *be numerous* Jr 15$_8$, כבד *be heavy* Jb 6$_3$; אֶל *to* Si 40$_{13(B)}$ (Bmg, M חַיִל *wealth*).

<COLL> חוֹל as abundant, + כּוֹכָב *star* Gn 22$_{17}$, צָבָא *host* of heaven Jr 33$_{22}$ (||), עָפָר *dust* Ps 78$_{27}$ (||), מָעָה *grain* Is 48$_{19}$, רֹב *multitude* Gn 32$_{13}$ Jos 11$_4$ Jg 7$_{12}$ 1 S 13$_5$ 2 S 17$_{11}$ 1 K 4$_{20}$, הַרְבֵּה מְאֹד *very much* Gn 41$_{49}$; חוֹל as heavy, + אֶבֶן *stone* Pr 27$_3$ (||).

<SYN> צָבָא *host* of heaven, עָפָר *dust*, אֶבֶן *stone*.*

חוֹל II 1 n.[m.] **phoenix,** <PREP> כְּ *as*, + רבה hi. *multiply* days Jb 29$_{18}$ (unless חוֹל I *sand*).

חוּל 2.0.1 pr.n.m. **Hul, 1.** son of Aram and grandson of Shem or brother of Aram and son of Shem, <NOM CL> בְּנֵי אֲרָם עוּץ וְחוּל *the sons of Aram were Uz and Hul* Gn 10$_{23}$ (Sam חוץ וחויל *Huz and Havil*), בְּנֵי שֵׁם ... עוּץ וְחוּל *the sons of Shem were ... Uz and Hul* 1 C 1$_{17}$ (or em. בְּנֵי אֲרָם עוּץ וְחוּל *the sons of Aram were Uz and Hul*). **2.** nation descended from the preceding, <NOM CL> עוץ חול ... אשר בעבר פורת *Uz and Hul ... which are beyond the Euphrates* 1QM 2$_{11}$. <APP> בֵּן *son* of Aram 1QM 2$_{11}$. <PREP> בְּ *against*, + לחם ni. *fight* 1QM 2$_{11}$.

חוּם 4 adj. **brown,** colour of sheep, **1.** used attributively of שֶׂה *sheep* Gn 30$_{32}$ (+ נָקֹד *speckled,* טלא pass. ptc. *spotted*). **2.** used as predicative adj. or noun, **brown (one),** <NOM CL> כֹּל אֲשֶׁר־אֵינֶנּוּ ... חוּם בַּכְּבָשִׂים *every one which is not ... (a) brown one among the sheep* Gn 30$_{33}$ (+ נָקֹד, טלא pass.). <OBJ> סור hi. *remove* Gn 30$_{35}$. <CSTR> כָּל־חוּם *every brown one* Gn 30$_{35}$ (+ בַּכְּבָשִׂים *among the sheep*) 30$_{40}$ (+ בְּצֹאן *in the flock of* Laban). <PREP> אֶל *to*, + נתן *give*, i.e. place Gn 30$_{40}$ (+ עָקֹד *striped*).*

חוֹמָה 133.0.11 n.f. **wall**—חֹמָה; cstr. חוֹמַת; sf. חוֹמָתָהּ; du. חֹמֹתַיִם (חֹמֹתָיִם); pl. חוֹמוֹת (חֹמוֹת); cstr. חוֹמוֹת (חֹמוֹת, חוֹמֹת); sf. חוֹמֹתַי, חוֹמֹתֶיךָ (חֹמֹתֶיךָ), חוֹמוֹתַיִךְ (חוֹמֹתַיִךְ, חֹמֹתַיִךְ, חוֹמוֹתַיִךְ), חוֹמֹתֶיהָ (חוֹמוֹתֶיהָ)—wall of city (e.g. Dt 28$_{52}$ Jos 2$_{15}$ 6$_{5.20}$ 1 S 31$_{10.12}$), of building (e.g. Ezk 40$_5$ 42$_{20}$ Lm 2$_7$), wall as description of Y. (Zc 2$_9$), of prophet (Jr 1$_{18}$ 15$_{20}$), of virtuous woman (Ca 8$_{9.10}$), of waters of Red Sea (Ex 14$_{22.29}$).

<SUBJ> היה *be* 1 S 25$_{16}$ Zc 2$_9$, שׁלם *be finished* Ne 6$_{15}$, קשׁר ni. *be joined together* Ne 3$_{38}$, בנה ni. *be built* Ne 7$_1$, בצר pass. *be fortified* Dt 28$_{52}$ Is 2$_{15}$ Jr 15$_{20}$, שׂגב ni. *be high* Is 30$_{13}$ Pr 18$_{11}$ 1QH 6$_{25}$ 7$_8$ 1QSb 5$_{23}$, זוע htpalp. *be moved to and fro* 1QH 7$_9$, הרס ni. *be torn down* Jr 50$_{15}$, פרץ pu. *be broken down* Ne 1$_3$, ערר htpalp. *be demolished* Jr 51$_{58}$, רעשׁ *quake* Ezk 26$_{10}$, נפל *fall* Jos 6$_{5.20}$ 1 K 20$_{30}$ Jr 51$_{44}$ Ezk 38$_{20}$.

<NOM CL> הַמַּיִם לָהֶם חֹמָה *the waters were to them (as) a wall* Ex 14$_{22.29}$ 4QPentPar$^b$ 6$_5$ ([המי]ם להם חומה]), מַיִם חוֹמָתָהּ *water was its wall* (the city No's) Na 3$_8$ (if em.), מים חו[מ]ותיה *water was its walls* 4QpNah 3.3$_{10}$, חו[מותיה] כעקרה *its walls are as a barren women* 4Qap

Lam$^{a}$ 2$_{6}$, חוֹמֹתַיִךְ נֶגְדִּי תָּמִיד *your walls are before me continually* Is 49$_{16}$=4QTanḥ 1.2$_{5}$ (חומותיך נג[די תמיד]), הִנֵּה חוֹמָה מִחוּץ לַבַּיִת *behold the wall is outside the house* Ezk 40$_{5}$, אֲנִי חוֹמָה *I am a wall* Ca 8$_{10}$, אִם־חוֹמָה הִיא *if she is a wall* Ca 8$_{9}$, היאה חומת הבחן *it is a wall of testing* 1QS 8$_{7}$, לוֹ חֹמָה *the wall belonged to it* Lv 25$_{30(Qr)}$, sim. Ezk 42$_{20}$, וְלַחוּצָה הַחוֹמָה הָאַחֶרֶת *and at the outside was the other wall* 2 C 32$_{5}$, אֵין לָהֶם חֹמָה *they do not have a wall* Lv 25$_{31}$.

<OBJ> עלה *go up on* Jl 2$_{7}$, שׁמר *keep* Ca 5$_{7}$, שׁית *place* Is 26$_{1}$, נצב hi. *set up* 4QTestim$_{26}$ (+ מִגְדָּל *tower*), בנה *build* 1 K 3$_{1}$ 9$_{15}$ Is 60$_{10}$ Ps 51$_{20}$ Ne 2$_{17}$ 3$_{15.33.38}$ 6$_{1.6}$ 2 C 32$_{5}$ 33$_{14}$ 1QH 6$_{26}$, בצר pi. *fortify* Is 22$_{10}$, אבל hi. *cause mourning* Lm 2$_{8}$, נפל hi. *bring down* 2 S 20$_{15}$, הרס *tear down* Ezk 26$_{12}$, נתץ *tear down* 2 K 25$_{10}$||Jr 39$_{8}$||52$_{14}$, pi. *tear down* 2 C 36$_{19}$, פרץ *tear down* Ne 3$_{35}$ 2 C 26$_{6.6.6}$, שׁחת pi. *ruin* Ezk 26$_{4}$, hi. *destroy* Lm 2$_{8}$, סגר hi. *deliver* Lm 2$_{7}$, טהר pi. *declare clean* Ne 12$_{30}$, קרא *call* Is 60$_{18}$.

<CSTR> חוֹמַת אַשְׁדּוֹד *wall of Ashdod* 2 C 26$_{6}$, בָּבֶל *of Babylon* Jr 51$_{44.58(mss)}$, בֵּית שָׁן *of Beth-shan* 1 S 31$_{10.12}$, דַּמֶּשֶׂק *of Damascus* Jr 49$_{27}$, גַּת *of Gath* 2 C 26$_{6}$, עַזָּה *of Gaza* Am 1$_{7}$, יַבְנֵה *of Jabneh* 2 C 26$_{6}$, יְרוּשָׁלַםִ *of Jerusalem* 1 K 3$_{1}$ 9$_{15}$ 2 K 14$_{13}$||2 C 25$_{23}$ Ne 1$_{3}$ 2$_{17}$ 12$_{27}$ 2 C 36$_{19}$, רַבָּה *of Rabbah* Am 1$_{14}$, צֹר *of Tyre* Am 1$_{10}$, הָעִיר *of the city* Jos 6$_{5}$ Ne 2$_{8}$, הָעֹפֶל *of Ophel* Ne 3$_{27}$ 2 C 27$_{3}$, בְּרֵכַת *of the pool of* Ne 3$_{15}$, בַּת *of the daughter of* Lm 2$_{8.18}$, אֵשׁ *of fire* Zc 2$_{9}$, נְחֹשֶׁת *of bronze* Jr 1$_{18}$ 15$_{20}$, אַבְנֵיהֶם *of their stones* Ne 3$_{35}$, עוז *of strength* 1QH 3$_{37}$ 5$_{37}$ ([חומת עו]ז) 6$_{26}$ ([חומת] עוז), אֲנָךְ *of tin* Am 7$_{7}$, בחן *of testing* 1QH 7$_{9}$ 1QS 8$_{7}$ (הבחן).

חוֹמֹת בָּבֶל *walls of Babylon* Jr 51$_{12.58}$ (חֹמוֹת), יְרוּשָׁלַםִ *of Jerusalem* 2 K 25$_{10}$||Jr 39$_{8}$ Ne 2$_{13}$ (mss חוֹמַת *wall of*) Ps 51$_{20}$ (חומות) Ne 4$_{1}$ (חֹמוֹת; mss חוֹמַת), אַרְמְנוֹתֶיהָ *of its fortresses* Lm 2$_{7}$ (or em. חֶמְדַּת אֹצְרוֹתֶיהָ *delight of its treasures*), חֹמוֹת צֹר *walls of Tyre* Ezk 26$_{4}$.

קִיר הַחוֹמָה *upper surface of the wall* Jos 2$_{15}$, מִשְׂגַּב חוֹמֹתַיִךְ *high* fortifications *of your walls* Is 25$_{12}$, מְלֶאכֶת הַחוֹמָה *work of the wall* Ne 5$_{16}$, חֲנֻכַּת חוֹמַת *dedication of wall of* Ne 12$_{27}$, כָּל־חוֹמָה *every wall* Is 2$_{15}$ Ezk 38$_{20}$, כָּל־הַחוֹמָה *all the wall* Ne 3$_{38}$ 2 C 32$_{5}$, כָּל־חוֹמֹת *all walls of* 2 K 25$_{10(ms)}$||Jr 52$_{10}$ כָּל־חוֹמֹתֶיהָ *all of its walls* Jr 1$_{15}$.

<APP> עִיר *city* Lv 25$_{29}$, נְחֹשֶׁת *bronze* Jr 1$_{18}$.

<ADJ> גְּבֹהָה *high* Dt 3$_{5}$ 28$_{52}$, רְחָבָה *broad* Jr 51$_{58}$ Ne 3$_{8}$ 12$_{38}$, חִיצוֹן *outer* 2 C 33$_{14}$, אַחֵר *other* 2 C 32$_{5}$, זֹאת *this* Ne 5$_{16}$.

<PREP> לְ of benefit, *to, for*, + קרה *happen* Ne 2$_{8}$; of possession, *(belonging to)* Ne 12$_{37}$; *as* 1QH 7$_{9}$, + היה *be* 1QH 3$_{37}$, נתן *give*, i.e. appoint Jr 1$_{18}$ 15$_{20}$; *with respect to* Ne 4$_{7}$, + עלה *go up, advance*, of progress in rebuilding wall Ne 4$_{1}$.

בְּ of place, *in, on, at, among* Is 30$_{13}$ 1QSb 5$_{23}$, + ישׁב *dwell* Jos 2$_{15}$, רוץ *run* Jl 2$_{9}$, שׁלח pi. *send* Am 1$_{7.10}$, עוז *seek refuge* 1QH 6$_{25}$, נתן *give* Is 56$_{5}$ (+ בַּיִת *house*), תקע *fasten* body 1 S 31$_{10}$, יצת hi. *kindle* fire Jr 49$_{27}$ Am 1$_{14}$.

בְּ *against, at*, + נתן *give*, i.e. direct, battering ram Ezk 26$_{9}$, בנה *build* Ne 4$_{4}$ (+ יכל *be able*) 4$_{11}$ 2 C 27$_{3}$; *of*, + חזק hi. *repair* Ne 3$_{13}$; introducing object, + בטח *trust* Dt 28$_{52}$, פרץ *tear down* 2 K 14$_{13}$||2 C 25$_{23}$, שׂבר *inspect* Ne 2$_{13.15}$.

כְּ *as* Pr 18$_{11}$, + שׂים *place* 1QH 7$_{8}$.

מִן of direction, *from*, + לקח *take* 1 S 31$_{12}$.

אֶל *to*, + נגשׁ ni. *go near* 2 S 11$_{21}$, שׁוב *go back* Ne 4$_{9(Qr)}$; *at, by, against*, + הלך *go* 2 S 18$_{24}$, נשׂא *raise* standard Jr 51$_{12}$.

עַל *upon* 2 K 18$_{26}$||2 C 32$_{18}$||Is 36$_{11}$ Ezk 27$_{11}$, + היה *be* 2 K 6$_{26}$ (+ עבר ptc. *pass by*), פרד ni. *be separated* Ne 4$_{13}$, סבב pol. *encircle* Ps 55$_{11}$, עבר *pass by* 2 K 6$_{30}$, ישׁב *sit* 2 K 18$_{27}$||Is 36$_{12}$, נצב ni. *stand* Am 7$_{7}$, פקד hi. *appoint* Is 62$_{6}$, תלה pi. *hang* Ezk 27$_{11}$, עלה hi. *offer* sacrifice 2 K 3$_{27}$; *against* Is 2$_{15}$ (+ מִגְדָּל *tower*), + נתן *give* Jr 1$_{15}$.

אֵין *without*, + פרץ pass. *be breached* Pr 25$_{28}$; בְּאֵין *without*, + ישׁב *dwell* Ezk 38$_{11}$; בֵּין *between* 2 K 25$_{4}$||Jr 39$_{4}$||52$_{7}$, + עשׂה *make* Is 22$_{11}$; בְּעַד *behind*, + שׁלך ho. *be thrown* through 2 S 20$_{21}$; מִחוּץ לְ *outside of*, + צור *besiege* Jr 21$_{4}$; נֶגֶד *opposite*, + לין *spend night* Ne 13$_{21}$; עַד *until* Ne 12$_{38}$, + עזב *forsake* Ne 3$_{8}$ (or em. עזר *restore*), חזק hi. *repair* Ne 3$_{27}$; מֵעַל *from (upon)*, + ירה hi. *shoot* arrow 2 S 11$_{20.24}$, שׁלך hi. *cast* 2 S 11$_{21}$; מֵעַל לְ *from (upon over)* Ne 12$_{31.38}$, + עלה hi. *bring up* Ne 12$_{31}$, תַּחַת *under* 3QTr 2$_{10}$.

<COLL> כָּל־אֵלֶּה עָרִים בְּצֻרוֹת חוֹמָה גְבֹהָה *all these were fortified cities (with) high wall(s)* Dt 3$_{5}$, שִׁשִּׁים עָרִים גְּדֹלוֹת חוֹמָה *sixty great cities (with) wall(s)* 1 K 4$_{13}$, יְמַהֲרוּ חוֹמָתָהּ *they will make haste (to) its walls* Na 2$_{6}$, עָרֵי מָצוֹר חוֹמוֹת *cities of fortification (with) walls* 2 C 8$_{5}$, וְנָסֵב חוֹמָה *and we will surround (them with) a wall* 2 C 14$_{6}$.*

[חוֹנִי] 0.0.4 pr.n.m. **Honi**—Q חני—**1.** landowner mentioned in deed of sale, <NOM CL> ת[חומי המ]קום ה[זה] מזרח חוני *the limits of this place are, at the east, Honi* Mur 22 $1_{11}$. **2.** son of Jonathan and father of Salome, mentioned in deed of sale, perh. ident. with preceding, <CSTR> בת חני *daughter of Honi* Mur 30 $1_{6}$ $2_{26}$ (חוני) $2_{33}$ (ברת חוני). <APP> בַּר *son* Mur 30 $1_{6}$ $2_{26}$. **3.** appar. father of Zadok, T. en-Naṣbeh inscr. 6 (חנ[י]).

[חוֹנָן] 0.0.0.1 pr.n.m. **Honan,** son of Jaazaniah, <APP> בֵּן *son* Seal 21. <PREP> לְ of possession, *(belonging) to* Seal 21.

חוס 25.0.2 vb. **pity—Qal** 24 Pf. חָסָה, חַסְתָּ, חָסְתָה; impf. יָחֹס (יָחוּס), 3fs תָּחוֹס (תָּחֹס, תָּחוּס), אָחוּס; + waw 3fs וַתָּחָס, 2ms Q ותחס; impv. חוּסָה—**pity, look with compassion (upon), spare,** <SUBJ> Y. Jr $13_{14}$ (|| חמל *spare,* רחם pi. *have compassion*) Ezk $24_{14}$ (|| פרע *let go,* נחם ni. *repent*) Jl $2_{17}$ Jon $4_{11}$ Ne $13_{22}$ (+ זכר *remember*) 4QDibHam$^{a}$ $1.2_{8}$, David 1 S $24_{11}$ (if em. וַתָּחָס *and she spared* to וָאָחֹס *and I spared*), Jonah Jon $4_{10}$, Nebuchadrezzar Jr $21_{7}$ (|| חמל, רחם pi.), מֶלֶךְ *king* Jr $21_{7}$ Ps $72_{13}$ (+ ישע hi. *save*), עַיִן *eye* Gn $45_{20}$ Dt $7_{16}$ $13_{9}$ (+ חמל) $19_{13.21}$=11QT $61_{12}$ Dt $25_{12}$ 1 S $24_{11}$ (if וַתָּחָס is *and* my eye *spared*) Is $13_{18}$ (+ רחם pi.) Ezk $5_{11}$ $7_{4.9}$ $8_{18}$ $9_{5.10}$ $16_{5}$ (all seven + חמל) $20_{17}$ (:: שחת pi. *destroy*); subj. not specified, 1 S $24_{11}$ (unless em.; see above).

<PREP> כְּ *according to,* + רֹב *abundance* of mercy Ne $13_{22}$; עַל *upon,* + Saul 1 S $24_{11}$, Nehemiah Ne $13_{22}$, Zedekiah Jr $21_{7}$, עַם *people* Dt $7_{16}$ Jr $21_{7}$ Jl $2_{17}$, אֲדָמָה *land* Ezk $7_{4}$, Israel Ezk $20_{17}$, Jerusalem Ezk $16_{5}$, Nineveh Jon $4_{11}$, עִיר *city* Jon $4_{11}$, אִישׁ *man* Dt $19_{13}$, אִשָּׁה *wife* Dt $13_{9}$, אָב *father* 4QDibHam$^{a}$ $1.2_{8}$, בֵּן *son* Dt $13_{9}$ Is $13_{18}$, בַּת *daughter* Dt $13_{9}$, אָח *brother* Dt $13_{9}$, מֶלֶךְ *king* Jr $21_{7}$, עֶבֶד *servant* Jr $21_{7}$, רֵעַ *friend* Dt $13_{9}$, דַּל *poor one* Ps $72_{13}$, אֶבְיוֹן *needy one* Ps $72_{13}$, שׁאר ni. ptc. *one who remains* Jr $21_{7}$, קִיקָיוֹן *castor oil plant* Jon $4_{10}$, כְּלִי *article of property* Gn $45_{20}$; לְמַעַן *for the sake of,* + בְּרִית *covenant* 4QDibHam$^{a}$ $1.2_{8}$.

<SYN> חמל *spare,* רחם pi. *have compassion,* פרע *let go,* נחם ni. *repent.*

<ANT> שׁחת pi. *destroy.**

חוֹף 7 n.[m.] **shore**—cstr. חוֹף—**shore, coast,** <CSTR> חוֹף הַיָּם *shore of the sea* Dt $1_{7}$ (+ עֲרָבָה *Arabah,* הַר *hill country,* שְׁפֵלָה *lowland,* נֶגֶב *Negeb*) Jos $9_{1}$ (+ הַר, שְׁפֵלָה) Jr $47_{7}$ (+ אַשְׁקְלוֹן *Ashkelon*) Ezk $25_{16}$ (+ פְּלִשְׁתִּי *Philistine,* כְּרֵתִי *Cherethite*), חוֹף יַמִּים *shore of the seas* Gn $49_{13}$ Jg $5_{17}$ (+ מִפְרָץ *landing place*), אֳנִיּוֹת *of ships,* i.e. harbour Gn $49_{13}$ (or em.; see Prep.); שְׁאֵרִית חוֹף *remainder of the coast of* Ezk $25_{16}$, כֹּל חוֹף *all the shore of* Jos $9_{1}$.

<PREP> לְ *at,* + שׁכן *dwell* Gn $49_{13}$ (unless em. יִשְׁכֹּן *he will dwell* to יִזְבֹּל *he will dwell*), זבל *dwell* Gn $49_{13}$ (if em.), ישׁב *dwell* Jg $5_{17}$; *as,* introducing predicate Gn $49_{13}$ (or em. לְחוֹף *as a shore* to חֹבֵל *a sailor* of ships, or חֹלֵף *one who passes* [in] ships); בְּ *of place, in* Dt $1_{7}$ Jos $9_{1}$; אֶל *against,* + צוה pi. *command* Jr $47_{7}$.

חוּפָם 1 pr.n.m. **Hupham,** son or descendant of Benjamin, appar. ident. with Huppim (חֻפִּים, חֻפָּם) at Gn $46_{21}$ 1 C $7_{12.15}$, and Huram at 1 C $8_{5}$, <SUBJ> היה *be* 1 C $8_{5}$ (if em. חוּרָם *Huram*). <NOM CL> בְּנֵי בִנְיָמִן ... חוּפָם *the sons of Benjamin were ... Hupham* Gn $46_{21}$ (if em. חֻפִּים), שֻׁפָּם וְחֻפָּם בְּנֵי עִיר *Shupham and Hupham were sons of Ir* 1 C $7_{12}$ (if em. שֻׁפִּם וְחֻפִּם *Shuppim and Huppim*). <PREP> לְ of possession, *(belonging) to* Nm $26_{39}$; of benefit, *to, for,* + לקח *take* 1 C $7_{15}$ (if em. לְחֻפִּים *for Huppim*).

→ חוּפָמִי *Huphamite.*

חוּפָמִי 1 gent. **Huphamite,** as collective sing. noun, of descendants of Hupham, <CSTR> מִשְׁפַּחַת הַחוּפָמִי *the family of the Huphamites* Nm $26_{39}$.

→ חוּפָם *Hupham.*

[חֹופֶשׁ], see חֹפֶשׁ II *freedom.*

*חוץ 1 vb. **be strong—Polel** Ptc. חֹצֵץ—**1. be massed** (unless חצץ Qal *divide oneself*), <SUBJ> אַרְבֶּה *locust* Pr $30_{27}$. <COLL> וַיֵּצֵא חֹצֵץ כֻּלּוֹ *it all goes out, en masse* Pr $30_{27}$. **2. strike up** tune, <OBJ> קוֹל *voice,* i.e. tune Jg $5_{11}$ (if em. מְחַצְצִים sound of *those distributing water* [חצץ pi.] to מְחֹצְצִים *striking up* tune).

→ חוץ *aloud.*

**חוץ** I 164.0.24 n.[m.] **outside**—cstr. חוץ (Q חיץ); pl. חוצות; cstr. חוצות (חֻצֹת, חוצֹת); sf. חוצֹתֶיהָ, חוצֹתָיו, חוצוֹתֶיךָ, חוצוֹתֵינוּ; חוצוֹתָם, (חוצֹתֶיהָ); + ה- of direction חוּצָה (חֻצָה).

**1.** as noun, **street, open field,** etc., p. 175a
**2–6.** as adverb, **outside, beyond,** etc.
  **2a.** חוץ (הַחוּץ), p. 176a
  **2b.** חוּצָה (הַחוּצָה), p. 176a
  **3a.** לַחוּץ, p. 176a
  **3b.** לַחוּצָה, p. 176a
  **4.** בַּחוּץ, p. 176a
  **5a.** מִחוּץ, p. 176b
  **5b.** מֵהַחוּץ, p. 176b
  **5c.** מִחוּצָה, p. 176b
  **5d.** מִבַּחוּץ, p. 176b
  **6a.** אֶל־הַחוּץ, p. 176b
  **6b.** אֶל־הַחוּצָה, p. 176b
**7–9.** as preposition, **outside,** etc.
  **7a.** חוּץ לְ, p. 176b
  **7b.** חוּצָה לְ, p. 176b
  **7c.** חוּץ מִן, p. 176b
  **7d.** חוּצָה מִן, p. 176b
  **8a.** לַחוּץ מִן, p. 176b
  **8b.** לַחוּצָה מִן, p. 177a
  **9a.** מִחוּץ לְ, p. 177a
  **9b.** מִחוּצָה לְ, p. 177a
  **9c.** אֶל־מִחוּץ לְ, p. 177a

**1.** as noun,* usu. **street,** less often **open field, countryside** (Ps $144_{13}$ Jb $5_{10}$ Pr $8_{26}$ Ezr $10_{13}$ perh. Jb $18_{17}$ Pr $24_{27}$ Ca $8_1$), **(the) outside** (Ezk $47_{2.2}$ CD $11_{8.8}$), perh. **bazaar** (1 K $20_{34}$); in plural except at Is $42_2$ $51_{23}$ Jr $9_{20}$ $37_{21}$ Ps $31_{12}$ Jb $18_{17}$ $31_{32}$ Pr $1_{20}$ $7_{12}$ $22_{13}$ $24_{27}$ Ca $8_1$ Ezr $10_{13}$, where, esp. if preceded by preposition, distinction from adverbial usage is uncertain.

<SUBJ> שׁמם ni. *be devastated* Jr $33_{10}$. <OBJ> עשׂה *make* Pr $8_{26}$ (or em. חָצִיר *grass;* + אֶרֶץ *earth*), שׂים *place,* i.e. establish certain streets/bazaars for yourself 1 K $20_{34}$, מלא pi. *fill* with corpses Ezk $11_6$, רמס *trample* Ezk $26_{11}$, חרב hi. *ruin* Zp $3_6$ (+ מִבְּלִי עוֹבֵר *so that there is no passerby;* || עִיר *city,* פִּנָּה *corner [tower]*).

<CSTR> חוּץ הָאֹפִים *the bakers' street* Jr $37_{21}$, חוצֹת אַשְׁקְלוֹן *streets of Ashkelon* 2 S $1_{20}$, חֻצוֹת יְרוּשָׁלַםִ *streets of Jerusalem* Jr $5_1$ (חוצות) $7_{17}$ (יְרוּשָׁלָםִ) $7_{34}$ $11_{6.13}$ $14_{16}$ $33_{10}$ $44_{6.9}$ (יְרוּשָׁלָםִ) $44_{17}$ (יְרוּשָׁלָםִ) $44_{21}$; דֶּרֶךְ חוּץ *way of outside,* i.e. along an outside way Ezk $47_2$ (unless both words are adverbs with סבב hi. *take around,* i.e. set on a way, outside), שַׁעַר הַחוּץ *the gate of outside,* i.e. the outer gate Ezk $47_2$ (or em. הֶחָצֵר gate of *the court*), טִיט חוצות *mud of streets* 2 S $22_{43}$||Ps $18_{43}$ (2 S טִיט־) Mc $7_{10}$ Zc $9_3$ $10_5$ 1QSb $5_{27}$ 4QPrFêtes[c] 1.13 (ט[י]ט), חֹמֶר *clay of* Is $10_6$, מִסְפַּר חֻצוֹת *number of streets of* Jr $11_{13}$, בְּרֹאשׁ כָּל־ חוצות *at the head of,* i.e. entrance to, *every street* Is $51_{20}$ (or del.) Na $3_{10}$=4QpNah 3.4₂ Lm $2_{19}$ (or del.) $4_1$, כָּל־ חוצות *every street* Am $5_{16}$, כָּל־חוצוֹתֶיךָ *all your streets* Ezk $26_{11}$ (+ מַצֵּבָה *pillar,* חוֹמָה *wall,* בַּיִת *house*).

<PREP> לְ of direction, *to,* + יצא hi. *take out* from house CD $11_8$; בְּ of place, *in, on, among* Is $24_{11}$ Jr $6_{11}$ (עוֹלָל בַּחוּץ *an infant in the street*) Pr $22_{13}$ (+ רְחוֹב *street*) 4QHymPr $8_2$, + אלף hi. *be numbered in the thousands* Ps $144_{13}$, רבב pu. *be numbered in the tens of thousands* Ps $144_{13}$, לין *pass night* Jb $31_{32}$ (+ אֹרַח *way*), עמד *stand* Ezr $10_{13}$, שׁלח pi. *send away,* i.e. release plague and bloodshed Ezk $28_{23}$ (or del. שׁלח, leaving nom. cl., 'plague and bloodshed are in her streets'), שׁלך hi. *throw* Ezk $7_{19}$, ho. *be thrown* Jr $14_{16}$, ארב *wait in ambush* Pr $7_{12}$ (|| פִּנָּה ,רְחוֹב *corner [tower]*), נוע *wander* Lm $4_{14}$, דקר pu. *be pierced* Jr $51_4$ (+ אֶרֶץ *land*), שׁמם ni. *be devastated* Lm $4_5$ (+ אַשְׁפֹּת *refuse heap*), נכר ni. *be recognized* Lm $4_8$, אמר *say* Am $5_{16}$ (|| רְחוֹב), בשׂר pi. *announce* 2 S $1_{20}$, קרא *call* Jr $11_6$ (|| עִיר *city*), שׁמע ni. *be heard* Jr $33_{10}$ (|| עִיר), hi. *proclaim* Is $42_2$, נשׂא *raise* voice Is $42_2$, רנן *exult* Pr $1_{20}$ (or em. רנה *rattle* or רִנָּה her *cry* is in the street; || רְחוֹב), ראה *see* Ps $31_{12}$, מצא *find* Ca $8_1$, חגר *be girded* Is $15_3$ (|| רְחוֹב), שׁוט pol. *roam about* Jr $5_1$ (|| רְחוֹב), בער *blaze* Jr $44_6$ (|| עִיר), הלל htpo. *act madly* Na $2_5$ (|| רְחוֹב), עשׂה *do* Jr $7_{17}$ (|| עִיר) $44_9$ (+ אֶרֶץ) $44_{17}$ (|| עִיר), כון hi. *prepare* Pr $24_{27}$ (|| שָׂדֶה *field*), קטר pi. *offer incense* Jr $44_{21}$ (|| עִיר); כְּ *as (though it were),* + שׂים *place* back Is $51_{23}$ (+ לַעֹבְרִים *for passersby;* + אֶרֶץ *earth,* i.e. ground); מִן of direction, *from,* + יצא hi. *take out* to house CD $11_8$, נתן *give* bread Jr $37_{21}$, שׁבת hi. *cause to cease* Jr $7_{34}$ (|| עִיר), כרת hi. *cut off* Jr $9_{20}$ (|| רְחוֹב); בְּקֶרֶב *in the middle of,* + היה *be* (of

corpses) Is 5$_{25}$=4QpIsa[b] 2$_9$; עַל־פְּנֵי *upon (the surface of)* Jb 18$_{17}$ (+ אֶרֶץ *earth*), + שׁלח *send* water Jb 5$_{10}$ (+ אֶרֶץ).

<COLL> חוּצוֹת ... שָׁכְבוּ *they lie down ... (in) the streets* Lm 2$_{21}$.

**2a.** חוּץ (הַחוּץ Jg 19$_{25}$ 2 S 13$_{18}$ Ne 13$_8$) as adverb, **outside,** + ילד ho. *be born* (of half-sister) Lv 18$_9$ (:: בַּיִת *[in the] house*, i.e. at home, into one's immediate family), יצא *go out* Dt 23$_{13}$ (Sam הַחוּצָה, as §2b), hi. *take out* Jg 19$_{25}$ 2 S 13$_{18}$, שׁלך hi. *throw* Ne 13$_8$ (+ מִן appar. throw outside, *away from* the chamber), ישׁב *sit* Dt 23$_{14}$ (Sam הַחוּצָה); מִן־הַחוּץ *from (the) outside*, i.e. from afar, from abroad, + בוא hi. *bring* Jg 12$_9$, שׁאל *ask* for vessels 2 K 4$_3$.

**2b.** הַחוּצָה (חוּצָה Ex 12$_{46}$ 1 K 6$_6$ Is 33$_7$ [חֻצָה] Pr 5$_{16}$ 2 C 24$_8$ 29$_{16}$) as adverb, **(to the) outside;** also **from** or **on, the outside** (1 K 8$_8$||2 C 5$_9$), **beyond** (Nm 35$_4$), **outwards** (Nm 35$_{4[Sam]}$ 1 K 6$_6$), **afar, abroad** (Jg 12$_9$), perh. **publicly** (Is 33$_7$ [unless חוּץ III *aloud*]), + היה *be*, i.e. go for marriage Dt 25$_5$, ראה ni. *be seen* 1 K 8$_8$||2 C 5$_9$, פוץ *be scattered* Pr 5$_{16}$ (+ רְחוֹב *street*, as §1), יצא *go out* Gn 39$_{12.13(Sam, mss).15.18(mss)}$ Dt 23$_{13(Sam)}$ Jos 2$_{19}$ 1 S 9$_{26}$, hi. *take out* Gn 15$_5$ 19$_{17}$ Ex 12$_{46}$ 2 C 29$_{16}$, רוץ *run* Gn 24$_{29}$, נוס *flee* Gn 39$_{12(mss).13.15(mss).18}$, ישׁב *sit* Dt 23$_{14}$ (Sam), שׁלח pi. *send away* Jg 12$_9$ 2 S 13$_{17}$, נתן *give*, i.e. place 1 K 6$_6$ 2 C 24$_8$, צעק *cry out* Is 33$_7$; in nom. cl., מִגְרְשֵׁי הֶעָרִים ... מִקִּיר הָעִיר וָחוּצָה אֶלֶף אַמָּה סָבִיב *the pastures of the cities are to be ..., from the wall of the city and beyond, a thousand cubits all around* Nm 35$_4$ (Sam הַחוּצָה from the wall of the city *outwards*; or em. אַלְפַּיִם *two thousand* cubits).

**3a.** לַחוּץ as adverb, **(on the) outside, beyond,** + יצא *go out* Ps 41$_7$ (unless לַחוּץ go out *onto the street*, as §1; or + דבר pi. if om. יצא, as ms) 11QT 41$_{12}$ 46$_{14}$; עַד־הַבַּיִת הַפְּנִימִי וְלַחוּץ *unto the inner house and beyond* Ezk 41$_{17}$, גָּדֵר אֲשֶׁר־לַחוּץ *a wall, which was outside* Ezk 42$_7$.

**3b.** לַחוּצָה as adverb, **(on the) outside, beyond,** + בנה *build* 2 C 32$_5$.

**4.** בַּחוּץ as adverb, **(on the) outside, outdoors** (but sometimes perh., as §1, חוּץ as noun, **open field, countryside,** with בְּ *in*), + הלך htp. *go about* Ex 21$_{19}$, נגד hi. *declare* Gn 9$_{22}$, עמד *stand* Gn 24$_{31}$ Dt 24$_{11}$, שׂים *place* 2 K 10$_{24}$, פשׁט *strip*, i.e. raid Ho 7$_1$, עשׂה *do*, i.e. make chambers 11QT 38$_{15(erased)}$; in nom. cl., Ezk 7$_{15}$ (ms מִחוּץ in same sense).

**5a.** מִחוּץ as adverb, **(on the) outside; perh. outwards** (Ezk 40$_{19}$), + כפר *cover* Gn 6$_{14}$ (:: מִבַּיִת *[on the] inside*), צפה pi. *overlay* Ex 25$_{11}$||37$_2$ (:: מִבַּיִת), גרר poal *be sawn* 1 K 7$_9$ (:: מִבַּיִת), שׁכל pi. *bereave* Dt 32$_{25}$ (:: מֵחֲדָרִים [Sam ms מֵהֲדָרִים] *[on the] inside*), שׁכל pi. *bereave* Lm 1$_{20}$ (+ בַּבַּיִת perh. *[on the] inside*), מדד *measure* Ezk 40$_{19}$, עשׂה *do*, i.e. make chambers 11QT 38$_{15}$ 40$_{10}$, appar. בוא *come* Ezk 46$_2$; in nom. cl., Ezk 7$_{15(ms)}$ (:: מִבַּיִת).

**5b.** מֵהַחוּץ as adverb, **(on the) outside,** עָב עֵץ אֶל־פְּנֵי הָאוּלָם מֵהַחוּץ perh. *thickness*, i.e. a thick piece, *of wood was in front of the vestibule on the outside* Ezk 41$_{25}$ (or em. עַל־פְּנֵי in same sense).

**5c.** מִחוּצָה as adverb, **(on the) outside,** אֶל־הַכָּתֵף מִחוּצָה *on the side outside* Ezk 40$_{40}$ (or em. עַל *upon* or *by*; + הַכָּתֵף הָאַחֶרֶת *the other side*).

**5d.** מִבַּחוּץ as adverb, **(on the) outside,** + צפה pi. *overlay* 11QT 31$_9$ ([ומ]בחוץ]; :: מִבַּיִת *[on the] inside*).

**6a.** אֶל־הַחוּץ as adverb, **(on the) outside,** הַקִּיר אֲשֶׁר־לַצֵּלָע אֶל־הַחוּץ *the wall of the chamber on the outside*, i.e. external wall Ezk 41$_9$.

**6b.** אֶל־הַחוּצָה as adverb, **(to) outside, abroad,** + פוץ hi. *scatter* Ezk 34$_{21}$.

**7a.** חוּץ לְ as preposition, **outside,** (1) followed by noun, עִיר *city* CD 10$_{21}$; (2) preceded by verb, הלך htp. *go about* CD 10$_{21}$.

**7b.** חוּצָה לְ as preposition, **outside,** (1) followed by noun, Jerusalem 4QMMT B$_{30}$ ([חוצה לירושלים]), עִיר *city* 2 C 33$_{15}$, מַחֲנֶה *camp* 4QMMT B$_{30}$ ([חו]צה); (2) preceded by verb, שׁלך hi. *throw* 2 C 33$_{15}$.

**7c.** חוּץ מִן as preposition, **outside, apart from,** (1) followed by pronoun in ref. to Koheleth Ec 2$_{25}$ (or em. מִמֶּנּוּ apart *from him* [Y.]), thirty-six royal counsellors 11QT 57$_{15}$; (2) followed by noun, עִיר *city* CD 11$_5$ 11QT 46$_{13}$, מַחֲנֶה *camp* 4QMMT B$_{31}$ ([ממ]חנה); (3) preceded by verb, הלך *go* CD 11$_5$, אכל *eat* Ec 2$_{25}$, חושׁ *feel* Ec 2$_{25}$ (or em. חוס *pity*), עשׂה *do* 11QT 46$_{13}$ 57$_{15}$.

**7d.** חוּצָה מִן, as preposition, **outside,** (1) followed by noun, מִשְׁפָּט *judgment*, i.e. illegally 4QD[e] 11.1$_{12}$; (2) with verb, אכל *eat* 4QD[e] 11.1$_{12}$.

**8a.** לַחוּץ מִן as preposition, **outside,** (1) followed by noun, חָצֵר *court* 11QT 46$_5$; (2) with verb, עשׂה *do* 11QT 46$_5$.

**8b.** לְחוּצָה מִן as preposition, **outside,** (in nom. cl.) followed by pronoun, זֶה *this (wall)* 11QT 42$_{04}$.

**9a.** מִחוּץ לְ as preposition, **outside,** (1) followed by noun, Jerusalem 2 K 23$_{4.6}$ Ne 13$_{20}$, עִיר *city* Gn 19$_{16}$ 24$_{11}$ Nm 35$_5$ 1 K 21$_{13}$ 2 C 32$_3$ 11QT$^b$ 44 [מהיץ ל[עיר]), מַחֲנֶה *camp* Ex 29$_{14}$||Lv 8$_{17}$ Ex 33$_{7.7}$ Lv 13$_{46}$ 17$_3$ Nm 12$_{14.15}$ 15$_{35}$ 19$_9$ 31$_{19}$ Dt 23$_{13}$ Jos 6$_{23}$ 4QMMT B$_{28}$, גְּבוּל *border* Nm 35$_{27}$, חוֹמָה *wall* Jr 21$_4$, אֹהֶל *tent* Lv 14$_8$= 4QMMT B$_{66}$ (מחוץ [לאוהלו]), פָּרֹכֶת *veil* Ex 26$_{35}$||40$_{22}$ (+ נֹכַח *opposite*) 27$_{21}$||Lv 24$_3$, בַּיִת *house* 4QMMT B$_{66}$ ([מחוץ לבית]), i.e. temple Ezk 40$_5$, מִקְדָּשׁ *sanctuary* Ezk 43$_{21}$; (2) preceded by verb, היה *be* Dt 23$_{13}$ 4QMMT B$_{66}$ ([יהיו מחוץ לבית]), יצא hi. *take out* 1 K 21$_{13}$ 2 K 23$_6$, שׂים *place* Ex 26$_{35}$||40$_{22(Sam)}$, נתן *give*, i.e. place Ex 40$_{22}$, נוח hi. *cause to rest*, i.e. place Gn 19$_{16}$ Nm 19$_9$ Jos 6$_{23}$, ערך *array* Ex 27$_{21}$||Lv 24$_3$, נטה *spread out* tent Ex 33$_7$, מדד *measure* Nm 35$_5$, מצא *find* Nm 35$_{27}$, ישׁב *sit* Lv 14$_8$=4QMMT B$_{66}$ ([י]שב מחוץ [לאוהלו]), לין *pass night* Ne 13$_{20}$, סגר ni. *be enclosed* Nm 12$_{14.15}$, חנה *encamp* Nm 31$_{19}$, ברך hi. *cause to kneel* Gn 24$_{11}$, שׂרף *burn* Ex 29$_{14}$||Lv 8$_{17}$ 2 K 23$_4$ Ezk 43$_{21}$ 11QT$^b$ 44 ([ישרפו] מהיץ ל[עיר]), שׁחט *slaughter* Lv 17$_3$ 4QMMT B$_{28}$ ([ישחט]), רגם *stone* Nm 15$_{35}$, appar. לחם ni. *fight* Jr 21$_4$ (unless צור *besiege*; + אֶל־תּוֹךְ *[to] inside*); (3) in nom. cl., Ex 33$_7$ Lv 13$_{46}$ Ezk 40$_5$ 2 C 32$_3$.

**9b.** מִחוּצָה לְ as preposition, **outside,** (1) followed by noun, שַׁעַר *gate* Ezk 40$_{44}$ (or em. שַׁעַר to חָצֵר *court*), מַחֲנֶה *camp* 4QM$^a$ 1$_9$; (2) with verb, יצא *go out* 4QM$^a$ 1$_9$ ([י]אצאו); (3) in nom. cl., Ezk 40$_{44}$.

**9c.** אֶל־מִחוּץ לְ as preposition, **(to) outside** (for difference from מִחוּץ לְ, see esp. Nm 15$_{35(L).36}$ 19$_{3.9}$), (1) followed by noun, עִיר *city* Lv 14$_{40.41.45.53}$, מַחֲנֶה *camp* Lv 4$_{12.21}$ 6$_4$ 10$_{4.5}$ 14$_3$ 16$_{27}$ 24$_{14.23}$ Nm 5$_{3.4}$ 15$_{35(mss).36}$ 19$_3$ 31$_{13}$ Dt 23$_{11}$ (:: אֶל־תּוֹךְ *[to] inside*) 2QapMoses 1$_4$ (מ[חו]ץ); (2) with verb, יצא *go out* Lv 14$_3$ appar. Nm 31$_{13}$ (unless קרא *meet*) Dt 23$_{11}$ 2QapMoses 1$_4$ (מ[חו]ץ), hi. *take out* Lv 4$_{12.21}$ 6$_4$ 14$_{45}$ 16$_{27}$ 24$_{14.23}$ Nm 15$_{36}$ 19$_3$, נשׂא *raise* Lv 10$_{4.5}$, שׁלח pi. *send away* Lv 14$_{53}$ Nm 5$_{3.4}$, שׁלך hi. *throw* Lv 14$_{40}$, שׁפך *pour* Lv 14$_{41}$, רגם *stone* Nm 15$_{35(mss)}$.

Also 4QM$^a$ 1$_6$ (מחוץ).

<SYN> §1 רְחוֹב pl. *streets*, עִיר *city*, פִּנָּה *corner (tower)*, שָׂדֶה *field*.

<ANT> §2a בַּיִת *(in the) house*, i.e. at home; §5a, §5d מִבַּיִת *(on the) inside*, מֵחֲדָרִים *(on the) inside*; §9c אֶל־תּוֹךְ *(to) inside*.

**[חוּץ] II** $_1$ pr.n.m. **Huz,** son of Aram and grandson of Shem, בני ארם חוץ *the sons of Aram were Huz* Gn 10$_{23(Sam)}$ (MT עוּץ *Uz and Hul*).

***[חוּץ] III** $_1$ adv. **loudly**—+ ה- חֻצָה—<COLL> צָעֲקוּ חֻצָה *they cried aloud* Is 33$_7$ (unless חוּץ I *outside*, used adverbially, *publicly*).

⇒ חוץ *be strong*.

***חוק** $_1$ vb. **gather—Qal** $_1$ Inf. חוּקוֹ—**gather,** <SUBJ> ״ *Y.* Pr 8$_{29}$. <OBJ> מוֹסָד *foundation* of earth Pr 8$_{29}$.

**[חוֹק]**, see חק *statute*.

*** [חוּק]** $_{0.1}$ n.[m.] **circle**—in ref. to vault of heaven, <OBJ> נקף hi. *surround* Si 43$_{12(B)}$ (unless חק *statute*, i.e. boundary; M חוג *circle*; Bmg הוד *splendour*).

**חוּקֹק** $_2$ pl.n. **Hukok**—+ ה- of direction חוּקֹקָה—**1.** town in Naphtali, perh. Šēḫ en-Nāši near Yāqūq, 6 km WNW of Chinnereth, <COLL> יָצָא מִשָּׁם חוּקֹקָה *it*, i.e. the border, *went out from there to Hukok* Jos 19$_{34}$. **2.** town in Asher, appar. ident. with חֶלְקַת *Helkath* at Jos 19$_{25.31}$, <OBJ> נתן *give* 1 C 6$_{60}$ (or em. חֶלְקַת *Helkath*).

**חור I** $_{1.0.1}$ vb. **be white—Qal** $_{1.0.1}$ Pf. Q חורו; impf. יֶחֱוָרוּ (Q יחוורו)—**be white, be pale, become pale** (unless at Is 29$_{22}$ חור III *turn* and at Is 24$_6$ חור II *be feeble*), <SUBJ> אֹרֵג *weaver* 1QIsa$^a$ 19$_9$ (MT חוֹרָי *white stuff*; || בושׁ *be ashamed*), יֹשֵׁב *inhabitant* perh. Is 24$_6$ (1QIsa$^a$ חורו), פָּנִים *face* Is 29$_{22}$=4QpIsa$^c$ 18$_5$ (פניו יחורו; + בושׁ). <SYN> בושׁ *be ashamed*.

⇒ חוּר *white*, חוֹרָי *white stuff*, חֹרִי *white bread*.

**חור II** $_1$ vb. **be feeble—Qal** $_1$ Pf. חָרוּ—**become feeble,**

dwindle away (unless חור I *be white*), <SUBJ> יֹשֵׁב *inhabitant* Is 24$_6$ (unless חרה *dwindle away;* 1QIsa[a] חורו perh. חור I *become pale*).

*חוּר III 1.0.1 vb. **turn—Qal** 1.0.1 Impf. יֶחֱוָרוּ (Q יחורו)—**go to and fro** (unless חור I *be white*), <SUBJ> פָּנִים *face* Is 29$_{22}$=4QpIsa[c] 18$_5$.

חוֹר, see חֹר I *noble*, II *hole*.

חוּר I 14 pr.n.m. **Hur, 1.** son of Judah or descendant of Judah and firstborn son of Caleb with second wife Ephrath, and father of Uri, appar. ident. with Ben-hur (בֶּן־חוּר) at 1 C 2$_{50}$, <SUBJ> ילד hi. *beget* 1 C 2$_{20}$. <NOM CL> בְּנֵי יְהוּדָה פֶּרֶץ ... וְחוּר *the sons of Judah were Perez ... and Hur* 1 C 4$_1$. <OBJ> ילד *give birth* 1 C 2$_{19}$. <CSTR> בֶּן־חוּר *son of Hur* Ex 31$_2$ 35$_{30}$ 38$_{22}$ 2 C 1$_5$, בְּנֵי־חוּר *sons of Hur* 1 C 4$_4$. <APP> בְּכוֹר *firstborn* 1 C 4$_4$, אָב *father* 1 C 4$_4$ (or em. הִיא *she*).

**2.** companion of Moses and Aaron at Sinai, <SUBJ> עלה *go up* Ex 17$_{10}$, תמך *support* Ex 17$_{12}$. <NOM CL> אַהֲרֹן וְחוּר עִמָּכֶם *Aaron and Hur are with you* Ex 24$_{14}$. <PREP> אֶל *to*, + נגשׁ *draw near* Ex 24$_{14}$. **3.** king or prince of Midian killed by Israelites under Moses, <SUBJ> ישׁב *dwell* Jos 13$_{21}$. <OBJ> הרג *kill* Nm 31$_8$, נכה hi. *strike* Jos 13$_{21}$. <APP> מֶלֶךְ *king* Nm 31$_8$, נָשִׂיא *prince* Jos 13$_{21}$, נָסִיךְ *prince* Jos 13$_{21}$. **4.** father or ancestor of Rephaiah, a wall-builder in Nehemiah's time, <CSTR> בֶּן־חוּר *son of Hur* Ne 3$_9$. **5.** father of Benaiah, <CSTR> בן חר *son of Hur* Seal 18 (others בן[]חר; Cyprus).*

חוּר II 2.0.1 n.[m.] **white** colour, <SUBJ> אחז pass. *be held* Est 1$_6$ (unless em.; see Cstr.). <CSTR> חוּר כַּרְפַּס *white of linen* Est 1$_6$ (or em. כַּרְפַּס חוּר *linen of white;* + תְּכֵלֶת *blue*); לְבוּשׁ מַלְכוּת תְּכֵלֶת וָחוּר *royal robes of blue and white* Est 8$_{15}$, כַּרְפַּס חוּר *linen of white* Est 1$_6$ (if em.), מראי חור *appearance of white* 4QShirShabb[f] 23.2$_9$. <SYN> תְּכֵלֶת *blue*.

⇒ חור *be white*.

[חוֹר] III, see חֹר *hole*.

חוֹרֵב, see חֹרֵב *Horeb*.

[חוֹרוֹן] 0.0.1 pl.n. **Horon,** site of hidden treasure, appar. ident. with בֵּית חוֹרוֹן *Beth-horon*, <CSTR> צריחי החורון *the cellars of Horon* 3QTr 9$_7$.

⇒ בֵּית חוֹרוֹן *Beth-horon*.

חוֹרִי, see חֹרִי I *Hori*.

[חוֹרָי] 1 n.[m.] **white stuff**—חוֹרָי—<OBJ> ארג *weave* Is 19$_9$=4QpIsa[c] 11.2$_1$ ([חורי]; 1QIsa[a] חורו *they have become pale;* or em. יֶחֱוָרוּ *they will become pale*).

⇒ חור *be white*.

חוּרַי 1 pr.n.m. **Hurai,** one of David's warriors, appar. ident. with Hiddai (הִדַּי) at 2 S 23$_{30}$, <COLL> חוּרַי מִנַּחֲלֵי גָעַשׁ *Hurai from the wadis of Gaash* 1 C 11$_{32}$.

חוּרִי 1 pr.n.m. **Huri,** descendant of Gad, son of Jaroah and father of Abihail, <CSTR> בֶּן־חוּרִי *son of Huri* 1 C 5$_{14}$. <APP> בֵּן *son* 1 C 5$_{14}$.

חוּרָם, see חִירָם *Hiram*.

חַוְרָן 2 pl.n. **Hauran,** territory SE of Bashan, <CSTR> גְּבוּל חַוְרָן *border of Hauran* Ezk 47$_{16}$. <PREP> מִבֵּין *from between* Ezk 47$_{18}$ (or em. וּבֵין *and between*).

חוֹרֹנַיִם, see חֹרֹנַיִם *Horonaim*.

[חוֹרָץ] 0.0.0.1 pr.n.m. **Horaz,** son of Paklal, <APP> בֵּן *son* Seal 22 (8th cent.). <PREP> לְ of possession, *(belonging) to* Seal 22 (8th cent.).

חוּשׁ I 21.2.6 vb. **hasten—Qal** 15.1.4 Pf. חָשׁ, 3fs Si חשתה; impf. Q יחושו; + waw וְחָשׁ; 3fs וַתָּחַשׁ; impv. חוּשָׁה (Kt חישה); ptc. pass. m. pl. חֲשִׁים; inf. חוּשִׁי, Q חושה—**1. hasten,** intrans., <SUBJ> Y. Ps 38$_{23}$ 40$_{14.18}$ (if em. יַחֲשָׁב לִי *he takes thought for me* to חוּשָׁה לִי *hasten to me*) 70$_{2.6}$ 71$_{12}$ (:: רחק *be distant*) 141$_1$, בֵּן *son* of Reuben and Gad Nm 32$_{17}$ (or em. חֲשִׁים appar. *hastening* to חֲמֻשִׁים *[being] in groups of fifty;* + חלץ ni. *be equipped for war*), נַעַר *lad*

1 S 20$_{38}$ (+ מְהֵרָה *quickly*; :: עמד *stand*, i.e. stay), worshipper Ps 119$_{60}$ (:: מהה htpalp. *delay*), רֶגֶל *foot* Jb 31$_{5}$ (unless hi.; + הלך *go*), גּוֹי *nation* Jl 4$_{11}$ (if em. עוּשׁוּ *lend aid* to חוּשׁוּ *hasten*), נֶשֶׁר *eagle* Hb 1$_{8}$= 1Qp Hab 3$_{8}$, מַחֲשָׁב *crafted thing* 4QShirShabb$^{d}$ 1.2$_{13}$, עָתִיד fem. pl. *future things* Dt 32$_{35}$, אֱיָלוּת *help*, in ref. to Y. Ps 22$_{20}$ (:: רחק), תְּשׁוּעָה *salvation* Ps 38$_{23}$, שְׂעִפִּים *disquieting thoughts* Jb 20$_{2}$ (if em. חוּשִׁי *my hastening* to יָחוּשׁוּ *they hasten*), צְעָקָה *cry* Si 32$_{20(B)}$ (צעקה ענן חשתה appar. *[his] cry hastens to the clouds*; unless from חשה *be silent*), עֵת *time* 1QM 1$_{12}$ (:: תמם *be complete*).

<PREP> לְ of direction, *to(wards)*, + worshipper Ps 40$_{18}$ (if em.; see Subj.) 70$_{6}$ 141$_{1}$, אֹיֵב *enemy* Dt 32$_{35}$, עֶזְרָה *help* Ps 22$_{20}$ 38$_{23}$ 40$_{14}$ 70$_{2}$ 71$_{12}$; בְּ of accompaniment, *with*, + תְּהִלָּה *psalm* 4QShirShabb$^{d}$ 1.2$_{13}$; לִפְנֵי *before*, + בֵּן *son* of Israel Nm 32$_{17}$ (or em.; see Subj.).

<COLL> חוּשִׁי בִּי *my hastening within me* Jb 20$_{2}$ (unless *my feeling*, i.e. חוש II; or em.; see Subj.); חִישׁ, חוּשׁ followed by inf. with לְ Hb 1$_{8}$=1QpHab 3$_{8}$ (אכל *eat*).

<ANT> מהה htpalp. *delay*, רחק *be distant*, עמד *stand*, תמם *be complete*.

**2. be dislodged,** <SUBJ> יְסוֹד *foundation* 4QS$^{e}$ 1.2$_{14}$ (=1QS 8$_{8}$ יחישו, i.e. hi.). <PREP> מִן of direction, *from*, + מָקוֹם *place* 4QS$^{e}$ 1.2$_{14}$.

**Hi.** 6.1.3 Pf. הֶחִישׁוּ; יָחִישׁ (יָחִישָׁה), 3fs Q תחיש, אָחִישָׁה (אֲחִישֶׁנָּה), Q יחישו; + waw 3fs וַתָּחַשׁ (unless qal); impv. Si החיש—**1. hasten** (intrans.), <SUBJ> רֶגֶל *foot* Jb 31$_{5}$ (+ הלך *go*), אֹרֵב *ambush party* Jg 20$_{37}$, חֶרֶב *sword* 1QH 6$_{29}$, מַעֲשֶׂה *work* Is 5$_{19}$ (unless §2, with Y. as subj.; + מהר pi. *hurry*), מַשְׁבֵּר *breach*, i.e. mouth of womb, in ref. to childbirth 1QH 3$_{10}$, חֵבֶל *labour pain* 1QH 3$_{10}$. <PREP> בְּ of time, *in*, + קֵץ *period* 1QH 6$_{29}$; עַל *upon*, i.e. towards + מִרְמָה *deceit* Jb 31$_{5}$.

**2.** trans. **make to hasten, seek with haste** (Ps 55$_{9}$), <SUBJ> Y. Is 5$_{19}$ (unless §1, with מַעֲשֶׂה *work* as subj.) 60$_{22}$ Si 33$_{10}$, worshipper Ps 55$_{9}$. <OBJ> מַעֲשֶׂה *work* Is 5$_{19}$ (unless §1), מִפְלָט *refuge* Ps 55$_{9}$, קֵץ *end* Si 33$_{10}$ (+ פקד *appoint* time), fulfilment of prophecy Is 60$_{22}$. <PREP> בְּ of time, *in*, + עֵת *time* Is 60$_{22}$.

**3. give way, be dislodged,** <SUBJ> אמן hi. ptc. *one who believes* Is 28$_{16}$,* יְסוֹד *foundation* 1QS 8$_{8}$ (=4QS$^{e}$ 1.2$_{14}$ יחושו, i.e. qal; || זוע htpalp. *be shaken*). <PREP> מִן of direction, *from*, + מָקוֹם *place* 1QS 8$_{8}$.

<SYN> זוע htpalp. *be shaken*.*

→ מַהֵר שָׁלָל חָשׁ בַּז *Maher-shalal-hash-baz*, חִישׁ *quickly*.

**חוש II** 2 vb. **feel—Qal** 2 Impf. יָחוּשׁ; inf. חוּשִׁי—**1. feel (pain), be painful,** <SUBJ> שְׂעִפִּים *disquieting thoughts* Jb 20$_{2}$ (if em. חוּשִׁי *my feeling* to יָחוּשׁוּ *they are painful*). <COLL> חוּשִׁי בִּי *my feeling within me* Jb 20$_{2}$ (unless *my hastening*, i.e. חוש I; or em.; see Subj.). **2. feel joyful** (unless חוש III *be anxious* or IV *be sated*). <SUBJ> מִי *who?* Ec 2$_{25}$ (|| אכל *eat*). <SYN> §2 אכל *eat*.

***חוש III** 1 vb. **be anxious—Qal** 1 Impf. יָחוּשׁ—**be anxious,** <SUBJ> מִי *who?* Ec 2$_{25}$ (|| אכל *eat*), שְׂעִפִּים *disquieting thoughts* Jb 20$_{2}$ (if em. חוּשִׁי *my feeling* to יָחוּשׁוּ *they are perturbed*). <COLL> חוּשִׁי בִּי *my feeling within me* Jb 20$_{2}$ (unless *my hastening*, i.e. חוש I; or em.; see Subj.). <SYN> אכל *eat*.

***חוש IV** 1 vb. **be sated—Qal** 1 Impf. יָחוּשׁ—**be sated,** <SUBJ> מִי *who?* Ec 2$_{25}$ (|| אכל *eat*). <SYN> אכל *eat*.

**חוש V** 0.0.1 vb. **cease—Qal** 0.0.1 Impf. Q יחושו—**cease,** perh. **be silent,** <SUBJ> appar. קוֹל *sound* of rams' horns 1QM 8$_{11}$.

**חוּשָׁה** 1 pr.n.m. **Hushah,** son of Ezer and descendant of Judah, <CSTR> אֲבִי חוּשָׁה *father of Hushah* 1 C 4$_{4}$.

→ חֻשָׁתִי *Hushathite*.

**חוּשַׁי** 14 pr.n.m. **Hushai**—חוּשָׁי—Archite servant and friend of David, <SUBJ> היה *be* 2 S 15$_{32.32}$ 16$_{18.18}$, הלך *go* 2 S 16$_{17}$, בוא *come* 2 S 15$_{37}$ 16$_{16}$ 17$_{6.8}$, שׁוב *return* 2 S 15$_{32}$, עבר *pass* 2 S 15$_{32}$, ישׁב *dwell* 2 S 16$_{18}$, קרא *meet* 2 S 15$_{32}$, שׁלח *send* 2 S 15$_{32(mss)}$ (MT שְׁלַחְתֶּם *you sent*), עבד *serve* 2 S 16$_{18.18}$, פרר hi. *break* 2 S 15$_{32}$, סחב *drag* 2 S 17$_{8}$, אמר *say* 2 S 15$_{32}$ 16$_{16.18}$ 17$_{7.8.15}$, דבר pi. *speak* 2 S 17$_{6}$, נגד hi. *tell* 2 S 15$_{32}$, יָעַץ *counsel* 2 S 17$_{15}$, שׁמע *hear* 2 S 15$_{32.32}$. <NOM CL> חוּשַׁי ... רֵעַ הַמֶּלֶךְ *Hushai was ... the king's friend* 1 C 27$_{33}$. <CSTR> עֲצַת חוּשַׁי *counsel of Hushai* 2 S 17$_{14}$. <APP> אַרְכִּי *Archite* 2 S 15$_{32}$ 16$_{16}$ 17$_{5.14}$ 1 C 27$_{33}$, רֵעָה *friend* 2 S 15$_{37}$ 16$_{16}$. <PREP> לְ of direction, *to*, + קרא *call* 2 S $17_5$; אֶל *to*, + אמר *say* 2 S $15_{32}$ $16_{17}$ $17_6$; עִם *with* 2 S $15_{32}$.

2. father of Baana, <CSTR> בֶּן־חוּשַׁי *son of Hushai* 1 K $4_{16}$.

3. <CSTR> [בן] חשי *son of Hushai* Arad ost. $57_2$ (others שי).

**חוּשִׁים** I $_2$ pr.n.f. **Hushim**—חֻשִׁים—wife of Shaharaim and mother of Abitub and Elpaal, <OBJ> שׁלח pi. *send away* 1 C $8_8$ (or em. אוֹתָם חוּשִׁים *them, Hushim* to אֶת־מַחְשָׁם/מַחְשָׁם *Mahsham/Mahsam*). <APP> אִשָּׁה *woman* 1 C $8_8$. <PREP> מִן of instrument, *by (means of)*, + ילד hi. *beget* 1 C $8_{11}$ (or em. מִמַּחְשָׁם/מִמַּחְשָׁם *by Mahsham/ Mahsam*).

**[חוּשִׁים]** II $_2$ pr.n.m. **Hushim**—חֻשִׁים, חֻשִׁם—**1.** son of Dan, appar. ident. with Shuham at Nm $26_{42}$, <NOM CL> וּבֶן־דָּן חֻשִׁים *and the son of Dan was Hushim* Gn $46_{23(Seb)}$. **2.** appar. son of Aher, <NOM CL> וְשֻׁפִּם וְחֻפִּם בְּנֵי עִיר חֻשִׁם בְּנֵי אַחֵר *and Shuppim and Huppim were the sons of Ir; Hushim was the son(s) of Aher* 1 C $7_{12}$ (or em. וְשֻׁפָם וְחֻפָם בְּנֵי דָן חֻשִׁם בְּנוֹ אֶחָד *Shupham and Hupham, sons of Dan; Hushim was his first son*, as §1).

**חוּשָׁם**, see חֻשָׁם *Husham*.

**[חוּשָׁתִי]**, see חֻשָׁתִי *Hushathite*.

***חות** vb. **be bold—Qal,** <SUBJ> עַם *people* Is $8_{9.9.9}$ (if em. in all three חֹתּוּ, from חתת *be dismayed* to חותו *be bold*).

**חוֹתָם** I $_{14.4.2.2}$ n.m. **seal**—cstr. mss חוֹתַם; חֹתָם; sf. חֹתָמְךָ, חֹתָמוֹ—**seal, signet ring,** <SUBJ> היה *be* Jr $22_{24}$, ידע ni. *be known* 1QH $8_{11}$ (unless חותם is qal ptc. or pu. pf. חתם *seal*), חתם pass. *be sealed* 4QMyst[b] $1.2_2$ ([ח]תם).

<NOM CL> סְגוּרוֹ חוֹתָם צָר *his breast is a seal of flint* Jb $41_7$ (if em. סָגוּר חוֹתָם צָר *closed [with] a tight seal*), חותם ברקת קול מזמור על נועם תירוש *the sound of stringed music with pleasant wine is a seal of emerald* Si $35_6$ (+ מִלֵּאָה *setting* of gold), חֹתָמְךָ ... אֲשֶׁר בְּיָדֶךָ *your signet ring ... which is upon your hand* Gn $38_{18}$ (+ פְּתִיל *cord*, מַטֶּה *staff*), לְמִי הַחוֹתָם *whose is the signet ring?* Gn $38_{25}$ (if em. הַחֹתֶמֶת *the signet ring*).

<CSTR> חוֹתַם תָּכְנִית *seal of proportion* Ezk $28_{12(mss)}$, צֹר *of flint* Jb $41_7$ (if em.; see Nom. Cl.), ברקת *of emerald* Si $35_6$, חוכם *of a wise one* Si $42_{6(B)}$, רזו *of its mystery* 1QH $8_{11}$ (unless *sealing its mystery*, i.e. חותם qal ptc. of חתם *seal*, or *its mystery has been sealed*, i.e. pu. pf. of חתם), [ח]תם החזון *seal of the vision* 4QMyst[b] $1.2_2$; חֹמֶר חוֹתָם *clay of*, i.e. under, *the seal* Jb $38_{14}$, פִּתּוּחֵי חֹתָם *engravings of a signet* Ex $28_{11.21.36}$||$39_{6.14.30}$ (חוֹתָם at $28_{21}$ $39_{6.30}$) Si $45_{11}$ (חותם), כול חותם *every seal* 1QH fr. $11_3$ (unless *everyone that is sealing*, i.e. qal ptc. חתם *seal*, or *everything has been sealed*, i.e. pu. pf. חתם).

<ADJ> צַר *narrow*, i.e. tight Jb $41_7$ (unless em.; see Nom. Cl.), אֵלֶּה *these* Gn $38_{25}$ (if em.; see Nom. Cl.).

<PREP> בְּ of instrument, *by (means of), with*, + חתם *seal* 1 K $21_8$ Arad ost. $13_3$ ([וחתם] בחתמך *and seal it with your seal*) $17_6$; כְּ *as* Hg $2_{23}$ Ca $8_{6.6}$ Si $35_5$.

<COLL> חוֹתָם עַל־יַד יְמִינִי *the signet ring on my right hand* Jr $22_{24}$, חוֹתָם עַל־לִבֶּךָ *a seal on your heart* Ca $8_6$, חוֹתָם עַל־זְרוֹעֶךָ *a seal upon your arm* Ca $8_6$, חותם על כיס זהב *a seal on a bag of gold* Si $35_5$, סָגוּר חוֹתָם צָר *closed (with) a tight seal* Jb $41_7$ (unless em.; see Nom. Cl.), אשה רעה חותם חכם appar. be ashamed of *a wicked woman (with) the seal of a wise person* Si $42_{6(B)}$ (Bmg אשה טפשה *a foolish woman*).*

→ חתם *seal*.

**חוֹתָם** II $_2$ pr.n.m. **Hotham, 1.** descendant of Asher, son of Heber and brother of Japhlet, Shomer and Shua, <OBJ> ילד hi. *beget* 1 C $7_{32}$. **2.** Aroerite, father of Shama and Jeiel, <CSTR> בְּנֵי חוֹתָם *sons of Hotham* 1 C $7_{35}$ (if em. בֶּן־חֵלֶם *son of Helem*) $11_{44}$. <APP> עֲרֹעֵרִי *Aroerite* 1 C $11_{44}$.

**חֲזָאֵל** $_{23}$ pr.n.m. **Hazael**—חֲזָהאֵל—king of Syria anointed by Elijah at time of Jehu, father of Ben-hadad, <SUBJ> הלך *go* 2 K $8_{8.9.10.14}$, בוא 2 K $8_{9.14}$, עלה *go up* 2 K $12_{18.19}$, עמד *stand* 2 K $8_9$, קרא *meet* 2 K $8_{8.9}$, דרשׁ *seek* 2 K $8_8$, לקח *take* 2 K $8_{8.9}$, שׁלח pi. *send* fire 2 K $8_{12}$, שׂים *set* face 2 K $12_{18}$, אמר *say* 2 K $8_{8.9.10.12.13}$ (חֲזָהאֵל) $8_{14}$, עשׂה *do* 2 K $8_{13}$, הרג *kill* 2 K $8_{12}$, רטשׁ pi. *dash in pieces* 2 K $8_{12}$, בקע pi. *tear apart* 2 K $8_{12}$, נכה hi. *strike* 2 K $10_{32}$, לחץ

*oppress* 2 K $13_{22}$, מלך *rule* 2 K $8_{15}$ (חֲזָהאֵל), מות *die* 2 K $13_{24}$. <OBJ> משׁח *annoint* 1 K $19_{15}$, לחם ni. *fight* 2 K $8_{29}$||2 C $22_{6}$ (both חֲזָהאֵל) $12_{18}$, לכד *capture* 2 K $12_{18}$. <CSTR> בֶּן־חֲזָאֵל *son of Hazael* 2 K $13_{3.25}$, יַד *hand of* 2 K $13_{3}$, חֶרֶב *sword of* 1 K $19_{17}$, בֵּית *house of* Am $1_{4}$. <APP> מֶלֶךְ *king* 2 K $8_{28}$||2 C $22_{5}$ $8_{29}$||2 C $22_{6}$ $9_{14.15}$ $12_{18.19}$ $13_{3.22.24}$. <PREP> לְ of direction, *to*, + אמר *say* 2 K $8_{14.14}$, שׁלח *send* 2 K $12_{19}$; אֶל *to*, + אמר *say* 2 K $8_{8}$ (חֲזָהאֵל, mss. חזאל) $8_{10}$; עַל *against* 2 C $22_{5}$; אֵת *with, against*, + לחם ni. *fight* 2 K $9_{15}$; עִם *with* 2 K $8_{28}$; מִפְּנֵי *because of*, + שׁמר *keep*, i.e. guard 2 K $9_{14}$.

→ חזה *see* + אֵל *God*.

**חזה I** $_{59.6.4}$ vb. **see—Qal** Pf. חָזָה, חָזִיתָ, חָזַת, חָזִתִי (חֲזִיתִיךְ), חָזוּ, חֲזִיתֶם, יֶחֱזוּ; impf. יֶחֱזֶה, אֶחֱזֶה, תֶּחֱזֶה, 3fs תֶּחַז, (אֶחַז), יֶחֱזוּ, תֶּחֱזוּ (יֶחֱזָיוּן), 3fpl תֶּחֱזֶינָה, נֶחֱזֶה; + waw וָאֶחֱזֶה, וַיֶּחֱזוּ; impv. חֲזֵה, חֲזוּ; ptc. חֹזֶה, חֹזִים; inf. חֲזוֹת—**see, perceive, gaze, select, cleave** (Jb $8_{17}$, unless here and at Ex $24_{11}$ Ps $63_{3}$ Jb $36_{25}$ חזה II *be opposite*; perh. at Jb $34_{32}$ חזה III *be vile*), <SUBJ> יי Y. Si $15_{18}$, Babylon Is $47_{13}$, בֵּית *house* of Jacob Is $48_{6}$, Amos Am $1_{1}$, Balaam Nm $24_{4.16}$=4QTestim$_{11}$, Ben Sira Si $42_{15}$, Eliphaz Jb $15_{17}$, Habakkuk Hb $1_{1}$=1QpHab $1_{1}$ ([חוזה]), Isaiah Is $1_{1}$=3QpIsa$_{1}$ ([חוזה])=4QpIsa$^{e}$ $1_{1}$ ([חוזה]) Is $2_{1}$ $13_{1}$ Si $48_{24}$, Job Jb $15_{17}$ $19_{26.27}$ $23_{9}$, Micah Mc $1_{1}$, Moses Ex $18_{21}$, אָדָם *human being* Jb $36_{25}$, אִישׁ *man* 4Q424 $3_{3}$, בֶּן *son* of human being, i.e. mortal Ezk $12_{27}$, בַּת *daughter* of Jerusalem Ezk $13_{23}$.

אָצִיל *leader* Ex $24_{11}$ (|| ראה *see*), נָבִיא *prophet* Ezk $13_{6.7}$ (+ אמר *say*) $13_{8}$ (+ דבר pi. *speak*) $13_{9.16}$ $22_{28}$ Lm $2_{14.14}$, יָשָׁר *upright one* Ps $11_{7}$, צַדִּיק *righteous one* Ps $58_{11}$, רָשָׁע *wicked one* Is $26_{11.11}$, wicked Is $57_{8}$.

ידע ptc. *one who knows* Jb $24_{1(Qr)}$, חֹזֶה *seer* Is $30_{10.10}$, seer Ezk $31_{24}$, קֹסֵם *diviner* Zc $10_{2}$, יֹעֵץ *counsellor* Si $37_{7(D)}$, worshipper Ps $17_{15}$ $27_{4}$ $46_{9}$ $63_{3}$, עַיִן *eye* Is $33_{17}$ Mc $4_{11}$=4QpMic $1_{5}$ ([ותחז]) Ps $11_{4}$ $17_{2}$, נֵפֶל *miscarriage* Ps $58_{9}$, perh. שֹׁרֶשׁ *root* Jb $8_{17}$, כֹּל *everyone* Jb $27_{12}$ 1QH $2_{15}$ 4QTohD$_{7}$; subj. not specified, Is $33_{20}$ Jb $34_{32}$ Pr $22_{29}$ $24_{32}$ $29_{20}$ Ca $7_{1.1}$ Si $44_{3}$ CD $2_{12}$ 1QH $4_{10.20}$ 1QM $11_{8}$ 4QBer$^{a}$ $3.2_{12}$ ([חוזין]) MurEpBarC$^{b}_{6}$.

<OBJ> Zion Is $33_{20}$, אֱלֹהִים *God* Ex $24_{11}$ Ps $63_{3}$, אֱלוֹהַּ *God* Jb $19_{26}$, אֵל *God* Ps $63_{3}$, מֶלֶךְ *king* Is $33_{17}$, אִישׁ *man* Ex $18_{21}$ Pr $22_{29}$ $29_{20}$, seer Ezk $21_{34}$, יָשָׁר *upright one* 4Q424 $3_{3}$, קִנְאָה *passion* Is $26_{11}$, יָד *hand* Is $57_{8}$ (unless יָד חָזִית = *erect* [חָזָה *prominent*] *penis*), פָּנִים *face* Ps $11_{7}$ $17_{15}$, מִפְעָל *deed* Ps $46_{9}$, אֱמֶת *truth* CD $2_{12}$ 4QTohD$_{7}$ 4QBer$^{a}$ $3.2_{12}$, נְכֹחָה *truth* Is $30_{10}$ 1QH $2_{15}$, מֵישָׁרִים *straightness* Ps $17_{2}$, נָקָם *vengeance* Ps $58_{11}$.

מַהֲתַלָּה *deception* Is $30_{10}$, שָׁוְא *falsehood* Ezk $13_{6.9.23}$ $21_{34}$ $22_{28}$ Lm $2_{14.14}$, שֶׁקֶר *lie* Zc $10_{2}$, כָּזָב *lie* Ezk $13_{8}$, תְּעוּת *error* 1QH $4_{20}$, רְמִיָּה *deceit* 1QH $4_{10}$, קֶסֶם *divination* Ezk $13_{6}$, תָּפֵל *worthless vision* Lm $2_{14}$, מַדּוּחִים *repudiation* Lm $2_{14}$, נְבוּאָה *prophetic word* Si $44_{3}$, מַחֲזֶה *vision* Nm $24_{4.16}$=4QTestim$_{11}$ Ezk $13_{7}$, חָזוֹן *vision* Is $1_{1}$=3QpIsa$_{1}$ Ezk $12_{27}$ $13_{16}$, דָּבָר *word* Is $2_{1}$ Am $1_{1}$ Mc $1_{1}$, מַשָּׂא *pronouncement* Is $13_{1}$ Hb $1_{1}$=1QpHab $1_{1}$ Lm $2_{14}$, שֶׁמֶשׁ *sun* Ps $58_{9}$, תְּעוּדָה *fixed time* 1QM $11_{8}$, יוֹם *day* Jb $24_{1}$, אַחֲרִית *end* Si $48_{24}$, זֶה *this* Jb $15_{17}$ Si $42_{15}$, כֹּל *everything* Is $48_{6}$.

<PREP> לְ of direction, *to*, + Israelite(s) Is $30_{10}$, יוֹם *day* Ezk $12_{27}$, עֵת *time* Ezk $12_{27}$; of benefit, *to, for*, + Zion Lm $2_{14.14}$, Jerusalem Ezk $13_{16}$ Lm $2_{14.14}$, Job Jb $19_{27}$, בֵּן *son* of Ammon Ezk $21_{34}$.

בְּ of place/time, *in*, + קֹדֶשׁ *sanctuary* Ps $63_{3}$, יוֹם *day* Is $1_{1}$ Am $1_{1}$; of instrument, *by (means of)*, + רוּחַ *spirit* Si $48_{24}$; of accompaniment, *in, with*, + יָפֶה *beauty* Is $33_{17}$, צֶדֶק *righteousness* Ps $17_{15}$; *because of*, + Zion Mc $4_{11}$=4QpMic $1_{5}$; introducing object, + נֹעַם *kindness* Ps $27_{4}$, פֹּעַל *deed* Jb $36_{25}$, כּוֹכָב *star* Is $47_{13}$, שׁוּלַמִּית *Shulammite* Ca $7_{1.1}$.

מִן of direction, *from*, + בָּשָׂר *flesh* Jb $19_{26}$; partitive, *some of, (any) one of*, + עַם *people* Ex $18_{21}$.

עַל *concerning*, + Israel Am $1_{1}$, Judah Is $1_{1}$=3QpIsa$_{1}$=4QpIsa$^{e}$ $1_{1}$ Is $2_{1}$, Samaria Mc $1_{1}$, Jerusalem Is $1_{1}$=3QpIsa$_{1}$=4QpIsa$^{e}$ $1_{1}$ Is $2_{1}$ Mc $1_{1}$.

בֵּית *among*, + אֶבֶן *stone* Jb $8_{17}$.

Also Si $46_{15}$.*

→ חֹזֶה *seer*, חָזֶה *vision*, חָזוֹן *vision*, חָזוּת *revelation*, חָזָה *vision*, חִזָּיוֹן *vision*, מַחֲזֶה *vision*.

***חזה II** $_{4}$ vb. **be opposite—Qal** $_{3}$ Pf. חָזוּ, חֲזִיתִיךָ; impf. יֶחֱזֶה; + waw וַיֶּחֱזוּ—**stand apart, stay away (from), confront** (unless חזה I *see* throughout), <SUBJ> worshipper Ps $63_{3}$, Moses, Aaron, Nadab, and Abihu Ex

24$_{11}$, אָדָם *human being* Jb 36$_{25}$, זָקֵן *elder* Ex 24$_{11}$. <OBJ> אֱלֹהִים *God* Ex 24$_{11}$ Ps 63$_{3}$, בַּיִת *house* Jb 8$_{17}$. <PREP> בְּ *against*, + אֵל *God* Jb 36$_{25}$.

*חזה III 1 vb. **be vile**—**Qal** 1 Impf. אֶחֱזֶה—<SUBJ> perh. אָדָם impious *human being* Jb 34$_{32}$.

[חָזָה] 1 n.f. **vision**—pl. cstr. חֲזוֹת—as title of prophetic book, <CSTR> חֲזוֹת יֶעְדּוֹ הַחֹזֶה *visions of Iddo the seer* 2 C 9$_{29}$ (or em. חָזוּת *vision of*, from חָזוּת *vision*; + דָּבָר *word*, נְבוּאָה *prophecy*). <PREP> בְּ of place, *in*, + כתב pass. *be written* 2 C 9$_{29}$.*

⇒ חזה *see*.

חָזֶה I 13.0.4 n.m. **breast**—cstr. חֲזֵה (Q חזי); pl. חָזוֹת—of sacrificial animal, <SUBJ> היה *be* Ez 29$_{26}$ (+ לְ *to* Moses, *as* a portion) Lv 7$_{31}$ (+ לְ *to* Aaron and his sons) 11QT 21$_{02}$, נוף ho. *be waved* Ex 29$_{27}$. <OBJ> בוא hi. *bring* Lv 10$_{15}$, נוף hi. *wave* Ex 29$_{26}$ Lv 7$_{30}$ 8$_{29}$ 9$_{21}$ (+ שׁוֹק) 11QT 20$_{15}$, לקח *take* Ex 29$_{26}$ Lv 7$_{34}$ 8$_{29}$, רום hi. *raise*, i.e. offer 11QT 20$_{15}$ 22$_{9}$, אכל *eat* Lv 10$_{14}$, קדשׁ pi. *consecrate* Ex 29$_{27}$. <CSTR> חֲזֵה הַתְּנוּפָה *breast of the wave offering* Ex 29$_{27}$ Lv 7$_{34}$ 10$_{14.15}$ Nm 6$_{20}$ 18$_{18}$ 11QT 21$_{02}$ ([התנופה]) 22$_{9}$ (חזי; all eight ‖ שׁוֹק *thigh*). <APP> תְּנוּפָה *wave offering* Ex 29$_{26}$ Lv 7$_{30}$ 8$_{29}$ 9$_{21}$ 11QT 20$_{15}$, תְּרוּמָה *offering* 11QT 20$_{15}$.

<PREP> כְּ *as*, + היה *be* Nm 18$_{18}$; עַל *upon, with*, Lv 7$_{30}$ (הַחֵלֶב עַל־הֶחָזֶה *the fat with the breast*) Nm 6$_{20}$, + שׂים *place* fat Lv 9$_{20}$. <COLL> הֶחָזֶה מֵאֵיל הַמִּלֻּאִים *the breast of the ram of the installation* Ex 29$_{26}$. Also 11QT 24$_{3}$. <SYN> שׁוֹק *thigh*.

*חָזֶה II 3 adj. **prominent**—fem. חָזִית, חָזוּת—**1. prominent, erect, protruding,** used attributively of יָד *hand*, i.e. penis Is 57$_{8}$ (unless חָזִית = *you saw* hand), קֶרֶן *horn* Dn 8$_{5}$ (unless חָזוּת = horn of *vision*, i.e. conspicuous horn; or em. אַחַת *one* horn). **2.** as noun, **protruding one**, i.e. horn (unless חָזוּת = *conspicuous one*), <SUBJ> עלה *go up* Dn 8$_{8}$ (or del. חָזוּת) <COLL> חָזוּת אַרְבַּע *four protruding ones* Dn 8$_{8}$ (or del. חָזוּת).

חֹזֶה I 16.1.3 n.m. **seer**—cstr. חֹזֵה (חוֹזֵה); pl. חֹזִים (Q חוזים); cstr. mss חוֹזֵי—<SUBJ> חזה *see* Is 30$_{10}$ (‖ רֹאֶה *seer*), אמר *say* 2 C 19$_{2}$, דבר pi. *speak* Is 30$_{10}$ 2 C 33$_{18}$, נבא ni. *prophesy* Am 7$_{12}$, בושׁ *be ashamed* Mc 3$_{7}$ (‖ קֹסֵם *diviner*), סור *turn aside* Is 30$_{10}$, נטה hi. *turn aside* Is 30$_{10}$, שׁבת hi. *remove* Is 30$_{10}$, הלך *go* Am 7$_{12}$, יצא *go out* 2 C 19$_{2}$, ברח *flee* Am 7$_{12}$, אכל *eat* Am 7$_{12}$, יסף *do again* Am 7$_{12}$, עטה *wrap oneself* Mc 3$_{7}$, דרשׁ pass. *be sought* Si 46$_{15}$ (ד[רושׁ]).

<CSTR> חֹזֵה דָוִד *seer of David* 2 S 24$_{11}$‖1 C 21$_{9}$ (דָּוִיד), הַמֶּלֶךְ *of the king* 1 C 25$_{5}$ 2 C 29$_{25}$ (+ נָבִיא *prophet*) 35$_{15}$ (חוֹזֵה; mss חוֹזֵי *seers of*); דִּבְרֵי ... הַחֹזֶה *words of ... the seer* 1 C 29$_{29}$ (‖ רֹאֶה *seer*) 2 C 12$_{15}$ (both ‖ נָבִיא) 29$_{30}$, דִּבְרֵי הַחֹזִים *words of the seers* 2 C 33$_{18.19(ms)}$ (חוֹזִים; L חוֹזָי *of Hozai*; or em. חוֹזָיו *of his seers*), חֲזוֹת ... הַחֹזֶה *visions of ... the seer* 2 C 9$_{29}$ (or em. חָזוּת *vision of*; + נָבִיא *prophet*), מִצְוַת ... חֹזֵה *command of ... the seer of* 2 C 35$_{15}$ (mss חוֹזֵי *of the seers of*), נְבִיאֵי כָל־חֹזֶה appar. *the prophets of every seer* 2 K 17$_{13(Qr)}$ 2 K 17$_{13(Kt, ms)}$, כול החוזים *all the seers* 4QMidrEschat$^{a}$ 4$_{9}$.

<APP> Asaph 2 C 29$_{30}$ 35$_{15(mss)}$, Gad 2 S 24$_{11}$‖1 C 21$_{9}$ 1 C 29$_{29}$ 2 C 29$_{25}$, Heman 1 C 25$_{5}$ 2 C 35$_{15(mss)}$, Iddo 2 C 9$_{29}$ 12$_{15}$, Jeduthun 2 C 35$_{15}$, Jehu 2 C 19$_{2}$, בֶּן *son* 2 C 19$_{2}$, נָבִיא *prophet* 2 S 24$_{11}$.

<PREP> לְ of direction, *to*, + אמר *say* Is 30$_{10}$; of possession, *of, (belonging) to* 1 C 25$_{5}$; בְּ of place, *among* 4QMidrEschat$^{a}$ 4$_{9}$; אֶל *to*, + היה *be* 2 S 24$_{11}$, דבר pi. *speak* 1 C 21$_{9}$; בְּיַד *by means of*, עוד hi. *testify* 2 K 17$_{13}$ (mss) (בְּיַד כָּל־נָבִיא וְכָל־חֹזֶה *by means of every prophet and every seer*), ידע hi. *make known* CD 2$_{12}$.

<COLL> אֶת־רָאשֵׁיכֶם הַחֹזִים כִּסָּה *he has covered your heads, the seers* Is 29$_{10}$=4QpIsa$^{c}$ 15$_{2}$ ([ח]זים; ‖ נָבִיא *prophet*).

Also perh. 5Q517 15 perh. 4Q518 2.

<SYN> נָבִיא *prophet*, רֹאֶה *seer*, קֹסֵם *diviner*.*

⇒ חזה *see*.

חֹזֶה II 1 n.[m.] **agreement**, <OBJ> עשׂה *make* with Sheol Is 28$_{15}$ (or em. חֹזֶה to חָזֶה or חזה with same meaning, or חֶסֶד *loyalty*; ‖ בְּרִית *covenant*). <SYN> בְּרִית *covenant*.

חֲזָהאֵל, see חֲזָאֵל *Hazael*.

חֲזוֹ 1 pr.n.m. **Hazo**, son of Nahor and Milcah and nephew of Abraham, <OBJ> ילד *give birth* Gn $22_{22}$. <APP> בֵּן *son* Gn $22_{22}$.

**חָזוֹן** I $_{35.2.11}$ n.m. **vision**—cstr. חֲזוֹן—**vision,** in ref. to vision during night, deceptive vision, etc. (e.g. 1 S $3_1$ Is $29_7$ Jr $14_{14}$ Ezk $13_{16}$ Dn $8_{15}$),* **revelatory word, inspired saying** (e.g. Is $1_1$ Ob$_1$ Na $1_1$),* sought from prophet (e.g. Ezk $7_{26}$ Lm $2_9$; unless at Ezk $7_{13}$ חָזוֹן II *pact* and at Pr $29_{18}$ חָזוֹן II *magistrate*).

<SUBJ> היה *be* Is $29_7$ Ezk $12_{24}$, פרץ ni. *be ordered* 1 S $3_1$, ראה ni. *appear* Dn $8_1$, שׁוב *go back* Ezk $7_{13}$, אבד *perish* Ezk $12_{22}$, דבר *speak* 11QPs$^a$ $22_{13}$.

<NOM CL> חָזוֹן לַיָּמִים *the vision is for the days* yet to come Dn $10_{14}$, הֶחָזוֹן ... לְיָמִים רַבִּים *the vision ... is for many days* Ezk $12_{27}$, חָזוֹן לַמּוֹעֵד *the vision is for the appointed time* Hb $2_3$=1QpHab $7_5$, לְעֶת־קֵץ הֶחָזוֹן *the vision is for the time of the end* Dn $8_{17}$, הואה חזון *that is the vision* 4Q417 $2.1_{16}$, עַד־מָתַי הֶחָזוֹן *how long is the vision?* Dn $8_{13}$, אֵין חָזוֹן *there is no vision* 1 S $3_1$ Pr $29_{18}$.

<OBJ> חזה *see* Is $1_1$=3QpIsa$_1$ Ezk $12_{27}$ $13_{16}$, ראה *see* Dn $8_{15}$, רבה hi. *multiply* Ho $12_{11}$, חתם *seal up* Dn $9_{24}$, סתם *keep secret* Dn $8_{26}$, פתח *open* 4QMyst$^b$ $1.2_3$, בקשׁ pi. *seek* Ezk $7_{26}$, מצא *find* Lm $2_9$, לקח *take,* i.e. accept 11QPs$^a$ $22_{13}$, עמד hi. *cause to stand,* i.e. fulfil Dn $11_{14}$, קום hi. *establish* Si $36_{20}$, כתב *write* Hb $2_2$=1QpHab $6_{15}$ ([חזון]), דבר pi. *speak* Jr $23_{16}$, נבא htp. *prophesy* Jr $14_{14}$.

<CSTR> חֲזוֹן יְשַׁעְיָהוּ *vision of Isaiah* Is $1_1$=3QpIsa$_1$ 2 C $32_{32}$, עֹבַדְיָה *of Obadiah* Ob$_1$, נַחוּם *of Nahum* Na $1_1$, שָׁלֹם *of peace* Ezk $13_{16}$, דַּעַת *of knowledge* 1QH $4_{18}$, לַיְלָה *of (the) night* Is $29_7$, שָׁוְא *of falsehood* Ezk $12_{24}$, שֶׁקֶר *of falsehood* Jr $14_{14}$, לִבָּם *of their heart* Jr $23_{16}$, נפשׁו *of his soul* Si $40_6$.

אנשי חזונכה *men of your vision* 1QH $14_7$, [ח]תם החזון *seal of the vision* 4QMyst$^b$ $1.2_2$, סֵפֶר חֲזוֹן *book of the vision of* Na $1_1$, דְּבַר כָּל־חָזוֹן *word of every vision* Ezk $12_{23}$, כָּל־חָזוֹן *every vision* Ezk $12_{22}$ Dn $1_{17}$ 4Q417 $2.1_{22}$ (כול), כֹּל הֶחָזוֹן *all the vision* 1 C $17_{15}$, כָּל־חֲזוֹן *every vision of* Ezk $12_{24}$.

<APP> חֲלוֹם *dream* Is $29_7$.

<ADJ> זֶה *this* 1 C $17_{15}$.

<PREP> לְ *concerning,* + אמר *say* 1QH $4_{18}$.

בְּ of instrument, *by (means of),* + דבר pi. *speak* Ps $89_{20}$; *in, with,* + ראה *see* Dn $8_{2.2}$ $9_{21}$, בין hi. *understand* Dn $1_{17}$ (‖ חֲלוֹם *dream*), כתב pass. *be written* 2 C $32_{32}$.

כְּ *as,* + דבר pi. *speak* 1 C $17_{15}$.

מִן privative, *without* Mc $3_6$; of cause, *because of* Si $40_6$.

<SYN> חֲלוֹם *dream.*

Also 1QH $6_4$ ([חזון]) fr. $29_2$ 4QMyst$^b$ $1.2_6$ (ח[זון]) 4Q410 $1_9$.

⇒ חזה *see.*

*__חָזוֹן__ II $_1$ n.m. **pact** (unless חָזוֹן I *vision*), <SUBJ> שׁוב *go back* Ezk $7_{13}$.

*__חָזוֹן__ III $_1$ n.[m.] **magistrate** (unless חָזוֹן I *vision*), <NOM CL> בְּאֵין חָזוֹן יִפָּרַע עָם *where there is no magistrate, the people cast off restraint* Pr $29_{18}$.

**חָזוּת** I $_{4.1}$ n.f. **vision**—cstr. חָזוּת—**1. vision,** of prophet (Is $21_2$ $29_{11}$ 2 C $9_{29}$ [if em.]), **(fleeting) glimpse** (Si $42_{22[M]}$), <SUBJ> היה *be* Is $29_{11}$=4QpIsa$^c$ $15_2$ (ח[זות]), נגד ho. *be told* Is $21_2$. <CSTR> חֲזוֹת יֶעְדּוֹ הַחֹזֶה *vision of Iddo the seer* 2 C $9_{29}$ (if em. חֲזוֹת *visions of*), חָזוּת הַכֹּל *vision of everything* Is $29_{11}$=4QpIsa$^c$ $15_2$ (ח[זות הכול]), חזות מראה *glimpse of a vision* Si $42_{22(M)}$ (+ נִיצוֹץ *spark*). <ADJ> קָשָׁה *hard* Is $21_2$. <PREP> בְּ of place, *in,* + כתב pass. *be written* 2 C $9_{29}$ (if em.; see Cstr.); עַד *unto* Si $42_{22(M)}$.

**2. conspicuousness, conspicuous one** (unless חָזוּת fem. of חָזֶה *prominent*), <SUBJ> עלה *grow* Dn $8_8$ (or del.). <CSTR> קֶרֶן חָזוּת *horn of conspicuousness,* i.e. conspicuous horn Dn $8_5$ (or em. אַחַת *one* horn). <COLL> חָזוּת אַרְבַּע *four conspicuous ones* Dn $8_8$ (or del. חָזוּת).*

⇒ חזה *see.*

[**חָזוּת**] II $_1$ n.f. **agreement**—sf. חָזוּתְכֶם—<SUBJ> קום *stand* Is $28_{18}$ (or em.; see Coll.; ‖ בְּרִית *covenant*). <COLL> חָזוּתְכֶם אֶת־שְׁאוֹל *your agreement with Sheol* Is $28_{18}$ (or em. חַסְדְּכֶם *your loyalty*). <SYN> בְּרִית *covenant.**

**חֲזִיאֵל** $_1$ pr.n.m. **Haziel,** Levite, son of Shimei and descendant of Gershom, <NOM CL> בְּנֵי שִׁמְעִי שְׁלֹמִית וַחֲזִיאֵל *the sons of Shimei were Shelomith and Haziel* 1 C $23_{9(Qr)}$ (Kt שׁלמות *Shelomoth*). ⇒ חזה *see* + אֵל *God.*

**חֲזָיָה** 1 pr.n.m. **Hazaiah,** son of Adaiah, father of Col-hozeh and descendant of Judah, <CSTR> בֶּן־חֲזָיָה *son of Hazaiah* Ne 11$_{5}$. <APP> בֵּן *son* Ne 11$_{5}$.
⇒ חזה *see* + יה *Y.*

**חֶזְיוֹן** 1 pr.n.m. **Hezion,** king of Syria and ancestor of Ben-hadad, <CSTR> בֶּן־חֶזְיוֹן *son of Hezion* 1 K 15$_{18}$.

**חִזָּיוֹן** 9 n.m. **vision**—cstr. חֶזְיוֹן; sf. חֶזְיֹנוֹ; pl. חֶזְיֹנוֹת; cstr. חֶזְיֹנוֹת—<OBJ> ראה *see* Jl 3$_{1}$ (|| חֲלוֹם *dream*). <CSTR> חֶזְיוֹן לַיְלָה *vision of the night* Jb 20$_{8}$ (לַיְלָה; + חֲלוֹם *dream*) 33$_{15}$, חֶזְיֹנוֹת לָיְלָה *visions of the night* Jb 4$_{13}$; גֵּיא חִזָּיוֹן *valley of vision* Is 22$_{1.5}$, כֹּל חִזָּיוֹן *all* this *vision* 2 S 7$_{17}$ (|| דָּבָר *word*). <APP> חֲלוֹם *dream* Jb 33$_{15}$, תְּנוּמָה *slumber* Jb 33$_{15}$. <ADJ> זֶה *this* 2 S 7$_{17}$. <PREP> בְּ of place, time, *in, during,* + גלה *uncover* ear Jb 33$_{15}$; כְּ *as,* + נדד ho. *be chased away* Jb 20$_{8}$; *according to,* + דבר pi. *speak* 2 S 7$_{17}$; מִן *from* Jb 4$_{13}$; of agent, *by (means of),* + בעת pi. *terrify* Jb 7$_{14}$ (|| חֲלוֹם *dream*); בוש מִן *be ashamed of* Zc 13$_{4}$. <SYN> חֲלוֹם *dream,* דָּבָר *word.**
⇒ חזה *see.*

[חֲזִיז] I 3.2 n.[m.] **thunderstorm**—cstr. חֲזִיז; pl. חֲזִיזִים—perh. specif. **thunderbolt, lightning, thundercloud** (unless at Zc 10$_{1}$ חֲזִיז II *dream*), <OBJ> עשׂה *make* Zc 10$_{1}$ (+ מְטַר גֶּשֶׁם *rain of rain*). <CSTR> חֲזִיז קֹלוֹת *lightning of thunder* Jb 28$_{26}$ (|| מָטָר *rain*) 38$_{25}$ (|| שֶׁטֶף *flood*) Si 40$_{13(B)}$ (קולות); עת חזיזים *time of thunderstorms* Si 32$_{26}$ (or em. כעת *as a time of* to כעב *as a cloud of*). <PREP> לְ of benefit, *to, for,* + עשׂה *make* a way Jb 28$_{26}$, פלג pi. *divide* a channel Jb 38$_{25}$; בְּ of time, *in, during* Si 40$_{13(B)}$. <SYN> מָטָר *rain,* שֶׁטֶף *flood.*

*[חֲזִיז] II 1 n.[m.] **dream**—pl. חֲזִיזִים—<OBJ> עשׂה *make* Zc 10$_{1}$ (unless חֲזִיז I *thunderstorm;* + מְטַר גֶּשֶׁם *rain of rain*).

**חֲזִיר** 7 n.m. **swine**—Q חוזיר (1QIsa$^{a}$)—**swine, wild boar,** prohibited as food (Lv 11$_{7}$||Dt 14$_{8}$), <SUBJ> כרסם pi. *tear off* Ps 80$_{14}$ (+ זִיז *moving thing*), פרס *divide* hoof Lv 11$_{7}$||Dt 14$_{8}$, שׁסע *divide* Lv 11$_{7}$ Dt 14$_{8}$ (if ins. שֹׁסַע שֶׁסַע פַּרְסָה *it divides the cleft of the hoof*), גרר *chew* cud Lv 11$_{7}$ Dt 14$_{8}$ (if ins. יָגוֹר or יִגֹּר). <OBJ> אכל *eat* Lv 11$_{7}$||Dt 14$_{8}$, חמד *desire* Is 66$_{3}$ (if em.; see Cstr.). <CSTR> בְּשַׂר הַחֲזִיר *flesh of the swine* Is 65$_{4}$ 66$_{17}$, דַּם־חֲזִיר *blood of a swine* Is 66$_{3}$ (or em. דַּם to חֹמֵד *one who desires*), אַף *nose of* Pr 11$_{22}$. <COLL> חֲזִיר מִיַּעַר *wild boar from the forest* Ps 80$_{14}$.*

**חֵזִיר** 2.0.11.1 pr.n.m. **Hezir, 1.** officer and head of priestly family at time of David, <PREP> לְ of benefit, *to, for,* + יצא *go out,* i.e. cast lot 1 C 24$_{15}$.

**2.** leader and co-signatory with Nehemiah, <NOM CL> רָאשֵׁי הָעָם ... חֵזִיר *the chiefs of the people were ... Hezir* Ne 10$_{21}$.

**3.** head of priestly family of (second and) first century BCE, <CSTR> בני חזיר *the sons of Hezir* Bene Ḥezir tomb inscr.$_{3}$ (Frey 1394).

**4.** title of priestly priestly course (and the period of its office), perh. in ref. to descendants of foregoing.

<NOM CL> [ב]שנית ... ח[זיר] *on the second (sabbath, is ... Hezir* 4QMishF$^{a}$ 1$_{3}$. <CSTR> ביאת ח[זיר] *arrival of Hezir* 4QMishC$^{c}$ 1$_{5}$, שבת חזיר *sabbath of Hezir* 4QMishD 2$_{2}$. <PREP> בְּ of time, *in, of* 4QS$^{e}$ 8$_{2}$ 4QMishA 1.3$_{11}$ 4.4$_{10}$ 4.6$_{1}$ 4QMishB$^{a}$ 1.2$_{5}$ ([ב]חזיר) 1.3$_{5.8}$ (בחוז[יר]) 2.1$_{1}$ 2.2$_{3.7.9}$ ([ב]חז[יר]) 2.3$_{2.9}$ (both [בחזיר]) 4QMishB$^{b}$ 1.1$_{9}$ ([בחזי]ר) 4QMishC$^{b}$ 2$_{1}$ (בחזו[י]ר) 4QMishC$^{c}$ 1$_{6}$ ([ב]חזיר).

Also 4QMishF$^{b}$ 1$_{1}$ ([חזיר]).

**חזק** I 293.13.91 vb. **be strong**—**Qal** 84.1.18 Pf. חָזַק (חָזָק), חָזְקָה (חָזְקָה), חֲזַקְתַּנִי, חָזְקוּ, (חָזְקוּ); impf. יֶחֱזַק (יֶחֱזָק), 3fs תֶּחֱזַק, תֶּחֶזְקוּ, יֶחֶזְקוּ (יֶחְזְקוּ), 3fpl תֶּחֱזַקְנָה, נֶחֱזַק; + waw וַיֶּחֱזַק (וַיֶּחֱזָק), 3fs וַתֶּחֱזַק; impv. וְחָזַקְתָּ, וְחָזְקוּ, וַחֲזַקְתֶּם; חֲזַק (חֲזָק), חִזְקוּ; ptc. חָזֵק; inf. חָזְקָה (חֶזְקָה)—**be strong, be firm, be powerful, be courageous, be confident** (in physical, political, moral, etc. contexts); **be hard** (of Pharaoh's heart, Ex 7$_{13.22}$ 8$_{15}$ 9$_{35}$), **be severe** (of famine Gn 41$_{56.57}$ 47$_{20}$ 2 K 25$_{3}$=Jr 52$_{6}$), **take hold of** branches of tree (of Absalom's head, 2 S 18$_{9}$); rarely with dir. obj.; or followed by prep. בְּ, מִן or עַל, **defeat, be stronger (than), prevail (against)** (e.g. Jg 19$_{4}$ 2 S 10$_{11}$ ||1 C 19$_{12}$ 1 K 16$_{22}$ Jr 20$_{7}$ [unless at Jr 20$_{7}$ חזק II *outwit*] 2 C 27$_{5}$), perh. **be too much (for)** (עַל) (Gn 47$_{20}$ Ml 3$_{13}$).*

<SUBJ> ׳׳ Y. Jr 20$_{7}$ (+ יכל *be able*, i.e. prevail), עַם *people* 1 K 16$_{22}$ Hg 2$_{4}$, Aramaeans 2 S 10$_{11}$||1 C 19$_{12}$ 1 K 20$_{23.25}$, Egyptians Ex 12$_{33}$ (+ מהר pi. *go quickly*), Israel Dt 31$_{6}$ (|| אמץ *be strong*; :: ירא *fear*, ערץ *dread*) Jos 23$_{6}$ Jg 1$_{28}$ 1 K 20$_{23}$, Israelite(s) Dt 11$_{8}$ 12$_{23}$ Ezr 9$_{12}$ 11QT 53$_{5}$, Benjamin 2 C 15$_{7}$ (+ רפה *be limp*), Judah 2 C 15$_{7}$.

Abishai 2 S 10$_{12}$||1 C 19$_{13}$, Amaziah 2 C 25$_{8}$, Amnon 2 S 13$_{14}$, Asa 2 C 15$_{7}$, David 1 S 17$_{50}$ 2 S 3$_{1}$, Ezra Ezr 10$_{4}$, Hezekiah Is 39$_{1}$ (1QIsa$^{a}$ ויחיה *and he revived*), Joshua, son of Nun Dt 31$_{7.23}$ Jos 1$_{6.7.9}$ (:: ערץ *dread*, חתת *be terrified*) 1$_{18}$ (all six || אמץ *be strong*) perh. 4QPsJos$^{a}$ 3.2$_{10}$ (+ חתת), Joshua, priest Hg 2$_{4}$, Jotham 2 C 27$_{5}$, Solomon 1 K 2$_{2}$ 1 C 22$_{13}$ (|| אמץ; :: ירא *fear*, חתת) 28$_{7.10.20}$ (:: ירא, חתת; both || אמץ) 2 C 8$_{3}$, Tilgath-pilneser 2 C 28$_{20}$ (or em. חֲזָקוֹ appar. *he prevailed against him* to חִזְּקוֹ *he strengthened him*, i.e. pi.), Uzziah 2 C 26$_{15}$, Zerubbabel Hg 2$_{4}$.

מֶלֶךְ *king* Dn 11$_{5}$ 2 C 25$_{8}$ 28$_{20}$ (or em.; see above), קָצִין *leader* Jos 10$_{25}$ (|| אמץ *be strong*; :: ירא *fear*, חתת *be terrified*), שַׂר *prince* Dn 11$_{5}$ (or del.) 2 C 32$_{7}$ (|| אמץ; :: ירא, חתת), כֹּהֵן *priest* Hg 2$_{4}$ 2 C 19$_{11}$ 31$_{4}$, לֵוִי *Levite* 2 C 19$_{11}$ 31$_{4}$, זָקֵן *elder* Jos 23$_{6}$, אִישׁ *man* Dn 10$_{19.19}$ (mss וֶאֱמָץ *and be strong*; or em. וְהִתְחַזֵּק *and take courage*, i.e. htp.; :: ירא), אָב *father* Jg 19$_{4}$ (mss וַיֶּחֱזַק־, i.e. hi.), בֵּן *son* 1 C 28$_{20}$ 1QM 1$_{13}$ (+ נגף *smite*) 1QM 17$_{16}$ ([יחזקו בני]), specif. *son* of Israel Jos 17$_{13}$, of Ammon 2 S 10$_{11}$||1 C 19$_{12}$, אָח *brother* Is 41$_{6}$, חֹתֵן *father-in-law* Jg 19$_{4}$ (mss וַיֶּחֱזַק־, i.e. hi.), נַעַר *lad* 2 S 13$_{28}$ (:: ירא; + היה לְבֶן־חַיִל *be son of valour*, i.e. valiant), שֹׁפֵט *judge* Jos 23$_{6}$, שֹׁטֵר *official* Jos 23$_{6}$, מהר ni. ptc. *hurried*, i.e. anxious, *one* Is 35$_{4}$ (:: ירא), יחל pi. ptc. *one who waits* Ps 31$_{25}$ (+ אמץ hi. *show courage*), מאס *one who refuses* 1QS 3$_{1}$ (unless pi.), worshipper Ps 27$_{14}$ (+ אמץ hi. *exhibit courage*).

ראשׁ *head* 2 S 18$_{9}$, *chief* Jos 23$_{6}$ 2 C 19$_{11}$, לֵב *heart* of Pharaoh Ex 7$_{13.22}$ 8$_{15}$ 9$_{35}$, יָד *hand* Jg 7$_{11}$ 2 S 2$_{7}$ (+ היה לְבֶן־חַיִל *be son of valour*, i.e. valiant) 16$_{21}$ Ezk 3$_{14}$ 22$_{14}$ Zc 8$_{9.13}$ (+ ירא *fear*) 4QPsJos$^{a}$ 3.2$_{11}$ ([ת]חזקנה), זְרוֹעַ *arm* Ezk 30$_{21}$ (or em. לְחָבְשָׁהּ לְחָזְקָה *to bind it that it may be strong* to לָשׂוּם חָזְקָה *to place strength*; or לְחַזְּקָהּ *to make it strong*), נֶפֶשׁ *soul* 1QH 2$_{28}$ (unless hi.), קוֹל *sound* of trumpet Ex 19$_{19}$, בַּיִת *house* 2 K 12$_{13}$ (or em. לְחָזְקָה *to be strong* to לְחַזְּקָהּ *to strengthen it*, i.e. pi.), מַמְלָכָה *kingdom* 2 K 14$_{5}$||2 C 25$_{3}$, רָעָב *famine* Gn 41$_{56.57}$ 47$_{20}$ 2 K 25$_{3}$||Jr 52$_{6}$, מִלְחָמָה *battle* 2 K 3$_{26}$ 11QT 58$_{10}$, מַעֲרָכָה *battle line* 1QM 15$_{7}$ (|| אמץ *be strong*, + היה לְבֶן חַיִל *be a son of valour*, i.e. valiant), מוֹסֵר *bond* Is 28$_{22}$, דָּבָר *word* 2 S 24$_{4}$||1 C 21$_{4}$ Ml 3$_{13}$, טוּב *goods* Si 34$_{11}$.

<OBJ> Ahaz 2 C 28$_{20}$ (or em.; see Subj.), Jeremiah Jr 20$_{7}$, עַם *people* 1 K 16$_{22}$ (ms מִן־הָעָם *than the people*).

<PREP> לְ of purpose, *for (the purpose of)*, + מִלְחָמָה *battle* 2 C 25$_{8}$, מָשׁוּב *repentance* 1QS 3$_{1}$ (unless pi.); *in*, + יוֹם *day* Ezk 22$_{14}$ (|| עמד *stand*).

בְּ introducing object, + אֵלָה *terebinth* 2 S 18$_{9}$; of place, *in, at, among*, + אֶרֶץ *land* Gn 41$_{56.57}$, עִיר *city* 2 K 25$_{3}$||Jr 52$_{6}$, יָד *hand* 2 K 14$_{5}$||2 C 25$_{3(mss)}$, גּוֹרָל *lot* 1QM 17$_{16}$ ([יחזקו]); of instrument, *by (means of), with*, + קֶלַע *sling* 1 S 17$_{50}$, אֶבֶן *stone* 1 S 17$_{50}$; of accompaniment, *with, in*, + תּוֹרָה *law* 2 C 31$_{4}$, בְּרִית *covenant* 1QH 2$_{28}$ (unless hi.), רוּחַ *spirit* of knowledge 6QHymn 5$_{3}$ ([י]חזקו); *against*, i.e. (prevail) *upon*, + אִישׁ *man* Jg 19$_{4}$ (mss וַיֶּחֱזַק־, i.e. hi.).

מִן of comparison, *(more) than*, + Aramaean 1 K 20$_{23}$, Israel 1 K 20$_{23.25}$, Philistine 1 S 17$_{50}$, Abishai 2 S 10$_{11}$||1 C 19$_{12}$, Joab 2 S 10$_{11}$||1 C 19$_{12}$, Tamar 2 S 13$_{14}$, מֶלֶךְ *king* 2 K 3$_{26}$, עַם *people* 1 K 16$_{22(ms)}$.

עַל prevail *over* 4QMidrEschat$^{b}$ 11$_{11}$ (עליה[ם]), + Amaziah 2 C 25$_{3}$ (mss בְּיָדוֹ *in his hand*), Ezekiel Ezk 3$_{14}$, Joab 2 S 24$_{4(mss)}$||1 C 21$_{4}$ (L אֶל in same sense), Hamath-zobah 2 C 8$_{3}$, Egypt Gn 47$_{20}$, עַם *people* Ex 12$_{33}$, מֶלֶךְ *king* Dn 11$_{5}$ 2 C 27$_{5}$ (mss lack מֶלֶךְ) 11QT 58$_{10}$, שַׂר *prince* 2 S 24$_{4}$, בֵּן *son* of Ammon 2 C 27$_{5}$; be strong (of words) *against*, + ׳׳ Y. Ml 3$_{13}$.

<COLL> with adverb, מְאֹד *exceedingly* Ex 19$_{19}$ Jos 23$_{6}$; וַיְהִי קוֹל הַשּׁוֹפָר הוֹלֵךְ וְחָזֵק *and the sound of the trumpet grew louder and louder* Ex 19$_{19}$, דָּוִד הֹלֵךְ וְחָזֵק *David became stronger and stronger* 2 S 3$_{1}$ (+ וּבֵית שָׁאוּל הֹלְכִים וְדַלִּים *and the house of Saul became weaker and weaker*), חֲזַק וְנִתְחַזַּק *be strong and let us be courageous* 2 S 10$_{12}$ ||1 C 19$_{13}$ (וְנִתְחַזְּקָה).

Also 4QD$^{a}$ 4$_{3}$ (חזק[ו]) 4QMyst$^{a}$ 6.1$_{15.17}$ 13$_{3}$ 4Q415 7$_{3}$ 4QM$^{a}$ 15$_{5}$ (|| אמץ *be strong*) 4Q525 27$_{3}$.

<SYN> אמץ *be strong*, עמד *stand*.

<ANT> ירא *fear*, ערץ *dread*, חתת *be terrified*.

**Pi.** $_{64.4.28}$ Pf. חִזַּק, Q חזקתה (חִזַּקְתָּנִי), חִזַּקְתִּי, חִזְּקוּ,

חִזַּקְתֶּם; impf. 2ms תְּחַזֵּק, אֲחַזֵּק, (אֲחַזְּקֶנּוּ) יְחַזְּקוּ, (יְחַזְּקוּם); + waw Q וחזק, וְחִזַּקְתִּי; וַיְחַזֵּק (וַיְחַזְּקֵנִי, וַיְחַזְּקֵהוּ, וַיְחַזְּקֵם), 2ms Q ותחזקני, וַיְחַזְּקוּ (וַיְחַזְּקוּם); impv. חַזֵּק (חַזְּקֵנִי), חַזְּקוּ), חַזְּקִי (חַזֵּק), חַזְּקֵהוּ; ptc. מְחַזֵּק, pl. מְחַזְּקִים, cstr. Q מחזקי, Q מחזקות; inf. חַזֵּק—**make strong, strengthen, fortify, encourage,** specif. **harden** heart (e.g. Ex $4_{21}$ $9_{12}$ Jos $11_{20}$ 4Q422 $10_{7}$), **fasten, hold firm** base of mast (Is $33_{23}$), idol (Is $41_{7}$), **bind with** girdle (Is $22_{21}$), **repair** temple (e.g. 2 K $12_{6.7.8.9.15}$ 2 C $34_{8}$), doors of temple (2 C $29_{3}$), wall (Ne $3_{19}$), **hold, grasp** (e.g. 1QS $5_{3}$ 1QSb $1_{2}$ 4QpNah $3.3_{8}$).

**<SUBJ>** Y. Ex $4_{21}$ $9_{12}$ $10_{20.27}$ $11_{10}$ $14_{4.8.17}$ Jos $11_{20}$ Jg $3_{12}$ $16_{28}$ (+ זכר *remember*) Is $22_{21}$ (|| לבשׁ hi. *clothe with*) Ezk $30_{24}$ $34_{16}$ (|| חבשׁ *bind*, שׁוב hi. *bring back*, בקשׁ pi. *seek*) Ho $7_{15}$ (|| יסר pi. *train*) Ps $147_{13}$ Pr $8_{29}$ (if em. בְּחוּקוֹ *when he marked out* to בְּחַזְּקוֹ *when he strengthened*) appar. Ne $6_{9}$ 1 C $29_{12}$ (|| גדל pi. *magnify*) GnzPs $1_{25}$ (+ תמך *support*) appar. 1QH $14_{5}$ $16_{15}$ (לחזקו]) 4QBark[c] $1_{4.6.8.9}$ 4QDibHam[a] $1.6_{9}$ perh. $4_{12}$, אֱלֹהִים *God* Ho $7_{15}$ Ps $147_{13}$ Si $45_{3}$ 4QJub[d] $21_{25}$ ([יחזק]), אֵל *God* Si $43_{15(M)}$ 1QH $1_{32}$ 4QJub[d] $21_{25}$ (אל ע]ליון ... יחזק] *may the most high God ... strengthen*) 4Q422 $10_{7.11}$ ([ויח]זק), אֲדֹנָי *Lord* 1QH $7_{7}$, Israelite(s) Is $35_{3}$ (|| אמץ pi. *strengthen*), יְהוּדִי *Jew* Ne $2_{18}$, Nineveh Na $2_{2}$ (|| אמץ pi.) $3_{14}$=4QpNah $5_{3}$ ([חזק]), David 1 C $26_{27}$, Ezer Ne $3_{19}$, Job Jb $4_{3}$ (|| יסר pi.), Hezekiah 2 C $29_{3}$ $32_{5}$ Si $48_{17}$, Jehoash 2 K $12_{8}$, Jeshua, son of Galgula MurEpBarC[b]$_{7}$, Joah 2 C $34_{8}$, Jonathan 1 S $23_{16}$, Josiah 2 C $35_{2}$, Maaseiah 2 C $34_{8}$, Moses Dt $1_{38}$ (Sam חזק hi. *make strong*) $3_{28}$ (|| אמץ pi.), Rehoboam 2 C $11_{11.12}$, Shaphan 2 C $34_{8}$, Simeon, the priest Si $50_{4}$, Tilgath-pilneser 2 C $28_{20}$ (if em. חֲזָקוֹ appar. *he prevailed against him* to חִזְּקוֹ *he strengthened him*), Uzziah 2 C $26_{9}$.

מֶלֶךְ *king* Ezr $6_{22}$ 1 C $26_{27}$ 2 C $28_{20}$ (if em.; see above), בַּעַל *lord* Jg $9_{24}$, חֹר *noble* Ne $2_{18}$, שַׂר *prince* 1 C $26_{27}$ 2 C $34_{8}$, סֶגֶן *prefect* Ne $2_{18}$, ראשׁ *head*, i.e. chief 1 C $26_{27}$, גִּבּוֹר *mighty one* 4QMyst[a] $10_{2}$ (גב]ו[רי; unless qal), כֹּהֵן *priest* 2 K $12_{6.7.8.9}$ Ne $2_{18}$ Si $50_{4}$ 1QM $7_{11}$ $15_{7}$ $16_{11}$ 1QSb $3_{23}$ perh. 4QM[a] $10.2_{14}$, נָבִיא *prophet* Jr $23_{14}$, לֵוִי *Levite* 2 C $29_{34}$, מַלְאָךְ *messenger* 2 S $11_{25}$, חָרָשׁ *artisan* Is $41_{7}$ Jr $10_{4}$ 2 C $24_{12}$ (+ חדשׁ pi. *renew*), פֶּתִי *simple one* 4QpNah $3.3_{8}$, רעע hi. ptc. *wicked one* Ps $64_{6}$ (or em. יְחַזְּקוּ *they strengthen* to יִתְחַזְּקוּ *they strengthen themselves*, i.e. htp.), פעל ptc. *doer* of evil Ps $64_{6}$ (or em.; see above), מאס ptc. *one who refuses* perh. 1QS $3_{1}$ (unless qal), רֹעֶה *shepherd* Ezk $34_{4}$ (|| רפא pi. *heal*), עֹשֶׂה *worker* 2 K $12_{15}$ $22_{5}$ 2 C $34_{10}$, חלק hi. ptc. *one who smoothes* Is $41_{7}$, נתן ptc. *one who gives* heart, i.e. intends 2 C $11_{17}$ (|| אמץ pi.), סָבִיב *neighbour* Ezr $1_{6}$, אָדָם *human being* Dn $10_{18.19}$ (both כְּמַרְאֵה אָדָם *like one having the appearance of a human being*), אִישׁ *man* Jr $5_{3}$ 1QS $5_{3}$, בֵּן *son* Ne $3_{19}$ 2 C $34_{8}$ Si $42_{11(M)}$ ([ח]זק) $50_{4}$ 1QSa $1_{17}$ 1QSb $3_{23}$, of Israel Lv $25_{35(Sam)}$ (L hi.), בַּת *daughter* Ezk $13_{22}$, אָח *brother* 2 C $29_{34}$, עָקָר *barren one* Is $54_{2}$, רוּחַ *spirit* 4QShirShabb[f] $23.2_{8}$, חֶבֶל *rope* Is $33_{23}$, יֶתֶר *remainder* of workmen Ne $2_{18}$, workmen 2 K $12_{13.13}$ (if em. לְחָזְקָה *to be strong* to לְחַזְּקָהּ *to strengthen it*); subj. not specified, $22_{6}$ Is $41_{7}$ Ezk $30_{21}$ (if em.; see Obj.) 2 C $24_{5}$ 1QSb $1_{2}$ 4QD[a] $18.3_{7}$ ([י]חזקו; =CD $14_{14}$ hi.).

**<OBJ>** Ahaz 2 C $28_{20}$ (if em.; see Subj.), Daniel Dn $10_{18.19}$, Eglon Jg $3_{12}$, Joab 2 S $11_{25}$ Joshua Dt $1_{38}$ $3_{28}$, Moses Si $45_{3}$, Samson Jg $16_{28}$, בֵּן *son* 4QJub[d] $21_{25}$ ([יחזק]), מֶלֶךְ *king* Jg $3_{12}$, כֹּהֵן *priest* 2 C $29_{34}$ $35_{2}$, עֶבֶד *servant* Is $22_{21}$, חלה ni. ptc. *diseased one* Ezk $34_{4}$, חלה ptc. *sick one* Ezk $34_{16}$, צרף ptc. *one who smelts* Is $41_{7}$, הלם ptc. *one who hammers* Is $41_{7}$, worshipper 1QH $7_{7}$, זְרוֹעַ *arm* Ezk $30_{21}$ (if em. לְחָבְשָׁהּ לְחָזְקָהּ *to bind it that it may be strong* to לְחַזְּקָהּ *to make it strong*) $30_{24}$ Ho $7_{15}$ GnzPs $1_{25}$, יָד *hand* Jg $9_{24}$ 1 S $23_{16}$ Is $35_{3}$ Jr $23_{14}$ Ezk $13_{22}$ Jb $4_{3}$ Ezr $1_{6(ms)}$ $6_{22}$ Ne $2_{18}$ $6_{9}$ 1QM $7_{11}$ $15_{7}$ ([ידיהם]) $16_{11}$ 4QM[a] $10.2_{14}$, רֶגֶל *foot* 4QBark[c] $1_{8}$, מָתְנַיִם *loins* Na $2_{2}$ 1QSa $1_{17}$, פָּנִים *face* Jr $5_{3}$, לֵב *heart* Ex $4_{21}$ $9_{12}$ $10_{20.27}$ $11_{10}$ $14_{4.8.17}$ Jos $11_{20}$ 4Q422 $10_{7.11}$ ([ויח]זק) 4QBark[c] $1_{1}$ 4QM[a] $11.2_{15}$ ([לב]) 4QDibHam[a] $4_{12}$, לֵבָב *heart* 1QM $16_{11}$ 4Q421 $9_{2}$ 4QDibHam[a] $1.6_{9}$, רוּחַ *spirit* 1QH $1_{32}$.

מַלְכוּת *kingdom* 2 C $11_{17}$, עִיר *city* 2 C $11_{12}$ Si $48_{17}$ $50_{4}$, מִבְצָר *fortress* Na $3_{14}$=4QpNah $5_{3}$ (חזקי מבצ]ריך]), מוּסָד *foundation* Pr $8_{29}$ (if em.; see Subj.), מְצוּרָה *fortification* 2 C $11_{11}$, מִגְדָּל *tower* 2 C $26_{9}$, בַּיִת *house*, i.e. temple 2 K $12_{13}$ (if em.; see Subj.) $12_{15}$ $22_{6}$ 2 C $24_{5.12}$ $34_{8.10}$, בֶּדֶק *breach* of temple 2 K $12_{6.7.8.9.13}$ $22_{5.6(mss)}$, מִלּוֹא *Millo* 2 C $32_{5}$, מָקוֹם *place* MurEpBarC[b]$_{7}$, מִדָּה *measured portion* Ne $3_{19}$, דֶּלֶת *door* 2 C $29_{3}$, בְּרִיחַ *bar* Ps $147_{13}$, כֵּן *base* of mast Is $33_{23}$, עֵץ *tree* Jr $10_{4}$, דָּבָר *word* Ps $64_{6}$ (or em.; see Subj.), image Is 41$_{7}$, עֵצָה *counsel* 4QpNah 3.3$_{8}$, חֹק *statute* 1QH 14$_{5}$, בְּרִית *covenant* 1QSb 3$_{23}$ 4QBark$^{c}$ 1$_{4}$, עֲבֹדָה *service* perh. 4QMyst$^{a}$ 6.1$_{3}$, מַעֲמָד *standing place* 4QShirShabb$^{f}$ 23.2$_{8}$, עָנָן *cloud* Si 43$_{15(M)}$, מִשְׁמָר *watch* Si 42$_{11(M)}$ (ח[ז]ק).

<PREP> לְ of benefit, *to, for,* + רעע hi. ptc. *wicked one* Ps 64$_{6}$ (or em.; see Subj.), פעל ptc. *doer* of evil Ps 64$_{6}$ (or em.; see Subj.); of purpose, *for (the purpose of),* + טוֹבָה *good* Ne 2$_{18}$, מָשׁוֹב *repentance* perh. 1QS 3$_{1}$ (unless qal); introducing object, + בַּיִת *house* of Y. 1 C 26$_{27}$, כֹּל *all* 1 C 29$_{12}$.

בְּ of instrument, *by (means of), through, with (the help of),* + אֱלֹהִים *God* 1 S 23$_{16}$, גְּבוּרָה *might* 1QM 16$_{11}$ (בן[גבורת]) 4QM$^{a}$ 10.2$_{14}$, כְּלִי *vessel* Ezr 1$_{6}$, זָהָב *gold* Ezr 1$_{6}$, כֶּסֶף *silver* 2 K 12$_{15}$ (בּוֹ lacking in mss), מִגְדָּנָה *precious thing* Ezr 1$_{6}$, רְכוּשׁ *possession* Ezr 1$_{6}$, בְּהֵמָה *beast* Ezr 1$_{6}$, יָד *hand* 4QBark$^{c}$ 1$_{9}$, מַקֶּבֶת *hammer* Jr 10$_{4}$, מַסְמֵר *nail* Is 41$_{7}$ Jr 10$_{4}$; of accompaniment, place, *with, in* 1QH 14$_{5}$ ([בהם]), + רַחֲמִים *compassion* 1QH 1$_{32}$, גֹּדֶל *greatness of* mercy 1QH 1$_{32}$, דֶּרֶךְ *way* 1QH 16$_{15}$ (לחו]זקו בכול דרכ[ו *to keep him in all his ways*), מִלְחָמָה *battle* 1QM 7$_{11}$ 15$_{7}$ ([במלחמ]ה) 16$_{11}$, יוֹם *day* 4QBark$^{c}$ 1$_{9}$; introducing object, + אָח *brother* Lv 25$_{35(Sam)}$ (L hi.), יָד *hand* Ezr 1$_{6}$, בְּרִית *covenant* 1QS 5$_{3}$, רוּחַ *spirit* 1QSb 1$_{2}$ (בר[וח]).

מִן of comparison, *(more) than,* + סֶלַע *rock* Jr 5$_{3}$; of instrument, *by means of, with,* + שָׂכָר *wages* 4QD$^{a}$ 18.3$_{7}$ ([שכר] ... ומממנו י[חזקו]; =CD 14$_{14}$ hi.); perh. of cause, *on account of,* + צַר *enemy* Si 50$_{4}$.

עַל *against,* + Israel Jg 3$_{12}$, גִּבּוֹר *mighty one* GnzPs 1$_{25}$; introducing object, + worshipper 4QBark$^{c}$ 1$_{6}$, לֵב *heart* 4QBark$^{c}$ 1$_{4}$ ([לבן]); strengthen watch *over,* + בַּת *daughter* Si 42$_{11(M)}$ (ח[וז]ק).

עַל־יַד *by (the hand of),* i.e. next to, + Bavvai Ne 3$_{19}$ (mss Binnui), בֵּן *son* Ne 3$_{19}$.

בְּעַד *on behalf of, for,* [י]חזקו בעד [הע]ני והאביון *they shall make strong for the needy and the poor* 4QD$^{a}$ 18.3$_{7}$= CD 14$_{14}$ (יחזיקו ביד *they shall strengthen the hand of,* i.e. hi.).

לִפְנֵי *before, in the face of,* + מֶלֶךְ *king* Si 45$_{3}$, נֶגַע *affliction* 1QH 1$_{32}$, מִלְחָמָה *battle* 1QH 7$_{7}$.

<COLL> חַזְּקֵנִי נָא אַךְ הַפַּעַם הַזֶּה *strengthen me, pray, also this once* Jg 16$_{28}$ (or em. הַזֶּה *this* to ״י *Y.*), אַבְנֵטְךָ אֲחַזְּקֶנּוּ *I will bind him with your girdle* Is 22$_{21}$, גבורתו חזק ענן *by his might he has strengthened the cloud* Si 43$_{15(M)}$, וַיְחַזְּקֵם לְהַרְבֵּה מְאֹד *and he strengthened them very greatly* 2 C 11$_{12}$; with adverb, עוֹד *still* 4QpNah 3.3$_{8}$.

<SYN> גדל pi. *magnify,* אמץ pi. *strengthen,* רפא pi. *heal,* חבשׁ *bind,* יסר pi. *train,* לבשׁ hi. *clothe with,* שׁוב hi. *bring back,* בקשׁ pi. *seek.*

**Pu.** 0.1 Pf. Si חזק—**be strengthened, be repaired,** <SUBJ> הֵיכָל *temple* Si 50$_{1}$ (|| פקד ni. *be visited,* i.e. renovated). <PREP> בְּ of place/time, *in, during,* + יוֹם *day* Si 50$_{1}$.

<SYN> פקד ni. *be visited,* i.e. renovated.

**Hi.** 117.6.31 Pf. הֶחֱזִיק (הֶחֱזִיקַךְ), הֶחֱזִיקָה (הֶחֱזַקְתַּנִי), הֶחֱזַקְתִּי (הֶחֱזַקְתִּיךָ, Q החזקתיכה [4QTanḥ 1.1$_{10}$; corrected from חזקתיכה, perh. pi.]), הֶחֱזַקְנוּ, הֶחֱזִיקַתְהוּ, הֶחֱזִיקוּ; impf. יַחֲזִיק (יַחֲזֵק, Q יחזיקנה), אַחֲזִיק (Q אחזיקה), יַחֲזִיקוּ (יַחֲזִקוּ); + waw וְהֶחֱזִיק, וְהֶחֱזִיקָה, וְהֶחֱזַקְתָּ (Si והחזקתה), וְהַחֲזַקְתִּי, וְהֶחֱזִיקוּ; וַיַּחֲזֵק (וַיַּחֲזֶק־), 3fs וַתַּחֲזֵק (וַתַּחֲזֶק־), וַיַּחֲזִיקוּ (וַיַּחֲזִקוּ); impv. הַחֲזֵק, הַחֲזִיקִי, הַחֲזִיקוּ; ptc. מַחֲזִיק (מַחֲזִקָה), מַחֲזֶקֶת, מַחֲזִיקִים, מַחֲזִיקֵי; inf. הַחֲזִיק (הֶחֱזִיקִי, Q לחזיק, Q החזק)—**make strong, strengthen, preserve, make severe, repair; take hold of, grasp, seize; be strong, be steadfast, prevail** (e.g. Jg 19$_{4[mss]}$ 2 K 4$_{8}$ Dn 11$_{7.32}$ 2 C 26$_{8}$), <SUBJ> ״י *Y.* Dt 1$_{38(Sam^{mss})}$ (אַחֲזִיק) Is 41$_{9}$=4QTanḥ 1.1$_{10}$ (+ קרא *call*) 41$_{13}$ 42$_{6}$ (+ קרא) 45$_{1}$ Jr 31$_{32}$ Ezk 30$_{25}$ (+ נפל *fall*) Ps 35$_{2}$, אֲדֹנָי *Adonai* Ezk 30$_{25}$ (or del. אֲדֹנָי), אֱלֹהִים *God* Is 41$_{13}$, אֵל *God* Mc 7$_{18}$ Jb 8$_{20}$ 1QM 17$_{3}$, צָבָא *host* of Y. Si 42$_{17(Bmg)}$, עַם *people* Jr 6$_{23}$=50$_{42}$ 8$_{5}$ Dn 11$_{32}$ (+ עשׂה *do*) 4QMidr Eschat$^{a}$ 4$_{4a}$, גּוֹי *nation* Jr 6$_{23}$=50$_{42}$, Israel 1 K 9$_{9}$||2 C 7$_{22}$ (+ שׁחה htpal *worship,* עבד *serve*), Medes Jr 51$_{12}$, Damascus Jr 49$_{24}$ (+ אחז *grasp;* unless em. הֶחֱזִיקָה *she has seized* panic, to הֶחֱזִיקָהּ *panic has seized her*), Nineveh Na 3$_{14}$, Sodom Ezk 16$_{49}$.

Absalom 2 S 15$_{5}$ (|| נשׁק *kiss*), Adonijah 1 K 1$_{50}$, Amnon 2 S 13$_{11}$, Azariah Ne 3$_{23}$, Baruch Ne 3$_{20}$, Benjamin Ne 3$_{23}$, Binnui Ne 3$_{24}$, Daniel Dn 11$_{1}$, David 1 S 17$_{35}$ 2 S 1$_{11}$ (+ קרע *tear*), Elisha 2 K 2$_{12}$ (+ קרע), Gideon Jg 7$_{8}$, Hagar Gn 21$_{18}$, Hananiah, the perfumer Ne 3$_{8}$, son of Shelemiah Ne 3$_{30}$, Hanun Ne 3$_{13.30}$,

Hashabiah Ne 3$_{17}$, Hasshub Ne 3$_{11.23}$, Hattush Ne 3$_{10}$, Hezekiah Si 48$_{22}$, Jadon Ne 3$_{7}$, Jedaiah Ne 3$_{10}$, Joab 2 S 11$_{25}$ 1 K 2$_{28}$, Job Jb 2$_{3.9}$ 27$_{6}$ (:: רפה hi. *release*), Joiada Ne 3$_{6}$, Malchijah son of Harim Ne 3$_{11}$, son of Rechab Ne 3$_{14}$, Melatiah Ne 3$_{7}$, Menahem 2 K 15$_{19}$, Meremoth Ne 3$_{4.21}$, Meshullam son of Berechiah Ne 3$_{4.30}$, son of Besodiah Ne 3$_{6}$, Moses Ex 4$_{4}$ Dt 1$_{38(Sam)}$ (הַחֲזֵק), Nehemiah son of Azbuk Ne 3$_{16}$, son of Hacaliah Ne 5$_{16}$, Palal Ne 3$_{25}$ (if ins. אַחֲרָיו הֶחֱזִיק), Rehum Ne 3$_{17}$, Rephaiah Ne 3$_{9}$, Saul 1 S 15$_{27}$, Shallum, son of Hallohesh Ne 3$_{12}$, son of Col-hozeh Ne 3$_{15(mss)}$ (L שַׁלּוּן *Shallun*), Shemiah Ne 3$_{29}$, Uzziah 2 C 26$_{8}$, Uzziel Ne 3$_{8}$, Zadok, son of Baana Ne 3$_{4}$, son of Immer Ne 3$_{29}$, Gibeonite Ne 3$_{7}$, Merothonite Ne 3$_{7}$, Shunammite 2 K 4$_{27}$, Tekoites Ne 3$_{5.27}$.

פַּרְעֹה *Pharaoh* Ex 9$_{2}$, אָדָם *human being* 4Q185 1.2$_{14}$, אִישׁ *man* Gn 19$_{16}$ Dt 22$_{25}$=11QT 66$_{5}$ (+ שׁכב *lie*) Jg 19$_{25.29}$ 2 S 2$_{16}$ Ezk 7$_{13}$ (if em. יִתְחַזָּקוּ *they take hold of* to יַחֲזִיק *he will take hold of*) Zc 8$_{23.23}$ 14$_{13}$ Ne 3$_{7.22.28}$ 2 C 28$_{15}$ CD 6$_{21}$ 1QM 5$_{4}$ 1QS 5$_{1}$ 1QSa 2$_{5}$ 4QD$^{a}$ 6.1$_{7}$ (... אנשי] [המחזי]קים), אִשָּׁה *woman* Dt 25$_{11}$ 2 K 4$_{8}$ Is 4$_{1}$ Pr 7$_{13}$ (+ נשק *kiss*) Ne 10$_{30}$, אָב *father* Jg 19$_{4(mss)}$ (וַיַּחֲזֶק־; L וַיֶּחֱזַק־), חֹתֵן *father-in-law* Jg 19$_{4}$, בֵּן *son* Pr 4$_{13}$ (:: רפה hi. *release*; + נצר *keep*) Ne 3$_{4+18t}$ 10$_{30}$ Si 6$_{27}$ (:: רפה hi.) 42$_{11(Bmg)}$, of Israel Lv 25$_{35}$ (Sam pi.), of human being Is 56$_{2}$ (+ עשׂה *do*), בַּת *daughter* Ne 10$_{30}$, אָחוֹת *sister* Ezk 16$_{49}$, נַעַר *lad* Jg 16$_{26}$.

סָרִיס *eunuch* Is 56$_{4}$ (+ שׁמר *keep*, בחר *choose*), עֶבֶד *servant* Jb 2$_{3}$ 1QH 5$_{29}$, שֹׁעֵר *gatekeeper* Ne 10$_{30}$, נָתִין *temple servant* Ne 10$_{30}$, זָקֵן *elder* Ezk 27$_{9}$, לֵוִי *Levite* Ne 3$_{17}$ 10$_{30}$, כֹּהֵן *priest* Ne 3$_{22.28}$ 10$_{30}$, חָכָם *wise one* Ezk 27$_{9}$, שַׂר *prince* Ne 3$_{9.12.15.16.17.18}$, ראשׁ *head*, i.e. company of men Jg 7$_{20}$, מַשְׂכִּיל *instructor* 1QS 9$_{14}$, אֹהֵב *friend* Si 37$_{5}$, חָבֵר *companion* Si 37$_{6(Bmg)}$, תָּמִים *perfect one* 1QH 1$_{36}$ (החזיק[ו]), בזה ni. ptc. *despised one* Dn 11$_{21}$, בדל ni. ptc. *one who is separated* Ne 10$_{30}$, יֹשֵׁב *inhabitant* Ne 3$_{13}$, ידע ptc. *one who knows* Ne 10$_{30}$, שׁמר ptc. *one who keeps* Ne 3$_{29}$, בוא ptc. *one who enters* covenant CD 6$_{21}$ 8$_{2(A)}$=19$_{14(B)}$, שׁכח *one who forgets* Jb 8$_{15}$ (+ שׁען ni. *lean*), עתד pass. ptc. *one prepared* for battle 1QM 10$_{5.6}$, מְשֹׁרֵר *singer* Ne 10$_{30}$, worshipper 1QH 15$_{11}$, enemy Is 27$_{5}$, שׁבה ptc. *one who takes captive* Jr 50$_{33}$, רכל ptc. *trader* Ne 3$_{32}$, צֹרֵף *smelter* Ne 3$_{8}$ (unless em. צוֹרְפִים *smelters* to חֶבֶר הַצּוֹרְפִים *the company of smelters*) 3$_{32}$, חָנֵף *profane one* Jb 8$_{15}$, נָדִיב *willing one* 1QM 10$_{5.6}$, פָּרָשׁ *cavalry officer* 1QM 6$_{14.15}$ ([פרשי ... יחזיקו]), חֶבֶר *company* Ne 3$_{8}$ (if em.), דֶּגֶל *battalion* 1QM 6$_{5.5}$, חֲצִי *half* of the lads Ne 4$_{10.15}$, שְׁאָר *remainder* of people Ne 10$_{30}$, אֲשֶׁר *who(ever)* CD 13$_{21}$ ([אשר ... יחזיקו]).

צָרָה *distress* Jr 6$_{24}$=50$_{43}$, שַׁמָּה *horror* Jr 8$_{21}$, רֶטֶט *panic* Jr 49$_{24}$ (if em.; see above), חִיל *pain* Jr 6$_{24}$=50$_{43}$ Mc 4$_{9}$=4QpMic 1$_{2}$ ([החז]יקכה), צַמִּים *snare* Jb 18$_{9}$ (+ אחז *grasp*), יָם *sea* 2 C 4$_{5}$ (+ כול hi. *contain*), יָד *hand* Ne 4$_{11}$, שָׂפָה *lip* 1QMyst 1.1$_{10}$ (unless pi.), לָשׁוֹן *tongue* 1QMyst 1.1$_{10}$ (unless pi.), נֵצֶר *branch* Dn 11$_{7}$, נֶפֶשׁ *soul* perh. 1QH 2$_{28}$ (but prob. qal), רוּחַ *spirit* 1QH 4$_{36}$; subj. not specified, 2 S 3$_{29}$* Is 51$_{18}$ (+ נהל pi. *guide*) 56$_{6}$ 64$_{6}$ Ezk 27$_{27}$ Pr 3$_{18}$ (+ תמך *hold*) 26$_{17}$ Dn 11$_{6}$ CD 3$_{12.20}$ 7$_{13}$ 20$_{27}$ 14$_{14}$ (=4QD$^{a}$ 18.3$_{7}$ [י]חזקו appar. pi.) 4Q418 69.2$_{8}$.

<OBJ> Israel Is 41$_{9}$=4QTanḥ 1.1$_{10}$, Eleazar 1QM 17$_{3}$ ([אלעזר]), Ithamar 1QM 17$_{3}$, Jacob Is 41$_{9}$=4QTanḥ 1.1$_{10}$ (יעק[ו]ב), מַמְלָכָה *kingdom* 2 K 15$_{19}$, מַלְכוּת *kingdom* Dn 11$_{21}$, בַּת *daughter* Dn 11$_{6}$, of Zion Jr 6$_{24}$ Mc 4$_{9}$=4QpMic 1$_{2}$ ([החז]יקכה), Damascus Jr 49$_{24}$ (if em.; see Subj.), מֶלֶךְ *king* Jr 50$_{43}$, גִּבּוֹר *mighty one* 1QM 10$_{6}$, עֶבֶד *servant* Is 41$_{9}$=4QTanḥ 1.1$_{10}$ (עב[די]), Jeremiah Jr 8$_{21}$, Joshua Dt 1$_{38(Sam)}$, זֶרַע *seed* Is 41$_{9}$=4QTanḥ 1.1$_{10}$ ([זרע]), מִלְחָמָה *battle* 2 S 11$_{25}$, מִשְׁמָר *watch* Jr 51$_{12}$, שִׁרְיוֹן *coat of armour* Ne 4$_{10}$, מָגֵן *shield* Ps 35$_{2}$ Ne 4$_{10}$ 1QM 5$_{4}$ 6$_{5.14.15}$ ([יחזיקו מגן]), צִנָּה *shield* Ps 35$_{2}$ Si 37$_{5.6(Bmg)}$, קֶשֶׁת *bow* Jr 6$_{23}$=50$_{42}$ Ne 4$_{10}$ 1QM 6$_{15}$ ([יחזיקו]), חֲנִית *spear* 1QM 6$_{5}$, כִּידוֹן *javelin* Jr 6$_{23}$=50$_{42}$ 1QM 6$_{5}$, זֶרֶק *javelin* 1QM 6$_{15}$ ([יחזיקו]), רֹמַח *lance* Ne 4$_{10}$ 1QM 6$_{14}$, שֶׁלַח *dart* Ne 4$_{11}$, חֵץ *arrow* 1QM 6$_{15}$ ([יחזיקו]), חֶרֶב *sword* Jg 7$_{20}$ (if em. הַשּׁוֹפָרוֹת לִתְקוֹעַ *the trumpets to blow* to הַחֶרֶב *the sword*), שׁוֹפָר *trumpet* Jg 7$_{20}$ (unless em.), זְרוֹעַ *arm* Ezk 30$_{25}$, יָמִין *right hand* Is 41$_{13}$, יָד *hand* Gn 21$_{18}$ Ezk 16$_{49}$ Zc 14$_{13}$, חַיָּה *life* Ezk 7$_{13}$ (if em.; see Subj.), מַלְבֵּן *brick mould* Na 3$_{14}$, בֶּדֶק *breach*, i.e. leak in ship Ezk 27$_{9.27}$, שַׁעַר *gate* Ne 3$_{6.13.14.15}$, מִדָּה *measured portion* Ne 3$_{11.20.21.24.27.30}$, בַּת *bath* 2 C 4$_{5}$, אַף *anger* Mc 7$_{18}$, רֶטֶט *panic* Jr 49$_{24}$ (or em.; see Subj.), מִשְׁמָר *watch* Si 42$_{11(Bmg)}$, מַעֲמָד *standing place* 1QH 1$_{36}$ (החזיק[ו מעמד]) 5$_{29}$ 1QSa 2$_{5}$, מוֹרָא *fear* 1QH 15$_{11}$ (מו[ראך]), מִשְׁפָּט *ordinance* 1QH 15$_{11}$

([משפטיכה]), רִשְׁעָה *wickedness* 4Q418 69.2$_{8}$, בְּרִית *covenant* 4QD$^{b}$ 3$_{4}$ ([מחזי]קי הברי[ת]), עֲבֹדָה *service* 4Q 416 2.2$_{12}$, חָכְמָה *wisdom* Si 6$_{27}$ perh. 4Q416 2.2$_{12}$, obj. not specified, but appar. wisdom 4Q185 1.2$_{14}$.

<PREP> לְ of benefit, *to, for,* + אֵל *God* 1QM 17$_{3}$; introducing object, + Tamar 2 S 13$_{11(ms)}$, אִישׁ *man* 2 S 15$_{5}$; לָעַד *for ever* Mc 7$_{18}$; לְ *as,* + בְּרִית *covenant* 1QM 17$_{3}$.

בְּ of place/time, *in, during,* + יוֹם *day* Is 4$_{1}$, עֵת *time* Dn 11$_{6}$ (unless בָּעִתִּים: *In the times*), יָד *hand* 2 K 15$_{19}$ (לְהַחֲזִיק הַמַּמְלָכָה בְּיָדוֹ *to strengthen the kingdom in his hand*, i.e. to confirm his authority over it).

בְּ of instrument, *by (means of), with,* + יָד *hand* Jg 7$_{20}$ 1QM 6$_{14}$, חֲלַקְלַק *intrigue* Dn 11$_{21}$, גְּבוּרָה *might* 1QM 10$_{5}$, חָלָק fem. pl. *smooth things* 4Q185 1.2$_{14}$; of accompaniment, *in, with,* + שֵׁם *name* 4QD$^{a}$ 6.1$_{7}$ (המחזי[קים]), אֱמֶת *truth* 1QMyst 1.1$_{10}$ (unless pi.); perh. *in accordance with,* + רָצוֹן *desire* 4Q416 2.2$_{12}$.

בְּ introducing object, *(hold) onto, strengthen, seize,* + י״ *Y.* Is 64$_{6}$ 11QapPs$^{a}$ 1$_{10}$ ([בי״]), אֱלֹהִים *gods* 1 K 9$_{9}$∥2 C 7$_{22}$, עַם *people* Ex 9$_{2}$, Tamar 2 S 13$_{11}$, אִישׁ *man* Jg 7$_{8}$ 19$_{4}$ 2 S 15$_{5(mss)}$ Is 4$_{1}$, אִשָּׁה *woman* 11QT 66$_{5}$, אָח *brother* Lv 25$_{35}$ (Sam pi.), בֵּן *son* of Israel Jr 50$_{33}$, of Judah Jr 50$_{33}$, נַעַר *lad* Gn 21$_{18}$ Pr 7$_{13}$, נַעֲרָה *girl* Dt 22$_{25}$, פִּלֶגֶשׁ *secondary wife* Jg 19$_{25.29}$, שִׁבְיָה *captive* 2 C 28$_{15}$, בָּחִיר *chosen one* 1QS 9$_{14}$.

נָחָשׁ *snake* Ex 4$_{4}$, רֹאשׁ *head* 2 S 2$_{16}$, זָקָן *beard* 1 S 17$_{35}$, יָד *hand* Gn 19$_{16}$ Jg 16$_{26}$ Is 42$_{6}$ 51$_{18}$ Jr 31$_{32}$ Zc 14$_{13(mss)}$ Jb 8$_{20}$ CD 6$_{21}$ 14$_{14}$ (=4QD$^{a}$ 18.3$_{7}$ [י]חזקו appar. pi.) perh. 4QMyst$^{a}$ 53$_{3}$ ([י]חזיקו), יָמִין *right hand* Is 45$_{1}$, רֶגֶל *foot* 2 K 4$_{27}$, אֹזֶן *ear* Pr 26$_{17}$ (or em. בְּאָזְנֵי *ears of* to בִּזְנַב *tail of*), מְבוּשִׁים *genitals* Dt 25$_{11}$ (Sam בָּשָׂר *flesh*), קֶרֶן *horn* 1 K 1$_{50}$ 2$_{28}$, לַפִּיד *torch* Jg 7$_{20}$, רֹמַח *lance* Ne 4$_{15}$, פֶּלֶךְ *spindle* 2 S 3$_{29}$, כָּנָף *skirt* of garment 1 S 15$_{27}$, of man Zc 8$_{23}$, בֶּגֶד *garment* 2 S 1$_{11}$ 2 K 2$_{12}$.

בְּרִית *covenant* Is 56$_{4.6}$ perh. 1QH 2$_{28}$ (but prob. qal), תֻּמָּה *integrity* Jb 2$_{3.9}$, צְדָקָה *righteousness* Jb 27$_{6}$, חָכְמָה *wisdom* Pr 3$_{18}$, מוּסָר *instruction* Pr 4$_{13}$, מִשְׁפָּט *judgment* CD 20$_{27}$, מִצְוָה *commandment* CD 3$_{12}$, תַּרְמִית *deceit* Jr 8$_{5}$, מָעוֹז *(place of) refuge* Is 27$_{5}$, בַּיִת *house* Jb 8$_{15}$ CD 3$_{20}$, מְלָאכָה *work* Ne 5$_{16}$, דֶּרֶךְ *way* Si 48$_{22}$, מַעֲמָד *standing place* 1QH 4$_{36}$, זֹאת *this* Is 56$_{2}$, אֵלֶּה *these* CD 8$_{2(A)}$= 19$_{14(B)}$, כֹּל *all* 1QS 5$_{1}$ (להחזיק בכול אשר צוה *to hold onto all that he has commanded*).

בְּ (be strong) *against*, i.e. prevail upon, + Elisha 2 K 4$_{8}$, אִישׁ *man* Jg 19$_{4(mss)}$ (וַיְחַזֶּק־; L וַיֶּחֱזַק־).

בְּ of cause, *on account of,* + עָוֹן *iniquity* Ezk 7$_{13}$ (if em.; see Subj.).

כְּ *as* Jr 6$_{24}$=50$_{43}$ Mc 4$_{9}$.

מִן of direction, *from,* + קָצֶה *end* of earth Is 41$_{9}$, בַּיִת *house* Ne 3$_{24}$, מִקְצוֹעַ *corner* Ne 3$_{20}$, פֶּתַח *entrance* Ne 3$_{21}$; of instrument, *by (means of), with,* + שָׂכָר *wages* CD 14$_{14}$ (=4QD$^{a}$ 18.3$_{7}$ [י]חזקו, i.e. pi.).

אֶל *against,* + עִיר *city* 2 S 11$_{25}$.

עַל introducing object, *(hold) onto, strengthen, seize,* + רָשָׁע *wicked one* Jb 18$_{9}$, אָח *brother* Ne 10$_{30}$; strengthen watch *over,* + בַּת *daughter* Si 42$_{11(Bmg)}$; *according to,* + רַב pl. *many* 1QH 15$_{11}$.

מֵעַל *above,* + שַׁעַר *gate* Ne 3$_{28}$ (mss מֵעַל לְ).

עַל פִּי *according to,* + רָצוֹן *desire* 1QS 9$_{14}$.

עַל יַד *beside, next to,* + name of person repairing wall Ne 3$_{4+8t}$.

נֶגֶד *opposite, against,* + עָר *enemy* Si 37$_{5.6(Bmg)}$, בַּיִת *house* Ne 3$_{10.23.28}$ (לְנֶגֶד) 3$_{29}$, נִשְׁכָּה *chamber* Ne 3$_{30}$.

מִנֶּגֶד *(from) opposite,* + מִגְדָּל *tower* Ne 3$_{25}$ (if em.; see Subj.) 3$_{27}$, מִקְצוֹעַ *corner* Ne 3$_{25}$ (if em.; see Subj.).

עַד נֶגֶד *as far as opposite,* + קֶבֶר *grave* Ne 3$_{16}$.

לִפְנֵי *in the face of, against,* + כָּבוֹד *glory* Si 42$_{17(Bmg)}$, נֶגַע *blow* 1QH 4$_{36}$.

בְּתוֹךְ *among,* + עֵדָה *congregation* 1QSa 2$_{5}$.

עַד *as far as,* + חוֹמָה *wall* Ne 3$_{27}$, בַּיִת *house* Ne 3$_{31}$, עֲלִיָּה *upper chamber* Ne 3$_{31}$, מִקְצוֹעַ *buttress* Ne 3$_{24}$, פִּנָּה *corner* Ne 3$_{24}$, פֶּתַח *entrance* Ne 3$_{20}$, תַּכְלִית *end* Ne 3$_{21}$.

עַד לְ *unto (to),* + מַעַל *above*, i.e. exceedingly 2 C 26$_{8}$.

בְּעַד *on behalf of, for,* ל[מחז]יק בעו[ד עני ואביון וגר] *to the one who is strong for the needy and the poor and the sojourner* 4QD$^{d}$ 4.2$_{3}$ (=CD 6$_{21}$ להחזיק ביד *to strengthen the hand of*).

אֵצֶל *beside,* + בַּיִת *house* Ne 3$_{23}$.

אַחֲרֵי *after,* + name of person repairing wall Ne 3$_{16+14t}$, אִישׁ *man* Ne 3$_{23}$, כֹּהֵן *priest* Ne 3$_{23.29}$.

<COLL> חזק hi. with adverb, יַחַד *together* 1QM 10$_{6}$. Also 4QMyst$^{a}$ 29$_{3}$ ([מ]חזיק).

<SYN> נשק *kiss*.

<ANT> רפה hi. *release*.

**Htp.** 27.2.13 Pf. הִתְחַזֵּק, הִתְחַזַּקְתִּי, הִתְחַזַּקְתֶּם; impf. Q נִתְחַזְּקָה) נִתְחַזֵּק (Q אתחזקה), Q אתחזק, יִתְחַזְּקוּ, יתחזק; + waw וַיִּתְחַזֵּק (וַיִּתְחַזֵּק); impv. הִתְחַזֵּק (התחזק [MurEp BarC$^{b}$7]), הִתְחַזְּקוּ; ptc. מִתְחַזֵּק, מִתְחַזְּקִים; inf. הִתְחַזֵּק—**strengthen oneself, show oneself strong, hold fast, take courage,** <SUBJ> Y. 2 C 16$_{9}$, צָבָא *host* of Y. Si 42$_{17(B, M)}$, עַם *people* Jg 20$_{22}$, Philistine 1 S 4$_{9}$ (+ היה לְאִישׁ *be as a man*), Abijah 2 C 13$_{21}$, Abishai 2 S 10$_{12}$||1 C 19$_{13}$, Abner 2 S 3$_{6}$ (+ היה *be*), Amaziah 2 C 25$_{11}$, Asa 2 C 15$_{8}$, Daniel Dn 10$_{19}$, David 1 S 30$_{6}$, Ezra Ezr 7$_{28}$, Hezekiah 2 C 32$_{5}$ (unless em.; see below; + בנה *build*), Israel (Jacob) Gn 48$_{2}$ (+ ישׁב *sit*), Jehoiada 2 C 23$_{1}$, Jehoram 2 C 21$_{4}$, Jehoshaphat 2 C 17$_{1}$, Jeshua, son of Galgula MurEpBarC$^{b}$7 (appar. התהזק is error for התחזק), Joab 2 S 10$_{12}$||1 C 19$_{13}$, Josiah 2 C 35$_{22}$ (if em.; הִתְחַפֵּשׂ *he disguised himself* to וַיִּתְחַזֵּק *and he strengthened himself*), Jotham 2 C 27$_{6}$, Rehoboam 2 C 12$_{13}$ (+ מלך *rule*) 13$_{7.8}$, Solomon 2 C 1$_{1}$, אִישׁ *man* Nm 13$_{20}$ (+ לקח *take*) Jg 20$_{22}$ Ezk 7$_{13}$ (or em. יַחֲזִיק *he will take hold of*, i.e. hi.) Dn 10$_{19}$ (if em. וַחֲזַק *and be strong* to וְהִתְחַזֵּק *and take courage*) 1QSa 2$_{7}$, בֵּן *son* Si 3$_{12}$ (+ עזב *forsake*) 1QH 18$_{9}$ ([בן]; + עמד *stand*) 1QM 17$_{9}$, מֶלֶךְ *king* 1 K 20$_{22}$ (+ הלך *go*) 2 C 12$_{13}$ 32$_{5}$ (if em. וַיִּתְחַזֵּק *and he strengthened himself* to וְיִתְחַזְּקוּ *and they will strengthen themselves*, and join to 32$_{4}$), רֹאשׁ *chief* 1 C 11$_{10}$, רעע hi. ptc. *wicked one* Ps 64$_{6}$ (if em.; see Prep.), פעל ptc. *doer* of evil Ps 64$_{6}$ (if em.; see Prep.), worshipper 1QH 4$_{39}$ 10$_{6}$ 12$_{35}$ ([את]חזק) perh. 16$_{7}$, מַעֲרָכָה *battle line* 1QM 15$_{12}$ 17$_{4}$ (:: ירא *fear*) 4QM$^{a}$ 11.2$_{13}$ (התחזקו ... [המער]כ[ה]), אֶחָד *one* Dn 10$_{21}$.

<PREP> לְ of purpose, *for (the purpose of)*, + מִלְחָמָה *battle* 1QM 15$_{12}$, דָּבָר *word* Ps 64$_{6}$ (if em. יְחַזְּקוּ לָמוֹ דָּבָר *they strengthen for themselves* an evil *word* to יִתְחַזְּקוּ לְדָבָר *they strengthen themselves for* an evil *word*); *in the presence of*, + אֵל *God* 1QH fr. 3$_{12}$.

בְּ of place/time, *in, at, among*, + Jerusalem 2 C 12$_{13}$, בַּיִת *house* of Saul 2 S 3$_{6}$, מַלְכוּת *kingdom* 1 C 11$_{10}$, מַצְרֵף *crucible* 1QM 17$_{9}$, שָׁנָה *year* 2 C 23$_{1}$; בְּ of instrument, *by (means of), with, through*, + ״ Y. 1 S 30$_{6}$, אֱלֹהִים *God* 1 S 30$_{6}$, רוּחַ *spirit* 1QH 16$_{7}$; of accompaniment, *in, with*, + כֹּחַ *strength* 1QH 12$_{35}$ ([את]חזק); of cause, *on account of*, + עָוֹן *iniquity* Ezk 7$_{13}$ (or em.; see Subj.); introducing object, *(hold) onto*, + בְּרִית *covenant* 1QH 4$_{39}$ 18$_{9}$; appar. *in respect of*, + כָּבוֹד *honour*, i.e. honouring father Si 3$_{12}$.

בְּתוֹךְ *among*, + עֵדָה *congregation* 1QSa 2$_{7}$.

עַל *over, in charge of*, + Israel 2 C 17$_{1}$, מַלְכוּת *kingdom* 2 C 1$_{1}$; *against*, + אֵלֶּה *these (princes)* Dn 10$_{21}$.

עַד *until*, + מוֹעֵד *appointed time* 1QH 4$_{39}$.

בְּעַד *on behalf of*, + עַם *people* 2 S 10$_{12}$||1 C 19$_{13}$, עִיר *city* 2 S 10$_{12}$||1 C 19$_{13}$.

לִפְנֵי *in the face of, against*, + אִישׁ *man* 2 C 13$_{7}$, בֵּן *son* of worthlessness 2 C 13$_{7}$, מַמְלָכָה *kingdom* 2 C 13$_{8}$, כָּבוֹד *glory* Si 42$_{17(B, M)}$.

עִם *with*, + David 1 C 11$_{10}$, אָדָם *human being* Dn 10$_{21}$ (כְּמַרְאֵה אָדָם *like one having the appearance of a human being*); *on behalf of*, + לֵב *heart* 2 C 16$_{9}$ (לְהִתְחַזֵּק עִם־לְבָבָם שָׁלֵם אֵלָיו *to show himself strong with*, i.e. in the presence of, *those whose heart is blameless toward him*).

<COLL> אִישׁ בַּעֲוֹנוֹ חַיָּתוֹ לֹא יִתְחַזָּקוּ *a man will not strengthen himself as to his life by means of his iniquity* Ezk 7$_{13}$ (or em.; see Subj.), חֲזַק וְנִתְחַזַּק *be strong and let us take courage* 2 S 10$_{12}$||1 C 19$_{13}$ (וְנִתְחַזְּקָה), var. Dn 10$_{19}$ (if em.; see Subj.); חזק htp. + adverb, תָּמִיד *continually* 4Q417 2.1$_{23}$ (ת[ת]חזק).

Also 4Q418 68$_{6}$ 4Q525 28$_{2}$.

<ANT> ירא *fear*.*

→ חָזָק *strong*, חֵזֶק *strength*, חֶזְקָה *strength*, חֹזֶק *strength*, חָזְקָה *strength*, חִזְקִי *Hizki*, חִזְקִיָּהוּ *Hezekiah*, יְחֶזְקֵאל *Ezekiel*.

***חזק II** 1 vb. **outwit—Qal** 1 Pf. חֲזַקְתַּנִי—**outwit** (unless חזק I *be strong*, i.e. prevail [against]), <SUBJ> ״ Y. Jr 20$_{7}$ (+ יכל *be able*, i.e. prevail). <OBJ> Jeremiah Jr 20 7.

**חָזָק I** 57.3.7 adj. **strong**—fem. חֲזָקָה; pl. חֲזָקִים; cstr. חִזְקֵי—**strong, hard, severe, 1.** used attributively of יָד *hand* Ex 3$_{19}$ 6$_{1.1}$ 13$_{9}$ 32$_{11}$ Nm 20$_{20}$ (|| כָּבֵד *heavy*) Dt 3$_{24}$ 4$_{34}$ 5$_{15}$ (both || נטה pass. ptc. *outstretched*) 6$_{21}$ 7$_{8.19}$ (|| נטה pass. ptc.) 9$_{26}$ 11$_{2}$ 26$_{8}$ (both || נטה pass. ptc.) 34$_{12}$ 1 K 8$_{42}$ Jr 32$_{11}$ Ezk 20$_{33.34}$ Ps 136$_{12}$ (all five || נטה pass. ptc.) Dn 9$_{15}$ Ne 1$_{10}$ 1 C 6$_{32}$ (|| נטה pass. ptc.; both || גָּדוֹל *great*),* זְרוֹעַ *arm* Jr 21$_{5}$ (|| נטה pass. ptc.), רוּחַ *wind* Ex 10$_{19}$ 1 K 19$_{11}$ (unless transfer to follow רַעַשׁ *earthquake*; || גָּדוֹל), רַעַשׁ *earthquake* 1 K 19$_{11}$ (if em.), קוֹל *sound* Ex

19$_{16}$, מִלְחָמָה *battle* 2 S 11$_{15}$, חֶרֶב *sword* (‖ גָּדוֹל, קָשֶׁה *hard*), חֳלִי *sickness* Si 34$_{2}$, נַחְשִׁיר *carnage* 1QM 1$_{9}$, מִשְׁבָּר *breach* 1QH 2$_{6}$ ([משברים]), גְּבוּרָה *might* 1QM 10$_{9}$ (‖ גָּדוֹל).

**2a.** in nom. cl. used predicatively of Y. Si 39$_{20}$ (אין ... חזק ממנו *there is no ... stronger one than he*; ‖ פלא ni. *wonderful one*), Caleb Jos 14$_{11}$, כְּנַעֲנִי *Canaanite* Jos 17$_{18}$, עַם *people* Nm 13$_{18}$ (:: רָפֶה *weak*) 13$_{31}$, אִישׁ *man* Si 8$_{12}$ (איש חזק ממך *a man [who is] stronger than you*), בַּיִת *house* of Israel Ezk 3$_{7}$ (‖ קָשֶׁה *hard*), בֵּן *son* Jg 18$_{26}$ Ezk 2$_{4}$ (‖ קָשֶׁה), גֹּאֵל *redeemer* Jr 50$_{34}$ Pr 23$_{11}$, יָד *hand* Jos 4$_{24}$, רֹב *multitude* Si 43$_{32}$ ([חז]ק), רָעָב *famine* 1 K 18$_{2}$, שַׁחַק *sky* Jb 37$_{18}$ (שְׁחָקִים חֲזָקִים *the skies [which are] strong*).

<COLL> חָזָק followed by preposition, כְּ *as*, + רְאִי molten *mirror* Jb 37$_{18}$; מִן of comparison, *(more) than*, i.e. stronger than, + Y. Si 39$_{20}$, Micah Jg 18$_{26}$, Jacob, i.e. Israel Jr 31$_{11}$, Israel Nm 13$_{31}$, גּוֹי *nation* 1QMyst 1.1$_{10}$, עָנִי *afflicted one* Ps 35$_{10}$ 1QH 2$_{35}$, רושׁ ptc. *poor one* 1QH 2$_{35}$, בֵּן *son* Si 8$_{12}$, אֵלֶּה *these* Si 43$_{32}$ ([א]לה)

חִזְקֵי־לֵב *strong of heart*, i.e. obstinate Ezk 2$_{4}$, חִזְקֵי־מֵצַח *hard of forehead* Ezk 3$_{7}$.

**2b.** with היה *be*, used predicatively of מִלְחָמָה *battle* 1 S 14$_{52}$, חֳלִי *sickness* 1 K 17$_{17}$, עִיר *city* Ezk 26$_{17}$.

**2c.** with נתן *give*, i.e. cause to be, used predicatively of פָּנִים *face* Ezk 3$_{8}$, מֵצַח *forehead* Ezk 3$_{8.9}$ (+ כְּשָׁמִיר *like adamant*). <COLL> חָזָק followed by preposition, מִן of comparison, *(more) than*, i.e. stronger than, + צֹר *flint* Ezk 3$_{9}$; לְעֻמַּת *against, in comparison with* פָּנִים *face* Ezk 3$_{8}$, מֵצַח *forehead* Ezk 3$_{8}$.

**3.** used as noun, **strong one, a.** חָזָק (masc.), <SUBJ> אמץ pi. *retain strength* Am 2$_{14}$, עשׁק *oppress* 1QMyst 1.1$_{10}$. <NOM CL> חָזָק ... לַאדֹנָי *a strong one is ... to the Lord* Is 28$_{2}$ (or em. חֹזֶק *strength*; ‖ אַמִּיץ *mighty one*). <CSTR> יַד חָזָק *hand of a strong one* Jr 31$_{11}$ Jb 5$_{15}$ 1QH 2$_{35}$. <PREP> בְּ of essence, *as*, + בוא *come* Is 40$_{10}$ (1QIsa$^{a}$ בחוזק *with strength*, i.e. חֹזֶק); מִן of direction, *from*, + נצל hi. *deliver* Ps 35$_{10}$ (+ גזל ptc. *one who robs*); עַל *against* 4QMyst$^{a}$ 50$_{8}$.

**b.** חֲזָקָה (fem.), in ref. to arm, sheep, <OBJ> שׁבר *break* Ezk 30$_{22}$ (:: שׁבר ni. ptc. *broken one*), שׁמד hi. *destroy* Ezk 34$_{16}$ (‖ שָׁמֵן *fat one*), שׁמר hi. *watch* Ezk 34$_{16(mss)}$. <APP> זְרוֹעַ *arm* Ezk 30$_{22}$. <PREP> בְּ רדה *rule over* Ezk 34$_{4}$ (if em. בְּחָזְקָה *with force*).

Also 4QMyst$^{a}$ 13$_{2}$ ([ח]זק[ות]) perh. 4QMyst$^{a}$ 50$_{6}$.

<SYN> §1 נטה pass. ptc. *outstretched*, גָּדוֹל *great*, קָשֶׁה *hard*, כָּבֵד *heavy*; §2a קָשֶׁה *hard*; §3a פלא ni. *wonderful one*, אַמִּיץ *mighty one*, שָׁמֵן *fat one*.

<ANT> §2a רָפֶה *weak*; §3b שׁבר ni. ptc. *broken one*.*

→ חזק *be strong*.

[חָזָק] II 0.0.0.1 pr.n.[m.] **Hazak**, <PREP> לְ of possession, *(belonging) to* Seal 756 (c. 700).

חָזֵק, see חזק *be strong*, Qal, Coll.

[חֵזֶק] 1 n.[m.] **strength**—sf. חִזְקִי—<OBJ> רחם *love* Ps 18$_{2}$. <APP> אֶרְחָמְךָ י׳ חִזְקִי *I love you, O Y. my strength* Ps 18$_{2}$.*

→ חזק *be strong*.

[חֹזֶק] 5.2.4 n.m. **strength**—Q חוזק; cstr. חֹזֶק (Q חוזק); sf. חָזְקֵנוּ—<NOM CL> טוב חזק appar. *strength is good* Si 41$_{3(Bmg)}$ (unless *a strong one is good*, from חָזָק *strong*; B חקיך *your decrees*). <OBJ> שׁמד hi. *destroy* Hg 2$_{22}$ (+ כִּסֵּא *throne*), עשׂה *make* 2 C 25$_{8}$ (if em. חֲזַק *be strong* to חֹזֶק *strength* for battle), נתן *give* 1QM 14$_{6}$ (‖ אֹמֶץ *might*). <CSTR> חֹזֶק יָד *strength of hand* Ex 13$_{3.14.16}$, מַמְלְכוֹת *of the kingdoms of* the nations Hg 2$_{22}$ (unless del. מַמְלְכוֹת), הַגּוֹיִם *of the nations* Hg 2$_{22}$ (if del. מַמְלְכוֹת), חוזק מותנים *strength of loins* 1QH 2$_{7}$ (‖ אֹמֶץ *might*, + כֹּחַ *strength*), ידים *of hands* 1QS 10$_{26}$, מעמד *of standing* 1QM 14$_{6}$. <PREP> בְּ of instrument, *by (means of), with*, + יצא hi. *bring out* Ex 13$_{3.14.16}$, לקח *take* Am 6$_{13}$, סמך *support* 1QH 2$_{7}$; of accompaniment, *with* 4QMyst$^{c}$ 2$_{3}$ (בלא חוזק *without strength*), + בוא *come* Is 40$_{10}$ (1QIsa$^{a}$; MT בְּחָזָק *as a strong one*), שׁאל *ask* Si 35$_{7(B)}$, נשׂא *bear*, i.e. permit Si 35$_{7(Bmg)}$.

<SYN> אֹמֶץ *might*.*

→ חזק *be strong*.

חזקא, see חִזְקִיָּהוּ *Hezekiah*.

[חֶזְקָה] 4.0.1 n.f. **strength**—cstr. חֶזְקַת; sf. חֶזְקָתוֹ—**strength**, i.e. **being strong** (Dn 11$_{2}$ 2 C 12$_{1}$ 26$_{16}$), **grasp-**

ing (Is $8_{11}$=4QMidrEschat$^{a}$ $3_{15}$), perh. inf. cstr. of חזק *be strong*, <CSTR> חֶזְקַת הַיָּד *grasping of the hand* Is $8_{11}$= 4QMidrEschat$^{a}$ $3_{15}$ ([היד]). <PREP> בְּ of accompaniment, *with*, + אמר *say* Is $8_{11(mss)}$; כְּ *according to*, + היה *be* 4QMidrEschat$^{a}$ $3_{15}$, אמר *say* Is $8_{11}$, עור hi. *stir* Dn $11_2$, עזב *forsake* 2 C $12_1$, גבה *be high*, i.e. proud 2 C $26_{16}$.*
→ חזק *be strong.*

**חָזְקָה** 5 n.f. **strength, force,** <PREP> בְּ of accompaniment, *with*, + לחץ *oppress* Jg $4_3$, רדה *rule* Ezk $34_4$ (or em. וּבַחֲזָקָה *and over the strong one;* + פֶּרֶךְ *severity*), ריב *strive* Jg $8_1$, לקח *take* 1 S $2_{16}$, קרא *cry* Jon $3_8$.*
→ חזק *be strong.*

**חִזְקִי** 1 pr.n.m. **Hizki,** son of Elpaal, descendant of Benjamin, <NOM CL> חִזְקִי וָחָבֶר : ... בְּנֵי אֶלְפָּעַל *Hizki and Heber ... were sons of Elpaal* 1 C $8_{17}$.

**חִזְקִיָּה**, see חִזְקִיָּהוּ *Hezekiah.*

**חִזְקִיָּהוּ** 125.2.3.4 pr.n.m. **Hezekiah**—חִזְקִיָּה 2 K $18_{1+7t}$ Zp $1_1$ Pr $25_1$ Ne $7_{21}$ $10_{18}$ 1 K $3_{23}$, יְחִזְקִיָּה Ho $1_1$ Mc $1_1$ Ezr $2_{16}$, יְחִזְקִיָּהוּ 2 K $20_{10}$ Is $1_1$ Jr $15_4$ 1 C $4_{41}$ 2 C $28_{12.27}$ $29_{1+4t}$ $30_{1+3t}$ $31_{2+5t}$ $32_{2+18t}$ $33_3$, Q חזקא—**1.** son of Ahaz and Abi, successor of Ahaz as king of Judah, and father of Manasseh, <SUBJ> היה *be* 2 K $18_1$, חיה *live* 2 K $20_1$||Is $38_1$ 2 K $20_{12(mss)}$ Is $38_{9.9}$, ילד hi. *beget* 2 K $20_{16}$ (or del.), יכל *be able* 2 K $18_{22}$||Is $36_7$ 2 K $18_{29}$||Is $36_{14}$, הלך *go* Is $38_9$, htp. *walk* 2 K $20_3$||Is $38_3$, בוא *come* 2 K $19_1$||Is $37_1$ 2 C $31_8$, hi. *bring* 2 K $20_{20}$ 2 C $29_{1.20}$, שׁוב hi. *bring back* 2 K $18_{22}$||Is $36_7$ 2 C $32_{25}$, יצא *go out* 2 K $18_1$, עלה *go up* 2 K $19_{14}$||$37_{10}$ 2 K $20_{5.8}$||Is $38_9$ 2 C $29_{20}$, hi. *raise* 2 C $32_2$, שׁכם hi. *rise* 2 C $29_{20}$, סור *depart* 2 K $18_1$, hi. *remove* 2 K $18_{4.22}$||Is $36_7$||2 C $32_{12}$, סבב hi. *turn* face 2 K $20_1$||Is $38_2$, נטה hi. *turn*, i.e. divert waters Si $48_{17}$ (יחזקיהו), ישׁר pi. *make straight* 2 C $32_{30(Qr)}$ (Kt ויישׁרם), ישׁב *dwell* 2 C $32_9$, רום hi. *raise* 2 C $30_{24}$, נשׂא *carry* 2 K $18_{14}$, ni. *be lifted up* 2 C $32_{23}$, אסף *gather* 2 C $29_{1.20}$, קבץ *gather together* 2 C $32_2$, שׁלח *send* 2 K $18_{14}$ $19_1$||Is $37_1$ 2 C $30_1$, נתן *give* 2 K $18_{15.16}$ 2 C $32_{2.11}$, לקח *take* 2 K $19_{14}$||$37_{14}$.

מלך *rule* 2 K $16_{20}$||2 C $28_{27}$ 2 K $18_{1.1}$||2 C $29_{1.1}$, עבד *serve* 2 K $18_1$, עמד hi. *station* 2 C $31_2$, עשׂה *do* 2 K $18_1$ ||2 C $29_1$ 2 K $20_3$||Is $38_3$ 2 K $20_{20}$ 2 C $31_{20.20.21}$ $32_{2.12.27.27}$ Si $48_{22(Segal)}$ (עשה יחז[קיהו]), חצב *hew* Si $48_{17}$, בנה *build* 2 C $32_2$, סתם *block* 2 C $32_{2.30}$ Si $48_{17}$, אבד pi. *destroy* 2 K $21_3$||2 C $33_3$ (נתץ pi. *tear down*), נכה hi. *strike* 2 K $18_1$, שׁבר pi. *break* 2 K $18_1$, כרת *cut* 2 K $18_1$, specif. make covenant 2 C $29_1$, קצץ pi. *cut off* 2 K $18_{16}$, כתת pi. *beat in pieces* 2 K $18_1$ (or em. וְאֵת *and* + object marker), ירא *fear* 2 K $19_5$||Is $37_5$ Jr $26_{19}$, מרד *rebel* 2 K $18_{1.19}$||Is $36_5$, חטא *sin* 2 K $18_{14}$, נשׁא hi. *deceive* 2 K $18_{29}$||Is $36_{14}$||2 C $32_{15}$, סות hi. *incite* 2 K $18_{32}$||Is $36_{18}$||2 C $32_9$ 2 C $32_{15}$, בטח *trust* 2 K $18_{1.19.19.19}$||Is $36_{4.4.4}$||2 C $32_9$ 2 K $18_{22}$||Is $36_7$ 2 K $18_{22}$ $19_{10}$||Is $37_{10}$, hi. *cause to trust* 2 K $18_{30}$||Is $36_{15}$, יעץ ni. *consult together* 2 C $32_2$, דבק *adhere* 2 K $18_1$, שׁמר *keep* 2 K $18_1$, נצל ni. *deliver oneself* 2 K $19_{10}$||Is $37_{10}$, hi. *take away* 2 K $18_{29}$, שׂכל hi. *prosper* 2 K $18_1$, צלח hi. *prosper* 2 C $31_{21}$ $32_{30}$.

ברך pi. *bless* 2 C $31_8$, פלל htp. *pray* 2 K $19_{15}$||Is $37_{15}$ 2 K $19_{20}$||Is $37_{21}$ 2 K $20_1$||Is $38_2$||2 C $32_{24}$ 2 C $30_{18}$ $32_{20}$, אמר *say* 2 K $18_{14.19}$||Is $36_5$ (if em.) 2 K $18_{22}$||Is $36_7$||2 C $32_{12.12}$ 2 K $18_{30}$||Is $36_{15}$ 2 K $18_{32}$||Is $36_{18}$||2 C $32_9$ $19_3$||Is $37_3$ 2 K $19_{10}$||Is $37_{10}$ $20_1$||Is $38_3$ 2 K $20_{8.10.14}$||Is $39_3$ 2 K $20_{15}$||Is $39_4$ 2 K $20_{19.19}$||Is $39_{8.8}$ Is $38_{9.9.22}$ 2 C $29_{1.20.27.30.31}$ $30_{18}$ $31_{11}$ $32_2$, דבר pi. *speak* Is $38_9$ 2 C $30_{22}$ $32_2$, ענה *answer* 2 C $29_{31}$, שׁמע *hear* 2 K $19_1$||Is $37_1$ 2 K $19_{10}$||Is $37_{10}$ 2 K $20_{13}$ (or em. with ||Is $39_2$ וַיִּשְׂמַח *he rejoiced*) 2 K $20_{16}$||Is $39_5$, קרא *call*, i.e. read 2 K $19_{14}$||Is $37_{14}$, שׁוע pi. *cry out* Is $38_9$, זעק *cry out* 2 C $32_{20}$, בכה *weep* 2 K $20_3$||Is $38_3$, צפף pilp. *chirp* Is $38_9$, הגה *moan* Is $38_9$, ידה hi. *praise* Is $38_9$, שׂמח *rejoice* Is $39_2$ (||2 K $20_{13}$ וַיִּשְׁמַע *he heard*) 2 C $29_{36}$, נגן pi. *play* music Is $38_9$.

ראה *see* Is $38_9$ 2 C $31_8$ $32_2$, hi. *show* 2 K $20_{13.13}$||Is $39_{2.2}$ 2 K $20_{15}$||Is $39_4$, נבט hi. *look at* Is $38_9$, פתח *open* 2 C $29_1$, קפד pi. *roll up* Is $38_9$, פרשׂ *spread out* 2 K $19_{14}$||Is $37_{14}$, כסה *cover* 2 K $19_1$||Is $37_1$, צפה pi. *overlay* with gold 2 K $18_{16}$, סמך *lay* hand upon 2 C $29_{20}$, קרע *tear* 2 K $19_1$||Is $37_1$, ערב htp. *make pledge* 2 K $18_{22}$||Is $36_7$, חלה pi. *entreat favour* Jr $26_{19}$, כנע ni. *humble oneself* 2 C $32_{26}$, צוה *put in order* 2 K $20_1$||Is $38_1$, פקד pu. *be deprived* Is $38_9$, חזק *be strong* Is $39_1$ (||2 K $20_{12}$ חִזְקִיָּהוּ; Q ויחיה *and he lived*), pi. *strengthen* 2 C $29_1$ $32_2$ Si $48_{17}$, hi. *hold* on to ways of David Si $48_{22}$ (חז[קיהו]), htp. *strengthen oneself* 2 C $32_2$

(unless עַם *people* is subj.), חלה *be weak* 2 K $20_{1}$||Is $38_{1}$||2 C $32_{24}$ 2 K $20_{12}$||Is $39_{1}$ Is $38_{9}$, מות *die* 2 K $20_{1.1}$||Is $38_{1.1}$||2 C $32_{24}$, hi. *kill* Jr $26_{19}$, שׁכב *lie down* 2 K $20_{21}$||2 C $32_{33}$, כתב *write* 2 C $30_{1}$, דרשׁ *seek* 2 C $31_{9.21}$, חלל hi. *begin* 2 C $31_{21}$.

<NOM CL> בְּנֵי־שְׁלֹמֹה ... חִזְקִיָּהוּ *the descendants of Solomon were ... Hezekiah* 1 C $3_{13(mss.)}$ (L בֶּן־ *son*).

<OBJ> ישׁע hi. *save* Is $38_{9}$ 2 C $32_{22}$, נצל hi. *deliver from* 2K $18_{30}$||2 C $32_{11}$ 2 K $20_{5}$||Is $38_{5}$, נהל pi. *give rest to* 2 C $32_{22}$ (or em. וַיָּנַח לָהֶם *and he gave rest to them*), עזר *help* 2 C $32_{8}$, ערב *go surety for* Is $38_{9}$, חלם hi. *restore to health* Is $38_{9}$, חיה hi. *make live* Is $38_{9}$, עזב *forsake* 2 C $32_{30}$, נסה pi. *test* 2 C $32_{30}$, נשׁא hi. *deceive* 2 K $19_{10}$||Is $37_{10}$, בצע pi. *cut off* Is $38_{9}$, שׁלם hi. *make an end of* Is $38_{9.9}$, קבר *bury* 2 C $32_{33}$, שׁמע *hear* 2 C $29_{1}$.

<CSTR> אֱלֹהֵי יְחִזְקִיָּהוּ *God of Hezekiah* 2 C $32_{17}$, אַנְשֵׁי חִזְקִיָּה *men of Hezekiah* Pr $25_{1}$, עבד חזקיהו Hilkiah, *servant of Hezekiah* Seal $321_{3}$ (Hebron, 8th/7th cent.), בֶּן־יְחִזְקִיָּהוּ *son of Hezekiah* Jr $15_{4}$, דִּבְרֵי חִזְקִיָּהוּ *words of Hezekiah* 2 K $20_{20}$||2 C $32_{32}$ 2 C $32_{8}$ (both יְחִזְקִיָּהוּ), יְמֵי *days of* Jr $26_{18}$ 1 C $4_{41}$ 2 C $32_{26}$ (יְחִזְקִיָּהוּ), יְמֵי ... יְחִזְקִיָּהוּ *days of ... Hezekiah* Is $1_{1}$ Ho $1_{1}$ (יְחִזְקִיָּה) Mc $1_{1}$ (יְחִזְקִיָּה), מִפְקַד יְחִזְקִיָּהוּ *appointment of Hezekiah* 2 C $31_{13}$.

<APP> בֵּן *son* 2 K $16_{20}$ $18_{1}$ 1 C $3_{13}$ 2 C $28_{27}$, אָב *father* 2 K $21_{3}$||2 C $33_{3}$, מֶלֶךְ *king* 2 K $18_{9.13}$||Is $36_{1}$ 2 K $18_{14.14.16.17}$||Is $36_{2}$||2 C $32_{9}$ 2 K $19_{1}$||Is $37_{1}$ 2 K $19_{5}$||Is $37_{5}$ 2 K $19_{10}$||Is $37_{10}$ 2 K $20_{14}$||Is $39_{3}$ Is $1_{1}$ $38_{9}$ Jr $26_{18.19}$ Ho $1_{1}$ Mc $1_{1}$ Pr $25_{1}$ 1 C $4_{41}$ 2 C $29_{18.20.30}$ $30_{24}$ $31_{13}$ $32_{8.20.23}$ perh. 4Q382 $41_{5}$ (יחזקיה מלך), נָגִיד *prince* 2 K $20_{5}$, עֶבֶד *servant* 2 C $32_{16}$.

<PREP> לְ of possession, *of, (belonging) to* 2 K $18_{9.10.13}$||Is $36_{1}$ 2 K $20_{8}$||Is $38_{5}$ Is $38_{9.9.9}$, + היה *be* 2 C $32_{27}$, of direction, *to(wards)*, + בוא hi. *bring* 2 C $32_{23}$, נתן *give* 2 K $18_{22.22}$||Is $36_{7.7}$ 2 C $32_{24.27}$, נגד hi. *declare* 2 K $18_{37}$, אמר *say* Is $38_{9}$ 2 C $32_{24}$, נוח hi. *give rest* 2 C $32_{22}$ (if em.), עשׂה *do* 2 C $32_{33}$, of benefit, *for*, עשׂה *do* 2 C $32_{27.27}$; אמן לְ hi. *trust in* 2 C $32_{15}$; רפא לְ *heal* 2 K $20_{5.8}$; מִן of direction, *from*, + יצא *go out* 2 K $20_{16}$ (or del.) ||Is $39_{5}$ (Q ממעיכה *from your innards*), שׁוב *go back* 2 C $29_{1}$, גלה ni. *be removed* Is $38_{9}$; לְבַד מִן *apart from*, + שׁחת hi. *be corrupt* Si $49_{4}$ (יחזקיהו); אֶל *to*, + אמר *say* 2 K $18_{19}$||Is $36_{4}$ $19_{10}$||Is $37_{10}$ $20_{1}$||Is $38_{1}$ 2 K $20_{5}$||Is $38_{5}$ 2 K $20_{14}$||Is $39_{3}$ 2 K $20_{16}$||Is $39_{5}$ 2 C $31_{9}$, שׁמע *hear*, i.e. obey 2 K $18_{31}$||Is $36_{16}$ 2 K $18_{32}$ 2 C $30_{20}$, בוא *come* 2 K $18_{37}$||Is $36_{22}$ 2 K $20_{1}$||Is $38_{1}$ 2 K $20_{14.14.14(mss)}$||Is $39_{3.3.3}$ 2 C $29_{18}$, שׁלח *send* 2 K $18_{17}$||Is $36_{2}$ $19_{9}$||Is $37_{9}$ 2 K $19_{20}$||Is $37_{21}$ $20_{12}$||Is $39_{1}$, קבץ *gather together* 2 C $32_{2}$; עַל *upon*, + היה *be* 2 C $32_{25}$, בוא *come* 2 C $32_{26}$, נתן *give* 2 K $18_{14}$, שׂים *set* 2 K $18_{14}$, *to* 2 C $32_{24}$, + שׁלח *send* 2 C $32_{9}$, pi. *send* 2 C $32_{30}$ (or em. pu. *be sent*), *against*, + דבר pi. *speak* Jr $26_{19}$ 2 C $32_{16}$; עִם *with* 2 C $32_{2.8}$, + היה *be* 2 K $18_{1}$; לִפְנֵי *before*, + נגשׁ hi. *cause to approach* 2 C $29_{20}$; תַּחַת *instead of*, + מלך *rule* 2 K $20_{21}$ ||2 C $32_{33}$.

**2.** father of Amariah and ancestor of Zephaniah the prophet, <CSTR> בֶּן־חִזְקִיָּה *son of Hezekiah* Zp $1_{1}$ (mss חלקיה *Hilkiah*).

**3.** ancestor of clan in postexilic Judah, and name in which clan head in Nehemiah's time signed document, <NOM CL> רָאשֵׁי הָעָם ... חִזְקִיָּה *the heads of the people were ... Hezekiah* Ne $10_{18}$. <PREP> לְ of possession, *of, belonging to* Ezr $2_{16}$||Ne $7_{21}$.

**4.** son of Neariah, descendant of Zerubbabel, <NOM CL> בְּנֵי נְעַרְיָה אֶלְיוֹעֵינַי וְחִזְקִיָּה *the sons of Neariah were Elioenai and Hezekiah* 1 C $3_{23(mss.)}$ (L בֶּן־ *son*).

**5.** **Jehizkiah,** Ephraimite chief, son of Shallum, <SUBJ> קום *arise* 2 C $28_{12}$, אמר *say* 2 C $28_{12}$. <APP> בֵּן *son* 2 C $28_{12}$. <PREP> לְ of possession, *of, belonging to* 2 C $28_{12}$; עַל *upon* 2 C $28_{12}$.

**6.** son or descendant of Kore (קראה), <APP> בֵּן *son* Ophel ost.$_{1}$ (ח[ז]קיהו or יח[ז]קיהו).

**7.** <PREP> לְ of possession, *of, (belonging) to* T. Beit Mirsim inscr. 3.

**8.** governor during Persian period, Stamp/Coin 43 44 (both יחזקיה; both 4th cent.), <APP> פֶּחָה *governor* Stamp/Coin 43 (4th cent.).

**9.** party to deed of sale Mur 22 $1_{2.4}$ (both חזקא) $1_{7}$ ([חז]קיה) $1_{10}$ (ח[ז]ק[יה]) $1_{23}$ (חזק[יה]), <CSTR> בר חזקא *(son of) Hezekiah*, i.e. Hezekiah himself Mur 22 $1_{4}$, <PREP> לְ of possession, *of (belonging) to* Mur 22 $1_{2}$ (את מקום שלחזקא *the place of Hezekiah*).

⇒ י״ *Y.* + חזק *be strong*.

**חזר** $_{0.1}$ vb. **turn around**—**Qal** $_{0.1}$ Ptc. חוזר—**turn around, revolve,** <SUBJ> אוֹפָן *wheel* Si $36_{5}$.

**חָח** 7 n.m. **hook**—sf. חַחִי; pl. חַחִים (Kt חיים Ezk 29$_{4}$)—**1. hook,** to lead away captives or animals, <OBJ> שׂים *place* in nose 2 K 19$_{28}$||Is 37$_{29}$ (|| מֶתֶג *bridle*), נתן *give*, i.e. place, in jaw Ezk 29$_{4}$ 38$_{4}$. <PREP> בְּ of instrument, *by (means of), with*, + בוא hi. *bring* Ezk 19$_{4}$, נתן *give*, i.e. place Ezk 19$_{9}$.

**2. fibula, brooch,** used collectively, <OBJ> בוא *bring* Ex 35$_{22}$ (|| נֶזֶם *earring*, טַבַּעַת *ring*, כּוּמָז *armlet*). <APP> כְּלִי *vessel* of gold Ex 35$_{22}$. <COLL> חָח וָנֶזֶם *fibulas and earrings* Ex 35$_{22}$.

<SYN> §1 מֶתֶג *bridle*; §2 נֶזֶם *earring*, טַבַּעַת *ring*, כּוּמָז *armlet*.

**[חַט]**, see חוּט *incisor*.

**חטא** $_{238.5.7}$ vb. **sin**—**Qal** $_{182.5.6}$ Pf. חָטָא, חָטְאָה (חָטָאָה), חָטָאתָ, חָטָאתִי, חָטְאוּ (חָטָאוּ), חֲטָאתֶם, חָטָאת [Ex 5$_{16}$]), חָטָאנוּ; impf. יֶחֱטָא (Gnz יֶחֱטָא Ex 19$_{4}$), 3fs תֶּחֱטָא, 2ms תֶּחֱטָא, אֶחֱטָא, יֶחֶטְאוּ, תֶּחֶטְאוּ (תֶּחֱטָאוּ); + waw וְחָטְאָה, וַנֶּחֱטָא, וַתֶּחֱטָא; 2ms וַחֲטָאתֶם, וְחָטָאתִי; a. חוֹטֵא (חֹטֵא, חוֹטֵא, חֹטֵא, חֹטְאִי), חֹטְאִים, חֹטֵאת; inf. חֲטֹא (חֲטוֹא, חֲטוֹ, חֲטֹאתוֹ).

**1a. sin, incur guilt** (e.g. Lv 4$_{14}$ 5$_{5}$), appar. **incur** (liability for a) sacrificial offering (Lv 5$_{7.11}$), **endanger** or **forfeit** life (Hb 2$_{10}$ [unless חוֹטֵא *sin* (noun)] Pr 20$_{2}$); **miss, fail to attain** (e.g. Is 65$_{20}$ Jb 5$_{24}$ Pr 8$_{36}$ 19$_{2}$ 24$_{9}$ [if em.; see Subj.] perh. Ec 2$_{26}$ 7$_{26}$*), <SUBJ> אֶרֶץ *land* Ezk 14$_{13}$, גּוֹי *nation* Is 1$_{4}$, עַם *people* Ex 5$_{16}$ (חָטָאת עַמֶּךָ appar. *your people have sinned*; or em. חָטָאתָ לְעַמֶּךָ *you have sinned against your people*) 20$_{20}$ 32$_{30.31}$ Lv 4$_{28.35}$ Nm 14$_{40}$ 21$_{7}$ 1 S 14$_{33.34}$ 1 K 8$_{33.35.46.47}$||2 C 6$_{24.26.36.37}$ (|| רשׁע *do wickedly*; + עוה hi. *commit iniquity*) 1 K 8$_{50}$||2 C 6$_{39}$ (1 K 8$_{50}$ + פשׁע *transgress*) Jr 2$_{35}$ 8$_{14}$ 16$_{10}$ 44$_{23}$ 50$_{7}$ Ho 4$_{7}$, Babylon Jr 50$_{14}$ (or del.), Samaria Ezk 16$_{51}$, Israel Dt 1$_{41}$ 9$_{16.18}$ Jos 7$_{11}$ (+ עבר *transgress*) 1 S 7$_{6}$ 1 K 8$_{33.35}$||2 C 6$_{24.26}$ Jr 33$_{8.8}$ (+ פשׁע *transgress*) Ho 10$_{9}$ (חָטָאתָ *you have sinned*; mss חַטַּאת *the sin of* Israel) Ps 78$_{32}$, Israelite(s) Dt 20$_{18}$ Is 42$_{24}$ 64$_{4}$ Jr 14$_{7}$ 40$_{3}$ Ps 106$_{6}$ (+ עוה hi. *commit iniquity*, רשׁע hi. *do wickedly*) Lm 5$_{16}$ Dn 9$_{5}$ (|| עוה *commit iniquity*, רשׁע hi., מרד *rebel*, + סור *turn aside*) 9$_{8.11.15}$ (|| רשׁע *do wickedly*), קָהָל *assembly* Lv 4$_{14}$, Jacob Ps 78$_{32}$, Judah 1 K 14$_{22}$ Jr 14$_{20}$ 33$_{8.8}$, Ephraim Ho 8$_{11}$ (or em. לַחֲטֹא *to sin* to לְחֵטְא *as a sin*) 8$_{11}$ (or del.) 13$_{2}$ (+ יסף hi. *do again*), Jerusalem Lm 1$_{8}$, Zion Jr 14$_{20}$, עִיר *city* Mc 7$_{9}$.

Aaron Nm 12$_{11}$ (|| יאל ni. *be foolish*), Abimelech Gn 20$_{6.9}$, Achan Jos 7$_{20}$, Baasha 1 K 16$_{13}$, Balaam Nm 22$_{34}$, David 1 S 19$_{4}$ 24$_{12}$ 2 S 12$_{13}$ 24$_{10}$||1 C 21$_{8}$ 2 S 24$_{17}$ (|| עוה hi. *commit iniquity*) 1 C 21$_{17}$ (+ רעע hi. *do evil*), Elah 1 K 16$_{13}$, Hezekiah 2 K 18$_{14}$, Jephthah Jg 11$_{27}$, Jeremiah Jr 37$_{18}$, Jeroboam 1 K 14$_{16}$ 15$_{30}$ Si 47$_{23}$ (ח[ט]א), Job Jb 1$_{22}$ 2$_{10}$ 7$_{20}$ 10$_{14}$ 35$_{6}$, Joseph Gn 39$_{9}$, Judah Gn 43$_{9}$ 44$_{32}$, Manasseh 2 K 21$_{17}$, Miriam Nm 12$_{11}$, Nehemiah Ne 1$_{6}$ 6$_{13}$, Obadiah 1 K 18$_{9}$, Samuel 1 S 12$_{23}$, Saul 1 S 15$_{24.30}$ 19$_{5}$ 26$_{21}$, Shimei 2 S 19$_{21}$, Solomon Ne 13$_{26}$, Zimri 1 K 16$_{19}$.

אָדָם *human being* Lv 5$_{22}$ 1 K 8$_{46}$||2 C 6$_{36}$ Zp 1$_{17}$ Jb 33$_{27}$ Ec 7$_{20}$ (:: עשׂה טוֹב *do good*), אֱנוֹשׁ *human being* Si 15$_{20}$, אִישׁ *man* Lv 19$_{22.22}$ Nm 6$_{11}$ 16$_{22}$ Dt 19$_{15}$=11QT 61$_{6}$ 1 S 2$_{25.25}$ 1 K 8$_{31}$||2 C 6$_{22}$ Dn 9$_{8}$, אִשָּׁה *woman* Nm 6$_{11}$, אָב *father* Is 43$_{27}$ (+ פשׁע *transgress*), specif. of Israel 1 S 12$_{10}$ Jr 3$_{25}$ Lm 5$_{7}$ Ne 9$_{29}$ 1QS 1$_{25}$ ([ח]טאנו ... [וא]בותינו), אָח *brother* Gn 42$_{22}$, בֵּן *son* 1 K 16$_{13}$ Jr 3$_{25}$ Ps 4$_{5}$ Jb 1$_{5}$ 8$_{4}$ Si 5$_{4}$ 16$_{21}$ 47$_{23}$ (ח[ט]א), specif. of Gad and Reuben Nm 32$_{23}$, of Ephraim Ps 78$_{17}$ (+ יסף hi. *do again*), of Israel Jg 10$_{10.15}$ 2 K 17$_{7}$ Ezk 37$_{23}$ Ne 1$_{6}$.

פַּרְעֹה *Pharaoh* Ex 5$_{16}$ (if em.; see above) 9$_{27.34}$ (+ יסף hi. *do again*) 10$_{16}$, מֶלֶךְ *king* 1 S 19$_{4}$ 2 K 18$_{14}$ Ezk 28$_{16}$ Ne 13$_{26}$, נָשִׂיא *prince* Lv 4$_{22.23}$, כֹּהֵן *priest* Lv 4$_{3.3}$, עֶבֶד *servant* 1QH 17$_{23.26}$ ([מ]חטוא]), בַּיִת *house* of my father Ne 1$_{6}$, צַדִּיק *righteous one* Ezk 3$_{21.21}$ 18$_{24}$ (|| מעל *be unfaithful*) 33$_{12}$, רָשָׁע *wicked one* Ezk 33$_{16}$, worshipper Ps 39$_{2}$ 41$_{5}$ 51$_{6}$ (+ עשׂה רַע *do evil*) 119$_{11}$ 1QH 14$_{17}$ (+ עשׂה *do* evil).

מַשְׁקֶה *butler* Gn 40$_{1}$, אֹפֶה *baker* Gn 40$_{1}$, בצע ptc. *one who makes (unjust) gain* Hb 2$_{10}$ (or em. וְחוֹטֵא *and sins* to בְּחֵטְא *by the sin of* your soul; =1QpHab 9$_{14}$ חוטי appar. *threads of* life), עבר htp. ptc. *one who provokes anger* Pr 20$_{2}$ (or em. חוֹטֵא *sins* to חוֹמֵס *does violence*), יֹשֵׁב *inhabitant* Dn 9$_{8}$, אוץ ptc. *one who hastens* Pr 19$_{2}$, בוז ptc. *one who despises* Pr 14$_{21}$, עבר *one who passes* into covenant 1QS 1$_{25}$ ([חט]אנו]), transgressor Lv 5$_{5.6.7.10.11.13.16.23}$ (|| אשׁם *be guilty*) Dt 9$_{15}$ Is 65$_{20}$ Jb 24$_{19}$ (or em. חָטָאוּ *[those who] have sinned* to יַנְחִיתוּ *they shall bring down*) Pr 8$_{36}$ (:: מצא *find*), אֲשֶׁר *one who* Si 38$_{15}$ 1QH 17$_{22}$, מִי אֲשֶׁר *who-*

*ever* Ex $32_{33}$, חֵךְ *palate*, i.e. mouth Jb $31_{30}$, נֶפֶשׁ *soul* Lv $4_{2.27}$ $5_{1.15}$ (+ מעל *be unfaithful*) $5_{17.21}$ Nm $15_{27}$ Ezk $18_{4.20}$ 4QD[a] $18.5_{2}$, זִמָּה *device* Pr $24_{9}$ (if em. חַטָּאת *sin* to חטאת *fails to attain [its goal]*).

<OBJ> חֲטָאָה *sin* Ex $32_{30.31}$, חַטָּאת *sin* Lv $4_{3.14.22.28.35}$ $5_{6.10.13}$ $19_{22.22}$ Nm $12_{11}$ Dt $9_{18}$ 1 K $14_{16.22}$ $15_{30}$ $16_{13.19}$ 2 K $21_{17}$ Jr $16_{10}$ Ezk $18_{24}$ $33_{16}$ Ne $1_{6}$, חֵטְא *sin* Dt $19_{15}$=11QT $61_{6}$ Lm $1_{8}$ (unless em. חֵטְא to חָטֹא, i.e. inf. abs.), עָוֹן *iniquity* Jr $33_{8.8}$, אָשָׁם incur *guilt offering* Lv $5_{7}$, קָרְבָּן incur *offering* Lv $5_{11}$, אֵת אֲשֶׁר *that which* Lv $5_{16}$, נֶפֶשׁ *soul*, i.e. endanger or forfeit one's life Hb $2_{10}$ (or em.; see Subj.; =1QpHab $9_{14}$ חוטי appar. *threads of* life) Pr $20_{2}$ (or em.; see Subj.), חָכְמָה miss *wisdom* Pr $8_{36}$.

<PREP> לְ *against* 4QPrQuot $81_{3}$ ([ח]טאנו ל[כה] *we have sinned against you*), + ׳׳ *Y.* Ex $10_{16}$ $32_{33}$ Nm $32_{23}$ Dt $1_{41}$ $9_{16}$ $20_{18}$ Jos $7_{20}$ Jg $10_{10}$ 1 S $2_{25}$ $7_{6}$ $12_{23}$ $14_{33.34}$ 2 S $12_{13}$ 1 K $8_{33.35.46.50}$||2 C $6_{24.26.36.39}$ 2 K $17_{7}$ Is $42_{24}$ Jr $3_{25}$ $8_{14}$ $14_{7.20}$ $16_{10}$ $33_{8.8}$ $40_{3}$ $44_{23}$ $50_{7.14}$ (or del.) Ezk $14_{13}$ Ho $4_{7}$ Mc $7_{9}$ Zp $1_{17}$ Ps $41_{5}$ $119_{11}$ Dn $9_{8.11}$ Ne $1_{6}$, אֲדֹנָי *Adonai* 1QH $14_{17}$ $17_{22.23.26}$ ([מ]חטוא) 4QDibHam[a] $1.2_{16}$, אֱלֹהִים *God* Gn $20_{6}$ $39_{9}$ Ex $10_{16}$ Dt $1_{41(mss)}$ $9_{16}$ $20_{18}$ Jos $7_{20}$ 1 K $8_{33.35.46.50}$||2 C $6_{24.26.36.39}$ 2 K $17_{7}$ Jr $3_{25}$ $16_{10}$ Ps $51_{6}$ $78_{17}$ Dn $9_{11}$ Ne $1_{6}$, אֵל *God* Jb $8_{4}$ Ne $1_{6}$, שַׁדַּי *Shaddai* Jb $8_{4}$, Aaron Ex $10_{16}$, Abraham Gn $20_{9}$, Israel (Jacob) Gn $43_{9}$, עַם *people* Ex $5_{16}$ (if em.; see Subj.), Moses Ex $10_{16}$, Saul 1 S $19_{4}$ $24_{12}$, Zedekiah Jr $37_{18}$, אִישׁ *man* 1 S $2_{25}$, אָב *father* Gn $44_{32}$, מֶלֶךְ *king* Gn $40_{1}$ Jg $11_{27}$ Jr $37_{18}$, אָדוֹן *lord* Gn $40_{1}$, עֶבֶד *servant* Jr $37_{18}$, רֵעַ *neighbour* 1 K $8_{31}$||2 C $6_{22}$, עַם *people* Jr $37_{18}$.

לְ introducing object, + אַשְׁמָה *guilt* Lv $4_{3}$.

בְּ of place, *in*, + מוֹשָׁב *settlement* Ezk $37_{23}$ (unless em. מוֹשְׁבֹתֵיהֶם *their settlements* to מְשׁוּבֹתֵיהֶם *their backslidings*).

בְּ of instrument, *by (means of), with*, + לָשׁוֹן *tongue* Ps $39_{2}$, שָׂפָה *lip* Jb $2_{10}$, שְׁגָגָה *error*, i.e. inadvertently Lv $4_{2.27}$ $5_{15}$ Nm $15_{27}$ 4QD[a] $18.5_{2}$, חַטָּאת *sin* Lv $4_{23}$, מְשׁוּבָה *backsliding* Ezk $37_{23}$ (if em.; see above), אַחַת מִכֹּל אֲשֶׁר־יַעֲשֶׂה הָאָדָם לַחֲטֹא בָהֵנָּה *one of any of the things that a human being does to sin by means of them* Lv $5_{22}$.

בְּ *against*, + David 1 S $19_{4}$, עֶבֶד *servant* 1 S $19_{4}$, יֶלֶד *child* Gn $42_{22}$, דָּם *blood* of innocent one 1 S $19_{5}$, מִשְׁפָּט *judgment* Ne $9_{29}$.

בְּ *despite*, + זֹאת *this* Jb $1_{22}$ $2_{10}$ Ps $78_{32}$ (all three בְּכָל־זֹאת *despite all this*).

כְּ *about*, כַּחֲצִי חַטֹּאתַיִךְ לֹא חָטָאָה *she has not committed about*, i.e. even, *half your sins* Ezk $16_{51}$.

מִן of time, *from, since*, + יוֹם *day* Ho $10_{9}$, נְעוּרִים *youth* Jr $3_{25}$.

מִן partitive, (sin in respect of) *some of, anyone of*, + מִצְוָה *commandment* Lv $4_{2}$, קֹדֶשׁ *holy thing* Lv $5_{15.16}$.

עַל (incur guilt) *on account of*, + נֶפֶשׁ *person*, i.e. dead body Nm $6_{11}$, חַטָּאת *sin* Lv $4_{14.28(Sam)}$, אֵלֶּה *these* Ne $13_{26}$, וְהִתְוַדָּה אֲשֶׁר חָטָא עָלֶיהָ *and he shall confess that (sin), on account of which he has incurred guilt* Lv $5_{5}$.

עִם *with*, + אָב *father* Ps $106_{6}$.

עַד *until*, + יוֹם *day* Jr $3_{25}$.

לִפְנֵי *before*, + עשׂה ptc. *maker* Si $38_{15}$.

<COLL> הַחוֹטֶא בֶּן־מֵאָה שָׁנָה יְקֻלָּל *he who fails to attain an age of a hundred years shall be deemed accursed* Is $65_{20}$, וְחָטָאתִי לְךָ כָּל־הַיָּמִים *and I will have sinned against you all the days* Gn $43_{9}$, sim. Gn $44_{32}$, חָטָאתִי הַפָּעַם *I have sinned (this) time* Ex $9_{27}$; חטא + adverb, עוֹד *still* Ps $78_{32}$, מְאֹד *much* 2 S $24_{10}$||1 C $21_{8}$.

חטא + verb specifying the sin, מעל *be unfaithful* Lv $5_{21}$ Ezk $14_{13}$, מרה hi. *rebel* Ps $78_{17}$, עבר *transgress* commandment 1 S $15_{24}$, עשׂה *make* gods, idols Ex $32_{31}$ Dt $9_{16}$ Ho $13_{2}$, *do* evil, etc. Lv $4_{22}$ $5_{17}$ Dt $4_{18}$ $20_{18}$ 2 S $24_{10}$||1 C $21_{8}$ 1 K $16_{19}$, כעס hi. *provoke* Dt $4_{18}$, עזב *forsake* Y. 1 S $12_{10}$, עבד *serve* Baal, etc. 1 S $12_{10}$, דבר pi. *speak* against Y. and Moses Nm $21_{7}$, ברך pi. *bless*, i.e. curse God Jb $1_{5}$, שׁאל *ask* for a life, i.e. someone's death Jb $31_{30}$, שׁמע *hear* Lv $5_{1}$, כבד hi. *harden* heart Ex $9_{34}$, הלך *walk* 1QS $1_{25}$ ([חט]אנו), in way of Jeroboam 1 K $16_{19}$, אכל *eat* (meat) with blood 1 S $14_{33.34}$, מות hi. *kill* 1 S $19_{5}$, חדל *cease* to pray 1 S $12_{23}$.

חטא + verb with negative, specifying default, שׁמע *listen* to voice, i.e. obey Jr $3_{25}$ $40_{3}$ $44_{23}$, הלך *walk* in law, etc. Jr $44_{23}$, אמן hi. *believe* in wonders Ps $78_{32}$.

**1b.** ptc. as noun, **sinner** (unless at Ec $9_{18}$ חוֹטֶא *sin*). <SUBJ> שׁלם pu. *be repaid* Pr $11_{31}$ (|| רָשָׁע *wicked one*; :: צַדִּיק *righteous one*), לכד ni. *be taken* Ec $7_{26}$,* אבד pi. *destroy* Ec $9_{18}$ (or em. חֵטְא *sin*), אסף *gather* Ec $2_{26}$,* כנס *collect* Ec $2_{26}$, עשׂה *do* Ec $8_{12}$, נתן *give* Ec $2_{26}$, ארך hi. *prolong* days Ec $8_{12}$. <CSTR> חֵיל חוֹטֵא *wealth of a sinner*

Pr $13_{22}$ (:: טוֹב *good one*), גורל חוטא *lot of a sinner* Si $25_{19}$. <PREP> לְ of direction, *to*, + נתן *give* Ec $2_{26}$; כְּ *as* Ec $9_2$ (:: טוֹב *good one*).

<SYN> §1 רשׁע qal & hi. *do wickedly*, עוה qal & hi. *commit iniquity*, מרד *rebel*, יאל ni. *be foolish*, מעל *be unfaithful*, אשׁם *be guilty*; §2 רָשָׁע *wicked one*.

<ANT> §1 עשׂה טוֹב *do good*, מצא *find*; §2 צַדִּיק *righteous one*, טוֹב *good one*.

**Pi.** 15 Pf. חִטְּאוּ; impf. 2ms אֲחַטֶּנָּה ,תְּחַטְּאֵנִי; + waw וַיְחַטְּאוּ, (וַיְחַטְּאֵהוּ) וַיְחַטֵּא ,וְחִטֵּאתָ ,וְחִטְּאוּ, (וְחִטְּאוֹ) וְחִטֵּא; ptc. מְחַטֵּא; inf. חַטֵּא—**1. purify, cleanse from sin,** Lv $8_{15}$ $14_{49.52}$ Nm $19_{19}$ Ezk $43_{20}$ (|| כפר pi. *make atonement for*) $43_{22.22.23}$ $45_{18}$ Ps $51_9$ (+ כבס pi. *wash*).

<SUBJ> אֱלֹהִים *God* Ps $51_9$, appar. Ezekiel Ezk $43_{20.23}$ $45_{18}$, Moses Lv $8_{15}$, שַׂר *prince*, i.e. commander of army Nm $31_{20}$ (if em. תִּתְחַטְּאוּ *you shall purify yourselves*, i.e. htp., to תְּחַטְּאוּ *you shall purify*), פקד pass. ptc. *appointed one* Nm $31_{20}$ (if em.), כֹּהֵן *priest* Lv $14_{49.52}$ Ezk $43_{22.22}$, טָהוֹר *clean one* Nm $19_{19}$.

<OBJ> בֶּגֶד *garment* Nm $31_{20}$ (if em.; see Subj.), כְּלִי *receptacle* of skin Nm $31_{20}$ (if em.; see Subj.), of wood Nm $31_{20}$ (if em.; see Subj.), מַעֲשֶׂה *product* of goats hair Nm $31_{20}$ (if em.; see Subj.), מִזְבֵּחַ *altar* Lv $8_{15}$ Ezk $43_{20.22}$, מִקְדָּשׁ *sanctuary* Ezk $45_{18}$, בַּיִת *house* Lv $14_{49.52}$, טָמֵא *unclean one* Nm $19_{19}$, worshipper Ps $51_9$.

<PREP> בְּ of time, *in, on*, + יוֹם *day* Nm $19_{19}$; of instrument, *by (means of)*, + פַּר *bull* Ezk $43_{22}$, צִפּוֹר *bird* Lv $14_{52}$, אֵזוֹב *hyssop* Lv $14_{52}$ Ps $51_9$, אֶרֶז cedar *wood* Lv $14_{52}$, שָׁנִי *scarlet stuff* Lv $14_{52}$, דָּם *blood* Lv $14_{52}$, מַיִם *water* Lv $14_{52}$.

**2. offer as sin offering,** Ex $29_{36}$ (unless §1a) Lv $6_{19}$ $9_{15}$ 2 C $29_{24}$ (+ כפר pi. *make atonement for*), <SUBJ> Aaron Lv $9_{15}$, Moses Ex $29_{36}$, כֹּהֵן *priest* Lv $6_{19}$ 2 C $29_{24}$. <OBJ> שְׂעִיר *goat* Lv $9_{15}$, חַטָּאת *sin offering* Lv $6_{19}$, דָּם *blood* 2 C $29_{24}$. <PREP> כְּ *as* Lv $9_{15}$; עַל *upon*, + מִזְבֵּחַ *altar* Ex $29_{36}$ (unless עַל introducing object); ה- of direction, *upon*, + מִזְבֵּחַ *altar* 2 C $29_{24}$.

**3. bear the loss of,** Gn $31_{39}$, <SUBJ> Jacob Gn $31_{39}$ (Sam$^{mss}$ אחיטנה *I would account for it*, i.e. חוט hi.). <OBJ> טְרֵפָה *torn animal* Gn $31_{39}$.

Also 4Q422 $10_7$ ([ל]חטוא).

<SYN> §1 כפר pi. *make atonement for*.

**Hi.** 32.0.1 Pf. הֶחֱטִיא (Kt החטי, mss הֶחֱטִיאָם [L הֶחֱטִיאָם 2 K $17_{21}$]), הֶחֱטִיאוּ (Q החטיום); impf. יַחֲטִא, 2ms תַּחֲטִיא, יַחֲטִיאוּ, Sam תחטיאו; + waw וַיַּחֲטִא, 2ms וַתַּחֲטִא; ptc. מַחֲטִיאֵי; inf. הַחֲטִיא (Kt החטי, לַחֲטִיא)—**1. cause to sin** (e.g. Ex $23_{33}$ 1 K $14_{16}$ 2 K $17_{21}$ Jr $32_{35}$). **2. declare guilty** (Dt $24_4$ Is $29_{21}$ Ec $5_5$). **3. miss the target,** in slinging of stones (Jg $20_{16}$), <SUBJ> Israelite(s) Dt $24_4$, Ahab 1 K $21_{22}$, Baasha 1 K $16_{2.13}$, Elah 1 K $16_{13}$, Jeroboam 1 K $14_{16}$ $15_{30.34}$ $16_{26}$ $22_{53}$ 2 K $3_3$ $10_{29.31}$ $13_{2.6.11}$ $14_{24}$ $15_{9.18.24.28}$ $17_{21}$ $23_{15}$ Si $47_{23}$ (ו[יח]טיא), Manasseh 2 K $21_{11.16}$, Zimri 1 K $16_{19}$, אָב *father*, i.e. ancestor 1 K $15_{26}$, אִישׁ *man* Jg $20_{16}$ Jr $32_{35}$, אִשָּׁה *women* Ne $13_{26}$, בֵּן *son* 1 K $22_{53}$ 2 K $3_3$ $10_{29}$ $13_{2.11}$ $14_{24}$ $15_{9.18.24.28}$ $23_{15}$ Si $47_{23}$ (ו[יח]טיא), of Israel Jr $32_{35}$, of Judah Jr $32_{35}$, מֶלֶךְ *king* 2 K $21_{11}$ Jr $32_{35}$, שַׂר *prince* Jr $32_{35}$, כֹּהֵן *priest* Jr $32_{35}$, נָבִיא *prophet* Jr $32_{35}$, יֹשֵׁב *inhabitant* Ex $23_{33}$ Jr $32_{35}$ 4Q522 $8.2_{10}$, wicked Is $29_{21}$=4QpIsa$^c$ $18_3$ ([מ]חטיאי), פֶּה *mouth* Ec $5_5$.

<OBJ> (1) person or thing caused to sin, אֶרֶץ *land* Dt $24_4$, עַם *people* 1 K $16_2$ 4Q522 $8.2_{10}$, Israel 1 K $14_{16}$ $15_{26.30.34}$ $16_{2.13.19.26}$ $21_{22}$ $22_{53}$ 2 K $3_3$ $10_{29.31}$ $13_{2.6.11}$ $14_{24}$ $15_{9.18.24.28}$ $17_{21}$ $23_{15}$ Si $47_{23}$ (ו[יח]טיא), Israelite(s) Ex $23_{33}$, Judah 2 K $21_{11.16}$ Jr $32_{35}$, Solomon Ne $13_{26}$, אָדָם *human being* Is $29_{21}$=4QpIsa$^c$ $18_3$ ([מ]חטיאי אדם), בָּשָׂר *flesh* Ec $5_5$.

(2) sin caused, חַטָּאת *sin* 1 K $14_{16}$ $15_{26.30.34}$ $16_{19}$ (if em. עָשָׂה לְהַחֲטִיא the sin *that he had committed, causing* Israel *to sin*, to הֶחֱטִיא that *he caused* Israel *to sin*) $16_{26}$ 2 K $3_3$ $10_{31}$ $13_{2.6.10}$ $14_{24}$ $15_{9.18.24.28}$ $21_{16}$, חֲטָאָה *sin* 2 K $17_{21}$, חֵטְא *sin* 2 K $10_{29}$.

<PREP> לְ *against*, + י׳ *Y.* Ex $23_{33}$, אֱלֹהִים *God* Ex $23_{33}$; בְּ of instrument, *by (means of)*, + גִּלּוּל *idol* 2 K $21_{11}$, דָּבָר *word* Is $29_{21}$=4QpIsa$^c$ $18_3$ ([מ]חטיאי ... בדבר).

**Htp.** 9 Impf. יִתְחַטָּא ,יִתְחַטְּאוּ ,תִּתְחַטְּאוּ (תִּתְחַטָּאוּ); + waw וַיִּתְחַטְּאוּ—**1. purify oneself, be purified (from sin),** <SUBJ> שַׂר *prince*, i.e. commander of army Nm $31_{20}$ (or em. תִּתְחַטְּאוּ *you shall purify yourselves* to תְּחַטְּאוּ *you shall purify*, i.e. pi.), לֵוִי *Levite* Nm $8_{21}$, אִישׁ *man* Nm $19_{20}$, פקד pass. ptc. *appointed one* Nm $31_{20}$ (or em.; see above), הרג ptc. *one who kills* Nm $31_{19}$, נגע ptc. *one who touches* corpse Nm $19_{12.12.13}$ $31_{19}$, דָּבָר *thing* Nm $31_{23}$.

<PREP> בְּ of time, *in, at, during*, + יוֹם *day* Nm $19_{12.12}$ $31_{19}$; of instrument, *by (means of), with*, + מַיִם *water* Nm

$19_{12}$ $31_{23}$.

**2. withdraw oneself,** <SUBJ> אֵל *god* Jb $41_{17}$ (unless em.; see Prep.), מִשְׁבָּר *wave* Jb $41_{17}$ (if em.; see Prep.). <PREP> מִן of cause, *on account of*, + שֶׁבֶר *breaking* Jb $41_{17}$ (unless em. מִשְּׁבָרִים to מִשְׁבְּרֵי יָם *waves of the sea*).*
→ חֵטְא *sin*, חַטָּא *sinful*, חֲטָאָה *sin*, חַטָּאָה *sin*, חַטָּאת *sin*.

**חַטָּא** 19.0.1 n.m. & adj. **sinner, sinful**—f.sg. חַטָּאָה; pl. חַטָּאִים; cstr. חַטָּאֵי; sf. חַטָּאֶיהָ—**1.** as noun, **sinner,** in ref. to **sinners** as class of individuals Gn $13_{13}$ Nm $17_3$ 1 S $15_{18}$ Is $1_{28}$ $13_9$ $33_{14}$ Am $9_{10}$ Ps $1_{1.5}$ $25_8$ $26_9$ $51_{15}$ $104_{35}$ Pr $1_{10}$ $13_{21}$ $23_{17}$; **2.** as adjective, **sinful,** Nm $32_{14}$ 1 K $1_{21}$ Am $9_8$.

**1.** <SUBJ> שׁוב *go back* Ps $51_{15}$, קום *arise* Ps $1_5$ (|| רָשָׁע *wicked one*), פתה pi. *persuade* Pr $1_{10}$, פחד *tremble* Is $33_{14}$, שׁבר ni. *be broken up* Is $1_{28}$ (if em.), pu. *be shattered* Is $1_{28}$ (if em.), תמם *be consumed* Ps $104_{35}$ (4QPs[d] 11QPs[a] חוטאים), מות *die* Am $9_{10}$.

<NOM CL> אַנְשֵׁי סְדֹם ... חַטָּאִים *the men of Sodom were ... sinners* Gn $13_{13}$. <OBJ> שׁוב hi. *bring back* 4Q393 $1_7$, רדף pi. *pursue* Pr $13_{21}$, ירה *throw down* Ps $25_8$, חרם hi. *devote to destruction* 1 S $15_{18}$, שׁבר pi. *shatter* Is $1_{28}$ (if em.), שׁמד hi. *exterminate* Is $13_9$.

<CSTR> חַטָּאֵי עַמִּי *sinners of my people* Am $9_{10}$; דֶּרֶךְ חַטָּאִים *way of sinners* Ps $1_1$ 4QMidrEschat[a] $3_{14}$ (דרך [חטאים]), שבילי חט[אים] *paths of sinners* 4QD[a] $2.2_3$, מַחְתּוֹת הַחַטָּאִים *censers of the sinners* Nm $17_3$, שֶׁבֶר ... חַטָּאִים *destruction of ... sinners* Is $1_{28}$ (or em. שׁבר ni. *be broken up*, or pu. *be shattered*, or pi. *shatter*), כֹּל חַטָּאֵי *all sinners of* Am $9_{10}$. <ADJ> אֵלֶּה *these* Nm $17_3$. <PREP> בְּ introducing object, + קנא pi. *be envious of* Pr $23_{17}$; עִם *with*, + אסף *gather*, i.e. remove, one's life Ps $26_9$. <SYN> רָשָׁע *wicked one*.

**2a.** as attributive adjective, **sinful,** + מַמְלָכָה *kingdom* Am $9_8$.

**2b.** as predicative adjective, **sinful,** <SUBJ> היה *be* 1 K $1_{21}$. <APP> אִישׁ *man* Nm $32_{14}$.*
→ חטא *sin*.

**חֵטְא** 33.5.8 n.m. **sin**—Si חט, Q חוט/חיט; cstr. חֵטְא; sf. חֶטְאוֹ, חֶטְאָהּ, חֶטְאָם; pl. חֲטָאִים; cstr. חֲטָאֵי; sf. חֲטָאַי (חֲטָאָי), Qr חֲטָאָיו, חֲטָאֵינוּ, חֲטָאֵיכֶם—**1. sin,** of sins against humans (Gn $41_9$ Ec $10_4$), sins against God (e.g. Is $31_7$ $38_{17}$ Ho $12_9$ Ps $51_{11}$ Lm $1_8$). **2. punishment for sin** (e.g. Lv $20_{20}$ $24_{15}$ Nm $9_{13}$ $18_{22}$ Is $53_{12}$ Ezk $23_{49}$). **3. guilt of sin** (e.g. Nm $27_3$ Dt $15_9$ $23_{22.23}$ $24_{15}$).

<SUBJ> היה *be* Dt $15_9$ $21_{22}$ $23_{22.23}$ $24_{15}$ Is $1_{18}$ 11QT $64_9$. <NOM CL> אֲשֶׁר־חֵטְא *which is a sin* Ho $12_9$ (or em. חָטָא *he has sinned*), אין לנערה חטא *the young woman does not have a sin* 11QT $66_6$, מי׳ ... חטא *sin is ... from Y.* Si $11_{15}$ (+ דֶּרֶךְ upright *path*), מקוה זדון חטא *sin is a reservoir of pride* Si $10_{13}$. <OBJ> שׁלח *send* 11QapPs[a] $2_8$, נשׂא *raise*, i.e. incur guilt Lv $19_{17}$=CD $9_8$ Lv $20_{20}$ $22_9$ $24_{15}$ Nm $9_{13}$ $18_{22.32}$ Ezk $23_{49}$, *bear* sin Is $53_{12}$ CD $15_4$ ([חטא]) Si $42_9$ 11QT $35_{15}$, שׁלך hi. *throw down* Is $38_{17}$, חטא *sin* Dt $19_{15}$ Lm $1_8$ (or em. חָטֹא inf. abs. *has greatly sinned*) 11QT $61_6$, נוח hi. *appease* Ec $10_4$, רפא pi. *heal* Ec $10_4$, זכר hi. *recount* Gn $41_9$, רבה hi. *multiply* Si $3_{11}$, שׁנה *repeat* Si $7_8$.

<CSTR> חֵטְא־רַבִּים *sin of many* Is $53_{12}$, חֲטָאֵי יָרָבְעָם *sins of Jeroboam* 2 K $10_{29}$, חֲטָאֵי גִּלּוּלֵיכֶן *sins of your idols* Ezk $23_{49}$, חֵטְא מָוֶת *sin of*, i.e. resulting in, *death* Dt $22_{26}$ 11QT $66_6$; כבד ... חטא *weighty of ... sin* 1QH $5_5$ ([חטא]), דבר חט *matter of sin* 11QT $57_{10}$, כָּל־חֵטְא *every sin* Dt $19_{15}$ 11QT $61_6$ (כול), כָּל־חֲטָאָי *all my sins* Is $38_{17}$. <ADJ> גָּדוֹל *great* Ec $10_4$.

<PREP> לְ *on account of*, + קום *arise*, i.e. prevail 11QT $61_6$; בְּ of accompaniment, *in, with*, + יחם pi. *conceive* Ps $51_7$ (|| עָוֹן *iniquity*); of cause, *be cause of* Dn $9_{16}$ (|| עָוֹן *iniquity*), + היה *be* 11QPs[a] $19_{10}$, מות *die* Nm $27_3$ 2 C $25_4$, ho. *be put to death* Dt $24_{16}$ 2 K $14_{6(Qr)}$; *on account of* Dt $19_{15}$; כְּ *as*, + עשׂה *deal with* Ps $103_{10}$ (|| עָוֹן *iniquity*); מִן of direction, *from*, + סתר hi. *hide* Ps $51_{11}$ 4Q393 $1_5$ ([חט]אינו); עַל *on account of*, + אנן htpol. *complain* Lm $3_{39(Qr)}$, כחשׁ pi. *feign submission* 4QapPs[b] $33_9$ (ח[טא]י).

<COLL> אֲשֶׁר עָשׂוּ לָכֶם יְדֵיכֶם חֵטְא *which your hands have made for you as a sin* Is $31_7$.

<SYN> עָוֹן *iniquity*.

Also perh. 4Q418 $101.2_2$ 4Q422 $2_8$ (חוט/חיט).*
→ חטא *sin*.

**[חִטָּא]** 0.0.3 pr.n.m. **Hitta**—Q חיטא—father of Eleazar, <CSTR> בן חיטא *son of Hitta* 5/6ḤevBA $44_2$, בר *son of* 5/6ḤevBA 45. <COLL> אלעזר חיטא *Eleazar (son of) Hitta* 5/6ḤevBA fr. 1.

**חֲטָאָה** 8 n.f. **sin—1.** of **sin** as an act (Gn 20$_{9}$ Ex 32$_{21.30.31}$ 2 K 17$_{21}$ Ps 32$_{1}$ 109$_{7}$). **2. sin offering** (Ps 40$_{7}$). <SUBJ> כסה pass. *be covered* Ps 32$_{1}$ (|| פֶּשַׁע *transgression*). <OBJ> בוא hi. *bring* Gn 20$_{9}$ Ex 32$_{21}$, חטא *sin* Ex 32$_{30.31}$, hi. *cause to sin* 2 K 17$_{21}$, שׁאל *ask* Ps 40$_{7}$ (mss חַטָּאת *sin*; || עוֹלָה *burnt offering*). <ADJ> גָּדוֹל *great* Gn 20$_{9}$ Ex 32$_{21.30.31}$ 2 K 17$_{21}$. <PREP> לְ *as*, + היה *be* Ps 109$_{7}$. <SYN> פֶּשַׁע *transgression*, עוֹלָה *burnt offering*.*

⇒ חטא *sin*.

**חַטָּאָה** 2.0.8 n.f. **sin,** Ex 34$_{7}$ Is 5$_{18}$, <SUBJ> היה *be* 11QT 53$_{12}$. <OBJ> נשׂא *raise*, i.e. forgive Ex 34$_{7}$ 1QH 17$_{12}$ (both || עָוֹן *iniquity*, פֶּשַׁע *transgression*), משׁך *drag* Is 5$_{18}$ (|| עָוֹן *iniquity*), עזב *forsake* 1QH 6$_{6}$. <CSTR> מבנה החטאה *the structure of sin* 1QH 1$_{22}$. <PREP> לְ of possession, *(belonging) to* 1QH 11$_{20}$; *as*, + היה *be* 11QT 53$_{12}$; בְּ *by (means of)*, + טמא pi. *defile* 11QT 51$_{15}$; עַל *on account of* 1QH fr. 4$_{14}$. <SYN> עָוֹן *iniquity*, פֶּשַׁע *transgression*.

Also 1QH 13$_{15}$ (ח[טא]ה).*

⇒ חטא *sin*.

**חֶטְאָה** 1 n.f. **sin,** of unintentional sinful act Nm 15$_{28}$, <PREP> בְּ of instrument, *by (means of)*, + שׁגג *commit error* Nm 15$_{28}$ (or em. חֶטְאָהּ *her sin*).*

⇒ חטא *sin*.

**חַטָּאת I** 291.5.52 n.f. **sin**—חַטָּאת (חַטָּת); cstr. חַטַּאת; sf. חַטָּאתִי, חַטָּאתְךָ, חַטָּאתוֹ (Q חטתו), חַטָּאתֵנוּ, חַטַּאתְכֶם, חַטָּאתָם (Q חטאתמה); pl. חֲטָאוֹת; cstr. חַטֹּאות (חַטֹּאת); sf. חַטֹּאותַי, חַטֹּאותֶיךָ (Q חטאותכה, חַטֹּאתֶיךָ, חַטֹּאתֶךָ), חַטֹּאתַיִךְ (חַטֹּאתֶיִךְ), חַטֹּאתָיו (חַטֹּאתָו), חַטֹּאטֶיהָ (Q חטותיהא), חַטֹּאוטֵינוּ (חַטֹּאתֵינוּ), חַטֹּאותֵיכֶם (חַטֹּאתֵיכֶם), חַטֹּאתֵיהֶם, חַטֹּאותָם (חַטֹּאתָם)—**1. sin,** of sins against humans (Gn 31$_{36}$ 50$_{17}$ Nm 5$_{6}$ 12$_{11}$ 1 S 20$_{1}$), sins against God (e.g. Lv 4$_{14.23.28}$ 1 S 2$_{17}$ Is 3$_{9}$ 30$_{1}$ Am 5$_{12}$). **2. sin offering** (e.g. Lv 7$_{37}$ 2 K 12$_{17}$ 2 C 29$_{21.23.24}$). **3. punishment for sin** (Zc 14$_{19}$). **4. guilt of sin** (Gn 18$_{20}$ Nm 16$_{26}$ 32$_{23}$ Jr 17$_{1}$ Ezk 3$_{20}$ 18$_{24}$). **5. purification from sin** (Nm 8$_{7}$ 19$_{9.17}$). **6.** appar. **sinner** (Pr 13$_{6}$).

<SUBJ> היה *be* Lv 14$_{22}$ 1 S 2$_{17}$ 14$_{38}$ Zc 14$_{19.19}$, כבד *be heavy* Gn 18$_{20}$, עצם *be numerous* Jr 30$_{14.15}$, pass. *be numerous* Am 5$_{12}$. ראה ni. *be seen* Ezk 21$_{29}$, ידע ni. *be known* Lv 4$_{14.23.28}$, זכר ni. *be remembered* Ezk 33$_{16}$, צפן pass. *be stored up* Ho 13$_{12}$, בקשׁ pu. *be sought* Jr 50$_{20}$ (|| עָוֹן *iniquity*), מצא ni. *be found* Jr 50$_{20}$ (|| עָוֹן), אכל ni. *be eaten* Lv 6$_{23}$.

מחה ni. *be wiped out* Ps 109$_{14}$ Ne 3$_{37}$, שׁחט ni. *be slaughtered* Lv 6$_{18}$ (|| עֹלָה *burnt offering*), שׁמד ni. *be destroyed* Ho 10$_{8}$, כפר pu. *be atoned for* Is 6$_{7}$ 1QS 3$_{8}$, כתב pass. *be written* 2 K 21$_{17}$ Jr 17$_{1}$, מצא *find* Nm 32$_{23}$, סתר hi. *hide* Is 59$_{2}$, רבץ *lie in wait* Gn 4$_{7}$, מנע *withhold* Jr 5$_{25}$, ענה *answer* Is 59$_{12}$.

<NOM CL> שְׂעִיר־עִזִּים אֶחָד חַטָּאת *one male goat is (the) sin offering* Nm 29$_{5.11.16.19}$, חֶסֶר לְאֻמִּים חַטָּאת *sin is a lack in peoples* Pr 14$_{34}$ (if em. חֶסֶד *loyalty* to חֶסֶר *lack*), נֵר רְשָׁעִים חַטָּאת *the light of the wicked is sin* Pr 21$_{4}$ (or em. מֵחַטָּאת *from sin*), זִמַּת אִוֶּלֶת חַטָּאת *(the) plan of foolishness is sin* Pr 24$_{9}$, חטאתי ... לסוד רמה *my sins ... belong to the assembly of maggots* 1QS 11$_{9}$, ... כול חטאתם בממשלתו *all their sins ... (are caused) by his dominion* 1QS 3$_{22}$, חַטֹּאתֵינוּ עָלֵינוּ *our sins are upon us* Ezk 33$_{10}$, חַטָּאתִי נֶגְדִּי תָמִיד *my sin is continually before me* Ps 51$_{5}$, מַה חַטָּאתִי *what is my sin?* Gn 31$_{36}$, חַטָּאת הוּא *it is a sin offering* Ex 29$_{14}$ Lv 4$_{24}$ 5$_{9}$, חטאת קהל הוא *it is a sin offering of the assembly* 11QT 16$_{18}$, חַטַּאת הַקָּהָל הוּא *it is the sin offering of the assembly* Lv 4$_{21}$ 11QT 26$_{9}$, חַטָּאת הִיא *it is a sin offering* Lv 5$_{11.12}$ Nm 19$_{9}$, [חטאת ורשע המה] *they are sin and wickedness* 4QJub$^{d}$ 21$_{21}$, מֶה־חַטָּאתִי *what is my sin?* 1 S 20$_{1}$, מֶה חַטָּאתֵנוּ *what is our sin?* Jr 16$_{10}$, כַּמָּה לִי עֲוֹנוֹת וְחַטָּאוֹת *how many are my iniquities and my sins* Jb 13$_{23}$.

<OBJ> אשׁם *be guilty (in respect of* or *so as to incur)* Nm 18$_{9(Sam)}$, בוא hi. *bring* Nm 15$_{25}$ (|| קָרְבָּן *offering*) 4QD$^{a}$ 18.5$_{3}$ 4QMMT B$_{32}$ ([חטאת]), שׁוב hi. *bring back* Nm 18$_{9}$ (|| אָשָׁם *guilt offering*, מִנְחָה *grain offering*, קָרְבָּן), קרב hi. *bring near* Lv 10$_{19}$ (|| עֹלָה) Ezk 44$_{27}$.

ראה *see* Ezk 18$_{14}$, כסה pi. *cover* Ps 85$_{3}$, נשׂא *raise*, i.e. forgive Gn 50$_{17}$ Ex 10$_{17}$ 32$_{32}$ 1 S 15$_{25}$, סלח *forgive* Gnz Ps 1$_{13}$, נוח hi. *place* Ezk 42$_{13}$ (|| אָשָׁם, מִנְחָה), לקח *take (away)* Dt 9$_{21}$.

סור hi. *remove* Is 27$_{9}$, עבר hi. *remove* 2 S 12$_{13}$, רחק hi. *remove far away* 11QPs$^{a}$ 24$_{11}$, מחה *wipe out* Is 44$_{22}$ Jr 18$_{23}$, ספה *sweep away* Is 30$_{1}$=4QpIsa$^{c}$ 21$_{10}$ ([חטאת]), שׁלך hi. *throw down* Mc 7$_{19}$, סלף *overturn* (unless

חַטָּאת III *step*, or em. חַטָּא *sinner*) Pr 13₆, שׂרף *burn* 4Q MMT B32 ([חטאת]), בשׁל pi. *boil* 11QT 37₁₄, שׁחט *slaughter* Lv 4₂₉ 14₁₃ (|| עֹלָה *burnt offering*) Ezk 40₃₉ (|| עֹלָה, אָשָׁם *guilt offering*), פקד *visit*, i.e. punish Ex 32₃₄ Jr 14₁₀ Ho 8₁₃ 9₉, שׂית *place*, i.e. punish Nm 12₁₁.

יאל *resolve to* Nm 12₁₁, עשׂה *do*, i.e. commit Nm 5₇ Dt 9₂₁ 1 K 15₃ 16₁₉ 2 K 17₂₂, *offer* Ex 29₃₆ Lv 9₇ (|| עֹלָה *burnt offering*) 9₂₂ (|| עֹלָה, שֶׁלֶם *peace offering*) 14₁₉ 15₁₅.₃₀ Nm 6₁₆ 8₁₂ Ezk 45₁₇ (|| מִנְחָה *grain offering*, עֹלָה, שֶׁלֶם) 45₂₃ (|| עֹלָה), חטא *sin* Lv 4₃.₁₄.₂₈.₂₈.₃₅ 5₆.₁₀.₁₃ 19₂₂.₂₂ Dt 9₁₈ 1 K 14₂₂ 16₁₉ 2 K 21₁₇ Jr 16₁₀ Ezk 16₅₁ 18₂₄ 33₁₆ Ne 1₆, תעב hi. *act abominably* Ezk 16₅₂.

ידה htp. *confess* Nm 5₇ Dn 9₂₀.₂₀, בשׁל pi. *boil* Ezk 46₂₀ (|| אָשָׁם), אכל *eat* Lv 10₁₇.₁₉ Ezk 44₂₉ (|| מִנְחָה, אָשָׁם) Ho 4₈, ידע *acknowledge* Nm 32₂₃, hi. *make known* Ps 32₅ Jb 13₂₃, זכר *remember* Is 43₂₅ Ps 25₇, אמר *say*, i.e. give command concerning 2 C 29₂₄, ספר pi. *relate* 1QH 1₂₅ 1QS 1₂₃ (|| עָוֺן *iniquity*, פֶּשַׁע *transgression*), נגד hi. *declare* Is 3₉ 58₁ Mc 3₈.

**<CSTR>** חַטַּאת מִצְרָיִם *sin of Egypt* Zc 14₁₉, יִשְׂרָאֵל *of Israel* Ho 10₈, יְהוּדָה *of Judah* Jr 17₁, חטאת העם *sin offering of the people* 11QT 35₁₂, חטאות העם *sin offerings of the people* 11QT 35₁₂, חַטַּאת עַמִּי *sin of my people* Ho 4₈ Dn 9₂₀, עַמְּךָ *of your people* 1 K 8₃₄, sim. 1 K 8₃₆, חַטַּאת הַקָּהָל *sin offering of the assembly* Lv 4₂₁ 11QT 16₁₈ (קהל) 26₉, חַטַּאת בֵּית *sin of the house of* 1 K 13₃₄, חַטֹּאות בֵּית *sins of the house of* 2 K 13₆ Mc 1₅=1QpMic 1₅ ([חט]אות) =8₂ ([חטאות]), חטאת בני *sin of the sons of* 4Q181 1₁, חַטֹּאות בְּנֵי *sins of the sons of* Ne 1₆.

חַטַּאת סְדֹם *sin of Sodom* Lm 4₆, חַטֹּאות בַּעְשָׁא *sins of Baasha* 1 K 16₁₃, אֵלָה *of Elah* 1 K 16₁₃, יָרָבְעָם *of Jeroboam* 1 K 14₁₆ 15₃₀ 16₃₁ 2 K 3₃ 10₃₁ 13₂ (חַטַּאת) 13₁₁ 14₂₄ 15₉.₁₈.₂₄.₂₈ 17₂₂, חַטֹּאת מְנַשֶּׁה *sins of Manasseh* 2 K 24₃, הכוהנים sin offering *of the priests* 11QT 35₁₁, עַבְדְּךָ sins *of your servant* 1 K 8₃₆(mss), עֲבָדֶיךָ *of your servants* 1 K 8₃₆.

חַטֹּאת אָבִיו *sins of his father* 1 K 15₃ Ezk 18₁₄, חַטַּאת אִמּוֹ *sin of my mother* Ps 109₁₄, בני *of the sons of* 1QS 11₁₅, הַנְּעָרִים *of the lads* 1 S 2₁₇, חטאת נעורי *sin of my youth* 11QPsª 24₁₁, חַטֹּאות נְעוּרַי *sins of my youth* Ps 25₇, חַטַּאת הַכִּפֻּרִים *sin offering of the atonement* Nm 29₁₁ 11QT 25₁₄.₁₅ (both חטאת הכפורים), חַטַּאת פִּימוֹ *sin of their mouths* Ps 59₁₃, נַפְשִׁי *of my soul* Mc 6₇, קֶסֶם *of divination* 1 S 15₂₃, כָּל־ *of all* Zc 14₁₉.

עֲוֺן חַטָּאתִי *guilt of my sin* Ps 32₅, משפט [החטאת] *judgment of the sin* 4QTohBᵇ 1₃, מעל חטאת *unfaithfulness of sin* 1QS 9₄, שבילי חטאת *paths of sin* 4Q181 1₁, חַבְלֵי חַטָּאתוֹ *snares of his sin* Pr 5₂₂.

פרת החטאת *cow of the sin offering* 4QMMT B13, פַּר הַחַטָּאת *bull of the sin offering* Lv 4₉.₂₀ 8₂.₁₄.₁₄ 16₆.₁₁.₁₁.₂₇ Ezk 43₂₁(mss) 45₂₂ (חַטָּאת), עֵגֶל *calf of* Lv 9₈, שְׂעִיר *goat of* Lv 9₁₅ 10₁₆ 16₁₅.₂₇ Nm 28₂₂ 29₂₂.₂₈.₃₁.₃₄.₃₈ Ezk 43₂₅ 11QT 20₀₁₂ ([חטאת]; all eight חַטָּאת), שְׂעִירֵי *goats of* 2 C 29₂₃, צְפִירֵי חַטָּאת *goats of sin offering* Ezr 8₃₅, חֵלֶב הַחַטָּאת *fat of the sin offering* Lv 16₂₅, דַּם הַחַטָּאת *blood of the sin offering* Lv 4₂₅.₃₄ 5₉ Ezk 45₁₉ 11QT 26₁₀, דַּם חַטַּאת *blood of the sin offering of* Ex 30₁₀, רֹאשׁ הַחַטָּאת *head of the sin offering* Lv 4₂₉.₃₃, [זבח החטאת] *sacrifice of the sin offering* 4QMMT B5, שְׂרֵפַת *burning of* Nm 19₁₇, כֶּסֶף חַטָּאוֹת *silver of sin offerings* 2 K 12₁₇, תּוֹרַת הַחַטָּאת *law of the sin offering* Lv 6₁₈, מֵי חַטָּאת *water of punishment (for sin)* Nm 8₇, [מי] החטאת *water of the punishment (for sin)* 4QMMT B15, מִשְׁנֵה ... חַטָּאתָם *double of ... their sin* Jr 16₁₈, רֵאשִׁית חַטָּאת *beginning of sin* Mc 1₁₃, חֲצִי חַטֹּאתַיִךְ *half of your sins* Ezk 16₅₁.

כָּל־חַטֹּאת *every sin* Lv 6₂₃ Dt 19₁₅, כָּל־חַטֹּאת *all sins* Nm 5₆ Ezk 18₁₄, כול חטאת *every sin offering of* 11QT 35₁₂, כָּל־חַטֹּאות *all the sins of* 1 K 15₃ 16₁₃ 2 K 10₃₁(mss) 13₁₁ 14₂₄ 15₁₈(mss) 17₂₂, כָּל־חַטֹּאותַי *all of my sins* Ps 25₁₈, כָּל־חַטֹּאותֶיךָ *all your sins* Jr 15₁₃, כָּל־חַטֹּאתְכֶם *all your sin* Dt 9₁₈, כֹּל חַטֹּאתֵיכֶם *all your sins* Lv 16₃₀ Dt 9₁₈(mss), כָּל־חַטָּאתוֹ *all his sin* 2 C 33₁₉, כָּל־חַטֹּאתָיו *all his sins* Ezk 18₂₁(Qr), כָּל־חַטֹּאתֶיהָ *all her sins* Is 40₂=4QTanḥ 1.1₆ (כול חטותיהא), כול חטאתנו *all our sin* 4QPrFêtesᵇ 41₁, כָּל־חַטֹּאתֵינוּ *all our sins* 1 S 12₁₉ GnzPs 1₁₃, כָּל־חַטֹּאתָם *all their sin* Lv 16₁₆.₂₁.₃₄ Nm 16₂₆ 4QDibHamª 1.2₁₁ ([כול חט]אתם), כָּל־חַטָּאתָם *all their sin* Nm 18₉ Ps 85₃ 11QT 26₁₂ (כול חטאתמה), כָּל־חַטֹּאותָם *all their sins* Mc 7₁₉.

**<APP>** פַּר *bull* Ex 29₃₆ Ezk 43₂₁, נִדָּה *pollution* 4QToh Bª 1₉ ([חטאת]), אֶחָד *one* Lv 14₃₁ 15₁₅.₃₀ Nm 8₁₂.

**<PREP>** לְ of direction, *to* Pr 10₁₆ (:: חַיִּים *life*; unless חַטָּאת II *penury*); of benefit, *to, for* Lv 7₃₇, + פתח ni. *be opened* Zc 13₁, בדל ho. *be separated* 11QT 16₁₂, קרב hi.

*bring near*, i.e. offer 11QT 25$_{15}$, עשׂה *make* 11QT 35$_{11.11.12}$, נתן *give* Ne 10$_{34}$, כפר pi. *make atonement* Lv 16$_{16}$.

לְ *as* Nm 7$_{16+12t}$ 28$_{15}$ 29$_{5(mss)}$ 11QT 15$_{2}$ ([חטאת]) 17$_{14}$ 18$_{4}$ 25$_{6}$ ([חטאת]) 25$_{14}$ 28$_{05}$ ([חטאת]) 28$_{4}$ (חטא[ת]) 28$_{8.11}$ 29$_{03}$ ([חטאת]) 29$_{05}$ ([חטאת]) 29$_{08}$ ([חטאת]), + היה *be* 1 K 12$_{30}$ 13$_{34}$, בוא *come* Lv 16$_{3}$, hi. *bring* Lv 4$_{32}$ 5$_{6.7.11}$ 12$_{6}$ 2 C 29$_{21}$, קרב hi. *bring near* Lv 4$_{14}$ 5$_{8}$ Nm 6$_{14}$ 15$_{27}$ Ezk 43$_{22}$, נתן *give* Ezk 43$_{19}$, לקח *take* Lv 9$_{2.3}$ 12$_{8}$ 16$_{5}$ Nm 8$_{8}$ 4QApocMosB 1.2$_{6}$, שׁחט *slaughter* Lv 4$_{33}$, עשׂה *do*, i.e. offer sacrifice Lv 23$_{19}$ Nm 6$_{11}$ 15$_{24}$ 11QT 14$_{10}$ ([חטאת]).

לְ introducing object, + סלח *forgive* Ex 34$_{9}$ (‖ עָוֹן) 1 K 8$_{34.36}$‖2 C 6$_{25.27}$ Jr 36$_{3}$ (‖ עָוֹן) 2 C 7$_{14}$ 4QDibHam[a] 4$_{7}$ (חו[טתנו]) 11QPs[a] 19$_{13}$, נשׂא *raise*, i.e. forgive Jos 24$_{19}$ (‖ פֶּשַׁע) Ps 25$_{18}$, זכר *remember* Jr 31$_{34}$, דרשׁ *seek* Jb 10$_{6}$, נתן *give*, i.e. place 11QT 26$_{12}$.

לְ *namely* Nm 18$_{9}$, + ידה htp. *confess* Lv 16$_{21}$; *concerning*, + קום *arise* Dt 19$_{15}$.

בְּ of instrument, *by (means of)*, + צדק *be righteous* Ezk 16$_{52}$, קנא pi. *make jealous* 1 K 14$_{22}$, עבד hi. *cause to serve* Is 43$_{24}$ 4QDibHam[a] 1.5$_{19}$ (חט[תנו]), כעס hi. *provoke to anger* 1 K 16$_{2}$, ספה ni. *be swept away* Nm 16$_{26}$, מקק ni. *waste away* Ezk 33$_{10}$, שׁגג *commit error* 11QT 35$_{14}$.

בְּ of accompaniment, *in, with* 4Q181 1$_{1}$, + הלך *go* 1 K 15$_{3.26.34}$ 16$_{19.26(Qr).31}$ 2 K 13$_{6.11}$ 17$_{22}$.

בְּ *because of* Mc 1$_{5}$=1QpMic 1$_{5}$ 8$_{2}$, + לקח *take* Is 40$_{2}$= 4QTanḥ 1.1$_{6}$, נתן *give* Ne 9$_{37}$, סור hi. *remove* 2 K 24$_{3}$, שׁמם hi. *make desolate* 4QMidrEschat[a] 3$_{6}$, מות *die* Ezk 3$_{20}$ 18$_{24(Qr)}$; *for, instead of*, + נתן *give* Jr 15$_{13}$ 17$_{3}$; introducing object, + דבק *cling to* 2 K 3$_{3}$.

כְּ *as* Lv 6$_{10}$ 7$_{7}$ 14$_{13}$, + עשׂה *make*, i.e. provide Ezk 45$_{25}$, שׁפט *judge* 11QPs[a] 24$_{7}$, נכה hi. *strike* Lv 26$_{21}$.

מִן of direction, *from* Lv 9$_{10}$ Pr 21$_{4}$ (if em.), + טהר *be clean* Lv 16$_{30}$ Ps 51$_{4}$ Pr 20$_{9}$, pi. *cleanse* 1QS 11$_{15}$ 4QDibHam[a] 1.6$_{3}$, נזר *abstain* CD 19$_{21}$, סור *depart* 2 K 3$_{3}$ 10$_{31(mss)}$ 13$_{6.11}$ 14$_{24}$ 15$_{9.18(mss).24.28}$ 17$_{22}$, שׁוב *go back* 1 K 8$_{35}$‖2 C 6$_{26}$ Ezk 18$_{21}$ 33$_{14}$, כפר pi. *make atonement* Lv 16$_{34}$, יעל hi. *profit* Jb 35$_{3}$.

מִן of cause, *because of* Lv 19$_{22}$ Lm 4$_{13}$ (‖ עָוֹן), + דאג *be anxious* Ps 38$_{19}$ (‖ עָוֹן), כפר pi. *make atonement* Lv 4$_{26}$ 5$_{6.10}$.

מִן partitive, *some of, anyone of*, + עשׂה *commit* Nm 5$_{6}$; of comparison, *(more) than*, + גדל *be great* Lm 4$_{6}$.

מִן privative, *without* 11QT 25$_{14}$.

אֶל *to*, + פנה *turn*, i.e. pay attention Dt 9$_{27}$ (‖ רֶשַׁע *wickedness* Dt 9$_{27}$; *on account of, because of* 1 K 16$_{13}$.

עַל *upon*, + יסף *add* 1 S 12$_{19}$, hi. *add* Jb 34$_{37}$ 2 C 28$_{13}$, שׁמר *keep* Jb 14$_{16}$ (unless חַטָּאת III *step*), עבר *pass by* 4Q417 1.1$_{15}$, ספה *sweep away* Is 30$_{1}$=4QpIsa[c] 21$_{10}$ ([חטאת]).

עַל *on account of, because of* 1 K 15$_{30}$ 16$_{19(Qr)}$ 4QPsJos[a] 6.1$_{4}$, + בוא hi. *bring* Lv 4$_{28}$ 5$_{6}$, קרב hi. *bring near* Lv 4$_{3}$, שׁוב *go back* 4QDibHam[a] 1.2$_{11}$, כפר pi. *make atonement* Lv 4$_{35}$ 5$_{13}$ 19$_{22}$ Ps 79$_{9}$, יסר pi. *chastise* Lv 26$_{18.28}$, נכה hi. *strike* Lv 26$_{24}$, שׁמם hi. *make desolate* Mc 6$_{13}$, אכל *eat* Dt 9$_{18}$, שׁתה *drink* Dt 9$_{18}$, גלה pi. *expose* Lm 4$_{22}$, ידה htp. *confess* Ne 1$_{6}$ 9$_{2}$, חנן htp. *make supplication* 1QH 1$_{25}$ ([חטאותי]).

אַחַר *after*, + הלך *go* 2 K 13$_{2}$; בִּגְלַל *on account of*, + נתן *give* 1 K 14$_{16}$; בְּעַד *on behalf of, for*, + כפר pi. *make atonement* Ex 32$_{30}$ 4QDibHam[a] 1.2$_{10}$; לְבַד מִן *besides, without regard to* 2 K 21$_{16}$; מֵעַל *from (upon)*, + סור *depart* 2 K 10$_{31}$ 15$_{18}$; נֶגֶד *before, opposite* 4QPrFêtes[b] 41$_{1}$; מִפְּנֵי *because of* Ps 38$_{4}$.

<COLL> וְעָשָׂהוּ חַטָּאת *and he shall offer it as a sin offering* Lv 16$_{9}$, וְלֹא־חַטָּאתִי י׳ *not (because of) my sin O Y.* Ps 59$_{4}$ (mss אֱלֹהָי *my God*).

<SYN> עָוֹן *iniquity*, רֶשַׁע *wickedness*, פֶּשַׁע *transgression*, עֹלָה *burnt offering*, אָשָׁם *guilt offering*, שֶׁלֶם *peace offering*, מִנְחָה *grain offering*, קָרְבָּן *offering*.

<ANT> חַיִּים *life*.

Also 1QDM 12$_{5}$ (חט[אותיך]) 4QapLam[a] 1.1$_{15}$ 4QAges 2.2$_{5}$ 4QD[a] 18.3$_{13}$ 4QSap[b] 4$_{2}$ perh. 4QPrFêtes[b] 5$_{2}$ (חטתנ[ו]) 4QShir[b] 181$_{2}$ ([ח]טאות) perh. 4QRitPur 29. 7$_{18}$ 28.8$_{4}$ 99$_{2}$ ([ חטת]) 4QMMT B$_{31}$ ([חטאת]) 4QOrd[b] 22$_{2}$ 11QT 16$_{13}$ (חט[את]).*

→ חטא *sin*.

***חַטָּאת II** 1 n.f. **penury** (unless חַטָּאת I *sin*), <PREP> לְ of direction, *to* Pr 10$_{16}$ (:: חַיִּים *life*, i.e. maintenance). <ANT> חַיִּים *life*, i.e. maintenance.

***חַטָּאת III** 2 n.f. **step**—sf. חַטָּאתִי—(perh. חַטָּאת I *sin*), <OBJ> סלף pi. *pervert* Pr 13$_{6}$. <PREP> עַל *over*, + שׁמר *keep (watch)* Jb 14$_{16}$ (‖ צַעַד *step*). <SYN> צַעַד *step*.

**חטב** 9 vb. **cut**—**Qal** 8 Impf. יַחְטְבוּ; ptc. חֹטֵב, חֹטְבִים, חֹטְבֵי; inf. לַחְטֹב—**1. cut, hew (wood),** <SUBJ> יֹשֵׁב *inhabitant* Ezk 39$_{10}$ (+ נשׂא *take* wood); subj. not specified, Dt 19$_5$. <OBJ> עֵץ *wood* Dt 19$_5$. <PREP> מִן of place, *out of,* + יַעַר *forest* Ezk 39$_{10}$.

**2.** ptc. as noun, **hewer (of wood),** <SUBJ> היה *be* Jos 9$_{21}$ (|| שֹׁאֵב *drawer* of water), כרת ni. *be cut off* Jos 9$_{23}$ (|| שֹׁאֵב; + עֶבֶד *servant*). <OBJ> נתן *give,* i.e. make into Jos 9$_{27}$ (|| שֹׁאֵב *drawer* of water). <CSTR> חֹטֵב עֵצֶיךָ *the hewer of your wood* Dt 29$_{10}$ (|| שֹׁאֵב *drawer* of water), חֹטְבֵי עֵצִים *hewers of wood* Jos 9$_{21.23.27}$ Jr 46$_{22}$. <APP> כֹּרְתֵ *cutter* of wood 2 C 2$_9$. <PREP> לְ of direction, *to,* + נתן *give* 2 C 2$_9$; כְּ *as,* + בוא *come* Jr 46$_{22}$; מִן *from,* מֵחֹטֵב עֵצֶיךָ עַד שֹׁאֵב מֵימֶיךָ *from the hewer of your wood to the drawer of your water,* i.e. both of them Dt 29$_{10}$.

<SYN> שֹׁאֵב *drawer (of water).*

**Pu.** 1 Ptc. מְחֻטָּבוֹת—**be cut, be carved,** <SUBJ> זָוִית *corner pillar* Ps 144$_{12}$. <COLL> זָוִיּת מְחֻטָּבוֹת תַּבְנִית הֵיכָל *corner pillars carved (according to) the construction of a palace* Ps 144$_{12}$.

**[חֲטֻבוֹת]** 1 n.f.pl. **multicoloured cloth**—cstr. חֲטֻבוֹת—<OBJ> רבד *spread with* Pr 7$_{16}$ (or em. חֲטֻבוֹת to הִטֵּיתִי *I have stretched out* linen, i.e. נטה hi.). <CSTR> חֲטֻבוֹת אֵטוּן *multicoloured cloth (consisting) of linen of,* i.e. from, Egypt Pr 7$_{16}$ (or em.; see Obj.). <APP> מַרְבַד *spread* Pr 7$_{16}$ (or em.; see Obj.).

**חִטָּה** 30.0.13.5 n.f. **wheat**—pl. חִטִּים (חִטִּין, Q חנטין); cstr. חִטֵּי—pl. as collective; sometimes **ears of wheat** (e.g. Jg 6$_{11}$), **wheat grain** (e.g. 1 K 5$_{25}$); **wheat crop** (e.g. Gn 30$_{14}$).

<SUBJ> נכה pu. *be destroyed* Ex 9$_{32}$ (+ כֻּסֶּמֶת *emmer-wheat*).

<NOM CL> יֶשׁ־לָנוּ ... חִטִּים *we have ... wheat* Jr 41$_8$.

<OBJ> שׂים *place* Is 28$_{25}$, נגשׁ hi. *bring near* 2 S 17$_{28}$, לקח *take* 2 S 4$_6$ Ezk 4$_9$, נתן *give* 1 K 5$_{25}$ 1 C 21$_{23}$ 2 C 2$_9$ 27$_5$ MurEpBarCb$_9$, מדד *measure out* Mur 24 5$_{11}$, שׁקל *weigh out* Mur 24 2$_{16}$ 3$_{15}$ 4$_{15}$, זרע *sow* Jr 12$_{13}$, חבט *beat* Jg 6$_{11}$, דושׁ *thresh* 1 C 21$_{20}$, אכל *eat* 4Q251 2$_5$, שׁלח *send* 2 C 2$_{14}$ MurEpBarCb$_3$ (חנטין), ספר *count* Arad ost. 1$_7$, אמר *speak of* 2 C 2$_{14}$.

<CSTR> חִטֵּי מִנִּית *wheat of (?) rice,* i.e. rice Ezk 27$_{17}$; אֶרֶץ חִטָּה *land of wheat* Dt 8$_8$ 4QPsJosa 11$_5$, עֲרֵמַת חִטִּים *heap of wheat* Ca 7$_3$, זרע חטים *seed of wheat* Mur 30 1$_2$ 2$_{14}$, דגן החטים *grain of the wheat* 11QT 43$_6$, סֹלֶת חִטִּים *flour of wheat* Ex 29$_2$, לחם חטים *bread of wheat* 11QT 18$_{14}$, קְצִיר־חִטִּים *harvest of wheat* Gn 30$_{14}$ Ex 34$_{22}$ Jg 15$_1$ 1 S 6$_{13}$ 12$_{17}$ Ru 2$_{23}$ (הַחִטִּים) 4QPsJosb 12$_7$, מנחת החטים *the offering of wheat* 11QT 11$_{11}$, כִּלְיוֹת חִטָּה *kidneys of wheat,* i.e. choicest wheat Dt 32$_{14}$, חֵלֶב חִטָּה *fat of wheat,* i.e. finest wheat Ps 81$_{17}$ 147$_{17}$ (חִטִּים), כֹּר חִטִּים *cor of wheat* 1 K 5$_{25}$, חֹמֶר חִטִּים *homer of wheat* Ezk 45$_{13}$.

<APP> מַכָּה *crushed* 2 C 2$_9$, כֹּר *cor* 2 C 27$_5$ Mur 24 4$_{15}$ MurEpBarCb$_3$.

<ADJ> חָדָשׁ *new* 4Q251 2$_5$, יָפֶה *appropriate* Mur 24 2$_{16}$ 3$_{15}$ 4$_{15}$ 5$_{11}$, נָקִי *pure* Mur 24 2$_{16}$ 3$_{15}$ 4$_{15}$ 5$_{11}$.

<PREP> בְּ of exchange, *for,* + נתן *give* Ezk 27$_{17}$; עַל *on account of,* + יבשׁ hi. *dry up* Jl 1$_{11}$, ילל hi. *wail* Jl 1$_{11}$; תַּחַת *underneath,* i.e. instead of, + יצא *go out* Jb 31$_{40}$.

<COLL> חמש חטים *five (measures of) wheat* Mur 30 1$_2$ 2$_{14}$, חטם סאה *seah of wheat* Arad ost. 33$_{1.6}$ (ח[ט]ם סאה), חטם לתך *lethech of wheat* Arad ost. 33$_3$.

Also Mur 24 1$_{11}$ (ח[נ]טין) Arad ost. 31$_1$ 33$_{2.4.7}$ (ח[ט]ם) 33$_7$ (ח[ט]ם]) 76$_1$ (ח[ט]ם]) Beersheba ost. 3$_1$ (ח[ט]ם]).

**חַטּוּשׁ** 5.0.0.1 pr.n.m. **Hattush**—I חטשׁ—**1.** Davidide family head, son of Shemaiah or Shecaniah, contemporary with Ezra, <NOM CL> מִבְּנֵי דָוִיד חַטּוּשׁ *of the sons of David was Hattush* Ezr 8$_2$, בְּנֵי שְׁמַעְיָה חַטּוּשׁ *the sons of Shemaiah were Hattush* 1 C 3$_{22}$ (or em. בְּנֵי שְׁכַנְיָה שְׁמַעְיָה וְחַטּוּשׁ *the sons of Shecaniah were Shemaiah and Hattush*).

**2.** name of priestly family or course, its head being attested in the time of Zerubbabel and of Nehemiah, <SUBJ> עלה *go up* Ne 12$_2$, חתם *affix seal* Ne 10$_5$. <NOM CL> עַל הַחֲתוּמִים ... חַטּוּשׁ *upon the sealed (documents) were ... Hattush* Ne 10$_5$ (or em. עַל הַחֲתוּמִים to הַחוֹתְמִים *those who sealed were,* or אֵלֶּה הַחוֹתְמִים *these are those who sealed*).

**3.** son of Hashabneiah and one who helped repair walls of Jerusalem, <SUBJ> חזק hi. *make strong* walls Ne 3$_{10}$. <APP> בֵּן *son* Ne 3$_{10}$.

**4.** perh. son of Shephatiah, <PREP> לְ of possession, *(belonging) to* Seal 576 (c. 700).

**חֲטִיטָא** 2 pr.n.m. **Hatita,** ancestor of temple gatekeepers, <CSTR> בְּנֵי חֲטִיטָא *sons of Hatita* Ezr 2$_{42}$||Ne 7$_{45}$.

**חֲטִיל** 2 pr.n.m. **Hattil,** postexilic temple servant, of the class of 'Solomon's servants', <CSTR> בְּנֵי־חַטִּיל *sons of Hattil* Ezr 2$_{57}$||Ne 7$_{59}$.

**חֲטִיפָא** 2 pr.n.m. **Hatipha,** postexilic temple servant, of the class of Nethinim, <CSTR> בְּנֵי חֲטִיפָא *sons of Hatipha* Ezr 2$_{54}$||Ne 7$_{56}$.

**חטם** 1 vb. **restrain—Qal** 1 Impf. אֶחֱטָם־—**restrain (anger),** with ellipsis of obj., <SUBJ> Y. Is 48$_9$ (or em. אֶחֱטָם־לָךְ *I will restrain [my anger] for you* to אֶחְמֹל עָלַיִךְ *I will spare you*, or em. אֶחֱטָם־ to אֶחָטֵם־ *I will restrain myself*, i.e. ni.; + ארך hi. *hold back* anger). <PREP> לְ of benefit, *for*, + Israel Is 48$_9$; לְמַעַן *for the sake of*, + תְּהִלָּה *praise* appar. Is 48$_9$ (unless transfer תְּהִלָּה to 48$_{11}$).

**Ni. restrain oneself,** see Qal.

**חטף** 4 vb. **seize—Qal** 4 Impf. יַחְטֹף (יַחְטֹף); + waw וַחֲטַפְתֶּם; inf. חֲטוֹף—**seize, snatch (away),** <SUBJ> Y. Jb 9$_{12(mss)}$ (L חתף *snatch away*), בֵּן *son* of Benjamin Jg 21$_{21}$, אִישׁ *man* Jg 21$_{21}$, רָשָׁע *wicked one* Ps 10$_{9.9}$. <OBJ> אִשָּׁה *wife* Jg 21$_{21}$, עָנִי *poor one* Ps 10$_{9.9}$. <PREP> לְ *for* Jg 21$_{21}$; מִן of direction, *from*, + בַּת *daughter* of Shilo Jg 21$_{21}$.

→ חֲטִיפָה *Hatipha.*

**חטר** 1 vb. **cut** 0.1—**Qal** 0.1 Ptc. Si חוטר—**cut,** <OBJ> תמך ptc. *that which supports*, i.e. neck Si 30$_{35}$ (unless חֹטֶר *shoot*).*

**חֹטֶר** 2.1.1 n.m. **shoot**—Si, Q חוטר; cstr. חֹטֶר—**shoot, rod,** <SUBJ> יצא *go out* Is 11$_1$=4QpIsa$^a$ 8$_{11}$ ([ויצא חטר]=4Q285 5$_2$; || נֵצֶר *branch*), תמך *support* Si 30$_{35}$. <CSTR> חֹטֶר גַּאֲוָה *rod of pride* Pr 14$_3$ (or em. גַּאֲוָה to גֵּוֹה rod of, i.e. for, *his back*).

**חַטָּת**, see חַטָּאת *sin*.

**חַי** I 249.16.52.2 adj. **living**—חַי (Am 8$_{14}$ +), חָי; cstr. חֵי (Dn 12$_7$); f. חַיָּה; sf. חַיֶּךָ; pl. חַיִּים; f. חַיּוֹת (rarely, distinction of certain forms from forms of חיה *be* and חַיִּים *life* unclear)—**1. living,** also specif. **fresh** (waters), **raw** (flesh); of persons, sometimes perh. **thriving** (e.g. Gn 43$_{7.27}$), **healthy** (Si 30$_{14}$); used attributively of אֱלֹהִים *God* Dt 5$_{26}$ 1 S 17$_{26.36}$ 2 K 19$_{4.16}$||Is 37$_{4.17}$ (all four אֱלֹהִים חַי, not אֱלֹהִים חַיִּים) Jr 10$_{10}$ 23$_{36}$ Ps 42$_{3(ms)}$ (אֱלֹהִים חַי), *gods* 4QShirShabb$^f$ 6$_5$ 14$_{5.6}$ 19$_{4.6}$ 20.2$_{11}$ ([א]לוהים), אֵל *God* Jos 3$_{10}$ Ho 2$_1$ Ps 42$_3$ 84$_3$ Si 35$_{14(Bmg)}$ 4QDibHam$^a$ 1.5$_9$ 8$_{12}$ 5QapMal 1$_4$, נֶפֶשׁ *soul*, i.e. creature Gn 1$_{20.21.24.30}$ 2$_{7.19}$ (or del.) 9$_{10.12.15.16}$ Lv 11$_{10.46}$ Ezk 47$_9$ CD 12$_{13}$, אָדָם *human being* Lm 3$_{39}$ (or em. יְהִי *may it be*), אִישׁ *man* 2 S 23$_{20(Kt)}$ (Qr חַיִל man of *valour*), יֶלֶד *child* 1 K 3$_{25.26(mss).27(mss)}$ (L יָלוּד [i.e. ילד pass. ptc.] *child*), מִסְכֵּן *pauper* Si 30$_{14}$ (see Coll.), שׁוֹר *ox* Ex 21$_{35}$, שָׂעִיר *goat* Lv 16$_{20.21}$ 11QT 26$_{11}$, צִפּוֹר *bird* Lv 14$_4$ (or del. חַי) 14$_{6.6.7.51.52.53}$, מַיִם *water(s)* Gn 26$_{19}$ Lv 14$_{5.6.50.51.52}$ 15$_{13}$ (or del. חַי) Nm 19$_{17}$ Jr 2$_{13}$ 17$_{13}$ Zc 14$_8$ Ca 4$_{15}$ 1QH 8$_{7.16}$ 4Q418 103.2$_6$ 4QDibHam$^a$ 1.5$_2$ 11QT 45$_{16}$, בָּשָׂר *flesh* Lv 13$_{10.14.15.16}$ 1 S 2$_{15}$ (with ellipsis of noun) 4QD$^a$ 9.1$_2$, עוֹר *skin* 4QD$^a$ 9.1$_3$, שֵׂעָר *hair* 4QD$^a$ 9.1$_{10}$ (:: מֵת *dead*), עֵת *time, as the living time*, i.e. at this time next year Gn 18$_{10.14}$ 2 K 4$_{16.17}$ (כָּעֵת חַיָּה). <COLL> כָּל־נֶפֶשׁ הַחַיָּה *every living soul* Gn 1$_{21}$ 9$_{10}$ Lv 11$_{10.46}$ (both כֹּל) CD 12$_{13}$, טוב מסכן וחי בעצמו *better is a pauper (and) alive in his body* Si 30$_{14}$.

**2. alive, a.** in nom. cl., used predicatively of Abraham Gn 25$_6$, Absalom 2 S 18$_{14}$ 19$_7$, Ben-hadad 1 K 20$_{32}$, Jonathan 1 S 20$_{14}$, Joseph Gn 45$_{26.28}$ 46$_{30}$, Moses Dt 5$_3$ 31$_{27}$, Naboth 1 K 21$_{15}$ (:: מֵת *dead*), אָב *father* Gn 43$_{7.27.28}$ 45$_3$, בֵּן *son* Gn 45$_{28}$ Dt 31$_{13}$ (if ins. בֵּן *son* of Israel) 1 S 20$_{31}$ 1 K 3$_{22.22.23.23}$ (all four :: מֵת) 3$_{26}$ 8$_{40}$||2 C 6$_{31}$ 1 K 17$_{23}$ 1QDM 1$_6$ ([חיים]), יֶלֶד *child* 2 S 12$_{21.22}$, אָח *brother* Ex 4$_{18}$, גֹּאֵל *redeemer* Jb 19$_{25}$, עֶבֶד *servant* 1 K 20$_{32}$, דָּבֵק *clinging (person)*, i.e. one who stays faithful to Y. Dt 4$_4$, חַי *living being* (הֵמָּה חַיִּים *those who are living* as §3) Ec 4$_2$, עַם *people* Dt 4$_{10}$, Israel Dt 5$_3$ 12$_1$ 31$_{13}$, רֶמֶשׂ *creeping creature* Gn 9$_3$, חָגָב *locust* CD 12$_{15}$ ([חי]ים), appar. עֻבָּרָה *foetus* 4QD$^e$ 9.2$_{15}$, כֹּל *all* Si 42$_{23(M)}$ (הכל חי וע[ומד] לעד *everything is alive and enduring for ever*), שֵׁם *name* Si 44$_{14(M)}$, unspecified subj. Si 30$_{29}$ (עד עודך חי ונשמה בך *while you are still alive and breath is in you*).

**2b.** with היה *be*, used predicatively of Solomon 1 K

12$_{6}$||2 C 10$_{6}$, אָב *father* 1 K 12$_{6}$||2 C 10$_{6}$, יֶלֶד *child* 2 S 12$_{18}$.

<COLL> (§2a–b) with עוֹד *still* (alive) Gn 25$_{6}$ 43$_{7.27.28}$ 45$_{3.26.28}$ 46$_{30}$ Ex 4$_{18}$ Dt 31$_{13}$ 1 S 20$_{14}$ 2 S 12$_{21}$ (if em. בַּעֲבוּר *on account of* to בְּעוֹד *while*) 12$_{22}$ 18$_{14}$ 1 K 20$_{32}$ Si 30$_{29}$.

2c. esp. in oaths,* חַי־י׳ *(as) Y. is alive* Jg 8$_{19}$ 1 S 14$_{39.45}$ 19$_{6}$ 20$_{3.21}$ 25$_{26.34}$ 26$_{10.16}$ 28$_{10}$ 29$_{6}$ 2 S 4$_{9}$ 11$_{11}$ (if em. חַיֶּךָ *[as] you* [David] *are alive*) 12$_{5}$ 14$_{11}$ 15$_{21}$ 1 K 1$_{29}$ 2$_{24}$ 17$_{1.12}$ 18$_{10.15}$ (both חַי י׳) 22$_{14}$||2 C 18$_{13}$ 2 K 2$_{2.4.6}$ 3$_{14}$ 4$_{30}$ 5$_{16.20}$ Jr 4$_{2}$ 5$_{2}$ 12$_{16}$ 16$_{14.15}$ 23$_{7.8}$ 38$_{16}$ Ho 4$_{15}$ Ru 3$_{13}$ Lachish ost. 3$_{9}$ (חיהוה) 6$_{12}$ 12$_{3}$ ([ח]י) Arad ost. 21$_{5}$ (חי[ה]וה]).

חַי־אֲדֹנָי י׳ *(as) my Lord Y. is alive* Jr 44$_{26}$, חַי הָאֱלֹהִים *(as) God is alive* 2 S 2$_{27}$, חַי־אֵל *(as) God is alive* Jb 27$_{2}$.

חַי־אָנִי *(as) I* (Y.) *am alive* Nm 14$_{21.28}$ Is 49$_{18}$ Jr 22$_{24}$ 46$_{18}$ Ezk 5$_{11}$ 14$_{16.18.20}$ 16$_{48}$ 17$_{16.19}$ 18$_{3}$ 20$_{3.31.33}$ 33$_{11.27}$ 34$_{8}$ 35$_{6.11}$ Zp 2$_{9}$, חַי אָנֹכִי *(as) I* (Y.) *am alive* Dt 32$_{40}$.

חֵי אֱלֹהֶיךָ *(as) your gods are alive* Am 8$_{14}$, חֵי דֶּרֶךְ *(as) the way of* Beer-sheba *is alive* Am 8$_{14}$ (or em. דֹּדְךָ *(as) your Dod* is alive, O Beer-sheba), חֵי פַרְעֹה *(as) Pharaoh is alive* Gn 42$_{15.16}$, חֵי אֲדֹנִי הַמֶּלֶךְ *(as) my lord the king is alive* 2 S 15$_{21}$, חֵי נַפְשְׁךָ *(as) your soul is alive* 1 S 1$_{26}$ 11$_{11}$ 17$_{55}$ 20$_{3}$ 25$_{26}$ 2 S 14$_{19}$ 2 K 2$_{2.4.6}$ 4$_{30}$ (and vars.), חַיֶּךָ appar. *(as) you* (David) *are alive* 2 S 11$_{11}$ (or em. הֵיךְ *how?* or חַי־י׳ *as Y. lives*).

3. as noun, **living being, one that is alive,** <SUBJ> ידה hi. *thank* Is 38$_{19.19}$ 11QPsa 19$_{2.2}$, ידע *know* Ec 9$_{5}$ (:: מֵת *dead*), צדק *be righteous* Ps 143$_{2}$ 11QPsa 24$_{7}$, הלך pi. *walk* Ec 4$_{15}$, נתן *give* Ec 7$_{2}$, מות *die* Ec 9$_{5}$. <NOM CL> הַחַיִּים אֲשֶׁר הֵמָּה חַיִּים עֲדֶנָה *the living, who are still alive* Ec 4$_{2}$. <OBJ> ראה *see* Ec 4$_{15}$, נכה hi. *strike* Gn 8$_{21}$.

<CSTR> חֵי־הָעוֹלָם *one that is alive of,* i.e. for, *eternity* Dn 12$_{7}$ perh. 4Q419 1$_{10}$ (חי עולם) 4QDibHama 8$_{2}$ ([חי עול[מים]) 6QHymn 2$_{5}$ (חי עולמים).

טובת חי *goodness of a living being* Si 41$_{13(B)}$ (M ט[ו]בת; Bmg טוב חי in same sense), אֶרֶץ חַיִּים *land of (the) living* (unless *land of life*) Is 38$_{11}$ (הַחַיִּים) 53$_{8}$ Jr 11$_{19}$ Ezk 26$_{20}$ 32$_{23.24.25.26.27.32}$ Ps 27$_{13}$ (mss הַחַיִּים) 52$_{7}$ 116$_{9}$ (אַרְצוֹת הַחַיִּים) 142$_{6}$ Jb 28$_{13}$ (both הַחַיִּים).

אֵם כָּל־חָי *mother of every living being* Gn 3$_{20}$ Si 40$_{1(B)}$ (Bmg אֵל *God* of every living being), מין כל חי *kind of every,* i.e. every kind of, *living being* Si 43$_{25(B)}$, נֶפֶשׁ כָּל־חָי *soul of every living being* Jb 12$_{10}$ GnzPs 3$_{22}$ 11QPsa 19$_{4}$ (כול; || בָּשָׂר *flesh*), רוח כול חי *spirit of every living being* 4QDibHama 6$_{22}$, עֵינֵי כָל־חָי *the eyes of every living being* Jb 28$_{21}$ (+ עלם מִן ni. *be hidden from*) Si 42$_{1}$ 44$_{23}$ (both + מצא חֵן בְּ *find grace in*) 46$_{20}$ (+ נבון נמצא ב *he was found intelligent in*).

דרך כול חי *way of every living being* 1QH 15$_{22}$, דרכי כל חי *ways of every living being* GnzPs 1$_{2}$, משפט כול חי *judgment of every living being* 1QS 10$_{17.18}$, נחלת כל חי *inheritance of every living creature* 4Q416 4$_{2}$ 4Q417 2.1$_{19}$ (בנחל[ת כול חי]) 4Q418 81$_{20}$ ([כ]ו[ל חי]).

כָּל־חַי *every living being* Gn 8$_{21}$ Ps 143$_{2}$ (חָי) 145$_{16}$ Jb 30$_{23}$ (חָי) Si 7$_{33}$ 42$_{8}$ 45$_{16}$ 49$_{16}$ CD 12$_{21}$ 13$_{22}$ ([כל חי]) 1QS 4$_{26}$ 9$_{12}$ (both כול) 4Q416 2.2$_{2}$ (=4Q417 1.2$_{3}$ לכ[ול חי]) 4Q417 7$_{2}$ (כ[ל חי]) 4QRitMar 39$_{2}$ (כול) 11QPsa 24$_{7}$ 26$_{13}$ (both כול), כָּל־הָחַי *every living being* Gn 6$_{19}$ (Sam חַיָּה every *beast*), כָּל־הַחַיִּים *all the living* Ec 4$_{15}$ 9$_{4}$ 1QH 4$_{29}$ (כול).

<PREP> לְ of direction, *to* perh. 6QHymn 2$_{5}$, + נתן *give* Si 7$_{33}$ 4Q416 2.2$_{2}$ ([ולתת טרף] לכל חי) *and to give prey to every living being;* =4Q417 1.2$_{3}$ ולתת טרף לכ[ול חי]), נפל hi. *cause to fall,* i.e. assign lot 1QS 4$_{26}$ (ו[ל]ה[פיל]), אמר *say* 1 S 25$_{6}$ (or em. לֶחָי appar. *to the one who is alive* to לְאַחַי *to my brothers* or [לְאָחִין] לְחִי *to my brother* or לוֹ וּלְחַיּוֹ *to him and to his kin,* from חַי II), ידע hi. *make known* 1QH 4$_{29}$; of possession, *of, (belonging) to* Jb 30$_{23}$; of benefit, *to, for,* + עטר pi. *crown* mountains with food 11QPsa 26$_{13}$; שׂבע לְ hi. *satisfy* Ps 145$_{16}$; כְּ *as (though it were),* + שׂער *blow away* Ps 58$_{10}$; מִן of direction, *from,* + יסף ni. *be added* 4QDa 9.14$_{11}$ ([מ]ן החיות [=4QDg 1.1$_{20}$ (מ)ן הח[יות]]; both :: מֵת *dead*); of comparison, *(more) than,* + שׁבח pi. *praise* Ec 4$_{2}$ (:: מֵת), בחר *choose* over Si 45$_{16}$; בֵּין *between* living and dead, + עמד *stand* Nm 17$_{13}$ (:: מֵת); אֶל *to,* + חבר pu. *be joined* Ec 9$_{4(Qr)}$, *for,* + בחר ni./pu. *be chosen* Ec 9$_{4(Kt)}$; עַל *over,* i.e. greater than Si 49$_{16}$; *against,* + פגע *encounter* Si 30$_{12}$ (or em. בְּ in same sense); אֵת *with* Ru 2$_{20}$ (:: מֵת); עִם *with,* + הלך htp. *go about* CD 12$_{21}$ 13$_{22}$ ([להתהלך בם עם כל חי] *to go about in them with every living being*) 1QS 9$_{12}$; בְּעַד *on behalf of,* + דרשׁ *seek* Is 8$_{19}$, i.e. ask, the dead (:: מֵת); לִפְנֵי *in the presence of,* + היה *be* Si 42$_{8}$; נֶגֶד *in the presence of,* + הלך *go* Ec 6$_{8}$.

<COLL> חַי as predicate, אִם ... תִּמָּצֵא בְיָדוֹ הַגְּנֵבָה ... חַיִּים *if ... the stolen item is found in his hand ... alive* Ex 22$_{3}$=4QBibPar 10$_{6}$ (only חיים extant), הַשָּׂעִיר ... יָעֳמַד־חַי *the goat ... will stand, alive* Lv 16$_{10}$ (or em. יַעֲמֹד to יַעֲמִיד אֹתוֹ *he will place it,* alive), וְיָרְדוּ חַיִּים שְׁאֹלָה *and they will go down to Sheol alive* Nm 16$_{30}$, sim. 16$_{33}$ Ps 55$_{16}$, אֶת־מֶלֶךְ הָעַי תָּפְשׂוּ חָי *the king of Ai they captured alive* Jos 8$_{23}$, sim. 1 S 15$_{8}$, חַיִּים תִּפְשׂוּם *capture them alive* 1 K 20$_{18}$, תִּפְשׂוּם חַיִּים *capture them alive* 1 K 20$_{18}$ 2 K 10$_{14}$, sim. 2 K 7$_{12}$ 10$_{14}$ (lacking in mss), חַיִּים שָׁבוּ *they captured alive* 2 C 25$_{12}$, בְּלָעוּנוּ חַיִּים *they swallowed us alive* Ps 124$_{3}$, sim. Pr 1$_{12}$, אשר יתלה אנשים חיים *who would hang people alive* 4QpNah 3.1$_{7}$, תלוי חי *one hanged alive* 4QpNah 3.1$_{8}$, נקרעו חיים *they have been ripped apart alive* CD 12$_{14}$.

Also 4QD$^{g}$ 1.1$_{5}$ (החי) 1.2$_{18}$ (ההיה) 4QMyst$^{a}$ 6.2$_{2}$ (החי).

<SYN> §3 בָּשָׂר *flesh.*

<ANT> §§1, 2a, 3 מֵת *dead*; §3 ״ *Y.**

⇒ חיה *live.*

**חַי** II 2 n.[m.] **kinsfolk**—sf. חַיַּי (חַיָּי)—<NOM CL> מִי חַיַּי *who are my kinsfolk?* 1 S 18$_{18}$ (or חַיִּי, i.e. sing. with same meaning). <CSTR> אֵל חַיָּי *God of my kinsfolk* perh. Ps 42$_{9}$ (unless *of my life,* from חַיִּים *life*). <APP> מִשְׁפָּחָה *family* 1 S 18$_{18}$. <PREP> לְ of direction, *to,* + אמר *say* 1 S 25$_{6}$ (if em. לֶחָי appar. *to the living one* to לוֹ וּלְחַיָּו *to him and his kinsfolk*).*

⇒ חיה *live.*

**חִיאֵל** 1 pr.n.m. **Hiel,** inhabitant of Bethel, builder of Jericho, <SUBJ> בנה *build* 1 K 16$_{34}$, יסד pi. *found* 1 K 16$_{34}$, נצב hi. *set up* 1 K 16$_{34}$. <APP> בֵּית הָאֱלִי *the Bethelite* 1 K 16$_{34}$.

⇒ חיה *live* + אֵל.

**[חַיָּב]** 0.1.0.1 adj. **guilty**—perh. cstr. I חיב; pl. Si חייבים—**guilty, indebted,** <NOM CL> זכר כי כלנו חייבים *remember that all of us are guilty* Si 8$_{5}$, לוי חיב קרקס perh. *Levi is indebted of,* i.e. to, *Karkas* Frey 1286$_{19(AHL)}$ (Frey lacks last two words). <CSTR> חיב קרקס *indebted of,* i.e. to,*Karkas* Frey 1286$_{19(AHL)}$.

⇒ חוב *be guilty.*

**[חִיד]** 0.0.1 n.[m.] **community** (appar. error for יַחַד *community*), <CSTR> אנשי החיד *men of the community* 1QS 6$_{3}$.

**חִידָה** 17.2.5 n.f. **riddle**—sf. חִידָתְךָ, חִידָתִי; pl. חִידוֹת (חִידֹת); sf. חִידֹתָם (Si חידתיהם)—**riddle, obscure saying,** or **problem** (Dn 8$_{23}$).

<OBJ> חוד *propound a riddle* Jg 14$_{12.13.16}$ Ezk 17$_{2}$ (|| מָשָׁל *parable*), נשׂא *take up* Hb 2$_{6}$ (or em. חִידוֹת *riddles* to יְחוּדוּ *they will recite a mocking poem;* + מְלִיצָה *mocking poem,* מָשָׁל), נגד hi. *tell,* i.e. explain Jg 14$_{12.14.15.17.19}$ 4QMyst$^{b}$ 1.2$_{1}$ (|| מָשָׁל), פתח *open* Ps 49$_{5}$ (+ מָשָׁל), נבע hi. *utter* Ps 78$_{2}$ (+ מָשָׁל), שׁמע *hear* Jg 14$_{13}$, מצא *find (out)* Jg 14$_{18}$, בין hi. *understand* Pr 1$_{6}$ (מְלִיצָה, מָשָׁל *figure,* דָּבָר *word*) Dn 8$_{23}$.

<NOM CL> מה החידה לכמה *what is the riddle to you?* 4QMyst$^{c}$ 2$_{1}$.

<CSTR> מַגִּידֵי הַחִידָה *tellers of the riddle* Jg 14$_{19}$, מליצי חידות *interpreters of riddles* 1QpHab 8$_{6}$.

<PREP> בְּ of accompaniment, *with, in,* + דבר pi. *speak* Nm 12$_{8}$ (+ מַרְאֶה *vision,* פֶּה אֶל־פֶּה *mouth to mouth*), רטשׁ htp. *abandon oneself,* i.e. occupy oneself Si 8$_{8}$ (+ שִׂיחָה *musing*), סער hi. *astound* Si 47$_{17}$ (|| מְלִיצָה *figure,* שִׁיר *song,* מָשָׁל *proverb*); of instrument, *by (means of), with,* + נסה pi. *test* 1 K 10$_{1}$||2 C 9$_{1}$.

Also 4QMyst$^{b}$ 9$_{1(WA)}$ (Schiffman סודות *secrets*) 4QMyst$^{c}$ 1$_{2}$.

<SYN> מָשָׁל *parable/proverb,* מְלִיצָה *figure/mocking poem,* שִׁיר *song.**

⇒ חוד *propound a riddle.*

**חיה** I 282.2.19 vb. **live—Qal** 203.2.14 Pf. חָיָה (חַי, חָי, חָי), חָיוּ; impf. יִחְיֶה (יְחִי, יֶחִי, וַיְחִי, יְחִי), 3fs תִּחְיֶה (תְּחִי), 2ms תִּחְיֶה (Si תחי), 2fs תִּחְיִי, אֶחְיֶה, יִחְיוּ, תִּחְיוּ (תִּחְיוּן), 3fpl תִּחְיֶינָה, נִחְיֶה; + waw וְחָיִיתָ, (וְחָיָה) וְחָיְתָה, 3fs (וְחֵי, וְחָי, וָחֵי, וְחַי) וְחָיָה, וַיְחִי (וַיֶּחִי) וַיְחִי; וִחְיִיתֶם, וְחָיוּ, (וְחָיִתָה), 3fs וַתְּחִי, וַיְחִיוּ; impv. חֲיֵה, חֱיִי, וִחְיוּ; inf. abs. חָיֹה (חָיוֹ), cstr. לִחְיוֹת (חֲיוֹתָם)—**1. live, remain alive** (e.g. Gn 5$_{3}$ 11$_{11}$ Ex 1$_{16}$ 33$_{20}$ Lv 25$_{36}$ Nm 4$_{19}$ Dt 30$_{16}$ 1 K 1$_{25}$ Is 55$_{3}$ Ezk 20$_{13}$ Ps 22$_{27}$ Jb 7$_{16}$ Ne 9$_{29}$ Si 15$_{15}$ CD 3$_{16}$ 2QJub$^{a}$ 23$_{8}$ 4QD$^{a}$ 18.5$_{12}$). **2. revive, recover** (intrans.) (e.g. Jg 15$_{19}$ 2 S 12$_{22}$ 2 K 13$_{21}$ Is 38$_{9}$ 39$_{1}$ [1QIsa$^{a}$] Jb 14$_{14}$).

<SUBJ> עַם *people* Dt 4$_{33}$ 2 K 18$_{32}$ (:: מות *die*) Jr 27$_{17}$ Ezk 37$_{14}$, גּוֹי *nation* Jos 5$_{8}$, Israel Dt 4$_{1.37}$ (if em. וְתַחַת *and because* to : וַתְּחִי *and you lived*) 5$_{33}$ 8$_{1}$ 16$_{20}$ 30$_{16}$ (or del.) 30$_{19}$ Ezk 18$_{32}$ 33$_{10}$ Ho 6$_{2}$ Am 5$_{4.6.14}$ Zc 10$_{9}$ (or em. וְחִיּוּ *and they shall rear*, or וְחִוּוּ pi. *and they shall gather*, i.e. חוה pi. *gather*) 11QT 51$_{15}$, Jerusalem Ezk 16$_{6.6}$* (or del.), Egyptians Gn 47$_{19}$ (:: מות), Reuben (tribe) Dt 33$_{6}$ (:: מות), שֵׁבֶט *tribe* of Kohathites Nm 4$_{19}$ (:: מות), בַּיִת *house* Jr 38$_{17}$.

Abimelech Gn 20$_{7}$, Abraham Gn 25$_{7}$ 2QJub$^{a}$ 23$_{8}$ ([אבר]הם), Adam Gn 5$_{3.5}$, Adonijah 1 K 1$_{25}$, Ahaziah 2 K 1$_{2}$, Amaziah 2 K 14$_{17}$||2 C 25$_{25}$, Arpachshad Gn 11$_{12.13}$, Benhadad 2 K 8$_{8.9.10.10}$ (:: מות *die*) 14$_{14.14}$, Caleb Nm 14$_{38}$, David 1 K 1$_{31}$, Eber Gn 11$_{16.17}$, Enoch Gn 5$_{21}$, Enosh Gn 5$_{9.10}$, Esau Gn 27$_{40}$, Hezekiah 2 K 20$_{1}$||Is 38$_{1}$ (:: מות) 20$_{7}$||Is 38$_{21}$ Is 38$_{9}$ 39$_{1}$ (1QIsa$^{a}$), Ishmael Gn 17$_{18}$, Jacob/Israel Gn 42$_{2}$ 43$_{8}$ (both :: מות) 47$_{28}$, Jared Gn 5$_{18.19}$, Job Jb 7$_{16}$ 42$_{16}$, Joseph Gn 50$_{22}$ 2QJub$^{b}$ 46$_{2}$ ([חיה]), Joshua Nm 14$_{38}$, Judah Gn 43$_{8}$, Kenan Gn 5$_{12.13}$, Lamech Gn 5$_{28.30}$, Mahalel Gn 5$_{15.16}$, Methuselah Gn 5$_{25.26}$, Nahor Gn 11$_{24.25}$, Noah Gn 9$_{28}$, Peleg Gn 11$_{18.19}$, Rahab Jos 6$_{17}$, Reu Gn 11$_{20.21}$, Samson Jg 15$_{19}$, Saul 2 S 1$_{10}$, Serug Gn 11$_{22.23}$, Seth Gn 5$_{6.7}$, Shelah Gn 11$_{14.15}$, Shem Gn 11$_{11}$, Solomon 1 K 1$_{34.39}$, Terah Gn 11$_{26}$, Zedekiah Jr 27$_{12}$ 38$_{17}$.

מֶלֶךְ *king* 1 S 10$_{24}$ 2 S 16$_{16.16}$ (lacking in 2 mss) 1 K 1$_{25.31.34.39}$ 2 K 11$_{12}$||2 C 23$_{11}$ 2 K 8$_{8.9.10.10}$ 14$_{17}$||2 C 25$_{25}$ Jr 27$_{12}$ Ps 72$_{15}$ Ne 2$_{3}$ 4QapPs$^{b}$ 31$_{5}$ ([מ]לך).*

אָדוֹן *lord* 1 K 1$_{31}$ 2 K 8$_{14.14}$, כֹּהֵן *priest* Jr 27$_{17}$, נָבִיא *prophet* Zc 1$_{5}$, worshipper Ps 118$_{17}$ (:: מות *die*) 119$_{17}$ (+ שׁמר *keep*) 119$_{77.116.144}$ Lm 4$_{20}$, צַדִּיק *righteous one* Ezk 3$_{21.21}$ 18$_{24}$ 33$_{12.13.13}$ =1QpHab 7$_{17}$ ([צדיק ... יחיה]), רָשָׁע *wicked one* Ezk 18$_{21.21}$ (:: מות) 18$_{22.23.28.28}$ (:: מות) 33$_{11.15.15}$ (:: מות) 33$_{16.16.19}$ Jb 21$_{7}$ (|| עתק *advance*, + גבר *be strong*), פֶּתִי *naïve one* Pr 9$_{6}$, חֲסַר *one lacking* sense Pr 9$_{6}$.

אָדָם *human being* Gn 3$_{22}$ Ex 33$_{20}$ Lv 18$_{5}$ Dt 5$_{24}$ 8$_{3.3}$ Is 38$_{16}$ (unless em. עֲלֵיהֶם יִחְיוּ וּלְכָל־בָּהֶן חַיֵּי רוּחִי perh. *by them do they live, and for everything in them is the life of my spirit* to עָלֶיוֹ יְחְיֶה־לְּךָ לִבִּי וְהָנַח י׳ לְרוּחִי *by them my heart shall live for you, so give rest, O Y., to my spirit*) Ezk 20$_{11.13.21}$ Ec 11$_{8}$ Ne 9$_{29}$ CD 3$_{16}$ 4QD$^{a}$ 18.5$_{12}$ 4QDibHam$^{a}$ 6$_{17}$, אִישׁ *man* Ex 19$_{13}$ Nm 21$_{9}$ 2 K 7$_{4}$ 13$_{21}$ Ezk 18$_{9.9}$ Zc 13$_{3}$ Ps 49$_{10}$ Ec 6$_{3.6}$ Est 4$_{11}$, גֶּבֶר *man* Ps 89$_{49}$ (:: ראה מָוֶת *see death*; + מלט נֶפֶשׁ pi. *deliver soul*) Jb 14$_{14}$, אִשָּׁה *woman* 2 K 4$_{7}$ (or em. אַתְּ וּבָנַיִךְ תִּחְיִי [Qr] *you and your sons shall live* to אֶת־בָּנַיִךְ תְּחַיִּי *you shall preserve you sons alive*, i.e. pi.) Est 4$_{11}$, אָב *father* Gn 43$_{8}$, אָח *brother* Gn 42$_{18}$ Lv 25$_{35.36}$, בֵּן *son* Gn 42$_{2}$ Nm 14$_{38}$ 2 K 4$_{7}$ (or em.; see above) 2 K 8$_{9.10.10}$ 14$_{17}$||2 C 25$_{25}$ Ezk 18$_{13.13.17.17.19.19}$ 20$_{25}$ Pr 4$_{4}$ (or del.) 7$_{2}$ Si 15$_{15}$ 40$_{28(Bmg)}$ (B מני appar. error for בני *my son*), specif. son of house of Rechab Jr 35$_{7}$, בַּת *daughter* Ex 1$_{16}$, יֶלֶד *child* 2 S 12$_{22}$ 1 K 17$_{22}$, טַף *infant* Gn 43$_{8}$, יצא ptc. *one who goes out* Jr 21$_{9}$=38$_{2}$ (:: מות *die*) 21$_{9(mss)}$=38$_{2}$, שׁוב ptc. *one who goes back* 4QpPs$^{a}$ 1.3$_{1}$, הלך htp. ptc. *one who walks* CD 7$_{6(A)}$=19$_{1(B)}$, יֹשֵׁב *inhabitant* Jos 9$_{21}$, זֹנָה *prostitute* Jos 6$_{17}$, מאס ptc. *one who despises* CD 3$_{17}$, שֹׂנֵא *one who hates* Pr 15$_{27}$, רֹצֵחַ *manslayer* Dt 4$_{42}$ 19$_{4}$, הרג pass. ptc. *one who is slain* Ezk 37$_{9.10}$ (+ עמד *stand*), נשך pass. ptc. *one who is bitten* Nm 21$_{8}$, מֵת *one who is dead* Is 26$_{14}$ (|| קום *rise*) 26$_{19}$ (+ קום).

זֶרַע *seed* Dt 30$_{19}$, בְּהֵמָה *beast* Ex 19$_{13}$, עֶצֶם *bone* Ezk 37$_{3.5.6}$ 4QpsEzek$^{a}$ 2$_{8}$ ([ויחיו]), לֵבָב *heart* Ps 22$_{27}$ 69$_{33}$, לֵב *heart* Is 38$_{16}$ (if em.; see below), נֶפֶשׁ *soul* Gn 12$_{13}$ 19$_{20}$ 1 K 20$_{32}$ Is 55$_{3}$ Jr 38$_{17.20}$ Ezk 13$_{19}$ 47$_{9}$ Ps 119$_{175}$, רוּחַ *spirit* Gn 45$_{27}$, בָּשָׂר *flesh* Dt 5$_{26}$.

מִי *who?* Nm 24$_{23}$ (Sam היה *be*) Ne 6$_{11}$, אֲשֶׁר *one who* Gn 31$_{32}$ Dt 19$_{5}$ Ne 5$_{2}$, כֹּל *all* Jos 6$_{17}$ 2 K 10$_{19}$ Ezk 47$_{9}$.

<OBJ> שָׁנָה *year* Gn 5$_{3+15t}$ 9$_{28}$ 11$_{11+13t}$ 48$_{28}$ 50$_{22}$ 2 K 14$_{17}$||2 C 25$_{25}$ Jb 42$_{16}$ Ec 6$_{3.6}$ 11$_{8}$ 2QJub$^{a}$ 23$_{8}$ ([שנים]), שָׁבוּעַ *week* 2QJub$^{a}$ 23$_{8}$ ([שבועי שנים] *weeks of years*), יוֹם *day* Gn 5$_{5}$ Jr 35$_{7}$ 2QJub$^{b}$ 46$_{2}$ ([חיה] ... י[מ]י חיי *days of the life* of Joseph which *he lived*), יוֹבֵל *jubilee* 2QJub$^{a}$ 23$_{8}$, חַיִּים *life* Si 40$_{28}$ (חיי מתן אל ח׳ *do not live the life of gifts*, i.e. of a beggar), דּוֹר *generation* CD 7$_{6(A)}$ (אלף דור *a thousand generations*; =19$_{1[B]}$ לאלפי דורות *for thousands of generations*) 4QpPs$^{a}$ 1.3$_{1}$.

<PREP> לְ of direction, *to, for*, + עוֹלָם *eternity* Gn 3$_{22}$ 1 K 1$_{31}$ Jb 7$_{16}$ Ne 2$_{3}$, עַד *perpetuity* Ps 22$_{27}$, נֶצַח *everlastingness* Ps 49$_{10}$, דּוֹר *generation* CD 19$_{1(B)}$.

בְּ of place, *in, among*, + אֶרֶץ *land* Gn 47$_{28}$, גּוֹי *nation* Lm 4$_{20}$, דָּם *blood* Ezk 16$_{6.6}$ (or del.); of instrument, *by (means of)* 4QDibHam$^{a}$ 6$_{17}$, + חֹק *statute* Ezk 20$_{11.13.21.25}$

4QDa 18.5$_{12}$, מִשְׁפָּט *ordinance* Ezk 20$_{11.13.21.25}$ Ne 9$_{29}$ 4QDa 18.5$_{12}$, עֵדָה *testimony* CD 3$_{16}$, דֶּרֶךְ *way* CD 3$_{16}$, חֵפֶץ *delight* of desire CD 3$_{16}$, צְדָקָה *righteousness* Ezk 18$_{22}$ 33$_{12}$, אֱמוּנָה *faithfulness* Hb 2$_{4}$=1QpHab 7$_{17}$ ([באמונתו יחיה]), יָשְׁרָה *uprightness* 4QpPsa 1.3$_{1}$.

מִן of direction, *from,* + חֳלִי *illness* 2 K 1$_{2}$ 8$_{8.9}$ Is 38$_{9}$; partitive, *(some) of, from (among),* + אִישׁ *man* Nm 14$_{38}$.

עַל *by (means of)* Is 38$_{16}$, + חֶרֶב *sword* Gn 27$_{40}$, לֶחֶם *bread* Dt 8$_{3}$, מוֹצָא *utterance* Dt 8$_{3}$, מִשְׁפָּט *ordinance* Ezk 33$_{19}$, צְדָקָה *righteousness* Ezk 33$_{19}$; *upon,* + פָּנִים *face* of earth Jr 35$_{7}$.

אַחַר *after,* + מַבּוּל *flood* Gn 9$_{28}$.

אַחֲרֵי *after,* + מָוֶת *death* 2 K 14$_{17}$‖2 C 25$_{25}$, אָב *father* 2QJubb 46$_{2}$ ([חיה אחרי]), זֹאת *this* Jb 42$_{16}$.

אֵת *with,* + בֵּן *son* Zc 10$_{9}$ (or em.; see Subj.).

בִּגְלַל *on account of,* + Sarai Gn 12$_{13}$.

לִפְנֵי *before,* + ײ Y. Ho 6$_{2}$, אֱלֹהִים *God* Gn 17$_{18}$.

עִם *with,* + בֵּן *son* of Israel Lv 25$_{35.36}$.

<COLL> + adverb עוֹד *still;* with inf. abs. חָיֹה תִחְיֶה *you shall surely live* (and vars.) 2 K 8$_{10.12}$ Ezk 3$_{21}$ 18$_{9.17.19.21.28}$ 33$_{13.15.16}$.

Also 1Q45 4$_{1}$ 4QpIsac 31$_{1}$ 4QDa 1$_{7}$ 4QapPsb 103$_{2}$ 4Q418 88$_{7}$ 6QapSam/Kings 27 ([ת]חיה).

<SYN> עתק *advance,* קום *rise.*

<ANT> מות *die,* ראה מָוֶת *see death.*

**Pi.** 56.0.4 Pf. חִיָּה, חִיִּתָנִי, חִיִּתַּנִי (חִיִּיתָנִי), חִיּוּ, חִיִּיתֶם; impf. יְחַיֶּה (יְחַיֵּנוּ, Q יחים), 3fs תְּחַיֶּה (תְּחַיֵּנִי), 2ms תְּחַיֶּה (Qr תְּחַיֵּינִי, תְּחַיֵּנִי, תְּחַיֵּנוּ, תְּחַיֵּינוּ), אֲחַיֶּה, יְחַיּוּ (יְחַיֻּנוּ), תְּחַיּוּן, תְּחַיֶּינָה, נְחַיֶּה; + waw וַיְחַיֶּהָ, 3fpl וַתְּחַיֶּיןָ, 2fpl וַתְּחַיֶּיןָ; impv. חַיֵּנִי (חַיֵּיהוּ); ptc. מְחַיֶּה; inf. חַיּוֹת (חַיֹּתוֹ, חַיֹּתֵנוּ, חַיּוֹתָם);—**1. keep alive, let live** (e.g. Gn 12$_{12}$ Ex 1$_{17}$ 22$_{17}$ Nm 31$_{15}$ Dt 6$_{24}$ Jos 9$_{15}$ 1 S 27$_{9}$ 2 K 7$_{4}$ 4QpPsa 1.3$_{3}$). **2. cause to live, revive** (e.g. Dt 32$_{29}$ 1 S 2$_{6}$ Ho 6$_{2}$* Ps 30$_{4}$ 71$_{20}$ Jb 33$_{4}$ 4Q521 2.2$_{12}$ 5.2$_{6}$), **repair** city (1 C 11$_{8}$). **3. cause** grain **to grow** (Ho 14$_{8}$), **rear** children (Zc 10$_{9}$ if em.; see Subj.), livestock (2 S 12$_{3}$ Is 7$_{21}$).

<SUBJ> Y. Dt 6$_{24}$ 32$_{39}$ 1 S 2$_{6}$ (both :: מות hi. *put to death*) Jr 49$_{11}$ Ho 6$_{2}$ (‖ קום hi. *raise up*) Hb 3$_{2}$ (or em. חַיֵּיהוּ *revive it* to חַוֵּהוּ *declare it*) Ps 30$_{4}$ 33$_{19}$ (+ נצל hi. *deliver*) 41$_{3}$ (‖ שׁמר *keep*) 71$_{20}$ 80$_{19}$ 85$_{7}$ 119$_{25+9t}$ 138$_{7}$ 143$_{11}$ Jb 36$_{6}$ Ne 9$_{6}$ 4QpPsa 1.3$_{3}$ 4QpsEzeka 2$_{8}$ ([חים]) 4Q521 2.2$_{12}$ (‖ רפא *heal*) 5.2$_{6}$.

עַם *people* Ex 1$_{22}$, Aramaean(s) 2 K 7$_{4}$ (:: מות hi. *put to death*), Egyptian(s) Gn 12$_{12}$ (:: הרג *kill*), Israelite(s) Ex 22$_{17}$ Dt 20$_{16}$=11QT 62$_{13}$ Ho 14$_{8}$ Zc 10$_{9}$ (if em. וְחָיוּ *and they shall live* to וְחִיּוּ *and they shall rear*), Jews Ne 3$_{34}$, עֵדָה *congregation* Jg 21$_{14}$, Ahab 1 K 18$_{5}$ (:: כרת hi. *allow to perish*), David 1 S 27$_{9.11}$, Ezekiel Ezk 3$_{18}$, Joab 1 C 11$_{8}$, Joshua Jos 9$_{15}$, Noah Gn 7$_{3}$, Obadiah 1 K 18$_{5}$.

מֶלֶךְ *king* 1 K 20$_{31}$, שַׂר *prince* Nm 31$_{15}$, רָשָׁע *wicked one* Ezk 18$_{27}$, אִישׁ *man* Is 7$_{21}$, אִשָּׁה *woman* 2 K 4$_{7}$ (if em.; see Qal Subj.), בַּת *daughter* Gn 19$_{32.34}$, פקד pass. ptc. *appointed one* Nm 31$_{15}$, מְיַלֶּדֶת *midwife* Ex 1$_{17.18}$, תפר pi. ptc. *one who sews* Ezk 13$_{18.19}$ (:: מות hi. *put to death*), רָשׁ *poor one* 2 S 12$_{3}$, חָכְמָה *wisdom* Ec 7$_{12}$, אִמְרָה *word* Ps 119$_{50}$, נְשָׁמָה *breath* Jb 33$_{4}$ (‖ עשׂה *make*); subj. not specified, Ps 22$_{30}$ (or em. חִיָּה *he has kept alive* to חַיָּה *alive*).

<OBJ> Israelite(s) Dt 6$_{24}$ Ho 6$_{2}$ Ps 71$_{20(Kt)}$ 80$_{19}$ 85$_{7}$ 4QpPsa 1.3$_{3}$, Elihu Jb 33$_{4}$, Sarai Gn 12$_{12}$.

אִישׁ *man* 1 S 27$_{9.11}$ 2 K 7$_{4}$, אִשָּׁה *woman* Jg 21$_{14}$ 1 S 27$_{9.11}$, נְקֵבָה *female* Nm 31$_{15}$, יֶלֶד *child* Ex 1$_{17.18}$, בֵּן 2 K 4$_{7}$ (if em.; see Qal Subj.) Zc 10$_{9}$ (if em.; see Subj.), בַּת *daughter* Ex 1$_{22}$, בַּעַל *possessor* Ec 7$_{12}$, רָשָׁע *wicked one* Ezk 3$_{18}$ Jb 36$_{6}$, worshipper Ps 30$_{4}$ Ps 71$_{20(Qr)}$ 119$_{25+10t}$ 138$_{7}$ 143$_{11}$, מְכַשֵּׁפָה *sorceress* Ex 22$_{17}$, שׂכל hi. ptc. *one who understands* Ps 41$_{3}$, ירא ptc. *one who fears* Ps 33$_{19}$, יֹשֵׁב *inhabitant* Jos 9$_{15}$, יחל pi. ptc. *one who waits* Ps 33$_{19}$, מֵת *dead one* 4Q521 2.2$_{12}$ 5.2$_{6}$.

סוּס *horse* 1 K 18$_{5}$, פֶּרֶד *mule* 1 K 18$_{5}$, עֶגְלָה *heifer* Is 7$_{21}$, צֹאן *sheep* Is 7$_{21}$, כִּבְשָׂה *lamb* 2 S 12$_{3}$, זֶרַע *seed* Gn 7$_{3}$ 19$_{32.34}$, דָּגָן *grain* Ho 14$_{8}$, עֶצֶם *bone* 4QpsEzeka 2$_{8}$ ([חים]), נְשָׁמָה *breath,* i.e. breathing thing Dt 20$_{16}$=11QT 62$_{13}$, נֶפֶשׁ *soul* 1 K 20$_{31}$ Ezk 13$_{18.19}$ 18$_{27}$ Ps 22$_{30}$ (or em.; see Subj.), פֹּעַל *deed* Hb 3$_{2}$ (or em.; see Subj.), אֶבֶן *stone* Ne 3$_{34}$, שְׁאָר *remainder* of city 1 C 11$_{8}$, כֹּל *everyone* Ne 9$_{6}$.

<PREP> לְ of benefit, *to, for,* + מְתַפֵּר *sewer* Ezk 13$_{18}$; *according to,* + אִמְרָה *word* Ps 119$_{154}$.

בְּ of time, *in, at, among,* + קֶרֶב *middle* of years Hb 3$_{2}$ (or em.; see Subj.); of instrument, *by (means of),* + צְדָקָה *righteousness* Ps 119$_{40}$, דֶּרֶךְ *way* Ps 119$_{37}$, דָּבָר *word* Ps 119$_{37(mss)}$, פִּקּוּד *precept* Ps 119$_{93}$, מִשְׁפָּט *judgment* Ps 119$_{149(mss)}$, חֶסֶד *loyalty* Ps 119$_{159}$; of accompaniment, *in, with,* + רָעָב *famine* Ps 33$_{19}$.

כְּ *according to*, + דָּבָר *word* Ps 119:25.107, חֶסֶד *loyalty* Ps 119:88.159, מִשְׁפָּט *judgment* Ps 119:149.156.

מִן *from, after*, + יוֹם *day* Ho 6:2; of agent, *by (means of)*, + אָב *father* Gn 19:32.34; partitive, *(some) of, from (among)*, + אִשָּׁה *woman* Jg 21:14, ירד ptc. *one who goes down* Ps 30:4.

לְמַעַן *for sake of*, + שֵׁם *name* Ps 143:11.

עַל־פְּנֵי *upon (face of)*, + אֶרֶץ *earth* Gn 7:3.

<SYN> קום hi. *raise up*, רפא *heal*, שׁמר *keep*, עשׂה *make*.

<ANT> מות hi. *put to death*, הרג *kill*, כרת hi. *allow to perish*.

**Hi.** 22.0.1 Pf. הֶחֱיִתֶם, הֶחֱיִתָנוּ, הֶחֱיָה, הֶחֱיֵיתִי; impv. הַחֲיֵינִי, הַחֲיוּ; inf. abs. הַחֲיֵה, cstr. הַחֲיוֹת (הַחֲיֹת), Q לחיות [unless pi.], הַחֲיֹתוֹ)—**1. keep alive, let live** (e.g. Gn 6:19 19:19 Nm 22:33 31:18 Jos 6:25 14:10 Jg 8:19). **2. cause to live, revive** (e.g. 2 K 5:7 8:1 Is 38:16 57:15 1QH 8:36).

<SUBJ> Y. Gn 50:20 Jos 14:10 Is 38:16 (|| חלם hi. *make healthy*), נשׂא ni. ptc. *exalted one* Is 57:15, רום ptc. *high one* Is 57:15, מַלְאָךְ *angel* Gn 19:19 Nm 22:33 (:: הרג *kill*), David 2 S 8:2 (:: מות hi. *put to death*), Elisha 2 K 8:1.5.5.5, Joseph Gn 45:7 47:25, Joshua Jos 6:25, Noah Gn 6:19.20, Zalmunna Jg 8:19, Zebah Jg 8:19, מֶלֶךְ *king* 2 K 5:7 (:: מות hi.), שַׂר *prince* Nm 31:15(Sam).18, אִישׁ *man* Jos 2:13, בֵּן *son* of Israel Jos 9:20, בַּת *daughter* Ezk 13:22, פקד pass. ptc. *appointed one* Nm 31:15(Sam).18, worshipper 1QH 8:36.

<OBJ> Egyptian(s) Gn 47:25, עַם *people* Gn 50:20, בַּיִת *house(hold)* Jos 6:25, פְּלֵיטָה *survivor* Gn 45:7(Sam), רָשָׁע *wicked one* Ezk 13:22, Caleb Jos 14:10, Hezekiah Is 38:16, Rahab Jos 6:25, אָב *father* Jos 2:13, אֵם *mother* Jos 2:13, אָח *brother* Jos 2:13 Jg 8:19, אָחוֹת *sister* Jos 2:13, בֵּן *son* Jg 8:19 2 K 8:1.5.5, טַף *small child* Nm 31:18, זֹנָה *prostitute* Jos 6:25, מֵת *dead one* 2 K 8:5, יֹשֵׁב *inhabitant* Jos 9:20, לֵב *heart* Is 57:15, רוּחַ *spirit* Is 57:15 1QH 8:36, נֶפֶשׁ *soul* Gn 19:19, אָתוֹן *she-ass* Nm 22:33, מְלֹא *fullness* of line 2 S 8:2, כֹּל *everyone* Jos 2:13 6:25.

<PREP> לְ of benefit, *to, for*, + שַׂר *prince* Nm 31:18, אָח *brother* Gn 45:7, פקד pass. ptc. *appointed one* Nm 31:18.

לְ introducing object, + פְּלֵיטָה *survivor* Gn 45:7.

אֵת *with*, + Noah Gn 6:19.

<COLL> הֶחֱיָה י׳ ... זֶה אַרְבָּעִים וְחָמֵשׁ שָׁנָה *Y. has kept me alive ... these forty five years* Jos 14:10.

<ANT> מות hi. *put to death*, הרג *kill*.

<SYN> חלם hi. *make healthy*.*

⇒ חַי *living*, חַי *kinsfolk*, חַיָּה I *beast*, חַיָּה II *life*, חָיֶה *lively*, חַיִּים *life*, חַיּוּת *living*, מִחְיָה *preservation of life*, חַיִּים *Hayyim*, חִיאֵל *Hiel*, יְחִיאֵל *Jehuel*, יְחִיאֵלִי *Jehieli*, יְחִיָּה *Jehiah*.

***חיה** II vb. **gather—Ni. be gathered, assemble,** אִיִּם יֵחָיֵ מִשְּׂמֹאל *the islands will be gathered from the north* Nm 24:23 (if em. אוֹי מִי יִחְיֶה מִשֻּׂמוֹ אֵל *woe [to] whoever lives apart from God's appointing it* [Sam יִהְיֶה whoever *is*]).

**Ho. be gathered, assemble,** אִיִּם יָחְיֵ מִשְּׂמֹאל *the islands will be gathered from the north* Nm 24:23 (if em.).

⇒ חַיָּה III *troop*.

**חַיָּה** I 96.3.23 n.f. **beast**—cstr. חַיַּת (Q חיית, חַיְתוֹ); sf. חַיָּתוֹ, חַיָּתָם; pl. חַיּוֹת—oft. collective, **beast(s), animal(s),** usu. wild; also **living being(s)** of Ezekiel's vision (Ezk 1:5+10t 3:13 10:15.17.20 4QpsEzek[a] 4:6.6.7.10.12.13).

<SUBJ> היה *be* Ezk 31:13 perh. 4QpsEzek[a] 4:12 (ו[ה]יה]), ברא ni. *be created* Si 39:30(B), רבב *be many* Ex 23:29, רבה *be many* Dt 7:22, שׁבת *cease* 11QBer 1:12, שׁלם ho. *be brought into peace* Jb 5:23, נשׂא ni. *be raised* Ezk 1:19, בחר ni. *be chosen* Si 39:30(Bmg).

בוא *come* Gn 7:14 Jb 37:8 Ezk 39:17, אתה *come* Is 56:9.9 Jr 12:9 (if em. הֵתָיוּ *bring* to אֵתָיוּ *come*, and אִסְפוּ *gather* to הֵאָסְפוּ *be gathered*), הלך *go* Lv 11:27 Ezk 1:19 4QpsEzek[a] 4:7, עבר *pass* 2 K 14:9||2 C 25:18, אסף ni. *be gathered* Jr 12:9 (if em. אִסְפוּ to הֵאָסְפוּ) Ezk 39:17, קבץ ni. *be gathered* Ezk 39:17 perh. 4QapPs[b] 76:1, רמשׂ *swarm* Gn 1:28 Ps 104:20, רוץ *run* Ezk 1:14 (or em. רָצוֹא *ran* to יָצוֹא *went out*), יצא *go out* Gn 8:19 (or em. הַבְּהֵמָה *the beasts*) Ezk 1:14 (if em.).

עמד *stand* Dn 8:4, שׁכן *dwell* Jb 37:8, נוח *rest* 2 S 21:10, רבץ *lie down* Zp 2:14, רעשׁ *quake* Ezk 38:20, רמס *trample* 2 K 14:9||2 C 25:18, דושׁ *trample* Jb 39:15, בקע pi. *tear* Ho 13:8 (or em. חַיַּת הַשָּׂדֶה תְּבַקְּעֵם *a beast of the field will tear them* to כְּחַיַּת הַשָּׂדֶה אֲבַקְּעֵם *like a beast of the field I shall tear them*), אכל *eat* Gn 37:20.33 Ex 23:11 Lv 25:7 Is 56:9.9 Jr 12:9 Ezk 33:27 34:28 39:17 Ho 2:14=4QpHos[a] 2:19 ([ח]ית]) Si 36:23, ni. *be eaten* Lv 11:47.47 17:13, רעה *graze* 1QH 8:8 ([חית]), שׁתה *drink* Ezk 39:17, שׂבע *be satisfied* Ezk 39:17,

שׁכל pi. *bereave* Lv 26:22 Ezk 5:17 14:15, כרת hi. *cut off* Lv 26:22, מעט hi. *make few* Lv 26:22, עבד *serve* Jr 27:6, כבד

pi. *honour* Is 43$_{20}$, הלל pi. *praise* Ps 148$_{10}$, ברך *bless* 4QShir$^{b}$ 1$_{4}$ ([יב]רכו[הו]), שׂחק pi. *play* Jb 40$_{20}$, ילד *give birth* Ezk 31$_{6}$ (or del.).

<NOM CL> הִיא הַחַיָּה *it was the beast* Ezk 10$_{15.20}$, זֹאת הַחַיָּה *this is the beast* Lv 11$_{2}$, חַיּוֹת ... שָׁם *there (are) ... beasts* Ps 104$_{25}$, חַיָּתוֹ אֵין דֵּי עוֹלָה *its beasts are not a sufficiency of*, i.e. sufficient for, *a burnt offering* Is 40$_{16}$, חַיַּת הַשָּׂדֶה אֲשֶׁר בַּלְּבָנוֹן *the beast of the field that was in Lebanon* 2 K 14$_{9}$‖2 C 25$_{18}$, לַחַיָּה אֲשֶׁר בְּאַרְצֶךָ *for the beast that is in your land* Lv 25$_{7}$, כָּל־הַחַיָּה אֲשֶׁר־אִתְּךָ *every beast that is with you* Gn 8$_{17}$, לִי כָל־חַיְתוֹ־יָעַר *every beast of the forest is mine* Ps 50$_{10}$.

<OBJ> שׁבת hi. *cause to cease* Lv 26$_{6}$ Ezk 34$_{25}$, ראה *see* Ezk 1$_{15}$ 10$_{15.20}$, אסף *gather* Jr 12$_{9}$ (unless em.; see Subj.), שׁלח pi. *send* Lv 26$_{22(Sam)}$ (unless qal) Ezk 5$_{17}$ 14$_{21}$, hi. *send* Lv 26$_{22}$, יצא hi. *bring out* Gn 1$_{24}$ 8$_{17}$, עבר hi. *cause to pass* Ezk 14$_{15}$.

עשׂה *make* Gn 1$_{25}$ 3$_{1}$, יצר *form* Gn 2$_{19}$, שׁקה hi. *give drink to* Ps 104$_{11}$, שׂבע hi. *satisfy* Ezk 32$_{4}$, אכל *eat* Lv 11$_{2}$, נתן *give* 2 S 21$_{10}$ Jr 27$_{6}$ 28$_{14}$, זכר *remember* Gn 8$_{1}$, גער *rebuke* Ps 68$_{31}$=1QpPs 9$_{2}$ ([חיית]).

<CSTR> חַיַּת הָאָרֶץ *beast(s) of the earth* Gn 1$_{25.26}$ (if ins. חַיַּת) 1$_{30}$ 9$_{2.10.10}$ (or del.) 1 S 17$_{46}$ Ezk 29$_{5}$ 32$_{4(mss)}$ (L כָּל־הָאָרֶץ *of all the earth*) 34$_{28}$ Jb 5$_{22}$ 4QJub$^{a}$ 2$_{13}$ (חי[ת] [הארץ]), חַיְתוֹ אֶרֶץ *beast(s) of the earth* Gn 1$_{24}$ Zp 2$_{14}$ (if em.; see below) Ps 79$_{2}$ (אָרֶץ), חַיְתוֹ־גוֹי *beast(s) of a nation* Zp 2$_{14}$ (or em. גּוֹי to גַּיְא *of the valley* or הַשָּׂדֶה *of the field* or הָאָרֶץ *of the land*), חַיַּת הַשָּׂדֶה *beast(s) of the field* Gn 2$_{19.20}$ 3$_{1.14}$ Ex 23$_{11.29}$ Lv 26$_{22}$ Dt 7$_{22}$ 2 S 21$_{10}$ 2 K 14$_{9}$‖2 C 25$_{18}$ Is 43$_{20}$ Jr 12$_{9}$ 27$_{6}$ 28$_{14}$ Ezk 31$_{6.13}$ 34$_{5.8}$ 38$_{20}$ 39$_{4.17}$ Ho 2$_{14}$=4QpHos$^{a}$ 2$_{19}$ ([ח]ית השדה) Ho 2$_{20}$ 4$_{3}$ 13$_{8}$ Zp 2$_{14}$ (חַיְתוֹ; if em.; see above) Jb 5$_{23}$ 39$_{15}$ 40$_{20}$ 1QDM 3$_{1}$ ([חית הש[דה]]), חיות השדה *beasts of the field* 4Q418 172$_{8}$ (בשדה erased), חַיְתוֹ שָׂדָי *beast(s) of (the) field* Is 56$_{9}$ Ps 104$_{11}$, חַיְתוֹ־יָעַר *beast(s) of the forest* Is 56$_{9}$ (בַּיָּעַר) Ps 50$_{10}$ 104$_{20}$ 1QH 8$_{8}$ ([חית]), חַיַּת קָנֶה *beast of the reed(s)* Ps 68$_{31}$=1QpPs 9$_{2}$ ([חיית קנה]) 1QpPs 9$_{3}$ ([ק]נה), חית שן *beast of tooth*, i.e. hungry beast Si 12$_{13}$ (ה[י]ת) 39$_{30}$.

רוּחַ הַחַיָּה *spirit of the living being(s)* Ezk 1$_{20.21}$ (or em. both רוּחַ אַחַת *one spirit*) 10$_{17}$, רָאשֵׁי *heads of* Ezk 1$_{22}$ (mss הַחַיּוֹת *the beasts*), כַּנְפֵי הַחַיּוֹת *wings of the living beings* Ezk 3$_{13}$, גבי *backs of* 4QpsEzek$^{a}$ 4$_{10}$, דְּמוּת *likeness of* Ezk 1$_{13}$ (or em. דְּמוּת to מִתּוֹךְ *from among*; or בְּתוֹךְ *among*), דְּמוּת אַרְבַּע חַיּוֹת *likeness of four living beings* Ezk 1$_{5}$, מעשי חיה *works (consisting) of beasts* 1QM 10$_{14}$.

פְּרִיץ חַיּוֹת *ravenous one of (the) beasts* Is 35$_{9}$, צֵיד חַיָּה *game of beast(s)* Lv 17$_{13}$, נִבְלַת *carcass of* Lv 5$_{2}$.

כָּל־הַחַיָּה *every beast* Gn 1$_{28}$ (חַיָּה; Sam החיה) 7$_{14}$ 8$_{1.17.19}$ 9$_{5}$ (חַיָּה) Lv 11$_{27}$ CD 12$_{12}$ 1QH 8$_{19}$ (כול חיה), כָּל־חַיּוֹת *all beasts* Dn 8$_{4}$, כָּל־חַיַּת *every beast of* Gn 1$_{26}$ (if em.; see above) 1$_{30}$ 2$_{19.20}$ 3$_{1.14}$ (all three כֹּל) 9$_{2.10.10}$ (כֹּל) Jr 12$_{9}$ Ezk 31$_{6.13}$ (both כֹּל) 32$_{4(mss)}$ 34$_{5.8}$ 39$_{4(mss).17}$ (כֹּל) Jb 40$_{20}$ 1QH 8$_{8}$ (כול [חית]) 4QJub$^{a}$ 2$_{13}$ ([חי]ת), כָּל־חַיְתוֹ *every beast of* Is 56$_{9}$ (כֹּל) 56$_{9}$ Zp 2$_{14}$ Ps 50$_{10}$ 104$_{11.20}$, כל חַיָּתָם *all their beasts* Nm 35$_{3}$ 4QShir$^{b}$ 1$_{4}$ (כול).

<APP> נֶפֶשׁ *soul*, i.e. living *being* Gn 1$_{24}$, בְּהֵמָה *beast* Ps 50$_{10}$, שֶׁפֶט *judgment* Ezk 14$_{21}$, צִפּוֹר *bird* Ezk 39$_{17}$, עֵדֶר *herd* Zp 2$_{14}$.

<ADJ> אֶחָד *one* 4QpsEzek$^{a}$ 4$_{7}$, טָמֵא *unclean* Lv 5$_{2}$ GnzPs 1$_{5}$, רַע *harmful* Gn 37$_{20.33}$ Lv 26$_{6}$ Ezk 5$_{17}$ 14$_{15.21}$ 34$_{25}$ 11QBer 1$_{12}$, קָטָן *small* Ps 104$_{25}$, גָּדוֹל *great* Ps 104$_{25}$.

<PREP> לְ of direction, *to*, + נתן *give* Gn 1$_{30}$ 1 S 17$_{46}$ Ezk 29$_{5}$ 33$_{27}$ 39$_{4}$ Ps 74$_{19}$ (or em. לַמָּוֶת *to death* or לְהַוּוֹת *to destruction*) 79$_{2}$, אמר *say* Ezk 34$_{17}$, קרא *call*, i.e. name Gn 2$_{20}$; of benefit, *to, for* 1QLitPr 3.1$_{4}$ ([ח[י]ת]), + היה *be* Lv 25$_{7}$ Ezk 34$_{5.8}$ 1QH 8$_{19}$ 1QDM 3$_{1}$ ([לחית]), זבח *sacrifice* Ezk 39$_{17}$.

לְ of possession, *of, (belonging) to* Gn 9$_{10}$ (or del.) Zp 2$_{15}$ (מַרְבֵּץ לַחַיָּה *a lair of [wild] beasts*) perh. 4QapLam$^{a}$ 1.1$_{9}$ 4QJub$^{e}$ 21$_{6}$ ([ד]ם לחיה *blood of a beast*), + היה *be* Nm 35$_{3}$ Is 46$_{1}$; *(consisting) of* 11QT 60$_{4.8}$.

בְּ of accompaniment, *with*, אבל *mourn* Ho 4$_{3}$; of instrument, *with, by (means of)*, + שׁקץ pi. *make detestable* CD 12$_{12}$; partitive, *some of, (any)one of* Gn 7$_{21}$ 9$_{10}$ Lv 11$_{27}$; רדה בְּ *rule over* Gn 1$_{26}$ (if em.; see Cstr.) 1$_{28}$, משׁל בְּ hi. *cause to rule over* 4QJub$^{a}$ 2$_{14}$ ([וימשילו]).

כְּ *as*, + בקע pi. *tear* Ho 13$_{8}$ (if em.; see Subj.).

מִן of comparison, *(more) than* perh. 4Q418 172$_{8}$, + היה *be* Gn 3$_{1}$ (+ עָרוּם *crafty*), ארר pass. *be cursed* Gn 3$_{14}$; partitive *(some) of*, + אכל *eat* CD 12$_{12}$; ירא מִן *be afraid of* Jb 5$_{22}$, טהר מִן pi. *cleanse of* GnzPs 1$_{5}$; מִיַּד *from (the hand of)*, + דרשׁ *require* Gn 9$_{5}$.

אֶל *to* 4Q422 2$_{2a}$, + קרב *draw near* Si 12$_{13}$(ה[י]ת); עַל *upon*, + היה *be* Gn 9$_{2}$; עַד *unto* 11QJub 5$_{2}$ ([ה]חיה).

אֵצֶל *beside* Ezk $1_{15}$; בֵּין *between* 4QpsEzek$^{a}$ $4_{13}$, + הלך htp. *go to and fro* Ezk $1_{13}$, בדל hi. *separate* Lv $11_{47.47}$; בְּתוֹךְ *(in) among* Ezk $1_{13}$ (if em.; see Cstr.); מִתּוֹךְ *(from) among* Ezk $1_{13}$ (if em.; see Cstr.); מִפְּנֵי *because of,* + היה *be* desolate Ezk $14_{15}$; עִם *with,* + כרת *make covenant* Ho $2_{20}$.

<COLL> אַרְבַּע חַיּוֹת *four living beings* Ezk $1_5$ 4QpsEzek$^{a}$ $4_6$.

בְּהֵמָה||חַיָּה *beast* Gn $1_{24.25}$ $2_{20}$ $3_{14}$ $7_{14.21}$ $8_{1.17}$ (+) $9_{10}$ Lv $5_2$ $11_2$ (+) $25_7$ $26_{22}$ Nm $35_3$ Is $46_1$ Ezk $14_{21}$ Ps $50_{10}$ (both +) $148_{10}$ 4QJub$^{e}$ $21_6$ 4QD$^{e}$ $9.2_{15}$.

עוֹף||חַיָּה *fowl* Gn $1_{28.30}$ $2_{19.20}$ $7_{14.21}$ $8_{17}$ (+) $8_{19}$ $9_{2.10}$ Lv $17_{13}$ 1 S $17_{46}$ 2 S $21_{10}$ Ezk $29_5$ $31_{6.13}$ $32_4$ $38_{20}$ Ho $2_{20}$ $4_3$ Ps $79_2$ 4QJub$^{e}$ $21_6$ 4QapPs$^{b}$ $76_1$ (+) 4Q418 $206_3$ (+) 11QT $60_{4.8}$.

שֶׁרֶץ||חַיָּה *swarming creature* Gn $7_{21}$ Lv $5_2$, צִפּוֹר *bird* Gn $7_{14}$ Ezk $39_4$ (+) $39_{17}$ Ps $148_{10}$, עַיִט *bird of prey* Ezk $39_4$ (+), בֶּן־כָּנָף *son of a wing,* i.e. bird 1QM $10_{14}$ (+), בַּת יַעֲנָה *ostrich* Is $43_{20}$.

רֶמֶשׂ||חַיָּה *creeping thing* Gn $1_{24.25.30}$ (רמשׂ ptc.) $7_{14}$ $8_{17}$ (+) $8_{19}$ Ezk $38_{20}$ Ho $2_{20}$ Ps $104_{25}$ (+) $148_{10}$ CD $12_{12}$ 4QJub$^{a}$ $2_{14}$ 4Q422 $1_8$ (+), עַקְרָב *scorpion* Si $39_{30(B)}$ (+), פֶּתֶן *viper* Si $39_{30(B)}$ (+).

דָּג||חַיָּה *fish* Gn $9_2$ (+) Ezk $38_{20}$ 11QT $60_{4.8}$, דָּגָה *fish* Gn $1_{28}$, אַבִּיר *bull* Ps $68_{31}$ (+), עֵגֶל *calf* Ps $68_{31}$ (+), אַרְיֵה *lion* Is $35_9$ (+), לָבִיא *lion* Ho $13_8$ (+), פֶּרֶא *wild ass* Ps $104_{11}$ (+), תַּן *jackal* Is $43_{20}$.

אָדָם||חַיָּה *human being* Gn $7_{21}$ (+) $9_5$ Ezk $38_{20}$ 1QM $10_{14}$ (+), אִישׁ *man* Gn $9_5$ (+), גּוֹי *nation* Jr $28_{14}$ Ezk $34_{28}$ (both +), Noah (and family) Gn $7_{14}$ $8_1$ (both +), כְּרוּב *cherub* Ezk $10_{15.20}$ (both +).

חֶרֶב||חַיָּה *sword* Lv $26_6$ (+) Ezk $5_{17}$ $14_{21}$ $33_{27}$ Si $39_{30(B)}$ (both +), רָעָב *famine* Ezk $5_{17}$ $14_{21}$, דֶּבֶר *pestilence* Ezk $5_{17}$ (+) $14_{21}$ $33_{27}$ (+), דָּם *blood* Ezk $5_{17}$ (+), אֶרֶץ *land* Jr $27_6$ (+), יָם *sea* 4QShir$^{b}$ $1_4$ (+), רְכוּשׁ *property* Nm $35_3$.

Also 4QpsEzek$^{a}$ $4_6$.*

<SYN> בְּהֵמָה *beast,* רֶמֶשׂ *creeping thing,* עוֹף *fowl,* צִפּוֹר *bird,* בַּת יַעֲנָה *ostrich,* שֶׁרֶץ *swarming creature,* דָּג *fish,* דָּגָה *fish,* תַּן *jackal,* אָדָם *human being,* חֶרֶב *sword,* רָעָב *famine,* דֶּבֶר *pestilence,* רְכוּשׁ *property.*

→ חיה *live.*

[חַיָּה] II $_{12.1.1}$ n.f. **life**—cstr. חַיַּת; sf. חַיָּתִי, חַיָּתוֹ, חַיָּתָם—**1. life,** Ezk $7_{13.13}$ Ps $74_{19}$ $78_{50}$ $143_3$ (both + נֶפֶשׁ *soul*) Jb $33_{18.22}$ (both || נֶפֶשׁ) $33_{28}$ (+ נֶפֶשׁ) $36_{14}$ Si $51_6$ (|| נֶפֶשׁ) 4Q 418 $126.2_9$. **2. appetite,** Jb $33_{20}$ (|| נֶפֶשׁ *soul,* i.e. appetite; unless §1) $38_{39}$.

<SUBJ> ראה *see* Jb $33_{28}$, קרב *draw near* Jb $33_{22}$, נגע *reach* Si $51_6$, מות *die* Jb $36_{14}$, זהם pi. *loathe* Jb $33_{20}$, עבר *pass* Jb $33_{18}$. <NOM CL> בַּחַיִּים חַיָּתָם *their life is among the living* Ezk $7_{13}$. <OBJ> חזק hi. *strengthen* Ezk $7_{13}$ (if em.; see Coll.), מלט pi. *deliver* Ps $107_{20}$ (if em. מִשְּׁחִיתוֹתָם *from their pits* to מִשַּׁחַת חַיָּתָם *their life from the pit*), מלא pi. *fill,* i.e. satisfy Jb $38_{39}$, מצא *find* Is $57_{10}$, חשׂך *hold back* Jb $33_{18}$, סגר hi. *deliver up* Ps $78_{50}$, דכא pi. *crush* Ps $143_3$, שׁכח *forget* Ps $74_{19}$.

<CSTR> חַיַּת עֲנִיֶּיךָ *life of your poor ones* Ps $74_{19}$, חַיַּת כְּפִירִים *appetite of young lions* Jb $38_{39}$, חַיַּת יָדֵךְ *life,* i.e. vigour, *of your hand* Is $57_{10}$ (or em. דֵּי חַיָּתֵךְ *sufficiency of your life*); בני חיה *sons of life* 4Q418 $126.2_9$, דֵּי חַיָּתֵךְ *sufficiency of your life* Is $57_{10}$ (if em.; see above).

<COLL> אִישׁ בַּעֲוֹנוֹ חַיָּתוֹ לֹא יִתְחַזָּקוּ *a man will not strengthen himself as to his life because of his iniquity* Ezk $7_{13}$ (or em. יִתְחַזָּקוּ *they will strengthen themselves* to יַחֲזִיק *he will strengthen*). <SYN> נֶפֶשׁ *soul.*

→ חיה *live.*

חַיָּה III $_3$ n.f. **troop**—cstr. חַיַּת; sf. חַיָּתְךָ—**troop, band,** perh. **tribe,** <SUBJ> חנה *camp* 2 S $23_{13}$ (or em.; see Cstr.), ישׁב *dwell* perh. Ps $68_{11}$ (but prob. חַיָּתְךָ *your dwelling place*). <CSTR> חַיַּת פְּלִשְׁתִּים *band of Philistines* 2 S $23_{13}$ (or em. חַוַּת *camp of,* from חַוָּה IV). <PREP> לְ of direction, *(in)to,* + אסף ni. *be gathered* 2 S $23_{11}$ (or em. לַחַיָּה to לֶחֱיָה *to Lehi*).

→ חיה II *gather.*

[חַיָּה] IV $_1$ n.f. **dwelling place**—sf. חַיָּתְךָ—**dwelling place,** or perh. **land,** <PREP> בְּ of place, *in,* + ישׁב *dwell* Ps $68_{11}$ (חַיָּתְךָ יָשְׁבוּ־בָהּ *your dwelling place, they dwelt in it*; or em. חַיַּת / חַוַּת תָּכִין יֵשֶׁב בָּהּ *you created for a dwelling place/tent village for him to dwell in*; or em. חַיָּתְךָ to מִחְיָתְךָ *your sustenance,* they dwelt by means of it), שׁוב *go back* Ps $68_{11(mss)}$ (or em.).

**[חָיֶה]** 1 adj. **lively**—f. pl. חָיוֹת—**lively, lifegiving,* etc.** <NOM CL> used predicatively of עִבְרִי *Hebrew* Ex 1₁₉.
⇒ חיה *live.*

**[חַיָּהוּ]** pr.n.m. **Haiah,** T. Qasile ost. 1₃ (others [א]חיהו *Ahijah*).
⇒ חיה *live* + ׳י *Y.*

**חַיּוּת I** 1 n.f. **living,** <CSTR> אַלְמְנוּת חַיּוּת *widowhood of living,* i.e. life of widowhood 2 S 20₃ (or em. אַלְמָנוֹת חַיּוֹת *living widows*). ⇒ חיה *live.*

***חַיּוּת II** 1 n.f. **shame,** <CSTR> אַלְמְנוּת חַיּוּת *widowhood of shame* 2 S 20₃.

**חַיִּים I** 147.39.57.2 n.m.pl. **life**—Q חיים, חַיִּין; cstr. חַיֵּי; sf. חַיַּי (חַיָּי), חַיֶּיךָ (חַיֶּךָ), Q חייכה, Q חיכה (חייך Q), 2fs חַיָּיִכִי (Q חייך), חַיֵּיהֶם, חַיֵּיכֶם, חַיֵּינוּ, חַיֶּיהָ, (חייהו Q, חַיָּו) חַיָּיו—(distinction from pl. of חַי *living* not alw. clear) **life,** in ref. to duration of life (e.g. Gn 7₁₁ Lv 18₁₈ Dt 28₆₆ Ps 49₁₉), eternal life (Dn 12₂ Si 37₂₆ CD 3₂₀ 1QS 4₇ 4Q181 14.₆ 4Q418 69. 2₁₃ 4QShir[b] 2.14 6QHymn 2₂), quality of life (Jr 21₈ Ml 2₅ Ps 56₁₄ Jb 10₁₂ Si 30₁₅ 34₂₀), etc.; perh. also **livelihood,** Pr 27₂₇ (or em.; see Nom. Cl.).

<SUBJ> היה *be* Gn 23₁ (+ שָׁנָה *year*) Dt 28₆₆ Ml 2₅ (+ בְּרִית *covenant;* ‖ שָׁלוֹם *peace*) Pr 3₂₂ (+ תּוּשִׁיָּה *wisdom,* מְזִמָּה *discretion;* ‖ חֵן *favour,* i.e. adornment), נגע hi. *draw near to* Ps 88₄ (+ נֶפֶשׁ *soul*) 1QH 8₂₉ ([חו]יי), עמד *stand* 1QH 9₆, תלא pass. *be suspended* Dt 28₆₆, כלה *be finished* Ps 31₁₁ (‖ שָׁנָה *year*), תמם *be finished* perh. 4Q418 103.2₉, מתק *be sweet* Si 40₁₈.

<NOM CL> יראת ׳י חיים *the fear of Y. is life* Si 50₂₉, רוּחַ חַיָּי *my life is breath* Jb 7₇, עֵקֶב ... חַיִּים *(the) reward is ... life* Pr 22₄ (‖ עֹשֶׁר *riches,* כָּבוֹד *honour*), חיים עולם נחלתם *their inheritance is eternal life* 4Q418 69.2₁₃, חַיֵּי בְשָׂרִים לֵב מַרְפֵּא *a mind of health is life of the flesh,* i.e. a healthy mind is life to the flesh Pr 14₃₀, שמחת לבב הם חיי איש appar. *the life of a man is gladness of heart* Si 30₂₂, חיים למי היין *to whom is wine life?* Si 34₂₇, חיי איש מספר ימים *the life of a man is a (small) number of days* Si 37₂₅(B) (D אנוש *of a human being*), חיי ישורון ימי אין מספר *the life of Jeshurun is days without number* Si 37₂₅(D), שְׁנֵי חַיֵּי שָׂרָה *(these were) the years of the life of Sarah* Gn 23₁, חַיִּים לְנַעֲרוֹתֶיךָ *there is life,* or *livelihood, to your servant girls* Pr 27₂₇ (or em. חֻקִּים *prescribed portions*), חַיִּים בִּרְצוֹנוֹ *in his favour is life* Ps 30₆, בְּאֹרַח־צְדָקָה חַיִּים *life is in the path of the righteous* Pr 12₂₈ (+ מָוֶת *death*), בְּאוֹר־פְּנֵי־מֶלֶךְ חַיִּים *in the light of the face of the king there is life* Pr 16₁₅, חַיִּים בְּיַד־לָשׁוֹן *life is in the power of the tongue* Pr 18₂₁ (:: מָוֶת *death*), לְכָל־בָּהֶן חַיֵּי רוּחִי perh. *for everything in them is the life of my spirit* Is 38₁₆ (or em. עֲלֵיהֶם יִחְיוּ וּלְכָל־בָּהֶן חַיֵּי רוּחִי *by them do they live, and for everything in them is the life of my spirit* to עָלֶימוֹ יְחְיֶה־לְךָ לִבִּי וְהָנַח ׳י לְרוּחִי *by them my heart shall live for you, so give rest, O Y., to my spirit*), חיים ... מי׳ הוא *life ... is from Y.* Si 11₁₄ (+ טוֹב *good,* עֹשֶׁר *riches,* :: מָוֶת), לפני אדם חיים *before a human being is life* (:: מָוֶת), הוּא חַיֶּיךָ *it is your life* Dt 30₂₀ (+ אֹרֶךְ יָמֶיךָ *your length of days*) 1QDM 2₅ ([חיי]כה), sim. Dt 32₄₇ Pr 4₁₃, חַיִּים הֵם *they are life* Pr 4₂₂, מה חיים חסר היין *what is life (to) one who lacks wine?* Si 34₂₇, חיי מה לחסר תירוש *what life is there to one who lacks new wine?* Si 34₂₇, לָמָּה לִי חַיִּים *what to me is life?,* i.e. what use is my life? Gn 27₄₆, אין חייו למנות חיים *his life is not to be counted a life* Si 40₂₉(B).

<OBJ> חיה *live* Si 40₂₈(B), חפץ *desire* Ps 34₁₃ (‖ יוֹם *day*), אוה pi. *desire* Si 30₁₅ (+ רוח טובה *good spirit,* :: פָּז *gold*), אהב *love* Si 4₁₂, ברך pi. *bless* Si 41₁(B) (חיים למות מה [מ]ר יברך appar. *how bitter it is that one should bless a life for death;* Bmg הוי למות *alas for death!*), ראה *see,* i.e. observe Ec 9₉, עשׂה *do* Jb 10₁₂ (‖ חֶסֶד *loyalty*), עלה hi. *bring up* Jon 2₇, נתן *give,* i.e. place Dt 30₁₅ (‖ טוֹב *good*) 30₁₉ (both :: מָוֶת *death*) Ml 2₅ Jb 3₂₀ (‖ אוֹר *light*), מָצָא *find* Pr 8₃₅ 21₂₁ (‖ צְדָקָה *righteousness,* כָּבוֹד *honour*), מנה *count* Si 40₂₉, יסף hi. *add* Si 37₃₁, רבה hi. *increase* 4QRit Mar 24₃ ([הר]בות), עזר *help* 1QH 5₆, נצר *preserve* Ps 64₂, גאל *redeem* Ps 103₄ Lm 3₅₈, שלם hi. *cause to be at peace* Si 34₁₀, חזק pi. *strengthen* 1QS 3₁, שׂנא *hate* Ec 2₁₇, מאס *reject* Jb 9₂₁ (+ נֶפֶשׁ *soul*), מרר pi. *make bitter* Ex 1₁₄, אסף *gather,* i.e. take away Ps 26₉ (‖ נֶפֶשׁ), קפד pi. *roll up* Is 38₁₂, גער *rebuke* 1QH 9₁₁ (‖ שָׁלוֹם *peace,* תִּקְוָה *hope*), רמס *trample* Ps 7₆ (+ נֶפֶשׁ), צמת *exterminate* Lm 3₅₃, הפך *overturn* 1QH 2₁₇, שׂמח pi. *gladden* Ec 10₁₉, שׁאל *ask* Ps 21₅ (+ אֹרֶךְ יָמִים *length of days*), צוה pi. *command* Ps 133₃.

<CSTR> חַיֵּי אַבְרָהָם *life of Abraham* Gn 25$_{7}$, שָׂרָה *of Sarah* Gn 23$_{1.1}$, יִשְׁמָעֵאל *of Ishmael* Gn 25$_{17}$, נֹחַ *of Noah* Gn 7$_{11}$ (חַיֵּי־) 4QpGen$^{a}$ 1.1$_{1.4}$ 1.2$_{1}$ (all three נוח), חיי יוסף *life of Joseph* 2QJub$^{b}$ 46$_{1}$ ([חיי יוסף]) 46$_{2.2}$ ([חיי יוסף]).

חיי איש *life of a man* Si 30$_{22}$ 37$_{25(B)}$, גבר *of a man* 1QH 2$_{17}$, אנוש *of a human being* Si 37$_{25(D)}$, עם *of the people of* Israel Si 37$_{25(B)}$, ישורון *of Jeshurun* Si 37$_{25(Bmg, D)}$, עני *of a poor one* Si 4$_{1}$ (+ נֶפֶשׁ *soul*).

חיי שוא *life of vanity* Si 30$_{17}$, חַיֵּי הֶבְלֶךָ *life of your vanity*, i.e. your vain life Ec 9$_{9}$, הֶבְלוֹ *of his vanity* Ec 6$_{12}$.

חיי שר *life of navel*, i.e. body Si 30$_{15(B)}$ (Bmg חיי בשר/ שאר *life of the flesh*), חַיֵּי בְשָׂרִים *life of flesh* Pr 14$_{30}$, רוּחִי *of my spirit* Is 38$_{16}$ (or em.; see Nom. Cl.).

חיי יין ושכר *life of wine and strong drink* Si 40$_{18(B)}$, יתר *of abundance* of remuneration Si 40$_{18(D)}$, יותר *of abundance* of wisdom Si 40$_{18(Bmg)}$, מתן *of gift(s)*, i.e. life of a beggar Si 40$_{28(B)}$.

חַיֵּי עוֹלָם *life of eternity* Dn 12$_{2}$ Si 37$_{26}$ 4Q181 1$_{4.6}$ ([עו]ל[ם]) HN133/Frey 1536$_{3}$, חיי נצח *life of eternity* CD 3$_{20}$ 1QS 4$_{7}$ 4QShir$^{b}$ 2.1$_{4}$ 6QHymn 2$_{2}$, חיי מה *life of what?*, i.e. what life? Si 34$_{27}$.

אֵל חַיָּי *God of my life* Ps 42$_{9}$ (unless from חַי II *kinsfolk*; mss חַי *living* God), נִשְׁמַת חַיִּים *breath of life* Gn 2$_{7}$ 4QDibHam$^{a}$ 8$_{5}$ ([נשמת חיים]), רוּחַ *spirit of* Gn 6$_{17}$ 7$_{15.22}$ 4QD$^{a}$ 9.1$_{12}$ (ר[וח החיים) 4QD$^{g}$ 1.1$_{7}$ (רו[ח החיים]) 4Q418 126.2$_{8}$.

אוֹר הַחַיִּים *light of life* Ps 56$_{14}$ Jb 33$_{30}$ 1QS 3$_{7}$, עֵץ הַחַיִּים *tree of life* Gn 2$_{9}$ 3$_{22.24}$ Pr 3$_{18}$ 11$_{30}$ 13$_{12}$ 15$_{4}$ (all four עֵץ חַיִּים), עצי חיים *trees of life* 1QH 8$_{6}$, מעין חיים *fountain of life* 1QH 8$_{12}$ 1QH$^{b}$ 2$_{1}$, מְקוֹר חַיִּים *fountain of life* Ps 36$_{10}$ (הַחַיִּים; + אוֹר *light*) Pr 10$_{11}$ 13$_{14}$ 14$_{27}$ (both :: מָוֶת *death*) 16$_{22}$ 1QH 8$_{14}$, תּוֹצְאוֹת חַיִּים *sources of life* Pr 4$_{23}$.

דֶּרֶךְ הַחַיִּים *way of life* Jr 21$_{8}$ (:: מָוֶת *death*) Pr 6$_{23}$ (חַיִּים; + אוֹר *light*, נֵר *lamp*), דרכי חיים *ways of life* GnzPs 3$_{26}$ 4QD$^{e}$ 9.2$_{20}$ (:: שַׁחַת *pit*), אֹרַח חַיִּים *path of life* Ps 16$_{11}$ Pr 5$_{6}$ 15$_{24}$, אָרְחוֹת *paths of* Pr 2$_{19}$ 4Q525 15$_{8}$ (אורחות), מָעוֹז־חַיַּי *stronghold of my life* Ps 27$_{1}$ Si 51$_{1}$, גבול [חיי]ם *border of life* 1QH 7$_{15}$, גבול חייהו *border of his life* 4Q416 2.4$_{6}$.

חֻקּוֹת הַחַיִּים *the statutes of life* Ezk 33$_{15}$, תורת חיים *law of life* Si 45$_{5}$, סֵפֶר חַיִּים *book of life* Ps 69$_{29}$ 4QapPs$^{b}$ 31$_{8}$ (החי[י]ם) 4QDibHam$^{a}$ 1.6$_{14}$ (החיים), תּוֹכַחַת חַיִּים *reproof of life*, i.e. life-giving reproof Pr 15$_{31}$, שכל חיים *insight of life* 1QS 2$_{3}$.

צְרוֹר הַחַיִּים *bundle of life* 1 S 25$_{29}$ Si 6$_{16}$ (חיים) 1QH 2$_{20}$ Antinoopolis inscr.$_{3}$ (HN 119/Frey 1534), חרט חיים *stylus of life*, i.e. life-imparting stylus 1QM 12$_{3}$, שנות חיים *sleep of life*, i.e. healthy sleep Si 34$_{20}$, שלום חייו *peace of his life* Si 34$_{10}$, ארך חיים *length of life* 4Q298 1$_{3}$ ([אורך]) 4QMyst$^{a}$ 75$_{3}$.

יְמֵי־חַיֵּי *days of the life of* Ec 6$_{12}$ 9$_{9}$ 2QJub$^{b}$ 46$_{1}$ ([ימי חיי]) 46$_{2}$ ([ימ]י) 46$_{2}$ ([ימי חיי]), יְמֵי חַיָּי *days of my life* Ps 23$_{6}$ 27$_{4}$ 4QJub$^{d}$ 21$_{2}$ ([ימי חיי]) 4QJub$^{g}$ 25$_{9}$ (erased חיא), יְמֵי חַיֶּיךָ *days of your life* Gn 3$_{14.17}$ Dt 4$_{9}$ 6$_{2}$ 16$_{3}$ Jos 1$_{5}$ Ps 128$_{5}$ Si 3$_{12}$, יְמֵי חַיָּיו *days of his life* Dt 17$_{19}$ Jos 4$_{14}$ 1 S 1$_{11}$ 7$_{15}$ 1 K 5$_{1}$ 11$_{34}$ 15$_{5.6}$ 2 K 25$_{29.30}$||Jr 52$_{33(mss).34}$ (חַיָּו at 2 K 25$_{30}$ Jr 52$_{33[L]}$) Jr 52$_{34}$ Ec 5$_{17(Gnz)}$ (L חַיָּו) 5$_{19}$ 8$_{15}$ Si 3$_{13}$ 2QJub$^{a}$ 23$_{8}$ ([ימי חייו]), יְמֵי חַיֶּיהָ *days of her life* Pr 31$_{12(mss)}$ (L חַיֶּיהָ) 11QT 57$_{18}$, יְמֵי חַיֵּינוּ *days of our life* Is 38$_{20}$, יְמֵי חַיֵּיהֶם *days of their life* Ec 2$_{3}$.

שְׁנוֹת חַיִּים *years of life* Pr 3$_{2}$ (+ אֹרֶךְ יָמִים *length of days*, שָׁלוֹם *salvation*) 4$_{10}$ 9$_{11}$, שְׁנֵי חַיֵּי *years of the life of* Gn 23$_{1}$ 25$_{7.17}$ 47$_{9}$ Ex 6$_{16.18.20}$, שְׁנֵי חַיַּי *years of my life* Gn 47$_{9}$ 2 S 19$_{35}$, שְׁנֵי חַיֶּיךָ *years of your life* Gn 47$_{8}$, שְׁנֵי חַיָּיו *years of his life* Gn 47$_{28}$, כל חייכה *all your life* 4Q416 2.2$_{5}$.

<APP> בְּרָכָה *blessing* Dt 30$_{19}$ Ps 133$_{3}$, עולם *eternity* 4Q418 69.2$_{13}$.

<ADJ> רַע *bad* Si 30$_{17(Bmg).17(B)}$.

<PREP> לְ of direction, *to* Pr 10$_{16}$ (:: חַטָּאת *sin*) 10$_{17}$ 11$_{19}$ (+ מָוֶת *death*) 19$_{23}$ 4Q185 1.2$_{2}$ (דרך לחיים *a path towards life*) HN133/Frey 1536$_{3}$ (נשמתה לחיי עולם *may her spirit have eternal life*), + היה *be* 2 S 15$_{21}$ (:: מָוֶת), קִיץ hi. *awake* Dn 12$_{2}$ (:: חֶרְפָּה *reproach*); of benefit, *to, for* perh. 1QS 1$_{1}$, + כתב pass. *be written* Is 4$_{3}$; of possession, *of, (belonging) to* Gn 7$_{11}$ CD 3$_{20}$ 4Q181 1$_{4.6}$ 4QpGen$^{a}$ 1.1$_{1.4}$ 1.2$_{1}$; introducing object, + לעג *mock* Si 4$_{1}$, בוז *despise* 4Q416 2.2$_{21}$.

בְּ of time, *in, at, during* Ezk 7$_{13}$ Ps 17$_{14}$ Ec 6$_{12}$ 9$_{3.9}$ 1QS 4$_{7}$ perh. 4Q418 71$_{3}$ perh. 89$_{1}$ Mur 22 1$_{6}$, + רשע hi. *act wickedly* 1QH fr. 45$_{7}$, פרד ni. *be separated* 2 S 1$_{23}$ (:: מָוֶת *death*), עשׂה *do* Ec 3$_{12}$ Si 48$_{14}$ (:: מָוֶת), עמל *toil* 4Q417 1.1$_{10}$, לקח *take* 2 S 18$_{18}$ CD 4$_{21}$, עמד *stand* Si 37$_{26(D)}$, נצב hi. *set up* 2 S 18$_{18}$, מצא *find* 4Q418 103.2$_{9}$, גלה pi. *expose* nakedness Lv 18$_{18}$, נסה pi. *test* Si 37$_{27(B)}$ (Bmg, D בחמר *with wine*), מות hi. *put to death* Jg 16$_{30}$ (:: מָוֶת),

רמם ho. *be decayed* Si $10_9$, שׁלם hi. perh. *cause to be at peace* 4Q418 $88_2$, ברך pi. *bless* Ps $49_{19}$ $63_5$, pu. *be blessed* Ps $49_{19(mss)}$, שׁיר *sing* Ps $104_{33}$ (|| עוֹד *continuance*), הלל pi. *praise* Ps $146_2$ (|| עוֹד); of direction, *in(to)*, + שִׂים *place* Ps $66_9$.

בְּ introducing object, + אמן hi. *have assurance of* Dt $28_{66}$ Jb $24_{22}$ Si $16_{3(A)}$ (|| עָקֵב *heel*, i.e. end) 4QPrFêtes[b] $39_2$, בחר *choose* Dt $30_{19}$, קוץ *loathe* Gn $27_{46}$, קוט ni. *loathe* Jb $10_1$; of instrument, *by (means of)*, + שׁלח pi. *send* appar. Si $37_{18(Bmg, D)}$; מֹשׁל בְּ *rule over* Si $37_{18(B)}$ (+ טוֹב *good*, :: מָוֶת *death*), hi. *rule over* Si $30_{28}$.

מִן of comparison, *(more) than* Jon $4_{3.8}$ (both :: מָוֶת *death*) Ps $63_4$ Si $30_{17(B)}$ (:: מָוֶת) $30_{17(Bmg)}$ (:: נוּחָה *rest*) $30_{17(B)}$ (:: מָוֶת), + בחר ni. *be chosen* Jr $8_3$ (:: מָוֶת *death*).

עַל *according to*, + חלק *apportion* Si $16_{26(Segal)}$ ([חלק]).

נֹכַח *before, opposite to* Si $36_{14}$ (:: מָוֶת *death*).

לְמַעַן *for sake of*, + אהב *love* Dt $30_6$, הדר *honour* 4Q416 $2.3_{19}$.

<COLL> אין תוכחות בשׁ[אול] חיים *there are no arguments in Sheol (concerning) life* Si $41_{4(Bmg)}$ (B אישׁ perh. *the man* of arguments concerning life is in Sheol), חיים עולם *eternal life* 4Q418 $69.2_{13}$.

Also perh. 1Q26 $3_1$ 4QpsJub[b] $7_3$ 4Q417 $1.1_{21}$ 4Q418 $71_2$ perh. 4QSap[b] $18_2$ 4QPrFêtes[b] $39_1$ 5Q16 $5_3$.

<SYN> נֶפֶשׁ *soul*, עוֹד *continuance*, עָקֵב *heel*, i.e. end, תִּקְוָה *hope*, יוֹם *day*, שָׁנָה *year*, שָׁלוֹם *peace*, טוֹב *good*, צְדָקָה *righteousness*, אוֹר *light*, חֵן *favour*, חֶסֶד *loyalty*, עֹשֶׁר *riches*, כָּבוֹד *glory*.

<ANT> מָוֶת *death*, שַׁחַת *pit*, נוּחָה *rest*, חַטָּאת *sin*, חֶרְפָּה *reproach*, פַּז *gold*.*

→ חיה *live*.

[חַיִּים] II, see חַיִּם *Haim*.

חיל I 46.3.3 vb. **be in pain—Qal** 30.1.1 Pf. חָלָה, חַלְתִּי, חָלוּ, חַלְנוּ; impf. Si יחיל, 3fs תָּחִיל (Q תחול), Qr אוחילה (Kt, mss אָחוּלָה; mss אָחִילָה), יָחִילוּן, יָחִילוּ, תְּחִילִין, תָּחִילוּ; + waw וַיָּחֶל, וְחָלוּ, 3fs וַתָּחֶל (וַתָּחִל); impv. חִילִי (חוּלִי), חִילוּ; ptc. f.sg. חוֹלָה; inf. חוּל—**be in pain, be in labour** (Is $13_8$), **writhe, travail.**

<SUBJ> עַם *people* Dt $2_{25}$ (|| רגז *tremble*) Jr $5_{22}$ Jl $2_6$, Israelite(s) Is $26_{18}$ (+ הרה *be pregnant*), Babylonian(s) Is $13_8$, Egyptian Is $23_5$, Gaza Zc $9_5$, Pelusium Ezk $30_{16.16}$, people of Judah Si $48_{19}$, Zion Is $66_8$, הַר *mountain* Hb $3_{10}$, Jerusalem Is $54_1$ $66_7$, אִשָּׁה *woman* Is $45_{10}$, Jeremiah Jr $4_{19(Qr, mss)}$, Saul 1 S $31_3$||1 C $10_3$, בַּת *daughter* of Zion Mc $4_{10}$=4QpMic $1_2$, הָרָה *pregnant one* Is $26_{17}$ (+ זעק *cry out*), wicked Jr $5_3$, אֶרֶץ *earth* Ps $96_9$ $97_4$ Jr $51_{29}$ Ps $114_7$ 4QShir[b] $37_3$, יָם *sea* Is $23_4$ (+ ילד *bear child*), מַיִם *water* Ps $77_{17}$, לֵב *heart* Ps $55_5$.

<PREP> בְּ *in*, + קֶרֶב *innard* Ps $55_5$; מִן of cause, *on account of*, + יָרָה *archer* 1 C $10_3$, מוֹרֶה *archer* 1 S $31_3$; מִפְּנֵי *from (before), because of*, + י׳ Y. Ps $96_9$, Israelite(s) Dt $2_{25}$, עַם *people* Jl $2_6$.

<SYN> רגז *tremble*.

**Hi.** 2.1.2 Impf. יָחִיל; inf. Q החיל—**cause to tremble, cause writhing,** <SUBJ> י׳ *Y.* Ps $29_8$, קוֹל *voice* Si $43_{19}$, *voice* of Y. Ps $29_8$; subj. not specified, 1QH $3_8$ 4Q 393 $3_8$. <OBJ> מִדְבָּר *steppe* Ps $29_{8.8}$.

**Ho.** 1 Impf. יוּחַל—**be brought to birth,** <SUBJ> אֶרֶץ *land* Is $66_8$. <PREP> בְּ of time, *in, during*, + יוֹם *day* Is $66_8$.

**Polel** 7 Impf. יְחוֹלֵל, 3fs תְּחוֹלֵל (תְּחוֹלֶלְכֶם); + waw וַתְּחוֹלֵל; ptc. מְחֹלֶלְךָ; inf. חֹלֵל—**bring into labour, bring to birth,** <SUBJ> אֵל *God* Dt $32_{18}$, אֲדֹנָי *Lord* Ps $90_2$, Sarah Is $51_2$, רַב perh. *archer* Pr $26_{10}$, אַיָּלָה *hind* Jb $39_1$, רוּחַ *wind* Pr $25_{23}$, קוֹל *voice* of Y. Ps $29_9$.

<OBJ> עַם *people* Dt $32_{18}$, רדף ptc. *one who pursues* Is $51_2$, בקשׁ pi. *one who seeks* Is $51_2$, אַיָּלָה *hind* Ps $29_9$, אֶרֶץ *earth* Ps $90_2$, תֵּבֵל *world* Ps $90_2$, גֶּשֶׁם *rain* Pr $25_{23}$, כֹּל *everyone* Pr $26_{10}$.

**Polal** 4 Pf. חוֹלָלְתָּ, חוֹלָלְתִּי; impf. יְחוֹלָלוּ—**1. be brought to birth, 2. be brought to trembling,** <SUBJ> Job Jb $15_7$, worshipper Ps $51_7$, רְפָאִים *shades* Jb $26_5$, חָכְמָה *wisdom* Pr $8_{24.25}$.

<PREP> בְּ of accompaniment, *in, with*, + עָוֹן *iniquity* Ps $51_7$; לִפְנֵי *before*, + גִּבְעָה *hill* Jb $15_7$ Pr $8_{25}$.

**Htpol.** 1.1 Ptc. מִתְחוֹלֵל—**writhe in fear** (unless חיל IV *to heed*, htpol. *boast*), <SUBJ> רָשָׁע *wicked one* Jb $15_{20}$, *stubborn one* Si $3_{27}$.

**Htpalp.** 1 + waw וַתִּתְחַלְחַל—**writhe in fear,** <SUBJ> מַלְכָּה *queen* Est $4_4$.*

→ חִיל *pain*, חִילָה *pain*.

**חיל II** $_{5.0.1}$ vb. **wait—Qal** $_3$ Pf. חָלָה; + waw וַיָּחֶל, וַיָּחִילוּ—**wait,** <SUBJ> Noah Gn $8_{10}$ (or em. וַיְיַחֵל *and he waited,* i.e. יחל pi.), עֶבֶד *servant* Jg $3_{25}$ (or em. וַיּוֹחִילוּ/וַיְיַחֲלוּ *and they waited,* i.e. יחל pi./hi.), יֹשֶׁב female *inhabitant* Mc $1_{12}$ (or em. כִּי חָלָה *for she has waited* to מִי יִחֲלָה *who has waited?* or אֵיךְ יִחֲלָה *how has he waited?,* i.e. יחל pi.). <PREP> לְ wait *for,* + טוֹב *good* Mc $1_{12}$ (or em.; see Subj.). <COLL> + עוֹד שִׁבְעַת יָמִים *another seven days* Gn $8_{10}$ (or em.; see Subj.); + עַד בּוֹשׁ *unto shaming,* i.e. until they were ashamed Jg $3_{25}$ (or em.; see Subj.).

**Pol.** $_1$ Impf. תְּחוֹלֵל—**wait,** <SUBJ> Job Jb $35_{14}$ (or em. וּתְחוֹלֵל *and you shall wait* to וְהוֹחֵל *and wait,* i.e. יחל hi. impv.). <PREP> לְ wait *for,* + Y. Jb $35_{14}$ (or em.; see Subj.).

**Htpol.** $_{1.0.1}$ Impv. הִתְחוֹלֵל—**wait longingly,** <SUBJ> Israel Ps $37_7$=4QpPs$^a$ $1.1_{17}$ (or em. וְהוֹחֵל *and wait,* i.e. יחל hi.; || דמם *be silent*). <PREP> לְ wait *for,* + Y. Ps $37_7$=4QpPs$^a$ $1.1_{17}$ (or em.; see Subj.). <SYN> דמם *be silent.*

**חיל III** $_2$ vb. **endure—Qal** $_2$ Impf. יָחִילוּ, יָחִיל—**endure, prosper,** <SUBJ> דֶּרֶךְ *way* Ps $10_5$ (or em. יַצְלִיחַ *it will prosper* or יַצְלִיחוּ *they will prosper*), טוּב *goodness,* i.e. prosperity Jb $20_{21}$. <PREP> בְּ of time, *at,* + עֵת *time* Ps $10_5$.

→ חַיִל *strength.*

*חיל **IV** $_{3.1}$ vb. **take heed—Qal** $_2$ Pf. חָלוּ; ptc. חֹלֶה—**take heed** (unless חלה I *be weak* or IV *be anxious*), <SUBJ> עֹשֶׂה ptc. *one who does* justice Jr $5_3$ (+ נכה hi. *strike*), subj. not specified, 1 S $22_8$. <PREP> עַל *for, concerning* Saul 1 S $22_8$.

**Htpol.** $_{1.1}$ Ptc. מִתְחוֹלֵל—**boast** (unless חיל I *writhe,* htpol. *writhe in fear*), <SUBJ> רָשָׁע *wicked one* Jb $15_{20}$; subj. not specified, Si $3_{27}$.

**חַיִל** $_{267.11.32.1}$ n.m. **power**—חַיִל (חָיִל); cstr. חֵיל; sf. חֵילִי, חֵילֶךָ (חֵילְךָ), חֵילֵךְ, חֵילוֹ, חֵילָם; pl. חֲיָלִים; sf. חֵילֵהֶם—**1. power, might,** in ref. to human **strength, ability** of men (e.g. Gn $47_6$ Ex $18_{21.25}$ Jg $11_1$ 1 S $2_4$ 1 K $1_{42}$ Pr $31_{29}$ 1 C $9_{13}$), and of women (e.g. Pr $12_4$ $31_{10}$ Ru $3_{11}$), to sexual **power** (e.g. Pr $31_3$), to **strength** of horse (e.g. Ps $33_{17}$).

<SUBJ> הלך *go* 1 S $10_{26}$.

<NOM CL> י׳ אֲדֹנָי חֵילִי *Y. the Lord is my strength* Hb $3_{19}$, עוד בנ[ו ח]יל *strength is still with him* Si $41_{1(B)}$, אין לך חיל *you do not have strength* Si $7_{6(A)}$.

<OBJ> אזר pi. *gird with* 2 S $22_{40}$||Ps $18_{40}$ Ps $18_{33}$, גבר pi. *make mighty* Ec $10_{10}$, עבה pi. *increase* Si $6_{2(A)}$, עשׂה *do,* i.e. increase in might, perform mighty acts Nm $24_{18}$ 1 S $14_{48}$ Ps $60_{14}$ $108_{14}$ $118_{15.16}$ Pr $31_{29}$ Ru $4_{11}$ 1QM $6_6$ $11_{5.7}$ $12_{11}$ $19_3$, נתן *give* Jl $2_{22}$ Pr $31_3$, ברך *bless* Dt $33_{11}$ =4QMidrEschat$^a$ $1_{12}$ ([חילו]).

<CSTR> גִּבּוֹר חַיִל *mighty one of strength, warrior* Jg $11_1$ 1 S $9_1$ (חָיִל) $16_{18}$ 1 K $11_{28}$ (חָיִל) 2 K $5_1$ Ru $2_1$ 1 C $12_{29}$ (חָיִל) $28_1$ 2 C $13_3$ $17_{16}$ (all three חָיִל) $17_{17}$ $25_6$ (חָיִל) 2 C $32_{21}$ 1QM $11_1$, גִּבּוֹר הֶחָיִל *warrior* Jg $6_{12}$, גִּבּוֹרֵי חַיִל *warriors* Ne $11_{14}$ 1 C $5_{24}$ $7_{2.9}$ (חָיִל) $8_{40}$ (גִּבֹּרֵי) $9_{13}$ (חָיִל) $12_{22.26.31}$ $26_{6.31}$ 2 C $14_7$ (חָיִל) $17_{13.14}$ $25_{6(mss)}$ $26_{12}$ (חָיִל) CD $2_{17}$ 1QM $10_6$ 4QMyst$^a$ $10_2$ (גב[ו]רי חיל) 11QT $57_9$, גִּבּוֹרֵי הַחַיִל *warriors* Jos $1_{14}$ $6_2$ (הֶחָיִל) $8_3$ $10_7$ (הֶחָיִל) 2 K $15_{20}$ $24_{14}$ 1 C $12_9$ (גִּבֹּרֵי) 11QT $58_{17}$, גִּבּוֹרֵי חֲיָלִים *mighty ones of valour(s), warriors* 1 C $7_{5.7.11.40}$, גִּבּוֹרֵי הַחֲיָלִים *the warriors* 1 C $11_{26}$.

אִישׁ חַיִל *warrior* Jg $3_{29}$ 1 S $31_{12}$||1 C $10_{12}$ 2 S $23_{20(Qr)}$ $24_9$ 1 K $1_{42}$ 1 C $11_{22}$ $26_8$ (all six חָיִל) 4Q424 $3_8$, אַנְשֵׁי־חַיִל *men of ability* Gn $47_6$ Ex $18_{21.25}$ Jg $20_{44.46}$ (both חָיִל) 2 S $11_{16}$ Is $5_{22}$ Jr $48_{14}$ Na $2_4$ Ps $76_6$ Ne $11_6$ (חָיִל) Si $44_{6(B)}$ 1QM $2_8$ $6_{13}$ 4QapPs$^b$ $48_9$ ([אנשי חיל]).

אֵשֶׁת־חַיִל *woman of might, doughty woman* Pr $12_4$ $31_{10}$ Ru $3_{11}$ Si $26_{2(G)}$.

בֶּן־חַיִל *son of might,* i.e. mighty man 1 S $14_{52}$ $18_{17}$ 2 S $17_{10}$ 1 K $1_{52}$ Si $46_{1(B)}$, בְּנֵי־חַיִל *sons of might,* i.e. mighty men Dt $3_{18}$ Jg $18_2$ (חָיִל) 1 S $10_{26}$ (4Q Sam$^a$) 2 S $2_7$ (חָיִל) $13_{28}$ $17_{10}$ 2 K $2_{16}$ (both חָיִל) 1 C $5_{18}$ $26_7$ (both חָיִל) $26_{9.30.32}$ (both חָיִל) 2 C $26_{17}$ $28_6$ 1QM $15_7$ (בני חיל), בְּנֵי הֶחָיִל *the sons of might,* i.e. mighty men Jg $21_{10}$.

מָעוּזִּי חָיִל *my refuge of might* 2 S $22_{33}$ (4Q Sam$^a$ מאזרני *he who girds me*), יוֹם חֵילֶךָ *day of your power* Ps $110_3$, כֹּחַ חָיִל *strength of might* 2 C $26_{13}$, עוז חילכה *strength of your might* 1QM $11_5$, רֹב חֵילוֹ *greatness of his might* Ps $33_{17}$.

<PREP> לְ of possession, *(belonging) to* 2 C $26_{12}$; בְּ of

instrument, *by (means of)* Zc $4_6$ (|| כֹּחַ *strength*), + נוע hi. *make unsteady* Ps $59_{12}$; *in*, + בטח *trust* Si $16_{3(B)}$; מִן of direction, *from*, + הלך *go* Ps $84_8$.

<SYN> כֹּחַ *strength.*

<COLL> אָזְרוּ חָיִל *they gird on strength* 1 S $2_4$.

**2. property, wealth** (e.g. Gn $34_{29}$ Nm $31_9$ Dt $8_{18}$ $33_{11}$ Jb $20_{18}$), <SUBJ> היה *be* Zp $1_{13}$=4QpZeph $1_1$ ([חילם]), אסף pu. *be gathered together* Zc $14_{14}$, בוא *come* Is $60_5$, קום *arise* Jb $15_{29}$, נוב *prosper* Ps $62_{11}$.

<NOM CL> רַב חֵילִי *my wealth is great* Jb $15_{29}$, חיל מחיל *wealth is from wealth* Si $40_{13(B)mg}$, חיל מעול *wealth is from injustice* Si $40_{13(M)}$.

<OBJ> בוא hi. *bring* Is $60_{11}$=1QM $19_6$, שׁאף *pant for* Jb $5_5$, רבה hi. *make great* Ezk $28_5$, שׂגה hi. *make great* Ps $73_{12}$, עשׂה *do*, i.e. gain, wealth Dt $8_{17.18}$ Ezk $28_4$, חרם hi. *devote* Mc $4_{13}$, עזב *forsake* Ps $49_{11}$ Si $14_{15(A)}$, נתן *give* Jr $15_{13}$ $17_3$ (both || אוֹצָר *treasure*), נשׂא *raise* Is $8_4$ $30_6$ (|| אוֹצָר *treasure*), בלע *swallow* Jb $20_{15}$, שׁבה *take captive* Gn $34_{29}$ $Ob_{11}$, בזז *plunder* Nm $31_9$, שׁלל *plunder* Ezk $26_{12}$, אכל *eat*, i.e. enjoy Is $61_6$.

<CSTR> חֵיל גּוֹיִם *wealth of nations* Is $60_{5.11}$ $61_6$ Zc $14_{14}$ (כָּל־ *of all*) GnzPs $3_{15}$ 1QM $12_{14}$ (חיל גואים) $19_6$, הָעַמִּים *of the peoples* Is $10_{14}$, of Damascus Is $8_4$, גבורים *of the mighty* 1QH $10_{24}$, חוֹטֵא *of a sinner* Pr $13_{22}$, תְּמוּרָתוֹ *of its trading* Jb $20_{18}$, כָּל־חֵילָם *all their wealth* Gn $34_{29}$ Nm $31_9$.

<PREP> לְ introducing object, + מצא *find* Is $10_{14}$.

בְּ of instrument, *by (means of)*, + עלס *gain enjoyment* Jb $20_{18(Mss)}$; of cause, *on account of*, + גבה *be proud* Ezk $28_5$; *against*, + שׁלח *stretch out* hand $Ob_{13}$.

כְּ *as* Jb $20_{18}$.

מִן of direction, *from* Si $40_{13(Bmg)}$; עַל *upon, in*, + בטח *trust* Ps $49_7$, שׁען *depend* Si $5_{1(A)}$.

<SYN> אוֹצָר *treasure.*

<COLL> גָּבְרוּ חָיִל *they have become mighty in respect of wealth* Jb $21_7$.

**3. army** (e.g. Ex $14_4$ 1 S $17_{20}$ 2 K $6_{14}$ Jr $32_2$ Ezk $17_{17}$), <SUBJ> היה *be* 2 C $14_7$ $26_{11}$, נפץ *be scattered* 2 K $25_5$||Jr $52_8$, דכה *be crushed* Ps $10_{10(mss; Qr)}$, אזר htp. *gird oneself* 1QM $1_{13}$, בוא *come* 2 K $25_1$||Jr $52_4$ Jr $39_1$ 2 C $24_{23.24}$, סבב *go around* 2 K $6_{15}$, עלה *go up* 2 C $24_{23}$, ni. *withdraw* Jr $37_{11}$, מלט ni. *escape* 2 C $16_7$, יצא *go out* 1 S $17_{20}$ Jr $37_{5.7}$ 2 C $26_{11}$, שׁוב *go back* Jr $37_7$, רדף *pursue* Ex $14_9$ 2 K $25_5$||Jr $52_8$ Jr $39_5$, שׁלח pi. *send away* 2 C $24_{23}$, עשׂה *wage war* 2 C $26_{11}$, שׁטף *be washed away* Dn $11_{26}$, נפל *fall* 1 K $20_{25}$, צור *besiege* Jr $32_2$ $39_1$, לחם ni. *fight* Jr $34_{1.7}$, נתץ *tear down* 2 K $25_{10}$||Jr $52_{14}$, שׁחת hi. *destroy* 2 C $24_{23}$, אכל *eat* Jl $2_{25}$.

<NOM CL> הַחַיִל אֲשֶׁר אַחֲרֵיהֶם *the army that was after them* 1 K $20_{19}$, כָּל־חֵילוֹ ... חַלְלֵי־חֶרֶב *all his army ... (shall be) slain of the sword* Ezk $32_{31}$, עַל־יָדָם חֵיל צָבָא *under their control (was) an army of warriors* 2 C $26_{13}$, חֵילֵם עַל־חוֹמוֹתַיִךְ *their army was upon your walls* Ezk $2_{11}$ (+ בְּנֵי אַרְוַד *sons of Arvad*; if em. חֵילֵךְ *Helech*).

<OBJ> קבץ *assemble* 1 K $20_1$, יצא hi. *bring out* Is $43_{17}$ Ezk $38_4$, שׁלח *send* 2 K $6_{14}$, pi. *send away* Jl $2_{25}$, נהג *lead* 1 C $20_1$, עבד hi. *cause one to work* Ezk $29_{18}$, נתן *give* 2 C $17_2$ $24_{24}$ GnzPs $3_{15}$, ירה *throw down* Ex $15_4$, נער pi. *shake off* Ps $136_{15}$, נכה hi. *strike* 2 S $8_9$||1 C $18_9$ Jr $37_{10}$, אבד pi. *destroy* Est $8_{11}$, מנה *count* 1 K $20_{25}$, שׁאל *ask* Ezr $8_{22}$.

<CSTR> חֵיל מִצְרַיִם *army of Egypt* Dt $11_4$, כַּשְׂדִּים *of the Chaldaeans* 2 K $25_5$||Jr $52_8$ 2 K $25_{10}$||Jr $39_5$ $52_{14}$ Jr $35_{11}$ $37_{10.11}$, אֲרָם *of Syria* Jr $35_{11}$ 2 C $24_{23.24}$, הכתיים *of the Kittim* 1QM $17_{13}$ 1QpHab $9_7$ (הכתיאים), פָּרַס *of Persia* Est $1_3$, שֹׁמְרוֹן *of Samaria* Ne $3_{34}$, עָם *of the people* Est $8_{11}$, פַּרְעֹה *of Pharaoh* Ex $14_{28}$ Jr $37_{5.7.11}$ $46_2$, בליעל *of Belial* 1QM $1_{1.13}$ $15_2$ fr. $1_3$ ([חו]יל בליעל), מֶלֶךְ *of the king of* Jr $32_2$ $34_7$ 2 C $16_7$, הַצָּבָא *of the warriors* 1 C $20_1$, sim. 2 C $26_{13}$ (צָבָא), חילי עצומי *armies of the mighty of* 4Q393 $3_8$ (unless החילי is vb. חול hi.), כאים *of dejected ones* Ps $10_{10(Qr)}$, כָּבֵד *of heaviness*, i.e. great army 2 K $18_{17}$||Is $36_2$, ממשלתו *of his dominion* 1QM $18_1$ (ח[י]ל ממשלתו), כול *of all of* 1QM $19_{10}$.

הֲמוֹן חֲיָלִים *multitude of armies* Dn $11_{10}$, פְּקֻדֵי הַחַיִל *appointed ones of the army*, i.e. officers of the army Nm $31_{14}$ (פְּקוּדֵי הַחַיִל) 2 K $11_{15}$||2 C $23_{14}$ (פְּקוּדֵי), שַׂר־הַחַיִל *commander of the army* 2 S $24_2$, שָׂרֵי חַיִל *commanders of the army* Ne $2_9$ 2 C $33_{14}$, שָׂרֵי הֶחָיִל *commanders of the army* 2 S $24_{4.4}$ 2 K $9_5$ (both חַיִל), שָׂרֵי הַחֲיָלִים *commanders of the armies* 1 K $15_{20}$||2 C $16_4$ 2 K $25_{23.26}$ Jr $40_{7.13}$ $41_{11.13.16}$ $42_{1.8}$ $43_{4.5}$, גדודי חילו *troops of his army* 4QpNah $3.1_{10}$, רשע[י חיל]ה *wicked ones of its army* 4QpNah $3.4_1$, אנשי חילו *men of its army* 4QpIsa[a] $1_3$, אנשי [ה]ילה *men of its army* 4QpNah $3.3_{11}$, אַנְשֵׁי הַחַיִל

men of the army 2 K 24$_{16}$ Ec 12$_{3}$ (הֶחָיִל), אנושי החיל the men of the army 1QSa 1$_{28}$, קוֹל חַיִל sound of the army 2 K 7$_{6}$, יַד חַיִל hand of the army of Jr 34$_{21}$ 38$_{3}$ 1QpHab 9$_{7}$, רָב־חָיִל greatness of an army Ps 33$_{16}$ (|| כֹּחַ strength), כֹּל חַיִל all the army of Ex 14$_{28}$ 2 S 8$_{9}$||1 C 18$_{9}$ Jr 37$_{10}$ Est 8$_{11}$ (both כָּל־) 1QM 15$_{2}$ (כול חיל) 18$_{1}$ (כול [ח]יל) fr. 1$_{3}$ (כול ח[יל]), כָּל־חֵילֵךְ all your army Ezk 38$_{4}$, כָּל־חֵילוֹ all his army Ex 14$_{4.17}$ 1 K 20$_{1}$ 2 K 25$_{1}$||Jr 52$_{4}$ 2 K 25$_{5}$||Jr 52$_{8}$ Jr 34$_{1}$ 39$_{1}$ Ezk 32$_{31}$.

<APP> מִצְרַיִם Egypt Ex 14$_{9}$, קָהָל assembly Ezk 38$_{15}$, אַרְבֶּה locust Jl 2$_{25}$.

<ADJ> גָּדוֹל great 2 K 7$_{6}$ Ezk 17$_{17}$ 37$_{10}$ Jl 2$_{25}$ Dn 11$_{13.25.25}$, רַב great Ezk 38$_{15}$ Dn 11$_{10}$, כָּבֵד heavy, i.e. great 2 K 6$_{14}$ Is 36$_{2(mss)}$.

<PREP> לְ of direction, to, + עשׂה do Dt 11$_{4}$; of benefit, to, for, + היה be Ezk 29$_{18.19}$; as, + היה be 2 C 16$_{8}$; namely, + כסה pi. cover Ex 14$_{28}$.

בְּ of instrument, by (means of), + הלך go Jr 46$_{22}$, עשׂה do Ezk 17$_{17}$, עור hi. stir up Dn 11$_{25}$, אסר join battle 2 C 13$_{3}$, גרה htp. fight Dn 11$_{25}$; of accompaniment, in, with, + היה be Ezk 27$_{10}$, בוא come 1 K 10$_{2}$||2 C 9$_{1}$ Dn 11$_{13}$, יצא go out 2 C 14$_{8}$, שׁלח send 2 K 18$_{17}$||Is 36$_{2}$; of authority, over, + כבד ni. appear in one's glory Ex 14$_{4.17}$; against, + חלל hi. begin 1QM 1$_{1}$, שׁלח stretch out hand 1QM 17$_{13}$.

כְּ as, + מנה count 1 K 20$_{25}$.

אֶל against, + בוא come Dn 11$_{7}$.

עַל against, + נשׂא ni. be raised 1QM 18$_{1}$.

לִפְנֵי before, + נתן give Jl 2$_{11}$; מִפְּנֵי because of, on account of, + בוא come Jr 35$_{11}$, עלה ni. withdraw Jr 37$_{11}$.

**4. upper classes** of city (Ne 3$_{34}$), <PREP> לִפְנֵי before, + אמר say Ne 3$_{34}$.

Also Si 40$_{26}$ Arad ost. 24$_{4}$ 1QM 1$_{2}$ (ח[יל]) 1Q49 2$_{2}$ 4QTestim$_{19}$ perh. 4QM$^{a}$ 11.1$_{10}$.*

חֵיל I, see חֵל rampart.

חֵיל II, see חַיִל power.

חִיל 6 n.m. **1. pain, writhing. 2. birth** (if em. Ps 110$_{3}$; see Cstr.).

<SUBJ> בוא come Jr 22$_{23}$, אחז seize Ex 15$_{14}$ Ps 48$_{7}$, חזק hi. seize Jr 6$_{24}$ 50$_{43}$ Mc 4$_{9}$=4QpMic 1$_{2}$ ([החז]יקכה [חיל]). <CSTR> יוֹם חִילֶךָ day of your birth Ps 110$_{3}$ (if em. חֵילֶךָ day of your power). <APP> חֵבֶל labour pains Jr 22$_{23}$, צָרָה distress Jr 50$_{43}$, רְעָדָה trembling Ps 48$_{7}$. <COLL> חִיל כַּיּוֹלֵדָה pain like (that of) one giving birth Jr 6$_{24}$ 22$_{23}$ 50$_{43}$ Mc 4$_{9}$=4QpMic 1$_{2}$ ([חיל כיולדה]) Ps 48$_{7}$.*

⇒ חיל be in pain.

[חִילָא] 0.0.0.2 pr.n.m. **Hela, 1.** father of Malchijah, <CSTR> בן חילא son of Hela Seal 326 (8th/7th cent.). **2.** Seal 327 (8th–6th cent.).

חִילָה 1 n.f. **pain, anguish,** <SUBJ> חמל spare perh. Jb 6$_{10}$ (בְּחִילָה לֹא יַחְמֹל in pain [which] spares not, unless in pain [in which] he spares not). <PREP> בְּ of accompaniment, with, in, + סלד pi. recoil Jb 6$_{10}$.*

⇒ חיל be in pain.

חִילֵז 1 pl.n. **Hilez,** town in Judah. appar. ident. with חֹלֹן Holon at Jos 15$_{51}$ 21$_{15}$, <OBJ> נתן give 1 C 6$_{43}$ (mss חִילֵן Hilen).

חֵילֵךְ 1 pl.n. **Helech,** perh. Cilicia, north of the Tarsus Mountains in SE Asia Minor, <CSTR> בְּנֵי אַרְוַד וְחֵילֵךְ sons of Arvad and Helech Ezk 27$_{11}$ (or em. חֵילָם their army, from חַיִל).

חֵילָם 2 pl.n. **Helam**—+ ־ה of direction חֵלָאמָה (mss חֵלָמָה)—a town near the northern boundary of Gilead, <PREP> ־ה of direction, to, + בוא come 2 S 10$_{17}$. <COLL> וַיָּבֹאוּ חֵילָם and they came to Helam 2 S 10$_{16}$.

חֵילֹן, see חֹלֹן Helon.

חִילֵן 1 pl.n. **Hilen,** town in Judah. appar. ident. with חֹלֹן Holon at Jos 15$_{51}$ 21$_{15}$, <OBJ> נתן give 1 C 6$_{43(mss)}$ (L חִילֵז Hilez).

[חַיִּם] 0.0.0.2 pr.n.[m.] **Haim**—I חים (perh. חַיִּם as abbreviated form of אֲחִיָּם Ahijam)—**1.** <PREP> לְ of possession, (belonging) to Seal 8 (T. el-Far'ah, 8th cent.). **2.** Samaria coin 28 (fourth cent.). ⇒ חיה be alive.

***חין** 1 vb. **die—Qal pass.** or **Pu.** 1 Impf. יֻחַן—die (unless חנן ho. *be shown favour*), <SUBJ> רָשָׁע *wicked one* Is $26_{10}$ (1QIsa[a] יחון appar. חנן qal).

**[חִין]** 1 n.[m.] **gracefulness**—cstr. חִין—<OBJ> חרשׁ hi. *be silent (concerning)* Jb $41_4$ (or em.; see Cstr.). <CSTR> חִין עֶרְכּוֹ *gracefulness of his proportion* Jb $41_4$ (or em. חֵיל *strength of* his proportion, or אֵין עֵרֶךְ *there is no comparison*, or אֵין עֲרוֹךְ *one cannot compare*).

→ חנן *be gracious.*

**חַיִץ** 1.0.3 n.m. **wall**—Q חוץ—<SUBJ> נפל *fall* Ezk $13_{10}$. <OBJ> בנה *build* Ezk $13_{10}$, טוח *smear* Ezk $13_{10}$. <CSTR> בוני החיץ *builders of the wall* CD $4_{19}$ (החוץ; =6QD $1_1$ [בוני החיץ]) $8_{12(A).18(A)}$ (both החוץ; $=19_{25[B].31[B]}$ both החיץ).

**חִיצוֹן** 25.0.5.1 adj. **outer**—f. חִיצֹנָה (חִיצוֹנָה, חִצֹנָה, חִצוֹנָה, Q חיצונא), I חיצונית—**outer, external,** 1. used attributively of מָבוֹא *entrance*, appar. 2 K $16_{18}$ (perh. em. הַחִיצוֹנָה to הַחִיצוֹן), שַׁעַר *gate* Ezk $44_1$, חָצֵר *court* Ezk $10_5$ $40_{17.20.31.34.37}$ $42_{1.3}$ (+ פְּנִימִי *inner*) $42_{7.8.9.14}$ $44_{19.19}$ (or del.) $46_{20.21}$ Est $6_4$ 11QT $21_3$ ([בחצר חיצו]נה) $22_{13}$ $46_{3.5}$, חוֹמָה *wall* 2 C $33_{14}$, קִיר *wall* 11QT $37_9$, מְלָאכָה *work* Ne $11_{16}$ 1 C $26_{29}$, גַּיְא *valley* 3QTr $8_4$.

2. used as noun, **outer one,** of room of temple (1 K $6_{29.30}$ Ezk $41_{17}$), court of temple (Ezk $42_6$ [if em.], coffin (Beth Shearim tomb inscr. $17_1$), <CSTR> עַמּוּדֵי הַחִיצוֹנָה *pillars of the outer one* Ezk $42_6$ (if em. הַחֲצֵרוֹת *of the courts*). <APP> אֲרוֹן *ark*, i.e. coffin Beth Shearim tomb inscr. $17_1$ (:: פְּנִימִי *inner*). <PREP> לְ *in*, 1 K $6_{29.30}$; בְּ of place, *in* Ezk $41_{17}$ (:: פְּנִימִי *inner*).

<ANT> פְּנִימִי *inner.*

→ חוּץ *outside.*

**חֵיק** 38.1.7 n.m. **fold**—חֵק; cstr. חֵיק (חֵק); sf. חֵיקִי (חֵקִי), חֵיקְךָ (חֵיקֶךָ), חֵיקוֹ, חֵיקָהּ, חֵיקָם—**fold** of garment above belt, i.e. **bosom** (Ex $4_{6.6.7.7.7}$ Nm $11_{12}$ 2 S $12_3$ 1 K $3_{20}$ $17_{19}$ Is $40_{11}$ Pr $5_{20}$ $6_{27}$ $16_{33}$ $17_{23}$ $21_{14}$ Ru $4_{16}$ Ec $7_9$ La $2_{12}$); **hollow** of chariot (1 K $22_{35}$), **inner part of body** (Jb $19_{27}$), **channel** or **rim** around altar (Ezk $43_{13.17}$).

<NOM CL> חֵיק הָאַמָּה *the channel is a cubit (high)* Ezk $43_{13}$, הַחֵיק־לָהּ *the channel belongs to it* Ezk $43_{17}$.

<OBJ> חבק pi. *embrace* Pr $5_{20}$.

<CSTR> חֵיק אִמֹּתָם *bosom of their mothers* Lm $2_{12}$, אומנתי *of my nurse* 1QH $9_{31}$, אומניו *of its nurse* 1QH $7_{21}$, בְּנֵיהֶם *of their sons* Jr $32_{18}$, כְּסִילִים *of fools* Ec $7_9$, נָכְרִיָּה *of a foreign woman* Pr $5_{20}$, חֵיק הָרֶכֶב *hollow of the chariot* 1 K $22_{35}$, חֵיק הָאָרֶץ *channel of the earth*, i.e. channel in ground Ezk $43_{14}$; אִישׁ חֵיקָהּ *husband of her bosom* Dt $28_{56}$, אֵשֶׁת חֵיקֶךָ *wife of your bosom* Dt $13_7$ Si $9_1$, אשת חיקכה *wife of your bosom* 4Q416 $2.4_{5.13}$ 11QT $54_{20}$, אֵשֶׁת חֵיקוֹ *wife of his bosom* Dt $28_{54}$, שֹׁכֶבֶת חֵיקֶךָ *the woman who lies in your bosom* Mc $7_5$, קֶרֶב *inside of* Ps $74_{11}$.

<PREP> בְּ *in, into* Pr $21_{14}$ 1QH $9_{31}$ 4QHod[b] $7_3$ ([חיק]) 4QSap[a] $_6$, + כלה *be weak* Jb $19_{27}$, טול ho. *be cast* Pr $16_{33}$, בוא hi. *bring* Ex $4_{6.6}$, יצא hi. *bring out* Ex $4_7$, שׁוב hi. *bring back* Ex $4_{7.7}$, נתן *give*, i.e. place Gn $16_5$ 2 S $12_8$, שׁית *place* Ru $4_{16}$, נוח *settle* Ec $7_9$, שׁכב *lie* 2 S $12_3$ 1 K $1_2$, hi. *cause to lie* 1 K $3_{20.20}$, שׁעע pilp. *play* 1QH $7_{21}$, נשׂא *raise* Nm $11_{12}$ Is $40_{11}$ Ps $89_{51}$, חתה *fetch* Pr $6_{27}$, כול pilp. *sustain* 1QH $9_{36}$.

מִן of direction, *from* Ezk $43_{14}$, + לקח *take* 1 K $17_{19}$ Pr $17_{23}$; אֶל *to*, + מדד *measure* Is $65_{7(Qr)}$ Jr $32_{18}$, יצק *spread* 1 K $22_{35}$, שׁפך htp. *expire* Lm $2_{12}$; עַל *upon*, + שׁוב *go back* Ps $35_{13}$, hi. *bring back* Ps $79_{12}$, שׁלם pi. *repay* Is $65_6$.

<COLL> אֵשֶׁת חֵיקוֹ *wife of his bosom*, i.e. dearly beloved wife (and vars.) Dt $13_7$ $28_{54}$ Si $9_1$ 4Q416 $2.4_{5.13}$ 11QT $54_{20}$, אִישׁ חֵיקָהּ *husband of her bosom* Dt $28_{56}$; נתן בְּחֵיק *give into the bosom of* (so as to be close to) Gn $16_5$ 2 S $12_8$, בְּחֵיקֶךָ *in your bosom*, i.e. close to you (and vars.) 1 K $1_2$ Is $65_{6.7}$ Jr $32_{18}$ Mc $7_5$ Ps $35_{13}$ $74_{11}$ $79_{12}$ $89_{51}$.

Also perh. 4QPrFêtes[c] $134_1$.*

**[חִיר]** 0.0.1 n.[m.] **den**—sf. Q חירה—of lion, <OBJ> מלא pi. *fill* with prey 4QpNah $3.1_6$ ([וימלא]; =Na $2_{13}$ חֹרָיו *his holes*, from חֹר; ‖ מְעֹנָה *lair*). <SYN> מְעֹנָה *lair.*

**חִירָה** I 2 pr.n.m. **Hirah,** Adullamite and friend of Judah, <SUBJ> עלה *go up* Gn $38_{12}$. <NOM CL> שְׁמוֹ חִירָה *his name was Hirah* Gn $38_1$. <APP> רֵעַ *friend* Gn $38_{12}$, עֲדֻלָּמִי *Adullamite* Gn $38_{12}$.

* [**חִירָה**] II $_{3.0.1}$ n.f. **court**—Q חרה; pl. חִירֹת—**court, desert tract,** at 3QTr 8$_{4}$ perh. **rock** (Milik; others הדר *the circle,* i.e. הַדּוּר or הַדּוֹר [Allegro], or *the cattle-shed, the sheepfold,* i.e. הַדִּיר [Luria]).

<CSTR> פִּי הַחִירֹת *mouth,* i.e. entrance, *of desert tracks* Ex 14$_{2.9}$ Nm 33$_{7}$ (unless pl.n. *Pi-hahiroth*). <PREP> בְּ of place, *in* Ps 84$_{11}$ (if em. בָּחַרְתִּי *I chose* to בְּחִרְתִי *in my court;* + חָצֵר *court*); בְּתוֹךְ *within,* + חפר *dig* 3QTr 8$_{4}$.

**חִירוֹם**, see חִירָם *Hiram.*

**חִירָם** $_{33}$ pr.n.m. **Hiram**—חִירוֹם, חוּרָם—**1.** king of Tyre at time of David.

<SUBJ> היה *be* 1 K 5$_{15.24}$ (חִירוֹם), שׁלח *send* 2 S 5$_{11}$||1 C 14$_{1}$ (Qr חוּרָם, Kt חירם) 1 K 5$_{15.22}$ 9$_{14.27}$||2 C 8$_{18}$ (unless em. וַיִּשְׁלַח *and he sent* to וַיָּשֶׂם *and he placed*) 2 C 2$_{10.11}$, יצא *go out* 1 K 9$_{12}$, נשׂא pi. *raise,* i.e. support 1 K 9$_{11}$, שׂים *place* 1 K 5$_{23}$ 2 C 8$_{18}$ (if em.; see above), נתן *give* 1 K 5$_{24}$ 2 C 8$_{2}$, צוה pi. *command* 1 K 5$_{16}$, קרא *call* 1 K 9$_{12}$, אמר *say* 1 K 5$_{16.21}$||2 C 2$_{11}$ 1 K 5$_{22}$ 9$_{12}$ 2 C 2$_{10}$ (חוּרָם), שׁמע *hear* 1 K 5$_{15.21.22}$, ראה *see* 1 K 9$_{12}$, ידע *know* 1 K 5$_{16.16}$, עשׂה *do* 1 K 5$_{22}$ 2 C 2$_{2}$, אהב *love* 1 K 5$_{15}$, שׂמח *rejoice* 1 K 5$_{21}$, נפץ pi. *break in pieces* 1 K 5$_{22}$, כרת *cut* covenant 1 K 5$_{26}$. <CSTR> בְּנֵי חִירוֹם *sons of Hiram* 1 K 5$_{32}$, עַבְדֵי חוּרָם *servants of Hiram* 2 C 9$_{10.21}$ (both Qr) (both Kt חירם), אֳנִי חִירָם *ships of Hiram* 1 K 10$_{11.22}$. <APP> מֶלֶךְ *king* 2 S 5$_{11}$ 1 K 5$_{15}$ 9$_{11}$ 2 C 2$_{2.10}$. <PREP> לְ of direction, *to(wards),* + נתן *give* 1 K 5$_{16.25.25}$ 9$_{11.12.12}$, שׁלח *send* 2 C 2$_{2}$; אֶל *to(wards),* + שׁלח *send* 1 K 5$_{16}$||2 C 2$_{2}$ (L חוּרָם, mss חִירָם) 1 K 5$_{22.22}$; בֵּין *between,* + היה *be* 1 K 5$_{26}$.

**2.** skilled craftsman in time of King Hiram, son of Tyrian father and Israelite mother.

<SUBJ> בוא *come* 1 K 7$_{13}$, קום hi. *raise* 1 K 7$_{13.13.13}$, נתן *give* 1 K 7$_{13.13}$, עשׂה *do* 1 K 7$_{13+8t}$ 7$_{40}$ (חִירוֹם)||2 C 4$_{11}$ (unless em. עָשָׂה *he made* to עֶשֶׂר *ten*) 1 K 7$_{40.40}$||2 C 4$_{11.11 (both Qr)}$ (Kt חוּרָם) 1 K 7$_{45}$||2 C 4$_{16}$ (חוּרָם) 2 C 4$_{11}$, צור *fashion* 1 K 7$_{13}$, קרא *call* 1 K 7$_{13.13}$, מלא ni. *be filled* 1 K 7$_{13}$, כלה pi. *complete* 1 K 7$_{40}$||2 C 4$_{11 (Qr)}$ (Kt חוּרָם). <OBJ> לקח *take* 1 K 7$_{13}$. <APP> אָב *father* 2 C 2$_{12}$ 4$_{16}$, אִישׁ *man* 2 C 2$_{12}$ (חוּרָם), יוֹדֵעַ *one who knows* 2 C 2$_{12}$. <PREP> לְ introducing object, + שׁלח *send* 2 C 2$_{12}$.

**3.** son of Bela, descendant of Benjamin, <SUBJ> היה *be* 1 C 8$_{5}$ (חוּרָם). <APP> בֵּן *son* 1 C 8$_{5}$.

**חִישׁ**, see חושׁ I *hasten.*

**חִישׁ** $_{1}$ adv. **quickly,** with verb גוז *pass away* Ps 90$_{10}$.*
→ חושׁ *hasten.*

**חֵךְ** I $_{18.3.1}$ n.m. **palate**—Si חיך; sf. חִכִּי, חִכְּךָ (חִכֵּךְ), חִכֵּךְ, חִכּוֹ, חִכָּהּ, חִכָּם—**palate, roof of mouth, mouth,** in connection with taste (e.g. Ps 119$_{103}$ Jb 12$_{11}$ 20$_{13}$ 34$_{3}$ Pr 24$_{13}$ Ca 2$_{3}$ Si 36$_{24}$ 49$_{1}$), or speech (e.g. Jb 31$_{30}$ 33$_{2}$ Pr 5$_{3}$ 8$_{7}$ Si 6$_{5}$).

<SUBJ> טעם *taste* Jb 12$_{11}$ 34$_{3}$ (both + אֹזֶן *ear*) Si 36$_{24 (C)}$, בין *understand* Jb 6$_{30}$ (+ לָשׁוֹן *tongue*), בחן *test* Si 36$_{24 (B)}$ (|| לֵב *heart*), הגה *utter* Pr 8$_{7}$ (+ שָׂפָה *lip*), רבה hi. *multiply* Si 6$_{5}$, חטא *sin* Jb 31$_{30}$, יבשׁ *be dry* Ps 22$_{16}$ (if em. כֹּחִי *my strength* to חִכִּי *my palate*), ערב *be sweet* Si 6$_{5}$ (+ שׂפה *lip*), הלך *go* Ca 7$_{10}$ (if em. חִכֵּךְ כְּיֵין הַטּוֹב הוֹלֵךְ לְדוֹדִי appar. *your mouth is like good wine going to my beloved* to חִכֵּךְ הֹלֵךְ לְחִכִּי *your mouth goes to my mouth*).

<NOM CL> חָלָק מִשֶּׁמֶן חִכָּהּ *her palate is smoother than oil* Pr 5$_{3}$ (+ שָׂפָה *lip*), חִכּוֹ מַמְתַקִּים *his mouth is sweetness* Ca 5$_{16}$ (unless חֵךְ II *disposition*), חִכֵּךְ כְּיֵין הַטּוֹב *your mouth is like good wine* Ca 7$_{10}$ (or em.; see Subj.).

<OBJ> נתן *give,* i.e. allow Jb 31$_{30}$.

<PREP> לְ of benefit, *to, for* Ca 2$_{3}$, + מליץ ni. *be smooth* Ps 119$_{103}$ (+ פֶּה *mouth*), טעם *taste* Jb 12$_{11}$; of direction, *to,* + דבק *cleave* Ps 137$_{6}$ Jb 29$_{10}$ 1QH 5$_{31}$, הלך *go* Ca 7$_{10}$ (if em.; see Subj.); בְּ of place, *in,* + מתק hi. *taste sweet* Si 49$_{1}$, דבר pi. *speak* Jb 33$_{2}$ (+ פֶּה *mouth*); אֶל *to* Ho 8$_{1}$, + דבק *cleave* Lm 4$_{4}$, hi. *cause to cleave* Ezk 3$_{26}$; עַל *upon* Pr 24$_{13}$; בְּתוֹךְ *within,* + מנע *withhold* Jb 20$_{13}$ (+ פֶּה *mouth,* לָשׁוֹן *tongue*).

<SYN> לֵב *heart.*

**חֵךְ** II $_{1}$ n.[m.] **disposition,** <NOM CL> חִכּוֹ מַמְתַקִּים *his disposition is sweetness* Ca 5$_{16}$ (unless חֵךְ I *palate*).

**חכה** $_{14.0.7}$ vb. **wait—Qal** $_{1.0.3}$ Ptc. חוֹכֵי (Q חכי)—**wait for.**

<SUBJ> pious, Is 30$_{18}$=4QpIsa[c] 23.2$_{9}$ (אַשְׁרֵי כָּל־חוֹכֵי לוֹ *happy are all those who wait for him*) 4QapPs[b] 31$_{7}$

([תגיר] לחכי עלידי חרב *you will hand over those who wait for me to the sword*) 4QShirShabb[d] $1.1_{23}$ (וברך לכול חוכי לו *and he will bless all who wait for him*)=4QShirShabb[f] $13_{6}$ ([וברך] לכול ח]וכי[ן לו[ן]).

<PREP> לְ wait *for*, + יי *Y.* Is $38_{18}$ 4QShirShabb[d] $1.1_{23}$, psalmist 4QapPs[b] $31_{7}$.

**Pi.** $_{13.0.4}$ Pf. חִכָּה, חִכְּתָה, חִכִּיתִי, חִכּוּ; impf. יְחַכֶּה, 2ms תְּחַכֶּה; + waw וַתְּחַכֶּה; impv. חַכֵּה, חַכּוּ; ptc. מְחַכֶּה (מְחַכֵּה־), מְחַכִּים, mss מְחַכֵּי; inf. חַכֵּי—**wait (for), delay** (intrans.), **lie in wait** (Ho $6_{9}$; or em.; see Subj.), <SUBJ> Y. Is $30_{18}$=4QpIsa[c] $23.2_{8}$ (+ לַחֲנַנְכֶם *to be gracious to you*), Israel Is $64_{3}$, Elihu Jb $32_{4}$, Habakkuk Hb $2_{3}$=1QpHab $7_{9}$, Isaiah Is $8_{17}$ (+ קוה pi. *wait*), Israel Zp $3_{8}$, אִישׁ *man* 2 K $7_{9}$ Ho $6_{9}$=4QpIsa[c] $23.2_{14}$ (or em. כְּחַכֵּי *as the lying in wait of* [4QpIsa[c] $23.2_{14}$ כיחכה appar. *as he lies in wait*] to כְּחֶבְא *as the hiding of*, or כְּחֶבֶר *as a company of*, or בְּכֹחַ *with the strength of*; or em. כְּחַכֵּי אִישׁ *as the lying in wait of men of* to יְכֻחֲדוּ כְּאִישׁ *they will be destroyed like men of*, or מְחַכֶּה כְאִישׁ *waiting like men of*), אָב *father* Ps $106_{13}$, בֵּן *son* of prophets 2 K $9_{3}$ (:: נוס *flee*), פעל ptc. *one who does* evil Ho $6_{9}$ (if em.; see above), עָמֵל *sufferer* Jb $3_{20}$, מַר *bitter one* Jb $3_{20}$, pious Dn $12_{12}$, נֶפֶשׁ *soul* Ps $33_{20}$, עִיר *city* Zp $3_{8}$ (if em. חַכּוּ *wait* [cpl] to חַכִּי *wait* [fs]).

<OBJ> Job Jb $32_{4}$.

<PREP> לְ wait *for*, + Y. Is $8_{17}$ $64_{3}$ Zp $3_{8}$ Ps $33_{20}$, חָזוֹן *vision* Hb $2_{3}$=1QpHab $7_{9}$, עֵצָה *counsel* Ps $106_{13}$, יוֹם *day* Zp $3_{8}$, מָוֶת *death* Jb $3_{20}$; בְּ of accompaniment, *with*, + דָּבָר *word* Jb $32_{4}$; כְּ *as*, + אִישׁ *man* Ho $6_{9}$ (if em.; see Subj.); עַד *until*, + אוֹר *light* of morning 2 K $7_{9}$.

Also perh. 4Q418 $34_{3}$.*

**חַכָּה** $_{3}$ n.f. **fish-hook,** <OBJ> שׁלך hi. *cast* Is $19_{8}$ (+ מִכְמֹרֶת *net*). <PREP> בְּ of instrument, *by (means of), with,* + עלה hi. *bring up* Hb $1_{15}$=1QpHab $5_{13}$ (בח]כה]; + חֵרֶם *net*, מִכְמֶרֶת *net*), משׁך *draw* Jb $40_{25}$ (+ חֶבֶל *cord*).

**[חָכוֹר]** $_{0.0.1}$ n.[m.] **rent,** i.e. money received in payment of rent, <OBJ> חכר *take in rent* 5/6ḤevBA 45 fr. 2.

<PREP> מִן partitive, *(some) of* 5/6ḤevBA 45 fr. 2.

⇒ חכר *rent.*

**חֲכִילָה** $_{3}$ pl.n. **Hachilah,** hill in Judaean desert, south of Jeshimon (1 S $23_{19}$) or east of Jeshimon (1 S $26_{1.3}$), perh. Ḍahret el-Kōla, 12 km ESE of Hebron, <CSTR> גִּבְעַת הַחֲכִילָה *hill of Hachilah* 1 S $23_{19}$ (mss הַחֲוִילָה *Havila*) $26_{1}$ (mss הַחֲבִילָה *Habilah*, and הַחֲוִילָה *Havila*) $26_{3}$ (mss הַחֲבִילָה).

**[חָכִיר]** $_{0.0.3}$ n.[m.] **rent,** i.e. money paid as rent, <OBJ> שׁקל *weigh*, i.e. pay Mur 24 $2_{15}$ (חכי]ר]) $3_{13}$ (חכ]יר]) $4_{14}$ ([חכיר]), מדד *measure* Mur 24 $5_{10}$. <PREP> בְּ perh. *in (exchange for)*, + חכר *rent* Mur 24 $1_{7}$ ([חכרתי בחכיר]) $2_{8}$ ([חכרת]י) $3_{8}$ (בחכ]יר]) $6_{7}$. ⇒ חכר *rent.*

**[חֲכִירוּת]** $_{0.0.0.1}$ n.f. **rent,** i.e. money paid as rent, <PREP> בְּ perh. *in (exchange for)*, + חכר *rent* Mur 24 $5_{6}$ (בחרתי; appar. error for בחכרתי); מִן *from* Mur 11.1 ([מ]ן חכר]ת]). ⇒ חכר *rent.*

**[חֵכֶל]** $_{0.0.0.1}$ pr.n.m. **Hechel,** father of Jeconiah, <CSTR> בן חכל *son of Hechel* Seal 746 (c. 700).

**חֲכַלְיָה** $_{2}$ pr.n.m. **Hacaliah, 1.** father of Nehemiah, <CSTR> בֶּן־חֲכַלְיָה *son of Hacaliah* Ne $1_{1}$ $10_{2}$. **2.** Lachish ost. $20_{2}$ (חכלי]הו]).

**[חַכְלִילוּת]** $_{1}$ n.f. **dullness**—cstr. חַכְלִלוּת—**dullness,** or perh. **sparkle,** or **redness,** of eyes after drinking wine, <NOM CL> לְמִי חַכְלִלוּת עֵינָיִם *to whom is there dullness of eyes?* Pr $23_{29}$ (+ פֶּצַע *wound*). <CSTR> חַכְלִלוּת עֵינָיִם *dullness of eyes* Pr $23_{29}$.

**[חַכְלִילִי]** $_{1}$ adj. **dull**—cstr. חַכְלִילִי—used as noun, **dull (one),** or perh. **sparkling (one),** or **red (one),** <CSTR> חַכְלִילִי עֵינַיִם *dull/sparkling/red one of eyes*, i.e. one who has dull/sparkling/red eyes Gn $49_{12}$ (+ מִיַּיִן *on account of wine*, or duller/redder *than wine*; ‖ לְבֶן *white*).

**חכם** $_{28.15.3}$ vb. **be wise**—**Qal** $_{18.6.2}$ Pf. חָכַם, חָכְמָה, חָכַמְתָּ, חָכַמְתִּי, חָכְמוּ; impf. יֶחְכַּם (יֶחְכָּם) תֶּחְכַּם (תֶּחְכָּם), אֶחְכָּם (אֶחְכָּמָה), יֶחְכָּמוּ; impv. חֲכַם (חֲכָם), חֲכָמוּ; ptc. Q חוכום—**be wise, act wisely,** <SUBJ> Sidon Zc $9_{2}$, Tyre Zc $9_{2}$, Israelite(s) Dt $32_{29}$ (+ שׂכל hi. *understand*), Solomon 1 K

$5_{11}$ Si $47_{14(B)}$, Koheleth Ec $2_{15.19}$ $7_{23}$, בֵּן *son* Pr $8_{33}$ $9_{12}$ $23_{19}$ $27_{11}$, רַב *great one* Jb $32_9$ (or em. רַבֵּי יָמִים *great ones of days*, i.e. aged ones), חָכָם *wise one* Pr $9_9$ Si $37_{22(B).23(D)}$, חָסִיד *pious one* 4Q370 $2_6$ ([חכמו]), פֶּתִי *simple one* Pr $21_{11}$, עָצֵל *lazy one* Pr $6_6$, הלך ptc. *one who goes* Pr $13_{20(Qr)}$, שׁגה ptc. *one who goes astray* Pr $20_1$, שׂנא ptc. *one who hates* Si $36_{2(B)}$, נתן ptc. *one who gives* Si $50_{28(B)}$, שׁמר ptc. *one who keeps* 4Q370 $2_6$ ([חכמו]), עבד *one who serves* GnzPs $2_{17}$, רֹפֵא *doctor* Si $38_{2(B)}$, addressee of proverb Pr $19_{20}$, לֵב *heart* Pr $23_{15}$; subj. not specified, 4QShir$^b$ $3_4$.

<PREP> לְ of benefit, *to, for*, + בֵּן *son* Pr $9_{12}$; בְּ of time, *in, at, during*, + נַעַר *youth* Si $47_{14(B)}$, אַחֲרִית *end* Pr $19_{20}$; of instrument, *by (means of)*, + פֶּסֶל *idol* GnzPs $2_{17}$; מִן of comparison, *(more) than*, + אָדָם *human being* 1 K $5_{11}$; *by (means of)*, + גְּבוּרָה *mighty act* 4Q370 $2_6$; תַּחַת *under*, + שֶׁמֶשׁ *sun* Ec $2_{19}$.

<COLL> חֲכָמָה מְאֹד *she is exceedingly wise* Zc $9_2$.

**Ni.** 0.3 Pf. Si נחכם—**be wise, show oneself wise,** <SUBJ> חָכָם *wise one* Si $37_{19(B).22(D).23(B)}$.

**Pi.** 3.1 Impf. יְחַכֵּם (Si יחכמך ,יְחַכְּמֵנוּ), תְּחַכְּמֵנִי—**make wise,** <SUBJ> אֱלוֹהַּ *God* Jb $35_{11}$, עֶלְיוֹן *Most High* Si $6_{37(A)}$, Joseph Ps $105_{22}$, מִצְוָה *commandment* Ps $119_{98}$. <OBJ> Elihu Jb $35_{11}$, Job Jb $35_{11}$, זָקֵן *elder* Ps $105_{22}$, בֵּן *son* Si $6_{37(A)}$, רֵעַ *friend* Jb $35_{11}$, worshipper Ps $119_{98}$. <PREP> מִן of comparison, *(more) than*, + אֹיֵב *enemy* Ps $119_{98}$, עוֹף *bird* Jb $35_{11}$.

**Pu.** 2 Ptc. מְחֻכָּם ,מְחֻכָּמִים—**be made wise,** <SUBJ> חָכָם *wise one* Pr $30_{24}$, חֹבֵר *conjuror* Ps $58_6$.

**Hi.** 1.0.1 Ptc. מַחְכִּימַת—**make wise,** <SUBJ> עֵדוּת *testimony* Ps $19_8$; subj. not specified, 4QapPs$^a$ $4_3$. <OBJ> פֶּתִי *simple one* Ps $19_8$.

**Htp.** 3.5 Impf. Si יתחכם ,תִּתְחַכַּם ,נִתְחַכְּמָה—**make oneself wise,** <SUBJ> עַם *people* Ex $1_{10}$, מֶלֶךְ *king* of Egypt Ex $1_{10}$, בֵּן *son* Si $6_{32(A)}$ $10_{26(A)}$ $35_{4(B)}$, תמך ptc. *one who holds* Si $38_{25(B)}$, הוּא *he* Si $38_{24(B)}$, addressee Ec $7_{16}$.

<PREP> לְ of benefit, *to, for*, + עַם *people* Ex $1_{10}$, בֵּן *son* of Israel Ex $1_{10}$.

<COLL> אַל־תִּתְחַכַּם יוֹתֵר *do not make yourself excessively wise* Ec $7_{16}$.*

→ חָכָם *wise*, חָכְמָה *wisdom*, חָכְמוֹת *wisdom*.

חָכָם 138.20.14 adj. **wise**—fem. חֲכָמָה; cstr. masc. חֲכַם, fem. חַכְמַת; pl. masc. חֲכָמִים; cstr. masc. חַכְמֵי, fem. חַכְמוֹת; sf. חֲכָמֶיהָ ,חֲכָמָיו ,חֲכָמַיִךְ ,חֲכָמֶיךָ—**wise, competent** in politics, administration (e.g. Gn $41_{33}$ 1 K $5_{21}$ Pr $20_{26}$), **astute** (e.g. 2 S $13_3$), **prudent** (e.g. Dt $4_6$ Jr $9_{11}$ Ho $13_{13}$), **skilful** (e.g. Is $3_3$ $40_{20}$ 2 C $2_{6.12}$), etc.

**1.** used attributively of אִישׁ *man* Gn $41_{33}$ (|| נָבוֹן *intelligent*) Ex $36_{1.2}$ (both חֲכַם־לֵב *wise of heart*) Dt $1_{13}$ (|| נָבוֹן) $1_{15}$ (both || יָדוּעַ *knowledgeable*) 2 S $13_3$ 1 K $2_9$ Jr $9_{11}$ (+ אֲשֶׁר דִּבֶּר פִּי־י׳ אֵלָיו *one to whom the mouth of Y. has spoken*) Pr $16_{14}$ $26_{12}$ $29_9$ (:: אֱוִיל *foolish*) Ec $9_{15}$ (|| מִסְכֵּן *poor*) 2 C $2_{6.12}$ Si $10_{23(A)}$ ([ח]כם]; B חָמָס man of *violence*) $35_{17(B)}$ (Bmg חָמָס) $35_{18}$, גֶּבֶר *man* Jb $34_{34}$ Pr $24_5$ (or em. גבר *be strong*, as §3), אִשָּׁה *woman* Ex $35_{25}$ (חַכְמַת־לֵב *wise of heart*) 2 S $14_2$ $20_{16}$, יֶלֶד *child* Ec $4_{13}$ (|| מִסְכֵּן), בֵּן *son* 1 K $5_{21}$ Ho $13_{13}$ Pr $10_1$ (+ כְּסִיל *fool*) $13_1$ (+ לֵץ *scoffer*) $15_{20}$ (+ כְּסִיל) 2 C $2_{11}$, יכח hi. ptc. *one who reproves* Pr $25_{12}$, חָרָשׁ *artisan* Is $40_{20}$, מֶלֶךְ *king* Pr $20_{26}$, עַם *people* Dt $4_6$ (|| נָבוֹן *intelligent*) $32_6$ (:: נָבָל *foolish*), לֵב *heart* 1 K $3_{12}$ (|| נָבוֹן) Si $3_{29}$, פֶּה *mouth* Si $15_{10(A)}$.

**2a.** in nom. cl., used predicatively of צֹר *Tyre* Ezk $28_3$, ׳׳ *Y.* Is $31_2$, אִישׁ rich *man* Pr $28_{11}$, אָדוֹן *lord*, i.e. David 2 S $14_{20}$, מֹשֵׁל *ruler* Si $9_{17}$ (מושׁ[ל]), בֵּן *son* Jr $4_{22}$ (+ נָבוֹן *intelligent*), עָצֵל *idler* Pr $26_{16}$ (or em. לֵץ *scoffer*), עַם *people* Jr $8_8$ (+ תּוֹרַת י׳ אִתָּנוּ *the law of Y. is with us*), מִי *who?* Ho $14_{10}$ (|| נָבוֹן, + יָשָׁר *upright*, צַדִּיק *righteous*) Ps $107_{43}$ 4Q411 $1_7$.

**2b.** with היה *be*, used predicatively of דָּוִד *David* 11QPs$^a$ $27_2$, קֹהֶלֶת *Koheleth* Ec $12_9$, בֵּן *son* Pr $3_7$ 11QPs$^a$ $27_2$, כְּסִיל *fool* Pr $26_5$.

**2c.** with חשׁב ni. **be reckoned,** used predicatively of אֱוִיל silent *fool* Pr $17_{28}$ (|| נָבוֹן *intelligent*).

<COLL> + מְאֹד *very* 2 S $13_3$, לֹא *not* Ho $13_{13}$; + כְּ *as*, + מַלְאָךְ *angel* 2 S $14_{20}$; מִן of comparison, *(more) than*, + Daniel Ezk $28_{3(Qr)}$, שׁוב hi. *one who takes back*, i.e. replies Pr $26_{16}$; בְּעֵינֵי *in the eyes*, i.e. opinion, *of*, + אִישׁ *man* Pr $26_{12}$ $28_{11}$, בֵּן *son* Pr $3_7$, עָצֵל *idler* Pr $26_{16}$ (or em.), כְּסִיל *fool* Pr $26_5$; חָכָם followed by לְ *to, at*, + inf. of רעע hi. *be evil* Jr $4_{22}$.

**3.** as noun, **wise one, sage, one who is wise** (Est $6_{13}$), **adviser** (e.g. Jr $10_9$ Si $42_{6(B)}$ 1 C $22_{15}$ 2 C $2_{6.13.13}$), **one who is skilful, skilled artisan** (e.g. Is $3_3$ $40_{20}$ Jr $10_9$), **skilled mourner** (e.g. Jr $9_{16}$).

**<SUBJ>** היה *be* Ezk 27$_{8}$ (or del.) 27$_{9}$ (or del. חָכָם; || זָקֵן *elder*) Ec 2$_{19}$ (+ אָדָם *human being*, :: סָכָל *fool*), מות *die* Ps 49$_{11}$ (+ כְּסִיל *fool*, בַּעַר *fool*) Ec 2$_{16}$ (:: כְּסִיל), גבר *be strong* Pr 24$_{5}$ (if em. גֶּבֶר wise *man*, as §1; + אִישׁ־דַּעַת *man of knowledge*), יכל *be able* Ec 8$_{17}$, שׂבע *be satisfied* Si 37$_{24(C,D)}$, בצר ni. *be cut off* Si 37$_{20}$, בושׁ hi. *be ashamed* Jr 8$_{9}$, חתת *be shattered* Jr 8$_{9}$, לכד ni. *be captured* Jr 8$_{9}$.

חכם *be wise* Pr 9$_{9}$ (|| צַדִּיק *righteous one*) Si 37$_{22(B,C).23(D)}$, ni. *be considered wise* Si 37$_{19(B,C,D).22(D).23(B)}$, pu. *be made wise* Pr 30$_{24}$ (or em. מְחֻכָּמִים *ones who are made wise* to מֵחֲכָמִים *wise*, i.e. wisest *of the wise*), יאל ni. *be considered foolish* Si 37$_{19(D)}$, ידע *know* Is 19$_{12}$=4QpIsa$^{c}$ 11.2$_{4}$ ([חכמיכה ... ויןדע[ו]) Ec 8$_{17}$ Est 1$_{13}$, שׂכל hi. *be intelligent* Pr 21$_{11}$ (if del. לְ introducing חָכָם as obj. of שׂכל hi. *make [more] intelligent*; + לֵץ *scoffer*) 4Q418 81$_{20}$, בין hi. *understand* Pr 1$_{5}$ 4Q302 2.2$_{2}$.

ראה *see* Jb 37$_{24}$, שׁמע *hear* Jb 34$_{2}$ (|| יֹדֵעַ *knowledgeable one*) Pr 1$_{5}$ (|| נָבוֹן *intelligent one*) 12$_{15}$ (+ אֱוִיל *fool*), אהב *love* Pr 9$_{8}$ (:: לֵץ *scoffer*), ירא *fear* Pr 14$_{16}$ (:: כְּסִיל *fool*), מאס *reject* Jr 8$_{9}$, ni. *be rejected* Si 37$_{20}$.

באר pi. *explain* 1QDM 2$_{8}$ ([חכמים]), יעץ *counsel* Is 19$_{11}$ (if em.; see Nom. Cl.), אמר *say* Ex 36$_{4.4}$ Ec 8$_{17}$ Est 6$_{13}$, דבר pi. *speak* Ex 36$_{4(Sam)}$, נגד hi. *tell* Is 19$_{12}$ (+ שַׂר *prince*) Jb 15$_{18}$, ענה *reply* Jg 5$_{29}$ Jb 15$_{2}$, יכח hi. *reprove* Jb 15$_{2}$, הלל *boast* because of wisdom Jr 9$_{22}$ (|| גִּבּוֹר *mighty one*, עָשִׁיר *wealthy one*), appar. שׂיח *meditate* 1QH 1$_{35}$ (+ מהר ni. ptc. *one who hastens*, perh. coward), כחד pi. *conceal* Jb 15$_{18}$, חרשׁ hi. *be silent* Si 20$_{7}$ (:: כְּסִיל *fool*).

בוא *come* Ex 35$_{10}$ 36$_{4}$ Jr 9$_{16}$ (|| מְקוֹנְנָה *female dirge singer*), סור *depart* Pr 14$_{16}$, עלה *go up* Pr 21$_{22}$, ירד hi. *take down* Pr 21$_{22}$, שׁוב hi. *take back*, i.e. divert anger Pr 29$_{8}$ (:: אִישׁ לָצוֹן *man of mockery*).

ישׁן *sleep* Jr 51$_{57}$ (|| שַׂר *prince*, גִּבּוֹר *mighty one*, פֶּחָה *governor*, סָגָן *prefect*), קיץ hi. *awake* intrans. Jr 51$_{57}$, גאל *redeem* soul Si 37$_{19(B,C)}$, נחל *inherit* glory Pr 3$_{35}$ (:: כְּסִיל *fool*) Si 37$_{26(D)}$, קדשׁ pi. *sanctify* Ex 28$_{3}$, שׁבח pi. *calm* Pr 29$_{11}$ (ms שׁכח *forget*; or em. חשׂך *withhold*; + כְּסִיל), חזק hi. *strengthen*, i.e. repair Ezk 27$_{9}$ (or del. חָכָם), מלא pi. *fill* Jb 15$_{2}$, יסף hi. *increase* Pr 1$_{5}$, צפן *store* Pr 10$_{14}$ (or ins. שִׂפְתֵי *lips of* wise ones; + אֱוִיל *fool*), מצא *find* Ec 8$_{17}$, לקח *take* Pr 10$_{8}$ (:: אֱוִיל) 11$_{30}$ (or em. חָמָס *violence*; + צַדִּיק *righteous one* [or em. צֶדֶק *righteousness*]) 21$_{11}$.

עשׂה *do* Ex 28$_{3}$ 31$_{6}$ 35$_{10}$ 36$_{4.4.8}$ 1QDM 2$_{8}$ (חכמים אשר] יעשו *wise ones, who will do*), חפר *dig* CD 6$_{3}$ (|| נָבוֹן *intelligent one*), בנה *build* Pr 14$_{1}$ (or em. חַכְמוֹת נָשִׁים to חָכְמוֹת תָּשִׁים בְּאֵיתָן בָּנְתָה *the wisest of women has built* Wisdom *places securely*; + אִוֶּלֶת *folly*), פגשׁ pi. *encounter* Jb 5$_{13}$, משׁשׁ pi. *grope* Jb 5$_{13}$.

**<NOM CL>** הַחֲכָמִים אֲשֶׁר עִמִּי בִּיהוּדָה *the skilled artisans who are with me in Judah* 2 C 2$_{6}$ (mss lack עִמִּי *with me*), חַכְמֵי יֹעֲצֵי פַרְעֹה עֵצָה *the wise ones among the counsellors of Pharaoh are*, i.e. give, foolish *counsel* Is 19$_{11}$= 4QpIsa$^{c}$ 11.2$_{2}$ ([חכמי יועצי] פרעוה עצ[ה]); or em. חַכְמֵי פַרְעֹה יָעֲצוּ *the wise ones of Pharaoh counsel* foolish counsel; + שַׂר *prince*), חכמיה כולמו כמלחים במצולות *its wise ones, all of them, are as sailors on the deeps* 1QH 3$_{14}$ (+ כי תתבלע כול חכמתם *for all their wisdom is swallowed up*), הַחֲכָמִים ... וַעֲבָדֵיהֶם בְּיַד הָאֱלֹהִים *the wise ones ... and their deeds are in the hand of God* Ec 9$_{1}$ (|| צַדִּיק *righteous one*), וְעִמְּךָ ... כָּל־חָכָם *and with you is ... every skilled artisan* 1 C 22$_{15}$, הֵמָּה חֲכָמִים *they are wise* Pr 30$_{24}$, אַיָּם אֵפוֹא חֲכָמֶיךָ *where are your wise ones?* Is 19$_{12}$=4QpIsa$^{c}$ 11.2$_{4}$ ([אפוא חכמיכה]), יש חכם *there is a wise one* who Si 37$_{19.20.22.23}$, אֵין ... חָכָם *there is not ... (such) a wise one* as you Gn 41$_{39}$ (|| נָבוֹן *intelligent one*).

**<OBJ>** ילד *give birth (to)* Pr 23$_{24}$ (|| צַדִּיק *righteous one*), קום hi. *raise* CD 6$_{3}$, שׁוב hi. *take*, i.e. turn, *back* Is 44$_{25}$ (+ דַּעְתָּם *their knowledge*), סור hi. *remove* Is 3$_{3}$ (|| נָבוֹן *intelligent one*, + גִּבּוֹר *mighty one*, אִישׁ מִלְחָמָה *man of war*, שֹׁפֵט *judge*, זָקֵן *elder*, שַׂר *prince*, יֹעֵץ *counsellor*, נשׂא pass. ptc. *one raised* of face, i.e. eminent, קֹסֵם *diviner*, נָבִיא *prophet*).

יהב *give*, i.e. appoint 1QDM 2$_{8}$ ([הבו לכם חכמים] *appoint for yourselves wise ones*), כון hi. *establish* 2 C 2$_{6}$, מצא *find* Jb 17$_{10}$, קרה *encounter* Ec 2$_{14}$ (:: כְּסִיל *fool*) 9$_{11}$ (|| נָבוֹן *intelligent one*, ידע ptc. *knowledgeable one*, + גִּבּוֹר *mighty one*, קַל *swift one*), מלא pi. *fill* with spirit Ex 28$_{3}$, שׁמע hi. *make known (to)* CD 6$_{3}$, ראה *see* perh. Ps 49$_{11}$ Si 37$_{24(D)}$, אשׁר pi. *pronounce happy* Si 37$_{24(B,C,D)}$, קרא *call* Gn 41$_{8}$ (|| חַרְטֹם *magician*), שׁכר hi. *inebriate* Jr 51$_{57}$, הלל po. *make mad* Ec 7$_{7}$, לכד *capture* Jb 5$_{13}$ (+ בְּעָרְמָם *despite their astuteness*; + נִפְתָּל *devious one*), אבד hi. *destroy* Ob 8 (+ תְּבוּנָה *understanding*).

**<CSTR>** חֲכַם־לֵב *one who is wise of heart* Ex 28$_{3(ms,}$

Sam) 31$_6$ 35$_{10}$ 36$_{1.2}$ (both §1) 36$_8$ Jb 9$_4$ (חֲכַם לֵבָב; || אַמִּיץ *mighty one*) Pr 10$_8$ 11$_{29}$ 16$_{21}$, חַכְמֵי־לֵב *those who are wise of heart* Ex 28$_3$ 36$_{8(Sam)}$ Jb 37$_{24}$ 4Q418 81$_{20}$, חכמי ידים *those who are wise of*, i.e. skilful with their, *hands* Si 9$_{17}$.

חָכָם חֲרָשִׁים *one who is wise of*, i.e. skilled in, *(magic) crafts* Is 3$_3$, חכמי שיח *ones wise of*, i.e. skilled in, *conversation* Si 44$_4$ (+ בספרתם *in their writing* [Bmg במספרתם appar. *in their counting*]; + מֹשֵׁל *ruler* or *teller of proverbs*, נשׂא ptc. *one who raises*, i.e. tells proverbs, יֹעֵץ *counsellor*, חֹזֶה *seer*, שַׂר *prince*, רֹזֵן *ruler*, אִישׁ חַיִל *man of valour*, שׁקט ptc. *one who is silent*, חֹקֵר *investigator*).

חכם עם *wise(st) one of (the) people* Si 37$_{26(D)}$, חַכְמֵי הַגּוֹיִם all *the wise(st) ones of the nations* Jr 10$_7$, חַכְמֵי אֲדֹנִי *skilled artisans of my lord* 2 C 2$_{13}$, חַכְמֵי יֹעֲצֵי פַרְעֹה *wise(st) ones of the counsellors of Pharaoh* Is 19$_{11}$=4QpIsa$^c$ 11.2$_2$ (or em.; see Nom. Cl.), חַכְמוֹת שָׂרוֹתֶיהָ *the wise(st) ones of her princesses* Jg 5$_{29}$ (ms חַכְמַת *wise[st] one of*), חַכְמוֹת נָשִׁים *the wise(st) one(s) of women* Pr 14$_1$ (or em. חָכְמוֹת תָּשִׁים *Wisdom places*), ח[כמי ]העדה *the wise(st) ones of the congregation* 1QSa 1$_{28}$ (+ נָבוֹן *intelligent one*), יֹדֵעַ *knowledgeable one*, תָּמִים *perfect one*).

חָכְמַת חֲכָמָיו *the wisdom of his wise ones* Is 29$_{14}$ (|| נָבוֹן), דִּבְרֵי חֲכָמִים *words of the wise* Pr 1$_6$ (+ חִידֹתָם *their riddles*) 22$_{17}$ Ec 9$_{17}$ 12$_{11}$, משלי חכמים *proverbs of the wise* Si 3$_{29}$, תּוֹרַת חָכָם *instruction of a wise one* Pr 13$_{14}$, גַּעֲרַת *rebuke of* Ec 7$_5$ (4QQoh$^a$ גַּעֲרוֹת), שיחת חכמים *conversation of wise ones* Si 8$_8$ (+ חידתיהם *their riddles*).

בֶּן־חֲכָמִים I am *a son of wise ones* Is 19$_{11}$ (=4QpIsa$^c$ 11.2$_3$ [בני חכמים] we are *sons of wise ones*; + מֶלֶךְ *king*), נחלת חכמ[ים] *inheritance of wise ones* 4QMyst$^c$ 2$_1$ (:: כְּסִיל *fool*).

מַעֲשֵׂה חֲכָמִים *work of skilled artisans* Jr 10$_9$ (+ חָרָשׁ *artisan*, צֹרֵף *refiner*), חותם חכם *seal of*, i.e. made by, *one who is skilful* Si 42$_{6(B)}$ (Bmg, M lack חָכָם), עֲטֶרֶת חֲכָמִים *crown of the wise* Pr 14$_{24}$ (:: כְּסִיל *fool*), נְוֵה חָכָם *abode of a wise one* Pr 21$_{20}$ (or em. פִּי *mouth of*; + כְּסִיל), perh. עול חכמ[] *yoke of a wise one* 4Q421 1.2$_{10}$.

לֵב חָכָם *heart of a wise one* Ex 31$_6$ (לֵב כָּל־חֲכַם־לֵב *heart of everyone who is wise of heart*) Pr 16$_{23}$ Ec 8$_5$ 10$_2$ (:: כְּסִיל *fool*), לֵב חֲכָמִים *heart of the wise* Ec 7$_4$ (:: כְּסִיל), פִּי חָכָם *mouth of a wise one* Pr 21$_{20}$ (if em. נְוֵה *abode of*) Ec 10$_{12}$ (+ כְּסִיל) Si 15$_{10(B)}$, עֵינֵי חֲכָמִים *eyes of the wise* Dt 16$_{19}$=11QT 51$_{14}$ (:: צַדִּיק *righteous one*), לְשׁוֹן חֲכָמִים *tongue of the wise* Pr 12$_{18}$ 15$_2$ (:: כְּסִיל), שִׂפְתֵי חֲכָמִים *lips of the wise* Pr 10$_{14}$ (if ins. שִׂפְתֵי) 14$_3$ (+ אֱוִיל *fool*) 15$_7$ (:: כְּסִיל), אֹזֶן חֲכָמִים *ear of the wise* Pr 18$_{15}$ (|| נָבוֹן *intelligent one*).

כָּל־חָכָם *every skilled artisan* 1 C 22$_{15}$, כָּל־הַחֲכָמִים *all the wise ones* Ex 36$_4$, כָּל־חֲכַם־לֵב *every wise one of heart* Ex 28$_{3(ms, Sam)}$ 31$_6$ 35$_{10}$ 36$_8$, כָּל־חַכְמֵי־ *all the wise ones of, all who are wise of* Ex 28$_3$ 36$_{8(Sam)}$ Jr 10$_7$ Jb 37$_{24}$ 1QSa 1$_{28}$ (ח[כמי]) 4Q418 81$_{20}$ (both כול), כָּל־חֲכָמֶיהָ *all its* (Egypt's) *wise ones* Gn 41$_8$.

<APP> כֹּל *all* 1QH 3$_{14}$, מִשְׁעָן *support* Is 3$_3$, מַשְׁעֵן *support* Is 3$_3$, מַשְׁעֵנָה *support* Is 3$_3$.

<PREP> לְ of direction, *to*, + נתן *give* Pr 9$_9$ 4QBark$^c$ 1$_2$ (+ יָשָׁר *upright one*), ni. *be given* Jb 15$_{18}$, אמר *say* Est 1$_{13}$, ספר pi. *relate* Gn 41$_8$, קרא *call* Ex 7$_{11}$ (|| מְכַשֵּׁף *sorcerer*, + חַרְטֹם *magician*); of benefit, *to, for* Jr 8$_9$, + עזז *be strong* Ec 7$_{19}$ (4QQoh$^a$ עזר לְ *help*); of possession, *of, (belonging) to* Pr 11$_{29}$ (+ אֱוִיל *fool*) 24$_{23}$ Ec 2$_{16}$ 6$_8$ (both :: כְּסִיל *fool*) 9$_{11}$; introducing object, + יכח hi. *reprove* Pr 9$_8$, שׂכל hi. *make (more) intelligent* Pr 21$_{11}$ (or del. לְ, leaving חָכָם as subj. of שׂכל hi. *be intelligent*), + קרא ni. *be called* intelligent Pr 16$_{21}$.

בְּ of place, *among* Jr 10$_7$; of instrument, *by (means of)*, + חשׁך ni. appar. *be maintained* Si 9$_{17}$ (or em. חשׁב ni. *be reckoned*, i.e. be held in esteem); of cause, *on account of*, + שׂמח *rejoice in* Pr 23$_{24}$; *in charge of, over*, + משׁל *rule* Is 3$_3$.

כְּ *as*, + יכח hi. *reprove* Ec 8$_1$ (if ins. יכח hi.).

מִן of direction, *from*, + אבד *die*, i.e. depart (of counsel) Jr 18$_{18}$=4QMidrEschat$^b$ 11$_6$ ([תואבד ... מחכם]; || כֹּהֵן *priest*, נָבִיא *prophet*); partitive, *of, from among* Pr 30$_{24}$ (if em. מְחֻכָּמִים *those who are made wise* to מֵחֲכָמִים *wise*, i.e. wisest *of the wise*).

אֶל *to*, + הלך *go* Pr 15$_{12}$ (or em. אֵת *with*; + לֵץ *scoffer*), שׁלח *send (messengers)* Jr 9$_{16}$, דבר pi. *speak* Ex 28$_3$; *against* Jr 50$_{35}$ (|| שַׂר *prince*), + קשׁה hi. *hold firm* Jb 9$_4$.

עִם *with*, + ישׁב *sit* 1QSa 2$_{16}$ ([חכמ]יהם), עשׂה *do* 2 C 2$_{6.13.13}$, פתח pi. *engrave* 2 C 2$_{6.13.13}$, חשׁב *fashion* 2 C 2$_{13.13}$, סוד htp. *act in secret*, i.e. be close to Si 9$_{14}$.

אֵת *with*, + הלך *go* Pr 13$_{20}$ (+ כְּסִיל *fool*) 15$_{12}$ (if em. אֶל *to*).

בְּתוֹךְ *among*, + עבר *pass* Jb $15_{18}$.

בְּקֶרֶב *among*, + לין *pass night* Pr $15_{31}$.

<COLL> חכמים *O wise ones* Jb $34_2$ 1QH $1_{35}$ 4Q302 $2.2_2$ (החכמים), הוֹי חֲכָמִים בְּעֵינֵיהֶם *woe (to) those who are wise in their (own) eyes* Is $5_{21}$ (|| נָבוֹן *intelligent one*), כָּל־חָכָם בְּכָל־מְלָאכָה *every skilled artisan in every trade* 1 C $22_{15}$, חכם במעט דבר נפשו *as for a wise one, in smallness of speech is his soul* Si $20_{13}$, הֶחָכָם עֵינָיו בְּרֹאשׁוֹ *as for the wise one, his eyes are in his head* Ec $2_{14}$.

Also 4QMyst[a] $2.2_4$ (|| צַדִּיק *righteous one*) 4QHod[b] $1_2$ (חכמים בערמתם *wise ones despite their astuteness*) 4Q525 $5_7$.

<SYN> §1 נָבוֹן *intelligent*, יָדוּעַ *knowledgeable*, מִסְכֵּן *poor*; 2a נָבוֹן *intelligent*; 2c נָבוֹן *intelligent*; §3 נָבוֹן *intelligent one*, יֹדֵעַ *knowledgeable one*, כֹּהֵן *priest*, נָבִיא *prophet*, זָקֵן *elder*, צַדִּיק *righteous one*, גִּבּוֹר *mighty one*, אַמִּיץ *mighty one*, שַׂר *prince*, פֶּחָה *governor*, סָגָן *prefect*, עָשִׁיר *wealthy one*, מְכַשֵּׁף *sorcerer*, חַרְטֹם *magician*, מְקוֹנְנָה female *dirge singer*.

<ANT> §1 נָבָל *foolish*, אֱוִיל *foolish*; §3 כְּסִיל *fool*, אֱוִיל *fool*, סָכָל *fool*, לֵץ *scoffer*, אִישׁ לָצוֹן *man of mockery*.*

⇒ חכם *be wise*.

**חָכְמָה** 153.25.44 n.f. **wisdom**—Q חוכמא; cstr. חָכְמַת; sf. חָכְמָתָהּ, חָכְמָתוֹ, חָכְמָתֵךְ, (חָכְמָתֵךְ) חָכְמָתְךָ, חָכְמָתִי, חָכְמָתָם, חָכְמַתְכֶם—**1. wisdom, prudence, skill,** in ref. to skill in technical work (e.g. Ex $28_3$ $31_6$ Is $10_{13}$ Ps $107_{27}$ 1 C $28_{21}$). **2.** personified **Wisdom** (Jb $28_{12-18}$ Pr $8_{1-36}$). **3. good sense, insight** (e.g. 2 S $20_{22}$ Is $47_{10}$ Jb $39_{17}$ Dn $1_{4.17.20}$), religious **wisdom** of Israel (e.g. Dt $4_6$ Is $33_6$ Ps $90_{12}$ Pr $10_{31}$), **wisdom** of God (e.g. Dt $34_9$ 2 S $14_{20}$ 1 K $3_{28}$).

<SUBJ> רבה *be numerous* 1 K $5_{10}$, נתן pass. *be given* 2 C $1_{12}$ (|| מַדָּע *knowledge*) 11QPs[a] $18_3$, כחד ni. *be hidden* 4QMyst[b] $1.2_4$ $5_5$, סתר ni. *be hidden* 4Q424 $3_6$, בזה pass. *be despised* Ec $9_{16}$, כתב pass. *be written* 1 K $11_{41}$, מצא ni. *be found* Jb $28_{12}$ Pr $10_{13}$, בלע htp. *be confused* Ps $107_{27}$ 1QH $3_{15}$, סרח ni. *be spoiled* Jr $49_7$.

בוא *come* Jb $28_{20}$ Pr $2_{10}$, יצא *go out* 4QapPs[b] $76_8$, נוח *rest* Pr $14_{33}$, עמד *stand* Ec $2_9$, שׁכן *dwell* Pr $8_{12}$, עזז *strengthen* Ec $7_{19}$, אור hi. *make shine* Ec $8_1$, חיה pi. *grant life* Ec $7_{12}$, שׁוב pol. *lead astray* Is $47_{10}$, אבד *perish* Is $29_{14}$, מות *die* Jb $12_2$, קרא *call* Pr $8_1$, בין hi. *understand* Pr $14_8$.

<NOM CL> חָכְמָה לְאִישׁ תְּבוּנָה *wisdom belongs to a man of understanding* Pr $10_{23}$, חָכְמַת אֱלֹהִים בְּקִרְבּוֹ *the wisdom of God (was) within him* 1 K $3_{28}$, בִּישִׁישִׁים חָכְמָה *wisdom is with the aged* Jb $12_{12}$, חכמתו בכל לבי *his wisdom is in all my heart* GnzPs $4_{19}$.

טוֹבָה חָכְמָה מִפְּנִינִים *wisdom is better than corals*, or *pearls* Pr $8_{11}$, טוֹבָה חָכְמָה מִגְּבוּרָה *wisdom is better than might* Ec $9_{16}$, טוֹבָה חָכְמָה מִכְּלֵי קְרָב *wisdom is better than weapons of war* Ec $9_{18}$, טוֹבָה חָכְמָה עִם־נַחֲלָה *wisdom is good with an inheritance* Ec $7_{11}$, אֶת־צְנוּעִים חָכְמָה *wisdom is with the humble* Pr $11_2$, אֶת־נוֹעָצִים חָכְמָה *wisdom is with those who take counsel together* Pr $13_{10}$, אֶת־פְּנֵי מֵבִין חָכְמָה *wisdom is with the face of the understanding one* Pr $17_{24}$, יִתְרוֹן הַכְשֵׁיר חָכְמָה *wisdom is an advantage for success* Ec $10_{10}$.

אֲנִי חָכְמָה *I am wisdom* Pr $8_{12}$, הִיא חָכְמָה *it is wisdom* Jb $28_{28}$ 4QMyst[b] $1.2_4$, הִיא חָכְמַתְכֶם *it is your wisdom* Dt $4_6$, חָכְמַת־מֶה לָהֶם *what wisdom is theirs?* Jr $8_9$, עִמּוֹ חָכְמָה *wisdom is with him* Jb $12_{13}$, לֹא חָכְמָה *there is no wisdom* Jb $26_3$, אֵין חָכְמָה *there is no wisdom* Pr $21_{30}$, sim. Ec $9_{10}$, הַאֵין עוֹד חָכְמָה בְּתֵימָן *is there no longer wisdom in Teman?* Jr $49_7$.

<OBJ> יסף hi. *add* 1 K $10_7$ Ec $1_{16}$ 4Q418 $137_2$, רבה hi. *multiply* GnzPs $4_7$, שׁית *place* Jb $38_{36}$, נצב hi. *set up* CD $2_3$, כון hi. *establish* 11QPs[a] $26_{14}$, נתן *give* Ex $31_6$ $36_1$ (|| תְּבוּנָה *understanding*) $36_2$ 1 K $5_9$ (|| תְּבוּנָה) $5_{26}$ $10_{24}$ Pr $2_6$ $29_{15}$ Ec $2_{26}$ (|| דַּעַת *knowledge*) 2 C $1_{10}$ (|| מַדָּע *knowledge*) 4Q525 $1_1$ ([חכמה]) $2_1$ (ח[כמה]).

בקשׁ pi. *seek* Pr $14_6$ Ec $7_{25}$, מצא *find* Jb $32_{13}$ 4Q424 $3_7$, פוק hi. *obtain* 4Q424 $3_7$, קנה *acquire* Pr $4_7$ $16_{16}$ $17_{16}$ $23_{23}$ (|| מוּסָר *instruction*, בִּינָה *insight*), נשׂג hi. *overtake* 4Q 525 $3.2_3$, נוב *prosper* Pr $10_{31}$.

נשׁה hi. *cause to forget* Jb $39_{17}$, בזה *despise* Pr $1_7$ (|| מוּסָר), גרע *limit* Jb $15_8$, שׁחת pi. *ruin* Ezk $28_{17}$.

ראה *see* 1 K $10_4$||2 C $9_3$ Ec $1_{16}$ (|| דַּעַת *knowledge*) $2_{12}$ (:: הוֹלֵלוֹת *folly*, סִכְלוּת *foolishness*) $9_{13}$, שׁמע *listen* 1 K $5_{14.14}$ $10_{8.24}$||2 C $9_{7.23}$, אהב *love* Pr $29_3$, שׁאל *ask* 2 C $1_{11}$ (|| מַדָּע *knowledge*), ידע *know* Pr $1_2$ (|| מוּסָר *instruction*) $24_{14}$ Ec $1_{17}$ (|| דַּעַת) $8_{16}$ 4Q417 $2.1_6$, hi. *make known* Ps $51_8$ Jb $32_7$, הגה *utter* Ps $37_{30}$=4QpPs[a] $3.4_3$, למד *learn* Pr $30_3$, pi. *teach* 4Q413 $1_1$, אלף pi. *teach* Jb $33_{33}$.

<CSTR> חָכְמַת אֱלֹהִים *wisdom of God* 1 K $3_{28}$, חָכְמַת *of Solomon* 1 K $5_{10.14}$ $10_4$, מַלְאַךְ *of the angel of* 2 S $14_{20}$, חֲכָמָיו *of his wise ones* Is $29_{14}$, עָרוּם *of the clever one* Pr $14_8$, הַמִּסְכֵּן *of the poor one* Ec $9_{16}$, אָדָם *of a human being* Ec $8_1$, בני *of the sons of* 1QS $4_{22}$, בִּינָה *of insight* Dn $1_{20}$ (or em. חָכְמָה וּבִינָה *wisdom and insight*), דעתכה *of your insight* 1QH $1_{19}$, לֵב *of heart* Ex $35_{35}$, לבו *of his heart* 4Q424 $3_6$, ידים *of hands* 4Q418 $81_{15}$ $137_2$ ([חכ]מת ידים), ידיכה *of your hands* 4Q418 $81_{19}$ $102_3$ $139_2$, ידיו *of his hands* 4Q424 $3_7$, כבודו *of his glory* 1QS $4_{18}$, גבורה *of might* 1QS $4_3$, עוזך *of your strength* GnzPs $1_6$, אוטו *of his storehouse* 4Q416 2.$2_{12}$, כָּל־ *of all* 1 K $5_{10}$.

רֵאשִׁית חָכְמָה *beginning of wisdom* Ps $111_{10}$ Pr $4_7$ (or em. רֵאשִׁית חֵילְךָ *beginning of your wealth*), דעת *knowledge of* 4Q 525 $22_6$, דֶּרֶךְ *way of* Pr $4_{11}$, מְקוֹר *fountain of* Pr $18_4$ (or em. חָכְמָה *wisdom* to חַיִּים *life*), שורש *root of* 4QMyst[b] 1.$2_3$, רוּחַ *spirit of* Ex $28_3$ Dt $34_9$ Is $11_2$=4QpIsa[a] $8_{12}$ ([רוח חכמ]ה), רוח ... חכמת *spirit of ... wisdom of* 1QS $4_3$, לְבַב חָכְמָה *heart of wisdom* Ps $90_{12}$, יְפִי חָכְמָתֶךָ *beauty of your wisdom* Ezk $28_7$, סוד חוכמא *secret of wisdom* 4QBer[a] $1_6$, תַּעֲלֻמוֹת חָכְמָה *secrets of wisdom* Jb $11_6$, רז חכמתכה *mystery of your wisdom* 1QH $9_{23}$, תְּחִלַּת חָכְמָה *beginning of wisdom* Pr $9_{10}$, מוּסַר *instruction of* Pr $15_{33}$ (or em. מוּסַד *foundation of*), מֶשֶׁךְ *pouch of*, i.e. for, wisdom Jb $28_{18}$.

צֵל הַחָכְמָה *the protection of wisdom* Ec $7_{12}$, דְּבַר חָכְמָה *matter of wisdom* Dn $1_{20}$ (if em.), דְּבַר חָכְמַת *matter of wisdom of* Dn $1_{20}$, יְשׁוּעֹת *salvation of* Is $33_6$, יְשׁוּעֹת חָכְמָה *salvation of wisdom* Is $33_6$ (if em.), רֹב *greatness of* Ec $1_{18}$, רֹב חָכְמָתְךָ *greatness of your wisdom* Ezk $28_5$, גבורת חכמ[ה] *greatness of wisdom* 4QapPs[a] 7.$2_2$, מַרְבִּית חָכְמָתֶךָ *great portion of your wisdom* 2 C $9_6$, כָּל־חָכְמָה *all wisdom* Dn $1_4$, sim. Dn $1_{17}$, כֹּל חָכְמַת *all wisdom of* 1 K $5_{10}$ $10_4$ (כָּל־) 4Q418 $102_3$, כָּל־חָכְמָתָם *all their wisdom* Ps $107_{27}$ 1QH $3_{15}$ 4QMyst[b] 1.$2_4$ (כל חוכמת[כ]ם) $3_3$ 4Q418 $115_3$ ([כול ח]כמתם).

<APP> אֱמֶת *truth* Pr $23_{23}$, דַּעַת *knowledge* 1QS $4_{18}$.

<ADJ> רבה hi. inf. *great* Ec $1_{16}$.

<PREP> לְ of direction, *to*, + קשב hi. *cause to pay attention* Pr $2_2$ $5_1$, שׂכל hi. *pay attention* 4QapPs[b] $76_8$, אמר *say* Pr $7_4$; of benefit, *to, for* Ec $2_{13}$ 1QH $9_{17}$ 4Qap Ps[b] $33_3$; *as*, + היה *be* Jb $13_5$; *in respect of*, + גדל *be great* 1 K $10_{23}$||2 C $9_{22}$ (+ עֹשֶׁר *wealth*).

בְּ of instrument, *by (means of)* Ec $2_{21}$ 4Q418 $81_{15}$ $139_2$ 4Q525 $1_1$, + בנה ni. *be built* Pr $24_3$, נשׂא *raise* Ex $35_{26}$, נהג *lead* Ec $2_3$, עשׂה *do* Is $10_{13}$ (+ כֹּחַ *strength*)=4QpIsa[c] 4.$2_3$ ([בחכמת]י), Ezk $28_4$ (|| תְּבוּנָה) Ps $104_{24}$, נתן *give* 1QS $4_{18}$, יסד *lay foundations of* Pr $3_{19}$, כון hi. *establish* Jr $10_{12}$=$51_{15}$, כון hi. *establish* 1QH $1_7$ (חכמתכ[ה]) $1_{14.19}$, מות *die* Jb $4_{21}$, מלט pi. *save* Ec $9_{15}$, תור *investigate* Ec $1_{13}$, נסה pi. *test* Ec $7_{23}$, ספר pi. *relate* Jb $38_{37}$; of accompaniment, *in, with*, + בוא *come* 2 S $20_{22}$; of cause, *because of, (consisting) of* Ex $31_3$||$35_{31}$ (|| תְּבוּנָה *understanding*, דַּעַת *knowledge*, מְלָאכָה *work*, + רוּחַ *spirit* of God) 1 C $28_{21}$; *in, of*, + הלך *go* Pr $28_{26}$, htp. *walk to and fro* 1QS $4_{24}$, פתח *open* Pr $31_{26}$, נתן *give* Dn $1_{17}$, הלל htp. *boast* Jr $9_{22}$, שׂמח *rejoice* 4Q411 $1_1$ (חכ[מת]), שׂכל hi. *have insight* Dn $1_4$, בין hi. *cause to understand* 1QS $4_{22}$.

כְּ *as* 2 S $14_{20}$ 1 K $2_6$.

מִן of direction, *from* perh. 4QMyst[a] 15.$1_2$, + שׁאל *ask* Ec $7_{10}$; of comparison, *(more) than* Ec $10_1$, + רבה *be numerous* 1 K $5_{10.10}$; *by (means of)*, + מלא *fill* 4Q418 $81_{19}$, שׂבע *be satiated* 4Q418 $81_{19}$.

עַל *concerning*, + שׁמע *hear* 1 K $10_6$||2 C $9_5$ (+ דָּבָר *word*).

<COLL> מִלֵּא אֹתָם חָכְמַת־לֵב *he filled them with wisdom of heart*, i.e. skill Ex $35_{35}$, וַיִּמָּלֵא אֶת־הַחָכְמָה *and he was filled with wisdom* 1 K $7_{14}$ (|| תְּבוּנָה *understanding*, דַּעַת *knowledge*), אַתָּה ... מָלֵא חָכְמָה *you (were) ... full of wisdom* Ezk $28_{12}$.

<SYN> תְּבוּנָה *understanding*, דַּעַת *knowledge*, מַדָּע *knowledge*, בִּינָה *insight*, מוּסָר *instruction*, מְלָאכָה *work*.

<ANT> הוֹלֵלוֹת *folly*, סִכְלוּת *foolishness*.

Also 1QH fr. $17_6$ 4QMyst[a] $39_4$ 4QapPs[a] $6_2$ 4Q421 1.$1_2$ 4QSap[b] $2_8$ (חוכ[מה]) 4QPrFêtes[c] 16.$4_7$ $55_2$ 4Q525 $1_2$ ([חכמה]) $2_2$.*

⇒ חכם *be wise*.

**חַכְמוֹנִי** I 2 pr.n.m. **Hachmoni** (unless gent., as II), **1.** father of Jashobeam, 1 C $11_{11}$. **2.** father of Jehiel, 1 C $27_{32}$. <CSTR> בֶּן־חַכְמוֹנִי *son of Hachmoni* 1 C $11_{11}$ $27_{32}$.

**[חַכְמוֹנִי]** II gent. **Hachmonite,** appar. in ref. to descendant of (unattested) Hachmon (unless at 1 C $11_{11}$ $27_{32}$

pr.n., as I), <CSTR> בֶּן־חַכְמוֹנִי *son of a Hachmonite* 1 C 11$_{11}$ 27$_{32}$. <APP> Ishbosheth 2 S 23$_{8}$ (if em. יֹשֵׁב בַּשֶּׁבֶת תַּחְכְּמֹנִי *Josheb-basshebeth a Tahchemonite* to יִשְׁבֹּשֶׁת הַחַכְמֹנִי *Ishbosheth the Hachmonite*).

**חָכְמוֹת** 4.1 n.f.pl. **wisdom,** esp. of personified **Wisdom,** (but see חָכְמָה § 2), <SUBJ> רנן *cry aloud* Pr 1$_{20}$, קרא *call* Pr 1$_{20}$, אמר *say* Pr 1$_{20}$, נבע hi. *pour out* Pr 1$_{20}$, ידע hi. *make known*, למד pi. *teach* Si 4$_{11}$, עוד hi. *admonish* Si 4$_{11}$, ענה *answer* Pr 1$_{20}$, נתן *give* Pr 1$_{20}$, שׁלח *send* Pr 9$_{1}$, שׂחק *laugh* Pr 1$_{20}$, לעג *mock* Pr 1$_{20}$, נטה *stretch out* hand Pr 1$_{20}$, בנה *build* Pr 9$_{1}$ 14$_{1}$ (if em. חָכְמוֹת נָשִׁים *wise ones of women*), חצב *hew* Pr 9$_{1}$, טבח *slaughter* Pr 9$_{1}$, ערך *arrange* Pr 9$_{1}$, רום *be high* perh. Pr 24$_{7}$ (see Nom. Cl.). <NOM CL> רָאמוֹת לֶאֱוִיל חָכְמוֹת appar. *wisdom is corals, or pearls, to a fool*, unless *wisdom is too high for a fool* Pr 24$_{7}$ (רום ptc. *be high*). <OBJ> דבר *speak* Ps 49$_{4}$ (+ תְּבוּנָה *understanding*), קרא *call* Pr 1$_{20}$, בקשׁ pi. *seek* Si 4$_{11}$, שׁחר pi. *seek early* Pr 1$_{20}$, אהב *love* Si 4$_{11}$, תמך *hold* Si 4$_{11}$, שׁרת pi. *serve* Si 4$_{11}$. <PREP> בְּ introducing object, + בין hi. *understand* Si 4$_{11}$.*

⇒ חכם *be wise.*

**חכר I** 0.0.10 vb. **rent—Qal** 0.0.9 Pf. חכרתי (חכרת), חכרו, חכרנו—**1. rent (from),** <SUBJ> Eleazar, son of the Shilonite Mur 24 2$_{7}$ ([אלעזר ... [חכרתי]) 2$_{9}$ ([חכרתי]) 2$_{13}$, Eleazar, son of Eleazar 5/6ḤevBA 44$_{5}$, Eliezer, son of Samuel 5/6ḤevBA 44$_{5}$, Halipha Mur 24 3$_{6.8.11}$ (all three [חליפא]), Judah, son of Rabbah Mur 24 5$_{5}$ (ח]כרת]) 5$_{7.8}$ (all three [י]הודה), perh. Niklah Mur 24 4$_{13}$ ([נק]ל[ה] ... חכו[ר]תי), Tehinnah 5/6ḤevBA 44$_{5}$. <OBJ> עָפָר *dust*, i.e. land Mur 24 5$_{5}$ (ח]כרת]) 5$_{8}$, מָקוֹם *place* 5/6ḤevBA 44$_{5}$. <PREP> בְּ perh. *in (exchange for)*, + חָכִיר *rent* Mur 24 2$_{7}$ ([חכרתי]) 3$_{8}$ ([בחכ]יר) Mur 24 6$_{5}$ ([חכרתי]), חֲכִירוּת *rent* Mur 24 5$_{5}$ ([ח]כרת]); מִן of direction, *from* Mur 24 1$_{6}$ ([חכרתי המך]) Mur 24 4$_{13}$ (חכו[ר]תי [המך]), + Hillel, son of Garis Mur 24 2$_{7}$ ([חכרתי ה]מך]) 2$_{13}$ 3$_{6.11}$ (both [ה]לל]) 5$_{5}$ ([ח]כרת]) 5$_{8}$ Mur 24 6$_{5}$ (הלל ...] [חכרתי המך]) 6$_{10}$ 8$_{4}$ ([הלל] ... [חכרתי המך]), Jonathan, son of Mahanaim 5/6ḤevBA 44$_{5}$, Simeon Mur 24 2$_{9}$ ([חכרתי מן ש]מעון]) 3$_{8}$ 5$_{7}$ 6$_{7}$ ([ח]כרתי מן שמעון]), בֵּן *son* 5/6ḤevBA 44$_{5}$, נָשִׂיא *prince* Mur 24 2$_{9}$ (חכרתי מן ש] מעון] [נ]סיא]) 3$_{8}$ ([נסיא]) 5$_{7}$ 6$_{7}$ ([ח]כרתי מן ... נשיא]), פַּרְנָס *administrator* 5/6ḤevBA 44$_{5}$, יוֹם *day* Mur 24 2$_{13}$ 3$_{8}$ ([מן היום]) 5$_{8}$; of instrument, *(by means) of*, + רָצוֹן *will* Mur 24 1$_{6}$ ([מרצוני חכרתי]) Mur 24 5$_{5}$ ([ח]כרת); מִקְצָת *some of*, + עָפָר *dust*, i.e. land Mur 24 1$_{6}$ ([חכרתי ... [מ]ן) [חכרתי ... מן] 6$_{5}$ ([מ]ן) 3$_{6}$ ([חכרתי]) 2$_{7}$ 24 ([קצת עפר]) 8$_{4}$ ([חכרתי] ... מן [קצת עפר]) (ק[צ]ת); עַד *unto*, + סוֹף *end* Mur 24 2$_{13}$ 3$_{8}$ ([ע]ד]) 5$_{8}$.

**2. take in rent,** <SUBJ> Eliezer, son of Samuel and Eleazar, son of Eleazar 5/6ḤevBA 45 fr. 2. <OBJ> חָכוֹר *rent* 5/6ḤevBA 45 fr. 2. <PREP> מִן of direction, *from*, + Jonathan, son of Mahanaim 5/6ḤevBA 45 fr. 2, בֵּן *son* 5/6ḤevBA 45 fr. 2, פַּרְנָס *administrator* 5/6ḤevBA 45 fr. 2.

Also Mur 24 6$_{8}$ ([חכר]ת).

**Hi.** 1 Pf. החכרתי—**let,** <SUBJ> Eleazar, son of Eleazar 5/6ḤevBA 45 fr. 1. <OBJ> גַּנָּה *garden* 5/6Ḥev BA 45 fr. 1. <PREP> לְ of direction, *to*, + Eliezer, son of Samuel 5/6ḤevBA 45 fr. 1.

⇒ חָכוֹר *rent*, חָכִיר *rent*, חֲכִירוּת *rent.*

**חכר II** 1 vb. **oppress**—Impf. mss תַּחְכְּרוּ—<SUBJ> Job's companions Jb 19$_{3(mss)}$ (L הכר *wonder at*). <PREP> לְ introducing object, Jb 19$_{3(mss)}$; בְּ introducing object, Jb 19$_{3(mss)}$.*

**חֵל** 9.0.3 n.m. **rampart**—חֵיל; cstr. חֵל; sf. חֵילָהּ ;חֵילֵךְ (חֵילָה)—**rampart, outer wall** of defences, **ditch** around the temple (11QT 46$_{9}$), perh. **fortress** (Ob$_{20}$; or em.; see Adj.) or in ref. to space in front of city walls (1 K 21$_{23}$ [||2 K 9$_{36}$ חֵלֶק *territory*] Ps 122$_{7}$).*

<SUBJ> אמל pulal *languish* Lm 2$_{8}$ (|| חוֹמָה *wall*).

<NOM CL> חֵיל יָם מִיָּם חוֹמָתָהּ appar. *its (of the city No) wall is a rampart of the sea from the sea* Na 3$_{8}$ (=4Qp Nah 3.3$_{10}$ חילה ים ומים ח[ו]מותיה *its rampart is the sea and water its walls*).

<OBJ> עשׂה *make* 11QT 46$_{9}$, אבל hi. *cause to mourn* Lm 2$_{8}$, נכה hi. *strike*, i.e. cast Zc 9$_{4}$ (unless חֵילָהּ *her wealth*, from חַיִל), שׁית *place*, i.e. make, salvation (into) Is 26$_{1}$ (|| חוֹמָה *wall*).

<CSTR> חֵל יִזְרְעֶאל *rampart of Jezreel* 1 K 21$_{23}$ (mss חֵלֶק *territory of*), חל בת *rampart of the daughter of* Zion

4QTestim$_{29}$, חֵיל יָם *rampart of the sea* Na $3_8$ (=4QpNah $3.3_{10}$ חילה ים *its rampart is the sea*); גָּלֻת הַחֵל *diaspora of the fortress* Ob$_{20}$ (or em.; see Adj.).

<ADJ> זֶה *this* Ob$_{20}$ (or em. לְ הַחֵל־הַזֶּה *this fortress of* to חֲלַח זֶה *Halah, which is*, or בַּחֲלַח יִזְבְּלוּ *[who] dwell in Halah*, or del.).

<PREP> לְ of direction, *to(wards)*, + שִׂית לֵב *place heart*, i.e. consider Ps $48_{14}$ (+ אַרְמוֹן *fortress*); בְּ of place, *in*, + היה *be* Ps $122_7$ (|| אַרְמוֹן), אכל *eat* 1 K $21_{23}$; *against*, + עמד *stand* 2 S $20_{15}$; אֶל *to*, + בוא *come* Dn $11_7$ (if em. הַחַיִל *the army* to הַחַיִל *strength*), הלך *go* Ps $84_8$ (if em. חַיִל *strength* to חֵיל *strength*); מִן of direction, *from*, + הלך *go* Ps $84_8$ (if em. מֵחַיִל *from strength* to מֵחֵיל *from [one] rampart*); עַל *upon*, + שׁפך *pour* blood 4QTestim$_{29}$ ((ושפכו]).

<COLL> חוֹמוֹת וָחֵל *walls and a rampart* Is $26_1$.

<SYN> חוֹמָה *wall*, אַרְמוֹן *fortress*.

**חֹל** 7.0.2 n.[m.] **profaneness**—Q חול—**profaneness, commonness,** as opposed to קֹדֶשׁ *holiness*, <NOM CL> חֹל הוּא לָעִיר *it is commonness*, i.e. for common use, *for the city* Ezk $48_{15}$. <CSTR> חֹל *bread of commonness*, i.e. common bread 1 S $21_5$, דֶּרֶךְ *journey of*, i.e. common journey 1 S $21_6$. <PREP> בֵּין קֹדֶשׁ לְ *between holiness and profaneness*, + בדל hi. *distinguish* Ezk $22_{26}$ $42_{20}$, ירה hi. *teach (the difference)* Ezk $44_{23}$, ידע hi. *make known (the difference)* CD $6_{18}$ $12_{20}$; בֵּין הַקֹּדֶשׁ וּבֵין הַחֹל *between holiness and profaneness*, + בדל hi. *distinguish* Lv $10_{10}$. <COLL> חֹל :: קֹדֶשׁ *holiness* Lv $10_{10}$ 1 S $21_5$ Ezk $22_{26}$ $42_{20}$ $44_{23}$; + קֹדֶשׁ 1 S $21_6$ Ezk $48_{15}$; + טָמֵא *unclean [thing]*, טָהוֹר *clean [thing]* Lv $10_{10}$ Ezk $22_{26}$ $44_{23}$ CD $6_{18}$ $12_{20}$.

Also perh. 4QMyst$^a$ $66_3$.

<ANT> קֹדֶשׁ *holiness*.*

→ חלל *profane*.

**חלא** I 2 vb. **be diseased—Qal** 1 + waw וַיֶּחֱלֶא (mss וַיֶּחֱלָא)—**become diseased,** <SUBJ> Asa 2 C $16_{12}$ (or em. וַיָּחַל *and he became diseased*, from חלה). <PREP> בְּ of time, place *in*, + שָׁנָה *year* 2 C $16_{12}$ (or em.; see Subj.), רֶגֶל *foot* 2 C $16_{12}$ (or em.).

**Hi.** 1 Pf. הֶחֱלִי—**make ill,** <SUBJ> Y. Is $53_{10}$ (unless הֶחֱלִי is חלה hi. *make sick*; or em. הֶחֱלִי אִם־תָּשִׂים *he made [him] sick; when you place* to חֲלָלִים אֶת־שָׂם *he healed the one who placed*, i.e. חלם hi.; 1QIsa$^a$ ויחללהו *and he wounded him*, i.e. חלל pi. *pierce*).

→ תַּחֲלֻאִים *diseases*.

**חלא** II 0.1 vb. **be rusty—Pi. cleanse of rust,** <SUBJ> perh. בַּיִת *house* of rebellion Ezk $24_{12}$ (if em. בְּאֵשׁ חֶלְאָתָהּ appar. *into a fire its rust (is to go)* to בְּאֵשׁ תְּחַלְאֶהָ *by fire you shall cleanse it of rust*). <OBJ> עִיר *city* Ezk $24_{12}$ (if em.; see Subj.). <PREP> בְּ of instrument, *by (means of), with*, + אֵשׁ *fire* Ezk $24_{12}$ (if em.; see Subj.).

**Hi.** 0.1 Impf. Si יחליא—**show rust,** <SUBJ> רֹעַ *evil* Si $12_{10}$. <PREP> כְּ *as*, + נְחֹשֶׁת *bronze* Si $12_{10}$.

→ חֶלְאָה *rust*.

**[חֶלְאָ]** 0.0.0.1 pr.n.[m.] **Hele,** <PREP> לְ perh. of possession, *(belonging) to* Samaria-Sebaste ost. $1266_1$.

**[חֶלְאָה]** I 5 n.f. **rust**—sf. חֶלְאָתָהּ (חֶלְאָתָה)—<SUBJ> יצא *go out* Ezk $24_6$, תמם *be consumed* Ezk $24_{11}$ (+ טֻמְאָה *uncleanness*). <NOM CL> סִיר אֲשֶׁר חֶלְאָתָהּ בָהּ *a pot whose rust is in it* Ezk $24_6$ (or em. חֶלְאָתָהּ *its rust* to חֶלְאָה *rust*), בְּאֵשׁ חֶלְאָתָהּ appar. *into a fire its rust (is to go)* Ezk $24_{12}$ (or em. בְּאֵשׁ תְּחַלְאֶהָ *by fire you shall cleanse it of rust*, i.e. חלא pi.), רַבָּה חֶלְאָתָהּ *its rust is great* Ezk $24_{12}$ (if em. רַבַּת חֶלְאָתָהּ *greatness of its rust*). <CSTR> רַבַּת חֶלְאָתָהּ *greatness of its rust* Ezk $24_{12}$ (if em.; see Nom. Cl.).*

→ חלא *be rusty*.

**חֶלְאָה** II 2 pr.n.f. **Helah,** wife of Ashhur and mother of Zereth, Izhar and Ethnan, <SUBJ> היה *be* 1 C $4_5$. <CSTR> בְּנֵי חֶלְאָה *sons of Helah* 1 C $4_7$. <APP> אִשָּׁה *woman* 1 C $4_5$.

**חֲלָאִים**, see חֲלִי I *ornament*.

**חֶלְאמָה**, see חֵילָם *Helam*.

**חָלָב** 44.2.2 n.m. **milk**—הֶחָלָב; cstr. חֲלֵב; sf. חֲלָבִי, חֲלָבֵךְ—in ref. to milk in various contexts (e.g. Gn $49_{12}$ Ex $3_{8.17}$ Is $55_1$ Ezk $25_4$ Pr $27_{27}$), to pieces of cheese (1 S $17_{18}$), to semen (Jb $10_{10}$), mentioned with דְּבַשׁ *honey* in descriptions of land of Canaan (see Coll.).

<NOM CL> דְּבַשׁ וְחָלָב תַּחַת לְשׁוֹנֵךְ *honey and milk are under your tongue* Ca 4$_{11}$.

<OBJ> מלא *be full of* Jb 21$_{24}$, עשׂה *produce* Is 7$_{22}$, נתן *give* Jg 5$_{25}$, לקח *take* Gn 18$_8$ (+ חֶמְאָה *curds*), שׁבר *buy* Is 55$_1$ (+ יַיִן *wine*), ינק *suck* Is 60$_{16}$, שׁתה *drink* Ezk 25$_4$.

<CSTR> חֲלֵב גּוֹיִם *milk of nations* Is 60$_{16}$, אִמּוֹ *of its mother* Ex 23$_{19}$=34$_{26}$=Dt 14$_{21}$, עִזִּים *of goats* Pr 27$_{27}$, צֹאן *of the flock* Dt 32$_{14}$; נֹאוד הֶחָלָב *the skin of milk* Jg 4$_{19}$, חֲרִצֵי *the slices of*, i.e. pieces of cheese 1 S 17$_{18}$, טְלֵה חָלָב *lamb of milk*, i.e. suckling lamb 1 S 7$_9$, מִיץ *pressing of* Pr 30$_{33}$, דֵּי חֲלֵב *sufficiency of milk of* Pr 27$_{27}$.

<PREP> בְּ *in*, + בשׁל pi. *boil* Ex 23$_{19}$=34$_{26}$=Dt 14$_{21}$, רחץ *bathe* Ca 5$_{12}$; כְּ *as*, + נתך hi. *pour out* Jb 10$_{10}$; מִן of instrument, *by (means of)*, + גמל pass. *be weaned* Is 28$_9$; of cause, *because of* Gn 49$_{12}$; of comparison, *(more) than*, + צחח *be white* Lm 4$_7$; עִם *with*, + שׁתה *drink* Ca 5$_1$.

<COLL> אֶרֶץ זָבַת חָלָב וּדְבָשׁ *a land flowing with milk and honey* Ex 3$_{8.17}$ 13$_5$ 33$_3$ Lv 20$_{24}$ Nm 14$_8$ 16$_{13.14}$ Dt 6$_3$ 11$_9$ 26$_{9.15}$ 27$_3$ Jos 5$_6$ Jr 11$_5$ 31$_{22}$ Ezk 20$_{6.15}$, sim. Nm 13$_{27}$ Dt 31$_{20}$, ארץ זבת חלב ודבשׁ *a land flowing with milk and honey* Si 46$_8$ 4QJub$^a$ 1$_7$ (ארץ זבת חלב ודב]שׁ]) 4QPsJos$^a$ 1$_{16}$, דְּבַשׁ וְחָלָב *honey and milk* Ca 4$_{11}$, וַיֵּנִקֵהוּ ... חֲלֵב צֹאן *and he nursed him with ... the milk of the flock* Dt 32$_{14}$, הַגְּבָעוֹת תֵּלַכְנָה חָלָב *the hills shall flow with milk* Jl 4$_{18}$.

Also Si 39$_{26}$ ([ח]לב) 5QRègle 24$_1$.*

**חֵלֶב** I 91.2.20 n.m. **fat**—cstr. חֵלֶב; sf. חֶלְבּוֹ, חֶלְבָּהּ, חֶלְבָּם; pl. חֲלָבִים; cstr. חֶלְבֵי; sf. חֶלְבְּהֶן, (חֶלְבָּמוֹ)—**fat, choice, best part,** in ref. to **fat** of human body (e.g. Jg 3$_{22}$ 2 S 1$_{22}$ Jb 15$_{27}$ Ps 17$_{10}$), **fat** of Edomites slaughtered as sacrifice (Is 34$_{6.6.7}$), **fat** of beasts (e.g. Ex 29$_{13}$ Lv 3$_{3.3.4}$ Dt 32$_{14}$ 1 S 15$_{22}$ Ezk 44$_{7.15}$), **choicest, best** products of land (Gn 45$_{18}$ Nm 18$_{12.29.30.32}$ Dt 32$_{14}$).

<SUBJ> עשׂה ni. *be prepared* Lv 7$_{24.24}$, רום ho. *be set apart* Si 47$_2$, סור ho. *be removed* Lv 4$_{31.35}$ (Sam hi. in both), לין *remain* Ex 23$_{18}$, סגר *shut* Jg 3$_{22}$.

<NOM CL> כָּל־חֵלֶב לַי׳ *all the fat belongs to Y.* Lv 3$_{16}$.

<OBJ> בוא hi. *bring* Lv 7$_{30}$, עלה hi. *bring up* 2 C 35$_{14}$, רום hi. *raise*, i.e. remove, set apart Lv 4$_{8.8.8.9.19}$ Nm 18$_{30.32}$, סור hi. *remove* Lv 4$_{31.35}$ 11QT 20$_6$ 23$_{16}$, סגר *shut* Ps 17$_{10}$ (or em. חֵלֶב לִבָּמוֹ *fat of their hearts*), כול hi. *hold*, i.e. receive 1 K 8$_{64}$‖2 C 7$_7$, לקח *take* Ex 29$_{13.13.22.22.22}$ Lv 8$_{16.16.25.25.25}$.

מצא hi. *present* Lv 9$_{19}$, שׂים *place* Lv 9$_{20}$, זרק *sprinkle* 16$_{17}$ ([חלב]), עשׂה *make*, i.e. offer 1 K 8$_{64}$‖2 C 7$_7$, נגשׁ hi. *offer* Si 45$_{16}$ CD 4$_2$, קרב hi. *offer* Lv 3$_{3+9t}$ 7$_{33}$ Ezk 44$_{7.15}$ 11QT 15$_6$ ([חלב]) 15$_{7.7}$ ([חלב]), קטר hi. *burn as incense* Lv 4$_{26}$ 6$_5$ 7$_{3.3.4.31}$ 9$_{10.20}$ 16$_{25}$ 17$_6$ Nm 18$_{17}$ 1 S 2$_{15.16}$ 4QJub$^d$ 21$_8$ ([חלב]) 21$_8$ ([חלב]) 21$_8$ (ח]לב]) 21$_8$ 4QJub$^e$ 21$_8$ ([חלב]) 21$_{8.8}$ (ח]לב]) 21$_8$ ([חלב]) 11QT 16$_6$ ([חלב]) 16$_{7.8.8}$ ([חלב]) 20$_4$ ([חלבם]) 20$_5$ ([חלב]) 20$_5$ (חל[ב]) 22$_{04}$ ([חלב]) 22$_6$ 23$_{14.14}$ 24$_5$ ([חלב]) 26$_7$ 52$_{21}$.

אכל *eat* Gn 45$_{18}$ Lv 3$_{17}$ 7$_{23.24.24.25}$ 9$_{24}$ Dt 32$_{38}$ Ezk 34$_3$ 39$_{19}$ 4QapPs$^b$ 1$_9$.

<CSTR> חֵלֶב גִּבּוֹרִים *fat of warriors* 2 S 1$_{22}$ (mss חֶרֶב *sword of*), ־חַגִּי *of my festival* Ex 23$_{18}$, זֶבַח *of sacrifice of* Lv 4$_{26}$ 4QJub$^d$ 21$_8$ 4QJub$^e$ 21$_8$ (both [חלב זבח]), חלבי זבח *fat portions of sacrifice* 1QS 9$_4$, חֵלֶב זְבָחֶיךָ *fat of your sacrifices* Is 43$_{24}$, זְבָחֵימוֹ *of their sacrifices* Dt 32$_{38}$, הַחַטָּאת *of the sin offering* Lv 16$_{25}$, חֶלְבֵי הַשְּׁלָמִים *fat portions of the peace offerings* Lv 6$_5$ 1 K 8$_{64}$‖2 C 7$_7$ 1 K 8$_{64}$ 2 C 29$_{35}$.

חֵלֶב הַכֶּשֶׂב *fat of the young ram* Lv 4$_{35}$, כָּרִים *of rams* Dt 32$_{14}$, אֵילִים *of rams* Dt 32$_{14}$ 1 S 15$_{22}$, שׁוֹר *of an ox* Lv 7$_{23}$, [הפר] *of the bull* 11QT 16$_6$ ([חלב]), מְרִיאִים *of fattened cattle* Is 1$_{11}$, חלבי מריא[ים] *fat portions of fattened cattle* 4QApocMosA 10$_4$, נְבֵלָה *of a carcass* Lv 7$_{24}$, טְרֵפָה *of a torn animal* Lv 7$_{24}$, כְּלָיוֹת *of the kidneys of* Is 34$_6$, כִּלְיוֹת חִטָּה *of the kidneys of wheat*, i.e. the choicest of wheat Dt 32$_{14}$, הָאָרֶץ *of the land* Gn 45$_{18}$, לִבָּמוֹ *of their hearts* Ps 17$_{10}$ (if em.).

חֵלֶב יִצְהָר *best of olive oil* Nm 18$_{12}$, תִּירוֹשׁ *of wine* Nm 18$_{12}$, חֵלֶב ... דָּגָן *best of ... grain* Nm 18$_{12}$, חִטָּה *of wheat* Ps 81$_{17}$, חִטִּים *of wheat* Ps 147$_{14}$, חלבי כל *choicest of all* 4QapPs$^b$ 1$_9$.

אִשֵּׁי הַחֲלָבִים *fire offerings of the fat portions* Lv 10$_{15}$, כָּל־חֵלֶב *all the fat* Lv 3$_{16.17}$, כָּל־חֵלֶב *all the fat of* Lv 4$_8$ 7$_{23}$, כָּל־הַחֵלֶב *all the fat* Ex 29$_{13}$ Lv 3$_{3.9.14}$ 4$_8$ 8$_{16.25}$ 4QJub$^d$ 21$_8$ ([כו]ל ה[ח]לב) 21$_8$ (כול חלב) 11QT 16$_7$ ([כול] החלב) 20$_5$ ([כול חל]ב), כֹּל חֵלֶב *all the best of* Nm 18$_{12.12}$ (כָּל־), כָּל־חֶלְבּוֹ *all its fat* Lv 4$_{19.26}$ 7$_3$ Nm 18$_{29}$, כָּל־חֶלְבָּהּ *all its fat* Lv 4$_{31.35(mss)}$.

<PREP> בְּ of instrument, *by (means of)*, + כסה pi. *cover* Jb 15$_{27}$, כפר pi. *make atonement* 11QT 16$_{15}$; of

accompaniment, *with* 2 C $29_{35}$; כְּ *as* Ps $119_{70}$ Si $47_{2}$, + קטר hi. *burn as incense* Lv $4_{26}$; מִן of direction, *from*, + בוא hi. *bring* Gn $4_{4}$, נשׂג *overtake* 2 S $1_{22}$, יצא *go out* Ps $73_{7}$, רום hi. *raise*, i.e. set apart Nm $18_{29}$; of comparison, *(more) than* 4QApocMosA $10_{4}$, + קשׁב hi. *pay attention* 1 S $15_{22}$; privative, *without* 1QS $9_{4}$; *with*, + דשׁן pu. *be made fat, saturated* Is $34_{7}$, hothpaal *make oneself fat, be satiated* Is $34_{6.6}$, אכל hi. *feed* Ps $81_{17}$; לְבַד מִן *besides, except*, + שׂרף *burn* 11QT $16_{13}$; עַל *upon, unto*, + אכל ni. *be eaten* 4QMMT $B_{11}$, שׂים *place* Lv $8_{26}$ 11QT $15_{10}$ ([חלבי]ם]), קטר hi. *burn as incense* $22_{7}$ ([חלבי]ם); עִם *with*, + ינק hi. *nurse* Dt $32_{14.14}$.

<COLL> שָׂבַעְתִּי ... חֵלֶב מְרִיאִים *I am satiated with ... the fat of fattened cattle* Is $1_{11}$, חֵלֶב זְבָחֶיךָ לֹא הִרְוִיתָנִי *you have not satisfied me with the fat of your sacrifices* Is $43_{24}$, חֵלֶב ... תִּשְׂבַּע נַפְשִׁי *my soul is satiated with ... fat* Ps $63_{6}$, חֵלֶב חִטִּים יַשְׂבִּיעֵךְ *he will satisfy you with the choicest of the wheat* Ps $147_{14}$.*

**חֵלֶב II** 1 pr.n.m. **Heleb,** son of Baanah, warrior and official of David, perh. ident. with חֵלֶד *Heled* and חֶלְדַּי *Heldai*, <APP> בֵּן *son* 2 S $23_{29}$ (mss. חֵלֶד *Heled*).

**חֶלְבָּה** 1 pl.n. **Helbah,** town assigned to, but not occupied by, Asher, <OBJ> ירשׁ hi. *dispossess* Jg $1_{31}$ (or del., as corrupt repetition of אַחְלָב *Ahlab*).

**חֶלְבּוֹן** 1 pl.n. **Helbon,** Ḥalbūn, town 18 km NNE of Damascus, <CSTR> יֵין חֶלְבּוֹן *wine of Helbon* Ezk $27_{18}$ Ho $14_{8}$ (if em. לְבָנוֹן *Lebanon*).

**חֶלְבְּנָה** 1 n.f. **galbanum,** a gum used in incense, <OBJ> לקח *take* Ex $30_{34}$ (|| נָטָף *stacte*, שְׁחֵלֶת *onycha*, + לְבֹנָה *frankincense*). <APP> סַם *spice* Ex $30_{34}$. <SYN> נָטָף *stacte*, שְׁחֵלֶת *onycha*.

**[חלד]** vb. **live,** <SUBJ> אִישׁ *man* Ps $49_{9}$ (if em. וְחָדַל *and it will cease*), אָדָם *human being* Jb $14_{6}$ (if em. חדל *cease*). <PREP> לְ of direction, *to*, + עוֹלָם *eternity* Ps $49_{9}$ (if em.; see Subj.).

**[חָלֵד]** adj. **everlasting,** used predicatively, אֲנִי מֶה־חָלֵד *I am not everlasting* Ps $89_{48}$ (if em. אֲנִי מֶה־חָלֶד *I, what is the duration of life?*).

**חֵלֶד** 2 pr.n.m. **Heled,** son of Baanah, warrior and official of David, perh. ident. with חֵלֶב *Heleb* and חֶלְדַּי *Heldai*, <NOM CL> גִּבּוֹרֵי הַחֲיָלִים ... חֵלֶד *the mighty men of the armies were ... Heled* 1 C $11_{30}$. <APP> בֵּן *son* 2 S $23_{29 (mss)}$||1 C $11_{30}$.*

**חֶלֶד** 5 n.[m.] **duration; world**—חָלֶד; sf. חֶלְדִּי—**1. duration of life, lifespan,** <SUBJ> היה *be* appar. Jb $11_{17}$ (unless em.; see below), קום *arise*, i.e. be bright Jb $11_{17}$, עוף *be dark* appar. Jb $11_{17}$ (unless em. תָּעֻפָה *it will be dark* to תְּעֻפָה *darkness*). <NOM CL> חֶלְדִּי כְאַיִן נֶגְדֶּךָ *my lifespan is as nothing before you* Ps $39_{6}$ (+ יוֹם *day*), מֶה־חָלֶד *what is the span of life?* Ps $89_{48}$ (mss חֶדֶל *lifespan*; or em. אֲנִי מֶה־חָלֶד *I, what is the duration of life?* to אֲנִי מֶה־חָלֵד *I am not everlasting*, or מֶה־חָדֵל אָנִי *how transient I am*). <OBJ> עשׂה *make* Jb $10_{12}$ (if em. וָחֶסֶד *and loyalty* to וָחֶלֶד *and duration of life*). <CSTR> יְמֵי חֶלְדִּי *days of my lifespan* Jb $10_{20}$ (if em. יָמַי יֶחְדָּל appar. *my days, let it cease*). <COLL> חַיִּים וָחֶלֶד *life and duration of life* Jb $10_{12}$ (if em.; see Obj.).

**2. world,** <CSTR> יֹשְׁבֵי חָלֶד *inhabitants of the world* Is $38_{11 (mss)}$ (יוֹשְׁבֵי חָדֶל; L חָדֶל *of the world*; + אֶרֶץ הַחַיִּים *land of the living*) Ps $49_{2}$ (mss חֶדֶל *of the world*). <PREP> לְ of direction, *to* Ps $11_{4}$ (if em. יֶחֱזוּ *they will see* to לְחֶלֶד *his eyes are to the world*); מִן *from* Ps $17_{14}$ (מֵחֶלֶד חֶלְקָם *their portion is from the world*, or em. מֵחֶלֶד חַלְּקֵם *destroy them from out of the world*, or em. מְמֻתִים מֵחֶלֶד *from men from the world* to מְמָתִים מַחֲלָה *caused to die [by] a disease*).*

**חֹלֶד** 1.0.1 n.[m.] **weasel**—Q חולד—in lists of unclean animals, <NOM CL> זֶה לָכֶם הַטָּמֵא בַּשֶּׁרֶץ ... הַחֹלֶד *this is what is unclean for you among the swarming things ... the weasel* Lv $11_{29}$. <OBJ> טמא pi. *declare unclean* 11QT $50_{20}$. <APP> שֶׁרֶץ *swarming thing* 11QT $50_{20}$.*

**חֻלְדָּה** 2 pr.n.f. **Huldah,** prophet and wife of Shallum, <SUBJ> ישׁב *dwell* 2 K $22_{14}$||2 C $34_{22}$, אמר *say* 2 K $22_{14}$||2 C $34_{22}$. <APP> אִשָּׁה *woman* 2 K $22_{14}$||2 C $34_{22}$,

נְבִיאָה *female prophet* 2 K 22$_{14}$||2 C 34$_{22}$. <PREP> אֶל *to*, + הלך *go* 2 K 22$_{14}$||2 C 34$_{22}$, שׁלח *send* 2 K 22$_{14}$||2 C 34$_{22}$, דבר pi. *speak* 2 K 22$_{14}$||2 C 34$_{22}$.*

**חֶלְדַּי** 2.0.0.2 pr.n.m. **Heldai, 1.** son of Baanah, warrior and official of David, perh. ident. with חֵלֶב *Heleb* and חֵלֶד *Heled*, <NOM CL> הַשְּׁנֵים עָשָׂר לִשְׁנֵים עָשָׂר הַחֹדֶשׁ חֶלְדַּי *the twelfth, for the twelfth month, was Heldai* 1 C 27$_{15}$. <APP> נְטוֹפָתִי *Netophathite* 1 C 27$_{15}$. **2.** returning exile from Babylon at time of Zechariah, <SUBJ> בוא *come* Zc 6$_{10}$. <PREP> לְ of benefit, *for, to*, + היה *be* Zc 6$_{14}$ (if em. לְחֶלְדַּי *to Heldai*); מִן of direction, *from*, + לקח *take* Zc 6$_{10}$. **3.** Arad ost. 27$_{5}$. **4.** father of Joab, <CSTR> בן חלדי *son of Heldai* Arad ost. 39$_{10}$.*

**חלה I** 59.0.5 vb. **be weak—Qal** 38.0.2 Pf. חָלָה, חָלִית, חָלוּ, חָלִיתִי; + waw וַיָּחַל, וְחָלִיתִי; ptc. חוֹלֶה (חֹלֶה), fs חוֹלָה, cstr. חוֹלַת; inf. חֲלוֹתָם, חֲלֹתוֹ—**1. be weak, be tired, be(come) ill, feel pain, regret** (perh. at 1 S 22$_{8}$ Is 57$_{10}$ Jr 5$_{3}$ Pr 23$_{35}$ חלה IV *be anxious*; perh. at 1 S 22$_{8}$ Jr 5$_{3}$ חיל IV *take heed*, perh. at Ec 5$_{12.15}$ חלה V *be alone*).

<SUBJ> Abijah 1 K 14$_{1}$, Ahaziah 2 K 1$_{2}$, Asa 1 K 15$_{23}$, Benhadad 2 K 8$_{7}$, David 1 S 19$_{14}$, Elisha 2 K 13$_{14}$, Hezekiah 2 K 20$_{1}$||Is 38$_{1}$||2 C 32$_{24}$ 2 K 20$_{12}$||Is 39$_{1}$ Is 38$_{9}$ (:: חיה *revive*), Joram 2 K 8$_{29}$||2 C 22$_{6}$, Nehemiah Ne 2$_{2}$, Samson Jg 16$_{7.11.17}$ (all three + היה *be*), Israelites Is 57$_{10}$ Jr 5$_{3}$, Benjaminite 1 S 22$_{8}$, מֶלֶךְ *king* 2 K 8$_{7}$, שָׁכֵן *inhabitant* Is 33$_{24}$, עֵד *witness* Ps 35$_{13}$, אָב *father* Gn 48$_{1}$, בֵּן *son* 1 K 14$_{5}$ 17$_{17}$, נַעַר *lad* 1 S 30$_{13}$, drunkard Pr 23$_{35}$, יָד *hand* Lm 4$_{6}$ (if em. חול I *whirl* or II *be weak*), רָעָה *evil* Ec 5$_{12.15}$; subj. not specified, 2QapProph 3$_{3}$ 4Q418 130$_{2}$ 5Q25 1$_{1}$.

<PREP> בְּ of place/time, *in*, + יוֹם *day* 2 K 20$_{1}$||Is 38$_{1}$|| 2 C 32$_{24}$; of instrument, *by (means of), through* Lm 4$_{6}$ (if em.); עַל *on account of*, + Saul 1 S 22$_{8}$; אֵת *with*, + חֳלִי *sickness* 2 K 13$_{14}$, רֶגֶל *feet* 1 K 15$_{23}$.

<COLL> חָלִיתִי הַיּוֹם שְׁלֹשָׁה *I became ill three day(s) ago* 1 S 30$_{13}$.

<ANT> חיה *revive*.

**2.** ptc. as noun, **weak one, sick one,** of humans (Ezk 34$_{4.16}$) or animals (Ml 1$_{8.13}$), <OBJ> בוא hi. *bring* Ml 1$_{13}$, נגשׁ hi. *bring near*, i.e. offer Ml 1$_{8}$, רפא pi. *heal* Ezk 34$_{4}$, חזק *strengthen* Ezk 34$_{16}$. <CSTR> חוֹלַת אַהֲבָה *one sick of love* Ca 2$_{5}$ 5$_{8}$. <PREP> כְּ *as* Jr 4$_{31}$.

**Ni.** 10 Pf. נֶחֱלוּ, נֶחֱלֵיתִי; ptc. נַחְלָה (נַחֲלָה), נַחֲלוֹת—**1. be made weak, be made sick** (perh. at Am 6$_{6}$ חלה IV *be anxious* and at Na 3$_{19}$ חלה V *be alone*, ni. *be unprecedented*), <SUBJ> Israel Jr 12$_{13}$, Daniel Dn 8$_{27}$, שׁכב ptc. *one who lies down* Am 6$_{6}$, מַכָּה *wound* Jr 10$_{19}$ 14$_{17}$ 30$_{12}$ Na 3$_{19}$, יוֹם *day* Is 17$_{11}$. <PREP> עַל *on account of, because of*, + שֶׁבֶר *breaking* Am 6$_{6}$. <COLL> נֶחֱלֵיתִי יָמִים *I was ill for days* Dn 8$_{27}$.

**2.** ptc. as noun, **one who is weak, sick,** <OBJ> חזק pi. *strengthen* Ezk 34$_{4}$, נגח pi. *thrust* Ezk 34$_{21}$. <CSTR> כָּל־הַנַּחְלוֹת *all the sick ones* Ezk 34$_{21}$.

**Pi.** 1 Pf. חִלָּה—**make sick,** <SUBJ> ״ *Y.* Dt 29$_{21}$. <OBJ> תַּחֲלֻאִים *diseases* Dt 29$_{21}$, מַכָּה *wound* Dt 29$_{21}$. <PREP> בְּ of place, *in*, + אֶרֶץ *land* Dt 29$_{21}$.

**Pu.** 1 Pf. חֻלֵּיתָ—**be made weak** (unless חלה V *be alone*, pu. *be left alone*, i.e. removed from human society), <SUBJ> מֶלֶךְ *king* of Babylon Is 14$_{10}$. <PREP> כְּ *as*, + מֶלֶךְ *king* of earth Is 14$_{10}$.

**Hi.** 3.0.3 Pf. הֶחֱלוּ, הֶחֱלֵיתִי; ptc. fs מַחֲלָה—**make sick,** <SUBJ> ״ *Y.* Mc 6$_{13}$ (unless חלה V *be alone*, hi. *make* wound *unique*; or em. חלל II hi. *begin*), שַׂר *prince* Ho 7$_{5}$, נֶגַע *plague* 1QH 11$_{22}$, hope deferred Pr 13$_{12}$; subj. not specified, 4QVisSam 3.3$_{1}$ 4Q411 1$_{4}$. <OBJ> לֵב *heart* Pr 13$_{12}$. <COLL> הֶחֱלוּ שָׂרִים חֲמַת מִיָּיִן *the princes became sick with their heat which was from wine* Ho 7$_{5}$ (if em. חֲמַת *heat of*).

**Ho.** 3 Pf. הָחֳלֵיתִי—**be wounded,** <SUBJ> Ahab 1 K 22$_{34}$||2 C 18$_{33}$, Josiah 2 C 35$_{23}$.

**Htp.** 3 + waw וַיִּתְחַל; impv. הִתְחָל; inf. הִתְחַלּוֹת—**feign sickness, make oneself ill,** <SUBJ> Amnon 2 S 13$_{2.5.6}$. <PREP> בַּעֲבוּר *on account of*, + Tamar 2 S 13$_{2}$, אָחוֹת *sister* 2 S 13$_{2}$.*

→ חֳלִי *sickness*, מַחֲלֶה *sickness*, מַחֲלָה *sickness*, תַּחֲלֻאִים *diseases*.

**חלה II** 16.2.1 vb. **entreat—Pi.** 16.2.1 Pf. חִלִּיתִי, חִלּוּ, חִלִּינוּ; impf. יְחַלּוּ; + waw וַיְחַל; impv. חַל, חַלּוּ; inf. חַלּוֹת—**appease, entreat favour of** (unless חלה V pi. *make* face *unique*, i.e. secure favour for oneself alone), <SUBJ> עַם *people* Zc 8$_{22}$, גּוֹי *nation* Zc 8$_{22}$, Israel Dn 9$_{13}$, Hezekiah

Jr 26$_{19}$, Jehoahaz 2 K 13$_{4}$, Manasseh 2 C 33$_{12}$, Moses Ex 32$_{11}$, Regem-melech Zc 7$_{2}$, Saul 1 S 13$_{12}$, Sharezer Zc 7$_{2}$.

אִישׁ *man* of God 1 K 13$_{6}$ (+ חלל htp. *pray*) 13$_{6}$, *man* Zc 7$_{2}$ Dn 9$_{13}$, בֵּן *son* Si 30$_{30}$, בַּת *daughter* of Tyre Ps 45$_{13}$, שַׂר *prince* Si 30$_{28}$ (+ שׁוב *do again*), רַב *great one* Jb 11$_{19}$ Pr 19$_{6}$, worshipper Ps 119$_{58}$ 1QH 16$_{11}$, יֹשֵׁב *inhabitant* Zc 8$_{21}$ Dn 9$_{13}$, מֹשֵׁל *ruler* Si 30$_{28}$ (+ שׁוב *do again*), כֹּהֵן *priest* Ml 1$_{9}$.

<OBJ> פָּנִים *face* of Y. Ex 32$_{11}$ 1 S 13$_{12}$ 1 K 13$_{6.6}$ 2 K 13$_{4}$ Jr 26$_{19}$ Zc 7$_{2}$ 8$_{21.22}$ Dn 9$_{13}$ 2 C 33$_{12}$, of God Ml 1$_{9}$, of another Ps 45$_{13}$ 119$_{58}$ Jb 11$_{19}$ Pr 19$_{6}$ Si 30$_{30}$ 1QH 16$_{11}$.

<PREP> בְּ of instrument, *by (means of)*, + לֵב *heart* Ps 119$_{58}$, רוּחַ *spirit* 1QH 16$_{11}$, מִנְחָה *grain offering* Ps 45$_{13}$.*

*חלה III vb. **adorn—Ni., be adorned,** <SUBJ> פֶּתִי *simple one* Pr 14$_{18}$ (if em. נָחֲלוּ the simple *inherit* folly to נֶחֱלוּ the simple *are adorned* [with] folly).

*חלה IV 5 vb. **be anxious—Qal** 4 Pf. חָלִית ,חָלִיתִי ,חָלוּ; ptc. חֹלֶה—**be aware, be concerned** (unless חלה I *be weak*), <SUBJ> Israelites Is 57$_{10}$ Jr 5$_{3}$, drunkard Pr 23$_{35}$ (|| ידע *know*), no one 1 S 22$_{8}$. <PREP> עַל *for, concerning* Saul 1 S 22$_{8}$ (unless חלה I *be weak* or חיל IV *take heed*).

**Ni.** 1 Pf. נֶחְלוּ—**be distressed** (unless חלה I *be weak*), <SUBJ> indolent Am 6$_{6}$. <PREP> עַל *on account of*, + שֵׁבֶר *breaking* Am 6$_{6}$.

*חלה V 20.2.1 vb. **be alone—Qal** 1 Ptc. חוֹלָה—**be alone, be unique** (Ec 5$_{12.15}$), **be disengaged** (Ps 77$_{11}$), **desist** (Ho 8$_{10}$), <SUBJ> Israel Ho 8$_{10}$ (if em. וַיָּחֵלּוּ *and they began*, from חלל II, to וְיֶחֱלוּ *and they will desist*), רָעָה *evil* Ec 5$_{12.15}$ (unless חלה I *weak*), יָמִין *right hand* Ps 77$_{11}$ (if em. חַלּוֹתִי הִיא *it is my being wounded*, i.e. my wound, from חלל III *be pierced*, to חָלְתָה *it* [right hand] *is disengaged*). <PREP> מִן *(away) from*, + מַשָּׂא *burden* Ho 8$_{10}$ (if em.).

**Ni.** 1 Ptc. נַחְלָה—**be unprecedented** (unless חלה I *be made weak*), <SUBJ> מַכָּה *wound* Na 3$_{19}$.

**Hi.** 1 Pf. הֶחֱלֵיתִי—**make** wound **unique** (unless חלה I *be weak*, hi. *make sick*; or em. חלל II hi. *begin*). <SUBJ> י׳ Y. Mc 6$_{13}$. <OBJ> מַכָּה *wound* Mc 6$_{13}$ (if em. נכה hi. inf. *striking*).

**Pi.** 16.2.1 **make** face **unique,** i.e. secure favour for oneself alone, <SUBJ> עַם *people* Zc 8$_{22}$, גּוֹי *nation* Zc 8$_{22}$, Israel Dn 9$_{13}$, Hezekiah Jr 26$_{19}$, Jehoahaz 2 K 13$_{4}$, Manasseh 2 C 33$_{12}$, Moses Ex 32$_{11}$, Regem-melech Zc 7$_{2}$, Saul 1 S 13$_{12}$, Sharezer Zc 7$_{2}$.

אִישׁ *man* of God 1 K 13$_{6}$ (+ חלל htp. *pray*) 13$_{6}$, *man* Zc 7$_{2}$ Dn 9$_{13}$, בֵּן *son* Si 30$_{30}$, בַּת *daughter* of Tyre Ps 45$_{13}$, שַׂר *prince* Si 30$_{28}$ (+ שׁוב *do again*), רַב *great one* Jb 11$_{19}$ Pr 19$_{6}$, worshipper Ps 119$_{58}$ 1QH 16$_{11}$, יֹשֵׁב *inhabitant* Zc 8$_{21}$ Dn 9$_{13}$, מֹשֵׁל *ruler* Si 30$_{28}$ (+ שׁוב *do again*), כֹּהֵן *priest* Ml 1$_{9}$.

<OBJ> פָּנִים *face* of Y. Ex 32$_{11}$ 1 S 13$_{12}$ 1 K 13$_{6.6}$ 2 K 13$_{4}$ Jr 26$_{19}$ Zc 7$_{2}$ 8$_{21.22}$ Dn 9$_{13}$ 2 C 33$_{12}$, of God Ml 1$_{9}$, of another Ps 45$_{13}$ 119$_{58}$ Jb 11$_{19}$ Pr 19$_{6}$ Si 30$_{30}$ 1QH 16$_{11}$.

<PREP> בְּ of instrument, *by (means of)*, + לֵב *heart* Ps 119$_{58}$, רוּחַ *spirit* 1QH 16$_{11}$, מִנְחָה *grain offering* Ps 45$_{13}$.

**Pu.** 1 Pf. חֻלֵּיתָ—**be left alone,** i.e. removed from human society (unless חלה I pu. *be made weak*), <SUBJ> מֶלֶךְ *king* of Babylon Is 14$_{10}$. <PREP> כְּ *as*, + מֶלֶךְ *king* of earth Is 14$_{10}$.

חַלָּה 14.0.4 n.f. **cake**—cstr. חַלַּת; pl. חַלּוֹת (חלת); cstr. חַלֹּת (חַלּוֹת)—**cake** of bread, used in offerings, <SUBJ> היה *be* Lv 24$_{5}$ (+ שְׁנֵי עֶשְׂרֹנִים *two tenths [of an ephah]*) 11QT 8$_{9}$ ([יהיה החלה]; + (שני [עשרונים] 18$_{15}$ ([תה[יה]; + [שני] עשרונים סולת *two tenths [of an ephah] of fine flour*), בלל pass. *be mixed* with oil Ex 29$_{2}$ (+ לֶחֶם *bread*, רָקִיק *wafer*) Lv 24 7$_{12}$ (both || רָקִיק) 7$_{12}$ Nm 6$_{15}$ (+ מַצָּה ,רָקִיק *unleavened bread*).

<NOM CL> [לחם] בכורים הוא חלות החמץ *the bread of the first fruits is the leavened cakes* 4Q251 2$_{4}$.

<OBJ> אפה *bake* Lv 24$_{5}$ 11QT 8$_{8}$ ([אפיתה ... חל[ות *you shall bake ... cakes*), בוא hi. *bring* 11QT 18$_{15}$ ([חלות]; + לֶחֶם *bread*), לקח *take* Ex 29$_{2.23}$ (|| כִּכָּר *loaf*) Lv 8$_{26}$ Nm 6$_{19}$ (all three || רָקִיק *wafer*) 11QT 15$_{9}$ ([ולקחו חלת] *and they shall take a cake of* unleavened bread) 15$_{9}$ (+ רָקִיק), קרב hi. *offer* Lv 7$_{12.12}$, רום *raise*, i.e. offer Nm 15$_{20}$, חלק pi. *apportion* 2 S 6$_{19}$ (+ אֲשִׁישָׁה *raisin cake*, אֶשְׁפָּר *date cake*).

<CSTR> חַלַּת לֶחֶם *cake of bread* 2 S 6$_{19}$, *of bread of*, i.e. with, oil Ex 29$_{23}$ Lv 8$_{26}$ 11QT 15$_{9}$, חַלֹּת לֶחֶם חָמֵץ *cakes of*

*bread of leaven*, i.e. leavened bread Lv $7_{13}$, חלות החמץ *the cakes of leaven*, i.e. leavened cakes 4Q251 $2_4$, חַלַּת מַצָּה *cake of unleavened bread* Lv $8_{26}$ Nm $6_{19}$ 11QT $15_9$ ([חלת מצה]), חַלֹּת מַצּוֹת *cakes of unleavened bread* Ex $29_2$ Lv $2_4$ (חַלּוֹת), חלות התרומה *cakes of the offering* 4QD$^e$ $6_{19}$; סֹלֶת חַלֹּת *fine flour (consisting) of cakes* (unless *fine flour, cakes*) Lv $2_4$ (חַלּוֹת *of cakes of* unleavened bread) Nm $6_{15}$.

<APP> סֹלֶת *fine flour* Lv $7_{12}$, תְּרוּמָה *offering* Nm $15_{20}$, רֵאשִׁית עֲרִסֹתֵיכֶם *cereal offering* 11QT $18_{15}$ ([חלות]), מִנְחָה *the first of your coarse meal* Nm $15_{20}$.

<ADJ> אֶחָד *one* Ex $29_{23}$ Lv $8_{26.26}$ $24_5$ Nm $6_{19}$ 2 S $6_{19}$ 11QT $8_9$ ([החלה האחת]) 11QT $15_9$ ([חלת ... אחת]) $15_9$ $18_{15}$.

<PREP> עַל *upon*, i.e. with, + קרב hi. *offer* Lv $7_{13}$.

<COLL> שְׁתֵּים עֶשְׂרֵה חַלּוֹת *twelve cakes* Lv $24_5$ 11QT $8_8$ ([שתים עשרה חל]ות) $18_{15}$ ([שתים] עשרה חלות]).

<SYN> רָקִיק *wafer*, כִּכָּר *loaf*.

**חֲלוֹם** 65.2.5 n.m. **dream**—חֲלֹם; cstr. חֲלוֹם (חֲלֹם); sf. חֲלֹמִי (חֲלֹמִי), חֲלֹמוֹ; pl. חֲלוֹמוֹת (חֲלֹמוֹת); cstr. חֲלוֹמוֹת; sf. חֲלֹמֹתָיו ,חֲלֹמֹתֵינוּ ,חֲלֹמֹתֵיכֶם ,חֲלֹמֹתָם—of ordinary **dreams** in sleep (e.g. Is $29_7$ Ps $73_{20}$ Jb $7_{14}$ Ec $5_2$), **dreams** with prophetic content (e.g. Gn $20_{3.6}$ $31_{10.11}$ Nm $12_6$ 1 K $3_5$ Jb $33_{15}$), **dreams** of false prophets (Dt $13_{2.4.6}$ Jr $23_{27.28.28.32}$ $27_9$ $29_8$ Zc $10_2$).

<SUBJ> היה *be* Gn $37_{20}$, רבב *be many* Ec $5_6$, שׁנא ni. *be repeated* Gn $41_{32}$, בעה htp. *be sought* 11QPs$^a$ $22_{14}$, בוא *come* Ec $5_2$ (or em. הַחֲלוֹם *the dream* to הֶחָלוּם *the one who is sound*, i.e. חלם *be healthy*, pass. ptc.)

<NOM CL> הוּא אִתּוֹ חֲלוֹם *the dream is with him* Jr $23_{28}$, חֲלוֹם פַּרְעֹה אֶחָד *the dream of Pharaoh is one* Gn $41_{25}$, sim. Gn $41_{26}$, מָה הַחֲלוֹם הַזֶּה *what is this dream?* Gn $37_{10}$, הִנֵּה חֲלוֹם *behold it was a dream* Gn $41_7$ 1 K $3_{15}$.

<OBJ> לקח *take*, i.e. accept 11QPs$^a$ $22_{14}$, חלם *dream* Gn $37_{5.9.9}$ $40_{5.8}$ $41_{11.15}$ Dt $13_{2.4.6}$ Jg $7_{13}$ Jl $3_1$ Dn $2_{1.3}$ 11QT $54_{8.11.15}$, זכר *remember* Gn $42_9$, שׁמע *hear* Gn $37_6$ $41_{15}$, ידע *know* Dn $2_3$, פתר *interpret* Gn $40_8$ $41_{12.15.15}$, ספר pi. *relate* Gn $37_9$ $40_9$ $41_8$ Jg $7_{13}$ Jr $23_{27.28}$, דבר pi. *speak* Zc $10_2$ (or em. חֲלוֹמָה *wise woman*, as subj. of דבר pi.), נגד hi. *declare* Dn $2_2$, נבא ni. *prophesy* Jr $23_{32}$.

<CSTR> חֲלוֹם פַּרְעֹה *dream of Pharaoh* Gn $41_{25}$, חֲלוֹם הַלָּיְלָה *dream of the night* Gn $20_3$ $31_{24}$ (חֲלֹם) 1 K $3_5$, חֲלֹמוֹת חלמות נביאים *dreams of the prophets* 11QPs$^a$ $22_{14}$, חֲלֹמוֹת שֶׁקֶר *dreams of falsehood* Jr $23_{32}$, הַשָּׁוְא *of falsehood* Zc $10_2$ (or em. חֲלוֹמָה *wise woman*).

בַּעַל הַחֲלֹמוֹת *the master of dreams*, i.e. expert in dreams Gn $37_{19}$, פִּתְרוֹן חֲלֹמוֹ *interpretation of his dream* Gn $40_5$ $41_{11}$, מִסְפַּר הַחֲלוֹם *the recounting of the dream* Jg $7_{15}$, נְבִיאֵי חֲלֹמוֹת *prophets of dreams of* Jr $23_{32(mss)}$, ... כָּל חֲלֹמוֹת *all ... dreams* Dn $1_{17}$.

<ADJ> זֶה *this* Gn $37_6$, הוּא *that* Dt $13_{4.6}$ 11QT $54_{11}$, אַחֵר *another* Gn $37_9$.

<PREP> בְּ *in, with* Gn $40_{9.16}$ $41_{17}$ Jb $33_{15}$, + ראה *see* Gn $31_{10}$ $41_{22}$, ni. *appear* 1 K $3_5$, בוא *come* Gn $20_3$ $31_{24}$, בין hi. *understand* Dn $1_{17}$ Si $40_6$ ([חלו]מות), אמר *say* Gn $20_6$ $31_{11}$; of instrument, *by (means of)*, + שׁכח hi. *cause to forget* Jr $23_{27}$, חתת pi. *scare* Jb $7_{14}$, ענה *answer* 1 S $28_6$ (+ נָבִיא *prophet*, אוּרִים *Urim*) $28_{15}$, דבר pi. *speak* Nm $12_6$; עַל *because of, on account of*, + שׂנא *hate* Gn $37_8$ (דָּבָר II *word*); כְּ *as* Gn $41_{12}$ Ps $73_{20}$ Jb $20_8$, + היה *be* Is $29_7$; אֶל *to*, + שׁמע *listen* Jr $27_9$ (or em. חֲלוֹמָה *wise woman*) $29_8$.

<COLL> וַיַּחַלְמוּ חֲלוֹם ... אִישׁ חֲלֹמוֹ *and they dreamt a dream ... each one his own dream* Gn $40_5$.

<SYN> דָּבָר *word*.

Also Si $31_1$ 11QapPs$^a$ $4_7$ (חל[ו]ם).*

⇒ חלם *dream*.

**[חָלוּם]**, see חלם II *be healthy*, Qal.

* **[חֲלוֹמָה]** n.f. **wise woman**, <SUBJ> דבר pi. *speak* Zc $10_2$ (if em. חֲלֹמוֹת הַשָּׁוְא *dreams of falsehood* to הַחֲלֹמוֹת שָׁוְא *the wise women* speak *falsehood*). <PREP> אֶל *to*, + שׁמע *hear*, i.e. listen Jr $27_9$ (if em. חֲלֹמֹתֵיכֶם *your dreams* to חֲלֹמֹתֵיכֶם *your wise women*).

**חַלּוֹן** 31.1.2 n.m. **window**—cstr. חַלּוֹן; pl. חַלּוֹנִים (חַלּוֹנוֹת, חַלֹּנוֹת); cstr. חַלּוֹנֵי; sf. חַלּוֹנֵינוּ ,חַלּוֹנָיו ,חַלּוֹנֵי—**window, opening**, <SUBJ> אטם pass. perh. *be recessed* 1 K $6_4$ Ezk $40_{16}$ $41_{26}$ 11QT $33_{11}$, כסה pu. *be covered* Ezk $41_{16}$.

<NOM CL> חַלּוֹנוֹת סָבִיב סָבִיב *the windows were all around* Ezk $40_{16}$, חַלּוֹנוֹת ... סָבִיב סָבִיב *the windows ... were all around* Ezk $40_{25}$ (חַלּוֹנִים) $40_{29.33.36}$, sim. Ezk $41_{16}$, [חלונים] בתוכימה *the windows were among them*

11QT 32$_{9}$, חַלּוֹנָיו ... כְּמִדַּת הַשַּׁעַר *its windows ... were as the measurement of the gate* Ezk 40$_{22(Qr)}$.

<OBJ> עשׂה *make* 1 K 6$_{4}$, פתח *open* Gn 8$_{6}$=4QpGen$^{a}$ 1.1$_{13}$ 2 K 13$_{17}$.

<CSTR> חַלּוֹן הַתֵּבָה *window of the ark* Gn 8$_{6}$=4QpGen$^{a}$ 1.1$_{13}$, בֵּיתִי *of my house* Pr 7$_{6}$, חַלּוֹנֵי שְׁקֻפִים *windows of frames* 1 K 6$_{4}$.

<APP> גֹּבַהּ *height* 11QT 5$_{7}$ ([החלונים]) 6$_{5}$ ([החל]ונים).

<ADJ> אֵלֶּה *these* Ezk 40$_{25}$.

<PREP> בְּ *in*, + עלה *go up* Jr 9$_{20}$, קשׁר *bind* Jos 2$_{18.21}$, שׁיר pol. *sing continuously* Zp 2$_{14}$; כְּ *as* Ezk 40$_{25}$; מִן of direction, *from*, + שׁגח hi. *gaze* Ca 2$_{9}$; אֶל *to*, + נשׂא *raise* 2 K 9$_{32}$; בְּעַד *through*, + שׁקף ni. *look down* Jg 5$_{28}$ 2 S 6$_{16}$||1 C 15$_{29}$ Pr 7$_{6}$, hi. *look down* Gn 26$_{8}$ 2 K 9$_{30}$ Si 14$_{23}$, בוא *come* Jl 2$_{9}$, ירד hi. *bring down*, i.e. let down Jos 2$_{15}$ 1 S 19$_{12}$; עַד *unto* Ezk 41$_{16}$.

Also 4QpGen$^{c}$ 1$_{2}$ (ח[לונים]).

⇒ חלל *pierce*.

**חֵלוֹן**, see חֵלֹן *Helon*.

**חֹלוֹן**, see חלן *Holon*.

**חֲלוֹף** 1 n.m. **passing away** or **opposition*** or **foolishness**, <CSTR> בְּנֵי חֲלוֹף *sons of passing away*, i.e. ones who pass away, or *sons of opposition*, i.e. legal opponents, or *sons of foolishness*, i.e. ones unable to mount legal defence Pr 31$_{8}$ (or em. חֳלִי *of sickness*, or עֲלוּף *of fainting*; + אִלֵּם *dumb one*).*

**חָלוּץ**, see חלץ II *equip (for war)*, Qal, §2.

**חֲלוּשָׁה** 1 n.f. **defeat**, perh. **defeated ones**, <OBJ> ענה *sing* Ex 32$_{18}$ (אֵין קוֹל עֲנוֹת חֲלוּשָׁה *there is no voice of singing [of] defeat*; :: גְּבוּרָה *might*). <ANT> גְּבוּרָה *might*.

⇒ חלשׁ *defeat*.

**[חֲלַח]** 3 pl.n. **Halah**—לְ/בַּחְלַח—city or district in northern Mesopotamia, <CSTR> גָּלֻת חֲלַח *diaspora of Halah* Ob 20 (if em. הַחֵל־הַזֶּה לְ *this fortress of* to חֲלַח זֶה *Halah, which is*). <PREP> לְ of direction, *to*, + בוא hi. *bring* 1 C 5$_{26}$ (mss לְהָלַח); בְּ of place, direction, *in(to)*, + זבל *dwell* Ob 20 (if em. הַחֵל־הַזֶּה לְ *this fortress of* to בַּחֲלַח יִזְבְּלוּ *[who] dwell in Halah*), ישׁב hi. *cause to dwell* 2 K 17$_{6}$, נוח hi. *place* 2 K 18$_{11}$ (if em. וַיַּנְחֵם *and he led them* to וַיַּנִּחֵם *and he placed them*), נחה hi. *lead* 2 K 18$_{11}$ (unless em.).

**חַלְחוּל** 1 pl.n. **Halhul**, town in Judah, mod. Ḥalḥūl, 6 km N of Hebron, <NOM CL> בָּהָר ... חַלְחוּל *in the hill country was ... Halhul* Jos 15$_{58}$.

**חַלְחָלָה** 4.0.2 n.f. **anguish**, <SUBJ> היה *be* Ezk 30$_{4}$ (+ חֶרֶב *sword*) 30$_{9}$ (both + בְּ *in* Ethiopia). <NOM CL> חַלְחָלָה בְּכָל־מָתְנַיִם *anguish is on all loins* Na 2$_{11}$ (+ פָּארוּר *paleness*) 4QMidrEschat$^{b}$ 10$_{3}$ ([בכול מתנ]ים). <OBJ> מלא *be full of* Is 21$_{3}$ (מָלְאוּ מָתְנַי חַלְחָלָה *my loins are full of anguish*; + צִיר *pang*). <PREP> בְּ of accompaniment, *with*, *in*, + הלל htpo. *act like a mad one* 1QH 10$_{33}$ (|| רְעָדָה *trembling*); of instrument, *by (means of)*, *with*, + דלל po. *make low* 4Q525 15$_{3}$ (בחלח[לות]). <SYN> רְעָדָה *trembling*.*

⇒ חול *writhe*.

**חלט** 1 vb. **accept—Qal** (or perh. **Hi.**) 1 + waw וַיַּחְלְטוּ (mss וַיַּחְלְטוּהָ)—**accept** as convincing, <SUBJ> אִישׁ *man* 1 K 20$_{33}$ (+ מהר pi. *be quick*). <OBJ> words of Ahab 1 K 20$_{33(mss)}$ (וַיַּחְלְטוּהָ *and they accepted it*). <PREP> מִן of direction, *from*, + מֶלֶךְ *king* 1 K 20$_{33(mss)}$ (וַיַּחְלְטוּהָ מִמֶּנּוּ *and they accepted it from him*; L וַיַּחְלְטוּ הֲמִמֶּנּוּ appar. *and they came to a decision as to whether [it was] from him*).

**[חֲלִי] I** 2 n.m. **ornament**—cstr. חֲלִי; pl. חֲלָאִים—item of jewellery, <NOM CL> חֲלִי־כֶתֶם מוֹכִיחַ חָכָם *a wise reprover is an ornament of gold* Pr 25$_{12}$, חַמּוּקֵי יְרֵכַיִךְ כְּמוֹ חֲלָאִים *the curves of your thighs are like ornaments* Ca 7$_{2}$. <CSTR> חֲלִי־כֶתֶם *ornament of gold* Pr 25$_{12}$ (|| נֶזֶם *ring*). <SYN> נֶזֶם *ring*.

**חֲלִי II** 1 pl.n. **Hali**, town in Asher, <SUBJ> היה *be* Jos 19$_{25}$ (וַיְהִי גְּבוּלָם חֶלְקַת וַחֲלִי *and their border was Helkath and Hali*; or em. מֵחֶלְקַת *from Helkath* and Hali). <PREP> מִן of direction, *from*, + היה *be* Jos 19$_{25}$ (if em.; see Subj.).

**חֳלִי** 24.3.3 n.m. **sickness**—חֳלִי (Si חולי); sf. חָלְיוֹ; pl. חֳלָיִם (חֳלָיִים, Q חוליים, mss חֳלָאִים); sf. חֳלָיֵנוּ—**sickness, illness, affliction** (e.g. Jr 10$_{19}$ Ec 6$_{2}$), <SUBJ> היה *be* 1 K 17$_{17}$ (+ חָזָק *severe*), כתב pass. *be written* Dt 28$_{61}$ (|| מַכָּה *affliction*, + מַדְוֶה *illness*), קנן pi. *nest* Si 37$_{30(B, D)}$, רנן *shout* Si 37$_{30(Bmg)}$.

<NOM CL> זֶה חֳלִי *this is affliction* Jr 10$_{19}$ (+ מַכָּה *affliction*, שֶׁבֶר *breaking*), הוּא ... חֳלִי *it is ... affliction* Ec 6$_{2}$ (|| הֶבֶל *vanity*), עַד־לְמַעְלָה חָלְיוֹ *his illness (became) severe* 2 C 16$_{12}$, עַל־פָּנַי תָּמִיד חֳלִי *sickness is continually before me* Jr 6$_{7}$ (|| מַכָּה), חָלְיוֹ וָקָצֶף appar. *(there is) his sickness and anger* Ec 5$_{16}$.

<OBJ> פלא hi. *make wonderful*, i.e. exceptional Dt 28$_{59}$ (|| מַכָּה *affliction*), עלה hi. *bring up* Dt 28$_{61}$, נשׂא *bear* Is 53$_{4}$ (|| מַכְאוֹב *pain*) Jr 10$_{19}$, סור hi. *remove* Dt 7$_{15}$=4QMidrEschat$^{b}$ 10$_{2}$ ([הסיר]; + מַדְוֶה *illness*), ידע *know* Is 53$_{3}$ (1QIsa$^{a,b}$; MT יְדוּעַ *known of*), חלה *be sick with* 2 K 13$_{14}$, ראה *see* Ho 5$_{13}$ (|| מָזוֹר *wound*).

<CSTR> בְּנֵי חֳלִי *sons of sickness*, i.e. the ill Pr 31$_{8}$ (if em. חֲלוֹף *of passing away*), יְדוּעַ חֳלִי *one known of*, i.e. by, *sickness* Is 53$_{3}$ (|| מַכְאוֹב *pain*), כָּל־חֳלִי *every sickness* Dt 7$_{15}$ (חֳלִי)=4QMidrEschat$^{b}$ 10$_{2}$ (כול) Dt 28$_{61}$.

<ADJ> רַע *bad*, i.e. severe Dt 28$_{59}$ Ec 6$_{2}$ 2 C 21$_{15(mss)}$ 4QDibHam$^{a}$ 1.3$_{8}$ (+ רָעָב *hunger*, צָמָא *thirst*, דֶּבֶר *pestilence*, חֶרֶב *sword*), רַב *great* 2 C 21$_{15}$, חָזָק *strong*, i.e. severe Si 34$_{2(B)}$, אמן ni. ptc. *enduring* Dt 28$_{59}$, זֶה *this* 2 K 1$_{2}$ 8$_{8.9}$.

<PREP> לְ introducing predicate Is 1$_{5}$ (+ דַּוָּי *faint*); *by (means of), with*, + נגף *strike* 2 C 21$_{18}$; בְּ of place, time, *in, during* 2 C 21$_{15}$ (+ מַחֲלֶה *disease*), + הפך *turn*, i.e. change Ps 41$_{4}$ (or em. בְּחָלְיוֹ *in his sickness* to בַּחֲלוֹתִי *when I am sick*, from חלה, or לְחֵיִל *into strength*; + דְּוַי *illness*), דרשׁ *seek* 2 C 16$_{12}$; עבר htp. *delay* Si 38$_{9(B)}$; of direction, *into*, + בוא *come* 2 C 21$_{15}$ (if ins. תָּבֹא *you will come*); *because of*, + מות *die*; מִן of direction, *from*, + חיה *live*, i.e. recover 2 K 1$_{2}$ 8$_{8.9}$ Is 38$_{9}$; of cause, *on account of*, + יצא *go out* 2 C 21$_{15}$; of comparison, *(more) than*, + פרע hi. *disturb* Si 34$_{2(B)}$; עִם *with*, i.e. because of, + יצא *go out* 2 C 21$_{19}$ (+ תַּחֲלֻאִים *diseases*), מגר pass. *be cast down* 1QH 8$_{26}$ (+ נֶגַע *plague*).

<COLL> חֳלִי לְאֵין מַרְפֵּא *an illness without cure* 2 C 21$_{18}$.

<SYN> מַכָּה *affliction*, מַכְאוֹב *pain*, מָזוֹר *wound*, הֶבֶל *vanity*.*

⇒ חלה *be sick*.

**[חֶלְיָה]** 1 n.f. **jewellery**—sf. חֶלְיָתָהּ—<OBJ> עדה *deck oneself with* Ho 2$_{15}$ (|| נֶזֶם *ring*). <SYN> נֶזֶם *ring*.

**[חֶלְיָה]** 0.0.1 n.f. **sediment**—Q חליא—either **sediment** at bottom of cistern or **(perforated) stone** covering top of cistern (Milik), <PREP> בְּ of instrument, *by (means of), with*, + סתם pass. *be stopped up*, i.e. concealed 3QTr 1$_{7}$ (Allegro בחלא *in a hole*).

**[חַלְיוֹ]** 0.0.0.1 pr.n.[m.] **Hallio,** Kuntillet ʿAjrud inscr. C3.

**חָלִיל** 6.1.4 n.m. **flute**—cstr. Q חליל; pl. חֲלִלִים (חֲלִילִים)—**flute, pipe,** <SUBJ> היה *be* Is 5$_{12}$=4QpIsa$^{b}$ 2$_{3}$ (|| נֵבֶל *harp*, תֹּף *tambourine*, כִּנּוֹר *lyre*, יַיִן *wine*), ערב hi. *make sweet* Si 40$_{21(Bmg)}$ (נֵבֶל || [ח]ל[י]ל). <NOM CL> לִפְנֵיהֶם ... חָלִיל *before them was ... a flute* 1 S 20$_{5}$ (|| נֵבֶל *harp*, תֹּף *tambourine*, כִּנּוֹר *lyre*). <OBJ> נשׂא *raise* 1QS 10$_{9}$. <CSTR> חליל תהלה *flute of praise* 1QH 11$_{23}$ (|| נֵבֶל *harp*, כִּנּוֹר *lyre*), שפתי *of my lips* 1QS 10$_{9}$ (+ כִּנּוֹר, נֵבֶל). <PREP> בְּ of accompaniment, *with*, + הלך *go* Is 30$_{29}$, זמר pi. *sing praises* 1QH 11$_{23}$; introducing object, + חלל pi. *play* 1 K 1$_{40}$ (or em. מְחַלְּלִים בַּחֲלִלִים *playing flutes* to מְחֹלְלִים בִּמְחֹלוֹת *dancing with dances*); כְּ *as* 4QBark$^{a}$ 2.1$_{10}$, + המה *moan* Jr 48$_{36.36}$. <COLL> חָלִיל וָיַיִן *flute and wine* Is 5$_{12}$. <SYN> נֵבֶל *harp*, תֹּף *tambourine*, כִּנּוֹר *lyre*, יַיִן *wine*.*

⇒ חלל *play the flute*.

**חָלִילָה** 21 interj. **may it not be**—חָלִלָה (Gn 18$_{25.25}$ Jb 34$_{10}$)—**1a.** followed by לִי *to me* (etc.), in ref. to יי *Y.* Gn 18$_{25.25}$ 1 S 2$_{30}$, יוֹסֵף *Joseph* Gn 44$_{17}$, שְׁמוּאֵל *Samuel* 1 S 12$_{23}$, דָּוִד *David* 1 S 20$_{2}$ (if em.; see §3) 20$_{9}$ 24$_{7}$, אֲחִימֶלֶךְ *Ahimelech* 1 S 22$_{15}$, יוֹאָב *Joab* 2 S 20$_{20}$, אִיּוֹב *Job* Jb 27$_{5}$, Reubenites, Gadites, and Manassites Jos 22$_{29}$, עַם *people* Jos 24$_{16}$, עֶבֶד *servant*, i.e. Joseph's brother Gn 44$_{7}$.

**1b.** followed by noun + לְ, לָאֵל *to God* Jb 34$_{10}$.

<COLL> לִי *to me* (etc.) followed by מֵיי *from Y.*, i.e. may Y. prevent me (from) 1 S 24$_{7}$ 26$_{11}$ 2 S 23$_{17(mss)}$ (L lacks מִן, i.e. 'may it not be, O Y., to me'; ||1 C 11$_{19}$

מֵאֱלֹהָי *from my God* [or del. מִן]) 1 K 21$_3$ (or em. מֵאֱלֹהַי); חָלִילָה חָלִילָה לִּי *may it not be, may it not be to me* 2 S 20$_{20}$ (mss lack second חָלִילָה), מִמֶּנּוּ *from us*, i.e. may we prevent ourselves (from) Jos 22$_{29}$.

**2.** followed by לִי *to me* (etc.) and **a.** מִן privative, *from*, i.e. so as not to (e.g. Gn 18$_{25}$ Jos 22$_{29}$ 1 S 12$_{23}$) + inf. of עשׂה *do* Gn 18$_{25}$ 44$_{7.17}$ 2 S 23$_{17}$‖1 C 11$_{19}$, מרד *rebel* Jos 22$_{29}$, חטא *sin* 1 S 12$_{23}$, עזב *abandon* Jos 24$_{16}$, חדל *cease* 1 S 12$_{23}$, שׁלח *send*, i.e. extend hand against 1 S 26$_{11}$, נתן *give* 1 K 21$_3$. **b.** מִן partitive, *(any) of, (some) of*, + רֶשַׁע *evil*, i.e. may there not be any evil (belonging) to God Jb 34$_{10}$. **c.** אִם *if*, + impf. (e.g. חָלִילָה לִּי מֵי׳ אִם־אֶעֱשֶׂה *may Y. prevent me from doing* 1 S 24$_7$), of עשׂה *do* 1 S 24$_7$, בלע pi. *destroy* 2 S 20$_{20}$, שׁחת hi. *destroy* 2 S 20$_{20}$, צדק hi. *justify* Jb 27$_5$. **d.** without following subordinate clause, Gn 18$_{25}$ 1 S 2$_{30}$ 20$_9$ 22$_{15}$.

**3.** without following prep. or subordinate clause, 1 S 14$_{45}$ (חָלִילָה חַי־י׳ *may it not be; as Y. is alive*) 20$_2$ (or ins. לְךָ *to you*, i.e. David, as §1).

[חֲלִיפָא] 0.0.2 pr.n.m. **Halipha, 1.** in deed of sale, **<NOM CL>** דרום חליפא *in the south is Halipha* Mur 22 1$_3$ ([חל]יפא) 1$_{12}$ ([דרום]). **<APP>** בַּר *son* Mur 22 1$_{12}$. **2.** son of Joseph and party to tenancy agreement, **<SUBJ>** היה *be* Mur 24 3$_{14}$ ([חליפא]), אמר *say* Mur 24 3$_4$ ([חליפא]), חכר *rent* Mur 24 3$_4$ ([חליפא]), שׁקל *weigh* Mur 24 3$_{14}$ ([חליפא]). **<APP>** בֵּן *son* Mur 24 3$_4$ ([חליפא בן]) 3$_{19}$ (חל]יפא).

[חֲלִיפָה] I 12.1.3 n.f. **change**—sf. חֲלִיפָתִי; pl. חֲלִיפוֹת; cstr. חֲלִיפוֹת (חֲלִפוֹת, חֲלִפֹת)—**change** of clothing (Gn 45$_{22.22}$ Jg 14$_{12.13.19}$ 2 K 5$_{5.22.23}$), of way of life (Ps 55$_{20}$), **relay** of forced labourers (1 K 5$_{28}$), **reserve** of troops (1QM 16$_{10}$ 4QM$^a$ 1$_{12}$), **relief** from hard service (Jb 10$_{17}$ 14$_{14}$).

**<SUBJ>** בוא *come* Jb 14$_{14}$, יצא *go out* 1QM 16$_{10}$ 4QM$^a$ 1$_{12}$ ([יצאו]). **<NOM CL>** חֲלִיפוֹת וְצָבָא עִמִּי perh. *relief, then hard service, is with me* Jb 10$_{17}$ (or em. תְּחַלֵּף צְבָאֶיךָ *you renew your hosts* against me), אֵין חֲלִיפוֹת לָמוֹ *there are no changes to them* Ps 55$_{20}$ (unless חֲלִיפָה II *oath*). **<OBJ>** נתן *give* Gn 45$_{22.22}$ Jg 14$_{12.13.19}$ 2 K 5$_{22}$, לקח *take* 2 K 5$_5$, צור *bind* 2 K 5$_{23}$, חוה pi. *declare* Si 42$_{19}$ (+ חֵקֶר *thing to be searched out*, סתר ni. ptc. *hidden thing*). **<CSTR>** חֲלִפוֹת שְׂמָלֹת *changes of garments* Gn 45$_{22.22}$ (חֲלִפֹת), חֲלִפֹת בְּגָדִים *changes of garments* Jg 14$_{12.13}$ 2 K 5$_5$ (both חֲלִיפוֹת) 5$_{22.23}$, חליפות נהיות *the changes of past events*, i.e. all the varied events of the past Si 42$_{19}$. **<APP>** מַעֲרָכָה *battle line* 1QM 16$_{10}$. **<COLL>** וַיִּשְׁלָחֵם ... עֲשֶׂרֶת אֲלָפִים בַּחֹדֶשׁ חֲלִיפוֹת *and he sent them ... ten thousand a month (in) relays* 1 K 5$_{28}$; חֲלִיפוֹת (and vars.) *changes of* garments + numeral שְׁתֵּי *two* 2 K 5$_{22.23}$, חָמֵשׁ *five* Gn 45$_{22}$, עֶשֶׂר *ten* 2 K 5$_5$, שְׁלֹשִׁים *thirty* Jg 14$_{12.13}$.

Also 3QJub 23$_{12}$ (חל]יפה).*

→ חלף *pass on*.

[חֲלִיפָה] II 1 n.f. **oath**—pl. חֲלִיפוֹת—**<NOM CL>** אֵין חֲלִיפוֹת לָמוֹ *there is no (respect for) oaths to them*, i.e. they have no respect for oaths Ps 55$_{20}$ (unless חֲלִיפָה I *change*).*

[חֲלִיצָה] 2 n.f. **spoil**—sf. חֲלִצָתוֹ; pl. sf. חֲלִיצוֹתָם—stripped from body, **<OBJ>** לקח *take* Jg 14$_{19}$ 2 S 2$_{21}$.

→ חלץ *loose*.

חֵלְכָה 3.0.5 adj. **wretched; wicked**—חֵלְכָה; pl. Kt, Q חלכאים (Qr חֵיל כָּאִים appar. *army of dejected ones*); cstr. Q חילכיא—used as noun, **1. wretched one, hapless one,** Ps 10$_8$ (+ נָקִי *innocent one*) 10$_{10.14}$ (+ יָתוֹם *orphan*).* **2. wicked one, tyrant,*** 1QH 3$_{25}$ (+ רִשְׁעָה *wickedness*) 3$_{26}$ 4$_{25.35}$ (‖ רָשָׁע *wicked one*) 4QapLam$^b$4 (unless §1).

**<SUBJ>** קום *rise* 1QH 4$_{35}$, נפל *fall* Ps 10$_{10(Kt)}$ (mss, Qr חֵיל כָּאִים appar. *army of dejected ones*), דכה *be crushed* Ps 10$_{10(Kt)}$ (unless insert צַדִּיק *righteous one* as subj. of דכה), שׁחח *be bowed down* Ps 10$_{10(Kt)}$ (unless insert צַדִּיק as subj. of שׁחח), עזב *leave*, i.e. commit oneself Ps 10$_{14}$, הפך ho. *be turned* 4QapLam$^b$4, סבב *surround* 4QapLam$^b$4. **<CSTR>** חילכיא עמכה *wicked ones of your people* 4QapLam$^b$4; יד חלכאים *hand of the wicked* 1QH 4$_{25}$, מכמרת *net of* 1QH 3$_{26}$. **<PREP>** לְ *for*, + צפן *hide in wait* Ps 10$_8$ (unless em. יִצְפְּנוּ *they hide in wait* to יְצַפּוּ *they look out*), צפה *look out* Ps 10$_8$ (if em.); עִם *with*, + יצב htp. *stand* 1QH 3$_{25}$.

**<SYN>** §2 רָשָׁע *wicked one*.

חלל I $_{79.3.17}$ vb. **profane**—**Ni.** $_{10.2}$ Pf. נִחַל; impf. יֵחַל, 3fs תֵּחֵל; + waw וְנִחַלְתְּ, וְנִחַלוּ, וָאֵחַל; inf. הֵחֵל (הֵחַלּוֹ)—**be profaned, profane, defile oneself,** <SUBJ> י׳ *Y.* Ezk 22$_{16(ms).26}$, Josiah Si 49$_{2}$, בֵּן *son* of Aaron Lv 21$_{4}$, בַּת *daughter* Si 42$_{10}$, *daughter* of priest Lv 21$_{9}$ (+ זנה *prostitute oneself*), Jerusalem Ezk 22$_{16}$, מִקְדָּשׁ *sanctuary* Ezk 7$_{24}$ 25$_{3}$, שֵׁם *name* Ezk 20$_{9.14.22}$; subj. not specified, Is 48$_{11}$ (1QIs$^{a}$ איחל).

<PREP> בְּ *because of,* + Jerusalem Ezk 22$_{16}$; עַל *on account of,* + מְשׁוּבָה *faithlessness* Si 49$_{2}$; בְּתוֹךְ *among,* + כֹּהֵן *priest* Ezk 22$_{26}$; לְעֵינֵי *in the presence of,* + גּוֹי *nation* Ezk 20$_{9.14.22}$ 22$_{16}$.

**Pi.** $_{66.1.12}$ Pf. חִלֵּל (חִלְּלוֹ), חִלַּלְתָּ, חִלַּלְתְּ, חִלַּלְתִּי, חִלְּלוּ (חִלְּלוּ, חִלְּלוּהוּ, חִלְּלוּהָ, חִלְּלָהּ), חִלַּלְתֶּם; impf. יְחַלֵּל (יְחַלְּלֵהוּ, יְחַלֵּלוּ) יְחַלְּלוּ, אֲחַלֵּל, תְּחַלֵּל (תְּחַלְּלֻנוּ), (יְחַלְּלֻנוּ); + waw וַתְּחַלֶּלְנָה, וָאֲחַלֶּלְךָ, וַתְּחַלְּלֶהָ, וַיְחַלְּלוּ, וְחִלַּלְתָּ; ptc. מְחַלֵּל, מְחַלֶּלֶת, מְחַלְּלִים (מְחַלְלֶיהָ); inf. חַלֵּל (חַלְּלוֹ, חַלְּלָם)—**profane, make profane use of** (Dt 20$_{6.6}$ 28$_{30}$ Jr 31$_{5}$), <SUBJ> י׳ *Y.* Is 23$_{9}$ 43$_{28}$ 47$_{6}$ Ezk 24$_{21}$ 28$_{16}$ Ps 89$_{35.40}$, אֲדֹנָי *Lord* Ezk 24$_{21}$ 28$_{16}$ Lm 2$_{2}$, אֵל *God* Ps 55$_{21}$, Israelite(s) Ex 20$_{25}$ Dt 28$_{30}$ Jr 34$_{16}$ Ml 2$_{10}$, Israel Am 2$_{7}$, בַּיִת *house* of Israel Ezk 20$_{13.16.21.24.39}$ 36$_{20.21.22.23}$ 44$_{7}$, עֵדָה *congregation* Lv 19$_{12.29}$, Judah Ml 2$_{11}$, Jerusalem Ezk 22$_{8}$.

Aaron Lv 22$_{2.9.15.32}$, Oholah Ezk 23$_{38.39}$, Oholibah Ezk 23$_{38.39}$, Reuben Gn 49$_{4}$ 4QpGen$^{a}$ 1.4$_{5}$, Solomon Si 47$_{20}$, אֱנוֹשׁ *human being* Is 56$_{2}$, אִישׁ *man* Lv 21$_{23}$ Dt 20$_{6.6}$ 11QT 35$_{7}$ (יחל]לו]), בֵּן *son* Ps 89$_{32}$, *son* of Israel Lv 18$_{21}$ 19$_{12.29}$ 20$_{3}$ 22$_{32}$ Jr 16$_{18}$ 11QT 46$_{11}$, *son* of Aaron Lv 21$_{6}$ 22$_{2.9.15.32}$, בַּת *daughter* Ezk 13$_{19}$, of priest Lv 21$_{9}$, בְּכֹר *firstborn* 1 C 5$_{1}$.

מֶלֶךְ *king* of Tyre Ezk 28$_{18}$, זְרוֹעַ *arm,* i.e. military force Dn 11$_{31}$, חֹר *noble* Ne 13$_{17.18}$, כֹּהֵן *priest* Lv 21$_{6.12.15}$ Ezk 22$_{26}$ Zp 3$_{4}$ Ml 1$_{12}$ 4QM$^{c}$ $_{5}$, לֵוִי *Levite* Nm 18$_{32}$, פָּרִיץ *robber* Ezk 7$_{22}$, זָר *stranger* Ezk 7$_{21(Qr).22}$ 28$_{7}$, אכל ptc. *one who eats* Lv 19$_{8}$, נטע ptc. *one who plants* Jr 31$_{5}$, בגד ptc. *one who is faithless* 1QpHab 2$_{4}$ ([ויחללו]), צֹרֵר *oppressor* Ps 74$_{7}$, sabbath-breaker Ex 31$_{14}$.

אַחֵר *another one* 11QT 62$_{1}$ ([יחללנו]), כֹּל *everyone* Is 56$_{6}$ CD 12$_{4}$; subj. not specified, CD 15$_{3}$ perh. 4QapLam$^{a}$ 3$_{2}$ 4QJub$^{c}$ 22$_{7}$ ([מחלל]) 4QD$^{a}$ 6.2$_{6}$ 4QD$^{e}$ 9.1$_{11}$ 4QApocJerC 1$_{11}$ ([וי]חללו[ן]) 4QpsMos$^{e}$ 2.1$_{10.10}$ (יחלל[ו]) 2.2$_{11}$ 4QOrd$^{b}$ 2.2$_{6}$.

<OBJ> י׳ *Y.* Ezk 13$_{19}$, אֲדֹנָי *Lord* Ezk 13$_{19}$, מֶלֶךְ *king* of Tyre Ezk 28$_{16}$, שַׂר *prince* Is 43$_{28}$ Lm 2$_{2}$, אָב *father* Lv 21$_{9}$, בַּת *daughter* Lv 19$_{29}$, זֶרַע *seed,* i.e. offspring Lv 21$_{15}$.

אֶרֶץ *land* Jr 16$_{18}$, מַמְלָכָה *kingdom* Lm 2$_{2}$, כֶּרֶם *vineyard* Dt 20$_{6.6}$ 28$_{30}$, נַחֲלָה *heritage* Is 47$_{6}$, חֹק *statute* Ps 89$_{32}$, בְּרִית *covenant* Ml 2$_{10}$ Ps 55$_{21}$ 89$_{35}$, מִקְדָּשׁ *sanctuary* Lv 21$_{12.23}$ Ezk 23$_{39}$ 24$_{21}$ 28$_{18}$ 44$_{7}$ Dn 11$_{31}$ 11QT 35$_{7}$ 46$_{11}$, בַּיִת *house,* i.e. temple Ezk 44$_{7}$, מִשְׁכָּן *dwelling-place* Ps 74$_{7}$, מָעוֹז *fortress* Dn 11$_{31}$, מוֹעֵד *appointed time* 4QpsMos$^{e}$ 2.1$_{10}$, מִזְבֵּחַ *altar* Ex 20$_{25}$, שֶׁמֶן *oil* 4QM$^{c}$ $_{5}$, יָצוּעַ *couch* 1 C 5$_{1}$ Si 47$_{20}$ 4QpGen$^{a}$ 1.4$_{5}$.

שַׁבָּת *sabbath* Ex 31$_{14}$ Is 56$_{2.6}$ Ezk 20$_{13.16.21.24}$ 22$_{8}$ 23$_{38}$ Ne 13$_{18}$ CD 12$_{4}$, יוֹם *day* of sabbath Ne 13$_{17}$, מוֹעֵד *appointed time* CD 12$_{4}$, קֹדֶשׁ *holy thing* Lv 19$_{8}$ 22$_{15}$ Nm 18$_{32}$ Ezk 22$_{26}$ Zp 3$_{4}$, *holy place* Ml 2$_{11}$, שֵׁם *name* Lv 20$_{3}$ 22$_{2.9.32}$ Jr 34$_{16}$ Ezk 20$_{39}$ 36$_{20.21.22}$ Am 2$_{7}$ Ml 1$_{12}$ CD 15$_{3}$ 1QpHab 2$_{4}$ 4QD$^{e}$ 9.1$_{11}$, *name* of God Lv 18$_{21}$ 19$_{12}$ 21$_{6}$ 4QApocJerC 1$_{11}$ ([וי]חללו[ן]).

גָּאוֹן *pride* Is 23$_{9}$, יִפְעָה *splendour* Ezk 28$_{7}$, צפן pass. ptc. *that which is stored up,* i.e. treasure Ezk 7$_{22.22}$, זָהָב *gold* Ezk 7$_{21}$, כֶּסֶף *silver* Ezk 7$_{21}$, נֵזֶר *diadem* Ps 89$_{40}$; obj. not specified, 11QT 62$_{1}$.

<PREP> לְ of direction, *to,* + אֶרֶץ *ground* Ps 89$_{40}$; בְּ of instrument, *by (means of),* + מַתָּנָה *gift* Ezk 20$_{39}$, גִּלּוּל *idol* Ezk 20$_{39}$, טֻמְאָה *impurity* 4QD$^{a}$ 6.2$_{6}$; *in, with, among,* + עַם *people* Lv 21$_{15}$, גּוֹי *nation* Ezk 36$_{21.22}$; מִן *at,* + הַר *mountain* Ezk 28$_{16}$; אֶל *to,* + עַם *people* Ezk 13$_{19}$; בְּתוֹךְ *among,* + גּוֹי *nation* Ezk 36$_{23}$.

**Pu.** $_{1}$ ptc. מְחֻלָּל—**be profaned,** <SUBJ> שֵׁם *name* Ezk 36$_{23}$; subj. not specified, perh. 4QpGen$^{c}$ 3$_{8}$.

<PREP> בְּ *in, with, among,* + גּוֹי *nation* Ezk 36$_{23}$.

**Hi.** $_{1.0.5}$ Pf. Q החל; impf. יַחֵל, Q יחלו; inf. החל—**make invalid, profane,** <SUBJ> אִישׁ *man* Nm 30$_{3}$=11QT 53$_{15}$ CD 11$_{15}$, כֹּהֵן *priest* 1QM 9$_{8}$; subj. not specified, 4QCat$^{b}$ 1$_{3}$ 4QOrd$^{b}$ 2.2$_{5}$.

<OBJ> שַׁבָּת *sabbath* CD 11$_{15}$, שֶׁמֶן *oil* 1QM 9$_{8}$, דָּבָר *word* Nm 30$_{3}$=11QT 53$_{15}$.

<PREP> עַל *on account of,* + הוֹן *wealth* CD 11$_{15}$, בֶּצַע *profit* CD 11$_{15}$.*

→ חֹל *profaneness,* חָלָל *profaned.*

**חלל II** 54.0.12 vb. **begin—Hi.** 53.0.12 Pf. הֵחֵל, הֵחֵלָּה, הַחִלּוֹתָ, הַחִלֹּתִי, הֵחֵלּוּ; impf. יָחֵל, 2ms תָּחֵל, אָחֵל, תָּחֵלּוּ; + waw וַיָּחֶל, 3fs וַתָּחֶל, וַיָּחֵלּוּ, וַתְּחִלֶּינָה; impv. הָחֵל; ptc. מֵחֵל; inf. הָחֵל (הַחִלָּם)—**begin,** usu. followed by infinitive, e.g. Gn 61 116 Dt 225 Jg 1619 1 S 1435 etc., rarely by finite verb Gn 920 Dt 224 1 S 312, **<SUBJ>** ׳י Y. Dt 225.31 (both + נתן *give*) 324 (+ ראה hi. *show*) Jos 37 (+ גדל pi. *make great*) 1 S 312 2 K 1032 (+ קצה pi. *trim off*) 1537 (+ שׁלח hi. *let loose*) Jr 2529 (+ רעע hi. *do evil*), רוּחַ *spirit* of Y. Jg 1325 (+ פעם *impel*).

עַם *people* Gn 116 (+ עשׂה *do*) Nm 251 (+ זנה *prostitute oneself*) 11QT 217 ([יחלו]; + שׁתה *drink*), Israel Ho 810 (or em. חדל *cease* or חלה V *be alone*, i.e. desist), Israelite(s) Dt 224.31 (both + ירשׁ *take possession*) 169 (+ ספר *count*), Jew Est 923 (+ עשׂה *do*), Benjamin (tribe of) Jg 2039 (+ נכה hi. *strike*).

Ahimelech 1 S 2215 (+ שׁאל *ask*), Delilah Jg 1619 (+ ענה pi. *humiliate*), Haman Est 613 (+ נפל *fall*), Hezekiah 2 C 3121, Jeshua Ezr 36 (+ עלה hi. *offer*) 38, Joab 1 C 2724 (+ מנה *count*), Jonah Jon 34 (+ בוא *come*), Josiah 2 C 343 (+ דרשׁ *seek*) 343 (+ טהר pi. *cleanse*), Nimrod Gn 108‖1 C 110 (both + היה *be*), Noah Gn 920, Samson Jg 135 (+ ישׁע hi. *save*), Saul 1 S 1435 (+ בנה *build*), Solomon 2 C 31.2 (both + בנה *build*), Zerubbabel Ezr 36 (+ עלה hi. *offer*) 38.

אִישׁ אָדָם *human being* Gn 61 (+ רבב *be numerous*), אִישׁ *man* Jg 1018 (+ לחם ni. *fight*) 1QM 1714 (+ נפל hi. *bring down*) 1QS 910 4QMa 113 10.29 4QMc7 ([הח]לו), אָח *brother* Ezr 36.6 (both + עלה hi. *offer*), בֵּן *son* 1QM 11, *son* of Benjamin, i.e. Benjaminite Jg 2031 (+ נכה hi. *strike*), *son* of Israel 2 C 317 (+ יסד *amass*), *son* of Judah 2 C 317 (+ יסד *amass*) 3110 (+ בוא hi. *bring*), נָבִיא *prophet* 4QpsMose 2.16 ([ח]לו]י; + ריב hi. *dispute*), לֵוִי *Levite* Ezr 38 2 C 2917 (+ קדשׁ pi. *sanctify*) 3110 (+ בוא hi. *bring*), חָלָל *slain one* 1QM 169 (+ נפל *fall*), אֲשֶׁר עַל־בֵּיתוֹ *one who was over his house*, i.e. overseer Gn 4412, שְׁאָר *remainder* of priests Ezr 38, בוא ptc. *one who comes* Ezr 38, חלל pi. ptc. *one who praises* 2 C 2022, מְשֹׁרֵר *singer* 2 C 2022, בקשׁ pi. ptc. *one who seeks* 4QJuba 112 ([ויחלו]; + עשׂה *do*) 4QTohA 1.11 (+ נפל hi. *bring down*), farmer Dt 169.

שֵׂעָר *hair* Jg 1622 (+ צמח pi. *grow*), עַיִן *eye* 1 S 32, יָד *hand* 1QM 91 167 (both + נפל hi. *bring down*), שָׁנָה *year* Gn 4154 (+ בוא *come*), נֶגֶף *plague* Nm 1711.12, מַשְׂאֵת *rising* cloud Jg 2040 (+ עלה *go up*), עוֹלָה *burnt offering* 2 C 2927, שִׁיר *song* 2 C 2927, פרץ pass. ptc. *that which is breached* Ne 41 (+ סתם ni. *be stopped up*), אֵלֶּה *these* Ezk 96.6; subj. not specified, 1QM 1716 ([יחלו]) 4Q3179 ([יחל]) perh. 4QApocMosA 163 4QMa 10.210 ([יחלו]) 184 ([יחלו]) 203 ([יחל]ו) 4QOrdc 1.14.7 (+ טהר *cleanse*) 11QJub 52 ([יחלו]) 11QT 2110 ([החלו]; + נסך *pour out*).

**<PREP>** בְּ *in, with, among,* + עַם *people* Nm 1712, אִישׁ *man* Ezk 96, חָלָל *slain one* 1QM 91 167 1714, רִנָּה *singing* 2 C 2022, תְּהִלָּה *praise* 2 C 2022; *against,* + גּוֹרָל *lot* 1QM 11; מִן *at,* + מִקְדָּשׁ *sanctuary* Ezk 96.

**<COLL>** וַיָּחֶל נֹחַ אִישׁ הָאֲדָמָה *and Noah began (to be) a man of the earth,* i.e. a farmer Gn 920.

**Ho.** 1 Pf. הוּחַל—**be begun, <SUBJ>** subj. not specified, Gn 426 (+ קרא *call*).

⇒ תְּחִלָּה *beginning.*

**חלל III** 8 vb. **be pierced—Qal** 2 Pf. חָלַל; inf. חַלּוֹתִי—**be pierced, be wounded, <SUBJ>** worshipper Ps 7711 (חַלּוֹתִי הִיא *it is my being wounded,* i.e. my wound; or em. חֲלוֹתִי *my being sick* or חָלְתָה *it* [right hand] *is sick,* from חלה I *be weak,* or *it is disengaged,* from חלה V *be alone*), לֵב *heart* Ps 10922 (unless חלל V *tremble;* or em. חֻלַּל *it has been made to tremble,* i.e. חיל pol.). **<PREP>** בְּקֶרֶב *within,* + worshipper Ps 10922 (unless em.; see Subj.).

**Pi.** 1.0.1 + waw Q ויחללהו; ptc. מְחַלְלֶיךָ—**pierce, <SUBJ>** Y. Is 5310 (1QIsaa; MT הֶחֱלִי *he made [him] sick,* from חלה; + דכא pi. *crush*) Ezk 289. **<OBJ>** נָגִיד *prince* of Tyre Ezk 289, עֶבֶד *servant* Is 5310 (1QIsaa).

**Pu.** 1 Ptc. מְחֻלְלֵי—ptc. used as noun, **pierced one, <NOM CL>** כֻּלָּם ... מְחֻלְלֵי חֶרֶב *all of them are ... pierced ones of the sword* Ezk 3226 (or em. חַלְלֵי *slain ones of;* ‖ עָרֵל *uncircumcised one*). **<CSTR>** מְחֻלְלֵי חֶרֶב *pierced ones of,* i.e. by, *the sword* Ezk 3226 (or em.; see Nom. Cl.). **<SYN>** עָרֵל *uncircumcised one.*

**Poel** 4 Pf. חֹלְלָה; ptc. מְחוֹלֵל, מְחֹלֶלֶת, ms מְחֹלְלֶיךָ—**pierce, <SUBJ>** Y.'s arm Is 519 (‖ חצב hi. *hew*) Ezk 289(ms) (L מְחַלְלֶיךָ, i.e. pi.), רַב appar. *archer* Pr 2610, יָד *hand* Jb 2613. **<OBJ>** נָגִיד *prince* of Tyre Ezk 289(ms), עבר

ptc. *one who passes* Pr 26$_{10}$ (if transfer עֹבְרִים *those who transgress, pass* to follow כֹּל *everyone*), תַּנִּין *sea-monster* Is 51$_9$, נָחָשׁ *serpent* Jb 26$_{13}$, כֹּל *everyone* Pr 26$_{10}$. <SYN> חצב hi. *hew*.

**Poal** $_1$ Ptc. מְחֹלָל—**be pierced, be wounded** <SUBJ> עֶבֶד *servant* Is 53$_5$ (‖ דכא pu. *be crushed*). <PREP> מִן of cause, *on account of*, + פֶּשַׁע *transgression* Is 53$_5$. <SYN> דכא pu. *be crushed*.*

→ חָלָל *slain one*, מְחִלָּה *hole*.

**חלל IV** $_2$ **play the flute—Qal** $_1$ Ptc. חֹלְלִים—ptc. used as noun, **flautist**), <PREP> בְּ of accompaniment, *with* Ps 87$_{7(ms)}$; כְּ *as* Ps 87$_7$ (or em. מְחֹלְלִים *dancers*, from חול I; + שָׁר *singer*).

**Pi.** $_1$ Ptc. מְחַלְּלִים—**play the flute,** <SUBJ> עַם *people* 1 K 1$_{40}$ (or em.; see Prep.).<PREP> בְּ introducing object, + חלל pi. *play* 1 K 1$_{40}$ (or em. מְחַלְּלִים בַּחֲלִלִים *playing flutes* to מְחֹלְלִים בִּמְחֹלוֹת *dancing with dances*, i.e. חול pol. *dance*).*

→ חָלִיל *flute*.

***חלל V** $_1$ vb. **tremble—Qal** Pf. חָלַל—**tremble, be disturbed,** <SUBJ> לֵב *heart* Ps 109$_{22}$ (unless חלל III *be pierced*; or em. חֹלַל *it has been made to tremble*, i.e. חיל pol.). <PREP> בְּקֶרֶב *within*, + worshipper Ps 109$_{22}$ (or em.).

**חָלָל I** $_{91.1.41}$ n.m. **slain one**—cstr. חֲלַל; pl. חֲלָלִים; cstr. חַלְלֵי; sf. חֲלָלֶיךָ, חֲלָלַיִךְ, חֲלָלָיו, חֲלָלֶיהָ, חֲלָלֵינוּ, חַלְלֵיכֶם, חַלְלֵיהֶם—**one slain** (e.g. Nm 19$_{18}$ Dt 21$_1$ Jg 9$_{40}$ 1 S 17$_{52}$), **one pierced** with sword (e.g. Is 22$_2$ Jr 14$_{18}$ Ezk 31$_{17}$), **one killed** by famine (Lm 4$_9$), **one deflowered** (Lv 21$_{7.14}$); in plural in 1QM, perh. **carnage, massacre.***

<SUBJ> היה *be* Jr 25$_{33}$ Ezk 6$_{13}$ Lm 4$_9$ Si 34$_{6(Bmg)}$, רבב *be numerous* Is 66$_{16}$, מצא ni. *be found* Dt 21$_1$, שׁלך ho. *be thrown down* Is 34$_3$, שׁכב *lie down* Ps 88$_6$, נפל *fall* Jg 9$_{40}$ 1 S 17$_{52}$ Jr 51$_{4.47.49}$ Ezk 6$_7$ 28$_{23(mss)}$ 30$_4$ 35$_8$ Dn 11$_{26}$ 1 C 5$_{22}$ 2 C 13$_{17}$ 1QM 9$_7$ 14$_3$ 16$_9$ 2QapProph 1$_{11}$ ([נפלו]) 4QM[a] 10.2$_{11}$, pilal *fall* Ezk 28$_{23}$, אנק *groan* Jr 51$_{52}$ Ezk 26$_{15}$.

<NOM CL> הַצְּבִי יִשְׂרָאֵל ... חָלָל *the glory, O Israel ... is a slain one* 2 S 1$_{19}$, יְהוֹנָתָן ... חָלָל *Jonathan is ... a slain one* 2 S 1$_{25}$, חֲלָלַיִךְ לֹא חַלְלֵי־חֶרֶב *your slain are not slain of the sword* Is 22$_2$, חַלְלֵי־חֶרֶב פַּרְעֹה וְכָל־חֵילוֹ *the slain of the sword are Pharaoh and all his army* Ezk 32$_{31}$, רַבִּים חֲלָלִים *many are the slain* Pr 7$_{26}$, כֻּלָּם חֲלָלִים *all of them are slain ones* Ezk 32$_{22.23.24}$, כֻּלָּם ... חַלְלֵי־חֶרֶב *all of them are ... slain of the sword* Ezk 32$_{25.26}$ (if em.; see Cstr.), הֶעָרִים אֲשֶׁר סְבִיבֹת הֶחָלָל *the cities that are all around the slain one* Dt 21$_2$, אַתָּה חָלָל *you are a slain one* Ezk 21$_{30}$, חֲלָלִים שָׁם הוּא *the slain are there* Jb 39$_{30}$, חַלְלֵי חַרְבִּי הֵמָּה *they are the slain of my sword* Zp 2$_{12}$, חַלְלֵיכֶם ... הֵמָּה הַבָּשָׂר *your slain ones ... they are the flesh* Ezk 11$_7$.

<OBJ> רבה hi. *make many* Jg 16$_{24}$ Ezk 11$_6$, לקח *take* Lv 21$_{7.14}$, שׂים *place* Ezk 11$_7$, פשׁט pi. *strip* 1 S 31$_8$‖1 C 10$_8$, hi. *strip off* 1QM 7$_2$, קבר pi. *bury* 1 K 11$_{15}$, נפל hi. *bring down* Ezk 6$_4$ Pr 7$_{26}$ 1QM 6$_{3.5}$ 8$_{11}$, נכה hi. *strike* Jg 20$_{31.39}$, אכל *eat*, i.e. destroy 1QM 6$_3$, רפא *heal* 4Q521 2.2$_{12}$, בכה *weep* Jr 8$_{23}$, כתב *write* 1QM 4$_7$.

<CSTR> חַלְלֵי י׳ *slain ones of Y.* Is 66$_{16}$ Jr 25$_{33}$, אל *of God* 1QM 4$_7$, יִשְׂרָאֵל *of Israel* Jr 51$_{49}$, הַפְּלִשְׁתִּים *of the Philistines* 1 S 17$_{52}$, כתיים *of the Kittim* 1QM 16$_7$ 19$_{13}$ ([ח]ללי כתי[ים]) 4Q285 5$_6$ ([ח]לל[י]) 4QM[a] 10.2$_9$, כָּל־הָאָרֶץ *of all the earth* Jr 51$_{49}$, רְשָׁעִים *of wicked ones* Ezk 21$_{34}$, האויב *of the enemy* 1QM 14$_3$, המצרף *of the refiner* 4QM[a] 10.2$_{11}$, בַּת *of the daughter of* Jr 8$_{23}$, חֲלַל־חֶרֶב *slain one of sword*, i.e. by the sword Nm 19$_{16}$ 11QT 50$_5$, חַלְלֵי־חֶרֶב *slain ones of sword* Is 22$_2$ Jr 14$_{18}$ Ezk 31$_{17}$ (חֶרֶב) 31$_{18}$ 32$_{20.21}$ (חֶרֶב) 32$_{25.26}$ (if em. מְחֻלְלֵי *pierced ones of*) 32$_{28}$ (חֶרֶב) 32$_{29}$ (חֶרֶב) 32$_{30.31.32}$ 35$_8$ Lm 4$_9$, חַרְבִּי *of my sword* Zp 2$_{12}$ (or em. חֶרֶב י׳ *sword of Y.*), חַלְלֵי רָעָב *slain ones of famine* Lm 4$_9$, חללי זהב *slain ones of gold* Si 34$_{6(Bmg)}$, מעל *of unfaithfulness* 1QM 3$_8$, און *of iniquity* 1QM 6$_3$, האשמה *of guilt* 4QM[a] 1$_{13}$ 11.2$_{23}$, אשמתם *of their guilt* 1QM 6$_{17}$, הבינים *of the interval* 1QM 16$_9$=4QM[a] 11.2$_9$.

דַּם חָלָל *blood of the slain* Dt 32$_{42}$, חֲלָלִים *of the slain* Nm 23$_{24}$ 2 S 1$_{22}$, החללים *of the slain* 4QM[c]$_5$ ([ח]ללי[ם]), חללי *of the slain of* 1QM 6$_{17}$, חֶרֶב חָלָל *sword of the slain* Ezk 21$_{19}$, חֲלָלִים *of the slain* Ezk 21$_{19}$, משׁפט *judgment of* 4QMMT B$_{73}$, צַוְּארֵי חַלְלֵי *necks of the slain of* Ezk 21$_{34}$, נֶפֶשׁ־חֲלָלִים *throat of the slain* Jb 24$_{12}$, תרועות החללים *alarms of the slain* 1QM 3$_1$, נַאֲקוֹת חָלָל *groans of a slain one* Ezk 30$_{24}$, מַכְאוֹב חֲלָלֶיךָ *pain of your slain* Ps 69$_{27}$, חצוצרות החללים *trumpets of the slain* 1QM 3$_{8}$ 8$_{9}$ 9$_{2}$ 16$_{6}$ (חצוצרות]ח]) 16$_{8}$ 17$_{13.15}$ ([חצוצרות החללי]ם) 4QMa 13$_{6}$ (חצוצרות]ח]) 4QMc$_{7}$ ([חללים]), מְמוֹתֵי חָלָל *deaths of the slain* Ezk 28$_{8}$, במותי *high places of* 1QM 12$_{10}$ 4QMb 1$_{3}$ ([במותי חלל]), רֹב חָלָל *abundance of the slain* Na 3$_{3}$=4Qp Nah 3.2$_{4}$, כלל חלליהם *total of their slain ones* 4QpNah 3.2$_{6}$, תוך החללים *middle of slain ones* 1QM 9$_{8}$, כול חללי *all the slain of* 1QM 3$_{8}$, כָּל־חֲלָלֶיהָ *all its slain ones* Jr 51$_{47}$, [כו]ל חלליה[ם] *all their slain* 4Q285 2$_{6}$.

<APP> אִשָּׁה *woman* Lv 21$_{7}$, אֵלֶּה *these* Lv 21$_{14}$.

<ADJ> רָשָׁע *wicked one* Ezk 21$_{30}$, רַב *great one* Dn 11$_{26}$ 1 C 5$_{22}$ 2QapProph 1$_{11}$.

<PREP> לְ *because of*, + נפל *fall* Jr 51$_{49}$.

בְּ *in, with*, + נפל hi. *bring down* 1QM 9$_{1}$ 16$_{7}$ 17$_{14}$ 4QMa 1$_{13}$ 10.2$_{9}$ 11.2$_{23}$ 18$_{4}$; introducing object, + נגע *touch* Nm 19$_{16.18}$ 31$_{19}$ 11QT 50$_{5}$.

כְּ *as* Lm 2$_{12}$, + היה *be* Ps 88$_{6}$, דכא pi. *crush* Ps 89$_{11}$= 4QapPsb 15$_{5}$.

מִן of comparison, *(more) than*, + היה *be* Lm 4$_{9}$.

אֶל *to, in addition to* Dt 21$_{6}$ 11QT 63$_{4}$, + היה *be* Dt 21$_{3}$, ירד *go down* Ezk 31$_{17}$, הרג *kill* Jos 13$_{22}$.

עַל *upon, above, on behalf of, in addition to* 1QM 19$_{13}$, + בוא *come* Gn 34$_{27}$ (or em. חֹל *profane one*), הרג *kill* Nm 31$_{8}$ Jos 13$_{22(mss)}$, בכה *weep* Jr 8$_{23(mss)}$.

מֵעַל *from (upon)*, + עלה ni. *depart* 1QM 14$_{2}$.

אֵת *with*, + נתן ni. *be given*, i.e. be appointed Ezk 32$_{29}$, שכב *lie down* Ezk 31$_{18}$ 32$_{28.30}$, ho. *be laid down* Ezk 32$_{32}$, ירד *go down* Ezk 32$_{30}$.

בְּתוֹךְ *among*, + נתן *give*, i.e. appoint Ezk 32$_{25}$, ni. *be given*, i.e. be appointed Ezk 32$_{25}$, נפל *fall* Ezk 32$_{20}$.

מִבֵּין *from among*, + יצא *go out* 4QMc$_{4}$.

<COLL> אָנֹכִי נֹתֵן אֶת־כֻּלָּם חֲלָלִים *I will give*, i.e. make, *all of them (into) slain ones* Jos 11$_{6}$, וַיִּפְּלוּ חֲלָלִים *and they fell (as) slain ones* 1 S 31$_{1}$||1 C 10$_{1}$, יָרְדוּ שָׁכְבוּ ... חַלְלֵי־חֶרֶב *they go down, they lie down ... (as) slain ones of the sword* Ezk 32$_{21}$.

אתו מִלֵּא ... חֲלָלִים *he filled it with ... slain ones* Jr 41$_{9}$, מַלְאוּ אֶת־הַחֲצֵרוֹת חֲלָלִים *fill the courts with slain ones* Ezk 9$_{7}$, מִלֵּאתֶם חוּצֹתֶיהָ חָלָל *you have filled its streets with slain one(s)* Ezk 11$_{6}$, מָלְאוּ אֶת־הָאָרֶץ חָלָל *they have filled the earth with slain one(s)* Ezk 30$_{11}$.

שְׁלֹשׁ מֵאוֹת חָלָל *three hundred slain* 2 S 23$_{18}$||1 C 11$_{20}$ 1 C 11$_{11}$, שְׁמֹנֶה מֵאוֹת חָלָל *eight hundred slain* 2 S 23$_{8}$.
Also 1QM 8$_{19}$ 16$_{13}$ 17$_{16}$ 19$_{3}$ ([חלל]) 19$_{10}$.
⇒ חלל *wound*.

**חָלָל II** $_{4}$ adj. **profane**—חֲלָלָה; pl. cstr. חַלְלֵי—**1.** used attributively of רָשָׁע *wicked one* Ezk 21$_{30}$ (unless חָלָל I *slain one*; or em. חֲלַל רֶשַׁע *profane one of wickedness*).

**2.** used as noun, **a. profane one,** <CSTR> חַלְלֵי רְשָׁעִים *profane ones of the wicked* Ezk 21$_{34}$ (unless *slain ones of*, i.e. חָלָל I), חֲלַל רֶשַׁע *profane one of wickedness* Ezk 21$_{30}$ (if em. חָלָל רָשָׁע *profane wicked one*); צַוְּארֵי חַלְלֵי *necks of profane ones of* Ezk 21$_{34}$ (unless חָלָל I). <APP> נָשִׂיא *prince* Ezk 21$_{30}$ (if em.; see Subj.). **b. defiled one,** of woman defiled sexually, <OBJ> לקח *take (in marriage)* Lv 21$_{7.14}$ (|| אַלְמָנָה *widow*, גְּרוּשָׁה *divorced woman*; both || זֹנָה *prostitute*). <APP> אִשָּׁה *woman* Lv 21$_{7.14}$. <SYN> §2b זֹנָה *prostitute*, אַלְמָנָה *widow*, גְּרוּשָׁה *divorced woman*.
⇒ חלל *pollute*.

**חָלִלָה**, see חָלִילָה *may it not be*.

**חלם I** $_{26.0.5}$ vb. **dream—Qal** $_{26.0.4}$ Pf. חָלַמְתִּי, חָלָמְתָּ, חָלָם (חָלַמְתִּי), (חָלָמְנוּ) חָלַמְנוּ; impf. יַחֲלֹמוּן, יַחֲלֹם; + waw וַיַּחֲלֹם, וַיַּחַלְמוּ, וַנַּחַלְמָה; ptc. חוֹלֵם (חֹלֵם)—**dream, 1a.** <SUBJ> Jacob Gn 28$_{12}$, Joseph Gn 37$_{5.6.9.9.10}$ 42$_{9}$, Nebuchadnezzar Dn 2$_{1.3}$, אִישׁ *man* Jg 7$_{13}$, Pharaoh Gn 41$_{1.5.15}$, נָבִיא *prophet* Jr 23$_{25.25}$, זָקֵן *elder* Jl 3$_{1}$, מַשְׁקֶה *cup-bearer* Gn 40$_{5.8}$ 41$_{11}$, אֹפֶה *baker* Gn 40$_{5.8}$ 41$_{11}$, רָעֵב *hungry one* Is 29$_{8}$, צָמֵא *thirsty one* Is 29$_{8}$, worshipper 11QPsa 24$_{17}$.

<OBJ> חֲלוֹם *dream* Gn 37$_{5.6.9.9.10}$ 40$_{5.8}$ 41$_{11.15}$ 42$_{9}$ Jg 7$_{13}$ Dn 2$_{1.3}$.

<PREP> לְ *concerning*, + אָח *brother* Gn 42$_{9}$; בְּ of time, *in, at, during*, + לַיְלָה *night* Gn 40$_{5}$ 41$_{11}$.

<COLL> וַיַּחֲלֹם שֵׁנִית *and he dreamt a second time* Gn 41$_{5}$.

**1b.** ptc. as noun, **dreamer,** <SUBJ> מות ho. *be put to death* Dt 13$_{6}$ 11QT 54$_{15}$, קום *arise* Dt 13$_{2}$ 11QT 54$_{8}$.

<CSTR> חֹלֵם חֲלוֹם *dreamer of dream(s)* Dt 13$_{2.4}$ (הַחֲלוֹם) 13$_{6}$ 11QT 54$_{8.11.15}$ (all three חולם).

<PREP> לְ of direction, *to*, + שמע *listen* 11QT 54$_{11}$; כְּ *as*, + היה *be* Ps 126$_{1}$; אֶל *to*, + שמע *listen* Dt 13$_{4}$.

**Hi.** 1 Ptc. מַחְלְמִים—**dream,** <SUBJ> נָבִיא *prophet* Jr 29$_8$ (if em.), קֹסֵם *one who divines* Jr 29$_8$ (if em.), גּוֹלה *exile* Jr 29$_8$ (or em. הֵם *they*).
<OBJ> חֲלוֹם *dream* Jr 29$_8$.*
⇒ חֲלוֹם *dream.*

**חלם** II 2.2.2 vb. **be healthy—Qal** 1 Impf. יַחְלְמוּ—**1.** active, **be healthy, be strong,** <SUBJ> בֵּן *son* Jb 39$_4$. **2.** passive ptc. as noun, **one who is sound,** <SUBJ> בוא *come* Ec 5$_2$ (if em. הַחֲלוֹם *the dream* to הֶחָלוּם *the one who is sound*).*

**Ni.** 0.0.1 Impv. Q החלמי—**be sure, be confident,** <SUBJ> אֵם *mother* 4QJub$^g$ 25$_{10}$.

**Hi.** 1.2.1 Pf. Si החלים, Si החלימו; impf. תַּחֲלִימֵנִי; inf. Q החלימם—**heal, make strong,** <SUBJ> Y. Is 38$_{16}$ (+ חיה hi. *cause to live*) Si 15$_{20(A)}$, נָבִיא *prophet* Si 49$_{10}$. <OBJ> Hezekiah Is 38$_{16}$, Jacob, i.e. Israel Si 49$_{10}$, אִישׁ *man* Si 15$_{20(A)}$.

Also 4Q470 3$_4$ (+ עזר *help*).*

**חֵלֶם** 1 pr.n.m. **Helem,** returning exile from Babylon at time of Zechariah, <PREP> לְ of benefit, *for, to,* + היה *be* Zc 6$_{14}$ (or em. חֶלְדַּי *Heldai*).

**[חֲלָמָה]** 0.0.1 n.f. **seamed robe,** <OBJ> כבס pi. *wash* 4QTohB$^b$ 1$_4$ ([ויכבסו]). <PREP> בְּ of accompaniment, *with, in,* + כפר pi. *make atonement* 4QTohB$^b$ 1$_4$.

**חַלָּמוּת** 1 n.f. **mallow,** plant with tasteless juice, perh. **common mallow** (*malva sylvestris*), **marsh mallow** (*althaea officinalis*), or **purslane** (*saeda asphaltica*), etc., unless **egg-yolk,** <CSTR> רִיר חַלָּמוּת *juice of mallow,* or *of egg-yolk,* i.e. white of egg Jb 6$_6$ (+ תָּפֵל *tasteless thing*).

**חַלָּמִישׁ** 5.0.2 n.m. **flint**—cstr. חַלְמִישׁ—as dry (Dt 8$_{15}$ 32$_{13}$ Ps 114$_8$), unyielding (Is 50$_7$ Jb 28$_9$ 1QH 3$_{31}$ 8$_{23}$), <OBJ> הפך *overturn,* i.e. change into springs of water Ps 114$_8$ (|| צוּר *rock*). <CSTR> חַלְמִישׁ צוּר *flint of rock,* i.e. flinty rock Dt 32$_{13}$; צוּר הַחַלָּמִישׁ *the rock of flint,* i.e. flinty rock Dt 8$_{15}$ 1QH 8$_{23}$ (צור חלמיש), שורשי חלמיש *roots of flint* 1QH 3$_{31}$ (|| הַר *mountain*). <PREP> בְּ *against,* + שׁלח *send* hand Jb 28$_9$ (+ הַר, צוּר, אֶבֶן *stone*); כְּ *as (though it were),* + שִׂים *place,* i.e. cause (face) to be Is 50$_7$; מִן of direction, *from,* + ינק hi. *suckle (with)* fat Dt 32$_{13}$. <SYN> צוּר *rock,* הַר *mountain.*

**חֵלֹן** 5 pr.n.m. **Helon**—חֵלוֹן, Sam חֵילֹן—descendant of Zebulun and father of Eliab, <CSTR> בֶּן־חֵלֹן *son of Helon* Nm 1$_9$ 2$_7$ 7$_{24.29}$ 10$_{16}$ (חֵלוֹן; all five Sam חֵילֹן).

**חֹלֹן** 3 pl.n. **Holon**—חלון—**1.** town in Judah, Kh. ʻAlīn, 18 km WSW of Bethlehem, appar. ident. with חִילֵז *Hilez* (mss חִילֵן *Hillen*) at 1 C 6$_{43}$, <NOM CL> בָּהָר ... חלֹן *in the hill country were ... Holon* Jos 15$_{51}$. <OBJ> נתן *give* Jos 21$_{15}$. **2.** town in Moab, <APP> אֶרֶץ הַמִּישֹׁר *land of the plain* Jr 48$_{21}$. <PREP> אֶל *to,* + בוא *come* Jr 48$_{21}$.

**חלף** I 28.5.4 vb. **pass—Qal** 15.4.3 Pf. חָלַף (חָלָף, Si חלפו), חָלְפוּ; impf. יַחֲלֹף, יַחַלְפוּ; + waw וְחָלַפְתָּ; inf. חֲלֹף—**pass on, pass by, pass away, be renewed** (Ps 90$_{5.6}$),* <SUBJ> אֵל *God* Jb 9$_{11}$ (|| עבר *pass by*), אֱלוֹהַּ *God* Jb 11$_{10}$, אֱלִיל *worthless god* Is 2$_{18}$ GnzPs 2$_{19}$, גּוֹי *nation* Hb 1$_{11}$=1QpHab 4$_9$ (both || עבר *pass by*), Chaldaean Hb 1$_{11}$=1QpHab 4$_9$ (both || עבר *pass by*), Saul 1 S 10$_3$, יֹשֵׁב *inhabitant* Is 24$_5$ (|| עבר *pass by*), רוּחַ *spirit* Jb 4$_{15}$, שָׁמַיִם *heaven* Ps 102$_{27}$, אֶרֶץ *earth* Ps 102$_{27}$, נָהָר *river* Is 8$_8$=4QpIsa$^c$ 2$_2$ ([חלף]), סוּפָה *whirlwind* Is 21$_1$, גֶּשֶׁם *rain* Ca 2$_{11}$ (|| הלך *go*), חָצִיר *grass* Ps 90$_{5.6}$, יוֹם *day* Jb 9$_{26}$, שַׁוְעָה *cry* Si 32$_{20(Bmg)}$, דָּבָר *word,* i.e. thought Si 42$_{20}$, זֶה *this one* Si 42$_{25}$; subj. not specified, Si 11$_{19}$ ([י]חלף) 4Q418 261$_2$.

<OBJ> עֶלְיוֹן *Most High* Si 42$_{20}$, חֹק *statute* Is 24$_5$, טוֹב *goodness* Si 42$_{25}$.

<PREP> בְּ of place, *in, at,* + Judah Is 8$_8$=4QpIsa$^c$ 2$_2$, בֹּקֶר *morning* Ps 90$_{5.6}$; מִן of direction, *from,* + שָׁם *there* 1 S 10$_3$; עַל *upon,* + פָּנֶה *face* Jb 4$_{15}$; *on behalf of,* + זֶה *this one* Si 42$_{25}$; עִם *with,* + אֳנִיָּה *ship,* i.e. skiff Jb 9$_{26}$.

<COLL> הָאֱלִילִים כָּלִיל יַחֲלֹף *the worthless gods shall utterly pas away* Is 2$_{18}$ GnzPs 2$_{19}$, אָז חָלַף רוּחַ *then he passes by (as) the wind* Hb 1$_{11}$.

<SYN> עבר *pass by,* הלך *go.*

**Pi.** 2 + waw וַיְחַלֵּף—**change,** <SUBJ> David 2 S 12$_{20}$, Joseph Gn 41$_{14}$.

<OBJ> שִׂמְלָה *mantle,* i.e. garment Gn 41$_{14}$ 2 S 12$_{20}$.

**Hi.** 10.1.1 Pf. הֶחֱלִף; impf. יַחֲלִיף (יַחֲלִיפֶנּוּ), 3fs תַּחֲלִיף,

2ms תַּחֲלִיפֵם, יַחֲלִיפוּ, Si תחליפו, נַחֲלִיף; + waw וַתַּחֲלֵף; impv. הַחֲלִיפוּ—**replace, substitute, renew, change,** <SUBJ> יי *Y.* 4Q521 2.$2_{6}$, אֵל *God* Ps $102_{27}$, לְאֹם *people* Is $41_{1}$, Ephraim Is $9_{9}$, Laban Gn $31_{41}$, אָב *father* Gn $31_{7}$, בַּיִת *household* of Jacob Gn $35_{2}$, worshipper Si $43_{30}$, offerer Lv $27_{10}$, יֹשֵׁב *inhabitant* Is $9_{9}$, קוה ptc. *one who waits* Is $40_{31}$, עֵץ *tree* Jb $14_{7}$, קֶשֶׁת *bow* Jb $29_{20}$.

<OBJ> אֱמוּנָה *faithful one* 4Q521 2.$2_{6}$, בְּהֵמָה *beast* Lv $27_{10}$, שִׂמְלָה *mantle,* i.e. garment Gn $35_{2}$, מַשְׂכֹּרֶת *wages* Gn $31_{7.41}$, כֹּחַ *strength* Is $40_{31}$ $41_{1}$ Si $43_{30}$, שָׁמַיִם *heaven* Ps $102_{27}$, אֶרֶץ *earth* Ps $102_{27}$, אֶרֶז *cedar* Is $9_{9}$.

<PREP> בְּ of instrument, *by (means of),* + כֹּחַ *strength* 4Q521 2.$2_{6}$; כְּ *as,* + לְבוּשׁ *garment* Ps $102_{27}$.*

→ חֵלֶף *exchange,* חֵלֶף *Heleph,* חֲלִיפָה *change,* מַחֲלָף *knife,* מַחְלָפָה *plait of hair.*

חלף II $2.1$ vb. **pierce through—Qal** $2.1$ Pf. חָלְפָה; impf. תַּחְלְפֵהוּ—<SUBJ> Jael Jg $5_{26}$ (+ הלם *strike,* מחק *crush,* מחץ *shatter*), קֶשֶׁת *bow,* i.e. arrow Jb $20_{24}$, שַׁוְעָה *cry* of poor Si $32_{21\text{Bmg}}$. <OBJ> רָשָׁע *wicked one* Jb $20_{24}$, חָנֵף *godless one* Jb $20_{24}$, רַקָּה *temple* Jg $5_{26}$, עָב *cloud* Si $32_{21}$ (Bmg).

*חלף III $1$ vb. **grow—Qal** $1$ + waw חָלַף—**grow, sprout,** <SUBJ> חָצִיר *grass* Ps $90_{6}$ (|| ציץ *flourish*). <SYN> ציץ *flourish.*

חֵלֶף I $2$ prep. **in return for,** שָׂכָר הוּא לָכֶם חֵלֶף עֲבֹדַתְכֶם *it is a reward for you in return for your service* Nm $18_{31}$, נָתַתִּי כָּל־מַעֲשֵׂר ... לְנַחֲלָה חֵלֶף עֲבֹדָתָם *I have given every tithe … as an inheritance in return for their service* Nm $18_{21}$.*

→ חלף *pass.*

חֵלֶף II $1$ pl.n. **Heleph,** town in Naphtali, perh. Kh. ʿIrbāda, 6 km NNE of Mount Tabor, <PREP> מִן of direction, *from,* + היה *be* Jos $19_{33}$.

[חֲלַפְתָּא] $0.0.0.1$ pr.n.m. **Halaphta,** perh. son of Kaddari (קד[ר]י; others קר[ק]ס *Karkas,* קרנו *Karno*), <CSTR> בן חלפתא *son of Halaphta* Frey $1285_{13}$.

חלץ I $23.0.4$ vb. **loosen—Qal** $5$ Pf. חָלַץ, חָלְצָה, חָלְצוּ; impf. יַחֲלֹץ; ptc. pass. חֲלוּץ—**loosen, expose** (Lm $4_{3}$), **take off, withdraw** (Ho $5_{3}$), <SUBJ> יי *Y.* Ho $5_{6}$, Isaiah Is $20_{2}$, יְבָמָה *brother's widow* Dt $25_{9}$, תַּן *jackal* Lm $4_{3}$; subj. of pass. נַעַל Dt $25_{10}$. <OBJ> שַׁד *breast* Lm $4_{3}$, נַעַל *sandal* Dt $25_{9}$ Is $20_{2}$. <PREP> מִן of direction, *from,* + Ephraim Ho $5_{6}$, Judah Ho $5_{6}$; מֵעַל *from (upon),* + רֶגֶל *foot* Dt $25_{9}$ Is $20_{2}$.

**Ni.** $4$ Impf. יֵחָלְצוּ (יֵחָלְצוּן); ptc. נֶחֱלָץ—**be delivered,** <SUBJ> יָדִיד *beloved one* Ps $60_{7}$ $108_{7}$, צַדִּיק *righteous one* Pr $11_{8.9}$. <PREP> בְּ of instrument, *by (means of),* + דַּעַת *knowledge* Pr $11_{9}$; מִן of direction, *from,* + צָרָה *distress* Pr $11_{8}$.

**Pi.** $13.0.4$ Pf. חִלֵּץ, חִלַּצְתָּ, חִלְּצוּ; impf. יְחַלֵּץ (יְחַלְּצֵנִי), אֲחַלֶּצְךָ (אֲחַלְּצֵהוּ); + waw וַיְחַלְּצֵם, וָאֲחַלְּצָה (וָאֲחַלְּצֶךָ); impv. חַלְּצָה (חַלְּצֵנִי)—**plunder** (Ps $7_{5}$); **pull out** (Lv $14_{40.43}$); **deliver,** <SUBJ> יי *Y.* 2 S $22_{20}$||Ps $18_{20}$ Ps $6_{5}$ $91_{15}$ $116_{8}$ $119_{153}$ $140_{2}$ 4QMidrEschat[b] $11_{8}$, אֱלֹהִים *God* Ps $50_{15}$ $81_{8}$, אֵל *God* Jb $36_{15}$ 1QS $11_{13}$, עֶלְיוֹן *Most High* Ps $91_{15}$, מַלְאָךְ *messenger* of Y. Ps $34_{8}$, worshipper Ps $7_{5}$; subj. not specified, Lv $14_{40.43}$ perh. 4QWiles $3_{1}$ 4QDibHam[b] $125_{3}$ 4Q525 14.$2_{12}$.

<OBJ> עַם *people* Ps $50_{15}$, Israel Ps $81_{8}$, עָנִי *poor one* Jb $36_{15}$, worshipper 2 S $22_{20}$||Ps $18_{20}$ Ps $91_{15}$ $119_{153}$, ירא ptc. *one who fears* Ps $34_{8}$, צֹרֵר *oppressor* Ps $7_{5}$, נֶפֶשׁ *soul* Ps $6_{5}$ $116_{8}$ 1QS $11_{13}$ 4QMidrEschat[b] $11_{8}$, אֶבֶן *stone* Lv $14_{40.43}$; obj. not specified, 4Q525 14.$2_{12}$.

<PREP> בְּ of instrument, *by (means of),* + עֳנִי *affliction* Jb $36_{15}$.

מִן of direction, *from,* + אָדָם *human being* Ps $140_{2}$, רַע *evil* 4Q525 14.$2_{12}$, מָוֶת *death* Ps $116_{8}$, שַׁחַת *pit* 1QS $11_{13}$.

<COLL> וָאֲחַלְּצָה צוֹרְרִי רֵיקָם *and I have plundered my oppressor without cause* Ps $7_{5}$.*

→ חֲלִיצָה *stripped off object,* מַחֲלָצָה *robe.*

חלץ II $21.0.2$ **equip (for war)—Qal** $17.0.2$ Impf. Q יחלוצו; ptc. pass. חָלוּץ, חָלוּץ, חֲלוּצִים, חֲלוּצֵי (חֲלֻצֵי)—**1. equip (for war), arm,** <SUBJ> Israel 1QM $2_{7.8}$ (both + לצאת לצבא *to go to war*). <OBJ> איש *man* of valour 1QM $2_{7}$. <PREP> לְ *for (oneself),* + Israel 1QM $2_{7}$.

**2a.** pass. ptc. as adj. **equipped (for war), armed,** used as predicate, with עבר *pass* Nm $32_{30.32}$ Dt $3_{18}$.

**2b.** pass. ptc. used as noun, **one equipped (for war), armed man,** sometimes collective, <SUBJ> עבר *pass* Nm 32$_{21.27.29}$ Jos 4$_{13}$ 6$_{7}$, הלך *go* Jos 6$_{9.13}$ (both + מְאַסֵּף *rearguard*), עזב *leave* 2 C 28$_{14}$, מסר ni. *be delivered over* Nm 31$_{5}$, רוע hi. *shout* Is 15$_{4}$ (or em. חֲלָצֵי מוֹאָב יָרִיעוּ *the armed ones of Moab shout* to חַלְצֵי מוֹאָב יָרֵעוּ *the loins of Moab tremble*). <NOM CL> עִמּוֹ ... חֲלוּצֵי צָבָא *with him were ... men equipped for war* 2 C 17$_{18}$. <CSTR> חֲלוּץ צָבָא *man equipped of,* i.e. for, *war* Nm 32$_{27}$, חֲלוּצֵי *men equipped of* Nm 31$_{5}$ Jos 4$_{12}$ (הַצָּבָא) 1 C 12$_{25}$ 2 C 17$_{18}$, חֲלֻצֵי מוֹאָב *armed men of Moab* Is 15$_{4}$ (or em.; see Cstr.); כָּל־חָלוּץ *every equipped man* Nm 32$_{21.29}$, רָאשֵׁי הֶחָלוּץ *heads of those equipped for war* 1 C 12$_{24}$, כָּל־חֲלוּץ *every equipped man of* Nm 32$_{27}$. <APP> בֵּן *son* Nm 32$_{29}$. <PREP> לִפְנֵי *before*, + יצא *go out* 2 C 20$_{21}$. <COLL> חָלוּץ לַמִּלְחָמָה *man equipped for war* Nm 32$_{29}$, הֶחָלוּץ לַצָּבָא *those equipped for war* 1 C 12$_{24}$; חֲלוּצֵי צָבָא *those equipped for war*, + number Nm 31$_{5}$ (12,000) Jos 4$_{13}$ (הַצָּבָא; 40,000) 1 C 12$_{25}$ (6,800) 2 C 17$_{18}$ (180,000).

**Ni.** 3.0.1 Impf. נֵחָלֵץ, תֵּחָלְצוּ, Q יחלצו; impv. הֵחָלְצוּ—**1. be equipped, equip oneself,** <SUBJ> עַם *people* Nm 31$_{3}$ (Sam$^{mss}$ hi.), בֵּן *son* of Reuben and Gad Nm 32$_{17.20}$. <PREP> לְ *for*, + מִלְחָמָה *war* Nm 32$_{20}$; לִפְנֵי *before*, + ′′ *Y.* Nm 32$_{20}$. <COLL> הֵחָלְצוּ מֵאִתְּכֶם אֲנָשִׁים לַצָּבָא appar. *be equipped from among you (as) men for war* Nm 31$_{3}$ (Sam$^{mss}$ hi.), נֵחָלֵץ חֲמֻשִׁים *we shall equip ourselves (in) groups of fifty* Nm 32$_{17}$ (if em. נֵחָלֵץ חֻשִׁים *we shall equip ourselves, hastening*).

**2.** appar. **be strong,** <SUBJ> עֶצֶם *bone* Is 58$_{11}$ (1QIsa$^{b}$; MT, 1QIsa$^{a}$ hi.).

**Hi.** 2.0.1 Impf. יַחֲלִיץ, Q יחילצו; impv. Sam$^{mss}$ הַחֲלִיצוּ—**1. equip,** <SUBJ> עַם *people* Nm 31$_{3(Sam^{mss})}$ (MT ni.). <OBJ> אִישׁ *man* Nm 31$_{3(Sam^{mss})}$ (MT ni.). <PREP> מֵאֵת *from*, + עַם *people* Nm 31$_{3(Sam^{mss})}$ (MT ni.). **2. make strong** (Is 58$_{11}$), appar. **be strong** (Is 58$_{11}$ 1QIsa$^{a}$), <SUBJ> ′′ *Y.* Is 58$_{11}$ (or em. יַחֲלִיף *he will renew*, i.e. חלף hi.), appar. עֶצֶם *bone* Is 58$_{11}$ (1QIsa$^{a}$). <OBJ> עֶצֶם *bone* Is 58$_{11}$.

**חֶלֶץ** 5.0.0.8 pr.n.m. **Helez**—חָלֶץ—**1.** son of Azariah, father of Eleasah and descendant of Judah, <SUBJ> ילד hi. *beget* 1 C 2$_{39}$. <OBJ> ילד hi. *beget* 1 C 2$_{39}$. **2.** Pelonite or Paltite warrior and official of David, <NOM CL> גִּבּוֹרֵי הַחֲיָלִים ... חֶלֶץ *the mighty men of the armies were ... Helez* 1 C 11$_{27}$, הַשְּׁבִיעִי לַחֹדֶשׁ הַשְּׁבִיעִי חֶלֶץ *seventh, for the seventh month, was Helez* 1 C 27$_{10}$. <APP> פַּלְטִי *Paltite* 2 S 23$_{26}$, פְּלוֹנִי *Pelonite* 1 C 11$_{27}$ (unless em. הַפְּלוֹנִי *the Pelonite* to הַפַּלְטִי *the Paltite*) 27$_{10}$. **3.** appar. recipient of goods at Samaria, <PREP> לְ of possession, *(belonging) to* Samaria ost. 26$_{2}$ (לחל[ץ]) 30$_{2}$ 31$_{2}$ 32$_{2}$ 33$_{2}$ (לחל[ץ]) 34$_{2}$ ([לחלץ]) 35$_{2}$ 49$_{2}$ ([לחל]ץ) 90$_{2}$ (לחל[ץ]). <COLL> חלץ מחצרת *Helez from Hazeroth* Samaria ost. 22$_{3}$ 23$_{3}$. **4.** son of Ahab, <APP> בֵּן *son* Seal 560 ([בן]; T. Beit Mirsim?, 7th/6th cent.). <PREP> לְ of possession, *(belonging) to* Seal 560 ([ל]חלץ; T. Beit Mirsim?, 7th/6th cent.). **5.** appar. father of Alijah, Seal 642 (T. Beit Mirsim?, 7th/6th cent.).

**[חֶלֶצְיָהוּ]** 0.0.0.5 pr.n.m. **Heleziah, 1.** appar. father of Malchijah Seal 176 (Judaea, 7th cent.). **2.** appar. father of Hoshaiah, Seal 547 (T. Beit Mirsim?, 7th/6th cent.) 909 (7th/6th cent.). **3.** father of Ishmael, <CSTR> בן [חל]ציה[ו] *son of Heleziah* Seal 579 (T. Beit Mirsim?, 7th/6th cent.). **4.** appar. father of Reaiah, Seal 657 (T. Beit Mirsim?, 7th/6th cent.). **5.** appar. father of Elishama, Seal 729 (7th cent.).

⇒ ′′ *Y.*

**[חֲלָצַיִם]** 10 n.[f.]du. **loins**—חֲלָצַיִם; חֲלָצֶיךָ, חֲלָצָיו (Kt חלצו)—<SUBJ> ברך pi. *bless* Jb 31$_{20}$, ירע *tremble* Is 15$_{4}$ (if em. חֲלֻצֵי מוֹאָב יָרִיעוּ *the armed ones of Moab shout* to חַלְצֵי מוֹאָב יָרֵעוּ *the loins of Moab tremble*). <OBJ> אזר *gird* Jb 38$_{3}$ 40$_{7}$, מחץ *shatter* Nm 24$_{8}$ (if em. חִצָּיו *his arrows* to חֲלָצָיו *his loins*). <CSTR> חַלְצֵי מוֹאָב *loins of Moab* Is 15$_{4}$ (if em.; see Subj.); אֵזוֹר חֲלָצָיו *girdle of his loins* Is 5$_{27}$ 11$_{5}$=4QpIsa$^{a}$ 8$_{16}$ ([אזור חלציו]; ‖ מָתְנַיִם *loins*). <PREP> מִן of direction, *from*, + יצא *go out* Gn 35$_{11}$ (+ מִמְּךָ *from you*) 1 K 8$_{19}$‖2 C 6$_{9}$; עַל *upon* Jr 30$_{6}$, + חגר *gird oneself* Is 32$_{11}$. <SYN> מָתְנַיִם *loins.**

**חלק I** 56.10.9 vb. **divide**—**Qal** Pf. חָלַק, חָלְקוּ; impf. יַחֲלֹק, יַחֲלְקוּ, תַּחְלְקוּ; + waw וַיֶּחֱלְקֵם, וַתַּחְלְקֵם, וַיַּחְלְקוּ (וַיַּחְלְקוּם); impv. חִלְקוּ; ptc. חוֹלֵק; inf. חֲלֹק—**divide, apportion, assign, distribute, share,** <SUBJ> ′′ *Y.* Dt

$4_{19}$* Dt $29_{25}$ Ne $9_{22}$ Si $16_{16}$ $39_{25}$ $45_{22}$, אֱלֹהִים *God* Dt $4_{19}$, אֱלוֹהַּ *God* Jb $39_{17}$, אֵל *God* Si $34_{13}$ $38_1$ $40_1$, עֶלְיוֹן *Most High* Si $44_2$, חֲצִי *half* tribe of Manasseh Jos $22_8$, Ahaz 2 C $28_{21}$ (unless חלק V *strip*; or em. חלץ pi. *plunder*), Ahimelech 1 C $24_3$ (if em. חלק ni. *be divided*) $24_{4.5}$, David 1 C $23_6$ (if em. חלק ni. *be divided*) $24_3$ (if em. חלק ni. *be divided*) $24_{4.5}$ 2 C $23_{18}$, Mephibosheth 2 S $19_{30}$, Zadok 1 C $24_3$ (if em. חלק ni. *be divided*) $24_{4.5}$, Ziba 2 S $19_{30}$, בֵּן *son* of Israel Jos $14_5$ $18_2$, עֶבֶד *slave* Pr $17_2$, נָקִי *innocent one* Jb $27_{17}$, warriors 1 S $30_{24}$, officials Ne $13_{13}$, friend of a thief Pr $29_{24}$.

**<OBJ>** אֱלֹהִים *gods* Dt $29_{25}$, שֶׁמֶשׁ *sun* Dt $4_{19}$, יָרֵחַ *moon* Dt $4_{19}$, כּוֹכָב *star* Dt $4_{19}$, צָבָא *host* of heaven Dt $4_{19}$, אוֹר *light* Si $16_{16}$, שֶׁבַח *praise* Si $16_{16}$, כָּבוֹד *glory* Si $44_2$, אָב Israelite *father* Ne $9_{22}$, בֵּן *son* of Aaron 1 C $24_3$ (if em.), *son* of Eleazar 1 C $24_{4.5}$, *son* of Ithamar 1 C $24_{4.5}$, כֹּהֵן *priest* 2 C $23_{18}$, לֵוִי *Levite* 1 C $23_6$ (if em.) 2 C $23_{18}$, רֹפֵא *healer* Si $38_1$, אֶרֶץ *land* Jos $14_5$, שָׂדֶה *field* 2 S $19_{30}$, בַּיִת *house* 2 C $28_{21}$, נַחֲלָה *heritage* Jos $18_2$ Pr $17_2$ Si $45_{22}$, כֶּסֶף *silver* Jb $27_{17}$, שָׁלָל *plunder* Jos $22_8$, רַע *evil* Si $34_{13}$, עֵסֶק *work* Si $40_1$.

**<PREP>** לְ of benefit, *to, for,* + עַם *people* Dt $4_{19}$, Israel Dt $29_{25}$, אִישׁ *man* Si $44_{2(Bmg)}$, אָח *brother*, i.e. associate Ne $13_{13}$, בֵּן *son* Si $16_{16}$, רְנָנָה *ostrich* Jb $39_{17}$, טוֹב *good* Si $39_{25}$; *according to,* + פֵּאָה *piece* of land, i.e. boundary Ne $9_{22}$, פְּקֻדָּה *appointment* of service 1 C $24_3$ (if em.); בְּ of instrument, *by (means of),* + גּוֹרָל *lot* 1 C $24_5$; *in, with,* + בִּינָה *understanding* Jb $39_{17}$; מִן of comparison, *(more) than,* + עַיִן *eye* Si $34_{13}$; עַל *in charge of,* + בַּיִת *house* of Y. 2 C $23_{18}$; עִם *with,* + אָח *brother* Jos $22_8$, גַּנָּב *thief* Pr $29_{24}$; בְּתוֹךְ *among* Si $45_{22}$.

**<COLL>** יַחְדָּו יַחֲלֹקוּ *they shall share together* 1 S $30_8$.

**Ni.** 8.3.3 Pf. Si נחלק, Si נחלקה; impf. יֵחָלֵק (יֵחָלֶק), 3fs תֵּחָלֵק; + waw וַיֵּחָלֵק, וַיֵּחָלְקֵם—**be divided, be apportioned, divide oneself** (unless at Gn $14_{15}$ חלק IV *surround*), **<SUBJ>** אֶרֶץ *land* Nm $26_{53.55}$, עַם *people* 1 K $16_{21}$, Abram Gn $14_{15}$, Ahimelech 1 C $24_3$ (or em. חלק qal *divide*), David 1 C $23_6$ (or em. חלק qal *divide*) $24_3$ (or em. חלק qal *divide*), Zadok 1 C $24_3$ (or em. חלק qal *divide*), כֹּהֵן *priest* 1QM $9_6$ ([נחל]קו), עֶבֶד *servant* Gn $14_{15}$, מִלְחָמָה *war* 1QM $2_{13.14}$, מַעֲרָכָה *battle-line* 1QM $18_4$, נַחֲלָה *heritage* Nm $26_{56}$, תְּהִלָּה *praise* Si $15_9$, אוֹר *light* Jb $38_{24}$, תִּירוֹשׁ *new wine* Si $34_{27}$, מלאכת עבדה *work of farming* Si $7_{15}$.

**<PREP>** לְ of benefit, *to, for,* + רָשָׁע *wicked one* Si $15_9$, גִּיל *rejoicing* Si $34_{27}$, אֵלֶּה *these* Nm $26_{53}$; *in(to),* + חֲצִי *half* 1 K $16_{21}$; *according to,* + פְּקֻדָּה *appointment* of service 1 C $24_3$; בְּ of instrument, *by (means of),* + גּוֹרָל *lot* Nm $26_{55}$; of essence, *as,* + נַחֲלָה *heritage* Nm $26_{53}$; מִן of agent, *by (means of),* + אֵל *God* Si $15_9$; עַל *against* 1QM $18_4$, + מֶלֶךְ *king* Gn $14_{15}$, בֵּן *son* 1QM $2_{13.14}$ ([בן]); עַל־פִּי *according to,* + גּוֹרָל *lot* Nm $26_{56}$.

**Pi.** 26.0.6 Pf. חִלֵּק, 3fs חִלְּקָה (חִלְּקָתַם) חִלְּקָם, חִלְּקוּ, חִלַּקְתֶּם; impf. יְחַלֵּק, 3fs תְּחַלֵּק, אֲחַלֵּק (אֲחַלֶּק־), אֲחַלְּקָה, יְחַלְּקוּ, (אֲחַלְּקֵם); + waw וַיְחַלֶּק־; impv. חַלֵּק; inf. חַלֵּק (חַלְּקָם)—**divide, apportion, assign, distribute, scatter,** **<SUBJ>** י׳ *Y.* Is $53_{12}$ Mc $2_4$, אֱלֹהִים *God* Ps $60_8$=4QPps[a] $13_3$ ([אחלקה]) Ps $108_8$, אֵל *God* Jb $21_{17}$ (unless חלק III pi. *destroy*), פָּנִים *face* of Y. Lm $4_{16}$ (unless חלק III pi. *destroy*), גּוֹי *nation* Jl $4_2$, Israelite(s) Ezk $47_{21}$, Kittim 1QpHab $6_6$, עֵדָה *congregation* of evildoers Ps $22_{19}$, Ahab 1 K $18_6$, Alma 5/6ḤevBA $44_1$, Benjamin Gn $49_{27}$, David 2 S $6_{19}$‖1 C $16_3$, Eleazar Jos $19_{51}$ 5/6ḤevBA $44_1$, Eliezer 5/6ḤevBA $44_1$, Jacob Gn $49_7$, Joshua Jos $13_7$ $18_{10}$ $19_{51}$, Obadiah 1 K $18_6$, Tehinnah 5/6ḤevBA $44_1$, מֶלֶךְ *king* Dn $11_{39}$, רֹאשׁ *head* of ancestral house Jos $19_{51}$, woman Ps $68_{13}$=1QpPs $3_3$ ([תחלק]), בֵּן *son* 5/6 ḤevBA $44_1$, *son* of human being, i.e. mortal Ezk $5_1$, עֶבֶד *servant* Is $53_{12}$, warrior Jg $5_{30}$ Is $9_2$ Pr $16_{19}$, worshipper 1QS $10_{25}$, אֹיֵב *enemy* Ex $15_9$, יָד *hand* Is $34_{17}$; subj. not specified, 1QpPs $3_5$ 4QMyst[c] $1_1$ 11QT $44_{3.5}$ ([תח]לק).

**<OBJ>** אֶרֶץ *land* Jos $13_7$ $18_{10}$ $19_{51}$ Ezk $47_{21}$ Jl $4_2$, אֲדָמָה *land* Dn $11_{39}$, land Is $34_{17}$, מָקוֹם *place* 5/6ḤevBA $44_1$, שָׂדֶה *field* Mc $2_4$, נִשְׁכָּה *room* 11QT $44_{3.5}$, חֶדֶר *chamber* 11QT $44_{3.5}$, Israelite(s) Lm $4_{16}$, Shechem Ps $60_8$=4QPps[a] $13_3$ Ps $108_8$, Levi Gn $49_7$, Simeon Gn $49_7$, חֶבֶל *destruction* Jb $21_{17}$, שָׁלָל *plunder* Gn $49_{27}$ Ex $15_9$ Jg $5_{30}$ Is $9_2$ $53_{12}$ Ps $68_{13}$=1QpPs $3_3$ Pr $16_{19}$, עֹל *yoke* 1QpHab $6_6$, מַס *forced labour* 1QpHab $6_6$, בֶּגֶד *garment* Ps $22_{19}$, חֹק *statute* 1QS $10_{25}$, דָּבָר *word* 4QMyst[c] $1_1$.

**<PREP>** לְ of benefit, *to, for* Is $34_{17}$, + עַם *people* 2 S $6_{19}$, Israelite(s) Ezk $47_{21}$, הָמוֹן *multitude* 2 S $6_{19}$, שֵׁבֶט *tribe* Jos $13_7$, עֵדָה *congregation* Ps $22_{19}$, חֲצִי *half* tribe Jos $13_7$, Ahab 1 K $18_6$, Obadiah 1 K $18_6$, אִישׁ *man* of Israel 1 C

16$_3$, בֵּן *son* Jos 18$_{10}$ 11QT 44$_5$, עֶבֶד *servant* Is 53$_{12}$, שׁוֹבֵב *faithless one* Mc 2$_4$ (or em. שׁוֹבֵינוּ *our captor*).

לְ *according to*, + שֵׁבֶט *tribe* of Israel Ezk 47$_{21}$; *at*, + עֶרֶב *evening* Gn 49$_{27}$.

בְּ of place, *in*, + Jacob Gn 49$_7$; of instrument, *by (means of)*, + קָו *line* Is 34$_{17}$ 1QS 10$_{25}$, אַף *anger* Jb 21$_{17}$; of accompaniment, *with*, + רַב *great one* Is 53$_{12}$; of essence, *as*, + נַחֲלָה *heritage* Jos 13$_7$; *for*, + מְחִיר *market price* Dn 11$_{39}$.

מִן of cause, *on account of*, + רָצוֹן *will* 5/6ḤevBA 44$_1$.

אֵת *with*, + גֵּאֶה *proud one* Pr 16$_{19}$, עצם pass. ptc. *one who is strong* Is 53$_{12}$.

בֵּין *among*, + Alma 5/6ḤevBA 44$_1$, Eleazar 5/6Ḥev BA 44$_1$, Eliezer 5/6ḤevBA 44$_1$, Tehinnah 5/6ḤevBA 44$_1$, בֵּן *son* 5/6ḤevBA 44$_1$.

**Pu.** 3 Pf. חֻלַּק; impf. 3fs תְּחֻלָּק—**be divided,** <SUBJ> אֲדָמָה *land* Am 7$_{17}$, עַד *prey* of plunder Is 33$_{23}$, שָׁלָל *plunder* Zc 14$_1$. <PREP> בְּ of instrument, *by (means of)*, + חֶבֶל *line* Am 7$_{17}$; בְּקֶרֶב *in, within*, + Jerusalem Zc 14$_1$.

**Hi.** 1 Inf. חֲלֵק—**participate in distribution,** <SUBJ> Jeremiah Jr 37$_{12}$ (unless חלק VII *flee*).

**Htp.** 1 + waw וְהִתְחַלְּקוּ—**divide with one another,** <SUBJ> אִישׁ *man* Jos 18$_5$. <OBJ> אֶרֶץ *land* Jos 18$_5$. <PREP> לְ *in(to)*, + שִׁבְעָה *seven* portions Jos 18$_5$.*

→ חֵלֶק *portion*, חֵלֶק *Helek*, חֶלְקִי *Helekite*, חֶלְקָה *portion*, חֲלֻקָּה *portion*, חֶלְקַי *Helkai*, חֶלְקַת *Helkath*, חֶלְקַת הַצֻּרִים *Helkath-hazzurim*, חִלְקִיָּהוּ *Hilkiah*, מַחֲלֹקֶת *division*.

## חלק II

10.0.2 vb. **be smooth—Qal** 2 Pf. חָלַק, חָלְקוּ—**be smooth, be slippery,** <SUBJ> לֵב *heart* Ho 10$_2$ (or em. חֻלַּק *it is divided*, i.e. חלק I pu.), מַחְמָאֹת *curds* Ps 55$_{22}$ (or em. חָלְקוּ מַחְמָאֹת פִּיו *the curds of his mouth are smooth* to חָלַק מֵחֶמְאוֹת פִּיו *his mouth is smoother than curds*), פֶּה *mouth* Ps 55$_{22}$ (if em.). <PREP> מִן of comparison, *(more) than*, + חֶמְאָה *curd* Ps 55$_{22}$ (if em.; see Subj.).

**Hi.** 8.0.2 Pf. הֶחֱלִיק, הֶחֱלִיקָה, Q החליקו; impf. יַחֲלִיקוּן (mss יַחֲלִיקוּן); מַחֲלִיק—**1. make smooth,** in metal working, <SUBJ> metal-worker Is 41$_7$. <COLL> חלק hi. + פַּטִּישׁ *smooth [with] a hammer* Is 41$_7$ (1QIsa[a] פלטיש *hammer*).

**2. make smooth** one's speech in flattery, **flatter, use flattery,** <SUBJ> גֶּבֶר *man* Pr 29$_5$, אִשָּׁה strange *woman* Pr 2$_{16}$ 7$_5$, נָכְרִי fem. *foreign woman* Pr 2$_{16}$ 7$_5$, זוֹנָה *prostitute* 4QWiles 1$_2$ ([הזונ]ה ... תחלו[י]ק), נָבִיא *prophet* Jr 23$_{31}$ (if em. הַלֹּקְחִים *who take* to מַחֲלִקִים *who make smooth* their tongue), שׁוֹרֵר *watcher*, i.e. enemy Ps 5$_{10}$, flatterer Pr 28$_{23}$ (+ יכח hi. *reprove*), perh. פֶּשַׁע *transgression* Ps 36$_3$. <OBJ> אֵמֶר *word* Pr 2$_{16}$ 7$_5$ 1QH 4$_7$ ([אמ]רים), לָשׁוֹן *tongue* Jr 23$_{31}$ (if em.; see Subj.) Ps 5$_{10}$ Pr 28$_{23}$, קֶלֶס *derision* 4QWiles 1$_2$ (תחלו[י]ק). <PREP> לְ of direction, *to*, + עַם *people* 1QH 4$_7$; בְּ of place, *in*, + עַיִן *eye*, i.e. sight Ps 36$_3$; אֶל *to*, i.e. with, + רָשָׁע *wicked one* Ps 36$_3$; עַל *upon*, + רֵעַ *neighbour* Pr 29$_5$.*

→ חָלָק I *smooth*, (?) חָלָק II *Halak*, חַלָּק *smooth*, חֵלֶק *smoothness*, חֶלְקָה *smoothness*, חֲלַקְלַקּוֹת *smoothness*.

## חלק III

2 vb. **destroy—Pi.** 1 Pf. חִלְּקָם; impf. יְחַלֵּק—**destroy** (unless חלק I *divide*), <SUBJ> Y. Ps 17$_{14}$ (if em. חֶלְקָם *their portion* to חַלְּקֵם *eradicate them*), אֵל *God* Jb 21$_{17}$, פָּנִים *face* of Y. Lm 4$_{16}$. <OBJ> כֹּהֵן *priest* Lm 4$_{16}$, נָבִיא *prophet* Lm 4$_{16}$, חֹבֵל *wrongdoer* Jb 21$_{17}$ (if em. חֶבֶל *destruction*). <PREP> בְּ of instrument, *by (means of)*, + אַף *anger* Jb 21$_{17}$; perh. *from*, + חַיִּים *life* Ps 17$_{14}$.*

→ חֲלַקּוֹת *perdition*.

## * חלק IV

1 **surround—Ni.** 1 + waw וַיֵּחָלֵק—**draw round, encircle** (unless חלק I *divide*, ni. *be divided*, i.e. deploy oneself), <SUBJ> Abram Gn 14$_{15}$, עֶבֶד *servant* Gn 14$_{15}$. <PREP> עַל *around*, + מֶלֶךְ *king* Gn 14$_{15}$.

## * חלק V

1 vb. **strip—Qal** 1 Pf. חָלַק—**strip** (unless חלק I *divide*; or em. חלץ pi. *plunder*), <SUBJ> Ahaz 2 C 28$_{21}$. <OBJ> בַּיִת *house* 2 C 28$_{21}$.

## * חלק VI

1 vb. **create—Ni.** 1 Impf. יֵחָלֵק—**be created,** <SUBJ> אוֹר *light* or *heat* Jb 38$_{24}$.

## * חלק VII

1 **flee—Hi.** 1 Inf. חֲלֵק—**flee, escape,** <SUBJ> Jeremiah Jr 37$_{12}$ (unless חלק I hi. *participate in distribution*). <PREP> מִן of direction, *from*, + שָׁם *there* Jr 37$_{12}$.

## חָלָק I

10.0.14 adj. **smooth**—pl. חֲלָקוֹת (חֲלָקוֹת), cstr. חַלְקֵי—**1a. smooth,** used attributively of אִישׁ *man* Gn

27$_{11}$ (:: שָׂעִר *hairy*). **1b. flattering,** used attributively of מִקְסָם *divination* Ezk 12$_{24(mss)}$, פֶּה *mouth* Pr 26$_{28}$ (+ לְשׁוֹן־שֶׁקֶר *tongue of deceit*).

2. in nom. cl. used predicatively of חֵךְ *palate* Pr 5$_{3}$ (חָלָק מִשֶּׁמֶן חִכָּהּ *her palate is smoother than oil*), שׁוֹק *thigh* 4QCrypt 2.1$_{5}$.

3. used as noun, **smooth one, a.** (masc. pl.) appar. **smooth stone** (Is 57$_{6}$), **b.** (fem. pl.) **slippery place** (Ps 73$_{18}$ [unless חֲלָקוֹת *perdition*]), **c.** (masc. sg.) **flattery** or perh. **flatterer** (Ezk 12$_{24}$), **d.** (fem. pl.) **smooth speech, flattery** (Is 30$_{10}$ Ps 12$_{3.4}$ Dn 11$_{32}$ 4QWiles 1$_{17}$ 4Q185 1.2$_{14}$), **e.** (fem. pl.) usu. at Qumran **smooth thing, easy interpretation,** attributed to sectarians' opponents (CD 1$_{18}$ 1QH 2$_{32}$ 1QH 4$_{10}$ 4QpIsa$^{c}$ 23.2$_{10}$ 4QpNah 3.1$_{2.6}$ 3.2$_{2.4}$ 3.3$_{3.7}$ 4QMidrEschat$^{b}$ 9$_{12}$).

<OBJ> דבר pi. *speak* Is 30$_{10}$ (‖ מַהֲתַלּוֹת *deceptions*), דרשׁ *seek* 1QH 2$_{15}$ ([חל]קות; + רְמִיָּה *deceit*) 2$_{32}$ (+ כָּזָב *lie*) 4QpIsa$^{c}$ 23.2$_{10}$ 4QpNah 3.1$_{2}$ 3.2$_{2}$ (+ כַּחַשׁ *deceit*) 3.2$_{4}$ 3.3$_{3.7}$ 4QMidrEschat$^{b}$ 9$_{12}$ (חו[ל]קות). <CSTR> דורשי חלקות *seekers of smooth things* 1QH 2$_{15}$ (חל[קות]) 2$_{32}$ 4QpIsa$^{c}$ 23.2$_{10}$ (ד[ורשי]) 4QpNah 3.1$_{2}$ 3.2$_{2.4}$ 3.3$_{3.7}$ 4Q MidrEschat$^{b}$ 9$_{12}$ (חו[ל]קות), מִקְסַם חָלָק *divination of flattery* Ezk 12$_{24}$ (‖ שָׁוְא *vanity*), שְׂפַת חֲלָקוֹת *lip of flattery* Ps 12$_{3}$ (+ שָׁוְא), שִׂפְתֵי *lips of* Ps 12$_{4}$ (+ גְּדוֹלוֹת *great things*); חַלְּקֵי־נַחַל *smooth ones of the valley* Is 57$_{6}$. <PREP> לְ of direction, *to*, + שׁפך *pour* libation Is 57$_{6}$, עלה hi. *bring up* cereal offering Is 57$_{6}$; בְּ of place, *in, among* Is 57$_{6}$, שׁית *place* Ps 73$_{18}$; of price, *(in exchange) for*, + מור hi. *exchange* law 1QH 4$_{10}$; of instrument, *by (means of), with*, + חנף hi. *make profane* Dn 11$_{32}$, פתה pi. *seduce* 4Q Wiles 1$_{17}$; of accompaniment, *with*, + חזק hi. *take hold of* 4Q185 1.2$_{14}$; introducing object, + דרשׁ *seek* CD 1$_{18}$ (‖ מַהֲתַלּוֹת *deceptions*).

<SYN> §3 מַהֲתַלּוֹת *deceptions*, שָׁוְא *vanity*.

<ANT> §1a שָׂעִר *hairy*.*

→ חלק *be smooth*.

***חָלָק** II $_{2}$ pl.n. **Halak,** name of mountain, הָהָר הֶחָלָק *Mount Halak*, perh. Ğebel Ḥalāq, 42 km WSW of Sodom, Jos 11$_{17}$ 12$_{7}$.

→ (?) חָלָק *smooth*.

**[חָלָק] III** $_{0.1}$ n.[m.] **creature,** <SUBJ> יצב htp. *stand* Si 36$_{13}$ (להתיצב מפניו חלק *that a creature may stand before him*).

→ חלק *create*.

**[חַלַּק]** $_{1}$ adj. **smooth**—pl. cstr. חַלְּקֵי—used as noun, **smooth one,** <OBJ> בחר *choose* 1 S 17$_{40}$. <CSTR> חַלְּקֵי־אֲבָנִים *smooth ones of stones*, i.e. smooth stones 1 S 17$_{40}$. <COLL> חֲמִשָּׁה חַלֻּקֵי *five smooth ones of* 1 S 17$_{40}$.*

→ חלק *be smooth*.

**חֵלֶק I** $_{66.6.7}$ n.m. **portion**—cstr. חֵלֶק; sf. חֶלְקִי, חֶלְקְךָ (חֶלְקֶךָ), חֶלְקוֹ, חֶלְקָם; pl. חֲלָקִים; sf. חֶלְקֵיהֶם—**portion, share,** of food or plunder (e.g. Gn 14$_{24.24}$ Lv 6$_{10}$ Nm 31$_{36}$ 1 S 30$_{24.24}$), of humankind (e.g. Dt 32$_{9}$), of inheritance (e.g. Gn 31$_{14}$ 2 S 20$_{1}$ Ne 2$_{20}$), of allotted territory (e.g. Dt 10$_{9}$ 12$_{12}$ Jos 19$_{9}$ Ezk 45$_{7}$); also **reward** for work (Ec 2$_{10}$).*

<SUBJ> היה *be* Nm 18$_{20}$ 31$_{36}$ Dt 10$_{9}$ 18$_{1}$ Jos 19$_{9}$ Ec 2$_{10}$ CD 20$_{13}$.

<NOM CL> חֶלְקִי י׳ *Y. is my portion* Ps 119$_{57}$ Lm 3$_{24}$, חֶלְקִי אֱלֹהִים *my portion is God* Ps 73$_{26}$, חֵלֶק י׳ עַמּוֹ *the portion of Y. is his people* Dt 32$_{9}$, י׳ מְנָת־חֶלְקִי *Y. is the portion of my share*, i.e. my chosen portion Ps 16$_{5}$, שָׁמֵן חֶלְקוֹ *his portion is fat* Hb 1$_{16}$=1QpHab 5$_{15}$=1Qp Hab 6$_{5}$, מעט הוא חלקו *small is his portion* Si 14$_{9}$, בְּחַלְּקֵי־נַחַל חֶלְקֵךְ *your portion is among the smooth stones* (חָלָק I) *of the river* Is 57$_{6}$, חֶלְקָם בַּחַיִּים *their portion is among the living* Ps 17$_{14}$, לֹא־כְאֵלֶּה חֵלֶק יַעֲקֹב *not like these is the portion of Jacob* Jr 10$_{16}$ 51$_{19}$ (יַעֲקוֹב), עִם מְנָאֲפִים חֶלְקֶךָ *your portion is with adulterers* Ps 50$_{18}$.

אֲנִי חֶלְקְךָ *I am your portion* Nm 18$_{20}$, אני חל[קכה] *I am your portion* 1Q26 1$_{7}$, אַתָּה ... חֶלְקִי *you are ... my portion* Ps 142$_{6}$, הוּא חֶלְקְךָ *that is your portion* Ec 9$_{9}$, הוא חלקכה *that is your portion* 4Q418 81$_{3}$, הוּא חֶלְקוֹ *that is his portion* Ec 3$_{22}$ 5$_{17}$ (חֶלְקוֹ), זֶה חֵלֶק *this is the portion* Is 17$_{14}$ Jb 20$_{29}$ 27$_{13}$ Si 41$_{4}$.

מֶה חֵלֶק אֱלוֹהַּ *what is the portion of God?* Jb 31$_{2}$, מַה־לָּנוּ חֵלֶק בְּדָוִד *what portion have we in David?* 1 K 12$_{16}$‖2 C 10$_{16}$ (דָּוִיד), הַעוֹד לָנוּ חֵלֶק *do we still have a portion?* Gn 31$_{14}$.

אֵין לוֹ אֵין־חֵלֶק *there is not a portion* Jos 18$_{7}$ Ne 2$_{20}$, אֵין לוֹ

חֵלֶק *he does not have a portion* Dt 12$_{12}$ 14$_{27.29}$, אֵין־לָכֶם חֵלֶק *you do not have a portion* Jos 22$_{25.27}$, אין להם חלק *they do have a share* CD 20$_{10}$, אֵין־לָנוּ חֵלֶק *we do not have a portion* 2 S 20$_{1}$, חֵלֶק אֵין־לָהֶם *they do not have a portion* Ec 9$_{6}$.

<OBJ> נתן *give* Jos 14$_{4}$ 15$_{13}$ Ec 11$_{2}$ Si 7$_{31}$(ח[לקם]), לקח *take* Gn 14$_{24}$ Si 14$_{9}$, נשׂא *raise*, i.e. accept Ec 5$_{18}$, מור hi. *change* Mc 2$_{4}$, אכל *eat* Dt 18$_{8}$ 11QT 60$_{14}$, i.e. devour Am 7$_{4}$, אבד pi. *destroy* Si 14$_{9}$, ענה *answer* Jb 32$_{17}$.

<CSTR> חֵלֶק י׳ *portion of Y.* Dt 32$_{9}$, אֱלוֹהַּ *of God* Jb 31$_{2}$, עַמִּי *of my people* Mc 2$_{4}$, יַעֲקֹב *of Jacob* Jr 10$_{16}$ 51$_{19}$ (יַעֲקוֹב), ח]לקי מלכי צ[דק *portions of Melchizedek* 11Q Melch$_{5}$, חֵלֶק־אָדָם *portion of a human* Jb 20$_{29}$ 27$_{13}$, הָאֲנָשִׁים *of the men* Gn 14$_{24}$, רעהו *of his neighbour* Si 14$_{9}$, הַיֹּרֵד *of the one who goes down* 1 S 30$_{24}$, הַיֹּצְאִים *of the ones who go out* Nm 31$_{36}$, הַיֹּשֵׁב *of the one who sits* 1 S 30$_{24}$, ירא *of one who fears* Si 26$_{3}$, שׁוֹסֵינוּ *of those who plunder us* Is 17$_{14}$.

חֵלֶק יִזְרְעֶאל *territory of Jezreel* 2 K 9$_{10.36.37}$.

אנשי חלו[ק] *men of lot* 6QBen 1$_{2}$, מְנָת־חֶלְקִי *portion of my share*, i.e. my chosen portion Ps 16$_{5}$, אַחַד הַחֲלָקִים *one of the portions* Ezk 45$_{7}$ 48$_{8}$.

<APP> מֶחֱצָה *half* Nm 31$_{36}$, שִׁבְעָה *seven* Jos 18$_{5.6.9}$.

<PREP> לְ of benefit, *to, for*, + נגד hi. *declare* Jb 17$_{5}$; *as*, + נצב hi. *establish* Si 44$_{23}$, *in(to)*, + חלק htp. *divide with one another* Jos 18$_{5}$; *according to*, + כתב *write* Jos 18$_{6(mss).9}$; בְּ of place, *in* 11QMelch$_{5}$ (ח[לקי]), + היה *be* 2 K 9$_{37}$, אכל *eat* 2 K 9$_{10.36}$; *in, with*, + נתן ni. *be given* Si 26$_{3}$; כְּ *as* Dt 18$_{8}$ 1 S 30$_{24.24}$ 11QT 60$_{14}$; אֵת *with*, + אכל *eat*, i.e. devour Ho 5$_{7}$; לְעֻמַּת *alongside* Ezk 48$_{21}$.

<COLL> חֶלְקָם נָתַתִּי אֹתָהּ *I have given it as their portion* Lv 6$_{10}$, יָרֹנּוּ חֶלְקָם *they shall rejoice in their lot* Is 61$_{7}$, וְנָחַל י׳ ... חֶלְקוֹ *and Y. shall inherit ... (as) his portion* Zc 2$_{16}$, יִתְּנֶנּוּ חֶלְקוֹ *he will give it (as) his portion* Ec 2$_{21}$.

Also Si 45$_{20}$.*

→ חלק *divide*.

**חֵלֶק** II 2.0.0.4 pr.n.m. **Helek, 1.** descendant of Manasseh and son of Gilead, <NOM CL> אֵלֶּה בְּנֵי גִלְעָד אִיעֶזֶר ... וְחֵלֶק *these were the sons of Gilead ... Iezer and Helek* Nm 26$_{30(mss, Sam)}$ (L לְחֵלֶק *to Helek* was the family of the Helekites). <CSTR> בְּנֵי־חֵלֶק *sons of Helek* Jos 17$_{2}$. <PREP> לְ of possession, *of, (belonging) to* Nm 26$_{30}$ (mss, Sam וְחֵלֶק *and Helek*).

**2.** father of Delethiah, Seal 331 (8th–6th cent.). **3.** son of Ezer, Seal 557 (T. Beit Mirsim?, 7th/6th cent.). **4.** appar. father of Malchijah, Seal 598 (T. Beit Mirsim?, 7th/6th cent.). **5.** father of Paltiah, Seal 649 (T. Beit Mirsim?, 7th/6th cent.). <CSTR> בן חלק *son of Helek* Seal 331 (8th–6th cent.) 557 649 (both T. Beit Mirsim?, 7th/6th cent.).

→ חֶלְקִי *Helekite*.

**חֵלֶק** III 0.0.0.3 pl.n. **Helek,** perh. ʿAṣīre eš-Šemāliye, 5 km NNW of Shechem, <PREP> מִן of direction, *from* Samaria ost. 22$_{1}$ 23$_{1}$ 24$_{1}$ (מח[לק]) 25$_{1}$ ([מחל]ק) 26$_{1}$ (מחל[ק]) 27$_{1}$.

**[חֵלֶק]** IV 1 n.[m.] **smoothness**—cstr. חֵלֶק—of speech, i.e. flattery, <CSTR> חֵלֶק שְׂפָתֶיהָ *smoothness of her lips* Pr 7$_{21}$ (+ לֶקַח *teaching*, i.e. persuasion). <PREP> בְּ of instrument, *(by means of), with*, + נדח hi. *compel* Pr 7$_{21}$.*

→ חלק *be smooth*.

**[חִלְקָא]** 0.0.0.1 pr.n.[m.] **Hilka,** appar. father of Azariah, Seal 728 (8th/7th cent.).

**[חֲלֻקָּה]** 1.0.1 n.f. **division**—cstr. חֲלֻקַּת; pl. sf. Q חלוקותמה—**division, part,** <NOM CL> וַחֲלֻקַּת בֵּית־אָב לַלְוִיִּם appar. *and part of a father's house is to the Levites* 2 C 35$_{5}$ (or em. וּלְכָל־בֵּית־אָב לִבְנֵי הָעָם חֲלֻקַּת *and to every father's house of the sons of the people is part of* a father's house of Levites). <CSTR> חֲלֻקַּת בֵּית־אָב *part of a father's house* 2 C 35$_{5}$. <PREP> בְּ of place, *in* 4QM$^{a}$ 1$_{6}$ (ב]חלוקותמה] *in their divisions*).*

→ חלק *divide*.

**חֶלְקָה** I 23.0.1 n.f. **plot of land**—cstr. חֶלְקַת; sf. חֶלְקָתִי, חֶלְקָתָם; pl. sf. Q חלקותיכה—**plot (of land), field,** <SUBJ> היה *be* 2 S 23$_{11}$‖1 C 11$_{13}$, יבשׁ *be dry* Am 4$_{7}$, מטר ni. *be rained upon* Am 4$_{7}$, קלל pu. *be cursed* Jb 24$_{18}$, ספן pass. appar. *be reserved* Dt 33$_{21}$=4QMidrEschat$^{a}$ 2$_{3}$ ([ספון] ... [חלקת]; unless em. סָפוּן וַיֵּתֵא *reserved, and he came to* וְהִתְאַסְּפוּן *and they gathered together*). <NOM CL>

חֶלְקַת יוֹאָב אֶל־יָדִי *the field of Joab is to my hand*, i.e. next to mine 2 S 14$_{30}$, הַחֶלְקָה אֲשֶׁר לִי *the field that is mine* 2 S 14$_{31}$, sim. Ru 4$_{3}$.

**<OBJ>** קנה *purchase* Gn 33$_{19}$, מכר *sell* Ru 4$_{3}$, נתן *give*, i.e. make, into desert Jr 12$_{10}$, נצל hi. *deliver* 2 S 23$_{12}$‖1 C 11$_{14}$, מלא pi. *fill* 2 K 3$_{25}$, קרה *chance upon* Ru 2$_{3}$, נשם *pant for*, i.e. desire Dt 33$_{21}$=4QMidr Eschat$^{a}$ 2$_{3}$ ([חלקת]; if em. שָׁם *there* to יִשֹּׁם *he pants for*), יצת hi. *set on fire* 2 S 14$_{30.31}$, כאב *mar* with stones 2 K 3$_{19}$, בוס pol. *trample* Jr 12$_{10}$ (mss נַחֲלָתִי *my heritage*; ‖ כֶּרֶם *vineyard*).

**<CSTR>** חֶלְקַת יוֹאָב *field/plot of Joab* 2 S 14$_{30}$, נָבוֹת *of Naboth* 2 K 9$_{21.25(mss)}$, מְחֹקֵק *of the commander* Dt 33$_{21}$=4QMidrEschat$^{a}$ 2$_{3}$ ([חלקת]), הַשָּׂדֶה *of the field*, i.e. plot of land Gn 33$_{19}$ Jos 24$_{32}$ 2 S 23$_{11}$‖1 C 11$_{13}$ Ru 2$_{3}$ 4$_{3}$, שָׂדֵה *of the field of* Naboth 2 K 9$_{25}$, חֶלְקָתִי *of my desire*, i.e. my desirable field Jr 12$_{10}$; תּוֹךְ הַחֶלְקָה *middle of the plot* 2 S 23$_{12}$‖1 C 11$_{14}$, כָּל־חֶלְקָה *every plot* 2 K 3$_{19}$ (כל הַחֶלְקָה) 3$_{25}$. **<ADJ>** טוֹב *good* 2 K 3$_{19.25}$, אֶחָד *one* Am 4$_{7}$, זֶה *this* 2 K 9$_{26}$. **<PREP>** בְּ of place, *in, on, at* 1QM 12$_{11}$ 19$_{4}$ ([בחלקותיכה]), + שלך hi. *throw* 2 K 9$_{25.26}$, קבר *bury* Jos 24$_{32}$, מצא *find* 2 K 9$_{21}$, שלם pi. *requite* 2 K 9$_{26}$; עַל *upon*, + מטר hi. *send rain* Am 4$_{7}$. **<COLL>** חֶלְקָה + שלך אֶבֶן hi. *throw a stone (on)* 2 K 3$_{25}$, חֶלְקַת הַשָּׂדֶה מְלֵאָה עֲדָשִׁים *a plot of land full of lentils* 2 S 23$_{11}$‖1 C 11$_{13}$.

**<SYN>** כֶּרֶם *vineyard*.*

→ חלק *divide*.

[חֶלְקָה] II 2 n.f. **smoothness**—cstr. חֶלְקַת—**1. smooth part** of neck, **<CSTR>** חֶלְקַת צַוָּארָיו *the smooth part of his neck* Gn 27$_{16}$ (+ יָד *hand*). **<PREP>** עַל *upon*, + לבשׁ hi. *clothe* Gn 27$_{16}$.

**2. smoothness** of tongue, i.e. flattery, **<CSTR>** חֶלְקַת לָשׁוֹן *smoothness of tongue* Pr 6$_{24}$ (or em. לְשׁוֹן *of the tongue of* the foreign woman). **<APP>** appar. נָכְרִיָּה Pr 6$_{24}$ (unless em.; see Cstr.). **<PREP>** מִן of direction, *from*, + שׁמר *keep* Pr 6$_{24}$.*

→ חלק *be smooth*.

חֲלַקְלַקּוֹת* 1 n.f.pl. **perdition** (unless חָלָק *smooth*, used as noun, *slippery places*), **<PREP>** לְ of direction, *to*, + שׁית *place* Ps 73$_{18}$ (or em. שׁתל *transplant*).

→ חלק *die*.

חֲלַקְלַקּוֹת, see חָלָק I *smooth*.

[חֶלְקַי] 1 pr.n.m. **Helkai**—חֶלְקָי—priest and family head at time of Joiakim, **<NOM CL>** לִמְרָיוֹת חֶלְקָי *(belonging) to Meraioth was Helkai* Ne 12$_{15}$ (or em. לִמְרָיוֹת to לִמְרֵמוֹת *to Meremoth* was Helkai; mss. חֶלְקִי).

חֶלְקִי I 1 gent. **Helekite,** descendant(s) of Helek, son of Gilead, as pl. noun **Helekites, <CSTR>** מִשְׁפַּחַת הַחֶלְקִי *family of the Helekites* Nm 26$_{30}$.

→ חֵלֶק *Helek.*

חֶלְקִי II 1 pr.n.m. **Helki,** priest and leader at time of Joiakim, **<NOM CL>** לִמְרָיוֹת חֶלְקִי *(belonging) to Meraioth was Helki* Ne 12$_{15(mss.)}$ (or em. לִמְרָיוֹת to לִמְרֵמוֹת *to Meremoth* was Helki; L חֶלְקָי).

חִלְקִיָּה, see חִלְקִיָּהוּ *Hilkiah.*

חִלְקִיָּהוּ 34.0.0.16 pr.n.m. **Hilkiah**—חִלְקִיָּה 2 K 18$_{37}$ 22$_{8.10.12}$ Jr 29$_{3}$ Ezr 7$_{1}$ Ne 8$_{4}$ 11$_{11}$ 12$_{7.21}$ 1 C 5$_{39.39}$ 6$_{30}$ 9$_{11}$ 2 C 35$_{8}$—**1.** son of Shallum or Meshullam, father of Azariah and high priest at time of Josiah, **<SUBJ>** ילד hi. *beget* 1 C 5$_{39}$, הלך *go* 2 K 22$_{12.14}$‖2 C 34$_{20.22}$, יצא hi. *bring out* 2 K 23$_{4}$, שׁוב hi. *bring back* 2 K 22$_{14}$, נתן *give* 2 K 22$_{8.10}$‖2 C 34$_{15.18}$ 2 C 35$_{8}$, מצא *find* 2 K 22$_{8}$‖2 C 34$_{15}$ 23$_{24}$ 2 C 34$_{14}$, אמר *say* 2 K 22$_{8.14}$‖2 C 34$_{22}$ 2 K 22$_{14}$‖2 C 34$_{22}$ 2 C 34$_{15}$, דבר pi. *speak* 2 K 22$_{14}$‖2 C 34$_{22}$, ענה *answer* 2 C 34$_{15}$, דרשׁ *seek* 2 K 22$_{12.14}$‖2 C 34$_{20.22}$, תמם hi. *complete*, i.e. calculate money 2 K 22$_{4}$, שׂרף *burn* 2 K 23$_{4}$ (if em.). **<OBJ>** ילד hi. *beget* 1 C 5$_{39}$, שׁלח *send* 2 K 22$_{14}$‖2 C 34$_{22}$ 2 K 22$_{14}$‖2 C 34$_{22}$, צוה pi. *command* 2 K 22$_{12}$‖2 C 34$_{20}$ 2 K 23$_{4}$. **<CSTR>** בֶּן־חִלְקִיָּה *son of Hilkiah* Ezr 7$_{1}$ Ne 11$_{11}$‖1 C 9$_{11}$. **<APP>** כֹּהֵן *priest* 2 K 22$_{4.8.10}$‖2 C 34$_{18}$ 2 K 22$_{12.14}$ 23$_{4.24}$ 2 C 34$_{9.14}$, נָגִיד *prince* 2 C 35$_{8}$, בֵּן *son* Ezr 7$_{1}$ Ne 11$_{11}$‖1 C 9$_{11}$. **<PREP>** אֶל *to*, + בוא *come* 2 C 34$_{9}$, עלה *go up* 2 K 22$_{4}$, אמר *say* 2 K 22$_{14}$‖2 C 34$_{22}$ (לְ *to*).

**2.** father of Eliakim, **<CSTR>** בֶּן־חִלְקִיָּהוּ *son of Hilkiah* 2 K 18$_{18}$‖Is 36$_{3}$ 2 K 18$_{26.37}$‖Is 36$_{22}$ Is 22$_{20}$ (1QIsa$^{a}$ חלקיה). **3.** father of Gemariah, **<CSTR>** בֶּן־חִלְקִיָּה *son of Hilkiah* Jr 29$_{3}$. **4.** Merarite, son of Amzi and father of

Amaziah, <CSTR> בֶּן־חִלְקִיָּה *son of Hilkiah* 1 C $6_{30}$. <APP> בֵּן *son* 1 C $6_{30}$. **5.** leader present at Ezra's reading of the Torah, <SUBJ> עמד *stand* Ne $8_{4}$. **6.** head of priestly family associated with Zerubbabel, <SUBJ> עלה *go up* Ne $12_{7}$. <APP> כֹּהֵן *priest* Ne $12_{7}$, רֹאשׁ *chief* Ne $12_{7}$. <PREP> לְ of possession, *of, (belonging) to* Ne $12_{21}$. **7.** father of the prophet Jeremiah, <CSTR> בֶּן־חִלְקִיָּהוּ *son of Hilkiah* Jr $1_{1}$. **8.** Merarite, second son of Hosah, <NOM CL> חִלְקִיָּהוּ הַשֵּׁנִי *Hilkiah was the second* 1 C $26_{11}$.

**9.** appar. father of Isaiah, Seal 52 (Palestine). **10.** son of Meapes (others Maas), Seal 150 (Lachish, 8th/7th cent.). **11.** father of Jehozarah, Seal 321 (Hebron, 8th/7th cent.). **12.** son of Dodiah (others Adaiah), Seal 325 (7th cent.). **13.** appar. father of Paltiah, Seal 379 (8th/7th cent.). **14.** son of Shema, Seal 416 (חלקיה[ו]; 8th/7th cent.). **15.** father of Ishmael, Seal 418, (8th/7th cent.). **16.** appar. father of Azariah, Seal 496 (7th cent.). **17.** Seal 558 (T. Beit Mirsim?, 7th/6th cent.). **18.** Seal 559 (T. Beit Mirsim?, 7th/6th cent.). **19.** appar. father of Maaseiah, Seal 607 (T. Beit Mirsim?, 7th/6th cent.). **20.** father of Rapha, Seal 723 (7th cent.). **21.** father of Hanan, Seal 734 (8th/7th cent.). **22.** son of Pedaiah, Seal 737 (8th/7th cent.). **23.** father of Azariah, Seal 827 (City of David, 7th/6th cent.). **24.** appar. father of Paltiah, Seal 888 (7th/6th cent.).

<CSTR> בן חלקיהו *son of Hilkiah* Seal 321 (חלק[י]הו; Hebron. 8th/7th cent.) 418, (8th/7th cent.) 723 (7th cent.) 734 (8th/7th cent.) 827 (City of David, 7th/6th cent.). <APP> בֵּן *son* Seal 150 (Lachish, 8th/7th cent.) 325 (7th cent.) 416 (חלקיה[ו]; 8th/7th cent.) 558 (ב[ן]) 559 (both T. Beit Mirsim?, 7th/6th cent.) 737 (8th/7th cent.). <PREP> לְ of possession, *(belonging) to* Seal 150 (Lachish, 8th/7th cent.) 325 (7th cent.) 416 (לחלקיה[ו]; 8th/7th cent.) 558 559 (both T. Beit Mirsim?, 7th/6th cent.) 737 (8th/7th cent.).

⇒ חלק *divide* + י״ *Y.*

חֲלַקְלַקּוֹת I 4 n.f.pl. **smoothness—1. slipperiness, slippery places** (unless at Ps $35_{6}$ חֲלַקְלַקּוֹת II *darkness*), <SUBJ> היה *be* Ps $35_{6}$ (+ דֶּרֶךְ *way,* חֹשֶׁךְ *darkness*). <PREP> כְּ *as,* + היה *be* Jr $23_{12}$ (+ דֶּרֶךְ *way*). <COLL> חֲלַקְלַקּוֹת בָּאֲפֵלָה *slippery places in the darkness* Jr $23_{12}$.

**2. smoothness** of speech, **flattery, intrigue,** <PREP> בְּ of instrument, *by (means of), with,* + חזק hi. *take hold of* kingdom Dn $11_{21}$, לוה ni. *join oneself* Dn $11_{34}$.*

⇒ חלק *be smooth.*

*חֲלַקְלַקּוֹת II 1 n.f.pl. **darkness** (unless חֲלַקְלַקּוֹת I *smoothness*), <SUBJ> היה *be* Ps $35_{6}$ (+ דֶּרֶךְ *way,* חֹשֶׁךְ *darkness*).

חֶלְקַת 2 pl.n. **Helkath**—חֶלְקָת—town in Asher, perh. Kh. Ḫirbet el-Harbağ, 12 km SE of Haifa, <SUBJ> היה *be* Jos $19_{25}$ (וַיְהִי גְּבוּלָם חֶלְקַת *and their border was Helkath;* or em. מֵחֶלְקַת *from Helkath*). <OBJ> נתן *give* Jos $21_{31}$ 1 C $6_{60}$ (if em. חוקק *Hukok*). <PREP> מִן of direction, *from,* + היה *be* Jos $19_{25}$ (if em.; see Subj.).

חֶלְקַת הַצֻּדִים pl.n. **Helkath-hazzidim,** i.e. *the side field,* place near the pool of Gibeon, <NOM CL> חֶלְקַת הַצֻּדִים אֲשֶׁר בְּגִבְעוֹן *Helkath-hazzidim, which is in Gibeon* 2 S $2_{16}$ (if em. חֶלְקַת הַצֻּרִים *Helkath-hazzurim*). <OBJ> קרא *call* 2 S $2_{16}$ (if em.; see Nom. Cl.).

⇒ חֶלְקָה *field.*

חֶלְקַת הַצֻּרִים 1 pl.n. **Helkath-hazzurim,** place near the pool of Gibeon, <NOM CL> חֶלְקַת הַצֻּרִים אֲשֶׁר בְּגִבְעוֹן *Helkath-hazzurim, which is in Gibeon* 2 S $2_{16}$ (or em. חֶלְקַת הַצֻּדִים *Helkath-hazzidim*). <OBJ> קרא *call* 2 S $2_{16}$ (or em.; see Nom. Cl.).

⇒ חֶלְקָה *field.*

חלשׁ I 2 vb. **defeat—Qal** 2 + waw וַיַּחֲלֹשׁ; ptc. חוֹלֵשׁ—**defeat*** (unless חלשׁ II trans. *weaken*), <SUBJ> Joshua Ex $17_{13}$, הֵילֵל *shining one* Is $14_{12}$ (unless em. הֵילֵל to הֵילֵל *morning star*), בֵּן *son* Is $14_{12}$. <OBJ> Amalek Ex $17_{13}$, עַם *people* Ex $17_{13}$, גּוֹי *nation* Is $14_{12}$ (if em.; see Prep.). <PREP> לְ *at,* i.e. with, + פֶּה *edge* of sword Ex $17_{13}$; עַל appar. inflict defeat *upon,* + גּוֹי *nation* Is $14_{12}$ (or em. עַל־ *upon* to כָּל־ *all* the nations).

**Ni. be carried off (dead),** <SUBJ> גֶּבֶר *man* Jb $14_{10}$ (if em. וַיֶּחֱלַשׁ *and he is weak* to וַיֵּחָלֵשׁ *and he is carried off*).

⇒ חֲלוּשָׁה *defeat.*

**חלשׁ** II $_{1}$ vb. **be weak—Qal** $_{1}$ + waw וַיֶּחֱלַשׁ—**be weak, powerless, pass away,** <SUBJ> גֶּבֶר *man* Jb 14$_{10}$ (or em. וַיֵּחָלֵשׁ *and he is carried off,* i.e. חלשׁ I *be carried off;* + מות *die,* גוע *expire*), worshipper Is 26$_{16}$ (if em. לחשׁ *whisper* to חָלַשְׁנוּ *we were weak*).*
⇒ חַלָּשׁ *weak.*

**חַלָּשׁ** $_{1}$ adj. **weak,** used as noun, **weak one,** <SUBJ> אמר *say* Jl 4$_{10}$ (הַחַלָּשׁ יֹאמַר גִּבּוֹר אָנִי *let the weak one say, I am mighty,* i.e. a warrior). <ANT> גִּבּוֹר *mighty.*
⇒ חלשׁ *be weak.*

**[חַם]** $_{2.0.2}$ adj. **hot**—חָם; pl. חַמִּים—**1.** used attributively of לֶחֶם *bread* 1 S 21$_{7}$ (if em. חֹם *heat*). **2.** in nom. cl. used predicatively of לֶחֶם *bread* Jos 9$_{12}$, בֶּגֶד *garment* Jb 37$_{17}$. **3.** used as noun, **hot water,** <CSTR> בית חמים *house of hot waters* 3QTr 10$_{15}$ (Allegro בית המים *the house of waters,* i.e. bathhouse or urinals). Also 4QPrQuot 94$_{2}$.*
⇒ חמם *be warm.*

**חָם** I $_{12.0.3}$ pr.n.m. **Ham,** son of Noah, brother of Shem and Japheth, father of Cush, Egypt, Put and Canaan, <SUBJ> היה *be* Gn 9$_{18}$, בוא *come* Gn 7$_{13}$, יצא *go out* Gn 9$_{18}$, ראה *see* Gn 9$_{22}$, נגד hi. *declare* Gn 9$_{22}$. <NOM CL> חָם הוּא אֲבִי כְנָעַן *Ham was the father of Canaan* Gn 9$_{18}$, אֵלֶּה תּוֹלְדֹת בְּנֵי־נֹחַ שֵׁם חָם וָיָפֶת *these are the generations of the sons of Noah: Shem, Ham and Japheth* Gn 10$_{1}$, בְּנֵי נֹחַ שֵׁם חָם וָיָפֶת *the sons of Noah were Shem, Ham and Japheth* 1 C 1$_{4}$ (if ins. בְּנֵי). <OBJ> ילד hi. *beget* Gn 5$_{32}$ 6$_{10}$, קלל pi. *curse* 4QpGen$^{a}$ 1.2$_{7}$. <CSTR> בְּנֵי חָם *sons of Ham* Gn 10$_{6.20}$ 1 C 1$_{8}$ 1QM 2$_{13}$, אָהֳלֵי חָם *men of Ham* 1 C 4$_{41}$ (if em. אָהֳלֵיהֶם *their tents* and אָהֳלֵי is from אֹהֶל II *man*). <APP> בֵּן *son* Gn 6$_{10}$ 7$_{13}$, אָב *father* Gn 9$_{22}$. <PREP> מִן of possession, *of, (belonging) to* 1 C 4$_{40}$.
Also 4Q462$_{2}$.

**חָם** II $_{4}$ pl.n. **Ham,** name for Egypt, <CSTR> אֶרֶץ־חָם *land of Ham* Ps 105$_{23}$ (+ מִצְרַיִם *Egypt*) 105$_{27}$ 106$_{22}$ (+ מִצְרַיִם) 4Q370 2$_{7}$ ([ארץ חם]), אָהֳלֵי חָם *tents of Ham* Ps 78$_{51}$ (+ מִצְרָיִם).

**[חָם]** III $_{4.1}$ n.m. **father-in-law**—sf. 2ms Si חמיך, חָמִיךָ, חָמִיהָ—husband's father (Gn 38$_{13.25}$ 1 S 4$_{19.21}$), wife's father (Si 37$_{10}$), <SUBJ> עלה *go up* Gn 38$_{13}$, גזז *shear sheep* Gn 38$_{13}$, מות *die* 1 S 4$_{19}$ (+ אִישׁ *husband,* כַּלָּה *daughter-in-law*) 4$_{21(mss)}$. <CSTR> מוֹת חָמִיהָ *death of her father-in-law* 1 S 4$_{21(mss)}$ (+ אִישׁ *husband*). <PREP> אֶל *to,* + שׁלח *send* Gn 38$_{25}$; *because of* 1 S 4$_{21}$; עִם *with,* + יעץ ni. *take counsel* Si 37$_{10}$ (unless חמיך *one who looks upon you,* from חמה *see,* or חָמִיךָ *unreliable guide*).

**חֹם** $_{6.1.6.1}$ n.m. **heat**—Q חום; cstr. חֹם (Q חום); pl. cstr. Q חומי—<SUBJ> בוא *come* Jr 17$_{8}$, שׁבת *cease* Gn 8$_{22}$, גזל *snatch* Jb 24$_{19}$ (‖ צִיָּה *drought*). <CSTR> חֹם קָצִיר *heat of harvest* Is 18$_{4}$ (mss יוֹם *day of*), [חום ה[שמש *heat of the sun* 4QPrQuot 1$_{4}$, חומי רשף *heat of,* i.e. for, *a flame* 4Q418 127$_{3}$; לֶחֶם חֹם *bread of heat,* i.e. hot bread 1 S 21$_{7}$ (or em. חַם *hot*), עת חום *time of heat* 1QH 8$_{23}$, מועדי *seasons of* 4QMyst$^{a}$ 5$_{3}$. <ADJ> צַח *dazzling* Is 18$_{4}$. <PREP> לְ of possession, *of, (belonging) to* 4QJub$^{a}$ 2$_{2}$ ([ל[חום), *as,* + היה *be* 4Q418 127$_{3}$; בְּ of place, time, *in* Is 18$_{4}$ (mss בְּיוֹם *in the day of*), קצר *reap* Meṣad Ḥashavyahu ost. 1$_{10}$; כְּ *as* Is 18$_{4}$ Si 3$_{15}$; לִפְנֵי *before* 1QH 8$_{26}$. <COLL> קֹר וָחֹם *cold and heat* Gn 8$_{22}$. <SYN> צִיָּה *drought*.*
⇒ חמם *be warm.*

**חֵמָא**, see חֵמָה *anger.*

**חֶמְאָה** $_{11}$ n.f. **curd**—חֶמָה; cstr. חֶמְאַת (Sam חמת); pl. mss חֲמָאוֹת—**curd(s), butter,** <OBJ> נגשׁ hi. *bring near* 2 S 17$_{29}$ (‖ דְּבַשׁ *honey*), קרב hi. *bring near* Jg 5$_{25}$ (+ חָלָב *milk*), יצא hi. *bring out* Pr 30$_{33}$ (+ חָלָב), לקח *take* Gn 18$_{8}$ (‖ חָלָב), ינק hi. *cause to suck* Dt 32$_{14}$ (‖ חָלָב), אכל *eat* Is 7$_{15}$ (‖ דְּבַשׁ) 7$_{22}$ (+ חָלָב) 7$_{22}$ (‖ דְּבַשׁ). <CSTR> חֶמְאַת בָּקָר *curds of,* i.e. from, *the herd* Dt 32$_{14}$; נַחֲלֵי ... חֶמְאָה *streams of curds* Jb 20$_{17}$ (‖ דְּבַשׁ *honey*). <PREP> בְּ of instrument, *by (means of), with,* + רחץ *wash* Jb 29$_{6}$; מִן of comparison, *(more) than,* + חלק *be smooth* Ps 55$_{22(mss)}$ (מֵחֲמָאוֹת; L מַחְמָאֹת *curd-like things;* or em. מֵחֶמְאָה *than butter*). <SYN> חָלָב *milk,* דְּבַשׁ *honey*.*

**חמד** $_{21.3.8}$ vb. **desire—Qal** $_{16.2.5}$ Pf. חָמַד, חָמְדוּ, חֲמַדְתֶּם; impf. יַחְמֹד (Q יחמוד), 2ms תַּחְמֹד (Si, Q תחמוד), Q תחמודו; + waw וָאֶחְמְדֵם, וַנֶּחְמְדֵהוּ; ptc. pass. Si חמוד,

חֲמוּדוֹ (mss חֲמֻדוֹ), חֲמוּדֵיהֶם—**1a.** transitive, **desire; 1b. delight in** (e.g. Pr 1$_{22}$ Is 1$_{29}$); **1c.** perh. **take, appropriate** (e.g. Ex 20$_{17}$ 34$_{24}$).*

<SUBJ> Y. Ps 68$_{17}$, Achan Jos 7$_{21}$ (|| לקח *take*), Israel(ite) Ex 20$_{17.17}$=4QBibPar 7$_2$ Dt 5$_{21}$ (|| אוה htp. *desire*) 7$_{25}$ (+ לקח) Is 1$_{29}$ (|| בחר *choose*) Is 53$_2$ (or em. וְחֶמְדָּה *and desirable thing*; || ראה *look at*) 11QT 2$_8$ (+ לקח), עַם *people* Jos 6$_{18}$ (if em. תַּחֲרִימוּ *you will devote* to תַּחְמְדוּ *you will desire*; + לקח), אִישׁ *man* Ex 34$_{24}$, בֵּן *son* Pr 6$_{25}$ Si 14$_{14}$, מֶלֶךְ *king* 11QT 57$_{20}$ (+ גזל *seize*), רָשָׁע *wicked one* Pr 12$_{12}$ (or em.; see Obj.), חשב ptc. *one who devises* iniquity Mc 2$_2$ (+ גזל, נשׂא *take*), פעל ptc. *one who does* evil Mc 2$_2$, לֵץ *scoffer* Pr 1$_{22}$ (+ אהב *love*), לֵבָב *heart* Ps 86$_{11}$ (if em. יַחֵד *unite* to יַחְמֹד *it desires*; + לְיִרְאָה *to fear* your name).

<OBJ> אִשָּׁה *wife* Ex 20$_{17}$=4QBibPar 7$_2$ Dt 5$_{21}$, עֶבֶד *servant* Ex 20$_{17}$ Is 53$_2$, אָמָה *female servant* Ex 20$_{17}$, שׁוֹר *ox* Ex 20$_{17}$, חֲמוֹר *ass* Ex 20$_{17}$, אֵלָה *terebinth* Is 1$_{29}$, בַּיִת *house* Ex 20$_{17}$ Dt 5$_{21(mss, Sam)}$ 11QT 57$_{20}$, אֶרֶץ *land* Ex 34$_{24}$, שָׂדֶה *field* Ex 20$_{17(mss, Sam)}$ Mc 2$_2$ 11QT 57$_{20}$, כֶּרֶם *vineyard* 11QT 57$_{20}$, הַר *mountain* Ps 68$_{17}$, כֶּסֶף *silver* Dt 7$_{25}$ Jos 7$_{21}$ 11QT 2$_8$, זָהָב *gold* Dt 7$_{25}$ 11QT 2$_8$, לָשׁוֹן *tongue*, i.e. bar, of gold Jos 7$_{21}$, הוֹן *wealth* 11QT 57$_{20}$, אַדֶּרֶת *cloak* Jos 7$_{21}$, מָצוֹד *net* Pr 12$_{12}$ (or em. חָמַד to חֶמֶד *desire* or חֶמְדָּה *desire*, or em. חָמַד רָשָׁע מְצוֹד רָעִים *the wicked one desires the net of evil ones* to חֹמֶר רֹעֵשׁ מְצוּדַת רָעִים *the fortress of evil ones is quaking clay*, or יִשָּׁמֵד יְסוֹד רָעִים *the foundation of evil ones will be destroyed*), יֳפִי *beauty* Pr 6$_{25}$, לָצוֹן *scorning* Pr 1$_{22}$, חמד pass. ptc. *desirable thing* Si 14$_{14}$ 11QT 57$_{20}$, כֹּל *everything* Ex 20$_{17}$.

<PREP> לְ of benefit, *to, for*, + לֵץ *scoffer* Pr 1$_{22}$; *as*, + שֶׁבֶת *dwelling-place* Ps 68$_{17}$; בְּ of place, *in*, + לֵבָב *heart* Pr 6$_{25}$.

<SYN> אוה htp. *desire*, בחר *choose*, לקח *take*, ראה *look at*.

**2.** pass. ptc. as noun, **desired thing,** i.e. **desirable thing,** of possessions, etc. (Ps 39$_{12}$ [or em.; see Obj.] Jb 20$_{20}$ Si 14$_{14}$ 11QT 57$_{21}$), **delightful thing,** of idols (Is 44$_9$), <SUBJ> יעל hi. *profit* Is 44$_9$. <OBJ> מסה hi. *cause to melt* Ps 39$_{12}$ (or em. חֶמְדוֹ *his desire*), חמד *desire* Si 14$_{14}$ 11QT 57$_{21}$. <ADJ> רַע *evil* Si 14$_{14}$. <PREP> בְּ partitive *(some) of*, + מלט pi. *rescue* Jb 20$_{20}$.

Also 4Q525 14.2$_5$.

**Ni.** 4.1.3 Ptc. נֶחְמָד, נֶחֱמָדִים—ptc. as adj. **desirable, delightful** (Si 42$_{22}$), **1.** used attributively of אוֹצָר *treasure* Pr 21$_{20}$, עֵץ *tree* 4Q423 2$_1$ (+ הַשְׂכִּיל *to make wise*). **2.** in nom cl. used predicatively of עֵץ *tree* Gn 2$_9$ (+ לְמַרְאֶה *to the sight*; || טוֹב *good*) 3$_6$ (+ הַשְׂכִּיל *to make wise*), מִשְׁפָּט *ordinance* Ps 19$_{11}$ (|| מָתוֹק *sweet*), מַעֲשֶׂה *work* Si 42$_{22}$ ([נחמד]ים). <PREP> מִן of comparison, (more desirable) *than*, + זָהָב *gold* Ps 19$_{11}$, פַּז *fine gold* Ps 19$_{11}$. <SYN> §2 טוֹב *good*, מָתוֹק *sweet*.

Also 4Q418 188$_5$ 4Q423 9$_1$.

**Pi.** 1 Pf. חִמַּדְתִּי—**delight greatly,** <SUBJ> female lover Ca 2$_3$. <PREP> בְּ of place, *in*, + צֵל *shadow* Ca 2$_3$ (בְּצִלּוֹ חִמַּדְתִּי וְיָשַׁבְתִּי *in his shadow I delighted greatly and sat*, i.e. I sat with great delight in his shadow).*

⇒ חֶמֶד *desire*, חֶמְדָּה *desire*, חֲמֻדוֹת *preciousness*, מַחְמַד *desirable thing*.

**חֶ֫מֶד** 6.0.2 n.[m.] **desire**—sf. Q חמדו—**desire, delight; beauty,** as desired or delighted in, <NOM CL> כָּל־חַמְדוֹ כְּצִיץ הַשָּׂדֶה *all its beauty is as the flower of the field* Is 40$_6$ (if em. חַסְדּוֹ *its loyalty*), חֶמֶד רָשָׁע מְצוֹד רָעִים *the desire of the wicked is a hunting of*, i.e. for, *evil things* Pr 12$_{12}$ (if em. חָמַד the wicked *has desired*). <OBJ> עשׂה *do* 4QApocJos$^b$ 2$_6$ (לע[שות]), מסה hi. *cause to melt* Ps 39$_{12}$ (if em. חֲמוּדוֹ *his desirable thing*). <CSTR> חֶמֶד רָשָׁע *the desire of the wicked* Pr 12$_{12}$ (if em.; see Nom. Cl.); שְׂדֵי־חֶמֶד *fields of desire* Is 32$_{12}$ (1QIsa$^a$ חמדה *of desire*), כֶּרֶם חֶמֶד *vineyard of* Is 27$_2$ (mss חֶמֶר *of wine*), כַּרְמֵי־ *vineyards of* Am 5$_{11}$, בַּחוּרֵי חֶמֶד *youths of desire* Ezk 23$_{6.12.23}$, כָּל־חֶמְדוֹ *all its beauty* Is 40$_6$ (if em.; see Nom. Cl.). Also perh. 1QH fr. 11$_6$.*

⇒ חמד *desire*.

**[חֶמְדָּא]** 0.0.0.1 pr.n.m. **Hemda,** <CSTR> בן חמדא *son of Hemda* Arad ost. 55$_1$.

**חֶמְדָּה** 17.1.4 n.f. **desire**—cstr. חֶמְדַּת; sf. חֶמְדָּתִי, חֶמְדָּתֵךְ, חֶמְדָּתָם—**1. desire. 2. beauty, preciousness,** of object or person, <SUBJ> בוא *come* appar. Hg 2$_7$. <NOM CL> לְמִי כָל־חֶמְדַּת יִשְׂרָאֵל *to whom is all the desire of Israel* 1 S 9$_{20}$, חֶמְדַּת רָשָׁע מְצוֹד רָעִים *the desire of the wicked is a* *hunting of*, i.e. for, *evil things* Pr 12$_{12}$ (if em. חָמַד the wicked one *has desired*).

<CSTR> חֶמְדַּת נָשִׁים *desirable one of*, i.e. by, *women* Dn 11$_{37}$, חֶמְדַּת רָשָׁע *desire of the wicked* Pr 12$_{12}$ (if em.; see Nom. Cl.), יִשְׂרָאֵל *of Israel* 1 S 9$_{20}$, כָּל־הַגּוֹיִם *of all the nations* Hg 2$_{7}$ (or em. חֲמֻדֹת *precious things of*), חמדת מלכים *preciousness*, i.e. treasure, *of kings* GnzPs 3$_{15}$ (‖ חַיִל *wealth*, אוֹצָר *treasure*), ארצם *of their land* 4QDibHam[a] 1.4$_{11}$; שְׂכִיּוֹת הַחֶמְדָּה perh. *ships of desire*, i.e. beautiful ships Is 2$_{16}$ (or em. שְׂכִיּוֹת to שְׂכִתֵי *ships of* or סְפִינוֹת *ships of*), אֶרֶץ חֶמְדָּה *land of desire*, i.e. a beautiful land Jr 3$_{19}$ (‖ צְבִי *beauty*) Zc 7$_{14}$ Ps 106$_{24}$ GnzPs 1$_{21}$ (א[רץ ח]מדה), חֶלְקַת חֶמְדָּתִי *field of my desire* Jr 12$_{10}$, שדי חמדה *fields of desire* Is 32$_{12}$ (1QIsa[a]; MT חֶמֶד *desire*), בָּתֵּי חֶמְדָּתֵךְ *houses of your desire* Ezk 26$_{12}$, כְּלִי חֶמְדָּה *vessel of preciousness* Jr 25$_{24}$ (or em. כְּלִי to אֵילֵי *rams of* or בִּבְלִי *without*) Ho 13$_{15}$ Na 2$_{10}$ GnzPs 2$_{26}$, כְּלֵי *vessels of* 2 C 32$_{27}$, כְּלֵי חֶמְדַּת *vessels of preciousness of* the house of Y. 2 C 36$_{10}$, כְּלֵי חֶמְדָּתָם *vessels of their preciousness* Dn 11$_{8}$, אוצרות חמדה *treasures of preciousness* Si 4$_{12(Bmg)}$ (B חכמה *of wisdom*), כָּל־חֶמְדַּת *all the desire of* 1 S 9$_{20}$ 4QDibHam[a] 1.4$_{11}$ (כול).

<PREP> עַל *introducing object*, + בין *understand* Dn 11$_{37}$; בְּלֹא *without*, + הלך *go* 2 C 21$_{20}$; בִּבְלִי *without*, + נפל *fall* Jr 25$_{34}$ (if em.; see Prep.).

<COLL> וַיֵּלֶךְ בְּלֹא חֶמְדָּה *and he departed (life) without desire*, i.e. without being regretted 2 C 21$_{20}$. <SYN> צְבִי *beauty*, חַיִל *wealth*, אוֹצָר *treasure*.

Also 4Q434a$_{8}$.*

⇒ חמד *desire*.

חֲמֻדוֹת 9.1.1 n.f.pl. **preciousness**—חֲמֻדֹת, חֲמוּדֹת, חֲמוּדוֹת; cstr. חֲמֻדוֹת (Si חמודות)—**preciousness, precious things; desirableness** (4QApocMos A 2.2$_{5}$), **desires** (Si 5$_{3}$), <SUBJ> בוא *come* Hg 2$_{7}$ (if em.; see Cstr.). <NOM CL> הַחֲמֻדֹת אֲשֶׁר אִתָּהּ בַּבָּיִת *the precious things that were with her in the house* Gn 27$_{15}$, חֲמוּדוֹת אָתָּה *you are preciousness*, i.e. precious Dn 9$_{23}$ (or em. אִישׁ חֲמוּדוֹת *man of preciousness*). <OBJ> לקח *take* Gn 27$_{15}$, שׁקל *weigh* Ezr 8$_{27}$.

<CSTR> חֲמֻדוֹת מִצְרָיִם *precious things of Egypt* Dn 11$_{43}$ (‖ מִכְמָן *treasure*, זָהָב *gold*, כֶּסֶף *silver*), חֶמְדַּת כָּל־הַגּוֹיִם *precious things of all the nations* Hg 2$_{7}$ (if em. חֶמְדַּת *desire of*), חומדות רעה *desires of evil*, i.e. evil desires Si 5$_{2}$; אִישׁ־חֲמֻדוֹת *man of preciousness*, i.e. precious man Dn 9$_{23}$ (חֲמוּדוֹת; if em.; see Nom. Cl.) 10$_{11.19}$, לֶחֶם חֲמֻדוֹת *bread of preciousness*, i.e. delicacies Dn 10$_{3}$, כְּלֵי חֲמֻדוֹת *vessels of preciousness*, i.e. precious vessels 2 C 20$_{25}$, ארץ חמדות *land of desirableness*, i.e. desirable land 4QApocMos A 2.2$_{5}$, כֹּל חֲמֻדוֹת *all the precious things of* Dn 11$_{43}$. <APP> בֶּגֶד *garment* Gn 27$_{15}$, כְּלִי *vessel* Ezr 8$_{27}$.

<PREP> בְּ of instrument, *by (means of), with*, + כבד pi. *honour* Dn 11$_{38}$ (‖ זָהָב *gold*, כֶּסֶף *silver*, אֶבֶן precious *stone*), of accompaniment, *with, in*, + הלך *walk* Si 5$_{2}$; בְּ *over*, + משׁל *rule* Dn 11$_{43}$. <COLL> חֲמוּדֹת כַּזָּהָב *precious things as gold*, i.e. as precious as Ezr 8$_{27}$.*

⇒ חמד *desire*.

חֶמְדָּן 2 pr.n.m. **Hemdan,** son of Dishon and descendant of Seir the Horite, appar. ident. with Hamran at 1 C 1$_{41}$, <NOM CL> אֵלֶּה בְּנֵי דִישָׁן חֶמְדָּן וְאֶשְׁבָּן *these are the sons of Dishan: Hemdan and Eshban* Gn 36$_{26}$ (Sam דִּישׁוֹן *Dishon*), בְּנֵי דִישׁוֹן חֶמְדָּן וְאֶשְׁבָּן *the sons of Dishon were Hemdan and Eshban* 1 C 1$_{41(mss)}$ (L חַמְרָן *Hamran*). <APP> בֵּן *son* Gn 36$_{26}$.*

חֶמְדַּת, see חֲמֻדוֹת *preciousness*.

חמה I 0.1 vb. **see—Qal** 0.1 Pt. Si חמיך—**see, look, look upon** with disdain (Si 37$_{10}$), **beware** (Jb 36$_{18}$ [if em.; see Subj.]), <SUBJ> Job 36$_{18}$ (if em. חֵמָה *wrath* to חֲמֵה *beware*), שֶׁמֶשׁ *sun* Ps 19$_{7}$ (if em. מֵחַמָּתוֹ *from its heat* to מֵחֶמְתוֹ *from its seeing*), אֲדָמָה Ps 76$_{11}$ (if em. חֲמַת אָדָם *wrath of human beings* to חָמְתָה אֲדָמָה *the earth saw*, unless חֵמָה II, *family*), אֱדֹם *Edom* Ps 76$_{11}$ (if em. חֲמַת אָדָם *wrath of human beings* to חָמְתָה אֱדֹם *Edom saw*), שְׁאֵרִית *remnant* Ps 76$_{11}$ (if em. חֵמֹת *wrath* to חָמְתָה *it saw*, unless חֵמָה pl. *families*); subj. not specified, Si 37$_{10}$ (unless חמיך *your father-in-law*, from חָם *father-in-law*; + קנא pi. *be jealous*). <OBJ> בֵּן *son* Si 37$_{10}$.

**Ni. be seen,** <SUBJ> עָקֵב *heel* Jr 13$_{22}$ (if em. נֶחְמְסוּ *they suffer violence* to נֶחֱמוּ *they are seen*).*

[חמה] II vb. **be hot—Qal, be hot, be inflamed,** <SUBJ>

סְעָרָה *storm* Jr $23_{19}$=$30_{23}$ (if em. סַעֲרַת י׳ חֵמָה *a storm of Y.* goes forth *(in) fury* to חַמָּה a storm of Y. *is hot*), יַיִן *wine* Jr $25_{15}$ (if em. הַיַּיִן הַחֵמָה *the wine, the anger* to הַיַּיִן הַחַמָּה *the hot wine*), שַׂר *prince*, i.e. officer Ho $7_5$ (if em. הֶחֱלוּ שָׂרִים חֲמוֹת מִיָּיִן *they made princes sick (through) poison of wine* to הֶחֱלוּ שָׂרִים חֲמוֹת מִיַּיִן *the officers began to be inflamed with wine*). <PREP> מִן of instrument, *by (means of), through*, + יַיִן *wine* Ho $7_5$ (if em.).

**חַמָּה** 6.1 n.f. **heat; sun**—sf. חַמָּתוֹ—**1. heat** of sun, <OBJ> נבע hi. *pour out* Si $43_{2(B)}$, יפע hi. *shine out* Si $43_{2(Bmg)}$. <PREP> מִן of direction, *from*, + סתר ni. *be hidden* Ps $19_7$ (or em. מֵחֶמְתוֹ *from its seeing*, from חמה I *see*).

**2. sun,** <SUBJ> בּוֹשׁ *be ashamed* Is $24_{23}$ (|| לְבָנָה *moon*). <CSTR> אוֹר הַחַמָּה *light of the sun* Is $30_{26}$ (|| לְבָנָה *moon*) $30_{26}$. <PREP> בְּ of accompaniment, *with*, + הלך pi. *go* Jb $30_{28}$ (בְּלֹא חַמָּה *without the sun*; or em. חֵמָה III *protection* or נֶחָמָה *comfort*); כְּ *as* Ca $6_{10}$ (|| לְבָנָה *moon*).

<SYN> §2 לְבָנָה *moon*.*

→ חמם *be warm*.

**חֵמָה I** 125.2.23 n.f. **anger**—חֵמָא; cstr. חֲמַת; sf. חֲמָתִי, חֲמָתְךָ (חֲמָתֶךָ), חֲמָתוֹ, חֲמָתָם; pl. חֵמוֹת (חֵמֹת)—**1. anger** of human beings (e.g. Gn $27_{44}$ 2 S $11_{20}$ 2 K $5_{12}$ Pr $16_4$ $19_{19}$ Est $1_{12}$) or God (e.g. 2 K $22_{13.17}$ Is $27_4$ Jr $4_4$ Ezk $5_{13}$ Lm $2_4$). **2. heat** of fever (Ho $7_5$). **3. poison** (Dt $32_{24.33}$ Ps $58_5$ $140_4$ Jb $6_4$).

<SUBJ> שׁפך pass. *be poured out* Ezk $20_{33.34}$, נתך ni. *be poured out* Jr $7_{20}$ $42_{18}$ (|| אַף *anger*) $42_{18}$ $44_6$ (|| אַף *anger*) Na $1_6$ 2 C $12_7$ $34_{21.25}$ 4QDibHam$^a$ $1.5_4$, עלה *go up* 2 S $11_{20}$ Ezk $38_{18}$ 2 C $36_{16}$, יצא *go out* Jr $4_4$ $21_{12}$ $23_{19}$=$30_{23}$ (or em. חַמָּה *hot*), שׁוב *go back* Gn $27_{44}$ Dn $9_{16}$ 4QDibHam$^a$ $1.2_{11}$ $1.6_{11}$ (all three || אַף *anger*), יצת ni. *break out* 2 K $22_{13.17}$ Si $16_6$, פרח *break out* 1QH $5_{27}$, יצב *take one's position* 4Q525 $15_4$, סמך *support* Is $63_5$ Ps $88_8$, שׁכך *abate* Est $2_1$ $7_{10}$, סות hi. *lead astray* Jb $36_{18}$ (or em. חֲמָה *beware*), בער *burn* Ps $89_{47}$ Est $1_{12}$, ידה hi. *praise* Ps $76_{11}$ (or em.; see Cstr.).

<NOM CL> חֲמַת תַּנִּינִם יֵינָם *the venom of serpents is their wine* Dt $32_{33}$=CD $8_{9(A)}$, חמת תנינים כול מזמותם *the venom of vipers are all their plans* 1QH $5_{10}$, חֵמָה עֲוֹנוֹת חֶרֶב *wrath (causes) the punishment of the sword* Jb $19_{29}$, חֲמַת־מֶלֶךְ מַלְאֲכֵי־מָוֶת *the anger of the king is messenger(s) of death* Pr $16_{14}$, אַכְזְרִיּוּת חֵמָה *anger is cruel* Pr $27_4$, גָּדוֹל ... הַחֵמָה *great is ... the wrath* Jr $36_7$, גְּדוֹלָה חֲמַת י׳ *great is the anger of Y.* 2 K $22_{13}$||2 C $34_{21}$, חמה גדולה בלהבי אש *great anger is with flames of fire* CD $2_5$, לכה חמה *you have wrath* 1QH fr. $3_{17}$, חֲמַת לָמוֹ *they have poison* Ps $58_5$, חֲמַת מִיָּיִן *the heat is from the wine* Ho $7_5$, חֵמָה עַל־כָּל־צְבָאָם *wrath is over all their hordes* Is $34_2$, חֲמַת עַכְשׁוּב תַּחַת שְׂפָתֵימוֹ *the venom of a viper is under their lips* Ps $140_4$, אַיֵּה חֲמַת הַמֵּצִיק *where is the fury of the oppressor?* Is $51_{13}$, חֵמָה אֵין לִי *I have no wrath* Is $27_4$.

<OBJ> קצף *be angry with* Dt $9_{19}$, עלה hi. *bring up* Ezk $24_8$, שׁוב hi. *bring back* Nm $25_{11}$ Jr $18_{20}$ Ps $106_{23}$ Pr $15_1$, ספח pi. *join* Hb $2_{15}$=1QpHab $11_6$ (or em. מִסַּף חֲמָתוֹ *from the goblet of his wrath*), עור hi. *rouse* Ps $78_{38}$, שׁלם pi. *repay* Is $59_{18}$, שׁפך *pour out* Is $42_{25}$ Jr $10_{25}$ Ezk $7_8$ $9_8$ $14_{19}$ $20_{8.13.21}$ $22_{22}$ $30_{15}$ $36_{18}$ Ps $79_6$ Lm $2_4$ Si $33_8$ (|| אַף *anger*), כלה pi. *complete* Ezk $5_{13}$ $6_{12}$ $13_{15}$ Lm $4_{11}$, עזב *forsake* Ps $37_8$=4QpPs$^a$ $1.2_1$, נוח hi. *appease* Ezk $5_{13}$ $16_{42}$ $21_{22}$ $24_{13}$, כפה *soothe* Pr $21_{14}$, שׁתה *drink* Jb $6_4$, דבר pi. *speak* Jr $36_7$ (|| אַף).

<CSTR> חֲמַת י׳ *wrath of Y.* 2 K $22_{13}$||2 C $34_{21}$ Is $51_{20}$ Jr $6_{11}$ 2 C $28_9$ $36_{16}$, [א]ל *of God* 1QpHab $11_{14}$, שַׁדַּי *of Shaddai* Jb $21_{20}$, הַמֵּצִיק *of the oppressor* Is $51_{13.13}$ 4QDibHam$^a$ $1.5_{18}$, הַמֶּלֶךְ *of the king* 2 S $11_{20}$ Pr $16_{14}$ Est $2_1$ $7_{10}$, גֶּבֶר *of a man* Pr $6_{34}$, אָדָם *of humanity* Ps $76_{11}$ (unless חֵמָה III *family* or em. חֲמָתָה אֲדָמָה *the earth saw* or חֲמַת אֲרָם *Hamath of Aram*), אָחִיךָ *of your brother* Gn $27_{44}$, קֶרִי *of hostility* Lv $26_{28}$, אפו *of his anger* 1QIsa$^a$ $42_{25}$, כֹּחוֹ *of his strength* Dn $8_6$, רוּחִי *of my spirit* Ezk $3_{14}$, חֲמַת זֹחֲלֵי *venom of crawling ones of* Dt $32_{24}$, נָחָשׁ *of a serpent* Ps $58_5$, [ח]מת תנין *venom of a serpent* 4Q525 $18_4$, חֲמַת תַּנִּינִם *venom of serpents* Dt $32_{33}$=CD $8_{9(A)}$=1QH $5_{10.27}$ 4Q525 $15_4$, עַכְשׁוּב *of a viper* Ps $140_4$.

כּוֹס חֲמָתִי *cup of my wrath* Is $51_{22}$, חֲמָתוֹ *of his wrath* Is $51_{17}$, כוס חמת *cup of wrath of* 1QpHab $11_{14}$, יֵין הַחֵמָה *wine of anger* (if em.) Jr $25_{15}$, תֹּכְחוֹת חֵמָה *reprimands of anger* Ezk $5_{15}$ $25_{17}$ (תּוֹכְחוֹת), כעס חמתו *vexation of his poison* 1QpHab $11_6$, חרוני חמתו *angers of his wrath* 4QBark$^a$ $2.1_6$, מתך חמה *outpouring of anger* 1QH $3_{28}$, דַּם חֵמָה *blood of anger* Ezk $16_{38}$, בַּעַל *master of* Na $1_2$ Pr $29_{22}$, אִישׁ *man of* Pr $15_{18}$, אִישׁ חֵמוֹת *man of wrath(s)* Pr

22₂₄, שְׁאֵרִית חֵמֹת *remnant of wrath(s)* Ps 76₁₁ (or em. חֲמָתְךָ *it saw*), דְּמוּת חֲמַת *likeness of venom of* a serpent Ps 58₅, גְּדָל־חֵמָה *greatness of wrath* Pr 19₁₉(Qr), רוב חמת[ו] *greatness of his wrath* 4QMyst^c 3₄, כָּל־חֲמָתוֹ *all his wrath* Ps 78₃₈.

<APP> יַיִן *wine* Jr 25₁₅ (or em. יֵין הַחֵמָה *wine of the anger*, or em. הַיַּיִן הַחֹמֶה *the hot wine*, from חמה II).

<ADJ> גָּדוֹל *great* Zc 8₂ Dn 11₄₄ CD 2₅ 1QM 1₄, עַז *strong* Pr 21₁₄, זֶה *this* Jr 25₁₅.

<PREP> לְ introducing object, + ירה *throw* 1QH 5₂₇ (לחמ[תם]).

בְּ of instrument, *by (means of)* Ezk 20₃₃.₃₄, + בהל ni. *be terrified* Ps 90₇, כמר ni. *be hot* 1QpHab 3₁₂, נסה ni. *test* 4QDibHam^a 1.5₁₈, כלה pi. *destroy* Ps 59₁₄, הפך *destroy* Dt 29₂₂ (|| אַף *anger*), נתשׁ *uproot* Dt 29₂₇ (|| אַף *anger*, קֶצֶף *rage*), רמס *trample* Is 63₃, שׁכר pi. *make drunk* Is 63₆, נדח hi. *scatter* Jr 32₃₇ (|| אַף, קֶצֶף), לחם ni. *fight* Jr 21₅ (|| אַף, קֶצֶף), נגע hi. *hurt* 4QDibHam^a 1.5₁₈, נכה hi. *strike* Jr 33₅ (|| אַף), עשׂה *do*, i.e. execute, judgments Ezk 5₁₅ (|| אַף), *act* Ezk 8₁₈ 23₂₅ Mc 5₁₄ (|| אַף), יסר pi. *discipline* Ps 6₂ 38₂, דבר pi. *speak* Ezk 36₆ (+ קִנְאָה *jealousy*) 1QS 7₂.

בְּ of accompaniment, *in, with*, + היה *be* Ezk 13₁₃, הלך *go* Lv 26₂₈ 2 K 5₁₂ Ezk 3₁₄, קום *arise* Est 7₇, רוץ *run* Dn 8₆, יצא *go out* Dn 11₄₄ 1QM 1₄, שׁוב hi. *bring back* Is 66₁₅, בקע pi. *cause to break out* Ezk 13₁₃.

בְּ *because of, for the sake of* 2 C 28₉, + נתשׁ ho. *be uprooted* Ezk 19₁₂, קבץ *gather* Ezk 22₂₀.

כְּ *as* 1QH 5₂₇, + עשׂה *do* Ezk 25₁₄.

מִן of direction, *from*, + שׁתה *drink* Jb 21₂₀.

עַל *because of*, עַל־אַפִּי ... הָיְתָה לִּי הָעִיר *the city has been ... a cause of my anger* Jr 32₃₁ (|| אַף *anger*).

אֵת *with*, + מלא *be full* Jr 6₁₁.

לִפְנֵי *before*, + יצב htp. *take one's stand* 1QH 7₂₉.

מִפְּנֵי *from (before)*, + יגר *be afraid* Dt 9₁₉ (|| אַף *anger*), פחד pi. *tremble* Is 51₁₃.

עִם *with*, + שׁלח pi. *send away* Dt 32₂₄.

<COLL> הַמְלֵאִים חֲמַת י׳ *who are full of the wrath of Y.* Is 51₂₀, הֶחֱלוּ שָׂרִים חֲמַת מִיָּיִן *the princes became ill with the heat that is from the wine* Ho 7₅ (or em. חֲמָתָם יַיִן with *their heat [which was caused by] wine*), חֵמָה גְדוֹלָה קִנֵּאתִי לָהּ *I am jealous for her with great anger* Zc 8₂, ... וַיִּמָּלֵא חֵמָה *and he was filled ... with anger* Est 3₅ 5₉.

<SYN> אַף *anger*, קֶצֶף *rage*.

Also 4QapPs^b 78₂.*

⇒ חמם *be warm*.

*[חֵמָה] II ₁ n.f. **family**—pl. חֵמֹת—<SUBJ> ידה hi. *praise* Ps 76₁₁ (if em.). <CSTR> חֲמַת אָדָם *families of humankind* Ps 76₁₁ (if em. חֲמַת *heat of*), חֲמַת אֲבִי *the family of the father of* 1 C 2₅₅ (if em. חַמַּת *Hammath*, father of); שְׁאֵרִית חֵמֹת *the remnant of the families*, i.e. nations. <PREP> מִן of direction, *from*, + בוא *come* 1 C 2₅₅ (if em.).

*[חֵמָה] III n.f. **protection**, <PREP> בְּ of accompaniment, *with*, + הלך pi. *go* Jb 30₂₈ (בְּלֹא חֵמָה *without protection*, if em. חַמָּה *sun*).

חֵמָה IV, see חֶמְאָה *curd*.

חַמּוּאֵל ₂ pr.n.m. **Hammuel, 1.** descendant of Simeon, son of Mishma, and father of Zaccur, <NOM CL> בְּנֵי מִשְׁמָע חַמּוּאֵל *the sons of Mishma were ... Hammuel* 1 C 4₂₆. <APP> בֵּן *son* 1 C 4₂₆. **2.** son of Perez and grandson of Judah, appar. ident. with Hamul at 1 C 2₅ Nm 26₂₁, <SUBJ> היה *be* Gn 46₁₂(Sam) (L חָמוּל *Hamul*).

⇒ אֵל *God*.

חֲמוּדוֹת, see חֲמֻדוֹת *preciousness*.

חֲמוּדֹת, see חֲמֻדוֹת *preciousness*.

חֲמוּטַל ₃ pr.n.f. **Hamutal,** mother of Jehoahaz, and daughter of Jeremiah of Libnah, <NOM CL> שֵׁם אִמּוֹ חֲמוּטַל *the name of his mother was Hamutal* 2 K 23₃₁(L) (mss חֲמִיטַל *Hamital*) 24₁₈(Qr) Jr 52₁(Qr) (both Kt חמיטל). <APP> בַּת *daughter* 2 K 23₃₁ 24₁₈ Jr 52₁.

חָמוּל ₃ pr.n.m. **Hamul,** son of Perez and grandson of Judah, <SUBJ> היה *be* Gn 46₁₂ (Sam. חַמּוּאֵל *Hammuel*). <NOM CL> בְּנֵי־פֶרֶץ חֶצְרוֹן וְחָמוּל *the sons of Perez were Hezron and Hamul* 1 C 2₅. <PREP> לְ of possession, *of, (belonging) to* Nm 26₂₁.

⇒ חָמוּלִי *Hamulite*.

**חָמוּלִי** 1 gent. **Hamulite,** descendant(s) of Hamul, son of Perez, as coll. noun **Hamulites,** <CSTR> מִשְׁפַּחַת הֶחָמוּלִי *family of the Hamulites* Nm 26$_{21}$.
⇒ חָמוּל *Hamul.*

**חַמּוֹן** 2 pl.n. **Hammon, 1.** town in Asher, perh. Kh. Umm el-ʿAwāmīd, 17 km SSW of Tyre, <PREP> אֶל *to,* + יצא *go out* Jos 19$_{28}$. **2.** town in Naphtali, appar. ident with Hammath at Jos 19$_{35}$ and Hammoth-dor at Jos 21$_{32}$, <OBJ> נתן *give* 1 C 6$_{61}$ (+ מִגְרָשׁ *pasture land*).

**חָמוֹץ** 1.0.1 n.m. **oppressor,** <SUBJ> אפס *cease* Is 16$_4$ (1QIsa$^a$; MT הַמֵּץ *the extortioner*). <OBJ> אשׁר pi. *correct* Is 1$_{17}$ (or em. חָמוּץ *oppressed one*).
⇒ חמץ *oppress.*

**[חָמוּץ]** 1 adj. **crimson**—cstr. חֲמוּץ—used as noun, **crimson one, one who is dyed red, winestained,** <SUBJ> בוא *come* Is 63$_1$. <CSTR> חֲמוּץ בְּגָדִים *one bright red of garments,* i.e. with bright red garments Is 63$_1$. <APP> זֶה *this (warrior)* Is 63$_1$.*

**[חַמּוּק]** 1 n.m. **curve**—pl. cstr. חַמּוּקֵי (Gnz חָמוּקֵי)—<NOM CL> חַמּוּקֵי יְרֵכַיִךְ כְּמוֹ חֲלָאִים *the curves of your thighs are like ornaments* Ca 7$_2$. <CSTR> חַמּוּקֵי יְרֵכַיִךְ *the curves of your thighs* Ca 7$_2$.

**חֲמוֹר I** 96.1.5.1 n.m. (sometimes f.) **ass**—חֲמֹר; cstr. חֲמוֹר (חֲמֹר); sf. חֲמֹרְךָ חֲמֹרֶךָ (חֲמֹרֶךָ), חֲמֹרוֹ; pl. חֲמוֹרִים (חֲמֹרִים, I חמרם); sf. חֲמוֹרֵינוּ (חֲמֹרֵינוּ), חֲמוֹרֵיכֶם, חֲמוֹרֵיהֶם (חֲמֹרֵיהֶם)—employed in, e.g. ploughing (Is 32$_{20}$), transportation of goods (Gn 22$_{3.5}$ 42$_{26.27}$ Jos 9$_4$ 1 S 25$_{18}$); as valuable property (e.g. Gn 12$_{16}$ 30$_{43}$ Ex 20$_{17}$ Jos 6$_{21}$); sg. used collectively (Gn 32$_6$ Is 21$_7$); female ass (2 S 19$_{27}$); burial of ass (Jr 22$_{19}$).

<SUBJ> היה *be* Gn 12$_{16}$ (+ לְ *[belonging] to* Abram; + גָּמָל *camel,* אָתוֹן *she-ass,* צֹאן *flock,* בָּקָר *cattle,* עֶבֶד *servant,* שִׁפְחָה *female servant*) 30$_{43}$ (+ לְ *[belonging] to* Jacob; + גָּמָל, צֹאן, עֶבֶד, שִׁפְחָה) 32$_6$ (+ שׁוֹר *ox*) Nm 31$_{34}$ (+ צֹאן, בָּקָר), אסר pass. *be bound* 2 K 7$_{10}$, חבשׁ pass. *be saddled* 2 S 16$_1$, גזל pass. *be stolen* Dt 28$_{31}$, שׁלח pu. *be sent away* Gn 44$_3$, שׁוב *go back* Dt 28$_{31}$, נוח *rest* Ex 23$_{12}$, עמד *stand* 1 K 13$_{24.28}$, עשׂה *do* Dt 5$_{14}$, נשׂא *raise* Gn 45$_{23}$, נפל *fall* Ex 21$_{33}$ (+ שׁוֹר), תעה *go astray* Ex 23$_4$, ידע *know* Is 1$_3$.

<NOM CL> חֲמֹרִים אֶחָד וְשִׁשִּׁים אָלֶף *the asses were sixty one thousand* Nm 31$_{34}$, חֲמֹרִים שְׁלֹשִׁים אֶלֶף וַחֲמֵשׁ מֵאוֹת *the asses were thirty thousand and five hundred* Nm 31$_{39.45}$, חֲמֹרִים שֵׁשֶׁת אֲלָפִים שְׁבַע מֵאוֹת וְעֶשְׂרִים *the asses were six thousand seven hundred and twenty* Ezr 2$_{67}$||Ne 7$_{68}$ (+ גָּמָל *camel*), יִשָּׂשכָר חֲמֹר גָּרֶם *Issachar is an ass of (strong) bone(s)* Gn 49$_{14}$, הַחֲמוֹרִים לְבֵית־הַמֶּלֶךְ *the asses are for the house of the king* 2 S 16$_2$.

<OBJ> לקח *take* Gn 34$_{28}$ 43$_{18}$ Jos 7$_{24}$ (+ שׁוֹר, צֹאן *flock*) 1 S 8$_{16}$ 12$_3$ 16$_{20}$ 27$_9$ (+ גָּמָל *camel,* צֹאן *flock,* בָּקָר *cattle,* בֶּגֶד *garment*), נתן *give* Gn 24$_{35}$ (+ גָּמָל, צֹאן, בָּקָר, עֶבֶד *servant,* שִׁפְחָה *female servant,* כֶּסֶף *silver,* זָהָב *gold*) Ex 22$_9$ Nm 31$_{30}$ (+ צֹאן, בָּקָר, בְּהֵמָה *beast*), נשׂא *raise* Nm 16$_{15}$, שׁאר hi. *leave over* Jg 6$_4$.

חבשׁ *saddle* Gn 22$_3$ 2 S 17$_{23}$ 19$_{27}$ 1 K 2$_{40}$ 13$_{13.13.23.27}$, רכב *ride* 1QIsa$^a$ 21$_7$ (MT רֶכֶב *chariotry;* || גָּמָל), פגע *encounter* Ex 23$_4$, נהג *drive* Jb 24$_3$, שׁלח *send* Gn 45$_{23}$, רעה *pasture* Gn 36$_{24}$.

עזב *forsake* 2 K 7$_7$, אוה htp. *crave* Dt 5$_{21}$, חמד *covet* Ex 20$_{17}$ (+ שׁוֹר), שׁבה *take captive* 1 C 5$_{21}$ (or em. שׁלל *plunder;* + גָּמָל *camel,* צֹאן *flock,* נֶפֶשׁ *person*), שׁבר *break,* i.e. attack 1 K 13$_{28}$, נכה hi. *strike* 1 S 22$_{19}$ (+ שׁוֹר *ox,* שֶׂה *sheep*), ראה *see* Ex 23$_5$ Dt 22$_4$=11QT 64$_{13}$.

<CSTR> חֲמֹר גָּרֶם *ass of (strong) bone(s)* Gn 49$_{14}$ (Sam גֵּרִים *of sojourners*), חֲמוֹר אָחִיךָ *ass of your brother* Dt 22$_4$, חֲמוֹר שֹׂנַאֲךָ *ass of one who hates you* Ex 23$_5$, חֲמוֹר לֶחֶם *ass of bread,* i.e. laden with bread (unless name of weight)* 1 S 16$_{20}$.

פֶּטֶר חֲמֹר *firstborn of an ass* Ex 13$_{13}$ 34$_{20}$, צֶמֶד חֲמֹרִים *team of asses* Jg 19$_{3.10}$ (חֲמוֹרִים) 2 S 16$_1$ Arad ost. 3$_5$ (חמרם), רֶכֶב חֲמוֹר *a chariotry of an ass* Is 21$_7$ (or em. רֹכֵב חֲמוֹר *one riding an ass*), בְּשַׂר־חֲמוֹרִים *flesh of asses* Ezk 23$_{20}$, רֹאשׁ־חֲמוֹר *head of an ass* 2 K 6$_{25}$, לְחִי־חֲמוֹר *jawbone of an ass* Jg 15$_{15.16.16}$ (both הַחֲמוֹר), רֶגֶל ... הַחֲמוֹר *foot of ... the ass* Is 32$_{20}$, קְבוּרַת חֲמוֹר *burial of an ass* Jr 22$_{19}$, מַגֵּפַת ... הַחֲמוֹר *plague of ... the ass* Zc 14$_{15}$ (|| סוּס *horse,* פֶּרֶד *mule,* גָּמָל *camel,* + בְּהֵמָה *beast*).

<APP> מִקְנֶה *cattle* Ex 9$_3$ (|| סוּס *horse,* גָּמָל *camel,* + צֹאן *flock,* בָּקָר *cattle*), מַלְקוֹחַ *war booty* Nm 31$_{34}$.

<PREP> לְ of direction, *to,* + נתן *give* Gn 42$_{27}$ 43$_{24}$, בלל

*feed* Jg 19$_{21}$; of benefit, *to, for* Jg 19$_{19}$ Pr 26$_{3}$ Si 30$_{33}$, + לקח *take* Jos 9$_{4}$; עשׂה לְ *do with respect to* Dt 22$_{3}$.

בְּ of instrument, *by (means of)*, + בוא hi. *bring* food 1 C 12$_{41}$ (|| גָּמָל *camel*, פֶּרֶד *mule*, + בָּקָר *cattle*), נהל pi. *help along* 2 C 28$_{15}$, חרשׁ *plough* Dt 22$_{10}$=11QT 52$_{13}$ 4Q 418 103.2$_{8}$ (ח[מו]ר); *against*, + היה *be* Ex 9$_{3}$; in exchange, *for, on behalf of*, + נתן *give* Gn 47$_{17}$.

כְּ *as* 4QD$^{f}$ 1.1$_{10}$.

מִן of direction, *from* Nm 31$_{40}$, מִגָּמָל וְעַד־חֲמוֹר *from camel (and) unto ass*, i.e. both of them 1 S 15$_{3}$ (+ שׁוֹר *ox*, שֶׂה *sheep*), + רום hi. *raise*, i.e. levy tax Nm 31$_{28}$.

אֶל *to, upon, over*, + נוח hi. *put* 1 K 13$_{29}$.

עַל *upon, over*, + לקח *take* Jg 19$_{28}$, שׂים *place* 1 S 25$_{18}$, נשׂא *raise* Gn 42$_{26}$, עמס *load* Gn 44$_{13}$ Ne 13$_{15}$, רכב *ride* 1 S 25$_{20.42}$ Zc 9$_{9}$, hi. *mount* Ex 4$_{20}$; *over*, i.e. in charge of 1 C 27$_{30}$ (+ גָּמָל *camel*, צֹאן *flock*, בָּקָר *cattle*); *concerning* Ex 22$_{8}$.

מֵעַל *from (upon)*, + ירד *go down* 1 S 25$_{23}$, צנח *dismount* Jos 15$_{18}$ Jg 1$_{14}$.

עַד *until* Jos 6$_{21}$, מִשּׁוֹר עַד־חֲמוֹר *from ox unto ass*, i.e. whether ox or ass Ex 22$_{3}$.

עִם *with*, + ישׁב *dwell*, i.e. wait Gn 22$_{5}$.

<COLL> חֲמוֹר אֶחָד *one ass* Nm 16$_{15}$, עֲשָׂרָה חֲמֹרִים *ten asses* Gn 45$_{23}$, חֲמוֹרִים אַלְפָּיִם *two thousand asses* 1 C 5$_{21}$.

<SYN> גָּמָל *camel*, פֶּרֶד *mule*, סוּס *horse*.

Also 4QBibPar 10$_{6}$ perh. 4QpGen$^{c}$ 3$_{4}$.*

**חֲמוֹר II** 13 pr.n.m. **Hamor,** Hivite and father of Shechem, <SUBJ> היה *be* Gn 34$_{13.13.20}$, לקח *take* Gn 34$_{4.20}$, נתן *give* Gn 34$_{20}$, בוא *come* Gn 34$_{20}$, יצא *go out* Gn 34$_{6}$, אמר *say* Gn 34$_{8.20}$, דבר pi. *speak* Gn 34$_{6.8.20}$, שׁמע *hear* Gn 34$_{13}$, אות ni. *consent to* Gn 34$_{20}$, מול ni. *circumcise* Gn 34$_{13.13.20}$. <OBJ> ענה *answer* Gn 34$_{13}$, הרג *kill* Gn 34$_{26}$. <CSTR> בֶּן־חֲמוֹר *son of Hamor* Gn 34$_{2.18}$ (Sam בְּנוֹ *his son*), בְּנֵי *sons of* Gn 33$_{19}$ Jos 24$_{32}$, אַנְשֵׁי *men of* Jg 9$_{28}$, עֵינֵי *eyes of* Gn 34$_{18}$. <APP> אָב *father* Gn 34$_{4.6.13}$ Jg 9$_{28}$. <PREP> לְ of possession, *of, (belonging) to* Gn 34$_{13.20.20}$; of direction, *to*, + נתן *give* Gn 34$_{8.13}$; of benefit, *to, for*, לקח *take* Gn 34$_{20}$; אות לְ ni. *consent to* Gn 34$_{13.20}$; אֶל *to*, + אמר *say* Gn 34$_{4.13}$, שׁמע *hear* Gn 34$_{24}$; אות ni. *consent to* Gn 34$_{13.20}$; אֵת *with* Gn 34$_{20}$, + חתן htp. *marry* Gn 34$_{8}$ (if em. אֹתָנוּ *us* to אִתָּנוּ *with us*), ישׁב *dwell* Gn 34$_{8.13.20.20}$.

**חֲמוֹר III** 2 n.[m.] **heap**—du. חֲמֹרָתָיִם—<COLL> חֲמוֹר חֲמֹרָתָיִם *a heap, two heaps* Jg 15$_{16}$ (or em. חָמוֹר חֲמַרְתִּים *I have utterly flayed them*, from חמר *flay*).

**[חָמוּשׁ]**, see חמשׁ *be five*, Qal.

**[חָמוֹת]** 11 n.f. **mother-in-law**—sf. חֲמוֹתָהּ, חֲמוֹתֵךְ (חֲמֹתָהּ)—of husband's mother, <SUBJ> אמר *say* Ru 2$_{19}$ 3$_{1}$, צוה pi. *command* Ru 3$_{6}$, ראה *see* Ru 2$_{18}$. <OBJ> ראה hi. *show* Ru 2$_{18(mss)}$. <APP> Naomi Ru 3$_{1}$. <PREP> לְ introducing object, + נשׁק *kiss* Ru 1$_{14}$, נגד hi. *tell* Ru 2$_{19}$; בְּ *against*, + קום *rise* Mc 7$_{6}$ (|| אֵם *mother*); אֶל *to*, + בוא *come* Ru 3$_{16.17}$, שׁוב *go back* Ru 2$_{23(mss)}$; אֵת *with*, + עשׂה *do* Ru 2$_{11}$, ישׁב *dwell* Ru 2$_{23}$.

**חֹמֶט** 1.0.1 n.[m.] **lizard,** in lists of unclean animals, <NOM CL> זֶה לָכֶם הַטָּמֵא בַּשֶּׁרֶץ ... הַחֹמֶט *this is what is unclean for you among the swarming things ... the lizard* Lv 11$_{30}$. <OBJ> טמא pi. *declare impure* 11QT 50$_{21}$. <APP> שֶׁרֶץ *swarming thing* 11QT 50$_{21}$.

**חֻמְטָה** 1 pl.n. **Humtah,** town in Judah, <NOM CL> בָּהָר ... וְחֻמְטָה *in the hill country were ... and Humtah* Jos 15$_{54}$. <APP> עִיר *city* Jos 15$_{54}$.

**[חֲמִיאֹהֶל]** 0.0.0.1 pr.n.f. **Hamiohel,** daughter of Menahem, <APP> בַּת *daughter* Seal 412 (Jerusalem, 7th cent.). <PREP> לְ of possession, *of, (belonging) to* Seal 412 (Jerusalem, 7th cent.).

**חֲמִיטַל** 3 pr.n.f. **Hamital,** mother of Jehoahaz, and daughter of Jeremiah of Libnah, <NOM CL> שֵׁם אִמּוֹ חֲמִיטַל *the name of his mother was Hamital* 2 K 23$_{31(mss)}$ (L חֲמוּטַל *Hamutal*) 24$_{18(Kt)}$ Jr 52$_{1(Kt)}$ (both Qr חֲמוּטַל). <APP> בַּת *daughter* 2 K 23$_{31}$ 24$_{18}$ Jr 52$_{1}$.

*[**חָמִיךְ**] 0.1 n.[m.] **unreliable guide**—Si חמיך—<PREP> עִם *with*, + יעץ ni. *take counsel* Si 37$_{10}$ (unless חמיך *your father-in-law*, from חָם III, or חֹמֶיךָ *those who look upon you*, from חמה I *see*).

**[חֲמִיעֲדָן]** 0.0.0.1 pr.n.f. **Hamiadan,** daughter of Ahimelech, <APP> בַּת *daughter* Seal 324 (7th cent.). <PREP> לְ of possession, *of, (belonging) to* Seal 324 (7th cent.).

**חָמִיץ** 1 n.[m.] **sorrel**—Q חמץ (1QIsa$^{a}$)—**sorrel,** plant with acid-tasting leaves, <CSTR> בְּלִיל חָמִיץ *fodder of sorrel* Is 30$_{24}$.*

⇒ חמץ *be sour.*

**חֲמִישִׁי** 34.0.33 adj. **fifth**—חֲמִשִׁי (Ezk 20$_{1}$ Zc 7$_{3}$), L חמישי (1 C 27$_{8}$); fem. חֲמִישִׁת, חֲמִשִּׁת, חֲמִישִׁית—used attributively of יוֹם *day* Gn 1$_{23}$ Nm 7$_{36}$ 29$_{26}$ Jg 19$_{8}$ 4QJub$^{a}$ 2$_{11}$ ([ביום החמישי]) 2$_{12}$ ([ביום החמישי]) 4QpGen$^{a}$ 1.1$_{9}$ 11QT 24$_{14}$ 29$_{01}$ ([ביום החמשי]) perh 4QPrQuot 51$_{19}$ ([ח]מיש׳), שָׁבוּעַ *week* 4Q247$_{2}$ ([המ]ישׁי) 4QMishC$^{a}$ 3$_{3}$ ([יום]) 11QJub 4$_{7}$ ([הח]מישי) 4$_{11}$ ([הח]מישי [בשבו]ע) 4$_{13}$ ([לשבוע החמישי]), חֹדֶשׁ *month* Nm 33$_{38}$ 2 K 25$_{8}$||Jr 52$_{12}$ Jr 1$_{3}$ 28$_{1}$ Zc 7$_{3}$ Ezr 7$_{8.9}$ 1 C 27$_{8}$, בֵּן *son* Gn 30$_{17}$, שָׁנָה *year* Lv 19$_{25}$ 1 K 14$_{25}$ Jr 36$_{9}$ (or em. שְׁמִינִי *eighth*) Ezk 1$_{2}$ 2 C 12$_{2}$ 4QMishH 1.2$_{3}$ ([ח]מישית), יֹבֵל *jubilee* 4QOtot 2$_{19}$ 2$_{19}$ 4QS$^{e}$ 1.6$_{19}$ (both [היובל החמש]י) 1.6$_{19}$ ([היובל החמש]) 11QJub 4$_{9}$ ([היובל החמ]שי), פַּעַם *time* Ne 6$_{5}$, גּוֹרָל *lot* Jos 19$_{24}$.

2. as noun, **fifth (one),** usu. in ref. to son, also to Gadite warrior 1 C 12$_{11}$, royal administrator 1 C 27$_{8}$, heavenly singer 4QShirShabb$^{d}$ 1.1$_{18}$ ([החמיש]י) 1.2$_{37}$ ([החמישי]) 4QShirShabb$^{f}$ 11$_{4.4}$ 13$_{2}$ ([החמ]יש׳) MasShir Shabb 2$_{12}$, lot 1 C 24$_{9}$ 1 C 25$_{12}$, battle standard 1QM 4$_{10}$, day 4QMishB$^{a}$ 1.2$_{1}$, month Ezk 20$_{1}$ Zc 7$_{5}$ 8$_{19}$ 4Q MMT A 3$_{10}$ 4QMishA 1.1$_{10}$ 1.2$_{9}$ 1.3$_{7}$ 4QMishB$^{a}$ 1.3$_{3}$ 2.2$_{1.5}$ 2.3$_{1.8}$ 2.4$_{3}$ 4QMishB$^{b}$ 1.1$_{9}$ 2$_{3}$ 4QMishF$^{a}$ 1$_{1.5}$ 4Q Mish F$^{b}$ 1$_{3}$, year 1QM 2$_{11}$ 4QOtot 1$_{13.15.19}$ 2$_{2.6.9.11.15.17}$ 3$_{2.5.10.13.16}$ 4QS$^{e}$ 1.5$_{13.15.19}$ 1.6$_{2.6.9.11.15.17}$ 1.7$_{2.5.9.10.13.16}$ 4QMish A 4.5$_{9}$ 4QMishB$^{a}$ 2.3$_{4.7}$ 4QMishG 1$_{5}$ 11QJub 12$_{16}$.

<SUBJ> ברך pi. *bless* 4QShirShabb$^{d}$ 1.1$_{18}$ ([החמיש]י) 4QShirShabb$^{f}$ 13$_{2}$ ([החמ]יש׳).

<NOM CL> רַדַּי הַחֲמִישִׁי *Raddai was the fifth (son)* 1 C 2$_{14}$, sim. 1 C 12$_{11}$ 26$_{3.4}$, הַחֲמִישִׁי שְׁפַטְיָה *the fifth (son) was Shephatiah* 2 S 3$_{4}$||1 C 3$_{3}$, sim. 1 C 8$_{2}$ 25$_{12}$ 29$_{8}$, לְמַלְכִּיָּה הַחֲמִשִׁי *to Malchijah was,* i.e. fell, *the fifth (lot)* 1 C 24$_{9}$, החמישי בפתחיה *the fifth (month) is in Pethahiah* 4QMish B$^{a}$ 2.2$_{5}$, var. 2.3$_{1}$ ([בפתחיה החמישי]), sim. 2.2$_{1}$ ([בבלגה] *in Bilgah*) 2.3$_{8}$ (בק[ו]ץ *in Koz*) 2.3$_{4}$ ([החמישי בחר]ים *the fifth is in Harim*) 2.4$_{3}$ ([החמישי באלישיב] *the fifth is in Eliashib*).

<CSTR> צוֹם הַחֲמִישִׁי *fast of the fifth (month)* Zc 8$_{19}$, לשון החמישי *tongue of the fifth (angel)* 4QShirShabb$^{d}$ 1.2$_{37}$ ([ל]שון החמישי) 4QShirShabb$^{f}$ 11$_{4.4}$ MasShirShabb 2$_{12}$ (=4QShirShabb$^{d}$ 1.1$_{3}$ [החמיש]י).

<PREP> בְּ of place/time, *in, during* 4QOtot 1$_{13}$ ([בחמ]ישית) 1$_{15.19}$ 2$_{2}$ ([בחמישית]) 2$_{6.9.11.15}$ ([בחמישית]) 2$_{17}$ ([בחמישית]) 3$_{2}$ ([ב]חמישית) 3$_{5}$ (ב[ח]מ[י]שית) 3$_{10}$ ([בחמישית]) 3$_{13.16}$ 4QS$^{e}$ 1.5$_{13}$ ([בחמישית]) 1.5$_{15.19}$ 1.6$_{2}$ ([בחמישית]) 1.6$_{6.9.11.15}$ ([בחמ]ישת) 1.6$_{17}$ ([בחמישית]) 1.7$_{2}$ ([בחמישית]) 1.7$_{5}$ (בח[מ]ישית) 1.7$_{10}$ ([בחמישית]) 1.7$_{13.16}$ 4QMishA 1.1$_{10}$ 1.2$_{9}$ 1.3$_{7}$ 4QMishB$^{a}$ 1.2$_{1}$ 1.3$_{3}$ 2.1$_{1}$ 4QMishB$^{b}$ 1.1$_{9}$ (all six [בחשימ]י) 2$_{3}$ 4QMMT A 3$_{10}$ (בחמ[י]ש[י]) 4QMishF$^{a}$ 1$_{1.5}$ 4QMishF$^{b}$ 1$_{3}$ (all three [בחמישית]) 11QJub 12$_{16}$ ([בחמש]ית), + היה *be* Ezk 20$_{1}$, צום *fast* Zc 7$_{5}$, ספד *mourn* Zc 7$_{5}$, לחם ni. *fight* 1QM 2$_{11}$; על *upon,* + כתב *write* 1QM 4$_{10}$.

<COLL> החמשית מעדיה *as for the fifth (year), its festivals (are)* 4QMishA 4.5$_{9}$ ([החמישית] מועדיה) 4QMishG 1$_{5}$, החמיש[י] בנש[יא]י רוש *the fifth among the princes of (the) head* 4QShirShabb$^{d}$ 1.1$_{18}$, sim. 4QShirShabb$^{f}$ 13$_{2}$ ([החמ]יש׳).

Also 4QS$^{e}$ 1.7$_{9}$ ([הח]מישי) 4QShirShabb$^{b}$ 3$_{5}$ ([ה]חמיש]י) 11QJub 4$_{16}$ ([הח]מישי).

⇒ חמש *be five.*

**[חֲמִישִׁית]** 11.0.2 n.f. **fifth**—חֲמִישִׁת, חֲמִשִׁית; cstr. חֲמִישִׁית, חֲמִשִּׁית; sf. חֲמִשִׁתוֹ, חֲמִישִׁיתוֹ) חֲמִישִׁתוֹ); pl. sf. חֲמִשְׁתָיו (Lv 5$_{24}$ [mss, Sam חֲמִשְׁתוֹ])—in ref. to fifth part of produce (תְּבוּאָה) Gn 47$_{24}$, silver (כֶּסֶף) Lv 27$_{15.19}$, valuation (עֵרֶךְ) Lv 5$_{16}$ 27$_{13.27}$, (value of) holy thing (קֹדֶשׁ) Lv 22$_{14}$, tithe (מַעֲשֵׂר) Lv 27$_{31}$, principal (רֹאשׁ) Lv 5$_{24}$ Nm 5$_{7}$, entrance (פֶּתַח) of shrine 1 K 6$_{31}$. <NOM CL> הָאַיִל מְזוּזוֹת חֲמִשִׁית *the pillar (and) doorposts were,* i.e. occupied, *a fifth* 1 K 6$_{31}$ (or em. הָאוּלָם וְהַמְּזוּזוֹת חֲמִשׁוֹת *the vestibule,* i.e. lintel, *and the doorposts were fivefold,* i.e. formed a pentagon). <OBJ> נתן *give* to Pharaoh Gn 47$_{24}$ (+ אַרְבַּע הַיָּדֹת *the [remaining] four portions*), יסף *add* to valuation, etc. Lv 5$_{16.24}$ 22$_{14}$ 27$_{13.15.19.27.31}$ Nm 5$_{7}$. <CSTR> חֲמִישִׁית כֶּסֶף־עֶרְכְּךָ *a fifth of the silver of your valuation* Lv 27$_{15.19}$ (חֲמִשִׁית), חמישית אנשי *a fifth of the*

*men of* war 11QT $58_{7}$, חמישית העם *a fifth of the people* 11QT $58_{16}$.
→ חמש *be five*.

חמל $_{41.4.7}$ vb. **spare—Qal** $_{41}$ Pf. חָמַל (חָמֵל), חָמַלְתָּ, Q חמלו, חֲמַלְתֶּם; impf. יַחְמֹל (יַחְמוֹל), 3fs Q תחמל, 2ms תַּחְמֹל, תַּחְמוֹל (תַּחְמְלוּ) תַּחְמֹלוּ, יַחְמְלוּ, (אֶחְמֹל) אֶחְמוֹל; + waw וַיַּחְמֹל, וָאֶחְמֹל, וַתַּחְמֹל, 3fs וַיַּחְמֹל; וְחָמַלְתִּי; inf. חֶמְלָה—**spare, have compassion,** <SUBJ> Y. Is $30_{14}$ (:: שׁבר *break*) Jr $13_{14}$ (|| חוס *pity*, רחם pi. *have compassion*, :: שׁחת hi. *destroy*) Ezk $5_{11}$ $7_{4.9}$ $8_{18}$ $9_{10}$ (all five + חוס) $36_{21}$ Jl $2_{18}$ (+ קנא pi. *be jealous*) Zc $11_{6}$ Ml $3_{17}$=4QpGen$^{b}$ $4.1_{3}$ ([חלמתי]) Jb $16_{13}$ $27_{22}$ Lm $2_{2}$ (:: בלע pi. *destroy*) $2_{17}$ (:: הרס *tear down*) $2_{21}$ (:: טבח *slaughter*) $3_{43}$ (both :: הרג *kill*) 2 C $36_{15}$ Si $16_{8}$ (+ נשׂא *forgive*) $16_{9}$ perh. 4Q416 $2.2_{13}$, Nebuchadrezzar Jr $21_{7}$ (|| חוס, רחם pi.), Saul 1 S $15_{3.9}$ (both :: חרם hi. *exterminate*), Israelites Dt $13_{9}$=11QT$^{b}$ $20_{5}$ (+ חוס *pity*), Ziphites 1 S $23_{21}$, Chaldaeans Hb $1_{17}$=1QpHab $6_{9}$ (:: הרג *slay*), עַם *people* 1 S $15_{9.15}$, אִישׁ 2 S $12_{4.6}$ Is $9_{18}$ Ml $3_{17}$=4QpGen$^{b}$ $4.1_{4}$ ([יחמול איש]), גֶּבֶר *man* Pr $6_{34}$, בַּת *daughter* Ex $2_{6}$, מֶלֶךְ *king* 2 S $21_{7}$ 2 C $36_{17}$ (:: הרג), זָר *foreigner* Jr $51_{3}$ (unless em. זָרִים *foreigners* to זֹרִים *winnowers*, i.e. זרה ptc.; :: חרם hi.), רֹעֶה *shepherd* Zc $11_{5}$ GnzPs $2_{5}$, דרך ptc. *one who treads*, i.e. bends bow Jr $50_{14}$, רָשָׁע *wicked one* Jb $20_{13}$ (+ מנע *withhold*; :: עזב *let go*), חָנֵף *impious one* Jb $20_{13}$, עָשִׁיר *rich one* Si $13_{4}$, נָדִיב *noble one* Si $13_{12}$, עַיִן *eye* Ezk $16_{5}$ (+ חוס *pity*) 11QPs$^{a}$ $18_{14}$, חִילָה *pain* perh. Jb $6_{10}$, אֵלֶּה *these* Ezk $9_{5}$ (+ חוס; :: נכה hi. *strike*), מִי *who?* Jr $15_{5}$ (+ נוד *show grief*), no one 1 S $22_{8}$ (if em. חֹלֶה *one who is sick* to חֹמֵל *one who has compassion*).

<PREP> בְּ of time, *in*, + יוֹם *day* Pr $6_{34}$; עַל *upon*, or introducing object 4Q416 $2.2_{13}$, + Amalek 1 S $15_{3}$, Agag 1 S $15_{9}$, Mephibosheth 2 S $21_{7}$, Saul 1 S $22_{8}$ (if em.; see Subj.) $23_{21}$, Jerusalem Jr $15_{5}$ Ezk $16_{5}$, עַם *people* Jl $2_{18}$ 2 C $36_{15}$, גּוֹי *nation* Si $16_{9}$, בֵּן *son* Ml $3_{17}$=4QpGen$^{b}$ $4.1_{4}$ ([יחמול ... על בנו]) Si $13_{4}$, יֶלֶד *child* Ex $2_{6}$, בָּחוּר *youth* 2 C $36_{17}$, בְּתוּלָה *young woman* 2 C $36_{17}$, זָקֵן *elder* 2 C $36_{17}$, יָשֵׁשׁ *aged one* 2 C $36_{17}$, יֹשֵׁב *inhabitant* Zc $11_{6}$, ירא ptc. *one who fears* Ml $3_{17}$=4QpGen$^{b}$ $4.1_{3}$ ([ליראי ... ] [חלמתי]), חשׁב ptc. *one who thinks* Ml $3_{17}$=4QpGen$^{b}$ $4.1_{3}$ ([ולחשבי ... ] [חלמתי]), טוֹב *good one* 11QPs$^{a}$ $18_{14}$, מֵיטָב *the best* of sheep and oxen 1 S $15_{9.15}$, צֹאן *flock* Zc $11_{5}$ GnzPs $2_{5}$, תְּנוּבָה *fruit* 4Q417 $19_{5}$ ([תנוב[תה]), מָעוֹן *dwelling place* 2 C $36_{15}$, מָגוֹר *sojourning place* Si $16_{8}$, הוֹן *wealth* 4Q418 $101.2_{4}$, טוֹב *good thing* 1 S $15_{9}$, רָעָה *evil* Jb $20_{13}$; *for the sake of*, + שֵׁם Ezk $36_{21}$; אֶל introducing object, + אָח *brother* Is $9_{18}$, בָּחוּר *youth* Jr $51_{3}$; חֵץ *arrow* Jr $50_{14}$.

<COLL> חמל + inf. of לקח *take* 2 S $12_{4}$; + adverb עוֹד *again* Zc $11_{6}$.

<SYN> חוס *pity*, רחם pi. *have compassion*.

<ANT> שׁחת hi. *destroy*, בלע pi. *destroy*, הרס *tear down*, טבח *slaughter*, הרג *kill*, חרם hi. *exterminate*, עזב *let go*, נכה hi. *strike*.*

→ חֶמְלָה *compassion*, יַחְמְלְיָהוּ *Jahmeliah*.

[חָמָל] $_{0.0.0.2}$ pr.n.m. **Hamal, 1.** appar. father of Darshiah, Seal 338 (8th–6th cent.). **2.** father of Jeshaiah, <CSTR> בן חמל *son of Hamal* Seal 583 (T. Beit Mirsim?, 7th/6th cent.).

[חֶמְלָה] $_{2}$ n.f. **compassion**—cstr. חֶמְלַת; sf. חֶמְלָתוֹ—<CSTR> חֶמְלַת י׳ *compassion of Y.* Gn $19_{16}$. <PREP> בְּ *on account of* Gn $19_{16}$; of accompaniment, *with, in*, + גאל *redeem* Is $63_{9}$ (|| אַהֲבָה *love*). <COLL> חֶמְלַת י׳ עָלָיו *the compassion of Y. for him* Gn $19_{16}$. <SYN> אַהֲבָה *love*.

→ חמל *spare*.

חֶמְלָה, see חמל inf. *spare*.

חמם $_{26}$ vb. **be warm—Qal** $_{23}$ Pf. חַם, Sam חַמָּה, חַמּוֹתִי; impf. יֵחַם (יֵחָם, יֵחַם), 3fs תֵּחַם, יֵחַמּוּ; + waw וַיֵּחַם, וַיִּחַם; inf. חֹם, חַמּוֹ, חֻמָּם (לַחְמָם)—**be** or **become warm, be** or **become hot, warm oneself** (Is $44_{15.16}$ $47_{14}$ [or em.; see Subj.]), <SUBJ> Israelites Ho $7_{7}$, Babylonians Jr $51_{39}$, אָדָם *human being* Is $44_{15.16.16}$, לֵבָב *heart* Dt $19_{6}$, לֵב *heart* Ps $39_{4}$, בָּשָׂר *flesh* 2 K $4_{34}$, יוֹם *day* Gn $18_{1}$ 1 S $11_{11}$ 2 S $4_{5}$, שֶׁמֶשׁ *sun* Ex $16_{21}$ 1 S $11_{9}$ Ne $7_{3}$, סִיר *pot* Ezk $24_{11}$ (+ חרה *burn*); subj. impersonal (e.g. לֹא יִחַם לוֹ *it was not warm for him*, i.e. he was not warm 1 K $1_{1}$), 1 K $1_{1.2}$ Hg $1_{6}$ Jb $6_{17}$ (+ זרב pu. *be scorched*) Ec $4_{11.11}$; subj. unspecified, Is $47_{14}$ (or em. לַחְמָם *to warm oneself* to לְחַמֵּם *to give out heat*, i.e. pi.) Jb $30_{4}$ (unless לַחְמָם *their bread*, from לֶחֶם). <PREP> לְ of benefit, *for* Hg $1_{6}$, + David 1 K

1$_{1}$, אָדוֹן *lord* 1 K 1$_{2}$, מֶלֶךְ *king* 1 K 1$_{2}$, אֶחָד *one* Ec 4$_{11}$, שְׁנַיִם *two* Ec 4$_{11}$; כְּ *as*, + תַּנּוּר *oven* Ho 7$_{7}$; בְּקֶרֶב *with*, + psalmist Ps 39$_{4}$.

**Ni.** 1 Ptc. נֵחָמִים—**inflame oneself,** <SUBJ> wicked Is 57$_{5}$. <PREP> בְּ of place, *among*, + אֵלָה *terebinth* Is 57$_{5}$; תַּחַת *under*, + עֵץ *tree* Is 57$_{5}$.

**Pi.** 1 Impf. 3fs תְּחַמֵּם—**keep eggs warm** (Jb 39$_{14}$), **give out heat** (Is 47$_{14}$ [if em.; see Subj.]), <SUBJ> רְנָנִים appar. *ostrich* Jb 39$_{14}$, גַּחֶלֶת *coal* Is 47$_{14}$ (if em. לַחְמָם *to warm oneself* to לְחַמֵּם *to give out heat*). <PREP> עַל *upon*, + עָפָר *dust* Jb 39$_{14}$.

**Htp.** 1 Impf. יִתְחַמָּם—**warm oneself,** <SUBJ> אֶבְיוֹן *poor one* Jb 31$_{20}$. <PREP> מִן of instrument, *by (means of)*, + גֵּז *fleece* Jb 31$_{20}$.*

⇒ חַם *hot*, חֹם *heat*, חַמָּה *heat; sun*.

[חַמָּן] 8 n.m. **incense altar**—pl. חַמָּנִים; sf. חַמָּנֵיכֶם—<SUBJ> קום *stand* Is 27$_{9}$ (|| אֲשֵׁרָה *Asherah*, + מִזְבֵּחַ *altar*), שׁבר ni. *be broken* Ezk 6$_{4}$ (|| מִזְבֵּחַ), גדע ni. *be hewn down* Ezk 6$_{6}$ (|| מִזְבֵּחַ, גִּלּוּל *idol*, מַעֲשֶׂה *work*, + בָּמָה *high place*). <OBJ> ראה *see* Is 17$_{8}$ (or del.; || אֲשֵׁרָה *Asherah* + מִזְבֵּחַ *altar*), כרת hi. *cut down* Lv 26$_{30}$ (|| בָּמָה *high place*), גדע pi. *hew down* 2 C 34$_{4}$ (+ מַסֵּכָה *molten image*) 34$_{7}$ (both + מִזְבֵּחַ, אֲשֵׁרָה, פָּסִיל *graven image*), סור hi. *remove* 2 C 14$_{14}$ (|| בָּמָה). <CSTR> כָּל־חַמָּנִים *all the incense altars* 2 C 34$_{7}$. <SYN> מִזְבֵּחַ *altar*, אֲשֵׁרָה *Asherah*, גִּלּוּל *idol*, בָּמָה *high place*, מַעֲשֶׂה *work*.*

[חַמֹּן] 0.0.0.2 pr.n.m. **Hammon, 1.** Seal 3 (Megiddo, 8th cent.). **2.** father of Nahum, Seal 202 (7th cent.). <CSTR> בן חמן *son of Hammon* Seal 202. <PREP> לְ of possession, *of, (belonging) to* Seal 3 (לחמן; others חמן).

חמס I 8.1.1 vb. **be violent**—**Qal** 7.1.1 Pf. חָמְסוּ; impf. יַחְמֹס, Q יחמס, תַּחְמְסוּ; + waw וַיַּחְמֹס; ptc. חֹמֵס (Si חומס)—**treat violently, do wrong** (Jb 21$_{27}$), <SUBJ> Y. Lm 2$_{6}$ (|| שׁחת pi. *destroy*), מֶלֶךְ *king* Jr 22$_{3}$ (|| ינה hi. *oppress*), עֶבֶד *servant* Jr 22$_{3}$, כֹּהֵן *priest* Ezk 22$_{26}$ Zp 3$_{4}$ (both || חלל pi. *profane*) 4QpsMos$^{e}$ 2.1$_{10}$, עַם *people* Jr 22$_{3}$, רָשָׁע *wicked one* Jb 15$_{33}$ (|| שׁלך hi. *cast*), רָכִיל *slanderer* Si 11$_{30}$, בֹּצֵעַ *extortioner* Si 11$_{30}$, חטא ptc. *one who misses* wisdom Pr 8$_{36}$ (+ אהב *love* death), Job's friends Jb 21$_{27}$ (unless חמס II *devise*; or em. תַּהְגּוּ *you cogitate*).

<OBJ> אַלְמָנָה *widow* Jr 22$_{3}$, יָתוֹם *orphan* Jr 22$_{3}$, גֵּר *sojourner* Jr 22$_{3}$, נֶפֶשׁ *soul* Pr 8$_{36}$, בֹּסֶר *unripe grape* Jb 15$_{33}$, שֹׂךְ *booth* Lm 2$_{6}$ (or em. כַּגַּן שֻׂכּוֹ *like a garden his booth* to מְכוֹן שִׁבְתּוֹ *the fixed place of his abode*), מָכוֹן *fixed place* Lm 2$_{6}$ (if em.), תּוֹרָה *law* Ezk 22$_{26}$ Zp 3$_{4}$.

<PREP> כְּ *as*, + גֶּפֶן *vine* Jb 15$_{33}$ Lm 2$_{6}$ (if em. כַּגַּן *as a garden* to כַּגֶּפֶן); עַל *against*, or introducing object, + Job Jb 21$_{27}$ (or em.; see Subj.).

<COLL> מְזִמּוֹת עָלַי תַּחְמֹסוּ *the devices with which you do me wrong* Jb 21$_{27}$ (or em.; see Subj.). <SYN> ינה hi. *oppress*, שׁחת pi. *destroy*, חלל pi. *profane*, שׁלך hi. *cast*.

**Ni.** 1 Pf. נֶחְמְסוּ—**suffer violence** <SUBJ> עָקֵב *heel* Jr 13$_{22}$ (|| גלה ni. *be uncovered*). <PREP> בְּ *on account of*, + רֹב *greatness* of iniquity Jr 13$_{22}$. <SYN> גלה ni. *be uncovered*.*

⇒ חָמָס *violence*.

חמס II 1 vb. **devise**—**Qal** 1 תַּחְמֹסוּ—<SUBJ> friends of Job Jb 21$_{27}$ (unless חמס I *do wrong*). <OBJ> מְזִמָּה *device* Jb 21$_{27}$. <PREP> עַל *against*, + Job Jb 21$_{27}$.

חמס III 1 vb. **make bare**—**Qal** 1 Ptc. חֹמֵס—<SUBJ> שׁלח ptc. *one who sends* Pr 26$_{6}$ (if em.; see Obj.). <OBJ> שֵׁת *buttocks* Pr 26$_{6}$ (if em. חָמָס שֹׁתֶה *drinks violence* to חֹמֵס שֵׁתוֹ *bares his buttocks*).

חָמָס 60.10.15 n.m. **violence**—cstr. חֲמַס; sf. חֲמָסִי, חֲמָסוֹ; pl. חֲמָסִים—**violence, wrong,** <SUBJ> שׁמע ni. *be heard* Is 60$_{18}$ (|| שֶׁבֶר *destruction*) Jr 6$_{7}$ (both || שֹׁד *devastation*), בוא *come* Jg 9$_{24}$, ירד *go down* Ps 7$_{17}$ (|| עָמָל *mischief*), קום *arise*, i.e. grow into Ezk 7$_{11}$, כסה pi. *cover* Hb 2$_{17}$=1Qp Hab 11$_{17}$ (+ שֹׁד), עטף *wrap* Ps 73$_{6}$, לקח *take* lives Pr 11$_{30}$ (if em. חָכָם *a wise one*).

<NOM CL> נֶפֶשׁ בֹּגְדִים חָמָס *the soul*, i.e. desire, *of the treacherous is violence* Pr 13$_{2}$, חָמָס בָּאָרֶץ *violence is in the land* Jr 51$_{46}$, לֹא־חָמָס בְּכַפַּי *no violence is in my hands* Jb 16$_{17}$, חֲמָסִי עָלֶיךָ *my wrong*, i.e. the wrong done to me, *is upon you* Gn 16$_{5}$, חֲמָסִי ... עַל־בָּבֶל *my violence*, i.e. the violence done to me, *is ... upon Babylon* Jr 51$_{35}$ (+ דָּם *blood*), חָמָס לְנֶגְדִּי *violence is before me* Hb 1$_{3}$=1Qp Hab 1$_{7}$ ([חמס לנגדי]; || שֹׁד *devastation*).

<OBJ> ראה *see* Ps $55_{10}$ (|| רִיב *strife*), אהב *love* Ps $11_5$, אצר *store up* Am $3_{10}$ (|| שֹׁד *devastation*), כלה pi. *accomplish* Gn $49_{5(Sam)}$, מלא *fill with* Ezk $8_{17}$ $28_{16}$ 4QDibHam[a] $8_{14}$ (למלוא ח[מס]), pi. Zp $1_9$ (|| מִרְמָה *deceit*), כסה pi. *cover (with)* Ml $2_{16}$ Pr $10_{6.11}$, פלס pi. *weigh out* Ps $58_3$ (unless em.; see Cstr.), חרשׁ *devise* Si $7_{12}$, קרא *cry* Jr $20_8$ (|| שֹׁד), זעק *cry* Hb $1_2$=1QpHab $1_4$ ([אזעק ... חמס]), צעק *cry* Jb $19_7$, פוח hi. *breathe*, i.e. utter Ps $27_{12}$ (if em.; see Cstr.), נגשׁ hi. *bring near* Am $6_3$ (if em.; see Cstr.), עשׂה *do* Is $53_9$ (+ מִרְמָה *deceit*), סור hi. *remove* Ezk $45_9$ (|| שֹׁד), טהר pi. *purify* 11QPs[a] $22_6$, שׁתה *drink* Pr $26_6$ (or em. חָמָס to חֶרְפָּה *reproach*, or em. חָמָס שֹׁתֶה *drinks violence* to חֹמֵס שֵׁתוֹ *bares his buttocks*, from חמס III *bare*).

<CSTR> חֲמַס כָּל־הַיֹּשְׁבִים *violence of all those who dwell* Ezk $12_{19}$, חֲמַס יְדֵיכֶם *violence of your hands* Ps $58_3$ (unless em. חֲמַס *violence of* to לְחָמָס *to violence*), חמס גאוה *violence of pride* Si $10_8$, חֲמַס שִׁבְעִים בְּנֵי־יְרֻבָּעַל *violence of*, i.e. done to, *the seventy sons of Jerubaal* Jg $9_{24}$, בְּנֵי יְהוּדָה *of*, i.e. done to, *the sons of Judah* Jl $4_{19}$, לְבָנוֹן *of*, i.e. done to, *the Lebanon* Hb $2_{17}$=1QpHab $11_{17}$, אָחִיךָ *of*, i.e. done to, *your brother* $Ob_{10}$, אֶרֶץ *of*, i.e. done to, *the earth* Hb $2_{8.17}$=1QpHab $9_8$ $12_{1.7}$ (both || דָּם *blood*) $12_9$; אִישׁ חָמָס *man of violence* Ps $18_{49}$ Ps $140_{12}$ Pr $3_{31}$ $16_{29}$ Si $10_{23}$, אִישׁ חֲמָסִים *man of violence* 2 S $22_{49}$ Ps $140_{2.5}$, אנשי חמס *men of violence* Si $13_{13}$ $15_{12}$ $35_{17(Bmg).18(B)}$ 1QpHab $1_5$ (אנשי] [חמס) $8_{11}$, עֵד חָמָס *witness of violence*, i.e. malicious witness Ex $23_1$ Dt $19_{16}$=11QT $61_7$ Pr $24_{28(ms)}$ (L חִנָּם *of needlessness*), עֵדֵי *witnesses of* Ps $35_{11}$, יָפֵחַ *witness of* Ps $27_{12}$ (unless em. וִיפֵחַ *and a witness of* to וְיָפִיחוּ *and they breathe*, i.e. utter, violence; || שֶׁקֶר *deceit*), נצר *shoot of* Si $40_{15(M)}$, כְּלֵי *weapons of* Gn $49_5$ (Sam כִּלּוּ *they have accomplished* violence) 4QTestim$_{25}$, שֶׁבֶת *seat of* Am $6_3$ (unless em. שֶׁבֶת to שְׁנַת *year of* or שֶׁבֶר וְ *destruction and* or שֹׁד וְ *devastation and*), פֹּעַל *deed of* Is $59_6$ (|| אָוֶן *iniquity*), נְאוֹת *habitations of* Ps $74_{20}$ (unless em. נְאוֹת to אֲנָחָה וְ *sighing and*), ממלכת *kingdom of* Si $47_{21}$, סוד *council of* 1QH $6_5$, ימי *days of* Si $49_3$, הון *wealth of*, i.e. gained by 1QH $10_{23}$ ([חמס]) 1QS $10_{19}$, יֵין חֲמָסִים *wine of violence* Pr $4_{17}$ (|| רֶשַׁע *wickedness*), שִׂנְאַת חָמָס *hatred of violence*, i.e. violent hatred Ps $25_{19}$, כול חמס *all violence* 4QBibPar $1_8$.

<PREP> לְ *for (the purpose of)*, + בוא *come* Hb $1_9$=1QpHab $3_8$, פלס pi. *weigh out* Ps $58_3$ (if em.; see Cstr.), גבר htp. *display might* 4QpsMos[e] $2.1_9$ ([לחמס]); בְּ of accompaniment, *with, in* perh. 4QApocJos[a] $3_3$; בְּלֹא *without* 1 C $12_{18}$; מִן of direction, *from* 1QpHab $9_8$ $12_7$, + שׁוב *turn* Jon $3_8$, ישׁע hi. *save* 2 S $22_3$, נצל hi. *deliver* 4QBibPar $1_8$, גאל *redeem* Ps $72_{14}$ (|| תֹּךְ *oppression*); *on account of*, + היה *be* a desolation Jl $4_{19}$, שׁמם *be desolate* Ezk $12_{19}$, שׁלל *plunder* Hb $2_8$, חתת hi. *terrify* Hb $2_{17}$=1QpHab $12_1$, כסה pi. *cover* $Ob_{10}$; *as a result of*, + יצר ni. *be formed* Si $40_{15(B)}$; בִּגְלַל *on account of*, + סבב *turn* intrans. Si $10_8$, אבד *perish* 4QMMT $C_5$ ([בגלל]).

<COLL> וַתִּמָּלֵא הָאָרֶץ חָמָס *and the earth was filled with violence* Gn $6_{11}$, sim. $6_{13}$ Ezk $7_{23}$ (+ דָּם *blood*) Mc $6_{12}$ Ps $74_{20}$ (if em.; see Cstr.), חָמָס וָשֹׁד *violence and devastation* Jr $6_7$ $20_8$ Ezk $45_9$ Am $3_{10}$.

Also 4QMMT $C_4$ (ח[מס]).

<SYN> שֹׁד *devastation*, שֶׁבֶר *destruction*, עָמָל *mischief*, רִיב *strife*, מִרְמָה *deceit*, שֶׁקֶר *deceit*, דָּם *blood*, אָוֶן *iniquity*, רֶשַׁע *wickedness*, תֹּךְ *oppression*.*

→ חמס *be violent*.

**חמץ I** 4 vb. **be sour—Qal** 3 Pf. חָמֵץ; impf. יֶחְמַץ; inf. sf. חֲמְצָתוֹ—**be leavened,** <SUBJ> בָּצֵק *dough* Ex $12_{34.39}$ Ho $7_4$.

**Htp.** 1 Impf. יִתְחַמֵּץ—**be soured, be embittered,** <SUBJ> לֵבָב *heart* Ps $73_{21}$ (+ שׁנן htpo. *be pierced*).*

→ חָמֵץ *leavened*, חֹמֶץ *vinegar*, חָמִיץ *sorrel*, מַחְמֶצֶת *leavened thing*.

**חמץ II** 1 vb. **oppress—Qal** 1 Ptc. חוֹמֵץ—**1.** ptc. used as noun, **oppressor,** <SUBJ> אפס *cease* Is $16_4$ (if em. הַמֵּץ *the extortioner* to חֹמֵץ *[the] oppressor*). <CSTR> ... כַּף חוֹמֵץ *hand of the oppressor* Ps $71_4$ (|| עול pi. ptc. *unjust one*, + רָשָׁע *wicked one*). **2.** pass. ptc. used as noun, **oppressed one,** <OBJ> אשׁר pi. *correct* Is $1_{17}$ (if em. חָמוֹץ *oppressor*). <SYN> עול pi. ptc. *unjust one*.

→ חָמוֹץ *oppressor*.

**[חמץ] III** vb. **be red,** <SUBJ> רֶגֶל *foot* Ps $68_{24}$ (if em. תִּמְחַץ appar. *you will shatter* to תֶּחֱמַץ *it will be red*). <PREP> בְּ *on account of*, + דָּם *blood* Ps $68_{24}$ (if em.; see Subj.).

חָמֵץ 11.0.3 adj. **leavened, 1.** used attributively of לֶחֶם *bread* Lv 7$_{13}$ 11QT 18$_{14}$ ([לחם]). **2.** used as noun, **leavened thing, leaven,** <SUBJ> אכל ni. *be eaten* Ex 13$_{3}$, ראה ni. *be seen* Ex 13$_{7}$ (|| שְׂאֹר *leaven*). <OBJ> אכל *eat* Ex 12$_{15}$ Dt 16$_{3}$. <CSTR> חלות החמץ *the cakes of leaven,* i.e. leavened cakes 4Q251 2$_{4}$. <PREP> מִן partitive, *(some) of,* + קטר pi. *offer a sacrifice* Am 4$_{5}$; עַל *upon,* i.e. with, + זבח *sacrifice* Ex 23$_{18}$, שחט *slaughter* Ex 34$_{25}$. <COLL> לֹא תֵאָפֶה חָמֵץ *it shall not be baked (with) leaven* Lv 6$_{10}$, var. 23$_{17}$, כָּל־מִנְחָה ... לֹא תֵעָשֶׂה חָמֵץ *no cereal offering ... shall be made (with) leaven* Lv 2$_{11}$, לוא תאכל חמץ *it shall not be eaten leavened* 11QT 20$_{12}$.*

חֹמֶץ 6.0.1.1 n.m. **vinegar**—Q חומץ; cstr. חֹמֶץ—<NOM CL> אם עוד חמץ *if there is yet vinegar* Arad ost. 2. <OBJ> שׁתה *drink* Nm 6$_{3.3}$, שׁקה hi. *give to drink* Ps 69$_{22}$ (+ רֹאשׁ *poisonous plant*) 1QH 4$_{11}$. <CSTR> חֹמֶץ יַיִן *vinegar of,* i.e. made from, *wine* Nm 6$_{3}$, שֵׁכָר *of,* i.e. made from, *strong drink* Nm 6$_{3}$. <PREP> בְּ of place, *in,* + טבל *dip* Ru 2$_{14}$; כְּ *as* Pr 10$_{26}$ (כְּחֹמֶץ לַשִּׁנַּיִם *as vinegar to the teeth;* || עָשָׁן *smoke*). <COLL> חֹמֶץ עַל־נָתֶר *vinegar upon natron* Pr 25$_{20}$ (or em. עַל־נֶתֶק *upon a wound,* or em. חֹמֶץ עַל־נֶתֶק וּמַיִם עַל־נֶתֶר *vinegar upon a scab and water upon natron*). <SYN> עָשָׁן *smoke.*

⇒ חמץ *be sour.*

חמק 2 vb. **turn—Qal** 1 Pf. חָמַק—intrans. **turn away,** <SUBJ> דּוֹד *beloved* Ca 5$_{6}$ (|| עבר *pass*). <SYN> עבר *pass.*

**Htp.** 1 Impf. תִּתְחַמָּקִין—**turn hither and thither,** i.e. **waver,** <SUBJ> בַּת *daughter* Jr 31$_{22}$.

חמר I 4.1 vb. **foam—Qal** 2 Pf. חָמַר; impf. יֶחֶמְרוּ—**foam,** <SUBJ> מַיִם *water* Ps 46$_{4}$ (|| המה *roar*), יַיִן *wine* Ps 75$_{9}$ (or em. חֶמֶר *wine*). <SYN> המה *roar.*

**Pealal** 2 Pf. חֳמַרְמְרוּ (חֳמַרְמָרוּ)—**ferment,** <SUBJ> מֵעֶה *bowel* Lm 1$_{20}$ (+ הפך ni. *be turned*) 2$_{11}$ (+ כלה *be finished,* שׁפך ni. *be poured out*).*

**Hi.** 0.1 Impf. 2ms Si תחמיר—**cause to ferment,** <SUBJ> בֵּן *son* Si 4$_{2}$. <OBJ> מֵעֶה *bowels* of oppressed one Si 4$_{2}$.*

⇒ חֶמֶר *wine,* חמר *foaming.*

חמר II 1 vb. **cover with bitumen—Qal** 1 + waw וַתַּחְמְרָה—<SUBJ> אִשָּׁה *woman* Ex 2$_{3}$. <PREP> בְּ of instrument, *by (means of), with,* + חֵמָר *bitumen* Ex 2$_{3}$, זֶפֶת *pitch* Ex 2$_{3}$.

⇒ חֵמָר *bitumen.*

חמר III 1 vb. **be red—Pealal** 1 Pf. Kt חמרמרה, Qr חֳמַרְמְרוּ—**be reddened,** <SUBJ> פָּנִים *face* Jb 16$_{16}$. <PREP> מִן *on account of,* + בְּכִי *weeping* Jb 16$_{16}$.

חמר IV vb. **flay,** <SUBJ> Samson Jg 15$_{16}$ (if em. חֲמוֹר חֲמֹרָתַיִם *a heap, two heaps* to חָמוֹר חֲמַרְתִּים *I have utterly flayed them*). <OBJ> אִישׁ *man* Jg 15$_{16}$ (if em.; see Subj.).

חֶמֶר 2.2 n.[m.] **wine**—חֶמֶר—**(fermenting) wine,** <OBJ> שׁתה *drink* Dt 32$_{14}$ (+ דַּם עֵנָב *blood of grape*), רבה hi. *increase* Si 34$_{30}$. <CSTR> כֶּרֶם חֶמֶר *vineyard of wine* Is 27$_{2(mss)}$ (1QIsa[a] חומר *of wine;* L חֶמֶד *of desire*), יַיִן *wine of* Ps 75$_{8}$ (if em. חָמַר *it has foamed*). <PREP> בְּ of instrument, *with,* + נסה pi. *test* Si 37$_{27(Bmg, D}$ (ח[מר]; B בחייך *in your life*).*

חֵמָר 3 n.[m.] **bitumen,** <SUBJ> היה *be* Gn 11$_{3}$ (+ לְ *as mortar*). <CSTR> בֶּאֱרֹת חֵמָר *pits of bitumen* Gn 14$_{10}$. <PREP> בְּ of instrument, *with,* + חמר *cover* Ex 2$_{3}$ (|| זֶפֶת *pitch*). <SYN> זֶפֶת *pitch.*

⇒ חמר *cover with bitumen.*

חֹמֶר I 17.1.13 n.m. **clay**—cstr. חֹמֶר—**1. clay,** as material of vessels* Is 29$_{16}$=4QpIsa[c] 17$_{1}$ ([חמר]) Is 45$_{9}$ 64$_{7}$ Jr 18$_{4.6}$ Jb 10$_{9}$ (+ עָפָר *dust*), material of the human body Jb 4$_{19}$ (+ עָפָר) 13$_{12}$ (+ אֵפֶר *ashes*) 33$_{6}$ Si 36$_{10}$ (+ עָפָר) 1QH 1$_{21}$ 3$_{24}$ 4$_{29}$ 7$_{17}$ ([חמר]) 11$_{3}$ (+ עָפָר) 12$_{24}$ ([חמר]) 12$_{26}$ (+ עָפָר) 12$_{32}$ 18$_{12.26}$ ([חמר]) fr. 1$_{8}$ fr. 2$_{8}$ fr. 3$_{11.18}$ (both [חמר]) 1QS 11$_{22.22}$ 4QHod[b] 15$_{2}$ 4QShir[b] 28$_{4}$ ([חמר]), material in which seal impression is made Jb 38$_{14}$.

**2. clay,** as substance in the earth, **mud,** Is 10$_{6}$ 41$_{25}$ (+ טִיט *mud*) Na 3$_{14}$ (|| טִיט) Jb 27$_{16}$ (|| עָפָר *dust*) 30$_{19}$ (+ עָפָר, אֵפֶר *ashes*) Pr 12$_{12}$ (if em.; see Nom Cl.) 1QH 3$_{30}$.

**3. mortar,** Gn 11$_{3}$ (|| אֶבֶן *stone*) Ex 1$_{14}$ (|| לְבֵנָה *brick*).

<SUBJ> אמר *say* Is 45$_9$, שׁוב hi. *reply* 1QS 11$_{22}$, רעשׁ *quake* Pr 12$_{12}$ (if em.; see Nom. Cl.), קרץ pu. *be pinched off* 1QS 11$_{22}$.

<NOM CL> אֲנַחְנוּ הַחֹמֶר *we are the clay* Is 64$_7$, Pr 12$_{12}$ (if em. חָמַד רָשָׁע מְצוֹד רָעִים *the wicked one desires the net of evil ones* to חֹמֶר רֹעֵשׁ מְצוּדַת רָעִים *the fortress of evil ones is quaking clay*).

<CSTR> חֹמֶר חוּצוֹת *mud of the streets* Is 10$_6$; בָּתֵּי חֹמֶר *houses of clay* Jb 4$_{19}$, גַּבֵּי־חֹמֶר *responses of clay* Jb 13$_{12}$, יצר החמר *creature of clay* 1QH 1$_{21}$ 3$_{24}$ 4$_{29}$ (חמר) 7$_{17}$ ([חמר]) 11$_3$ 12$_{26.32}$ 18$_{12}$ (all four חמר) 18$_{26}$ ([ה]חמר) fr. 1$_8$ fr. 2$_8$ (י]צר חמר]) fr. 3$_{11.18}$ (both ה]חמר]) 4QHod$^b$ 15$_2$ 4QShir$^b$ 28$_4$ ([חמר]), אושי חמר *foundations of clay* 1QH 3$_{30}$, כ]לי חמר] *vessel of clay* Si 36$_{10}$.

<PREP> לְ of direction, *(in)to*, + ירה hi. *cast* Jb 30$_{19}$ (unless em. הוֹרַנִי *he has cast me* to הוֹרִדַנִי *he has brought me down*, i.e. ירד hi.); *as*, + היה *be* Gn 11$_3$ (+ חֵמָר *bitumen*); בְּ of place, *in*, + רמס *tread* Na 3$_{14}$; of instrument, *by (means of), with*, + עשׂה *make* Jr 18$_4$, מרר pi. *make* life *bitter* Ex 1$_{14}$; כְּ *as* Is 10$_6$ 41$_{25}$ Jr 18$_6$ Jb 10$_9$ 27$_{16}$ 38$_{14}$, חשׁב ni. *be reckoned* Is 29$_{16}$=4QpIsa$^c$ 17$_1$ ([כחמר ... יחשב]), שׁחת ni. *be spoilt* Jr 18$_{4(mss)}$; מִן of direction, *from*, + קרץ pu. *be pinched* Jb 33$_6$ 1QH 12$_{24}$ ([מחמר קו]רצתי]).

<SYN> §2 טִיט *mud*, עָפָר *dust*; §3 אֶבֶן *stone*, לְבֵנָה *brick*.*

**חֹמֶר II** 12.0.0.2 n.m. **homer**—cstr. חֹמֶר; pl. חֳמָרִים—unit of dry measure, sometimes liquid measure (Arad ost. 2$_5$), about 400 litres, equal to ten ephahs (Ezk 45$_{11}$), or ten baths of liquid measure (Ezk 45$_{11.14}$), <NOM CL> עֲשֶׂרֶת הַבַּתִּים חֹמֶר *ten baths are a homer* Ezk 45$_{14}$ (or del.) 45$_{14}$ (or em. הַכֹּר *the cor*). <OBJ> אסף *gather* Nm 11$_{32}$. <CSTR> חֹמֶר שְׂעֹרִים *homer of barley* Lv 27$_{16}$ Ezk 45$_{13}$ (הַשְּׂעֹרִים) Ho 3$_2$ (+ לֶתֶךְ *lethech*), הַחִטִּים *of wheat* Ezk 45$_{13}$; זֶרַע חֹמֶר *seed of*, i.e. measuring, *homer of* Lv 27$_{16}$ Is 5$_{10}$, מַעְשַׂר הַחֹמֶר *tenth of a homer* Ezk 45$_{11}$, עֲשִׂירִת *tenth of* Ezk 45$_{11}$, מלא החמר *fullness of a homer*, i.e. a full homer Arad ost. 2$_5$. <PREP> בְּ of price, *(in exchange) for*, + כרה *buy* Ho 3$_2$; מִן partitive, *(some) of, from* Ezk 45$_{13.13}$ 4QD$^f$ 1.2$_2$ ([החומר]), + ירד hi. *bring down* 4QD$^f$ 1.2$_1$ (ה[חו]מר]); אֶל *according to*, + היה *be* Ezk 45$_{11}$. <COLL> עֲשָׂרָה חֳמָרִים *ten homers* Nm 11$_{32}$, מלא החמר יין *a full homer of wine* Arad ost. 2$_5$.

Also perh. Kh. Rosh Zayit jar inscr.

**[חֹמֶר] III** 2 n.[m.] **foaming**—Q חומר; cstr. חֹמֶר—**1. foaming,** <CSTR> חֹמֶר מַיִם *foaming of waters* Hb 3$_{15}$. <PREP> בְּ of place, *in*, + דרך *tread* Hb 3$_{15}$. **2. (fermenting) wine,** <CSTR> כרם חומר *vineyard of wine* Is 27$_2$ (1QIsa$^a$; mss חֶמֶר *of wine*; L חֶמֶד *of desire*).*

→ חמר I *foam*.

**[חֹמֶר] IV** 2 n.[m.] **heap**—pl. חֳמָרִם—<COLL> וַיִּצְבְּרוּ אֹתָם חֳמָרִם חֳמָרִם *and they gathered them in heaps* Ex 8$_{10}$.*

**חַמְרָן** 1 pr.n.m. **Hamran,** son of Dishon and descendant of Seir, appar. ident. with Hemdan at Gn 36$_{26}$, <NOM CL> בְּנֵי דִישׁוֹן חַמְרָן וְאֶשְׁבָּן *the sons of Dishon were Hamran and Eshban* 1 C 1$_{41}$ (mss חֶמְדָּן *Hemdan*).

**חמשׁ** 5 vb. **be five—Qal** 4 Ptc. חֲמֻשִׁים—**1.** (masc.) **be grouped in fifties** in battle-readiness,* <SUBJ> בֵּן *son* of Israel Ex 13$_{18}$ (חֲמֻשִׁים עָלוּ *they went up grouped in fifties*; Sam mss חֲמִשִּׁים appar. *in fifties*), Reubenites, Gadites (and Manassites) Nm 32$_{17}$ (if em. נֵחָלֵץ חֻשִׁים *we shall equip ourselves, hastening* to נֵחָלֵץ חֲמֻשִׁים *we shall equip ourselves grouped in fifties*) Jos 1$_{14}$ (תַּעַבְרוּ חֲמֻשִׁים *you are to cross grouped in fifties*) 4$_{12}$ ( ... וַיַּעַבְרוּ חֲמֻשִׁים *and they crossed … grouped in fifties*), בֹּנֶה *builder* Ne 4$_{11}$ (if em. עֹמְשִׂים *were carrying*), נֹשֵׂא *bearer* Ne 4$_{11}$ (if em.), troops Jg 7$_{11}$ (אֶל־קְצֵה הַחֲמֻשִׁים אֲשֶׁר בַּמַּחֲנֶה *to the end*, i.e. edge, *of those who were grouped in fifties*, i.e. battle-ready troops, *who were in the camp*; or em. אֶל־קְצֵה to לְצַפּוֹת *to spy on*; ms חֲמִשִּׁים *fifty*). **2.** (fem.) **be grouped in fives, be fivefold, form pentagon,** הָאוּלָם וְהַמְּזוּזוֹת חֲמִשׁוֹת *the vestibule*, i.e. lintel, *and the doorposts were fivefold*, i.e. formed a pentagon 1 K 6$_{31}$ (if em. הָאַיִל מְזוּזוֹת חֲמִשִׁית *the pillar [and] doorposts were*, i.e. occupied, *a fifth*).

**Pi.** 1 + waw וְחִמֵּשׁ—**take a fifth (part of produce of),** <SUBJ> פַּרְעֹה *Pharaoh* Gn 41$_{34}$ (or em. וִיחַמְּשׁוּ *and let them* [officers] *take a fifth*), פָּקִיד *officer* Gn 41$_{34}$ (if em.). <OBJ> אֶרֶץ *land* of Egypt Gn 41$_{34}$. <PREP> לְ of benefit, *to, for*, + פַּרְעֹה *Pharaoh* Gn 47$_{26}$ (if em. לְפַרְעֹה לַחֹמֶשׁ

appar. *for Pharaoh a fifth* to לְחַמֵּשׁ לְפַרְעֹה *to take a fifth for Pharaoh*); בְּ of place/time, *in, during*, + שָׁנָה *year* Gn 41$_{34}$.

⇒ חָמֵשׁ *five*, חֲמִשִּׁים *fifty*, חֲמִישִׁי *fifth* (adj.), חֲמִישִׁית *fifth* (noun), חֹמֶשׁ *fifth* (noun).

**חָמֵשׁ** 344.0.34.2 n.m. and f. **five**—cstr. חֲמֵשׁ (L חָמֵשׁ); masc. חֲמִשָּׁה; cstr. חֲמֵשֶׁת—**1.** חָמֵשׁ/חֲמִשָּׁה (and חֲמֵשׁ/חֲמֵשֶׁת) **five** (or part of a larger number); alw. before pl. noun (unless otherwise noted), שָׁנָה *year* Gn 5$_{6.10}$ (sing.) 5$_{11.15}$ 5$_{17.21.23.26(Sam).28(Sam).30.30.31(Sam).32}$ 11$_{11.11.32}$ (all twelve sing.) 12$_4$ 25$_7$ (sing.) 45$_{6.11}$ Lv 27$_{5.6}$ Nm 8$_{24}$ Jos 14$_{10.10}$ (all three sing.) 2 S 4$_4$ 1 K 22$_{42.42}$||2 C 20$_{31.31}$ 2 K 14$_{2.17}$||2 C 25$_{1.25}$ 2 K 14$_{23}$ 15$_{33}$||2 C 27$_1$ 2 K 18$_2$||2 C 29$_1$ 2 K 20$_6$||Is 38$_5$ 2 K 21$_1$||2 C 33$_1$ 2 K 23$_{36}$||2 C 36$_5$ Is 7$_8$ 2 C 27$_8$ CD 10$_6$ (all twenty-two sing.) 1QM 2$_9$ 7$_3$ 1QSa 1$_{12}$ (both sing.) 2QJub$^a$ 23$_8$ ([חמש שנים]) 4QpGen$^a$ 1.2$_{9.10}$ ([חמש]) 4Q464 7$_1$ ([שנה]; all three sing.) Mur 24 2$_{10}$ ([ח]מ[ש שנים]) 3$_{13}$ ([שנים חמש]) 5$_{10}$ (numeral follows in both), יוֹם *day* Nm 11$_{19}$ Dn 12$_{12}$ (numeral follows) 4QD$^a$ 18.4$_{13}$, פַּעַם *occasion* 2 K 13$_{19}$.

אַמָּה *cubit* Gn 7$_{20}$ (sing.) Ex 27$_{1.1}$||38$_{1.1}$ 27$_{14}$||38$_{14}$ (both sing.) 27$_{18}$ 38$_{15}$ (sing) 38$_{18}$ 1 K 6$_{10.24.24}$||2 C 3$_{11.11}$ (numeral follows in both) 1 K 7$_{16}$||2 C 3$_{15}$ (numeral follows) 1 K 7$_{16}$ 2 K 25$_{17}$||Jr 52$_{22}$ (if em. שָׁלֹשׁ *three* in 2 K; 2 K Kt sing, Qr pl.) Ezk 40$_{7.13.25}$ (sing.) 40$_{29.30.33.36}$ (both sing.) 40$_{48}$ 41$_{2.2.9.11.12}$ 42$_{16(Kt)}$ 2 C 3$_{12.12.35}$ (numeral follows in all three; at 3$_{25}$ perh. em. 26; ||1 K 7$_{15}$ 25$_{17}$ 18) 6$_{13}$ (or del.) 6$_{13}$ 3QTr 2$_8$ (numeral follows) 11QT 7$_8$ ([אמ]ות]), תְּרוּמָה (cubits of) *contribution* Ezk 48$_{21}$ (sing.; or em. תְּרוּמָה to קָדִימָה *to the east*, as §3), טֶפַח *span* 1QM 5$_{14}$, קָנֶה *reed* (as unit of measurement) Ezk 42$_{16(Qr).17.18.19}$ (or del. קָנִים *reeds* in all four, as §3), יָד *hand*, i.e. portion Gn 43$_{34}$, סְאָה *seah* 1 S 25$_{18}$ Mur 30 2$_{14}$, כֹּר *kor* MurEpBarC$^b$$_2$, שֶׁקֶל *shekel* Ex 38$_{25}$ Lv 27$_{6.7}$ (sing.; or em. כֶּסֶף *silver*) Nm 3$_{47.47}$ 18$_{16}$ 1 S 17$_5$ Ezk 45$_{12}$ (if em. עֶשְׂרִים *twenty*) 45$_{12.12}$ (sing.; or em. חֲמִשִּׁים *fifty*) 4QOrd$^a$ 1.2$_9$ (sing.), כִּכָּר *talent* 1 C 29$_7$, מָנֶה *mina* Ezr 2$_{69}$ (5,000; ||Ne 7$_{70}$ 2,200) Ne 7$_{69}$ (if ins. מָנֶה; numeral follows in both), כֶּסֶף (piece of) *silver* Lv 27$_3$ (if em. שֶׁקֶל *shekel*) 2 K 6$_{25}$ Ho 3$_2$ 4QOrd$^a$ 1.2$_9$ ([חמ]שה [כ]סף; all four sing.), זָהָב (bar of) *gold* 3QTr 2$_4$ (sing., with numeral following), גּוֹרָל *lot* 4QPrQuot 1$_{21}$ ([חמש]ה גור[ל]ות).

חֲלִיפָה *change* of clothing Gn 45$_{22}$, מֹר (unit of) *myrrh* Ex 30$_{23}$ (singular, with numeral following), קִדָּה *cassia* Ex 30$_{24}$ (sing., with numeral following), עֵץ *tree* Jos 10$_{26}$, כְּתֹנֶת *tunic* Ne 7$_{69}$ (numeral follows; or ins. מָנֶה *mina*), יְרִיעָה *curtain* Ex 26$_{3.3.9}$||36$_{10.10(Sam).16}$, קֶלַע *curtain* Ex 27$_{15}$, בְּרִיחַ *bar* Ex 26$_{27.27}$||36$_{32.32}$, עַמּוּד *pillar* Ex 26$_{37}$||36$_{38}$ (numeral follows) 1 K 7$_3$ (numeral follows; or ins. וּמִסְפַּר הָעַמּוּדִים *and the number of the pillars* was forty-five, as §3), חַלָּק *smooth (stone)* 1 S 17$_{40}$, עִיר *city* Is 19$_{18}$ 1 C 4$_{32}$ (numeral follows), נִשְׁכָּה *chamber* 11QT 45$_2$ (sing.; [חמש ... נשכה]), טְחוֹר *haemorrhoid* 1 S 6$_{4(Qr)}$, עֹפֶל *tumour* 1 S 6$_{4(Kt)}$, לֶחֶם (loaf of) *bread* 1 S 21$_4$ (sing.).

אִישׁ *man* Gn 47$_2$ Jos 8$_{12}$ 1 S 22$_{18}$ (or em. 85 to 350; both sing.) 2 K 25$_{19}$ (or em. 50; ||Jr 52$_{25}$ 7) 1 C 4$_{42}$ (numeral follows) Ezk 8$_{16}$ (or del. חֲמִשָּׁה) 11$_1$ Est 9$_{6.12}$ 2 C 13$_{17}$ (all five sing.), נֶפֶשׁ *soul*, i.e. person Jr 52$_{30}$ (sing., with numeral following), נַעֲרָה *girl* 1 S 25$_{42}$, בֵּן *son* 2 S 19$_{18}$ 21$_8$ 2 S 9$_{10}$, מֶלֶךְ *king* Nm 31$_8$ Jos 10$_{5.16.17.22.23}$ Jg 18$_{2.7.14.17}$ 20$_{35.45.46}$ (all three sing.), סֶרֶן *governor* Jos 13$_3$ Jg 3$_3$ 1 S 6$_{16.18}$, נִצָּב *prefect* 1 K 5$_{29}$ (if em. 3,300 to 3,500), מְשֹׁרֵר *singer* Ezr 2$_{66}$||Ne 7$_{67}$ (if del. פֶּרֶד *mule* in Ezr; numeral follows in both), סוּס *horse* 2 K 7$_{13(mss)}$.

גָּמָל *camel* Ne 7$_{68}$ (or em. גְּמַלִּים 435 *camels* to גְּמַלֵּיהֶם *their camels* were, i.e. numbered 435, as §3 and ||Ezr 2$_{67}$; numeral follows), חֲמוֹר *ass* Nm 31$_{39.45}$ (numeral follows in both), אָתוֹן *she-ass* Jb 1$_3$, אַיִל *ram* Nm 7$_{17+11t}$ (numeral follows in all twelve), כֶּבֶשׂ *lamb* Nm 7$_{17+11t}$ (numeral follows in all twelve), עַתּוּד *goat* Nm 7$_{17+11t}$ (numeral follows in all twelve), בָּקָר (unit of) *cattle* Ex 21$_{37}$ (sing.) Nm 31$_{37(Sam)}$ 2 C 35$_9$ (sing., with numeral following), צֶמֶד (member of) *yoke* of cattle Jb 1$_3$ (sing.), צֹאן (member of) *flock* Nm 31$_{32}$ (sing., with numeral following) 1 S 25$_{18}$ (sing.) 2 C 35$_9$ (sing.; if ins. צאן), עַכְבָּר *mouse* 1 S 6$_4$ (lacking in 4QSam$^a$).

<CSTR> חֲמֵשֶׁת אֲלָפִים *five (of) thousand(s)* Nm 31$_{32}$ Jos 8$_{12}$ Jg 20$_{45}$ 1 S 17$_5$ (חֲמֵשֶׁת־) Ezk 45$_6$ 48$_{15}$ Ezr 1$_{11}$ 2$_6$ 2$_{67}$ (if em. שֵׁשֶׁת אֲלָפִים שְׁבַע מֵאוֹת וְעֶשְׂרִים *six thousand seven hundred and twenty* to חֲמֵשֶׁת אֲלָפִים חֲמִשָּׁה וְעֶשְׂרִים *five thousand and twenty-five*) 1 C 29$_7$ (חֲמֵשֶׁת־) 2 C 35$_9$.

חֲמֵשׁ מֵאוֹת *five (of) hundred(s)* Gn 5$_{30}$ (מֵאת) 5$_{32}$ 11$_{11}$ Ex 30$_{23.24}$ 38$_{26}$ Nm 1$_{21.33.41.46}$ 2$_{11.19.28.32}$ 3$_{22}$ 4$_{48}$ 26$_{18.22.27.37}$ 31$_{28(Sam)}$ (MT הַמֵּאוֹת) 31$_{36.39.43.45}$ 2 S 24$_{9}$ (חֲמֵשׁ־) 1 K 9$_{23}$ Ezk 42$_{17.18.19}$ (all three חֲמֵשׁ־) 42$_{20}$ 45$_{2.2}$ 48$_{16.16(Qr).16.16.30.32.33.34}$ Jb 1$_{3.3}$ Est 9$_{6.12}$ Ne 7$_{69}$ 1 C 4$_{42}$ 2 C 13$_{17}$ (חֲמֵשׁ־) 2 C 35$_{9}$.

חֲמֵשׁ עֶשְׂרֵה *five of ten,* i.e. fifteen Gn 5$_{10}$ 7$_{20}$ Ex 27$_{14.15}$||38$_{14.15}$ (38$_{14}$ חֲמֵשׁ־; L 27$_{15}$ חָמֵשׁ) 2 K 14$_{15}$||2 C 15$_{10}$ 2 K 14$_{23}$ 20$_{6}$||Is 38$_{5}$ 2 C 15$_{10}$ 3QTr 2$_{8}$ (ח[מ]ש עסרא).

חֲמֵשֶׁת עָשָׂר *five of ten,* i.e. fifteen Jg 8$_{10}$ 2 S 19$_{18}$.

חֲמֵשׁ הַיְרִיעֹת *five of the curtains* Ex 26$_{3.9}$||36$_{10.16}$ 36$_{10}$ (Sam).

חֲמֵשֶׁת שְׁקָלִים *five (of) shekels* Nm 3$_{47}$ 18$_{16}$.

חֲמֵשֶׁת מַלְכֵי *five (of) kings of* Nm 31$_{8}$ Jos 10$_{5.16.17.22.23}$ (all four חֲמֵשֶׁת הַמְּלָכִים *the five kings*), חֲמֵשֶׁת סַרְנֵי פְלִשְׁתִּים *five (of) lords of (the) Philistines* Jos 13$_{3}$, חֲמֵשֶׁת הַסְּרָנִים *the five governors* 1 S 6$_{18}$, חֲמֵשֶׁת הָאֲנָשִׁים *the five men* Jg 18$_{7.14.17}$, חֲמֵשֶׁת בְּנֵי מִיכַל *the five sons of Michal* 2 S 21$_{8}$ (or em. מֵירַב of *Merab*), חֲמֵשֶׁת עָשָׂר בָּנָיו *his fifteen sons* 2 S 19$_{18}$, חמשת כורין *five (of) kors* MurEpBarC$^{b}_{2}$.

[ימים] חמשת *five (of) days* 4QD$^{a}$ 18.4$_{13}$, שְׁנַת חֲמֵשׁ־עֶשְׂרֵה שָׁנָה *year of fifteen years,* i.e. the fifteenth year 2 K 14$_{23}$.

**2.** ordinal number, **fifth,** etc., esp. in dates, with noun in singular, יוֹם *day* Ex 16$_{1}$ Lv 23$_{6.34.39}$ Nm 28$_{17}$ 29$_{12}$ 33$_{3}$ 1 K 12$_{32.33}$ Ezk 45$_{25}$ (all ten בַּחֲמִשָּׁה עָשָׂר יוֹם *on the fifteenth day*) Est 9$_{21}$ (יוֹם־חֲמִשָּׁה עָשָׂר *fifteenth day*) 4QpGen$^{a}$ 1.1$_{7}$ (יום חמש *fifth day,* i.e. Thursday) 4QPrQuot 37.12$_{13}$ (יום חמשה [עשרים לחודש] *the twenty-fifth day of the month*), שָׁנָה *year* Ezk 40$_{1}$; with ellipsis of noun, גּוֹרָל *lot* 1 C 24$_{14}$ 25$_{22}$, שַׁעַר *gate* 4QPrQuot 1$_{14}$ ([בח]משה עשר שער[י] *in the fifteenth of the gates of* light), יוֹם *day* Jr 52$_{31}$ (or em. twenty-fifth to twenty-fourth; ||2 K 25$_{27}$ twenty-seventh [ms twenty-eighth]) Ezk 1$_{1.2}$ 8$_{1}$ 32$_{17}$ 33$_{21}$ (all six + לַחֹדֶשׁ *of the month*) Est 9$_{18}$ (+ בּוֹ *of it* [month]) Ne 6$_{15}$ (+ לֶאֱלוּל *of Elul*) 4Q317$_{1}$ ([בח]משה) 4QMishB$^{a}$ 1.1$_{1}$ ([בחמשה]) 1.1$_{3.7.8}$ 1.2$_{1.3}$ (all four [בחמשה]) 1.2$_{3}$ ([בח]משה) 1.2$_{4.7}$ ([בחמשה]) 2.1$_{2.3.3}$ 1.3$_{2.3.4.5.5}$ 4QMishB$^{b}$ 1.1$_{8.9}$ 1.2$_{3}$ 2$_{1.3.6.7.7}$ (all thirteen [בחמשה]) 3$_{1}$ ([בן]חמשה) 3$_{2.2}$ (both [בחמשה]) 4QMishC$^{b}$ 2$_{3}$ ([וחמשה]) 4QMishD 1$_{2}$ 4QMishE$^{b}$2.3$_{7}$ 4QMMT A 1$_{15}$ 3$_{7}$ 4QShirShabb$^{b}$ 1$_{1}$ ([בחמש]) (all thirty-five + בְּ *of* month) 4QPrQuot 1$_{6}$ 11QT 17$_{10}$ 27$_{10}$ (all three + לחודש *of the month*).

**3.** with elipsis of noun, **five persons, things, units,** etc. **a. units of measurement,** cubits 1 K 6$_{6}$ 7$_{23}$||2 C 4$_{2}$ Ezk 40$_{21}$ 1 C 11$_{23}$ (lacking in ||2 S 23$_{21}$) Ezk 42$_{16.17.18.19}$ (if del. קָנִים five hundred *reeds,* as §1, in all four) 42$_{20.20}$ 45$_{1.2.2.3.5.6.6}$ 48$_{8.9.10.10.13.13.15.15.20.20.21}$ (if em. תְּרוּמָה [cubits of] *contribution,* as §1, to קָדִימָה *to the east*) 48$_{21.30.32.33.34}$ 11QT 36$_{6}$ 40$_{7}$ ([שו]שים וחמש מאות), years 2 K 8$_{16}$ 2 C 15$_{10.19}$ 1QM 6$_{13.17}$ (חמש).

**b. human beings and beasts,** kings Gn 14$_{9}$, righteous Sodomites Gn 18$_{28.28.28}$, those who left Egypt Ex 38$_{26}$ Lv 26$_{8}$, members of tribes or tribal armies Nm 1$_{21.25.33.37.41.46}$ 2$_{11.15.19.23.28.32}$ Nm 26$_{18.22.27.37.41.50}$, post-exilic Judaeans Ezr 2$_{5}$ 2$_{8.20}$||Ne 7$_{13.25}$ Ezr 2$_{33}$ 2$_{34}$||Ne 7$_{36}$ Ne 7$_{20}$, Gershonite males Nm 3$_{22}$, Levites Nm 4$_{48}$, sons of Judah 1 C 2$_{4}$, sons of Perez 1 C 2$_{6}$, sons of Pedaiah (or em. Shealtiel) 1 C 3$_{20}$, sons of Izrahiah 1 C 7$_{3}$ (or del. וּבְנֵי יִזְרַחְיָה *and the sons of Izrahiah,* leaving בְּנֵי עֻזִּי *the* five *sons of Uzzi*), sons of Bela 1 C 7$_{7}$, followers of Zebah and Zalmunna Jg 8$_{10}$, Assyrian warriors 2 K 19$_{35}$||Is 37$_{36}$ Is 30$_{17}$=4QpIsa$^{c}$ 23.2$_{7}$, Uzziah's warriors 2 C 26$_{13}$, people of Judah 2 S 24$_{9}$, enemies of Jews Est 9$_{16}$, Solomon's foremen 1 K 9$_{23}$ (550; ||2 C 8$_{10}$ 250, =1 K 5$_{27}$ 3,300 [or em. 3,600, 3,700, or 3,500), souls of captive humans and beasts Nm 31$_{28}$ (or del. נֶפֶשׁ *soul*), horses 2 K 7$_{13}$, mules Ezr 2$_{66}$ (or del. פֶּרֶד *mule*), asses Ezr 2$_{67}$ (if em. 6,720 to 5,025), camels Ezr 2$_{67}$||Ne 7$_{68}$ (if em.), sheep Nm 31$_{36.37.43}$ 2 C 35$_{9}$ (or ins. צֹאן *flock,* as §1).

**c. items of furniture, etc.,** pillars 1 K 7$_{3}$ (if em.), cedar planks 1 K 7$_{3}$, bars Ex 26$_{26}$||36$_{31}$, shekels Ex 38$_{28}$ Nm 3$_{50}$, (laver) stands 1 K 7$_{39.39}$||2 C 4$_{6.6}$, lampstands 1 K 7$_{49.49}$ 2 C 4$_{7.7}$, tables 2 C 4$_{8.8}$, berries Is 17$_{6}$, songs 1 K 5$_{12}$.

<SUBJ> היה *be* Nm 1$_{46}$ 4$_{48}$ 31$_{37.43}$ 2 S 24$_{9}$ 1 K 5$_{12}$ Ezk 45$_{2}$ 1QM 6$_{10}$, יתר ni. *remain* Ezk 48$_{15}$, רדף *pursue* warriors Lv 26$_{8}$, רדה *rule* 1 K 9$_{23}$, עשׂה *do,* i.e. practise, valour 2 C 26$_{13}$, עזר *help* 2 C 26$_{13}$.

<NOM CL> (1) as subj. of nom. cl. with predicate introduced by לְ of benefit, *to, for* Ex 26$_{26}$||36$_{31}$, בְּ *in* Is 17$_{6}$, מִן *to* right, left 1 K 7$_{49.49}$, אֶל *at* corner Ezk 48$_{32}$ (or ins. מִדָּה *measurement* as subj. of nom. cl. and/or em.

אֶל to עַל), עַל *at* (right-hand, left-hand) side, corner 1 K 7$_{39.39}$ Ezk 48$_{32}$ (if em.), *under (charge of)* 2 C 26$_{13}$, אַחֲרֵי *after* 1 C 3$_{20}$ (if em. חֲשֻׁבָה *Hashubah* to אַחֲרֵי שׁוּבוֹ *after his return*), צָפוֹנָה *to the north* Ezk 48$_{10}$, נֶגְבָּה *to the south* Ezk 48$_{10}$ (if del. אֹרֶךְ its *length* is to be).

(2) as predicate of nom. cl., with subject בֵּן *son* Ezr 2$_{5}$ (775; or em. 756; ||Ne 7$_{10}$ 652 [or em. 752 or 672]) 2$_{8}$||Ne 7$_{13}$ (Ezr 945; or em. 970; Ne 845; or em. 840 or 854) Ezr 2$_{20}$||Ne 7$_{25}$ (or em. אִישׁ *man* in Ne) Ezr 2$_{33}$ (or em. אִישׁ; 725; ||Ne 7$_{37}$ 721 [mss 921 or 941]) 2$_{34}$||Ne 7$_{36}$ (or em. אִישׁ) Ne 7$_{20}$ (655; or em. 654; ||Ezr 2$_{15}$ 454) 1 C 2$_{4}$ 3$_{20}$ (or em.; see preceding section) 7$_{3}$ (or em. אַרְבָּעָה *four*) 7$_{7}$, אִישׁ *man* Ezr 2$_{33}$ Ne 7$_{25.36}$ (if em. בֵּן in all three), פקד pass. ptc. *mustered one* Nm 1$_{21.25.33.37.41}$ 2$_{11.15.19.23.28}$ 3$_{22}$ 26$_{41.50}$ (or in both em. לִפְקֻדֵיהֶם *according to their mustered ones*), צָבָא *army* Nm 2$_{11.15.19.23.28}$, גָּמָל *camel* Ezr 2$_{67}$||Ne 7$_{68}$ (if em. Ne; see last paragraph of §1), פֶּרֶד *mule* Ezr 2$_{66}$ (or del. פֶּרֶד, leaving מְשֹׁרֵר *singer*), חֲמוֹר *ass* Ezr 2$_{67}$ (if em. שֵׁשֶׁת אֲלָפִים שְׁבַע מֵאוֹת וְעֶשְׂרִים *six thousand seven hundred and twenty* to חֲמֵשֶׁת אֲלָפִים חֲמִשָּׁה וְעֶשְׂרִים *five thousand and twenty-five*; ||Ne 7$_{68}$ 6,720 [or em. 2,700 or 6,000]), מִסְפָּר *number* Nm 31$_{36}$ 1 K 7$_{3}$ (if ins. וּמִסְפַּר הָעַמּוּדִים *and the number of the pillars* was forty-five), קוֹמָה *height* 1 K 7$_{23}$||2 C 4$_{2}$, גֹּבַהּ *height* 11QT 36$_{6}$ (וגוב[הו]), רֹחַב *width* Ezk 40$_{21}$ 42$_{20}$ 45$_{6}$ 48$_{8}$ 11QT 40$_{7}$ ([רו]חב ... שו[שים וחמש מאות]), אֹרֶךְ *length* Ezk 42$_{20}$ 45$_{1.3.5.6}$ 48$_{9.10}$ (or del.) 48$_{13.13}$, מִדָּה *measurement* Ezk 48$_{30.32}$ (if ins. מִדָּה) 48$_{33.34}$ (if ins. מִדָּה), פֵּאָה *corner* Ezk 48$_{34}$ (or ins. מִדָּה), יָצִיעַ *first storey* 1 K 6$_{6(Qr)}$ (or em. צֵלָע *rib*, i.e. side chamber and/or ins. עשׂה *make* first storey/side chamber five [cubits]), טוּר *row* 1 K 7$_{3}$, חֹל *profane(ness)* Ezk 48$_{15}$, תְּרוּמָה *contribution* Ezk 48$_{20}$, כְּלִי *vessel* Ezr 1$_{11}$, כֹּל *all* 1 C 2$_{6}$.

**<OBJ>** חסר *lack* Gn 18$_{28}$, מצא *find* Gn 18$_{28}$, לקח *take* Nm 3$_{50}$ 2 K 7$_{13}$, רום hi. *raise*, i.e. take 2 C 35$_{9}$ (or ins. צֹאן *flock*, as §1), נתן *give*, i.e. place 2 C 4$_{6.6.7.7}$, נוח hi. *cause to rest*, i.e. place 2 C 4$_{8.8}$, מדד *measure* Ezk 42$_{16.17.18.19}$ (if del. קָנִים *reeds*, as §1, in all four), נכה hi. *strike* 2 K 19$_{35}$||Is 37$_{36}$, הרג *kill* Est 9$_{16}$ (or em. חֲמִשָּׁה שִׁבְעִים אֶלֶף *seventy-five thousand* to שִׁבְעִים אֶלֶף וּמֵאָה *seventy thousand, one hundred*), עשׂה *make* into hooks Ex 38$_{28}$.

**<CSTR>** גַּעֲרַת חָמֵשׁ *rebuke of five (warriors)* Is 30$_{17}$= 4QpIsa[c] 23.2$_{7}$, שְׁנַת חָמֵשׁ *year (of) five (years)*, i.e. (in) the fifth year 2 K 8$_{16}$ 2 C 15$_{10}$ (חֲמֵשׁ־עֶשְׂרֵה *fifteen*) 15$_{19}$ (שְׁנַת־שְׁלֹשִׁים וְחָמֵשׁ *year of thirty-five*), בן חמש וארבעים *a son of*, i.e. person aged, *forty-five (years)* 1QM 6$_{13.17}$ (בן חמש] [וארבעים).

**<APP>** names of children 1 C 3$_{20}$ 7$_{3.7}$, ראשׁ *head* 1 C 7$_{7}$, גִּבּוֹר *mighty one* 1 C 7$_{7}$, כֶּסֶף *silver* Nm 3$_{50}$, חַיִל *force* 2 C 26$_{13}$, רוּחַ *spirit*, i.e. side Ezk 42$_{16.17.18.19}$ (if del. קָנִים *reeds*, as §1, in all four).

**<PREP>** לְ *in respect of* Ex 38$_{26}$; בְּ of place, *in*, + היה *be* Ezk 45$_{3}$; of cause, *on account of*, + שׁחת hi. *destroy* Gn 18$_{28}$; of instrument, *(multiplied) by* Ezk 48$_{20}$, + היה *be* Ezk 45$_{2}$; כְּ *as*, i.e. approximately Jg 8$_{10}$; מִן partitive, *(some) of, from among, out of*, + רום hi. *raise*, i.e. take one (human being or beast) Nm 31$_{28}$; אֵת *against* Gn 14$_{9}$; עַל־פְּנֵי *in front of* Ezk 48$_{15.21}$ (if em. תְּרוּמָה [cubits of] *contribution*, as §1, to קָדִימָה *to the east*) 48$_{21}$.

**<COLL>** §3 חָמֵשׁ בָּאַמָּה *five (in) cubit(s)* 1 K 6$_{6}$ 7$_{23}$||2 C 4$_{2}$ 1 C 11$_{23}$ Ezk 40$_{21}$ (חָמֵשׁ וְעֶשְׂרִים *twenty-five*) 11QT 36$_{6}$ (חמש [וארבעים באמה] *forty-five in cubit[s]*) 40$_{7}$ (שו[שים] [וחמש מאות באמה] *five hundred and sixty in cubit[s]*).

§1 חֲמֵשֶׁת חֲמֵשֶׁת שְׁקָלִים לַגֻּלְגֹּלֶת *five shekels for each person* Nm 3$_{47}$, חָמֵשׁ נַעֲרֹתֶיהָ *her five girls* 1 S 25$_{42}$, חָמֵשׁ אוֹ־שֵׁשׁ *five or six* times 2 K 13$_{19}$, אַרְבָּעָה חֲמִשָּׁה *four [or] five* berries Is 17$_{6}$.

§§1–3 חֲמִשָּׁה, חָמֵשׁ as part of larger numbers: 15 Gn 7$_{20}$ Ex 27$_{14.15}$||38$_{14.15}$ Lv 27$_{7}$ 2 S 9$_{10}$ 19$_{18}$ (both + 20) 1 K 7$_{3}$ 2 K 14$_{17}$||2 C 25$_{25}$ 2 K 20$_{6}$||Is 38$_{5}$ Ezk 45$_{12}$ (if em. 25) Ho 3$_{2}$ 3QTr 2$_{8}$ 4QMishB[a] 1.2$_{3}$ ([בחמשה עשר]) 1.2$_{4}$ ([חמשה [עשר]) (בחמשה [עשר]) 4QMishB[b] 1.1$_{8}$ 3$_{1.2}$ (all three חמשה [עשר]) 4QMMT A 1$_{15}$ 4QPrQuot 1$_{14}$ ([בח]משה עשר) 11QT 17$_{10}$ 27$_{10}$.

25 Nm 8$_{24}$ 1 K 22$_{42}$||2 C 20$_{31}$ 2 K 14$_{2}$||2 C 25$_{1}$ 2 K 15$_{33}$||2 C 27$_{1}$ 2 K 18$_{2}$||2 C 29$_{1}$ 2 K 23$_{36}$||2 C 36$_{5}$ Jr 52$_{31}$ (or em. 24; ||2 K 25$_{27}$ 27 [ms 28]) Ezk 8$_{16}$ (or em. 20) 11$_{1}$ 40$_{25.29.33.36}$ 45$_{12}$ (or em. 15) 2 C 27$_{8}$ CD 10$_{6}$ 1QM 7$_{3}$ 1QSa 1$_{12}$ (חמש ועש[ר]ים) 4QOrd[a] 1.2$_{9}$ ([עשרים ו]חמשה) 4QMishB[a] 1.1$_{1}$ ([בחמשה] ועש[רים]) 4QMishC[b] 2$_{3}$ ([בעש]רים וחמשה) 4QMishD 1$_{2}$ 4QMMT A 3$_{7}$ 4QShir Shabb[b] 1$_{1}$ ([בחמש] ועשרים) 4Q464 7$_{1}$ (חמש עשרא) 4QPr Quot 37.12$_{13}$ ([חמשה] [עשרים]).

35 Gn 11$_{12}$ (Sam 135) 1 K 22$_{42}$||2 C 20$_{31}$ 2 C 3$_{15}$ (or em. 26; ||1 K 7$_{15}$, =1 K 25$_{17}$ 18) 1QM 2$_{9}$; 45 Gn 18$_{28}$ Jos 14$_{10}$ 1 K 7$_{3}$ Ne 7$_{25(ms)}$ 1QM 6$_{13.17}$ ([חמש וארבעים]) 11QT 36$_{6}$ (חמש [וארבעים]).

53 Gn 5$_{28(Sam)}$ (MT 182); 55 2 K 21$_{1}$||2 C 33$_{1}$; 65 Gn 5$_{15.21}$ Is 7$_{8}$ 3QTr 2$_{4}$ 4QpGen$^{a}$ 1.2$_{10}$ ([ששי]ם וחמש); 75 Gn 12$_{4}$, 85 Jos 14$_{10}$ 1 S 22$_{18}$ (or em. 305 or 350); 95 Ezr 2$_{20}$||Ne 7$_{25}$ (or em. 3005; ms [Ne] 45).

105 Gn 5$_{6}$; 135 Gn 11$_{12(Sam)}$ (MT 35); 145 Gn 11$_{32(Sam)}$ (MT 205); 175 Gn 25$_{7}$ 2QJub$^{a}$ 23$_{8}$ ([מאה ושבעים] [וחמש]); 195 Gn 5$_{6}$.

205 Gn 11$_{32}$ (Sam 145); 245 Ezr 2$_{34}$ (if em. 345) 2$_{66}$||Ne 7$_{67}$; 305 1 S 22$_{18}$ (if em. 85); 345 Ezr 2$_{34}$||Ne 7$_{36}$ (or em. 245 in Ezr); 365 Gn 5$_{23}$; 435 Ezr 2$_{67}$||Ne 7$_{68}$.

500 Gn 5$_{32}$ 11$_{11}$ Ex 30$_{23.24}$ Nm 31$_{28}$ Ezk 42$_{16(Qr).17.18.19.20.20}$ 45$_{2.2}$ Jb 1$_{3.3}$ Est 9$_{6.12}$ Ne 7$_{69}$ (if em. 530) 1 C 4$_{42}$ 2 C 35$_{9}$; 530 Ne 7$_{69}$ (or ins. כֶּסֶף מָנִים thirty tunics and five hundred *silver minas*); 550 1 K 9$_{23}$; 560 11QT 40$_{7}$ ([ש]שים וחמש מאות); 586 11QT 45$_{2}$ ([שש ושמונים וחמש מאות]); 595 Gn 5$_{30}$ (Sam 600); 653 Gn 5$_{26(Sam)}$ (MT 782; or em. 802]) 5$_{31(Sam)}$ (MT 777); 654 Ne 7$_{20(ms)}$; 655 Ne 7$_{20}$ (||Ezr 2$_{15}$ 454), 675 Nm 31$_{37}$; 725 Ezr 2$_{33}$ (||Ne 7$_{37}$ 721 [mss 921, 941]); 745 Jr 52$_{30}$; 775 Ezr 2$_{5}$ (or em. 756; ||Ne 7$_{10}$ 652 [or em. 672 or 752]).

815 Gn 5$_{10}$; 845 Ne 7$_{13}$ (or em. 840 or 854; ||Ezr 2$_{8}$ 945); 895 Gn 5$_{17}$; 945 Ezr 2$_{8}$ (or em. 970; ||Ne 7$_{13}$ 845); 995 Gn 5$_{11}$.

1,005 1 K 5$_{12}$ (or em. 5,000); 1,335 Dn 12$_{12}$; 1,365 Nm 3$_{50}$; 1,775 Ex 38$_{25.28}$; 3,500 1 K 5$_{29}$ (if em. 3,300); 4,500 Ezk 8$_{16.16.16.16.30.32.33.34}$.

5,000 Jos 8$_{12}$ Jg 20$_{45}$ 1 S 17$_{5}$ 1 K 5$_{12}$ (if em. 1,005) Ezk 45$_{6}$ 48$_{15}$ Ezr 2$_{69}$ 1 C 29$_{7}$ 2 C 35$_{9}$; 5,025 Ezr 2$_{67}$ (if em. 6720; ||Ne 7$_{68}$ 6,720 [or em. 2700 or 6,000]); 5,469 Ezr 1$_{11}$; 5,500 2 C 35$_{9}$; 6,500 1QM 6$_{10}$; 7,500 Nm 3$_{22}$; 8,580 Nm 4$_{48}$; 15,000 Jg 8$_{10}$ Est 9$_{16}$ (if em. 75,000).

25,000 Jg 20$_{46}$ Ezk 45$_{1.3.5.6}$ 48$_{8.9.10.10.13.13.15.20.21.21}$; 25,100 Jg 20$_{35}$; 30,500 Nm 31$_{39.45}$; 32,500 Nm 26$_{37}$; 35,400 Nm 1$_{37}$ 2$_{23}$; 40,500 Nm 2$_{19}$ 26$_{18}$; 41,500 Nm 1$_{41}$ 2$_{28}$; 45,400 Nm 26$_{50}$; 45,500 Nm 1$_{33}$; 45,600 Nm 2$_{11}$ 26$_{41}$; 46,500 Nm 1$_{21}$ 2$_{11}$; 45,650 Nm 1$_{25}$ 2$_{15}$; 60,500 Nm 26$_{27}$.

75,000 Est 9$_{16}$ (or em. 15,000 or 70,100); 76,500 Nm 26$_{22}$; 185,000 2 K 19$_{35}$||Is 37$_{36}$; 307,500 2 C 26$_{13}$; 337,500 Nm 31$_{36.43}$; 500,000 2 S 24$_{9}$ 2 C 13$_{17}$; 603,550 Ex 38$_{26}$ Nm 1$_{46}$ 2$_{32}$; 675,000 Nm 31$_{32}$.

Also 4QPrQuot 1$_{20}$ 37.12$_{19}$ ([חמשה]) Eshtemoa jug inscr. Weight 53 (Samaria, 8th cent.).

⇒ חמש *be five*.

**חֹמֶשׁ** I 1.0.2 n.[m.] **fifth**—sf. Q חומשה; pl. Q חומשים—**a.** in ref. to fifth part of produce of Egypt, <PREP> לְ appar. introducing object, + שׂים *place*, i.e. appoint for Pharaoh Gn 47$_{26}$ (or em. הַחֹמֶשׁ *the fifth*, or לַחְמֹשׁ לְפַרְעֹה *to take a fifth for Pharaoh*). **b.** appar. of fifth part of Pentateuch or Psalter and in pl. to Pentateuch or Psalter as a whole, <APP> [ס]פרים חומשים *books (of the) Pentateuch/Psalter* 1Q30 1$_{4}$. **c.** of fifth part of redemption fee, <NOM CL> וחומשה עליה *and its fifth is to be added to it* 4QD$^{e}$ 9.2$_{10}$

⇒ חמש *be five*.

**חֹמֶשׁ** II 4 n.[m.] **abdomen**, <PREP> אֶל *in(to)*, + נכה hi. *strike* 2 S 2$_{23}$ 3$_{27}$ (if ins. אֶל; mss עַל *against*; 4QSam$^{a}$ עַד *unto*) 4$_{6}$ (or em. וַיַּכֻּהוּ אֶל־הַחֹמֶשׁ *and they struck him in the abdomen* to וַתָּנָם וַתִּישָׁן *and she fell asleep and was [still] sleeping*) 20$_{10}$ (4QSam$^{a}$ עַל). <COLL> וַיַּכֵּהוּ שָׁם הַחֹמֶשׁ *and they struck him there, in the abdomen* 2 S 3$_{27}$ (or ins. אֶל *in[to]*).*

**חֲמִשִׁי**, see חֲמִישִׁי *fifth*.

**חֲמִשִּׁים** 165.0.30 n.m. and f. **fifty**—Sam חמישים; sf. חֲמִשֶּׁיךָ, חֲמִשָּׁיו, חֲמִשֵּׁיהֶם—**1. fifty**, preceding noun in plural unless otherwise noted, שָׁנָה *year* Gn 9$_{28.29}$ Lv 25$_{10.11}$ Nm 4$_{3.23.30.35.39.43.47}$ 8$_{25}$ (all eight + בֶּן *son* of, i.e. person aged, fifty years) 2 K 15$_{2}$||2 C 26$_{3}$ 2 K 15$_{23.27}$ 21$_{1}$||2 C 33$_{1}$ CD 14$_{9}$ 1QM 2$_{4}$ 7$_{1}$ (erased ששים *sixty*; all three + בֶּן; alw. sing.), יוֹם *day* Gn 7$_{24}$ 8$_{3}$ Lv 23$_{16}$ Ne 6$_{15}$ 4QpGen$^{a}$ 1.1$_{7.8}$ 11QT 18$_{13}$ ([חמשים]) 19$_{13}$ 21$_{14}$ (alw. sing.).

אַמָּה *cubit* Gn 6$_{15}$ Ex 27$_{12.13}$||38$_{12(Sam).13}$ 1 K 7$_{2.6}$ Ezk 40$_{15.21.25.29.33.36}$ 42$_{2.7.8}$ 45$_{2}$ Est 5$_{14}$ 7$_{9}$ 11QT 31$_{11}$ (sing. except at Ezk 42$_{2}$), שֶׁקֶל *shekel* Lv 27$_{3.16}$ Nm 31$_{52}$ (all three sing.) Jos 7$_{21}$ 2 K 15$_{20}$ 24$_{24}$ (numeral follows) Ezk

45$_{12}$ (sing.; if em. חֲמִשָּׁה *five*), כִּכָּר *talent* Ezr 8$_{26}$ (numeral follows) 2 C 8$_{18}$ (sing.; ||2 K 9$_{28}$ עֶשְׂרִים *twenty*), כֶּסֶף (piece of) *silver* Dt 22$_{29}$=11QT 66$_{10}$ (sing.).

לוּלִי *loop* Ex 26$_{5.5.10.10}$||36$_{12.12.17}$ (numeral follows at 36$_{17}$), קֶרֶס *hook* Ex 26$_{6.11}$||36$_{13.18}$ (numeral follows at 26$_{11}$||36$_{18}$), מַחְתָּה *fire holder* Nm 16$_{17}$, מִזְרָק *bowl* Ne 7$_{69}$ (numeral follows), פּוּרָה *winepress* Hg 2$_{16}$ (+ עֶשֶׂר *ten*, עֶשְׂרִים *twenty*), מָגֵן *shield* 1QM 7$_{14}$ (sing.), נִשְׁכָּה *chamber* 11QT 44$_{8.12}$ (sing. at 44$_{8.12[erased]}$).

אִישׁ *man* Nm 16$_2$ (numeral follows) 16$_{35}$ 26$_{10}$ 1 S 6$_{19}$ (lacking in mss) 1 S 22$_{18}$ (if em. 85 to 350) 2 S 15$_1$ 1 K 1$_5$ 18$_{22}$ 18$_{4.13}$ 2 K 2$_7$ (sing. in all ten) 2$_{16.17}$ 15$_{25}$ (sing. in both) 2 K 25$_{19}$ (if em. 5; ||Jr 52$_{25}$ 7) Ne 5$_{17}$ (sing.), שַׂר *prince* 1 K 9$_{23}$||2 C 8$_{10}$ (numeral follows) 1QM 7$_{15.15}$ ([חמשים], with ellipsis of noun), פָּרָשׁ *rider* 2 K 13$_7$, עֶבֶד *servant* 2 K 1$_{13}$, צַדִּיק *righteous one* Gn 18$_{24.24.26.28}$, נָבִיא *prophet* 1 K 18$_{19}$ (numeral follows).

גָּמָל *camel* 1 C 5$_{21}$ (numeral follows), צֹאן (member of) *flock* 1 C 5$_{21}$ (sing.; numeral follows).

שִׁיר *song* 11QPs$^a$ 27$_7$.

**2.** with ellipsis of noun, **fifty persons, things, units,** etc. **a. units of measurement,** cubits Ex 27$_{12}$||38$_{12(Sam)}$ 27$_{18}$ 30$_{23.23}$ 38$_{12}$ Ezk 48$_{17.17.17.17}$ appar. 4Qp254a 1$_2$ ([חמ]שים) 11QT 40$_{12}$, pieces of cinnamon and cane Ex 30$_{23}$, pieces of silver 1 K 10$_{29}$||2 C 1$_{17}$, watches 4QM$^d$$_3$, years 1QM 6$_{13}$ 7$_{1.7(erased).2}$, tithes 11QT 60$_9$.

**b. human beings and beasts,** warriors Jg 7$_{11(ms)}$ 2 K 1$_{9+12t}$ 1 C 12$_{34}$ 1QM 2$_{16}$ 3$_{17.17}$ (all three [חמשים]) 4$_{3.4}$ 6$_{10}$ 4QPsJos$^a$ 3.2$_7$ ([חמ]שים) 4QM$^a$ 1$_{10}$ 11QT 57$_4$, those who left Egypt Ex 13$_{18(Sam mss)}$ 18$_{21.25}$ 38$_{26}$ Nm 1$_{46}$ 2$_{32}$, members of tribes or tribal armies Nm 1$_{23.25.29.31.43}$ 2$_{6.8.13.15.16.16.30.31}$ 26$_{34.47}$, inhabitants of postexilic Judaea Ezr 2||Ne 7 Ezr 8$_{3.6}$ 1 C 9$_8$, Kohathites Nm 4$_{36}$, those bound by covenant CD 13$_1$ 1QS 2$_{22}$ 1QSa 1$_{14}$ (ח[מ]שים) 2$_1$, descendants of Ulam 1 C 8$_{40}$, resident aliens 2 C 2$_{16}$, redeemed persons 4QOrd$^a$ 1.2$_9$, human beings and beasts Nm 31$_{30.47}$.

**c. items of furniture, etc.,** curtains Ex 38$_{12}$.

**d. David's compositions,** 11QPs$^a$ 27$_{7.10}$.

<SUBJ> היה *be* Nm 4$_{36}$ (§2b) Ezk 48$_{17.17.17.17}$ (all four §2a) 11QPs$^a$ 27$_{10}$ (§2d), יחשׂ htp. *be genealogically enrolled* Ezr 8$_3$ (§2b), עלה *go up* 2 K 1$_9$ (§2b; if em. וַיַּעַל *and he* [commander] *went up* to וַיַּעֲלוּ *and they went up*).

<NOM CL> §§2a and 2c [רוחבה ... חמ]שים perh. *fifty (cubits) ... was its width* 4Qp254a 1$_2$, רֹחַב חֲמִשִּׁים בַּחֲמִשִּׁים appar. *(its) width is to be fifty (cubits) in (all) fifty (cubits),* i.e. fifty cubits throughout Ex 27$_{18}$ (Sam בָּאַמָּה fifty units *in cubit[s]*, רוחב השערים חמשים באמה *the width of the gates was fifty (in) cubits* 11QT 40$_{12}$, לִפְאַת־יָם קְלָעִים חֲמִשִּׁים בָּאַמָּה *to the south were curtains, fifty (units) in cubits* Ex 38$_{12}$ (Sam, ||27$_{12}$ חֲמִשִּׁים אַמָּה *fifty cubits*), משמרות [ראשי אבות העדה שנים וחמשים] *the watches of the heads of the fathers of the congregation are to be fifty-two* 4QM$^d$$_3$ (=1QM$^a$ 2$_1$ lacks משמרות).

§2b אֲחֵיהֶם ... חֲמִשִּׁים וְשִׁשָּׁה *their brothers ... were,* i.e. numbered, nine hundred and *fifty-six* 1 C 9$_8$ (or em. תִּשְׁעִים וְתִשְׁעָה nine hundred and *ninety-nine*), וְעִמּוֹ חֲמִשִּׁים הַזְּכָרִים *and with him fifty were,* i.e. numbered, *the males* Ezr 8$_6$, פְּקֻדֵיהֶם ... תִּשְׁעָה וַחֲמִשִּׁים אֶלֶף *their mustered ones ... were fifty-nine thousand* Nm 1$_{23}$ 2$_{13}$, sim. Nm 1$_{29.31.43}$ 2$_{6.8}$ (in both צְבָאוֹ וּפְקֻדָיו *his army and his mustered ones* [or em. וּפְקֻדֵיהֶם *and their mustered ones*]) 2$_{16}$ (כָּל־הַפְּקֻדִים *all the mustered ones*) 2$_{30}$ (צְבָאוֹ וּפְקֻדֵיהֶם) 2$_{31}$ (כָּל־הַפְּקֻדִים) 26$_{34}$ (or em. לִפְקֻדֵיהֶם *according to their mustered ones*), פְּקֻדֵיהֶם ... וַחֲמִשִּׁים *their mustered ones ... were* forty-five thousand six hundred and *fifty* (members of tribe) Nm 1$_{25}$ 2$_{15}$, sim. 2$_{16}$ (כָּל־הַפְּקֻדִים) 2$_{32}$ (כָּל־פְּקֻדֵי הַמַּחֲנֹת *all the mustered ones of the camps*), בְּנֵי עֵילָם ... חֲמִשִּׁים *the sons of Elam were* one thousand, two hundred and *fifty*-four (inhabitants of Judaea) Ezr 2$_{7.30}$||Ne 7$_{12.34}$ (or em. 1,854 at 7$_{12}$ and/or 2,250 at 7$_{30}$), sim. Ezr 2$_{14.15}$||Ne 7$_{20}$ Ezr 2$_5$||Ne 7$_{10}$ (if em. 775 at 2$_5$; or em. 672) Ezr 2$_{22}$ 2$_{29.37.60}$||Ne 7$_{33.40.62}$ (if em. 642 at 7$_{62}$), יוֹצְאֵי צָבָא ... חֲמִשִּׁים *those who go out to war ... were,* i.e. numbered, *fifty* thousand (warriors) 1 C 12$_{34}$, חמשים למערכה [הא]חת *fifty (warriors) are to the one battle line* 1QM 6$_{10}$, הַחֲמִשִּׁים אֲשֶׁר בַּמַּחֲנֶה *the fifty (warriors) who were in the camp* Jg 7$_{11}$ (or em. אֶל־קְצֵה to לְצַפּוֹת *to spy on*; L הַחֲמֻשִׁים *those who were grouped in fifties*).

<OBJ> (mainly §2b) מצא *find* 2 C 2$_{16}$, לקח *take* Ex 30$_{23.23}$ (both §2a), שׁלח *send* 2 K 1$_{9.11.13}$, אכל *eat,* i.e. destroy 2 K 1$_{10.10.12.12.14}$.

<CSTR> §2a בן חמשים *son of fifty (years),* i.e. fifty-year

old man 1QM 6$_{13}$ 7$_1$ (both + אַרְבָּעִים *forty*) 7$_{1(erased).2}$.

§2b שַׂר־חֲמִשִּׁים *prince*, i.e. commander, *of fifty (warriors)* 2 K 1$_{9.10}$ (שַׂר הַחֲמִשִּׁים) 1$_{11.13.13}$ (שַׂר־הַחֲמִשִּׁים [or del.]) Is 3$_3$ 1QM 3$_{17}$ ([שר החמשים]) 4$_4$ (שר החמשים), שָׂרֵי חֲמִשִּׁים *princes of fifty* Ex 18$_{21.25}$ Dt 1$_{15}$ 1 S 8$_{14}$ (all four + אֶלֶף *thousand*, מֵאָה *hundred*, עֶשֶׂר *ten* [if ins. מֵאָה and עֶשֶׂר at 1 S]) 1 K 1$_{14}$ (הַחֲמִשִּׁים) 1QSa 1$_{14}$ (שרי ח[מ]שים) 4QPsJosa 3.2$_7$ ([שרי הח]משים) 11QT 57$_4$ (both + עֶשֶׂר, מֵאָה, אֶלֶף), אות החמשים *standard of the fifty (warriors)* 1QM 3$_{17}$ ([אות החמשים]) 4$_3$ (+ מֵאָה, אֶלֶף, עֶשֶׂר) 4$_{17}$ ([אות החמשים]), אֶל־קְצֵה הַחֲמִשִּׁים *to the end*, i.e. edge, *of fifty (warriors)* Jg 7$_{11(ms)}$ (L חֲמֻשִׁים *those who were grouped in fifties*; or em. אֶל־קְצֵה to לִצְפּוֹת *to spy on*).

<APP> §2a קִנְּמָן־בֶּשֶׂם מַחֲצִיתוֹ חֲמִשִּׁים ... וּקְנֵה־בֹשֶׂם חֲמִשִּׁים *fragrant cinnamon, half as much, (that is)* two hundred and *fifty (units), and fragrant cane*, two hundred and *fifty (units)* Ex 30$_{23}$.

§2b עבר ptc. *one who passes*, i.e. is entered into records Ex 38$_{26}$, בֵּן *son* 1 C 8$_{40}$ (or em. תִּשְׁעִים *ninety*).

<ADJ> (§2b) אַחֵר *other* 2 K 1$_{11}$ (if em. אַחֵר *another* commander to אֲחֵרִים *another* fifty), שְׁלִישִׁי *third* 2 K 1$_{13}$ (or em. שְׁלֹשִׁים *third* fifty to שְׁלִישִׁי *third* commander or שְׁלִישִׁית *a third time*), perh. רִאשׁוֹן *first* 2 K 1$_{14}$ (unless רִאשׁוֹן qualifies שַׂר *commander*).

<PREP> §2b לְ of possession, *of, (belonging) to* 1QSa 2$_1$ (שר[י]ם ... לחמשים *princes ... of fifties*; + אֶלֶף *thousand*, מֵאָה *hundred*, עֶשֶׂר *ten*); of benefit, *to, for* 4QOrda 1.2$_9$; *in accordance with* Ex 38$_{26}$, + עבר *pass* 1QS 2$_{22}$ (+ אֶלֶף, מֵאָה, עֶשֶׂר); *by*, i.e. in groups of CD 13$_1$ 1QM 2$_{16}$ ([ל ... חמשים]) 4QMa 1$_{10}$ (all three + אֶלֶף, מֵאָה, עֶשֶׂר).

§2a בְּ appar. of place, *in*, רֹחַב חֲמִשִּׁים בַּחֲמִשִּׁים appar. *(its) width is to be fifty (cubits), in (all) fifty (cubits)*, i.e. fifty cubits throughout Ex 27$_{18}$ (Sam בָּאַמָּה fifty units *in cubit[s]*); *at the cost of*, סוּס בַּחֲמִשִּׁים וּמֵאָה *a horse was at the cost of one hundred and fifty (pieces of silver)* 1 K 10$_{29}$||2 C 1$_{17}$ (or del. וּמֵאָה).

§2a–b מִן partitive, *(some) of, from among* 11QT 60$_9$, + לקח *take* one (human being or beast) Nm 31$_{30.47}$, עשׂה *do*, i.e. cause to be employed as 2 C 2$_{16}$; אֶל *to*, + דבר pi. *speak* 2 K 1$_{12}$ (or em. אֲלֵיהֶם *to them* to אֵלָיו *to him* [commander]).

<COLL> §2a חֲמִשִּׁים בָּאַמָּה *fifty (units) in cubits* Ex 27$_{18(Sam)}$ 38$_{12}$.

§2b חֲמִשִּׁים עָלוּ appar. *in fifties they went up* Ex 13$_{18(Sam mss)}$ (MT חֲמֻשִׁים *being grouped in fifties*).

§1 חֲמִשִּׁים הַצַּדִּיקִם *the fifty righteous* Gn 18$_{24.28}$, הַחֲמִשִּׁים ... אִישׁ *the fifty ... men* Nm 16$_{35}$ (Sam חֲמִשִּׁים), גְּמַלֵּיהֶם חֲמִשִּׁים *fifty* thousand *of their camels* 1 C 5$_{21}$, בִּשְׁנַת חֲמִשִּׁים שָׁנָה לַעֲזַרְיָה *in the year of fifty years*, i.e. in the fiftieth year, *of (the reign of) Azariah* 2 K 15$_{23}$ (or em. אַרְבָּעִים *forty*), שְׁנַת הַחֲמִשִּׁים שָׁנָה *the year of fifty years*, i.e. the fiftieth year Lv 25$_{10.11}$, חֲמִשִּׁים חֲמִשִּׁים אִישׁ בַּמְּעָרָה appar. *fifty men to a cave* or *men in groups of fifty throughout the cave country* or *men by fives to a cave** 1 K 18$_4$ (if ins. חֲמִשִּׁים) 18$_{13}$ (or em. בִּמְעָרָתַיִם *in two caves* in both).

§§1–2 חֲמִשִּׁים as part of larger numbers: 52 2 K 15$_2$ ||2 C 26$_3$ 2 K 15$_{27}$ Ezr 2$_{29}$||Ne 7$_{33}$ Ne 6$_{15}$ 1QM 2$_4$ 11QT 44$_{12}$ 11QPsa 22$_7$; 54 11QT 44$_8$; 55 2 K 21$_1$||2 C 33$_1$; 56 Ezr 2$_{22}$ (or em. 55); 150 Gn 7$_{24}$ 8$_3$ 1 K 10$_{29}$||2 C 1$_{17}$ (or em. 50) Ezr 8$_3$ Ne 5$_{17}$ 1 C 8$_{40}$ (or em. 190) 4QpGena 1.1$_{7.8}$; 250 Ex 30$_{23.23}$ Nm 16$_{2.17.35}$ 26$_{10}$ Ezk 48$_{17.17.17.17}$ Ezr 8$_6$ (if em 50) 2 C 8$_{10}$; 350 Gn 9$_{28}$ 1 S 22$_{18}$ (if em. 85); 450 2 K 18$_{19.22}$ 2 C 8$_{18}$ (||2 K 9$_{28}$ 420); 454 Ezr 2$_{15}$ (||Ne 7$_{20}$ 655).

550 1 K 9$_{23}$; 650 Ezr 8$_{26}$; 652 Ezr 2$_{60}$||Ne 7$_{62}$ (if em. 642 at 7$_{62}$) Ne 7$_{10}$ (||Ezr 2$_5$ 775; or em. 672 or 752); 654 Ne 7$_{20(ms)}$; 655 Ne 7$_{20}$ (||Ezr 2$_{15}$ 454); 752 Ne 7$_{10}$ (if em. 652; ||Ezr 2$_5$ 775); 756 Ezr 2$_5$ (if em. 775; ||Ne 7$_{10}$ 655); 950 Gn 9$_{29}$; 956 1 C 9$_8$ (or em. 999).

1,052 Ezr 2$_{37}$||Ne 7$_{40}$ (or em. 254); 1,254 Ezr 2$_{7.30}$||Ne 7$_{12.34}$ (or em. 1,854 at 7$_{12}$ and/or 2,250 at 7$_{30}$); 2,056 Ezr 2$_{14}$ (||Ne 7$_{19}$ 2,067); 1,854 Ne 7$_{12}$ (if em.); 2,750 Nm 4$_{36}$; 4,050 11QPsa 27$_{10}$; 16,750 Nm 31$_{52}$; 45,650 Nm 1$_{25}$ 2$_{15}$; 50,000 1 S 6$_{19}$ (lacking in mss) 1 C 5$_{21}$ 12$_{34}$; 52,700 Nm 26$_{34}$ ; 53,400 Nm 1$_{43}$ 2$_{30}$ 26$_{47}$; 54,400 Nm 1$_{29}$ 2$_6$; 57,400 Nm 1$_{31}$ 2$_8$; 59,300 Nm 1$_{23}$ 2$_{13}$; 151,450 Nm 2$_{16}$; 153,600 2 C 2$_{16}$; 157,600 Nm 2$_{31}$; 250,000 1 C 5$_{21}$; 603,550 Ex 38$_{26}$ Nm 1$_{46}$ 2$_{32}$.

→ חמשׁ *be five*.

**חֲמֻשִׁים**, see חמשׁ *be five*, Qal.

**חַמַּת I** $_1$ pr.n.m. **Hammath,** ancestor of the Rechabites (unless חַמָּה III *family*), <APP> אָב *father* 1 C 2$_{55}$. <PREP> מִן of direction, *from*, + בוא *come* 1 C 2$_{55}$.

**חַמַּת II** $_1$ pl.n. **Hammath,** town in Naphtali, perh. El-Ḥammām, 2 km S of Tiberias, appar. ident. with Hammon at 1 C 6$_{61}$ and Hammoth-dor at Jos 21$_{32}$, <NOM CL> עָרֵי הַמִּבְצָר ... חַמַּת *the fortified cities are ... Hammath* Jos 19$_{35}$.

**חֲמָת** $_{36}$ pl.n. **Hamath**—+ ה- of direction חֲמָתָה—city in Syria, on River Orontes, 214 km NNE of Damascus, <SUBJ> גבל *border* Zc 9$_2$, בושׁ *be ashamed* Jr 49$_{23}$, ידה hi. *praise* Ps 76$_{11}$ (if em.; see Cstr.). <NOM CL> אִם־לֹא כְאַרְפַּד חֲמָת *or is not Hamath like Arpad?* Is 10$_9$, זֶה גְּבוּל הָאָרֶץ ... חֲמָת *this is the border of the land ... Hamath* Ezk 47$_{16}$ (or transfer before לְבוֹא at 47$_{15}$). <OBJ> שׁוב hi. *recover* 2 K 14$_{28}$. <CSTR> חֲמָת אֲרָם *Hamath of Aram* Ps 76$_{11}$ (if em. חֲמַת אָדָם *wrath of humanity*); אֱלֹהֵי חֲמָת *gods of Hamath* 2 K 18$_{34}$||Is 36$_{19}$, מֶלֶךְ *king of* 2 S 8$_9$ 2 K 19$_{13}$||Is 37$_{13}$ 1 C 18$_9$, אַנְשֵׁי *men of* 2 K 17$_{30}$, יַד *hand*, i.e. side, *of* Ezk 48$_1$, אֶרֶץ *land of* 2 K 23$_{33}$ 2 K 25$_{21}$||Jr 52$_{27}$ Jr 39$_5$ 52$_9$, גְּבוּל *border of* Ezk 47$_{16.17}$, לְבוֹא חֲמָת perh. *entrance of Hamath*, but prob. name of area *Lebo-hamath* Nm 13$_{21}$ 34$_8$ (both לְבֹא) Jos 13$_5$ Jg 3$_3$ 1 K 8$_{65}$ 2 K 14$_{25}$ Ezk 47$_{16}$ (if em.; see Nom. Cl.) Ezk 47$_{20}$ 48$_1$ Am 6$_{14}$ 1 C 13$_5$ 2 C 7$_8$. <ADJ> רַב *great* Am 6$_2$. <PREP> בְּ of place, *in*, + בנה *build* 2 C 8$_4$; מִן of direction, *from*, + בוא hi. *bring* 2 K 17$_{24}$, קנה *buy* Is 11$_{11}$ (or em. מֵחִתִּים *from the Hittites* or מֵאַחְמְתָא *from Ecbatana*). <COLL> חֲמָת + הלך *go (to)* Am 6$_2$, נכה hi. *defeat (towards)* 1 C 18$_3$

⇒ חֲמָת צוֹבָה *Hamath-zobah*, לְבוֹא חֲמָת *Lebo-hamath*

**חֵמֶת** $_3$ n.[m.] **skin (bottle)**—cstr. חֵמַת—<OBJ> לקח *take* Gn 21$_{14}$, מלא pi. *fill* with water Gn 21$_{19}$. <CSTR> חֵמַת מַיִם *skin of water* Gn 21$_{14}$. <PREP> מִן of direction, *from*, + כלה *be finished* Gn 21$_{15}$.

**חַמֹּת דֹּאר** $_1$ pl.n. **Hammoth-dor,** town in Naphtali, appar. ident. with Hammath at Jos 19$_{35}$ and Hammon at 1 C 6$_{61}$, <OBJ> נתן *give* Jos 21$_{32}$ (+ מִגְרָשׁ *pasture land*).

**חֲמָתִי** $_2$ gent. **Hamathite,** collective, inhabitant of Hamath, <OBJ> ילד *give birth*, i.e. beget Gn 10$_{18}$||1 C 1$_{16}$.

⇒ חֲמָת *Hamath.*

**חֲמָת צוֹבָה** $_1$ pl.n. **Hamath-zobah,** perh. the combined regions of Hamath and Zobah, <PREP> עַל *against*, + חזק *be strong*, i.e. prevail 2 C 8$_3$ (or em. בֵּית צוֹבָה *Beth-zobah*). <COLL> חֲמָת צוֹבָה + הלך *go (to)* 2 C 8$_3$ (or em.; see Prep.)

⇒ חֲמָת *Hamath*, צוֹבָה *Zobah.*

**חֵן I** $_{69.11.3}$ n.m. **favour**—cstr. חֵן; sf. חִנּוֹ—**favour, grace,** with human beings (e.g. Gn 30$_{27}$ 32$_6$ 34$_{11}$ 39$_4$ 50$_4$ Ex 3$_{21}$ Nm 32$_5$ Dt 24$_1$ 1 S 1$_{18}$ 16$_{22}$ 20$_3$ 27$_5$ 2 S 14$_{22}$ 1 K 11$_{19}$ Pr 3$_4$ 22$_1$ Ru 2$_2$ Ec 9$_{11}$ Est 2$_{15}$ 5$_8$ Si 4$_{21}$ 42$_1$ 44$_{23}$), with God (e.g. Gn 6$_8$ Ex 33$_{12}$ 34$_9$ Nm 11$_{11}$ 2 S 15$_{25}$ Jr 31$_2$ Pr 3$_4$ Si 3$_{18[C]}$), **charm, elegance,** of woman (Na 3$_4$=4QpNah 3.2$_7$ Pr 11$_{16}$ 31$_{30}$ Si 7$_{19}$ 9$_8$ 26$_{15}$), of doe (Pr 5$_{19}$), of ornament (Pr 1$_9$ 3$_{22}$ 4$_9$), of stone (Pr 17$_8$), of speech (Ps 45$_3$ Pr 22$_{11}$ Si 6$_5$).

<SUBJ> היה *be* Pr 3$_{22}$ (+ לְגַרְגְּרֹתֶיךָ *for your neck*; || חַיִּים *life*), כון ni. *be established* Si 36$_{24(Bmg)}$ (appar. error for חךְ *palate*), יצק ho. *be poured* Ps 45$_3$, נצח *flash* Si 35$_{10}$.

<NOM CL> שֶׁקֶר הַחֵן *charm is deception* Pr 31$_{30}$ (|| יֹפִי *beauty*), דִּבְרֵי פִי־חָכָם חֵן *the words of the mouth of a wise one are favour* Ec 10$_{12}$, חֵן שְׂפָתָיו רְצוֹן מֶלֶךְ *grace of lips is*, i.e. wins, *the favour of a king* Pr 22$_{11}$ (if em. רֵעֵהוּ *his friend* to רְצוֹן *favour of*), מִכֶּסֶף וּמִזָּהָב חֵן טוֹב *favour is better than silver or gold* Pr 22$_1$, לֹא לַיֹּדְעִים חֵן *favour is not to those who know* Ec 9$_{11}$ (|| עֹשֶׁר *riches*, לֶחֶם *bread*), חֵן חֵן לָהּ *grace, grace be to it* Zc 4$_7$.

<OBJ> מצא *find* Gn 6$_8$ 18$_3$ 19$_9$ 30$_{27}$ 32$_6$ 33$_{8.10.15}$ 34$_{11}$ 39$_4$ 47$_{25.29}$ 50$_4$ Ex 33$_{12.13.13.16.17}$ 34$_9$ Nm 11$_{11.15}$ 32$_5$ Dt 24$_1$ Jg 6$_{17}$ 1 S 1$_{18}$ 16$_{22}$ 20$_{3.29}$ 25$_8$ 27$_5$ 2 S 14$_{22}$ 15$_{25}$ 16$_4$ 1 K 11$_{19}$ Jr 31$_2$ Pr 3$_4$ (+ שֵׂכֶל *insight*) 28$_{23}$ Ru 2$_{2.10.13}$ Est 5$_8$ 7$_3$ 8$_5$ Si 3$_{18(C)}$ 42$_1$ 44$_{23}$ 4QDibHam$^c$ 125$_3$ (וימצ[או]), נתן *give* Gn 39$_{21}$ Ex 3$_{21}$ 11$_3$ 12$_{36}$ Ps 84$_{12}$ (|| כָּבוֹד *honour*) Pr 3$_{34}$ 13$_{15}$, נשׂא *bear* Est 2$_{15.17}$ (|| חֶסֶד *favour*) 5$_2$.

<CSTR> חֵן הָעָם *favour of*, i.e. for, *the people* Ex 3$_{21}$ 11$_3$ 12$_{36}$, חֵן שְׂפָתָיו *grace of lips* Pr 22$_{11}$ (unless *one who is gracious of speech*, i.e. חנן *be gracious*, §2); אֵשֶׁת־חֵן *woman of charm* Pr 11$_{16}$ Si 9$_8$ (+ יֳפִי *beauty*), טוֹבַת *a good one of*

Na $3_{4}$=4QpNah $3.2_{7}$ (+ כֶּשֶׁף *sorcery*) Si $7_{19}$, בושי appar. *those ashamed of* Si $35_{10}$, יַעֲלַת־ *doe of* Pr $5_{19}$ (|| אַהַב *loved one*), שפתי *lips of* Si $6_{5}$, רוּחַ *spirit of* Zc $12_{10}$ (|| תַּחֲנוּנִים *supplication*),* לִוְיַת *garland of* Pr $1_{9}$ $4_{9}$ (|| תִּפְאֶרֶת *beauty*), אֶבֶן *stone of* Pr $17_{8}$, בשת חן וכבוד *a shame (worthy) of favour and honour* Si $4_{21}$(C) (A כבוד וחן *honour and favour*).

<PREP> לְ introducing predicate, or *as*, + היה *be* Zc $6_{14}$ (if em. וּלְחֵן בֶּן־צְפַנְיָה לְזִכָּרוֹן *and to Hen the son of Zephaniah as a memorial* to וּלְבֶן־צְפַנְיָה לְחֵן וּלְזִכָּרוֹן *and to the son of Zephaniah as favour and a memorial,* i.e. a favourable memorial).

<COLL> חֵן *favour* + בְּעֵינֵי *in the sight of* Gn $6_{8}$ $18_{3}$ $19_{9}$ $30_{27}$ $32_{6}$ $33_{8.10.15}$ $34_{11}$ $39_{4.21}$ $47_{25.29}$ $50_{4}$ Ex $3_{21}$ $11_{3}$ $12_{36}$ $33_{12.13.13.16.17}$ $34_{9}$ Nm $11_{11.15}$ $32_{5}$ Dt $24_{1}$ Jg $6_{17}$ 1 S $1_{18}$ $16_{22}$ $20_{3.29}$ $25_{8}$ $27_{5}$ 2 S $14_{22}$ $15_{25}$ $16_{4}$ 1 K $11_{19}$ Pr $3_{4}$ Ru $2_{2.10.13}$ Est $2_{15}$ $5_{2.8}$ $7_{3}$ Si $3_{18}$(C) $42_{1}$ $44_{23}$ 4QDibHam^c $12_{5.3}$ (בע[יניכה]), לִפְנֵי *before* Est $2_{17}$ $8_{5}$; חֵן וָחֶסֶד *grace and favour* Est $2_{17}$, חֵן וְכָבוֹד *favour and honour* Ps $84_{12}$ Si $4_{21}$(C), כבוד וחן *honour and favour* Si $4_{21}$(A), חֵן וְתַחֲנוּנִים *favour and supplication* Zc $12_{10}$, חֵן וְשֵׂכֶל טוֹב *favour and good insight* Pr $3_{4}$.

Also Si $26_{15}$ 4Q415 $28_{1}$.

<SYN> יְפִי *beauty*, תִּפְאֶרֶת *beauty*, כָּבוֹד *honour*, חֶסֶד *favour*, חַיִּים *life*, עֹשֶׁר *riches*, לֶחֶם *bread*, אַהַב *loved one*, תַּחֲנוּנִים *supplication*.*

→ חנן *be gracious.*

**חֵן II** 1 pr.n.m. **Hen,** son of Zephaniah, <APP> בֵּן *son* Zc $6_{14}$ (or em.; see Prep.). <PREP> לְ of benefit, *to, for,* + היה *be* Zc $6_{14}$ (or em. וּלְיֹאשִׁיָּה *and to Josiah*, or em. וּלְחֵן בֶּן־צְפַנְיָה לְזִכָּרוֹן *and to Hen the son of Zephaniah for a memorial* to לְבֶן־צְפַנְיָה לְחֵן וּלְזִכָּרוֹן *to the son of Zephaniah for favour and as a memorial*).

**[חַנָּא]** 0.0.0.1 pr.n.[m.]. **Hanna,** recipient of goods, Samaria ost. $30_{3}$ (others חנאב *Hanniab*)

→ חנן *be gracious.*

**[חַנִּאָב]** 0.0.0.1 pr.n.[m.]. **Hanniab,** recipient of goods, Samaria ost. $30_{3}$ (others חנא *Hanna*)

→ חנן *be gracious* + אָב *father.*

**חנג** 0.1 vb. **dance—Htp.** 0.1 Impf. Si 2ms תתחנג—**dance,** <SUBJ> בֵּן *son* Si $37_{29}$(Bmg, D) (perh. error for ענג htp. *take delight*; B שׁפך pu. *be poured,* i.e. be caused to slip). <PREP> עַל *on account of, for* + מַטְעָם *delicacy* Si $37_{29}$ (Bmg, D).

**חֵנָדָד** 4 pr.n.m. **Henadad,** father of Bavvai and Binnui, <CSTR> בֶּן־חֵנָדָד *son of Henadad* Ne $3_{18.24}$, בְּנֵי *sons of* Ezr $3_{9}$ Ne $10_{10}$.

**חנה I** 143.3.7 vb. **encamp—Qal** 143.3.7 Pf. חָנָה, חָנִיתִי, חָנוּ; impf. תַּחֲנֶה, תַּחֲנוּ, יַחֲנוּ; + waw וַיִּחַן, וַיַּחֲנוּ (וַיִּחֲנוּן), וַנַּחֲנֶה; impv. חֲנֵה, חֲנוּ; ptc. חֹנֶה (Q חונה, חֹנֵךְ), fs. חֹנָה, pl. חוֹנִים (חֹנִים); inf. חֲנוֹת (חֲנֹת, חֲנֹתֵנוּ, חֲנֹתְכֶם)—**encamp,** in encampment of any sort (e.g. Gn $26_{17}$ $33_{18}$ Ex $14_{9}$ 1 S $11_{1}$ Is $29_{1}$ Zc $9_{8}$); **decline,** of day towards evening (Jg $19_{9}$).

<SUBJ> ׳י *Y.* Is $29_{3}$ Zc $9_{8}$, אֵל *God* 4Q421 $12_{3}$, מַלְאַךְ *angel* of Y. Ps $34_{8}$.

עַם *people* Ex $15_{27}$ Nm $12_{16}$ Jos $4_{19}$ $8_{11}$ Jg $7_{1}$ 1 S $26_{5}$ 1 K $16_{15.16}$ 1 C $19_{7}$, Amalekites Jg $6_{4.33}$, Midianites Jg $6_{4.33}$, Philistines Jg $15_{9}$ 1 S $4_{1}$ $13_{5.16}$ $17_{1}$ $28_{4}$ 2 S $23_{13}$, Sihon Jg $11_{20}$, Israel Ex $19_{2}$ Nm $10_{31}$ Jos $10_{31.34}$ Jg $11_{18}$ 1 S $4_{1}$ $28_{4}$ $29_{1}$ 2 S $17_{26}$, Israelite(s) Nm $10_{5.6}$, מַחֲנֶה *army* Nm $2_{3}$ Jos $10_{5}$ Ps $27_{3}$ 1 C $11_{15}$, חַיִל *army* 2 K $25_{1}$||Jr $52_{4}$, גְּדוּד *troop* Jb $19_{12}$, enemy Ps $53_{6}$, עֵדָה *congregation* Ex $17_{1}$, מַטֶּה *tribe* Nm $2_{5.12.27.34}$, מִשְׁפָּחָה *family* Nm $3_{23.29.35}$, מִשְׁמָר *division* perh. 11QT $45_{5}$, רֹאשׁ *head* of ancestral house Ezr $8_{15}$.

Aaron Nm $3_{38}$, Abimelech Jg $9_{50}$, Absalom 2 S $17_{26}$, David 2 S $12_{28}$ Is $29_{1}$, Ezra Ezr $8_{15}$, Gideon Jg $7_{1}$, Hobab Nm $10_{31}$, Isaac Gn $26_{17}$, Jacob Gn $33_{18}$, Joab 2 S $11_{11}$ $24_{5}$, Joshua Jos $10_{31.34}$, Moses Ex $18_{5}$ Nm $3_{38}$ $10_{31}$, Nahash 1 S $11_{1}$, Nebuchadnezzar 2 K $25_{1}$||Jr $52_{4}$, Saul 1 S $17_{2}$ $26_{3.5}$ $28_{4}$, Sennacherib 2 C $32_{1}$.

מֶלֶךְ *king* Jos $10_{5.5.5.5.5}$ $11_{5}$ 1 C $19_{7}$ 2 C $32_{1}$, אָדוֹן *lord* 2 S $11_{11}$, שַׂר *prince,* i.e. commander of army Nm $31_{19.19}$ 2 S $24_{5}$, לֵוִי *Levite* Nm $1_{50.53}$ $2_{17}$, גִּבּוֹר *mighty one* 1QH $2_{25}$, archer Jr $50_{29}$, wise Si $4_{13}$(A), עֶבֶד *servant* 2 S $11_{11}$, אֱנוֹשׁ *human being* Si $14_{24}$(A), אִישׁ *man* Jg $18_{12}$ 1 S $17_{1}$, בֵּן *son* of Israel Ex $13_{20}$ $14_{2.2.9}$ $17_{1}$ $19_{2}$ Nm $1_{52}$ $2_{2.2}$ $9_{17.18.18.20.22.23}$ $21_{10.11.12.13}$ $22_{1}$ $33_{5+41t}$ Dt $1_{33}$ Jos $5_{10}$ Jg $10_{17}$

$20_{19}$ 2 K $20_{27}$, of Aaron Nm $3_{38}$, of Judah Ne $11_{30}$, of east Jg $6_{4.33}$, of Ammon Jg $10_{17}$, of light 1QM $1_3$, אזן hi. ptc. *one who listens* Si $4_{15(A)}$, פקד pass. ptc. *one who is appointed* Nm $31_{19}$, עָתוּד *one who is ready* 1QM $15_2$.

מִשְׁכָּן *tabernacle* Nm $1_{51}$, יוֹם *day* Jg $19_9$, רֶכֶב *chariot* 1 C $19_7$, גֹּבַי *locusts* Na $3_{17}$, אֵלֶּה *these* 1 K $20_{29}$; subj. not specified, 4Q421 $11_4$ 4QMª $1_6$.

<PREP> לְ *beside*, + צָבָא *host* Nm $1_{52}$.

לְ *at*, + בַּיִת *house* Zc $9_8$.

חנה סָבִיב לְ *encamp around*, + אֹהֶל *tent* Nm $2_2$ Jb $19_{12}$.

בְּ of place, *in, at, among*, + עַבְרֹנָה *Abronah* Nm $33_{34}$, עַלְמֹן דִּבְלָתַיִם *Almon-diblathaim* Nm $33_{46}$, אָלוּשׁ *Alush* Nm $33_{13}$, אֲפֵק *Aphek* 1 S $4_1$, עֲרוֹעֵר *Aroer* 2 S $24_5$, בְּנֵי יַעֲקָן *Bene-jaakan* Nm $33_{31}$, דִּיבֹן גָּד *Dibon-gad* Nm $33_{45}$, דָּפְקָה *Dophkah* Nm $33_{12}$, אֵתָם *Etham* Ex $13_{20}$ Nm $33_6$, עֶצְיוֹן גֶּבֶר *Ezion-geber* Nm $33_{35}$, גִּלְבֹּעַ *Gilboa* 1 S $28_4$, גִּלְעָד *Gilead* Jg $10_{17}$, גִּלְגָּל *Gilgal* Jos $4_{19}$ $5_{10}$, חֲרָדָה *Haradah* Nm $33_{24}$, חַשְׁמֹנָה *Hashmonah* Nm $33_{29}$, חֲצֵרֹת *Hazeroth* Nm $33_{17}$, הֹר *Hor* Nm $33_{37}$, חֹר הַגִּדְגָּד *Horhag-gidgad* Nm $33_{32}$, עִיֵּי הָעֲבָרִים *Iye-abarim* Nm $21_{11}$ $33_{44}$, יָהְצָה *Jahaz* Jg $11_{20}$, יָטְבָתָה *Jotbathah* Nm $33_{33}$, יְהוּדָה *Judah* Jg $15_9$, קְהֵלָתָה *Kehelathah* Nm $33_{22}$, קִבְרֹת הַתַּאֲוָה *Kibroth-hattaavah* Nm $33_{16}$, קִרְיַת יְעָרִים *Kiriath-jearim* Jg $18_{12}$.

לִבְנָה *Libnah* Nm $33_{20}$, מַקְהֵלֹת *Makheloth* Nm $33_{25}$, מָרָה *Marah* Nm $33_8$, מִכְמָשׂ *Michmash* 1 S $13_{5.16}$, מִתְקָה *Mithkah* Nm $33_{28}$, מִצְפָּה *Mizpah* Jg $10_{17}$, מֹסֵרוֹת *Moseroth* Nm $33_{30}$, אֹבֹת *Oboth* Nm $21_{10}$ $33_{43}$, פּוּנֹן *Punon* Nm $33_{42}$, רְפִידִים *Rephidim* Ex $17_1$ Nm $33_{14}$, רִמֹּן פֶּרֶץ *Rimmon-perez* Nm $33_{19}$, רִסָּה *Rissah* Nm $33_{21}$, רִתְמָה *Rithmah* Nm $33_{18}$, שׁוּנֵם *Shunem* 1 S $28_4$, סֻכֹּת *Succoth* Nm $33_5$, תַּחַת *Tahath* Nm $33_{26}$, תֵּבֵץ *Thebez* Jg $9_{50}$, תֶּרַח *Terah* Nm $33_{27}$, צַלְמֹנָה *Zalmonah* Nm $33_{41}$.

הַר *mountain* Nm $33_{23.47}$, גִּבְעָה *hill* 1 S $26_3$, מִדְבָּר *steppe* Ex $19_2$ Nm $10_{31}$ $12_{16}$ $33_{11.15.36}$ 1QM $1_3$, עֲרָבָה *desert* Nm $22_1$ $33_{48}$, עֵמֶק *valley* Jg $6_{33}$ 1 S $17_2$ 2 S $23_{13}$ 1 C $11_{15}$, נַחַל *wadi* Gn $26_{17}$ Nm $21_{12}$, עַיִן *spring* 1 S $29_1$, גְּדֵרָה *fence* Na $3_{17}$, חֶדֶר *innermost chamber* Si $4_{15(A)}$.

בְּ of accompaniment, *with, in*, + בְּרָכָה *blessing* of Y. Si $4_{13(A)}$.

מִן *from*, + בְּאֵר־שֶׁבַע *Beersheba* Ne $11_{30}$; *at*, + מָקוֹם *place* 4Q421 $11_4$; *at*, + צָפוֹן *north* Jos $8_{11}$.

אֶל *at*, + מַיִם *water* Jos $11_5$.

עַל *upon*, + Nahshon Nm $2_5$, Elizur Nm $2_{12}$; *in, at, by, against*, + בָּבֶל *Babylon* Jr $50_{29}$, יִשְׂרָאֵל *Israel* Jg $6_4$, הָאֶבֶן הָעֵזֶר *Ebenezer* 1 S $4_1$, עֶגְלוֹן *Eglon* Jos $10_{34}$, גִּבְּתוֹן *Gibbethon* 1 K $16_{15}$, גִּבְעָה *Gibeah* Jg $20_{19}$, גִּבְעוֹן *Gibeon* Jos $10_5$, יָבֵשׁ גִּלְעָד *Jabesh-gilead* 1 S $11_1$, יְרוּשָׁלַםִ *Jerusalem* 2 K $25_1$||Jr $52_4$, לָכִישׁ *Lachish* Jos $10_{31}$, עִיר *city* 2 S $12_{28}$ Is $29_3$ 2 C $32_1$, יָם *sea* Ex $14_{2.9}$ Nm $33_{10}$, יַרְדֵּן *Jordan* Nm $33_{49}$, מַיִם *water* Ex $15_{27}$, עַיִן *spring* Jg $7_1$, worshipper Ps $27_3$ 1QH $2_{25}$; *according to, by*, + מַחֲנֶה *camp* Nm $1_{52}$, דֶּגֶל *standard* Nm $1_{52}$, פֶּה *mouth*, i.e. command, of Y. Nm $9_{18.\,20.23}$.

עַל יֶרֶךְ *upon (side of)*, + מִשְׁכָּן *tabernacle* Nm $3_{29.35}$.

עַל־פְּנֵי *upon (face of)*, + שָׂדֶה *field* 2 S $11_{11}$.

אֶת־פְּנֵי *before, in the presence of*, + עִיר *city* Gn $33_{18}$.

בֵּין *between*, + שׂוֹכֹה *Socoh* 1 S $17_1$ (+ עֲזֵקָה *Azekah*).

לִפְנֵי *before*, + מֵידְבָא *Medeba* 1 C $19_7$, מִגְדֹּל *Migdol* Nm $33_7$, פִּי הַחִירֹת *Pi-ha-hiroth* Ex $14_2$, מִשְׁכָּן *tabernacle* Nm $3_{38}$.

מִחוּץ לְ *outside of*, + מַחֲנֶה *camp* Nm $31_{19}$.

נֶגֶד *before, opposite*, + Aramaeans 1 K $20_{27}$, הַר *mountain* Ex $19_2$, מֶלֶךְ *king* 1QM $15_2$, חַיִל *army* 1QM $15_2$.

נֹכַח *opposite*, + אֵלֶּה *these* 1 K $20_{29}$.

בְּעֵבֶר *at (the other side)*, + אַרְנוֹן *Arnon* Jg $11_{18}$.

מֵעֵבֶר *from (the other side)*, + אַרְנוֹן *Arnon* Nm $21_{13}$.

עַד *as far as*, + גַּיְא *valley* Ne $11_{30}$.

<COLL> הוּא חֹנֶה שָׁם הַר הָאֱלֹהִים *he encamped there, at the mountain of God* Ex $18_5$, וַיִּחַן ... אֶרֶץ הַגִּלְעָד *and* Israel *encamped ... in the land of Gilead* 2 S $17_{26}$, קִרְיַת חָנָה דָוִד *the city where David encamped* Is $29_1$, סָבִיב לַמִּשְׁכָּן יַחֲנוּ *they will encamp around (at) the tabernacle* Nm $1_{50}$, sim. Nm $1_{53}$, הַחֹנִים קֵדְמָה *those encamping on the east* Nm $2_3$ $10_5$, sim. Nm $3_{38}$ 1 S $13_5$, יַחֲנוּ יָמָּה *they shall encamp on the west* Nm $3_{23}$, יַחֲנוּ ... תֵּימָנָה *they shall encamp ... on the south* Nm $3_{29}$, הַחֹנִים תֵּימָנָה *those encamping on the south* Nm $10_6$, יַחֲנוּ צָפֹנָה *they shall encamp on the north* Nm $3_{35}$.*

⇒ חָנוּת *cell*, חֲנִית *spear*, מַחֲנֶה *camp*, מַחֲנֵה־דָן *Mahaneh-dan*, מַחֲנַיִם *Mahanaim*, תַּחַן *Tahan*, תַּחֲנִי *Tahanite*, תַּחֲנָה *encampment*.

**חנה II** 1 vb. **have compassion—Pi.** 1 Inf. חַנּוֹת—**have**

**compassion,** <SUBJ> אֵל *God* Ps $77_{10}$ (unless חֲנוֹת is qal of חנן *be gracious;* + שׁכח *forget*).

**חַנָּה** 13.0.3.2 pr.n.f. **Hannah, 1.** wife of Elkanah and mother of the prophet Samuel, <SUBJ> הרה *conceive* 1 S $1_{20}$ $2_{21}$, ילד *give birth* 1 S $1_{20}$ $2_{21}$, הלך *go* 1 S $1_{15}$, בוא *come* 1 S $1_{19}$, hi. *bring* 1 S $1_{22}$, שׁוב *go back* 1 S $1_{19}$, עלה *go up* 1 S $1_{22}$, קום *arise* 1 S $1_{9}$, שׁכם hi. *rise early* 1 S $1_{19}$, ישׁב *remain* 1 S $1_{22}$, סור hi. *remove* 1 S $1_{13}$, בכה *weep* 1 S $1_{5.8.9}$, אכל *eat* 1 S $1_{5.8.9}$, שׁתה *drink* 1 S $1_{9.15}$, שׁכר htp. *make oneself drunk* 1 S $1_{13}$, אמר *say* 1 S $1_{9.15.15.22}$ $2_{1}$, דבר pi. *speak* 1 S $1_{13.15}$, קרא *call,* i.e. name 1 S $1_{20}$, שׁאל *ask* 1 S $1_{15.20}$, ענה *answer* 1 S $1_{15}$, נדר *vow* 1 S $1_{9}$, פלל htp. *pray* 1 S $1_{9.9}$ $2_{1}$, שׁחה htp. *bow down* 1 S $1_{19}$, שׂמח *rejoice* 1 S $2_{1}$, נתן *give* 1 S $1_{9}$, רבה hi. *make many,* i.e. continue 1 S $1_{9}$, שׁפך *pour out* 1 S $1_{15}$, עשׂה *do* 1 S $1_{22}$, גמל *wean* 1 S $1_{22}$. <NOM CL> שֵׁם אַחַת חַנָּה *the name of one was Hannah* 1 S $1_{2}$ (mss הָאַחַת *the first one*). <OBJ> אהב *love* 1 S $1_{5}$, ידע *know,* i.e. have intercourse with 1 S $1_{19}$, כעס pi. *anger* 1 S $1_{5.5}$, רעם hi. *cause to tremble* 1 S $1_{5}$, זכר *remember* 1 S $1_{19.19}$, חשׁב *think of* 1 S $1_{13}$, פקד *visit* 1 S $2_{21}$. <APP> אִשָּׁה *woman,* i.e. wife 1 S $1_{2.19}$. <PREP> לְ of possession, *of, (belonging) to* 1 S $1_{2}$; of direction, *to* 1 S $1_{8}$, + נתן *give* 1 S $1_{5}$, אמר *say* 1 S $1_{8.22}$; אֶל *to,* + אמר 1 S $1_{13}$; מֵעַל *from upon,* סור hi. 1 S $1_{13}$.

**2.** mother of Bilhah, <OBJ> הרה *conceive* 4QTNaph $1.1_{2}$ ([ותהר חנה]), ילד *give birth* 4QTNaph $1.1_{2}$ ([חנה ותלד]), קרא *call,* i.e. name 4QTNaph $1.1_{4}$, נתן *give* 4QTNaph $1.1_{2}$, נהג *lead* 4QTNaph $1.1_{8}$. <APP> אֵם *mother* 4QTNaph $1.1_{8}$, אֶחָד *one* 4QTNaph $1.1_{2}$.

**3.** Seal 351 (8th cent.). **4.** daughter of Azariah, Seal 733 (Jerusalem, 7th cent.). <APP> בַּת *daughter* Seal 733 (Jerusalem, 7th cent.). <PREP> לְ of possession, *(belonging) to, of* Seal 351 (8th cent.) 733 (Jerusalem, 7th cent.).

→ חנן *be gracious.*

**חֲנוֹךְ I** 16.1.2 pr.n.m. **Enoch**—חֲנֹךְ—**1.** son of Cain and father of Irad, <SUBJ> היה *be* Gn $5_{21}$, ילד hi. *beget* Gn $5_{21.22.22}$, הלך htp. *walk* Gn $5_{22.24}$ Si $44_{16}$, מצא ni. *be found* blameless Si $44_{16}$, לקח ni. *be taken* Si $44_{16}$ $49_{14}$ (if em.; see Prep.), למד pi. *teach* 4QpsJub$^{c}$ $2_{1}$ ([ח]נוך). <OBJ> ילד *give birth* Gn $4_{17}$, hi. *beget* Gn $5_{18.19}$, לקח *take* Gn $5_{24}$. <CSTR> יְמֵי חֲנוֹךְ *the days of Henoch* Gn $5_{23}$. <APP> בֵּן *son* Gn $4_{17}$. <PREP> לְ of benefit, *to, for,* + ילד ni. *be born* Gn $4_{18}$, כְּ *as,* + יצר ni. *be formed* Si $49_{14}$ (if em. כהניך appar. error for כחנוך *as Enoch*). <COLL> חֲנוֹךְ מְתוּשֶׁלַח לָמֶךְ *Enoch, Methuselah, Lamech* 1 C $1_{3}$.

**2. Hanoch,** son of Reuben, <NOM CL> בְּנֵי רְאוּבֵן חֲנוֹךְ וּפַלּוּא *the sons of Reuben were Hanoch and Pallu* Gn $46_{9}$, sim. 1 C $5_{1}$, אֵלֶּה רָאשֵׁי בֵית־אֲבֹתָם ... חֲנוֹךְ וּפַלּוּא *these are the heads of their fathers' house(s) ... Hanoch and Pallu* Ex $6_{14}$. <PREP> לְ of possession, *(belonging) to, of* Nm $26_{5}$ (if em. חֲנוֹךְ *Hanoch* to לַחֲנוֹךְ *of Hanoch*).

**3. Hanoch,** son of Midian, and grandson of Abraham and Keturah, <NOM CL> בְּנֵי מִדְיָן עֵיפָה ... וַחֲנֹךְ *the sons of Midian were Ephah ... and Hanoch* Gn $25_{4}$||1 C $1_{33}$ (חֲנוֹךְ).

Also 5QRègle $3_{2}$ 11QJub $4_{9}$ (§1).*

→ חֲנֹכִי *Hanochite.*

**חֲנוֹךְ II** 1 pl.n. **Enoch,** city built by Cain and named after Enoch his son, <OBJ> קרא *call* Gn $4_{17}$.

**חָנוּן** 11 pr.n.m. **Hanun, 1.** son of Nahash, and king of the Ammonites at time of David, <SUBJ> מלך *rule* 2 S $10_{1}$, לקח *take* 2 S $10_{4}$||1 C $19_{4}$, שׁלח *send* 1 C $19_{6}$, pi. *send away* 2 S $10_{4}$||1 C $19_{4}$, גלח pi. *shave* 2 S $10_{4}$||1 C $19_{4}$, כרת *cut* 2 S $10_{4}$||1 C $19_{4}$, שׂכר *hire* 1 C $19_{6.6}$. <OBJ> נחם pi. *console* 2 S $10_{2}$||1 C $19_{2.2}$. <APP> בֵּן *son* 2 S $10_{1.2}$||1 C $19_{2}$, אָדוֹן *lord* 2 S $10_{3}$. <PREP> לְ of direction, *to,* + שׁלח *send* 2 S $10_{3}$||1 C $19_{3}$; שׂכר לְ *hire for* 1 C $19_{6.6}$; אֶל *to,* + בוא *come* 1 C $19_{2.3}$, אמר *say* 2 S $10_{3}$||1 C $19_{3}$ (לְ); עִם *with,* + עשׂה *do* 2 S $10_{2}$||1 C $19_{2}$.

**2.** one who helped repair gates of Jerusalem, <SUBJ> חזק hi. *strengthen* Ne $3_{13}$, בנה *build* Ne $3_{13}$, עמד hi. *set* Ne $3_{13}$. **3.** sixth son of Zalaph, repairer of walls of Jerusalem, <SUBJ> חזק hi. *strengthen* Ne $3_{30}$. <APP> בֵּן *son* Ne $3_{30}$.

→ חָנַן *be gracious.*

**חַנּוּן** 13.0.2 adj. **gracious, 1.** used attributively of אֵל *God* Ex $34_{6}$ Jon $4_{2}$ Ps $86_{15}$ (all three || רַחוּם *compassionate*) Ne $9_{31}$ 4QShir$^{b}$ $57.3_{1}$ ([אל חנון]) Kh. Beit Lei graf. $6_{2}$ (others אתה חננת *you have been gracious*).

**2.** in nom. cl. used predicatively of Y. Ex 22$_{26}$ Jl 2$_{13}$ Ps 103$_{8}$ 111$_{4}$ (all three || רַחוּם *compassionate*) 116$_{5}$ (|| צַדִּיק *righteous;* + רחם *have compassion*) 145$_{8}$ Ne 9$_{17}$ (+ אֱלוֹהַּ סְלִיחוֹת *God of forgiveness,* i.e. forgiving God) 2 C 30$_{9}$ all three || רַחוּם) 1QH 16$_{16}$ ([חנון]) 4QapPs[b] 47$_{1}$ (|| רַחֲמוֹן *compassionate*), perh. אִישׁ *man* Ps 112$_{4}$ (|| רַחוּם, צַדִּיק).

<COLL> חַנּוּן וְרַחוּם *gracious and compassionate* Jl 2$_{13}$ Jon 4$_{2}$ Ps 111$_{4}$ 112$_{4}$ 145$_{8}$ Ne 9$_{17.31}$ 2 C 30$_{9}$ 1QH 16$_{16}$ ([חנון] ורחום) 4QShir[b] 57.3$_{1}$ ([חנון ורחום]), רַחוּם וְחַנּוּן *compassionate and gracious* Ex 34$_{6}$ Ps 86$_{15}$ 103$_{8}$, רחמון וחנון *compassionate and gracious* 4QapPs[b] 47$_{1}$; חַנּוּן + אֶרֶךְ אַפַּיִם *long of,* i.e. slow to, *anger* Ex 34$_{6}$ Jl 2$_{13}$ Jon 4$_{2}$ Ps 86$_{15}$ 103$_{8}$ 145$_{8}$ Ne 9$_{17}$ 1QH 16$_{16}$ ([חנון] ... [אר]ך אפים) 4QShir[b] 57.3$_{1}$ ([חנון] ... וארוך אפים), רַב־חֶסֶד *abundant of,* i.e. abounding in, *loyalty* Ex 34$_{6}$ Jl 2$_{13}$ Jon 4$_{2}$ Ps 86$_{15}$ 103$_{8}$ Ne 9$_{17}$ 1QH 16$_{16}$ ([חנון]) 4QShir[b] 57.3$_{1}$ ([חנון] ... רב החסד), גְּדָל־חָסֶד *great of loyalty* Ps 145$_{8}$.

Also 4QHymPr 5$_{3}$.

<SYN> רַחוּם *compassionate,* רַחֲמוֹן *compassionate,* צַדִּיק *righteous.**

⇒ חנן *be gracious.*

**[חָנוּת]** 1 n.f. **vault,** perh. cellar—pl. חֲנֻיוֹת—<PREP> אֶל *to,* + בוא *come* Jr 37$_{16}$ (+ בֵּית הַבּוֹר *house of the pit,* i.e. dungeon).*

**חנט I** 3 vb. **embalm—Qal** 1 + waw וַיַּחַנְטוּ; inf. חֲנֹט—**embalm,** <SUBJ> רֹפֵא *physician* Gn 50$_{2.2.26}$, עֶבֶד *servant* Gn 50$_{2}$. <OBJ> Israel, i.e. Jacob Gn 50$_{2}$, Joseph Gn 50$_{26}$, אָב *father* Gn 50$_{2}$.*

⇒ חֲנֻטִים *embalming.*

**חנט II** 1 vb. **ripen—Qal** 1 Pf. חָנְטָה—**make ripe,** perh. **make red,** <SUBJ> תְּאֵנָה *fig tree* Ca 2$_{13}$. <OBJ> פַּגָּה *early fig* Ca 2$_{13}$.*

**חֲנֻטִים** 1 n.[m.]pl. **embalming,** <CSTR> יְמֵי הַחֲנֻטִים *the days of embalming* Gn 50$_{3}$.*

⇒ חנט *embalm.*

**[חֹנִי]**, see חוֹנִי *Honi.*

**[חָנְיָא]** 0.0.0.2 pr.n.m. **Honia**—I חניה— **1.** son of Joseph and descendent of Hezir, Bene Ḥezir tomb inscr. (Frey 1394). **2.** father of Joseph and Eleazar and descendent of Hezir, Bene Ḥezir tomb inscr. (Frey 1394). <CSTR> בני חניה *sons of Honia* Bene Ḥezir tomb inscr. (Frey 1394). <APP> בֵּן *son* Bene Ḥezir tomb inscr. (Frey 1394). <PREP> לְ of possession, *(belonging) to, of* Bene Ḥezir tomb inscr. (Frey 1394).

**חַנִּיאֵל** 2 pr.n.m. **Hanniel, 1.** son of Ephod, and prince of Manasseh, <APP> נָשִׂיא *prince* Nm 34$_{23}$ (Sam. חנאל), בֵּן *son* Nm 34$_{23}$. **2.** son of Ulla, and brother of Arah and Rizia, <NOM CL> בְּנֵי עֻלָּא אָרַח וְחַנִּיאֵל *the sons of Ulla were Arah and Hanniel* 1 C 7$_{39}$

⇒ חנן *be gracious* + אֵל *God.*

**[חָנְיָה]**, see חָנְיָא *Honia.*

**[חֲנַנְיָהוּ]** 0.0.0.1 pr.n.m. **Hanniah,** father of Sheariah, <CSTR> בן חניהו *son of Hanniah* Seal 359 (8th/7th cent.)

⇒ חנן *be gracious* + 'י *Y.*

**חֲנֻיוֹת**, see חָנוּת *vault.*

**[חָנִיךְ]** 1 n.[m.] **retainer**—<OBJ> ריק hi. *empty,* i.e. lead out Gn 14$_{14}$, דוק hi. *muster* Gn 14$_{14 (Sam)}$. <APP> יָלִיד *one born* Gn 14$_{14}$. <COLL> חָנִיךְ + number שְׁמוֹנָה עָשָׂר וּשְׁלֹשׁ מֵאוֹת *three hundred and eighteen* Gn 14$_{14}$.*

⇒ חנך *dedicate.*

**[חָנִין]** 0.0.4.1 pr.n.m. **Hanin, 1.** son of Hanina, Mur 22 1$_{3.12}$. **2.** son of Jonathan, Mur 30 1$_{4}$ 2$_{17}$. **3.** Beshanite, Frey 1373. <NOM CL> צפון חנין *in the north is Hanin* Mur 22 1$_{3.12}$, דרום חנין *in the south is Hanin* Mur 30 1$_{4}$ 2$_{17}$. <APP> בַּר *son* Mur 22 1$_{3.12}$ Mur 30 1$_{4}$ 2$_{17}$. <ADJ> בֵּישָׁנִי *Beshanite* Frey 1373.

⇒ חנן *be gracious.*

**[חֲנִינָא]** 0.0.2 pr.n.m. **Hanina,** father of Hanin, <CSTR> בר חנינא *son of Hanina* Mur 22 1$_{3.12}$

⇒ חנן *be gracious.*

**חֲנִינָה** 1.0.2 n.f. **grace, favour,** <OBJ> נתן *give* Jr 16$_{13}$. <NOM CL> אין חנינה *there is no grace* 3QJub fr. 2$_{1}$. <CSTR> אל הרחמים והחנינה *God of compassion and grace* 1QH 11$_{29}$.

→ חנן *be gracious*.

**חֲנִית** 47.1.7 n.f. **spear**—cstr. חֲנִית; sf. חֲנִיתוֹ, חֲנִיתֶךָ; pl. חֲנִיתִים; sf. חֲנִיתֹתֵיהֶם (חֲנִיתוֹתֵיהֶם)—<SUBJ> מצא ni. *be found* 1 S 13$_{22}$ (|| חֶרֶב *sword*), מעך pass. *be pressed* 1 S 26$_{7}$, יצא *go out* 2 S 2$_{23}$, נשׂג hi. *reach* Jb 41$_{18}$ (|| שִׁרְיָה *lance*, מַסָּע *dart*, חֶרֶב), קום *stand*, i.e. be effective Jb 41$_{18}$.

<NOM CL> שִׁנֵּיהֶם חֲנִית *their teeth are a spear* Ps 57$_{5}$ (|| חֵץ *arrow*, חֶרֶב *sword*), אִין יֶשׁ־פֹּה תַחַת־יָדְךָ חֲנִית *is there not here under your hand a spear?* 1 S 21$_{9}$ (|| חֶרֶב *sword*), אֵי חֲנִית הַמֶּלֶךְ *where is the spear of the king?* 1 S 26$_{16}$, הִנֵּה חֲנִית הַמֶּלֶךְ *here is the spear of the king* 1 S 26$_{22(Qr, mss)}$ (Kt החנית here is *the spear,* O king!), בְּיַד הַמִּצְרִי חֲנִית *in the hand of the Egyptian was a spear* 2 S 23$_{21}$||1 C 11$_{23}$, var. 1 S 18$_{10}$ 19$_{9}$ 22$_{6}$.

<OBJ> עשׂה *make* 1 S 13$_{19}$ (|| חֶרֶב *sword*), גזל *snatch* 2 S 23$_{21}$||1 C 11$_{23}$, לקח *take* 1 S 26$_{11.12}$, נתן *give* 2 K 11$_{10}$||2 C 23$_{9}$ (|| שֶׁלֶט *shield,* [2 C] מָגֵן *shield*), עור pol. *rouse,* i.e. wield 2 S 23$_{18}$||1 C 11$_{20}$ 1 C 11$_{11}$, חזק hi. *hold* 1QM 6$_{5}$ (|| מָגֵן *shield,* + כִּידוֹן *javelin*), ריק hi. *empty,* i.e. draw Ps 35$_{3}$, טול hi. *throw* 1 S 18$_{11}$ 20$_{33}$, נכה hi. *strike* 1 S 19$_{10}$, כתת pi. *beat* Is 2$_{4}$||Mc 4$_{3}$ (|| חֶרֶב), קצץ pi. *cut off* Ps 46$_{10}$ (|| קֶשֶׁת *bow*).

<CSTR> חֲנִית הַמֶּלֶךְ *spear of the king* 1 S 26$_{16.22(Qr, mss)}$; אַחֲרֵי הַחֲנִית *back of the spear* 2 S 2$_{23}$, בְּרַק חֲנִית *flash of the spear* Na 3$_{3}$=4QpNah 3.2$_{4}$ (|| חֶרֶב *sword*), חֲנִיתֶךָ *of your spear* Hb 3$_{11}$ (|| חֵץ *arrow*), ברקת חנית *flash of a spear* 1QM 6$_{2}$ (+ זֶרֶק *javelin*), עֵץ חֲנִית *wood,* i.e. shaft, *of a spear* 2 S 23$_{7}$, חֲנִיתוֹ *of his spear* 1 S 17$_{7(Qr, mss)}$ (Kt חֵץ appar. *arrow of* his spear) 2 S 21$_{19}$||1 C 20$_{5}$ (2 S mss חֵץ), לַהַב חֲנִית *flame,* i.e. head, *of a spear* Jb 39$_{23}$ (|| כִּידוֹן *javelin,* + אַשְׁפָּה *quiver*), לְהֶבֶת להוב *flame of* 1QH 2$_{26}$, לֶהָבֶת חֲנִיתוֹ *flame,* i.e. head, *of his spear* 1 S 17$_{7}$. <ADJ> חד *sharp* 1QH 5$_{10}$.

<PREP> בְּ of accompaniment, *with* 1 C 12$_{35}$ (|| צִנָּה *shield*), + בוא *come* 1 S 17$_{45}$ (|| חֶרֶב *sword,* כִּידוֹן *javelin,* :: שֵׁם *name* of Y.), פאר htp. *glorify oneself* Si 38$_{25}$ (+ מַלְמַד *ox-goad*); of instrument, *by (means of), with* 2QapProph 1$_{5}$ (|| חֶרֶב), + ישׁע hi. *save* 1 S 17$_{47}$ (|| חֶרֶב), הרג *kill* 2 S 23$_{21}$, נכה hi. *strike* 1 S 19$_{10}$ 26$_{8}$; בטח בְּ *trust in* 1QM 11$_{2}$ (|| חֶרֶב, :: שֵׁם); כְּ *as* 1QH 5$_{10}$ (|| חֶרֶב); עַל *upon,* + שׁען ni. *lean* 2 S 1$_{6}$.

<SYN> חֶרֶב *sword,* כִּידוֹן *javelin,* שִׁרְיָה *lance,* מַסָּע *dart,* חֵץ *arrow,* קֶשֶׁת *bow,* מָגֵן *shield,* שֶׁלֶט *shield,* צִנָּה *shield.*

<ANT> שֵׁם *name.*

**חנך** 5 vb. **dedicate; train**—Pf. חֲנָכוּ; impf. יַחְנְכֶנּוּ; + waw וַיַּחְנְכוּ; impv. חֲנֹךְ—**1. dedicate,** <SUBJ> אִישׁ *man* Dt 20$_{5.5}$, בֵּן *son* of Israel 1 K 8$_{63}$, עַם *people* 2 C 7$_{5}$, מֶלֶךְ *king* 1 K 8$_{63}$|| 2 C 7$_{5}$. <OBJ> בַּיִת *house* Dt 20$_{5.5}$, i.e. temple 1 K 8$_{63}$|| 2 C 7$_{5}$.

**2. train,*** <PREP> לְ introducing object, + נַעַר *lad* Pr 22$_{6}$.

→ חֲנֻכָּה *dedication,* חָנִיךְ *trained.*

**חֲנֻכָּה** 8 n.f. **dedication**—cstr. חֲנֻכַּת—**dedication, dedication offering,** <NOM CL> זֹאת חֲנֻכַּת הַמִּזְבֵּחַ *this was the dedication offering of,* i.e. for, *the altar* Nm 7$_{84.88}$. <OBJ> קרב hi. *bring near,* i.e. offer Nm 7$_{10}$, עשׂה *make,* i.e. celebrate Ne 12$_{27}$ 2 C 7$_{9}$. <CSTR> חֲנֻכַּת הַבַּיִת *dedication of the house* Ps 30$_{1}$, חוֹמַת *of the wall of* Jerusalem Ne 12$_{27}$, חֲנֻכַּת הַמִּזְבֵּחַ *dedication (offering) of the altar* Nm 7$_{84.88}$ 2 C 7$_{9}$; שִׁיר־חֲנֻכַּת *song of,* i.e. for, *the dedication of* the house Ps 30$_{1}$. <PREP> לְ of direction, *to,* + קרב hi. *bring near,* i.e. offer Nm 7$_{11}$; בְּ of place, time, *in, at,* + בקשׁ pi. *seek* Ne 12$_{27}$.*

→ חנך *dedicate, train.*

**חֲנֹכִי** 1 gent. **Hanochite,** as noun, in ref. to descendant(s) of Hanoch, <CSTR> מִשְׁפַּחַת הַחֲנֹכִי *family of the Hanochites* Nm 26$_{5}$

→ חֲנוֹךְ *Enoch.*

**חִנָּם** 32.1.4 adv. **for nothing, 1.** as adverb, **needlessly,** i.e. without purpose, for no good reason, 1 S 19$_{5}$ 25$_{31}$ Ezk 14$_{23}$ Ps 35$_{19}$ 69$_{5}$ Jb 1$_{9}$ 2$_{3}$ Pr 1$_{11}$ (or em.) 3$_{30}$ 23$_{29}$ Si 20$_{23}$ 1QS 7$_{11}$ 4QD$^{a}$ 18.4$_{7}$ (וח[נם]) 4Q416 2.2$_{17}$=4Q417 1.2$_{22}$ (appar. not *gratis,* although + במחיר *for a price*); **without warrant, illegally, unjustly,** Ps 35$_{7.7}$ (or del. in both) 109$_{3}$ 119$_{161}$ Jb 9$_{17}$ (+ בִּשְׂעָרָה *for the sake of a hair,* i.e. for no good reason) 22$_{6}$ Lm 3$_{52}$ 4QJub$^{d}$ 21$_{19}$ ([חנם]; + [בלי משפט] *without judgment*); **in vain,** i.e. without the intended result, Pr 1$_{17}$ CD 6$_{12.14}$=4QD$^{a}$ 3.3$_{6}$ 1QM 16$_{13}$ ([חנם]); **at no cost, gratis,** Gn 29$_{15}$ Ex 21$_{2.11}$ (+ אֵין־כֶּסֶף *without silver*) Nm 11$_{5}$ 2 S 24$_{24}$‖1 C 21$_{24}$ (+ בִּמְחִיר *at a price,* בְּכֶסֶף *with silver*) Is 52$_{3}$=4QTanḥ 8$_{4}$ ([חנם]; + בְּכֶסֶף) Is 52$_{5}$ Jr 22$_{13}$ (+ וּפֹעֲלוֹ לֹא יִתֶּן־לוֹ *and he does not give him his wage*).

**a.** with verb, שׂנא *hate* Ps 35$_{19}$ 69$_{5}$, ירא *fear* Jb 1$_{9}$, מכר ni. *be sold* Is 52$_{3}$=4QTanḥ 8$_{4}$ ([חנם נמכרתם]), זרה pu. *be scattered* Pr 1$_{17}$ (or em. מזר pass. *be spread*), יצא *go out* Ex 21$_{2.11}$, פטר ni. *disappear* 1QS 7$_{11(mg)}$ (or em. וחנם appar. *and needlessly* to והנם *and whoever sleeps*) 4QD$^{a}$ 18.4$_{7}$ (וח]נם ... [והנפ]טר]), נפל *fall* 1QM 16$_{13}$ ([חנם נפלו]), לקח pu. *be taken* Is 52$_{5}$, קנה *acquire* enemy Si 20$_{23}$, רדף *pursue* Ps 119$_{161}$, צוד *hunt* Lm 3$_{52}$ (unless איב *be at enmity*), ריב *strive* Pr 3$_{30(Qr)}$, לחם ni. *fight* Ps 109$_{3}$, רבה hi. *increase* wounds Jb 9$_{17}$, מות hi. *kill* 1 S 19$_{5}$, שׁפך *pour* blood 1 S 25$_{31}$ 4QJub$^{d}$ 21$_{19}$ ([חנם]), חבל *exact pledge* Jb 22$_{6}$, אכל *eat* Nm 11$_{5}$, בלע pi. *destroy* Jb 2$_{3}$, עלה hi. *raise,* i.e. offer sacrifice 2 S 24$_{24}$‖1 C 21$_{24}$, עשׂה *do* Ezk 14$_{23}$, עבד *serve* Gn 29$_{15}$ 4Q416 2.2$_{17}$=4Q417 1.2$_{22}$ ([תע[בוד]), specif. have work done by another Jr 22$_{13}$, אור hi. *kindle* (fire on) altar Ml 1$_{10}$ CD 6$_{12.14}$=4QD$^{a}$ 3.3$_{6}$ ([תא[ירו]), חפר *dig* Ps 35$_{7}$ (or del. חִנָּם), טמן *conceal* Ps 35$_{7}$ (or del. חִנָּם) Pr 1$_{11}$ (or em. לְתָם *for an innocent one*).

**<COLL>** preceded by לֹא *not* Ezk 14$_{23}$ Ml 1$_{10}$ CD 6$_{14}$=4QD$^{a}$ 3.3$_{6}$ ([ולו תא[ירו]) 1QM 16$_{13}$ ([חנם נפלו]).

**b.** with nom. cl., לְמִי פְּצָעִים חִנָּם *who has (suffered) wounds needlessly?* Pr 23$_{29}$.

**2.** as noun, **needlessness, <CSTR>** דְּמֵי חִנָּם *blood of needlessness,* i.e. innocent blood, 1 K 2$_{31}$, appar. עֵד־חִנָּם *witness of needlessness* Pr 24$_{28}$ (or rd. עֵד חִנָּם *a witness without cause*; ms חָמָס witness of *violence*), קִלְלַת חִנָּם *curse of needlessness,* i.e. a curse without cause Pr 26$_{2}$.

**3.** אֶל־חִנָּם **needlessly, without cause,** + דבר pi. *speak* Ezk 6$_{10}$.*

**חֲנַמְאֵל** 4 pr.n.m. **Hanamel,** son of Shallum, and cousin or uncle of the prophet Jeremiah, **<SUBJ>** בוא *come* Jr 32$_{7.8}$, אמר *say* Jr 32$_{7.8}$. **<CSTR>** עֵינֵי חֲנַמְאֵל *eyes of Hanamel* Jr 32$_{12}$. **<APP>** בֵּן *son* Jr 32$_{7.8.9.12(mss)}$ (L דֹּד), דּוֹד *uncle* Jr 32$_{12}$. **<PREP>** לְ of direction, *to,* + שׁקל *weigh* Jr 32$_{9}$; מֵאֵת *from,* + קנה *acquire* Jr 32$_{9}$.

**[חֲנָמַל]** 1.0.1 n.[m.] **frost**—חֲנָמַל—**frost (?), flood (?), <PREP>** בְּ of instrument, *by (means of), with,* + הרג *kill* Ps 78$_{47}$ (‖ בָּרָד *hail*), נכה hi. *strike* 4Q422 10$_{10}$ ( ... [ויך] בח[נמל]). **<SYN>** בָּרָד *hail.*

**[חַנַּמֶּלֶךְ]** 0.0.0.1 pr.n.[m.] **Hannimelech,** appar. son of Jobanah, **<PREP>** לְ of possession, *(belonging) to, of* Seal 788 (Jerusalem, 8th cent.)

⇒ חנן *be gracious* + מלך *reign.*

**חנן I** 78.4.26.1 vb. **be gracious—Qal** 55.1.22 Pf. חנן (חַנַּנִי), Q חנותני, חָנָנוּ; impf. יָחֹן (Q יחון, יְחֻנַּן, יְחָנְךָ, Q יחונך, Q יחונכה, יְחָנֵּנוּ), 2ms תָּחֹן (תְּחָנֵּם), אָחֹן; + waw Qr וחנני, וַחֲנֹתִי; וַיָּחָן (וַיְחֻנֶּךָּ, וַיְחָנֵּנוּ, L וַיְחָנֵּנוּ, וִיחָנֵּנוּ), 2ms Q ותחון, Q ותחוננו; impv. חָנֵּנִי (Q חונני, חָנְנֵנִי, חָנֵּנוּ), חָנֵּנִי (חָנּוּנוּ); ptc. חוֹנֵן (חֹנֵן, חֵן?) inf. abs. חָנוֹן, cstr. חֶנְנָה (Q חונכה, חֲנַנְכֶם,* Q חונכם).

**1. be gracious (to), show favour (to), spare; graciously give to** (Gn 33$_{5}$ Jg 21$_{22}$ Ps 119$_{29}$ 11QPs$^{a}$ 19$_{14}$ Kuntillet ʿAjrud add. inscr. 2).

**<SUBJ>** Y. Gn 33$_{5.11}$ 43$_{29}$ Ex 33$_{19.19}$ Nm 6$_{25}$ 2 S 12$_{22}$ 2 K 13$_{23}$ Is 30$_{18}$=4QpIsa$^{c}$ 23.2$_{8}$ (לחנ[נכ]מה; both ‖ רחם pi. *have compassion*) 30$_{19.19}$=4QpIsa$^{c}$ 23.2$_{15}$ ([חנון יחנכה]) Is 33$_{2}$ Am 5$_{15}$ Ml 1$_{9}$ (+ נשׂא פָּנִים *lift face,* i.e. have regard for) Ps 4$_{2}$ (+ שׁמע *hear* prayer) 6$_{3}$=4QMidrEschat$^{b}$ 11$_{7}$ ([חנני]; ‖ רפא *heal*) Ps 9$_{14}$ (+ ראה *see* affliction) 25$_{16}$ (+ פנה אֶל *turn to*) 26$_{11}$ (‖ פדה *redeem*) 27$_{7}$ (‖ ענה *answer,* + שׁמע *hear* voice) 30$_{11}$ (+ שׁמע, היה *be* helper) 31$_{10}$ 41$_{5}$ (+ רפא) 41$_{11}$ (‖ קום hi. *raise up*) 51$_{3}$ (+ מחה *blot out* transgressions) 56$_{2}$ 57$_{2.2}$ 59$_{6}$ 67$_{2}$ (‖ ברך pi. *bless*) 77$_{10}$ (unless חַנּוֹת is pi. of חנה *have compassion*) 86$_{3.16}$=4QapPs$^{b}$ 15$_{2}$ ([חנני]; + פנה אֶל) Ps 102$_{14}$ (+ רחם pi. *have compassion*) 119$_{29.58.132}$ (+ פנה אֶל) 123$_{2.3.3}$ Si 4$_{10}$ (+ נצל hi. *deliver*) GnzPs 2$_{1}$ 1QH 1$_{6}$ ([חנ[ות]) 14$_{25}$ 1QS 2$_{3.8}$ (+ סלח *forgive*) 1QSb 2$_{22.23}$ ([יחוננ[כה]) 2$_{24.25.26.27}$ 4QMidrEschat$^{b}$ 11$_{8}$ 4QTohD3 4QBark$^{a}$ 2.1$_{3}$ 4QDibHam$^{a}$ 1.5$_{11}$ 11QPs$^{a}$ 19$_{14.17}$ Kuntillet ʿAjrud add. inscr. 2 Kh. Beit Lei graf. 6$_{1}$ (others אל חנן *gracious God*).

Israel Dt 7$_{2}$, גּוֹי *nation* Dt 28$_{50}$ (+ נשׂא פָּנִים *lift face,* i.e.

have regard for), אִישׁ *man* Ps 112$_{5}$ (|| לוה hi. *lend*), אָב *father* Jg 21$_{22}$, אָח *brother* Jg 21$_{22}$, רֵעַ *friend* Jb 19$_{21.21}$, יצר ptc. *one who forms* Is 27$_{11}$ (|| רחם pi. *have compassion*), צַדִּיק *righteous one* Ps 37$_{21}$=4QpPs$^{a}$ 1.3$_{9}$ (|| נתן *give*) Ps 37$_{26}$=4QpPs$^{a}$ 1.3$_{18}$ (|| לוה hi.), מַלְאָךְ *angel* Jb 33$_{24}$, מֵלִיץ *mediator* Jb 33$_{24}$, גּוֹי *nation* perh. Lm 4$_{16}$ (+ נשׂא פָּנִים); subj. not specified, appar. Is 26$_{10}$ (1QIsa$^{a}$; MT ho.) Ps 109$_{12}$ (+ משׁך חֶסֶד *extend kindness*) Pr 14$_{31}$ (:: עשׁק *oppress*) 19$_{17}$ 28$_{8}$.

<OBJ> David 2 S 12$_{22}$, Jacob Gn 33$_{11}$, Job Jb 19$_{21.21}$, Melkiresha 4QTohD$_{3}$, Israel(ite) Nm 6$_{25}$ 2 K 13$_{23}$ Is 30$_{18}$=4QpIsa$^{c}$ 23.2$_{8}$ (לחננ[כמה]) Ml 1$_{9}$ 4QDibHam$^{a}$ 1.5$_{11}$, Zion Ps 102$_{14}$, Canaanite Dt 7$_{2}$, Girgashite Dt 7$_{2}$, Hittite Dt 7$_{2}$, Hivite Dt 7$_{2}$, Jebusite Dt 7$_{2}$, Perizzite Dt 7$_{2}$, גּוֹי *nation* Dt 7$_{2}$, עַם *people* Is 27$_{11}$ 30$_{19}$=4QpIsa$^{c}$ 23.2$_{15}$ ([חנון יחנכה]) 4QDibHam$^{a}$ 1.5$_{11}$, אִישׁ *man* 1QS 2$_{3.8}$, אָדָם *human being* Jb 33$_{24}$, בֵּן *son* Gn 43$_{29}$ Si 4$_{10}$, of Benjamin Jg 21$_{22}$, בַּת *daughter* Jg 21$_{22}$, יֶלֶד *child* Gn 33$_{5}$, נַעַר *lad* Dt 28$_{50}$, עֶבֶד *servant* Gn 33$_{5}$, זָקֵן *elder* Lm 4$_{16}$ 4QapPs$^{b}$ 79$_{2}$, בגד ptc. *treacherous one* Ps 59$_{6}$, אֶבְיוֹן *poor one* Pr 14$_{31}$, דַּל *poor one* Pr 19$_{17}$ 28$_{8}$ 4QpsEzek$^{b}$ 3.3$_{1}$, עָנָו *humble one* 4QBark$^{a}$ 2.1$_{3}$, שְׁאֵרִית *remnant* Am 5$_{15}$, worshipper Is 33$_{2}$ Ps 4$_{2}$ 6$_{3}$=4QMidrEschat$^{b}$ 11$_{7}$ ([חנני]) Ps 9$_{14}$ 25$_{16}$ 26$_{11}$ 27$_{7}$ 30$_{11}$ 31$_{10}$ 41$_{5.11}$ 51$_{3}$ 56$_{2}$ 57$_{2.2}$ 67$_{2}$ 86$_{3.16}$=4QapPs$^{b}$ 15$_{2}$ ([חנני]) Ps 119$_{29.58.132}$ 123$_{2.3.3}$ GnzPs 2$_{1}$ 1QH 14$_{25}$ 16$_{9}$ 11QPs$^{a}$ 19$_{14}$, ירא ptc. *one who fears* Y. 1QSb 2$_{22.23}$ (יחוננ[כה]) 2$_{24.25.26.27}$, שׁמר ptc. *one who keeps* commandments 1QSb 2$_{22.23}$ (יחוננ[כה]) 2$_{24.25.26.27}$, חזק pi. ptc. *one who grasps* holy spirit 1QSb 2$_{22.23}$ (יחוננ[כה]) 2$_{24.25.26.27}$, הלך ptc. *one who walks* perfectly 1QSb 2$_{22.23}$ (יחוננ[כה]) 2$_{24.25.26.27}$, אֲשֶׁר *one who, (that) which* Ex 33$_{19.19}$ Kuntillet ʿAjrud add. inscr. 2, רוּחַ *spirit* 11QPs$^{a}$ 19$_{14}$, תּוֹרָה *law* Ps 119$_{29}$, נָוֶה *habitation* 2 Kh. Beit Lei graf. 7, מֹרִיָּה *(Mount) Moriah* 2 Kh. Beit Lei graf. 7.

<PREP> לְ *at*, + קוֹל *sound* Is 30$_{19}$; כְּ *according to*, + חֶסֶד *loyalty* Ps 51$_{3}$, אִמְרָה *word* Ps 119$_{58}$, מִשְׁפָּט *custom* Ps 119$_{132}$; בְּ of place, *in*, + אֶרֶץ *land* 4QDibHam$^{a}$ 1.5$_{11}$; of accompaniment, *with, in*, + רוּחַ *spirit* 1QH 14$_{25}$ 16$_{9}$ 1QSb 2$_{22}$ (ב[רוח]) 2$_{24}$, דַּעַת *knowledge* 1QS 2$_{3}$, מִשְׁפָּט *judgment* 1QSb 2$_{26}$, מַעֲשֶׂה *deed* 1QSb 2$_{27}$.

<SYN> רחם pi. *have compassion*, נתן *give*, פדה *redeem*, רפא *heal*, ענה *answer*, קום hi. *raise up*, ברך pi. *bless*, לוה hi. *lend*.

**2.** ptc. (חַן) as noun, **one who is gracious,** חֵן שְׂפָתָיו רֵעֵהוּ מֶלֶךְ *one who is gracious of speech—their friend is the king* Pr 22$_{11}$.*

Also 1QSb 2$_{3}$ (יחו[ננכה]).

**Ni.** 1 Pf. נֵחַנְתְּ—**be pitied,** <SUBJ> יֹשֵׁב *inhabitant* of Lebanon Jr 22$_{23}$ (or em. נֶאֱנַחְתְּ or נֶאֱנַחַתְּ *you groan*, i.e. אנח ni.).

**Pi.** 1 Impf. יְחַנֵּן—**make gracious,** <SUBJ> שׂנא ptc. *one who hates* Pr 26$_{25}$. <OBJ> קוֹל *voice* Pr 26$_{25}$.

**Po.** 2 Impf. יְחֹנֵנוּ; ptc. מְחוֹנֵן—**have pity on,** <SUBJ> עֶבֶד *servant* Ps 102$_{15}$ (|| רצה *be pleased with*), neighbour Pr 14$_{21}$ (:: בוז *despise*). <OBJ> עָנִי *poor one* Pr 14$_{21(Kt)}$, עָנָו *humble one* Pr 14$_{21(Qr)}$, עָפָר *dust* Ps 102$_{15}$. <SYN> רצה *be pleased with*. <ANT> בוז *despise*.

**Ho.** (or **Qal pass.**) 2.2 Impf. יֻחַן (Si יוחן), Si יחנו—**be shown favour** (unless Qal pass.), <SUBJ> רָשָׁע *wicked one* Is 26$_{10}$ (unless חין pu. *die*; 1QIsa$^{a}$ יחון appar. חנן qal), רֵעַ *neighbour* Pr 21$_{10}$, תמך ptc. *one who holds* wisdom Si 4$_{13}$, חֹבֵר *(snake) charmer* Si 12$_{13}$. <PREP> בְּ of place, *in*, + עַיִן *eye* Pr 21$_{10}$; of instrument, *by (means of), with*, + בְּרָכָה *blessing* Si 4$_{13}$.

**Htp.** 17.1.4 Pf. הִתְחַנַּנְתִּי, הִתְחַנְּנָה; impf. 2ms Si יתחנן, תִּתְחַנַּן, אֶתְחַנַּן (אֶתְחַנֵּן־); + waw וַיִּתְחַנֵּן (וַיִּתְחַנֶּן־), וָהִתְחַנְּנוּ; 3fs וַתִּתְחַנֶּן־, וָאֶתְחַנַּן (mss וָאֶתְחַנֵּן); inf. הִתְחַנֵּן־ (הִתְחַנְּנוֹ)—**make supplication, implore favour, seek pity,** <SUBJ> Esther Est 4$_{8}$ (+ בקשׁ pi. *seek*) 8$_{3}$, Jacob Ho 12$_{5}$, Job Jb 8$_{5}$ (|| שׁחר pi. *seek*) 9$_{15}$ 19$_{16}$ (+ קרא *call*), Joseph Gn 42$_{21}$, Moses Dt 3$_{23}$, Solomon 1 K 8$_{58}$ 9$_{3}$, Israel 1 K 8$_{33}$||2 C 6$_{24}$ (+ פלל htp. *pray*), עַם *people* 1 K 8$_{33.47}$||2 C 6$_{24.37}$, שַׂר *captain* 2 K 1$_{13}$, worshipper Ps 30$_{9}$ (+ קרא) 142$_{2}$ (|| זעק *cry*) 1QH 12$_{4}$ (+ נפל htp. *prostrate oneself*) 17$_{18}$, אִישׁ *man* 1QH 16$_{6}$ (להת[חנן]), דַּל *poor one* Si 13$_{3}$.

<PREP> לְ of direction, (make supplication) *to*, + מֶלֶךְ *king* Est 4$_{8}$ 8$_{3}$, עֶבֶד *servant* Jb 19$_{16}$, מַלְאָךְ *angel* Ho 12$_{5}$, שׁפט po. ptc. *opponent at law* Jb 9$_{15}$; בְּ of instrument, *by (means of), with*, + פֶּה *mouth* Jb 19$_{16}$; מִן of direction, *from*, מקץ לקץ *from end to end*, i.e. for evermore 1QH 12$_{4}$; אֶל (make supplication) *to*, + Y. Dt 3$_{23}$ 1 K 8$_{33.47}$|| 2 C 6$_{37}$ Ps 30$_{9}$ 142$_{2}$ Jb 8$_{5}$, Elijah 2 K 1$_{13}$, אָח *brother* Gn 42$_{21}$; עַל *for, on account of*, + חַטָּאת *sin* 1QH 17$_{18}$, מַעַל *unfaithful act* 1QH 16$_{6}$ (להת[חנן על מע]ל), רַע *evil* 1QH

$17_{18}$ ([רוע]), עוה ni. ptc. *perverseness* 1QH $17_{18}$; סתר ni. *hidden deed* perh. 4QRitPur $34.5_{15}$ (תחתן[ ]); עִם *with*, i.e. at, + מָבוֹא *coming* of light 1QH $12_4$; לִפְנֵי *before*, + Y. 1 K $8_{59}$ $9_3$ 2 C $6_{24}$.

<COLL> חנן htp. + noun without preposition, *make supplication (with)* 1 K $9_3$ (תְּחִנָּה *supplication*) Ps $142_2$ (קוֹל *voice*); + inf. cstr. of עבר hi. *cause to pass* Est $8_3$.

<SYN> שׁחר pi. *seek*, זעק *cry*.

Also 4QWiles $2_4$.*

⇒ חֵן *grace*, חֲנִינָה *grace, favour*, חַנּוּן *gracious*, תְּחִנָּה *supplication*, תַּחֲנוּנִים *supplications*, חָנָן *Hanan*, חַנָּא *Hanna*, חַנָּה *Hannah*, חָנוּן *Hanun*, חָנִין *Hanin*, חֲנִינָא *Hanina*, חֲנָנָה *Hananah*, חֲנָנִי *Hanani*, חֲנִיָּהוּ *Hanniah*, חַנִּמֶלֶךְ *Hannimelech*, חֲנַנְיָה *Hananiah*, אֶלְחָנָן *Elhanan*, חַנִּאָב *Hanniab*, חַנִּיאֵל *Hanniel*, חֲנַנְאֵל *Hananel*, יְהוֹחָנָן *Jehohanan*.

**חנן II** 1 vb. **be loathsome—Qal** 1 + waw וְחַנֹּתִי—**be loathsome,** <SUBJ> Job Jb $19_{17}$ (|| זור *be loathsome*). <PREP> לְ of direction, *to*, + בֵּן *son* Jb $19_{17}$. <SYN> זור *be loathsome*.

**חָנָן** 12.0.0.11 pr.n.m. **Hanan, 1.** son of Maacah, and soldier in David's army, <NOM CL> גִּבּוֹרֵי הַחֲיָלִים ... חָנָן *the mighty men of the armies were ... Hanan* 1 C $11_{43}$. <APP> בֶּן *son* 1 C $11_{43}$.

**2.** Levite, co-signatory with Nehemiah, and law-interpreter, <SUBJ> בין *understand* Ne $8_7$, hi. *explain* Ne $8_7$, קרא *read* Ne $8_7$, שׂים *put* Ne $8_7$. <NOM CL> ... אֲחֵיהֶם חָנָן *their brothers were ... Hanan* Ne $10_{11}$.

**3.** family head at time of Nehemiah, <NOM CL> רָאשֵׁי הָעָם ... חָנָן *the chiefs of the people were ... Hanan* Ne $10_{23}$.

**4.** chief of people at time of Nehemiah, <NOM CL> רָאשֵׁי הָעָם ... חָנָן *the chiefs of the people were ... Hanan* Ne $10_{27}$ (or em. חֲנָנִי *Hanani*).

**5.** son of Zaccur, a singer, and assistant to Shelemiah, Zadok and Pedaiah, <SUBJ> אמן ni. *be trustworthy* Ne $13_{13}$, חלק *divide* Ne $13_{13}$. <NOM CL> עַל־יָדָם חָנָן *over their hand*, i.e. as their assistant, *was Hanan* Ne $13_{13}$. <APP> בֶּן *son* Ne $13_{13}$.

**6.** chief, descendant of Benjamin and son of Shashak, <NOM CL> זִכְרִי וְחָנָן ... בְּנֵי שָׁשָׁק *Zichri and Hanan ... were the sons of Shashak* 1 C $8_{23}$.

**7.** one of six sons of Azel, <NOM CL> ... אֵלֶּה שְׁמוֹתָם עֹבַדְיָה וְחָנָן *these were their names: ... Obadiah and Hanan* 1 C $8_{38}$||1 C $9_{44}$.

**8.** ancestor of Nethinim, temple servants, <CSTR> בְּנֵי חָנָן *sons of Hanan* Ezr $2_{46}$||Ne $7_{49}$.

**9.** son of Igdaliah or Gedaliah, and father of temple officials, <CSTR> בְּנֵי חָנָן *sons of Hanan* Jr $35_{4(L)}$ (ms יְחָנָן Jehanan; mss בֶּן־ *son of*). <APP> בֶּן *son* Jr $35_4$.

**10.** father of Shual, Arad ost. $38_2$. **11.** appar. recipient of goods, Samaria ost. $43_2$ $45_2$ $46_2$ $47_1$. **12.** appar. son of Jedaliah, Seal 49 (Jerusalem 8th/7th cent.). **13.** son of Uzziah, Seal 563 (T. Beit Mirsim?, 7th/6th cent.). **14.** son of Shemaiah, Seal 564 (T. Beit Mirsim?, 7th/6th cent.). **15.** son of Hilkiah, Seal 734 (8th/7th cent.). **16.** Arad ost. $38_6$. **17.** Arad ost. 92. **18.** T. Batash bowl rim inscr. **19.** Seal 918 (8th cent.).

<CSTR> בן חנן *son of Hanan* Arad ost. $38_2$ ([ב]ן חנ[ן]; others אן appar. error for בן) T. Batash bowl rim inscr. ([ב]ן). <APP> בֶּן *son* Seal 563 564 (both T. Beit Mirsim?, 7th/6th cent.) 734 (8th/7th cent.), כֹּהֵן *priest* perh. Seal 734 (8th/7th cent.). <PREP> לְ of possession, *(belonging) to, of* Arad ost. 92 Samaria ost. $43_2$ (ל[ח]נן) $45_2$ $46_2$ $47_1$ Seal 49 (Jerusalem 8th/7th cent.) 563 (לחנ[ן]) 564 (both T. Beit Mirsim?, 7th/6th cent.) 734 (8th/7th cent.) 918 (8th cent.).

⇒ חנן *be gracious*.

**חֲנַנְאֵל I** 4 pl.n. **Hananel,** name of tower in Jerusalem, in northern part of city wall, <CSTR> מִגְדַּל חֲנַנְאֵל *tower of Hananel* Jr $31_{38}$ Zc $14_{10}$ Ne $3_1$ $12_{39}$.

⇒ חנן *be gracious* + אֵל *God*.

**חֲנַנְאֵל II** 0.0.0.1 pr.n.m. **Hananel,** husband of Alijah, <CSTR> אשת חננאל *wife of Hananel* Seal 157 (others אמת *official of*; Amman c. 600).

⇒ חנן *be gracious* + אֵל *God*.

**[חֲנָנָה]** 0.0.0.1 pr.n.f. **Hananah,** Stamp 9 (5th/4th cent.).

⇒ חנן *be gracious*.

**חֲנָנִי** 12.0.0.1 pr.n.m. **Hanani, 1.** seer at time of Asa, <SUBJ> בוא *come* 2 C 16$_7$, אמר *say* 2 C 16$_7$. <CSTR> בֶּן־חֲנָנִי *son of Hanani* 1 K 16$_{1.7}$ 2 C 19$_2$ 20$_{34}$. <APP> רֹאֶה *seer* 2 C 16$_7$.

**2.** brother of Nehemiah, and governor of Jerusalem,* <SUBJ> בוא *come* Ne 1$_2$, אמר *say* Ne 1$_2$, עמד hi. *set* Ne 7$_{2(L)}$ (ms אַעֲמִיד with Nehemiah as subj.). <OBJ> שׁאל *ask* Ne 1$_2$, צוה pi. *give charge over* Ne 7$_2$. <APP> אֶחָד *one* Ne 1$_2$, אָח *brother* Ne 7$_2$. <PREP> לְ of direction, *to*, + אמר *say* Ne 7$_2$.

**3.** musician and relative of Zechariah son of Jonathan, <NOM CL> חֲנָנִי בִּכְלֵי־שִׁיר דָּוִיד *Hanani was with David's instruments of song* Ne 12$_{36}$. <APP> אָח *brother* Ne 12$_{36}$.

**4.** son of Heman the seer, <NOM CL> לְהֵימָן ... חֲנָנִי *(belonging) to Heman were ... Hanani* 1 C 25$_4$. <APP> בֵּן *son* 1 C 25$_4$. <PREP> לְ of direction, *to*, + יצא *go out* (of lot) 1 C 25$_{25}$.

**5.** priest, descendant of Immer, and husband of foreign wife, <NOM CL> מִבְּנֵי אִמֵּר חֲנָנִי וּזְבַדְיָה *of the sons of Immer were Hanani and Zebadiah* Ezr 10$_{20}$ (mss Zechariah).

**6.** family head at time of Nehemiah, <NOM CL> רָאשֵׁי הָעָם ... חֲנָנִי *the chiefs of the people were ... Hanani* Ne 10$_{27}$ (if em. חָנָן *Hanan*).

**7.** Seal 650 (T. Beit Mirsim?, 7th/6th cent.).

⇒ חנן *be gracious*.

**חֲנַנְיָה** 28.0.3.33 pr.n.m. **Hananiah**—חֲנַנְיָהוּ—**1.** son of Azzur, and prophet from Gibeon, <SUBJ> לקח *take* Jr 28$_{10}$, אמר *say* Jr 28$_{1.1.11.11}$, דבר pi. *speak* Jr 28$_{15}$, שׁמע *hear* Jr 28$_{5.15}$, נבא ni. *prophesy* Jr 28$_5$, שׁבר *break* Jr 28$_{10.12.13}$, עשׂה *do* Jr 28$_{13}$ (or em.), בטח hi. *cause to trust* Jr 28$_{15}$, מות *die* Jr 28$_{15.17}$. <OBJ> שׁלח *send* Jr 28$_{15}$, pi. *send away* Jr 28$_{15}$. <APP> בֵּן *son* Jr 28$_1$, נָבִיא *prophet* Jr 28$_{1.5.10.12.15.17}$. <PREP> אֶל *to*, + אמר *say* Jr 28$_{5.13.15}$; לִפְנֵי *before*, + היה *be* Jr 28$_5$.

**2.** descendant of Judah and companion of Daniel, <SUBJ> היה *be* Dn 1$_6$, עמד *stand* Dn 1$_{19}$. <OBJ> מצא *find* Dn 1$_{19}$. <PREP> לְ of direction, *to*, + שׂים *put* Dn 1$_{7.7}$; כְּ *as* Dn 1$_{19}$; מִן of direction, *from*, + בקשׁ pi. *seek* Dn 1$_{19}$; עַל *over*, + מנה pi. *appoint* Dn 1$_{11}$.

**3.** father of Shelemiah, <CSTR> בֶּן־חֲנַנְיָה *son of Hananiah* Jr 37$_{13}$.

**4.** son of Zerubbabel, and father of Pelatiah and Jeshaiah, <NOM CL> בֶּן־זְרֻבָּבֶל מְשֻׁלָּם וַחֲנַנְיָה *the son of Zerubbabel was Meshullam and Hananiah* 1 C 3$_{19}$ (mss בְּנֵי־ *sons of*). <CSTR> בֶּן־חֲנַנְיָה *son of Hananiah* 1 C 3$_{21}$ (or em. בְּנֵי *sons of*).

**5.** chief, descendant of Benjamin and son of Shashak, <NOM CL> חֲנַנְיָה וְעֵילָם ... : בְּנֵי שָׁשָׁק *Hananiah and Elam ... were the sons of Shashak* 1 C 8$_{24}$ (or ins. וְעָמְרִי *and Omri*).

**6.** son of Heman the seer, <NOM CL> לְהֵימָן ... חֲנַנְיָה *(belonging) to Heman were ... Hananiah* 1 C 25$_4$, לְשִׁשָּׁה עָשָׂר לַחֲנַנְיָהוּ *the sixteenth (lot) was (for) Hananiah* 1 C 25$_{23}$. <APP> בֵּן *son* 1 C 25$_4$.

**7.** father of Zedekiah, <CSTR> בֶּן־חֲנַנְיָהוּ *son of Hananiah* Jr 36$_{12}$.

**8.** commander in Uzziah's army, <CSTR> יַד־חֲנַנְיָהוּ *hand of Hananiah* 2 C 26$_{11}$.

**9.** son of Bebai, <NOM CL> מִבְּנֵי בֵּבָי ... חֲנַנְיָה *of the sons of Bebai were ... Hananiah* Ezr 10$_{28}$.

**10.** perfumer and repairer of walls of Jerusalem, <SUBJ> חזק hi. *strengthen* Ne 3$_8$, עזב *restore* Ne 3$_8$. <APP> בֵּן *son* Ne 3$_8$.

**11.** son of Shelemiah, <SUBJ> חזק hi. *strengthen* Ne 3$_{30}$. <APP> בֵּן *son* Ne 3$_{30}$.

**12.** governor at time of Nehemiah, <SUBJ> עמד hi. *set* Ne 7$_{2(L)}$ (ms אַעֲמִיד, subj. Nehemiah), ירא *fear* Ne 7$_2$. <OBJ> צוה pi. *give charge over* Ne 7$_2$*. <APP> שַׂר *prince* Ne 7$_2$. <PREP> לְ of direction, *to*, + אמר *say* Ne 7$_2$.*

**13.** family head at time of Nehemiah, <NOM CL> רָאשֵׁי הָעָם ... חֲנַנְיָה *the chiefs of the people were ... Hananiah* Ne 10$_{24}$.

**14.** priestly family head at time of Joiakim, <NOM CL> לְיִרְמְיָה חֲנַנְיָה *(belonging) to Jeremiah was Hananiah* Ne 12$_{12}$.

**15.** temple musician, son of Jonathan, descendant of Asaph, <NOM CL> הַכֹּהֲנִים ... זְכַרְיָה חֲנַנְיָה בַּחֲצֹצְרוֹת *the priests were ... Zechariah (and) Hananiah, with trumpets* Ne 12$_{41}$.

**16.** son of Simeon (שמ[עון]), 4Q477 2.2$_{5.9}$. **17.** father of Jonathan, Mur 30 2$_{10}$. **18.** son of Tiriah (others

Todiah), Seal 23 (Babylonia?, 8th/7th cent.). **19.** appar. father of Ahima, Seal 845 (City of David 7th/6th cent.). **20.** official, Arad ost. 3$_3$ 16$_1$. **21.** Arad ost. 36$_4$. **22.** appar. son of Neriah, Gibeon jar handle inscr. 22 24 (חננ]יהו]) 32 33 35 37 (חנ]ניהו]) 38 40 41 42 (ח]נניהו]) 43 (חנני]הו]) 44 (חנניה]ו]) 45 46 (both חנניהו]) 47 (ח]נניהו]) 48 49 (both חנניהו]) 50 51 (חננ]יהו]) 52 57 62 (חנניה]ו]). **23.** Kh. el-Meshash ost. 1543.1$_3$. **24.** son of Azariah, Seal 24 (Jerusalem, 7th cent.). **25.** son of Achbor, Seal 25 (Jerusalem, 7th cent.). **26.** appar. son of Neriah, Seal 50 (Jerusalem, 7th cent.). **27.** Seal 218 (6th cent.). **28.** appar. father of Hizziliah, Seal 419 (6th cent.). **29.** appar. father of Uriah, Seal 429 (8th/7th cent.). **30.** appar. son of Nehemiah, Seal 561 (T. Beit Mirsim?, 7th/6th cent.). **31.** appar. son of Zerah, Seal 562 (T. Beit Mirsim?, 7th/6th cent.). **32.** appar. father of Menahem, Seal 600 (T. Beit Mirsim?, 7th/6th cent.). **33.** son of Kolaiah, Seal 715 (7th/6th cent.). **34.** son of Aha, Seal 834 (City of David, 7th/6th cent.). **35.** governor of Samaria, coin 29 30 (חננ]יה]; both 4th cent.).

<SUBJ> צוה pi. *command* Arad ost. 3$_3$, שׁלח *send* Arad ost. 16$_1$. <OBJ> יכח hi. *reprove* 4Q477 2.2$_{5.9}$ ([הוכיחו]). <CSTR> בר חנניה *son of Hananiah* Mur 30 2$_{10}$. <APP> בֵּן *son* 4Q477 2.2$_9$ Kh. el-Meshash ost. 1543.1$_3$ (בן]) Seal 23 (Babylonia?, 8th/7th cent.) 24 25 (both Jerusalem, 7th cent.) 218 (6th cent.) 715 (7th/6th cent.) 834 (City of David. 7th/6th cent.), אָח *brother* Arad ost. 16$_1$. <PREP> לְ of possession, *(belonging) to, of* Gibeon jar handle inscr. 51 Seal 23 (Babylonia?, 8th/7th cent.) 24 25 50 (all three Jerusalem, 7th cent.) 218 (6th cent.) 561 (T. Beit Mirsim?, 7th/6th cent.) 715 (7th/6th cent.) 834 (City of David, 7th/6th cent.).*

→ חנן *be gracious* + ׳י *Y.*

**חֲנַנְיָהוּ**, see חֲנַנְיָה *Hananiah.*

**חָנֵס** 1.0.1 pl.n. **Hanes,** city in Egypt, perh. Aḥnās, on Nile W of Beni Suef, <OBJ> נגע *reach* Is 30$_4$=4QpIsa$^c$ 21$_{14}$.

**חנף I** 11 vb. **be polluted—Qal** 7 Pf. חָנְפוּ, חָנְפָה; impf. 3fs תֶּחֱנַף (תֶּחְנַף); + waw 3fs וַתֶּחֱנַף; inf. abs. חָנוֹף—**1. be polluted,** <SUBJ> בַּת *daughter* of Zion Mc 4$_{11}$=4QpMic 1$_5$ ([תח]נף]; or em. תֶּחֱנַף *be violated,* i.e. חנף III ni., or תֶּחְשַׂף *let her be stripped,* i.e. חשׂף ni.), אֶרֶץ *land* Is 24$_5$ (unless חנף III *suffer outrage*) Jr 3$_{1.1}$ Ps 106$_{38}$ (or em. תֶּחֱנַף). <PREP> בְּ of instrument, *by (means of), with,* + דָּם *blood* Ps 106$_{38}$ (or em.); תַּחַת *on account of,* + יֹשֵׁב *inhabitant* Is 24$_5$.

**2. be impious,** <SUBJ> נָבִיא *prophet* Jr 23$_{11}$, כֹּהֵן *priest* Jr 23$_{11}$.

**3. pollute,** <SUBJ> Judah Jr 3$_9$ (or em. hi.), מְשׁוּבָה *apostate one* Jr 3$_9$ (or em.). <OBJ> אֶרֶץ *land* Jr 3$_9$ (or em.).

**Hi.** 4 Impf. תַּחֲנִיפוּ, יַחֲנִיף; + waw וַתַּחֲנִיפִי—**pollute,** <SUBJ> Israel(ites) Nm 35$_{33.33}$ Jr 3$_2$ (unless חנף III hi. *violate* in all three), Judah 3$_9$ (if em. qal, but then perh. חנף III), מֶלֶךְ *king* Dn 11$_{32}$ (unless em. יַחֲנִיף *he will pollute* to יַחֲנִיפוּ *they will pollute*), מַרְשִׁיעַ *wicked one* Dn 11$_{32}$ (if em.), מְשׁוּבָה *apostate one* Jr 3$_9$ (if em.), דָּם *blood* Nm 35$_{33}$ (unless חנף III) 4QJub$^d$ 21$_{19}$ ([הדם ... מחניף]). <OBJ> אֶרֶץ *land* Nm 35$_{33.33}$ Jr 3$_{2.9}$ (if em.) 4QJub$^d$ 21$_{19}$ ([מחניף את ארץ]), מַרְשִׁיעַ *wicked one* Dn 11$_{32}$ (unless em.; see Subj.). <PREP> בְּ of instrument, *by (means of), with,* + זְנוּת *fornication* Jr 3$_2$, רָעָה *evil* Jr 3$_2$, חֲלָק *smooth thing,* i.e. flattery Dn 11$_{32}$.*

→ חָנֵף *profane,* חֹנֶף *profaneness, hypocrisy,* חֲנֻפָּה *profanity.*

**[חנף] II** vb. **limp,** <SUBJ> worshipper Ps 35$_{16}$ (if em. בְּחַנְפֵי appar. *as profane ones of* to בְּחַנְפִי *when I limped*).

***[חנף] III** 4 vb. **be outraged—Qal** 1 Pf. חָנְפָה—**suffer outrage,** <SUBJ> אֶרֶץ *land* Is 24$_5$. <PREP> תַּחַת *on account of,* + יֹשֵׁב *inhabitant* Is 24$_5$ (unless חנף I *be polluted*).

**Ni. suffer outrage, be violated**—<SUBJ> בַּת *daughter* of Zion Mc 4$_{11}$ (if em. תֶּחֱנָף *is polluted,* i.e. חנף I qal), אֶרֶץ *land* Ps 106$_{38}$ (if em. תֶּחֱנַף). <PREP> בְּ of instrument, *by (means of), with,* + דָּם *blood* Ps 106$_{38}$ (if em.).

**Hi.** 3 Impf. תַּחֲנִיפוּ, יַחֲנִיף; + waw וַתַּחֲנִיפִי—**subject to outrage, violate,** <SUBJ> Israel Jr 3$_2$, Judah Jr 3$_9$ (if em. וַתֶּחֱנַף *and it* [land] *was polluted,* i.e. חנף I, qal, to וַתַּחֲנִף *and she violated* the land), בֵּן *son* of Israel Nm 35$_{33}$, דָּם *blood* Nm 35$_{33}$. <OBJ> אֶרֶץ *land* Nm 35$_{33.33}$ Jr 3$_{2.9}$ (if em.). <PREP> בְּ of instrument, *by (means of), with,* + זְנוּת *fornication* Jr 3$_2$, רָעָה *evil* Jr 3$_2$.

→ חֹנֶף *shame.*

**חָנֵף I** 13.3.1 adj. **profane**—pl. חֲנֵפִים; cstr. חַנְפֵי—**profane, impious, 1.** as adjective, used attributively of אָדָם *human being* Jb 34$_{30}$, גּוֹי *nation* Is 10$_{6}$ Si 16$_{6}$ (+ עדת רשעים *company of wicked ones*).

2. as adjective, in nom. cl. used predicatively of כֹּל *everyone* Is 9$_{16}$ (+ מֵרַע *wicked*); in verbal clause, with מצא ni. *be found* 4Q424 1$_{12}$.

3. as noun, **profane one, impious one,** <SUBJ> בוא *come* Jb 13$_{16}$, שׁוב *go back* Si 41$_{10}$, שׂים *place* anger Jb 36$_{13}$ (unless חָנֵף II *haughty;* or em. יָשִׂימוּ *they place* to יִשְׁמוּ *they breathe* from כשם *pant*), שׁוע pi. *cry for help* Jb 36$_{13}$, שׁחת hi. *destroy* Pr 11$_{9}$ (unless em. בְּפֶה חָנֵף יַשְׁחִת רֵעֵהוּ *with [his] mouth the impious would destroy his neighbour* to בְּפִי חָנֵף יָשְׁחַת רֵעֵהוּ *by the mouth of the wicked is his neighbour destroyed,* or בְּפִי חָנֵף שַׁחַת רָעָה *in the mouth of the impious is an evil pit*). <OBJ> אסר *bind* Jb 36$_{13}$, אחז *seize* Is 33$_{14}$ (+ חַטָּא *sinner*). <CSTR> חַנְפֵי־לֵב *those impious of heart* Jb 36$_{13}$ (or *those haughty of heart,* i.e. חָנֵף II); תִּקְוַת חָנֵף *hope of a impious one* Jb 8$_{13}$ (+ שׁכח ptc. *one who forgets* God) 27$_{8}$, שִׂמְחַת *joy of* Jb 20$_{5}$ (|| רָשָׁע *wicked one*), עֲדַת *company of* Jb 15$_{34}$, פֶּה *mouth of* Pr 11$_{9}$ (if em.; see Subj.), עַצְמוֹת *bones of* Ps 53$_{6}$ (if em. חֹנֵךְ *of him who camps against you*), שורש *root of* Si 40$_{15}$. <PREP> בְּ *as,* בְּחַנְפֵי לַעֲגֵי מָעוֹג appar. *as profane ones of mockers of a cake* Ps 35$_{16}$ (or em. בְּחַנְפִי *when I limped,* from חנף II *limp,* or בְּחָנֻנִי *they tested me,* or בְּהִנָּפְלִי *when I prostrated myself*); עַל *against,* + עור htpol. *rouse oneself* Jb 17$_{8}$ (or em. חֹנֶף *shame*).

<SYN> §3 רָשָׁע *wicked one.**

→ חנף *be polluted.*

* **[חָנֵף] II** 1 adj. **haughty,** used as noun, **haughty one,** <SUBJ> שׂים *place* anger Jb 36$_{13}$ (unless חָנֵף I *profane;* or em. יָשִׂימוּ *they place* to יִשְׁמוּ *they breathe* from כשם *pant*), שׁוע pi. *cry for help* Jb 36$_{13}$. <CSTR> חַנְפֵי־לֵב *those haughty of heart* Jb 36$_{13}$ (unless *those impious of heart,* i.e. חָנֵף I *profane*).

**חֹנֶף** 2.0.1 n.[m.] **profaneness,** <OBJ> עשׂה *do* Is 32$_{6}$=4QpIsa$^{c}$ 26$_{3}$=4QpIsa$^{e}$ 6$_{3}$ (C [לעשות חנף], E [לעשות חנף]; + תּוֹעָה *error*). <CSTR> רוב חנף *abundance of profaneness* 1QS 4$_{10}$. <PREP> עַל *against,* + עור htpol. *rouse oneself* Jb 17$_{8}$ (if em. חָנֵף *profane one*).*

→ חנף *be polluted.*

**חֲנֻפָּה** 1.0.1 n.f. **impiousness**—Q חנופה—**impiousness, profaneness,** <SUBJ> יצא *go out* Jr 23$_{15}$. <OBJ> עשׂה *do* 4QTestim$_{28}$ (|| נְאָצָה *contempt*). <SYN> נְאָצָה *contempt.**

→ חנף *be polluted.*

**חנק** 2.0.1 vb. **strangle**—**Ni.** 1 + waw וַיֵּחָנַק—**hang oneself,** <SUBJ> Ahithophel 2 S 17$_{23}$.

**Pi.** 1.0.1 Ptc. מְחַנֵּק—**strangle,** of lion strangling prey, <SUBJ> אַרְיֵה *lion* Na 2$_{13}$=4QpNah 3.1$_{4}$ (ארי; + טרף *tear*). <PREP> לְ of benefit, *for,* + לְבִיא *lioness* Na 2$_{13}$=4QpNah 3.1$_{4}$.

→ מַחֲנָק *strangling.*

**חַנָּתֹן** 1 pl.n. **Hannathon,** town in Zebulun, perh. T. el-Bedēwīye, 27 km W of Tiberias, <COLL> וְנָסַב ... מִצְּפוֹן חַנָּתֹן *and it* (border) *turns … on the north to Hannathon* Jos 19$_{14}$.

**חסד I** 2 vb. **be loyal**—**Htp.** 2 Impf. 2ms תִּתְחַסָּד—**show oneself loyal,** <SUBJ> Y. 2 S 22$_{26}$||Ps 18$_{26}$ (|| תמם htp. *show oneself blameless*). <PREP> עִם *with,* + חָסִיד *loyal one* S 22$_{26}$||Ps 18$_{26}$. <SYN> תמם htp. *show oneself blameless.*

→ חֶסֶד *loyalty,* חָסִיד *loyal,* חַסְדָּא *Hasda,* חֲסַדְיָה *Hasadiah.*

**חסד II** 1 **be ashamed**— **Pi.** 1 יְחַסֶּדְךָ—**bring shame upon, reproach,** <SUBJ> שׁמע ptc. *one who hears* Pr 25$_{10}$, נֶפֶשׁ *soul* Si 14$_{2}$ (if em. חסרתו *it has* not *caused him to lack;* to חסדתו *it has* not *reproached him*). <OBJ> Israelite Pr 25$_{10}$, אִישׁ *man* Si 14$_{2}$ (if em.; see Subj.).

→ חֶסֶד II *shame.*

**חֶסֶד I** 246.26.104.1. n.m. **loyalty**—cstr. חֶסֶד (חֲסֶד); sf. חַסְדִּי, חַסְדָּם, חַסְדְּכֶם, חַסְדּוֹ, חַסְדֵּךְ (חַסְדֵּךְ, Q חסדכה), חַסְדֶּךָ; pl. חֲסָדִים; cstr. חַסְדֵי; sf. חֲסָדַי, חֲסָדֶיךָ (חֲסָדֶךָ, Q חסדיכה), חֲסָדָיו—**loyalty, faithfulness, kindness, love, mercy,** pl. **mercies, (deeds of) kindness,** of Y. to humans (e.g. Ex 15$_{13}$ Nm 14$_{18}$ Is 63$_{7}$ Jr 31$_{3}$ Mc 7$_{20}$ Ps 25$_{7}$ 33$_{22}$ 89$_{2}$ Jb

$10_{12}$ 1QS $11_{12}$), of humans to Y. (e.g. Jr $2_2$ Ho $6_{4.6}$), between humans (e.g. Gn $32_{11}$ 1 S $20_{15}$ 2 S $16_{17}$ Ps $141_5$ Pr $19_{22}$), of things (Is $40_6$ 4Q185 $1.1_{10}$).

<SUBJ> היה *be* Ps $33_{22}$ $119_{76}$, אפס *cease* Ps $77_9$ (+ אֹמֶר *word*), תמם *cease* Lm $3_{22(ms)}$ (‖ רַחֲמִים *compassion*), גמר *cease* Ps $21_2$ (if em. חָסִיד *loyal one* to חֶסֶד), מוּשׁ *depart* Is $54_{10}$=4QTanḥ $8_{12}$ (+ בְּרִית *covenant*), סור *turn aside* 2 S $7_{15}$, מוט ni. *be moved* Si $40_{17(B)}$ (‖ צְדָקָה *righteousness*), כרת ni. *be cut off* Si $40_{17(M)}$, פרח *flourish* 4Q185 $1.1_{10}$, גבר *be mighty* Ps $103_{11}$ (unless em. גָּבַר *it is mighty* to גִּבַּר *he has made mighty*, or גָּבְהָ *it is high*) $117_2$ (+ אֱמֶת *truth*), אמן ni. *be established* Is $55_3$ Si $50_{24}$, בנה ni. *be built*, i.e. established Ps $89_3$ (+ אֱמוּנָה *faithfulness*), ברך pass. *be blessed* Ps $144_2$ (or em. חָסְנִי *my stronghold* or סַלְעִי *my rock*), ספר pu. *be recounted* Ps $88_{12}$ (+ אֱמוּנָה), כתב pass. *be written* 2 C $32_{32}$ $35_{26}$ (both + דָּבָר *word*), קדם pi. *meet* Ps $89_{15}$ (‖ אֱמֶת, + צֶדֶק, מִשְׁפָּט *justice*), פגשׁ ni. *meet one another* Ps $85_{11}$ (‖ אֱמֶת, + צֶדֶק, שָׁלוֹם *peace*), בוא *come* Ps $119_{41}$, סבב pol. *encircle* Ps $32_{10}$, רדף *pursue* Ps $23_6$ (‖ טוֹב *goodness*), עזב *forsake* Pr $3_3$ (‖ אֱמֶת), נטשׁ *forsake* Si $47_{22}$, נחם pi. *comfort* Ps $119_{76}$, סעד *support* Ps $94_{18}$, נצר *guard* Ps $40_{12}$ (+ רַחֲמִים *compassion*) $61_8$ Pr $20_{28}$ (unless em. יִצְּרוּ *they keep* to יִצֹּר *he keeps*, with חֶסֶד as obj.; all three ‖ אֱמֶת).

<NOM CL> כָּל־אָרְחוֹת י׳ חֶסֶד וֶאֱמֶת *all the paths of Y. are loyalty and truth* Ps $25_{10}$, חסדי אל ישועתי *the mercies of God are my salvation* 1QS $11_{12}$, חֶסֶד וֶאֱמֶת חֹרְשֵׁי טוֹב *loyalty and truth are (to) those who plan good* Pr $14_{22}$ (or em. לְחֹרְשֵׁי *to those who plan*), חֶסֶד י׳ מֵעוֹלָם *the faithfulness of Y. is from eternity* to eternity Ps $103_{17}$ (+ צְדָקָה *righteousness*), חסדיו אשר מעולם *his mercies which are from eternity* Si $51_8$, חֶסֶד אֵל כָּל־הַיּוֹם *the faithfulness of God is*, i.e. remains, *all the day* Ps $52_3$ (or em.; see Cstr.), חַסְדִּי עִמּוֹ *my faithfulness is with him* Ps $89_{25}$ (+ אֱמוּנָה *faithfulness*), חסדי ברכה [לאלפיכה] *mercies of blessing are to your thousands* 1QM $12_3$, חַסְדְּךָ לְעוֹלָם *your faithfulness is to eternity* Ps $138_8$, חַסְדְּךָ לְנֶגֶד עֵינָי *your faithfulness is before my eyes* Ps $26_3$ (+ אֱמֶת *truth*), בְּהַשָּׁמַיִם חַסְדֶּךָ *your faithfulness is in the heavens* Ps $36_6$ (+ אֱמוּנָה), תַּאֲוַת אָדָם חַסְדּוֹ *the desire of a human is one's loyalty* Pr $19_{22}$ (or em. סַחְרוֹ *one's profit*), חַסְדְּכֶם כַּעֲנַן־בֹּקֶר *your loyalty is as a cloud of the morning* Ho $6_4$, כָּל־חַסְדּוֹ כְּצִיץ הַשָּׂדֶה *all its loyalty*, i.e. *constancy, is as the flower of the field* Is $40_6$ (or em. הֲדָרוֹ *its glory*, or חֶמְדּוֹ *its desirability*). גָּדוֹל חַסְדְּךָ *your faithfulness is great* Ps $86_{13}$, sim. Ps $57_{11}$‖$108_5$ (+ אֱמֶת), טוֹב חַסְדְּךָ *good is your faithfulness* Ps $63_4$ $69_{17}$ $109_{21}$ (or em.; see Cstr.).* לְךָ־אֲדֹנָי חָסֶד *to you, O Lord, is faithfulness* Ps $62_{13}$, מֵרֵעֵהוּ חָסֶד *loyalty is (due) from his friend* Jb $6_{14}$ (or em.; see Obj.), עִם־י׳ חֶסֶד *with Y. is faithfulness* Ps $130_7$, עִמָּךְ חֶסֶד *faithfulness be with you* 2 S $15_{20}$ (or em. וַי׳ יַעֲשֶׂה עִמְּךָ חֶסֶד *may Y. do kindness with you*; ‖ אֱמֶת). כִּי־לְעוֹלָם חַסְדּוֹ *for his mercy is to eternity* Jr $33_{11}$ Ps $100_5$ (+ אֱמוּנָה *faithfulness*) $106_1$‖1 C $16_{34}$ Ps $107_1$ $118_{1.2.3.4.29}$ $136_{1+25t}$ (לְעֹלָם at Ps $136_3$) Ezr $3_{11}$ 1 C $16_{41}$ 2 C $5_{13}$ $7_{3.6}$ $20_{21}$ Si $51_{12(14t)}$, חסדי עולם לכול קצ[יהם] *eternal mercies are to all their end times* 1QH $13_5$, חסד ואמת סביב פניו *faithfulness and truth are around his presence* 11QPs$^a$ $26_{10}$ (+ מִשְׁפָּט *justice*, צֶדֶק *justice*). זֶה חַסְדֵּךְ *this is your kindness* Gn $20_{13}$, var. 2 S $16_{17}$, אַיֵּה חֲסָדֶיךָ *where are your acts of mercy?* Ps $89_{50}$ (+ אֱמוּנָה), מַה־יָּקָר חַסְדְּךָ *how precious is your faithfulness* Ps $36_8$ 1QH $1_6$ (מה [יקר חסדך]), אֵין־חֶסֶד ... בָּאָרֶץ *there is no loyalty ... in the land* Ho $4_1$ (‖ אֱמֶת, + דַּעַת *knowledge* of God), [אין בהם חסד] *there is no loyalty among them* 4Q Jub$^f$ $23_{23}$.

<OBJ> גדל pi. *make great* 11QPs$^a$ $18_{14}$, hi. *make great* Gn $19_{19}$, גבר pi. *make mighty* Ps $103_{11}$ (if em.; see Subj.), שׂבע pi. *satisfy* Ps $90_{14}$, חפץ *delight in* Ho $6_6$ (+ דַּעַת *knowledge*, :: זֶבַח *sacrifice*) Mc $7_{18}$, ראה hi. *show* Ps $85_8$ (+ יֶשַׁע *salvation*), אהב *love* Mc $6_8$ (‖ מִשְׁפָּט *justice*) 4Q298 $3_7$ Ketef Hinnom inscr. $1_5$ ([א]הב), עטר pi. *crown with* Ps $103_4$ (‖ רַחֲמִים *compassion*), יטב hi. *make good* Ru $3_{10}$, שׁלח *send* Ps $57_4$ (‖ אֱמֶת *truth*), רדף *pursue* Pr $21_{21}$ (‖ צְדָקָה *righteousness*), נשׂא *raise*, i.e. win favour Est $2_{9.17}$ (‖ חֵן *grace*), נתן *give* Mc $7_{20}$ (‖ אֱמֶת) 4QapPs$^b$ $33_5$ ([ו]תתן), גמל *repay* Si $37_{11(B)}$, מנה pi. *appoint* Ps $61_8$ (מַן *appoint* is lacking in mss), מנע *withhold* Si $7_{33}$.

עשׂה *do*, i.e. perform Gn $19_{19}$ $20_{13}$ $24_{12.14.49}$ (‖ אֱמֶת *truth*) $32_{11}$ (‖ אֱמֶת) $40_{14}$ $47_{29}$ (‖ אֱמֶת) Ex $20_6$‖Dt $5_{10}$ Jos $2_{12.12.14}$ (‖ אֱמֶת) Jg $1_{24}$ $8_{35}$ 1 S $15_6$ $20_{8.14}$ 2 S $2_{5.6}$ (‖ אֱמֶת) $3_8$ $9_{1.3.7}$ $10_{2.2}$‖1 C $19_{2.2}$ 2 S $22_{51}$‖Ps $18_{51}$ 2 S $15_{20}$ (if em.; see Nom. Cl.) 1 K $2_7$ $3_6$‖2 C $1_8$ 1 K $3_6$ Jr $9_{23}$ (‖ מִשְׁפָּט *judgment*, צְדָקָה *righteousness*) $32_{18}$ Zc $7_9$ (‖ רַחֲמִים *com-*

*passion*) Ps 109$_{16}$ Jb 10$_{12}$ (|| חַיִּים *life*) Ru 1$_{8}$ Ne 13$_{14}$ 2 C 24$_{22}$ Si 46$_{7}$ 49$_{3}$ CD 20$_{21}$ 1QH 16$_{9}$ ([לעש]ות]) 16$_{13}$ ([חסד]) 4QJub$^{f}$ 23$_{31}$ ([עושה חסד]), פלא hi. *make wonderful* Ps 17$_{7(Gnz, mss)}$ 31$_{22}$ (or em. חֲסִידוֹ *his faithful one*) 1QM 14$_{9}$, פלה hi. *make distinct* Ps 4$_{4}$ (if em. חָסִיד לוֹ *the loyal one to him* to חֶסֶד לִי *[his] loyalty to me*) 17$_{7}$, שׁלם hi. *make complete* 1QH 16$_{12}$ ([חס]דיך]), משׁך *extend* Jr 31$_{3}$ (+ אַהֲבָה *love*) Ps 36$_{11}$ (|| צְדָקָה *righteousness*) 109$_{12}$, נטה *extend* Gn 39$_{21}$, hi. *extend* Ezr 7$_{28}$ 9$_{9}$, שׁמר *keep* Dt 7$_{9.12}$ (both || בְּרִית *covenant*) 1 K 8$_{23}$||2 C 6$_{14}$ (|| בְּרִית) Ho 12$_{7}$ (|| מִשְׁפָּט *judgment*) Ps 89$_{29}$ (+ בְּרִית) Dn 9$_{4}$ Ne 1$_{5}$ 9$_{32}$ CD 19$_{1}$ (all four || בְּרִית) 1QM 14$_{4}$ 4Q370 2$_{6}$ (שמרי ... [חסדיו) 4Q393 3$_{2}$ (|| בְּרִית) 4QShir$^{b}$ 10$_{10}$ ([שומר חס]ד]), נצר *keep* Ex 34$_{7}$ Pr 20$_{28}$ (if em.; see Subj.) 1QH 16$_{8}$ ([חסד]כה]), קשׁר *bind* Pr 3$_{3}$.

כחד pi. *hide* Ps 40$_{11}$ (|| אֱמֶת *truth*), מאס *reject* Jb 6$_{14}$ (if em. לְמָס מֵעֵהוּ [mss למאס] *to the despairing one* loyalty is [due] *from his friend* to לֹא מָאַס מֵרֵעַ *a friend does not reject* loyalty), עזב *forsake* Gn 24$_{27}$ (|| אֱמֶת) Jon 2$_{9}$ Ru 2$_{20}$ 11QPs$^{a}$ 19$_{6}$, אסף *take away* Jr 16$_{5}$, סור hi. *remove* Ps 66$_{20}$ (+ תְּפִלָּה *prayer*) 89$_{34(mss)}$ (+ אֱמוּנָה *faithfulness*) 1 C 17$_{13}$, פרר hi. *violate* Ps 89$_{34}$ 4Q463 1$_{3}$ (|| בְּרִית), מחה *wipe out* Ne 13$_{14}$, כרת *cut*, i.e. make, covenant Is 55$_{3}$, hi. *cut off* 1 S 20$_{15}$, דמה pi. *ponder* Ps 48$_{10}$, בין htpol. *consider* Ps 107$_{43}$, זכר *remember* Jr 2$_{2}$ Ps 25$_{6}$ (|| רַחֲמִים *compassion*) 98$_{3}$ (|| אֱמוּנָה *faithfulness*) 2 C 24$_{22}$ Si 51$_{8}$ (|| רַחֲמִים) 11QPs$^{a}$ 22$_{5}$, hi. *mention* Is 63$_{7}$, צוה pi. *command* Ps 42$_{9}$, רנן pi. *shout joyfully about* Ps 59$_{17}$ (+ עֹז *strength*), שׁיר *sing* Ps 89$_{2}$ (+ אֱמוּנָה *faithfulness*) 101$_{1}$ (|| מִשְׁפָּט *judgment*), ידע hi. *make known* 11QPs$^{a}$ 19$_{3}$ (+ צְדָקָה *righteousness*), שׁמע hi. *announce* Ps 143$_{8}$ 1QS 1$_{22}$, נגד hi. *declare* Ps 92$_{3}$ (|| אֱמוּנָה), ספר pi. *recount* 1QS 9$_{26}$ (יספ[ר] [חסדיו]) 11QPs$^{a}$ 19$_{1}$, כתב *write* Pr 3$_{3}$.

**<CSTR>** חֶסֶד י׳ *mercy of Y.* Ps 33$_{5}$ 103$_{17}$, חַסְדֵי י׳ *mercies of Y.* Is 63$_{7}$ Ps 89$_{2}$ (or em. חֲסָדֶיךָ *your mercies*) 107$_{43}$ Lm 3$_{22}$, חֶסֶד אֱלֹהִים *mercy of God* 2 S 9$_{3}$ Ps 52$_{10}$, חסדי אלו[הים] *mercies of God* 4QShirShabb$^{a}$ 1.2$_{20}$, חֶסֶד אֵל *mercy of God* Ps 52$_{3}$ (or em. חֶסֶד אֵל to אֶל־חָסִיד *to a godly one*), חסדי אל *mercies of God* 1QS 11$_{12}$, חֶסֶד עֶלְיוֹן *mercy of the Most High* Ps 21$_{8}$, חַסְדֵי דָוִד *mercies of*, i.e. shown to, *David* Is 55$_{3}$ 2 C 6$_{42}$ (דָּוִיד), חסדי נביאיך *loyalties of your prophets* 11QPs$^{a}$ 22$_{5}$, חֶסֶד נְעוּרַיִךְ *loyalty of your youth* Jr 2$_{2}$, חֶסֶד עוֹלָם *mercy of eternity*, i.e. eternal mercy Is 54$_{8}$, חסדי עולם *mercies of eternity*, i.e. eternal mercies 4QS$^{d}$ 4.1$_{1}$ (=1QS 10$_{4}$ חסדיו עולם) 4Q Tanḥ 8$_{10}$ 1QH 13$_{5}$, חסד אמ[תכה] *mercy of your truth* 1QH 13$_{8}$, חסדי אמת *mercies of truth* 4QBer$^{a}$ 1$_{8}$ (+ רַחֲמִים *compassion*, רָז *mystery*), חסדי ברכה *mercies of blessing* 1QM 12$_{3}$, חסדי רחמים *mercies of compassion* 1QS 1$_{22}$.

אל החסדים *God of mercies* 1QM 14$_{8}$, אֱלֹהֵי חַסְדִּי *God of my loyalty* Ps 59$_{11(Qr).18}$, חַסְדּוֹ *of his loyalty* Ps 59$_{11(Kt)}$, מַלְכֵי חֶסֶד *kings of loyalty* 1 K 20$_{31}$, אִישׁ חֶסֶד *man of loyalty* Pr 11$_{17}$ (mss חָסִיד *loyal one*), איש חסדים *man of loyalties* 4QMMT C$_{25}$, אִישׁ חַסְדּוֹ *man of his loyalty* Pr 20$_{6}$ (or em. חָסִיד), חַסְדֶּךָ *of your loyalty* Dt 33$_{8}$ (if em. חֲסִידֶךָ *your loyal one*), אַנְשֵׁי־חֶסֶד *men of loyalty* Is 57$_{1}$ Si 44$_{1(B).10}$, בני *sons of* 1QH 7$_{20}$, אביוני *poor ones of*, i.e. loyal poor ones 1QH 5$_{22}$, יד חסדיכה *hand of your mercies* 1QM 18$_{10}$, פני חסדיו *face of his mercies*, i.e. his merciful face 1QS 2$_{4}$, רוח קודש וחס[ד] *spirit of holiness and loyalty* 1QSb 2$_{24}$, שם חסד *name of*, i.e. for, *kindness* Si 41$_{11}$, תּוֹרַת־חֶסֶד *law of kindness* Pr 31$_{26}$, חק חסדך *statute of your kindness* 4Q521 2.3$_{1}$ (corrected from חסדיך), [נסתרות אמת] וחסד *hidden things of truth and kindness* 1QH 11$_{17}$.

רַב־חֶסֶד *great of mercy* Ex 34$_{6}$ (|| אֱמֶת *truth*) Nm 14$_{18}$ Jl 2$_{13}$ Jon 4$_{2}$ Ps 86$_{5.15}$ (|| אֱמֶת) 103$_{8}$ (חֶסֶד) Ne 9$_{17(Qr)}$ 1QH 10$_{14}$ ([רב ה]חסד; + רַחֲמִים *compassion*) 16$_{16}$ (|| אֱמֶת) 4Q Shir$^{b}$ 52.3$_{1}$ (החסד), רוב חסד *abundance of mercy* 1QH 12$_{14}$, רוב חסדים *abundance of mercies* 1QS 4$_{5}$, רֹב חַסְדְּךָ *abundance of your mercy* Ps 5$_{8}$ 69$_{14}$ (רָב־חַסְדֶּךָ) Ps 106$_{7(mss)}$ (חַסְדֶּךָ) Ne 13$_{22}$ (חַסְדֶּךָ) Si 51$_{3}$ (רוב) 4QDib Ham$^{a}$ 1.2$_{10}$ ([רוב חסדכ[ה]; + כֹּחַ *strength*), רֹב חֲסָדֶיךָ *abundance of your mercies* Ps 106$_{7}$ 1QH 6$_{32}$ (רוב [חסדיכה]) 11$_{28}$ fr. 2$_{5}$ (both רוב חסדיכה) 4QapPs$^{b}$ 46$_{2}$ (ר[וב]), רוב חסדו *abundance of his mercy* 1QS 4$_{4}$, רֹב חֲסָדָיו *abundance of his mercies* Is 63$_{7}$ (|| רַחֲמִים *compassion*) Ps 106$_{45(Qr)}$ Lm 3$_{32(Qr)}$ (both Kt חסדו *of his mercy*) 4QHod$^{a}$ 7.2$_{13}$ ([רוב חס[דיו]), המו[ן] חסדיכה *abundance of your mercies* 1QH 11$_{30}$, גְּדָל־חֶסֶד *great of mercy* Ps 145$_{8}$, גדול [החס]דים *great of mercies* 1QH 14$_{24}$, גֹּדֶל חַסְדֶּךָ *greatness of your mercy* Nm 14$_{19}$, גדול חסדיכה *great of your mercies* 1QH 13$_{2}$ (+ רַחֲמִים *compassion*) 7$_{18}$ ([גדול]) 16$_{12}$ (חסדיך), טוּב חַסְדְּךָ *goodness of your mercy*

Ps $109_{21}$ (if em. טוֹב חַסְדְּךָ *good is your mercy*), אהבת חסד *love of loyalty* CD $13_{18}$ 1QS $2_{24}$ (+ צֶדֶק *righteousness*, טוֹב *good*, אֱמֶת *truth*) $5_4$ (+ צְדָקָה *righteousness*, מִשְׁפָּט *justice*, אֱמֶת) $5_{25}$ (+ עֲנָוָה *humility*) $8_2$ (+ צְדָקָה, מִשְׁפָּט, אֱמֶת) $10_{26}$ 4QMyst$^{a}$ $51_3$ 4Q418 $169_3$ ([אהבן]ת חסד]) $170_3$ ([אהבת [ח]סד]) 4QRitMar $14_5$, רחמי חסדו *compassion of his mercy* 1QS $2_1$ 4QShirShabb$^{f}$ $3.2_{15}$ $13_7$ ([רחמי חסדו]), [רחמי] חסדיו *compassion of his mercies* 4QShir Shabb$^{d}$ $1.1_{23}$, גמילות חסד *recompense of*, i.e. for, *loyalty* Si $37_{11(Bmg, D)}$, ברית חסד *covenant of loyalty* 1QH fr. $7_7$ 1QS $1_8$, מפתח חסדיו *opening of his mercies* 1QS $10_4$, משוב חסדים *withdrawal of mercy* 1QM $3_6$ (unless *shameful retribution*, i.e. from חֶסֶד II *shame*).

כָּל־חַסְדּוֹ *all its faithfulness* Is $40_6$, כֹּל הַחֲסָדִים *all the mercies* Gn $32_{11}$, כול חסדי *all mercies of* 1QS $1_{22}$.

<APP> י׳ *Y.* Ps $144_2$ (or em.; see Subj.), צוּר *rock* Ps $144_2$ (or em.; see Subj.), מְצוּדָה *fortress* Ps $144_2$ (or em.; see Subj.), מִשְׂגָּב *refuge* Ps $144_2$ (or em.; see Subj.), מְפַלֵּט *deliverer* Ps $144_2$ (or em.; see Subj.), מְלַמֵּד *teacher* Ps $144_2$ (or em.; see Subj.), מָגֵן *shield* Ps $144_2$ (or em.; see Subj.), בְּרִית *covenant* Is $55_3$, תְּהִלָּה *praise* Is $63_7$, אַהֲבָה *love* Jr $2_2$, תְּשׁוּעָה *salvation* Ps $119_{41}$, שָׁלוֹם *peace*, רַחֲמִים *compassion*).

<ADJ> גָּדוֹל *great* 1 K $3_6$||2 C $1_8$ 1 K $3_6$, טוֹב *good* 4Q185 $1.2_1$ 4Q370 $2_6$ ([כחסדיו הטובים]), רִאשׁוֹן *former* Ps $89_{50}$ Ru $3_{10}$, אַחֲרוֹן *last* Ru $3_{10}$, זֶה *this* 2 S $2_5$ 1 K $3_6$.

<PREP> לְ of benefit, *to, for*, + מצא hi. *cause to come* Jb $37_{13}$ (unless em. יְמַצְאֵהוּ *he causes it to come* to יְאַמְּצֵהוּ *he strengthens it*); of possession, *(belonging) to*, 4Q416 $3_4$ ([לחסדיו]); introducing object, + זכר *remember* 2 C $6_{42}$; יחל לְ pi. *wait for* Ps $33_{18}$ $147_{11}$ 1QH $4_{40}$ ( ... איחל] לחסד]יכה) $9_{10}$ $10_{16}$ ([יחלתי]), hi. *wait for* 1QH fr. $4_{17}$ ([לחסד]כה), קוה לְ pi. *wait for* 1QH $11_{31}$ (|| טוּב *goodness*), נתן לְ *give*, i.e. make, *into* an object of kindness Dn $1_9$ (|| רַחֲמִים *compassion*), בוא לְ hi. *bring*, i.e. lead, *in* 1QH $7_{35}$ (ותבי]אני לחסדיכה] *and you lead me in your kindness*; =4QHod$^{b}$ $7_1$ [ותקראני [לחסדיכה *and you meet me in your kindness*).

בְּ of instrument, accompaniment, *by (means of), through, with, in* 1QH $2_{25}$ $7_{27}$ (+ רַחֲמִים *compassion*) $9_{14}$ (בו[ח]סדיכה; + כֹּחַ *strength*) $9_{18}$ ([בחסדכה]) $11_{18}$ 4Q418 $81_8$ (+ רַחֲמִים) 4Q423 $21_2$ ([בחסדיכ[ה]) 4QHod$^{a}$ $7.1_{22}$ (+ צֶדֶק, רַחֲמִים *righteousness*) 4Q525 $29_3$, + כון ho. *be established* Is $16_5$ (+ אֱמֶת *truth*), סעד *be upheld* Pr $20_{28}$ (or em. בְּצֶדֶק *by righteousness*), פתח ni. *be opened* 1QH $12_{13}$ ([נפתח ... בחס]דיך), גלה *uncover* ear 1QH $12_{21}$ ([בח]סדיכה גליתה]), חנן *be gracious* Ps $51_{3(mss)}$, ארשׂ pi. *betroth oneself* Ho $2_{21}$ (|| צֶדֶק *righteousness*, מִשְׁפָּט *justice*, רַחֲמִים *compassion*), בוא hi. *bring* 1QS $11_{13}$ (+ רַחֲמִים), נחה *lead* Ex $15_{13}$ (+ עֹז *strength*), רחם pi. *have compassion* Is $54_8$=4QTanḥ $8_{10}$, פדה *redeem* 1QH $6_3$ ( ... פדיתה [בחסדיכה] *you have redeemed ... in your mercies*), כפר pu. *be atoned for* Pr $16_6$ (|| אֱמֶת), ישׁע hi. *save* Ps $31_{17}$ $109_{26(mss)}$ 1QH $2_{23}$, שׁפט *judge* 1QH $6_9$ (+ אֱמֶת, רַחֲמִים), שׁלם pi. *repay* 4Q521 $2.2_9$ ([ישלם]), מוט ni. *be moved* Ps $21_8$, צמת hi. *exterminate* Ps $143_{12}$, זנח hi. *reject* 1QH $9_7$, שׁמע *hear* Ps $119_{149(mss)}$, שׂמח *rejoice* Ps $31_8$, ידע hi. *make known* 1QH $13_8$ ([הודעתם]), שׁעע *dandle* 1QH $9_{31}$ ([תשעשעני בחסדכ[ה]), בטח בְּ *trust in* Ps $13_6$ (+ יְשׁוּעָה *salvation*) $52_{10}$, שׁען בְּ ni. *lean upon* 1QH $4_{37}$ ([נשענ]תי]; + רַחֲמִים *compassion*) 1QH fr. $1_9$ ([ח]סדיכה]), חסה בְּ *take refuge in* Ps $144_2$ (or em.; see Subj.), זמר בְּ pi. *sing praises of* 1QH $11_5$ (|| גְּבוּרָה *might*).

כְּ *according to* 4Q185 $1.2_1$ 4Q370 $2_8$ ([כחסדיו]), + חנן *be gracious* Ps $51_3$ (+ רַחֲמִים *compassion*), עשׂה *do* Gn $21_{23}$ Ps $119_{124}$, גמל *repay* Is $63_7$, שׁפט *judge* 4QapPs$^{b}$ $33_6$ ([תשפט]), ישׁע hi. *save* Ps $109_{26}$, חיה pi. *preserve alive* Ps $119_{88.159}$, שׁמע *hear* Ps $119_{149}$ (+ מִשְׁפָּט *justice*); *according to*, + זכר *remember* Ps $25_7$.

מִן of comparison, *(more) than*, + קטן *be small*, i.e. unworthy Gn $32_{11}$.

עַל *upon*, + שׁען ni. *lean* 1QS $10_{16}$, סמך ni. *lean* 11QPs$^{a}$ $19_{13}$; *on account of*, + נתן *give* glory Ps $115_1$ (|| אֱמֶת *truth*), ידה hi. *give thanks* Ps $138_2$ (|| אֱמֶת).

לְמַעַן *for the sake of*, ישׁע hi. *save* Ps $6_5$, פדה *redeem* Ps $44_{27}$, נצל hi. *deliver* 4QBark$^{a}$ 2.14.

לְפִי *according to*, + קצר *reap* Ho $10_{12}$ (+ צְדָקָה *righteousness*).

<COLL> חֶסֶד וֶאֱמֶת, and vars. *loyalty and truth*, i.e. reliability Gn $24_{27.49}$ $32_{11}$ $47_{29}$ Ex $34_6$ Nm $14_{18(mss, Sam)}$, Jos $2_{14}$ 2 S $2_6$ $15_{20}$ Ps $25_{10}$ $40_{11.12}$ $57_4$ $61_8$ $85_{11}$ $86_{15}$ $89_{15}$ $115_1$ Pr $3_3$ $14_{22}$ $16_6$ $20_{28}$ 1QH $16_{16}$ 11QPs$^{a}$ $26_{10}$, ... אֱמֶת חֶסֶד *truth ... loyalty* Ho $4_1$ Mc $7_{20}$ 1QH $11_{17}$ ([אמת] וחסד), חַיִּים וָחֶסֶד *life and loyalty* Jb $10_{12}$, טוֹב וָחֶסֶד *good-

*ness and loyalty* Ps 23$_{6}$, צְדָקָה וָחֶסֶד *righteousness and loyalty* Pr 21$_{21}$, חֵן וָחֶסֶד *grace and kindness* Est 2$_{17}$, הַבְּרִית וְהַחֶסֶד *covenant and loyalty* Ne 1$_{5}$ (mss וְהַחֶסֶד), אֶרֶךְ אַפַּיִם וְרַב־חֶסֶד *long of,* i.e. slow to, *anger and great of loyalty* Ex 34$_{6}$ Nm 14$_{18}$ Jl 2$_{13}$ Jon 4$_{2}$ Ps 86$_{15}$ 103$_{8}$ Ne 9$_{17(Qr)}$ 1QH 16$_{16}$ ([אר]ך) 4QShir[b] 52.3$_{1}$ (ארוך ... החסד), var. Ps 145$_{8}$ (גְּדָל־חָסֶד *great of loyalty*).

יוֹדוּ לַי׳ חַסְדּוֹ *let them give thanks to Y. (for) his faithfulness* Ps 107$_{8.15.21.31}$ (all four || נִפְלָא *wonder*), var. 11QPs[a] 19$_{9}$, יֶהֶלְמֵנִי־צַדִּיק חֶסֶד *let the righteous one strike me (in) loyalty* Ps 141$_{5}$ (or em. חָסִיד *loyal one*), אֱלֹהֵי חַסְדּוֹ יְקַדְּמֵנִי *my God will meet me (with) his faithfulness* Ps 59$_{11(mss, Kt)}$ (mss אֱלֹהִים *God;* L, Qr אֱלֹהֵי חַסְדִּי *the God of my faithfulness,* i.e. my faithful God), מעטר חסידיו חסד *(he) crowns his loyal ones with kindness* 11QPs[a] 19$_{8}$ (|| רַחֲמִים *compassion*), חֶסֶד י׳ מָלְאָה הָאָרֶץ *the earth is full of the faithfulness of Y.* Ps 33$_{5}$, var. 119$_{64}$, היככה יתשלמו חסדם *how will they be rewarded for their loyalty?* 4QpsEzek[a] 2$_{3}$, חסדיו עולם *his eternal mercies* 1QS 10$_{4}$ (=4QS[d] 4.1$_{1}$ חסדי עולם).

Also 1QH fr. 5$_{9}$ 1QpPs 2$_{2}$ (חסד[ו]) 4QMidrEschat[b] 8$_{13}$ 4Q185 1.2$_{13}$ 4QBer[a] 1$_{8}$ (חסד[י]ם) 4QPsJos[a] 22.1$_{5}$ 4QapPs[a] 1.2$_{9}$ 4QShirShabb[a] 1.1$_{18}$ ([ח]סדיו) 4Q413 1$_{4}$ 4Q415 13$_{4}$ 4Q434[a] $_{11}$ 4QRitMar 254$_{1}$ 4QPrFêtes[c] 3.1$_{5}$ ([ח]סדיכה) 4QShir[b] 26$_{2}$ 36$_{2}$ (חסד[י]ו) 4QShir[b] 148$_{3}$ 4Q RitPur 56$_{6}$ 5QRègle 23$_{2}$.

<SYN> בְּרִית *covenant,* אֱמֶת *truth,* אֱמוּנָה *faithfulness,* חֵן *grace,* צֶדֶק *righteousness,* צְדָקָה *righteousness,* טוּב *goodness,* טוֹב *goodness,* מִשְׁפָּט *justice,* שָׁלוֹם *peace,* רַחֲמִים *compassion,* גְּבוּרָה *might,* נִפְלָא *wonder,* חַיִּים *life,* תְּפִלָּה *prayer.*

<ANT> זֶבַח *sacrifice.**

⇒ חסד *be loyal.*

**חֶסֶד II** 2.1.1 n.m. **shame**—cstr. חֶסֶד; pl. Q חסדים—**shameful thing,** of incest (Lv 20$_{17}$), **reproach,** <NOM CL> חֶסֶד הוּא *it is a shameful thing* Lv 20$_{17}$, חֶסֶד לְאֻמִּים חַטָּאת *sin is a reproach of peoples* Pr 14$_{34}$ (or em. חֶסֶר *lack of*). <CSTR> חֶסֶד לְאֻמִּים *reproach of peoples,* i.e. a reproach to any people Pr 14$_{34}$ (or em.; see Nom. Cl.); דברי חסד *words of reproach* Si 41$_{22(Bmg, M)}$ (B חרפה *reproach*), משוב חסדים *retribution of shame,* i.e. shameful retribution 1QM 3$_{6}$ (unless *withdrawal of mercy,* i.e. from חֶסֶד *loyalty*).

⇒ חסד *be ashamed.*

**חֶסֶד III**, see בֶּן־חֶסֶד *Ben-hesed.*

**[חַסְדָּא]** 0.0.0.1 pr.n.[m.] **Hasda,** appar. son of Jeremiah, Seal 411 (Beth-Shemesh, 7th/6th cent.).

⇒ חסד *be loyal.*

**חַסְדָה**, see חַסְרָה *Hasrah.*

**חֲסַדְיָה** 1.0.0.2 pr.n.m. **Hasadiah**—I חסדיהו—**1.** son of Zerubbabel, <NOM CL> וּבְנֵי־זְרֻבָּבֶל ... וַחֲסַדְיָה *and the sons of Zerubbabel were ... and Hasadiah* 1 C 3$_{20(mss)}$ (L וּבֶן־ *and the son of*). **2.** appar. father of Ahijah, Ramat Raḥel ost. **3.** appar. father of Seal 220 (c. 200 BCE).

⇒ חסד *be loyal* + י׳ *Y.*

**[חֲסַדְיָהוּ]**, see חֲסַדְיָה *Hasadiah.*

**[חֲסִדִין]**, see מְצַד חֲסִידִין *Mezad-hasidin.*

**חסה** 37.2.3 vb. **seek refuge—Qal** 37 Pf. 3fs חָסָיָה, חָסִיתִי, חָסָיו (חָסוּ); impf. אֶחֱסֶה (אחסה), תֶּחְסֶה, יֶחֱסֶה, 2ms תֶּחֱסֶה, Q אחסיה, (יֶחֱסָיוּן) יֶחֱסוּ; + waw וְחָסוּ, וְחָסָה; impv. חֲסוּ; ptc. חֹסֶה (חוֹסֶה), חֹסִים (חוֹסִים), חֹסֵי (חוֹסֵי); inf. חֲסוֹת (לַחֲסוֹת)—**seek refuge, take refuge,** <SUBJ> Israelites Dt 32$_{37}$, עַם *people* Zp 3$_{12}$, Ruth Ru 2$_{12}$, worshipper 2 S 22$_{3}$||Ps 18$_{3}$ Ps 7$_{2}$ 11$_{1}$=4QMidrEschat[b] 8$_{7}$ (חסית[י]) Ps 16$_{1}$ 25$_{20}$ 31$_{2}$ 57$_{2}$ 61$_{5}$ (|| גור *sojourn*) 71$_{1}$ 141$_{8}$ 144$_{2}$ 1QH 9$_{29}$ 11QPs[a] 19$_{12}$ 24$_{17}$ ([חסיתי]), אֱנוֹשׁ *human being* Si 14$_{27}$ (|| שכן *dwell*), גֶּבֶר *man* Ps 34$_{9}$, בֵּן *son* Is 30$_{2}$=4QpIsa[c] 21$_{12}$ ([בנים] ... [לחסו]ת; || עוז *take refuge*) Ps 36$_{8}$, עָנִי *afflicted one* Is 14$_{32}$, צַדִּיק *righteous one* Ps 37$_{40}$=4QpPs[a] 3.4$_{20}$ ([חסו]) Ps 64$_{11}$ Pr 14$_{32}$, יֹשֵׁב *inhabitant* Ps 91$_{4}$, חזק hi. ptc. *one who holds* CD 20$_{34}$, pious 2 S 22$_{31}$||Ps 18$_{31}$ Is 57$_{13}$ Na 1$_{7}$ Ps 2$_{12}$ 5$_{12}$ 17$_{7}$ 31$_{20}$ 34$_{23}$ 118$_{8.9}$ (both || בטח *trust*) Pr 30$_{5}$ Si 51$_{8}$, נֶפֶשׁ *soul* Ps 57$_{2}$, עֵץ *tree* Jg 9$_{15}$.

<PREP> בְּ of place, *in,* + Y. 2 S 22$_{3.31}$||Ps 18$_{3.31}$ Is 57$_{13}$ Na 1$_{7}$ Ps 2$_{12}$ 5$_{12}$ 7$_{2}$ 11$_{1}$=4QMidrEschat[b] 8$_{7}$ (חסית[י]) Ps 16$_{1}$ 17$_{7}$ (if em. חוֹסִים *the ones who seek refuge* to חוֹסֶה־בָּךְ

*the one who seeks refuge in you*) 25$_{20}$ 31$_{2.20}$ 34$_{9.23}$ 37$_{40}$=4QpPs$^a$ 3.4$_{20}$ ([חסו בו]) Ps 57$_2$ 64$_{11}$ 71$_1$ 118$_{8.9}$ 141$_8$ 144$_2$ Pr 30$_5$ Si 51$_8$ 11QPs$^a$ 24$_{17}$ ([חסיתי בכה]), שֵׁם *name* of Y. Zp 3$_{12}$ CD 20$_{34}$, צוּר *rock* Dt 32$_{37}$ Ps 18$_3$ 144$_2$, Zion Is 14$_{32}$, צֵל *shade* Jg 9$_{15}$ Is 30$_2$=4QpIsa$^c$ 21$_{12}$ ([לחסו]ת) Ps 36$_8$ 57$_2$ Si 14$_{27}$ 11QPs$^a$ 19$_{12}$, סֵתֶר *hiding place* Ps 61$_5$, מָוֶת *death* Pr 14$_{32}$ (unless em. בְּמוֹתוֹ *in his death* to בְּתוּמּוֹ *in his integrity*), תֹּם *integrity* Ps 14$_{32}$ (if em.); מִן of direction, *from*, + קום htpol. ptc. *one who rises up* Ps 17$_7$, חֹרֶב *heat* Si 14$_{27}$, מַדְהֵבָה *destruction* 1QH 9$_{29}$ (מכול מ[דהבה]); תַּחַת *under*, + כָּנָף *wing* Ps 91$_4$ Ru 2$_{12}$.

<SYN> גור *sojourn*, שׁכן *dwell*, עוז *take refuge*, בטח *trust*.

⇒ חָסוּת *refuge*, מַחֲסֶה *refuge*, מַחְסֵיָה *Mahseiah*, חֹסָה I *Hosah*.

חֹסָה I 4 pr.n.m. **Hosah**, Merarite, gatekeeper of temple, <NOM CL> עֹבֵד אֱדֹם ... וְחֹסָה לְשֹׁעֲרִים *Obed-edom ... and Hosah were gatekeepers* 1 C 16$_{38}$. <PREP> לְ of direction, *to*, + נפל (of lot) *fall* 1 C 26$_{16}$; of possession, *(belonging) to, of* 1 C 26$_{10.11}$.*

⇒ חסה *seek refuge*.

חֹסָה II 1 pl.n. **Hosah**, town in Asher, perh. Kh. el-Ḥōš, 6 km SE of Tyre, <COLL> שָׁב הַגְּבוּל חֹסָה *the border turns to Hosah* Jos 19$_{29}$.

חָסוּת 1 n.f. **refuge**, <SUBJ> היה *be* Is 30$_3$=4QpIsa$^c$ 21$_{13}$ ([חסו]ת]; + לִכְלִמָּה *as a shame*, מָעוֹז *protection*). <COLL> הֶחָסוּת בְּצֵל־מִצְרַיִם *the shelter in the shade of Egypt* Is 30$_3$ =4QpIsa$^c$ 21$_{13}$ ([החסו]ת בצל מצרי[ם]).*

⇒ חסה *seek refuge*.

חָסִיד 32.1.9 adj. **loyal**—sf. חֲסִידְךָ (חֲסִידֶךָ), Kt, Q חסידו; pl. חֲסִידִים; sf. חֲסִידַי, חֲסִידֶיךָ, חֲסִידָיו, חֲסִידֶיהָ—**loyal, godly, kind, 1.** used attributively of גּוֹי *nation* (גּוֹי לֹא־חָסִיד *an ungodly nation*), אִישׁ *man* 2 S 22$_{26}$||Ps 18$_{26}$ (if insert אִישׁ).

**2.** in nom. cl. used predicatively of Y. Jr 3$_{12}$ Ps 145$_{17}$ (|| צַדִּיק *righteous*), psalmist Ps 86$_2$.

**3.** used as noun, **loyal one, godly one,** <SUBJ> אבד *perish* Mc 7$_2$ (+ יָשָׁר *upright one*), גמר *be ended* Ps 12$_2$ (or em. חֶסֶד *loyalty*; || אֱמֻן *faithful one*), אהב *love* Ps 31$_{24}$ (+ אֱמֻן), פלל htp. *pray* Ps 32$_6$, רנן pi. *shout for joy* Ps 132$_{9.16}$ (both + כֹּהֵן *priest*) 149$_5$, עלז *exult* Ps 149$_5$, שׂמח *rejoice* 2 C 6$_{41}$, זמר pi. *sing praise* Ps 30$_5$, ידה hi. *give thanks* Ps 30$_5$, ברך pi. *bless* Ps 145$_{10}$ (|| מַעֲשֶׂה *work*), כרת *cut*, i.e. make, covenant Ps 50$_5$, יכח hi. *reprove* Ps 141$_5$ (if em. חֶסֶד וְיוֹכִיחֵנִי *loyalty and let him reprove me* to וְחָסִיד יוֹכִיחֵנִי *and let a godly one reprove me*).

<OBJ> פלה hi. *set apart* Ps 4$_4$ (or em. חַסְדּוֹ *his loyalty*), נתן *give*, i.e. permit Ps 16$_{10}$, עזב *forsake* Ps 37$_{28}$, אסף *gather* Ps 50$_5$, בקר pi. *seek* 4Q521 2.2$_5$ (+ צַדִּיק *righteous one*), כבד pi. *honour* 4Q521 2.2$_7$, עטר pi. *crown* 11QPs$^a$ 19$_7$, פדה *redeem* 11QPs$^a$ 24$_{17}$ ([פדה ... חסידיכה]).

<CSTR> אִישׁ חֲסִידֶךָ *man of your godly one* Dt 33$_8$=4Q Testim$_{14}$=4QMidrEschat$^a$ 1$_9$ ([איש חסידכה]; mss, Gnz חֲסִידֶיךָ *your godly ones*; or em. חַסְדֶּךָ *your loyalty*), רַגְלֵי חֲסִידָיו *feet of his godly ones* 1 S 1$_{9(Qr, mss)}$ (Kt חסידו *his godly one*; + רָשָׁע *wicked one*), בְּשַׂר חֲסִידֶיךָ *flesh of your godly ones* Ps 79$_2$ (|| עֶבֶד *servant*), נַפְשׁוֹת חֲסִידָיו *souls of his godly ones* Ps 97$_{10}$, רוח חסידו *spirit of his godly one* GnzPs 3$_{25}$ (+ אהב ptc. *one who loves*), קְהַל חֲסִידִים *congregation of godly ones* Ps 149$_1$ (ms קְדוֹשִׁים *of holy ones*) 11QPs$^a$ 18$_{10}$ (|| צַדִּיק *righteous one*), דורות חסידים *generations of godly ones* 11QPs$^a$ 22$_3$, דֶּרֶךְ חֲסִידָיו *way of his godly ones* Pr 2$_{8(Qr)}$ (Kt חסידו *of his godly one*), מעשי חסידיך *deeds of your godly ones* 11QPs$^a$ 22$_6$ (+ נָבִיא *prophet*), כָּל־חָסִיד *every godly one* Ps 32$_6$, כָּל־חֲסִידָיו *all his godly ones* Ps 31$_{24}$ (mss lack כָּל־) 148$_{14}$=Si 51$_{12}$ Ps 149$_9$.

<APP> בֵּן *son* of Israel Ps 148$_{14}$, עַם *people* Ps 148$_{14}$, יִשְׂרָאֵל *Israel* 11QPs$^a$ 24$_{17}$ ([ישראל חסידיכה]).

<PREP> לְ of direction, *to*, + דבר pi. *speak* Ps 89$_{20}$, רום hi. *raise* praise Ps 148$_{14}$=Si 51$_{12}$, חנן *be gracious* 4QapPs$^a$ 2$_5$ (ל[ח]סיד); of possession, *of, (belonging) to* Ps 116$_{15}$ 149$_9$; אֶל *to*, + דבר pi. *speak* peace Ps 85$_9$ (|| עַם *people*); *against* Ps 52$_3$ (if em. חֶסֶד אֵל *mercy of God* to אֶל־חָסִיד *against the godly one*); עִם *with*, + חסד htp. *show oneself loyal* 2 S 22$_{26}$||Ps 18$_{26}$ (unless em. אִישׁ חָסִיד *a loyal man*); נֶגֶד *before*, + קוה pi. *wait for* Ps 52$_{11}$ (unless em. וַאֲקַוֶּה *and I will wait for* to וַאֲחַוֶּה *and I will proclaim*), חוה pi. *declare* Ps 52$_{11}$ (if em.); בַּעֲבוּר *for the sake of*, + מחה ni. *be blotted out* 4QTNaph 1.2$_3$ (חסי[ד]יו).

Also 4QPrFêtes$^{c}$ 50$_{2}$.
<SYN> §2 צַדִּיק *righteous;* §3 אֱמֻן *faithful one,* צַדִּיק *righteous one,* עֶבֶד *servant,* עַם *people,* מַעֲשֶׂה *work.**
⇒ חסד *be loyal.*

**חֲסִידָה** 6 n.f. **stork,** among birds prohibited as food (Lv 11$_{19}$ Dt 14$_{18}$), <SUBJ> ידע *know* Jr 8$_{7}$ (+ תֹּר *turtledove,* סוס *swallow,* עָגוּר *crane*). <OBJ> שׁקץ pi. *abominate* Lv 11$_{19}$, אכל *eat* Dt 14$_{18}$=11QT 48$_{1}$ ([והחסידה]). <CSTR> כַּנְפֵי הַחֲסִידָה *wings of the stork* Zc 5$_{9}$. <COLL> חֲסִידָה בְּרוֹשִׁים בֵּיתָהּ *as for the stork, the fir trees are her house* Ps 104$_{17}$ (+ צִפּוֹר *bird*), אֶבְרָה חֲסִידָה וְנֹצָה appar. *the wing (of) the stork and (her) plumage* Jb 39$_{13}$.*

**חָסִיל** 6.0.1 n.m. **locust**—Q חסל—as collective, <SUBJ> היה *be* 1 K 8$_{37}$‖2 C 6$_{28}$ (‖ אַרְבֶּה *locust,* שִׁדָּפוֹן *blight,* יֵרָקוֹן *mildew*), אכל *eat* Jl 1$_{4}$ (‖ יֶלֶק *locust,* אַרְבֶּה, + גָּזָם *locust*) 2$_{25}$ (‖ אַרְבֶּה, יֶלֶק, גָּזָם) 4Q422 10$_{10}$, כסה pi. *cover* 4Q422 10$_{10}$. <OBJ> בוא hi. *bring* 4Q422 10$_{10}$, שׁלח pi. *send* Jl 2$_{25}$. <CSTR> אֹסֶף הֶחָסִיל *swarm of the locusts* Is 33$_{4}$ (+ גֵּב *locust*). <APP> אַרְבֶּה *locust* 4Q422 10$_{10}$, חַיִל *army* Jl 2$_{25}$. <ADJ> כָּבֵד *heavy* 4Q422 10$_{10}$. <PREP> לְ of direction, *to,* + נתן *give* Ps 78$_{46}$ (‖ אַרְבֶּה *locust*). <SYN> אַרְבֶּה *locust,* גָּזָם *locust,* יֶלֶק *locust,* שִׁדָּפוֹן *blight,* יֵרָקוֹן *mildew.**
⇒ חסל *consume.*

**חֲסִין** 1 adj. **strong,** used predicatively, מִי־כָמוֹךָ חֲסִין יָהּ *who is strong like you, O Y.* Ps 89$_{9}$ (or em. חֲסִין יָהּ to חָסְנְךָ *your stronghold,* or יֶחֱסַן your faithfulness *is strong*).
⇒ חסן *be strong.*

**[חָסִיר]**, see חָסֵר *lacking.*

**חסל** 1 vb. **consume—Qal** 1 (or **Hi.**) Impf. יַחְסְלֶנּוּ—<SUBJ> אַרְבֶּה *locust* Dt 28$_{38}$. <OBJ> זֶרַע *seed* Dt 28$_{28}$.
⇒ חָסִיל *locust.*

**[חָסַל]**, see חָסִיל *locust.*

**חסם** 2.1.1 vb. **stop up—Qal** 2.1.1 Impf. 2ms תַּחְסֹם (Q תחסום); + waw Si ויחסום; ptc. חֹסֶמֶת—**1. block (the way of),** <SUBJ> גַּיְא *valley* Ezk 39$_{11}$ (unless em. וְחֹסֶמֶת הִיא אֶת־הָעֹבְרִים *and it will block (the) way of those who pass through* to וְחָסְמוּ אֶת־הַגַּיְא *and they will block the valley*), קֶבֶר *grave* Ezk 39$_{11}$ (if em.). <OBJ> עבר ptc. *one who passes* Ezk 39$_{11}$ (unless em.; see Subj.), גַּיְא *valley* Ezk 39$_{11}$ (if em.; see Subj.). **2. dam,** <SUBJ> Hezekiah Si 48$_{17}$. <OBJ> הַר *mountain* Si 48$_{17}$ (+ מקוה *[for a] reservoir*). **3. muzzle,** <SUBJ> Israelite Dt 25$_{4}$ (+ בְּדִישׁוֹ *when it threshes*) 11QT 52$_{12}$. <OBJ> שׁוֹר *ox* Dt 25$_{4}$ 11QT 52$_{12}$. <PREP> עַל *upon,* i.e. during, + דִּישׁ *threshing* 11QT 52$_{12}$.
⇒ מַחְסוֹם *muzzle.*

**חסן** 1 vb. **be strong—Ni.** 1 Impf. יֵחָסֵן—**be secured, be hoarded,** <SUBJ> סַחַר *gain* Is 23$_{17}$ (‖ אצר ni. *be stored up*), אֶתְנַן *fee* Is 23$_{18}$. <SYN> אצר ni. *be stored up.*
⇒ חֲסִין *strong,* חֹסֶן *wealth, stronghold, strength,* חָסֹן *strong.*

**חָסֹן** I 2 adj. **strong**—Q החסנכם—**1.** in nom. cl. used predicatively of אֱמֹרִי *Amorite* Am 2$_{9}$ (+ כָּאַלּוֹנִים *as the oaks*). **2.** used as noun, **strong one,** <SUBJ> היה *be* Is 1$_{31}$ (+ לִנְעֹרֶת *as tow;* 1QIsa$^{a}$ החסנכם appar. *your strong one,* unless *your strength,* from חֹסֶן).
⇒ חסן *be strong.*

**חָסֹן** II n. m. **flax** <SUBJ> היה *be* Is 1$_{31}$ (+ לִנְעֹרֶת *as tow;* 1QIsa$^{a}$ החסנכם appar. *your strong one,* unless *your strength,* from חֹסֶן).*

**חֹסֶן** 5.0.2 n.m. **wealth; stronghold; strength**—cstr. חֹסֶן; sf. Q חסנכה, Q החסנכם—**1. wealth, treasure, abundance,** <SUBJ> היה *be* Is 33$_{6}$. <NOM CL> בֵּית צַדִּיק חֹסֶן רָב *(in) the house of the righteous is great treasure* Pr 15$_{6}$ (or em. בֵּית to בְּבֵית *in the house of;* + תְּבוּאָה *income*). <OBJ> נתן *give* Jr 20$_{5}$ (‖ אוֹצָר *treasure,* יְגִיעַ *gain,* יְקָר *precious object*), לקח *take* Jr 20$_{5}$ Ezk 22$_{25}$ (‖ יְקָר), בוא hi. *bring* Jr 20$_{5}$, בזז *plunder* Jr 20$_{5}$. <CSTR> חֹסֶן יְשׁוּעֹת חָכְמַת וָדָעַת *abundance of salvation, wisdom and knowledge* Is 33$_{6}$ (mss חָכְמָה), חֹסֶן הָעִיר *wealth of the city* Jr 20$_{5}$, כָּל־חֹסֶן *all the wealth of* Jr 20$_{5}$. <APP> אֱמוּנָה *faithfulness* Is 33$_{6}$, חֹסֶן לֹא לְעוֹלָם *wealth is not for ever* Pr 27$_{24}$ (+ נֵזֶר *crown*). <ADJ> רַב *great* Pr 15$_{6}$. <PREP> כְּ *as* Is 33$_{6}$ (if em. to

כְּחֹסֶן *as abundance of*). Also 4QpIsa$^c$ 27$_3$.

**2. stronghold, <SUBJ>** ברך pass. *be blessed* Ps 144$_2$ (if em. חַסְדִּי *my loyalty* to חָסְנִי *my stronghold*). **<NOM CL>** חָסְנֵךְ וֶאֱמוּנָתֵךְ סְבִיבוֹתֶיךָ *your stronghold and your faithfulness are round about you* Ps 89$_9$ (if em. חֲסִין יָהּ *strong, O Y.* to חָסְנֵךְ *your stronghold*). **<APP>** יי *Y.* Ps 144$_2$ (if em.; see Subj.), צוּר *rock* Ps 144$_2$ (if em.; see Subj.), מְצוּדָה *fortress* Ps 144$_2$ (if em.; see Subj.), מִשְׂגָּב *refuge* Ps 144$_2$ (if em.; see Subj.), מְפַלֵּט *deliverer* Ps 144$_2$ (if em.; see Subj.), מְלַמֵּד *teacher* Ps 144$_2$ (if em.; see Subj.), מָגֵן *shield* Ps 144$_2$ (if em.; see Subj.). **<PREP>** בְּ חסה *take refuge in* Ps 144$_2$ (if em.; see Subj.).

**3. strength, <SUBJ>** היה *be* perh. Is 1$_{31}$ (1QIsa$^a$, but prob. החסנכם *your strong one*, from חָסֹן *strong*; MT הֶחָסֹן *the strong one*; + לִנְעֹרֶת *as tow*).

**<SYN>** אוֹצָר *treasure*, יְגִיעַ *gain*, יְקָר *precious object*.

→ חסן *be strong*.

**חסף** 1 vb. **be scaly—Pualal** 1 Ptc. pass. מְחֻסְפָּס—ptc. pass. as attributive adj., **scaly,** דַּק מְחֻסְפָּס *a fine, scaly, thing*, in ref. to manna Ex 16$_{14}$.

**חסר** 25.6.6 vb. **lack—Qal** 21.4.6 Pf. חָסֵר, חָסַרְתָּ, חָסֵרוּ, חָסָרְנוּ; impf. יֶחְסַר (יֶחְסָר), 3fs תֶּחְסַר, 2ms תֶּחְסַר, אֶחְסָר, יַחְסְרוּ (יֶחְסָרוּן), Si תחסרון; + waw וַיֶּחְסְרוּ; inf. abs. חָסוֹר; ptc. חָסֵר—**1a.** trans. **lack, need, <SUBJ>** Israel(ites) Dt 2$_7$ 8$_9$ Jr 44$_{18}$ Ezk 4$_{17}$ 4Q417 1.1$_{17.19.19}$, Hadad 1 K 11$_{22}$, אִישׁ *man* Ec 6$_2$, אָח *brother* Dt 15$_8$ (unless §2), בַּעַל *husband* Pr 31$_{11}$, צַדִּיק *righteous one* Gn 18$_{28}$, דרשׁ ptc. *one who seeks* Ps 34$_{11}$ (+ רושׁ *be in want*, רעב *be hungry*), אַגָּן *bowl* Ca 7$_3$. **<OBJ>** מַחְסֹר *need* Dt 15$_8$, לֶחֶם *bread* Ezk 4$_{17}$, טֶרֶף *prey*, i.e. food 4Q417 1.1$_{17}$, מַיִם *water* Ezk 4$_{17}$, מֶזֶג *mixed wine* Ca 7$_3$, דָּבָר *thing* Dt 2$_7$, שָׁלָל *gain* Pr 31$_{11}$, חָמֵשׁ *five* (righteous ones) Gn 18$_{28}$, טוֹב *good thing* Ps 34$_{11}$, כֹּל *everything* Dt 8$_9$ Jr 44$_{18}$, מָה *what?* 1 K 11$_{22}$. **<PREP>** לְ *for (oneself)*, Dt 15$_8$ (unless §2); of benefit, *for*, + נֶפֶשׁ *soul* Ec 6$_2$; מִן partitive, *(some) of*, + אֵלֶּה *these* Si 51$_{24}$, אֵינֶנּוּ חָסֵר ... מִכֹּל אֲשֶׁר־יִתְאַוֶּה *he does not lack (anything) ... of all that he desires* Ec 6$_2$.

**1b.** abs. **lack anything, be in need, <SUBJ>** Israelites Ne 9$_{21}$, worshipper Ps 23$_1$, רדף pi. ptc. *one who pursues* Pr 12$_{11}$ (if em. חֲסַר־לֵב *one lacking of sense* to חָסֵר *he is in need*), בֶּטֶן *belly* of the wicked Pr 13$_{25}$.

**2.** intrans. **be lacking, fail, <SUBJ>** לֶחֶם *bread* Is 51$_{14}$, שֶׁמֶן *oil* Ec 9$_8$, צַפַּחַת *flask* of oil 1 K 17$_{14.16}$ (both ‖ כלה *fail*), לֵב *heart*, i.e. mind, of fool Ec 10$_3$, מַדָּע *mind* Si 3$_{13}$, חָכְמָה *wisdom* Si 3$_{25}$, אוֹר *light* Si 3$_{25}$, אוֹצָר *treasure* perh. 4Q417 1.1$_{19}$, מַחְסֹר *need* Dt 15$_8$ (unless §1). **<PREP>** לְ of direction, *to*, + אָח *brother* Dt 15$_8$ (unless §1); עַל *upon*, + רֹאשׁ *head* Ec 9$_8$.

**3. diminish, abate, <SUBJ>** מַיִם *water* Gn 8$_3$ (+ שׁוב *go back*) 8$_5$ 4QpGen$^a$ 1.1$_{9.11}$. **<PREP>** בְּ of place, time, *in*, + סוֹף *end* 4QpGen$^a$ 1.1$_9$; מִן of place, time, *from*, + קָצֶה *end* Gn 8$_3$; עַד *until*, + חֹדֶשׁ *month* Gn 8$_5$ 4QpGen$^a$ 1.1$_{11}$. **<COLL>** הַמַּיִם הָיוּ הָלוֹךְ וְחָסוֹר *the waters continually abated* Gn 8$_5$ 4QpGen$^a$ 1.1$_{11}$ ([הי]ו).

Also 4QMyst$^a$ 61$_3$.

**<SYN>** §2 כלה *fail*.

**Pi.** 2.2 Pf. Si חסרתו; + waw וַתְּחַסְּרֵהוּ; ptc. מְחַסֵּר—**cause to lack, cause to be less (than),** perh. at Si 14$_2$ **dishonour** (or em. חסד pi. *reproach*),* **<SUBJ>** Y. Ps 8$_6$, אֶחָד *one (person)* Ec 4$_8$, נֶפֶשׁ *soul* Si 14$_2$ (or em.), מַרְבֶּה *abundance* of wine Si 34$_{30}$ (:: ספק pi. *make sufficient*). **<OBJ>** אֱנוֹשׁ *human being* Ps 8$_6$ Si 14$_2$ (or em.), בֵּן *son* of human being Ps 8$_6$, נֶפֶשׁ *soul* Ec 4$_8$, כֹּחַ *strength* Si 34$_{30}$. **<PREP>** מִן of comparison, *than*, + אֱלֹהִים *God* Ps 8$_6$; partitive, *(some) of* Ec 4$_8$. **<COLL>** + מְעַט *a little* Ps 8$_6$. **<ANT>** ספק pi. *make sufficient*.

**Hi.** 2 Pf. הֶחְסִיר; impf. יַחְסִיר—**1.** abs. **lack anything, <SUBJ>** מעט hi. ptc. *one who makes*, i.e. gathers, *little* Ex 16$_{18}$. **2. cause to lack, <SUBJ>** נָבָל *fool* Is 32$_6$=4QpIsa$^e$ 6$_4$ ([יחסיר]; + ריק hi. *make empty*). **<OBJ>** (1) person lacking, צָמֵא *thirsty one* Is 32$_6$=4QpIsa$^e$ 6$_4$ ([צמא יחסיר]). (2) object lacked, מַשְׁקֶה *drink* Is 32$_6$=4QpIsa$^e$ 6$_4$ ([משקה ... ) [יחסיר]).*

→ חָסֵר *lacking*, חֶסֶר *want*, חֹסֶר *lack*, חֶסְרוֹן *deficiency*, מַחְסֹר *need*, חַסְרָה *Hasrah*.

**חָסֵר** 16.9.6.1 adj. **lacking**—cstr. חֲסַר; Si חסירה; Si חֲסֵירֵי (Q חסרי)—**1.** used attributively of נֶפֶשׁ *soul* Si 4$_2$.

**2.** used predicatively or as noun, **(one) lacking (in), <SUBJ>** תקע *clap* hands Pr 17$_{18}$, ערב *stand surety* Pr 17$_{18}$, כרת ni. *be cut off* 2 S 3$_{29}$, כול pilp. *endure* Si 6$_{20}$, חכם htp. *be wise* Si 38$_{24}$.

<NOM CL> חָסֵר מְשֻׁגָּעִים אָנִי *I am lacking in madmen* 1 S 21$_{16}$, נֹאֵף ... חֲסַר־לֵב *one who commits adultery ... is lacking in sense* Pr 6$_{32}$, מְרַדֵּף רֵיקִים חֲסַר־לֵב *one who pursues worthless things is lacking in sense* Pr 12$_{11}$ (or em.; see Cstr.), בָּז־לְרֵעֵהוּ חֲסַר־לֵב *one who despises his neighbour is lacking in sense* Pr 11$_{12}$, מִי ... חֲסַר־לֵב *who ... is lacking in sense?* Pr 9$_{4.16}$, כול עצם ש[היא חסרה] *every bone which is lacking (in flesh)* 4QMMT B$_{73}$.

<OBJ> בין hi. *perceive* Pr 7$_{7}$.

<CSTR> חֲסַר־לֵב *(one) lacking of heart*, i.e. in sense Pr 6$_{32}$ 7$_{7}$ 9$_{4.16}$ 10$_{13.21}$ (or em.; see Prep.) 11$_{12}$ 12$_{11}$ (or em. חָסֵר *he is in need*) 15$_{21}$ 17$_{18}$ 24$_{30}$ Si 6$_{20}$, חסרי לבב *those lacking of heart*, i.e. in sense 11QPs$^{a}$ 18$_{5}$.*

חֲסַר־תְּבוּנוֹת *(one) lacking of*, i.e. in, *understanding* Pr 28$_{16}$ (or em. תְּבוּאוֹת *of income*), חסר בינה *(one) lacking of*, i.e. in, *understanding* Si 47$_{23}$ (:: רְחַב *one broad* of folly), חֲסֵרֵי מַדָּע *those lacking of*, i.e. in, *knowledge* Si 13$_{8}$.

חֲסַר מְשֻׁגָּעִים *(one) lacking of*, i.e. in, *madmen* 1 S 21$_{16}$, חֲסַר־לָחֶם *(one) lacking of*, i.e. in, *bread* 2 S 3$_{29}$ Pr 12$_{9}$ 4Q416 2.2$_{20}$, חסר היין *(one) lacking of*, i.e. in, *wine* Si 34$_{27}$, תירוש *of*, i.e. in, *new wine* Si 34$_{27}$, עסק *of*, i.e. in, *toil* Si 38$_{24}$, מתן *a gift*, i.e. in sustenance Si 10$_{27}$ ([ח]ס[ר]), עצמה *of*, i.e. in, *might* Si 41$_{2}$, הון *of*, i.e. in, *wealth* 4Q424 3$_{10}$, חסר כל *(one) lacking of*, i.e. in, *everything* Si 11$_{12}$, חסר דינרין ששה עשר *lacking of*, i.e. minus, *sixteen denars* 5/6ḤevBA 44 fr. 1.

גֵּו חָסֵר *back of one lacking of* Pr 10$_{13}$, ... כֶּרֶם *vineyard of* Pr 24$_{30}$, כל חסרי *all those lacking of* 4Q424 3$_{10}$.

<APP> אָדָם *human being* Pr 17$_{18}$ 24$_{30}$, נַעַר *lad* Pr 7$_{7}$, נָגִיד *leader* Pr 28$_{16}$, מָנוֹן *offspring* Si 47$_{23}$.

<PREP> לְ of direction, *to*, + שׂכל hi. *explain* 11QPs$^{a}$ 18$_{5}$; of benefit, *to, for* Pr 15$_{21}$ Si 34$_{27}$ 41$_{2}$; בְּ of place, *among* Si 13$_{8}$; *as*, + מות *die* Pr 10$_{21}$ (or em. בְּחֹסֶר/בְּחֶסֶר *on account of lack of*).

<COLL> מה חיים חסר היין *what is life (to) one lacking in wine?* Si 34$_{27}$, יתיר או חסר *remaining or lacking*, i.e. more or less Mur 22 1$_{11}$ ([יתיר]) Mur 30 1$_{3}$ (א[ו חס]ר) 2$_{14}$ ([ח]סר).

Also perh. 4QRitMar 3$_{2}$ Arad inscr. 98.

<ANT> רָחָב *broad*.*

→ חסר *lack*.

**חֶ֫סֶר** 2 n.m. **want, lack,** <SUBJ> בוא *come* Pr 28$_{22}$. <CSTR> חֶסֶר לֵב *lack of heart*, i.e. sense Pr 10$_{21}$ (if em.; see Prep.). <NOM CL> חֶסֶר לְאֻמִּים חַטָּאת *lack of peoples is sin* Pr 14$_{34}$ (if em. חֶסֶד *reproach of*). <CSTR> חֶסֶר לְאֻמִּים *lack of peoples* Pr 14$_{34}$ (if em.; see Nom. Cl.). <PREP> בְּ of cause, *on account of*, + ערק *gnaw* Jb 30$_{3}$ (‖ כָּפָן *hunger*), מות *die* Pr 10$_{21}$ (if em. בַּחֲסַר *as one lacking of*). <SYN> כָּפָן *hunger*.*

→ חסר *lack*.

**[חֹ֫סֶר]** 3.3.2 n.[m.] **lack**—cstr. חֹסֶר (Q חסור)—**lack, want, need,** <OBJ> נתן *give* Am 4$_{6}$. <CSTR> חֹסֶר לֶחֶם *lack of bread* Am 4$_{6}$ (+ נִקְיוֹן שִׁנַּיִם *cleanness of teeth*), לֵב *of heart*, i.e. sense Pr 10$_{21}$ (if em.; see Prep.), כֹּל *of everything* Dt 28$_{48}$ (+ צָמָא *thirst*, עֵירֹם *nakedness*) 28$_{57}$ Si 35$_{12}$ 11QT 59$_{3}$ (חסור כול), חסר ביתו *need of his house* Si 34$_{4}$, כחו *of his strength* Si 34$_{4}$; [כ]ול חסרו *all his lack* 4Q418 7$_{16}$. <PREP> לְ of benefit, *for*, + יגע *labour* Si 34$_{4}$, עמל *toil* Si 34$_{4}$; בְּ of accompaniment, *with, in* 11QT 59$_{3}$, + עבד *serve* Dt 28$_{48}$, דבר pi. *speak* Si 34$_{12}$; of cause, *on account of*, + אכל *eat* Dt 28$_{57}$, מות *die* Pr 10$_{21}$ (if em. בַּחֲסַר *as one lacking of*).*

→ חסר *lack*.

**חַסְרָה** 1 pr.n.m. **Hasrah,** father of Tokhath, appar. ident. with Harhas at 2 K 22$_{14}$, <CSTR> בֶּן־חַסְרָה *son of Hasrah* 2 C 34$_{22}$ (mss חַסְדָּה *Hasdah*).

→ חסר *lack*.

**חֶסְרוֹן** 1 n.m. **deficiency,** <SUBJ> חֶסְרוֹן לֹא־יוּכַל לְהִמָּנוֹת *a deficiency cannot be counted* Ec 1$_{15}$ (or em. לְהִמָּנוֹת to לְהִמָּלוֹת cannot *be filled*; ‖ עות pu. ptc. *crooked thing*).*

→ חסר *lack*.

**חַף** I 1 adj. **pure,** in nom. cl. used predicatively of Job Jb 33$_{9}$ (‖ זַךְ *pure*; + לֹא עָוֹן לִי *I have no iniquity*). <SYN> זַךְ *pure*.

**[חַף]** II pr.n.m. **Apis,** Egyptian bull-god, <SUBJ> נוס *flee* Jr 46$_{15}$ (if em. נִסְחַף *is swept away* to נָס חַף *Apis has fled*), עמד *stand* Jr 46$_{15}$ (if em.). <OBJ> הדף *thrust* Jr 46$_{15}$ (if em.; see Subj.). <APP> אַבִּיר *bull* Jr 46$_{15}$ (if em.; see

Subj.).

**חפא** $_1$ vb. **hide—Pi.** $_1$ + waw וַיְחַפְּאוּ—**do secretly,** <SUBJ> בֵּן *son* of Israel 2 K $17_9$. <OBJ> דָּבָר *thing* 2 K $17_9$. <PREP> עַל *against,* + ׳י *Y.* 2 K $17_9$, אֱלֹהִים *God* 2 K $17_9$.*

**חפה** $_{12}$ vb. **cover—Qal** $_6$ Pf. חָפוּ; ptc. pass. חָפוּי, חֲפוּי—**1. cover, veil,** <SUBJ> עַם *people* 2 S $15_{30}$, צָעִיר *servant* Jr $14_3$, palace servants Est $7_8$ (or em. חָפְרוּ *they were ashamed* or חָוְרוּ *they were pale*), אִכָּר *farmer* Jr $14_4$. <OBJ> ראשׁ *head* 2 S $15_{30}$ Jr $14_{3.4}$, פָּנִים *face* of Haman Est $7_8$ (or em.; see Subj.).

**2.** pass. **be covered,** <SUBJ> ראשׁ *head* 2 S $15_{30}$ Est $6_{12}$.

**Ni.** $_1$ Ptc. נֶחְפָּה—**be covered,** <SUBJ> כָּנָף *wing* of dove Ps $68_{14}$. <PREP> בְּ *with,* + כֶּסֶף *silver* Ps $68_{14}$.

**Pi.** $_5$ Pf. חִפָּה; + waw וַיְחַף (וַיְחַפֵּהוּ)—**overlay,** <SUBJ> Solomon 2 C $3_{5.5.7.8.9}$. <OBJ> בַּיִת *house,* i.e. temple 2 C $3_7$, *house,* i.e. nave 2 C $3_{5.5}$, *house,* i.e. most holy place 2 C $3_8$, עֲלִיָּה *upper chamber* 2 C $3_9$. <COLL> חִפָּה עֵץ *he overlaid it with wood* 2 C $3_5$, חִפָּה זָהָב *he overlaid (it) with gold* 2 C $3_9$, וַיְחַפֵּהוּ זָהָב *he overlaid it with gold* 2 C $3_{5.8}$, וַיְחַף ... זָהָב *and he overlaid (it) ... with gold* 2 C $3_7$.

⇒ חֻפָּה *chamber.*

**חֻפָּה I** $_{3.1}$ n.f. **shelter**—sf. חֻפָּתָהּ, חֻפָּתוֹ—**shelter, bridal chamber,** <SUBJ> היה *be* Is $4_5$. <NOM CL> עַל־כָּל־כָּבוֹד חֻפָּה *a shelter will be over all the glory* Is $4_5$, [על כל כ]בוד חפתה *its canopy is over all the glory* Si $40_{27(M)}$. <PREP> מִן of direction, *from,* + יצא *go out* Jl $2_{16}$ Ps $19_6$.

⇒ חפה *cover.*

**חֻפָּה II** $_{1.0.9}$ pr.n.m. **Huppah**—Q חופה (חופא, חפא)—**1.** head of priestly family at time of David, <PREP> לְ of direction, *to,* + יצא (of lot) *go out* 1 C $24_{13}$.

**2.** name of priestly course (derived from §1) and the period during which it holds office, <NOM CL> [חופה ב]שנית ידעיה *Huppah is on the second of Jedaiah* 4QMishFa $1_3$. <CSTR> [באית חופה] *arrival of Huppah* 4QMishCc $1_2$. <PREP> בְּ of time, *in, at, during* 4QMishA 1.$2_7$ 1.$3_{10}$ 4.$4_1$ ([ח]פא) 4.$5_6$ 4QMishBa 1.$1_8$ ([חופה]) 1.$3_5$ ([חופה]) 2.$2_{3.5}$ ([חו]פה) 2.$2_7$ 2.$3_5$ 2.$4_5$ 4QMishBb 1.$1_8$ ([חופ]ה) $2_7$ ([חופ]ה) $3_7$.

Also 4QMishFb $2_2$.

⇒ חפה *cover.*

**חפז** $_{9.0.3}$ vb. **hurry—Qal** $_{6.0.3}$ Impf. יַחְפּוֹז, תַּחְפְּזוּ; + waw ויחפוזו Q; inf. חָפְזִי (חָפְזָהּ, חָפְזָם)—**make haste, hurry away, be alarmed,** <SUBJ> Aramaean 2 K $7_{15(Qr)}$, Israel 1QM $10_4$ (תח[פזו]), Israelite(s) Dt $20_3$, אָח *brother* 1QM $15_8$, worshipper Ps $31_{23}$ $116_{11}$, אֹמֶנֶת *nurse* 2 S $4_4$ (+ נוס *flee*), Behemoth Jb $40_{23}$, רוּחַ *spirit* 1QH $12_{19}$ ( ... רוחות] [י]חפזו ), כֹּל *all* 4QShira $1_3$. <PREP> מִן of direction, *from,* + הָדָר *splendour* 4QShira $1_3$. <COLL> 4QShirb $37_5$ (יבהלו [ויחפ]זו *they shall be alarmed and dismayed*).

**Ni.** $_3$ Pf. נֶחְפָּזוּ; impf. יֵחָפֵזוּן; ptc. נֶחְפָּז; inf. הֵחָפְזָם—**hurry away,** <SUBJ> David 1 S $23_{26}$ (+ הלך *go*), מֶלֶךְ *king* Ps $48_6$, מַיִם *water* Ps $104_7$.*

⇒ חִפָּזוֹן *haste.*

**[חֵפֶז]** pr.n.[m.] **Hephez,** Seal 2 (חפז; others חגי *Haggai* or חגז *Hegez*).

**חִפָּזוֹן** $_3$ n.m. **haste, hurried flight,** <PREP> בְּ of accompaniment, *in, with,* + יצא *go out* Dt $16_3$ Is $52_{12}$ (|| מְנוּסָה *flight*), אכל *eat* Ex $12_{11}$. <SYN> מְנוּסָה *flight.**

⇒ חפז *make haste.*

**חֻפִּים** $_3$ pr.n.m. **Huppim**—חֻפִּם—**1.** son of Benjamin who went down to Egypt with Jacob, appar. ident. with Hupham Nm $26_{39}$, <NOM CL> בְּנֵי בִנְיָמִן ... חֻפִּים *the sons of Benjamin were ... Huppim* Gn $46_{21}$. **2.** leader of the tribe of Benjamin, <NOM CL> שֻׁפִּם וְחֻפִּם בְּנֵי עִיר *Shuppim and Huppim were sons of Ir* 1 C $7_{12}$. <PREP> לְ of benefit, *to, for,* + לקח *take* 1 C $7_{15}$.

⇒ חפה *cover.*

**חֹפֶן** $_6$ n.m. **hollow of the hand**—du. חָפְנַיִם; cstr. חָפְנֵי; sf. חָפְנָיו, חָפְנֵיכֶם, חָפְנֶיךָ—<OBJ> מלא pi. *fill* Ezk $10_2$. <CSTR> מְלֹא חָפְנַיִם *fullness of both hands* Ec $4_6$, חָפְנָיו *of his hands* Lv $16_{12}$, חָפְנֵיכֶם *of your hands* Ex $9_8$. <PREP> בְּ of instrument, *by (means of),* + אסף *gather* Pr $30_4$; אֶל *to,* + נתן *give* Ezk $10_7$.

**חָפְנִי** 5 pr.n.m. **Hophni,** priest at sanctuary at Shiloh and son of Eli, <SUBJ> מות *die* 1 S 2$_{34}$ 4$_{11.17}$. <NOM CL> חָפְנִי וּפִנְחָס כֹּהֲנִים לַי׳ *Hophni and Phineas were priests to Y.* 1 S 1$_{3}$. <APP> בֵּן *son* 1 S 1$_{3}$ 4$_{4.11.17}$. <PREP> אֶל *to,* + בוא *come* 1 S 2$_{34}$.

**חפף** 1 vb. **shelter—Qal** 1 Ptc. חֹפֵף—<SUBJ> י׳ *Y.* Dt 33$_{12}$. <PREP> עַל *upon,* + Benjamin Dt 33$_{12}$.
→ חֻפַּפְיוֹ *Haphaphiah.*

**[חֻפַּפְיוֹ]** 0.0.0.1 pr.n.[m.] **Haphaphiah,** <PREP> לְ of possession, *of, (belonging) to* Seal 912 (8th cent.).
→ חפף *shelter.*

**חפץ I** 86.7.12 vb. **desire—Qal** 86.7.12 Pf. חָפֵץ, חָפְצָה, חָפַצְתָּ, חָפַצְתִּי (חָפָצְתִּי), חֲפַצְתֶּם, חָפָצְנוּ; impf. יַחְפֹּץ (יֶחְפָּץ), 3fs תֶּחְפָּץ, 2ms תַּחְפֹּץ (Si תחפוץ), אֶחְפֹּץ (אֶחְפָּץ), יַחְפְּצוּ (יֶחְפָּצוּ, יֶחְפָּצוּן); impv. Si חפוץ; ptc. חָפֵץ; inf. חֲפֹץ—**desire, delight (in), take pleasure (in); be willing, be pleased** (to do).

<SUBJ> י׳ *Y.* Nm 14$_{8}$ Jg 13$_{23}$ 1 S 2$_{25}$ (both + מות hi. *kill*) 2 S 15$_{26}$ 22$_{20}$||Ps 18$_{20}$ 1 K 10$_{9}$||2 C 9$_{8}$ Is 1$_{11}$ 42$_{21}$ 53$_{10}$ (+ דכא pi. *crush*) 55$_{11}$ 56$_{4}$ 62$_{4}$ 65$_{12}$ 66$_{4}$ Jr 9$_{23}$ Ezk 18$_{23.32}$ 33$_{11}$ Ho 6$_{6}$ Jon 1$_{14}$ Ml 2$_{17}$ Ps 22$_{9}$ 35$_{27}$ 37$_{23}$=4QpPs$^{a}$ 1.3$_{14}$ Ps 40$_{7}$ 41$_{12}$ 135$_{6}$ 147$_{10}$ Pr 21$_{1}$ GnzPs 1$_{3}$ 4$_{5}$ appar. 4QpsMos$^{e}$ 2.1$_{8}$, אֱלֹהִים *God* 1 K 10$_{9}$||2 C 9$_{8}$ Is 1$_{11}$ Ps 51$_{8.18.21}$ 115$_{3}$, אֵל *God* Mc 7$_{18}$ Ps 5$_{5}$ GnzPs 1$_{3}$ 1QH 10$_{5}$.

Israelite(s) Dt 21$_{14}$ Ml 3$_{1}$, Medes Is 13$_{17}$, גּוֹי *nation* 1QMyst 1.1$_{10}$, עַם *people* Is 58$_{2}$ (+ ידע *know*) 58$_{4}$ Jr 42$_{22}$ Ps 68$_{31}$, בַּיִת *house* of Jacob Is 58$_{2}$ (+ ידע *know*) 58$_{4}$, שְׁאֵרִית *remnant* of Israel Jr 6$_{10}$.

אָדוֹן *lord* 2 S 24$_{3}$, מֶלֶךְ *king* 1 S 18$_{22}$ 2 S 24$_{3}$ Ec 8$_{3}$ Est 2$_{14}$ 6$_{6.6}$ (+ עשׂה *do*) 6$_{7.9.9.11}$, שַׂר *prince* Jr 42$_{22}$, מַשְׂכִּיל *instructor* 1QS 9$_{24}$, Ben Sira Si 51$_{13}$, Elihu Jb 33$_{32}$ (+ צדק pi. *declare righteous*), Job Jb 13$_{3}$ (+ יכח hi. *reprove*), Johanan Jr 42$_{22}$, Jonathan 1 S 19$_{1}$, Naboth 1 K 21$_{6}$, Solomon 1 K 9$_{1}$ (+ עשׂה *do*).

אָדָם *human being* Si 15$_{17}$, אֱנוֹשׁ *human being* Jb 9$_{3}$ (+ ריב *contend*), אִישׁ *man* Dt 25$_{7.8}$ (both + לקח *take*) Ps 34$_{13}$ 112$_{1}$ 1QS 9$_{24}$, בֵּן *son* 1 S 19$_{1}$ Si 6$_{32.35}$ 7$_{13}$ (+ כחשׁ pi. *lie*) 15$_{15}$ (+ שׁמר *keep*) 15$_{16}$ (+ שׁלח *stretch out* hand), נַעַר *lad* Gn 34$_{19}$, עֶבֶד *servant* Ne 1$_{11}$ 1QH 10$_{30}$ ([יחפו]ץ), worshipper Ps 40$_{9}$ 41$_{12}$ 73$_{25}$ 109$_{17}$ 119$_{35}$ 1QH 7$_{1}$ ([אחפו]ץ), psalmist's friends Ps 35$_{27}$, psalmist's enemies Ps 40$_{15}$=70$_{3}$, כְּסִיל *fool* Pr 18$_{2}$, רָשָׁע *wicked one* Jb 21$_{14}$ (+ ידע *know*), גֹּאֵל *redeemer* Ru 3$_{13}$ (+ גאל *redeem*), נֶפֶשׁ *soul* Is 66$_{3}$ 1 C 28$_{9}$ perh. 4Q302 3.1$_{5}$ 4QpsEzek$^{a}$ 4$_{2}$ ([חפצה]), מִי *whoever* 2 S 20$_{11}$ 1QMyst 1.1$_{11}$, כֹּל *everyone* Ps 111$_{2}$, אַהֲבָה *love* Ca 2$_{7}$ 3$_{5}$ 8$_{4}$; subj. not specified, 1 K 13$_{333}$ 1QLitPr 3.2$_{4}$ 4QapPs$^{a}$ 1.2$_{6}$ (+ עשׂה *do*) Mur 30 2$_{23}$ MurEpBarC$^{b}$$_{6}$.

<OBJ> דָּם *blood* Is 1$_{11}$, אֱמֶת *truth* Ps 51$_{8}$, צֶדֶק *righteousness* Ps 35$_{27}$, שָׁלוֹם *peace* Ps 35$_{27}$, חֶסֶד *loyalty* Ho 6$_{6}$ Mc 7$_{18}$, רַע *evil* Ps 40$_{15}$=70$_{3}$, רֶשַׁע *wickedness* Ps 5$_{5}$, רָצוֹן *will* of God 1QS 9$_{24}$, חַיִּים *life* Ps 34$_{13}$, מָוֶת *death* Ezk 18$_{23}$, שִׂיחָה *discourse* Si 6$_{35}$, דֶּרֶךְ *way* Ps 37$_{23}$=4QpPs$^{a}$ 1.3$_{14}$, זֶבַח *sacrifice* Ps 40$_{7}$ 51$_{18.21}$, מִנְחָה *offering* Ps 40$_{7}$, קְרָב *battle* Ps 68$_{31}$, אֵלֶּה *these (things)* 1QH 7$_{1}$ ([אחפו]ץ).

<PREP> לְ of benefit, *to, for,* + מַשְׂכִּיל *master* 1QS 9$_{24}$, אִישׁ *man* 1QS 9$_{24}$.

בְּ (delight) *in,* + Zion Is 62$_{4}$, אֶרֶץ *earth* Ps 73$_{25}$, Jerusalem Is 62$_{4}$, עֵדָה *congregation* Nm 14$_{8}$, מָקוֹם *place* Jr 42$_{22}$, David 1 S 18$_{22}$ 19$_{1}$ 2 S 22$_{20}$||Ps 18$_{20}$, Joab 2 S 20$_{11}$, Solomon 1 K 10$_{9}$||2 C 9$_{8}$, מֶלֶךְ *king* 2 S 15$_{26}$, אִשָּׁה *woman* Dt 21$_{14}$, בַּת *daughter* Gn 34$_{19}$, נַעֲרָה *young girl* Est 2$_{14}$, worshipper Ps 22$_{9}$, עשׂה ptc. *one who does* evil Ml 2$_{17}$, רוּם *height* 1QH 10$_{30}$, גְּבוּרָה *might* Ps 147$_{10}$, בְּרָכָה *blessing* Ps 109$_{17}$, חָכְמָה *wisdom* Si 51$_{13}$, צֶדֶק *righteousness* GnzPs 1$_{3}$, טוֹב *welfare* GnzPs 4$_{5}$, יְקָר *honour* Est 6$_{6.7.9.9.11}$, זָהָב *gold* Is 13$_{17}$, נָתִיב *path* Ps 119$_{35}$, מָוֶת *death* Ezk 18$_{23(mss)}$ 18$_{32}$ 33$_{11}$, עַוְלָה *wickedness* 1QLitPr 3.2$_{4}$ (עו[ל]ה), שִׁקּוּץ *abominable object* Is 66$_{3}$, טֻחוֹת *inward parts* Ps 51$_{8}$, תְּבוּנָה *understanding* Pr 18$_{2}$, מִצְוָה *commandment* Ps 112$_{1}$, דָּבָר *word* Jr 6$_{10}$, *matter* 2 S 24$_{3}$, אֲשֶׁר *that which* 4QpsMos$^{e}$ 2.1$_{8}$, אֵלֶּה *these* Jr 9$_{23}$.

<COLL> הֶחָפֹץ אֶחְפֹּץ מוֹת רָשָׁע *do I have any pleasure in the death of the wicked?* Ezk 18$_{23}$.*
→ חֵפֶץ *desire,* חֵפֶץ *Hephez,* חֶפְצִי־בָהּ *Hephzi-bah.*

**חפץ II** 1 vb. **stretch out—Qal** 1 Impf. יַחְפֹּץ—**stretch out, let** (tail) **hang,** <SUBJ> Behemoth Jb 40$_{17}$. <OBJ> זָנָב *tail* Jb 40$_{17}$.

**חָפֵץ**, see חפץ I *desire.*

**חֵ֫פֶץ** I $_{40.8.39}$ n.m. **desire**—cstr. חֵ֫פֶץ; sf. חֶפְצִי, חֶפְצְךָ (Q חפצכה), חֶפְצוֹ, חֶפְצָהּ, חֶפְצָם; pl. חֲפָצִים; cstr. Si חפצי; sf. חֲפָצַ֫יִךְ (Q חפציכה), חֲפָצֶ֫יהָ—**delight, desire, pleasure, will, requirement; affair** (Ec $3_{1.17}$ $5_{7}$ $8_{6}$), <SUBJ> שׁוה *be like* Pr $3_{15}$ $8_{11}$, צלח *be successful* Is $53_{10}$.

<NOM CL> בְּתוֹרַת י׳ חֶפְצוֹ *his delight is the law of Y.* Ps $1_{2}$, כָּל־חֶפְצִי־בָם *all my delight is in them* Ps $16_{3}$=4QMidr Eschat[b] $10_{2}$, זה חפצי *this is my delight* GnzPs $3_{2}$, מַה־חֶפְצוֹ *what is his delight?* Jb $21_{21}$, הַחֵפֶץ לַי׳ *is it a delight to Y?* 1 S $15_{22}$, הַחֵפֶץ לְשַׁדַּי *is it a delight to Shaddai?* Jb $22_{3}$, אֵין־חֵפֶץ לַמֶּלֶךְ *it is not a delight to the king* 1 S $18_{25}$, אֵין לִי חֵפֶץ *I have no delight* Ml $1_{10}$ Ec $12_{1}$ Si $15_{12}$, אֵין־חֵפֶץ *there is no delight* Jr $22_{28}$ $48_{38}$ Ho $8_{8}$= 4QpHos[b] $1_{18}$ ([חפץ]) Ec $5_{3}$, sim. 4QapLam[a] $1.2_{10}$.

<OBJ> כון hi. *establish* 4Q418 $88_{1}$, מצא *find* Is $58_{3.13}$ 4Q416 $2.2_{8}$, דרשׁ *seek* Si $35_{14}$ 4Q418 $81_{18}$ $102_{4}$ $126.2_{12}$, תכן *measure* 4Q416 $1_{2}$ (unless לתכן חפצו *for the measurement of his pleasure*), נתן *give* 1 K $5_{24}$ $10_{13}$‖2 C $9_{12}$, עשׂה *do* 1 K $5_{22.23}$ Is $46_{10}$ $48_{14}$ $58_{13}$ (1QIsa[b] חֶפְצְךָ) Si $10_{26(B)}$ $11_{23}$ ([חפצ[י) CD $3_{15}$ $11_{2}$ 4Q418 $127_{5}$ $158_{3}$, עבד *serve* Si $10_{26(A)}$, צמח hi. *cause to prosper* 2 S $23_{5}$, שׁלם hi. *complete* Is $44_{28}$.

<CSTR> חֵפֶץ י׳ *pleasure of Y.* Is $53_{10}$, חפצי אל *pleasures of God* Si $35_{14(B)}$, מלכים *of kings* GnzPs $2_{27}$, חֵפֶץ דַּלִּים *desire of the poor* Jb $31_{16}$, חֵפֶץ כַּפֶּיהָ *delight of her hands* Pr $31_{13}$, חפצי רצונך *desires of your will* GnzPs $1_{6}$ $3_{1.4}$, חפצי רצונו *desires of his will* CD $3_{15}$.

אֶרֶץ חֵפֶץ *land of delight* Ml $3_{12}$, מְחוֹז חֶפְצָם *the haven of their desire* Ps $107_{30}$, אַבְנֵי־חֵפֶץ *stones of delight* Is $54_{12}$ Si $45_{11}$ $50_{9}$ 1QM $5_{6.9.14}$ $12_{12}$ $19_{5}$ ([אבני חפץ]) 4Q525 $3.3_{3}$, עבודת חפצו *work of his desire* CD $10_{20}$, דִּבְרֵי־חֵפֶץ *words of delight* Ec $12_{10}$, רזי חפצו *mysteries of his delight* 1QH fr $3_{7}$.

כָּל־חֵפֶץ *all desire* 2 S $23_{5}$, *every matter* Ec $3_{1.17}$ $8_{6}$, כָּל־חֲפָצִים *all desires* Pr $3_{15(ms)}$ $8_{11}$, כָּל־חֶפְצִי *all my purpose* Is $44_{28}$ $46_{10}$, *all my delight* Ps $16_{3}$=4QMidrEschat[b] $10_{2}$, כָּל־חֶפְצְךָ *all your desire* 1 K $5_{22}$, כָּל־חֲפָצַיִךְ *all your desires* Pr $3_{15}$ (ms חֲפָצִים *all desires*) 4Q418 $88_{1}$ ([כו[ל חפציכה) $138_{3}$ (כול חפציכה), כָּל־חֶפְצוֹ *all his desire* 1 K $5_{24}$ $9_{11}$ 4Q418 $127_{5}$, כָּל־חֶפְצָהּ *all her desire* 1 K $10_{13}$‖2 C $9_{12}$, כל חפציהם *all their requirements* CD $14_{12}$, *all their affairs* 1QS $3_{17}$.

<APP> מַרְגָּלִית *jewel* GnzPs $2_{27}$, אֶבֶן precious *stone* GnzPs $2_{27}$.

<PREP> לְ of benefit, *to, for* Ec $3_{1.17}$ $8_{6}$ 1QH $1_{13}$ ([חפציה[ם), + היה *be* 4Q417 $1.1_{12}$; *according to* 1 K $9_{11}$ 1QH $13_{20}$ 4Q418 $46_{3}$ $126.2_{4}$ 4QHod[f] $21_{1}$ ([חפציה[ם), + תכן *regulate* 4Q424 $1_{11}$.

בְּ of instrument, *by (means of)*, + עשׂה *do* Pr $31_{13}$; *in, with* 4Q 418 $107_{4}$, + כול pilp. *sustain* 1QS $3_{17}$, מצא *find* GnzPs $3_{1}$.

כְּ *as* GnzPs $1_{6}$, + עשׂה *do* GnzPs $3_{2}$.

מִן of direction, *from*, + שׂים *place* 4Q418 $126.2_{14}$, מנע *withhold* Jb $31_{16}$; of comparison, *(more) than* GnzPs $2_{27}$.

עַל *on behalf of*, + תמה *be astounded* Ec $5_{7}$.

<COLL> תותיר הובל למחיו חפצו *you shall leave what grows for his subsistence (according to) his desire* 4Q417 $1.1_{18}$.

Also Si $43_{7(B)}$ perh. 4Q418 $94_{3}$ $102_{2}$ $103.2_{5}$ $106_{1}$ $127_{4}$ $128_{3}$ 4Q419 $8.2_{1}$.*

→ חפץ *desire.*

**[חֵ֫פֶץ]** II pr.n.m. **Hephez,** Seal 2 (others חגי *Haggai*, or חגז *Hegez*).

→ חפץ *desire.*

**חֶפְצִי־בָהּ** $_{2}$ pr.n.f. **Hephzi-bah, 1.** wife of Hezekiah and mother of Manasseh, <NOM CL> שֵׁם אִמּוֹ חֶפְצִי־בָהּ *the name of his mother was Hephzi-bah* 2 K $21_{1}$. **2.** name given by Isaiah to land of Israel, *my desire is in,* i.e. for, *it*, <SUBJ> קרא ni. *be called* Is $62_{4}$.

→ חפץ *desire.*

**חפר** I $_{22.0.27}$ vb. **search—Qal** $_{23.0.27.1}$ Pf. חָפַר, חָפַרְתִּי, חָפְרוּ (חֲפָרוּהָ, חָפְרוּ) חֲפָרוּ; impf. יַחְפְּרוּ; + waw וְחָפַרְתָּ (וַיַּחְפְּרֵהוּ וַיַּחְפֹּר, (וְחָפַרְתָּה), Q ויחפרו (Q ויחפורו, וַיַּחְפְּרֵהוּ, וָאֶחְפֹּר; impv. Q חפור; ptc. חֹפֵר (Q חופריה); inf. לַחְפֹּר—usu. **dig;** also **search (out), explore** (Dt $1_{22}$ Jos $2_{2.3}$ Jb $3_{21}$ $39_{29}$ 1 C $19_{3}$ [if em.; see Subj.]), <SUBJ> Egyptian Ex $7_{24}$, Israel CD $3_{16}$, Israelite(s) Dt $23_{14}$, Abraham Gn $21_{30}$, Isaac Gn $26_{18.22}$, Jeremiah Jr $13_{7}$, Job Jb $11_{18}$ (or em. וְחָפַרְתָּ appar. *and you will search* to וְחֻפַּרְתָּ *and you will be protected*, from חפר *protect*), אִישׁ *man* Dt $1_{22}$ Jos $2_{2.3}$, עֶבֶד *servant* Gn $26_{15.19.21.32}$ 1 C $19_{3}$

(if em. לַהֲפֹךְ *to overthrow* to לַחְפֹּר *to search out*), Abraham's servants Gn 26$_{18}$, שַׂר *prince* Nm 21$_{18}$ CD 6$_{3}$, חָכָם *wise one* CD 6$_{3}$, wicked Ps 7$_{16}$, לֹחֵם *combatant* Ps 35$_{7}$, סוּס *horse* Jb 39$_{21}$, נֶשֶׁר *eagle* Jb 39$_{29}$, עָמֵל *sufferer* Jb 3$_{21}$, מַר *bitter one* Jb 3$_{21}$; subj. not specified, Ec 10$_{8}$ CD 6$_{4}$ 3QTr 2$_{14}$ 3$_{6}$ 4$_{7.13}$ 5$_{3.10.14}$ 6$_{3.9.12}$ 7$_{1.9.12.15}$ 8$_{5.9.12.14}$ 9$_{2.5.8.12}$ 10$_{13}$ Lachish ost. 13$_{2}$ ([]ויחפרהו; others [א]ת עבדה ה[] *the service of the*).

<OBJ> בְּאֵר *well* Gn 21$_{30}$ 26$_{15.18.21.22.32}$ Nm 21$_{18}$ CD 3$_{16}$ 6$_{3.3.4}$, בּוֹר *cistern* Ps 7$_{16}$, גּוּמָּץ *pit* Ec 10$_{8}$, אֶרֶץ *land* Dt 1$_{22}$ Jos 2$_{2.3}$ 1 C 19$_{3}$ (if em.; see Subj.), מָוֶת *death* Jb 3$_{21}$, אֹכֶל *food* Jb 39$_{29}$, אַמָּה *cubit* 3QTr 2$_{14+14t}$ (see Coll).

<PREP> לְ of benefit, *to, for,* + Israelite(s) Dt 1$_{22}$, נֶפֶשׁ *soul* Ps 35$_{7}$.

בְּ of place/time, *in, at, among, during,* + יוֹם *day* Gn 26$_{15.18}$, עֵמֶק *valley* Jb 39$_{21}$, גַּיְא *valley* 3QTr 8$_{5}$, מְעָרָה *cave* 3QTr 6$_{3.9}$ 7$_{9}$, מִשְׁכָּן *dwelling place* 3QTr 6$_{12}$, קֶרֶב *tomb* 3QTr 5$_{14}$, נַחַל *wadi* Gn 26$_{19}$, ראשׁ *head* of water conduit 3QTr 5$_{3}$, בְּרֵכָה *pond* 3QTr 2$_{14}$; of instrument, *by (means of),* + יָתֵד *nail* Dt 23$_{14}$.

מִן of comparison, *(more) than,* + מַטְמוֹן *hidden treasure* Jb 3$_{21}$.

עַל *at,* + פֶּה *mouth* of water exit 3QTr 7$_{15}$.

תַּחַת *under,* + יָד *hand,* i.e. monument, of Absalom 3QTr 10$_{13}$.

<COLL> וַיַּחְפְּרוּ ... סְבִיבֹת הַיְאֹר *and they dug ... around the Nile* Ex 7$_{24}$, חפור אמות שלוש *dig for three cubits* 3QTr 4$_{7}$ 5$_{10}$ 6$_{3}$ 7$_{15}$ 8$_{9}$, חפור אמות ארבע *dig for four cubits* 3QTr 2$_{14}$, חפר אמות שש *dig for six cubits* 3QTr 3$_{6}$ 7$_{9}$, חפור אמות שבע *dig for seven cubits* 3QTr 5$_{14}$ 7$_{12}$ 8$_{5}$ 9$_{12}$, חפור אמות שמונא *dig for eight cubits* 3QTr 9$_{5}$, חפר אמות תשע *dig for nine cubits* 3QTr 6$_{9}$ 7$_{1}$.*

→ חֵפֶר *Hepher.*

**חפר II** 17.1 vb. **be ashamed—Qal** 13 Pf. חָפְרָה (חָפֵרָה), חָפְרוּ; impf. יַחְפְּרוּ (יֶחְפָּרוּ), תַּחְפְּרוּ—**be ashamed, be confounded,** <SUBJ> Zion Is 1$_{29}$, ילד ptc. *one who bears* Jr 15$_{9}$ 50$_{12}$, בקשׁ pi. ptc. *one who seeks* Ps 40$_{15}$ 70$_{3}$ 71$_{24}$, אֹיֵב *enemy* Ps 83$_{18}$ (+ אבד *perish*), חֹשֵׁב *schemer* Ps 35$_{4}$, קֹסֵם *diviner* Mc 3$_{7}$, שׂמח ptc. *one who rejoices* Ps 35$_{26}$, הֲלִיכָה *caravan* Jb 6$_{20}$, לְבָנָה *full moon* Is 24$_{23}$, פָּנִים *face* Ps 34$_{6}$ Est 7$_{8}$ (if em. חָפוּ *they covered* to חָפְרוּ *they were ashamed*). <PREP> מִן of cause, *because of,* + גַּנָּה *garden* Is 1$_{29}$. <COLL> חפר || בושׁ *be ashamed* Is 1$_{29}$ 24$_{23}$ Jr 15$_{9}$ 50$_{12}$ Mc 3$_{7}$ Ps 35$_{26}$ 40$_{15}$ 70$_{3}$ 71$_{24}$. <SYN> בושׁ *be ashamed.*

**Hi.** 4.1.0 Pf. הֶחְפִּיר; impf. יַחְפִּיר, תַּחְפִּירִי; ptc. מַחְפִּיר, Si מחפרת—**be ashamed, act shamefully,** <SUBJ> Lebanon Is 33$_{9}$, Jerusalem Is 54$_{4}$=4QTanh 8$_{5}$ ([ת]חפירי), בֵּן *son* Pr 19$_{26}$ (|| בושׁ hi. *act shamefully*), בַּת *daughter* Si 42$_{14(Bmg)}$, רָשָׁע *wicked one* Pr 13$_{5}$ (|| באשׁ hi. *be odious*). <SYN> באשׁ hi. *be odious,* בושׁ hi. *act shamefully.*

**[חפר] III** vb. **protect—Pu. be protected,** <SUBJ> Job Jb 11$_{18}$ (if em. וְחָפַרְתָּ appar. *and you will search* to וְחֻפַּרְתָּ *and you will be protected*).

**חֵפֶר I** 2 pl.n. **Hepher, 1.** Canaanite royal town defeated by Joshua, <CSTR> מֶלֶךְ חֵפֶר *king of Hepher* Jos 12$_{17}$. **2.** administrative district of Solomon administered by Ben-hesed, <CSTR> אֶרֶץ חֵפֶר *land of Hepher* 1 K 4$_{10}$.

→ חפר *search.*

**חֵפֶר II** 7.0.0.1 pr.n.m. **Hepher, 1.** son of Gilead and grandson of Manasseh, <CSTR> בֶּן־חֵפֶר *son of Hepher* Nm 26$_{33}$ 27$_{1}$ Jos 17$_{3}$. בְּנֵי־חֵפֶר *sons of Hepher* Jos 17$_{2}$. <APP> בֵּן *son* Nm 26$_{32}$.

**2.** Judahite, son of Asshur, <OBJ> ילד *bear child* 1 C 4$_{6}$.

**3.** warrior in David's army, <NOM CL> גִּבּוֹרֵי הַחֲיָלִים ... חֵפֶר *... the warriors of the armies were ... Hepher* 1 C 11$_{36}$.

**4.** Seal 75$_{3}$.

→ חפר *search.*

**חֶפְרִי** 1 gent. **Hepherite,** used as sing. collective noun, **Hepherites,** <CSTR> מִשְׁפַּחַת הַחֶפְרִי *family of the Hepherites* Nm 26$_{32}$.

→ חפר *search out.*

**חֲפָרַיִם** 1 pl.n. **Hapharaim,** in territory of Issachar, perh. eṭ-Ṭaiyibe E of Sōlem, <SUBJ> היה *be* Jos 19$_{19}$.

→ חפר *search out.*

**חָפְרַע** 1 pr.n.m. **Hophra,** Egyptian pharaoh defeated by Nebuchadnezzar, <OBJ> נתן *give* Jr 44$_{30}$. <APP>

פַּרְעֹה *pharaoh* Jr 44$_{30}$.

[חֲפַרְפָּרָה] $_{1}$ n.f. **mole**—pl. mss חֲפַרְפָּרוֹת (Q חפרפרים)—**mole,** or perh. **shrew,** or **bat,** <PREP> לְ of direction, *to,* שׁחה htpal. *bow down* Is 2$_{20}$ (לַחְפֹּר פֵּרוֹת; mss לַחֲפַרְפָּרוֹת; 1QIsa[a] לחפרפרים; || עֲטַלֵּף *bat*). <SYN> עֲטַלֵּף *bat*.

חפשׂ I $_{23.0.2}$ vb. **search**—**Qal** $_{4}$ Impf. יַחְפְּשׂוּ, 2ms תַּחְפְּשֶׂנָּה, נַחְפְּשָׂה; ptc. חֹפֵשׂ—**search (out),** <SUBJ> בֵּן *son* Pr 2$_{4}$, worshipper Lm 3$_{40}$, enemy Ps 64$_{7}$, נֵר *lamp* Pr 20$_{27}$. <OBJ> עוֹלָה *wickedness* Ps 64$_{7}$, חֶדֶר *chamber,* i.e. innermost part, of body Pr 20$_{27}$, דֶּרֶךְ *way* Lm 3$_{40}$. <PREP> כְּ *as,* + מַטְמוֹן *hidden treasure* Pr 2$_{4}$.

**Ni.** $_{1.0.2}$ Pf. נֶחְפְּשׂוּ—**be searched out, hide oneself,** <SUBJ> Esau Ob$_{6}$, רוּחַ *spirit* 1QH 8$_{29}$, נְהָמָה *groaning* 1QH 10$_{34}$.

<PREP> בְּ of place, *in,* + חֶדֶר *chamber,* i.e. recesses of Sheol 1QH 10$_{34}$.

עִם *with,* + מֵת *dead one* 1QH 8$_{29}$.

**Pi.** $_{8}$ Pf. חִפְּשׂוּ; impf. אֲחַפֵּשׂ; + waw וַיְחַפֵּשׂ; וְחִפַּשְׂתִּי; impv. חַפְּשׂוּ—**search (for), trace out,** <SUBJ> ״ *Y.* Am 9$_{3}$ Zp 1$_{12}$, Laban Gn 31$_{35}$, Saul 1 S 23$_{23}$, עֶבֶד *servant* 1 K 20$_{6}$ 2 K 10$_{23}$, אֲשֶׁר עַל־בֵּיתוֹ *one who was over his house,* i.e. steward Gn 44$_{12}$, רוּחַ *spirit* Ps 77$_{7}$.

<OBJ> David 1 S 23$_{23}$, בַּיִת *house* 1 K 20$_{6.6}$, Jerusalem Zp 1$_{12}$, כָּלָה *destruction* 4Q185 1.3$_{12}$.

<PREP> בְּ of instrument, *by (means of),* + נֵר *lamp* Zp 1$_{12}$; *in, among,* + אֶלֶף *thousand* of Judah 1 S 23$_{23}$.

**Pu.** $_{2}$ Impf. יְחֻפַּשׂ; ptc. מְחֻפָּשׂ—**be sought, be devised** (unless at Ps 88$_{6}$ [if em.] Pr 28$_{12}$ חפשׂ II pu. *be prostrated*), <SUBJ> אָדָם *human being* Pr 28$_{12}$ (or em. יִתְחַפֵּשׂ htp. *he hides himself*), worshipper Ps 88$_{6}$ (if em. חָפְשִׁי *free* to חֻפַּשְׂתִּי *I was sought*), חֵפֶשׂ *plot* Ps 64$_{7}$ (or em. הִתְחַפְּשׂוּ htp. *they hide themselves*). <PREP> בְּ of place, *among,* + מֵת *dead one* Ps 88$_{6}$ (if em.; see Subj.).

**Htp.** $_{8}$ Pf. הִתְחַפֵּשׂ; impf. יִתְחַפֵּשׂ; inf. הִתְחַפֵּשׂ—**disguise oneself, hide oneself,** <SUBJ> Josiah 2 C 35$_{22}$, Saul 1 S 28$_{8}$, אָדָם *human being* Pr 28$_{12}$ (if em. יְחֻפַּשׂ *he is sought for*), מֶלֶךְ *king* 1 K 22$_{30.30}$||2 C 18$_{29.29}$, נָבִיא *prophet* 1 K 20$_{38}$, מֵרַע *evildoer* Ps 64$_{7}$ (if em. חֵפֶשׂ מְחֻפָּשׂ *a plot devised*), פעל ptc. *one who does* evil Ps 64$_{7}$ (if em.), לְבוּשׁ *garment* Jb 30$_{18}$. <PREP> בְּ of instrument, *by (means of), with,* + אֲפֵר *bandage* 1 K 20$_{38}$.*

⇒ חֵפֶשׂ *plot.*

*חפשׂ II $_{2}$ vb. **throw**—**Pu.** Impf. יְחֻפַּשׂ—**be prostrated** (unless חפשׂ I pu. *be sought, be devised*), <SUBJ> אָדָם *human being* Pr 28$_{12}$, מֵת *one who is dead* Ps 88$_{6}$ (if em. בַּמֵּתִים חָפְשִׁי *free among the dead* to כְּמֵתִים מְחֻפָּשִׂים *like prostrate dead*).

חֵ֫פֶשׂ $_{1}$ n.m. **plot,** or (if em.; see Coll.) **disguise,** <SUBJ> חפשׂ pu. *be devised* Ps 64$_{7}$. <OBJ> תמם *complete* Ps 64$_{7}$. <COLL> חֵפֶשׂ + חפשׂ htp. *disguise oneself with a disguise* Ps 64$_{7}$ (if em. מְחֻפָּשׂ *devised* to הִתְחַפְּשׂוּ *they disguise themselves*).*

⇒ חפשׂ *search out.*

חפשׁ $_{1.1}$ vb. **be free**—**Qal** $_{0.1}$ Inf. Si חפשׁ—**be free,** <SUBJ> בֵּן *son* Si 13$_{11}$. <PREP> עִם *with,* + נָדִיב *noble* Si 13$_{11}$.

**Pu.** $_{1}$ Pf. חֻפָּשָׁה—**be freed,** <SUBJ> שִׁפְחָה *female servant* Lv 19$_{20}$.*

⇒ חֹפֶשׁ *freedom,* חֻפְשָׁה *freedom,* חָפְשִׁי *free,* חָפְשִׁית *freedom.*

חֹ֫פֶשׁ I $_{1}$ n.m. **woven material**—for saddlecloths Ezk 27$_{20}$, <CSTR> בִּגְדֵי־חֹפֶשׁ *garments of woven material* Ezk 27$_{20}$.

חֹ֫פֶשׁ II $_{0.1}$ n.m. **freedom**—Si חופש—<OBJ> מנע *withhold* Si 7$_{21}$.

⇒ חפשׁ *be free.*

*[חֹ֫פֶשׁ] III $_{1}$ n.[m.] **prison**—sf. חָפְשִׁי—<NOM CL> בַּמֵּתִים חָפְשִׁי *among the dead ones is my prison* Ps 88$_{6}$ (unless חָפְשִׁי *free*).

חֻפְשָׁה $_{1}$ n.f. **freedom**—<SUBJ> נתן ni. *be given* Lv 19$_{20}$.*

⇒ חפשׁ *free.*

חָפְשׁוּת $_{2}$ n.f. **freedom**—Qr חָפְשִׁית—from normal human contact, perh. as euphemistic of isolation or exclusion on account of leprosy, <CSTR> בֵּית הַחָפְשׁוּת *the house of freedom* 2 K 15$_{5(mss)}$||2 C 26$_{21(Kt)}$ (L, Qr חָפְשִׁית in same sense).*

⇒ חפשׁ *be free.*

**חָפְשִׁי** 17 adj. **free**—pl. חָפְשִׁים—**1a.** in nom. cl. used predicatively of עֶבֶד *slave* Jb 3$_{19}$. **1b.** with היה *be*, used predicatively of worshipper Ps 88$_{6}$ (unless חָפְשִׁי *my prison*, i.e. חֹפֶשׁ III; or em. נַפְשִׁי *my soul*, or הֲשִׁבֹתִי *I was brought back*, from שׁוב ho., or חֻפַּשְׂתִּי *I was sought*).

**2.** used as noun, **freed one,** <PREP> לְ *as*, + יצא *go out* Ex 21$_{2}$, שׁלח pi. *send away*, i.e. let go Ex 21$_{26.27}$.

**3. freely, in freedom,** predicate of שׁלח pi. *send away*, i.e. let go Dt 15$_{12.13.18}$ Is 58$_{6}$ Jr 34$_{9.10.11.14.16}$ Jb 39$_{5}$, יצא *go out* Ex 21$_{5}$, עשׂה *make* 1 S 17$_{25}$.*

⇒ חפשׁ *free.*

**חָפְשִׁית**, see חָפְשׁוּת *freedom.*

**חֵץ** 53.1.5 n.m. **arrow**—cstr. חֵץ; sf. חִצָּם, חִצּוֹ, חִצַּי, חִצֵּי; pl. חִצִּים; cstr. חִצֵּי; sf. חִצַּי, חִצֶּיךָ (חֲצָצֶיךָ), חִצָּיו—usu. as weapon, also as instrument of divination (2 K 13$_{15.15.17.17.18}$ Ezk 21$_{26}$)*, perh. also of **lightning** (Ps 144$_{6}$).

<SUBJ> ברר pass. *be sharp* Is 49$_{2}$, שׁנן pass. *be sharp* Is 5$_{28}$ Ps 45$_{6}$ 120$_{4}$ Pr 25$_{18}$, שׁחט *slaughter* Jr 9$_{7(Kt)}$, pass. *be hammered*, i.e. sharpened Jr 9$_{7(Qr)}$, הלך htp. *go to and fro* Ps 77$_{18}$, יצא *go out* Zc 9$_{14}$, עוף *fly* Ps 91$_{5}$, htpol. *fly away* 1QH 3$_{27}$, נחת ni. *penetrate* Ps 38$_{3}$, פלח pi. *split open* Pr 7$_{23}$.

<NOM CL> חֵץ תְּשׁוּעָה *(it is) the arrow of deliverance* 2 K 13$_{17.17}$, שִׁנֵּיהֶם ... חִצִּים *their teeth are ... arrows* Ps 57$_{5}$, אָנוּשׁ חִצִּי *incurable is my arrow*, i.e. its effects Jb 34$_{6}$, חֵץ שָׁנוּן אִישׁ עֹנֶה *a sharp tooth is (as) a man who answers* against his neighbour Pr 25$_{18}$.

חֵץ חֲנִיתוֹ כִּמְנוֹר אֹרְגִים *the shaft of his spear was as the beam of weavers* 1 S 17$_{7}$, חִצָּיו כְּגִבּוֹר *his arrows are as a warrior*, i.e. like a warrior's Jr 50$_{9}$, הַחִצִּים מִמְּךָ וָהֵנָּה *the arrows are from you and over there*, i.e. on this side of you 1 S 20$_{21}$, הַחִצִּים מִמְּךָ וָהָלְאָה *the arrows are from you and beyond*, i.e. beyond you 1 S 20$_{22}$, חִצֵּי שַׁדַּי עִמָּדִי *the arrows of the Almighty are with me* Jb 6$_{4}$.

<OBJ> פעל *make* Ps 7$_{14}$, ברר hi. *sharpen* Jr 51$_{11}$, לקח *take* 2 K 13$_{15.15.18}$, חזק hi. *take hold of* 1QM 6$_{15}$, כון pol. *fix* on string Ps 11$_{2}$=4QMidrEschat[b] 8$_{8}$ (hi.).

שׁלח *send* 2 S 22$_{15}$||Ps 18$_{15}$ Ps 144$_{6}$, pi. *send out* Ezk 5$_{16}$, ירה *shoot* 1 S 20$_{20.37(mss)}$ 2 K 19$_{32}$||Is 37$_{33}$ Ps 64$_{8}$ Pr 26$_{18}$, פוץ hi. *scatter* 2 S 22$_{15}$||Ps 18$_{15}$, מצא *find* 1 S 20$_{21.36}$, לקט pi. *gather* 1 S 20$_{38(Qr)}$.

כלה pi. *use up* Dt 32$_{23}$, שׁכר hi. *make drunk* Dt 32$_{42}$, דרך *tread*, i.e. bend bow Ps 58$_{8}$ 64$_{4}$, בער pi. *burn* Ezk 39$_{9}$, נפל hi. *bring down* Ezk 39$_{3}$, פרר hi. appar. *let loose* 1QH 2$_{26}$.

<CSTR> חִצֵּי שַׁדַּי *arrows of the Almighty* Jb 6$_{4}$, גִּבּוֹר *of a warrior* Ps 120$_{4}$, חֵץ תְּשׁוּעָה *arrow of salvation* 2 K 13$_{17.17}$, חִצֵּי הָרָעָב *the arrows of famine* Ezk 5$_{16}$, שׁחת *of the pit* 1QH 3$_{16.27}$, חֵץ חֲנִיתוֹ *arrow*, i.e. shaft, *of his spear* 1 S 17$_{7(Kt)}$ (Qr, mss עֵץ *wood of*), חצי לשון *arrows of a tongue* Si 51$_{6}$.

בַּעֲלֵי חִצִּים *masters of arrows*, i.e. archers Gn 49$_{23}$, אוֹר חִצֶּיךָ *light of your arrows* Hb 3$_{11}$, מְקוֹם הַחִצִּים *place of the arrows* 1 S 20$_{37(mss)}$, שְׁלֹשֶׁת הַחִצִּים *three of the arrows* 1 S 20$_{20}$, כול חצי *all arrows of* 1QH 3$_{16.27}$ 6$_{28}$ ([חן[צין).

<PREP> לְ of benefit, *to, for*, + נצב hi. *set up* Lm 3$_{12}$; *as*, + שׂים *place*, i.e. make Is 49$_{2}$.

בְּ of accompaniment, *in, with*, + בוא *come* Is 7$_{24}$, ימן hi. *use right hand* 1 C 12$_{2}$, שׂמאל hi. *use left hand* 1 C 12$_{2}$; of instrument, *by (means of) with*, + ירה *shoot* 2 C 26$_{15}$; introducing object, + נשׂק hi. *set on fire* Ezk 39$_{9}$, קלל pilp. *shake* for casting lots Ezk 21$_{26}$.

כְּ *as* Ps 127$_{4}$.

מִן of direction, *from*, + ישׁע hi. *save* Si 51$_{6}$; of cause, *because of*, + ירא *fear* Ps 91$_{5}$.

אֶל introducing object, + חמל *spare* Jr 50$_{14}$.

<COLL> חִצָּיו יִמְחָץ *he will strike them down with his arrows* Nm 24$_{8}$.*

⇒ חֵצִי I *arrow.*

**חצב I** 25.1.1.4 vb. **hew**—**Qal** 22.1.1.3 Pf. חָצַב, חָצְבָה, חָצַבְתָּ, חָצַבְתִּי; impf. 2ms תַּחְצֹב; + waw וַיַּחְצֹב; ptc. חֹצֵב (I חצבך), חֹצְבִי, חֹצְבִים, חֹצְבֵי, חֲצוּבִים—**1a. hew (out), quarry, mine** (Dt 8$_{9}$); **strike down** (Ho 6$_{5}$),* **divide** (Ps 29$_{7}$, unless חצב *rake*), <SUBJ> י׳ Y. Ho 6$_{5}$, קוֹל *voice* of Y.

Ps $29_{7}$ (unless חצב *rake*), עַם *people* Jr $2_{13}$, Israelite(s) Dt $6_{11}$=1QDM $2_{4}$ ([ח]צבתה) Dt $8_{9}$, יָדִיד *beloved* Is $5_{2}$, Hezekiah Si $48_{17}$, Shebna Is $22_{16.16}$ (+ חקק *cut*), Uzziah 2 C $26_{10}$, חֹצֵב *stonemason* 1 C $22_{2}$, axeman Is $10_{15}$, חָכְמָה *wisdom* Pr $9_{1}$; subj. not specified, Kh. el-Qom tomb inscr. $4_{1}$ (unless חצבך = *your stonemason*, as §2).

<OBJ> קֶבֶר *grave* Is $22_{16.16}$ perh. Kh. el-Qom tomb inscr. $4_{1}$, יֶקֶב *wine-vat* Is $5_{2}$, בּוֹר *cistern* Jr $2_{13}$ 2 C $26_{10}$, עַמּוּד *pillar* Pr $9_{1}$, צוּר *rock* Si $48_{17}$, נְחֹשֶׁת *bronze* Dt $8_{9}$, אֶבֶן *stone* 1 C $22_{2}$, לֶהָבָה *flame* Ps $29_{7}$.

<PREP> לְ of benefit, *to, for*, + Shebna Is $22_{16}$, עַם *people* Jr $2_{13}$; בְּ of place, *in*, + כֶּרֶם *vineyard* Is $5_{2}$; of instrument, *by (means of), with*, + נָבִיא *prophet* Ho $6_{5}$, גַּרְזֶן *axe* Is $10_{15}$; כְּ *as*, נְחֹשֶׁת *bronze* Si $48_{17}$; מִן of direction, *from*, + הַר *mountain* Dt $8_{9}$.

<COLL> + מָרוֹם *(on the) height* Is $22_{16}$.

**1b.** pass. **be hewn out,** <SUBJ> בּוֹר *cistern* Dt $6_{11}$= 1QDM $2_{3}$ (חצוב[ים]) Ne $9_{25}$.

**2.** ptc. as noun, **stonemason,** <SUBJ> היה *be* 1 K $5_{29}$, נוף hi. *wield* Siloam tunnel inscr.$_{1}$, נכה hi. *strike* Siloam tunnel inscr.$_{4}$.

<OBJ> עשׂה *do*, i.e. assign 2 C $21_{7}$, עמד hi. *appoint* 1 C $22_{2}$, שׂכר *hire* 2 C $24_{12}$, ספר *register* 2 C $2_{1}$.

<CSTR> ראש החצב[ם] *head of the masons* Siloam tunnel inscr.$_{6}$.

<APP> עשׂה ptc. *one who does* work 1 C $22_{15}$, אִישׁ *man* 2 C $2_{1}$.

<PREP> לְ of direction, *to*, + יצא hi. *bring out* 2 K $12_{13}$, נתן *give* Ezr $3_{7}$.

**Ni.** 1 Impf. יֵחָצְבוּן—**be hewn,** <SUBJ> מִלָּה *word* Jb $19_{24}$. <PREP> לְ of direction, *to*, + עַד *eternity* Jb $19_{24}$; בְּ of place, *in*, + צוּר *rock* Jb $19_{24}$.

**Pu.** 1 Pf. חֻצַּבְתֶּם—**be hewn out,** <SUBJ> רדף ptc. *one who pursues* Is $51_{1}$, בקשׁ pi. ptc. *one who seeks* Is $51_{1}$. <COLL> הַבִּיטוּ אֶל־צוּר חֻצַּבְתֶּם *look to the rock from which you were hewn* Is $51_{1}$.

**Hi.** 1 Ptc. מַחְצֶבֶת—**hew in pieces,** <SUBJ> זְרוֹעַ *arm* of Y. Is $51_{9}$ (1QIsa[a] המחצת *the one who strikes through*). <OBJ> Rahab Is $51_{9}$.*

⇒ מַחְצֵב *hewing*.

**חצב II** 1 vb. **rake—Qal** 1 Ptc. חֹצֵב—**rake (fire),** <SUBJ> קוֹל *voice* of Y. Ps $29_{7}$ (unless חצב *hew*, i.e. divide). <OBJ> לֶהָבָה *flame* Ps $29_{7}$.

**[חַצָּבִי]** n.m. **stonemason,** <APP> בֵּן *son* Ezr $2_{57}$‖Ne $7_{59}$ (if em. בְּנֵי פֹּכֶרֶת הַצְּבָיִים *the sons of Pochereth-hazzabaim* to בְּנֵי פֹּכֶרֶת חַצְּבָיִים *the sons of Pochereth, the stonemasons*).

**[חָצָד]** 0.0.1 n.m. **date,** or a variety of date, appar. used collectively, <NOM CL> החצד שבכפר *the dates that are in the village* 5/6ḤevBA 46.

**חצה I** 14.0.2 vb. **divide—Qal** 11.0.2 Pf. חָצוּ ,חָצִיתָ ,חָצָה; impf. (יֶחֱצוּהוּ ,יֶחֱצוּן) יֶחֱצוּ ,יֶחֱצֶה; + waw (וַיֶּחֱצֵם) וַיַּחַץ— **divide,** <SUBJ> Abimelech Jg $9_{43}$, Gideon Jg $7_{16}$, Jacob Gn $32_{8}$ $33_{1}$, Moses Nm $31_{27.42}$, אִישׁ *man* Ex $21_{35.35}$=4QBibPar $10_{3}$ ([יחצו]ן) Ps $55_{24}$, שַׂר *prince* 11QT $58_{14}$, חַבָּר *trader* Jb $40_{30}$; subj. not specified, 11QT $15_{4}$.

<OBJ> עַם *people* Gn $32_{8}$, אִישׁ *man* Jg $7_{16}$ $9_{43}$, בֵּן *son* of Israel Nm $31_{42}$, יֶלֶד *child* Gn $33_{1}$, מֵת *dead one* Ex $21_{35}$=4QBibPar $10_{3}$, לִוְיָתָן *Leviathan* Jb $40_{30}$, אַיִל *ram* 11QT $15_{4}$, כֶּסֶף *money*, i.e. price Ex $21_{35}$, מַלְקוֹחַ *booty* Nm $31_{27}$, יוֹם *day* Ps $55_{24}$, סַל *basket* 11QT $15_{4}$, מַחֲצִית *half* 11QT $58_{14}$.

<PREP> לְ *for (the duration of)*, + יוֹם *day* 11QT $15_{4}$; *in(to)*, + רֹאשׁ *head*, i.e. company Jg $9_{43}$.

מִן of direction, *from*, + אִישׁ *man* Nm $31_{42}$.

עַל *among*, + Leah Gn $33_{1}$, Rachel Gn $33_{1}$, שִׁפְחָה *female servant* Gn $33_{1}$.

בֵּין *between*, + תפשׂ ptc. *one who seizes*, i.e. takes part in, war Nm $31_{27}$ (+ עֵדָה *congregation*) 11QT $58_{14}$, כְּנַעֲנִי *merchant* Jb $40_{30}$.

<COLL> וַיַּחַץ ... הָאִישׁ שְׁלֹשָׁה רָאשִׁים *and he divided ... the men into three companies* Jg $7_{16}$.

**Ni.** 4 Impf. 3fs תֵּחָץ ,יֵחָצוּ; + waw וַיֵּחָצוּ—**be divided,** <SUBJ> בֵּן *son* of Israel Ezk $37_{22}$, מַלְכוּת *kingdom* Dn $11_{4}$, מַיִם *water* 2 K $2_{8.14}$.

<PREP> לְ of direction, *to*, + רוּחַ *wind* of heaven Dn $11_{4}$; *in(to)*, + מַמְלָכָה *kingdom* Ezk $37_{22}$.

<COLL> וַיֵּחָצוּ הֵנָּה וָהֵנָּה *and they were divided here and here*, i.e. on this side and on that 2 K $2_{8.14}$.

⇒ חֲצוֹת *middle*, חֲצִי *half*, מֶחֱצָה *half*, מַחֲצִית *half*.

**חצה II** $_{1}$ vb. **reach to—Qal** Impf. יֶחֱצֶה—<SUBJ> נַחַל *stream* Is 30$_{28}$. <PREP> עַד *until*, + צַוָּאר *neck* Is 30$_{28}$.

**חֲצוֹצְרָה** $_{29.1.51}$ n.f. **trumpet**—חֲצֹצְרָה; pl. חֲצוֹצְרוֹת (חֲצוֹצְרֹת, חֲצֹצְרוֹת); cstr. חֲצֹצְרוֹת (חֲצוֹצְרֹת)—**1. trumpet,** sounded during worship (e.g. Ps 98$_{6}$ Ezr 3$_{10}$ 1 C 13$_{8}$ 15$_{28}$ 16$_{6.42}$), in coronation ceremony (2 K 11$_{14}$‖2 C 23$_{13}$), as alarm or in battle (e.g. Ho 5$_{8}$ 1QM 2$_{15.16}$ 3$_{1}$ 7$_{12}$), etc. **2. trumpeter** (2 K 11$_{14}$‖2 C 23$_{13}$ 2 C 29$_{28}$).

**1.** <SUBJ> היה *be* Nm 10$_{8}$ 1QM 7$_{12.12.12.12.12}$ 8$_{1}$, עשׂה ni. *be made* 2 K 12$_{14}$, חלל hi. *begin* 2 C 29$_{27}$, רוע hi. *sound* CD 11$_{22}$ 1QM 8$_{1}$.

<NOM CL> [הח]צו[צרה הי]אה ספר התורה שנית *the trumpet is the book of the second law* 4QMidrEschat[b] 10$_{14}$, חֲצֹצְרוֹת הַתְּרוּעָה בְּיָדוֹ *the trumpets of the alarm were in his hand* Nm 31$_{6}$, [חצוצרה ברמה] *the trumpet is in Ramah* 4QMidrEschat[b] 10$_{14}$, עִמָּנוּ ... חֲצֹצְרוֹת *with us are ... the trumpets* 2 C 13$_{12}$, עִמָּהֶם ... חֲצֹצְרוֹת *with them were ... trumpets* 1 C 16$_{42}$.

<OBJ> עשׂה *make* Nm 10$_{2}$, תקע *blow* Ho 5$_{8}$, שׁמע *hear* 4QMa 1$_{13}$.

<CSTR> חֲצֹצְרוֹת הַתְּרוּעָה *trumpets of the alarm* Nm 31$_{6}$ 1QM 2$_{15}$ (חצוצר[ות]) 7$_{12}$ (חצוצרות) 1QM 17$_{11}$ (חצוצרות תרועה) 4QMa 13$_{4}$ ([חצוצרות תרועה]) 4QMa 1$_{13}$ ([חצוצרות התר]ועה]) 4QMc 11 (חצוצרות), חצוצרות תרועות *trumpets of the alarms of* 1QM 3$_{1}$, המלחמה *of the war* 4QMc 3, השבתות *of the sabbaths* 4QMc 13 ([חצוצרו]ת).

חצוצרות מסעיהם *trumpets of their journeyings* 1QM 3$_{5}$, המארב *of the ambush* 1QM 3$_{1.8}$, המרדף *of the pursuit* 1QM 3$_{2.9}$ 7$_{12}$ 9$_{6}$ (המרדוף), המאסף *of the withdrawal* 1QM 3$_{2}$ 7$_{12}$ 4QMc 11 ([חצוצרות]), המשוב *of the return* 1QM 3$_{10}$ 8$_{2.13.17}$ ([חצוצ]רות) 4QMc 8 (חצו[צ]רות), דרך *of the way of* 1QM 3$_{10}$, המסורות *of the formations* 1QM 3$_{3}$, סדרי *of the arrays of* 1QM 3$_{6}$ 7$_{17}$ ([חצוצרות]), המחנות *of the camps* 1QM 3$_{4}$, אנשי *of the men of* 1QM 3$_{3}$, החללים *of the slain* 1QM 3$_{8}$ 8$_{8}$ 16$_{6.8}$ 17$_{12.15}$ ([חצוצרות]) 4QMa 13$_{6}$ ([ח]צוצרות) 4QMc 7.

חֲצוֹצְרֹת כֶּסֶף *trumpets of silver* Nm 10$_{2}$, חצצרות מקשה *trumpets of hammered metal* Si 50$_{16}$, חצוצרות הזכרון *trumpets of remembrance* 1QM 7$_{12}$ 16$_{2}$ 18$_{4}$ ([חצוצר]ות) 4QMc 2, המקרא *of summoning* 1QM 2$_{15}$ ([חצוצרות]) 7$_{12.14}$ 8$_{3.18}$ ([חצוצרות]) 9$_{3}$ 16$_{10}$ ([ח]צו[צרות]) 4QMa 10.2$_{11}$ ([חצוצרות]) 4QMc 10, מקראם *of their summoning* 1QM 3$_{1}$, מקרא *of summoning of* 1QM 3$_{2.3.7}$.

[סרך חצוצרות] *order of the trumpets of* 1QM 2$_{15}$, קול החצוצרות *sound of the trumpets* 1QM 16$_{4}$ 17$_{10}$ 4QMa 13$_{4}$ ([חצו]צרות).

<PREP> בְּ of instrument, *by (means of), with*, or introducing object, + רום hi. *raise* sound 2 C 5$_{13}$, רוע hi. *give a blast* Nm 10$_{9}$ Ps 98$_{6}$ (‖ שׁוֹפָר *ram's horn*) Si 50$_{16}$ 1QM 10$_{7}$ 1QM 8$_{8.11.19}$ ([חצוצרות]) 9$_{1}$ 16$_{6.8}$ 17$_{12.15}$ 18$_{4}$ 4QMa 1$_{17}$ 4QMc 2.3, תקע *give a blast* Nm 10$_{8.10}$ 2 K 11$_{14}$‖2 C 23$_{13}$ 1QM 7$_{12.16.17}$ (both [חצוצרות]) 8$_{2.3.5.13.17.18}$ 9$_{3.6}$ 16$_{2.10}$ 17$_{11}$ 4QMa 10.2$_{11}$ 13$_{4}$ 4QMc 8.10.11, חצצר hi. *sound* 1 C 15$_{24(Kt)}$ 2 C 5$_{12(Kt)}$ 13$_{14(Kt)}$, pi. 2 C 5$_{13(Kt)}$.

בְּ of accompaniment, *with, in* 1 C 16$_{6}$, + עמד *stand* Ne 12$_{41}$ 2 C 29$_{26}$, hi. *position* Ezr 3$_{10}$, בוא *come* 2 C 20$_{28}$, הלך *go* Ne 12$_{35}$, קרב htp. *draw near* 4QMc 7, עלה hi. *bring up* 1 C 15$_{28}$, שׂחק pi. *make merry* 1 C 13$_{8}$, שׁבע ni. *swear oath* 2 C 15$_{14}$, מלא pi. *complete* service 4QMc 11.

עַל *upon* 1QM 2$_{16}$ ([חצוצרות]) 4QMf 9.3$_{2}$ ([חצו]צרות), + כתב *write* 1QM 3$_{2+12t}$ 4QMc 13 ([חצוצרו]ת).

<COLL> שְׁתֵּי חֲצוֹצְרֹת *two trumpets of* Nm 10$_{2}$ 1QM 7$_{12}$ (חצוצרות), שש חצוצרות *six trumpets of* 1QM 8$_{8}$ 18$_{4}$ ([שש חצוצר]ות).

<SYN> שׁוֹפָר *ram's horn*.

Also 4Q285 8$_{1}$ ([חצ]וצרות) 4QMf 17$_{2}$ ([חצו]צרות) 58$_{5}$ ([חצוצר]ו[ת]).

**2.** <SUBJ> חצצר pi. *blow trumpet* 2 C 29$_{28}$.

<NOM CL> חֲצֹצְרוֹת אֶל־הַמֶּלֶךְ *the trumpeters were towards the king* 2 K 11$_{14}$‖2 C 23$_{13}$ (עַל *beside*).

⇒ חצצר *sound trumpet*.

**חָצוֹר I** $_{16}$ pl.n. **Hazor**—חָצֹר—**1.** in territory of Naphtali, T. el Qedaḥ, 6 km SW of Lake Huleh,* <NOM CL> חָצוֹר לְפָנִים הִיא רֹאשׁ כָּל־הַמַּמְלָכוֹת הָאֵלֶּה *Hazor was formerly head of all these kingdoms* Jos 11$_{10}$. <OBJ> בנה *build* 1 K 9$_{15}$, לקח *take* 2 K 15$_{29}$, לכד *capture* Jos 11$_{10}$, שׂרף *burn* Jos 11$_{11.13}$.

<CSTR> מֶלֶךְ־חָצוֹר *king of Hazor* Jos 11$_{1}$ 12$_{19}$ Jg 4$_{17}$, צְבָא חָצוֹר *army of Hazor* 1 S 12$_{9}$. <APP> עִיר *city* Jos 19$_{36}$. <PREP> בְּ *over*, + מלך *reign* Jg 4$_{2}$.

**2.** in territory of Benjamin, perh. Kh. Ḥazzūr, 7 km NW of Jerusalem, <NOM CL> בְּנֵי בִנְיָמִן ... חָצוֹר *the sons* *of Benjamin were … (at) Hazor* Ne 11$_{33}$.

**3.** in territory of Judah, <APP> עִיר *city* Jos 15$_{23}$.

**4.** in territory of Judah, another name for Kerioth-hezron, <NOM CL> קְרִיּוֹת חֶצְרוֹן הִיא חָצוֹר *Kerioth-hezron, that is Hazor* Jos 15$_{25}$.

**5.** in Arabian desert, <SUBJ> היה *be* Jr 49$_{33}$. <CSTR> מַמְלְכוֹת חָצוֹר *kingdoms of Hazor* Jr 49$_{28}$, יֹשְׁבֵי חָצוֹר *inhabitants of Hazor* Jr 49$_{30}$.

* [חָצוֹר] II adj. **green**, used attributively of בִּין *tamarisk* Is 44$_4$ (if em. בְּבֵין חָצִיר sprout up *among grass* to כְּבִין חָצוֹר sprout up *like a green tamarisk*).

חָצוֹר חֲדַתָּה 1 pl.n. **Hazor-hadattah,** in territory of Judah, <SUBJ> היה *be* Jos 15$_{25}$. <APP> עִיר *city* Jos 15$_{25}$.

חֲצוֹת 3 n.f. **middle**—cstr. חֲצוֹת (חֲצֹת)—<CSTR> חֲצוֹת הַלַּיְלָה *middle of the night* Ex 11$_4$ (חֲצֹת) Ps 119$_{62}$ Jb 34$_{20}$.

<PREP> כְּ *as* Ex 11$_4$.

<COLL> חֲצוֹת־לַיְלָה אָקוּם *(in) the middle of the night I will arise* Ps 119$_{62}$, חֲצוֹת לַיְלָה יְגֹעֲשׁוּ עָם *(in) the middle of the night people are shaken* Jb 34$_{20}$ (unless em. יְגֹעֲשׁוּ עָם to יִגְוְעוּ שׁוֹעִים *nobles expire*).

⇒ חצה *divide*.

חֲצוֹת, see חוּץ *outside*.

חֲצִי 126.0.9.3 n.m. **half**— cstr. חֲצִי (חֲצִי, וַחֲצִי, בַּחֲצִי, לַחֲצִי); sf. חֶצְיוֹ, חֶצְיָהּ, חֶצְיֵנוּ, חֶצְיָם—**1.** in absolute, <SUBJ> נגד ho. *be reported* 1 K 10$_7$.

<NOM CL> אֹרֶךְ אַמָּה אַחַת וָחֵצִי *(the) length was one cubit and a half* Ezk 40$_{42}$, אורך כידן אמה וחצי *the length of the spear was a cubit and a half* 1QM 5$_{12}$, אַמָּתַיִם וָחֵצִי אָרְכּוֹ *two cubits and a half was its length* Ex 25$_{10}$ 37$_1$, אַמָּתַיִם וָחֵצִי אָרְכָּהּ *two cubits and a half was its length* Ex 25$_{17}$ 37$_6$ 11QT 7$_{10}$ ([אמתים וחצי אורכה]), אורך המגן אמתים וחצי *the length of the shield was two cubits and a half* 1QM 5$_6$, אַמָּה וָחֵצִי רָחְבּוֹ *one cubit and a half was its breadth* Ex 25$_{10}$ 37$_1$, רוחבו אמה וחצי *its breadth was a cubit and a half* 1QM 5$_6$, אַמָּה וָחֵצִי רָחְבָּהּ *one cubit and a half was its breadth* Ex 25$_{17}$ 37$_6$ 11QT 7$_{10}$ ([אמה וחצי] רוחבה), רֹחַב אַמָּה אַחַת וָחֵצִי *(the) breadth was one cubit and a half* Ezk 40$_{42}$, אַמָּה וָחֵצִי קֹמָתוֹ *one cubit and a half was its height* Ex 25$_{10.23}$ 37$_{1.10}$ 11QT 8$_6$ ([אמה וחצי] קומתו), אמות וחצי רמו *cubits and a half was his height* 4QApocJos$^c$ 1$_3$, לְמוֹעֵד מוֹעֲדִים וָחֵצִי it will be *for a time, times and half (a time)* Dn 12$_7$.

<PREP> בְּ *in*, + כרת *cut* 1 C 19$_4$.

<COLL> אַמָּה וָחֵצִי *one cubit and a half* Ex 25$_{10.10.17.23}$ 37$_{1.1.6.10}$ 1QM 5$_{6.12}$ 11QT 7$_{10}$ ([אמה וחצי]) 11QT 8$_6$ ([אמה] וחצי), אַמָּה אַחַת וָחֵצִי *one cubit and a half* Ezk 40$_{42.42}$, אַמָּתַיִם וָחֵצִי *two cubits and a half* Ex 25$_{10.17}$ 37$_{1.6}$ 1QM 5$_6$ 11QT 7$_{10}$ ([אמתים וחצי]), ([ארבע עשרא וחצי]) *fourteen and a half* 4Q317$_{8a}$, אמות וחצי *cubits and a half* 4QApocJos$^c$ 1$_3$, מוֹעֲדִים וָחֵצִי *times and half (a time)* Dn 12$_7$.

**2.** with suffix or in construct, <SUBJ> היה *be* Nm 28$_{14}$ Jos 13$_{25.31}$ 1 K 16$_{21}$, אכל ni. *be eaten* Nm 12$_{12}$, נגד ho. *be reported* 2 C 9$_6$.

הלך *go* Jos 22$_9$ Ne 12$_{32}$, ירד *go down* 4QJub$^a$ 24 ([חצים]), עלה *go up* 4QJub$^a$ 24 ([חצים]), יצא *go out* Zc 14$_{2.8.8}$, מושׁ *remove* Zc 14$_4$, עבר *pass by* Jos 4$_{12}$, hi. *bring over* 2 S 19$_{41(Qr)}$, סרח *project* Ex 26$_{12}$.

עשׂה *do*, i.e. work Ne 4$_{10}$, בנה *build* Jos 22$_{10.11}$, לקח *take* Nm 34$_{14.15}$ Jos 18$_7$, חזק hi. *take hold of* Ne 4$_{10.15}$, מות *die* 2 S 18$_3$, ענה *answer* Jos 22$_{21}$, דבר pi. *speak* Ne 13$_{24}$.

<NOM CL> שֶׁמֶן חֲצִי הַהִין *the oil is half of the hin* Nm 15$_9$, sim. 11QT 14$_2$ ([חצי ההין שמן]), יַיִן … חֲצִי הַהִין *the wine (is) … half of the hin* Nm 15$_{10}$, הַגְּבוּל … חֲצִי הָאַמָּה *the border … is half a cubit* Ezk 43$_{17}$, הלוהב חצי האמה *the spike was half of a cubit* 1QM 5$_7$, חצי למלך *a half was to the king* Beersheba jug inscr.$_1$, חֶצְיוֹ אֶל־מוּל הַר־גְּרִזִים *its half was to the front of Mount Gerizim* Jos 8$_{33}$, חֶצְיוֹ אֶל־מוּל הַר־עֵיבָל *its half was to the front of Mount Ebal* Jos 8$_{33}$, הַחֲצִי אַחֲרֵי עָמְרִי *the half (went) after Omri* 1 K 16$_{21}$, חֲצִי הָעָם מֵעַל לְהַחוֹמָה *half of the people were upon the wall* Ne 12$_{38}$, חֶצְיוֹ־נֶגְבָּה *its half is to the south* Zc 14$_4$.

<OBJ> לקח *take* Ex 24$_6$, נתן *give* Dt 3$_{12}$ 1 K 3$_{25.25}$ 13$_8$, שׁקל *pay* 5/6ḤevBA 44 fr. 1$_{1.2}$, זרק *sprinkle* Ex 24$_6$, גלח pi. *shave* 2 S 10$_4$, שׂרף *burn* Is 44$_{16.19}$.

<CSTR> חֲצִי הַשָּׁמַיִם *half of the heaven*, i.e. mid-heaven Jos 10$_{13}$, אֶרֶץ *of the land of* Jos 13$_{25}$, הָהָר *of the mountain* Zc 14$_4$, הַר *of the mountain of* Dt 3$_{12}$, הַגִּלְעָד *of Gilead* Jos 12$_{2.5}$ 13$_{31}$, פֶּלֶךְ *of the district of* Ne 3$_{9.12.16.17.18}$, הָעִיר *of the city* Zc 14$_2$, בֵּיתֶךָ *of your house* 1 K 13$_8$.

חֲצִי הָעָם *half of the people* 1 K $16_{21}$ Ne $12_{38}$, עַם *of the people of* 2 S $19_{41}$, מְנַשֶּׁה *of Manasseh* 1 C $6_{46}$ $27_{21}$, הַמַּטֶּה *of the tribe* Nm $34_{13.15}$ Jos $14_{2.3}$, מַטֵּה *of the tribe of* Nm $34_{14}$ Jos $21_{5.\,6.27}$ $22_{1}$ 1 C $6_{56}$ $12_{32}$, שֵׁבֶט *of the tribe of* Nm $32_{33}$ Dt $3_{13}$ $29_{7}$ Jos $1_{12}$ $4_{12}$ $12_{6}$ $13_{7.29}$ $18_{7}$ $22_{7.9.10.11.21.13}$ 1 C $5_{18.23.26}$ $12_{38}$ $26_{32}$ $27_{20.21(mss)}$ 4QpPs$^{a}$ $13_{5}$, הַסְּגָנִים *of the governors* Ne $12_{40}$, שָׂרֵי *of the princes of* Ne $12_{32}$, נְעָרַי *of the servants of* Ne $4_{10}$, בְּנֵי *of the sons of* Jos $13_{31}$.

חֲצִי זְקָנָם *half of their beard* 2 S $10_{4}$, הַדָּם *of the blood* Ex $24_{6.6}$ 4QBibPar $4_{5}$ (חצ]י ה[דם), בְּשָׂרוֹ *of his flesh* Nm $12_{12}$, הַמִּזְבֵּחַ *of the altar* Ex $27_{5}$, הַיְרִיעָה *of the curtain* Ex $26_{12}$, חַטֹּאתַיִךְ *of your sins* Ezk $16_{51}$, הַמַּלְכוּת *of the kingdom* Est $5_{3.6}$ $7_{2}$, הָאַמָּה *of the cubit* Ex $36_{21}$ 1 K $7_{31.32.35}$ Ezk $43_{17}$ 1QM $5_{7}$, מַעֲנָה *of a furrow* 1 S $14_{14}$, הכסף *of the silver* 5/6ḤevBA 44 fr. $1_{1.2}$, הַהִין *of the hin* Nm $15_{9.10}$ $28_{14}$ 11QT $14_{2.3}$ (ח]צי ההין]) $28_{6.6}$ (both [חצי ההין]), הלג *of the log* Susa inscribed measure $1_{1}$, מַרְבִּית *of the greatness of* 2 C $9_{6}$.

חֲצִי הַלַּיְלָה *half of the night*, i.e. midnight Ex $12_{29}$ Jg $16_{3.3}$ Ru $3_{8}$, יָמַי *of my days*, i.e. in the middle of my days Ps $102_{25}$, יָמָיו *of his days*, i.e. in the middle of his days Jr $17_{11(Qr)}$, הַשָּׁבוּעַ *of the seven*, i.e. in the middle of the week Dn $9_{27}$.

נַחֲלַת ... חֲצִי *inheritance of ... half of* Jos $14_{3}$, שַׂר חֲצִי *prince of half of* Ne $3_{9.12.16.17.18}$, בְּנֵי חֲצִי *sons of half of* 1 C $5_{23}$, מַטֵּה חֲצִי *of tribe of half of* 1 C $6_{46}$, מִשְׁפַּחַת חֲצִי *family of half of* 1 C $6_{56}$ (or em. לְמִשְׁפְּחֹתָם מֵחֲצִי *according to their families, from half of*).

<PREP> לְ of direction, *to*, + היה *be* Jos $13_{29}$, נתן *give* Nm $32_{33}$ $34_{13}$ Dt $3_{13}$ $29_{7}$ Jos $12_{6}$ $13_{29}$ $22_{7}$, חלק pi. *divide* Jos $13_{7}$, קרא *call* Jos $22_{1}$, אמר *say* Jos $1_{12}$.

לְ of benefit, *to, for* 1 C $27_{20.21}$, + היה *be* Jos $13_{31}$, צוה pi. *command* Jos $14_{2}$; *into*, + חלק ni. *be divided* 1 K $16_{21}$; introducing object, + גלה hi. *exile* 1 C $5_{26}$.

בְּ of place/time, *in, at, during, among*, + היה *be* Ex $12_{29}$ Ru $3_{8}$, עמד *stand* Jos $10_{13}$, קום *arise* Jg $16_{3}$, עלה hi. *bring up* Ps $102_{25}$, עזב *forsake* Jr $17_{11}$; of accompaniment, *with, in* 11QT $14_{2}$ $28_{6}$.

כְּ *as*, + חטא *sin* Ezk $16_{51}$.

מִן of direction, *from* 1 C $6_{56}$ (if em.) $12_{32}$, + היה *be* Jos $21_{5.6.27}$.

בקע מִן ni. *be split in half* Zc $14_{4}$.

אֶל *to*, + בוא *come* Jos $22_{15}$, שלח *send* Jos $22_{13}$; עַל *over, upon*, + צלה *roast* meat Is $44_{16}$; כְּבַחֲצִי *about half* 1 S $14_{14}$; עַד *until* Ex $38_{4}$ Est $5_{6}$ $7_{2}$, + היה *be* Ex $27_{5}$, נתן ni. *be given* Est $5_{3}$, קשר ni. *be joined together* Ne $3_{38}$, שכב *lie down* Jg $16_{3}$.

<COLL> הן 1 וחצי הלג וארבעת הלג *one hin and a half and a quarter of a log* Susa inscribed measure $1_{1}$.

Also Arad inscr. $101_{1}$.

⇒ חצה *divide*.

**חֵץִי I** $_{4}$ n.m. **arrow**—<SUBJ> יצא *go out* 2 K $9_{24}$.

<NOM CL> הֲלוֹא הַחֵצִי מִמְּךָ *is not the arrow from*, i.e. beyond, *you* 1 S $20_{37}$.

<OBJ> ירה *shoot* 1 S $20_{36.37}$.

<CSTR> מְקוֹם הַחֵצִי *place of the arrow* 1 S $20_{37}$.

⇒ חֵץ *arrow*.

**[חֵצִי] II** $_{0.0.0.2}$ pr.n.m. **Hezi, 1.** son of Gemaliah, <APP> בֵּן *son* Seal 169 (Judaea, 7th cent). <PREP> לְ of possession, *(belonging) to, of* Seal 169 (Judaea, 7th cent). **2.** father of Micaiah ([מכי]הו), <CSTR> בן חצי *son of Hezi* Seal 808 (city of David, 7th/6th cent.).

**[חָצִין]** n.[m.] **battle-axe**, <OBJ> עור pol. *rouse*, i.e. brandish 2 S $23_{8}$ (if em. עֲדִינוֹ הָעֶצְנִי [Qr] perh. *Adino the Eznite* to עֹרֵר חֲצִינוֹ *he brandished his battle-axe*).

**חָצִיר I** $_{18.1}$ n.m. **grass**—cstr. חֲצִיר—<SUBJ> היה *be* 2 K $19_{26}$||Is $37_{27}$, יבשׁ *wither* Is $15_{6}$=4QpIsa$^{e}$ $4_{2}$ ([חציר]) Is $34_{13}$ (1QIsa$^{a}$ חצר appar. חָצֵר *court*) $40_{7.8}$, גלה *go away* Pr $27_{25}$. <NOM CL> כָּל־הַבָּשָׂר חָצִיר *all flesh is grass* Is $40_{6}$, חָצִיר הָעָם *the people is grass* Is $40_{7}$. <OBJ> צמח hi. *make grow* Ps $104_{14}$ $147_{8}$, מצא *find* 1 K $18_{5}$, אכל *eat* Jb $40_{15}$. <CSTR> חֲצִיר גַּגּוֹת *grass of rooftops* 2 K $19_{26}$||Is $37_{27}$. <PREP> כְּ *as* Ps $37_{2}$ $90_{5}$ $103_{15}$ 4Q185 $1.1_{10}$ (ח[צ]יר), + היה *be* Ps $129_{6}$. <COLL> חָצִיר יִנָּתֵן *he is given*, i.e. made, *like grass* Is $51_{12}$. Also Si $40_{16}$ (חצ[י]ר) 4Q370 $2_{4}$ ([חציר]).*

**חָצִיר II** $_{3}$ n.[m.] **reed** (if not חָצִיר I *grass*), collective, <NOM CL> בִּנְוֵה תַנִּים ... חָצִיר *in the haunt of jackals ... are reeds* Is $35_{7}$ (or em.; see Coll.). <CSTR> מֵאֲרַב חֲצֵרִים

*ambush of*, i.e. among, *the reeds* Ps 10₈ (if em. חֲצֵרִים *of*, i.e. in, *villages*), כָּל־חָצִיר *all reeds* Jb 8₁₂. <PREP> בְּבֵין *in (among)*, + צמח *sprout* Is 44₄ (or em. בְּבֵין חָצִיר sprout up *among grass* to כְּבִין חָצוֹר sprout up *like a green tamarisk*); לִפְנֵי *before*, + יבשׁ *wither* Jb 8₁₂. <COLL> חָצִיר לְקָנֶה וָגֹמֶא *reeds, namely cane and papyrus* Is 35₇ (or em. חָצֵר *a settlement* for).

**חָצִיר** III 1 n.[m.] **leek,** collective, <OBJ> זכר *remember* Nm 11₅ (‖ בָּצָל *onion,* שׁוּם *garlic,* אֲבַטִּיחַ *melon,* קִשֻּׁאָה *cucumber,* + דָּגָה *fish*). <SYN> בָּצָל *onion,* שׁוּם *garlic,* אֲבַטִּיחַ *melon,* קִשֻּׁאָה *cucumber.*

**חֹצֶן** I 3 n.m. **fold**—sf. חָצְנִי, חִצְנוֹ—**fold** of garment, <OBJ> מלא pi. *fill* Ps 129₇=4QpPs[b] 4₁ ([חצנו]), נער *shake out* Ne 5₁₃. <PREP> בְּ *in,* + בוא hi. *bring* Is 49₂₂.

**חֹצֶן** II 1 n.[m.] **war-horses,** collective, <COLL> בָּאוּ עָלַיִךְ חֹצֶן *they will come against you (with) war-horses* Ezk 23₂₄ (mss) (L הֹצֶן *arms*; or em. הֲמוֹן *multitude of* chariots or מִצָּפוֹן *from the north*).*

**[חָצָף]** 0.1 adj. **impudent,** used as noun, **impudent one, impudence,** <CSTR> פני חצף *face of an impudent one* Si 40₂₈(M) (B סלל htpo. ptc. *one who grovels*) <APP> דֵּי בִּזָּיוֹן חָצָף *a sufficiency, contempt and impudence* Est 1₁₈ (if em. קָצֶף *wrath*).*

**חצץ** 3 vb. **divide**—**Qal** 1 Ptc. חֹצֵץ—intrans. **divide,** of locusts dividing themselves into swarms, <SUBJ> אַרְבֶּה *locust* Pr 30₂₇ (or em.; see Coll.). <COLL> וַיֵּצֵא חֹצֵץ כֻּלּוֹ *and they all go out, dividing (into swarms)* Pr 30₂₇ (unless חֹצֵץ *massing,* from חוץ pol. *be massed* or em. to חָלַץ *armed*).

**Pi.** 1 Ptc. מְחַצְצִים—ptc. as noun, **one who distributes water,** <CSTR> קוֹל מְחַצְצִים *sound of those distributing water* Jg 5₁₁ (or em. מְחַצְצְרִים *of the trumpeters* or מְחֹצְצִים *striking up* tune, from חוץ pol.).

**Pu.** 1 Pf. חֻצָּצוּ—**be cut off, be at an end,** <SUBJ> חֹדֶשׁ *month* Jb 21₂₁.

⇒ חָצָץ *gravel.*

**חָצָץ** 2 n.m. **gravel,** <PREP> בְּ *on,* + גרס hi. *cause to grind* Lm 3₁₆. <COLL> יִמָּלֵא־פִיהוּ חָצָץ *his mouth will be filled with gravel* Pr 20₁₇.

⇒ חצץ *divide.*

**חַצְצוֹן תָּמָר** 2 pl.n. **Hazazon-tamar,** perh. ʿĒn Ḥoṣb, 32 km SW of southern end of Dead Sea, but ident. with En-gedi at 2 C 20₂, <NOM CL> חַצְצוֹן תָּמָר הִיא עֵין גֶּדִי *Hazazon-Tamar, that is En-gedi* 2 C 20₂. <PREP> בְּ of place, *at* 2 C 20₂, + ישׁב *dwell* Gn 14₇.

**חצצר** 6 vb. **sound trumpet**—**Pi.** 1 Ptc. Kt מחצצרים (Qr מְחַצְּרִים)—**sound trumpet,** <SUBJ> trumpeters 2 C 5₁₃. <PREP> בְּ of instrument, *by (means of), with,* or introducing object, + חֲצוֹצְרָה *trumpet* 2 C 5₁₃.

**Hi.** 5 Ptc. Kt מחצצרים (Qr מַחְצְרִים)—**sound trumpet,** <SUBJ> כֹּהֵן *priest* 1 C 15₂₄ 2 C 5₁₂ 7₆ 13₁₄, חֲצוֹצְרָה *trumpeter* 2 C 29₂₈. <PREP> בְּ of instrument, *by (means of), with,* or introducing object, + חֲצוֹצְרָה *trumpet* 1 C 15₂₄ 2 C 5₁₂ 13₁₄; לִפְנֵי *before,* + אָרוֹן *ark* of God 1 C 15₂₄; נֶגֶד *opposite,* + לֵוִי *Levite* 2 C 7₆.

⇒ חֲצוֹצְרָה *trumpet.*

**חֲצֹצְרָה**, see חֲצוֹצְרָה *trumpet.*

**חָצֵר** 190.0.19 n.m. & f. **court**—+ ה- of direction חָצֵרָה; cstr. חֲצַר; sf. חֲצֵרוֹ; pl. חֲצֵרִים, חֲצֵרוֹת, חֲצֵרֹת (חֲצֵרֹת); cstr. חַצְרוֹת, חַצְרֵי; sf. חֲצֵרָי, חֲצֵרוֹתַי, חֲצֵרֶיךָ, חֲצֵרוֹתָיו, חַצְרֹתֵיהֶם, חַצְרֵיהֶם, חֲצֵרֶיהָ, חֲצֵרֵיהֶן, (חֲצֵרֹתָיו)—**court, enclosure,** of house (e.g. Ex 8₉ 2 S 17₁₈), of palace (e.g. 1 K 7₈ 2 K 20₄ Jr 36₂₀ Est 1₅), of tabernacle (e.g. Ex 27₉ 35₁₇ Lv 6₉), of temple (e.g. 1 K 6₃₆ 7₁₂ Ezk 40₁₄ 41₁₅ 2 C 24₂₁); **settlement, village** (e.g. Gn 25₁₆ Lv 25₃₁ Dt 2₂₃ Jos 15₃₂ Ne 11₂₅).

<SUBJ> היה *be* 1 K 7₈ 4QapLam[a] 1.1₇, מלא *be full* Ezk 10₄, נשׂא *raise* Is 42₁₁, קטר pass. perh. *be enclosed* Ezk 46₂₂ (if em.; see Nom. Cl.), קצר pass. *be shortened* Ezk 46₂₂ (if em.; see Nom. Cl.).

<NOM CL> חָצֵר הַגְּדוֹלָה סָבִיב שְׁלֹשָׁה טוּרִים גָּזִית *the great court all around was (of) three rows (of) hewn stone* 1 K 7₁₂, הִנֵּה חָצֵר בְּמִקְצֹעַ הֶחָצֵר *behold a court was in the corner of a court* Ezk 46₂₁.₂₁, בְּאַרְבַּעַת מִקְצוֹעוֹת הֶחָצֵר

חֲצֵרוֹת קְטֻנוֹת *in the four corners of the court were small courts* Ezk 46$_{22}$ (if em. קְטֻרוֹת perh. *enclosed* to קְטֻנּוֹת *small*, or em. קְצֻרוֹת *shortened*), כָּל־הַחֲצֵרִים אֲשֶׁר סְבִיבוֹת הֶעָרִים *all the villages that were round about the cities* Jos 19$_{8}$.

<OBJ> עשׂה *make* Ex 27$_{9}$ 38$_{9}$ 2 C 4$_{9}$ 11QT 38$_{12}$ 40$_{5}$, שׂים *place* Ex 40$_{8}$, קום hi. *erect* Ex 40$_{33}$, בנה *build* 1 K 6$_{36}$ Ne 12$_{29}$ 1 C 28$_{6}$, נתן *give* Jos 21$_{12}$=1 C 6$_{41}$, מלא *fill* Ezk 9$_{7}$ 10$_{3}$, שׁמר *keep* Zc 3$_{7}$, רמס *trample* Is 1$_{12}$, מדד *measure* Ezk 40$_{47}$.

<CSTR> חַצְרוֹת י׳ *courts of Y.* Ps 84$_{3}$, אֱלֹהֵינוּ *of our God* Ps 92$_{14}$, חֲצַר הַמִּשְׁכָּן *court of the tabernacle* Ex 27$_{9}$, בֵּית *of the house of* 1 K 7$_{12}$ Jr 19$_{14}$ 26$_{2}$ Ezk 8$_{16}$ Est 2$_{11}$ 5$_{1}$ 6$_{4}$ 2 C 24$_{21}$ 29$_{16}$, בתי *of the houses of* 3QTr 2$_{5}$, חַצְרֵי בֵית *courts of the house of* Ne 13$_{7}$, חַצְרוֹת בֵּית *courts of the house of* 2 K 21$_{5}$||2 C 33$_{5}$ 2 K 23$_{12}$ Ps 116$_{19}$ 135$_{2}$ Ne 8$_{16}$ 1 C 28$_{12}$ 2 C 23$_{5}$, חֲצַר אֹהֶל *court of the tent of* Lv 6$_{9.19}$, הפרסטלין *of the little colonnade* 3QTr 1$_{6}$, גִּנַּת *of the garden of* Est 1$_{5}$, הַכֹּהֲנִים *of the priests* 2 C 4$_{9}$, הַמַּטָּרָה *of the guard* Jr 32$_{2.8.12}$ 33$_{1}$ 37$_{21.21}$ 38$_{6.13.28}$ 39$_{14.15}$ Ne 3$_{25}$, חצרות [ה]קודש *courts of the sanctuary* 11QT 17$_{9}$, קָדְשִׁי *of my sanctuary* Is 62$_{9}$, קודשנו *of our sanctuary* 4QapLam$^{a}$ 1.1$_{7}$, חַצְרֵי נְטֹפָתִי *villages of the Netophathites* Ne 12$_{28}$ 1 C 9$_{16}$.

בָּתֵּי הַחֲצֵרִים *houses of the villages* Lv 25$_{31}$, מַאְרַב *ambush of*, i.e. in, the villages Ps 10$_{8}$ (or em. חֲצִרִים *of*, i.e. among, *the reeds*).

רֹחַב הֶחָצֵר *width of the court* Ex 27$_{12.13}$, אֹרֶךְ *length of* Ex 27$_{18}$, תּוֹךְ *middle of* 1 K 8$_{64}$||2 C 7$_{7}$ 11QT 36$_{14}$, דֶּרֶךְ *way of* Ezk 42$_{7}$, שַׁעַר *gate of* Ex 27$_{16}$ 35$_{17}$ 38$_{15.18.31}$ 39$_{40}$ 40$_{8.33}$ Nm 4$_{26}$ Ezk 45$_{19}$ (or em. שַׁעֲרֵי *gates of*) 46$_{1}$, שער חצרו *gate of his court* 4Q421 11$_{3}$, שַׁעֲרֵי הֶחָצֵר *gates of the court* Ezk 44$_{17.17}$ 45$_{19}$ (if em.), פֶּתַח *entrance of* Nm 3$_{26}$ Ezk 8$_{7}$, מִקְצֹעַ *corner of* Ezk 46$_{21.21}$, מִקְצוֹעֵי *corners of* Ezk 46$_{21}$ (or em. מִקְצוֹעוֹת *corners of*), מִקְצוֹעוֹת *corners of* Ezk 46$_{21}$ (if em.) 46$_{22}$ 11QT 37$_{13}$, אֵלַמֵּי *porches of* Ezk 41$_{15}$ (or em. הָאֻלָם הַחִצוֹן *the outer porch* or אֵלַמּוֹ הַחִצוֹן *its outer porch*).

קַלְעֵי הֶחָצֵר *curtains of the court* Ex 35$_{17}$ 38$_{9.16.18}$ 39$_{40}$ Nm 3$_{26}$ 4$_{26}$, גֶּדֶר *wall of* Ezk 42$_{10}$, קיר החצר *wall of the court* 11QT 37$_{9}$ (קיר [החצר]) 41$_{12.13}$, אֵיל הֶחָצֵר *pillar of* Ezk 40$_{14}$, עַמּוּדֵי *pillars of* Ex 27$_{17}$ 38$_{17}$ Nm 3$_{37}$ (both עַמֻּדֵי) 4$_{32}$, עַמּוּדֵי הַחֲצֵרוֹת *pillars of the courts* Ezk 42$_{6}$, יִתְדֹת הֶחָצֵר *pegs of the court* Ex 27$_{19}$ 35$_{18}$ 38$_{31}$, אַדְנֵי *bases of* Ex 38$_{31}$.

רֹמְסֵי חֲצֵרָי *trampling ones of*, i.e. those who trample, *my courts* Is 1$_{12}$ (if em. רְמֹס *to trample*), כָּל־הַחֲצֵרִים *all the villages* Jos 19$_{8}$, כָּל־חַצְרֵיהֶם *all their villages* 1 C 4$_{33}$.

<ADJ> גָּדוֹל *great* 1 K 7$_{9.12}$, קָטָן *small* Ezk 46$_{22}$ (if em.; see Nom. Cl.), חָדָשׁ *new* 2 C 20$_{5}$, אַחֵר *other* 1 K 7$_{8}$, עֶלְיוֹן *upper* Jr 36$_{10}$, תִּיכוֹן *middle* 2 K 20$_{4(\text{Qr, mss})}$ 11QT 33$_{6}$ ([החצר התיכונה]) 40$_{7}$, פְּנִימִי *inner* 1 K 6$_{36}$ Ezk 10$_{3}$ 40$_{19.23.27.28.32.44}$ 42$_{3}$ 43$_{5}$ 44$_{17.17.21.27}$ 45$_{19}$ 46$_{1}$ Est 4$_{11}$ 11QT 11$_{14}$ ([חצר הפנ]ימית) 19$_{5}$ ([הצו]ר הפנימית) 20$_{11}$ (חצר [הפני]מ[י]ת) 11QT 36$_{14}$ 37$_{4}$ ([החצר] הפנימית) 38$_{7}$ ([חצר הפנימית]) 38$_{12}$ ([חצר הפנ]ימית), חִיצוֹן *outer* Ezk 10$_{5}$ 40$_{17.20.31.34.37}$ 42$_{1.7.8.9.14}$ 44$_{19.19}$ (or del.) 46$_{20.21}$ 11QT 21$_{3}$ ([חצר החצו]נה) 22$_{13}$ 37$_{9}$ ([חצר] החיצון) 46$_{3.5}$, שֵׁנִי *second* 11QT 38$_{12}$ ([ח]צר), שְׁלִישִׁי *third* 11QT 40$_{5}$ (שליש[י]ת), זֹאת *this* 11QT 39$_{4.11}$ ([ח]צר הזואת) 40$_{4}$ ([החצ]ר הזואת).

<PREP> לְ of direction, *to* Ezk 40$_{34.37}$, + בוא *come* Ps 96$_{8}$ (mss לְפָנָיו *before him*) Est 6$_{4}$ 11QT 38$_{7}$, יצא hi. *bring out* 2 C 29$_{16}$.

לְ of benefit, *to, for* 1 C 28$_{12}$, + עשׂה pass. *be made* Ezk 40$_{17}$.

לְ of possession, *(belonging) to, of* Ex 27$_{9}$ 38$_{20}$ 1 K 7$_{12}$ Ezk 40$_{20.23.27}$ 42$_{3.8}$ 11QT 36$_{12.14}$ 38$_{12}$ 39$_{11}$ 40$_{7}$ 46$_{3}$ perh. 11QT$^{b}$ 22$_{3}$.

לְ *at* Ne 3$_{25}$; כלה לְ *fail (with longing) for* Ps 84$_{3}$, כסף לְ ni. *long for* Ps 84$_{3}$.

בְּ of place, *in, at, among* Gn 25$_{16}$ (|| טִירָה *encampment*) 2 S 17$_{18}$ Jr 36$_{10}$ 38$_{6}$ Ezk 40$_{44}$ Ps 84$_{11}$ Est 6$_{4}$ 1 C 9$_{25}$ 2 C 23$_{5}$ 3QTr 1$_{6}$ 2$_{5}$ 3$_{1}$ ([חצ]ר), + כלא pass. *be detained* Jr 32$_{2}$, עצר pass. *be imprisoned* Jr 33$_{1}$ 39$_{15}$, ישׁב *dwell* Dt 2$_{23}$ Jr 32$_{12}$ 37$_{21}$ 38$_{13.28}$ Ne 11$_{25.30}$ 1 C 9$_{16}$, עמד *stand* Jr 19$_{14}$ 26$_{2}$ Ps 135$_{2}$ Est 5$_{1.2}$ 6$_{5}$.

פקד hi. *commit* Jr 37$_{21}$, פרח hi. *flourish* Ps 92$_{14}$, עשׂה *make* Ne 8$_{16.16}$ 13$_{7}$ Est 1$_{5}$ 11QT 37$_{8}$, רגם *stone* 2 C 24$_{21}$, אכל *eat* Lv 6$_{9}$ 11QT 17$_{9}$ 19$_{5}$ 20$_{11}$ 21$_{3}$ 22$_{13}$, ni. *be eaten* Lv 6$_{19}$, שׁתה *drink* Is 62$_{9}$, הלל pi. *praise* Ps 116$_{19}$, יחשׂ htp. *be enrolled by genealogy* 1 C 9$_{22}$.

מִן of direction, *from* 11QT 46$_{5}$, + בוא Ezk 42$_{9}$, אסף ni. *be gathered* Ne 12$_{28}$, לקח *take* Jr 39$_{14}$, מות *die* Ex 8$_{9}$.

אֶל *to* Ezk 40$_{31}$, + בוא *come* Jr 32$_{8}$ Ezk 44$_{21.27}$ Est 4$_{11}$, hi. *bring* Ezk 8$_{16}$ 40$_{17.28.32}$ 43$_{5}$, יצא *go out* Ezk 42$_{14}$ 44$_{19}$.

19 (or del.) 11QT $33_{6}$, hi. *bring out* Ezk $42_{1}$ $46_{20.21}$; *concerning* Ne $11_{25}$.

עַל *in charge of* 1 C $23_{28}$; עַד *unto* 1 K $7_{9}$, + שׁמע ni. *be heard* Ezk $10_{5}$; לִפְנֵי *before* Ezk $40_{19}$, + הלך htp. *go to and fro* Est $2_{11}$, עמד *stand* 2 C $20_{5}$.

חָצֵר with ה- of direction, *to the court*, + בוא *come* Jr $36_{20}$.

<COLL> לֹא יָצָא חָצֵר הַתִּיכֹנָה *he had not gone out of the middle court* 2 K $20_{4(Qr, mss)}$, יִשְׁכֹּן חֲצֵרֶיךָ *he will dwell in your courts* Ps $65_{5}$, בֹּאוּ ... חֲצֵרֹתָיו *enter into ... his courts* Ps $100_{4}$ (|| שַׁעַר *gate*), עָרִים ... וְחַצְרֵיהֶן *cities ... and their villages* and vars. Jos $13_{23.28}$ $15_{32+9t}$ $16_{9}$ $18_{23.28}$ $19_{6+7t}$ 1 C $4_{32}$, עֶקְרוֹן וּבְנֹתֶיהָ וַחֲצֵרֶיהָ *Ekron and its villages and settlements* Jos $15_{45}$, var. $15_{47.47}$, כֹּל אֲשֶׁר עַל־יַד אַשְׁדּוֹד וְחַצְרֵיהֶן *all that were at the side of Ashdod and their settlements* Jos $15_{46}$, שְׁתֵּי חַצְרוֹת *two courts of* 2 K $21_{5}$||2 C $33_{5}$ 2 K $23_{12}$.

<SYN> טִירָה *encampment*, שַׁעַר *gate*.*

⇒ חֲצַר אַדָּר *Hazar-addar*, חֲצַר גַּדָּה *Hazar-gaddah*, חָצֵר הַתִּיכוֹן *Hazar-hatticon*, חֲצַר סוּסָה *Hazar-susa*, חֲצַר סוּסִים *Hazar-susim*, חֲצַר עֵינוֹן *Hazar-enon*, חֲצַר עֵינָן *Hazar-enan*, חֲצַר שׁוּעָל *Hazar-shual*.

**חֲצַר אַדָּר** 1 pl.n. **Hazar-addar,** town on southern border of Judah near Kadesh-barnea, perh. 'Ēn el-Qudērat, and perh. ident. with Hezron and Addar at Jos $15_{3}$, <COLL> וְיָצָא חֲצַר־אַדָּר *and it* (border) *goes out to Hazar-addar* Nm $34_{4}$.

⇒ חָצֵר *court*.

**[חֲצַר אֲסָם]** 0.0.0.1 pl.n. **Hazar-asam,** <PREP> בְּ of place, *in* Meṣad Ḥashavyahu ost. $1_{3}$.

**חֲצַר גַּדָּה** 1 pl.n. **Hazar-gaddah,** town in territory of Judah, appar. near Beer-sheba, <APP> עִיר *city* Jos $15_{27}$.

⇒ חָצֵר *court*.

**חָצֵר הַתִּיכוֹן** 1 pl.n. **Hazer-hatticon,** town on northern border of Israel, near Hauran, <NOM CL> חָצֵר הַתִּיכוֹן אֲשֶׁר אֶל־גְּבוּל חַוְרָן *Hazer-hatticon which is on the border of Hauran* Ezk $47_{16}$.

⇒ חָצֵר *court*.

**חֶצְרוֹ** 2 pr.n.m. **Hezro,** a Carmelite warrior in David's army, <NOM CL> גִּבּוֹרֵי הַחֲיָלִים ... חֶצְרוֹ *the warriors of the armies were ... Hezro* 1 C $11_{37}$. <ADJ> כַּרְמְלִי *Carmelite* 2 S $23_{35(Kt)}$||1 C $11_{37}$ (2 S Qr חֶצְרַי *Hezrai*).

**חֶצְרוֹן I** 16 pr.n.m. **Hezron, 1.** son of Reuben, <NOM CL> בְּנֵי רְאוּבֵן ... חֶצְרוֹן *the sons of Reuben were ... Hezron* Gn $46_{9}$ Ex $6_{14}$ 1 C $5_{3}$. <PREP> לְ of possession, *(belonging) to, of* Nm $26_{6}$.

**2.** son of Perez and grandson of Judah, <SUBJ> היה *be* Gn $46_{12}$, ילד hi. *beget* Ru $4_{19}$, בוא *come* 1 C $2_{21}$. <NOM CL> בְּנֵי־פֶרֶץ חֶצְרוֹן *the sons of Perez were Hezron* 1 C $2_{5}$, בְּנֵי יְהוּדָה ... חֶצְרוֹן *the sons of Judah were ... Hezron* 1 C $4_{1}$. <OBJ> ילד hi. *beget* Ru $4_{18}$. <CSTR> אֵשֶׁת חֶצְרוֹן *wife of Hezron* 1 C $2_{24}$, בְּכוֹר *firstborn of* 1 C $2_{25}$, בֶּן־ *son of* 1 C $2_{18}$, בְּנֵי *sons of* 1 C $2_{9}$, מוֹת־ *death of* 1 C $2_{24}$. <PREP> לְ of possession, *(belonging) to, of*, + היה *be* Nm $26_{21}$.

**חֶצְרוֹן II** 1 pl.n. **Hezron,** town on southern border of Judah, perh. 'Ēn el-Qudērat, and perh. ident. with חֲצַר אַדָּר at Nm $34_{4}$. <COLL> עָבַר חֶצְרוֹן *it passes by Hezron* Jos $15_{3}$.

⇒ חָצֵר *court*, קְרִיּוֹת חֶצְרוֹן *Kerioth-hezron*.

**חֶצְרוֹנִי** 2 gent. **Hezronite**—הַחֶצְרֹנִי—collective, of descendants of Hezron, son of Reuben (Nm $26_{6}$), and Hezron son of Perez (Nm $26_{21}$), <CSTR> מִשְׁפַּחַת הַחֶצְרוֹנִי *family of the Hezronites* Nm $26_{6.21}$ (הַחֶצְרֹנִי).

⇒ חֶצְרוֹן *Hezron*.

**חֲצֵרוֹת** 6.0.0.4 pl.n. **Hazeroth**—חֲצֵרֹת—**1.** station of exodus in Sinai peninsula, perh. 'Ēn Ḥudrat NE of Ğebel Musa, <PREP> בְּ of place, *in, at, among*, + היה *be* Nm $11_{35}$, חנה *encamp* Nm $33_{17}$; מִן of direction, *from* + נסע *set out* Nm $12_{16}$ $33_{18}$; בֵּין *between* Dt $1_{1}$. <COLL> נָסְעוּ ... חֲצֵרוֹת *they journeyed ... to Hazeroth* Nm $11_{35}$ (Sam הַחֲצֵרוֹת).

**2.** mentioned in connection with recipient of goods, perh. 'Aṣīret el-Ḥaṭab, 4 km NNW of Shechem, <PREP> מִן of direction, *from* Samaria ost. $15_{1}$ (ח[צרת]) $18_{1}$ $22_{3}$ $23_{3}$ $24_{2}$ (ח[צרת]) $25_{3}$ $26_{2}$ (ח[צרת]).

⇒ חָצֵר *court*.

**חֶצְרַי** 1 pr.n.m. **Hezrai, 1.** Carmelite warrior in David's army, <ADJ> כַּרְמְלִי *Carmelite* 2 S $23_{35(Qr)}$ (Kt חצרו *Hezro*). **2.** <CSTR> [בן] חצרי *son of Hezrai* Frey 1286 (others בן הציד *son of the hunter*, others בן הציר *son of the artist*).

**חֲצַרְמָוֶת** 2 pr.n.m. **Hazarmaveth,** son of Joktan and great-grandson of Shem, <OBJ> ילד *bear* Gn $10_{26}$‖1 C $1_{20}$.

**חֲצַר סוּסָה** 2.0.0.1 pl.n. **Hazar-susa**—חֲצַר סוּסִים (1 C $4_{31}$)—town in territory allocated to Simeon, perh. Kh. Abū Sūsēn, 14 km S of Beer-sheba, <SUBJ> היה *be* Jos $19_5$. <CSTR> חדש [חצר]סוסה *month of Hazar-Susa* Arad ost. $32_1$. <PREP> בְּ of place, *in*, + ישׁב *dwell* 1 C $4_{31}$.
⇒ חָצֵר *court.*

**חֲצַר סוּסִים**, see חֲצַר סוּסָה *Hazar-susa.*

**חֲצַר עֵינָן**, see חֲצַר עֵינוֹן *Hazar-enon.*

**חֲצַר עֵינוֹן** 4 pl.n. **Hazar-enon**—חֲצַר עֵינָן—town on northern border of Canaan, perh. el-Qaryatēn, 13 km E of Damascus, <SUBJ> היה *be* Nm $34_9$. <NOM CL> חֲצַר עֵינָן גְּבוּל דַּמֶּשֶׂק צָפוֹנָה *Hazar-Enon is (on) the northern border of Damascus* Ezk $48_1$. <PREP> מִן of direction, *from*, + תאה pi. *mark out* Nm $34_{10}$. <COLL> וְהָיָה גְבוּל מִן־הַיָּם חֲצַר עֵינוֹן *and the border shall be from the sea to Hazar-enon* Ezk $47_{17}$.
⇒ חָצֵר *court.*

**חֲצַר שׁוּעָל** 4 pl.n. **Hazar-shual,** town in territory of Judah, perh. Kh. Waṭan, 7 km E of Beer-sheba, <SUBJ> היה *be* Jos $19_3$. <APP> עִיר *city* Jos $15_{28}$. <PREP> בְּ of place, *in, at, among,* + ישׁב *dwell* Ne $11_{27}$ 1 C $4_{28}$.
⇒ חָצֵר *court.*

**חֹק** 129.19.107 n.m. **statute**—Si, Q חוק; cstr. חֹק (חָק־, חֹק־); sf. חֻקִּי (Q חוקי), חָקְךָ (Si חוקך, Q חוקכה), חָקְךָ, חֻקּוֹ (Si חוקו), חָקְכֶם, חֻקָּם; pl. חֻקִּים (Q חוקים); cstr. חֻקֵּי (חוּקֵי), חֻקֵּי־; sf. חֻקַּי (חֻקָּי), חֻקֶּיךָ (Q חוקיך, חוקיכה), חֻקָּיו (Q חוקיו, חוקוהי), חֻקֶּיהָ (Q חוקיה), Q חוקיהם.

**1.** usu. **statute, decree, law, rule, instruction,** issued by God (e.g. Ex $18_{16}$ Dt $4_5$ Ps $119_{83}$ Ne $10_{30}$), Wisdom (4Q525 $3.2_1$), or human ruler or superior (e.g. Gn $47_{26}$ Ex $5_{14}$ Is $10_1$), or social **convention, custom** (e.g. Jg $11_{39}$ 1 S $30_{25}$). **2. institution** (e.g. Ex $12_{24}$ $30_{21}$), arising from regular observance of statute, and, similarly, legal or conventional **right** to, or expected **allocation** of, food (e.g. Pr $30_8$ perh. $31_{15}$), food and territory (e.g. Gn $47_{22}$), sacrifice (e.g. Lv $6_{11}$ $10_{13.14}$), protection, of wife (Ezk $16_{27}$), or royal rights (Si $47_{11}$). **3. lot, appointed destiny** (1QH $7_{34}$), appar. in ref. to death (Si $41_3$), **appointed time** of death or resurrection (Jb $14_{13}$ Si $14_{12}$). **4. law** in general (e.g. Mc $7_{11}$ Ezr $7_{10}$), **legal instruction** (4Q424 $1_4$); **law of nature** (e.g. Jr $31_{36}$ Jb $28_{26}$). **5.** perh. **prescription, will, intention** of person or God (Jb $23_{12}$ [or em.] $23_{14}$). **6. boundary** of earth (Si $43_{12}$ [unless חוּג *circle*] 1QM $10_{12}$), sea (e.g. Jb $26_{10}$ $38_{10}$ Pr $8_{29}$), **limit** of Sheol's appetite (Is $5_{14}$). **7.** appar. **metre** of psalms (Si $44_5$).

<SUBJ> היה *be* Ex $30_{21}$ Lv $24_9$ Jg $11_{39}$ Ps $119_{54}$ 1QS $10_{8.10}$, מצא ni. *be found* 4QD[a] $18.5_6$, נגד ho. *be told* Si $14_{12}$, חרת pass. *be engraved* 1QS $10_{6.8.11}$ 4Q417 $2.1_{14}$, רחק *be distant* Mc $7_{11}$ Si $16_{22}$ (if em. יצק appar. *pour,* perh. issue, statute) CD $4_{12}$, כון ni. *be established* 1QH $18_{23}$, שׁלם ni. *be complete* 1QS $10_6$, עמד *stand* Si $43_{10}$, בוא *come* 4QTNaph $1.2_5$ 4Q417 $2.1_{14}$, מושׁ *depart* Jr $31_{36}$, נשׂג hi. *overtake* Zc $1_6$ (‖ דָּבָר *word*).

<NOM CL> טוב חוקו *death is his decree* Si $41_{2(Bmg)}$, חֹק לַכֹּהֲנִים *prescribed territory was,* i.e. belonged, *to the priests* Gn $47_{22}$, אֲשֶׁר־לוֹ חֻקִּים *to which are,* i.e. that are governed by, *statutes* Dt $4_8$, ממנו חוק *from him is a statute* Si $43_{7(Bmg)}$ (M חַג *pilgrim festival*), הוּא ... חֹק *it is ... a decree* Ps $81_5$, הוא חקך *it is your decree* Si $38_{22(B)}$, כן חקך *thus is your decree* Si $38_{22(Bmg)}$, חָקְךָ וְחָק־בָּנֶיךָ הִיא *it is your due and the due of your sons* Lv $10_{13(Qr)}$, זֹאת ... מָה ... הַחֻקִּים *what are ... the statutes?* Dt $6_{20}$, ... הַחֻקִּים *this is ... the statutes* Dt $6_1$, אֵלֶּה הַחֻקִּים *these are the statutes* Lv $26_{46}$ Dt $4_{45}$ (אֵלֶּה ... הַחֻקִּים) $12_1$=CD $19_{14}$ $12_{20}$ 1QS $9_{12}$ 4QD[a] $6.1_{15}$ (אלה החו[ק]ים).

<OBJ> נתן *give,* i.e. issue (statute) Dt $11_{32}$ (‖ מִשְׁפָּט *judgment*) Ps $99_7$ (or em. שׁמע *hear;* ‖ עֵדָה *testimony*) $148_6$ Ne $9_{13}$ (‖ מִשְׁפָּט, תּוֹרָה *law,* מִצְוָה *commandment*) Si

$47_{11}$ 4QDᵃ $18.5_{11}$ (|| מִשְׁפָּט) 4QapPsᵇ $69_5$ (ח[קים] נתן]; || תּוֹרָה, מִצְוָה), provide (allocation of food) Gn $47_{22}$ Pr $31_{15}$.

שׂים *place*, i.e. issue (statute) Ex $15_{25}$=4QPentParᵇ $6.2_{11}$ (|| מִשְׁפָּט *judgment* [4Q (משפט)]) Jos $24_{25}$ (|| מִשְׁפָּט), assign (lot) 1QH $7_{34}$, establish (boundary) Pr $8_{29}$, שׁית *place*, i.e. assign (appointed time) Jb $14_{13}$.

עשׂה *do*, i.e. fulfil Dt $4_{14}$ (|| מִשְׁפָּט *judgment*) $5_{31}$ (|| מִצְוָה *commandment*, מִשְׁפָּט) $6_1$ (|| מִשְׁפָּט) $6_{24}$ $7_{11}$ (|| מִצְוָה, מִשְׁפָּט) $11_{32}$ (|| מִשְׁפָּט) $16_{12}$ $17_{19}$ $26_{16.16}$ (|| מִשְׁפָּט) $27_{10}$ (|| מִצְוָה) 2 K $17_{37}$ (|| מִשְׁפָּט, מִצְוָה, תּוֹרָה *law*) Ps $119_{112}$ Jb $14_5$ Ne $10_{30}$ (|| מִצְוָה, מִשְׁפָּט) 1 C $22_{13}$ (|| מִשְׁפָּט) 1QS $1_7$ $5_{22}$ 1QDM $2_1$ ([חוקי] ... ת]עשה אותם]) 4QDᵃ $18.5_{11}$ (|| מִשְׁפָּט), issue Jb $28_{26}$, prepare sacrifice Lv $6_{15}$.

שׁמר *keep* Ex $15_{26}$ Dt $4_{40}$ (both || מִצְוָה *commandment*) $6_{17}$ (|| מִצְוָה, עֵדָה *testimony*) $7_{11}$ (|| מִצְוָה, מִשְׁפָּט *judgment*) $16_{12}$ $17_{19}$ (+ דָּבָר *word* of covenant) $26_{16}$ (|| מִשְׁפָּט) $26_{17}$ (|| מִצְוָה, מִשְׁפָּט [lacking in ms, Sam]) 1 K $3_{14}$ (|| מִצְוָה) $8_{58}$ (|| מִצְוָה, מִשְׁפָּט) $9_4$||2 C $7_{17}$ (|| מִשְׁפָּט) 2 K $17_{37}$ (|| מִשְׁפָּט, מִצְוָה, תּוֹרָה *law*) Am $2_4$ (|| תּוֹרָה) Ps $99_7$ (or em. שׁמע *hear*; || עֵדָה) $105_{45}$ (|| תּוֹרָה) $119_{5.8}$ Ne $1_7$ $10_{30}$ (both || מִצְוָה, מִשְׁפָּט) 1 C $22_{13}$ (|| מִצְוָה) $29_{19}$ (|| מִצְוָה, עֵדוּת *testimony*) 2 C $34_{31}$ (||2 K $23_3$ חֻקָּה *statute*; || מִצְוָה, עֵדוּת) 1QDM $2_1$ ([ושׁ]מרתה חוקי]; || מִצְוָה [ומצוו]תי], עֵדוּת) 4QApocMosB $1.1_2$ ([ההח]קים]).

נצר *keep* Ps $119_{145}$ Si $16_{22}$ (if em. יצק appar. *pour*, perh. issue, statute), פקד *visit*, i.e. observe 1QS $5_{22}$ 1QSb $3_{24}$, כלה pi. *fulfil* Ex $5_{14}$, שׁלם hi. *complete*, i.e. fulfil Jb $23_{14}$ 11QT $39_8$.

שׁנה hi. *change* 4QWiles $1_{15}$ ([ח]וק; + מִצְוָה *commandment*), עבר *pass*, i.e. transgress perh. Ps $148_6$ 1QpHab $8_{17}$ 1QS $5_7$ 1QLitPr $3.2_2$, חלף *pass*, i.e. transgress Is $24_5$, פרר hi. *(cause) to frustrate*, i.e. transgress CD $1_{20}$ (|| בְּרִית *covenant*), שׁוב hi. *take back*, appar. reject CD $20_{33}$, מאס *reject* 2 K $17_{15}$ (|| בְּרִית *covenant*, עֵדוּת), תעב pi. *abominate* CD $2_6$ (מתאבי חק), עזב *abandon* 1Q38 $2_1$ ([ח]וקיכה]), רפה hi. *release* 4Q416 $2.2_8$, גרע *diminish*, i.e. cut off (right) Ezk $16_{27}$ (|| מִשְׁפָּט *judgment*).

שׁכח *forget* Ps $119_{83}$ 4QpsMoseᵉ $1_8$ (|| בְּרִית *covenant*, שַׁבָּת *sabbath*, מוֹעֵד *appointed time*) 4QBarkᶜ $1_5$ 4Q422 $1_{11}$ ([חקיו]).

זכר *remember* Si $38_{22}$, דרשׁ *seek* Ps $119_{155}$, שׁמע *hear* Dt $4_6$ $5_1$ (|| מִשְׁפָּט *judgment*) Ps $99_7$ (if em. שׁמר *keep*; || עֵדָה *testimony*) CD $20_{33}$ 4QMMT $B_{52}$ (|| מִשְׁפָּט, טָהֳרָה *purity regulation*).

כתב *write* 2 K $17_{37}$ (|| מִשְׁפָּט *judgment*, מִצְוָה *commandment*, תּוֹרָה *law*), חקק *engrave*, i.e. decree Is $10_1$, חרת *engrave* 4QShirShabbᵃ $1.1_{5.15}$ ([חוקי]) 4QShir Shabbᶜ $4_3$ ([ח]וקי]) 4QShirᵇ $63.2_3$, כרת *cut*, i.e. inscribe Si $44_{20}$ (|| מִצְוָה).

קרא *read* 1QSa $1_5$ (+ מִשְׁפָּט *judgment* [משפ(טיה)מה]), אמר *say*, i.e. recite 1QS $10_{10}$ (+ בְּרִית *covenant*), דבר *say*, i.e. state Dt $5_1$ (|| מִשְׁפָּט), pi. *speak* Lv $10_{11}$ (Gnz דָּבָר *word*) Dt $5_{31}$ (|| מִצְוָה *commandment*, מִשְׁפָּט), ספר pi. *relate* Ps $50_{16}$ 1QH $18_{23}$, נגד hi. *declare* Ps $147_{19}$ (|| דָּבָר, מִשְׁפָּט), חלק perh. *divide*, i.e. promulgate 1QS $10_{26}$, יצק appar. *pour*, perh. issue, statute Si $16_{22}$ (or em. נצר *keep* statute or רחק *be distant*, with חק as subj.).

ידע hi. *make known* Ex $18_{16}$ (|| תּוֹרָה *law*), ירה hi. *teach* Lv $10_{11}$ (Gnz דָּבָר *word*), למד *learn* Ps $119_{71}$, pi. *teach* Dt $4_{5.14}$ (both || מִשְׁפָּט) $5_{31}$ (|| מִצְוָה, מִשְׁפָּט) $6_1$ (|| מִשְׁפָּט) Ps $119_{12.26.64.68.124.135.171}$ Ezr $7_{10}$ (|| מִשְׁפָּט) Si $45_5$ (|| מִשְׁפָּט, עֵדָה *testimony*, + תּוֹרָה, מִצְוָה *law*) $45_{17}$ (|| מִשְׁפָּט), זהר hi. *teach* Ex $18_{20}$ (|| תּוֹרָה *law*).

צוה pi. *command* Dt $4_{40}$ (|| מִצְוָה *commandment*) $6_1$ (|| מִשְׁפָּט *judgment*) $6_{17.20}$ (both || מִצְוָה, עֵדָה *testimony*) $7_{11}$ (|| מִצְוָה, מִשְׁפָּט) $27_{10}$ (|| מִצְוָה) 1 K $8_{58}$ (|| מִצְוָה, מִשְׁפָּט [or del.]) Ml $3_{22}$ (|| מִשְׁפָּט) Ne $1_7$ (|| מִצְוָה, מִשְׁפָּט) $9_{14}$ (|| מִצְוָה, תּוֹרָה *law* [or del. one of these]) 1 C $22_{13}$ (|| מִשְׁפָּט) 1QS $5_{22}$ 1QDM $2_1$ ([חוקי]).

לקח *take*, i.e. accept, instruction 4Q424 $1_4$, תמך *hold* 4Q525 $3.2_1$, חוג *draw* boundary Jb $26_{10}$ (or em. חַג־חֹק *he drew a boundary* to חַק חוּג *he drew a circle*), שׁבר *break*, perh. enforce, boundary Jb $38_{10}$, קום hi. *establish* Si $45_{24}$ (|| בְּרִית *covenant*), נקף hi. *surround* boundary Si $43_{12(B)}$ (unless חוק *circle*; Bmg הוֹד *splendour*; M חוג *vault [of heaven]*), חזק pi. *strengthen*, perh. enforce 1QH $14_5$, גבר pi. *strengthen*, i.e. confirm 4QShirShabbᵃ $1.1_9$, ברא *create* 1QM $10_{12}$, ילד *give birth (to)* Zp $2_2$ (or em. לֶדֶת חֹק appar. before *one gives birth to a statute*, i.e. before a decree is issued, to לֹא תִּדָּחֲקוּ before *you are crushed*), אכל *eat* Gn $47_{22}$ (allocation of food).

<CSTR> חק י׳ *decree of Y.* Ps $2_7$, חֻקֵּי הָאֱלֹהִים *statutes of God* Ex $18_{16}$, חוקי אל *statutes of God* 1QpHab $2_{15}$ (חוקי

[א]ל) 8$_{17}$ (חוקי [אל]) 1QS 1$_{7.12}$ 3$_{8}$ 11QMelch$_{12}$, חוקי הגוים *the ordinances of the nations* CD 9$_{1}$, חָק־בָּנֶיךָ *due of your sons* Lv 10$_{13.14}$, חוקי פיכ[ה] *statutes of your mouth* 4QRitPur 82$_{2}$.

חוקי הודות *statutes of thanksgiving* 4QShir$^{b}$ 63.2$_{3}$, האמת *of truth* 4QTNaph 1.2$_{5}$, אמתכה *of your truth* 4QD$^{a}$ 18.5$_{11}$, אמתו *of his truth* 1QS 1$_{15}$, הצדק *of righteousness* CD 20$_{11.33}$ (both חקי), חק חסדך *statute of your loyalty* 4Q521 2.3$_{1}$, [חוקי קוד]שים *statutes of holiness* 4QShirShabb$^{a}$ 1.1$_{15}$, חוקי קודו[ש] *statutes of holiness* 4Q414 1.2$_{1}$, קוד[שכה] *of your holiness* 4QRitPur 64$_{6}$, קדשו *of his holiness* CD 20$_{30}$ (חקי), חוק כבוד *statute of glory* 4Q414 4$_{3}$, חִקְקֵי־אָוֶן *decrees of iniquity* Is 10$_{1}$, חוקי חושך *statutes of darkness* 1QM 13$_{12}$.

חֹק הַשֶּׁמֶן *portion of the oil* Ezk 45$_{14}$, חִקְקֵי־לֵב *decrees of the heart* Jg 5$_{15}$ (or em. חִקְרֵי *searchings of heart*), חק ממלכת *statute of kingship* Si 47$_{11}$, חוקי ברית *statutes of covenant (of)* CD 5$_{12}$ 20$_{29}$ (חקי) 1QSa 1$_{5}$ (הברית) 1$_{7}$ (חוק[י] הברית) 4Q414 1.2$_{1}$ ([חוקי בר]ית), בריתך *of your covenant* 1QH 16$_{15}$, מפלגיה *of its divisions* 1QM 10$_{12}$, חוק תכונם *statute of their abode* 1QS 10$_{6}$ 4QMyst$^{a}$ 18$_{1}$, חוק ירושלם *boundary of Jerusalem* 4QTestim$_{29}$.

חוק העת *statute of the time* 1QS 9$_{14}$, חָק־עוֹלָם *statute/due of eternity* Ex 29$_{28}$ 30$_{21}$ Lv 6$_{11.15}$ 7$_{34}$ 10$_{15}$ 24$_{9}$ Nm 18$_{8.11.19}$ Jr 5$_{22}$ Si 14$_{17}$ 45$_{7}$ CD 15$_{5}$ (חוק) 4QPrFêtes$^{b}$ 2$_{3}$ ([חוק עו]לם) 11QT 21$_{04}$ ([חוק]) 21$_{05}$ (חוק) 21$_{9}$ (חוק] [עולם) 11QT 39$_{8}$ (חוק), חוקי עולמ[ים] *statutes of eternities* 4QShirShabb$^{b}$ 12$_{2}$.

מלומדי חוק *instructed ones of statute* 1QM 10$_{10}$, מתאבי חק *ones who abominate (the) statute(s)* CD 2$_{6}$, דֶּרֶךְ חֻקֶּיךָ *way of your statutes* Ps 119$_{33}$, מעון חוקו *dwelling of its statute* 1QS 10$_{1}$, לֶחֶם חֻקִּי *bread of my prescription* Pr 30$_{8}$, אמת חוקי *truth of the statutes of* 1QS 1$_{12}$, דִּבְרֵי ... חֻקָּיו *words of ... his statutes* Ezr 7$_{11}$, ספר חוקיך *book of your statutes* 4Q434a$_{13}$, כלי חוקכה *vessel of your statute* 4Q416 2.2$_{21}$, זמני חק *times of statute*, i.e. appointed times Si 43$_{7(B)}$.

כָּל־הַחֻקִּים *all the statutes* Lv 10$_{11}$ Dt 4$_{6}$ 6$_{24}$ 11$_{32}$, sim. Dt 5$_{31}$ 2 C 33$_{8}$, כול החוקים *all the statutes* 1QS 5$_{7.20}$ 4QD$^{a}$ 18.5$_{6}$ 4QApocMosB 1.1$_{2}$ ([כול החו]קים) 4QDibHam$^{a}$ 3.2$_{14}$ (כול החו[ק]ים), כול חוק *every statute* 4QToh A 3.1$_{2}$, כול חוקי *all the statutes of* 1QS 3$_{8}$ 1QSa 1$_{5}$ (כ]ול חוקי) 4QM$^{h}$ 3$_{4}$ 4QDibHam$^{a}$ 6$_{3}$ (כול חוק[י]), כול חוקיך *all your statutes* 1QH 15$_{12}$, כָּל־חֻקָּיו *all his statutes* Ex 15$_{26}$, כול חוקיו *all his statutes* 1QS 5$_{22}$ 1QSb 3$_{24}$ 4QSap$^{b}$ 1.1$_{4}$.

<APP> תּוֹרָה *law* Ml 3$_{22}$, מָוֶת *death* Si 41$_{3}$.

<ADJ> טוֹב *good* Ezk 16$_{27}$ Ne 9$_{13}$, צַדִּיק *righteous* Dt 4$_{8}$, זֶה *this* 1QSa 2$_{21}$, אֵלֶּה *these* Dt 4$_{6}$ 6$_{24}$ 16$_{12}$ 17$_{19}$ 26$_{16}$ Jr 31$_{36}$ 1QS 5$_{20}$ 4QApocMosB 1.1$_{2}$ ([החו]קים).

<PREP> לְ of direction, *to*, + ענה pi. *humble* 1QS 3$_{8}$; *as* 4Q414 1.2$_{1}$ 4Q417 6.2 11QT 21$_{04}$ ([חוק]), + היה *be* Ex 29$_{28}$ Lv 10$_{15}$, בוא *come* CD 15$_{5}$, שׂים *place*, i.e. make Gn 47$_{26}$ 1 S 30$_{25}$ (‖ מִשְׁפָּט *ordinance*) Si 45$_{7}$, שׁמר *keep* Ex 12$_{24}$, נתן *give* Lv 7$_{34}$ Nm 18$_{8.11.19}$ 2 C 35$_{25}$, עמד hi. *confirm* Ps 105$_{10}$‖1 C 16$_{17}$ (‖ בְּרִית *covenant*); *concerning* 2 C 19$_{10}$ (‖ מִצְוָה *commandment*, מִשְׁפָּט) 33$_{8}$ (‖ תּוֹרָה *law*, מִשְׁפָּט); *according to* 1QH 1$_{10}$; קנא לְ pi. *be zealous for* 1QS 9$_{23}$.

בְּ of instrument, *by (means of), with*, + כול htpal. *be steadfast* 4QShirShabb$^{f}$ 20.2$_{2}$ (ח]וק ית[כלכלו), דין *judge* 11QMelch$_{9}$, מות hi. *cause to die* CD 9$_{1}$, יסר htp. *be disciplined* 1QH 7$_{20}$ ([את]יסר בחוקיכה), דרשׁ *seek* 1QS 5$_{11}$; of accompaniment, *with, in* 1Q51 1$_{2}$ 4QMyst$^{a}$ 58$_{2}$ 4QShirShabb$^{a}$ 1.1$_{9}$ (חוק בחוק *a statute with a statute*, i.e. every statute) 4QShirShabb$^{b}$ 12$_{2}$ 4Q416 2.3$_{20}$ (בלוא חוק *without statute*) 4QM$^{h}$ 3$_{4}$ 4QSap$^{b}$ 1.1$_{4}$, + היה *be* Ps 119$_{80}$, משׁל hi. *give dominion* Si 45$_{17}$ (‖ מִשְׁפָּט *judgment*), הלך *go* 1 K 8$_{61}$ Ezk 11$_{12}$ 20$_{18}$ 36$_{27}$, htp. 1QM 13$_{12}$, עמד *stand* Si 11$_{20}$, מרה hi. *rebel* Si 39$_{31}$, שׂכל hi. *give insight* 1QSa 1$_{7}$.

בְּ introducing object, + בגד *betray* 1QpHab 8$_{10}$, בין htpol. *consider* 1QH 10$_{2}$ ([חו]קיך) 4QDibHam$^{a}$ 6$_{3}$ (חוק[י]), אמן hi. *believe* 1QpHab 2$_{15}$, שׁעה *have regard for* Ps 119$_{117}$ (or em. שׁעע htpalp. *delight oneself*), מאס *reject* CD 19$_{6}$.

בְּ of place, *in*, + שׁפך *pour out* 4QTestim$_{29}$; *against* 4QD$^{a}$ 1$_{17}$, + הלך *go* CD 20$_{29}$; שׂיח בְּ *meditate on* Ps 119$_{23.48}$.

כְּ *as, according to* 1QS 10$_{11}$ 4Q418 123.1$_{3}$, + עשׂה *do* 1QS 5$_{20}$ 1QSa 2$_{21}$, טהר *be clean* 11QT 50$_{6}$, ברך pi. *bless* 1QS 10$_{6}$.

מִן of direction, *from* 4QShirShabb$^{f}$ 43$_{3}$, + סור *depart* Ml 3$_{7}$ 1QS 1$_{15}$ 11QMelch$_{12}$, עזב *forsake* 1QH 15$_{12}$, שׁגה *go astray* Ps 119$_{118}$, כשׁל *stumble* 1QH 16$_{15}$; of comparison, *more (than)*, + צפן *treasure* Jb 23$_{12}$ (or em. מֵחֻקִּי *than my [own] will* to בְּחֵקִי *in my bosom*); of cause, *(on account) of*, or, *concerning*, + פחד *fear* Si 41$_{3}$; *according to*, + ראה pass. *be fit* 11QT 66$_{9}$.

אֶל *to*, + שמע *listen* Dt 4$_{1}$ (‖ מִשְׁפָּט *judgment*); *concerning*, + ספר pi. *relate* Ps 2$_{7}$.

עַל *over*, + דלג *leap*, i.e. omit 4QShirShabb[f] 23.1i$_{10}$ (+ אֹמֶר *word*); *by (means of)*, + יצר *form* trouble Ps 94$_{20}$; *according to* 1QS 5$_{7}$ 4QDibHam[a] 3.2$_{14}$, + הלך *go* 4Q458 2.2$_{4}$ ([החו]קים), חקר *search* Si 44$_{5}$; *against*, + רום hi. *raise* hand CD 20$_{30}$, פתח *open* mouth CD 5$_{12}$, דבר pi. *speak* CD 20$_{11}$; *(because) of*, + בוש *be ashamed* Si 42$_{2}$.

לִבְלִי *without*, i.e. beyond (limit), + פער *open* mouth Is 5$_{14}$=4QpIsa[b] 2$_{5}$.

לְפִי *according to*, + מצא ni. *be found* 1QS 9$_{14}$.

עַל פִּי *according to* 4QD[a] 18.5$_{6}$.

<COLL> יֹאכְלֶנָּה חָק־עוֹלָם *he shall eat of it (as) a perpetual due* Lv 6$_{11}$, חָקְךָ וְחָק־בָּנֶיךָ נִתְּנוּ *they have been given as your allocation and as the allocation of your sons* Lv 10$_{14}$, שַׂמְתִּי חוֹל ... חָק־עוֹלָם *I made the sand ... (as) an eternal boundary* Jr 5$_{22}$, וָאֶקַּח אֶת־סֵפֶר הַמִּקְנָה ... הַמִּצְוָה וְהַחֻקִּים *and I took the deed of the purchase ... (which contained) the commandment and the statutes* Jr 32$_{11}$.

<SYN> מִשְׁפָּט *judgment*, מִצְוָה *commandment*, בְּרִית *covenant*, תּוֹרָה *law*, עֵדָה *testimony*, עֵדוּת *testimony*, דָּבָר *word*, טָהֳרָה *purity regulation*, שַׁבָּת *sabbath*, מוֹעֵד *appointed time*.

Also 1QH 2$_{37}$ 17$_{23}$ perh. 4QMidrEschat[a] 16$_{2}$ 4QWiles 5$_{5}$ 4QD[a] 5$_{3}$ 4QD[b] 3$_{4}$ (חו[ק]י) perh. 4QMyst[a] 66$_{1}$ 4QapPs[b] 46$_{3}$ 86$_{1}$ 4QShirShabb[a] 2$_{11}$ perh. 4Q425 5$_{5}$ perh. 4QSap[b] 21$_{3}$ 4QRitMar 1$_{2}$ 4QPrFêtes[c] 31$_{4}$ 4Q515 2$_{1}$ 4Q525 5$_{9}$ 8QPhyl 31$_{6}$ 11QT 22$_{01}$.*

⇒ חקק *engrave*.

**חקה** 4.0.1 vb. **carve—Pu.** 3.0.1 Ptc. מְחֻקֶּה, Q cstr. מחקת—**be carved, be engraved, 1a.** <SUBJ> בְּהֵמָה *beast* Ezk 8$_{10}$, רֶמֶשׂ *reptile* Ezk 8$_{10}$, גִּלּוּל *idol* Ezk 8$_{10}$, שֶׁקֶץ *detestable object* Ezk 8$_{10}$. <PREP> עַל *upon*, + קִיר *wall* Ezk 8$_{10}$.

**1b.** ptc. as noun, **carved thing, engraving,** <CSTR> אַנְשֵׁי מְחֻקֶּה *men of engraving*, i.e. men who are engraved Ezk 23$_{14}$ (or em. אֲנָשִׁים חֲקֻקִים *men engraved*), כול מחקת *every engraving* 4QShirShabb[f] 15.2$_{4}$. <PREP> עַל *upon*, + ישר pu. *be made even* 1 K 6$_{35}$.

**Htp.** 1 Impf. תִּתְחַקֶּה—**engrave for oneself,** <SUBJ> אֵל *God* Jb 13$_{27}$. <PREP> עַל *upon*, + שֹׁרֶשׁ *root*, i.e. sole, of foot Jb 13$_{27}$.*

**חֻקָּה** 100.0.19 n.f. **statute**—cstr. חֻקַּת (Q חוקת); pl. חֻקּוֹת (Q חוקות); cstr. חֻקּוֹת (חֻקֹּת); sf. חֻקּוֹתַי (חֻקֹּתַי, חֻקֹּתָי), חֻקֹּתֶיךָ (Q חוקתיך), חֻקּוֹתָיו (חֻקֹּתָיו), חֻקֹּתָם (חֻקֹּתֵיהֶם)—**1. statute, ordinance, law, decree,** issued by God (e.g. Ex 12$_{14}$ Lv 23$_{41}$ Nm 31$_{21}$ Dt 6$_{2}$ 1 K 6$_{12}$ Jr 44$_{10}$ Ps 89$_{32}$), as regulation for natural order, **fixed time** (e.g. Jr 5$_{24}$ 31$_{35}$ 33$_{25}$ Jb 38$_{33}$ 1QH 12$_{5}$). **2. statute, custom** of human beings (e.g. Lv 18$_{3.30}$ 1 K 3$_{3}$ 2 K 17$_{8}$ Jr 10$_{3}$ Mc 6$_{16}$).

<SUBJ> היה *be* Lv 17$_{7}$ Nm 9$_{14}$ 11QT 18$_{8}$, כתב pass. *be written* Dt 30$_{10}$, שמר htp. *be kept* Mc 6$_{16}$=1QpMic 17$_{3}$ ([שתמר חוקות]י; unless em. וְיִשְׁתַּמֵּר *and it is kept* to וַתִּשְׁמֹר qal *and you have kept*).

<NOM CL> חֻקָּה אַחַת לָכֶם *one statute shall be to you* Nm 15$_{15}$, חֻקַּת עוֹלָם לוֹ *it is an eternal statute to him* Ex 28$_{43}$, חֻקַּת עוֹלָם לְדֹרֹתָם *it is an eternal statute for their generations* Ex 27$_{21}$ Lv 7$_{36}$, sim. Lv 3$_{17}$ 10$_{9}$ 23$_{14.21.31.41}$ 24$_{3}$ Nm 15$_{15}$ 18$_{23}$, חֻקּוֹת הָעַמִּים הֶבֶל הוּא *the statutes of the peoples are vanity* Jr 10$_{3}$ (or em.; see Cstr.), זֹאת חֻקַּת הַפָּסַח *this is the ordinance of the passover* Ex 12$_{43}$, זֹאת חֻקַּת הַתּוֹרָה *this is the statute of the law* Nm 19$_{2}$ 31$_{21}$, אֵלֶּה חֻקּוֹת הַמִּזְבֵּחַ *these are the regulations of the altar* Ezk 43$_{18}$.

<OBJ> עשׂה *do*, i.e. practise Lv 19$_{37}$ (‖ מִשְׁפָּט *judgment*) 20$_{8.22}$ 25$_{18}$ (both ‖ מִשְׁפָּט) Dt 28$_{15}$ (‖ מִצְוָה *commandment*) 1 K 11$_{33}$ (‖ מִשְׁפָּט) Ezk 18$_{19}$ 37$_{24}$ 43$_{11}$, שׁמר *keep* Gn 26$_{5}$ (‖ מִצְוָה, תּוֹרָה *law*) Ex 13$_{10}$ Lv 18$_{4.5.26}$ (both ‖ מִשְׁפָּט) 19$_{19.37}$ (‖ מִשְׁפָּט) 20$_{8.22}$ 25$_{18}$ (both ‖ מִשְׁפָּט) Dt 6$_{2}$ (‖ מִצְוָה) 8$_{11}$ (‖ מִשְׁפָּט, מִצְוָה) 10$_{13}$ (‖ מִצְוָה) 11$_{1}$ (‖ מִשְׁפָּט, מִצְוָה) 28$_{45}$ 30$_{10}$ (both ‖ מִצְוָה) 30$_{16}$ (‖ מִשְׁפָּט, מִצְוָה) 1 K 2$_{3}$ (‖ מִשְׁפָּט, מִצְוָה, עֵדוּת *testimony*) 11$_{11}$ (‖ בְּרִית *covenant*) 11$_{34.38}$ 2 K 17$_{13}$ (all three ‖ מִצְוָה) 23$_{3}$ (‖ מִצְוָה, עֵדוּת) Ezk 18$_{19.21}$ 37$_{24}$ 43$_{11}$ 44$_{24}$ (‖ תּוֹרָה *law*) Mc 6$_{16}$ (if em.; see Subj.) 4QPentPar[b] 6.2$_{13}$, נתן *give* Jr 5$_{24}$ 1 K 9$_{6}$ (‖ מִצְוָה) Jr 31$_{35}$ Ezk 20$_{11}$ 2 C 7$_{19}$, שׂים *place* Jr 33$_{25}$, דרשׁ *seek* 4QApocJer C 2$_{8}$ (‖ מִצְוָה).

געל *abhor* Lv 26$_{43}$, שׁכח *forget* 4QJub[a] 1$_{14}$ ([וישכחו ... חקותי]), עזב *forsake* 2 C 7$_{19}$ (‖ מִצְוָה *commandment*) 4Q

Jub[a] $1_{10}$ ([עזבו]), מאס *refuse* Ezk $20_{24}$ 4QpsEzek[b] $4_{4}$ (+ תּוֹרָה *law*), מרה hi. *rebel against* Ezk $5_{6}$ (|| מִשְׁפָּט), חלל pi. *profane* Ps $89_{32}$, סור hi. *remove* Ps $18_{23}$, פרר hi. *break* 4QpsMos[e] $2.1_{5}$ (|| מִצְוָה).

צוה pi. *command* Dt $8_{11}$ $10_{13}$ $28_{15.45}$ (all three || מִצְוָה *commandment*) 1 K $11_{11}$ (|| בְּרִית), ידע *know* Jb $38_{33}$, hi. *make known* Ezk $43_{11}$, חרת *engrave* 4QShirShabb[f] $23.2_{13}$ ([חרת] ... [חו]קות]).

<CSTR> חֻקּוֹת הָעַמִּים *statutes of the peoples* Jr $10_{3}$ (or em. חִתַּת *terror of*) 4QpIsa[c] $4.2_{5}$ (עמים), הַגּוֹי *of the nation* Lv $20_{23}$ (חֻקֹּת), הַגּוֹיִם *of the nations* Lv $20_{23(ms)}$ (חֻקֹּת) 2 K $17_{8}$, יִשְׂרָאֵל *of Israel* 2 K $17_{19}$, דָּוִד *of David* 1 K $3_{3}$, עָמְרִי *of Omri* Mc $6_{16}$=1QpMic $17_{3}$ ([חוקות עומרי]).

חֻקּוֹת הַחַיִּים *statutes of life* Ezk $33_{15}$, חֻקַּת הַתּוֹרָה *statute of the law* Nm $19_{2}$ (or em. הַתּוֹרָה to הַפָּרָה *the cow*) $31_{21}$, חֻקַּת מִשְׁפָּט *statute of judgment* Nm $27_{11}$ $35_{29}$, חוקות מקדשיו *ordinances of his sanctuaries* 4QShirShabb[d] $1.2_{21}$, חֻקַּת הַפָּסַח *ordinance of the passover* Ex $12_{43}$ (הַפָּסַח) Nm $9_{12.14}$, חֻקּוֹת הַמִּזְבֵּחַ *ordinances of the altar* Ezk $43_{18}$, בַּיִת *of the house of* Ezk $44_{5}$, [חו]קות מסרותם *statutes of their divisions* 4QShirShabb[f] $23.2_{13}$.

חֻקּוֹת הַתּוֹעֵבֹת *the customs of abominations*, i.e. abominable customs Lv $18_{30}$, חֻקַּת הַפָּרָה *statute of the cow* Nm $19_{2}$ (if em.; see above), חֻקּוֹת קָצִיר *fixed times of harvest* Jr $5_{24}$, חוקות מאור *fixed times of the luminary* 1QH $12_{5}$, חֻקֹּת יָרֵחַ *fixed time of the moon* Jr $31_{35}$, חֻקּוֹת שָׁמַיִם *ordinances of heaven* Jr $33_{25}$ Jb $38_{33}$, אֶרֶץ ... חֻקּוֹת *ordinances of ... earth* Jr $33_{25}$, חֻקַּת עוֹלָם *statute of eternity*, i.e. eternal statute Ex $12_{14.17}$ $27_{21}$ $28_{43}$ $29_{9}$ Lv $3_{17}$ $7_{36}$ $10_{9}$ $16_{29.31.34}$ $17_{7}$ $23_{14.21.31.41}$ $24_{3}$ Nm $10_{8}$ $15_{15}$ $18_{23}$ $19_{10.21}$ Ezk $46_{14(mss)}$ 4QD[b] $12_{2}$ 4QTohB[a] $1_{9}$ (חוקת] [עולם) 11QT $40_{3}$ (all three [חוקת עולם]), חֻקּוֹת עוֹלָם *statutes of eternity* Ezk $46_{14}$ 1QS $8_{10}$ 1QDM $4_{4}$ (חוקו]ת [עול]ם) 11QT $9_{14}$ ([חוקות עול]ם) $17_{3}$ ([חוקות עולם]) $18_{8}$ ([חו]קות עולם) $19_{8}$ ([חוקות עו]לם) $22_{14}$ $24_{8}$ (חוקות [עולם]) $25_{8}$ $27_{4}$.

כָּל־חֻקַּת שְׁבֻעוֹת חֻקּוֹת *weeks of fixed times of* Jr $5_{24}$, כָּל־חֻקַּת *every statute of* Nm $9_{12}$, כָּל־חֻקּוֹת *all statutes of* Ezk $44_{5}$, כָּל־חֻקֹּתַי *all my statutes* Lv $19_{37}$ Ezk $18_{19.21}$ (both חֻקּוֹתַי) 4QJub[a] $1_{14}$ ([כל חקותי]) 4QpsMos[e] $2.1_{5}$, כָּל־חֻקֹּתָיו *all his statutes* Nm $9_{3}$ Dt $6_{2}$ Ezk $43_{11.11}$ 4QPent Par[b] $6.2_{13}$ (כול חוקותיו).

<ADJ> אֶחָד *one* Nm $9_{14}$ $15_{15}$, זֶה *this* Ex $13_{10}$.

<PREP> לְ *as*, or introducing predicate, + היה *be* Ex $29_{9}$ Lv $16_{29.34}$ Nm $10_{8}$ $19_{10.21}$ $27_{11}$ $35_{29}$ 4QD[b] $12_{2}$, נוח hi. *place*, i.e. establish 4QTohB[a] $1_{9}$; *according to* 1QH $12_{5}$, קום hi. *raise up*, i.e. establish 1QS $8_{10}$.

בְּ of accompaniment, *with, in*, + הלך *go* Lv $18_{3}$ $20_{23}$ $26_{3}$ 1 K $3_{3}$ $6_{12}$ 2 K $17_{8.19}$ Jr $44_{10}$ (|| תּוֹרָה *law*) $44_{23}$ (|| תּוֹרָה, עֵדוּת *testimony*) Ezk $5_{6.7}$ $11_{20}$ $18_{9}$ (if em.) $18_{17}$ $20_{13.16.19.21}$ $33_{15}$ 4QpHos[b] $7_{2}$ 11QT $59_{16}$, pi. *go* Ezk $18_{9}$ (or em. Qal); שׁעע בְּ htpalp. *delight in* Ps $119_{16}$; introducing object, + מאס *refuse* Lv $26_{15}$; *according to* 4QShir Shabb[d] $1.2_{21}$.

כְּ *according to*, + עשׂה *do* Nm $9_{3.12.14}$ 2 K $17_{34}$.

מִן of direction, *from*, + סור *depart* 2 S $22_{23}$; partitive, *some of*, + עשׂה *do* Lv $18_{30}$.

<SYN> תּוֹרָה *law*, מִצְוָה *commandment*, עֵדוּת *testimony*, מִשְׁפָּט *judgment*, בְּרִית *covenant*.

<COLL> חֻקַּת עוֹלָם תְּחָגֻּהוּ *you will celebrate it (as) an eternal statute* Ex $12_{14}$, חֻקַּת עוֹלָם ... שְׁמַרְתֶּם *you will keep it ... (as) an eternal statute* Ex $12_{17}$.

Also 1Q57$_{2}$ 4QJub[e] $21_{5}$ ([חקותיו]) 4QapPs[b] $20_{2}$.*

⇒ חקק *engrave*.

**חֲקוּפָא** 2 pr.n.m. **Hakupha,** name of family of Nethinim, postexilic temple servants, <CSTR> בְּנֵי־חֲקוּפָא *sons of Hakupha* Ezr $2_{51}$||Ne $7_{53}$.

**חקק** 19.1.19 vb. **engrave—Qal** 9.0.11 Pf. Q חקק (Q חקקא), Q חקותה, חַקֹּתִיךָ; + waw וְחַקּוֹתָ; impv. חֻקָּה; ptc. sf. חֹקְקִי, pl. חֹקְקִים, cstr. חוֹקְקֵי; ptc. pass. Q חקוק, pl. חֲקֻקִים; inf. חוּקוֹ (חוקו)—**1. cut, engrave, decree,** <SUBJ> יי *Y.* Is $49_{16}$=4QTanh $1.2_{4}$ ([חקותי]ך) Pr $8_{27.29}$ 4Q185 $1.2_{4}$ perh. 1Q25 $1_{4}$ 1QH $18_{11.27}$, אֵל *God* 1QpHab $7_{13}$ 1QS $10_{1}$ 4QD[e] $9.2_{18}$, appar. Isaiah Is $30_{8}$, Shebna Is $22_{16}$, בֶּן *son* of human being Ezk $4_{1}$, wicked Is $10_{1}$, מְחֹקֵק *staff* CD $6_{9}$.

<OBJ> Zion Is $49_{16}$, עִיר *city* Ezk $4_{1}$, מִשְׁכָּן *dwelling place* Is $22_{16}$, מוֹסָד *foundation* of earth Pr $8_{29}$ (perh. חוק II *gather*)*, חֹק *decree* Is $10_{1}$, מִצְוָה *commandment* 1Q25 $1_{4}$ ([המ]צות), קָו *measuring line* 1QH $18_{11}$ ([קו]ים), חוּג *circle* Pr $8_{27}$, קֵץ *time* 1QS $10_{1}$, מְחֹקֵק *staff* CD $6_{9}$.

<PREP> לְ of direction 1Q25 $1_{4}$, *to*, + אִישׁ *man* 1Qp

Hab 7$_{13}$; of benefit, *to, for*, + Isaac 4Q185 1.2$_{4}$.

בְּ of place, *in, on* 4QDe 9.2$_{18}$, + לָשׁוֹן *tongue* 1QH 18$_{11}$, סֶלַע *rock* Is 22$_{16}$, רָז *mystery* 1QpHab 7$_{13}$.

עַל *upon, in*, + סֵפֶר *inscription* Is 30$_{8}$, לְבֵנָה *brick* Ezk 4$_{1}$, כַּף *palm* of hand Is 49$_{16}$, פָּנֶה *face* of deep Pr 8$_{27}$; *concerning*, + קָו *line* 1QH 18$_{11}$.

**2.** pass. **be decreed** (4Q247$_{1}$ 4QDa 2.1$_{3}$), **be engraved** (Ezk 23$_{14}$ 1QH 1$_{24}$ 4Q417 2.1$_{14}$), <SUBJ> קֵץ *time* 4Q247$_{1}$ (קץ ח]קוק]) 4QDa 2.1$_{3}$, צֶלֶם *image* Ezk 23$_{14}$, פְּקֻדָּה *visitation* 4Q417 2.1$_{14}$, כֹּל *everything* 1QH 1$_{24}$. <PREP> לְ of direction, *to* + קֵץ *time* 1QH 1$_{24}$; of benefit, *to, for*, + עַם *people* 4QDa 2.1$_{3}$; בְּ of instrument, *by (means of), with* + שָׁשַׁר *vermilion* Ezk 23$_{14}$, חֶרֶת *ink* of remembrance 1QH 1$_{24}$; לִפְנֵי *before*, + Y. 1QH 1$_{24}$.

**3.** ptc. as noun, **commander,** <SUBJ> נדב htp. *volunteer oneself* Jg 5$_{9}$. <CSTR> חוֹקְקֵי יִשְׂרָאֵל *commanders of Israel* Jg 5$_{9}$. <PREP> לְ of direction Jg 5$_{9}$.

**Pu.** 1.0.2 Ptc. מְחֻקָּק (מחוקק), Q מחוקקי—**1. be engraved,** <SUBJ> בְּדָן *form* 4QShirShabbf 19$_{5}$. <PREP> סָבִיב לְ *round about*, + לְבֵן *brickwork* 4QShirShabbf 19$_{5}$.

**2.** ptc. used as noun, **decree,** <SUBJ> חרת pass. *be engraved* 4Q417 2.1$_{15}$. <OBJ> שׁכח *forget* Pr 31$_{5}$.

**Po.** 8.1.6 Impf. יְחֹקְקוּ; ptc. מְחֹקֵק (Si, Q מחוקק), sf. מְחֹקְקִי, מְחֹקְקֵנוּ, pl. מְחֹקְקִים, Q מחוקקות—**decree,** <SUBJ> רֹזֵן *ruler* Pr 8$_{15}$. <OBJ> צֶדֶק *righteousness* Pr 8$_{15}$.

**2.** ptc. used as noun, **commander** (Dt 33$_{21}$=4QMidr Eschata 2$_{4}$ Jg 5$_{14}$ Is 33$_{22}$ Si 10$_{5}$), **commander's staff, sceptre** (Gn 49$_{10}$ Nm 21$_{18}$ Ps 60$_{9}$=108$_{9}$ CD 6$_{4.7.9.9}$ 4QpGena 1.5$_{2}$ unless *portion* in Gn 49$_{10}$ Nm 21$_{18}$ Ps 60$_{9}$=108$_{9}$*), <SUBJ> ירד *go down* Jg 5$_{14}$, סור *depart* Gn 49$_{10}$, חקק *decree* CD 6$_{9}$. <NOM CL> י' מְחֹקְקֵנוּ *Y. is our commander* Is 33$_{22}$, יְהוּדָה מְחֹקְקִי *Judah is my sceptre* Ps 60$_{9}$=108$_{9}$, המחקק היא ברית המלכות *the staff is the covenant of royalty* 4QpGena 1.5$_{2}$, המחוקק הוא דורש התורה *the staff is the seeker of the law* CD 6$_{7}$. <CSTR> חֶלְקַת מְחֹקֵק *portion of the commander* Dt 33$_{21}$=4QMidrEschata 2$_{4}$ (חלקת] מחקק]). <PREP> בְּ of instrument, *by (means of)*, + כרה *dig* Nm 21$_{18}$ CD 6$_{4.9}$; לִפְנֵי *before*, + שִׁית *place* Si 10$_{5}$.

**Ho.** 1 Impf. יֻחָקוּ—**be inscribed,** <SUBJ> מִלָּה *word* Jb 19$_{23}$. <PREP> בְּ *of place, in, on*, + סֵפֶר *book* Jb 19$_{23}$.*

⇒ חֹק *statute*, חֻקָּה *statute*, חוּקֹק *Hukok*.

**חקר I** 27.8.8 vb. **search—Qal** 22.8.7. Pf. חָקַר (Si חקר, Si חקרך), חֲקָרוֹ, חֲקָרָהּ, חֲקַרְתַּנִי, חֲקַרְנוּהָ; impf. יַחְקֹר (Si יחקר), יַחְקְרוּ, אֶחְקְרֵהוּ, אֶחְקֹר (Si תחקור), Si תחקר, יַחְקְרֻנוּ, נַחְקְרָה (Si נחקור), תַּחְקְרוּן; impv. חִקְרֵנִי (Si חקר), חִקְרוּ; ptc. חֹקֵר (חוקר), חֹקְרֵי (Si חוקרי); inf. חֲקוֹר (חָקְרָהּ, לַחְקֹר, לַחְקוֹר, חֲקֹר)—**search (out), explore, investigate.**

<SUBJ> י' Y. Jr 17$_{10}$ Ps 139$_{1}$ (+ ידע *know*), אֱלֹהִים *God* Ps 44$_{22}$ Si 42$_{18}$ 4Q392 1$_{4}$, אֵל *God* Ps 139$_{23}$ (+ ידע *know*) Jb 13$_{9}$ 28$_{27}$ 1QM 16$_{13}$ (חוקר אל]]), Israelite(s) Dt 13$_{15}$=11QT 55$_{5}$ (|| דרשׁ *seek*, שׁאל *ask*) Lm 3$_{40}$ Si 43$_{28.30(Bmg)}$ 11QT 55$_{19}$, Eliphaz Jb 5$_{27}$, Job Jb 29$_{16}$, Jonathan 1 S 20$_{12}$, אִישׁ *man* Jg 18$_{2.2}$ Ezk 39$_{14}$, בֵּן *son* Si 3$_{21}$ 6$_{27}$ 11$_{7.27}$, מֶלֶךְ *king* Pr 25$_{2}$, עֶבֶד *servant* 2 S 10$_{3}$||1 C 19$_{3}$, נָדִיב *noble one* Si 13$_{11}$, דַּל *poor one* Pr 28$_{11}$ (unless חקר II *despise*), friend of Job Jb 5$_{27}$ 32$_{11}$, רֵעַ *friend* Pr 18$_{17}$, בוא ptc. *one who comes* Pr 23$_{30}$, miner Jb 28$_{3}$, poet Si 44$_{5}$; subj. not specified, 4QMystc 1$_{2}$ 2$_{1}$.

<OBJ> אֶרֶץ *land* Jg 18$_{2.2}$ 1 C 19$_{3}$, עִיר *city* 2 S 10$_{3}$, אָדָם *human being* Si 11$_{27}$, אָב *father* 1 S 20$_{12}$, בֵּן *son* Si 13$_{11}$, עָשִׁיר *rich one* Pr 28$_{11}$ (unless חקר II *despise*), worshipper Ps 139$_{1.23}$, friends of Job Jb 13$_{9}$, רִאשׁוֹן *former one* Pr 18$_{17}$, לֵב *heart* Jr 17$_{10}$ Si 42$_{18}$, גָּדוֹל *great deed* 4QDibHama 6$_{21}$, חָכְמָה *wisdom* Jb 28$_{27}$, רִיב *case* Jb 29$_{16}$, דָּבָר *word* Pr 25$_{2}$, מִלָּה *word* Jb 32$_{11}$, מִזְמוֹר *psalm* Si 44$_{5}$, דֶּרֶךְ *way* Lm 3$_{40}$ 4Q185 1.2$_{1}$ 4Q392 1$_{4}$, אֶבֶן *stone* Jb 28$_{3}$, שֹׁרֶשׁ *root* 4QMystc 1$_{2}$, מִמְסָךְ *mixed wine* Pr 23$_{30}$, תְּהוֹם *deep* Si 42$_{18}$, כסה pu. ptc. *that which is concealed* Si 3$_{21}$, זֹאת *this* Ps 44$_{22}$ Jb 5$_{27}$.

<PREP> לְ of direction, *to*, + תַּכְלִית *extremity* Jb 28$_{3}$; of benefit, *to, for* 4Q185 1.2$_{1}$.

בְּ of accompaniment, *with, in*, + צֶדֶק *righteousness* 1QM 16$_{13}$ (חוקר ... בצדק]]); introducing object, + שֹׁרֶשׁ *root* 4QMystc 2$_{1}$.

מִן *at*, + קֵץ *end* Ezk 39$_{14}$.

עַל *according to*, + חֹק *statute* Si 44$_{5}$.

Also perh. 4Q298 1$_{4}$.

<SYN> דרשׁ *seek*, שׁאל *ask*.

**Ni.** 4 Pf. נֶחְקַר; impf. יֵחָקֵר, יֵחָקְרוּ—**be searched out, be ascertained,** <SUBJ> יַעַר *forest* Jr 46$_{23}$, מוֹסָד *foundation* of earth Jr 31$_{37}$, מִשְׁקָל *weight* of bronze 1 K 7$_{47}$||2 C 4$_{18}$.

**Pi.** 1.0.1 Pf. חִקֵּר; inf. לחקיר—**search out,** <SUBJ> Koheleth Ec 12$_{9}$ (|| אזן pi. *weigh*). Also 4QPsJosa 1$_{18}$. <OBJ> מָשָׁל *proverb* Ec 12$_{9}$. <SYN> אזן pi. *weigh.**
→ חֵקֶר *searching,* מֶחְקָר *exploration.*

* **חקר II** 1 vb. **despise—Qal** 1 Impf. יַחְקְרֶנּוּ—<SUBJ> דַּל *poor one* Pr 28$_{11}$ (unless חקר I *search*), <OBJ> עָשִׁיר *rich one* Pr 28$_{11}$ (unless חקר I *search*).

**חֵ֫קֶר** 12.2.11 n.m. **searching**—pl. cstr. חִקְרֵי—**searching (out); (object of) searching out, depth** of ocean (Jb 38$_{16}$), of God (Jb 11$_{7}$), of hidden things (Si 42$_{19}$).

<NOM CL> גְּדוֹלִים חִקְרֵי־לֵב *great were the searchings of heart* Jg 5$_{16}$, חֵקֶר כְּבֹדָם כָּבוֹד *the searching of their glory is glory* Pr 25$_{27}$ (or em. הֹקַר דִּבְרֵי כָבוֹד *and be sparing with,* or *value, honourable words*), אֵין חֵקֶר *there is no searching,* i.e. it cannot be found Is 40$_{28}$ Jb 5$_{9}$ 9$_{10}$ Ps 145$_{3}$ Pr 25$_{3}$ 1QH 3$_{20}$ 6$_{3.17}$ ([אין]) 8$_{17}$ 18$_{30}$ (both חן[קר]) fr. 2$_{15}$ ([אין חקר]) 4Q181 2$_{6}$ 4Q185 1.2$_{15}$ 4QapPsb 33$_{3}$ 76$_{4}$ (חן[קר]) 4Q392 1$_{7}$ 2$_{4}$ 4QHodb 4$_{2}$ ([אין חקר]) 11QPsa 19$_{9}$.

<OBJ> גלה pi. *reveal* Si 42$_{19}$, מצא *find* Jb 11$_{7}$.

<CSTR> חֵקֶר אֲבוֹתָם *searching of their fathers* Jb 8$_{8}$, חִקְרֵי־לֵב *searchings of heart* Jg 5$_{16}$, חֵקֶר כְּבֹדָם *searching of their glory* Pr 25$_{27}$, חֵקֶר אֱלוֹהַּ *depth of God* Jb 11$_{7}$, חֵקֶר תְּהוֹם *depth of ocean* Jb 38$_{16}$, חקר נסתרות *searching of hidden things,* i.e. hidden things to be searched out Si 42$_{19}$.

<PREP> לְ introducing object, + כון pol. *consider* Jb 8$_{8}$. בְּ of place, *in, at, among,* + הלך htp. *walk to and fro* Jb 38$_{16}$; of accompaniment, *with, in,* + יצא *go out* Si 14$_{22}$.

<COLL> יָרֹעַ כַּבִּירִים לֹא־חֵקֶר *he breaks the mighty ones (without) searching,* perh. without prior investigation or without number Jb 34$_{24}$, מִסְפַּר שָׁנָיו לֹא־חֵקֶר *the number of his years is (beyond) searching* Jb 36$_{26}$.

Also 1QH fr. 15$_{5}$ 1QMyst 13$_{3}$ (חקרן[י]).*
→ חקר *search.*

**[חִקָּר]** 0.0.1 pl.n. **Hikkar,** in list of place names, 4Q522 1.1$_{13}$.

**חֹר I** 13.1 n.m. **noble**—pl. חֹרִים (חוֹרִים); cstr. חֹרֵי; sf. חֹרֶיהָ—**noble,** as leading member of community, <SUBJ> ישׁב *dwell* 1 K 21$_{11}$ (+ זָקֵן *elder*), עשׂה *do* 1 K 21$_{11}$, רבה hi. *increase* Ne 6$_{17}$, עבד *serve* Si 10$_{25(B)}$, קרא *call* Is 34$_{12}$ (or em. חֹרֶיהָ *its nobles* to חֲדֶיהָ *its limits,* as obj. of נטה *extend*). <OBJ> קבץ *assemble* Ne 7$_{5}$, גלה *exile* Jr 27$_{20}$, שׁחט *slaughter* Jr 39$_{6}$. <CSTR> חֹרֵי יְהוּדָה *nobles of Judah* Jr 39$_{6}$ Ne 6$_{17}$ 13$_{17}$; בֶּן־חוֹרִים *son of nobles* Ec 10$_{17}$, כָּל־חֹרֵי *all the nobles of* Jr 27$_{20}$ 39$_{6}$. <APP> אִישׁ *man* 1 K 21$_{11}$. <PREP> לְ of direction, *to,* + נגד hi. *declare* Ne 2$_{16}$; אֶל *to,* + שׁלח *send* 1 K 21$_{8}$ (+ זָקֵן *elder*), אמר *say* Ne 4$_{8.13}$; אֶת *with,* + ריב *dispute* Ne 5$_{7}$ 13$_{17}$.*

**חֹר II** 7 n.[m.] **hole**—mss חוֹר; pl. חֹרִים; cstr. חֹרֵי; sf. חֹרָיו, חֹרֵיהֶם—as hiding place (1 S 14$_{11}$), dwelling place (Jb 30$_{6}$), den of lions (Na 2$_{13}$), socket of eye (Zc 14$_{12}$), in wall (Ezk 8$_{7}$), in lid of chest (2 K 12$_{10}$), perh. in door (Ca 5$_{4}$), <NOM CL> הִנֵּה חֹר־אֶחָד בַּקִּיר *behold, there was a hole in the wall* Ezk 8$_{7}$. <OBJ> נקב *bore* 2 K 12$_{10}$, מלא pi. *fill* with prey Na 2$_{13}$ (|| מְעֹנָה *lair*). <CSTR> חֹרֵי עָפָר וְכֵפִים *holes of,* i.e. in, *dust and rocks* Jb 30$_{6}$. <APP> עָרוּץ perh. *slope* of wadi Jb 30$_{6}$. <ADJ> אֶחָד *one* Ezk 8$_{7}$. <PREP> בְּ of place, *in,* + שׁכן *dwell* Jb 30$_{6}$, מקק ni. *rot* Zc 14$_{12}$; מִן of direction, *from,* + יצא *go out* 1 S 14$_{11}$, שׁלח *send* Ca 5$_{4}$. <COLL> הַחֹרִים אֲשֶׁר הִתְחַבְּאוּ־שָׁם *the holes where they hid* 1 S 14$_{11}$. <SYN> מְעֹנָה *lair.*

**[חֻר]** 2 n.[m.] **hole**—cstr. חֻר; pl. חוּרִים—of snake (Is 11$_{8}$), as hiding place of people (Is 42$_{22}$), <CSTR> חֻר פָּתֶן *hole of the asp* Is 11$_{8}$ (|| מְאוּרָה *light-hole*). <PREP> בְּ of place, *in,* + פחח hi. *ensnare* Is 42$_{22}$ (or em. הָפֵחַ בַּחוּרִים *ensnaring in holes* to הֻפַּחוּ בְחוּרִים *ensnared in holes,* from חור *hole*); עַל *over,* + שׁעע pilp. *play* Is 11$_{8}$. <SYN> מְאוּרָה *light-hole.*

**[חֲרָא]** 0.0.1 adv. perh. **afterwards,** <COLL> לחרא (perh. = לְאַחֲרָא) *for afterwards* 4Q422 2$_{11}$.

**[חֶ֫רֶא]** 3 n.[m.] **dung**—cstr. Kt חרי; sf. חריהם; pl. sf. חראיהם (Q חריהמה)—<OBJ> אכל *eat* 2 K 18$_{27(Kt)}$||Is 36$_{12}$ (Qr צֹאָה *filth;* || שַׁיִן *urine*). <CSTR> חריונים *doves' dung,* perh. carob pods or star of Bethlehem as medicinal plant 2 K 6$_{25(Kt)}$ (Qr דִּבְיוֹנִים *dove's dung*). <APP> רֹבַע *quarter* kab 2 K 6$_{25}$. <SYN> שַׁיִן *urine.**

**חרב I** $_{37.1.6}$ vb. **be dry, be desolate—Qal** $_{15.1.1}$ Pf. חָרְבוּ; impf. יֶחֱרַב, 3fs תֶּחֱרַב (תֶּחֱרָב), יֶחֶרְבוּ (יֶחֱרָבוּ), תֶּחֱרַבְנָה; + waw וַיֶּחֱרַב, וְחָרְבוּ; impv. חָרְבִי, חָרְבוּ; inf. abs. חָרֹב—**be dry, be dried up, be wasted away, be desolate,** <SUBJ> Edom Is 34$_{10}$, גּוֹי *nation* Is 60$_{12}$, עִיר *city* Jr 26$_{9}$ Ezk 6$_{6}$ 12$_{20}$ Si 16$_{4}$, מִקְדָּשׁ *sanctuary* Am 7$_{9}$, מִזְבֵּחַ *altar* Ezk 6$_{6}$, שָׁמַיִם *heaven* Jr 2$_{12}$ (|| שׁמם *be desolated*), צוּלָה *abyss* Is 44$_{27}$, יָם *sea* Ps 106$_{9}$, נָהָר *river* Is 19$_{5}$ Jb 14$_{11}$ (both || יבשׁ *be dry*), יְאֹר *branch of Nile* Is 19$_{6}$ (+ דלל *be small*), מַיִם *water* Gn 8$_{13}$ 4QpGen$^a$ 1.1$_{21.22}$ ([חרבו]), מַעְיָן *fountain* Ho 13$_{15}$, פָּנֶה *face*, i.e. surface, of the ground Gn 8$_{13}$.

<PREP> לְ of direction, *to*, + דּוֹר from generation to *generation* Is 34$_{10}$; מִן of direction, *from*, + דּוֹר *generation* Is 34$_{10}$; of agent, *by (means of)*, + מִשְׁפָּחָה *family* of traitors Si 16$_{4}$; מֵעַל *from (upon)*, + אֶרֶץ *earth* Gn 8$_{13}$ 4QpGen$^a$ 1.1$_{21}$. <SYN> יבשׁ *be dry*, שׁמם *be desolate.*

**Ni.** $_{2}$ Ptc. נֶחֱרֶבֶת, נֶחֱרָבוֹת—**be laid waste,** <SUBJ> עִיר *city* Ezk 26$_{19}$ 30$_{7}$.

**Pu.** $_{2}$ Pf. חֹרְבוּ—**be dried up,** <SUBJ> יֶתֶר *cord* Jg 16$_{7.8}$.

**Hi.** $_{13.0.5}$ Pf. הֶחֱרִיב, הֶחֱרַבְתִּי, הֶחֱרִיבוּ; impf. אַחֲרִיב (אַחְרִב); + waw וְהַחֲרַבְתִּי; ptc. מַחֲרִיב, מַחֲרֶבֶת, מַחֲרִבֵךְ; inf. Q לחריב, להחריבה—**dry up, lay waste,** <SUBJ> appar. Kittim 1QpHab 6$_{8}$, י׳ *Y.* Is 11$_{15}$ (if em. וְהֶחֱרִים *and he will destroy* to וְהֶחֱרִיב *and he will dry up*) 42$_{15}$ 50$_{2}$ Jr 51$_{36}$ Na 1$_{4}$ Zp 3$_{6}$, זְרוֹעַ *arm* of Y. Is 51$_{10}$, Sennacherib 2 K 19$_{24}$||Is 37$_{25}$, Samson Jg 16$_{24}$, מֶלֶךְ *king* 2 K 19$_{17.24}$||Is 37$_{18.25}$, perh. נָשִׂיא *prince* 1QSb 5$_{24}$, enemies Is 49$_{17}$=4QTanḥ 1.2$_{5}$ ([חרביך]), כְּפִיר *young lion* Ezk 19$_{7}$, perh. חֵמָה *anger* 4QDibHam$^a$ 1.5$_{5}$.

<OBJ> אֶרֶץ *land* Jg 16$_{24}$ 2 K 19$_{17}$||Is 37$_{18}$ 1QpHab 6$_{8}$ 1QSb 5$_{24}$ 4QDibHam$^a$ 1.5$_{5}$, גּוֹי *nation* 2 K 19$_{17}$||Is 37$_{18}$, Zion Is 49$_{17}$=4QTanḥ 1.2$_{5}$, הַר *mountain* Is 42$_{15}$, גִּבְעָה *hill* Is 42$_{15}$, עִיר *city* Ezk 19$_{7}$, חוּץ *street* Zp 3$_{6}$, יָם *sea* Is 50$_{2}$ 51$_{10}$ Jr 51$_{36}$, נָהָר *river* Na 1$_{4}$, יְאֹר *branch of Nile* 2 K 19$_{24}$||Is 37$_{25}$, מַיִם *water* Is 51$_{10}$, לָשׁוֹן *tongue* of sea of Egypt Is 11$_{15}$ (if em.; see Subj.).

<PREP> בְּ of instrument, *by (means of)*, + כַּף *sole* of foot 2 K 19$_{24}$||Is 37$_{25}$, גְּעָרָה *rebuke* Is 50$_{2}$.

Also 4Q458 1$_{9}$.

**Ho.** $_{2}$ Pf. הָחֳרָבָה; ptc. מָחֳרָבוֹת—**be laid waste,** <SUBJ> Jerusalem Ezk 26$_{2}$ (or em. אִמָּלְאָה הָחֳרָבָה *I [Tyre] am full, she [Jerusalem] has been laid waste* to מְלֵאַת הַחֲרֵבָה *the full one of ruin*, from חָרֵב *devastated*), עִיר *city* Ezk 29$_{12}$ (or em. מָחֳרָבוֹת *ruined* to חֲרֵבוֹת, from חָרֵב).*

⇒ חָרֵב *dry*, חֹרֶב *drought*, חָרָבָה *dry ground*, חֲרָבוֹן *drought*, חָרְבָּה *waste*.

**חרב II** $_{4}$ vb. **destroy—Qal** $_{2}$ Impv. חֲרֹב, חֲרֹבוּ—<SUBJ> enemies Jr 50$_{21}$ (+ חרם hi. *put to ban*) 50$_{27}$. <OBJ> יֹשֵׁב *inhabitant* Jr 50$_{21}$, פַּר *bull* Jr 50$_{27}$ (or em. פְּרִי *fruit*).

**Ni.** $_{1}$ Pf. נֶחֶרְבוּ—**be destroyed,** <SUBJ> מֶלֶךְ *king* 2 K 3$_{23}$. <COLL> see Ho. Coll.

**Ho.** $_{1}$ Inf. abs. הָחֳרֵב—**be destroyed,** <COLL> הָחֳרֵב נֶחֶרְבוּ *they must have been destroyed* 2 K 3$_{23}$ (or em. הָחֳרֵב to הֵחָרֵב, i.e. ni. inf. abs., or to הַחֶרֶב *[of] the sword*).*

**חָרֵב** $_{10.0.2}$ adj. **dry, devastated**—fem. חֲרֵבָה; pl. חֲרֵבוֹת—**1a. dry,** used attributively of מִנְחָה *grain offering* Lv 7$_{10}$ (+ בְּלוּלָה בַשֶּׁמֶן *mixed with oil*), פַּת *morsel* Pr 17$_{1}$. **1b. devastated, in ruins,** used attributively of עִיר *city* Ezk 29$_{12}$ (if em. מָחֳרָבוֹת ho. ptc. *ruined* to חֲרֵבוֹת) 36$_{35}$ (|| שׁמם ni. ptc. *devastated*, הרס ni. ptc. *overthrown*) 36$_{38}$, מָקוֹם *place* Jr 33$_{12}$ (+ מֵאֵין אָדָם וְעַד־בְּהֵמָה *without human beings or beasts*).

**2a. dry,** in nom. cl. used predicatively of מִנְחָה *grain offering* 11QT 20$_{10}$ ([כו]ל מחנה [א]שר קרב עליה לבונה או חרבה *every grain offering with which frankincense is offered or [that is] dry*). **2b. devastated, in ruins,** in nom. cl. used predicatively of Jerusalem Ne 2$_{17}$, עִיר *city* Ne 2$_{3}$, בַּיִת *house*, i.e. graveyard Ne 2$_{3}$, i.e. temple Hg 1$_{4.9}$, מָקוֹם *place* Jr 33$_{10}$.

**3.** as noun, **ruin,** <NOM CL> perh. וקברכה חרב *and your grave will be a ruin* Ḥorvat 'Uza bowl inscr.$_{15}$. <CSTR> מְלֵאַת הַחֲרֵבָה *the full one of ruin*, i.e. the one full of ruins (in ref. to Jerusalem) Ezk 26$_{2}$ (if em. אִמָּלְאָה הָחֳרָבָה *I [Tyre] am full, she [Jerusalem] has been laid waste*).

<SYN> §1b שׁמם ni. ptc. *devastated*, הרס ni. ptc. *overthrown*.*

⇒ חרב *be dry*

**חֶ֫רֶב** 411.2.55 n.f. **sword**—cstr. חֶרֶב (חֲרֶב); sf. חַרְבִּי, חַרְבְּךָ, חַרְבֵּךְ (Q חרבכה), חַרְבּוֹ, חַרְבְּכֶם, חַרְבָּם; pl. חֲרָבוֹת; cstr. חַרְבוֹת; sf. חַרְבוֹתָיו, חַרְבוֹתָם (חַרְבֹתֵיהֶם)—**1. sword,** used in war (e.g. Gn 48$_{22}$ Jg 7$_{14.20}$ 1 S 21$_{9}$ Ps 149$_{6}$). **2. knife,** for circumcision (Jos 5$_{2.3}$), shaving (Ezk 5$_{1}$). **3. sharp tool,** for hewing stone (Ex 20$_{25}$=4QBibPar 7$_{8}$), etc.

<SUBJ> היה *be* 1 S 14$_{20}$ Jr 14$_{15}$ (|| רָעָב *famine*) Ezk 38$_{21}$, קרא *befall* Is 51$_{19}$ (|| רָעָב *famine*, שֶׁבֶר *destruction*, שֹׁד *devastation*), מלא *be full* Is 34$_{6}$, תמם *cease* 4QHod$^{c}$ 2.2$_{12}$ ([ח]רבות), שׂבע *be sated* Jr 46$_{10}$, חוש *make haste* 1QH 6$_{29}$, חול *whirl* Ho 11$_{6}$, לוט pass. *be wrapped* 1 S 21$_{10}$, אסר pass. *be bound* Ne 4$_{12}$, צמד pu. *be fastened* 2 S 20$_{8}$, עור be awake Zc 13$_{7}$=CD 19$_{7}$, חדד ho. *be sharpened* Ezk 21$_{14.14.16}$, לטשׁ pass. *be sharpened* Is 21$_{15}$=4QpIsa$^{e}$ 5$_{5}$ (if em. נְטוּשָׁה *drawn* to לְטוּשָׁה), מרט pass. *be polished* Ezk 21$_{14}$ (or em. מְרוּטָה to מֹרָטָה, i.e. pu.) 21$_{33}$, pu. *be polished* Ezk 21$_{16}$ (or em. מֹרָטָה *it has been polished* to מְרָטָהּ *he has polished it*), כפל ni. *be doubled* Ezk 21$_{19}$, שׁלשׁ pu. *be trebled* Ezk 21$_{19}$ (if em. שְׁלִישִׁתָה perh. *thrice* to וְשֻׁלְּשָׁה *and it shall be trebled*).

שׁלף pass. *be drawn* Nm 22$_{23.31}$ Jos 5$_{13}$ 1 C 21$_{16}$, נטשׁ pass. *be drawn* Is 21$_{15}$=4QpIsa$^{e}$ 5$_{5}$ (unless em.; see above; || קֶשֶׁת *bow*, + מִלְחָמָה *battle*), פתח pass. *be drawn* Ezk 21$_{33}$, מצא ni. *be found* 1 S 13$_{22}$ (|| חֲנִית *spear*), נתן ni. *be given* Ezk 32$_{20}$ (or em. נִתָּנָה to אִתּוֹ a sword is *with him*), בוא *come* Ezk 21$_{24.25}$ 30$_{4}$ 32$_{11}$ 33$_{3.4.6}$ Ps 37$_{15}$=4QpPs$^{a}$ 1.2$_{16}$ (+ קֶשֶׁת *bow*) 2 C 20$_{9}$ (|| שְׁפוֹט *judgment*, רָעָב *famine*, דֶּבֶר *pestilence*), מושׁ *depart* 4QpNah 3.2$_{5}$ (+ שְׁבִי *captives*, בַּז *plunder*, חַרְחֻר *violent heat*), הלך *go* Jr 48$_{2}$, עבר *pass* Lv 26$_{6}$ Ezk 14$_{17}$ 11QBer 1$_{13}$ (חרב לוא תעבו[ר]), נשׂג hi. *overtake* Jr 42$_{16}$ Jb 41$_{18}$ (+ חֲנִית, מַסָּע *dart*, שִׁרְיָה *javelin*) 1 C 21$_{12}$, נגע *reach* Jr 4$_{10}$, שׁוב *go back* 2 S 1$_{22}$ (|| קֶשֶׁת) Ezk 21$_{10}$, יצא *go out* Ezk 21$_{9}$, סור *depart* 2 S 12$_{10}$, חדר *penetrate deeply* Ezk 21$_{19}$, perh. ינה *oppress* Jr 25$_{38(mss)}$ 46$_{16}$ 50$_{16}$ (but prob. חֶרֶב הַיּוֹנָה is *sword of the oppressor*), נקם *avenge* Lv 26$_{25}$ CD 1$_{17}$ 19$_{13}$, לקח *take* Ezk 33$_{4}$, שׁכל pi. *bereave of children* Dt 32$_{25}$ 1 S 15$_{33}$ Lm 1$_{20}$.

אכל *eat*, i.e. destroy Dt 32$_{42}$ (+ חֵץ *arrow*) 2 S 2$_{26}$ 11$_{25}$ 18$_{8}$ Is 31$_{8}$=1QM 11$_{11}$ Jr 2$_{30}$ 12$_{12}$ 46$_{10.14}$ Ho 11$_{6}$ Na 2$_{14}$=4QpNah 3.1$_{9}$ 1QM 6$_{3}$ 12$_{10}$ 19$_{4}$, כרת hi. *destroy* Na 3$_{15}$ (|| אֵשׁ *fire*), כלה pi. *destroy* Ho 11$_{6}$, טבח *slaughter* Ezk 21$_{14}$, הרג *kill* Jr 15$_{3}$ (+ כֶּלֶב *dog*, עוֹף *bird*, בְּהֵמָה *beast*) Am 9$_{4}$, חרם hi. *exterminate* Si 39$_{30(B)}$ (+ חַיָּה *wild animal*, עַקְרָב *scorpion*, פֶּתֶן *viper*), רום hi. *raise* Si 39$_{30(Bmg)}$, ישׁע hi. *save* Ps 44$_{7}$, רוה *drink one's fill* Is 34$_{5}$ (1QIsa$^{a}$ תראה *it will be seen*) Jr 46$_{10}$.

<NOM CL> חַרְבוֹת שִׁנָּיו *his teeth are swords* Pr 30$_{14}$, חַרְבּוֹ גַּאֲוָתֶךָ *his sword is your pride* Dt 33$_{29}$ (if em. וַאֲשֶׁר חֶרֶב גַּאֲוָתֶךָ *and who is the sword of your pride*; or em. וְשַׁדַּי חֶרֶב גַּאֲוָתֶךָ *and the Almighty is the sword of your pride*; Sam גֵּאֻתְךָ *your pride*), אִישׁ ... חֶרֶב *a man* who bears false witness ... *is a sword* Pr 25$_{18}$ (|| חֵץ *arrow*, מֵפִיץ *scatterer*), לְשׁוֹנָם חֶרֶב *their tongue is a sword* Ps 57$_{5}$ (+ חֵץ *arrow*, חֲנִית *spear*).

חֲרָבוֹת בְּשִׂפְתוֹתֵיהֶם *swords are within their lips* Ps 59$_{8}$ (unless חֶרְבָּה *deceit*), חֶרֶב ... בְּיָדָם *a sword ... is in their hands* Ps 149$_{6}$, חַרְבּוֹ ... בְּיָדוֹ *his sword ... is in his hand* Nm 22$_{23.31}$ Jos 5$_{13}$ 1 C 21$_{16}$, חַרְבּוֹ בְּצַד *his sword was in the side of* his neighbour 2 S 2$_{16}$, הַחֶרֶב בַּחוּץ *the sword is on the outside* Ezk 7$_{15}$ (ms מִחוּץ *from the outside*; + דֶּבֶר *pestilence*, רָעָב *famine*).

חֶרֶב אִתּוֹ *a sword is with him* Ezk 32$_{20}$ (if em.; see Subj.).

חַרְבּוֹ עַל־יְרֵכוֹ *his sword is upon his thigh* Ca 3$_{8}$, חֶרֶב עַל־כַּשְׂדִּים *a sword is against the Chaldaeans* Jr 50$_{35}$, חֶרֶב עַל־זְרוֹעוֹ *a sword is upon his arm* Zc 11$_{17}$.

חֶרֶב אֶל־הַבַּדִּים *a sword is to the prattlers* Jr 50$_{36}$, חֶרֶב אֶל־גִּבּוֹרֶיהָ *a sword is to its warriors* Jr 50$_{36}$, חֶרֶב אֶל־סוּסָיו *a sword is to his horses* Jr 50$_{37}$, חֶרֶב אֶל־אוֹצְרֹתֶיהָ *a sword is to its treasuries* Jr 50$_{37}$, חֶרֶב אֶל־מֵימֶיהָ *a sword is to its waters* Jr 50$_{38}$ (if em. חֹרֶב *drought*).

חֶרֶב לַי״ *there is a sword for Y.* Jg 7$_{20}$ (or em. הַחֶרֶב *the sword*) Is 34$_{6}$ Jr 12$_{12}$ 47$_{6}$, חֶרֶב לְאֹיֵב *a sword is to the enemy* Jr 6$_{25}$.

המה החרב *they are the sword* 4QMidrEschat$^{b}$ 10$_{16}$, חֶרֶב חֲלָלִים הִיא *it is the sword of the slain* Ezk 21$_{19}$, זֹאת ... חֶרֶב גִּדְעוֹן *this is ... the sword of Gideon* Jg 7$_{14}$.

יֶשׁ־חֶרֶב בְּיָדִי *there is a sword in my hand* Nm 22$_{29}$, אֵין חֶרֶב בְּיַד־דָּוִד *there was no sword in the hand of David* 1 S 17$_{50}$, אֵין יֶשׁ־פֹּה ... חֶרֶב *here there is not ... a sword* 1 S 21$_{9}$ (mss אֵין; or em. אַיִן *where is?* or אִם *is?* or הֵן *behold*; || חֲנִית *spear*), חרב *(there is) a sword* Si 40$_{9}$ (|| דָּם *blood*,

חַרְחֻר *violent heat*, שֹׁד *devastation*, שֶׁבֶר *ruin*, רָעָה *evil*, מָוֶת *death*).

**<OBJ>** בוא hi. *bring* Ezk $14_{17}$ Lv $26_{25}$ 1 K $3_{24}$ Ezk $5_{17}$ (+ רָעָב *famine*, דֶּבֶר *pestilence*, חַיָּה wild *beast*, דָּם *blood*) $6_3$ $11_8$ $14_{17}$ $29_8$ $33_2$, שׁוב hi. *bring back* Ps $89_{44}$ (if em.; see Cstr.) 1 C $21_{27}$, נגשׁ hi. *bring near* Jb $40_{19}$ (or em. חֲבֵרוֹ *his companion*), יצא hi. *bring out* Ezk $21_{8.10}$, פקד *summon* Jr $15_3$, נשׂא *raise* Is $2_4$=Mc $4_3$ 1 C $5_{18}$ (‖ מָגֵן *shield*, + קֶשֶׁת *bow*), עוף pol. *cause to fly* Ezk $32_{10}$ (or em. נוף pol. *wave*), ראה *see* Jr $5_{12}$ (‖ רָעָב, + רָעָה *evil*) $14_{13}$ (+ רָעָב) Ezk $33_{3.6}$, עשׂה *make* Jos $5_{2.3}$ Jg $3_{16}$ 1 S $13_{19}$ (‖ חֲנִית), חגר *gird oneself with* Jg $3_{16}$ 1 S $17_{39}$ $25_{13.13.13}$ Ps $45_4$, נתן *give* Ex $5_{21}$ 1 S $22_{10.13}$ (+ לֶחֶם *bread*) Is $41_2$ (‖ קֶשֶׁת) Ezk $21_{14.16}$ $30_{24.25}$ $32_{27}$.

שׁלח pi. *send* Jr $9_{15}$ $24_{10}$ $29_{17}$ (both ‖ רָעָב, דֶּבֶר *pestilence*) $49_{37}$ Ezk $14_{21}$ (‖ דֶּבֶר, רָעָב, חַיָּה wild *beast*), שׁלף *draw* Jg $3_{22}$ $8_{10.20}$ $9_{54}$ $20_{2.15.17.25.35.46}$ 1 S $17_{51}$ $31_4$‖1 C $10_4$ 2 S $24_9$‖1 C $21_5$ 2 K $3_{26}$ 1 C $21_5$, ריק hi. *draw* Ex $15_9$ Lv $26_{33}$ Ezk $5_{2.12}$ $12_{14}$ $28_7$ $30_{11}$ 1QpHab $6_8$, פתח *open*, i.e. draw Ps $37_{14}$=4QpPs$^a$ $1.2_{15}$ (+ קֶשֶׁת), שׂים *place* Ex $32_{27}$ Jg $7_{22}$, תפשׂ *take hold of* Ezk $38_4$, לקח *take* Gn $34_{25}$ Jg $3_{21}$ 1 S $17_{51}$ $21_9$ (+ כְּלִי *weapon*) $31_4$‖1 C $10_4$ 1 K $3_{24}$ Ezk $5_1$ (+ תַּעַר *razor*), נוף hi. *wave* Ex $20_{25}$=4QBibPar $7_8$, תקע *thrust* Jg $3_{21}$, מרט *polish* Ezk $21_{14}$ (if em. לְמָרְטָה *to polish* to לְמֹרְטָהּ *to the one who polishes it*) $21_{16}$ (if em.; see Subj.).

ירא *fear* Ezk $11_8$, מנע *hold back* Jr $48_{10}$, נפל hi. *cause to fall* Ezk $30_{22}$, שׁבר *break* Ho $2_{20}$ (‖ קֶשֶׁת *bow*, מִלְחָמָה *war*), pi. *shatter* Ps $76_4$ (‖ מָגֵן *shield*, מִלְחָמָה *war*, + קֶשֶׁת), לטשׁ *sharpen* Ps $7_{13}$ (+ קֶשֶׁת), כתת pi. *beat* Is $2_4$= Mc $4_3$ (‖ חֲנִית, :: אֵת *ploughshare*), קרא *call* Jr $25_{29}$ Ezk $38_{21}$ (or em. הָרַי חֶרֶב *my mountains a sword* to חֲרָדָה *fear*) 1QM $16_1$, צוה pi. *command* Am $9_4$.

**<CSTR>** חֶרֶב י׳ *sword of Y.* Is $34_5$ (if em. חַרְבִּי *my sword*) Zp $2_{12}$ (if em. חַרְבִּי הֵמָּה *they are* slain ones of *my sword*) 1 C $21_{12}$, אל *of God* 1QH $6_{29}$ 1QM $15_3$ $19_{11}$ (both חרבאל), מַלְאַךְ *of the angel of* 1 C $21_{30}$, מֶלֶךְ־ *of the king of* Ezk $21_{24}$ $32_{11}$, פַּרְעֹה *of Pharaoh* Ex $18_4$, גִּבּוֹר *of a warrior* Zc $9_{13}$, חַרְבוֹת גִּבּוֹרִים *swords of warriors* Ezk $32_{12}$, חֶרֶב אוֹיִבְךָ *sword of your enemies* 1 C $21_{12}$, אֹיְבֵיהֶם *of their enemies* Jr $20_4$, הַיּוֹנָה *of the oppressor* Jr $25_{38(mss)}$ $46_{16}$ $50_{16}$ (unless *sword that oppresses*), גִּדְעוֹן *of Gideon* Jg $7_{14}$, גָּלְיָת *of Goliath* 1 S $21_{10}$ $22_{10}$, חֲזָאֵל *of Hazael* 1 K $19_{17}$, יֵהוּא *of Jehu* 1 K $19_{17}$, שָׁאוּל *of Saul* 2 S $1_{22}$.

חֶרֶב אִישׁ *sword of a man* Jg $7_{22}$ 1 S $14_{20}$ Ezk $38_{21}$, לֹא־אִישׁ *of no man* Is $31_8$=1QM $11_{11}$, לֹא־אָדָם *of no human being* Is $31_8$=1QM $11_{11}$, אָחִיו *of his brother* Hg $2_{22}$, גוים *of the nations* 4QpNah $3.2_5$, גַּאֲוָתֶךָ *of your pride* Dt $33_{29}$ (or em.; see Nom. Cl.; Sam גֵּאוּתֶךָ *of your pride*), חָלָל *of the slain* Ezk $21_{19}$ (or em. חָלָל הַגָּדוֹל *the great slain one* to חֲלָלִים גְּדוֹלָה *great* sword *of the slain*), חֲלָלִים *of the slain* Ezk $21_{19.19}$ (if em.; see above), הַמִּדְבָּר *of the desert* Lm $5_9$, נקמות *of vengeance* Si $39_{30(B)}$, ח[רבות מלחמות] *swords of battles of* wickedness 4QHod$^c$ $2.2_{12}$, חֶרֶב פִּיפִיּוֹת *sword of mouths*, i.e. edges Ps $149_6$ Pr $5_{4(mss)}$ (L פִּיּוֹת), חַרְבוֹת צֻרִים *knives of flint* Jos $5_{2.3}$.

מְנֻסַת־חֶרֶב *flight of*, i.e. from, *the sword* Lv $26_{36}$, שְׂרִידֵי *survivors of* Jr $31_2$ (חָרֶב), פְּלִיטֵי *fugitives of* Jr $44_{28}$ Ezk $6_8$, שְׁבֻיוֹת *(female) captives of* Gn $31_{26}$ (חָרֶב), חֲלַל־ *slain one of* Nm $19_{16}$ 11QT $50_5$, חַלְלֵי־ *slain ones of* Is $22_2$ (‖ מִלְחָמָה *war*) Jr $14_{18}$ (‖ רָעָב *famine*) Ezk $31_{17}$ (חָרֶב) $31_{18}$ $32_{20.21}$ (חָרֶב) $32_{25.26}$ (if em. מְחֻלְלֵי *pierced ones of* to חַלְלֵי *slain ones of*) $32_{28}$ (חָרֶב) $32_{29}$ (חָרֶב) $32_{30.31.32}$ $35_8$ Lm $4_9$ (‖ רָעָב), חַלְלֵי־חַרְבִּי *slain ones of my sword* Zp $2_{12}$ (or em. חַרְבִּי הֵמָּה slain ones of *my sword they are* to חֶרֶב י׳ *of the sword of Y.*), מֻגְּרֵי־חֶרֶב *slain ones of the sword* Jr $18_{21}$ (‖ מָוֶת *death*), מְטֹעֲנֵי *pierced ones of* Is $14_{19}$ (חָרֶב), מלמדי *ones trained (in use) of* 4QM$^h$ $1_7$ (ח[רב]), חֲגוֹר *girdle of*, i.e. with, a sword 2 S $20_8$.

מַכַּת־חֶרֶב *stroke of the sword* Est $9_5$ (+ הֶרֶג *slaughter*, אַבְדָן *destruction*), עֲוֹנוֹת *punishments of* Jb $19_{29}$ (חָרֶב), אִבְחַת־ *slaughter of* Ezk $21_{20}$ (חָרֶב; or em. טִבְחַ or טֶבַח *slaughter of*), מַדְקְרוֹת *thrusts of* Pr $12_{18}$ (חָרֶב), לַהַט הַחֶרֶב *the flame of the sword* Gn $3_{24}$, לַהַב חֶרֶב *flash of the sword* Na $3_3$ (‖ חֲנִית *spear*), שלהובת *flash of* 1QM $6_3$, בְּרַק חַרְבִּי *flash of my sword* Dt $32_{41}$, צוּר חַרְבּוֹ *rock of his sword* Ps $89_{44}$ (or em. צוּר to צֹר *flint of*, or מִצָּר *from the enemy*), פִּי־חֶרֶב *mouth*, i.e. edge, *of sword* Gn $34_{26}$ (חָרֶב) Ex $17_{13}$ (חָרֶב) Nm $21_{24}$ (חָרֶב) Dt $13_{16}$ (חָרֶב) $13_{16}$ =11QT $55_{7.8}$ Dt $20_{13}$=11QT $62_9$ Jos $6_{21}$ (all three חָרֶב) $8_{24.24}$ (חָרֶב) $10_{28.30.32.35.37.39}$ $11_{11.12.14}$ $19_{47}$ Jg $1_{8.25}$ (both חָרֶב) $4_{15}$ (or del.) $4_{16}$ $18_{27}$ (חָרֶב) $20_{37}$ (חָרֶב) $20_{48}$ $21_{10}$ 1 S $15_8$ (חָרֶב) $22_{19.19}$ 2 S $15_{14}$ (both חָרֶב) 2 K $10_{25}$ (חָרֶב) Jr $21_7$ Jb $1_{15.17}$ (both חָרֶב) 2QapDavid $1_1$ 4QApocJos$^c$ $1_6$ (both פִּי

[חרב]) 11QT $58_{12}$, יְדֵי־חֶרֶב *hands*, i.e. power, *of the sword* Jr $18_{21}$ (+ רָעָב) Ezk $35_5$ Ps $63_{11}$ (both חֶרֶב) Jb $5_{20}$ (חֶרֶב) 4QapPs$^{b}$ $31_7$, [כל ח]רבות *all swords of* 4QHod$^{c}$ $2.2_{12}$.

<APP> שְׁנַיִם *two* Is $51_{19}$, שֶׁפֶט *act of judgment* Ezk $14_{21}$, רָעָה *evil* 2 C $20_9$.

<ADJ> גָּדוֹל *great* Is $27_1$ Ezk $21_{19}$ (if em.; see Cstr.), קָשָׁה *hard* Is $27_1$, חָזָק *strong* Is $27_1$, חַד *sharp* Is $49_2$ Ezk $5_1$ Ps $57_5$ 4QBark$^{c}$ $1_7$, רַע *evil* Ps $144_{10}$.

<PREP> לְ of direction, *to* Jr $15_{2.2}$ $43_{11.11}$ (all four ‖ מָוֶת *death*, רָעָב *famine*, שְׁבִי *captivity*), + מנה *appoint* Is $65_{12}$ (+ טֶבַח *slaughter*), נתן *give* Jr $15_9$ $25_{31}$ (or em. נִתְּנוּ *they are given*, i.e. ni.) Mc $6_{14}$ CD $1_4$ 4QpsEzek$^{b}$ $4_{11}$, סגר ni. *be delivered over* CD $3_{11}$, hi. *deliver over* Ps $78_{62}$ CD $1_{17}$ $8_1$ $19_{13}$ 4QpsMos$^{e}$ $1_{10}$ ([והסגרת]ים) $2.1_4$, ho. *be delivered over* CD $7_{13}$, מסר ni. *be delivered over* CD $19_{10}$.

לְ of possession, *of, (belonging) to* Jg $3_{16}$, + היה *be* Ezk $21_{14}$; of agent, *by (means of)*, + נפל *fall* Lv $26_{7.8}$, רדף *persecute* CD $1_{21}$.

לְ כתת pi. *beat* Jl $4_{10}$ (:: אֵת *ploughshare*, ‖ רֹמַח *spear*).

לְמוֹ *to, for* Jb $27_{14}$.

בְּ of instrument, *by (means of), with* 1QM $15_3$ perh. 2QapProph $1_5$ (‖ חֲנִית *spear*) perh. 4QpIsa$^{c}$ $21_4$ perh. 4QMidrEschat$^{b}$ $10_{16}$ perh. 4Q418 $172_{14}$ perh. 6QHymn $11_2$, + גרשׁ pi. *drive out* Jos $24_{12}$, שׁפט *judge* 4QpIsa$^{a}$ $8_{21}$, ni. *enter into dispute* Is $66_{16}$ (1QIsa$^{a}$ יבוא לשפוט *he will come to judge*; + אֵשׁ *fire*; or em. וּבְחַרְבּוֹ *and with his sword* to וּבָחַר בָּהּ *and he will test it*), ירשׁ *take possession of* Ps $44_4$ (+ זְרוֹעַ *arm*), רעה *pasture*, i.e. rule Mc $5_5$, ישׁע hi. *save* 1 S $17_{47}$ (‖ חֲנִית) Ho $1_7$ (‖ קֶשֶׁת *bow*, מִלְחָמָה *war*, סוּס *horse*, פָּרָשׁ *rider*), רדף *pursue* Jr $29_{18}$ (‖ רָעָב *famine*, דֶּבֶר *plague*) Am $1_{11}$, נתן ni. *be given* Jr $32_{36}$ (‖ רָעָב, דֶּבֶר) Ezr $9_7$ (+ שְׁבִי *captivity*, בִּזָּה *plunder*, בֹּשֶׁת *shame*), לקח *take* Gn $48_{22}$, שׁבה *take captive* 2 K $6_{22}$ (‖ קֶשֶׁת), קום *rise* Am $7_9$, פגע *meet* Ex $5_3$ (‖ דֶּבֶר), ירד *go down* Hg $2_{22}$, כשׁל ni. *stumble* Dn $11_{33}$ (‖ לֶהָבָה *flame*, + שְׁבִי, בִּזָּה), נפל *fall* Nm $14_{3.43}$ 2 S $1_{12}$ $3_{29}$ Is $3_{25}$ (‖ מִלְחָמָה *battle*) $13_{15}$ $31_8$ =1QM $11_{11}$ Jr $20_4$ $39_{18}$ Ezk $5_{12}$ (+ רָעָב, דֶּבֶר) $6_{11.12}$ (both ‖ רָעָב, דֶּבֶר) $11_{10}$ $17_{21}$ $23_{25}$ $24_{21}$ $25_{13}$ $28_{23(mss)}$ (+ דֶּבֶר, דָּם *blood*) $30_{5.6.17}$ (+ שְׁבִי) $32_{22.23.24}$ $33_{27}$ $39_{23}$ Ho $7_{16}$ $14_1$ Am $7_{17}$ Ps $78_{64}$ Lm $2_{21}$ 2 C $29_9$ (+ שְׁבִי) 1QM $19_{11}$, pilal appar. *fall* Ezk $28_{23}$, hi. *cause to fall* 2 K $19_7$‖Is $37_7$ Jr $19_7$ Ezk $32_{12}$ 2 C $32_{21}$, דקר *pierce* 1 S $31_4$‖1 C $10_4$, כרת *cut* 1 S $17_{51}$, גדד htpo. *cut oneself* 1 K $18_{28}$ (‖ רֹמַח *spear*), פקד *punish* Is $27_1$ Jr $27_8$ $44_{13}$ (both ‖ רָעָב, דֶּבֶר), בתק pi. *massacre* Ezk $16_{40}$ $23_{47}$ (if em.), הרג *kill* Ex $22_{23}$ Nm $31_8$ Jos $10_{11}$ $13_{22}$ 2 S $12_9$ 1 K $2_{32}$ $19_{1.10.14}$ 2 K $8_{12}$ Ezk $23_{10}$ $26_{8.11}$ Am $4_{10}$ (+ שְׁבִי, דֶּבֶר) $9_1$ 2 C $21_4$ $36_{17}$, ni. *be killed* Ezk $26_6$, ברא III *cut down* Ezk $23_{47}$, נכה hi. *strike* Dt $28_{22}$ (or em. בַּחֹרֶב *with drought*; ‖ שַׁחֶפֶת *consumption*, קַדַּחַת *fever*, דַּלֶּקֶת *inflammation*, חַרְחֻר *violent heat*, שִׁדָּפוֹן *blight*, יֵרָקוֹן *mildew*) Jos $11_{10}$ 2 S $12_9$ $20_{10}$ 2 K $19_{37}$‖Is $37_{38}$ Jr $20_4$ $26_{23}$ $41_2$ $42_{17}$ (‖ רָעָב, דֶּבֶר) Ezk $5_2$, מות *die* Jr $11_{22}$ (+ רָעָב) $21_9$ $27_{13}$ $38_2$ (all three ‖ דֶּבֶר) $44_{12}$ (all four ‖ רָעָב) Ezk $7_{15}$ (+ דֶּבֶר, רָעָב) Am $7_{11}$ $9_{10}$, hi. *put to death* 1 K $1_{51}$ $2_8$ 2 K $11_{20}$‖2 C $23_{21}$, ho. *be put to death* 2 C $23_{14}$, תמם *be consumed* Jr $14_{15}$ $44_{12.18.27}$ (all four ‖ רָעָב), אכל pu. *be destroyed* Is $1_{20}$ (1QIsa$^{a}$), כלה *be destroyed* Jr $16_4$ (‖ רָעָב), pi. *destroy* Jr $14_{12}$ (‖ דֶּבֶר, רָעָב), אבד *perish* 4QpNah $3.4_{4(Horgan)}$ ([יובדו]; + שְׁבִי *captivity*) 4QpPs$^{a}$ $1.2_1$ (‖ דֶּבֶר, רָעָב) Mur $45_7$, pi. *destroy* 1QpHab $2_{13}$ ([חרב]) $6_{10}$, רשׁשׁ pol. *batter down* Jr $5_{17}$, נתץ *tear down* Ezk $26_9$, pi. *tear down* perh. 2 C $34_{6(Qr)}$ (but prob. בחרבתיהם = *in their ruins*, from חָרְבָּה *ruin*).

בְּ of accompaniment, *in, with*, + בוא *come* 1 S $17_{45}$ (‖ חֲנִית *spear*, כִּידוֹן *javelin*, :: שֵׁם *name*), יצא *go out* Nm $20_{18}$; בטח בְּ *trust in* 1QM $11_2$ (‖ חֲנִית, :: שֵׁם).

בְּ introducing object, + תפשׂ *take hold of* Ezk $30_{21}$; שׁמר בְּ ni. *be on guard against* 2 S $20_{10}$; נתן בְּ *give to (the power of)* 4QJub$^{f}$ $23_{22}$ ([ויתן]; + מִשְׁפָּט *judgment*).

כְּ *as* Is $49_2$ Zc $9_{13}$ Ps $64_4$ Pr $5_4$ 1QH $5_{10}$ (‖ חֲנִית *spear*) $5_{13.15}$ 4QBark$^{c}$ $1_7$.

מִן of direction, *from* Jr $51_{50}$ 2 C $36_{20}$, + נצל hi. *deliver* Ex $18_4$ Ps $22_{21}$ (+ כֶּלֶב *dog*), פצה *set free* Ps $144_{10}$, ישׁע hi. *save* Jb $5_{15}$, מלט ni. *escape* 1 K $19_{17.17}$, שׁאר ni. *remain* Jr $21_7$ (‖ רָעָב *famine*, דֶּבֶר *plague*), יתר hi. *leave (over)* Ezk $12_{16}$ (‖ רָעָב, דֶּבֶר), שׁוב pol. *be brought back* Ezk $38_8$.

מִן of agent, *by (means of)*, + אכל pu. *be destroyed* Is $1_{20}$ (if em.).

אֶל *to* Jr $34_{17}$ (‖ רָעָב *famine*, דֶּבֶר *plague*), + צפה pass. *be looked out*, i.e. destined Jb $15_{22(Qr)}$, דבק *cling* 2 S $23_{10}$, נתץ pass. *be torn down* Jr $33_4$ (or em. הֶחָרֶב to הַחֵל *the bulwark*; or חִנָּם *without cause*; ‖ סֹלְלָה *siege mound*), מגר pass. *be thrown* Ezk $21_{17}$ (or em. מְגֻרֵי *those poured out of*, i.e. by, from נגר).

עַל upon, + עמד stand, i.e. rely on Ezk 33₂₆, נפל fall 1 S 31₄.₅||1 C 10₄.₅, תמך support GnzPs 1₂₅; by (means of), + חיה live Gn 27₄₀.

מִפְּנֵי from (before), on account of Lm 5₉ 4QpIsa[b] 2₁, + היה be Jr 25₃₈(mss), הלל htpo. act like a mad one Jr 25₁₆, געשׁ htpo. be put in turmoil Jr 25₁₆ (or em. געשׁ htpo. to קיא vomit), בעת ni. be terrified 1 C 21₃₀, כשׁל stumble Lv 26₃₇, פנה turn Jr 50₁₆, שׁוב go back Jr 46₁₆ Jb 39₂₂, שׁלך ho. be cast out Jr 14₁₆ (|| רָעָב famine), שׁתה drink Jr 25₁₆.₂₇, שׁכר be drunk Jr 25₂₇, קיא vomit Jr 25₁₆ (if em.) 25₂₇, נפל fall Jr 25₂₇, נתן ni. be given 32₂₄ (|| רָעָב, דֶּבֶר plague), נדד flee Is 21₁₅=4QpIsa[e] 5₅ₐ, נוס flee Is 31₈, גור fear Jb 19₂₉.

עַד unto 1 S 18₄ (|| קֶשֶׁת bow, חֲגוֹר girdle, + מַד garment).

עִם with, + עמד hi. cause to stand Ne 4₇ (|| רֹמַח spear, קֶשֶׁת bow).

<COLL> חֶרֶב תְּאֻכְּלוּ you will be destroyed by the sword Is 1₂₀ (IQIsa[a] בחרב by the sword; or em. מֵחֶרֶב by the sword, or חֳרָבוֹת [so as to be] ruins, or rd. חֲרוּב תֹּאכֵלוּ you will eat carob-beans), פַּלְּטָה נַפְשִׁי מֵרָשָׁע חַרְבֶּךָ deliver my soul from the wicked one (by) your sword Ps 17₁₃, אֲחֻזֵי חֶרֶב held of (the) sword Ca 3₈, חוליים רעים ורעב וצמא ודבר וחרב evil diseases and famine and thirst and pestilence and sword 4QDibHam[a] 1.3₇.

Also perh. 1Q38 10₁ perh. 2Q31 1₁ 4QapPs[b] 78₃ (+ רֹמַח spear) perh. 4QM[a] 24₂ perh. 5Q21.

<SYN> קֶשֶׁת bow, חֲנִית spear, רֹמַח spear, כִּידוֹן javelin, חֵץ arrow, מָגֵן shield, מֵפִיץ scatterer, חֲגוֹר girdle, סוּס horse, פָּרָשׁ rider, סֹלְלָה siege mound, מִלְחָמָה war, דֶּבֶר pestilence, רָעָב famine, שְׁבִי captivity, אֵשׁ fire, לֶהָבָה flame, שֶׁבֶר ruin, שֹׁד devastation, דָּם blood, חַרְחֻר violent heat, שַׁחֶפֶת consumption, קַדַּחַת fever, דַּלֶּקֶת inflammation, שִׁדָּפוֹן blight, יֵרָקוֹן mildew, רָעָה evil, מָוֶת death, שְׁפוֹט judgment.

<ANT> אֵת ploughshare, שֵׁם name.*

⇒ חרב slaughter.

**חֹ֫רֶב I** 16.4 n.m. **dryness, desolation**—Si חורב; sf. Si חרבו—**1. dryness** of ground (Jg 6₃₇.₃₉.₄₀ Jr 50₃₈), **drought** (Hg 1₁₁), **heat, warmth** of sun (Gn 31₄₀ Is 4₆ 25₄.₅.₅ Jr 36₃₀ Si 3₁₅ 14₂₇ 43₃.₂₁) or of fever (Jb 30₃₀). **2. desolation** (Is 61₄ Jr 49₁₃ Ezk 29₁₀. <SUBJ> היה be Jg 6₃₇.₃₉.₄₀, אכל eat, i.e. consume Gn 31₄₀. <NOM CL> חֹרֶב בַּסַּף drought is on the threshold Zp 2₁₄ (unless חֹרֶב II bustard; or em. עֹרֵב raven), חֹרֶב אֶל־מֵימֶיהָ a drought is upon its waters Jr 50₃₈ (or em. חֶרֶב sword), חורב על קרח heat is against the cold, i.e. heat disperses the cold Si 3₁₅. <OBJ> קרא call Hg 1₁₁. <CSTR> עָרֵי חֹרֶב cities of desolation Is 61₄, חָרְבוֹת חֹרֶב wastes of desolation Ezk 29₁₀ (or em. חָרְבוֹת חֹרֶב to חָרְבָּה ruin). <PREP> לְ of direction, to, + שׁלך ho. be cast out Jr 26₃₀; as, + היה be Jr 49₁₃ (or del. חֹרֶב; + חֶרְפָּה reproach, קְלָלָה curse); כְּ as Is 25₅ Si 3₁₅ 43₂₁(B); מִן of direction, from, + היה be Is 4₆ 25₄, חסה seek refuge Si 14₂₇; with, + חרר burn Jb 30₃₀; לִפְנֵי before, + כלכל htp. endure Si 43₃(B), כול htpol. withstand Si 43₃(M).*

⇒ חרב be dry, desolate.

* **חֹ֫רֶב II** n.[m.] perh. **bustard,** <NOM CL> חֹרֶב בַּסַּף a bustard is on the threshold Zp 2₁₄ (unless חֹרֶב I drought, or em. עֹרֵב raven).

**חֹרֵב** 17.1 pl.n. **Horeb**—חוֹרֵב; + ה- of direction חֹרֵ֫בָה—mountain where law of Y. was given, appar. ident. with Sinai, <CSTR> הַר חוֹרֵב mountain of Horeb Ex 33₆, מדברי חור[ב] steppes of Horeb 4QBer[a] 2₃.

<PREP> בְּ of place, in, at, among, + נתן give, i.e. place 2 C 5₁₀, שׂים place 1 K 8₉, עמד stand Ex 17₆ Dt 4₁₀, עשׂה make Ps 106₁₉, קצף hi. provoke Dt 9₈, כרת make covenant Dt 5₂ 28₆₉ 4QDibHam[a] 3.2₁₃ ([חו[רב]), שׁמע hi. proclaim Si 48₇ (|| סִינַי Sinai), שׁאל ask Dt 18₁₆ 11QT 61₀₃ ([חורב]), דבר pi. speak Dt 1₆ 4₁₅, צוה pi. command Ml 3₂₂.

מִן of direction, from Dt 1₂, + נסע set out Dt 1₁₉; עַד as far as, + הלך go 1 K 19₈.

חֹרֵ֫בָה (with ה- of direction), to, in, at, + בוא come Ex 3₁.

<SYN> סִינַי Sinai.

**חָרְבָּה** 41.1.3 n.f. **waste**—pl. חֳרָבוֹת (הֶחֳרָבוֹת); cstr. חָרְבוֹת; sf. חָרְבֹתֶ֫יהָ (חָרְבוֹתֶ֫יהָ), חָרְבֹתָיו, חָרְבֹתַ֫יִךְ, Si חרבתינו, חָרְבוֹתֵיהֶם—**waste, desolation, ruin,** of cities (e.g. Lv $26_{31.33}$ Is $44_{26}$ $49_{19}$ Jr $25_{18}$ $27_{17}$), land (e.g. Is $5_{17}$ Jr $7_{34}$ $44_{22}$ Ezk $33_{24.27}$ $36_{4}$), temple (Ezr $9_{9}$).

<SUBJ> היה *be* Lv $26_{33}$ Jr $27_{17}$, צרר *be narrow* Is $49_{19}$, בנה ni. *be built* Ezk $36_{10.33}$, ישׁב ni. *be inhabited* Ezk $38_{12}$, רנן pi. *shout joyfully* Is $52_{9}$.

<NOM CL> חרבה [א]רצם *their land is a desolation* 4QpsEzek[b] $3.3_{5}$, הִנָּם חָרְבָּה *behold they are a desolation* Jr $44_{2}$, חֳרָבוֹת מֵעוֹלָם *desolations that are from eternity* Ezk $26_{20}$.

<OBJ> בנה *build* Is $58_{12}$ $61_{4}$ Ml $1_{4}$ Jb $3_{14}$ GnzPs $1_{17}$, עמד hi. *cause to stand*, i.e. erect Ezr $9_{9}$, קום pol. *raise up* Is $44_{26}$, hi. *raise up* Si $49_{13}$, נחם pi. *comfort* Is $51_{3}$.

<CSTR> חָרְבוֹת עוֹלָם *desolations of eternity* Is $58_{12}$ $61_{4}$ Jr $25_{9}$ $49_{13}$, יְרוּשָׁלָםִ *of Jerusalem* Is $52_{9}$ (יְרוּשָׁלֶםִ) Dn $9_{2}$, חָרְבוֹת חֹרֶב *wastes of desolation* Ezk $29_{10}$; כּוֹס חֳרָבוֹת *owl of ruins* Ps $102_{7}$, יֹשְׁבֵי הֶחֳרָבוֹת *inhabitants of the desolations* Ezk $33_{24}$, כָּל־חָרְבֹתֶיהָ *all its desolations* Is $51_{3}$.

<PREP> לְ of direction, *to*, + אמר *say* Ezk $36_{4}$.

לְ *as* 4Q462 $_{14}$ (|| בִּזָּה *plunder*), + היה *be* Is $64_{10}$ Jr $7_{34}$ $22_{5}$ $25_{11}$ $44_{6}$ (|| שְׁמָמָה *desolation*) $44_{22}$ $49_{13}$ Ezk $29_{9}$ (|| שְׁמָמָה) $38_{8}$ 11QT $59_{4}$, שׂים *place* Jr $25_{9}$, נתן *give*, i.e. make Jr $25_{18}$ Ezk $5_{14}$ $29_{10}$.

לְ introducing object, + מלא pi. *complete* Dn $9_{2}$.

בְּ of place, *in*, Ezk $26_{20(mss)}$, + היה *be* Ezk $13_{4}$, הלך hi. *bring* Is $48_{21}$, נפל *fall* Ezk $33_{27}$.

כְּ *as* Ezk $26_{20}$.

מִן of direction, *from*, + דרשׁ *seek* Ps $109_{10}$.

עַל *against*, + שׁוב hi. *bring back* Ezk $38_{12}$.

<COLL> וְנָתַתִּי אֶת־עָרֵיכֶם חָרְבָּה *and I will make your cities a waste* Lv $26_{31}$, נְתַתִּיהָ חָרְבָּה *I have made it a waste* Ezk $25_{13}$, עָרֶיךָ חָרְבָּה אָשִׂים *I will make your cities a waste* Ezk $35_{4}$, יֹאכֵלוּ ... חָרְבוֹת *they shall eat ... (among) the desolations* Is $5_{17}$, הָאוֹיֵב תַּמּוּ חֳרָבוֹת לָנֶצַח *the enemies have perished (in) ruins that are endless* Ps $9_{7}$.

<SYN> שְׁמָמָה *desolation*, בִּזָּה *plunder*.

Also perh. 4QapPs[b] $75_{1}$.*

⇒ חרב *be dry*.

**חָרָבָה** 8.0.2 n.f. **dry land**—הֶחָרָבָה—<OBJ> רעשׁ hi. *shake* Hg $2_{6}$. <PREP> לְ *as*, + שׂים *place*, i.e. make Ex $14_{21}$; בְּ of place, *in, at, among* Gn $7_{22}$ 4Q370 $1_{6}$, + היה *be* CD $2_{20}$, עמד *stand* Jos $3_{17}$, עבר *pass by* Jos $3_{17}$ 2 K $2_{8}$; אֶל *to*, + נתק ni. *be lifted up* Jos $4_{18}$. <COLL> וְנָתַתִּי יְאֹרִים חָרָבָה *and I will make the branches of the Nile as dry ground* Ezk $30_{12}$.*

⇒ חרב *be dry*.

***[חֶרְבָּה]** 1 n.f. **deceit**—pl. cstr. חַרְבוֹת—<NOM CL> חֲרָבוֹת בְּשִׂפְתוֹתֵיהֶם *deceits*, i.e. deceitful words, *are on their lips* Ps $59_{8}$ (unless חֶרֶב *sword*).

**[חֲרָבוֹן]** 1 n.m. **dry heat**—pl. cstr. חַרְבֹנֵי—<CSTR> חַרְבֹנֵי קַיִץ *dry heat(s) of summer* Ps $32_{4}$. <PREP> בְּ of instrument, *by (means of)*, + הפך ni. *be overturned* Ps $32_{4}$.*

⇒ חרב *be dry*.

**חַרְבוֹנָא** 2 pr.n.m. **Harbona**—חַרְבוֹנָה—eunuch of Ahasuerus, <SUBJ> אמר *say* Est $7_{9}$. <APP> סָרִיס *eunuch* Est $1_{10}$, אֶחָד *one* Est $7_{9}$ (אֶחָד מִן־הַסָּרִיסִים *one of the eunuchs*). <PREP> לְ of direction, *to*, + אמר *say* Est $1_{10}$.

**[חָרְבָּן]** 0.0.2 n.[m.] **desolation,** <CSTR> חרבן הארץ *desolation of the land* CD $5_{20}$ 4QD[a] $1_{4}$ ([חרבן הארץ]) 4QpsMose[e] $1_{8}$; קץ חרבן *time of desolation of* CD $5_{20}$ 4QD[a] $1_{4}$ ([קץ חרבן]). <PREP> לְ of possession, *(belonging) to, of* 4QpsMose[e] $1_{8}$.

⇒ חרב *be dry*.

**חרג** 1 vb. **come fearfully—Qal** 1 Impf. יַחְרְגוּ—<SUBJ> בֵּן *son* of foreigner Ps $18_{46}$. <PREP> מִן of direction, *from*, + מִסְגֶּרֶת *dungeon* Ps $18_{46}$.*

**חַרְגֹּל** 1.0.1 n.[m.] **locust**—Q חרגול (corrected to חורגול)—an edible species (Lv $11_{22}$=11QT $48_{3}$), <OBJ> אכל *eat* Lv $11_{22}$=11QT $48_{3}$ (+ לְמִינֵהוּ *according to its kind*, || אַרְבֶּה *locust*, סָלְעָם *locust*, חָגָב *locust*). <SYN> אַרְבֶּה *locust*, סָלְעָם *locust*, חָגָב *locust*.

**חרד I** 39.0.2 vb. **tremble—Qal** 30.0.1 Pf. חָרַד, חָרְדָה, חָרַדְתְּ, חָרְדוּ; impf. יֶחֱרַד, יֶחֶרְדוּ, יֶחֶרְדוּ (יֶחֱרָדוּ); + waw וַיֶּחֱרַד, וַיֶּחֶרְדוּ; impv. חִרְדוּ—**tremble, quake, come trembling; take trouble** (unless חרד III *separate*).

<SUBJ> עַם *people* Ex $19_{16}$ 1 S $13_{7}$ Am $3_{6}$, Egyptian Is

19$_{16}$ (|| פחד *fear*), Ahimelech 1 S 21$_2$ (+ קרא *meet*), Isaac Gn 27$_{33}$ (unless חרד II *be angry*), אִישׁ *man* Gn 42$_{28}$ Ezk 32$_{10}$ Ru 3$_8$, אִשָּׁה *woman* 2 K 4$_{13}$, בֵּן *son* Ho 11$_{10.11}$, אָח *brother* Gn 42$_{28}$, מֶלֶךְ *king* Ezk 32$_{10}$, נָשִׂיא *prince* Ezk 26$_{16}$, זָקֵן *elder* 1 S 16$_4$, שַׁאֲנָן *one at ease* Is 32$_{11}$, מַשְׁחִית *destroyer* 1 S 14$_{15}$, קרא ptc. pass. *invited one* 1 K 1$_{49}$.

קֵץ *end* of earth Is 41$_5$, אִי *island* Ezk 26$_{18}$, הַר *mountain* Ex 19$_{18}$, Ramah Is 10$_{29}$=4QpIsa$^a$ 5$_5$ ([חר]דה), מַצָּב *outpost* 1 S 14$_{15}$, לֵב *heart* 1 S 28$_5$ Jb 37$_1$, כל יוסדו appar. *all who are founded* 4QapPs$^a$ 2$_3$.

<OBJ> חֲרָדָה *trembling* Gn 27$_{33}$ (וַיֶּחֱרַד יִצְחָק חֲרָדָה גְּדֹלָה *and Isaac trembled with great trembling*; unless חרד II *be angry* and חֲרָדָה II *anger*), *trouble* 2 K 4$_{13}$ (חָרַדְתְּ אֵלֵינוּ אֶת־כָּל־הַחֲרָדָה הַזֹּאת *you have taken all this trouble for us*; unless חרד III *provide [separate accommodation]* and חֲרָדָה III *lodging*).

<PREP> לְ *at, for*, + רֶגַע *moment* Ezk 26$_{16}$ 32$_{10}$; *for (the sake of)*, + נֶפֶשׁ *life* Ezk 32$_{10}$; *because of*, + זֹאת *this* Jb 37$_1$; כְּ *as*, + צִפּוֹר *bird* Ho 11$_{11}$; אֶל *to, for, on account of*, + אָח *brother* Gn 42$_{28}$, Elisha 2 K 4$_{13}$, Gehazi 2 K 4$_{13}$; מִן of direction, *from*, + יָם *sea*, i.e. west Ho 11$_{10}$; אַחַר *after*, + Saul 1 S 13$_7$.

Also 4QpIsa$^a$ 5$_{11}$ ([חר]דה).

<SYN> פחד *fear*.

**Hi.** $_{16.0.1}$ Pf. הֶחֱרִיד; + waw וְהַחֲרַדְתִּי; ptc. מַחֲרִיד; inf. הַחֲרִיד—**startle, disturb,** <SUBJ> Ahithophel 2 S 17$_2$, Gideon Jg 8$_{12}$ (unless חרד III hi. *disperse* in both), מַלְאָךְ *messenger* Ezk 30$_9$, חָרָשׁ *smith* Zc 2$_4$, enemy Lv 26$_6$ Dt 28$_{26}$ Is 17$_2$ Jr 7$_{33}$ 30$_{10}$ 46$_{27}$ Ezk 34$_{28}$ 39$_{26}$ Mc 4$_4$ Na 2$_{12}$=4QpNah 3.1$_2$ ([מחריד]) Zp 3$_{13}$ Jb 11$_{19}$. <OBJ> Ethiopian Ezk 30$_9$, מַחֲנֶה *army* Jg 8$_{12}$, David 2 S 17$_2$, קֶרֶן *horn* of nation Zc 2$_4$ (unless חרד IV hi. *re-unite*). Also 2QapDavid 1$_3$. <COLL> וְאֵין מַחֲרִיד *and none shall frighten (them)*, etc. Lv 26$_6$ Dt 28$_{26}$ Is 17$_2$ Jr 7$_{33}$ 30$_{10}$ 46$_{27}$ Ezk 34$_{28}$ 39$_{26}$ Mc 4$_4$ Na 2$_{12}$ Zp 3$_{13}$ Jb 11$_{19}$.

⇒ חָרֵד *trembling*, חֲרָדָה *trembling*.

* חרד II $_2$ vb. **be angry—Qal** $_1$ Impf. יֶחֱרַד—<SUBJ> Isaac Gn 27$_{33}$ (unless חרד I *tremble*), <OBJ> חֲרָדָה *anger* Gn 27$_{33}$ (וַיֶּחֱרַד יִצְחָק חֲרָדָה גְּדֹלָה *and Isaac was angry with great anger*; unless חרד I *tremble* and חֲרָדָה I *trembling*).

⇒ חֲרָדָה *anger*.

* חרד III $_5$ vb. **separate—Qal** $_3$ Pf. חָרַדְתְּ, impf. יֶחֶרְדוּ—**1. provide (separate accommodation)** (unless חרד I *tremble*), <SUBJ> אִשָּׁה *woman* 2 K 4$_{13}$. <OBJ> חֲרָדָה *lodging* 2 K 4$_{13}$. <PREP> אֶל *for* Elisha and Gehazi 2 K 4$_{13}$. **2. make haste,** <SUBJ> בֵּן *son* Ho 11$_{10.11}$. <PREP> כְּ *as*, + צִפּוֹר *bird* Ho 11$_{11}$; מִן of direction, *from*, + יָם *sea*, i.e. west Ho 11$_{10}$.

**Hi.** $_2$ Pf. הַחֲרַדְתִּי, הֶחֱרִיד—**1.** intrans., **disperse, scatter** (unless חרד I *tremble*), <SUBJ> מַחֲנֶה *camp*, i.e. army Jg 8$_{12}$. **2.** trans., **separate, isolate,** <SUBJ> Ahithophel 2 S 17$_2$. <OBJ> David 2 S 17$_2$.

⇒ חֲרָדָה *lodging*.

* חרד IV $_1$ vb. **weave—Hi.** $_1$ Inf. הַחֲרִיד—**re-unite** (unless חרד I hi. *startle*), <SUBJ> חָרָשׁ *smith* Zc 2$_4$. <OBJ> קֶרֶן *horn* of nation Zc 2$_4$.

⇒ חֲרָדָה *loincloth*.

חָרֵד $_6$ adj. **trembling**—pl. חֲרֵדִים—**1a.** in nom cl. used predicatively of מִי *who?* Jg 7$_3$ (+ יָרֵא *fearful*). **1b.** with היה *be* as predicate of לֵב *heart* 1 S 4$_{13}$.

**2.** used as noun, **trembling one,** <SUBJ> אסף ni. *be gathered* Ezr 9$_4$, שׁמע *hear* Is 66$_5$. <CSTR> עֲצַת ... הַחֲרֵדִים *counsel of ... those who trembled* Ezr 10$_3$, כֹּל חָרֵד *everyone who trembles* Ezr 9$_4$. <PREP> אֶל *to*, + נבט hi. *look* Is 66$_2$ (+ עָנִי *poor one*, נְכֵה רוּחַ *contrite one of spirit*). <COLL> הַחֲרֵדִים אֶל־דְּבָרוֹ *those who tremble at his word* Is 66$_5$, חָרֵד עַל־דְּבָרִי *one who trembles at my word* Is 66$_2$, חָרֵד בְּדִבְרֵי אֱלֹהֵי־יִשְׂרָאֵל *one who trembles at the words of the God of Israel* Ezr 9$_4$, הַחֲרֵדִים בְּמִצְוַת אֱלֹהֵינוּ *those who tremble at the commandment of our God* Ezr 10$_3$.*

⇒ חרד *tremble*.

חֲרֹד $_1$ pl.n. **Harod,** camping place of Gideon, appar. ʿĒn Ğālūd, 3 km ESE of Jezreel, <CSTR> עֵין חֲרֹד *spring of Harod* Jg 7$_1$ Ps 83$_{11}$ (if em. עֵין דֹּאר *En-dor*).

חֲרָדָה I $_9$ n.f. **trembling**—cstr. חֶרְדַּת; pl. חֲרָדוֹת—**trembling, fear; trouble, care** (2 K 4$_{13}$), <SUBJ> היה *be* 1 S 14$_{15}$, נתן *give*, i.e. yield Pr 29$_{25}$, נפל *fall* Dn 10$_7$.

<OBJ> חרד *tremble (with)* Gn 27$_{33}$ (וַיֶּחֱרַד יִצְחָק חֲרָדָה גְּדֹלָה *and Isaac trembled with great trembling,* or חֲרָדָה II *anger*), *trouble oneself (for)* 2 K 4$_{13}$ (חָרַדְתְּ אֵלֵינוּ אֶת־כָּל־הַחֲרָדָה הַזֹּאת *you have taken all this trouble for us,* or חֲרָדָה III *lodging*), לבשׁ *clothe oneself (with)* Ezk 26$_{16}$ (or חֲרָדָה IV *loincloth*). <CSTR> חֶרְדַּת אֱלֹהִים *trembling of God,* i.e. perh. trembling like that inspired by God 1 S 14$_{15}$, אָדָם *of human being* Pr 29$_{25}$; קוֹל חֲרָדָה *sound of trembling* Jr 30$_{5}$, כָּל־הַחֲרָדָה *all the trouble* 2 K 4$_{13}$. <ADJ> גָּדוֹל *great* Gn 27$_{33}$ Dn 10$_{7}$. <PREP> לְ *as,* + היה *be* 1 S 14$_{15}$, שׂים *place,* i.e. make Is 21$_{4}$.
⇒ חרד *tremble.*

***חֲרָדָה** II $_{1}$ n. f. **anger,** <OBJ> חרד *be angry (with)* Gn 27$_{33}$ (וַיֶּחֱרַד יִצְחָק חֲרָדָה גְּדֹלָה *and Isaac was angry with great anger;* unless חרד I *tremble* and חֲרָדָה I *trembling*), <ADJ> גָּדוֹל *great* Gn 27$_{33}$.
⇒ חרד *be angry.*

***חֲרָדָה** III $_{1}$ n.f. **lodging,** <OBJ> חרד *provide (separate accommodation)* 2 K 4$_{13}$ (unless חרד I *tremble, take trouble* and חֲרָדָה I *trembling*)
⇒ חרד *separate.*

**[חֲרָדָה]** IV $_{1}$ n.f. **loincloth**—pl. חֲרָדוֹת—<OBJ> לבשׁ *clothe oneself (with)* (unless חֲרָדָה I *trembling*) Ezk 26$_{16}$.
⇒ חרד *weave.*

**חֲרָדָה** V $_{2}$ pl.n. **Haradah,** station of exodus, perh. el-Ḥarada, 85 km S of Aqaba, <PREP> בְּ of place, *at,* + חנה *encamp* Nm 33$_{24}$; מִן of direction, *from,* + נסע *set out* Nm 33$_{25}$.

**חֲרֹדִי** $_{1}$ gent. **Harodite,** inhabitant of Harod, perh. Kh. el-Harēdan in W. en-Nār, 6 km SE of Jerusalem, <APP> אֱלִיקָא הַחֲרֹדִי *Elika the Harodite* 2 S 23$_{25}$.

**חרה** I $_{96.4.13}$ vb. **burn—Qal** $_{85.1.11}$ Pf. חָרָה, Si חריתי; impf. יֶחֱרֶה (יִחַר); + waw וַיִּחַר; inf. חֲרֹה, חֲרוֹת—**1.** intrans. **burn, be kindled** (with אַף *anger* as subj.), **be angry** (with impersonal subj., e.g. וַיִּחַר לוֹ *and he was angry,* lit. *and it was kindled to him*), <SUBJ> אַף *anger* Gn 30$_{2}$ 39$_{19}$ 44$_{18}$ Ex 4$_{14}$ 22$_{23}$ 32$_{10.11.19.22}$ Nm 11$_{1.10.33}$ 12$_{9}$ 22$_{22.27}$ 24$_{10}$ 25$_{3}$ 32$_{10.13}$ Dt 6$_{15}$ 7$_{4}$ 11$_{17}$ 29$_{26}$ 31$_{17}$ Jos 7$_{1}$ 23$_{16}$ Jg 2$_{14.20}$ 3$_{8}$ 6$_{39}$ 9$_{30}$ 10$_{7}$ 14$_{19}$ 1 S 11$_{6}$ 17$_{28}$ 20$_{30}$ 2 S 6$_{7}$||1 C 13$_{10}$ 2 S 12$_{5}$ 24$_{1}$ 2 K 13$_{3}$ 23$_{26}$ Is 5$_{25}$=4QpIsa$^{b}$ 2$_{8}$ Ho 8$_{5}$ Hb 3$_{8}$ Zc 10$_{3}$ Ps 106$_{40}$ 124$_{3}$ Jb 19$_{11}$ (if em. וַיַּחַר *and he kindled* to וַיִּחַר *and* his anger *was kindled*) 32$_{2.2.3.5}$ 42$_{7}$ 2 C 25$_{10.15}$ CD 1$_{21}$ 2$_{21}$ 3$_{8}$ 5$_{16}$ 8$_{13(A).18(A)}$=19$_{26(B).31(B)}$ 20$_{15}$ 1QDM 2$_{9}$ 4Q415 11$_{7}$; subj. impersonal, Gn 4$_{5.6}$ 18$_{30.32}$ 31$_{35.36}$ 34$_{7}$ 45$_{5}$ Nm 16$_{15}$ 1 S 15$_{11}$ 18$_{8}$ 20$_{7}$ 2 S 3$_{8}$ 6$_{8}$||1 C 13$_{11}$ 2 S 13$_{21}$ 19$_{43}$ 22$_{8}$||Ps 18$_{8}$ Jon 4$_{1.4.9.9}$ Ne 3$_{33}$ (|| כעס *be angry*) 4$_{1}$ 5$_{6}$ 4QapPs$^{b}$ 24$_{10}$.

<PREP> לְ *on the part of,* + י׳ *Y.* 2 S 22$_{8}$||Ps 18$_{8}$, אֱלֹהִים *God* 2 S 22$_{8}$||Ps 18$_{8}$, אֲדֹנָי *Lord* Gn 18$_{30.32}$, Arabs Ne 4$_{1}$, Ammonite Ne 4$_{1}$, Ashdodite Ne 4$_{1}$, Abner 2 S 3$_{8}$, Cain Gn 4$_{5.6}$, David 2 S 6$_{8}$||1 C 13$_{11}$ 2 S 13$_{21}$, Jacob Gn 31$_{36}$, Jonah Jon 4$_{1.4.9.9}$, Moses Nm 16$_{15}$, Nehemiah Ne 5$_{6}$, Samuel 1 S 15$_{11}$, Sanballat Ne 3$_{33}$ 4$_{1}$, Saul 1 S 18$_{8}$ 20$_{7}$, Tobiah Ne 4$_{1}$, אִישׁ *man* Gn 34$_{7}$ 2 S 19$_{43}$.

בְּ of time, *in,* + יוֹם *day* Nm 32$_{10}$ Dt 31$_{17}$.

בְּ *against,* + אֶרֶץ *land* Dt 29$_{26}$, עַם *people* Ex 32$_{10.11}$ Nm 11$_{33}$ Dt 31$_{17}$ Is 5$_{25}$=4QpIsa$^{b}$ 2$_{8}$ Ps 106$_{40}$ 1QDM 2$_{9}$, עֵדָה *congregation* CD 1$_{21}$ 3$_{8}$ 8$_{13(A)}$=19$_{26(B)}$, Israel Nm 25$_{3}$ 32$_{13}$ Dt 6$_{15}$ 7$_{4}$ 11$_{17}$ Jos 7$_{1(mss)}$ 23$_{16}$ Jg 2$_{14.20}$ 3$_{8}$ 10$_{7}$ 2 S 24$_{1}$ 2 K 13$_{3}$ Ps 124$_{3}$ CD 20$_{15}$, Judah 2 K 23$_{26}$ 2 C 25$_{10}$, Samaria Ho 8$_{5}$, Aaron Nm 12$_{9}$, Amaziah 2 C 25$_{15}$, David 1 S 17$_{28}$, Eliphaz Jb 42$_{7}$, Gideon Jg 6$_{39}$, Job Jb 32$_{2}$, Jonathan 1 S 20$_{30}$, Miriam Nm 12$_{9}$, Moses Ex 4$_{14}$, Rachel Gn 30$_{2}$, Uzzah 2 S 6$_{7}$||1 C 13$_{10}$, אִישׁ *man* 2 S 12$_{5}$, בֵּן *son* of Israel Jos 7$_{1}$, רֹאשׁ *head,* i.e. principal officer Jos 23$_{16}$, זָקֵן *elder* Jos 23$_{16}$, שֹׁפֵט *judge* Jos 23$_{16}$, שֹׁטֵר *official* Jos 23$_{16}$, בֹּנֶה *builder* CD 8$_{18(A)}$=19$_{31(B)}$, עֶבֶד *servant* Gn 44$_{18}$, רֵעַ *friend* Jb 32$_{3}$ 42$_{7}$, בָּשָׂר *flesh* CD 2$_{21}$, חָכְמָה *wisdom* Si 51$_{19}$, עֲלִילָה *deed* CD 5$_{16}$, נָהָר *river* Hb 3$_{8}$.

אֶל *against,* + Balaam Nm 24$_{10}$.

עַל *against,* + רֹעֶה *shepherd* Zc 10$_{3}$.

בְּעֵינֵי *in eyes of,* i.e. before, + אָדוֹן *lord* Gn 31$_{35}$, אָח *brother* Gn 45$_{5}$.

**2.** trans. **kindle,** <SUBJ> Ben Sira Si 51$_{19}$ (11QPs$^{a}$). <OBJ> נֶפֶשׁ *soul,* i.e. desire Si 51$_{19}$ (11QPs$^{a}$). <PREP> בְּ *for (the sake of),* + appar. חָכְמָה *wisdom* Si 51$_{19}$ (11QPs$^{a}$).

<SYN> כעס *be angry.*

**Ni.** $_{3.2}$ Pf. נִחֲרוּ; impf. Si 2ms תאחר; + waw Si ויחרו;

ptc. נֶחֱרִים—**be angry, be incensed,** <SUBJ> בֵּן *son* Ca $1_{6}$ Si $11_{9}$, זָר *foreigner* Si $45_{18}$, כֹּל *everyone* Is $41_{11}$ (or em. נחר *rage;* + בושׁ *be ashamed,* כלם ni. *be disgraced*) $45_{24}$ (or em. נחר *rage;* + בוא *come,* בושׁ *be ashamed*). <PREP> בְּ *against* Ca $1_{6}$, + י״ *Y.* Is $45_{24}$, אֱלֹהִים *God* Is $41_{11}$, Aaron Si $45_{18}$.

**Hi.** 2.0.1 Pf. הֶחֱרָה; + waw וַיַּחַר—**1.** intrans. **burn with zeal,** <SUBJ> Baruch Ne $3_{20}$ (or del.). **2.** trans. **kindle,** <SUBJ> אֱלוֹהַּ *God* Jb $19_{11}$ (or em. וַיִּחַר *and he kindled* to וַיִּחַר *and* his anger *was kindled,* i.e. qal), אֲדֹנָי *Lord* 4QBark$^{a}$ $2.1_{5}$ ([ה]חרה). <OBJ> אַף *anger* Jb $19_{11}$ (or em.; see Subj.), עֶבְרָה *rage* 4QBark$^{a}$ $2.1_{5}$. <PREP> עַל *against,* + Job Jb $19_{11}$ (or em.; see Subj.), עָנִי *humble one* 4QBark$^{a}$ $2.1_{5}$, דַּל *dejected one* 4QBark$^{a}$ $2.1_{5}$.

**Htp.** 4.1.2 Impf. 2ms תִּתְחַר—**show oneself angry, be vexed,** <SUBJ> בֵּן *son* Pr $24_{19}$ Si $38_{16(Bmg)}$, worshipper Ps $37_{1.7.8}$=4QpPs$^{a}$ $1.1_{17}$ $1.2_{2}$. <PREP> בְּ of cause, *on account of, for sake of,* + צלח hi. ptc. *one who prospers* Ps $37_{7}$=4QpPs$^{a}$ $1.1_{17}$, מֵרַע *evildoer* Ps $37_{1}$ Pr $24_{19}$, גְּוַיַּע *death* Si $38_{16(Bmg)}$.

**Tiphel** 2 Impf. תְּתַחֲרֶה; ptc. מְתַחֲרֶה—**compete,** <SUBJ> appar. Jeremiah Jr $12_{5}$, appar. Jehoiakim Jr $22_{15}$. <PREP> בְּ *in, with,* + אֶרֶז *cedar* Jr $22_{15}$; אֵת *with,* + סוּס *horse* Jr $12_{5}$.*

⇒ חָרוֹן *burning,* חֳרִי *heat.*

**חרה II** 1 vb. **dwindle away—Qal** 1 Pf. חָרוּ—**dwindle away,** <SUBJ> יֹשֵׁב *inhabitant* Is $24_{6}$ (unless חור II *become feeble;* 1QIsa$^{a}$ חורו perh. חור II *become feeble* or חור I *become pale*).

**[חָרָה]**, see חִירָה *court.*

**חֹר הַגִּדְגָּד** 2 pl.n. **Hor-hagidgad,** station of exodus, appar. ident. with Gudgodah at Dt $10_{7}$, perh. in W. el-Ĝerāfī (Naḥal Pārān), <PREP> בְּ of place, *at,* + חנה *encamp* Nm $33_{32}$; מִן of direction, *from,* + נסע *set out* Nm $33_{33}$.

**חַרְהֲיָה** 1 pr.n.m. **Harhaiah**—mss חַרְחֲיָה—father of Uzziel, goldsmith, and repairer of wall of Jerusalem, <CSTR> בֶּן־חַרְהֲיָה *son of Harhaiah* Ne $3_{8}$ (or em. חֶבֶר son, i.e. member, of *the company of* smiths).

**[חָרוּב]** 0.0.2 n.[m.] **carob**—Q pl. חרובים (Q חרבי[ם])—**carob-tree, carob-bean,** <OBJ> אכל Is $1_{20}$ (if em. חֶרֶב תְּאֻכְּלוּ *you will be destroyed by the sword* to חָרוּב תֹּאכֵלוּ *you will eat carob-beans*). <COLL> המכר הזה בתחומו והחרובים *this sale in its boundary and the carob trees* Mur 22 $1_{12}$.

Also Mur 22 $1_{3}$ (חרבי[ם]).

**[חֲרוּבָה]** n.f. **fortress,** <NOM CL> חרובה שבעמק עכור *a fortress that is in the Valley of Achor* 3QTr $1_{1(\text{Allegro})}$ (erased חרובא *fortress;* others חֲרִיבָה *ruin* or חֳרֶבָּה *Horebbah*). <PREP> בְּ of place, *in* $1_{1}$.

⇒ חרב *be dry.*

**חָרוּז** 1 n.m. **necklace**—pl. חֲרוּזִים—<PREP> בְּ *with,* + נאה *be comely* Ca $1_{10}$.

**חָרוּל** 3.0.1 n.m. **nettles** or **thistles**—pl. חֲרֻלִים—in field and orchard (Zp $2_{9}$ Pr $24_{31}$), in a salt waste (1QH $8_{24}$), as bed for poor desert dwellers (Jb $30_{7}$), <CSTR> מִמְשַׁק חָרוּל *ground of the nettle,* i.e. ground overrun with nettles Zp $2_{9}$. <PREP> כְּ *as,* + היה *be* 1QH $8_{24}$; תַּחַת *under,* + ספח pu. *huddle together* Jb $30_{7}$. <COLL> כָּסּוּ פָנָיו חֲרֻלִּים *its surface was covered with nettles* Pr $24_{31}$.

**[חָרוּם]**, see חרם II, Qal *split.*

**חֲרוּמַף** 1 pr.n.m. **Harumaph,** father of Jedaiah, a builder of the wall of Jerusalem, <CSTR> בֶּן־חֲרוּמַף *son of Harumaph* Ne $3_{10}$.*

**חָרוֹן** 41.2.32 n.m. **burning**—cstr. חֲרוֹן; sf. חֲרוֹנִי, חֲרֹנְךָ (Q חרונכה), חֲרוֹנוֹ; pl. cstr. Q חרוני; sf. חֲרוֹנֶיךָ—**burning, anger, wrath,** alw. of divine anger, <SUBJ> שׁפך ni. *be poured out* 4QDibHam$^{a}$ $1.5_{5}$, בוא *come* Is $13_{9}$ (+ עֶבְרָה *fury*) Zp $2_{2}$=1QpZeph$_{3}$, שׁוב *go back* Nm $25_{4}$ Jr $4_{8}$ $30_{24}$ 2 C $29_{10}$ $30_{8}$, עבר *pass by* Ps $88_{17}$, נשׂג *overtake* Ps $69_{25}$, יעף *abate* 4QBark$^{a}$ $2.1_{6}$.

<NOM CL> חָרוֹן אֶל־כָּל־הֲמוֹנָהּ *wrath is towards all its multitude* Ezk $7_{12}$, sim. Ezk $7_{14}$, חרון בכל *the wrath is*

*against all* 4Q416 3₃, חֲרוֹן אַף־י׳ עֲלֵיכֶם *the burning of the anger of Y. is upon you* 2 C 28₁₁, חֲרוֹן אַף עַל־יִשְׂרָאֵל *the burning of anger is upon Israel* 2 C 28₁₃ (mss אַף י׳ *anger of Y.*).

<OBJ> בוא hi. *bring* Jr 49₃₇ 4QBarkª 2.1₁₃, שׁוב hi. *avert* Ezr 10₁₄ Si 46₇, שׁלח pi. *send away* Ex 15₇ Ps 78₄₉ Jb 20₂₃, עשׂה *do*, i.e. execute 1 S 28₁₈ Ho 11₉, שׁפך *pour out* Zp 3₈ Lm 4₁₁.

<CSTR> חֲרוֹן אַף *burning of anger of* Nm 25₄ 32₁₄ Is 13₉ (אָף) Jr 4₈ 12₁₃ 25₃₇ 30₂₄ 51₄₅ Zp 2₂=1QpZeph₃ Ezr 10₁₄ 2 C 28₁₁ CD 10₉ 11QapPsª 3₁₁, חרן אף 1QpHab 3₁₂, חֲרוֹן אַפִּי *burning of my anger* Jr 49₃₇ Ho 11₉ Zp 3₈ 11QT 55₁₁, חֲרוֹן אַפֶּךָ *burning of your anger* Ex 32₁₂ Ps 69₂₅ (אַפְּךָ) Ps 85₄ (אַפֶּךָ), חרון אפכה *burning of your anger* 4QDibHamª 1.3₁₁, חרוני אפכה *burnings of your anger* 4QDibHamª 1.5₅, חֲרוֹן אַפּוֹ *burning of his anger* Dt 13₁₈ Jos 7₂₆ 1 S 28₁₈ 2 K 23₂₆ Is 13₁₃ Jr 4₂₆ 25₃₈ Jon 3₉ Na 1₆=4QpNah 1₁₁ Ps 78₄₉ Jb 20₂₃ (אַפּוֹ) Lm 1₁₂ 4₁₁ 2 C 29₁₀ 30₈ Si 45₁₉ CD 9₄.₆ 1Q36 18₁ 4QApocMos B 1.1₃ 11QapPsª 3₅, חֲרוֹן הַיּוֹנָה *burning of the oppressor* Jr 25₃₈ (mss חֶרֶב *sword*).

כור חרון *oven of wrath* 4Q525 22₄, כפיר החרון *young lion of wrath* 4QpHosᵇ 2₂ 4QpNah 3.1₅.₆, כל[ת חרו]נו *annihilation of his wrath* 4QShirShabbᶠ 23.1₁₂, יוֹם חֲרוֹן *day of burning of* Is 13₁₃ Lm 1₁₂, קץ חרון *time of wrath* CD 1₅ 1QH 3₂₈ 4QDª 2.1₃, קץ חרונכה *time of your wrath* 1QH 15₁₇ ([קץ חר]ונכה) 17₁₀ ([קץ [חרונכה), קצי חרון *times of wrath* 1QH fr. 1₅ 4QpHosª 1₁₂ 4QDª 18.5₁₉ (החרון), כֹּל חֲרוֹן *all burning of* Zp 3₈ 4QDibHamª 1.3₁₁, כל חרוני *all burnings of* 4QBarkª 2.1₆.

<APP> יוֹם *day* Is 13₉.

<PREP> בְּ of instrument, *by (means of)*, + שׁלח *send* 11QapPsª 3₅, שׁפך *pour out* 4QDibHamª 1.3₁₁, בהל pi. *terrify* Ps 2₅ 11QapPsª 3₁₁, כלה pi. *destroy* Si 45₁₉ 4Q Barkª 2.1₆, אבד hi. *exterminate* 4QMidrEschatᵇ 11₈; *against*, + קום *arise* Na 1₆=4QpNah 1₁₁; *in, with* CD 10₉, + בוא *bring* CD 9₄, דבר pi. *speak* CD 9₆ 1QpHab 3₁₂.

כְּ *as* Ps 58₁₀.

מִן of direction, *from*, + שׁוב *go back* Ex 32₁₂ Dt 13₁₈ Jos 7₂₆ 2 K 23₂₆ Jon 3₉ Ps 85₄ 4QApocMos B 1.1₃ 11QT 55₁₁, מלט pi. *deliver* Jr 51₄₅; מִן of cause, *because of*, + בושׁ *be ashamed* Jr 12₁₃.

מִפְּנֵי *because of, on account of*, + היה *be* Jr 25₃₈.₃₈, נתץ ni. *be torn down* Jr 4₂₆ (mss יצת ni. *be burned up*), דמם ni. *be devastated* Jr 25₃₇.

עַל *upon, above, in addition to*, + יסף *add* Nm 32₁₄.

Also 4QMidrEschatᵇ 11₅ 4Q416 4₁ 4Q525 21₈.*

→ חרה *burn*.

**חֹרֹנַיִם** 4 pl.n. **Horonaim**—חוֹרֹנַיִם, חֹרוֹנַיִם—town in Moab, perh. T. el-Mēdān, 14 km NE of southern end of Dead Sea, <CSTR> דֶּרֶךְ חוֹרֹנַיִם *road of*, i.e. to, *Horonaim* 2 S 13₃₄ (if em. אַחֲרָיו *behind him* to חֹרֹנַיִם) Is 15₅=4Qp Isaᵉ 4₂ ([דרך חורנים]), מוֹרַד *descent of* Jr 48₅. <PREP> מִן of direction, *from* Jr 48₃ (or em. מֵהַר עֲבָרִים *from Mount Abarim*); עַד *unto, as far as*, + נתן *give* voice Jr 48₃₄ (+ מִצֹּעַר *from Zoar*).

**חֲרוּפִי** 1 gent. **Haruphite**—Kt. החריפי—as sing. noun, <APP> שְׁפַטְיָהוּ הַחֲרוּפִי *Shephatiah the Haruphite* 1 C 12₆₍Qr₎.

**חָרוּץ I** 6.2 n.m. **gold,** <SUBJ> נאה *be comely* Si 14₃, בחר ni. *be chosen*, i.e. choice Pr 8₁₀. <OBJ> רדף *pursue* Si 34₅, צבר *pile up* Zc 9₃. <CSTR> יְרַקְרַק חָרוּץ *greenness of gold* Ps 68₁₄. <PREP> מִן of comparison, *(more) than* Pr 3₁₄ 8₁₀.₁₉ 16₁₆.*

**חָרוּץ II** 4 n.m. **threshing sledge**—pl. חֲרֻצוֹת—<OBJ> רפד *stretch out* Jb 41₂₂. <CSTR> חֲרֻצוֹת הַבַּרְזֶל *threshing sledges of iron* Am 1₃. <APP> מוֹרַג *threshing sledge* Is 41₁₅ (unless חָרוּץ adj. *sharp*). <PREP> לְ *as*, + שׂים *place* Is 41₁₅ (unless חָרוּץ adj. *sharp*); בְּ of instrument, *by (means of)*, + דושׁ *thresh* Am 1₃, ho. *be threshed* Is 28₂₇.*

→ חרץ *sharpen*.

**חָרוּץ III** 1 n.m. **channel, moat,** <PREP> מֵעַל *from (upon)*, + חפר *dig* 3QTr 5₈₍Allegro₎ (others חָרִיץ *channel*). <COLL> נִבְנְתָה רְחוֹב וְחָרוּץ *it shall be (re)built (with) a square and a moat* Dn 9₂₅.

→ חרץ *sharpen*.

**חָרוּץ IV** 1 pr.n.m. **Haruz,** father of Meshullemeth and grandfather of Amon, king of Judah, <CSTR> בַּת־חָרוּץ

*daughter of Haruz* 2 K 21$_{19}$.

**חָרוּץ V** 1 adj. **mutilated,** as noun, **mutilated one,** <OBJ> קרב hi. *bring near,* i.e. offer Lv 22$_{22}$. <APP> אֵלֶּה *these* Lv 22$_{22}$.
→ חרץ *sharpen.*

**חָרוּץ VI** 5 adj. **diligent**—pl. חָרוּצִים (חָרֻצִים)—**1.** used attributively of אָדָם *human being* Pr 12$_{27}$ (if em.; see §2).

**2.** in nom. cl. used predicatively of הוֹן *wealth* Pr 12$_{27}$ (הוֹן אָדָם ... חָרוּץ) appar. *the wealth of a person is ... diligent;* or em. יְקַר הוֹן אָדָם חָרוּץ *precious is the wealth of a diligent person,* or הוֹן יָקָר לְאָדָם חָרוּץ *a diligent person has precious wealth*).

**3.** used as noun, **diligent one,** <CSTR> מַחְשְׁבוֹת חָרוּץ *plans of a diligent one* Pr 21$_{5}$, יַד חָרוּצִים *hand of the diligent* Pr 10$_{4}$ 12$_{24}$, נֶפֶשׁ חָרֻצִים *soul of the diligent* Pr 13$_{4}$.
→ חרץ *sharpen.*

* **חָרוּץ VII** 1 adj. **sickly,** used attributively of כִּלָּיוֹן *emaciation* Is 10$_{22}$ (unless כִּלָּיוֹן חָרוּץ = *destined destruction,* i.e. חָרוּץ VIII).

**חָרוּץ VIII**, see חרץ *decide,* Qal, §2.

**חָרוּץ IX**, see עֵמֶק חָרוּץ *Valley of Decision.*

**חָרוּת**, see חרת *engrave,* Qal, §2.

**[חַרְחוּר] I** 1.1.1 n.m. **burning**—חַרְחֻר—of **burning fever** (Dt 28$_{22}$), **heated strife** (4QpNah 3.2$_{5}$ Si 40$_{9}$), <NOM CL> חרחר perh. *(there is) heated strife* Si 40$_{9}$, חרחור בינותם *heated strife is among them* 4QpNah 3.2$_{5}$. <PREP> בְּ *with,* + נכה hi. *strike* Dt 28$_{22}$.
→ חרר *burn.*

**חַרְחוּר II** 2 pr.n.m. **Harhur,** ancestor of family of Nethinim, postexilic temple servants, <CSTR> בְּנֵי חַרְחוּר *sons of Harhur* Ezr 2$_{51}$||Ne 7$_{51}$.

**חַרְחֲיָה**, see חַרְהֲיָה *Harhaiah.*

**חַרְחַס** 1 pr.n.m. **Harhas,** grandfather of Shallum, the husband of Huldah the prophetess, appar. ident. with Hasrah at 2 C 34$_{22}$, <CSTR> בֶּן־חַרְחַס *son of Harhas* 2 K 22$_{14}$.

**חַרְחֻר**, see חַרְחוּר I *burning.*

**חֶרֶט** 2.0.1 n.m. **stylus,** <CSTR> חֶרֶט אֱנוֹשׁ *stylus of a human being,* i.e. in common script Is 8$_{1}$, חרט חיים *stylus of life* 1QM 12$_{3}$. <PREP> בְּ of instrument, *by (means of),* + יצר *form* Ex 32$_{4}$, כתב *write* Is 8$_{1}$, חרת *engrave* 1QM 12$_{3}$.*

**חַרְטֹם** 11.0.1 n.m. **magician**—pl. חַרְטֻמִּים (חַרְטֻמִּם); cstr. חַרְטֻמֵּי—**magician, soothsayer,** or perh. **minister (of state).***

<SUBJ> יכל *be able* Ex 9$_{11}$ (+ עמד *stand*), למד pu. *be instructed* 4QMyst$^{b}$ 1.2$_{1}$ ([חר]טמים), עשׂה *do* Ex 7$_{11.22}$ 8$_{3.18}$, אמר *say* Ex 8$_{15}$ 4QMyst$^{b}$ 1.2$_{1}$. <OBJ> קרא *call* Gn 41$_{8}$. <CSTR> חַרְטֻמֵּי מִצְרַיִם *magicians of Egypt* Gn 41$_{8}$ Ex 7$_{11.22}$; כָּל־חַרְטֻמֵּי *all magicians of* Gn 41$_{8}$, כָּל־הַחַרְטֻמִּים *all the magicians* Dn 1$_{20}$. <PREP> לְ of direction, *to,* + קרא *call* Dn 2$_{2}$; בְּ of accompaniment, *in, with,* + היה *be* Ex 9$_{11}$; אֶל *to,* + אמר *say* Gn 41$_{24}$; עַל *above,* i.e. better than, + מצא *find* Dn 1$_{20}$.*

**[חֲרִי]**, see חֶרֶא *dung.*

**חֹרִי I** 3 pr.n.m. **Hori**—חוֹרִי—**1.** Edomite, eldest son of Lotan, and grandson of Seir Gn 36$_{22}$ 1 C 1$_{39}$.

**2.** father of Shaphat, one of twelve spies sent out by Moses Nm 13$_{5}$.

<SUBJ> היה *be* Gn 36$_{22}$. <NOM CL> בְּנֵי לוֹטָן חֹרִי וְהוֹמָם *sons of Lotan were Hori and Homam* 1 C 1$_{39}$. <CSTR> בֶּן־חוֹרִי *son of Hori* Nm 13$_{5}$.

**חֹרִי II** 7 gent. **Horite**—pl. חֹרִים—ancient inhabitant of mountains of Seir, perh. **Hurrian, 1.** as collective sing. noun, **Horites,** <SUBJ> ישׁב *dwell* Dt 2$_{12(mss, Sam)}$. <NOM CL> הַחֹרִי בְּהַרְרָם *the Horites were in their mountain* Gn 14$_{6}$. <OBJ> נכה hi. *strike* Gn 14$_{6}$, שׁמד hi. *exterminate* Dt 2$_{22}$. <CSTR> אַלּוּפֵי הַחֹרִי *chiefs of the Horites* Gn 36$_{21.29.30}$.

**2.** as plural noun, **Horites,** <SUBJ> ישׁב *dwell* Dt 2$_{12}$.

**3.** as sing. noun, a particular **Horite,** <CSTR> ... בְּנֵי הַחֹרִי *sons of ... the Horite* Gn 36$_{20}$. <APP> שֵׂעִיר הַחֹרִי *Seir the Horite* Gn 36$_{20}$.

**חֹרִי** III 1 n.[m.] **white bread,** <CSTR> סַלֵּי חֹרִי *baskets of white bread* Gn 40$_{16}$.
⇒ חור *be white.*

**חֳרִי** 6.0.1 n.m. **heat**—cstr. חֳרִי—alw. with אַף, of heat of anger, <NOM CL> מֶה חֳרִי הָאַף הַגָּדוֹל הַזֶּה *what is the heat of this great anger?* Dt 29$_{23}$. <CSTR> חֳרִי־אַף *heat of anger* Ex 11$_{8}$ Dt 29$_{23}$ (הָאַף) 1 S 20$_{34}$ (אָף) Is 7$_{4}$ Lm 2$_{3}$ 2 C 25$_{10}$ (אָף). <PREP> בְּ of instrument, *by (means of),* + גדע *cut down* Lm 2$_{3}$; *in, with* 4QpPs$^{a}$ 1.1$_{14}$, + קום *arise* 1 S 20$_{34}$, יצא *go out* Ex 11$_{8}$, שׁוב *go back* 2 C 25$_{10}$; *because of* Is 7$_{4}$.*
⇒ חרה *burn.*

**[חֲרִיבָה]** 0.0.1 n.f. **ruin,** <NOM CL> חריבה שבעמק עכור *a ruin that is in the Valley of Achor* 3QTr 1$_{1}$ (García Martínez; Allegro חֲרוּבָה *fortress*). <PREP> בְּ of place, *in* 1$_{1}$.
⇒ חרב *be dry.*

**[חֹרֶיבָּה]** 0.0.1 pl.n. **Horebbah,** <NOM CL> חריבה שבעמק עכור *Horebbah, which is in the Valley of Achor* 3QTr 1$_{1}$ (erased חריבא *Horebbah*). <PREP> בְּ of place, *in* 1$_{1}$.

**חָרִיט** 2 n.m. **purse**—pl. חֲרִיטִים (חֲרִטִים)—**purse** or perh. **coat,*** <OBJ> סור hi. *remove* Is 3$_{22}$. <CSTR> שְׁנֵי חֲרִטִים *two purses* 2 K 5$_{23}$.

**[חָרִים]**, see חָרִם *Harim.*

**חריונים**, see חֶרֶא *dung.*

**חָרִיף** 2 pr.n.m. **Hariph,** head of family of postexilic Judaeans Ne 7$_{24}$ (appar. ident. with Jorah at Ezr 2$_{18}$) Ne 10$_{19}$.

<SUBJ> חתם pass. *be sealed* Ne 10$_{19}$. <CSTR> בְּנֵי חָרִיף *sons of Hariph* Ne 7$_{24}$.

**חָרִיץ** I 2 n.m. **pickaxe**—pl. cstr. חֲרִיצֵי (חֲרִצֵי)—<CSTR> חֲרִצֵי הַבַּרְזֶל *the pickaxes of iron* 2 S 12$_{31}$ 1 C 20$_{3}$ (חֲרִיצֵי). <PREP> בְּ *with,* + שׂים *place,* i.e. set to work 2 S 12$_{31}$; of instrument, *by (means of),* + שׂור *saw* 1 C 20$_{3}$.*
⇒ חרץ *sharpen.*

**[חָרִיץ]** II 0.0.1 n.[m.] **channel,** <PREP> מֵעַל *from (upon),* + חפר *dig* 3QTr 5$_{8}$ (Allegro חָרוּץ *channel*).
⇒ חרץ *sharpen.*

**חָרִיץ** III 1 n.m. **slice**—pl. cstr. חֲרִצֵי—<OBJ> בוא hi. *bring* 1 S 17$_{18}$. <CSTR> חֲרִצֵי הֶחָלָב *slices of the cheese* 1 S 17$_{18}$.*

**[חָרִיץ]** IV 0.1 n.[m.] **gold,** <OBJ> רדף *pursue* Si 34$_{5(Bmg)}$ (B חרוץ *gold*).

**חָרִישׁ** 3 n.m. **ploughing** (1 S 8$_{12}$), **ploughing time** (Gn 45$_{6}$ Ex 34$_{21}$), <NOM CL> אֵין־חָרִישׁ *there is no ploughing* Gn 45$_{6}$. <OBJ> חרשׁ *plough* 1 S 8$_{12}$. <PREP> בְּ of time, *in, at during,* + שׁבת *cease,* i.e. take rest Ex 34$_{21}$.
⇒ חרשׁ *plough.*

**[חֲרִישִׁי]** 1.0.1 adj. **sultry**—f. sg. חֲרִישִׁית—**1.** used attributively of רוּחַ *wind* Jon 4$_{8}$ (+ קָדִים *east*). **2.** used as noun, **sultry wind,** <CSTR> זעף חרישית *rage of sultry wind* 1QH 7$_{5}$.

**חרך** 1 vb. **roast**—**Qal** 1 Impf. יַחֲרֹךְ—<SUBJ> רְמִיָּה *lazy one* Pr 12$_{27}$. <OBJ> צַיִד *game* Pr 12$_{27}$.

**[חָרָךְ]** 1 n.m. **lattice**—pl. חֲרַכִּים; Gnz חֲרָכִים—<PREP> מִן of direction, *from,* + צוץ hi. *look* Ca 2$_{9}$ (|| חַלּוֹן *window*). <SYN> חַלּוֹן *window.*

**חרם** I 51.1.9 vb. **destroy**—**Hi.** 48.1.8 Pf. הֶחֱרִים (הֶחֱרִם, הֶחֱרַמְנוּ, הֶחֱרַמְתֶּם, הֶחֱרִימוּ, (הַחֲרַמְתִּים) הֶחֱרַמְתִּי, (הֶחֱרִימָם; impf. יַחֲרִם, 2ms תַּחֲרִים (תַּחֲרִימֵם), תַּחֲרִימוּ; + waw וַיַּחֲרֵם, וְהַחֲרַמְתֶּם, וְהַחֲרַמְתִּי, 2fs וְהַחֲרַמְתִּי, וְהַחֲרַמְתָּה (וַיַּחֲרִימָהּ), וַנַּחֲרֵם (וַיַּחֲרִימֵם), וַיַּחֲרִימוּ; impv. הַחֲרֵם, הַחֲרִימוּ (הַחֲרִימוּהָ); inf. הַחֲרִים, הַחֲרֵם (הַחֲרִימָם)—usu. **devote to ban of destruction, destroy;** also **dedicate** to

Y., thereby excluding redemption (Lv 27$_{28}$ Mc 4$_{13}$).

<SUBJ> ׳י Y. Jos 11$_{20}$ Is 11$_{15}$ (unless חרם hi. *divide*) 34$_{2}$ Jr 25$_{9}$, עַם *people* Jos 6$_{21}$ 1 S 15$_{9.9.15}$, Israel Nm 21$_{2}$ Jos 10$_{39}$ 1 S 15$_{3}$, Israelite(s) Dt 2$_{34}$ 3$_{6.6}$ 7$_{2}$ 13$_{16}$ 20$_{17}$ Jos 2$_{10}$ 11QT 62$_{14}$, בֵּן *son* of Israel Jos 6$_{18}$ (+ לקח *take*) Jg 21$_{11}$ 1 K 9$_{21}$, of Ammon 2 C 20$_{23}$ (+ שׁמד hi. *exterminate*), of Moab 2 C 20$_{23}$ (+ שׁמד hi. *exterminate*), בַּת *daughter* of Zion Mc 4$_{13}$.

Joshua Jos 8$_{26}$ 10$_{1.28.35.37.39.40}$ 11$_{11.12.21}$, Judah Jg 1$_{17}$, Saul 1 S 15$_{3.8.9.9.15.18.20}$, Simeon Jg 1$_{17}$, אִישׁ *man* Lv 27$_{28}$, אָדָם *human being* CD 9$_{1}$, אָב Assyrian *father* 2 C 32$_{14}$, מֶלֶךְ *king* 2 K 19$_{11}$||Is 37$_{11}$ Dn 11$_{44}$, warrior Jr 50$_{21.26}$ 51$_{3}$, חֶרֶב *sword* Si 39$_{30}$, אֵלֶּה *these* 1 C 4$_{41}$; subj. not specified, 1QM 9$_{7}$ 18$_{5}$ 4QTNaph 3$_{1}$ 11QT 55$_{7}$ 60$_{5}$ 62$_{14}$.

<OBJ> אֶרֶץ *land* 2 K 19$_{11}$||Is 37$_{11}$ Jr 50$_{26}$ 4QTNaph 3$_{1}$, גּוֹי *nation* Dt 7$_{2}$ Is 34$_{2}$ Jr 25$_{9}$ 2 C 32$_{14}$, עַם *people* 1 S 15$_{3}$, Amalekite 1 S 15$_{20}$, Anakim Jos 11$_{21}$, Amorite Dt 20$_{17}$ 11QT 62$_{14}$, Canaanite Nm 21$_{3}$ 11QT 62$_{14}$, Girgashite 11QT 62$_{14}$, Hittite Dt 20$_{17}$ 11QT 62$_{14}$, Hivite Dt 20$_{17}$ 11QT 62$_{14}$, Jebusite Dt 20$_{17}$ 11QT 62$_{14}$, Kittim 1QM 18$_{5}$, Menunim 1 C 4$_{41}$, Perizzite Dt 20$_{17}$ 11QT 62$_{14}$, צָבָא *host* Is 34$_{2}$ Jr 51$_{3}$, עִיר *city* Nm 21$_{2.3}$ Dt 2$_{34}$ 3$_{6.6}$ 13$_{16}$ Jos 11$_{12.20}$ 11QT 55$_{7}$, Ai Jos 8$_{26}$, Hebron Jos 10$_{37}$, Makkedah Jos 10$_{28}$, Zephath Jg 1$_{17}$.

Agag 1 S 15$_{9}$, Og Jos 2$_{10}$, Sihon Jos 2$_{10}$, אָדָם *human being* CD 9$_{1}$, בֵּן *son*, i.e. descendant 1 K 9$_{21}$, זָכָר *male* Jg 21$_{11}$, מֶלֶךְ *king* Jos 10$_{28}$ 11$_{12.20}$, חַטָּא *sinner* 1 S 15$_{18}$, יתר ptc. *one who remains* 1 S 15$_{15}$, רַב *great one* Dn 11$_{44}$, יֹשֵׁב *inhabitant* Jos 8$_{26}$, נֶפֶשׁ *soul* Jos 10$_{28.35.37.39}$, נְשָׁמָה *breath*, i.e. every living person Jos 10$_{40}$, בְּהֵמָה *beast* 11QT 55$_{7}$, צֹאן *sheep* 1 S 15$_{9}$, בָּקָר *cattle* 1 S 15$_{9}$, מִשְׁמָן *fatling* 1 S 15$_{9}$, כַּר *lamb* 1 S 15$_{9}$, בֶּצַע *profit* Mc 4$_{13}$, חַיִל *wealth* Mc 4$_{13}$, חֵרֶם *devoted object* Lv 27$_{28}$, מְלָאכָה *article* 1 S 15$_{9}$, לָשׁוֹן *tongue* of sea Is 11$_{15}$ (unless חרם II hi. *divide*), כָּל־אֲשֶׁר *all those* Dt 13$_{16}$, *all that* Jos 6$_{21}$ 1 S 15$_{3}$ 11QT 55$_{7}$, כֹּל *everything* 11QT 60$_{5}$.

<PREP> לְ of direction, *to*, + ׳י Y. Lv 27$_{28}$ Mc 4$_{13}$, אָדוֹן *Lord* Mc 4$_{13}$; of agent, *by (means of)*, + פָּנֶה *face*, i.e. edge of sword 1 S 15$_{8}$; בְּ of instrument, *by (means of)*, + חָרוֹן *wrath* 4QTNaph 3$_{1}$; מִן of direction, *from*, + כָּל־אֲשֶׁר *all that* Lv 27$_{28}$; partitive, *some of, (any)one of*, + אָדָם *human being* CD 9$_{1}$; אַחַר *after*, + יֹשֵׁב *inhabitant* Jr 50$_{21}$; עַד *until*, + יוֹם *day* 1 C 4$_{41}$; עִם *with*, + עִיר *city* Jos 11$_{21}$.

<SYN> שׁמד hi. *exterminate*.

**Ho.** 3.0.1 Impf. יָחֳרַם (יָחֳרָם)—**be devoted to ban of destruction,** <SUBJ> חֵרֶם *devoted one* Lv 27$_{29}$, זבח ptc. *one who sacrifices* Ex 22$_{19}$, רְכוּשׁ *property* Ezr 10$_{8}$. <PREP> מִן partitive, *some of, (any)one of*, + אָדָם *human being* Lv 27$_{29}$.

Also 4QpGen[a] 1.3$_{4}$.*

→ חֵרֶם *devoted object*.

**חרם II** 2 vb. **split—Qal** 1 Ptc. חָרֻם—passive participle as adjective in list of disqualifying defects, **split, mutilated** (perh. specif. in connection with nose), used attributively of אִישׁ *man* Lv 21$_{18}$.*

**Hi.** 1 + waw וְהֶחֱרִים—**divide,** <SUBJ> Y. Is 11$_{15}$ (unless חרם hi. *destroy*; or em. וְהֶחֱרִיב *and he will dry up*). <OBJ> לָשׁוֹן *tongue* of sea of Egypt Is 11$_{15}$ (or em.; see Subj.).*

**חָרִם** 11.0.4 pr.n.m. **Harim**—Q חרים—**1.** priest who served in tabernacle in David's time, 1 C 24$_{8}$.

**2.** head of family of postexilic Judaeans, Ezr 2$_{32}$||Ne 7$_{35}$ Ezr 10$_{31}$ Ne 3$_{11}$ 10$_{28}$.

**3.** priestly head of family in postexilic Judaea, Ezr 2$_{39}$||Ne 7$_{42}$ Ezr 10$_{21}$ Ne 10$_{5}$ 12$_{15}$.

**4.** as name of priestly course (derived from §2) and the period during which it holds office 4QMishA 1.3$_{2}$ ([חרים]) 4QMishB[a] 1.1$_{7}$ ([חרים]) 1.2$_{7}$ ([חרים]) 1.3$_{3}$ ([חר]ים) 2.1$_{3}$ 2.3$_{5}$ (חר[י]ם) 2.3$_{8}$ 2.4$_{3}$ ([חרם]) 4QMishB[b] 2$_{4}$ ([חרים]) 3$_{3}$ ([חרי]ם) 4QMishD 1$_{4}$ 4QMishF[a] 1$_{6}$ ([חרם]) 4QMishF[b] 1$_{3}$ (ח[רים]) 1$_{5}$ ([חרם]) 2$_{1}$.

<SUBJ> חתם pass. *be sealed* Ne 10$_{5.27}$. <NOM CL> [בחמישית ... חרם] *in the fifth ... is Harim* 4QMishF[a] 1$_{6}$, [ברביעית] ... [ח]רים *in the fourth ... is Harim* 4QMishF[b] 1$_{3}$, [בשנ]י ... חרם *in the year of ... is Harim* 4QMishF[b] 1$_{5}$. <CSTR> בֶּן־חָרִם *son of Harim* Ne 3$_{11}$, בְּנֵי חָרִם *sons of Harim* Ezr 2$_{32}$||Ne 7$_{35}$ Ezr 10$_{31}$ Ezr 2$_{39}$||Ne 7$_{42}$ Ezr 10$_{21}$, שבת חרים *sabbath of Harim* 4QMishD 1$_{4}$. <PREP> לְ of benefit, *to, for*, + יצא *go out* 1 C 24$_{8}$; of possession, *(belonging) to*, + היה *be* Ne 12$_{15}$; בְּ of time, *in, at, during* 4QMishA 1.3$_{2}$ ([חרים]) 4QMishB[a] 1.1$_{7}$ ([חרים]) 1.2$_{7}$ ([חרים]) 1.3$_{3}$ ([חר]ים) 2.1$_{3}$ 2.3$_{5}$ (חר[י]ם) 2.3$_{8}$ 2.4$_{3}$ ([חרם])

4QMishBb 24 ([חרים]) 33 (ם[חר[י]]); מִן partitive, *some of, (any) one of* Ezr $10_{21}$.

Also 4QMishFb $2_1$.

**חֵרֶם I** 29.2.7 n.m. **devoted object**—cstr. חֵרֶם; sf. חֶרְמִי—**devoted object, that which is banned,** i.e. excluded from profane use and devoted to Y. for destruction (e.g. Dt $13_{17}$ Jos $6_{17}$ $22_{20}$ 1 S $15_{21}$ 11QT $55_{11}$) or religious use (e.g. Lv $27_{28}$ Nm $18_{14}$ Ezk $44_{29}$ 3QTr $9_{16}$ $11_7$); **ban, devotion** to destruction (e.g. 1 K $20_{42}$ Is $34_5$ Is $43_{28}$ Zc $14_{11}$ Ml $3_{24}$ Si $16_9$ $46_6$) or to religious use (Lv $27_{21}$), <SUBJ> היה *be* Nm $18_{14}$ Dt $7_{26}$ Jos $6_{17}$ Ezk $44_{29}$ Zc $14_{11}$ 11QT $2_{10}$ ([והייתה]), פדה ni. *be redeemed* Lv $27_{29}$, מכר ni. *be sold* Lv $27_{28}$.

<NOM CL> חֵרֶם בְּקִרְבְּךָ *the devoted thing is among you* Jos $7_{13}$, כל שבה חרם *everything that is in it is devoted* 3QTr $9_{16}$, תחת המסמא הגדולא ... חרם *under the great closing stone ... are the devoted things* 3QTr $11_7$, חֵרֶם הוּא *it is a devoted thing* Dt $7_{26}$ 11QT $2_{11}$, כָּל־חֵרֶם קֹדֶשׁ־קָדָשִׁים הוּא *every devoted thing is most holy* Lv $27_{28}$, חֵרֶם הִיא *it is a devoted thing* Jos $6_{17}$.

<OBJ> סור hi. *remove* Jos $7_{13}$, שׁמד hi. *exterminate* Jos $7_{12}$.

<CSTR> עַם חֶרְמִי *people of my ban,* i.e. people devoted to destruction Is $34_5$, גוי חרם *nation of ban,* i.e. nation devoted to destruction Si $16_9$ $46_6$, אִישׁ־חֶרְמִי *man of my ban,* i.e. man devoted to destruction 1 K $20_{42}$, שְׂדֵה הַחֵרֶם *field of the ban,* i.e. field that has been devoted Lv $27_{21}$, רֵאשִׁית הַחֵרֶם *first of the ban,* i.e. the first of that which was devoted 1 S $15_{21}$, כָּל־חֵרֶם *every devoted thing* Lv $27_{28.28.29}$ Nm $18_{14}$ Ezk $44_{29}$.

<PREP> לְ *as,* + היה *be* Jos $7_{12}$, שׂים *place,* i.e. make Jos $6_{18}$, נתן *give,* i.e. make Is $43_{28}$; בְּ of instrument, *by (means of)* CD $6_{15}$; of accompaniment, *in, with,* + לכד ni. *be taken* Jos $7_{15}$; *with regard to,* + מעל *be unfaithful* Jos $7_1$ $22_{20}$ 1 C $2_7$; מִן of direction, *from* Dt $13_{18}$ 11QT $55_{11}$, + שׁמר *keep* Jos $6_{18}$, לקח *take* Jos $6_{18}$ $7_{1.11}$.

<COLL> וְהִכֵּיתִי אֶת־הָאָרֶץ חֵרֶם *and I will strike the earth with a ban of destruction* Ml $3_{24}$, איש את רעיהו יצ[ו]דו חרם *every man hunts his neighbour with a ban* CD $16_{15}$.

⇒ חרם *destroy.*

**חֵרֶם II** 9.0.3 n.m. **net**—sf. חֶרְמוֹ, חֶרְמִי; pl. חֲרָמִים—used by fishermen or hunters, <NOM CL> הִיא מְצוֹדִים וַחֲרָמִים לִבָּהּ *her heart is snares and nets* Ec $7_{26}$. <OBJ> ריק *empty out* Hb $1_{17}$. <CSTR> מִשְׁטַח חֲרָמִים *drying-yard of nets* Ezk $26_{5.14}$. <PREP> לְ of direction, *to,* + זבח pi. *sacrifice* Hb $1_{16}$=1QpHab $5_{14}$=1QpHab $6_2$; of benefit, *to, for,* + היה *be* Ezk $47_{10}$; בְּ of accompaniment, *in, with,* + גרר *drag out* Hb $1_{15}$=1QpHab $5_{13}$, עלה hi. *bring up* Ezk $32_3$. <COLL> יָצוּדוּ חֵרֶם *they shall hunt with a net* Mc $7_2$.*

⇒ חרם *split.*

**חֳרֵם** 1 pl.n. **Horem,** town in territory of Naphtali, perh. Kh. Qaṭamūn, 23 km W of Lake Hule, <APP> עִיר *city* Jos $19_{38}$.

**חָרְמָה** 9 pl.n. **Hormah**—הַחָרְמָה—city in territory of Judah, formerly called Zephath Jg $1_{17}$, perh. T. el-Mšāš, 5 km E of Beer-sheba, <SUBJ> היה *be* as inheritance Jos $19_4$. <OBJ> קרא *call* Nm $21_3$ Jg $1_{17}$. <CSTR> מֶלֶךְ חָרְמָה *king of Hormah* Jos $12_{14}$. <APP> עִיר *city* Jos $15_{30}$. <PREP> בְּ of place, *in, at, among* 1 S $30_{30}$, + ישׁב *dwell* 1 C $4_{30}$; עַד *until, as far as,* + כתת hi. *disperse* Nm $14_{45}$ Dt $1_{44}$.

**חֶרְמוֹן** 14 pl.n. **Hermon**—pl. חֶרְמוֹנִים—mountain and mountain range stretching from southern Syria to northern Palestine, <SUBJ> רנן pi. *shout joyfully* Ps $89_{13}$ (+ Tabor). <NOM CL> הוּא חֶרְמוֹן *it is Hermon* Dt $4_{48}$. <CSTR> אֶרֶץ ... חֶרְמוֹנִים *land of ... Hermon* Ps $42_7$, רֹאשׁ ... חֶרְמוֹן *head,* i.e. peak, *of ... Hermon* Ca $4_8$, הַר חֶרְמוֹן *mountain of Hermon* Dt $3_8$ Jos $11_{17}$ $12_{1.5}$ $13_{5.11}$ 1 C $5_{23}$, טַל־חֶרְמוֹן *dew of Hermon* Ps $133_3$. <PREP> לְ introducing object, + קרא *call* Dt $3_9$; תַּחַת *under, beneath* Jos $11_3$.

**חֶרְמֵשׁ** 2 n.[m.] **sickle,** <SUBJ> perh. חלל hi. *begin* Dt $16_9$ (מֵהָחֵל חֶרְמֵשׁ בַּקָּמָה perh. *from [when] a sickle begins [to work] against the standing grain;* Sam מֵהַחִלְּךָ *from your starting* [to use] a sickle against the standing grain). <OBJ> נוף hi. *wave* against standing grain Dt $23_{26}$, לטשׁ *sharpen* 1 S $13_{20}$ (if em. מַחֲרֵשָׁה *ploughshare;* + אֵת *axe,* קַרְדֹּם *spade*).

**חָרָן I** $_{10.0.7}$ pl.n. **Haran**—+ ה- of direction חָרָנָה—city in northern Mesopotamia, perh. Altinbazak, 40 km SE of Urfa, <SUBJ> רכל *conduct trade* Ezk $27_{23}$. <OBJ> שׁחת pi. *wipe out* 2 K $19_{12}$, hi. *destroy completely* Is $37_{12}$. <PREP> בְּ of place, *in, at*, 4Q464 $7_{2}$, + ישׁב *dwell* 4Qps Jub[a] $2.1_{2}$ 4QpGen[a] $1.2_{10}$, עשׂה *make*, i.e. acquire Gn $12_{5}$, מות *die* Gn $11_{32}$; מִן of direction, *from* Gn $29_{4}$, + יצא *go out* Gn $12_{4}$ 11QJub fr. $8_{2}$ ([חרן]); עַד *until, as far as*, + בוא *come* Gn $11_{31}$; אֶל *to*, + הלך *go* 1QJub[b] $35_{10}$; חָרָנָה (+ ה- of direction), *to, in, at*, + הלך *go* Gn $28_{10}$, ברח *flee* Gn $27_{43}$. <COLL> חָרָן (without preposition or ה- of direction), *to, in, at Haran*, + בוא *come* 4QpGen[a] $1.2_{9}$, הלך *go* 1Q Jub[a] $27_{19}$ 4Q464 $1_{2}$. Also perh. 4Q516 $9_{1}$.

**חָרָן II** $_{2}$ pr.n.m. **Haran,** son of Caleb and Ephah, <SUBJ> ילד hi. *be father of* 1 C $2_{46}$. <OBJ> ילד *bear child* 1 C $2_{46}$.

**חַרְנֶפֶר** $_{1}$ pr.n.m. **Harnepher,** son of Zophah and descendant of Asher, <NOM CL> בְּנֵי צוֹפַח ... חַרְנֶפֶר *the sons of Zophah were ... Harnepher* 1 C $7_{36}$.

**חֶרֶס I** $_{2}$ n.m. **sun**—חֶרֶס; + ה- of direction הַחַרְסָה—<SUBJ> בוא *come* Jg $14_{18}$. <PREP> לְ of direction, *to*, + אמר *say* Jb $9_{7}$.

**חֶרֶס II** $_{1}$ n.m. **itch**—חֶרֶס—<PREP> בְּ *with*, + נכה hi. *strike* Dt $28_{67}$.

**חֶרֶס III** $_{1}$ pl.n. **Heres**—חֶרֶס—place in territory of Gad E of Jordan Jg $8_{13}$. <CSTR> מַעֲלֵה הֶחָרֶס *ascent of Heres* Jg $8_{13}$.
⇒ הַר־חֶרֶס.

**חַרְסִית** $_{1}$ n.f. **potsherd**—Kt חרסות—<CSTR> שַׁעַר הַחַרְסִית *gate of the potsherd* Jr $19_{2(Qr)}$.

**חרף I** $_{39.3.2.1}$ vb. **reproach**—**Qal** $_{4.0.0.1}$ Impf. יֶחֱרַף; ptc. חֹרְפִי, pl. sf. חוֹרְפֶיךָ—**1. reproach, taunt,** <SUBJ> לֵבָב *heart* Jb $27_{6}$; subj. not specified, Kh. Beit Lei graf $3_{1}$ ([חרפד]). <OBJ> obj. not specified, Kh. Beit Lei graf $3_{1}$. <PREP> מִן of cause, *because of*, + יוֹם *day* Jb $27_{6}$.

**2.** ptc. as noun, **one who reproaches, taunts,** <OBJ> ענה *answer* Ps $119_{42}$, שׁוב hi. *bring back* word, i.e. answer Pr $27_{11}$. <CSTR> חֶרְפּוֹת חוֹרְפֶיךָ *the taunts of those who taunt you* Ps $69_{10}$.

**Pi.** $_{35.3.2}$ Pf. חֵרֵף, חֵרַפְתָּ, חֵרַפְתִּי, חֵרְפוּ, (חֵרְפוּנִי), חֵרְפוּךָ, (חֵרַפְתֶּם); impf. יְחָרֵף, (יְחָרְפֵנִי), Si תחרף, יְחָרְפוּנִי; + waw וַיְחָרֵף; ptc. מְחָרֵף, Si מחרפת; inf. חָרֵף, (חָרְפָם)—**reproach, revile,** <SUBJ> אֱלֹהִים *God* Ps $57_{4}$, עֶלְיוֹן *Most High* Ps $57_{4}$, Moab Zp $2_{8.10}$, עַם *people* Jg $5_{18}$, Philistine 1 S $17_{10.26.36.45}$ 11QPs[a] $28_{14}$, David 2 S $23_{9}$, Eleazar 2 S $23_{9}$, Rabshakeh 2 K $19_{4}$||Is $37_{4}$, Sennacherib 2 K $19_{16.22.23}$||Is $37_{17.23.24}$ 2 C $32_{17}$, Tobiah and Sanballat Ne $6_{13}$, אִישׁ *man* Jg $8_{15}$ 1 S $17_{25}$ 2 S $21_{21}$||1 C $20_{7}$, אִשָּׁה *woman* Si $42_{14}$, בֵּן *son* Si $41_{22}$, שָׁכֵן *inhabitant* Ps $79_{12}$, מֶלֶךְ *king* 2 K $19_{22.23}$||Is $37_{23.24}$ 2 C $32_{17}$, צַר *oppressor* Ps $74_{10}$, עֹשֵׁק *oppressor* Pr $14_{31}$, צֹרֵר *oppressor* Ps $42_{11}$, לעג *mocker* Pr $17_{5}$, אוֹיֵב *enemy* Ps $44_{17}$ $55_{13}$ $74_{18}$ $89_{52.52}$ $102_{9}$, אֵימָה *terror* Si $43_{16(B)}$; subj. not specified, 1QpHab $10_{13}$.

<OBJ> ' *Y.* 2 C $32_{17}$, אֱלֹהִים *God* 2 K $19_{4.16}$||Is $37_{4.17}$ 2 C $32_{17}$, אָדוֹן *Lord* 2 K $19_{23}$||Is $37_{24}$ Ps $79_{12}$, Israel 1 S $17_{25}$ 2 S $21_{21}$||1 C $20_{7}$, עַם *people* Zp $2_{8}$, Philistine 2 S $23_{9}$, מַעֲרָכָה *battle-line* of Israel 1 S $17_{10.45}$, of God 1 S $17_{26.36}$, Gideon Jg $8_{15}$, Nehemiah Ne $6_{13}$, worshipper Ps $42_{11}$ $55_{13}$ $102_{9}$, בָּחִיר *chosen one* 1QpHab $10_{13}$, עשׂה ptc. *one who makes*, i.e. creator Pr $14_{31}$ $17_{5}$, שׁאף ptc. *one who tramples* Ps $57_{4}$, נֶפֶשׁ *soul* Jg $5_{18}$, עָקֵב *footprint* Ps $89_{52}$.

<PREP> מִן of direction, + מַעֲרָכָה *battle-line* of Philistines 11QPs[a] $28_{14}$ (ממ[ערכות פלשתים]).

<COLL> חֶרְפָּתָם אֲשֶׁר חֵרְפוּנִי *their reproach with which they reproached me* Ps $79_{12}$.

Also Si $34_{31(Bmg)}$.*

⇒ חֶרְפָּה *reproach.*

**חרף II** $_{1.1}$ vb. **spend winter**—**Qal** $_{1}$ Impf. 3fs תֶּחֱרָף—**spend winter,** <SUBJ> בְּהֵמָה *beast* Is $18_{6}$. <PREP> עַל *upon*, + נְטִישׁוֹת *shoots* Is $18_{6}$.*

**Pi.** $_{0.1}$ Impf. Si 3fs תחרף (Si תחריף)—**make cold,** <SUBJ> אִמְרָה *word* Si $43_{16(M)}$, אֵימָה *fear* Si $43_{16(B)}$. <OBJ> תֵּימָן *south wind* Si $43_{16}$.

⇒ חֹרֶף *winter.*

**חרף III** $_{1.0.1}$ vb. **designate**—**Qal** $_{0.0.1}$ Ptc. pass. Q חרופה—pass. **be designated,** <SUBJ> שִׁפְחָה *female ser-*

*vant* 4QD$^{e}$ $8_{14}$.

**Ni.** 1 Pf. נֶחֱרֶפֶת—**be betrothed,** <SUBJ> שִׁפְחָה *female servant* Lv $19_{20}$. <PREP> לְ of benefit, *to, for,* + אִישׁ *man* Lv $19_{20}$.

**חָרֵף** 1.0.0.1 pr.n.m. **Hareph, 1.** son of Hur and descendant of Judah, <NOM CL> חָרֵף אֲבִי בֵית־גָּדֵר *Hareph was the father of Beth-gader* 1 C $2_{51}$. <APP> בֵּן *son* 1 C $2_{51}$. **2.** father of Azariah, <CSTR> בן חרף *son of Hareph* Seal 37.

**[חֶרֶף]** 0.0.1 n.m. **catapult**—<CSTR> יד החרף *hand,* i.e. side, *of the catapult* 4QM$^{c}$5.

**חֹרֶף** I 6.0.2 n.m. **winter,** <SUBJ> שׁבת *cease* Gn $8_{22}$ (+ קַיִץ *summer*). <OBJ> יצר *form* Ps $74_{17}$. <CSTR> בֵּית הַחֹרֶף *the house of winter* Jr $36_{22}$ Am $3_{15}$, יְמֵי חָרְפִּי *days of my winter,* i.e. youth, as time of sowing (if not חרף II *youth*). <PREP> לְ of possession, *(belonging) to* 4QJub$^{a}$ $2_{2}$; בְּ of time, *in, during,* + היה *be* Zc $14_{8}$; מִן *during,* + חרשׁ *plough* Pr $20_{4}$. מִלִּפְנֵי *because of* 4QapLam$^{a}$ $1.2_{6}$.*
⇒ חרף *spend winter.*

* **חֹרֶף** II 1 n.[m.] **youth**—sf. חָרְפִּי—<CSTR> יְמֵי חָרְפִּי *days of my youth* Jb $29_{4}$.

**חֶרְפָּה** I 73.9.13 n.f. **reproach**—cstr. חֶרְפַּת; sf. חֶרְפָּתִי, חֶרְפָּתְךָ, חֶרְפָּתֵךְ, חֶרְפָּתוֹ, חֶרְפָּתֵנוּ, חֶרְפָּתָם, חֶרְפָּתָם; pl. חֲרָפוֹת; cstr. חֶרְפוֹת—**1. reproach, taunt** of enemy (e.g. 1 S $17_{26}$ Is $51_{7}$ Ezk $21_{33}$ Ho $12_{15}$ Ps $15_{3}$). **2.** condition of **reproach, shame, disgrace** (e.g. Gn $30_{23}$ 2 S $13_{13}$ Is $54_{4}$ Jb $19_{5}$). **3.** object of **reproach** (e.g. Is $30_{5}$ Jr $6_{10}$ Ps $22_{7}$ $44_{14}$).

<SUBJ> היה *be* Ezk $5_{15}$ $16_{57}$ (if em.; see Cstr.) Ps $31_{12}$ $79_{4}$ $89_{42}$ $109_{25}$ Ne $2_{17}$, ראה ni. *be seen* Is $47_{3}$, מחה ni. *be wiped out* Pr $6_{33}$, בוא hi. *bring* 4Q525 $14.2_{8}$, נפל *fall* Ps $69_{10}$, שׁבר *break* Ps $69_{21}$, נוד hi. *make destitute* Si $34_{2}$.

<NOM CL> חרפה רעהו בעל שתים *a lord of two (tongues),* i.e. a duplicitous person, *is a reproach (to) his neighbour* Si $5_{14}$, חרפה לכל בשר *reproach (will be) to all flesh* 1QLitPr $3.1_{3}$, מַשְׂאֵת עָלֶיהָ חֶרְפָּה *a burden on her was reproach* Zp $3_{18}$, עִם־קָלוֹן חֶרְפָּה *disgrace comes with dishonour* Pr $18_{3}$, אָנֹכִי ... חֶרְפַּת אָדָם *I am ... a reproach of human beings* Ps $22_{7}$, חֶרְפָּה הִיא *it is a disgrace* Gn $34_{14}$.

<OBJ> שׂים *place,* i.e. make 1 S $11_{2}$ Ps $39_{9}$ $44_{14}$ 1QH $2_{9}$, נתן *give,* i.e. make Jr $23_{40}$ Ezk $22_{4}$ Jl $2_{19}$ Ps $78_{66}$, רבה hi. *make great* 4Q416 $2.2_{16}$, לקח *take* Ezk $36_{30}$, אסף *take away* Gn $30_{23}$ Is $4_{1}$, עבר hi. *turn away* Ps $119_{39}$, סור hi. *remove* 1 S $17_{26}$ Is $25_{8}$ Si $47_{4}$, גלל *roll away* Jos $5_{9}$ Ps $119_{22}$, שׁבת hi. *cause to cease* Dn $11_{18}$.

ירשׁ hi. *take possession* Si $6_{1}$, הלך hi. *cause to go* 2 S $13_{13}$, שׁוב hi. *bring back* Ho $12_{15}$ Ps $79_{12}$ Dn $11_{18}$ Ne $3_{36}$, נבע hi. *pour out* Si $42_{14(Bmg)}$, נשׂא *raise* Jr $15_{15}$ $31_{19}$ Ezk $36_{15}$ Mc $6_{16}$ Ps $15_{3}$ $69_{8}$, ירא *fear* Is $51_{7}$, ראה *see* Lm $5_{1}$ 4QapLam$^{b}$5, שׁמע *hear* Jr $51_{51}$ Zp $2_{8}$ Lm $3_{61}$, זכר *remember* Is $54_{4}$=4QTanḥ $8_{6}$ Ps $74_{22}$ $89_{51}$, ידע *know* Ps $69_{20}$, כסה pi. *cover* 4Q418 $177_{3}$, יכח hi. *reprove* Jb $19_{5}$.

<CSTR> חֶרְפַּת הַגּוֹיִם *taunt of the nations* Ne $5_{9}$, חֶרְפַּת מִצְרַיִם *reproach of Egypt* Jos $5_{9}$, מוֹאָב *of Moab* Zp $2_{8}$, עַמִּים *of peoples* Ezk $36_{15}$, עַמִּי *of my people* Mc $6_{16}$, עַמּוֹ *of his people* Is $25_{8}$, אָדָם *of humans* Ps $22_{7}$, אֱנוֹשׁ *of humans* Is $51_{7}$, בני *of sons of* 4QapLam$^{b}$5, בְּנוֹת *of daughters of* Ezk $16_{57}$, נְעוּרַי *of my youth* Jr $31_{19}$, אַלְמְנוּתַיִךְ *of your widowhood* Is $54_{4}$, ארמלותך *of your widowhood* 4QTanḥ $8_{6}$, עֲבָדֶיךָ *of your servants* Ps $89_{51}$, נָבָל *of a fool* Ps $39_{9}$, שונא *of one who hates* 4Q525 $14.2_{8}$, חֶרְפּוֹת חוֹרְפֶיךָ *the reproaches of those who reproached you* Ps $69_{10}$, חֶרְפַּת רָעָב *reproach of famine* Ezk $36_{30}$, חֶרְפַּת עוֹלָם *reproach of eternity* Jr $23_{40}$ Ps $78_{66}$ Si $47_{4}$ ([חר]פת ע[ו]לם), עד *of eternity* 1QS $4_{12}$, חרפה ש]חת] *reproach of the pit* 4QBer$^{a}$ $3.2_{9}$.

רִיב חֶרְפָּתִי *case of my disgrace* 1 S $25_{39}$, ריב חרפתך *case of your disgrace* Si $6_{9}$, דבר חרפה *word of reproach* Si $34_{31}$, עֵת חֶרְפַּת *time of reproach of* Ezk $16_{57}$ (or em. עַתָּ הָיִית *now you have become*), כול חרפה *every disgrace* Si $42_{14(M)}$.

<PREP> לְ of benefit, *to, for* Is $30_{5}$ Dn $12_{2}$; *as* Dn $9_{16}$, + היה *be* Jr $6_{10}$ $20_{8}$ $42_{18}$ $44_{8.12}$ $49_{13}$ Ps $69_{11}$ 4QpHos$^{a}$ $2_{13}$, נתן *give,* i.e. make Jr $24_{9}$ $29_{18}$ Ezk $5_{14}$ Jl $2_{17}$, שׂים *place,* i.e. make 1QH $23_{4}$; בְּ of accompaniment, *in (a state of), with* Ne $1_{3}$; of instrument, *by (means of), with,* + שׂבע *be sated* Lm $3_{30}$, נכה hi. *strike* Jb $16_{10}$; of cause, *on account of* 4Q416 $2.2_{3}$ (חרפת[נו]); מִן privative, *without* Ne $5_{9}$; of cause, *on account of* 4Q417 $1.1_{23}$; *at,* + פחד *be in dread* Si $42_{14(M)}$; אֶל *to, concerning,* + אמר *say* Ezk $21_{33}$; אַחַר *after,* + הלך *go* 4QJub$^{a}$ $1_{9}$ (חרפת[ם]).

<COLL> יַעֲטוּ חֶרְפָּה *may they be covered with reproach* Ps 71$_{13}$, חֶרְפָּתָם אֲשֶׁר חֵרְפוּנִי *their reproach with which they reproached me* Ps 79$_{12}$.

Also Si 41$_{6.22}$ 4Q415 1.1$_{5}$ perh. 4Q 416 2.4$_{13}$ ([ חרפּ]) 4Q418 178$_{4}$ 4Q 525 15$_{7}$.*

⇒ חרף *reproach.*

*חֶרְפָּה II 1 n.f. **knife** (unless חֶרְפָּה I *reproach*), <PREP> בְּ of instrument, *by (means of), with,* + נכה hi. *strike* cheek Jb 16$_{10}$.

חרץ 11.0.11 vb. **decide—Qal** 5.0.4 Pf. חָרַץ, חָרַצְתָּ; impf. יֶחֱרַץ, 2ms תֶּחֱרַץ; ptc. pass. חָרוּץ, חֲרוּצִים, Q חרוצי; inf. Q חרוץ—**1.** active, usu. **decide, settle,** also **take decisive action** (2 S 5$_{24}$), **sharpen** tongue (Ex 11$_{7}$ Jos 10$_{21}$), <SUBJ> David 2 S 5$_{24}$, אִישׁ *man* Jos 10$_{21}$ 1QS 8$_{10}$, נָבִיא *prophet* 1 K 20$_{40}$, כֹּהֵן *priest* 1QS 8$_{10}$, כֶּלֶב *dog* Ex 11$_{7}$.

<OBJ> לָשׁוֹן *tongue* Ex 11$_{7}$ Jos 10$_{21}$, מִשְׁפָּט *judgment* 1 K 20$_{40}$ 1QS 8$_{10}$.

<PREP> לְ of direction, *to,* + בֵּן *son* of Israel Jos 10$_{21}$.

**2a.** passive, **be decided, be destined,** <SUBJ> כֹּהֵן *priest* 1QM 15$_{6}$ , כִּלָּיוֹן *destruction* Is 10$_{22}$=4QpIsa$^{a}$ 2$_{3}$ ([כליון חר[וץ])=4QpIsa$^{c}$ 4.2$_{18}$ ([כליון חרוץ]) (unless חָרוּץ VII *sickly* emaciation), יוֹם *day* Jb 14$_{5}$, <PREP> לְ *for,* + מוֹעֵד *appointed time* 1QM 15$_{6}$.

**2b.** pass. ptc. used as noun, **appointed one, destined one,** <OBJ> בחן *test* 1QM 16$_{9}$. <CSTR> כול חרוצי מלחמה *all the appointed ones of,* i.e. those appointed for, *battle* 1QM 16$_{9}$.

Also 4QPrFêtes$^{c}$ 187$_{3}$.

**Ni.** 5.0.6 Ptc. נֶחֱרָצָה (נֶחֱרֶצֶת)—**1. be determined,** <SUBJ> שְׁמָמָה *desolation* Dn 9$_{26}$, מִשְׁפָּט *judgment* 1QS 4$_{20}$, קֵץ *time* 1QS 4$_{25}$.

**2.** ptc. used as noun, **that which is determined,** <SUBJ> עשׂה ni. *be accomplished* Dn 11$_{36}$, נתך *be poured out* Dn 9$_{27}$. <OBJ> עשׂה *do,* i.e. accomplish Is 10$_{23}$=4Qp Isa$^{c}$ 4.2$_{18}$ ([נחרצה]), שׁמע *hear* Is 28$_{22}$. <PREP> לְ of direction, *to,* + עַד *eternity* 1QH 3$_{36}$. <COLL> כָּלָה וְנֶחֱרָצָה *the end and that which is determined,* i.e. determined end Is 10$_{23}$=4QpIsa$^{c}$ 4.2$_{18}$ ([כלה ונחרצה]) Is 28$_{22}$ Dn 9$_{27}$ 1QH 3$_{36}$.

Also 4Q426 9$_{2}$ 4Q518 1$_{2}$, 4Q525 22$_{2}$.

**Pu.** 0.0.1 Ptc. Q מחורץ—**be cut, be fluted,** <SUBJ> סָגָר *socket* 1QM 5$_{9}$. <PREP> בֵּין *between,* + צָמִיד *ring* 1QM 5$_{9}$.*

⇒ חָרוּץ *diligent,* חָרוּץ *moat,* חָרוּץ *mutilated,* חָרוּץ *threshing sledge.*

חַרְצֻבָּה 2.0.1 n.f. **fetter**—pl. חַרְצֻבּוֹת—**1. fetter,** <OBJ> פתח pi. *loosen* Is 58$_{6}$, נתר hi. *break* fetter CD 13$_{10}$. <CSTR> חַרְצֻבּוֹת רֶשַׁע *fetters of wickedness* Is 58$_{6}$; כל חרצובות *all fetters* CD 13$_{10}$.

**2. torment,** <NOM CL> אֵין חַרְצֻבּוֹת *there are no torments* Ps 73$_{4}$.

חַרְצָן 1 n.m. **sour grape**—pl. חַרְצַנִּים—<PREP> מִן of direction, *from,* + אכל *eat* Nm 6$_{4}$.

חרק I 5.0.3 vb. **gnash—Qal** 5.0.3 Pf. חָרַק; impf. יַחֲרֹק, Q יחרוקו; + waw וַיַּחַרְקוּ; ptc. חֹרֵק, Q חורק; inf. חָרֹק—<SUBJ> אֵל *God* Jb 16$_{9}$, עֵד *witness* Ps 35$_{16}$, רָשָׁע *wicked one* Ps 37$_{12}$=4QpPs$^{a}$ 1.2$_{12}$ Ps 112$_{10}$, עָרִיץ *violent one* 1QH 13$_{9}$ 2$_{11}$, אֹיֵב *enemy* Lm 2$_{16}$. <OBJ> שֵׁן *tooth* Ps 35$_{16}$ 37$_{12}$=4QpPs$^{a}$ 1.2$_{12}$ Ps 112$_{10}$ Lm 2$_{16}$ 1QH 13$_{9}$ 2$_{11}$. <PREP> בְּ *with,* + שֵׁן *tooth* Jb 16$_{9}$; עַל *against,* + Job Jb 16$_{9}$, צַדִּיק *righteous one* Ps 37$_{12}$=4QpPs$^{a}$ 1.2$_{12}$.

*חרק II vb. **break—Ni. be broken,** <SUBJ> חֶבֶל *rope,* i.e. silver cord Ec 12$_{6}$ (if em. רחק ni. *be distant*).

חרר 10 vb. **burn—Qal** 3 Pf. חָרָה, חָרוּ—**be scorched, glow,** <SUBJ> יֹשֵׁב *inhabitant* Is 24$_{6}$ (1QIsa$^{a}$ חורו *they are pale*), עֶצֶם *bone* Jb 30$_{30}$, נְחֹשֶׁת *copper* Ezk 24$_{11}$. <PREP> מִן of cause, *because of,* + חֹרֶב *dryness* of skin Jb 30$_{30}$.

**Ni.** 6 Pf. נִחַר (נָחָר), נִחָרוּ; impf. יֵחָרוּ; + waw וַיֵּחַר—**be set aglow, be hoarse,** <SUBJ> מַפֻּחַ *bellows* Jr 6$_{29}$, עֵץ *wood* Ezk 15$_{5}$, עֶצֶם *bone* Ezk 24$_{10}$ Ps 102$_{4}$, גָּרוֹן *throat* Ps 69$_{4}$, תָּוֶךְ *middle* of charred wood Ezk 15$_{4}$.

**Pilp.** 1 Inf. חַרְחַר—**cause to glow,** <SUBJ> אִישׁ *man* Pr 26$_{21}$. <OBJ> רִיב *dispute* Pr 26$_{21}$.

⇒ חָרֵר *parched place,* חַרְחוּר *burning fever.*

[חָרָר] 0.0.1 n.[m.] **dispute,** <CSTR> כל חרר *every dispute* Mur 30 2$_{25}$. <PREP> מִן *against* Mur 30 2$_{25}$.

**חָרֵר** 1 n.m. **parched places, lava stretches**—pl. חֲרֵרִים—<COLL> וְשָׁכַן חֲרֵרִים בַּמִּדְבָּר *and he shall dwell in parched places in the steppe* Jr 17$_{6}$.
⇒ חרר *burn*.

* **חרשׁ** 0.1 vb. **provoke—Qal** 1 Impf. תחרשׁ—**provoke** (unless חרשׁ *plough*, i.e. devise, against, <SUBJ> בֵּן *son* Si 8$_{2}$. <PREP> עַל introducing object, + אִישׁ wealthy *man* Si 8$_{2}$ ([עו]ל).

**חֶ֫רֶשׂ** 17.0.4 n.m. **pot**—cstr. חֶ֫רֶשׂ (חֲרָשׂ); pl. cstr. חַרְשֵׂי; sf. חֲרָשֶׂ֫יהָ—**pot, potsherd, earthenware,** <SUBJ> מצא ni. *be found* Is 30$_{14}$, ריב *dispute* Is 45$_{9}$. <OBJ> גרם *gnaw* Ezk 23$_{34}$ (or em. גמר *bring to an end*), לקח *take* Jb 2$_{8}$. <CSTR> חַרְשֵׂי אֲדָמָה *potsherds of earth* Is 45$_{9}$; כְּלִי־חֶרֶשׂ *vessel of earthenware* Lv 6$_{21}$ 11$_{33}$ 14$_{5.50}$ 15$_{12}$ Nm 5$_{17}$ Jr 32$_{14}$ 4QTohA 3.2$_{10}$ 4QTohB[b] 1$_{3}$ 11QT 49$_{8}$ 50$_{18}$, נִבְלֵי־חֶרֶשׂ *jars of earthenware* Lm 4$_{2}$, חַדּוּדֵי חָ֫רֶשׂ *sharpness of potsherds* Jb 41$_{22}$. <APP> בַּקְבֻּק *flask* Jr 19$_{1}$. <PREP> כְּ *as* Ps 22$_{16}$; עַל *upon*, + צפה pu. *be overlaid* Pr 26$_{23}$; אֵת *with*, + ריב *dispute* Is 45$_{9}$.

**חרשׁ I** 27.4.3 vb. **plough—Qal** 24.2.3 Pf. חָרְשׁוּ, חֲרַשְׁתֶּם; impf. יַחֲרוֹשׁ (יַחֲרֹשׁ), 2ms תַּחֲרֹשׁ (Si, Q תחרושׁ); ptc. חוֹרֵשׁ (חֹרֵשׁ), חֹרְשִׁים, חֹרְשֵׁי, חֹרְשׁוֹת, pass. חֲרוּשָׁה; inf. חֲרֹשׁ—**1. plough** (e.g. Dt 22$_{10}$ Ju 14$_{18}$ 1 S 8$_{2}$ 1 K 19$_{19}$ Jb 1$_{14}$ 11QT 52$_{13}$). **2. engrave** (Jr 17$_{1}$). **3. devise** (e.g. Pr 3$_{29}$ 12$_{20}$ 14$_{22}$ Jb 4$_{8}$ Si 7$_{12}$).

<SUBJ> Israelite(s) Dt 22$_{10}$ Ho 10$_{13}$ 11QT 52$_{13}$, Judah Ho 10$_{11}$, שַׂר *prince* 1 S 8$_{12}$, Elisha 1 K 19$_{19}$, אָדָם *human being* Pr 6$_{14}$, אִישׁ *man* Jg 14$_{18}$ Pr 6$_{14}$, בֵּן *son* Pr 3$_{29}$ Si 7$_{12}$ 8$_{2}$ (or em. תריב do not *contend*), בָּקָר *oxen* Jb 1$_{14}$, חֹרֵשׁ *ploughman* Is 28$_{4}$ Ps 129$_{3}$, ploughman Am 6$_{12}$ Si 6$_{19}$ 25$_{8}$, good Pr 14$_{22}$, wicked Jb 4$_{8}$ (|| זרע *sow*) Pr 12$_{20}$ 14$_{22}$, לֵב *heart* Pr 6$_{18}$.

<OBJ> חָרִישׁ *ploughing* 1 S 8$_{12}$, טוֹב *good* Pr 14$_{22}$, אָוֶן *iniquity* Jb 4$_{8}$, רַע *evil* Pr 6$_{14}$ 12$_{20}$ 14$_{22}$, רָעָה *evil* Pr 3$_{29}$, רֶשַׁע *wickedness* Ho 10$_{13}$, חָמָס *violence* Si 7$_{12}$, מַחֲשָׁבָה *plan* Pr 6$_{18}$.

<PREP> בְּ of time, *in, at, during,* + עֵת *time* Pr 6$_{14}$; of instrument, *by (means of), with,* + בָּקָר *cattle* Am 6$_{12}$, שׁוֹר *ox* Dt 22$_{10}$ Si 25$_{8}$ 11QT 52$_{13}$, חֲמוֹר *ass* Dt 22$_{10}$ 11QT 52$_{13}$, עֶגְלָה *heifer* Jg 14$_{18}$; עַל *upon*, + לוּחַ *tablet* Jr 17$_{1}$, גַּב *back* Ps 129$_{3}$; *against*, + אִישׁ *man* Si 8$_{2}$ ([עו]ל; or em.; see Subj.), אָח *brother* Si 7$_{12}$, רֵעַ *neighbour* Pr 3$_{29}$ Si 7$_{12}$, חָבֵר *companion* Si 7$_{12}$.

<COLL> הֲכֹל הַיּוֹם יַחֲרֹשׁ *does he plough continually?* Is 28$_{24}$.

**2.** pass. **be engraved** (Jr 17$_{1}$), **be designated** (4QM[a] 10.2$_{13}$), <SUBJ> כֹּהֵן *priest* 4QM[a] 10.2$_{13}$, חַטָּאת *sin* Jr 17$_{1}$ (|| כתב pass. *be written*). <PREP> לְ *for*, + מִלְחָמָה *war* 4QM[a] 10.2$_{13}$; בְּ of instrument, *by (means of), with,* + צִפֹּרֶן *stylus* Jr 17$_{1}$.

**3.** ptc. as noun, **ploughman** (Is 28$_{24}$ Am 9$_{13}$ Ps 129$_{3}$), **artisan** (Gn 4$_{22}$ 1 K 7$_{14}$), <SUBJ> נגשׁ ni. *draw near* 9$_{13}$, חרשׁ *plough* Is 28$_{24}$ Ps 129$_{3}$, זרע *sow* Is 28$_{24}$, פתח pi. *open* Is 28$_{24}$, שׂדד pi. *harrow* Is 28$_{24}$. <NOM CL> אָבִיו ... חֹרֵשׁ נְחֹשֶׁת *his father was ... an artisan of bronze* 1 K 7$_{14}$. <CSTR> חֹרֵשׁ נְחֹשֶׁת *artisan of,* i.e. in, *bronze* Gn 4$_{22}$ (+ וּבַרְזֶל *and iron*) 1 K 7$_{14}$; לֹטֵשׁ כָּל־חֹרֵשׁ *sharpener,* i.e. instructor, *of every artisan of* Gn 4$_{22}$. <APP> אִישׁ *man* of Tyre 1 K 7$_{14}$. <SYN> §1 זרע *sow*; §2 כתב pass. *be written*. Also 4Q482 2$_{1}$.

**Ni.** 2 Impf. 3fs תֵּחָרֵשׁ—**be ploughed,** <SUBJ> Zion Jr 26$_{18}$ Mc 3$_{12}$. <COLL> צִיּוֹן שָׂדֶה תֵחָרֵשׁ *Zion shall be ploughed (as) a field* Jr 26$_{18}$ Mc 3$_{12}$.

**Hi.** 1 Ptc. מַחֲרִישׁ—**plan, devise,** <SUBJ> Saul 1 S 23$_{9}$. <OBJ> רָעָה *evil* 1 S 23$_{9}$. <PREP> עַל *against*, + David 1 S 23$_{9}$.*
⇒ חָרָשׁ *artisan*.

**חרשׁ II** 47.5.3 vb. **be silent—Qal** 7 Impf. יֶחֱרַשׁ, 2ms תֶּחֱרַשׁ, תֶּחֱרַ֫שְׁנָה—**be deaf,** <SUBJ> י׳ *Y.* Ps 28$_{1}$ 35$_{22}$ 39$_{13}$, אֱלֹהִים *God* Ps 50$_{3}$ 109$_{1}$, אֵל *God* Ps 83$_{2}$, אֹזֶן *ear* Mc 7$_{16}$. <PREP> מִן of direction, *from*, + worshipper Ps 28$_{1}$; אֶל *to*, + דִּמְעָה *tears* Ps 39$_{13}$.

**Hi.** 39.4.3 Pf. הֶחֱרִישׁ (הֶחֱרִשׁ), הֶחֱרַ֫שְׁתִּי, הֶחֱרִ֫ישׁוּ; impf. יַחֲרִישׁ, 3fs תַּחֲרִישׁ, 2ms תַּחֲרִשׁ, תַּחֲרִ֫ישִׁי, אַחֲרִישׁ, יַחֲרִ֫ישׁוּ, תַּחֲרִישׁוּן; + waw וַיַּחֲרִשׁוּ (וַיַּחֲרִישׁוּ); impv. הַחֲרֵשׁ (Si החריש), הַחֲרִ֫ישִׁי, הַחֲרִ֫ישׁוּ; ptc. מַחֲרִישׁ, מַחֲרִשִׁים; inf. הַחֲרֵשׁ—**be silent, cease speaking; make silent** (Jb 11$_{3}$), <SUBJ> י׳ *Y.* Is 42$_{14}$ Hb 1$_{13}$=1QpHab 5$_{8}$ Zp 3$_{17}$ (or em. חדשׁ pi. *renew*) Jb 41$_{4}$, אֱלֹהִים *God* Ps 50$_{21}$, אִי *island* Is 41$_{1}$, עַם *people* Ex 14$_{14}$ 2 S 19$_{11}$ 2 K 18$_{36}$||Is 36$_{21}$, שַׂר

*prince* Jr 38$_{27}$, חֹר *noble* Ne 5$_{8}$, סֶגֶן *prefect* Ne 5$_{8}$, כֹּהֵן *priest* Jg 18$_{19}$, Esther Est 4$_{14}$ 7$_{4}$, Jacob Gn 34$_{5}$, Jeremiah Jr 4$_{19}$, Job Jb 6$_{24}$ 13$_{19}$ 33$_{31.33}$, Samuel 1 S 7$_{8}$, Saul 1 S 10$_{27}$, Tamar 2 S 13$_{20}$, אִישׁ *man* Gn 24$_{21}$ Nm 30$_{8.12.15.15}$ Pr 11$_{12}$, אָב *father* Nm 30$_{5}$=11QT 53$_{18}$, חָכָם *wise one* Si 20$_{7}$, אֱוִיל *fool* Pr 17$_{28}$, worshipper Ps 32$_{3}$, friends of Job Jb 13$_{5.13}$, addressee of instruction Si 35$_{8}$, בַּד *empty talk* Jb 11$_{3}$; subj. not specified, Si 20$_{6}$ 41$_{20(M)}$ CD 9$_{6}$ 4QapPs$^{b}$ 85$_{2}$ ([ה]חרש). <OBJ> מַת *man* Jb 11$_{3}$.

<PREP> לְ of direction, *to*, + רֵעַ *neighbour* CD 9$_{6}$; *with respect to*, + אִשָּׁה *woman* Nm 30$_{5}$=11QT 53$_{18}$ Nm 30$_{8.12.15.15}$; בְּ *with*, + אַהֲבָה *love* Zp 3$_{17}$; מִן of direction, *from*, + Jeremiah Jr 38$_{27}$, Job Jb 13$_{13}$, בֵּן *son* of Israel 1 S 7$_{8}$, שׁאל inf. as noun, *one who asks* Si 41$_{20(Bmg\ M)}$, יוֹם *day* CD 9$_{6}$; אֶל *to*, perh. *(come silently) before*,* + ׳׳ *Y.* Is 41$_{1}$; עַד *until*, + עֵת *time* Si 20$_{7}$, בוא inf. as noun, *coming* Gn 34$_{5}$.

**Htp.** 1 Pf. Si התחרישו; + waw וַיִּתְחָרְשׁוּ—**keep still,** <SUBJ> עַזָּתִי *Gazite* Jg 16$_{2}$; subj. not specified, Si 41$_{20(Bmg)}$. <PREP> מִן of direction, *from*, + שׁאל inf. as noun, *one who asks* Si 41$_{20(Bmg)}$. <COLL> וַיִּתְחָרְשׁוּ כָל־הַלַּיְלָה *and they kept still all the night* Jg 16$_{2}$.*

⇒ חֵרֵשׁ *deaf*, חֶרֶשׁ *sorcery*, חֶרֶשׁ *secret.*

**חָרָשׁ** 37.1.6 n.m. **artisan**—cstr. חָרַשׁ; pl. חָרָשִׁים (חֲרָשִׁים); cstr. חָרָשֵׁי—worker in stone (e.g. Ex 28$_{11}$ 2 S 5$_{11}$), in wood (e.g. 2 S 5$_{11}$ 2 K 12$_{12}$ 22$_{6}$ Is 44$_{13}$), in metal (e.g. Dt 27$_{10}$ 1 S 13$_{19}$ Ho 8$_{6}$ 13$_{2}$); maker of idols (e.g. Is 45$_{16}$ Jr 24$_{1}$); one skilled in destruction Ezk 21$_{36}$.

<SUBJ> היה *be* 1 C 4$_{14}$, מצא ni. *be found* 1 S 13$_{19}$, הלך *go* Is 45$_{16}$, יצא *go out* Jr 29$_{2}$, נטה *stretch out* Is 44$_{13}$, עשׂה *make* Ho 8$_{6}$=4QpHos$^{b}$ 11$_{3}$ Si 38$_{27}$ ([חו]רש), פעל *work* Is 44$_{12}$, נסך *pour out*, i.e. cast idol Is 40$_{19}$, חזק pi. *encourage* Is 41$_{7}$.

<NOM CL> אָהֳלִיאָב ... חָרָשׁ *Oholiab was ... an artisan* Ex 38$_{23}$, חָרָשִׁים הֵמָּה מֵאָדָם *the artisans are from among human beings* Is 44$_{11}$.

<OBJ> ברא *create* Is 54$_{16}$, בקשׁ pi. *seek* Is 40$_{20}$, בוא hi. *bring* 2 K 24$_{16}$, שׁלח *sent* 2 S 5$_{11}$‖1 C 14$_{1}$, גלה hi. *exile* 2 K 24$_{14}$ Jr 24$_{1}$, שׂכר *hire* 2 C 24$_{12}$, ראה hi. *show* Zc 2$_{3}$.

<CSTR> חָרַשׁ עֵצִים *artisan of wood*, i.e. carpenter Is 44$_{13}$ 1 C 14$_{1}$, חָרָשֵׁי עֵץ *artisans of wood*, i.e. carpenters 2 S 5$_{11}$ 2 K 12$_{12}$ (הָעֵץ) 1 C 22$_{15}$ (... עֵץ), חָרַשׁ אֶבֶן *artisan of (precious) stone*, i.e. jeweller Ex 28$_{11}$, חָרָשֵׁי אֶבֶן *artisans of stone*, i.e. masons 2 S 5$_{11}$ 1 C 22$_{15}$, קִיר *of the wall*, i.e. masons 1 C 14$_{1}$, חָרַשׁ בַּרְזֶל *artisan of iron*, i.e. ironsmith Is 44$_{12}$. חָרָשֵׁי בַרְזֶל *artisans of iron* 2 C 24$_{12}$, חָרָשֵׁי ... נְחֹשֶׁת *... artisans of ... copper*, i.e. coppersmiths 2 C 24$_{12}$, צִירִים *of idols* Is 45$_{16}$, מַשְׁחִית *of destruction*, i.e. those skilled in bringing about destruction Ezk 21$_{36}$.

מַעֲשֵׂה חָרָשׁ *work of an artisan of* Ex 28$_{11}$ Jr 10$_{9}$ (חָרָשׁ) 1QM 5$_{6}$, מעשי חרש *works of an artisan* 1QM 5$_{9.10.11}$, מַעֲשֵׂה חָרָשִׁים *work of artisans* Ho 13$_{2}$, מְלֶאכֶת חָרָשׁ *work of an artisan* Ex 35$_{35}$, אנשי החרש *men of the artisans* 4QM$^{a}$ 1$_{7}$, יַד חָרָשִׁים *hand of artisans* 1 C 29$_{5}$, יְדֵי חָרָשׁ *hands of an artisan* Dt 27$_{15}$ Jr 10$_{3}$, גֵי הַחֲרָשִׁים *valley of the artisans* Ne 11$_{35}$ 1 C 4$_{14}$ (גֵּיא).

<ADJ> חָכָם *wise*, i.e. expert Is 40$_{20}$.

<PREP> לְ of direction, *to*, + יצא hi. *bring out* 2 K 12$_{12}$, נתן *give* 2 K 22$_{6}$‖2 C 34$_{11}$ Ezr 3$_{7}$; introducing object, + שׂכר *hire* 2 C 24$_{12}$.

<COLL> אַרְבָּעָה חָרָשִׁים *four artisans* Zc 2$_{3}$.

Also perh. 5Q20 1$_{1}$.*

⇒ חרשׁ *work.*

**חֵרֵשׁ** 9.0.3 adj. **deaf**—pl. חֵרְשִׁים—**1.** used attributively of פֶּתֶן *cobra* Ps 58$_{5}$.

**2.** in nom. cl. used predicatively of מִי *who?* Is 42$_{19}$ (+ עִוֵּר *blind*).

**3.** used as noun, **deaf one,** <SUBJ> שׁמע *hear* Is 29$_{18}$ 42$_{18}$ (+ עִוֵּר *blind one*) 4QMMT B$_{52}$, בוא *come* 1QSa 2$_{6}$ ([יבו]או; + עִוֵּר, פִּסֵּחַ *lame one*, אִלֵּם *dumb one*) 4QD$^{a}$ 17.1$_{8}$ ([יבוא]; + פִּסֵּחַ, חִגֵּר *lame one*), יצב htp. *take one's stand* 1QSa 2$_{6}$. <OBJ> יצא hi. *bring out* Is 43$_{8}$ (+ עִוֵּר *blind*), קלל pi. *curse* Lv 19$_{14}$ (+ עִוֵּר). <CSTR> אָזְנֵי חֵרְשִׁים *ears of the deaf* Is 35$_{5}$ (+ עִוֵּר *blind one*). <PREP> כְּ *as* Ps 38$_{14}$ (+ אִלֵּם *dumb one*); עַל *concerning* 4QMMT B$_{52}$.

**4.** used adverbially of שׂים *place*, i.e. make Ex 4$_{11}$ (+ אִלֵּם *dumb*, פִּקֵּחַ *seeing*, עִוֵּר *blind*).

⇒ חרשׁ *be silent.*

**חֶרֶשׁ I** 1 n.m. **sorcery**—pl. חֲרָשִׁים—**sorcery, magic,** <CSTR> חֲכַם חֲרָשִׁים *wise one of sorceries*, i.e. one expert in magic or sorcery Is 3$_{3}$.

⇒ חרשׁ *be silent.*

חֶרֶשׁ II 1 adv. **secretly,** + שׁלח *send* Jos 2$_1$.
⇒ חרשׁ *be silent.*

חֶרֶשׁ III 1 pr.n.m. **Heresh,** Levite and descendant of Asaph, who settled in Jerusalem after the exile, <NOM CL> בֶּן־אָסָף ... חֶרֶשׁ *Heresh was … a son of Asaph* 1 C 9$_{15}$.

חֹרֶשׁ I 3 n.m. **wood**—pl. חֳרָשִׁים—**wood (land),** <SUBJ> צלל hi. *give shade* Ezk 31$_3$. <CSTR> עֲזוּבַת הַחֹרֶשׁ *deserted places of the woodland* Is 17$_9$. <PREP> בְּ of place, *in,* + בנה *build* 2 C 27$_4$.

חֹרֶשׁ II 4 pl.n. **Horesh**—+ ה- of direction חֹרְשָׁה—perh. Ḥorēša, 10 km S of Hebron, <PREP> בְּ of place, *in, at, among* 1 S 23$_{15}$, + ישׁב *dwell* 1 S 23$_{18}$, סתר htp. *hide oneself* 1 S 23$_{19}$. <COLL> חֹרְשָׁה (with ה- of direction), *to, in, at,* + הלך *go* 1 S 23$_{16}$.

חַרְשָׁא 2 pr.n.m. **Harsha,** name of family of Nethinim, temple servants in postexilic Judaea Ezr 2$_{52}$ Ne 7$_{54}$, <CSTR> בְּנֵי חַרְשָׁא *sons of Harsha* Ezr 2$_{52}$||Ne 7$_{54}$.

חֹרְשָׁה, see חֹרֶשׁ *Horesh.*

חֲרֹשֶׁת 4 n.f. **carving**—cstr. חֲרֹשֶׁת—<CSTR> חֲרֹשֶׁת אֶבֶן *carving of stone,* i.e. cutting of stones Ex 31$_5$=Ex 35$_{33}$, חֲרֹשֶׁת עֵץ *carving of wood* Ex 31$_5$=Ex 35$_{33}$. <PREP> בְּ of accompaniment, *in, with,* + עשׂה *do,* i.e. work Ex 31$_5$=Ex 35$_{33}$.
⇒ חרשׁ *plough.*

חֲרֹשֶׁת הַגּוֹיִם 3 pl.n. **Harosheth-ha-goiim,** perh. T. ʻAmr near El-Ḥāriṯīye, 15 km SE of Haifa, <PREP> בְּ of place, *in,* + ישׁב *dwell* Jg 4$_2$; מִן of direction, *from,* + זעק *call out* Jg 4$_{13}$; עַד *until,* + רדף *pursue* Jg 4$_{16}$.

חרת 1.1.12 vb. **engrave—Qal** 1.1.12 Pf. Q חרתה ,חרת; impf. Q אחורתם; ptc. pass. חָרוּת—**1.** active, **engrave,** <SUBJ> אֱלֹהִים *God* 4QShirShabb$^a$ 1.1$_{5.15}$, אֵל *God* 1QM 12$_3$. <OBJ> בְּרִית *covenant* 1QM 12$_3$, חֹק *statute* 4QShirShabb$^a$ 1.1$_{5.15}$ ([חוק]) 4QShirShabb$^c$ 4$_3$ (חו[קי]) 4QShir$^b$ 63.2$_3$, חֻקָּה *statute* 4QShirShabb$^f$ 23.2$_{13}$ ([חו]קות ... [חרת]), מִשְׁפָּט *judgment* 4QShirShabb$^a$ 1.1$_5$, כָּבוֹד *glory* 4QShirShabb$^f$ 23.2$_3$, נִפְלָא *wonder* 4QShir$^b$ 63.2$_3$. <PREP> לְ of benefit, *for* 4QShirShabb$^a$ 1.1$_{15}$, + אֱלֹהִים *god* 4Q ShirShabb$^a$ 1.1$_5$, עַם *people* 4QShirShabb$^a$ 1.1$_5$, בָּחִיר *elect one* 1QM 12$_3$, יסד pi. ptc. *one who establishes* knowledge 4QShirShabb$^a$ 1.1$_5$ ([מ׳סדי]), מַעֲשֶׂה *creature* 4QShir Shabb$^a$ 1.1$_5$, קָרוֹב *one near* 4QShirShabb$^a$ 1.1$_5$; בְּ of instrument, *by (means of),* + חֶרֶט *stylus* 1QM 12$_3$; of accompaniment, *with, in,* + דַּעַת *knowledge* 4QShir Shabb$^f$ 23.2$_{13}$, שֵׂכֶל *insight* 4QShirShabb$^f$ 23.2$_{13}$.

**2.** passive, **be engraved,** <SUBJ> מִכְתָּב *writing* Ex 32$_{16}$, אֶבֶן *stone* Si 45$_{11}$, חֹק *statute* 1QS 10$_{6.8.1}$, מְחֹקֵק *decree* 4Q417 2.1$_{15}$. <PREP> לְ of direction, *to,* + עַד *eternity* 1QS 10$_6$; *as,* + זִכָּרוֹן *remembrance* Si 45$_{11}$; *according to,* + מִסְפָּר *number* Si 45$_{11}$; בְּ of accompaniment, *with, in,* + כְּתָב *writing* Si 45$_{11}$; עַל *upon,* + לוּחַ *tablet* Ex 32$_{16}$. <COLL> חרות החוקים appar. *engraved one of the statutes* 4Q417 2.1$_{14}$. Also 4QAges 1$_3$.
⇒ חֶרֶת *ink.*

חֶרֶת I 1 pl.n. **Hereth**—חָרֶת—place in Judah, perh. near Kh. Ḥarās, 3 km E of Keilah, <CSTR> יַעַר חָרֶת *forest of Hereth* 1 S 22$_5$.

[חֶרֶת] II 0.0.2 n.f. **ink**—<PREP> בְּ of instrument, *by (means of),* + חקק pass. *be engraved* 1QH 12$_4$; כְּ *as,* + כתב ni. *be written* 4QD$^a$ 18.5$_{16}$.
⇒ חרת *engrave.*

חָשׂוּף, see חשׂף I *make bare.*

חֲשׂוּפָא 2 pr.n.m. **Hasupha,** head of family of Nethinim, temple servants in postexilic Judaea, <CSTR> בְּנֵי־ חֲשׂוּפָא *sons of Hasupha* Ezr 2$_{43}$||Ne 7$_{46}$.

[חָשִׂיף] 1 n.m. **little flock**—cstr. חֲשִׂפֵי—<CSTR> חֲשִׂפֵי עִזִּים *little flocks of goats* 1 K 20$_{27}$; שְׁנֵי חֲשִׂפֵי *two little flocks of* 1 K 20$_{27}$. <PREP> כְּ *as,* + חנה *encamp* 1 K 20$_{27}$.

חשׂך I 28.2.1 vb. **withhold—Qal** 26.1 Pf. חָשַׂךְ (חָשָׂךְ), חָשַׂכְתָּ ,חָשַׂכְתִּי ,חָשְׂכוּ (חָשָׂכוּ); impf. יַחְשֹׂךְ ,תַּחְשֹׂךְ (תַּחְשׂוֹךְ),

חוֹשֵׂךְ ,אֶחֱשֹׂךְ ,תַּחְשְׂכִי; + waw וָאֶחְשֹׂךְ; impv. חֲשֹׂךְ; ptc. חוֹשֵׂךְ (חָשֵׂךְ)—**withhold, hold back, spare, refrain, fail to appear** (Ezk 30$_{18}$).

**<SUBJ>** ׳י *Y.* 1 S 25$_{39}$ Ps 19$_{14}$ Jb 38$_{23}$, אֲדֹנָי *Lord* Is 38$_{17}$ (if em. חָשַׁקְתָּ *you have loved*), אֱלֹהִים *God* Gn 20$_{6}$ Ps 78$_{50}$ Ezr 9$_{13}$ Si 51$_{2}$, אֵל *God* Jb 33$_{18}$, עַם *people* Jr 14$_{10}$, Abraham Gn 22$_{12.16}$, Job Jb 7$_{11}$, אָדוֹן *lord* Gn 39$_{9}$ 2 K 5$_{20}$, prophet Is 58$_{1}$, father Pr 13$_{24}$, בֵּן *son* of a fool Jb 30$_{10}$, righteous one Pr 21$_{26}$ 24$_{11}$, wise one Pr 10$_{19}$ 17$_{27}$, miser Pr 11$_{24}$, עָקָר fem. sing. *barren one* Is 54$_{2}$, מֻרְדָּף *persecution* Is 14$_{6}$, יוֹם *day* Ezk 30$_{18}$.

**<OBJ>** Abimelech Gn 20$_{6}$, Naaman 2 K 5$_{20}$, בֵּן *son* Gn 22$_{12.16}$, עֶבֶד *servant* 1 S 25$_{39}$ Ps 19$_{14}$, מוט ptc. *one who totters* Pr 24$_{11}$, שֵׁבֶט *rod* Pr 13$_{24}$, רֹק *spittle* Jb 30$_{10}$, אוֹצָר *storehouse* Jb 38$_{23}$, נֶפֶשׁ *soul* Ps 78$_{50}$ Jb 33$_{18}$, בָּשָׂר *flesh* Si 51$_{2}$, רֶגֶל *foot* Jr 14$_{10}$, פֶּה *mouth* Jb 7$_{11}$, שָׂפָה *lip* Pr 10$_{19}$, נִיד *solace* of lips Jb 16$_{5}$ (unless חשך II *be continuous*, with נִיד *movement*, as subj.), אִמְרָה *word* Pr 17$_{27}$, דַּעַת *knowledge* perh. 4Q418 95$_{3}$, מְאוּמָה *anything* Gn 39$_{9}$.

**<PREP>** לְ of benefit, *to, for*, + עֵת *time* Jb 38$_{23}$; *as*, + מַטָּה *less*, i.e. less punishment than deserved Ezr 9$_{13}$.

בְּ of place, *in*, + Tehaphnehes Ezk 30$_{18}$.

מִן of direction, *from*, + מַלְאָךְ *angel* of God Gn 22$_{12}$, Joseph Gn 39$_{9}$, חטא inf. as noun, *sinning* Gn 20$_{6}$, רָעָה *evil* 1 S 25$_{39}$, זֵד *presumptuous sins* Ps 19$_{14}$, מָוֶת *death* Ps 78$_{50}$, שַׁחַת *pit* Is 38$_{17}$ (if em.; see Subj.) Jb 33$_{18}$ Si 51$_{2}$; of cause, *because of*, + יֹשֶׁר *honesty* Pr 13$_{24}$; *at*, + פָּנִים *face* Jb 30$_{10}$.

**Ni.** 2.1 Impf. יֵחָשֵׂךְ ,יֵחָשֵׂךְ—**be withheld, be assuaged, be spared, <SUBJ>** רַע *evil one* Jb 21$_{30}$, יֹשֶׁר *uprightness* Si 9$_{17}$, כְּאֵב *pain* Jb 16$_{6}$. **<PREP>** לְ *at, on*, + יוֹם *day* Jb 21$_{30}$; בְּ of instrument, *by (means of)*, + חָכָם *wise one* Si 9$_{17}$.*

*חשך II 1 vb. **be continuous—Qal** 1 Impf. יַחְשֹׂךְ—**be continuous, be unceasing, <SUBJ>** נִיד *movement* of lips Jb 16$_{5}$ (unless חשך I *withhold*).

* [חֶשְׁכָּה] n.f. **abundance, <OBJ>** שִׁית *place* Ps 18$_{12}$ (if em. חֲשֵׁכָה *darkness*). **<CSTR>** חֶשְׁכַּת־מַיִם *abundance of water* Ps 18$_{12}$ (if em. חֶשְׁכַת־ *darkness of*; ms, ||2 S 22$_{12}$ חַשְׁרַת *sieve of* water).

חשף I 11.2 vb. **make bare—Qal** 11.2 Pf. חָשַׂף (חֲשָׂפָהּ), חָשַׂפְתִּי; impf. Si יחשוף; + waw וַיֶּחֱשֹׂף; impv. חֶשְׂפִּי־; ptc. pass. חֲשׂוּפָה, pl. cstr. חֲשׂוּפֵי; inf. חָשֹׂף (לַחְשֹׂף, Si חסוף)—**1. make bare, strip, skim** (Is 30$_{14}$ Hg 2$_{16}$).

**<SUBJ>** ׳י *Y.* Is 52$_{10}$ Jr 13$_{26}$ 49$_{10}$, קוֹל *voice* of Y. Ps 29$_{9}$, גּוֹי *nation* Jl 1$_{7}$, בַּת *daughter* of Babylon Is 47$_{2}$, בְּתוּלָה *virgin* Is 47$_{2}$, אהב ptc. *one who loves* Si 6$_{9}$, farmer Hg 2$_{16}$ (unless חשף II *scoop up*), addressee of instruction Si 42$_{1}$, חֶרֶשׂ *shard* Is 30$_{14}$ (unless חשף II *scoop up*).

**<OBJ>** Esau Jr 49$_{10}$, יַעַר *forest* Ps 29$_{9}$, תְּאֵנָה *fig tree* Jl 1$_{7}$, מַיִם *water* Is 30$_{14}$, שׁוּל *skirt* Jr 13$_{26}$, שֹׁבֶל *hem of skirt* Is 47$_{2}$, זְרוֹעַ *arm* Is 52$_{10}$, פּוּרָה *winepress* Hg 2$_{16}$ (unless חשף II *scoop up*), רִיב *dispute* Si 6$_{9}$, סוֹד *secret* Si 42$_{1(B)}$, דְּבַר עֵצָה *word of counsel, secret* Si 42$_{1(M)}$.

**<PREP>** לְ *before*, + עַיִן *eye*, i.e. sight, of nations Is 52$_{10}$; מִן of direction, *from*, + גֶּבֶא *cistern* Is 30$_{14}$ (unless חשף II *scoop up*); עַל *upon*, + פָּנֶה *face* Jr 13$_{26}$.

**2.** pass. **be made bare, be stripped, <SUBJ>** זְרוֹעַ *arm* Ezk 4$_{7}$, שֵׁת *buttock* Is 20$_{4}$.

* חשף II 2 vb. **scoop up, Qal** 2 Inf. לַחְשֹׂף—**scoop up** (unless חשף I *make bare*), **<SUBJ>** farmer Hg 2$_{16}$, חֶרֶשׂ *shard* Is 30$_{14}$. **<OBJ>** מַיִם *water* Is 30$_{14}$, פּוּרָה *winepress*, i.e. liquid from the winepress Hg 2$_{16}$. **<PREP>** מִן of direction, *from*, + גֶּבֶא *cistern* Is 30$_{14}$.

חשב 123.10.55 vb. **think—Qal** 65.8.25 Pf. חָשַׁב (חֲשָׁבָהּ), חָשַׁבְתָּ (חָשַׁבְתָּה) חָשַׁבְתִּי, חָשַׁבוּ חָשְׁבוּ (חֲשָׁבוּ), חֲשַׁבְתֶּם; impf. יַחְשֹׁב (Si יחשוב ,יַחְשָׁב ,יַחֲשָׁב־ ,יַחְשְׁבֵנִי), תַּחְשֹׁב (תַּחְשְׁבֵנִי), שְׁבוּ) תַּחְשְׁבוּ (Q יחשבוני ,יַחְשְׁבוּן Q ,יחשובו ,יַחְשְׁבוּ) יַחְשְׁבוּ ;וַנַּחְשְׁבָה ,וְחָשַׁבְתָּ ;תַּחְ ,תַּחְשְׁבֵנִי) ,נַחְשְׁבָה (חֲשַׁבְנֻהוּ); + waw וַיַּחְשְׁבֶהָ) וַיַּחְשְׁבֵנִי ,ויחשוב Q); impv. Si. חשב[והו]; ptc. חֹשֵׁב (חוֹשֵׁב), חֹשְׁבִים (Q חושבים), cstr. חֹשְׁבֵי; inf. לַחְשֹׁב (Q חשוב)—**1a. think, consider, plan, invent, value, <SUBJ>** ׳י *Y.* Gn 15$_{6}$ Jr 18$_{8}$ (+ עשׂה *do*) 26$_{3}$ 29$_{11}$ 36$_{3}$ 49$_{20}$ 50$_{45}$ Mc 2$_{1.3}$ Ps 32$_{2}$ 40$_{18(mss)}$ Lm 2$_{8}$, אֲדֹנָי *(my) Lord* Ps 40$_{18}$, אֱלֹהִים *God* Gn 50$_{20}$ 2 S 14$_{14}$, אֱלוֹהַּ *God* Jb 19$_{11}$, אֵל *God* Jb 13$_{24}$ 33$_{10}$.

אַשּׁוּר *Assyria* Is 10$_{7}$ (+ דמה pi. *intend*), גּוֹג *Gog* Ezk 38$_{10}$, מָדַי *Medes* Is 13$_{17}$, Amorites Jr 48$_{2}$, בַּיִת *house* of Israel Jr 11$_{19}$, of Judah Jr 11$_{19}$, יְהוּדִי *Jew* Ne 6$_{6}$ (+ מרד *revolt*), Israelite(s) Zc 7$_{10}$ 8$_{17}$.

אָדוֹן *lord* 2 S 19$_{20}$, מֶלֶךְ *king* Jr 49$_{30}$, אָמָה *female servant* Jb 19$_{15}$, נָבִיא *prophet* Jr 23$_{27}$ (+ שׁכח hi. *cause to forget*), אִישׁ *man* Jr 18$_{18}$ Ezk 11$_{2}$ (|| יעץ *counsel*) Ps 140$_{3.5}$ (+ דחה *push*) 5$_{26}$, אָח *brother* Gn 50$_{20}$, בֵּן *son* Ex 31$_{4}$ 2 C 2$_{13}$ Si 30$_{39}$ ([חשבנ]הו) 42$_{7(Bmg)}$ 4QMidrEschat$^{a}$ 3$_{9}$ 4QpsEzek$^{b}$ 3.2$_{3}$, מוֹדָע *relative* 1QH 4$_{9}$.

Ben Sira Si 51$_{18}$ (+ יטב hi. *cause to be good*), Bezalel Ex 31$_{4}$||35$_{32}$, David 2 S 14$_{13}$, Eli 1 S 1$_{13}$, Geshem Ne 6$_{2}$ (+ עשׂה *do*), Haman Est 8$_{3}$ 9$_{24}$ (+ אבד pi. *destroy*) 9$_{25}$, Job Jb 35$_{2}$, Huram-abi 2 C 2$_{13}$, Judah Gn 38$_{15}$, Nebuchadnezzar Jr 49$_{30}$, Nehemiah Ne 6$_{6}$ (+ מרד *revolt*), Sanballat Ne 6$_{2}$ (+ עשׂה *do*), Saul 1 S 18$_{25}$ (+ נפל hi. *cause to fall*).

רֵעַ *friend* 1QH 4$_{9}$, Job's friends Jb 6$_{26}$ (+ יכח hi. *reprove*), worshipper Is 53$_{3.4}$ 1QH 10$_{5}$, pious Ml 3$_{16}$=CD 20$_{19}$=4QpGen$^{b}$ 4.1$_{2}$ ([חשבי]), גִּבּוֹר *mighty one* Ps 52$_{4}$ Si 16$_{23(Amg)}$, רָשָׁע *wicked one* Ps 10$_{2}$ 36$_{5}$, wicked Na 1$_{11}$, צַר *adversary* Si 12$_{16}$.

יֹשֵׁב *inhabitant* Jr 18$_{18}$, יֹצֵר *potter* Jr 18$_{11}$, יֹעֵץ *counsellor* Si 37$_{8(B)}$, שׁכב ptc. *one who lies* Am 6$_{5}$, דרשׁ ptc. *one who seeks* 1QH 2$_{32}$ (+ תמם hi. *finish*), פתה ptc. *one who is foolish* Si 16$_{23(Amg)}$, עצם ptc. *one who closes* his eyes Pr 16$_{30}$ (if em. עצה ptc. *one who narrows* his eyes), עצה ptc. *one who narrows* his eyes Pr 16$_{30}$ (or em. עצם ptc. *one who closes* his eyes), enemy Ps 21$_{12}$ 35$_{4.20}$ Is 33$_{8}$, שׂנא ptc. *one who hates* Ps 35$_{20}$ 41$_{8}$, בוזה *one who despises* 1QH 4$_{23}$, נַעֲלָם *dissembler* 1QH 4$_{14}$.

אֲנַחְנוּ *we*, i.e. authors of halakhic epistle 4QMMT B$_{2}$ ([א]נ[ח]נו) B$_{8}$ ([אנחנו חושבים]) B$_{29.36}$ ([אנחנו חושבים]) B$_{37}$ ([אנח]נו) B$_{42}$ ([חוש[בים]) C$_{27}$, לִוְיָתָן *Leviathan* Jb 41$_{19.24}$, perh. לֵבָב *heart* Is 10$_{7}$; subj. not specified, Dn 11$_{25}$ 1QH 4$_{8}$ 8$_{14}$.

<OBJ> Hannah 1 S 1$_{13}$, Job Jb 13$_{24}$ 19$_{11.15}$ 33$_{10}$, Tamar Gn 38$_{15}$, אֱנוֹשׁ *human being* Is 33$_{8}$, אִישׁ *man* Is 53$_{3.4}$ 4Q417 1.1$_{7}$, עֶבֶד *servant* Si 30$_{39}$, worshipper 1QH 4$_{8.9.23}$.

עָוֹן *iniquity* 2 S 19$_{20}$ Ps 32$_{2}$, אָוֶן *iniquity* Ezk 11$_{2}$ Mc 2$_{1}$ Ps 36$_{5}$, רָעָה *evil* Gn 50$_{20.20}$ Jr 18$_{8.11}$ 36$_{3}$ 48$_{2}$ Mc 2$_{3}$ Na 2$_{11}$ Zc 7$_{10}$ 8$_{17}$ Ps 35$_{4}$ 41$_{8}$ 140$_{3}$, הַוָּה *ruin* Ps 52$_{4}$ 1QH 5$_{26}$, תַּהְפֻּכֹת *perversity* Pr 16$_{30}$.

כְּלִי *instrument* Am 6$_{5}$, כֶּסֶף *silver* Is 13$_{17}$, בַּרְזֶל *iron* Jb 41$_{19}$, מַחֲשָׁבָה *plan* 2 S 14$_{14}$ Jr 11$_{19}$ 18$_{11.18}$ 29$_{11}$ 49$_{20}$ 50$_{45}$ Ezk 38$_{10}$ Est 8$_{3}$ 9$_{25}$ Dn 11$_{25}$ 4QMidrEschat$^{a}$ 3$_{9}$, *invention* Ex 31$_{4}$ 35$_{32}$ 2 C 2$_{13}$, מְזִמָּה *plot* Ps 10$_{2}$ 21$_{12}$, תְּהוֹם *deep* Jb 41$_{24}$, מַהֲמֹרָה *pit* Si 12$_{16}$, דָּבָר *word* Ps 35$_{20}$, trust Gn 15$_{6}$, מִפְקָד *counting* of hand Si 42$_{7(Bmg)}$, שֵׁם *name* Ml 3$_{16}$=CD 20$_{19}$=4QpGen$^{b}$ 4.1$_{2}$, כֵּן *so* Is 10$_{7}$, אֶחָד *one* Si 30$_{39}$, זֹאת *this* Jb 35$_{2}$ Si 16$_{23}$.

<PREP> לְ of benefit, *to, for*, + Abram Gn 15$_{6}$, Shimei 2 S 19$_{20}$, אָדָם *human being* Ps 32$_{2}$, worshipper Ps 40$_{18}$ 41$_{8}$, שׁכב *one who lies* Am 6$_{5}$, טוֹבָה *good* Gn 50$_{20}$, נֶפֶשׁ *soul* Si 37$_{8(B)}$; *as*, + זָר *stranger* Jb 19$_{15}$, זוֹנָה *prostitute* Gn 38$_{15}$, שֵׂיבָה *grey-haired one* Jb 41$_{24}$, שִׁכֹּר *drunken one* 1 S 1$_{13}$, אֹיֵב *enemy* Jb 13$_{24}$ 33$_{10}$, מִשְׁפָּט *judgment* Jb 35$_{2}$, כְּלִי *vessel* 1QH 4$_{9}$, תֶּבֶן *straw* Jb 41$_{19}$; בְּ of place, *in, at, among*, + Heshbon Jr 48$_{2}$, לֵבָב *heart* Zc 7$_{10}$ 8$_{17}$, לֵב *heart* Ps 140$_{3}$ Si 12$_{16}$; כְּ *as*, + אָח *brother* Si 30$_{39}$, צַר *adversary* Jb 19$_{11}$, זֹאת *this* 2 S 14$_{13}$; אֶל *to, against*, + אֶרֶץ *land* Jr 50$_{45}$, יֹשֵׁב *inhabitant* Jr 49$_{20}$; עַל *upon*, + מִשְׁכָּב *couch* Ps 36$_{5}$; *against*, + י׳ Y. Na 1$_{11}$, Kedar Jr 49$_{30(Qr; mss)}$, Moab Jr 48$_{2}$, Jew Est 8$_{3}$ 9$_{24.25}$, עַם *people* of God 2 S 14$_{13}$, מִשְׁפָּחָה *family* Mc 2$_{3}$, מֶלֶךְ *king* Dn 11$_{25}$, Jeremiah Jr 11$_{19}$ 18$_{18}$, Joseph Gn 50$_{20}$, אִישׁ *man* Jr 18$_{11}$, בֵּן *son* of light 4QMidrEschat$^{a}$ 3$_{9}$, *son* of east Jr 49$_{30(Qr; mss)}$, יֹשֵׁב *inhabitant* Jr 18$_{11}$ 49$_{30(mss)}$; *on behalf of, on account of*, + גּוֹלָה *exile* Jr 29$_{11}$.

<COLL> וַיַּחְשְׁבֶהָ לּוֹ צְדָקָה *and he reckoned it to him (as) righteousness* Gn 15$_{6}$, איש עול אל תחשוב עזר *and do not consider the man of injustice as a help* 4Q417 1.1$_{7}$, אנחנו חושבים ש- *we are of the opinion that* 4QMMT B$_{29.36}$ ([אנחנו חושבים ש-]) B$_{37}$ ([אנח]נו חושבים ש-]), sim. B$_{42}$ ([חוש[בים אנחנו [ש-]).*

**1b. ptc. as noun, designer, planner,** <OBJ> עשׂה *make* Si 38$_{27(B)}$ ([חו[שב]). <CSTR> מעשה חשב *work of the designer* Si 45$_{10}$ 1QM 5$_{5.14}$ 7$_{10}$ 4QM$^{a}$ 1$_{18}$ (all four חושב).

Also 4QMyst$^{a}$ 10$_{4}$ 4Q417 2.2$_{15}$ 4QSap$^{b}$ 14$_{3}$ 4QDibHam$^{a}$ 1.3$_{2}$ 4QPrFêtes$^{c}$ 141$_{1}$.

<SYN> §1a יעץ *plan*.

**Ni.** 30.1.17 Pf. נֶחְשַׁב, Q נחשבה ,נֶחְשַׁבְתִּי ,נֶחְשָׁבוּ (נֶחְשָׁבוּ), Q נחשבתם ,נֶחְשַׁבְנוּ; impf. יֵחָשֵׁב, 3fs תֵּחָשֵׁב (תֵּחָשֵׁב), יֵחָשְׁבוּ; + waw וַתֵּחָשֵׁב ;וְנֶחְשַׁב; ptc. נֶחְשָׁב—**be accounted, be reckoned, be considered,** <SUBJ> perh. Y. 4QM$^{a}$ 11.1$_{18}$, אֵמִים *Emim* Dt 2$_{11}$, Israelite(s) Ps 44$_{23}$, גּוֹי *nation* Is 40$_{15.17}$ 4QDibHam$^{a}$ 1.3$_{3}$ ([נחשב]ו), אֶרֶץ Dt 2$_{20}$ Jos 13$_{3}$, Lebanon 4QpIsa$^{c}$ 22$_{1}$, כַּרְמֶל *fruitful field* Is 29$_{17}$

$32_{15}$, בְּאֵרוֹת *Beeroth* 2 S $4_{2}$.

Hanan Ne $13_{13}$, Leah Gn $31_{15}$, Pedaiah Ne $13_{13}$, Rachel Gn $31_{15}$, Shelemiah Ne $13_{13}$, Zadok Ne $13_{13}$, אָדָם *human being* Is $2_{22}$ 1QS $5_{17}$, בֵּן *son* of Zion Lm $4_{2}$, worshipper Ps $88_{5}$ 1QH $3_{24}$ $18_{26}$, friends of Job Jb $18_{3}$, אֱוִיל *foolish one* Pr $17_{28}$, יֹצֵר *potter* Is $29_{16}$=4QpIsa$^{c}$ $17_{1}$ ([יחשב]), ברך pi. ptc. *one who blesses* Pr $27_{14}$, מאס ptc. *one who refuses* 4QD$^{a}$ $18.5_{6}$.

בַּיִת *house* Lv $25_{31}$, כֶּלֶא *imprisonment* 1QH $5_{38}$, מַעֲשֶׂה *product* 11QT $7_{14}$ ([חוש]ב), תּוֹרָה *law* Ho $8_{12}$, זֶבַח *sacrifice* Lv $7_{18}$, תְּרוּמָה *offering* Nm $18_{27.30}$, prayer Ps $106_{31}$, דָּם *blood* Lv $17_{4}$ 4QTohA $1.1_{8}$, כֶּסֶף *silver* 1 K $10_{21}$||2 C $9_{20}$ 2 K $22_{7}$, נֵצֶר *shoot* 1QH $8_{11}$, פַּרְסָה *hoof* Is $5_{28}$, תּוֹתָח *cudgel* Jb $41_{21}$, אֵפֶר *dust* 4QHod$^{a}$ $7.2_{16}$, עָפָר *dust* 4QHod$^{a}$ $7.2_{16}$, אֶלֶף *thousand* 11QJub $4_{30}$, מִי *who?* 4QM$^{a}$ $11.1_{15}$, כֹּל *everyone* 1QS $5_{18}$; subj. not specified, 4QMMT $C_{31}$.

<PREP> לְ of benefit, *to, for,* + כְּנַעֲנִי *Canaanite* Jos $13_{3}$, לֵוִי *Levite* Nm $18_{27.30}$, Phinehas Ps $106_{31}$, אִישׁ *man* Lv $17_{4}$, קרב hi. ptc. *one who offers* sacrifice Lv $7_{18}$, worshipper 4QMMT $C_{31}$; *as,* + צְדָקָה *righteousness* Ps $106_{31}$ 4QMMT $C_{31}$, בּוּז *contempt* 4QM$^{a}$ $11.1_{15}$, יַעַר *forest* Is $29_{16}$ $32_{15}$, נֵבֶל *storage jar* Lm $4_{2}$, מְאוּמָה *anything* 1 K $10_{21}$||2 C $9_{20}$; of agent, *by (means of),* + ׳י *Y.* Is $40_{17}$, Laban Gn $31_{15}$, רֵעַ *friend* Pr $27_{14}$; בְּ of place/time, *in, at, during,* + יוֹם *day* 1 K $10_{21}$; of accompaniment, *in, with,* + בְּרִית *covenant* 1QS $5_{18}$, בֵּן *son* 4QD$^{a}$ $18.5_{6}$; כְּ *as,* + חֹמֶר *clay* Is $29_{16}$=4QpIsa$^{c}$ $17_{1}$, קַשׁ *stubble* Jb $41_{21}$, שַׁחַק *dust* Is $40_{15}$, צֹר *flint* Is $5_{28}$ (if em. כַּצָּר *as the adversary*), בְּהֵמָה *beast* Jb $18_{3}$, צֹאן *sheep* Ps $44_{23}$, תְּבוּאָה *produce* Nm $18_{30.30}$, זוֹב *discharge* 4QTohA $1.1_{8}$, זָר *strange thing* Ho $8_{12}$, אֶפֶס *nothingness* 4QDibHam$^{a}$ $1.3_{3}$ ([נחשב[ו]), תֹּהוּ *nothing* 4QDibHam$^{a}$ $1.3_{3}$ ([נחשב[ו] ... [כ]תהוו); מִן of comparison *(less) than,* + אֶפֶס *nothingness* Is $40_{17}$; עַל *upon, on, with,* + Benjamin 2 S $4_{2}$; *according to, as,* + שָׂדֶה *field* Lv $25_{31}$; אֵת *with,* + חָרָשׁ *artisan* 2 K $22_{7}$, בֹּנֶה *builder* 2 K $22_{7}$, גֹּדֵר *mason* 2 K $22_{7}$; לִפְנֵי *before,* + Y. 4QDibHam$^{a}$ $1.3_{3}$ ([נחשב[ו]); עַד *until,* + זֹאת *this* 1QH $18_{26}$; עִם *with,* + אֵל *God* 4QM$^{a}$ $11.1_{18}$, ירד ptc. *one who goes down* Ps $88_{5}$, תְּהוֹם *deep* 1QH $5_{38}$.

<COLL> הֲלוֹא נָכְרִיּוֹת נֶחְשַׁבְנוּ לוֹ *are not we regarded by him as foreigners?* Gn $31_{15}$, רְפָאִים יֵחָשְׁבוּ אַף־הֵם *even they are reckoned as the Rephaim* Dt $2_{11}$, אֶרֶץ־רְפָאִים תֵּחָשֵׁב אַף־הִיא *even it is reckoned as the land of the Rephaim* Dt $2_{20}$, גַּם אֱוִיל ... חָכָם יֵחָשֵׁב *even the foolish one ... is considered as wise* Pr $17_{28}$, קְלָלָה תֵּחָשֶׁב לוֹ *it will be reckoned to him as a curse* Pr $27_{14}$, נֶאֱמָנִים נֶחְשָׁבוּ *they were reckoned as faithful ones* Ne $13_{13}$.

Also Si $20_{5}$ 1QH fr $13_{5}$ 4QpHos$^{b}$ $14_{2}$ ([נ]חשב[ו]) 4QHod$^{a}$ $7.1_{13}$ 4Q471$^{a}$ $1_{5}$ 4QPrQuot $27_{3}$.

**Pi.** 16.0.4 Pf. חִשֵּׁב, חִשְּׁבָה, חִשַּׁבְתִּי; impf. יְחַשֵּׁב, יְחַשְּׁבוּ, תְּחַשְּׁבוּן; + waw וָאֲחַשְּׁבָה, וַתְּחַשְּׁבֵהוּ; ptc. מְחַשֵּׁב (Q מחשביה)—**calculate, consider, plan, be about to** (Jon $1_{4}$), <SUBJ> ׳י *Y.* Ps $144_{3}$, Ephraim Ho $7_{15}$, אִישׁ *man* Lv $25_{27}$, אָח *brother* Lv $25_{50.52}$, מֶלֶךְ *king* Dn $11_{24}$, כֹּהֵן *priest* Lv $27_{18.23}$ 2 K $12_{16}$, סֹפֵר *scribe* 2 K $12_{16}$, אֹיֵב *enemy* Na $1_{9}$, worshipper Ps $73_{16}$ $77_{6}$ $119_{59}$, wicked Pr $24_{8}$ (+ רעע hi. *do evil*), אֳנִיָּה *ship* Jon $1_{4}$ (+ שבר ni. *be broken up*), לֵב *heart* Pr $16_{9}$; subj. not specified, 1QH $3_{32.33}$ 4QDibHam$^{a}$ $1.7_{7}$ 4QShir$^{b}$ $37_{4}$.

<OBJ> אִישׁ *man* 2 K $12_{16}$, בֵּן *son* Ps $144_{3}$, רַע *evil* Ho $7_{15}$, הַוָּה *ruin* 1QH $3_{33}$, דֶּרֶךְ *way* Ps $119_{59}$ Pr $16_{9}$, מַחֲשָׁבָה *plan* Dn $11_{24}$, שָׁנָה *year* Lv $25_{27}$ Ps $77_{6}$, תְּהוֹם *deep* 1QH $3_{32}$, יוֹם *day* Ps $77_{6}$, כֶּסֶף *silver* Lv $27_{18}$, מִכְסָה *valuation* Lv $27_{23}$; obj. not specified, 4QDibHam$^{a}$ $1.7_{7}$ 4QShir$^{b}$ $37_{4}$.

<PREP> לְ of benefit, *to, for,* + אִישׁ *man* Lv $27_{18.23}$, אָח *brother* Lv $25_{50}$; מִן of direction, *from,* + שָׁנָה *year* Lv $25_{50}$, קֶדֶם *antiquity* Ps $77_{6}$; אֶל *to,* + ׳י *Y.* Ho $7_{15}$ Na $1_{9}$; עַל *against,* + מִבְצָר *fortress* Dn $11_{24}$; עַל־פִּי *according to,* + שָׁנָה *year* Lv $27_{18}$; עִם *with,* + קנה ptc. *one who acquires* Lv $25_{50}$.

**Hi.** 0.1.1 Impf. Q יחשיבוני, Si תחשיבך—**count, esteem,** <SUBJ> בֵּן *son* Si $7_{16}$; subj. not specified, 1QH $3_{6}$. <OBJ> בֵּן *son* Si $7_{16}$, worshipper 1QH $3_{6}$. <PREP> בְּ of accompaniment, *in, with,* + מַת *man* Si $7_{16}$.

**Ho.** 0.0.1 Pf. Q החשבו—**be counted, be reckoned,** <SUBJ> אִישׁ *man* 1QS $5_{11}$. <PREP> בְּ of accompaniment, *in, with,* + בְּרִית *covenant* 1QS $5_{11}$.

**Htp.** 1.0.7 Impf. יִתְחַשָּׁב, Q אתחשב, Q נתחשב—**reckon oneself,** <SUBJ> appar. Y. 4QM$^{a}$ $11.1_{14}$, עָם *people* Nm $23_{9}$ 4QDibHam$^{a}$ $6_{9}$, מאס ptc. *one who refuses* 1QS $3_{1.4}$, בֵּן *son* 4Q 181 $1_{3}$, worshipper 4QShirShabb$^{a}$ $2_{6}$; subj. not specified, 4QpsJub$^{a}$ $2.1_{8}$.

<PREP> לְ of benefit, *to, for,* + Abraham 4QpsJub$^{a}$ 2.1$_{8}$; בְּ of place, *in, at, among,* + סוֹד *council* 4Q 181 1$_{3}$; of accompaniment, *in, with,* + אֱלֹהִים *gods* 4QShirShabb$^{a}$ 2$_{6}$, גּוֹי *nation* Nm 23$_{9}$ 4QDibHam$^{a}$ 6$_{9}$, עַיִן *fountain* of perfect ones 1QS 3$_{4}$; עִם *with,* + אֵל *God* 4Q 181 1$_{3}$ 4QM$^{a}$ 11.1$_{14}$, יָשָׁר *upright one* 1QS 3$_{1}$.*

<COLL> ויתחשב לו צדקה *and it was reckoned to him as righteousness* 4QpsJub$^{a}$ 2.1$_{8}$.

→ חֵשֶׁב *girdle,* חֲשֻׁבָה *Hashubah,* חַשּׁוּב *Hasshub,* חֶשְׁבּוֹן *account,* חִשָּׁבוֹן *device,* חֲשַׁבְיָהוּ *Hashabiah,* חֲשַׁבְנָה *Hashabnah,* חֲשַׁבְנְיָה *Hashabneiah,* מַחֲשָׁבָה *thought.*

**חֵשֶׁב** 8.0.1 n.m. **girdle**—cstr. חֵשֶׁב—**girdle, band** of ephod (Ex 28$_{8.27.28}$ 29$_{5}$ 39$_{5.20.27}$ Lv 8$_{7}$); **artistry** of woven work (4QShirShabb$^{f}$ 23.2$_{10}$), <SUBJ> היה *be* Ex 28$_{8}$. <NOM CL> חֵשֶׁב אֲפֻדָּתוֹ ... כְּמַעֲשֵׂהוּ *the decorated band of its ephod ... was according to its craft* Ex 39$_{5}$, כול מחשביהם ... חשב *all their crafted garments ... are an artistry* 4QShirShabb$^{f}$ 23.2$_{10}$. <CSTR> חֵשֶׁב הָאֵפֹד *decorated band of,* i.e. around, *the ephod* Ex 28$_{27.28}$ (both הָאֵפוֹד) 29$_{5}$||Lv 8$_{7}$ Ex 39$_{20.21}$, אֲפֻדָּתוֹ *its ephod* Ex 28$_{8}$||Ex 39$_{5}$. <PREP> בְּ *with,* + אפד *dress in ephod* Ex 29$_{5}$, חגר *gird* Lv 8$_{7}$; עַל *upon,* + היה *be* Ex 28$_{28}$||Ex 39$_{21}$; מִמַּעַל לְ *above* Ex 28$_{27}$||Ex 39$_{20}$. <COLL> חשב כמעשי אורג *an artistry as (of) the work of a weaver* 4QShirShabb$^{f}$ 23.2$_{10}$.

→ חשׁב *think.*

**חֲשַׁבְדָּנָה** 1 pr.n.m. **Hashbaddana,** leader of Judah present at Ezra's reading of the Torah, <SUBJ> עמד *stand* Ne 8$_{4}$.

→ חשׁב *think.*

**חֲשֻׁבָה** 1 pr.n.m. **Hashubah,** son of Zerubbabel, <APP> בֵּן *son* 1 C 3$_{20}$.

→ חשׁב *think.*

**חֶשְׁבּוֹן I** 3.5.2 n.m. **reckoning**—sf. Si חשבונך, Si חשבונו, Q חשבונם—**1. reckoning, sum** (Ec 7$_{25.27}$ Si 42$_{3.4}$ 1QH 1$_{29}$ 4Q254$^{a}$ 1$_{2}$). **2. thought** (Ec 9$_{10}$). **3. conversation** (Si 9$_{15}$ 27$_{5.6}$), <SUBJ> היה *be* Si 9$_{15}$ 27$_{6}$. <NOM CL> זה חשבון *this is the reckoning* 4Q254$^{a}$ 1$_{2}$, אֵין ... חֶשְׁבּוֹן ... בִּשְׁאוֹל *there is no ... thought ... in Sheol* Ec 9$_{10}$. <OBJ> בקשׁ pi. *seek* Ec 7$_{25}$ (+ חָכְמָה *wisdom*), מצא *find* Ec 7$_{27}$. <CSTR> חשבון מעשה *reckoning of work of* 4Q254$^{a}$ 1$_{2}$. <PREP> לְ *according to,* + יצא hi. *bring out* 1QH 1$_{29}$; עַל *according to* Si 27$_{5}$; *on account of,* + בושׁ *be ashamed* Si 42$_{3}$ 42$_{4(Bmg)}$.*

→ חשׁב *think.*

**חֶשְׁבּוֹן II** 38 pl.n. **Heshbon,** city of Amorite king, later in territory of Gad, perh. Ḥesbān, 34 km E of Jericho, <SUBJ> בנה ni. *be built* Nm 21$_{27}$, אבד *perish* Nm 21$_{30}$, זעק *call out* Is 15$_{4}$, ילל hi. *wail* Jr 49$_{3}$.

<NOM CL> חֶשְׁבּוֹן עִיר סִיחֹן מֶלֶךְ הָאֱמֹרִי הִיא *Heshbon was the city of Sihon, king of the Amorites* Nm 21$_{26}$.

<OBJ> בנה *build* Nm 32$_{37}$, נתן *give* Jos 21$_{39}$ 1 C 6$_{66}$, רוה pi. *drench* Is 16$_{9}$.

<CSTR> מֶלֶךְ חֶשְׁבּוֹן *king of Heshbon* Dt 2$_{24.26.30}$ 3$_{6}$ 29$_{6}$ Jos 9$_{10}$ 12$_{5}$ 13$_{27}$ Jg 11$_{19}$ Ne 9$_{22}$, שַׁדְמוֹת חֶשְׁבּוֹן *fields of Heshbon* Is 16$_{8}$, צֵל חֶשְׁבּוֹן *shadow of Heshbon* Jr 48$_{45}$, זַעֲקַת חֶשְׁבּוֹן *cry of Heshbon* Jr 48$_{34}$.

<APP> אֶרֶץ *land* Nm 32$_{3}$, עִיר *city* Jos 13$_{17}$.

<PREP> בְּ of place, *in, at, among* Ca 7$_{5}$, + ישׁב *dwell* Nm 21$_{25.34}$ Dt 1$_{4}$ 3$_{2}$ 4$_{46}$ Jos 12$_{2}$ Jg 11$_{26}$, מלך *rule* Jos 13$_{10.21}$, חשׁב *invent* Jr 48$_{2}$; מִן of direction, *from,* + היה *be* Jos 13$_{26}$, יצא *go out* Nm 21$_{28}$ Jr 48$_{45}$; without preposition or ה- of direction, *to, in, at,* + בוא *come* Nm 21$_{27}$.

→ חשׁב *think.*

**[חִשָּׁבוֹן]** 2.0.1 n.m. **device**—pl. חִשְּׁבֹנוֹת—**device** (Ec 7$_{29}$), **scheme** (1QMyst 1.2$_{2}$); **war engine** (2 C 26$_{15}$), <SUBJ> היה *be* 2 C 26$_{15}$, ירה *shoot* 2 C 26$_{15}$, שׁוה *be equal* 1QMyst 1.2$_{2}$ ([ת]חשבונו). <OBJ> עשׂה *make* 2 C 26$_{15}$, בקשׁ pi. *seek* Ec 7$_{29}$. <APP> מַחֲשָׁבָה *device* 2 C 26$_{15}$. <ADJ> רַב pl. *many* Ec 7$_{29}$.*

→ חשׁב *think.*

**חֲשַׁבְיָה** 15 pr.n.m. **Hashabiah**—חֲשַׁבְיָהוּ—**1.** Levite, Merarite, son of Amaziah, <CSTR> בֶּן־חֲשַׁבְיָה *son of Hashabiah* 1 C 6$_{30}$.

**2.** son of Jeduthun, and musician in temple, <APP> בֵּן *son* 1 C 25$_{3}$. <PREP> לְ of direction, *to,* + יצא *go out* 1 C 25$_{19}$.

**3.** Hebronite officer in time of David, <NOM CL> לַחֶבְרוֹנִי חֲשַׁבְיָהוּ *of the Hebronites was Hashabiah* 1 C

26$_{30}$.

**4.** Levite overseer of tribe of Levi in time of David, son of Kemuel, <NOM CL> לַלֵּוִי חֲשַׁבְיָה *for Levi was Hashabiah* who was the son of Kemuel 1 C 27$_{17}$.

**5.** Levite chief in time of Josiah, <SUBJ> רום hi. *present* 2 C 35$_{9}$.

**6.** Levite, son of Bunni, <CSTR> בֶּן־חֲשַׁבְיָה *son of Hashabiah* 1 C 9$_{14}$ Ne 11$_{15}$.

**7.** Levite, who accompanied Ezra on his return (perh. identical with §8), <OBJ> בוא hi. *bring* Ezr 8$_{19}$, בדל hi. *separate* Ezr 8$_{24}$ (if del. לְ).

**8.** head of family of priests, <NOM CL> לְחִלְקִיָּה חֲשַׁבְיָה *belonging to Hilkiah was Hashabiah* Ne 12$_{21}$. <PREP> לְ *namely*, + בדל hi. *separate* Ezr 8$_{24}$ (or del.).

**9.** Levite chief who helped repair walls of Jerusalem, co-signatory with Nehemiah, <SUBJ> חתם pass. *be sealed* Ne 10$_{12}$, חזק hi. *repair* Ne 3$_{17}$. <NOM CL> חֲשַׁבְיָה שַׂר־חֲצִי־פֶּלֶךְ קְעִילָה *Hashabiah was prince of half of the district of Keilah* Ne 3$_{17}$, רָאשֵׁי הַלְוִיִּם חֲשַׁבְיָה *the heads of the Levites were Hashabiah* Ne 12$_{24}$.

**10.** Levite, son of Mattaniah, <CSTR> בֶּן־חֲשַׁבְיָה *son of Hashabiah* Ne 11$_{22}$.

**11.** Meṣad Ḥashavyahu ost. 1, <SUBJ> בוא *come* Meṣad Ḥashavyahu ost. 1$_{7}$ (others Hoashaiah), לקח *take* Meṣad Ḥashavyahu ost. 1$_{7}$ (others Hoashaiah). <NOM CL> חשביהו בן שב[י] *Hashabiah was the son of Shobi* Meṣad Ḥashavyahu ost. 1$_{7}$.

**12.** Meṣad Ḥashavyahu graf., <PREP> לְ of benefit, *to, for* Meṣad Ḥashavyahu graf.

⇒ חשב *think* + יי *Y.*

**חֲשַׁבְיָהוּ**, see חֲשַׁבְיָה *Hashabiah.*

**חֲשַׁבְנָה** 1 pr.n.m. **Hashabnah,** priestly head of a family, and co-signatory with Nehemiah, <SUBJ> חתם pass. *be sealed* Ne 10$_{26}$.

⇒ חשב *think.*

**חֲשַׁבְנְיָה** 2 pr.n.m. **Hashabniah, 1.** father of Hattush, <CSTR> בֶּן־חֲשַׁבְנְיָה *son of Hashabniah* Ne 3$_{10}$. **2.** Levite, <SUBJ> אמר *say* Ne 9$_{5}$. <APP> לֵוִי *Levite* Ne 9$_{5}$.

⇒ חשב *think* + יי *Y.*

**חשה** 16.2.2 vb. **be silent—Qal** 7.2.2 Pf. Si חשתה; impf. יֶחֱשׁוּ, אֶחֱשֶׁה, תֶּחֱשֶׁה; + waw וַיֶּחֱשׁוּ; inf. חֲשׁוֹת—**be silent, keep silence,** <SUBJ> יי *Y.* Is 64$_{11}$ 65$_{6}$ Ps 28$_{1}$, עַם *people* 1QM 9$_{1}$ 16$_{8}$ 4QMa 18$_{4}$ ([חו]שו ... העם]), worshipper Is 62$_{1}$, שֹׁמֵר ptc. *one who keeps* Is 62$_{6}$, גַּל *wave* Ps 107$_{29}$, perh. צְעָקָה *cry for help* Si 32$_{20}$; subj. not specified, Ec 3$_{7}$ Si 41$_{21(M)}$ (מ[ח]שא[ו]ת).

<PREP> מִן of direction, *from,* + worshipper Ps 28$_{1}$; of cause, *because of,* + קוֹל *voice* 1QM 9$_{1}$; לְמַעַן *for sake of,* + Zion Is 62$_{1}$.

<COLL> תָּמִיד לֹא יֶחֱשׁוּ *they shall not continue in silence* Is 62$_{6}$, העם יחשו קול התרועה *the people will keep silent at the sound of the alarm* 1QM 16$_{8}$, עֵת לַחֲשׁוֹת *a time to keep silence* Ec 3$_{7}$.

**Hi.** 9 Pf. הֶחֱשֵׁיתִי; impv. הַחֲשׁוּ; ptc. מַחְשֶׁה, מַחְשִׁים—**be silent** (2 K 2$_{3.5}$ 7$_{9}$ Is 42$_{14}$ 57$_{11}$* Ps 39$_{3}$); trans. **silence** (Ne 8$_{11}$), **delay** (Jg 18$_{9}$ 1 K 22$_{3}$), <SUBJ> יי *Y.* Is 42$_{14}$ 57$_{11}$, מֶלֶךְ *king* 1 K 22$_{3}$, לֵוִי *Levite* Ne 8$_{11}$, עֶבֶד *servant* 1 K 22$_{3}$, אָח *brother* Jg 18$_{9}$, בֵּן *son* of prophet 2 K 2$_{3.5}$, worshipper Ps 39$_{3}$, מְצֹרָע *leper* 2 K 7$_{9}$.

<PREP> לְ introducing object, + עַם *people* Ne 8$_{11}$; מִן of direction, *from,* + עוֹלָם *eternity* Is 42$_{14}$ 57$_{11}$; privative, *without,* + טוֹב *good* Ps 39$_{3}$, לקח inf. as noun, *taking* 1 K 22$_{3}$.

**חַשּׁוּב** 5 pr.n.m. **Hasshub, 1.** father of Shemaiah, <CSTR> בֶּן־חַשּׁוּב *son of Hasshub* Ne 11$_{15}$ 1 C 9$_{14}$.

**2.** one who helped to rebuild Jerusalem, son of Pahath-moab, <SUBJ> חזק hi. *strengthen* wall Ne 3$_{11}$. <NOM CL> חַשּׁוּב בֶּן־פַּחַת מוֹאָב *Hasshub was the son of Pahath-moab* Ne 3$_{11}$.

**3.** another who helped to rebuild Jerusalem, <SUBJ> חזק hi. *strengthen* wall Ne 3$_{23}$.

**4.** family head and co-signatory with Nehemiah, <SUBJ> חתם *seal* Ne 10$_{24}$ (if em. הַחֲתוּמִים *the ones who were sealed* to הַחוֹתְמִים *the ones who sealed*).

⇒ חשב *think.*

**חָשׁוּק** 8 n.m. **band**—sf. חֲשׁוּקֵיהֶם (חֲשֻׁקֵיהֶם)—ring or bar on pillars of tabernacle, <NOM CL> חֲשֻׁקֵיהֶם כָּסֶף *their bars were of silver* Ex 27$_{10.11}$ 38$_{10.11.12.17}$ (חֲשׁוּקֵיהֶם) 38$_{19}$. <OBJ> צפה pi. *overlay* Ex 36$_{38}$.* ⇒ חשק *cling to.*

**חִשּׁוּק** 1 n.m. **spoke**—sf. חִשֻּׁקֵיהֶם—of wheel, <SUBJ> יצק ho. *be cast* 1 K $7_{33}$.

**חִשּׁוּר** 1 n.m. **hub**—sf. חִשֻּׁרֵיהֶם—of wheel, <SUBJ> יצק ho. *be cast* 1 K $7_{33}$.

[חֻשַׁי], see חוּשַׁי *Hushai*.

חֲשֵׁיכָה, see חֲשֵׁכָה *darkness*.

חֻשִׁים, see חוּשִׁים I, II *Hushim*.

**חשׁך** 17.0.1 vb. **be dark**—**Qal** 11.0.1 Pf. חָשַׁךְ, חָשְׁכָה, חָשְׁכוּ; impf. 3fs תֶּחְשַׁךְ, תֶּחְשְׁכוּ, יֶחְשְׁכוּ, תֶּחְשַׁכְנָה; + waw Q ויחשך, וַתֶּחְשַׁךְ—**be dark, be dim; be gloomy** (Ec $12_3$),* <SUBJ> אֶרֶץ *land* Ex $10_{15}$, שֶׁמֶשׁ *sun* Is $13_{10}$ Ec $12_2$, יָרֵחַ *moon* Ec $12_2$, כּוֹכָב *star* Jb $3_9$ Ec $12_2$, מָאוֹר *light* 1QH $5_{32}$, אוֹר *light* Is $5_{30}$=4QpIsa$^b$ $3_2$ ([חשך]) Jb $18_6$ Ec $12_2$, night Mc $3_6$ (or em. חֲשֵׁכָה *darkness*), ראה ptc. *one who sees* Ec $12_3$, עַיִן *eye* Ps $69_{24}$ Lm $5_{17}$, תֹּאַר *appearance* Lm $4_8$.

<PREP> לְ of direction, *(in)to*, + אֲפֵלָה *darkness* 1QH $5_{32}$; of benefit, *to, for*, + רֹאשׁ *head* of Jacob Mc $3_6$ (or em.; see Subj.), קָצִין *leader* of house of Israel Mc $3_6$ (or em.; see Subj.); בְּ of place, *in*, + אֹהֶל *tent* Jb $18_6$; of instrument, *by (means of)*, + עָרִיף *cloud* Is $5_{30}$; מִן of comparison, *(more) than*, + שְׁחוֹר *soot* Lm $4_8$; privative, *without*, + ראה inf. as noun, *sight* Ps $69_{24}$, קסם inf. as noun, *divination* Mc $3_6$; עַל *on account of*, + אֵלֶּה *these* Lm $4_{17}$.

**Hi.** 6 Pf. הֶחְשִׁיךְ; impf. יַחְשִׁיךְ (יַחְשִׁךְ); + waw וְהַחֲשַׁכְתִּי; וַיַּחְשִׁךְ; ptc. מַחְשִׁיךְ—**be dark** (Ps $139_{12}$), **make dark**, <SUBJ> ״ *Y.* Jr $13_{16}$ Am $5_8$ $8_9$ Ps $105_{28}$, אֱלֹהִים *God* Jr $13_{16}$, חֹשֶׁךְ *darkness* Ps $139_{12}$, זֶה *this one* Jb $38_2$. <OBJ> יוֹם *day* Am $5_8$, עֵצָה *counsel* Jb $38_2$. <PREP> לְ introducing object, + אֶרֶץ *earth* Am $8_9$; בְּ of time, *in, during*, + יוֹם *day* Am $8_9$; of instrument, *by (means of)*, + מִלָּה *word* Jb $38_2$; מִן of direction, *from*, + ״ *Y.* Ps $139_{12}$. <COLL> יוֹם לַיְלָה הֶחְשִׁיךְ *he has darkened the day (as) the night* Am $5_8$.*

→ חֹשֶׁךְ *darkness*, חֲשֵׁכָה *darkness*, חָשֹׁךְ *obscure*, מַחְשָׁךְ *dark place*.

*[חָשָׁךְ] n.[m.] **thorn hedge**, <OBJ> שׂים *place* Jb $19_8$ (if em. חֹשֶׁךְ *darkness*).

[חָשֹׁךְ] 1 adj. **obscure**—pl. חֲשֻׁכִּים—used as noun, **obscure one**, <PREP> לִפְנֵי *before*, + יצב htp. *take one's stand* Pr $22_{29}$.*

→ חשׁך *be dark*.

**חֹשֶׁךְ** 80.2.57 n.m. **darkness**—Q חושך; cstr. חֹשֶׁךְ (Q חושך); sf. חָשְׁכִּי—**darkness, obscurity**, <SUBJ> היה *be* Ex $10_{21.22}$ $14_{20}$ (+ עָנָן *cloud*) Ps $35_6$ Jb $3_4$, יצר ni. *be formed* Si $11_{16}$, חשׁך hi. *be dark* Ps $139_{12}$, טמן pass. *be hidden* Jb $20_{26}$, כסה pi. *cover* Is $60_2$, שׁוּף *cover* Ps $139_{11}$ (or em. שׂכך *cover*, or סכך *cover*), גאל *reclaim* Jb $3_5$ (|| צַלְמָוֶת *darkness*), בהל pi. *terrify* Jb $22_{11}$, גלה *reveal* 1QMyst $1.1_5$ ([ח]ושך), אבד *perish* 1QH $18_{29}$ ([אבד]).

<NOM CL> [ח]ושך תשוקתנ[ו] *darkness is our longing* 6QHymn $2_4$, הָהָר ... חֹשֶׁךְ *the mountain ... was (in) darkness* Dt $4_{11}$, אתה חושך *you are darkness* 11QapPs$^a$ $4_7$, הוּא חֹשֶׁךְ *it is darkness* Am $5_{18}$, חשך [בתהום ר]בה *darkness is in the great deep* 11QapPs$^a$ $3_8$, חֹשֶׁךְ עַל־פְּנֵי תְהוֹם *darkness was upon the face of the deep* Gn $1_2$, נוכח האור [ח]ושך *the opposite of light is darkness* Si $36_{14}$, הִנֵּה־חֹשֶׁךְ *behold, (there is) darkness* Is $5_{30}$=4QpIsa$^b$ $3_2$ ([חשך]) Is $59_9$, הֲלֹא־חֹשֶׁךְ *is it not darkness?* Am $5_{20}$, אֵין־חֹשֶׁךְ *there is no darkness* Jb $34_{20}$ 4Q185 $1.2_6$.

<OBJ> ברא *create* Is $45_7$ 4Q392 $1_4$ (both :: אוֹר *light*), נתן *give*, i.e. place Ezk $32_8$, שׂים *place* Is $5_{20}$ Jb $19_8$ (or em. חָשָׁךְ *thorn hedge*), שׁית *place* 2 S $22_{12}$||Ps $18_{12}$ Ps $104_{20}$, שׁלח *send* Ps $105_{28}$, משׁשׁ hi. *feel* Ex $10_{21}$, פגשׁ pi. *meet* Jb $5_{14}$, שׁפל hi. *humiliate* 1QM $13_{15}$, נגה hi. *brighten* 2 S $22_{29}$||Ps $18_{29}$, נבט hi. *consider* 1QS $3_3$.

<CSTR> חֹשֶׁךְ־אֲפֵלָה *darkness of*, i.e. deepest, *darkness* Ex $10_{22}$, חושך מעשיכה *darkness of your deeds* 1QS $2_7$.

ממשלת חושך *dominion of darkness* 1QH $12_6$ 4Q408 $1_{10}$ ([חושך]), ממשל *dominion of* 4QPrQuot $33.10_{19}$ ([ח]ושך), רוחות *spirits of* 1QM $3_{25}$, מלאך *angel of* 1QS $3_{21.21}$, [ע]בדי *servants of* 4QM$^h$ $2_5$, בני *sons of* 1QM $1_{1.7}$ ([בנ]י) $1_{10.14}$ ([בני חושך]) $1_{16}$ $3_{7.9}$ $13_{16}$ $14_{17}$ ([ב]ני) $16_9$ 1QS $1_{10}$ (חושך), יֹשְׁבֵי חֹשֶׁךְ *those who sit in darkness* Is $42_7$ Ps $107_{10}$ (|| צַלְמָוֶת *darkness*).

משכבי חושך *couches of darkness* 4QWiles $1_6$, מדור

*dwelling of* 1QH $12_{26}$, אשמורי *watches of* 1QS $10_{2}$, דַּרְכֵי חֹשֶׁךְ *ways of darkness* Pr $2_{13}$ 1QS $3_{21}$ $4_{11}$ (both חושכ) 4QMyst$^{a}$ $5_{2}$ ([חושו[ך]) 4QMyst$^{a}$ $5_{2}$ ([חושו[ך]), מקור חושך *fountain of darkness* 1QS $3_{19}$, בור *pit of* 4QCrypt $1.2_{8}$ (החושך), הויות *abysses of* 1QS $4_{13}$, תהום *deep of darkness* 11QapPs$^{a}$ $1_{6}$ (תהו[ם חוש[ך]), בית *house of* 4QCrypt $1.3_{6}$ ([החושך]), מוסדי *foundations of* 4QWiles $1_{4}$, אֶרֶץ חֹשֶׁךְ *land of darkness* Is $45_{19}$ Jb $10_{21}$ (ǁ צַלְמָוֶת *darkness*), אוֹצְרוֹת *treasures of* Is $45_{3}$, חוקי חושך *statutes of darkness* 1QM $13_{12}$.

גורל חושך *lot of darkness* 1QM $1_{11}$ $13_{5}$ 4QBer$^{a}$ $3.2_{4}$, גורלי *lots of* 4QPrQuot $76_{4}$ $215_{4}$ ([חו]שך]), גורלות *lots of* 4QPrQuot $39.13_{2}$, מועדי *appointed times of* 1QM $1_{8}$, קץ *time of* 4Q462$_{10}$ (ק[ץ]), יוֹם חֹשֶׁךְ *day of darkness* Jl $2_{2}$ Zp $1_{15}$ (both ǁ אֲפֵלָה *darkness*) Jb $15_{23}$, יְמֵי הַחֹשֶׁךְ *days of the darkness* Ec $11_{8}$, תשובת חושך *return of darkness* 1QH fr $2_{11}$, אֱשׁוּן חֹשֶׁךְ *beginning of darkness* Pr $20_{20(Qr)}$ (Kt אישׁוֹן *the pupil*, i.e. middle, *of*), כָּל־חֹשֶׁךְ *all darkness* Jb $20_{26}$.

<APP> מָקוֹם *place* Jb $38_{19}$.

<PREP> לְ of direction, *to* 4Q419 $8.2_{5}$ 6QHymn $2_{4}$, + בדל hi. *separate* 4QJub$^{a}$ $2_{8}$ ([חשך]) 4Q392 $1_{6}$; of benefit, *to, for*, + שׂים *place* Jb $28_{3}$; *as*, + שׂים *place* Is $5_{20}$; *in(to)*, + הפך ni. *be turned* Jl $3_{4}$; קרא לְ *call*, i.e. name Gn $1_{5}$.

בְּ of place/time, *in, at, during, among* 1QM $13_{11}$ $15_{9}$ 4QJub$^{a}$ $2_{16}$ ([חשך]) 4QMyst$^{a}$ $28_{3}$ 4QHod$^{b}$ $16_{5}$, + ידע ni. *be known* Ps $88_{13}$, דמם ni. *be destroyed* 1 S $2_{9}$, ישׁב *dwell* Mc $7_{8}$, בוא *come* Is $47_{5}$, הלך *go* Is $9_{1}$ Ec $2_{14}$ $6_{4}$, עשׂה *do* Ezk $8_{12}$, רפד pi. *spread out* Jb $17_{13}$, חתר *break through* Jb $24_{16}$, סגר *shut* Jos $2_{5}$, זרח *shine* Is $58_{10}$ Ps $112_{4}$, אכל *eat* Ec $5_{16}$, אמר *say* Is $49_{9}$.

בְּ of instrument, *by (means of), with*, + כסה pu. *be covered* Ec $6_{4}$;* מֹשׁל בְּ *rule* 4QMidrEschat$^{b}$ $10_{8}$ ([חושך]) 11QapPs$^{a}$ $3_{11}$.

כְּ *as* 1QS $2_{7}$.

מִן of direction, *from* 4QHod$^{b}$ $16_{3}$ 4QShir$^{b}$ $28_{4}$, + ראה *see* Is $29_{18}$ (ǁ אֹפֶל *darkness*), שׁוּב *go back* Jb $15_{22}$, יצא hi. *bring out* Ps $107_{14}$ (ǁ צַלְמָוֶת *darkness*), סור *remove* Jb $15_{30}$, נצל hi. *deliver* 11QapPs$^{a}$ $4_{7}$ ([חו]שך]), גלה pi. *disclose* Jb $12_{22}$, אור hi. *cause to shine* 1QH $9_{26}$; of comparison, *more (than)* Ec $2_{13}$.

אֶל *to*, + הדף *drive away* Jb $18_{18}$.

עִם *with* Jb $26_{10}$.

בֵּין *between*, + בדל hi. *separate* Gn $1_{4.18}$ (+ אוֹר *light*) GnzPs $1_{4}$ (+ לְאוֹר *to light*) 4QJub$^{a}$ $2_{10}$ ([חשך]; + אור) 11QapPs$^{a}$ $1_{13}$ (חוש[ך]).

מִפְּנֵי *from (before)* Jb $17_{12}$, + צמת ni. *be silenced* Jb $23_{17}$, ערך *arrange* Jb $39_{17}$.

מִתּוֹךְ *from (among)*, + שׁמע *hear* Dt $5_{23}$.

<COLL> [חושך ואפ[לה *darkness and gloom* 6QHymn $2_{3}$, אֹיְבָיו יְרַדֶּף־חֹשֶׁךְ *he pursues his enemies (into) darkness* Na $1_{8}$ (or em. הדף *drive away*), אֵלֶךְ חֹשֶׁךְ *I went (in) darkness* Jb $29_{3}$, וַיֹּלַךְ חֹשֶׁךְ *and he brought (me into) darkness* Lm $3_{2}$, הולכי חושך *those who walk in darkness* 1QS $11_{10}$, יְמַשְׁשׁוּ־חֹשֶׁךְ *they grope in darkness* Jb $12_{25}$.*

<SYN> אֹפֶל *darkness*, אֲפֵלָה *darkness*, צַלְמָוֶת *darkness*.

<ANT> אוֹר *light*.

Also 1QH fr. $5_{13}$ 1QM $17_{16}$ 4QMidrEschat$^{b}$ $32_{2}$ 4QBer$^{a}$ $1_{13}$ ([חש[ך]) 4QMyst$^{a}$ $6.2_{10}$ ([חוש[ך]) $28_{.3}$ ([ח]ושך]) 4Q303 $1_{5}$ ([חוש[ך]) 4Q422 $10_{9}$ ([חו]שך]) 4QHod$^{b}$ $53_{1}$ ([ח]ושך]) 4Q525 $15_{6}$ ([ח]ושך]) 11QShirShabb $1_{4}$.*

⇒ חשך *be dark*.

**חֲשֵׁכָה** 6 n.f. **darkness**—חֲשֵׁיכָה; cstr. חֶשְׁכַת; pl. חֲשֵׁכִים— <SUBJ> נפל *fall* Gn $15_{12}$. <NOM CL> הִנֵּה צָרָה וַחֲשֵׁכָה *behold, there is distress and darkness* Is $8_{22}$. <OBJ> שׁית *place*, i.e. make Ps $18_{12}$ (or em. חֶשְׁכָּה *abundance*). <CSTR> חֶשְׁכַת־מַיִם *darkness of water* Ps $18_{12}$ (or em. חֶשְׁכַּת־ *abundance of*). <ADJ> גָּדוֹל *great* Gn $15_{12}$. <PREP> בְּ *in*, + הלך htp. *walk about* Ps $82_{5}$; כְּ *as* Ps $139_{12}$. <COLL> הָלַךְ חֲשֵׁכִים *he has walked in darkness* Is $50_{10}$.*

⇒ חשך *be dark*.

**חשל** 1 vb. **be feeble—Ni.** 1 Ptc. נֶחֱשָׁלִים—**be feeble, lag behind,** <SUBJ> כֹּל *all* Dt $25_{18}$. <PREP> אַחַר *after*, + Israelite(s) Dt $25_{18}$.

**חָשֻׁם** 5 pr.n.m. **Hashum—1.** family head in postexilic Judaea, <CSTR> בְּנֵי חָשֻׁם *sons of Hashum* Ezr $2_{19}$ǁNe $7_{22}$ Ezr $10_{33}$. **2.** leader of Judah present at Ezra's reading of the Torah, <SUBJ> עמד *stand* Ne $8_{4}$. **3.** leader of Judah and co-signatory with Nehemiah, <SUBJ> חתם *seal* Ne $10_{18}$ (if em. הַחֲתוּמִים *the ones who were sealed* to הַחוֹתְמִים *the ones who sealed*).

**חֻשָׁם** 4 pr.n.m. **Husham**—חוּשָׁם—Edomite king, <SUBJ> מלך *reign* Gn 36₃₄‖1 C 1₄₅ (חוּשָׁם), מות *die* Gn 36₃₅‖1 C 1₄₆ (חוּשָׁם). <PREP> תַּחַת *instead of*, + מלך *reign* Gn 36₃₅‖1 C 1₄₆ (חוּשָׁם). <COLL> חֻשָׁם מֵאֶרֶץ הַתֵּימָנִי *Husham from the land of the Temanites* Gn 36₃₄‖1 C 1₄₅ (חוּשָׁם).*

**חֶשְׁמוֹן** 1 pl.n. **Heshmon,** appar. in SW of territory of Judah, <APP> עִיר *city* Jos 15₂₇.

**חַשְׁמַל** 3 n.m. **amber**—הַחַשְׁמַלָה—amber, or perh. bronze, <CSTR> עֵין חַשְׁמַל *appearance of amber* Ezk 1₄.₂₇, עֵין הַחַשְׁמַלָה *the appearance of amber* Ezk 8₂.*

**[חַשְׁמַן]** 1 n.m. **envoy**—pl. חַשְׁמַנִּים—perh. **envoy,** or **bronze,** or **red cloth,** <SUBJ> אתה *come* Ps 68₃₂.

**חַשְׁמֹנָה** 2 pl.n. **Hashmonah,** station of exodus, <PREP> בְּ of place, *at*, + חנה *encamp* Nm 33₂₉; מִן of direction, *from*, + נסע *set out* Nm 33₃₀.

**חֹשֶׁן** 25.2.2 n.m. **breastpiece**—cstr. חֹשֶׁן; pl. cstr. Q חשני—**breastpiece, pouch** containing the Urim and the Thummim, worn by the high priest in the sanctuary.

<SUBJ> זחח ni. *be displaced* Ex 28₂₈‖39₂₁.

<OBJ> עשׂה *make* Ex 28₄.₁₅ 39₈.₉, רכס *bind* Ex 28₂₈‖39₂₁, שׂים *place* Lv 8₈, לבשׁ hi. *put on* Ex 29₅ Si 45₁₀.

<CSTR> חֹשֶׁן מִשְׁפָּט *breastpiece of judgment* Ex 28₁₅‖39₈ Ex 28₂₉.₃₀ Si 45₁₀; קְצוֹת הַחֹשֶׁן *ends*, i.e. edges, *of the breastpiece* Ex 28₂₃.₂₄.₂₆‖Ex 39₁₆.₁₇.₁₉, תבנית חשני *form of breastpieces of* 11QShirShabb 7₄.

<APP> בֶּגֶד *garment* Ex 28₄.

<PREP> לְ of benefit, *to, for* Ex 25₇, + בוא hi. *bring* Ex 35₉.₂₇; בְּ *in*, + נשׂא *raise*, i.e. bear name in remembrance Ex 28₂₉; אֶל *to*, + נתן *give*, i.e. place Ex 28₃₀‖Lv 8₈; עַל *on account of, on behalf of* Si 45₁₁, + עשׂה *make* Ex 28₂₂‖Ex 39₁₅ Ex 28₂₃.*

Also 4QShirShabb[f] 41₂.

**חשׁק** 11.2.1 vb. **desire**—**Qal** 8.1.1 Pf. חָשַׁק, חָשְׁקָה, חָשַׁקְתָּ (Q חשקתה); + waw וְחָשַׁקְתָּ—**desire, cling to, love,** <SUBJ> י׳ *Y.* Dt 7₇ 10₁₅ Is 38₁₇ (or em. חָשַׂכְתָּ *you have withheld*), Israelite(s) Dt 21₁₁=11QT 63₁₁, Solomon 1 K 9₁₀‖2 C 8₆, worshipper Ps 91₁₄, נֶפֶשׁ *soul* Gn 34₈ Si 51₁₉. <OBJ> נֶפֶשׁ *soul* Is 38₁₇. <PREP> בְּ introducing object, or (cling) *to*, + י׳ *Y.* Ps 91₁₄, Israelite(s) Dt 7₇, אִשָּׁה *woman* Dt 21₁₁=11QT 63₁₁, אָב *father*, i.e. ancestor Dt 10₁₅, בַּת *daughter* Gn 34₈, חָכְמָה *wisdom* Si 51₁₉; מִן of direction, *from*, + שַׁחַת *pit* Is 38₁₇ (or em.; see Subj.).

**Ni.** 0.1 Ptc. Si נחשקת—**be desired, be loved,** <SUBJ> אִשָּׁה *woman* Si 40₁₉.

**Pi.** 1 Pf. חִשַּׁק—**bind,** <SUBJ> Bezalel Ex 38₂₈. <OBJ> ראשׁ *head*, i.e. capital Ex 38₂₈.

**Pu.** 2 Ptc. מְחֻשָּׁקִים—**be bound,** <SUBJ> עַמּוּד *pillar* Ex 27₁₇‖Ex 38₁₇. <COLL> מְחֻשָּׁקִים כֶּסֶף *they were bound with silver* Ex 27₁₇‖Ex 38₁₇.*

⇒ חָשׁוּק *band*, חֵשֶׁק *desire.*

**חֵשֶׁק** 4 n.m. **desire**—cstr. חֵשֶׁק; sf. חִשְׁקִי—<OBJ> חפץ *delight* 1 K 9₁, חשׁק *desire* 1 K 9₁₉‖2 C 8₆. <CSTR> חֵשֶׁק שְׁלֹמֹה *desire of Solomon* 1 K 9₁.₁₉‖2 C 8₆; נֶשֶׁף חִשְׁקִי *twilight of my desire* Is 21₄, כָּל־חֵשֶׁק *all desire of* 1 K 9₁‖2 C 8₆.*

⇒ חשׁק *desire.*

**[חִשֻּׁק]**, see חִשּׁוּק *spoke.*

**[חָשֻׁק]**, see חָשׁוּק *band.*

**[חִשֻּׁר]**, see חִשּׁוּר *hub.*

**חַשְׁרָה** 1 n.f. **sieve**—cstr. חַשְׁרַת—**sieve, strainer,** <OBJ> שׁית *place*, i.e. make 2 S 22₁₂. <CSTR> חַשְׁרַת־מַיִם *strainer of water* 2 S 22₁₂ (‖Ps 18₁₂ חֶשְׁכַת־ *darkness of*).

**חֲשַׁשׁ** 2 n.m. **dried grass,** <SUBJ> רפה *sink down* Is 5₂₄. <OBJ> הרה *conceive* Is 33₁₁.

**חֻשָׁתִי** 5 gent. **Hushathite,** as noun, descendant of Hushah, <SUBJ> נכה hi. *strike* 2 S 21₁₈‖1 C 20₄. <NOM CL> הַשְּׁמִינִי ... הַחֻשָׁתִי *the eighth was ... the Hushathite* 1 C 27₁₁. <APP> Mebunai 2 S 23₂₇, Sibbecai 2 S 21₁₈‖1 C 20₄ 1 C 11₂₉ 27₁₁.

⇒ חוּשָׁה *Hushah.*

**חַת I** $_2$ n.m. **terror**—חַת; sf. חִתְּכֶם—<SUBJ> היה *be* Gn 9$_2$. <PREP> לִבְלִי *without* Jb 41$_{25}$.
⇒ חתת *be dismayed.*

**חַת II** $_2$ adj. **shattered**—pl. חַתִּים—**shattered, broken** (1 S 2$_4$), **dismayed** (Jr 46$_5$), in nom. cl., used predicatively, קֶשֶׁת גִּבֹּרִים חַתִּים *the bows of the mighty are broken* 1 S 2$_4$, הֵמָּה חַתִּים *they are dismayed* Jr 46$_5$.*
⇒ חתת *be dismayed.*

**חֵת** $_{14}$ pr.n.m. **Heth,** son of Canaan and ancestor of the Hittites, <OBJ> ילד *bear child* Gn 10$_{15}$‖1 C 1$_{13}$. <CSTR> בְּנֵי־חֵת *sons of Heth* Gn 23$_{3+7t}$ 25$_{10}$ 49$_{32}$, בְּנוֹת חֵת *daughters of Heth* Gn 27$_{46.46}$ (בְּנוֹת־).

**[חתא]** vb. **destroy—Qal pass., be destroyed,** <SUBJ> הֲלִיכָה *orbit* Hb 3$_7$ (if em. הֲלִיכוֹת עוֹלָם לוֹ : תַּחַת אָוֶן רָאִיתִי *its eternal orbits; instead of iniquity, I saw* to הֲלִיכוֹת עוֹלָם תֻּחֳתְאָנָּה : רָאִיתִי *the eternal orbits were destroyed; I saw*).

**Ni. be carried off,** <SUBJ> אֹהֶל *tent* of Cushan Hb 3$_7$ (if em. תַּחַת אָוֶן *instead of iniquity* to תֻּחָתְאוּן *they were carried off*).

**חתה I** $_{4.0.1}$ vb. **take—Qal** $_{4.0.1}$ Impf. יַחְתֶּה (יַחְתְּךָ); ptc. חֹתֶה; inf. לַחְתּוֹת—**take (away), snatch** (Is 30$_{14}$ Pr 6$_{27}$ 25$_{22}$), **destroy** (Ps 52$_7$ 1QpHab 12$_1$), <SUBJ> אֵל *God* Ps 52$_7$ Jb 9$_{12}$ (if em. יַחְתֹּף *he snatches away* to יַחְתְּ פָּמִי if *he snatches away then who* can resist him?),* אִישׁ *man* Pr 6$_{27}$ (unless חתה II *kindle*), righteous Pr 25$_{22}$ (unless חתה II *kindle*), שֹׁד *destruction* 1QpHab 12$_1$ ([שוד]; =MT יְחִיתַן appar. *it will terrify them*, from חתת I hi.); subj. not specified, Is 30$_{14}$. <OBJ> גִּבּוֹר *mighty one* Ps 52$_7$, אֵשׁ *fire* Is 30$_{14}$ (unless חתה II *kindle*) Pr 6$_{27}$, גַּחֶלֶת *coal* Pr 25$_{22}$. <PREP> בְּ *in, with,* + חֵיק *bosom* Pr 6$_{27}$; מִן of direction, *from,* + יָקוּד *hearth* Is 30$_{14}$; *on account of,* + דָּם *bloodshed* 1QpHab 12$_1$; עַל *upon,* + רֹאשׁ *head* Pr 25$_{22}$.
⇒ מַחְתָּה *censor.*

***חתה II** $_3$ vb. **kindle—Qal** $_3$ Impf. יַחְתֶּה ; ptc. חֹתֶה; inf. לַחְתּוֹת—**kindle** (unless חתה I *take*), <SUBJ> אִישׁ *man* Pr 6$_{27}$, righteous Pr 25$_{22}$, חֶרֶשׂ *shard* Is 30$_{14}$. <OBJ> אֵשׁ *fire* Is 30$_{14}$ Pr 6$_{27}$, גַּחֶלֶת *coal* Pr 25$_{22}$. <PREP> בְּ of place, *in,* + חֵיק *bosom* Pr 6$_{27}$; מִן of direction, *from,* + יָקוּד *hearth* Is 30$_{14}$; עַל *upon,* + רֹאשׁ *head* Pr 25$_{22}$.

**חִתָּה** $_1$ n.f. **terror**—cstr. חִתַּת—<SUBJ> היה *be* Gn 35$_5$. <CSTR> חִתַּת אֱלֹהִים *terror of God* Gn 35$_5$.*
⇒ חתת *be dismayed.*

**חִתּוּל** $_1$ n.m. **bandage** or **splint** for broken arm, <OBJ> שִׂים *place* Ezk 30$_{21}$.
⇒ חתל *be swaddled.*

**חָתוּם**, see חתם Qal, §2b *sealed thing.*

**[חַתְחַת]** $_1$ n.m. **terror**—pl. חַתְחַתִּים—<NOM CL> חַתְחַתִּים בַּדֶּרֶךְ *terrors are in the way* Ec 12$_5$. <OBJ> ירא *fear* Ec 12$_5$.*
⇒ חתת *be dismayed.*

**חִתִּי** $_{48.0.1}$ gent. **Hittite**—fem. חִתִּית; pl. חִתִּים, חִתִּיּת—**1.** as collective sing. noun, **Hittites,** <SUBJ> ישׁב *dwell* Nm 13$_{29}$, לחם ni. *fight* Jos 9$_1$ 24$_{11}$, שׁמע *hear* Jos 9$_1$, קבץ htp. *gather* (intrans.) Jos 9$_1$. <OBJ> נתן *give* Gn 15$_{20}$ Jos 24$_{11}$, ירשׁ hi. *dispossess* Jos 3$_{10}$, נשׁל *clear away* Dt 7$_1$, גרשׁ *expel* Ex 34$_{11}$=11QT 2$_3$ ([גורש ... חתי]), pi. *expel* Ex 23$_{28}$ 33$_2$, נכה hi. *strike* Jos 12$_8$, חרם hi. *destroy* Dt 20$_{17}$=11QT 62$_{14}$.

<CSTR> אֶרֶץ ... הַחִתִּי *land of ... the Hittites* Ex 3$_{17}$ 13$_5$ Ne 9$_8$, מְקוֹם ... הַחִתִּי *place of ... the Hittites* Ex 3$_8$.

<APP> אֶרֶץ *land* Gn 15$_{20}$, גּוֹי *nation* Dt 7$_1$, מֶלֶךְ *king* Jos 9$_1$.

<PREP> לְ of possession, *of, (belonging) to* Ezr 9$_1$; מִן partitive, *from among,* + יתר ni. *remain* 1 K 9$_{20}$‖2 C 8$_7$; אֶל *to,* + שׁלח *send* Jos 11$_3$, בוא hi. *bring* Ex 23$_{23}$; בְּקֶרֶב *among,* + ישׁב *dwell* Jg 3$_5$.

**2.** as plural noun, **Hittites,** once, **Hittite women** (1 K 11$_1$). <OBJ> אהב *love* 1 K 11$_1$. <CSTR> אֶרֶץ הַחִתִּים *land of the Hittites* Jos 1$_4$ Jg 1$_{26}$, מַלְכֵי הַחִתִּים *kings of the Hittites* 1 K 10$_{29}$‖2 C 1$_{17}$ 2 K 7$_6$. <APP> אִשָּׁה *woman* 1 K 11$_1$.

**3.** as sing. noun, a particular **Hittite,** <NOM CL> אִמֵּךְ חִתִּית *your mother was a Hittite* Ezk 16$_3$, אִמְּכֶן חִתִּית *your mother was a Hittite* Ezk 16$_{45}$. <APP> אֲחִימֶלֶךְ הַחִתִּי *Ahimelech the Hittite* 1 S 26$_6$, בְּאֵרִי הַחִתִּי *Beeri the Hittite*

Gn 26$_{34}$, אֵילֹן הַחִתִּי *Elon the Hittite* Gn 26$_{34}$ 36$_2$, עֶפְרוֹן הַחִתִּי *Ephron the Hittite* Gn 23$_{10}$ 49$_{29.30}$ 50$_{13}$ (עֶפְרֹן), עֶפְרֹן ... הַחִתִּי *Ephron ... the Hittite* Gn 25$_9$, אוּרִיָּה הַחִתִּי *Uriah the Hittite* 2 S 11$_{3.6.17.21.24}$ 12$_{9.10}$ 23$_{39}$||1 C 11$_{41}$ 1 K 15$_5$.

[חֲתִים] 2 n.[m.] **signet ring**—sf. Sam חתימך—<NOM CL> חתימך ... אשר בידך *your signet ring ... which is upon your hand* Gn 38$_{18(Sam)}$ (MT חוֹתָם *signet ring*; + פָּתִיל *cord*, מַטֶּה *staff*), למי החתים *whose is this signet ring?* Gn 38$_{25(Sam)}$ (MT חֹתֶמֶת *signet ring*; + מַטֶּה, פָּתִיל). <ADJ> אֵלֶּה *these* Gn 38$_{25(Sam)}$.

⇒ חתם *seal.*

[חֲתִימָה] 0.0.1 n.f. **seal,** appar. inscribed with formula, <OBJ> חקק *inscribe* 4Q185 1.2$_4$ (חתימה חקק לישחק *the seal he inscribed for Isaac*; AHL נתיבה *path*).

⇒ חתם *seal.*

חִתִּית 8 n.f. **terror**—cstr. חִתִּית; sf. חִתִּיתָם, חִתִּיתִי—<SUBJ> נתן ni. *be given,* i.e. be placed Ezk 32$_{25}$. <NOM CL> חִתִּית גִּבּוֹרִים בְּאֶרֶץ חַיִּים *the terror of the mighty was in the land of the living* Ezk 32$_{27}$. <OBJ> נתן *give,* i.e. place Ezk 32$_{17.23.24.26.32}$. <CSTR> חִתִּית גִּבּוֹרִים *the terror of the mighty* Ezk 32$_{27}$. <PREP> בְּ *despite* Ezk 32$_{30}$.*

⇒ חתת *be dismayed.*

חתך 1.0.1 vb. **determine—Ni.** 1.0.1 Pf. נֶחְתַּךְ; + waw Q ויחתכו—**be determined,** <SUBJ> שָׁבוּעַ *week* Dn 9$_{24}$, יוֹם *day* 4QpGen$^a$ 1.1$_2$. <PREP> עַל *concerning,* + עַם *people* Dn 9$_{24}$, עִיר *city* Dn 9$_{24}$; עַד *until,* + קֵץ *end* 4QpGen$^a$ 1.1$_2$.

חתל 2 vb. **wrap—Pu.** 1 Pf. חֻתָּלְתְּ—**be swaddled,** <SUBJ> Jerusalem Ezk 16$_4$.

**Ho.** 1 Inf. הָחְתֵּל—**be swaddled,** <SUBJ> Jerusalem Ezk 16$_4$.*

⇒ חִתּוּל *bandage,* חֲתֻלָּה *swaddling band.*

חֲתֻלָּה 1 n.f. **swaddling band**—sf. חֲתֻלָּתוֹ—<OBJ> שִׂים *place,* i.e. make Jb 38$_9$.

⇒ חתל *wrap.*

חֶתְלֹן 2 pl.n. **Hethlon**—חֶתְלֹן—on northern border of territory of Israel, <CSTR> דֶּרֶךְ חֶתְלֹן *way of Hethlon* Ezk 47$_{15}$ 48$_1$.

חתם 28.0.12.2 vb. **seal—Qal** 23.0.12 Pf. Q חתמתה; impf. יַחְתֹּם (יַחְתּוֹם); + waw וַיַּחְתֹּם, 3fs וַתַּחְתֹּם, וָאֶחְתֹּם; impv. חֲתֹם (חֲתוֹם), חִתְמוּ; ptc. חוֹתֵם, Q חותמים; ptc. pass. חָתוּם (חָתֻם), חֲתֻמִים (חֲתוּמִים); inf. abs. חָתוֹם, cstr. לַחְתֹּם (Q חתום)—**1. seal, set one's seal, seal up,** <SUBJ> Y. perh. Is 8$_{16}$ (|| צרר *bind*) Jb 9$_7$ 33$_{16}$ (or em. יַחְתֹּם *he seals* to יְחִתֵּם *he terrifies them,* from חתת hi.) 37$_7$ 4QShir$^b$ 30$_3$, Daniel Dn 12$_4$ (|| סתם *shut up*), Eliashib Arad ost. 4$_2$ 7$_8$ ([חת]ם), Esther Est 8$_8$, Jeremiah Jr 32$_{10}$, Jezebel 1 K 21$_8$, Jonathan, son of Joseph Mur 29 2$_9$ Mur 30 2$_9$, son of Eleazar Mur 30 2$_9$ ([בר] אלעז[ר]), son of Hanniah Mur 30 2$_9$, Judah Mur 29 2$_9$, Mordecai Est 8$_{8.10}$, Nahum Arad ost. 17$_6$, Simeon, son of Shimai Mur 30 2$_9$, son of Shobai Mur 29 2$_9$, son of Zechariah Mur 29 2$_9$, מֶלֶךְ *king* Ezk 28$_{12(L)}$ (mss חוֹתֵם *seal of* proportion), בַּר *son* Mur 29 2$_9$ Mur 30 2$_9$, purchaser Jr 32$_{44}$, נֵצֶר *shoot* 1QH 8$_{11}$ (unless חותם is pu. pf. or noun חוֹתָם *seal;* + סתר *conceal*), כֹּל *everyone* 1QH fr. 11$_3$ (unless noun חותם *seal,* or pu. pf. חתם); subj. not specified, Dn 9$_{24(Kt)}$ (Qr וּלְהָתֵם *and to put an end to,* i.e. תמם hi.; + כלא pi. *finish,* כפר pi. *atone for*) 9$_{24}$ Ne 10$_2$ (if em.; see §2b Prep.) 4QHod$^a$ 7.1$_{19}$ (ל[חתום]; || גלה *reveal*).

<OBJ> נָבִיא *prophet* Dn 9$_{24}$ (+ משח *anoint*), סֵפֶר *book* Dn 12$_4$, תּוֹרָה *teaching* Is 8$_{16}$, רָז *mystery* 1QH 8$_{11}$ (unless חותם is pu. pf. or noun חוֹתָם *seal*) 4QHod$^a$ 7.1$_{19}$, חָזוֹן *vision* Dn 9$_{24}$, שֶׁמֶן *(jar of) oil* Arad ost. 7$_8$ ([חת]ם) 17$_6$, תָּכְנִית *proportion* Ezk 38$_{12(L)}$ (mss חוֹתֵם תָּכְנִית *seal of proportion*), חַטָּאת *sin* Dn 9$_{24(Kt)}$.

<PREP> בְּ of instrument, *by (means of), with,* + חוֹתָם *seal* 1 K 21$_8$ Arad ost. 13$_3$ ([וחתם]) 17$_6$, טַבַּעַת *signet ring* Est 8$_{8.10}$; of accompaniment, *with,* + מוּסָר *discipline* Jb 33$_{16}$ (or em.; see Subj.); of place, *among,* + לִמֻּד *disciple* Is 8$_{16}$; introducing object, + יָד *hand* Jb 37$_7$ (unless em. בְּיַד to בְּעַד introducing object אָדָם *human being*).

בְּעַד introducing object, + כּוֹכָב *star* Jb 9$_7$, אָדָם *human being* Jb 37$_7$ (if em.; see above), כֹּל *all* 4QShir$^b$ 30$_3$.

עַד *until,* + עֵת *time* of the end Dn 12$_4$.

**2a.** pass. **be sealed,** <SUBJ> חוֹתָם *seal* 4QMyst$^b$ 1.2$_2$

([ח]תם]), סֵפֶר *book* Is 29$_{11}$=4QpIsa$^c$ 15$_3$ ([הספר הח]תום]) 29$_{11}$=4QpIsa$^c$ 15$_4$ CD 5$_2$,* דָּבָר *word* Dn 12$_9$ (|| סתם pass. *be shut up*), פֶּשַׁע *transgression* Jb 14$_{17}$ (+ טפל *smear* over), מַעְיָן *fountain* Ca 4$_{12}$ (|| נעל pass. *be locked*), הוּא *it*, i.e. wickedness of nation or vengeance of Y. Dt 32$_{34}$ (|| כמס pass. *be stored up*). <PREP> בְּ of place, *in*, + אוֹצָר *treasury* Dt 32$_{34}$, צְרוֹר *bag* Jb 14$_{17}$; מִן of direction, *from* 4QMyst$^b$ 1.2$_2$; עַד *until*, + עֵת *time* of the end Dn 12$_9$.

**2b.** pass. ptc. as noun, **sealed thing**, in ref. to copy of deed of sale, <OBJ> לקח *take* Jr 32$_{11}$ (:: גלה pass. ptc. *opened one*) 32$_{14}$ (+ סֵפֶר הַגָּלוּי *document of the opened one*, i.e. the open document), נתן *give*, i.e. place Jr 32$_{14}$. <APP> סֵפֶר *document* Jr 32$_{11}$. <PREP> עַל *upon* Ne 10$_{1.2}$ (or em. עַל הַחֲתוּמִים *upon the sealed ones* to הַחוֹתְמִים *those who seal* or אֵלֶּה הַחוֹתְמִים *these are those who seal*).

Also 4QD$^a$ 1$_9$ 4QShir$^b$ 30$_1$ 4QPrFêtes$^c$ 217$_1$.

<SYN> §1 צרר *bind*, סתם *shut up*, גלה *reveal*; § 2a סתם pass. *be shut up*, נעל pass. *be locked*, כמס pass.

<ANT> גלה pass. ptc. *opened one*.

**Ni.** 2 Pf. נֶחְתָּם; inf. abs. נַחְתּוֹם—**be sealed,** <SUBJ> כְּתָב *edict* Est 8$_8$, edict Est 3$_{12}$. <PREP> טַבַּעַת *signet ring* Est 3$_{12}$ 8$_8$.

**Pi.** 1 Pf. חִתְּמוּ—**keep (house) sealed,** i.e. **shut,** <SUBJ> רֹצֵחַ *murderer* Jb 24$_{16}$, נֹאֵף *adulterer* Jb 24$_{16}$. <PREP> לְ of benefit, *to, for*, + רֹצֵחַ *murderer* Jb 24$_{16}$, נֹאֵף *adulterer* Jb 24$_{16}$.

**Pu.** 0.0.2 Pf. Q חותם—**be sealed,** <SUBJ> רָז *mystery* 1QH 8$_{11}$ (unless חותם is qal ptc. or noun חוֹתָם *seal*), כֹּל *everything* 1QH fr. 11$_3$ (unless חותם is qal ptc. or noun חוֹתָם).

**Hi.** 2 Pf. הֶחְתִּים—**be blocked,** <SUBJ> בָּשָׂר *flesh*, i.e. penis Lv 15$_{3.3(Sam)}$. <PREP> בְּ of cause, *because of*, + זוֹב *discharge* Lv 15$_{3.3(Sam)}$.*

⇒ חוֹתָם *seal*, חֲתִים *signet ring*, חֲתִימָה *seal*, חֹתֶמֶת *signet ring*.

**חֹתָם**, see חוֹתָם *seal*.

**חֹתֶמֶת** 1 n.f. **signet ring,** <NOM CL> לְמִי הַחֹתֶמֶת *whose is the signet ring?* Gn 38$_{25}$ (or em. הַחוֹתָם *the signet ring*; + פָּתִיל *cord*, מַטֶּה *staff*). <ADJ> אֵלֶּה *these* Gn 38$_{25}$.

⇒ חתם *seal*.

**חתן** 11 vb. **marry—Htp.** 11 Pf. הִתְחַתַּנְתֶּם; impf. תִּתְחַתֵּן; + waw וַיִּתְחַתֵּן; impv. הִתְחַתְּנוּ, הִתְחַתֵּן; inf. הִתְחַתֵּן—of a man, **become related by marriage to, become son-in-law,** <SUBJ> Israel Jos 23$_{12}$, Israelite(s) Dt 7$_3$ Ezr 9$_{14}$, David 1 S 18$_{21.22.23.26.27}$, Hamor Gn 34$_9$, Jacob Gn 34$_9$, Jehoshapat 2 C 18$_1$, Solomon 1 K 3$_1$.

<OBJ> Hivite(s) Gn 34$_9$.

<PREP> לְ *to*, + Ahab 2 C 18$_1$; בְּ *with, to*, + גּוֹי *nation* Dt 7$_3$ Jos 23$_{12}$, עַם *people* Ezr 9$_{14}$, מֶלֶךְ *king* 1 S 18$_{22.23.26.27}$, Saul 1 S 18$_{21}$; אֵת *with*, + פַּרְעֹה *Pharaoh* 1 K 3$_1$.*

⇒ חֹתֵן *father-in-law*, חֹתֶנֶת *mother-in-law*, חָתָן *bridegroom*, חֲתֻנָּה *marriage*.

**חָתָן** 20 n.m. **bridegroom**—cstr. חֲתַן; sf. חֲתָנוֹ; pl. sf. חֲתָנָיו—**bridegroom** (e.g. Ex 4$_{25}$ Is 61$_{10}$ Jr 7$_{34}$ 25$_{10}$), **son-in-law,** i.e. **daughter's husband** (e.g. Gn 19$_{14}$ Jg 15$_6$ 1 S 18$_{18}$); of man, **relative by marriage** (2 K 8$_{27}$).

<SUBJ> היה *be* 1 S 18$_{18}$, יצא *go out* Jl 2$_{16}$ Ps 19$_6$.

<NOM CL> חֲתַן־דָּמִים אַתָּה *you are a bridegroom of blood* Ex 4$_{25}$, שִׁמְשׁוֹן חֲתַן הַתִּמְנִי *Samson was son-in-law of the Timnite* Jg 15$_6$, מִבְּנֵי יוֹיָדָע ... חָתָן לְסַנְבַלַּט *(one) of the sons of Jehoiada ... was son-in-law of Sanballat* Ne 13$_{28}$, חָתָן הוּא *he was a son-in-law* Ne 6$_{18}$, חֲתַן בֵּית־אַחְאָב הוּא *he was a relative by marriage of the house of Ahab* 2 K 8$_{27}$.

<OBJ> יצא hi. *bring out* Gn 19$_{12}$.

<CSTR> חֲתַן מֹשֶׁה *son-in-law of Moses* Nm 10$_{29}$ Jg 4$_{11}$ (both if em. חֹתֵן *father-in-law of*), הַתִּמְנִי *of the Timnite* Jg 15$_6$, הַמֶּלֶךְ *of the king* 1 S 22$_{14}$, חֲתַן בֵּית־אַחְאָב *relative by marriage of the house of Ahab* 2 K 8$_{27}$, חֲתַן־דָּמִים *bridegroom of blood* Ex 4$_{25.26}$.

בְּנֵי ... חֲתַן *sons of ... the father-in-law of* Moses Jg 4$_{11}$ (if em.; חֹתֵן), קוֹל חָתָן *voice of the bridegroom* Jr 7$_{34}$ 16$_9$ 25$_{10}$ 33$_{11}$, עֵינֵי חֲתָנָיו *eyes of his sons-in-law* Gn 19$_{14}$, מְשׂוֹשׂ חָתָן *joy of a bridegroom* Is 62$_5$.

<APP> Hobab Nm 10$_{29}$ 4$_{11}$ (if em. both; see Cstr.), בֵּן *son* Nm 10$_{29}$ (if em.; see Cstr.), מִדְיָנִי *Midianite* Nm 10$_{29}$ (or em.; see Cstr.).

<PREP> לְ of direction, *to*, + אמר *say* Nm 10$_{29}$ (if em.; see Cstr.); כְּ *as* Is 61$_{10}$ Ps 19$_6$ 4Q434a$_6$ ([חתן]); אֶל *to*, + אמר *say* Jg 19$_5$, דבר pi. *speak* Gn 19$_{14}$.*

⇒ חתן *marry*.

**חֹתֵן** 21 n.m. **father-in-law**—cstr. חֹתֵן; sf. חֹתֶנְךָ, חֹתְנוֹ—wife's father, **<SUBJ>** בוא *come* Ex 18$_{5.6}$, הלך *go* Ex 18$_{27}$, שׁמע *hear* Ex 18$_{1}$, ראה *see* Ex 18$_{14}$, אמר *say* Ex 18$_{14.17}$ Jg 19$_{9}$, חזק *be strong*, i.e. prevail Jg 19$_{4}$, hi. Jg 19$_{4(mss)}$, פצר *press*, i.e. urge Jg 19$_{7}$, לקח *take* Ex 18$_{2.12}$.

**<NOM CL>** אֲנִי חֹתֶנְךָ appar. *I am your father-in-law* Ex 18$_{6}$ (Sam הִנֵּה *behold* your father-in-law).

**<OBJ>** קרא *meet* Ex 18$_{7}$, שׁלח pi. *let go* Ex 18$_{27}$.

**<CSTR>** חֹתֵן מֹשֶׁה *father-in-law of Moses* Ex 18$_{1.2.5.12.12.14.17}$ Nm 10$_{29}$ (or em. חֲתַן *son-in-law of*) Jg 1$_{16}$ 4$_{11}$ (or em. חֲתַן); בְּנֵי ... חֹתֵן *sons of ... the father-in-law of* Moses Jg 1$_{16}$ 4$_{11}$ (or em. חֲתַן), קוֹל חֹתְנוֹ *voice of his father-in-law* Ex 18$_{24}$, צֹאן ... חֹתְנוֹ *flock of his father-in-law* Ex 3$_{1}$.

**<APP>** Jether Ex 4$_{18}$, Jethro Ex 3$_{1}$ 4$_{18(ms, Sam)}$ 18$_{1.2.5.6.12}$, Hobab Nm 10$_{29}$ 4$_{11}$ (or em. both; see Cstr.), אָב *father* Jg 19$_{4.9}$, בֵּן *son* Nm 10$_{29}$ (or em.; see Cstr.), כֹּהֵן *priest* Ex 3$_{1}$ 18$_{1}$, מִדְיָנִי *Midianite* Nm 10$_{29}$ (or em.; see Cstr.), קֵינִי *Kenite* Jg 1$_{16}$.

**<PREP>** לְ of direction, *to*, + הלך *go* Ex 18$_{27}$, אמר *say* Ex 4$_{18}$ 18$_{15}$ Nm 10$_{29}$ (or em.; see Cstr.), ספר pi. *recount* Ex 18$_{8}$; introducing object, + נשׁק *kiss* Ex 18$_{7}$; אֶל *to*, + שׁוב *go back* Ex 4$_{18}$; עִם *with*, + אכל *eat* Ex 18$_{12}$.*

→ חתן *marry*.

**חֲתֻנָּה** 1 n.f. **wedding**—sf. חֲתֻנָּתוֹ—**<CSTR>** יוֹם חֲתֻנָּתוֹ *day of his wedding* Ca 3$_{11}$.

→ חתן *marry*.

**[חֹתֶנֶת]** 1 n.f. **mother-in-law**—sf. חֹתַנְתּוֹ—**<PREP>** עִם *with*, + שׁכב *lie* Dt 27$_{23}$.*

→ חתן *marry*.

**[חַתֻּס]** 0.0.0.1 pr.n.m. **Hattus,** father of Uzza, **<CSTR>** בן חתס *son of Hathas* Seal 179 (7th cent.).

**חתף** 1.1.2 vb. **snatch away**—**Qal** 1.1.2 Impf. יַחְתֹּף; ptc. Si חותפו; inf. Q חתוף (Q לחתף)—**snatch away, <SUBJ>** אֵל *God* Jb 9$_{12}$ (unless em. to יַחַת פָּמִי *if he snatches away* [חתה] *then who* can resist him?), ירה ptc. *one who throws (oneself)* 4QHod$^c$ 1.3$_{10}$, wicked Si 15$_{14}$, כְּפִיר *young lion* 1QH 5$_{10}$. **<OBJ>** אָדָם *human being* Si 15$_{14}$, מַבְלָגָה *gleam* 4QHod$^c$ 1.3$_{10}$. → חֶתֶף *robber*.

**חֶתֶף** 1.2 n.m. **robber**—**robber; perh. robbery, prey, <PREP>** בְּ of purpose, *for (the purpose of)* robbery, + ארב *wait in ambush* Pr 23$_{28(mss)}$; כְּ *as* a robber, or *as (for)* prey, + ארב *wait in ambush* Pr 23$_{28}$; מִן of cause, *on account of*, + בטח *trust* Si 35$_{21(B)}$; *against*, + דאג *be anxious*, i.e. care for people, so as to protect them from Si 50$_{4}$.

→ חתף *snatch away*.

**חתר** 8 vb. **dig**—**Qal** 8 Pf. חָתַר, חָתַרְתִּי; impf. יַחְתְּרוּ; + waw וָאֶחְתֹּר; impv. חֲתָר־—**dig, break through; row** (Jon 1$_{13}$), **<SUBJ>** Israel Am 9$_{2}$, Ezekiel Ezk 8$_{8}$ 12$_{7}$, נָשִׂיא *prince* Ezk 12$_{12}$ (if em. יַחְתֹּר *he will dig through*), אִישׁ *man* Jon 1$_{13}$ (+ שׁוב hi. *bring back*), בֵּן *son* of mortal Ezk 8$_{8}$ 12$_{5}$, נֹאֵף *adulterer* Jb 24$_{16}$; subj. not specified, Ezk 12$_{12}$.

**<OBJ>** בַּיִת *house* Jb 24$_{16}$.

**<PREP>** לְ *with respect to*, + Ezekiel Ezk 12$_{5.7}$; בְּ of place, time, *in(to), through, during*, + קִיר *wall* Ezk 8$_{8.8}$ 12$_{5.7.12}$, חֹשֶׁךְ *darkness* Jb 24$_{16}$, שְׁאוֹל *Sheol* Am 9$_{2}$, עֶרֶב *evening* Ezk 12$_{7}$; לְעֵינֵי *in the sight of*, + בַּיִת *house* of Israel Ezk 12$_{5}$.

→ מַחְתֶּרֶת *housebreaking*.

**חתת I** 57.0.3 vb. **be shattered**—**Qal** 21 Pf. חַת, חַתָּה (חָתָּה), חַתּוּ (חָתּוּ, חָתּוּ); impv. חֹתּוּ—**be dismayed, be terrified, <SUBJ>** Merodach Jr 50$_{2}$, גִּלּוּל *idol* Jr 50$_{2}$, עַם *people* Is 8$_{9.9.9}$ (or em. חֹתּוּ *be dismayed* to חוּתוּ *be bold*, from חות), Moab Jr 48$_{20.39}$, שַׂר *prince* Is 31$_{9}$, גִּבּוֹר *mighty one* Jr 50$_{36}$ Ob$_{9}$, חָכָם *wise one* Jr 8$_{9}$, friends of Job Jb 32$_{15}$, יֹשֵׁב *inhabitant* 2 K 19$_{26}$||Is 37$_{27}$ Is 20$_{5}$, מִשְׂגָּב *retreat* Jr 48$_{1}$, אֲדָמָה *ground* Jr 14$_{4}$ (unless חתת II *be dry*).

**<PREP>** מִן cause, *on account of, at*, + נֵס *banner* Is 31$_{9}$.

**Ni.** 29.0.1 Pf. נִחַת; impf. יֵחַת (יֵחָת), תֵּחַת (תֵּחָת), אֵחַתָּה, יֵחַתּוּ, תֵּחַתּוּ (תֵּחָתּוּ)—**be shattered,** of Ephraim (Is 7$_{8}$), of righteousness (Is 51$_{6}$); **be terrified, be disheartened, <SUBJ>** Assyria Is 30$_{31}$, Israel 1 S 17$_{11}$ Jr 30$_{10}$ 46$_{27}$, גּוֹי *nation* Jr 10$_{2}$ 4QpIsa$^a$ 8$_{4}$, Ephraim Is 7$_{8}$, Judah 2 C 20$_{15.17}$, בַּיִת *house* of Israel Jr 10$_{2}$, Jerusalem 2 C 20$_{17}$, Israelite(s) Dt 1$_{21}$, שְׁאֵרִית *remnant* Jr 23$_{4}$, Jehoshaphat 2 C 20$_{15}$, Jeremiah Jr 1$_{17}$ 17$_{18}$, Joshua Dt 31$_{8}$ Jos 1$_{9}$ 8$_{1}$, Levi Ml 2$_{5}$, Saul 1 S 17$_{11}$, Solomon 1 C 22$_{13}$ 28$_{20}$, מֶלֶךְ

*king* 2 C 20 15, שַׂר *prince* 2 C 32 7, קָצִין *leader* Jos 10 25, גִּבּוֹר *mighty one* 4QpIsa[a] 8 4, בֶּן *son* of mortal Ezk 2 6 3 9, רָשָׁע *wicked one* Jb 21 13 (unless em. יֵחָתּוּ *they go down*, from נחת), ידע ptc. *one who knows* Is 51 7, יֹשֵׁב *inhabitant* 2 C 20 15, ריב hi. ptc. *one who strives* 1 S 2 10, רדף ptc. *persecutor* Jr 17 18, עתד pass. ptc. *one ready* for battle 1QM 15 8 ([ע]תודי[ן] ... תח[תו]), אַרְיֵה *lion* Is 31 4, סוּס *horse* Jb 39 22, צְדָקָה *righteousness* Is 51 6.

<PREP> בְּ of time, *in, at, during,* + רֶגַע *moment* Jb 21 13 (unless em.; see Subj.).

מִן privative, *from (being), so as not to be,* + עַם *people* Is 7 8; of cause, *on account of,* + גִּדּוּפָה *reviling* Is 51 7, אוֹת *sign* Jr 10 2, קוֹל *voice* Is 30 31 31 4, פָּנִים *face* Ezk 2 6 3 9.

מִפְּנֵי *from (before), because of,* + מֶלֶךְ *king* 2 C 32 7, מִשְׁפָּחָה *family* Jr 1 17, שֵׁם *name* Ml 2 5.

**Pi.** 2 Pf. חִתְּתָה, חִתְּתַנִי—**be shattered** (Jr 51 56); **dismay** (Jb 7 14), <SUBJ> appar. אֵל *God* Jb 7 14, קֶשֶׁת *bow* Jr 51 56. <PREP> בְּ of instrument, *by (means of),* + חֲלוֹם *dream* Jb 7 14.

**Hi.** 5.0.2 Pf. הֵחִתֹּת (Q החתיתני); impf. יָחֵת (Q יחתה, יְחִתֵּנִי, יְחִיתַן), אֲחִתְּךָ; + waw וְהַחִתֹּתִי—**shatter** (Is 9 13), **dismay, terrify** (Jr 1 17 49 37 Jb 31 34 Hb 2 17 1QH 2 35 7 8 9 19), <SUBJ> יי *Y.* Is 9 3 Jr 1 17 49 37, אֲדֹנָי *Lord* 1QH 7 8, אֵל *God* 1QH 2 35 9 19 ([ה]חתיתני), בּוּז *contempt* Jb 31 34, שֹׁד *destruction* Hb 2 17.

<OBJ> Elam Jr 49 37, Jeremiah Jr 1 17, Job Jb 31 34, worshipper 1QH 2 35 9 19, שׁקה hi. ptc. *one who makes drink* Hb 2 17 (perh. em. יְחִיתַּן *it will terrify them* to יְחִתֶּךָ *it will terrify you*), מַטֶּה *staff* Is 9 3.

<PREP> בְּ of cause, *on acount of,* + גִּדּוּפָה *reviling* 1QH 2 35, פַּחַד *fear* 1QH 9 19 ([ה]חתיתני מפחד); כְּ *as,* + יוֹם *day* Is 9 3; מִן of direction, *(away) from,* + בְּרִית *covenant* 1QH 7 8; לִפְנֵי *before,* + מִשְׁפָּחָה *family* perh. Jr 1 17, אֹיֵב *enemy* Jr 49 37.*

⇒ חַת I *terror,* II *shattered,* חִתָּה *terror,* חַתְחַת *terror,* חֲתַת *terror,* מְחִתָּה *terror.*

***חתת** II 1 vb. **be dry—Qal** 1 Pf. חַתָּה—**be parched, be dried up,** <SUBJ> אֲדָמָה *ground* Jr 14 4 (unless חתת I *be dismayed*), מֶגְרָפָה *water hole* Jl 1 17 (if em. תַּחַת *under* to תַּחַת *was dried up*).

**חֲתַת** I 1 n.[m.] **terror,** <OBJ> ראה *see* Jb 6 21.*
⇒ חתת *be dismayed.*

**חֲתַת** II 1 pr.n.m. **Hathath,** son of Othniel and leader of tribe of Judah, <APP> בֵּן *son* 1 C 4 13.*

# ט

**טאטא** I 1 vb. **sweep—Pilp.** 1 + waw וְטֵאטֵאתִיהָ—**sweep (away),** <SUBJ> ״י *Y.* Is 14$_{23}$. <OBJ> בָּבֶל *Babylon* Is 14$_{23}$. <PREP> בְּ of instrument, *by (means of), with,* + מַטְאֲטֵא *broom* Is 14$_{23}$ (+ הַשְׁמֵד broom of *destruction*).
⇒ מַטְאֲטֵא *broom.*

**טאטא** II 0.0.1 vb. **be muddy—Polp.** 0.0.1 Inf. Q טאטאיי—perh. **be muddied, be sunk in mud,** <COLL> ועם ענוים בטאטאיי רגל[הם] perh. *and with the humble when their foot is sunk in mud* 1QH 5$_{21}$.
⇒ טִיט *mud.*

**טָבְאַל** 1 pr.n.m. **Tabeel,** father of proposed Aramaean usurper of Ahaz's throne (or em. טָבְאֵל *Tabeel*), <CSTR> בֶּן־טָבְאַל *son of Tabal* Is 7$_{6}$.

**טָבְאֵל** 1.0.0.1 pr.n.m. **Tabeel—1.** signatory of letter to Artaxerxes I warning of plans to rebuild temple in Jerusalem, <SUBJ> כתב *write* Ezr 4$_{7}$. **2.** appar. son of Pedaiah (פדי), Seal 376 (8th cent.).
⇒ טוב *be good* + אֵל *god.*

**[טבב]** 1 vb. **speak—Qal** 1 Inf. טוֹב—**speak,** <SUBJ> לָשׁוֹן *tongue* of wise Pr 15$_{2}$ (if em. תֵּיטִיב *improves* knowledge to תָּטֵב/תָּטֹב *speaks* knowledge).* <OBJ> דַּעַת *knowledge* Pr 15$_{2}$ (if em.). <PREP> מִן privative, *so as not to, from,* + חשה hi. *be silent,* i.e. refrain Ps 39$_{3}$ (הֶחֱשֵׁיתִי מִטּוֹב *I refrained from speaking,* unless טוֹב *good*).
⇒ טִבָּה *word.*

**[טִבָּה]** n.f. **word, report, rumour,** <OBJ> אמר *say,* i.e. mention Ne 6$_{19}$ (if em. טוֹבֹתָיו *his good deeds* to טִבֹּתָיו *rumours about him;* + דָּבָר *word*).*
⇒ טבב *speak.*

**טָבָה**, see טוֹבָה *goodness.*

**[טְבוּל]** 1 n.[m.] **turban**—pl. טְבוּלִים—worn by Chaldaean military officers, <CSTR> סְרוּחֵי טְבוּלִים *loosened ones of turbans,* perh. overhanging turbans Ezk 23$_{15}$.

**[טַבּוּר]** 2 n.[m.] **navel, centre**—cstr. טַבּוּר (Gnz טיבור)—<CSTR> טַבּוּר הָאָרֶץ *centre of the land,* perh. in ref. to intersection of north–south and east–west routes east of Shechem Jg 9$_{37}$ (Gnz טיבור), *middle of the world,* appar. in ref. to Jerusalem Ezk 38$_{12}$. <PREP> עַל *above* or *at,* + ישׁב *dwell* Ezk 38$_{12}$; מֵעִם *from (with),* + ירד *go down* Jg 9$_{37}$.

**טבח** 11.0.4 vb. **slaughter—Qal** 11.0.3 Pf. טָבַחְתָּ, טָבְחָה, טָבַחְתִּי; + waw וּטְבָחוֹ; impv. טְבֹחַ; ptc. Q טֹבֵחַ, טובחים; inf. טְבֹחַ (טְבוֹחַ)—**1.** active, **slaughter** beast for consumption (Gn 43$_{16}$ Ex 21$_{37}$=4QBibPar 10$_{4}$ 1 S 25$_{11}$ Jr 11$_{19}$ 51$_{40}$ Pr 9$_{2}$) or sacrifice (11QT 34$_{7}$), **kill** human being (Ezk 21$_{15}$ Ps 37$_{14}$=4QpPs$^{a}$ 1.2$_{16}$ Lm 2$_{21}$) or beast (Jr 25$_{34}$).

<SUBJ> ״י *Y.* Lm 2$_{21}$ (|| הרג *kill,* + חמל not *pity*), חָכְמוֹת *Wisdom* Pr 9$_{2}$ (|| מסך *mix* wine), נָבָל *Nabal* 1 S 25$_{11}$, אִישׁ *man* Ex 21$_{37}$=4QBibPar 10$_{4}$ (|| מכר *sell* 4Q [מ]כרו), אֲשֶׁר עַל־הַבַּיִת *one who is over the house* Gn 43$_{16}$ (|| כון hi. *prepare* beast for eating), חֶרֶב *sword* Ezk 21$_{15}$ Ps 37$_{14}$=4QpPs$^{a}$ 1.2$_{16}$ (or del. טבח in MT), קֶשֶׁת *bow* Ps 37$_{14}$=4QpPs$^{a}$ 1.2$_{16}$ (or del. טבח in MT); subj. not specified, Jr 11$_{19}$ 25$_{34}$ 51$_{40}$.

<OBJ> כֶּבֶשׂ *lamb* Jr 11$_{19}$, כַּר *lamb* Jr 51$_{40}$, שֶׂה *sheep* Ex 21$_{37}$=4QBibPar 10$_{4}$ 1QIsa$^{a}$ 53$_{7}$ (כשה לטבוח יובל *like a sheep for slaughtering, he is brought* or *like a sheep, he is brought for slaughtering;* MT טֶבַח *slaughter*), שׁוֹר *ox* Ex 21$_{37}$=4QBibPar 10$_{4}$, פַּר *bull* 11QT 34$_{7}$, שׁוֹר *ox* Dt 28$_{31}$ (|| גזל *steal*), יָשָׁר *upright one* Ps 37$_{14}$=4QpPs$^{a}$ 1.2$_{16}$ (or del. MT; || נפל hi. *fell*), זָקֵן *elder* Lm 2$_{21}$, נַעַר *lad* Lm 2$_{21}$, בָּחוּר *youth* Lm 2$_{21}$, בְּתוּלָה *young woman* Lm 2$_{21}$, טִבְחָה *slaughter* 1 S 25$_{11}$, טֶבַח *slaughter* Gn 43$_{16}$ Ezk 21$_{15}$ Pr 9$_{2}$.

<PREP> לְ of benefit, *to, for,* + גזז ptc. *shearer* 1 S $25_{11}$; לְעֵינֵי *in the presence of,* + עַם *people* of Israel; Dt $28_{31}$. <SYN> נפל hi. *fell,* הרג *kill,* כון hi. *prepare* beast for eating, מסך *mix* wine, מכר *sell.*

<COLL> טבח טֶבַח/טִבְחָה *to slaughter slaughter,* i.e. to perform great slaughter Gn $43_{16}$ 1 S $25_{11}$ (טִבְחָה) Ezk $21_{15}$ Pr $9_{2}$.

2. passive, **be slaughtered,** <SUBJ> shepherds Jr 25 $_{34}$.

<SYN> גזל pass. *be stolen.**

⇒ טַבָּח *butcher,* טַבָּחָה *cook,* טִבְחַת *Tibhath,* (?) טֶבַח *Tebah,* טֶבַח *slaughter,* טִבְחָה *slaughter,* מַטְבֵּחַ *slaughter-house.*

**טַבָּח** 32.0.1 n.m. **butcher, cook**—pl. טַבָּחִים—**1. cook,** at Samuel's feast in honour of Saul, <SUBJ> נתן *give* meat 1 S $9_{23}$, שׂים *place* meat $9_{23.24}$, רום hi. *raise* meat $9_{24}$. <PREP> לְ of direction, *to,* + אמר *say* $9_{23}$, נתן *give* meat $9_{23}$; אֶל *to,* + אמר *say* $9_{23}$; עִם *with,* + שׂים *place,* i.e. keep meat $9_{23}$.

**2. domestic servant,** <CSTR> שַׂר הַטַּבָּחִים *prince of the domestic servants,* i.e. chief steward Gn $37_{36}$ $39_{1}$ (both Potiphar, a eunuch of Pharaoh) $40_{3}$ (L הַטַּבָּחִים; + מִשְׁמַר בֵּית in the *prison of the house of* the chief steward) $40_{4}$ $41_{10}$ (+ מִשְׁמַר בֵּית) $41_{12}$.

**3. (body)guard,** <CSTR> רַב־טַבָּחִים *captain of (the body)guard(s)* (as title of Nebuzaradan, head of the Babylonian forces who captured Jerusalem) 2 K $25_{8.10}$ ||Jr $52_{12.14}$ 2 K $25_{11.12}$||Jr $52_{15.16}$||Jr $39_{9.10}$ 2 K $25_{15.18.20}$||Jr $52_{19.24.26}$ Jr $39_{11.13}$ (+ סָרִיס *eunuch*) $40_{1.2.5}$ $41_{10}$ $43_{6}$ $52_{30}$ 4QApocJer C 1.4.*

⇒ טבח *slaughter.*

**טֹבַח**, see טֶבַח I *slaughter.*

**טֶבַח** I 12 n.m. **slaughter**—L טֹבַח (Pr $7_{22}$), טָבַח; sf. טִבְחָהּ—**slaughter** of beasts for food (Is $53_{7}$ Pr $7_{22}$) or sacrifice (Is $34_{6}$) or in war (Jr $50_{27}$) and of human beings in war, etc. (Is $34_{2}$ $65_{12}$ Jr $48_{15}$ Ezk $21_{15.20.33}$).

<NOM CL> טֶבַח גָּדוֹל בְּאֶרֶץ אֱדוֹם there will be *a great slaughter in the land of Edom* Is $34_{6}$ (|| זֶבַח *sacrifice*).

<OBJ> טבח *slaughter* Gn $43_{16}$ Ezk $21_{15}$ (לְמַעַן טְבוֹחַ טֶבַח *in order to slaughter slaughter,* i.e. to perform great slaughter; + חֶרֶב *sword*) Pr $9_{2}$ (|| יַיִן *wine*), perh. כון hi. *prepare* for eating Gn $43_{16}$. <ADJ> גָּדוֹל *great* Is $34_{6}$.

<PREP> לְ of direction, *to,* + יבל ho. *be brought* Is $53_{7}$, ירד *go down* Jr $48_{15}$ $50_{27}$ (or em. פָּרֶיהָ *its bulls* to פִּרְיָהּ *its fruit*), נתן *give,* i.e. hand over Is $34_{2}$; of purpose, *for (the purpose of),* + פתח pass. *be opened,* i.e. unsheathed Ezk $21_{33}$ (+ כול hi. inf. appar. *endurance* [or em. כָּלָה *destruction*], חֶרֶב *sword*), appar. עטה pu. *be sharpened* Ezk $21_{20}$ (or em. מְעֻטָּה *sharpened* to מְרֻטָּה/מֹרָטָה/מָרְטָה *polished;* + לְבָרָק *as lightning,* חֶרֶב), כרע *kneel* Is $65_{12}$ (+ חֶרֶב); אֶל *to,* + בוא *come* Pr $7_{22}$ (or em. ho. *be brought*).

<COLL> טָבַח טֶבַח *slaughter a slaughter,* i.e. perform great slaughter, לְמַעַן טְבוֹחַ טֶבַח *in order to slaughter slaughter,* i.e. to perform great slaughter Ezk $21_{15}$, טָבְחָה טִבְחָהּ *she has slaughtered a slaughter,* i.e. performed great slaughter Pr $9_{2}$.

<SYN> זֶבַח *sacrifice,* יַיִן *wine.**

⇒ טבח *slaughter.*

**טֶבַח** II 1 pr.n.[m.] **Tebah,** son of Nahor and Reumah, <OBJ> ילד *give birth (to)* Gn $22_{24}$.

⇒ (?) טבח *slaughter.*

**טֶבַח** III, see טִבְחַת *Tibhath.*

**[טַבָּחָה]** 1 n.f. **cook**—pl. טַבָּחוֹת—<PREP> לְ *as, in the function of,* + לקח *take* daughter 1 S $8_{13}$ (|| רַקָּחָה *perfumer,* אֹפָה *female baker*). <SYN> רַקָּחָה *perfumer,* אֹפָה *female baker.*

⇒ טבח *slaughter.*

**טִבְחָה** 3 n.f. **slaughter**—sf. טִבְחָתִי— **slaughter,** <OBJ> נתן *give* 1 S $25_{11}$ (|| לֶחֶם *bread,* מַיִם *water*), i.e. determine Ezk $21_{20}$ (if em. אִבְחַת appar. *destruction of* to טִבְחַת *slaughter of*), טבח *slaughter* 1 S $25_{11}$. <CSTR> טִבְחַת־חֶרֶב *slaughter of,* i.e. by, *sword* Ezk $21_{20}$ (if em.); צֹאן טִבְחָה *flock of,* i.e. destined for, *slaughter* Ps $44_{23}$ (mss לְטִבְחָה *for slaughter*). <PREP> לְ *(ready, destined) for* Jr $12_{3}$ Ps $44_{23(mss)}$ (both צֹאן לְטִבְחָה *flock for slaughter*). <SYN> לֶחֶם *bread,* מַיִם *water.**

⇒ טבח *slaughter.*

**טִבְחַת** 1 pl.n. **Tibhath,** city of Hadadezer in Aram-zobah, pillaged by David, appar. ident. with Betah (בֶּטַח) at ||2 S $8_{8}$ (or em. טֶבַח *Tebah* in both), <APP> עִיר *city* 1 C $18_{8}$ (+ כּוּן *Cun*). <PREP> מִן *from*, + לקח *take* bronze 1 C $18_{8}$.
→ טבח *slaughter.*

**טְבִיָּה**, see טוֹבִיָּה *Tobiah.*

**[טְבִיָּהוּ]**, see טוֹבִיָּה *Tobiah.*

**[טְבִילָה]** 0.0.1 n.f. **immersion,** <CSTR> ניקרת הטבילה *the cave of immersion* 3QTr $1_{12}$.*
→ טבל *immerse.*

**טבל** 16.0.2 vb. **immerse—Qal** 15.0.2 Impf. Q יטבול, תִּטְבְּלֵנִי; + waw וְטָבַל, וְטָבַלְתָּ, וּטְבַלְתֶּם, וַיִּטְבֹּל, וַיִּטְבְּלוּ; ptc. טֹבֵל—**immerse, dip,** appar. **wet** (Lv $4_{17}$ $14_{16}$; see Prep.), **immerse oneself** (2 K $5_{14}$ 4QTohA $2.1_{5}$), <SUBJ> Aaron Lv $9_{9}$, Asher Dt $33_{24}$, Hazael 2 K $8_{15}$, Jonathan 1 S $14_{27}$, Naaman 2 K $5_{14}$, Ruth Ru $2_{14}$, אֵל *God* Jb $9_{31}$, אִישׁ pure *man* Nm $19_{18}$, נגע ptc. *one who touches* semen 4QTohA $2.1_{4}$, נשׂא ptc. *one who raises,* i.e. carries something with semen on it 4QTohA $2.1_{5}$, כֹּהֵן *priest* Lv $4_{6.17}$ $14_{6.16.51}$, זָקֵן *elder* of Israel Ex $12_{22}$, בֵּן *son* of Israel Ex $12_{22}$ (if ins. בֵּן), אָח *brother* of Joseph Gn $37_{31}$.

<OBJ> Job Jb $9_{31}$, פַּת *crust* Ru $2_{14}$, אֶצְבַּע *finger* Lv $4_{6.17}$ $9_{9}$ $14_{16}$, רֶגֶל *foot* Dt $33_{24}$, מַטֶּה *rod* 1 S $14_{27}$ (קְצֵה הַמַּטֶּה *the end of the stick*), מִכְבָּר *netting* 2 K $8_{15}$, כְּתֹנֶת *tunic* Gn $37_{31}$, בֶּגֶד *vessel* 4QTohA $2.1_{5}$, כְּלִי *vessel* 4Q TohA $2.1_{4.5}$, צִפּוֹר *bird* Lv $14_{6.51}$, עֵץ cedar *wood* Lv $14_{6.51}$, אֵזוֹב *hyssop* Ex $12_{22}$ (אֲגֻדַּת אֵזוֹב *bunch of hyssop*) Lv $14_{6.51}$ Nm $19_{18}$, שָׁנִי *scarlet (cloth)* Lv $14_{6.51}$.

<PREP> בְּ of place, *in(to),* + Jordan 2 K $5_{14}$, חֹמֶץ *vinegar* Ru $2_{14}$, שַׁחַת *pit* Jb $9_{31}$ (or em. שֻׁחֹת, pl. of סוּחָה *dung*), יַעְרָה *(honey)comb* 1 S $14_{27}$, דָּם *blood* Gn $37_{31}$ Ex $12_{22}$ Lv $4_{6}$ $9_{9}$ $14_{6.51}$, מַיִם *water* Lv $14_{51}$ Nm $19_{18}$ 2 K $8_{15}$; מִן appar. of instrument, *by (means of), with,* + דָּם *blood* Lv $4_{17}$, שֶׁמֶן *oil* Lv $14_{16}$ Dt $33_{24}$.

<COLL> וַיִּטְבֹּל ... שֶׁבַע פְּעָמִים *and he immersed himself ... seven times* 2 K $5_{14}$; טבל followed by נזה hi. *sprinkle* Lv $4_{6.17}$ $14_{6.16.51}$ Nm $19_{18}$, נגע hi. *apply* Ex $12_{22}$, נתן *give,* i.e. place, יצק *pour* Lv $9_{9}$. Also 4QTohA $2.1_{5}$ (יטבו[ל]).

<SYN> נזה hi. *sprinkle,* נגע hi. *apply.*

**Ni.** 1 Pf. נִטְבְּלוּ—appar. **touch (water)** (without becoming immersed in it), <SUBJ> רֶגֶל *foot* of priests carrying ark across Jordan Jos $3_{15}$. <PREP> בְּ appar. make contact *with,* + קָצֶה *end,* i.e. edge of water Jos $3_{15}$.*
→ טְבִילָה *immersion.*

**טְבַלְיָהוּ** 1 pr.n.m. **Tebaliah,** gatekeeper (at time of David), son of Hosah, descendant of Merari, <NOM CL> טְבַלְיָהוּ הַשְּׁלִשִׁי *Tebaliah was the third (son)* 1 C $26_{11}$ (or em. טָבַלְיָהוּ *Tabliah*).

**טבע** 10.0.2 vb. **sink—Qal** 6.0.1 Pf. טָבַעְתִּי, טָבְעוּ; impf. אֶטְבָּעָה; + waw וַיִּטְבַּע, 3fs Q ותטבע—**sink, slip, fall,** <SUBJ> Jeremiah Jr $38_{6}$ (or em. טבע to היה *be*). worshipper Ps $69_{3}$ (+ וְאֵין מָעֳמָד *and there is no foothold;* + בוא *enter* watery depths [מַעֲמַקֵּי־מַיִם]) $69_{15}$ (+ מַעֲמַקֵּי־מַיִם), גּוֹי *nation* Ps $9_{16}$ (+ לכד ni. *be captured*), רֶגֶל *foot* of worshipper 1QH $7_{2}$, שַׁעַר *gate* Lm $2_{9}$, אֶבֶן *stone,* i.e. slingshot 1 S $17_{49}$. <PREP> בְּ of place, *in(to),* + יָוֵן *mire* Ps $69_{3}$, טִיט *mud* Jr $38_{6}$ (or em.), בֹּץ *mud* 1QH $7_{2}$, מֵצַח *forehead* 1 S $17_{4}$, שַׁחַת *pit* (as trap) Ps $9_{16}$, אֶרֶץ *earth* Lm $2_{9}$. <COLL> הַצִּילֵנִי מִטִּיט וְאַל־אֶטְבָּעָה *rescue me from (the) mud that I may not sink (into it)* Ps $69_{15}$, אַךְ לֹא־בְטֹבֵעַ יִשְׁלַח־יָד *surely he would not extend a hand against one who is sinking?* Jb $30_{24}$ (if em. בְּעִי *against a ruin*).

**Pi.** 0.0.1 Pf. Q וטבעת—**drown** (trans.), דַּיָּן eternal *judge* GnzPs $1_{24}$ (+ שׁבר pi. *shatter*), שֹׁפֵט righteous *judge* $1_{24}$. <OBJ> שׂנא ptc. *one who hates* $1_{24}$. <PREP> בְּ of place, *in,* + מְצוּלָה *deep* $1_{24}$.

**Pu.** 1 Pf. טֻבְּעוּ—**be drowned,** מִבְחַר *choice(st)* officers Ex $15_{4}$ (or em. טִבַּע pi. *he* [Y.] *has drowned* choicest officers). <PREP> בְּ of place, *in,* + יָם *sea* $15_{4}$.

**Hi., sink** (trans.), <SUBJ> אִישׁ *man* of one's peace, i.e. ally Jr $38_{22}$ (if em. ho. *be sunk,* of feet). <OBJ> רֶגֶל *foot* Jr $38_{22}$ (if em.). <PREP> בְּ of place, *in(to),* + בֹּץ *mud* Jr $38_{22}$ (if em.).

**Ho.** 3 Pf. הָטְבְּעוּ (הָטְבָּעוּ)—as Qal, **sink** (Jr $38_{22}$), perh. **be sunk, be set, be established** (Jb $38_{6}$ Pr $8_{25}$), <SUBJ> רֶגֶל *foot* Jr $38_{22}$ (or em. hi. *sink* feet), הַר *moun-*

tain Pr $8_{25}$, אֶדֶן *base* of world Jb $38_6$. <PREP> בְּ of place, *in(to)*, + בֹּץ *mud* Jr $38_{22}$ (or em.); עַל *upon*, + מָה *what?* Jb $38_6$.

**טַבָּעוֹת** 2 pr.n.m. **Tabbaoth,** head of family of Nethinim, temple servants in postexilic Judaea, <CSTR> בְּנֵי טַבָּעוֹת *sons of Tabbaoth* Ezr $2_{43}$||Ne $7_{46}$.

**טַבַּעַת** 49.0.2 n.f. **ring**—cstr. טַבַּעַת; sf. טַבַּעְתּוֹ; pl. טַבָּעוֹת (טַבָּעֹת); cstr. טַבְּעוֹת (טַבְּעֹת); sf. טַבְּעֹתָיו (Kt טבעתו), טַבְּעֹתָם (טַבְּעֹתֵיהֶם)—usu. as means of support for curtains, poles, bars, breastplate, etc., also as decorative, precious, or symbol of authority (Gn $41_{42}$ Ex $35_{22}$ Nm $31_{50}$ Est $3_{10.12}$ $8_{2.8.8.10}$) or as means of restraining head of bull (11QT $34_6$).

<SUBJ> היה *be* Ex $25_{27}$||$37_{14}$ (+ בַּיִת *house,* i.e. container for poles).

<NOM CL> שְׁתֵּי טַבָּעֹת עַל־צַלְעוֹ *two rings are on its* first/second *side* Ex $25_{12.12}$||$37_{3.3}$ (טַבָּעוֹת)

<OBJ> בוא hi. *bring* as gift Ex $35_{22}$ (Sam, mss lack טַבַּעַת; || חָח ear *ring,* נֶזֶם nose *ring,* כּוּמָז *bead,* עָגִיל *anklet* [Sam, mss]), קרב hi. *bring near,* i.e. present as gift Nm $31_{50}$ (|| אֶצְעָדָה *bracelet,* צָמִיד *bracelet,* עָגִיל, כּוּמָז), סור hi. *remove* (from hand) Gn $41_{42}$ Is $3_{21}$ (in list of fine clothing and jewellery) Est $3_{10}$ $8_2$, נתן *give* Est $3_{10}$ $8_2$, specif. place Ex $25_{26}$||$37_{13}$ $28_{23.27}$||$39_{16.20}$, place on hand Gn $41_{42}$, שׂים *place* Ex $28_{26}$||$39_{19}$, יצק *pour,* i.e. cast Ex $25_{12}$||$37_3$ $37_{13}$ $38_5$, עשׂה *make* Ex $25_{26}$ $26_{29}$||$36_{34}$ (both + זָהָב make ring [of] *gold,* בַּיִת make ring as *house,* i.e. container for bars) $27_4$ $28_{23.26.27}$||$39_{16.19.20}$ $30_4$||$37_{27}$.

<CSTR> טַבַּעַת הַמֶּלֶךְ *the king's (signet) ring* Est $3_{12}$ $8_{8.8.10}$, טַבְּעֹת הָאָרֹן *the rings of the ark* Ex $25_{15}$, טַבְּעֹת הָאֵפֹד *the rings of the ephod* Ex $28_{28}$||$39_{21}$, טַבְּעֹת זָהָב *rings of gold* Ex $25_{12.26}$||$37_{3.13}$ $28_{23.26.27}$||$39_{16.19.20}$ ($28_{23.26.27}$ טַבָּעוֹת) $30_4$||$37_{27}$, טַבְּעֹת נְחֹשֶׁת *of bronze* Ex $27_4$; שְׁתֵּי טַבָּעֹת *two rings* Ex $25_{12.12}$||$37_{3.3}$ (טַבָּעוֹת) $27_4$, שְׁתֵּי טַבְּעֹת *two rings of* Ex $28_{23.26.27}$||$39_{16.19.20}$ ($28_{23.26.27}$ טַבָּעוֹת) $30_4$||$37_{27}$, שְׁתֵּי הַטַּבָּעֹת *the two rings* Ex $28_{23.24}$||$39_{16.17}$ (Ex $28_{23}$ טַבָּעוֹת [Sam lacks שְׁתֵּי]), אַרְבַּע טַבָּעֹת *four rings* Ex $38_5$, אַרְבַּע טַבְּעֹת *four rings of* Ex $25_{12.26}$||$37_{3.13}$ $27_4$.

<APP> כְּלִי *vessel,* i.e. article, of gold Ex $35_{22}$ Nm $31_{50}$.

<ADJ> אֶחָד *one* Ex $26_{24}$||$36_{29}$.

<PREP> בְּ of place, *in(to)*, + היה *be* Ex $25_{15}$, בוא hi. *bring,* i.e. cause to pass through Ex $25_{14}$||$37_5$ $27_{7(\text{Sam})}$ ||$38_7$ (MT ho. *be brought*); of instrument, *by (means of), with* perh. 11QT $34_6$, + חתם *seal* Est $8_{8.10}$, ni. *be sealed* Est $3_{12}$ $8_8$; מִן of direction, *from,* or perh. of instrument, *by (means of), with,* + רכס *bind* breastplate Ex $28_{28}$||$39_{21}$; אֶל *to,* + אסר *bind* 11QT $34_6$, רכס *bind* breastplate Ex $28_{28}$||$39_{21}$; *at,* i.e. through, + תאם *be joined* Ex $26_{24}$||$36_{29}$ (if em. תַּמִּים *perfect* to תֹּאֲמִים *joining*); עַל *upon,* + נתן *give,* i.e. place Ex $28_{24}$||$39_{17}$.

<SYN> חָח ear *ring,* נֶזֶם nose *ring,* אֶצְעָדָה *bracelet,* צָמִיד *bracelet,* עָגִיל *anklet,* כּוּמָז *bead.*

**טַבְרִמֹּן** 1 pr.n.m. **Tabrimmon,** son of Hezion (or em. Hazael) and father of Ben-hadad (mss Ben-hadar), king of Aram, <CSTR> בֶּן־טַבְרִמֹּן *son of Tabrimmon* 1 K $15_{18}$. <APP> בֵּן *son* 1 K $15_{18}$.

⇒ טוב *be good* + רִמּוֹן *Rimmon.*

**[טֹבְשָׁלֵם]** 0.0.0.3 pr.n.m. **Tob-shalom, 1.** father of Jaazaniah, <CSTR> בן טבשלם *son of Tob-shalom* Lachish ost $1_2$. **2.** son of Zaccur (זכר), <APP> בֵּן *son* Seal 804 ([טבשלם]) 828 (both City of David, 7th/6th cent.). **3.** Seal 731 (En-Gedi, 7th/6th cent.).

⇒ טוב *be good* + שׁלם *be complete.*

**טַבָּת** 1 pl.n. **Tabbath**—טַבָּת—place to which Midianites fled pursued by Gideon, near Abel-Meholah in Gilead, <PREP> עַל *by, near* Jg $7_{22}$ (mss, Seb עַד flee *unto*).

**טֵבֵת** 1 pr.n.[m.] **Tebeth**—טֵבֵת—tenth month of Babylonian-based calendar, corresponding to December/January, <CSTR> חֹדֶשׁ טֵבֵת *month of Tebeth* Est $2_{16}$ (or em. אֲדָר *Adar;* + עֲשִׂירִי *tenth* month [or em. שְׁנֵים עָשָׂר *twelfth*]).

**טָהוֹר** 95.0.48 adj. **pure**—טָהֹר, טְהוֹרָה (טְהֹרָה); cstr. טְהוֹר (־טְהָר, Qr ־טְהַר); pl. טְהוֹרִים (טְהֹרִים), טְהוֹרוֹת (Q טהורות); cstr. Q טהורי—esp. in ritual contexts, **pure, purified, clean, cleansed, free** (of impurity) (e.g. 11QT $47_4$), **(in a) fit (state)** (e.g. 1 S $20_{26}$), perh. **radiant*** (e.g. Ps $19_{10}$).

# טָהוֹר

**1.** used attributively of אִישׁ *man* Nm 19$_{9.18}$ 4QTohB$^{b}$ 1$_{2}$ ([איש]) 11QT 49$_{8}$, בֵּן *son* 4QJub$^{g}$ 25$_{12}$ ([בן טהור]), כֹּהֵן *priest* 4QTohB$^{b}$ 1$_{6}$ ([טה]ור), עַם *people* 4Q414 3$_{3}$ ([ט]הור]), דּוֹר *generation* Pr 30$_{12}$, בְּהֵמָה *beast* Gn 7$_{2.8}$ 8$_{20}$ Lv 20$_{25}$ (:: טָמֵא *impure*) CD 12$_{9}$ 4QMMT B$_{23}$ ([הבהמה]) B7$_{6}$ (בה]מתו הטהור]ה) 11QT 47$_{7}$ 52$_{17}$, עֵז *goat* 11QT 52$_{13}$, שֶׂה *sheep* 11QT 52$_{13}$, שׁוֹר *ox* 11QT 52$_{13}$, עוֹף *fowl* Gn 8$_{20}$ Lv 20$_{25}$ (with ellipsis of noun; :: טָמֵא) Dt 14$_{20}$ (perh. עוֹף = *winged creature*), *bird* CD 12$_{9}$, צִפּוֹר *bird* Lv 14$_{4}$ (or del. טָהוֹר) Dt 14$_{11}$, זָהָב *gold* Ex 25$_{11+7t}$ 28$_{14.22.36}$ 30$_{3}$ 37$_{2+8t}$ 39$_{15.25.30}$ 1 C 28$_{17}$ 2 C 3$_{4.5(mss).8(mss)}$ (L טוֹב *good* in both) 9$_{17}$ 1QM 5$_{10.12}$ 11QT 3$_{8}$ ([טהו]ר) 3$_{9.12}$ 5$_{11}$ 6$_{9}$ 8$_{6}$ 9$_{1.12}$ 13$_{4}$ (all six [זהב טהור]) 36$_{11}$ 41$_{17}$, כֶּתֶם *gold* Jb 28$_{19}$, בַּרְזֶל *iron* 1QM 5$_{11}$, נְחֹשֶׁת *bronze* 11QT 3$_{15}$ ([נחו]שת]), קְטֹרֶת *incense* Ex 30$_{35}$ (unless of רֹקַח *powder*; || מלח pu. ptc. *salted*) 37$_{29}$, מַיִם *water* Ezk 36$_{25}$, מִנְחָה *cereal offering* Ml 1$_{11}$ (or del.), שֻׁלְחָן *table* Lv 24$_{6}$ 2 C 13$_{11}$, מְנֹרָה *lampstand* Ex 31$_{8}$||39$_{37}$ (||35$_{14}$ מְנֹרַת הַמָּאוֹר *the lampstand of light*) Lv 24$_{4}$, כְּלִי *vessel* Is 66$_{20}$, צָנִיף *turban* Zc 3$_{5.5}$, מָקוֹם *place* Lv 4$_{12}$ 6$_{4}$ 10$_{14}$ (or em. קָדוֹשׁ *holy*) Nm 19$_{9}$, לֵב *heart* Ps 51$_{12}$ 4QBark$^{c}$ 1$_{10}$ 4Q525 3.2$_{1}$, אִמְרָה *word* Ps 12$_{7}$=4QMidrEschat$^{b}$ 9$_{1}$ ([אמרות טהרות]). <COLL> דּוֹר טָהוֹר בְּעֵינָיו *a generation pure in its (own) eyes* Pr 30$_{12}$.

**2a.** in nom. cl., used predicatively of David 1 S 20$_{26.26}$, אָדָם *person* with skin disease Lv 13$_{13.17}$, אִישׁ *man* Nm 9$_{13}$, specif. man with lesion on head, face, or chin Lv 13$_{37.39}$, with baldness Lv 13$_{40.41}$, אִשָּׁה *woman* with lesion on head, face, or chin Lv 13$_{37.39}$, accused of adultery Nm 5$_{28}$, זוב ptc. fem. *woman suffering a discharge* 4QTohA 1.1$_{7}$ ([זבה]), לֵוִי *Levite* Ezr 6$_{20}$, כֹּהֵן *priest* Ezr 6$_{20}$ (or del. כֹּהֵן), בְּהֵמָה *beast* Gn 7$_{2.8}$, נְבֵלָה *carcase* Lv 11$_{37}$, בָּשָׂר *flesh* 4QTohB$^{b}$ 1$_{10}$ (וט]הור ב]שרם *and their flesh will be pure*), יִרְאָה *fear* of Y. Ps 19$_{10}$ (or em. אִמְרָה *word*), אֹמֶר *word* Pr 15$_{26}$.

<COLL> with לֹא *not*, i.e. impure Gn 7$_{2}$ 1 S 20$_{26}$ (בִּלְתִּי טָהוֹר הוּא כִּי־לֹא טָהוֹר *he is not clean, to be sure, he is not clean*; or em. second טָהוֹר to טֹהָר [i.e. טהר pu.] for *he has not been purified*), אַיִן *not* Gn 7$_{8}$, בִּלְתִּי *not* 1 S 20$_{6}$.

**2b.** with היה *be*, used predicatively of אִישׁ *man* Dt 23$_{11}$ (+ מִקְּרֵה לָיְלָה *[due to] a happening of*, i.e. involuntary ejaculation in, *the night*) 1QM 7$_{6}$=4QM$^{a}$ 1$_{10}$ ([טהור]),* בֵּן *son* 4QJub$^{d}$ 21$_{16}$ ([בני ... הייה טהור] *my son ..., be pure*), שׂרף ptc. *one who burns* red heifer 4QMMT B$_{15}$, אסף ptc. *one who gathers* ashes of red heifer 4QMMT B$_{15}$, נזה hi. ptc. *one who sprinkles* water 4QMMT B$_{15}$, יַיִן *wine* 11QT 47$_{7}$, שֶׁמֶן *oil* 11QT 47$_{7}$, אֹכֶל *food* 11QT 47$_{7}$, מַשְׁקֶה *wet food* or *vessel* 11QT 47$_{7}$ (unless מושקה = מַשְׁקֶה *drink*), בּוֹר *cistern* Lv 11$_{36}$, מַעְיָן *spring* Lv 11$_{36}$, עִיר *city* 11QT 47$_{3}$ (והיו) 47$_{4}$ (+ קֹדֶשׁ *holiness*, i.e. holy), כֹּל *all* 11QT 47$_{6.6}$. <COLL> with לֹא *not*, i.e. impure Dt 23$_{11}$ 1QM 7$_{6}$, לוא יהיה טהור ממקורו *he is impure on account of his source*, i.e. involuntary ejaculation 1QM 7$_{6}$=4QM$^{a}$ 1$_{10}$ ([טהור ממקורו]), טהורה מכול דבר *free of any* impure *thing* 11QT 47$_{4}$, [הייה טהור בבשרכה] *be pure in your flesh* 4QJub$^{d}$ 21$_{16}$.

**3.** as noun, **pure, purified one, one who** or **something that is pure, purified**, <SUBJ> היה *be* 4QMMT B$_{16}$, טמא *be impure* Lv 15$_{8}$, יסף hi. *increase* strength Jb 17$_{9}$ (+ צַדִּיק *righteous one*), אכל *eat* Lv 7$_{19}$ Nm 18$_{11.13}$ Dt 12$_{15}$=11QT 52$_{11}$ Dt 12$_{22}$=11QT 53$_{4}$ Dt 15$_{22}$ (all five :: טָמֵא *impure one*), כבס pi. *launder* Lv 15$_{8}$, רחץ *wash (oneself)* Lv 15$_{8}$, נזה hi. *sprinkle* Nm 19$_{19}$ 4QMMT B$_{16}$ (both :: טָמֵא), נבט hi. *look* Hb 1$_{13}$=1QpHab 5$_{1}$.

<OBJ> אהב *love* Pr 22$_{11}$ (unless טָהוֹר is subj. of אהב), נתן *give*, i.e. produce Jb 14$_{4}$ (ms lacks entire verse), טהר pi. *purify* 4QShirShabb$^{a}$ 1.1$_{15}$.

<CSTR> טְהָר־לֵב *one who is pure of heart* Pr 22$_{11(Qr)}$, טְהָר־יָדַיִם *one who is pure of hands* Jb 17$_{9}$, טְהוֹר עֵינַיִם *one who is pure of eyes* Hb 1$_{13}$=1QpHab 5$_{1.6}$, טהורי מועדו *the pure ones of his festival*, i.e. those fit to attend 4Q414 1.1$_{2}$, טהורי [אור] *pure ones of light* 4QShir Shabb$^{a}$ 1.1$_{15}$, טהורי עולמים *pure ones of ages* 4QShir Shabb$^{d}$ 1.1$_{13}$; טוהר טהורים *purity of pure ones* 4QShir Shabb$^{d}$ 1.1$_{42}$ (erased זוהר *brightness of*), יוֹם הַטָּהֹר *the day of the pure one* Lv 14$_{57}$ (unless טֹהַר *purity*; :: טָמֵא *impure one*), מלך הטהור *king of the pure one* 4QShirShabb$^{d}$ 1.2$_{26}$ (unless in last two טֹהַר *purity, splendour*), כָּל־טָהוֹר *every pure one* Lv 7$_{19}$ Nm 18$_{11.13}$ 2 C 30$_{17}$ (כֹּל לֹא טָהוֹר *every impure one*) 4QShirShabb$^{d}$ 1.1$_{13}$ ([כול] טהורי).

<PREP> לְ of benefit, *to, for* 2 C 30$_{17}$; of possession, *of, (belonging) to* Ec 9$_{2}$ (|| טוֹב *good one* [or del.], צַדִּיק *righteous one*, :: טָמֵא *impure one*, רָשָׁע *evil one*, + זבח ptc. *one who sacrifices*); introducing object, + ברך pi. *bless* 4QShirShabb$^{d}$ 1.1$_{13}$ ([וברך ... לכול] טהורי); =4QShir

Shabbf 3.23 ([וברך ... לכול טהו]רי]); בְּ at, against, + רקק spit Lv 158; בֵּין between, + בדל hi. separate Lv 1010 (|| קֹדֶשׁ holiness, :: טָמֵא impure one [Gnz lacks טָמֵא], חֹל profaneness) 1147 (:: טָמֵא; + חַיָּה beast) GnzPs 14 (בין ... לטהור; || אוֹר light, צֶדֶק righteousness, :: טָמֵא, חֹשֶׁךְ darkness, שֶׁקֶר deceit) CD 617 1220 (both בין ... לטהור; || קֹדֶשׁ holiness, :: טָמֵא impure, חֹל) 4QMMTB57 (בין ... ל]טהור; :: טָמֵא) 4QRitPur 414 (טהור [והב]דל ...; :: טָמֵא), ידע hi. make (distinction) known Ezk 2226 (בֵּין ... לְטָהוֹר; :: טָמֵא) 4423 (בֵּין ... לְטָהוֹר; || קֹדֶשׁ, :: טָמֵא, חֹל).

<COLL> with לֹא not, i.e. impure 2 C 3017; טְהוֹר עֵינַיִם מֵרְאוֹת רָע too pure of eyes to look upon evil Hb 113 (=1QpHab 51.6, ברע at evil), מִי־יִתֵּן טָהוֹר מִטָּמֵא who can produce the pure from the impure? Jb 144 (ms lacks entire verse).

Also 4Q185 1.14 4QpGenb 23 4QTohA 3.24 4Q414 1.14 (טהורים לפניכה those who are pure before you) 4Q418 1862 4QDibHama 616 (טהור[ים]) 93 4QRitPur 15.95 (טהורי[ם]) 51.29 1332.

<SYN> §1 מלח pu. ptc. salted; §3 טוֹב good one, צַדִּיק righteous one, קֹדֶשׁ holiness, אוֹר light, צֶדֶק righteousness.

<ANT> §1 טָמֵא impure; §3 טָמֵא impure one, רָשָׁע evil one, חֹל profaneness, חֹשֶׁךְ darkness, שֶׁקֶר deceit.*

⇒ טהר be pure.

**טהר** 94.1.65 vb. **be pure—Qal** 34.0.20 Pf. טָהֵרָה, טָהֲרָה, טָהַרְתְּ, טָהַרְתִּי; impf. יִטְהַר (יִטְהָר), 3fs תִּטְהַר, Q יטהרו, 2mpl תִּטְהָרוּ, תִּטְהֲרִי; + waw וְטָהֵר, וְטָהֲרָה (וְטָהֵרָה), Q וטהרו, וְטָהַרְתִּי, וּטְהַרְתֶּם, וַיִּטְהַר, וָאֶטְהַר; inf. Q טהור; impv. טְהָר—**be (regarded as) pure, be purified, be (regarded as) clean, cleansed, be (regarded as) healed** (e.g. 2 K 510), **be healthy, be free**, physically (e.g. Ex 2410), ritually (e.g. Gn 352 Lv 128) or ethically (e.g. Pr 209).

<SUBJ> Naaman 2 K 510.12.13 (all three + רחץ wash oneself) 514, אָדָם human being suffering from skin disease Lv 136 (+ כבס pi. launder, רחץ wash oneself), נֶפֶשׁ soul, i.e. person who eats unslaughtered beast Lv 1715 (:: טמא be impure [lacking in Sam], + כבס pi. launder, רחץ), who touches one unclean through contact with a corpse 11QT 508 (+ כבס pi., רחץ), i.e. priest who touches swarming thing or unclean person Lv 227 (+ רחץ, אכל not eat, :: טמא).

אִישׁ man suffering from skin disease or discharge Lv 224 (+ אכל not eat), who has had an ejaculation 4QOrdc 1.14.7 (both + אכל), suffering from lesion on head, face, or chin Lv 1334 (+ כבס pi. launder), who has returned from battle Nm 3124 (+ כבס pi., בוא come, i.e. enter camp), who finds corpse or remains of body 11QT 506.7, גֶּבֶר man Jb 417 (|| צדק be righteous).

אִשָּׁה woman suffering from lesion on head, face, or chin Lv 1334, נְקֵבָה female who has recently given birth Lv 127 (or em. וְטָהֲרָה and she will be considered cleansed to וְטִהֲרָהּ and he [priest] will declare her clean) 128, דָּוָה menstruant 4QTohA 1.17.

אֶבְיוֹן poor one 4QHodc 1.23 ([אביון]), טהר htp. ptc. one who undergoes purification Lv 147 (if em. וְטִהֲרוֹ and he will declare him cleansed to וְטָהֵר and he will be [considered] clean) 148.9 (+ כבס pi. launder, רחץ wash oneself, גלח pi. shave, ישׁב sit outside camp seven days) 1420, טָמֵא one who is unclean 4QOrdc 1.16.9 (both + כבס pi., רחץ, אכל eat) perh. 4QTohBb 18 (יט]ה[רו) 110, specif. one who is unclean through contact with a corpse Nm 1919 (or del. טהר; + כבס pi., רחץ).

זוב ptc. one suffering a discharge Lv 1513.13 (+ כבס pi. launder, רחץ wash oneself, ספר count, i.e. wait, seven days) 1528.28 (+ כבס pi., רחץ, ספר) 4QTohA 1.17 ([זבה]), נגע ptc. one who touches a corpse Nm 1912.12 (both + חטא htp. purge oneself), specif. the corpse of a swarming animal 11QT 513 ([כול הנוגע]; + כבס pi., רחץ), a house entered by a woman who has suffered a miscarriage 11QT 5016 (+ כבס pi., רחץ, נזה hi. sprinkle), נשׂא ptc. one who raises, i.e. carries away, part of the corpse of a swarming animal 11QT 515.

מִי who? Pr 209 (+ זכה pi. purify), כֹּל all, i.e. anyone who enters house in which there is a corpse 11QT 4920 (+ כבס pi. launder, רחץ wash oneself) perh. 504 ([וטהר]ו), Israelite Lv 1630, worshipper Ps 519 (+ לבן hi. be white, + חטא hi. purge with hyssop).

Jerusalem Jr 1327, עִיר city, i.e. Jerusalem Ezk 2413 (or del.) 2413, בַּיִת house of Israel Ezk 3625, אֶרֶץ land Ezk 3916 (if em. וְטִהֲרוּ and they will purify the land to וְטָהֲרָה and it will be pure), זרק scatter, i.e. sprinkle, pure water), בַּיִת house Lv 1453, בֶּגֶד garment in which there is disease Lv 1358 (+ כבס pu. be laundered), in unclean house 11QT $50_{18}$, כְּלִי *vessel* in unclean house 11QT $50_{18}$, i.e. anything touched by dead lizard, etc. Lv $11_{32}$ (:: טמא *be impure*), i.e. garment Lv $13_{58}$, דָּבָר *thing*, i.e. metal Nm $31_{23}$ (+ עבר hi. *cause to pass* through fire), מַעֲשֶׂה *thing* 11QT $50_8$.

בָּשָׂר *flesh* of human being 1QS $3_8$, of sacrificial beast 11QT $47_{16.16}$, עוֹר *skin* of sacrificial beast 11QT $47_{15}$, in unclean house 11QT $50_{18}$.

<PREP> לְ of instrument, *by (means of)*, + נזה hi. inf. *sprinkling* 1QS $3_8$; *in respect of*, i.e. for use in, + מִקְדָּשׁ *sanctuary* 11QT $47_{16}$, עִיר *city* 11QT $47_{16}$; *at, by*, + עֶרֶב *evening* 11QT $49_{20}$ $50_4$ (וטהר]ו לע[רב) $50_8$; כְּ *as*, perh. + כֶּסֶף *silver* 4QHodc $1.2_3$ ([וככסף]); *in accordance with*, + חֹק *statute* 11QT $50_6$, מִשְׁפָּט *judgment*, 11QT $50_7$; מִן of agent, be regarded as pure *by*, + עֹשֶׂה *maker* Jb $4_{17}$; be free (etc.) *of*, + חַטָּאת *sin* Pr $20_9$, טֻמְאָה *impurity* Ezk $24_{13}$ (or del. מִטֻּמְאָתֵךְ *of your impurity*) 4QTohBb $1_8$ (יט]ה[רו), נִדָּה *(menstrual) impurity* 4QTohA $1.1_7$ ([מנד]תה), מָקוֹר *(impurity emanating from) source*, i.e. ejaculation 4Q Ordc $1.1_4$ (ממקו]ר[ו) $1.1_7$; עַד לְ *unto*, i.e. for, + עוֹלָם *eternity* 11QT $50_{18}$; לִפְנֵי *before* or *in the estimation of* Y. Lv $16_{30}$.

<COLL> with עוֹד not be pure *again* Ezk $24_{13}$ 11QT $50_8$, אַחַר be pure *afterwards* 11QT $51_5$; [לטהורן שבעתים] *to be purified seven times* 4QHodc $1.2_3$.

Also 4QPrFêtesc 307 4QRitPur $15.1_{12}$ ([ט]הרתי) 11Q Tb $17_3$.

<SYN> צדק *be righteous*.

<ANT> טמא *be impure*.

**Pi.** 39.1.25 Pf. Q טהרני, טִהַרְתִּיךָ, Q טהרתה (טהרתני), טִהַרְנוּ; impf. Q יטהר (ויטהרם), 2ms אֲטַהֵר, תטהר, Q יטהרו, 2mpl תטהרו; + waw וְטִהֵר (וְטִהֲרוֹ), וְטִהַרְתָּ, וְטִהַרְתִּי (וְטִהַרְתִּים), וְטִהֲרוּ; וַיְטַהֵר, 3fs וַתְּטַהֲרֵם, וַיְטַהֲרוּ; impv. טַהֲרֵנִי; ptc. מְטַהֵר, Q מטהרים, מטהרי; inf. טַהֵר (טַהֲרָם, טַהֲרָהּ, טַהֲרוֹ, Q טהרני, טַהֲרִי)—**purify, cleanse, declare purified** (e.g. Lv $13_{13.17.28.34}$); esp. in Scrolls, perh. **save, release, absolve** from (or **fortify** against) sin (1QH $1_{32}$ $3_{21}$ $4_{37}$ $7_{30}$ $11_{10}$ 1QS $4_{21}$ $11_{14}$ 4Q370 $2_3$ 4Q DibHama $1.6_2$ 4QRitPur $29.7_9$ 11QPsa $19_{14}$ $24_{13}$); **refine** precious metal (Ml $3_3$), **clear away, remove** clouds (Jb $37_{21}$), violence (11QPsa $22_5$).

<SUBJ> Y. Jr $33_8$ (+ סלח *forgive*) Ezk $24_{13}$ (or del.) $36_{25.33}$ $37_{23}$ (+ ישׁע hi. *save*) 11QPsa $19_{14}$ (+ סלח) $24_{13}$ (+ רחק hi. *distance* evil) perh. Lv $16_{30}$ (or em. יְכַפֵּר *he* [Y.] *will make atonement* to free you to יְכֻפַּר *atonement will be made*) 4Q370 $2_3$ 4QapPsb $46_5$, 4Q414 $4_7$, אֱלֹהִים *God* Ps $51_4$ (|| כבס pi. *launder*, i.e. clean worshipper) 4Q Shirb $20.1_1$ ([יטה]רני) $36_2$ 4QShirShabba $1.1_{15}$ ([אלוהי]), אֵל *God* 1QH $1_{32}$ ([טה]רתה; + חזק pi. *strengthen*) $4_{37}$ ([לט]הר; + כפר pi. *atone*) $6_5$ ([ותטהרני]) $11_{10.30}$ fr. $1_8$ ([תטהרנו ... א]לי) 1QS $4_{21}$ (ברר pi. *purify*, זקק pi. *refine*) $11_{14}$ (+ כפר pi.) 4QRitPur $39.2_2$ ([אל]) $29.7_9$ ([אל]) perh. 1QH $5_{16}$, אָדוֹן *lord* 1QH $3_{21}$ $7_{30}$ ([לטהר]ם) $14_{13}$ ([תטהרנו]) $16_{12}$ $17_{11}$ ([אדוני ... ותטהר]) $17_{15}$ ([אדוני ( ... ]לטהרם]) 4QDibHama $1.6_2$ (ות]ט[הרנו); unless in all five אד]ו[ני = *Adonai*; + נגשׁ hi. *bring* worshipper *near*), דַּיָּן eternal *judge* GnzPs $1_5$, שֹׁפֵט *judge* GnzPs $1_5$, רוּחַ *spirit* of God 1QH fr. $2_{14}$ ([רוח ... לטהר]).

Aaron Lv $16_{19}$ (+ קדשׁ pi. *sanctify*) Nm $8_{21}$ (+ כפר pi. *atone*), Moses Nm $8_{6.7.15}$, Josiah 2 C $34_{3.5}$, Nehemiah Ne $13_{30}$ (or del.), Zion 11QPsa $22_5$ (+ כרת ni. *be cut off*).

מַלְאָךְ Y.'s *messenger* Ml $3_3$ (|| צרף pi. *refine*) $3_3$ (|| זקק pi. *purify*; or del. $3_3$), כֹּהֵן *priest* Lv $12_{7(Sam, ms)}$ (if em. qal; see Obj.) $13_{6.13.23.28.34}$ $14_7$ (or em. וְטִהֲרוֹ *and he will declare him cleansed* to וְטָהֵר *and he will be [considered] clean*) $14_{11.48}$ Ezk $43_{26}$ Ne $12_{30}$ 2 C $29_{16}$ (+ יצא hi. *take out* impurity) $29_{18}$ 4QTohBb $1_9$ ([הכו]הן), לֵוִי *Levite* Ne $12_{30}$ 2 C $29_{15.18}$, perh. מִשְׁמָר *watch*, i.e. priestly course 11QT $45_5$.

אִישׁ *man* CD $10_{12}$, בֵּן *son* Si $38_{10}$, בַּיִת *house* of Israel Ezk $39_{12}$, רוּחַ *wind* Jb $37_{21}$, perh. מַיִם *water* 4QRitPur $1.12_6$; subj. not specified, Ne $13_9$ 1QM $7_2$ (see Coll.)* 11QT $47_{14}$ $49_{14}$.

<OBJ> Israelite Lv $16_{30}$ 4QDibHama $1.6_2$ (ות]ט[הרנו), worshipper Ps $51_4$ 1QH $6_5$ ([ותטהרני]) $16_{12}$ 1QS $11_{14}$ 4QShirb $20.1_1$ ([יטה]רני) 4QRitPur $39.2_2$ $29.7_9$ 11QPsa $19_{14}$ $24_{13}$, עֶבֶד *servant*, i.e. worshipper 1QH $11_{30}$ (+ שׂמח pi. *gladden*) $17_{11}$ ([ותטהר]), עבד ptc. *one who serves*, i.e. worshipper 1QH $17_{15}$ ([לטהרם]), בחר pass. ptc. *chosen one* 4QapPsb $46_5$.

בֵּן *son* of Israel Ezk $37_{23}$, of Levi Ml $3_3$ (or del.), of truth 1QH $7_{30}$ ([לטהר]ם) 1QH fr. $2_{14}$ ([ולטהר את בני אמתכה]), אֱנוֹשׁ *human being* 1QH $4_{37}$ ([לט]הר) $11_{10}$, אָדָם *person* suffering from skin disease, rash, or burn Lv

$13_{6.23.28}$, אִישׁ *man* 1QH $14_{13}$ ([א]יש תטהרנו]) fr. $1_{8}$ ([תטהרנו]), suffering from lesion on head, face, or chin Lv $13_{34.37}$, appointed to bury dead Ezk $39_{14}$, אִשָּׁה *woman* suffering from lesion on head, face, or chin Lv $13_{34.37}$, נְקֵבָה *female* who has recently given birth Lv $12_{7}$ (if em. וְטָהֲרָה *and she will be considered cleansed* to וְטִהֲרָהּ *and he* [the priest] *will declare her clean*).

נֶגַע *(person suffering) wound* Lv $13_{13}$, עבר ptc. *one who passes* through land, burying dead Ezk $39_{16}$ (or em. וְטִהֲרוּ *and they will purify* to וְטָהֲרָה *and it* [the land] *will be pure*), טהר htp. ptc. *one who undergoes purification* Lv $14_{7}$ (or em. וְטִהֲרוֹ *and he will declare him cleansed* to וְטָהֵר *and he will be [considered] clean*), טָהוֹר *pure one* 4QShirShabb[a] $1.1_{15}$, perh. טָמֵא *one who is impure* 4QTohB[b] $1_{9}$ 4QRitPur $1.12_{6}$, כֹּהֵן *priest* Ne $13_{30}$ (or del.), לֵוִי *Levite* Nm $8_{6.7.15.21}$ Ne $13_{30}$ (or del.), אֶבְיוֹן *poor one* 1QH $5_{16}$.

Israel Jr $33_{8}$, Judah Jr $33_{8}$ 2 C $34_{3.5}$, Jerusalem 2 C $34_{3.5}$, עַם *people* 4Q414 $4_{7}$, specif. lay people Ne $12_{30}$, צֹאן *flock*, i.e. Israel GnzPs $1_{5}$, עִיר *city* 11QT $47_{14}$, i.e. Jerusalem Ezk $24_{13}$ (or del.), בַּיִת *house* of Israel Ezk $36_{25.33}$, of Y. 2 C $29_{15.16.18}$, suffering disease Lv $14_{48}$ (+ כִּי נִרְפָּא הַנָּגַע *for the infection has been cured*), in which corpse has lain 11QT $49_{14}$, אֶרֶץ *land* Ezk $39_{12.14.16}$ (or em. וְטִהֲרוּ *and they will purify* the land to וְטָהֲרָה *and it will be pure*) 1QM $7_{2}$ (see Coll.).

שַׁחַק *cloud* Jb $37_{21}$, לִשְׁכָּה *chamber* Ne $13_{9}$, נִשְׁכָּה *chamber* 11QT $45_{5}$, מִזְבֵּחַ *altar* Lv $16_{19}$ Ezk $43_{26}$ (+ כפר pi. *atone*) 2 C $29_{18}$, שֻׁלְחָן *table* 2 C $29_{18}$, שַׁעַר *gate* Ne $12_{30}$, חוֹמָה *wall* Ne $12_{30}$, בֶּגֶד diseased *garment* Lv $13_{59}$ (:: טמא pi. *declare impure*), רֵחַיִם *mill* in unclean house 11QT $49_{14}$, מְדֹכָה *mortar* in unclean house 11QT $49_{14}$, כְּלִי *vessel* CD $10_{12}$, specif. vessel in unclean house 11QT $49_{14.14.14}$, of temple 2 C $29_{18.18.18}$, diseased garment Lv $13_{59}$, לֵב *heart* Si $38_{10}$, perh. בָּשָׂר *flesh* 1QS $4_{21}$, רוּחַ errant *spirit* 1QH $1_{32}$ ([טה]רתה ... רוח]) $3_{21}$, חָמָס *violence* 11QPs[a] $22_{6}$.

<PREP> בְּ of place, *in*, or of instrument, *by (means of)*, *with*, + מַיִם *water* CD $10_{12}$ 4Q414 $4_{7}$; of accompaniment, *in (a state of)*, *with* or of instrument, *by (means of)*, *through*, + רַחֲמִים *compassion* 1QH $1_{32}$ ([טה]רתה]), צְדָקָה *righteousness* 1QH $4_{37}$ ([לט]הר]) $11_{30}$ 1QS $11_{14}$ 4QShir[b] $20.1_{1}$ ([בצד]קתו יטה[רני]), גָּדוֹל *great one*, i.e. great loyalty 1QH $1_{32}$ ([טה]רתה]), רֹב *abundance* of goodness 1QH $7_{30}$ ([לטהר[ם]), הָמוֹן *abundance* of mercy $17_{11}$ ([ותטהר ... בהמון]), רוּחַ *spirit* of holiness 1QH $14_{13}$ ([תטהרנו בר]וח) $16_{12}$ 1QS $4_{21}$; of cause, *on account of*, + רָצוֹן *desire* 1QH $14_{13}$ ([תטהרנו]); כְּ *as* 4QapPs[b] $46_{5}$; מִן of direction, remove *from*, + גֵּו *midst* 11QPs[a] $22_{6}$; free (Israelites, etc.) *of*, + טֻמְאָה *impurity* Lv $16_{19}$ Ezk $36_{25}$, חַטָּאת *sin* Lv $16_{30}$ Ps $51_{4}$ 1QS $11_{14}$ 4QDibHam[a] 1.6$_{2}$ פֶּשַׁע *sin* 1QH $3_{21}$ $7_{30}$ ([לטהר[ם]) $11_{10}$ $17_{11}$ ([ותט]הרנו), אַשְׁמָה *sin* 1QH $4_{37}$ ([לטהרם מפ]שע) $17_{15}$ ([ותטהר]), עָוֹן *sin* Jr $33_{8}$ Ezk $36_{33}$ 4Q370 $2_{3}$ 11QPs[a] $19_{14}$, רֹב *abundance* of sin 1QH $1_{32}$ ([טה]רתה]), עֲלִילָה *(wicked) deed* 1QS $4_{21}$, נִדָּה *impurity* 1QS $11_{14}$, עֶרְוָה *nakedness*, perh. indecency 4QRitPur $29.7_{9}$, גֹּעַל *abhorrence* 1QH fr. $1_{8}$ ([תטהרנו מ]געל), נֶגַע *blow*, i.e. scourge of sin 11QPs[a] $24_{13}$, נֵכָר *foreignness*, i.e. foreign elements Ne $13_{30}$ (or del.), חַיָּה impure *beast* GnzPs $1_{5}$, גִּלּוּל *idol* Ezk $36_{25}$, פֶּסֶל *idol* 2 C $34_{3}$, מַסֵּכָה *idol* 2 C $34_{3}$, אֲשֵׁרָה *Asherah* 2 C $34_{3}$, בָּמָה *high place* 2 C $34_{3}$; לִפְנֵי *in the presence of*, appar. + Y. 4QapPs[b] $46_{5}$, *despite*, + נֶגַע *blow* 1QH $1_{32}$ ([טה]רתה]); לְמַעַן *on account of*, + כָּבוֹד *glory* 1QH $11_{10}$.

<COLL> מטהרי הארץ *those who purify the land*, buriers of battle victims 1QM $7_{2}$, לטהר שבעתים *to purify [him] seven times* 1QH $5_{16}$, טהרתה ... לספר *you have absolved* from sin ... *in order to declare*, i.e. so that one might declare your wonders 1QH $1_{32}$ ([טה]רתה]) $3_{21}$ $11_{10}$.

Also 1QH fr. $65_{3}$ 4QRitPur $64_{8}$ ([וטה]ר]).

<SYN> זקק pi. *purify*, צרף pi. *refine*, כבס pi. *launder (clothes)*.

<ANT> טמא pi. *declare impure*.

**Pu.** $_{1}$ Ptc. מְטֹהָרָה—**be pure, purified,** <SUBJ> David 1 S $20_{6}$ (if em. טָהוֹר *pure* to טֹהַר *he has been purified*), אֶרֶץ *land* Ezk $22_{14}$ (or em. מטר pu./ho. *be rained upon*; + גשם pu. *be rained upon* [if em. גֻּשְׁמָהּ *her rain* to גֻּשְּׁמָה *she was rained upon*]). <COLL> with לֹא *not*, i.e. be impure 1 S $20_{6}$ (if em.) Ezk $22_{14}$ (or em.).

**Htp.** $_{20.0.19}$ Pf. הִטַּהַרְנוּ ,(הִטֶּהָרוּ) הִטַּהֲרוּ; impf. Q יטהר, 3fs תטהר, ואטהר, יטהרו; + waw וַיִּטַּהֲרוּ ,וְהִטֶּהָרוּ; ptc. מִטַּהֵר, מִטַּהֲרִים; inf. Q הטהר; impv. הִטַּהֲרוּ—**1. purify**

**oneself, cleanse oneself, absolve oneself** (1QS $3_{4.5.7}$), **be purified** (4QapPs$^{b}$ $69_{6}$ 4Q393 $3_{5}$), <SUBJ> worshipper 4QapPs$^{b}$ $45_{1}$ (+ פחד *fear*), אִישׁ *man* suffering discharge 11QT $45_{15}$ (+ כבס pi. *launder*, רחץ *wash oneself*, ספר *count*, i.e. wait, seven days), of injustice 1QS $5_{13}$, טָמֵא *one who is impure* through contact with a corpse 11QT $45_{17}$ perh. 4QRitPur $1.12_{2}$ ([טמאי]), צָרֻעַ *leper* 11QT $45_{18.18}$, נגע pu. ptc. *plague victim* 11QT $45_{18.18}$, מאס ptc. *one who refuses* to enter covenant 1QS $3_{4}$ (∥ קדשׁ htp. *sanctify oneself*, זכה htp. *purify oneself*) $3_{5.7}$ (+ כפר pu. *be expiated*), כֹּהֵן *priest* Ezr $6_{20}$ (or del. כֹּהֵן) Ne $12_{30}$, לֵוִי *Levite* Nm $8_{7}$ (+ כבס pi., עבר hi. *cause* razor *to pass* over body) Ezr $6_{20}$ Ne $12_{30}$ $13_{22}$, wicked Is $66_{17}$ (∥ קדשׁ htp.), perh. עַם *people* 4Q393 $3_{5}$, עֵדָה *congregation* of Israel Jg $22_{17}$, מִחְיָה *community* 1QH $6_{8}$ (+ זקק pi. *refine*), בַּיִת *house(hold)* of Jacob Gn $35_{2}$ (+ חלף hi. *change* clothes, סור hi. *remove* heathen gods), מַרְבִּית *majority* of people 2 C $30_{18}$, שְׁאֵרִית *remnant* of people 1QH $6_{8}$, perh. נַחֲלָה *inheritance* 4Q393 $3_{5}$, אֶרֶץ *earth* 4QJub$^{d}$ $21_{19}$ ([ל]הטהר), *land* 4QapPs$^{b}$ $69_{6}$; subj. not specified, CD $10_{10}$ (על הטהר *concerning purification*).

<PREP> בְּ of place, *in*, or of instrument, *by (means of), with*, + מַיִם *water* CD $10_{10}$ 1QS $3_{3.4}$ $5_{13}$ 4QRitPur $42.2_{5}$; of instrument, *by (means of), through*, + אֱמֶת *truth* 1QS $3_{7}$, דָּם *blood* of murderer 4QJub$^{d}$ $21_{19}$ ([ל]הטהר ... בדם); כְּ *as*, + אֶחָד *one*, i.e. at the same time; מִן free oneself *of*, + עָוֹן *sin* Jg $22_{17}$ 1QS $3_{7}$, טֻמְאָה *impurity* 4Q414 $1.2_{4}$, נִדָּה *impurity* 4QRitPur $1.12_{2}$ ([מ]נדת), אַשְׁמָה *sin* 1QH $6_{8}$, תּוֹעֵבָה *abomination* 4QapPs$^{b}$ $45_{1}$, זוֹב *discharge* 11QT $45_{15}$, דָּם *blood* of murder victim 4QJub$^{d}$ $21_{19}$ ([ל]הטהר [מדם]); אֶל perh. *in*, + גַּנָּה *garden* Is $66_{17}$; עַד *unto*, i.e. until, + יוֹם *day* Jg $22_{17}$; לִפְנֵי *before* 4Q414 $4_{2}$ ([לפנ]). <COLL> with לֹא *not*, i.e. be impure Jg $22_{17}$ 1QS $3_{3.4}$ $5_{13}$ 4Q393 $3_{5}$, בַּל *not* 4QRitPur $42.2_{5}$; אז תטהר *then it will be purified* 4QapPs$^{b}$ $69_{6}$.

Also 4Q414 $1.1_{6}$ 4QRitPur$181_{3}$.

**2.** ptc. as noun, **one who undergoes/is required to undergo purification,** <SUBJ> טהר *be (regarded as) pure* Lv $14_{7}$ (if em. וְטִהֲרוֹ *and he will declare him cleansed* to וְטָהֵר *and he will be [considered] clean*) $14_{8.8.19}$, בוא *come* into camp Lv $14_{8}$, hi. *bring* items for sacrifice Lv $14_{19}$, לקח *take* items for sacrifice Lv $14_{8.19}$, יָשַׁב *sit* outside tent seven days Lv $14_{8}$, כבס pi. *launder* Lv $14_{8.8}$, רחץ *wash oneself* Lv $14_{8.8}$, גלח pi. *shave* Lv $14_{8.8.8}$ עשׂה *do*, i.e. prepare as sacrifice Lv $14_{29}$. <OBJ> טהר pi. *declare pure* Lv $14_{7}$ (or em; see Subj.). <CSTR> תְּנוּךְ אֹזֶן הַמִּטַּהֵר *the* right *earlobe of the one undergoing purification* Lv $14_{14.17.25}$ (אֹזֶן) $14_{28}$, רֹאשׁ הַמִּטַּהֵר *the head of the one undergoing purification* Lv $14_{18.29}$. <PREP> לְ of benefit, *to, for*, + לקח *take* items for use in purification Lv $14_{4}$; עַל *upon*, + נזה hi. *sprinkle* blood Lv $14_{7}$; *for (the benefit of)*, + כפר pi. *atone* Lv $14_{18.19.19.19.29.31}$. <COLL> הַמִּטַּהֵר מִן־הַצָּרַעַת *the one who is to be purified of* (or *on account of*) *a skin disease* Lv $14_{7}$.

**3.** ptc. as adjective, **undergoing purification,** used attributively of אִישׁ *man* Lv $14_{11}$.

<SYN> §1 קדשׁ htp. *sanctify oneself*, זכה htp. *purify oneself*.*

⇒ טָהוֹר *pure*, טְהָר *purity*, טֹהַר *purity*, טָהֳרָה *purity*.

**טָהֹר**, see טָהוֹר *pure*.

**[טְהָר]** 1 n.[m.] **purity**—(perh. the same as טֹהַר)—<PREP> מִן perh. partitive, *(some) of*, + שׁבת hi. *cause to cease* Ps $89_{45}$ (or em. הִשְׁבַּתָּ מִטְּהָרוֹ *you caused some of his purity to cease* to שָׁבַרְתָּ מַטֵּה הֹדוֹ *you broke his rod of majesty* or שָׁבַרְתָּ חֻטְרוֹ *you broke his rod* or הִשְׁבַּתָּ מִטְהָרוֹ *you caused his splendour to cease* or הִשְׁבַּתָּ־ם טָהֳרוֹ in same sense; + כִּסֵּא *throne*).*

⇒ טהר *be pure*.

**טֹ֫הַר** 3.1.16 n.[m.] **purity**—Q טוהר, טהור; cstr. Q טוהר; sf. Q טוהרו; טָהֳרָה (Q טוהרה)—**1. purity, clarity; splendour** (Ex $24_{10}$ Ps $89_{45}$ [if em.] Si $43_{1}$ 4QShir$^{b}$ $52.3_{2}$ 4QBer$^{a}$ $3.1_{6}$ 4Q303 $1_{4}$ 4QShirShabb$^{a}$ $3.1_{2}$ 4QShirShabb$^{d}$ $1.1_{19}$ 4QShirShabb$^{f}$ $13_{3}$ $23.1_{7}$ $23.2_{9}$). **2. (process of) purification** undergone by woman after childbirth (Lv $12_{4.6}$), by man with discharge (4QRitPur $7.11_{2}$), etc.

<OBJ> שׁבת hi. *cause to cease* Ps $89_{45}$ (if em.; see טְהָר), נשׂא *raise* 4QShirShabb$^{f}$ $6_{3}$ (למשׂא *for the exaltation of*; =4QShirShabb$^{d}$ $1.1_{42}$ ל[משׂ]א).

<CSTR> טוהר טהורים *purity of pure ones* 4QShirShabb$^{d}$ $1.1_{42}$ (erased זוהר *brightness of*); אלי טוהר *gods*, i.e. angels, *of purity* 4QBer$^{a}$ $3.1_{6}$, רוחי צבעי [טוהר] *spir-*

*its (dressed in) colours of purity* 4QShirShabb[f] 23.2$_{9}$, שמי טוה[ר] *heavens of purity* 4Q303 1$_{4}$, רקי[ע]י הטוהר *the firmaments of purity* 4QShirShabb[f] 23.1$_{7}$, [רזי בינ]ת טוהר *secrets of the knowledge of purity* 4QShirShabb[d] 1.1$_{19}$, דברי רום טוהר seven *words of loftiness of purity* 4QShirShabb[f] 13$_{3}$ (=4QShirShabb[d] 1.1$_{20}$ אֱמֶת *truth* for טֹהַר), יְמֵי טָהֳרָהּ *the days of her purification* Lv 12$_{4.6}$, מועדי טהור *appointed times of purification* 4Q414 3$_{6}$, לשון הטוהר *the tongue of purity* 4QShirShabb[a] 3.1$_{2}$, דְּמֵי טָהֳרָהּ *blood of her purification* Lv 12$_{4.5}$ (if em. in both טָהֳרָה *purity*), מקור הטוהר *source of purity* 4QShir[b] 52.3$_{2}$ (‖ כָּבוֹד *glory*).

<PREP> לְ *in respect of*, כְּעֶצֶם הַשָּׁמַיִם לָטֹהַר *like the bone of the*, i.e. the very, *heavens/sky in respect of purity* Ex 24$_{10}$; of possession, *of, (belonging) to*, תאר מרום ורקיע לטהר *(as for) the form*, i.e. beauty, *of the heights and the firmament of purity* Si 43$_{1(M)}$; מִן purification *from*, + זוֹב *discharge* 4QRitPur 7.11$_{2}$; עַל *over*, + רקע *spread* trans. Si 43$_{1(Bmg)}$ (תואר מרום רקע על טה[ר] *the beauty of the heights he has spread over purity*, i.e. pure air/light).

<COLL> ממולח טוהר perh. *salted (in) purity*, i.e. purified with salt 4QShirShabb[f] 19$_{4}$ 20.2$_{11}$ (טוה) 23.2$_{10}$ 11QShirShabb 7$_{5}$ (unless טוהר is for טָהוֹר *pure*).

Also 4QShirShabb[f] 17$_{4}$ 4Q414 4$_{9}$ (טו[הר]כה בכבוד *your purification in glory [of]*) 4QRitPur 33.4$_{10}$ 29.7$_{10}$ (+ דָּם *blood* of sacrifice) 15.1$_{9}$ 11QShirShabb 3$_{4}$ 7$_{3}$ (+ קוד[ש] *holiness*) 11QShirShabb[c]$_{4}$ (טוה[ר]).*

<SYN> §1 כָּבוֹד *glory*.

⇒ טהר *be pure*.

**[טְהָר]**, see טֹהַר *purity*.

**טָהֳרָה** 13.1.48 n.f. **purity**—Q טוהרה; cstr. טָהֳרַת; sf. טָהֳרָתוֹ, Q טהרתמה—**1.** usu. **(process of) purification, purification ritual,** perh. **purification regulation(s)** (4QMMT B$_{13.52}$), **period of purification** (4QD[a] 11$_{4}$ 4QD[f] 1.2$_{8}$ 4QTohA 1.1$_{9}$ 10.11$_{2}$) for woman after childbirth, Nazirite, priest attending deceased relative, person with skin disease or with discharge. **2. purity,** 1 C 23$_{28}$ Si 51$_{20}$ 4QOrd[c] 1.1$_{6}$ 1QS 4$_{5}$ 6$_{22}$ (unless *pure food*, as §4) 4QTohA 3.1$_{6}$ 4QMMT B$_{56}$ 4QShir[b] 35$_{3}$ 4QRitPur 41$_{5}$ 11QT 47$_{10.15}$ perh. 4Q414 3$_{8}$ 4$_{4}$ 4QRitPur 7.11$_{2}$ 4QOrd[b] 10.2$_{6}$. **3. (ritually) pure thing(s),** 4QMMT B$_{54}$ (unless *pure food*, as §4) 11QT 47$_{17}$ 49$_{21}$ 63$_{14}$. **4. pure food,** i.e. the meals of the elect CD 9$_{21.23}$ 1QS 5$_{13}$ 6$_{16.25}$ 7$_{3.16.19.20(erased).25}$ 8$_{17.24}$ 4QS[d] 1.1$_{7}$ 4QD[d] 13$_{3}$ 4QD[e] 11.1$_{7}$ 4QTohA 1.1$_{2}$ 2.1$_{3}$ perh. 4QD[e] 7$_{21}$ 4QMMT B$_{23.65.68}$ 4QOrd[b] 2.2$_{1}$.

<SUBJ> היה *be* according to kind of flesh 11QT 47$_{10}$, פרש ni. *be made clear*, i.e. decreed 4QRitPur 42.2$_{4}$, perh. תעב pi. *abominate* 1QS 4$_{5}$.

<NOM CL> כול כלים אשר יש להמה טהרה *all vessels that have (the possibility of undergoing) purification* or *to which (the law of) purity applies* 11QT 49$_{15}$, אין בהם [ט]הרה *there is no purity in them*, i.e. they are impure 4QMMT B$_{56}$, וטהרה בנברים *and purity will be (among) the elect* 4QShir[b] 35$_{3}$.

<OBJ> בוא hi. *bring* 11QT 47$_{17}$, בדל hi. *separate*, i.e. exclude from CD 9$_{23}$, שמע *hear* 4QMMT B$_{52}$ (‖ מִשְׁפָּט *judgment*, חֹק *statute*).

<CSTR> טהרת כול *the purification of all* 4QRitPur 42.2$_{4}$, טָהֳרַת הַקֹּדֶשׁ *purification of holiness*, i.e. purification required to enter sanctuary 2 C 30$_{19}$, perh. *the pure food of holiness* 4QMMT B$_{23}$ ([טהרת הקודש]) B$_{65}$ (הקוד[ש]) B$_{68}$ 4QOrd[b] 2.2$_{1}$ (ה[קו]דש), טָהֳרַת לְכָל־קֹדֶשׁ *the purity of all holiness*, i.e. of every holy thing 1 C 23$_{28}$, טהרת עתים *purification of times*, i.e. temporary purification 4QRitPur 1.12$_{5}$.

טהרת המקדש *the pure thing(s) of the sanctuary* 4QMMT B$_{54}$ (טה[ר]ת) 11QT 47$_{17}$, טהרת אנשי הקודש *the pure food of the men of holiness* 1QS 5$_{13}$ 8$_{17}$ 4QS[d] 1.1$_{7}$ (הקד[ש]), טהרת הרבים *the pure food of the many* 1QS 6$_{16.25}$ 7$_{3}$ (both טהרת רבים) 7$_{16.19.20(erased)}$ (main text מַשְׁקֶה *drink*).

טהרת כבוד *of purity of glory*, i.e. honourable purity 1QS 4$_{5}$, טהרת צ[דקה] *purity of righteousness*, perh. perfect righteousness 4Q414 4$_{4}$, sim. 4QRitPur 41$_{5}$ (צֶדֶק), [י]שראל *of Israel* 4Q414 3$_{8}$ 4QRitPur 7.11$_{2}$ ([ט]הרת) (ישר[אל]), בשרו *of its flesh* 11QT 47$_{15}$.

טהרת פרת החטאת *the purification regulation(s) of the red heifer (ritual)* 4QMMT B$_{13}$.

מִשְׁמֶרֶת הַטָּהֳרָה observe *observation*, i.e. perform rituals, *of purification* Ne 12$_{45}$, משפט ה[ט]הרה *the judgment*, i.e. law, *of purity* 4QOrd[c] 1.1$_{6}$, רוח ... טהרת *a spirit of ... purity of* 1QS 4$_{5}$.

יוֹם טָהֳרָתוֹ *the day of his purification*, i.e. the day he is to undergo purification, Lv 14$_{2}$ Nm 6$_{9}$ 4QOrd$^{c}$ 1.1$_{3}$ (י[ו]ם טהרת[ו]), יום [ט]הרתם *the day of their purification* 4QOrd$^{c}$ 1.1$_{5.9}$ ([ט]הרת[ם]), שבעת ימי טה[רתו] *the seven days of his period of purification* 4QTohA 1.1$_{9}$ 4QRitPur 10.11$_{2}$ (טה[רתו]).

מי טהר[ה] *waters of purification* 11QT 50$_{2}$, דְּמֵי טָהֳרָה *blood of*, perh. requiring, *purification* Lv 12$_{4.5}$ (or em. in both טָהֳרָהּ [i.e. טֹהַר] *of her purification*) 4QSD 7.2$_{16}$ ([דמי] טהרה), דם טוהרה appar. *blood of purification* (not טָהֳרָהּ *her purification*) 4QSD 7.2$_{17}$.

כול טהרת *every pure thing of* 11QT 47$_{17}$, כול טהרתמה *all their pure thing(s)* 11QT 49$_{21}$.

<PREP> לְ of direction, *to*, + בוא *come* 4QMMT B$_{54}$ (לטה[ר]ת), נגע לְ *approach* 4QS$^{b}$ 5$_{8}$ ([יגעו לטהרת]) 4QS$^{d}$ 1.1$_{7}$, hi. *bring near* to 4QOrd$^{b}$ 2.2$_{1}$, נגשׁ לְ *approach* 4Q MMT B$_{23}$ ([יגשׁ לטהרת]); of purpose, *for (the purpose of)* perh. 4QRitPur 29.7$_{7}$, + ראה hi. *be seen*, i.e. present oneself Lv 13$_{7}$; of possession, *of, (belonging) to* Lv 14$_{23}$ 15$_{13}$ 11QT 45$_{15}$ (all three + יוֹם *day[s]* of purification) 4QRitPur 1.12$_{5}$ (+ מַיִם *water*); *in respect of* or *in accordance with*, + כתב *write*, i.e. register 1QS 6$_{22(mg)}$ (|| תּוֹרָה *law*, מִשְׁפָּט *judgment*).

בְּ perh. of place/time, *in/during* 4QD$^{a}$ 11$_{4}$ (טוה[רת/ה]), + perh. בוא hi. *bring* 4QD$^{f}$ 1.2$_{8}$; of accompaniment, *in (a state of), with* 4Q414 3$_{8}$ 4QOrd$^{b}$ 10.2$_{6}$, + היה *be* 4Q414 4$_{4}$, מצא *find* Wisdom Si 51$_{20}$, עבד *serve* 4QRitPur 41$_{5}$ ([ב]טהרת), אכל *eat* 4QTohA 3.1$_{6}$; partitive, *(some) of, (any) of*, + ערב htp. *share* 1QS 7$_{25}$ (|| הוֹן *wealth*); *for (the cost of)*, + נשׂג hi. *reach*, i.e. find sufficient funds Lv 14$_{32}$; *against*, + נגע *strike*, i.e. touch 1QS 5$_{13}$ 6$_{16}$ 7$_{19.20}$ 8$_{17}$ 4QTohA 2.1$_{3}$ 11QT 49$_{21}$ 63$_{14}$.

כְּ *in accordance with* 2 C 30$_{19}$, + טהר *be pure* 11QT 47$_{15}$.

מִן of direction, *from* 4QTohA 1.1$_{2}$ (רָחוֹק מִן twelve cubits *away from*), + בדל hi. *separate*, i.e. exclude 1QS 7$_{16}$ 4QS$^{d}$ 3.1$_{1}$ (|| עֵצָה *council*, מִשְׁפָּט *judgment*) 4QD$^{d}$ 13$_{3}$ ([והבדילוהו]) 4QS$^{e}$ 11.1$_{7}$ ([והבדילה]ו), ho. *be separated*, i.e. excluded CD 9$_{21}$ 1QS 7$_{3}$ 8$_{24}$ (|| עֵצָה).

אֶל *to*, + בוא hi. *bring* iron and lead 4QD$^{e}$ 7$_{21}$.

עַל *in charge of, over* 1 C 23$_{28}$; *concerning* 4QMMT B$_{13}$.

עִם *with*, + בוא *come*, i.e. be mixed with 4QMMT B$_{65}$ ([י]בואו) B$_{68}$ (באים ע[ם]).

אַחֲרֵי *after*, + פשׂה *spread* (of skin disease) Lv 13$_{35}$, ספר *count*, i.e. make someone wait seven days Ezk 44$_{26}$.

מִתּוֹךְ *from (among)*, + בדל hi. *separate*, i.e. exclude 1QS 6$_{25}$.

Also 4QD$^{f}$ 1.2$_{12}$ (טה[רתו]) 4QMMT B$_{3}$.

<SYN> תּוֹרָה *law*, מִשְׁפָּט *judgment*, חֹק *statute*, עֵצָה *council*, הוֹן *wealth*.*

⇒ טהר *be pure*.

**טוב** $_{113.6}$ vb. **be good—Qal** $_{106.5}$ Pf. טוֹב, טוֹבָה, טֹ֫בוּ; + waw וְטוֹב; inf. טוֹב (but for most forms, a distinction from טוֹב adj. is unclear)—**be good, be pleasing, be appropriate** (e.g. Est 1$_{19}$), **be happy, be in good spirits, be healthy** (e.g. 1 S 16$_{16.23}$), **be worthwhile** (e.g. Jb 10$_{3}$); oft. in the impersonal construction טוֹב לְ, **go well (for)**.

<SUBJ> Y. Ps 106$_{1}$||1 C 6$_{34}$ Ps 107$_{1}$ 118$_{1.29}$ 135$_{3}$ 136$_{1}$ 147$_{1}$ (+ נָעִים *pleasant*) Ezr 3$_{11}$ 2 C 5$_{13}$ 7$_{3}$ Si 51$_{12}$, Samuel 1 S 2$_{26}$, מֶלֶךְ *king* Jg 11$_{25}$, צַדִּיק *righteous one* Is 3$_{10}$, נַעַר *lad* 1 S 2$_{26}$.

לֵב *heart* Jg 16$_{25}$ 1 S 25$_{36}$ 2 S 13$_{28}$, דּוֹד *love* Ca 4$_{10}$ (or em. דַּד *breast*; || יפה *be beautiful*), אֹהֶל *tent* Nm 24$_{5}$, מִשְׁכָּן *tabernacle* Nm 24$_{5}$, אֶרֶץ *land* Jg 18$_{9}$ Ho 10$_{1}$ (if em. כְּטוֹב לְאַרְצוֹ *when it went well for his land* to כְּטוֹב לוֹ אַרְצוֹ *when his land was good to him*).

אוֹר *light* Gn 1$_{4}$, דָּבָר *word* Jr 42$_{16}$ (:: רעע *be evil*), שֵׁם *name* Ps 52$_{11}$ (or del. כִּי־טוֹב *for it is good* to לְדוֹר דּוֹרִים *for generation of generations*) 54$_{8}$, נֶעֱלָם *hidden (deed)* Ec 12$_{14}$ (:: רעע), מְנוּחָה *rest* Gn 49$_{15}$ (|| נעם *be pleasing*), רַע *evil* Is 5$_{20}$ (:: רעע), כֹּל *all* Gn 1$_{31}$ 2 S 3$_{19.36}$ (or del.), אֲשֶׁר *what(ever)* 2 S 19$_{38}$.

impersonal subj. + inf. (e.g. טוֹב הֱיוֹת *it is good to be* Gn 2$_{18}$), + היה *be* Gn 2$_{18}$ Jg 18$_{19}$, הלך *go* Ec 7$_{2}$, בוא *come* 1 S 29$_{6}$, יצא *go out* 1 S 29$_{6}$, שׁוב *go back* Nm 14$_{3}$, נטה hi. *take back* Pr 18$_{5}$ (with ellipsis of טוב), נשׂא *raise* Pr 18$_{5}$, ישׁב *dwell* Ps 133$_{1}$ (+ נָעִים *pleasant*) Pr 21$_{9.19}$ 25$_{24}$, נתן *give* Gn 29$_{19}$, עבד *serve* Ex 14$_{12}$, שׁמע *hear* 1 S 15$_{22}$ Ec 7$_{5}$, קשׁב hi. *attend* 1 S 15$_{22}$, נכר hi. *recognize* Pr 24$_{23}$ 28$_{21}$, אמר *say* Pr 25$_{7}$, ידה hi. *praise* Ps 92$_{2}$, זמר pi. *sing (praises)* Ps 92$_2$, חסה *take refuge* Ps 118$_8$ (4QPs$^b$ בטח *trust*) 118$_9$, ענשׁ *punish* Pr 17$_{26}$, נכה hi. *strike* Pr 17$_{26}$ (with ellipsis of טוב), אכל *eat* Pr 25$_{27}$.

impersonal subj. (e.g. טוֹב לָנוּ בְּמִצְרָיִם *it was good for us in Egypt* Nm 11$_{18}$), Gn 1$_{10.12.18.21.25}$ 2$_{18}$ (see Coll. for all six) Nm 11$_{18}$ 24$_1$ Dt 5$_{33}$ (+ ארך יָמִים hi. *prolong days*) 6$_{24}$ 10$_{13}$ 15$_{16}$ 19$_{13}$ 1 S 16$_{16.23}$ 20$_7$ (see Coll.) 20$_{12}$ 2 S 3$_{13}$ (see Coll.) 14$_{32}$ 15$_{26}$ 18$_3$ 1 K 2$_{18.42}$ (or del.; see Coll. for both) 21$_2$ Jr 22$_{15.16}$ 32$_{39}$ 40$_{4.5}$ (if em. in 40$_4$ אֶל־טוֹב *to a good [place]*, i.e. טוֹב noun, to אִם־טוֹב בְּעֵינֶיךָ *if it seems good to you*) Ho 2$_9$=4QpHos$^a$ 1$_{16}$ ([טוב לי]) Ho 10$_1$ (or em. כְּטוֹב לְאַרְצוֹ *when it went well for his land* to כְּטוֹב לוֹ אַרְצוֹ *when his land was good to him*)* Zc 11$_{12}$ Ps 119$_{71}$ Jb 10$_3$ 13$_9$ Pr 16$_{16}$ (if em.; see Coll.) 24$_{13}$ Ru 2$_{22}$ 3$_{13}$ Ec 5$_4$ Lm 3$_{26}$ (see Coll.) 3$_{27}$ Est 1$_{19}$ 3$_9$ 5$_{4.8}$ 7$_3$ 8$_5$ 9$_{13}$ Ne 2$_{5.7}$ Ps 128$_2$ Ec 7$_{18}$ 11$_7$ 1 C 13$_2$ Si 30$_{17.17.30}$ 46$_{10}$.

<PREP> לְ of benefit, *to, for*, + אֱלוֹהַּ *God* Jb 10$_3$, Saul 1 S 16$_{16.23}$, Absalom 2 S 14$_{32}$, worshipper Ps 119$_{71}$, גֶּבֶר *man* Lm 3$_{27}$, אָב *father* Jr 22$_{15.16}$ (or del.), אֵם *mother* Ho 2$_9$, אָח *brother* Dt 15$_{16}$, בֵּן *son* Ex 2$_2$ 14$_{12}$ Nm 14$_3$ Jr 32$_{39}$, ירא ptc. *one who fears* Y. Ps 128$_2$, הלך ptc. *one who walks* in Y.'s ways Ps 128$_2$, עַיִן *eye* Ec 11$_7$, עִיר *(inhabitants of) city* Jr 32$_{39}$, עַם *people* Nm 11$_{18}$, אֶרֶץ *land* Ho 10$_1$ (or em. כְּטוֹב לְאַרְצוֹ *when it went well for his land* to כְּטוֹב לוֹ אַרְצוֹ *when his land was good to him*), יִשְׂרָאֵל *Israel* Dt 5$_{33}$ 6$_{24}$ 10$_{13}$ 19$_{13}$ Ho 10$_1$ (if em.).

בְּ of place, *in*, + מִצְרַיִם *Egypt* Nm 11$_{18}$; of instrument, *by (means of), with*, + יַיִן *wine* 2 S 13$_{28}$ Est 1$_{10}$.

בְּעֵינֵי *in the eyes*, i.e. opinion, *of*, + ״ *Y.* Nm 24$_1$ 2 S 15$_{26}$, Achish 1 S 29$_6$, Naboth 1 K 21$_2$, Jeremiah Jr 40$_{4.5}$ (if em.; see Subj.), מֶלֶךְ *king* 2 S 19$_{38}$, עָנִי *poor one* Zc 11$_{12}$ (or em. כֵּן עֲנִיֵּי *so the poor of* the flock to כְּנַעֲנִיֵּי *traders of* the flock), יִשְׂרָאֵל *Israel* 2 S 3$_{19}$, בִּנְיָמִן *Benjamin* 2 S 3$_{19}$, עַם *people* 2 S 3$_{36}$ (or del. טוב).

מִן of comparison, *(more) than*, i.e. better than Ec 5$_4$, + בָּלָק *Balak* Jg 11$_{25}$, מֶלֶךְ *king* Jg 11$_{25}$, אִישׁ *man* Ec 7$_5$, אִשָּׁה *woman* Pr 21$_{9.19}$ 25$_{24}$, בֵּן *son* Jg 11$_{25}$, יַיִן *wine* Ca 4$_{10}$, חֵלֶב *fat* 1 S 15$_{22}$, זֶבַח *sacrifice* 1 S 15$_{22}$, חָרוּץ *gold* Pr 16$_{16}$ (if em.; see Coll.), חַיִּים *(to live) life* Si 30$_{17.17}$, הלך inf. *going* Ec 7$_2$, מות inf. *dying* Ex 14$_{12}$, נתן inf. *giving* Gn 29$_{19}$, נבט hi. inf. *looking* Si 30$_{30}$, בטח inf. *trusting* Ps 118$_{8.9}$, שׁפל hi. inf. *humbling* Pr 25$_7$, עַתָּה better for me then than *now* Ho 2$_9$=4QpHos$^a$ 1$_{16}$ ([טוב לי אז מעתה]).

אֶל *to, for, with*, + דָּוִד *David* 1 S 20$_{12}$.

עִם *with*, + ״ *Y.* 1 S 2$_{26}$, יִשְׂרָאֵל *Israel* Dt 15$_{16}$, אִישׁ *man* 1 S 2$_{26}$.

עַל appar. *within*, + נָבָל *Nabal* 1 S 25$_{36}$; *to, for, in the opinion of*, + מֶלֶךְ *king* Est 1$_{19}$ 3$_9$ 5$_{4.8}$ 7$_3$ (both + מצא חֵן בְּעֵינֵי *find grace in the eyes of*) 8$_5$ (+ מצא חֵן לִפְנֵי *find grace before*, כשׁר *be appropriate*) 9$_{13}$ Ne 2$_5$ (+ יטב *be good*) 2$_7$, קָהָל *assembly* 1 C 13$_2$.

<COLL> מַה־טֹּבוּ *how good are* Nm 24$_5$ Ca 4$_{10}$, מַה־טּוֹב *how good it is* Ps 133$_1$, *how much better it* (wisdom) *is* than gold Pr 16$_{16}$.

הֲטוֹב טוֹב אַתָּה מִבָּלָק *are you really any better than Balak?* Jg 11$_{25}$, הָלֵךְ וְגָדֵל וָטוֹב *growing ever greater and better* 1 S 2$_{26}$.

אָז טוֹב *then it went well* Jr 22$_{15.16}$, sim. Ho 2$_9$, וְהִנֵּה־טוֹב מְאֹד *and behold, it was very good* Gn 1$_{31}$, sim. Jg 18$_9$, אִם־טוֹב וְאִם־רָע *be it good or be it bad* Jr 42$_6$ Ec 12$_{14}$ (רָע), לֹא־טוֹב *it is not good* Pr 17$_{26}$ 18$_5$ 25$_{27}$ 28$_{21}$, בַּל־טוֹב *it is not good* Pr 24$_{23}$.

טוֹב followed by (1) לְ *to* + inf. *it is good to* (e.g. טוֹב לָתֵת *it is good to give* Est 5$_8$), with ברך pi. *bless* Nm 24$_1$, נתן *give* Est 5$_8$, עשׂה *do* Est 5$_8$, חלה pi. *sweeten* face, i.e. appease Si 30$_{30}$, מלא pi. *fill*, i.e. wholeheartedly pursue Si 46$_{10}$, מות *die* Si 30$_{17.17}$; (2) כִּי *that* + verbal sentence, (e.g. טוֹב לִי כִּי *it is good for me that*), 2 S 18$_3$ Ps 119$_{71}$ Jb 10$_3$ 13$_9$ Ru 2$_{22}$ Lm 3$_{27}$; (3) שֶׁ *that* + verbal sentence Ec 5$_4$; (4) אֲשֶׁר *that* + verbal sentence Ec 7$_{18}$; (5) וְ *and*, טוֹב וְיָחִיל וְדוּמָם appar. *it is good: (and) waiting (and) in silence* Lm 3$_{26}$ (or em. וְיָחִיל וְדָמַם חַסְדּוֹ *and he waits but his loyalty has ceased*).

וַיַּרְא אֱלֹהִים אֶת־הָאוֹר כִּי־טוֹב *and God saw the light, (saw) that it was good* Gn 1$_4$ (unless טוֹב adj. *good*), sim. Ex 2$_2$, וַיַּרְא אֱלֹהִים כִּי־טוֹב *and God saw that it* (the result of the actions described) *was good* Gn 1$_{10.12.18.21.25}$.

אִם־כֹּה יֹאמַר טוֹב *if he says, It is good*, i.e. that's all right 1 S 20$_7$, sim. 2 S 3$_{13}$ 1 K 2$_{18.42}$ (or del.), אִם־יִגְאָלֵךְ טוֹב יִגְאָל *if he redeems you, that's all right, let him redeem* Ru 3$_{13}$.

<SYN> יפה *be fair*, נעם *be pleasing*.

<ANT> רעע *be evil*.

**Hi.** 7.1 Pf. הֵטִיבֹתָ (הֱטִיבוֹתָ); + waw וְהֵטַבְנוּ; ptc. מֵטִיב

(מֵטִב) (unless יטב *do well*)—**be right, do well, act benevolently;** also transitive, **please** (Si $26_{13}$), <SUBJ> י׳ *Y.* Ps $119_{68}$, מֹשֶׁה *Moses* and Israelites Nm $10_{29.32}$, דָּוִד *David* 1 K $8_{18}$||2 C $6_8$, יֵהוּא *Jehu* 2 K $10_{30}$, שָׁר *singer* Ezk $33_{32}$ (if em. שִׁיר *song*), חֵן woman's *grace* Si $26_{13}$ ([חן]). <OBJ> אִישׁ *man* Si $26_{13}$. <PREP> לְ of benefit, *to, for,* + חֹבָב *Hobab* Nm $10_{29.32}$, בֵּן *son* Nm $10_{29.32}$. <COLL> followed by כִּי *because, in that* 1 K $8_{18}$||2 C $6_8$, לְ *by, in* doing 2 K $10_{30}$; מֵטִב נַגֵּן *doing well (in) playing (an instrument)* Ezk $33_{32}$.*

→ טוב I–II (adj. and noun) *good,* טוּב *good,* טוֹבָה *good,* טִיב *character,* יטב *be good,* טוֹבִיָּהוּ *Tobijah,* טוֹב אֲדֹנִיָּה *Tob-adonijah,* טֹבְשָׁלֹם *Tob-shalom,* טָבְאַל *Tabal,* טָבְאֵל *Tabeel,* טַבְרִמֹּן *Tabrimmon.*

**טוֹב I** $_{262.30.32.2}$ adj. **good**—טוֹבָה (טֹבָה); sf. טוֹבָם (Mc $7_4$); pl. טוֹבִים (טֹבִים), טֹבוֹת (טֹבֹת); cstr. טוֹבֵי—many exx. of טוב (verb) *be good* and טוֹב (noun) *good* may be טוֹב (adj.) *good*—**virtuous, kind, happy, content** (e.g. Jr $44_{17}$ Ps $112_5$ Si $13_{26}$; see also §4), **ripe** (old age), **correct** (e.g. Jb $34_4$), **prosperous, plentiful** (e.g. Gn $41_{35}$ Ex $3_8$), **well-fed, healthy** (e.g. Gn $41_{26}$; see also §3b), **luxurious, good-quality** (e.g. Jos $7_{21}$), **precious** stone (GnzPs $2_{27}$), **festive** day, time (1 S $25_8$ Zc $8_{19}$ $8_{17}$ $9_{19.22}$), **kind, well-disposed** (e.g. 1 S $25_{15}$), **pleasing** (e.g. 2 S $18_{27}$), **well-situated** (2 K $2_{19}$), **sweet** (perh. Ca $1_2$ Ps $34_9$),* **sweet-smelling** (Jr $6_{20}$), **favourable** (e.g. Jr $29_{10}$ $33_{14}$), **well-finished, well-polished** (Ezr $8_{27}$).

**1.** used attributively of י׳ *Y.* 2 C $30_{18}$ Si $45_{25}$, אִשָּׁה *woman* 1 K $20_3$ (or del. טוֹב) Pr $18_{22(mss)}$ Si $7_{19}$ $26_{1.3}$ (ט[ובה]), בְּתוּלָה *young woman* Est $2_{2.3}$, נַעֲרָה *girl* Est $2_{2.3}$, רְעוּת *female companion* Est $1_{19}$, שִׁפְחָה *female servant* 1 S $8_{16}$, זֹנָה *prostitute* Na $3_4$=4QpNah 3.$2_7$.

אִישׁ *man* 1 K $2_{32}$ (|| צַדִּיק *righteous*) Pr $14_{14}$ Si $36_{14}$, בָּחוּר *youth* 1 S $8_{16}$, יֶלֶד *child* Dn $1_4$, אֹהֵב *friend* Si $37_5$ (unless טוֹב [noun] *good*), רֵעַ *companion* 1 S $15_{28}$, עֶבֶד *servant* 1 S $8_{16}$, אָח *brother* 2 C $21_{13}$, בֵּן *son* 1 S $9_2$ (בֵּן ... בָּחוּר וָטוֹב *a son ... a youth and good*), specif. in ref. to young of cattle Gn $18_7$ (|| רַךְ *soft*) 1 K $20_3$ (or del. טוֹב), גְּדִי *kid* Gn $27_9$, פָּרָה *cow* Gn $41_{16}$.

אֶרֶץ *land* Ex $3_8$ (|| רָחָב *wide*) Dt $1_{35}$ $3_{25}$ $4_{21}$ (or del. טוֹב) $4_{22}$ $6_{18}$ $8_7$=4QPsJos$^a$ $1_{14}$ ([הארץ]; Sam, ms || רָחָב *wide*) $8_{10}$ $9_6$ $11_{17}$ Jos $23_{16}$ (or del.) 1 C $28_8$ 4QPsJos$^a$ $1_{14}$, אֲדָמָה *land* Jos $23_{13.15}$ 1 K $14_{15}$, הַר *mountain* Dt $3_{25}$, שָׂדֶה *field* 1 S $8_{14}$ Ezk $17_8$ (|| רַב *great*), חֶלְקָה *field* 2 K $3_{19.25}$, מִרְעֶה *pasture* Ezk $34_{14.18}$ 1 C $4_{40}$ (|| שָׁמֵן *fat*), נָוֶה *pasture* Ezk $34_{14}$ (|| שָׁמֵן), כֶּרֶם *vineyard* 1 S $8_{14}$ 1 K $21_2$, זַיִת *olive (grove)* 1 S $8_{14}$, תְּאֵנָה *fig tree* Jr $24_{2.3}$ (both :: רַע *evil*) $24_5$, דֶּקֶל *palm tree* 5/6ḤevBA 46, עֵץ *tree* Gn $2_9$ (|| חמד ni. ptc. *desirable*) 2 K $3_{19.25}$ Ezk $31_{16}$ (see Cstr.) 4Q302 2.$2_3$, שִׁבֹּלֶת *ear of grain* Gn $41_5$ (|| בָּרִיא *fat*) $41_{22}$ (|| מָלֵא *full*) $41_{24}$ (:: דַּק *thin*) $41_{26}$, תְּנוּבָה *produce* Jg $9_{11}$, אֹכֶל *food* 4Q426 1.$1_{11}$ 11QPs$^a$ $26_{13}$, פְּרִי *fruit* 4Q370 $1_1$, בֹּשֶׂם *spice* 2 K $20_{13}$||Is $39_2$, קָנֶה *reed*, i.e. cane Jr $6_{20}$ (but perh. טוֹב V *perfume*), שֶׁמֶן *oil* 2 K $20_{13}$||Is $39_2$ Ps $133_2$ (but perh. in all three טוֹב V *perfume*) Ec $7_1$, נֵתַח *piece (of meat)* Ezk $24_4$, אֶבֶן *stone* GnzPs $2_{27}$.

עִיר *city* Dt $6_{10}$=1QDM $2_3$ ([ער]ים ... [וטובו]ת]; || גָּדוֹל *great*), בַּיִת *house* Dt $8_{12}$ Is $5_9$ (|| רַב, גָּדוֹל *great*), שֶׁכֶן *dwelling* Si $14_{25}$, מַעֲשֶׂה *deed* 4Q521 2.$2_{10}$ ([מעש]ה), פֹּעַל *deed* Si $3_{31}$, אַדֶּרֶת *cloak* Jos $7_{21}$, קִנְיָן *possession* Si $51_{21}$, הוֹן *wealth* 4Q416 2.$2_{17}$, אוֹצָר *treasure* Dt $28_{12}$ 11QBer $1_7$=4Q285 $1_4$ ([את אוצרו ה]טוב), זָהָב *gold* 2 C $3_{5.8}$ (mss טָהוֹר *pure* in both; ||1 K $6_{20}$ סָגוּר *closed*, appar. of old or select gold) 2 K $20_{13}$||Is $39_2$ 11QT $36_{11}$ $39_4$ ([ז]הב [טוב]), כֶּתֶם *gold* Lm $4_1$ 4QapLam$^a$ 1.$2_{11}$, כֶּסֶף *silver* 2 K $20_{13}$||Is $39_2$, נְחֹשֶׁת *bronze* Ezr $8_{27}$ (|| צהב ho. ptc. *gleaming*), זוז *zuz* Mur 22 $1_2$ ([זוזין]), זֶבֶד *gift* Gn $30_{20}$, מַחְמַד *desire*, i.e. precious item Jl $4_5$, שָׂכָר *payment* Ec $4_9$, perh. אֶשְׁכָּר *payment* Kadesh Barnea add. ost.

דָּבָר *word* Jos $21_{45}$ $23_{14.15}$ (:: רַע *evil*) 1 K $8_{56}$ $12_7$||2 C $10_7$ 1 K $14_{13}$ Jr $29_{10}$ $33_{14}$ Zc $1_{13}$ (+ נִחוּם *consolation*) Ps $45_2$=4QpPs$^a$ $3_{24}$ Pr $12_{25}$ $13_{15}$ 2 C $12_{12}$ $19_3$, שֵׁם *name* Is $56_5$, שְׁמוּעָה *report* Pr $15_{30}$ $25_{25}$ Si $5_{11}$, חֹק *statute* Ezk $20_{25}$ Ne $9_{13}$, מִצְוָה *commandment* Ne $9_{13}$ (|| יָשָׁר *upright*), בְּשׂוֹרָה *news* 2 S $18_{27}$, עֵצָה *counsel* 2 S $17_{14}$.

דֶּרֶךְ *way* 1 S $12_{23}$ (if em. בְּדֶרֶךְ הַטּוֹבָה וְהַיְשָׁרָה *in the way of goodness and uprightness* to בַּדֶּרֶךְ *in the* good and upright *way*) $24_{20}$ 1 K $8_{36}$||2 C $6_{27}$ Is $65_2$ Jr $6_{16}$ (unless דֶּרֶךְ הַטּוֹב = *the way of goodness* [i.e. the noun טוֹב]) Ps $36_5$ Pr $16_{29}$ 1QH $15_{18}$, אַחֲרִית *end* Si $16_3$, שָׁנָה *year* Gn $41_{35}$, יוֹם *day* 1 S $25_8$ Est $8_{17}$ $9_{19.22}$,* מוֹעֵד *appointed time* Zc $8_{19}$.

שֵׂיבָה *greyness* Gn $15_{15}$ $25_8$ Jg $8_{32}$ 1 C $29_{28}$, לֵב *heart* Pr

$13_{15}$ (or em. טוּב *goodness* of heart) Ec $9_7$ Si $13_{26}$ $33_{13}$ 4QpsEzek$^a$ $4_2$, רוּחַ *spirit* Ps $143_{10}$ Ne $9_{20}$ Si $30_{15}$, עַיִן *eye* Si $14_{10}$ (+ עין רע *eye of an evil one*), יָד *hand* Ezr $7_9$ $8_{18}$ Ne $2_8$, שֵׂכֶל *intelligence* Ps $111_{10}$ Pr $3_4$ 2 C $30_{22}$ 4Q303 $1_8$ (+ רַע *evil*), לֶקַח *understanding* Pr $4_2$, חֶסֶד *loyalty* 4Q185 $1.2_1$ 4Q370 $2_8$ ([כחסדיו הטבים]), עֲנוּת *humility* 1QS $2_{24}$.

<CSTR> טוֹבַת חֵן *good of grace*, i.e. attractive Na $3_4$=4QpNah $3.2_7$ Si $7_{19}$ (+ שׂכל hi. ptc. *intelligent*), טוֹבַת־שֶׂכֶל *good of intelligence.*, i.e. intelligent 1 S $25_3$, טוֹבַת מַרְאֶה *good of vision*, i.e. attractive Gn $24_{16}$ $26_7$ 2 S $11_2$ Est $1_{11}$ $2_2$ (טוֹבוֹת) $2_{3.7}$ Dn $1_4$ (טוֹבֵי), טוֹב רֳאִי *good of appearance*, i.e. attractive 1 S $16_{12}$, טוֹב־תֹּאַר *good of form*, i.e. attractive 1 K $1_6$, מִבְחַר וְטוֹב־לְבָנוֹן *the choicest and best of Lebanon* Ezk $31_{16}$ (or del. וְטוֹב).

<COLL> שֶׁבַע פָּרֹת הַטֹּבֹת *the seven good*, i.e. well-fed, *cows* Gn $41_{26}$ (Sam הַפָּרֹת), וְאֵת שֶׁמֶן הַטּוֹב *and the good oil* 2 K $20_{13}$ (mss, ||Is $39_2$ הַשֶּׁמֶן; but perh. טוֹב V *perfume*), קָנֶה הַטּוֹב *(the) sweet-smelling cane* Jr $6_{20}$ (unless טוֹב V *perfume*), רוּחֲךָ טוֹבָה *your good spirit* Ps $143_{10}$ (ms הַטּוֹבָה), שְׁמָנֶיךָ טוֹבִים *your good oils* Ca $1_3$ (6QCant שְׁמָנִים), ענות טוב *humility of good*, i.e. virtuous humility 1QS $2_{24}$.

**2a.** in nom. cl., used predicatively of Y. Jr $33_{11}$ Na $1_7$ Ps $25_8$ (|| יָשָׁר *upright*) $34_9$ $86_{5(mss)}$ (L אֲדֹנָי *the Lord*; || סַלָּח *forgiving*) $100_5$ $119_{68}$ $135_3$ (if not טוב [verb] *be good*) $145_9$ Lm $3_{25}$, אֱלֹהִים *God* Ps $73_1$, אֵל *God* Ps $73_1$ (if em. טוֹב לְיִשְׂרָאֵל אֱלֹהִים *God is good to Israel* to טוֹב לַיָּשָׁר אֵל *God is good to the upright*).

Adonijah 1 K $1_6$, David 1 S $29_9$, Elijah 1 K $19_4$, Elkanah 1 S $1_8$, Esther Est $8_5$, Rebekah Gn $26_7$, Vashti Est $1_{11}$, rivers Amanah and Pharpar 2 K $5_{12(Qr)}$, rulers of Samaria Am $6_2$ (if em. הֲטוֹבִים appar. *are they good?*, i.e. better, to הַאַתֶּם טוֹבִים or הֲיֵטַבְתֶּם *are you good?*).

אִשָּׁה *woman* 1 S $25_3$ (|| יָפֶה *beautiful*, + קָשֶׁה *hard*, רַע *evil*) 2 S $11_2$, בַּת *daughter* Gn $6_2$, כַּלָּה *daughter-in-law* Ru $4_{15}$, אָחוֹת *sister* Jg $15_2$, נַעֲרָה *girl* Gn $24_{16(Qr)}$ Est $2_7$ (|| יָפֶה).

נֶפֶשׁ *soul*, i.e. person Pr $19_2$, אָדָם *human being* Ec $2_{26}$, אִישׁ *man* 1 S $9_2$ $25_{15}$ 2 S $18_{27}$ Ps $112_5$ Si $41_{15}$, יֶלֶד *child* Ec $4_{13}$, אֶחָד *one* child Si $16_3$, נֵפֶל *miscarried child* Ec $6_3$, קָטָן *little one*, i.e. youngest 1 S $16_{12}$ (|| יְפֵה *beautiful*), שָׁכֵן *neighbour* Pr $27_{10}$, עֹבֵד *worker* Si $10_{27}$, עשׂה ptc. *one who does* evil Ml $2_{17}$, קנה ptc. *one who acquires* Pr $16_{16}$ (if em. קְנֹה inf. *acquisition*), אסף ni. ptc. *one who is gathered*, i.e. dead Si $40_{28}$, אֶרֶךְ *one who is long* of anger, i.e. patient Pr $16_{32}$ Ec $7_8$, משׁל ptc. *one who rules*, i.e. controls, his temper Pr $16_{32}$ (with ellipsis of טוֹב), מִסְכֵּן *pauper* Si $30_{14}$, רָשׁ *pauper* Pr $19_{1.22}$ $28_6$, קלה ni. ptc. *one who is scorned* Pr $12_9$, שְׁפַל־רוּחַ *low of spirit*, i.e. humble Pr $16_{19}$, שְׁנַיִם *two* persons Ec $4_9$, activities Ec $11_6$, כֶּלֶב *dog* Ec $9_4$.

זָהָב *gold* Gn $2_{12}$, עֹשֶׁר *wealth* Si $13_{24}$ (:: רַע *evil*), סַחַר *value* Pr $3_{14}$ $31_{18}$, מְעַט *a little* Ps $37_{16}$=4QpPs$^a$ $1.2_{21}$ Pr $15_{16}$* $16_8$, מְלֹא *fullness* Ec $4_6$, אֲרֻחָה *ration (of food)* Pr $15_{17}$, פַּת *crust* Pr $17_1$, תַּעֲנוּג *delicacy* Si $37_{28(Bmg, D)}$.

אֶרֶץ *land* Nm $13_{19}$ (:: רַע *evil*) $14_7$ Dt $1_{25}$, מוֹשָׁב *location* 2 K $2_{19}$ (+ רַע), נָהָר *river* 2 K $5_{12}$, תְּאֵנָה *fig tree* Jr $24_3$ (:: רַע), עֵץ *tree* Gn $3_6$ (|| חמד ni. ptc. *desirable*), תְּבוּאָה *produce* Jb $22_{21}$ (if em. תְּבוֹאָתְךָ good *will come to you*) Pr $8_{19}$, פְּרִי *fruit* Pr $8_{19}$, עוֹלֵלוֹת *gleaning* Jg $8_2$, צֵל *shade* Ho $4_{13}$, אוֹר *light* 4Q408 $1_9$.

דָּבָר *word* 1 S $9_{10}$ 2 S $15_3$ (|| נָכֹחַ *straight*) 1 K $2_{38}$ $18_{24}$ $22_{13}$||2 C $18_{12}$ (or em. דִּבְרֵי הַנְּבִיאִים ... טוֹב *the words of the prophets are good* to דִּבְּרוּ הַנְּבִיאִים ... טוֹב *the prophets have spoken good* [טוֹב noun]) 2 K $20_{19}$||Is $39_8$ Pr $15_{23}$ Lachish ost. $6_6$, *deed* Ex $18_{17}$ Dt $1_{14}$ 1 S $26_{16}$ Ne $5_9$, קָדוֹשׁ *holy one* of, i.e. holy, words GnzPs $2_{26}$, שֵׁם *name* Ec $7_1$, שְׁמוּעָה *report* 1 S $2_{24}$, עֵצָה *counsel* 2 S $17_{7.14}$, תּוֹרָה *law* Ps $119_{72}$ GnzPs $2_{25}$, חֹק *statute* Si $41_{2(B, Bmg)}$, מִצְוָה *commandment* GnzPs $2_{27}$, מִשְׁפָּט *judgment* Ps $119_{39}$, מַעֲשֶׂה *deed* 1 S $19_4$ Si $39_{16(Segal)}$ ([מעשי]) $39_{33}$, מַעֲלָל *deed* Ezk $36_{31}$, מַרְאֶה *appearance* Ec $6_9$.

דֶּרֶךְ *way* Si $37_9$ (if em. מטוב appar. *of good* [טוֹב noun] to מה טוב *how good* is your way; mg להביט *to look at* your way), קִרְבָה *approach* Ps $73_{28}$, יוֹם *day* Ps $84_{11}$ Ec $7_1$ 4Q185 $1.2_4$ 4Q411 $1_3$, אַחֲרִית *end* Ec $7_8$, מָוֶת *death* Jon $4_{3.8}$ Si $16_{3(B)}$ (ט[וב]).

חֶסֶד *loyalty* Ps $63_4$ $69_{17}$ $109_{21}$ (or em. in both כִּי־טוֹב *for great is* your loyalty to כְּטוּב *in accordance with the goodness of* your loyalty), חָכְמָה *wisdom* Pr $8_{11}$ Ec $7_{11}$ $9_{18}$, חֵן *grace* Pr $22_1$, perh. חֹזֶק *strength* Si $41_{2(Bmg)}$ (unless חָזָק *strong one*), תּוֹכַחַת *reproof* Pr $27_5$, כַּעַס *anger* Ec $7_3$, דּוֹד *love* Ca $1_2$ (or em. דַּד *breast*), תַּאֲוָה *desire* Pr $11_{23}$ (+ עֶבְרָה *anger*, unless em. אָבְדָה *vanishes* or עָבְרָה

transgresses), רַע *evil* Si $42_{14(Bmg, M)}$.

מֹאזְנַיִם *scales* Pr $20_{23}$, דֶּבֶק *joint*, i.e. soldering Is $41_7$, יָד *hand* Ne $2_{18}$.

מָה *what?* Jg $9_2$ Mc $6_8$ (+ וּמָה־י׳ דּוֹרֵשׁ מִמְּךָ *and what Y. seeks from you*) Jb $34_4$ Ec $6_{12}$ 4Q410 $1_6$ (:: רַע *evil*) 4Q418 $69.2_4$,* אֵי־זֶה *which?* Ec $2_3$, אֲשֶׁר *one who* Ec $4_3$, כֹּל *all* Si $37_{28(B)}$ $39_{16.33}$.

<COLL> (1) טוֹב followed by preposition, לְ of benefit, *to, for* perh. 4Q521 $5.1_6$, + Hannah 1 S $1_8$, Naomi Ru $4_{15}$, Saul 1 S $19_4$, worshipper Ps $73_{28}$ GnzPs $2_{25.26.27}$, Israel Ps $73_1$ (or em. לְיִשְׂרָאֵל *to Israel* to לַיָּשָׁר אֵל *God is* good *to the upright*), יָשָׁר *upright person* Ps $73_1$ (if em.), חכה pi. ptc. *one who awaits* Na $1_7$ (if em. לְמָעוֹז *as a refuge* to לִמְחַכֵּי־לוֹ מָעוֹז *to those who wait for him as a refuge*), קוה ptc. *one who awaits* Lm $3_{25}$, דרשׁ ptc. *one who seeks* Lm $3_{25}$, אָדָם *human being* Ec $6_{12}$, כֹּל *all* Ps $145_9$ Si $37_{28}$.

לְ *for (the purpose of), as*, + מַאֲכָל *food* Gn $2_9$ $3_6$.

כְּ *as*, אִם שְׁנֵיהֶם כְּאֶחָד טוֹבִים *if the two of them are, as one*, i.e. equally, *good* Ec $11_6$.

מִן of comparison, *(more) than*, i.e. better than 4Q185 $1.2_4$, + Jehoram 2 C $21_{13}$, Joab 1 K $2_{32}$, Saul 1 S $9_2$ $15_{28}$, Vashti Est $1_{19}$.

אִישׁ *man* Pr $19_{22}$ (or em. עָשִׁיר *wealthy person*) Ec $6_3$ Si $41_{15}$, אִשָּׁה *woman* Jg $15_2$, סלל htpo. ptc. *supplicant* Si $40_{28(B)}$, אָב *father* 1 K $19_4$, אָח *brother* Pr $27_{10}$, בֵּן *son* 1 S $1_8$ $9_2$ Is $56_5$ Ru $4_{15}$.

מֶלֶךְ *king* Ec $4_{13}$, גִּבּוֹר *mighty one* Pr $16_{32}$, לכד ptc. *one who captures* Pr $16_{32}$, עָשִׁיר *wealthy person* Pr $19_{22}$ (if em. אִישׁ *man*) Si $30_{14}$, גְּבַהּ *one exalted* of spirit Ec $7_8$, כבד htp. ptc. *one who boasts* Pr $12_{9(mss)}$ (L appar. mixed form) Si $10_{27(A)}$ (מ[מת]כבד), פָּנִים *face* of impudent person Si $40_{28(M)}$, עִקֵּשׁ *one perverting* Pr $19_1$ $28_6$.

אֶחָד *one (person)* Ec $4_9$, שְׁנַיִם *two (categories of persons)*, i.e. the living and the dead Ec $4_3$, אֶלֶף *thousand* children Si $16_3$, days Ps $84_{11}$, pieces of gold and silver Ps $119_{72}$, כִּכָּר thousand thousand *talents* of gold GnzPs $2_{25}$, זָהָב *gold* Pr $22_1$, חָרוּץ *gold* Pr $8_{19}$ $16_{16}$, פַּז *(fine) gold* Pr $8_{19}$, כֶּסֶף *silver* Pr $8_{19}$ $22_1$, פְּנִינִים *corals* or *pearls* Pr $8_{11}$ Si $30_{15}$, אֶבֶן precious *stone* GnzPs $2_{27}$, כְּלִי desirable *instrument* GnzPs $2_{26}$, אוֹצָר *treasure* Pr $15_{16}$, חלל pi. inf. *dividing* spoil Pr $16_{19}$, רֹב *abundance* Pr $16_8$, הָמוֹן *tumult*, i.e. abundance Ps $37_{16}$=4QpPs[a] $1.2_{21}$.

שׁוֹר *ox* Pr $15_{17}$, אַרְיֵה *lion* Ec $9_4$, מַמְלָכָה *kingdom* Am $6_2$, בַּיִת *house* Pr $17_1$, כֶּרֶם *vineyard* 1 K $21_2$, בָּצִיר *grape harvest* Jg $8_2$, יַיִן *wine* Ca $1_2$, מַיִם *water* 2 K $5_{12}$, שֶׁמֶן *oil* Ec $7_1$.

מְלֹא *fulness* Ec $4_6$, גְּבוּרָה *might* Ec $9_{16}$, כְּלִי *instrument* of war Ec $9_{18}$, עֵצָה *counsel* 2 S $17_{14}$, אַהֲבָה *love* Pr $27_5$ (or em. אֵיבָה *enmity*), סַחַר *value* Pr $3_{14}$, טוֹב *good* Si $42_{14}$ (Bmg), טִיב *character* Si $42_{14(M)}$, שׂחק inf. *laughing* Ec $7_3$, חַיִּים *life* Jon $4_{3.8}$ Ps $63_4$, יוֹם *day* Ec $7_1$, רֵאשִׁית *beginning* Ec $7_8$, הלך inf. *going* Ec $6_9$.

עִם *with*, appar. as good as, + נַחֲלָה *inheritance* Ec $7_{11}$.

עַל *upon*, i.e. (favourable) towards, + Ezra (and leading exiles) Ezr $7_9$ $8_{18}$ (both §1), Nehemiah Ne $2_8$ (§1) $2_{18}$.

טוֹב אַתָּה בְּעֵינַי *you are good in my eyes*, i.e. in my opinion 1 S $29_9$, sim. Ml $2_{17}$ Est $8_5$, אָדָם שֶׁטּוֹב לְפָנָיו *a person that is good before him*, i.e. in God's estimation Ec $2_{26}$.

(2) other colls. לֹא־טוֹב way *(which is) not good* Is $65_2$ Ps $36_5$ Pr $16_{29}$ 1QH $15_{18}$, sim. Ezk $20_{25}$ (all four §1), לֹא־טוֹב *is not good* Pr $19_2$ $20_{23}$, לֹא־טוֹבִים *were not good* Ezk $36_{31}$ Lachish ost. $6_6$ (לא טבם), מַה־טּוֹב *how good* Pr $15_{23}$ $16_{16}$ (or del.) Si $37_9$ (if em.) $41_{2(M)}$,* טוֹב מְאֹד *very good* (and vars.) Gn $1_{31}$ (see verb טוב, Coll.) $2_{12(Sam)}$ $24_{16}$ Nm $14_7$ Jg $18_9$ (see verb טוב, Coll.) 1 S $19_4$ 2 S $11_2$ 1 K $1_6$ Jr $24_2$ $24_3$.

**2b.** with the verb היה *be*, used predicatively of חָלָל *one who is killed* by sword Lm $4_9$, אִישׁ *man* Jr $44_{17}$, אִשָּׁה *woman* Jr $44_{17}$, עַם *people* Jr $44_{17}$, יוֹם *day* Ec $7_{10}$. <PREP> מִן of comparison, *(more) than*, i.e. better than, + חָלָל *one who is killed* by famine Lm $4_9$, אֵלֶּה *these (days)* Ec $7_{10}$.

**2c.** with the verb ראה ni. *appear*, used predicatively of מַרְאֶה *appearance* Dn $1_{15}$ (+ בָּרִיא *fat*).

**2d.** in verbal clause used predicatively with verb הלך *go* 1 K $8_{66}$ Est $5_9$ (both ‖ שָׂמֵחַ *happy*), שׁלח *send away* 2 C $7_{10}$ (‖ שָׂמֵחַ). <COLL> וַיֵּלְכוּ ... שְׂמֵחִים וְטוֹבֵי לֵב *and they went ... happy and good of heart* 1 K $8_{66}$, sim. ‖2 C $7_{10}$ Est $5_9$.

**3.** used as noun, **a. good person,** <SUBJ> ברך pu. *be blessed* Pr $22_9$, פוק hi. *produce*, i.e. obtain Pr $12_2$ (+ אִישׁ מְזִמּוֹת *a man of [evil] plans*), נחל hi. *bequeath* Pr $13_{22}$

(+ צַדִּיק *righteous [person]*, חטא ptc. *sinner*), perh. שׁמע hi. *make known* 11QMelch$_{19}$ ([טוב משמי[ע perh. *a good person who makes* salvation *known*).

<OBJ> ברך pi. *bless* Si 34$_{33}$, ראה *see* 2 K 10$_{3}$ (|| יָשָׁר *upright [person]*), צפה *watch* Pr 15$_{3}$ (:: רַע *evil [person]*).

<CSTR> טוֹב־עַיִן *one who is good of eye*, i.e. generous Pr 22$_{9}$; דֶּרֶךְ טוֹבִים *way of good people* Pr 2$_{20}$ (|| צַדִּיק *righteous*).

<PREP> לְ of direction, *to*, + נתן *give* Si 12$_{4}$ (:: רַע); of possession, *of, (belonging) to* Ec 9$_{2}$ (or del. טוֹב; + צַדִּיק, טָהוֹר *pure person*, זבח ptc. *one who sacrifices*, רָשָׁע *evil person*, טָמֵא *impure person*), + היה *be(come)* wife Nm 36$_{6}$; of benefit, *to, for*, + חלק *apportion* or *create* Si 39$_{25}$ (:: רַע), יטב hi. *do good* Ps 125$_{4}$ (|| יָשָׁר) Si 39$_{27}$ (לַ[ט]ובים); חבר לְ pi. *unite* soul *with* 11QPs$^a$ 18$_{1}$ ([חברו]); כְּ *as*, כַּטּוֹב כַּחֹטֵא *the sinner is like the good person* Ec 9$_{2}$ (mss כַּחֹטֵא); חמל עַל *have mercy on* 11QPs$^a$ 18$_{14}$; עִם *with*, + היה *be* 2 C 19$_{11}$ (or ins. עֹשֵׂי with *those who do* good [i.e. the noun טוֹב]); לִפְנֵי *before*, + שׁחה *bow down* Pr 14$_{19}$ (|| צַדִּיק, :: רַע, רָשָׁע *evil person*).

<COLL> לַטּוֹב בְּעֵינֵיהֶם *to one who is good in their eyes*, i.e. to whomsoever they please Nm 36$_{6}$, טוב על לחם *one who is good*, i.e. generous, *with food* Si 34$_{23}$, טוֹבָם כְּחֵדֶק appar. *their best one is like a thornbush* Mc 7$_{4}$ (|| יָשָׁר; or em. וַיְעַבְּתוּהָ appar. *and they twist it*, at end of 7$_{3}$, to יְעַבְּתוּ *they twist* or יְעַוְּתוּ *they pervert* or יְתַעֲבוּ *they make abominable*).

**3b. healthy,** of beast, <OBJ> מור hi. *exchange* for unhealthy beast Lv 27$_{10}$ (:: רַע *evil*, i.e. unhealthy), חלף hi. *exchange* for unhealthy beast Lv 27$_{10}$ (:: רַע). <PREP> בְּ *(in exchange) for*, + מור hi. *exchange* unhealthy beast Lv 27$_{10}$ (:: רַע), חלף hi. *exchange* unhealthy beast Lv 27$_{10}$ (:: רַע); בֵּין *between* (בֵּין טוֹב וּבֵין רַע), + ערך hi. *assess whether it is good or bad* Lv 27$_{12}$ (:: רַע).

**4.** as adverb, **well, happily,** of פתר *interpret* Gn 40$_{16}$.

Also 1QH$^b$ 1$_{12}$ (טובה) 4Q178 9$_{3}$ 4Q185 1.3$_{14}$ 4Q408 1$_{11}$ ([טובה]) 4Q415 9$_{4}$ 4Q426 1.2$_{10}$ 4Q434a$_{4}$ 4QSap$^b$ 24$_{3}$ 4QDibHam$^a$ 3.2$_{15}$ ([וחטוב[ים).

<SYN> צַדִּיק *righteous*, יָשָׁר *upright*, נָכֹחַ *straight*, סַלָּח *forgiving*, רַךְ *soft*, יָפֶה *fair*, גָּדוֹל *great*, רָחָב *wide*, רַב *great*, מָלֵא *full*, שָׁמֵן *fat*, בָּרִיא *fat*, חמד ni. ptc. *desirable*, צהב ho. ptc. *gleaming*.

<ANT> רַע *evil*, רָשָׁע *evil*; דַּק *thin*.*
→ טוב *be good*.

**טוֹב II** n.[m.] $_{141.11.29.3}$ n.m. **good**—cstr. טוֹב (Est 3$_{11}$)—**good, good thing(s), prosperity** (e.g. 1 K 10$_{7}$ Ps 23$_{6}$ Jb 21$_{13}$), **well-being** (e.g. Ps 122$_{9}$ Ec 2$_{3.24}$), **good news** (e.g. 1 K 14$_{2}$ 22$_{8}$), **good deeds** (e.g. Ps 34$_{13}$ 37$_{27}$), **good location** (Gn 20$_{15}$ Dt 23$_{17}$ Jr 40$_{4}$ Est 2$_{9}$), moral **goodness** (e.g. Pr 2$_{9}$ Ec 7$_{20}$ 1QS 1$_{5}$).*

<SUBJ> היה *be* Nm 10$_{32}$ Ec 8$_{12.13}$, רעע *be evil* Is 5$_{20}$ (:: רַע *evil*), בוא *come* Jr 17$_{6}$, יצא *go out* Lm 3$_{38}$ (:: רָעָה *evil*), רדף *pursue* Ps 23$_{6}$ (|| חֶסֶד *loyalty*).

<NOM CL> טוב ... מיי הוא *good ... is from Y.* Si 11$_{14}$ (|| חַיִּים *life*, :: רַע *evil*, מָוֶת *death*), טוב [נוכח רע] *opposite evil is good* Si 36$_{14(Segal)}$ (|| חַיִּים :: רַע, מָוֶת), אֵין טוֹב *there is no good* Jr 8$_{15}$ 14$_{19}$ (both + שָׁלוֹם *peace*, מַרְפֵּא *healing*), אֵין־לִי טוֹב כִּי הִמָּלֵט אִמָּלֵט *I have no good thing except to escape* 1 S 27$_{1}$ (or del. הִמָּלֵט), sim. Ec 2$_{24}$ 3$_{12.22}$ 8$_{15}$.

<OBJ> עשׂה *do* Gn 16$_{6}$ 26$_{29}$ (:: רַע *evil*) Dt 12$_{28}$=11QT 53$_{7}$ (|| יָשָׁר *upright[ness]*) Dt 13$_{19(Sam)}$=11QT 55$_{14}$ (|| יָשָׁר) Jg 19$_{24}$ 1 S 1$_{23}$ 3$_{18}$ 11$_{10}$ (if del. כְּ do *in accordance with* the good) 14$_{36}$ 2 S 10$_{12}$||1 C 19$_{13}$ 2 S 19$_{19.28.39}$ 2 K 10$_{5}$ 20$_{3}$||Is 38$_{3}$ Ezk 18$_{18}$ (+ עשׁק *oppress*, גזל *rob*) Ps 14$_{1.3}$ 34$_{15}$ (|| שָׁלוֹם *peace*; :: רַע) 37$_{3}$ (|| אֱמוּנָה *faithfulness* [or em. הֲמוֹנָהּ *its multitude*]) 37$_{27}$ (:: רַע) 53$_{2.4}$ 119$_{65}$ perh. Pr 3$_{27}$ Ec 3$_{12}$ 7$_{20}$ 1 C 21$_{23}$ 2 C 14$_{1}$ (|| יָשָׁר; ||1 K 15$_{11}$ lacks טוֹב) 19$_{11}$ (if ins. עֹשֵׂי with *those who do* good) 31$_{20}$ (|| יָשָׁר, אֱמֶת *truth* [or del.]) Si 48$_{22(Segal)}$ ([עשה] ... הט[וב]) 1QH 17$_{24}$ ([ולעשות]) 1QS 1$_{2}$ (|| יָשָׁר) 1QapPs$^a$ 1.2$_{5}$ (or em. טוֹבָה *good* [noun]) 4QMMT C$_{31}$ (|| יָשָׁר) 4Q521 5.2$_{4}$ 11QT 59$_{17}$ 63$_{8}$ (both || יָשָׁר).

חלק *apportion* or *create* Si 39$_{25(Segal)}$ ([טוב]) 39$_{25}$ (:: רַע *evil*), הפך *overturn*, i.e. turn good into evil Si 11$_{31}$ (:: רַע), פרח *blossom (into)* Si 37$_{18}$ (|| חַיִּים *life*, :: רַע, מָוֶת *death*), מלא pi. *fill (with)* Ps 107$_{9}$ (or del. טוֹב) Jb 22$_{18}$, לקח *take* 2 S 24$_{22}$, עלה hi. *raise*, i.e. offer in sacrifice 2 S 24$_{22}$.

חסר *lack* Ps 34$_{11}$, חרם hi. *put to ban* 1 S 15$_{9}$, אכל *eat* Is 55$_{2}$ Pr 13$_{2}$ (|| חָמָס *violence*; or em. יֹאכַל *he will eat* to יִשְׂבַּע *he will be satisfied*).

דרשׁ *seek* Am 5$_{14}$ (:: רַע *evil*) Est 10$_{3}$, בקשׁ pi. *seek* Ps 122$_{9}$ (|| שָׁלוֹם *peace*), שׁחר *diligently seek* Pr 11$_{27}$ (or em.

חרש *devise*; || רָצוֹן *pleasure*, :: רָעָה *evil*), רדף *pursue* Ps $38_{21}$, מצא *find* Pr $16_{20}$ $17_{20}$ (:: רָעָה) $18_{22}$ (|| אִשָּׁה *woman*) $19_{8}$.

נתן *give* Dt $26_{11}$ $30_{15}$ (|| חַיִּים *life*, :: רַע *evil*, מָוֶת *death*) Jr $29_{32}$ Ps $85_{13}$ (|| יְבוּל *produce*), יסף hi. *add* 1 K $10_{7}$ (|| חָכְמָה *wisdom*), גמל *repay* Pr $31_{12}$ (:: רַע) Est $7_{9}$ (if em. דבר pi. *speak* good), שׁלם pi. *repay* Pr $13_{21}$ (+ רָעָה *evil*; or em. יְשַׁלֶּם־טוֹב *he repays good* to שָׁלוֹם *peace* or יַשְׁלִים טוב *he completes prosperity*), מנע *withhold* Jr $5_{25}$ Ps $84_{12}$ Pr $3_{27}$.

לקח *take* Ho $14_{3}$ (but perh. טוֹב IV *word*), קבל pi. *receive* Jb $2_{10}$ (:: רָעָה *evil*), נחל *inherit* Pr $28_{10}$ (or del.).

אהב *love* Am $5_{15}$ (:: רַע *evil*), שׂנא *hate* Mc $3_{2}$ (:: רַע [Qr], רָעָה [Kt] *evil*), זנח *reject* Ho $8_{3}$, ראה *see* Ps $34_{13}$ Jb $7_{7}$ Ec $3_{13}$ appar. $5_{17}$, hi. *show* Ps $4_{7}$ (+ אוֹר *light*) Ec $2_{24}$, שׁמע *hear* 2 S $14_{17}$, קוה pi. *await* Jb $30_{26}$ (|| אוֹר, :: רַע, אֹפֶל *darkness*).

חרשׁ *devise* Pr $11_{27}$ (if em. שׁחר *diligently seek*; :: רָעָה *evil*) $14_{22}$ (:: רַע *evil*; + חֶסֶד *loyalty*, אֱמֶת *truth*), ידע *know* Gn $2_{9.17}$ (both עֵץ הַדַּעַת טוֹב וָרָע *the tree of knowing good and evil*)* $3_{5.22}$ Dt $1_{39}$ (all five :: רַע) Si $12_{1}$ (or em. תדיע *you know* to תריע [i.e. רעע hi.] *you injure* a good person) 1QS $4_{26}$ 1QSa $1_{10}$ ([טוב]; :: רע) 4Q418 $221_{5}$ 4Q422 $1_{10}$ (עץ הד[עת טוב ורע]) 4Q423 $1.1_{7}$, hi. *make known* 4Q419 $1_{4}$ ([את הט]וב).

דבר pi. *speak* Gn $24_{50}$ (:: רַע *evil*) Nm $10_{29}$ 1 S $19_{4}$ 1 K $22_{13}$||2 C $18_{12}$ (or em. טוֹב ... דִּבְרֵי הַנְּבִיאִים *the words of the prophets are good* to טוֹב ... דִּבְּרוּ הַנְּבִיאִים *the prophets have spoken good* [טוֹב noun]) Est $7_{9}$ (or del. טוֹב or em. דבר pi. to גמל *repay*), בשׂר pi. *announce* 1 K $14_{2}$ 11QMelch$_{16}$ ([מב]שר טוב), נבא htp. *prophesy* 1 K $22_{8}$ (||2 C $18_{7}$ טוֹבָה *goodness*) $22_{18}$||2 C $18_{17}$ (all three :: רַע) Is $52_{7}$ (|| שָׁלוֹם *peace*, יְשׁוּעָה *salvation*).

<CSTR> טוֹב בֵּית הַנָּשִׁים *the best place of the house of women*, i.e. the harem Est $2_{9}$.

מעשי טוב *deeds of goodness* 1QS $1_{5}$, [דב]רי טוב seven *words of goodness* 4QShir Shabb$^{f}$ $13_{2}$ (=4QShirShabb$^{d}$ $1.1_{18}$ צֶדֶק *of righteousness*), שמעת טב *report of good*, i.e. good news Lachish ost. $4_{2}$ $5_{2}$ (שמעת של[ם וטב]) *report of peace and good*) $8_{2}$ (טב [שמ]עת), בִּרְכַּת־טוֹב *blessing of prosperity* Pr $24_{25}$, בִּרְכוֹת טוֹב *blessings of prosperity* Ps $21_{4}$ (|| פָּז *gold*), ממשל הטוב *the rule of goodness* 4QTNaph $1.2_{9}$ (erased הצדק *of righteousness*), מלך הטוב *king of goodness* MasShirShabb $2_{15}$, אל [ה]טוב *God of goodness* 4QShirShabb$^{d}$ $1_{5}$, יֵין הַטּוֹב appar. *wine of goodness*, i.e. good wine Ca $7_{10}$ (but perh. טוֹב V *perfume*), כָּל־מַעְגַּל־טוֹב *every path of goodness* Pr $2_{9}$ (+ צֶדֶק *righteousness*, מִשְׁפָּט *judgment*, מֵישָׁר *uprightness*), דֶּרֶךְ הַטּוֹב *the way of goodness* Jr $6_{16}$, מדו[ת ט]וב *measure of goodness* 4Q185 $1.2_{10}$, עדת טוב *congregation of goodness* 4QBer$^{a}$ $1_{8}$ (+ אֱמֶת *truth*), כָּל־טוֹב *every good thing* Ps $34_{11}$ 1QH $10_{26}$ ([כול טוב]) 1QS $2_{3}$ (כול; :: רַע *evil*) 1QMyst $1.2_{5}$, כָּל־הַטּוֹב *all the good (things)* Dt $26_{11}$ 1 S $11_{10}$ $14_{36.40}$ $15_{9}$ (Gnz lacks כָּל־) Jg $10_{15}$ 4QM$^{h}$ $2_{9}$.

<APP> שֵׁבֶט *rod*, i.e. branch Si $37_{18(B)}$ (D שַׁרְבִיט *rod*), perh. מָמוֹן *wealth* 1QMyst $1.2_{5}$.

<ADJ> הַטּוֹב הַהוּא *that good* Nm $10_{32}$.

<PREP> לְ of direction, *to*, + שׁנה pi. *change*, i.e. move Est $2_{9}$; of purpose, *for (the purpose of)*, + היה *be* 2 C $10_{7}$ (אִם־תִּהְיֶה לְטוֹב לְהָעָם־הַזֶּה *if you will be for the benefit of this people*; ||1 K $12_{7}$ עֶבֶד if you will be *a servant*), עשׂה *do* 4QMMT $C_{31}$, רדף *pursue* 4QS$^{f}$ $2_{5}$, צפה *watch* Si $10_{27}$, חשׁב *reckon* 4QMMT $C_{27}$, שׁנה pi. *change* face Si $13_{25}$ (:: רַע *evil*), ערב *guarantee* Ps $119_{122}$, שׂים *place* 4QMyst$^{b}$ $4_{4}$ ([לט]וב), שׁרה pi. *release* Jr $15_{11(Qr)}$ (or em. שׁרר *vex*, or ישׁר pi. *straighten*, or אשׁר pi. *pronounce happy*, or שׁרת pi. *serve*, or שְׁאֵרִית your *remnant* is for good); perh. of cause, *on account of*, *at* prosperity, + שׂישׂ *rejoice* Dt $30_{9}$; *concerning*, + אמר Is $5_{20}$.

יתר לְ hi. *cause to abound in* Dt $28_{11(Sam)}$ (MT טובה in same sense), חול לְ *writhe (in expectation) of*, i.e. wait for Mc $1_{12}$ (or em. יחל pi. *await*, with לְ introducing object).

בְּ of place, *in*, *among*, + ישׁב *dwell* Gn $20_{15}$ Dt $23_{17}$, שׁלח pi. *send away* Si $37_{18(Bmg, D)}$; of accompaniment, *with*, *in (a state of)*, + היה *be* Ec $7_{14}$ (or em. חיה *live*), לין *pass night* Ps $25_{13}$, צדק hi. *act righteously* 4QHod$^{a}$ $7.2_{13}$ ([ומצדיק] בדעת ... וטוב) *who acts righteously in knowledge ... and goodness*); of instrument, *by (means of)*, *with*, + שׂבע hi. *satisfy* Ps $103_{5}$, ברך pi. *bless* 1QS $2_{3}$, רדף *pursue* 1QS $10_{18}$, כלה pi. *complete* days Jb $21_{13(Qr)}$ $36_{11}$ (|| נְעִים *pleasant[ness]*), מלא pi. *fill* days 4Q525 $14.2_{13}$ (+ שָׁלוֹם *peace*), בלה *wear out* days Jb $21_{13(Kt)}$ $36_{11(mss)}$; perh. of cause, *on account of*, *at*, + שׂמח *rejoice* Dt $26_{11}$

2 C $6_{41}$; *over, in charge of*, + משׁל *rule* Si $37_{18(B)}$; *in preference to*, + בחר *choose* 1QH $10_{26}$ ([בח]רו בכול טוב); קנא בְּ pi. *be zealous for* 11QPsa Si $51_{18}$, דבק בְּ *cling to* 1QH $16_{18}$ ([ולדבקה בך ו]טוב *to cling to you and that which is good* in your eyes), בחר בְּ *choose* Is $7_{15.16}$ (both :: רַע *evil*), מאס בְּ *despise* 4QMh $2_7$ ([למאוס בטו]ב; :: רַע), ראה בְּ *see* Jr $29_{32}$ Ec $2_1$ (+ שִׂמְחָה *joy*) 4QapPsb $33_{10}$ (unless hi. *show* soul good or טוב נפשי = *the good of my soul*, i.e. טוֹב).

כְּ *in accordance with*, + עשׂה *do* Gn $19_8$ Jos $21_{45}$ (‖ יָשָׁר *upright[ness]*) Jg $10_{15}$ $19_{24(mss)}$ 1 S $11_{10}$ (or del. כְּ) Jr $26_{14}$ (‖ יָשָׁר) Est $3_{11}$, כתב *write* Est $8_8$.

מִן of comparison, *(more) than*, + אהב *love* evil Ps $52_5$ (‖ דבר pi. inf. *speaking* righteousness, or em. דָּבָר *word* of righteousness; :: רַע *evil*, שֶׁקֶר *falsehood*); partitive, *(some) of* perh. Si $37_9$ (or em. מטוב appar. *of good* to מה טוב *how good* is your way [טוֹב adj.]; mg להביט *to look at* your way), + דבר pi. *speak* Gn $31_{24.29}$; פוץ מִן *overflow with* Zc $1_{17}$, חשׁה מִן hi. *be silent from*, appar. refrain from doing Ps $39_3$ (unless טוֹב inf. of טבב *speak*).

אֶל *to*, + הלך *go* Jr $40_4$ (‖ יָשָׁר *upright[ness]*; or em.; see the verb טוב, Subj.).

עַל *for the purpose of*, + היה *be* protection 4QJubd $21_{20}$ ([ע]ל הטוב); חמל עַל *take pity on* 1 S $15_9$.

עַד *unto*, i.e. either ... *or* 2 S $13_{22}$ (:: רַע *evil*).

בֵּין *between* good and evil, + ידע *know* 2 S $19_{36}$ (:: רַע *evil*) 4QMystb $3_2$ ([ט]וב לרע) 4Q370 $2_4$ ([בי]ן טוב לרע) 4Q417 $2.1_8$ ([טו]ב ל[רע]) $2.1_{18}$ ([טו]ב; :: רַע), בין hi. *understand* 1 K $3_9$ (:: רַע), *explain (how to distinguish)* 4Q418 $2_7$ (=4Q416 $1_{15}$ כון hi. *establish*; :: רַע), בקר pi. *seek*, i.e. distinguish Lv $27_{33}$ (:: רַע), *whether it be* a good house or a bad house, + ערך hi. *assess* Lv $27_{14}$ (:: רַע), פלג pi. *divide* 1QH $14_{12}$ ([פלגתה]; :: רֶשַׁע *evil*).

<COLL> יִשְׂבְּעוּן טוֹב *they will be satisfied with good things* Ps $104_{28}$ Pr $12_{14}$ (־יִשְׂבַּע) $13_2$ (if em. יֹאכַל *he will eat*).

הַטּוֹב בְּעֵינֶיךָ *(the) good in your eyes*, i.e. what seems good to you Gn $16_6$ (בְּעֵינַיִךְ) 1 S $1_{23}$ (בְּעֵינַיִךְ), sim. Gn $19_8$ $20_{15}$ Dt $6_{18}$ $13_{19(Sam)}$ Jos $9_{25}$ Jg $10_{15}$ $19_{24}$ 1 S $3_{18}$ $11_{10}$ $14_{36.40}$ 2 S $10_{12}$‖1 C $19_{13}$ 2 S $19_{19.28.39}$ $24_{22}$‖1 C $21_{23}$ 2 K $10_5$ $20_3$‖Is $38_3$ Jr $26_{14}$ $40_4$ (or em. אֶל־טוֹב *to a good place* to אִם־טוֹב בְּעֵינֶיךָ *if it seems good to you*) Est $3_{11}$ $8_8$ 1QH $16_{18}$ $17_{24}$, וַיַּעַשׂ הַטּוֹב ... לִפְנֵי י׳ *and he did good ... before Y.* 2 C $31_{20}$, sim. 1QS $1_2$ 4QMMT $C_{31}$ 4Q521 $5.2_4$ 11QT $53_7$ $55_{14}$ $59_{17}$ $63_8$, טוב על פניהמה acting righteously in *goodness before them* 4QHoda $7.2_{13}$, טוב לך *what is good for you* 4QMMT $C_{27.31}$.

Also 4Q423 $5_7$ (+ רַע *evil*) 4QRitMar $163_2$ ([הטו]ב והישר *goodness and uprightness*).

<SYN> חֶסֶד *loyalty*, יָשָׁר *upright(ness)*, אֱמֶת *truth*, אֱמוּנָה *faithfulness*, שָׁלוֹם *peace*, חָכְמָה *wisdom*, יְשׁוּעָה *salvation*, רָצוֹן *pleasure*, נָעִים *pleasant(ness)*, אוֹר *light*, חַיִּים *life*, אִשָּׁה *woman*, יְבוּל *produce*, פַּז *gold*.

<ANT> רַע *evil*, רָעָה *evil*, רֶשַׁע *evil*, שֶׁקֶר *falsehood*, מָוֶת *death*, אֹפֶל *darkness*.

⇒ טוב *be good*.

**טוֹב III** 4 pl.n. **Tob**, appar. Aramaean territory near Gilead, to which Jephthah fled, <CSTR> אֶרֶץ טוֹב *the land of Tob* Jg $11_{3.5}$, אִישׁ טוֹב *man*, i.e. warriors or perh. ruler, *of Tob* 2 S $10_{6.8}$ (־אִישׁ; unless in both pr.n.m., *Ishtob*; 4QSama $10_8$ אישטוב appar. as pr.n.m.).

⇒ טוב *be good*.

**טוֹב IV** 2 n.[m.] **word**, <OBJ> לקח *take*, i.e. receive in sacrifice Ho $14_3$ (+ פְּרִי שְׂפָתֵינוּ *fruit of lips*; if em. פָּרִים *calves*, namely our lips). <PREP> לְ *with respect to*, + שׁרה pi. perh. *strengthen* Jr $15_{11}$.*

**טוֹב V** 2 n.[m.] **perfume**, <CSTR> קְנֵה הַטּוֹב *cane of perfume* Jr $6_{20}$ (if em. קָנֶה הַטּוֹב appar. *[the] good*, i.e. pleasant, *cane*), שֶׁמֶן הַטּוֹב *oil of perfume* 2 K $20_{13}$‖Is $39_2$ (if em. in Is הַשֶּׁמֶן הַטּוֹב *the good oil*) Ps $133_2$ (if em. הַשֶּׁמֶן), יֵין הַטּוֹב *wine of perfume* Ca $7_{10}$ (unless *the wine of goodness*, i.e. a good wine).

***טוֹב VI** 6 n.m. **rain**, <SUBJ> בוא *come* Jr $17_6$. <OBJ> נתן *give* Ps $85_{13}$, ראה hi. *show* Ps $4_7$, מנע *withhold* Jr $5_{25}$. <CSTR> אוֹצָרוֹ הַטּוֹב perh. *his treasury of rain* Dt $28_{12}$. <PREP> כְּ *as* Ho $10_1$.

**טוּב I** n.m. **good** 32.12.35—cstr. טוּב; sf. טוּבִי, טוּבְךָ (Q טובכה), טוּבוֹ, טוּבָהּ, טוּבָם; pl. sf. Q טוביך—**property** (e.g. Gn $45_{20}$ Si $34_{11}$ $44_{11}$); **health, prosperity, well-**

**being** (e.g. Ps 128$_5$ Jb 20$_{21}$ Si 37$_{11}$ GnzPs 2$_8$), **prospering** (Pr 11$_{10}$), **happiness** (e.g. 4QDibHam$^c$ 131$_9$); **beauty** (Ho 10$_{11}$=CD 1$_{19}$ Zc 9$_{17}$); **goodness, virtue** as moral attribute (e.g. 1QH 13$_{17}$).

<SUBJ> חזק *be strong* Si 34$_{11}$ (+ תְּהִלָּה *praise*), חיל *be strong* Jb 20$_{21}$, אמן ni. *be trustworthy*, i.e. enduring Si 44$_{11}$, שכח ni. *be forgotten* Si 45$_{26}$ (+ גְּבוּרָה *strength*).

<NOM CL> טוּב־לֵב מִשְׁתֶּה תָמִיד *happiness of heart is (like) a continuous feast* Pr 15$_{15}$ (if em. טוֹב־לֵב *a happy heart*), טוב חי ימי מספר *the happiness of a life is (measured in) days of (great) number* Si 41$_{13(Bmg)}$, sim. 41$_{13(Bmg)}$, כָּל־טוּב אֲדֹנָיו בְּיָדוֹ appar. *all his master's property was in his charge* Gn 24$_{10}$ (or em. מִכָּל־ *some of all*), לֹא בְיָדָם טוּבָם *is not their prosperity within their own power?* Jb 21$_{16}$, טוּב כָּל־אֶרֶץ מִצְרַיִם לָכֶם הוּא *the good*, i.e. property, *of all the land of Egypt is yours* Gn 45$_{20}$, הלוא לכה טובו *do not his good things belong to you?* 4Q418 81$_6$, מַה־טּוּבוֹ *what*, i.e. how great, *is his beauty*, or *goodness* Zc 9$_{17}$ (|| יָפְיוֹ *beauty*), מָה רַב־טוּבְךָ *how great is your goodness*, or *benefit* Ps 31$_{20}$.

<OBJ> נתן *give* Gn 45$_{18}$ Ne 9$_{35}$ (+ מַלְכוּת *kingship*), appar. חלף *exchange* Si 42$_{25}$ (unless טוב is subj. of חלף *succeed*), עבר hi. *transfer* Ex 33$_{19}$, צפן *store* Ps 31$_{20}$, גמל *repay* Is 63$_7$ (or em.; see Cstr.), שלם hi. *complete* Pr 13$_{21}$ (if em. יְשַׁלֶּם־טוֹב *he repays good* to יַשְׁלִם טוּב *he completes prosperity*), כון hi. *establish* 1QS 10$_{12}$ (מכין טובי; =4QS$^d$ 4.1$_{12}$ מכון טובי *foundation of my goodness*), למד pi. *teach* Ps 119$_{66}$ (unless טוּב II *word*; or del. טוּב), ספר pi. *relate* 1QH 18$_{14}$ ([לספר]), אכל *eat* Is 1$_{19}$ Jr 2$_7$ (|| פְּרִי *fruit*) Ezr 9$_{12}$ Ne 9$_{36}$ (|| פְּרִי; or del. טוּב) 4Q434a5 (|| פְּרִי), אהב *love* 4Q477 2.2$_{10}$, פרר hi. *frustrate* 4QHod$^a$ 7.1$_{23}$, עבת pi. *twist* or עות pi. *pervert* or תעב pi. *make abominable* Mc 7$_4$ (if em.; see טוֹב adj., §3a, Coll.).

<CSTR> טוב נפשי *the good of my soul* 4QapPs$^b$ 33$_{10}$ (unless *my soul* will not see *good* or you will not show *my soul good*, i.e. the noun טוֹב), טוּב לֵבָב *goodness of heart* Dt 28$_{47}$ Is 65$_{14}$ (לֵב; :: כְּאֵב *pain*) Si 30$_{16}$, טוב לב[בם *happiness of their heart* 4QDibHam$^c$ 131$_8$, טוב שאר *health of flesh* Si 30$_{16(Bmg)}$, בשר *of flesh* Si 37$_{11}$ (+ תַּגְמוּל חֶסֶד *repayment of loyalty*), טוּב עַיִן *goodness of eye* Si 32$_{12}$ (+ הַשָּׂגַת יָד *reaching of hand*; mg הַגִּישׁ יָד/הַגָּשַׁת יָד *extending of hand*), טוּב צַוָּארָהּ *beauty of her neck* Ho 10$_{11}$ (= CD 1$_{19}$ טוב הצואר *beauty of the neck* = 4QD$^a$ 2. 1$_{22}$ [טוב ה]צור = 4Q477 2.2$_{10}$ [טובן הצואר]), טוּב טַעַם *quality of taste*, i.e. good judgment Ps 119$_{66}$ (unless טוּב II *word*; or del. טוּב), טוּב שֵׁם *goodness of a name* Si 41$_{13(Bmg)}$ (B טובת שם in same sense [M lacks שם]).

טוּב י׳ *good things of Y.* Jr 31$_{12}$ Ps 27$_{13}$, טוּב צַדִּיקִים *prospering of the righteous* Pr 11$_{10}$ (:: אבד inf. *dying*), טוב קדושים *goodness of the holy* 1QH fr. 15$_7$, טוב עמו *prospering of his people* GnzPs 4$_5$, טוב [בח]יריו *prosperity of his elect* 4QapPs$^a$ 1.1$_{10}$, טוב אשה *a woman's goodness* Si 42$_{14(Bmg)}$, טוב רוע איש appar. *the good of the evil of a man* Si 42$_{14(B)}$ (or rd. טוב רע איש *better is the wickedness of a man* than the goodness of a woman, as Bmg), טוּב חַסְדְּךָ *goodness of your loyalty* Ps 69$_{17}$ (חַסְדְּךָ) 109$_{21}$ (if em. in both כִּי־טוֹב *for* your loyalty *is good* to כְּטוּב *in accordance with the goodness of*), טוב גודלו *goodness of his greatness* 4QHod$^a$ 7.1$_{23}$, טוּב אֲדֹנָיו *the property of his master* Gn 24$_{10}$, טוב חי *goodness of a living being* Si 41$_{13(Bmg)}$ (B טובת חי in same sense [M (ט)ובת]).

טוב אדמתו *good things of his land* CD 1$_8$, טוּב הָאָרֶץ *good things of the land* Is 1$_{19}$ Ezr 9$_{12}$ 4QMidrEschat$^a$ 2$_2$ ([הא]רץ]), טוּב אֶרֶץ מִצְרַיִם *good things of the land of Egypt* Gn 45$_{18.20}$ (טוּב כָּל־אֶרֶץ *good things of all the land of* Egypt) 45$_{23}$ (טוּב מִצְרַיִם *good things of Egypt*), טוּב דַּמֶּשֶׂק *good things of Damascus* 2 K 8$_9$, טוּב יְרוּשָׁלָםִ *prosperity of Jerusalem* Ps 128$_5$, טוּב בֵּיתֶךָ *good things of your house* Ps 65$_5$, טוב העולם *benefit of the world* GnzPs 2$_8$ (+ אוֹר *light*), טוב עולמים *goodness of worlds*, i.e. eternal goodness 1QS 4$_3$.

רוח ... טוב *spirit of ... goodness of* 1QS 4$_3$, מכון טובי *foundation of my goodness* 4QS$^d$ 4.1$_{12}$ (=1QS 10$_{12}$ מכין טובי *establisher of my goodness*), עדות טובו *testimony of his goodness* Si 34$_{23}$, גדול טובכה *great one*, i.e. greatness, *of your goodness* 1QH 10$_{16}$ 11$_{29}$ ([גדו[ל]), רוב טובכה *abundance of your goodness* 1QH 7$_{30}$ 11$_7$ 14$_{17}$ (טובך), רוב טובו *abundance of his goodness* 1QS 11$_{14}$, רַב־טוּב *great one*, i.e. abundance, *of goodness* Is 63$_7$ (or em. רָב־ טוּב *abundance of goodness* or רַב־/רָב־טוּבוֹ *abundance of his goodness*) זֵכֶר רַב־טוּבְךָ *memory of the great one*, i.e. abundance, *of your goodness* Ps 145$_7$ (or em. רָב־), 4Q434a4, רוב טוב *abundance of goodness* 4Q418 81$_{19}$ (+ חָכְמָה *wisdom*), *abundance of goodness of* 1QH fr. 15$_7$,

[רצון טו]בכה *desire of your goodness* 4QRitPur $41_6$, כָּל־טוּב *every good thing* Dt $6_{11}$=1QDM $2_3$=4Q393 $3_9$ (1Q [כו]ל טוב; 4Q [כול טוב]) 4Q418 $127_1$, כָּל־טוּב *all the good of* Gn $24_{10}$ 2 K $8_9$, כָּל־הַטּוּב *every good thing* Dt $26_{11}$ Ne $9_{25}$, כָּל־טוּבִי *all my good thing(s)* Ex $33_{19}$.

<APP> מַשָּׂא *burden* 2 K $8_9$, קָדוֹשׁ *holy one* Ps $65_5$ (or em. קְדֹשׁ *holy one of* your temple to קֹדֶשׁ *holiness of* or קָדוֹשׁ *holy one*, in app. to בַּיִת *house*), כֶּרֶם *vineyard* 1Q DM $2_3$, זַיִת *olive (grove)* 1QDM $2_3$, בּוֹר *cistern* 1QDM $2_3$ (כו]ל טוב כרמים וזיתים ... ובו]רות) 4Q393 $3_9$ (כול טוב] [בורות).

<ADJ> טוּבְךָ הָרָב *your great goodness* Ne $9_{35}$.

<PREP> לְ of possession, *of, (belonging) to* 4Q181 $2_6$; of purpose, *for (the purpose of)* perh. 4QPrFêtes[c] $215_2$, + עמד hi. *establish* GnzPs $2_8$, יחל לְ pi. *wait for* 1QH $4_{40}$ ([ואיחל לטובכה]) $11_{31}$ (+ צְדָקָה *righteousness*), צפה לְ pi. *look for* 1QH $12_{21}$.

בְּ of accompaniment, *with, in (a state of)*, + נתן *give* Si $32_{12}$ 4QDibHam[c] $131_8$ (נת]תה לו בטו]וב לב]בם *you have given to him in the happiness of his heart*); of cause, *on account of* 1QH $11_9$, + עלץ *rejoice* Pr $11_{10}$; of instrument, *by (means of), with, through*, + שׂבע *be satisfied* Ps $65_5$, דשׁן pi. *fatten* CD $1_8$, צדק *be righteous* 1QH $13_{17}$; *despite*, + עבד *serve* Ne $9_{35}$, שׁוב *go back* Ne $9_{35}$; ראה בְּ *see* Ps $27_{13}$ $128_5$, hi. *show* 4QapPs[a] $1.1_{10}$, חפץ בְּ *desire* GnzPs $4_5$, בחר בְּ *choose* CD $1_{19}$.

כְּ *in accordance with*, + עשׂה *do* 11QPs[a] $19_5$ (+ רַחֲמִים *mercy*), ענה *reply* Ps $69_{17}$ (if em. כִּי־טוֹב *for* your loyalty *is good* to כְּטוּב *in accordance with the goodness of*), נצל hi. *rescue* Ps $109_{21}$ (if em.), פתח *open* gates of salvation 1QM $18_8$.

מִן partitive, *(some) of* Gn $24_{10}$ (if ins. מִן) $42_{14(B)}$, + לקח *take* 2 K $8_9$ (if em. וְכָל־ *and all* to מִכָּל־ *some of all*), נשׂא *raise* Gn $45_{23}$; of cause, *on account of*, + רנן *exult* Is $65_{14}$; of comparison, *more than* Si $42_{14(Bmg)}$, perh. privative, *without, for lack of*, + דאב *languish* 4Q418 $127_1$.

אֶל *on account of* or *concerning*, + נהר *shine*, i.e. rejoice Jr $31_{12}$, פחד *fear* Ho $3_5$.

עַל *over*, + עבר *pass* Ho $10_{11}$ (or em. hi. *cause* yoke *to pass*); *upon*, + שׁען ni. *lean* 1QH fr. $4_{13}$; *more than* Si $30_{16}$; *concerning*, + יעץ ni. *take advice* Si $37_{11}$.

עִם *with* 4Q418 $126.2_9$ (+ כָּבוֹד *glory*).

לְפִי *in accordance with* 4Q181 $1_3$.

לְמַעַן *for the sake of* Ps $25_7$.

<COLL> מְלֵאִים כָּל־טוּב houses *full of every good thing* Dt $6_{11}$=1QDM $2_3$=4Q393 $3_9$ (1Q [כו]ל טוב; 4Q [כול טוב]) Ne $9_{25}$ (מְלֵאִים־), וְעַמִּי אֶת־טוּבִי יִשְׂבָּעוּ *and my people will be satisfied with my goodness* Jr $31_{14}$, ׳׳ יְ ... טוּבוֹ *Y. and ... his goodness* Ho $3_5$, כטובכה בנו *in accordance with your goodness towards us* 1QM $18_8$.

Also 1QH fr. $4_{19}$ ([וט]ובכה) 4Q302 $1_5$ (טוביך).

<SYN> יֳפִי *beauty*, פְּרִי *fruit*.

<ANT> כְּאֵב *pain*, אבד inf. *dying*.*

→ טוב *be good*.

* **טוּב II** 1 n.[m.] **word**—למד pi. *teach* Ps $119_{66}$ (unless טוּב I *goodness*; or del. טוּב; + טַעַם *taste, judgment*, דַּעַת *knowledge*).

→ טבב *speak*.

**טוֹב אֲדֹנִיָּה** 1 pr.n.m. **Tob-adonijah,** Levitical teacher at time of Jehoshaphat, <SUBJ> למד pi. *teach* 2 C $17_8$, סבב *go around* 2 C $17_8$. <NOM CL> עִמָּהֶם ... טוֹבִיָּהוּ וְטוֹב אֲדֹנִיָּה *with them were ... Tobijah and Tob-adonijah* 2 C $17_8$ (or del. Tobijah and/or Tob-adonijah). <APP> לֵוִי *Levite* 2 C $17_8$. <PREP> עִם *with* 2 C $17_8$.

→ טוב *be good* + אָדוֹן *lord* + ׳׳ *Y.*

**טוֹבָה I** n.f. **good** $_{66.23.2}$—טֹבָה (Gn $50_{20}$); sf. טוֹבָתִי, (טֹבָתָם) טוֹבָתָם, (טוֹבָתֶךָ) טוֹבָתֵךְ; pl. (טוֹבוֹת) טֹבוֹת; sf. טוֹבֹתָיו—**good(ness), good deed(s),** in moral sense (e.g. GnzPs $1_9$); **good things, good news** (e.g. 2 C $18_7$), **kind, pleasant words** (2 K $25_{28}$||Jr $52_{32}$ Jr $12_6$); **prosperity** (Si $6_{11}$ $12_8$), **property** (Si $11_{30}$), **value** (Si $6_{15}$), **bounty** (Ps $65_{12}$); **happiness, pleasure, satisfaction** (e.g. Jb $21_{25}$ Lm $3_{17}$ Si $8_{19}$), perh. **success** (Ne $6_{19}$ [or em.]), etc.; **(treaty of) friendship** (Dt $23_7$ 2 S $2_6$).*

<SUBJ> רבה *be great* Ec $5_{10}$, שׁכח pi. *cause to forget* evil Si $11_{25}$ (טוב[ת]; :: רָעָה *evil*), שׁפך pass. *be poured* Si $30_{18}$, בוא *come* Jb $22_{21}$ (or em. תְּבוֹאָתְךָ good *will come to you* to תְּבוּאָתְךָ *your produce* is good).

<NOM CL> טובה ... תנופה *good things ... are (like) a wave offering* Si $30_{18}$, טובת חי ימי מספר *the goodness of a life is (measured in) days of (great) number*, or *the good*

*things of life last only for days that can be numbered* Si 41$_{13(B)}$, sim. 41$_{13(B)}$, אין טובה *there is no good* Si 12$_{3}$ 30$_{16}$, אֲדֹנָי אָתָּה טוֹבָתִי בַּל־עָלֶיךָ appar. *you are my Lord; my goodness is not upon you* Ps 16$_{2}$ (or em. to כֻּלָּהּ עָלֶיךָ as for my goodness, *all of it is on account of you* or בַּל־בִּלְעָדֶיךָ *is none other than you*, or אֲדֹנָי אַתָּה טוֹבָתִי *you are my Lord, my goodness*).

<OBJ> עשׂה *do* Ex 18$_{9}$ Nm 24$_{13}$ (:: רָעָה *evil*) Jg 8$_{35}$ 9$_{16}$ 1 S 24$_{19}$ perh. 2 S 2$_{6}$ (or em. הַזֹּאת אֲשֶׁר *this* good *that* you have done to תַּחַת אֲשֶׁר *because* you have done this thing) 1 K 8$_{66}$‖2 C 7$_{10}$ Jr 33$_{9}$ 2 C 24$_{16}$ 1QapPs$^{a}$ 1.2$_{5}$ (if em. טוֹב *good thing*), פעל *do* GnzPs 1$_{9}$, אכל *eat*, i.e. benefit from Ec 5$_{10}$, אבד pi. *destroy* Ec 9$_{18}$, כון hi. *establish* Ps 68$_{11(ms)}$, בוא hi. *bring* Jr 32$_{42}$ (:: רָעָה), נגע hi. *extend* Si 12$_{5}$, נדח hi. *expel* Si 8$_{19}$, שׁוב hi. *take back*, i.e. repay 2 S 16$_{12}$ (:: קְלָלָה *curse*), גמל *repay* 1 S 24$_{18}$ (:: רָעָה), שׁלם pi. *repay* 1 S 24$_{20}$, נתן *give* 4Q418 81$_{6}$, אהב *love* Si 3$_{26}$, נשׁה *forget* Lm 3$_{17}$, שׁכח pi. *cause to forget* Si 11$_{25}$ (:: רָעָה), דרשׁ *seek* Dt 23$_{7}$ Ezr 9$_{12}$ (both ‖ שָׁלוֹם *peace*), בקשׁ pi. *seek* Ne 2$_{10}$, שׁפך *pour* Si 20$_{13}$, אמר *say*, i.e. mention Jr 18$_{10}$ (+ רַע *evil* [Qr], רָעָה *evil* [Kt]) Ne 6$_{19}$ (or em. טֹבָה *word*; + דָּבָר *word*), דבר *say*, i.e. mention Jr 32$_{42}$, pi. *speak* 1 S 25$_{30}$ 2 S 7$_{28}$‖1 C 17$_{26}$ 2 K 25$_{28}$‖Jr 52$_{32}$ Jr 12$_{6}$ 18$_{20}$, שׁמע *hear* Jr 33$_{9.9}$, ראה *see* Jb 9$_{25}$ Ec 5$_{17}$ 6$_{6}$.

<CSTR> טוֹבַת יוֹם *bounty of a day* Si 11$_{25}$ 14$_{14}$, טובת חי *the happiness of a living being* Si 41$_{13(B)}$ (M ט[ו]בת; Bmg טוב חי in same sense), טוֹבַת בְּחִירֶיךָ *bounty of your chosen ones* Ps 106$_{5}$ (+ שִׂמְחָה *joy*), טובת שם *bounty of a name* Si 41$_{13(B)}$ (Bmg טוב שם in same sense), טובת כסילים *bounty of fools* Si 20$_{13}$; פועלי טובתם *those who do their goodness* GnzPs 1$_{9}$, יוֹם טוֹבָה *day of prosperity* Ec 7$_{14}$ (:: רָעָה *evil*), שְׁנַת טוֹבָתֶךָ *year of your bounty* Ps 65$_{12}$, בְּדֶרֶךְ הַטּוֹבָה וְהַיְשָׁרָה *in the way of goodness and uprightness* 1 S 12$_{23}$ (or em. בַּדֶּרֶךְ *in the* good and upright *way*), כל טובה *every good deed* Si 12$_{5}$, כָּל־הַטּוֹבָה *all the good* Ex 18$_{9}$ Jg 8$_{35}$ 1 K 8$_{66}$‖2 C 7$_{10(mss)}$ (L lacks כָּל־) Jr 32$_{42}$ 33$_{9.9}$, כל [טו]בתם *all their property* Si 11$_{30}$.

<ADJ> הַטּוֹבָה הַזֹּאת *this good* 2 S 2$_{6}$ (or em. הַזֹּאת אֲשֶׁר *this* good *that* you have done to תַּחַת אֲשֶׁר *because* you have done) 7$_{28}$‖1 C 17$_{26}$.

<PREP> לְ of possession, *of, (belonging) to* Si 6$_{15}$, + היה *be* Si 12$_{1}$; of purpose, *for (the purpose of)* Ezr 8$_{22}$, + פלל htp. *intercede* Jr 14$_{11}$, נכר hi. *recognize*, i.e. select Jr 24$_{5}$, זכר *remember* Ne 5$_{19}$ 13$_{31}$, בוא hi. *bring* Jr 39$_{16}$ (:: רָעָה *evil*), שׂים *place* face, eyes Jr 21$_{10}$ (:: רָעָה) 24$_{6}$ Am 9$_{4}$ (:: רָעָה), שׁוב hi. *take back*, i.e. repay, convert Gn 50$_{20}$ (:: רָעָה), שׁקד *keep watch* Jr 44$_{27}$ (:: רָעָה), חזק hi. *strengthen* hand Ne 2$_{18}$, עשׂה *do*, i.e. give sign Ps 86$_{17}$=4QapPs$^{b}$ 15$_{3}$ ([לטובה]); perh. *concerning*, + נבא htp. *prophesy* 2 C 18$_{7}$ (:: רָעָה; ‖1 K 22$_{8}$ טוֹב *good*), *as* Si 45$_{1}$; שׂים לְ *make* contention *out of* Si 11$_{30}$ (ט[ו]בתם), יתר לְ hi. *cause to abound in* Dt 28$_{11}$ 30$_{9}$.

בְּ of place/time, *in, during* Si 6$_{11}$ 12$_{9}$ (:: רָעָה *evil*), + ידע ni. *be known* Si 12$_{8}$ (:: רָעָה); of accompaniment, *with, in (a state of)*, + אכל *eat* Jb 21$_{25}$ (unless בְּ partitive, eat *some of*, i.e. anything, good); of instrument, *by (means of), through*, + נהג *lead (life)* Si 3$_{26}$, קרא ni. *be called* or *be encountered* Si 14$_{5}$ (or em. חדה or שׂמח *rejoice* in, on account of), כון hi. *establish* Ps 68$_{11}$ (or בְּ of cause, *on account of*); *in accordance with* or *despite*, + נשׂג hi. *reach* Si 12$_{5}$; בוע בְּ htpalp. *delight in* Si 14$_{4}$, ראה בְּ *see* Ps 106$_{5}$.

כְּ *in accordance with*, + עשׂה *do* Jg 8$_{35}$.

מִן of instrument, *by (means of), with*, + רוה pi. *drench* Si 35$_{13}$; partitive, *(some) of, (any) of*, + אכל *eat* Si 11$_{19}$ ([מ]טובתי)), שׂבע *be satisfied (with)* Ec 6$_{3}$, מנע *withhold*, i.e. deprive oneself of Si 14$_{14}$ ([ת]מנע)), חסר pi. *deprive* Ec 4$_{8}$.

עַל *on account of* or *concerning* 1 K 8$_{66}$‖2 C 7$_{10}$, + חדה *rejoice* Ex 18$_{9}$, פחד *fear* Jr 33$_{9}$, נחם pi. *repent* Jr 18$_{10}$, רגז *quake* Jr 33$_{9}$.

תַּחַת *instead of*, + שׁלם pi. *repay* evil Gn 44$_{4}$ Ps 35$_{12}$ 38$_{21}$ (all three :: רָעָה *evil*), pu. *be repaid* Jr 18$_{20}$ (:: רָעָה), שׁוב hi. *take back*, i.e. repay evil 1 S 25$_{21}$ Ps 109$_{5}$ (if em. שִׂים *place* upon me) Pr 17$_{13}$ (all three :: רָעָה).

<COLL> טוֹבָה הַרְבֵּה *much good* Ec 9$_{18}$.

<SYN> שָׁלוֹם *peace*, יְשָׁרָה *uprightness*.

<ANT> רָעָה *evil*, קְלָלָה *curse*.

⇒ טוב *be good*.

* **טֹבָה II** $_{1}$ n.f. **word**—sf. טוֹבָתָיו—<OBJ> אמר *say* Ne 6$_{19}$.

**טוֹבִיָּה** 18.0.0.4 pr.n.m. **Tobijah**—טֹבִיָּה (Ne 2$_{19}$), טוֹבִיָּהוּ

(2 C $17_{8}$), I (all four) טביהו.

**1.** Ammonite governor of Samaria at time of Nehemiah, son-in-law of Shecaniah, father of Jehohanan (Ne $6_{18}$), and relative of Eliashib, a priest ($13_{4}$).

<SUBJ> שׁמע *hear* Ne $2_{10.19}$ $4_{1}$, אמר *say* $2_{19}$ $3_{35}$, שׁלח *send* letters $6_{19}$, לעג hi. *mock* $2_{19}$, בזה *despise* $2_{19}$ (or em. בוא *come*), חרף pi. *reproach* $6_{12}$, ירא pi. *frighten* $6_{19}$, קשׁר *plot* $4_{1}$, בוא *come* $2_{19}$ (if em.) $4_{1}$, לחם ni. *fight* $4_{1}$, שׂכר *hire* $6_{12}$, עשׂה *do* $4_{1}$. <NOM CL> טוֹבִיָּה ... אֶצְלוֹ *Tobiah ... was next to him* $3_{35}$. <OBJ> שׁוב hi. *take back*, i.e. reply $2_{19}$. <CSTR> כָּל־כְּלֵי בֵית־טוֹבִיָּה *all the vessels of the house of Tobiah* $13_{8}$. <APP> עַמֹּנִי *Ammonite* $3_{35}$, עֶבֶד Ammonite *servant, official* $2_{10.19}$. <PREP> לְ of direction, *to*, + אמר *say* $2_{19}$; of benefit, *to, for*, + רעע *be evil*, i.e. displeasing $2_{10}$, חרה *be hot, angry* $4_{1}$, עשׂה *do* $13_{7}$, *prepare* room $13_{7}$, *against*, + זכר *remember* $6_{14}$; of possession, *of, (belonging) to* $2_{19}$ $6_{12}$ (or em. לִי *to me*) $6_{17.17}$ $13_{4}$; of agent, *by*, + שׁמע ni. *be heard* $6_{1}$; עַל *against*, + עמד hi. *establish* guard $4_{1}$ (or em. עָלֶיהָ *over it*); מִפְּנֵי *on account of*, + פלל htp. *pray* $4_{1}$, *to*, + הלך *go* (of letter) $6_{17}$. <COLL> + Sanballat $2_{10.19}$ $3_{35}$ $4_{1}$ $6_{1.12}$ (or del.) $6_{14}$, Geshem $2_{19}$ $6_{1}$, Noadiah $6_{14}$.

**2.** exile returned from Babylon Zc $6_{10}$, <PREP> לְ of possession, *of, (belonging) to*, + היה *be* $6_{14}$ (+ Helem [or em. Heldai], Jedaiah, Hen [or em. Josiah]); מֵאֵת *from (with)*, + לקח *take* $6_{10}$ (+ Heldai, Jedaiah).

**3.** ancestor of postexilic Judaean family that could not prove its genealogy, <CSTR> בְּנֵי־טוֹבִיָּה *sons of Tobiah* Ezr $2_{60}$‖Ne $7_{62}$ (+ Delaiah, Nekoda).

**4.** Levitical teacher at time of Jehoshaphat, <SUBJ> למד pi. *teach* 2 C $17_{8}$, סבב *go around* $17_{8}$. <NOM CL> עִמָּהֶם ... טוֹבִיָּהוּ וְטוֹב אֲדוֹנִיָּה *with them were ... Tobijah and Tob-adonijah* $17_{8}$ (or del. Tobijah and/or Tob-adonijah). <APP> לֵוִי *Levite* $17_{8}$. <PREP> עם *with* $17_{8}$.

**5.** royal officer, <SUBJ> בוא hi. *bring* seed Lachish ost. $5_{10}$ (א[ב]ן; others [ ]יא). <CSTR> ספר טביהו *the letter of Tobiah* Lachish ost. $3_{19}$. <APP> עֶבֶד *servant* of the king Lachish ost. $3_{19}$.

**6.** father of Ahikam, <CSTR> בן[ ] טביהו *son of Tobiah* Seal 514 (T. Beit Mirsim?, 7th/6th cent.).

**7.** appar. son of Abda (עבדא), <PREP> לְ of possession, *of, (belonging) to* Seal 565 (לטבי[הו]; T. Beit Mirsim?, 7th/6th cent.).

**8.** Seal 393 (Buqei'ah Valley, 7th cent.; others בדיהו *Bedaiah*).

⇒ טוב *be good* + יְ Y.

**טוֹבִיָּ֫הוּ**, see טוֹבִיָּה *Tobiah*.

**טוה** 2 vb. **spin—Qal** 2 Pf. טָווּ—**spin,** <SUBJ> אִשָּׁה *woman* Ex $35_{25}$ (וְכָל־אִשָּׁה חַכְמַת־לֵב בְּיָדֶיהָ טָווּ *and all the women who were wise of heart*, i.e. who had skill, *spun with their hands*) $35_{26}$. <OBJ> עֵז *goat*, i.e. goat-hair Ex $35_{26}$. <PREP> בְּ of instrument, *by (means of), with*, + יָד *hand* Ex $35_{25}$.

**Pi.** 1 Pf. Sam טוו—as Qal, <SUBJ> אִשָּׁה *woman* Ex $35_{26(Sam)}$. <OBJ> עֵז *goat*, i.e. goat-hair Ex $35_{26(Sam)}$.

⇒ מַטְוֶה *cloth*, טַוָּה *cloth*.

**[טַוָּה]** 2 n.f. **cloth**—Sam טוה—<NOM CL> בְּיָדֶיהָ טַוָּה (as for) every skilful woman, *in her hands was cloth* Ex $35_{25(Sam)}$ (MT טָווּ with their hands *they spun*). <PREP> מִן partitive, *(some) of*, + בוא hi. *bring* Ex $35_{25(Sam)}$ (מִטַּוָּה *some of the cloth*; MT מַטְוֶה bring *cloth*).

⇒ טוה *spin*.

**[טוֹהַר]**, see טֹהַר *purity*.

**טוח** 11.0.4 vb. **cover—Qal** 9.0.4 Pf. Q טח, טחתה, טָחוּ, טַחְתֶּם; + waw וְטָח, Sam וטחו; ptc. טחים, טָחֵי, טָחִים, pass. Q טוח; inf. טוֹחַ—**1.** active, **(re)plaster** infected house with new plaster (עָפָר *dust*) (Lv $14_{42}$), **daub (with), plaster (with),** of covering wall with plaster or whitewash (תָּפֵל *whitewash* Ezk $13_{10.11.12.14.15.15}$ $22_{28}$ 4Q424 $1_{3}$), perh. **decorate** walls of temple (1 C $29_{4}$), **cover** face in shame (1QH $4_{23}$), eye to prevent seeing (Is $44_{18}$ [if em.; see Subj.]).

<SUBJ> Y. Is $44_{18}$ (if em. טַח *is covered*, from טחח, to טָח *he has covered*), אֵל *God* 1QH $4_{23}$, כֹּהֵן *priest* Lv $14_{42}$, נָבִיא *prophet* Ezk $13_{10.11.12.14.15.15}$ $22_{28}$; subj. not specified, Lv $14_{42(Sam)}$ Ezk $13_{11}$ 1 C $29_{4}$ CD $8_{12(A)}$=$19_{25(B)}$ Is $44_{18}$ (if em.).

<OBJ> (1) thing overlaid, בַּיִת *house* Lv $14_{42}$, קִיר *wall* Ezk $13_{14.15.15}$ 1 C $29_{4}$ 4Q424 $1_{3}$, חַיִץ *wall* Ezk $13_{10}$, פָּנִים *face* 1QH $4_{23}$, עַיִן *eye* Is $44_{18}$ (if em.); (2) material used

in overlaying, טִיחַ *plaster* Ezk 13$_{12}$, תָּפֵל *whitewash* Ezk 13$_{10.11}$ (טָחֵי תָפֵל *daubers of whitewash*) 13$_{14.15}$ 22$_{28}$ CD 8$_{12(A)}$=19$_{25(B)}$ (8 טחי תפל; 19 טחי התפל; + בנה *build* wall) 4Q424 1$_{3}$, בֹּשֶׁת *shame* 1QH 4$_{23}$.

<PREP> לְ of benefit, *to, for,* + שַׂר *prince* Ezk 22$_{28}$, נָשִׂיא *prince* Ezk 22$_{28}$ (if em. נָבִיא *prophet*) 22$_{28}$, כֹּהֵן *priest* Ezk 22$_{28}$; מִן privative, *from, so as not to,* + ראה inf. *see(ing)* Is 44$_{18}$ (if em.).

**2.** passive, appar. **be sealed with pitch,** <SUBJ> כְּלִי *vessel* CD 11$_{9}$=4QD$^{f}$ 3.1$_{5}$.

**Ni.** $_{2}$ Inf. הִטּוֹחַ (הִטֹּחַ)—**be re-covered, be replastered,** <SUBJ> בַּיִת infected *house* Lv 14$_{43}$ (+ קצה hi. *scrape* house of old covering [or em. קצע hi. *scrape*]) 14$_{48}$. <COLL> אַחֲרֵי הִטּוֹחַ *after being replastered* Lv 14$_{43.48}$ (אַחֲרֵי הִטֹּחַ אֶת־הַבָּיִת *after the replastering of the house*).*

⇒ טחח *be covered,* טִיחַ *plaster.*

**[טוֹטֶפֶת]** $_{3}$ n.f. **symbol**—pl. טוֹטָפֹת (טֹטָפֹת)—**symbol, amulet, headband,*** <NOM CL> ותורה לו טט[פת] קש[יר]ת [י]ד *and the law is to him an amulet, a binding of,* i.e. something bound upon, *(his) hand* Si 36$_{3(Smend)}$. <PREP> לְ *as,* + היה *be, function* Ex 13$_{16}$ Dt 6$_{8}$ (both + בֵּין עֵינֶיךָ *between your eyes,* i.e. on your forehead) 11$_{18}$ (+ בֵּין עֵינֵיכֶם *between your eyes*; all three || אוֹת *sign*). <APP> קְשִׁירָה *binding* Si 36$_{3(Smend)}$. <SYN> אוֹת *sign.**

**טול** $_{14.0.2}$ vb. **throw**—**Hi.** $_{9.0.1}$ Pf. הֵטִיל; impf. אֲטִילֶךָ, Q יטילו; + waw (וַיְטִלֵהוּ) וַיָּטִלוּ, וַיָּטֶל, וְהֵטַלְתִּי; impv. הֲטִילֻנִי—**1. fling, hurl** spear, javelin (1 S 18$_{11}$ 20$_{33}$ 1QM 6$_{4}$). **2. throw** Pharaoh, as sea monster, to ground (Ezk 32$_{4}$), persons and things into sea (Jon 1$_{5.12.15}$). **3. send** wind (Jon 1$_{4}$). **4. eject, expel** person (Jr 16$_{13}$ 22$_{26}$).

<SUBJ> ״ *Y.* Jr 16$_{13}$ 22$_{26}$ Ezk 32$_{4}$ (אֲדֹנָי י״ || נטשׁ *forsake,* i.e. drop on ground) Jon 1$_{4}$, שָׁאוּל *Saul* 1 S 18$_{11}$ 20$_{33}$ (or em. in both וַיָּטֶל *and he flung* to וַיִּטֹּל, from נטל, *and he raised,* i.e. picked up), אִישׁ *man* Jon 1$_{5.12.15}$ (both || נשׂא *raise*), מַלָּח *sailor* Jon 1$_{5}$, דֶּגֶל *battalion* 1QM 6$_{4}$.

<OBJ> כָּנְיָהוּ *Coniah* Jr 22$_{26}$, יוֹנָה *Jonah* Jon 1$_{12.15}$, פַּרְעֹה *Pharaoh* Ezk 32$_{4}$, מֶלֶךְ *king* Jr 22$_{26}$ Ezk 32$_{4}$, בֵּן *son* Jr 22$_{26}$, אֵם *mother* Jr 22$_{26}$, עַם *people* Jr 16$_{13}$, רוּחַ *wind* Jon 1$_{4}$, חֲנִית *spear* 1 S 18$_{11}$ 20$_{33}$ (or em. in both), כְּלִי *vessel* Jon 1$_{5}$.

<PREP> אֶל *(in)to,* + יָם *sea* Jon 1$_{4.5.12.15}$; עַל *to(wards),* + יְהוֹנָתָן *Jonathan* 1 S 20$_{33}$, אֶרֶץ *land* Jr 16$_{13}$ 22$_{26}$; מֵעַל *from (upon),* + אֶרֶץ *land* Jr 16$_{13}$; עַל־פְּנֵי *onto (the surface of),* + שָׂדֶה *field* Ezk 32$_{4}$.

<COLL> יטילו שבע פעמים *they will fling (their weapons) seven times* 1QM 6$_{4}$. <SYN> נטשׁ *forsake, drop,* נשׂא *raise.*

**Ho.** $_{4.0.1}$ Pf. הוּטְלוּ; impf. יוּטָל (יֻטַל, יוּטָל)—**be thrown down, fall** (Ps 37$_{24}$=4QpPs$^{a}$ 1.3$_{15}$), **throw oneself down** (Jb 41$_{1}$), **be ejected, expelled** from land (Jr 22$_{28}$), **be cast,** of lot (Pr 16$_{33}$), <SUBJ> כָּנְיָהוּ *Coniah* Jr 22$_{28}$ (|| שׁלך ho. *be thrown*), אִישׁ *man* Jr 22$_{28}$ (or del. אִישׁ), גֶּבֶר *man* Ps 37$_{24}$=4QpPs$^{a}$ 1.3$_{15}$ (+ נפל *fall*; 4Q [גבר] ... יו[פול]), זֶרַע *seed,* i.e. offspring Jr 22$_{28}$, עֶצֶב *vessel* Jr 22$_{28}$ (or del. עֶצֶב), גּוֹרָל *lot* Pr 16$_{33}$, anyone Jb 41$_{1}$. <PREP> בְּ of place, *in(to),* + חֵיק *fold of garment* Pr 16$_{33}$; אֶל *at, before,* + מַרְאֶה *appearance* Jb 41$_{1}$; עַל *to(wards),* + אֶרֶץ *land* Jr 22$_{28}$. <COLL> יוּטַל אֶת־הַגּוֹרָל *the lot is cast* Pr 16$_{33}$. <SYN> שׁלך ho. *be thrown.*

**Pilp.** $_{1}$ Ptc. מְטַלְטֶלְךָ—**hurl** or perh. **shake,** <SUBJ> ״ *Y.* Is 22$_{17.17}$ (if em. טַלְטֵלָה גָּבֶר is hurling/shaking you *with a hurling/shaking,* i.e. violently, *O man* to טַלְטֵל הַגֶּבֶר [i.e. inf. of טול pilp.] in the same sense or כְּטַלְטֵל הַבֶּגֶד *as shaking,* i.e. as he might shake, *a garment*; + עטה *wrap oneself*). <OBJ> גֶּבֶר *man* 22$_{17.17}$ (if em.), בֶּגֶד *garment* Is 22$_{17}$ (if em.).

⇒ טַלְטֵלָה *hurling* or *shaking,* הֵטֵל *throwing* or *troop.*

**טוּר I** $_{26.0.1}$ n.m. **row**—cstr. טוּר; pl. טוּרִים; cstr. טוּרֵי—**row** of jewels, columns, etc., **course** of stone or wood in construction of temple, etc.; supporting **wall,* parapet** (3QTr 7$_{15}$).

<NOM CL> טוּר אֹדֶם ... הַטּוּר הָאֶחָד *a row of ruby ... is the first row* Ex 28$_{17}$||39$_{10}$ (or em. הַטּוּר הָרִאשׁוֹן *the first row* is ruby ..., that was the first row), הַטּוּר הַשֵּׁנִי נֹפֶךְ סַפִּיר וְיָהֲלֹם *the second row is turquoise, sapphire and amethyst* 28$_{18}$||39$_{11}$ (mss וְיַהֲלֹם), הַטּוּר הַשְּׁלִישִׁי לֶשֶׁם שְׁבוֹ וְאַחְלָמָה *the third row is opal, agate and amethyst* 28$_{19}$||39$_{12}$, הַטּוּר הָרְבִיעִי תַּרְשִׁישׁ וְשֹׁהַם וְיָשְׁפֵה *the fourth row is beryl, lapis lazuli, and jasper* 28$_{20}$||39$_{13}$ (mss וְיָשְׁפָה; 39$_{13}$ שֹׁהַם), חָצֵר ... טוּרִים גָּזִית וְטוּר כְּרֻתֹת אֲרָזִים *the court was (made of) ... three courses (of) hewn stone and a course of cedar beams* 1 K 7$_{12}$ (or em. הֶחָצֵר *the court*), חֲמִשָּׁה

עָשָׂר הַטּוּר *fifteen (planks long) was the*, i.e. each, *row* 1 K 7$_{3}$, טוּר סָבִיב בָּהֶם *a row (of masonry) was around among them* Ezk 46$_{23}$ (mss לָהֶם *to them*, i.e. they had a row of masonry all around), שְׁנֵי טוּרִים סָבִיב *two rows were around* 1 K 7$_{18}$, הָרִמּוֹנִים מָאתַיִם טֻרִים סָבִיב *the pomegranates were two hundred, (in) rows all around* 1 K 7$_{20}$ (or del. or ins. שְׁנֵי *two* rows), שְׁנֵי טוּרִים הַפְּקָעִים *the gourds were (in) two rows* 1 K 7$_{24}$ (or del.), שְׁנַיִם טוּרִים הַבָּקָר *the cattle were (in) two rows* 2 C 4$_{3}$.

<OBJ> מלא pi. *fill (with)* Ex 39$_{10}$, בנה *build* 1 K 6$_{36.36}$ 7$_{2}$ (if del. עַל build *upon*), עשׂה *do* 1 K 7$_{42}$‖2 C 4$_{13}$.

<CSTR> טוּר אֹדֶם פִּטְדָה וּבָרֶקֶת *a row of ruby, topaz and emerald* Ex 28$_{17}$‖39$_{10}$, טוּרֵי גָזִית *rows of hewn stone* 1 K 6$_{36}$, טוּר כְּרֻתֹת אֲרָזִים *a row of beams of cedars* 1 K 6$_{36}$ 7$_{12}$, טוּרֵי עַמּוּדֵי אֲרָזִים *rows of columns of cedars* 1 K 7$_{2}$, טוּרֵי אָבֶן *rows of stone(s)* Ex 39$_{10}$; שְׁנֵי טוּרִים *two rows* 1 K 7$_{18.20}$ (if ins. שְׁנֵי) 7$_{24}$ (or del.) 7$_{42}$ (שְׁנֵי־).

<APP> אֶבֶן precious *stone* Ex 28$_{17.17}$ (lacking in Sam), גָּזִית *hewn stone* 1 K 7$_{12}$, טוּר *row* Ex 28$_{17}$‖39$_{10}$ (if em.; see Nom. Cl.), חָצֵר *court* 1 K 6$_{36.36}$, בַּיִת *house* 7$_{2}$ (if del. עַל build house *upon*), שָׁקוּף *window* 1 K 7$_{4}$, רִמּוֹן bronze *pomegranate* 1 K 7$_{18}$ (if ins. רִמּוֹן) 7$_{42}$‖2 C 4$_{13}$, מְלָאכָה *work* 1 K 7$_{42}$‖2 C 4$_{13}$.

<ADJ> רִאשׁוֹן *first* Ex 28$_{17}$‖39$_{10}$ (if em.; see Nom. Cl.), שֵׁנִי *second* 28$_{18}$‖39$_{11}$, שְׁלִישִׁי *third* 28$_{19}$‖39$_{12}$, רְבִיעִי *fourth* 28$_{20}$‖39$_{13}$, אֶחָד *one*, i.e. first Ex 28$_{17}$‖39$_{10}$.

<PREP> עַל *upon*, + בנה *build* 1 K 7$_{2}$ (or del. עַל, leaving טוּר in app. to בַּיִת *house* as obj. of בנה); עַד *unto*, *three cubits up to the wall* 3QTr 7$_{15}$ (אמות שלוש עד הטור; unless טוּר II *rock*, or rd. טִיר *wall*, Allegro טִיף *channel*).

<COLL> אַרְבָּעָה טוּרִים *four rows* Ex 28$_{17}$‖39$_{10}$ (טוּרֵי) 1 K 7$_{2}$ (טוּרֵי; or em. עַל אַרְבָּעָה *upon four* rows to וּשְׁלֹשָׁה *and three* rows), שְׁלֹשָׁה טוּרִים *three rows* 1 K 6$_{36}$ (טוּרֵי) 7$_{2}$ (טוּרֵי; if em.) 7$_{4.12}$, שְׁנַיִם טוּרִים *two rows* 2 C 4$_{3.13}$.

⇒ טִיר *wall*, טִירָה *row*.

**[טוּר]** II 0.0.1 n.[m.] **rock,** <PREP> עַד *unto*, אמות שלוש עד הטור *three cubits up to the rock* 3QTr 7$_{15}$ (unless טוּר I *wall*).

**טוּשׁ** 1 vb. **rush**—**Qal** Impf. יָטוּשׁ—**swoop,** and/or perh. **flutter, hover** (if em. at Nm 11$_{31}$), <SUBJ> נֶשֶׁר *eagle* Jb 9$_{26}$ (+ קלל *be swift*, ברח *flee*, חלף *exchange*), שְׂלָו *quail* Nm 11$_{31}$ (if em. וַיִּטֹּשׁ, from נטשׁ, *and* the wind *let* the quail *drop* onto the camp to וַיָּטֻשׁ *and* the quail *hovered* above the camp). <PREP> עַל *upon*, + אֹכֶל *food* Jb 9$_{26}$; *over*, + מַחֲנֶה *camp* Nm 11$_{31}$ (if em.).

Also 4Q415 12$_{4}$ (התטשו htp., unless טושׁ htp. *be besmeared, be dirtied*).

**טושׁ** 0.0.1 vb. **cover**—**Htp.** 0.0.1 perh. Pf. Q התטשו—**be besmeared, dirtied,** 4Q415 12$_{4}$ (unless טוּשׁ htp. *rush*).

**טחה** 1 vb. **throw**—**Pil.** Ptc. מְטַחֲוֵי—**shoot (arrow),** <COLL> וַתֵּשֶׁב ... הַרְחֵק כִּמְטַחֲוֵי קֶשֶׁת *and she sat down ... distant, as those who shoot a bow*, i.e. at the distance of an archer from a target Gn 21$_{16}$ (unless מִטַּחֲוֵה *shooting* of a bow).

**טְחוֹן** 1 n.[m.] **millstone,** <OBJ> נשׂא *raise*, i.e. carry (of youths) Lm 5$_{13}$ (+ כשׁל *stumble*; or em. לִטְחוֹן *to grind*, i.e. for hard labour).

⇒ טחן *grind*.

**[טְחוֹר]**, see טְחֹר *haemorrhoid*.

**טֻחוֹת** I 2 n.f. perh. **innards,** unless at Ps 51$_{8}$ טֻחוֹת II *darkness* and/or at Jb 38$_{36}$ טֻחוֹת III *ibis*, <PREP> בְּ of place, *in*, + שִׁית *place* wisdom Jb 38$_{36}$ (+ שֶׂכְוִי *mind* or *cock*), חפץ *desire* truth Ps 51$_{8}$ (unless טֻחוֹת II *darkness*, and em. מִטֻּחוֹת *more than darkness*, i.e. secrecy), ידע hi. *make known* Ps 51$_{8}$.*

**טֻחוֹת** II 1 n.f. perh. **darkness,** <PREP> בְּ of place, *in*, + חפץ *desire* truth Ps 51$_{8}$ (or em. מִטֻּחוֹת *more than darkness*, i.e. secrecy; or טֻחוֹת I *innards*).

**טֻחוֹת** III 1 n.f. perh. **ibis** or another bird, <PREP> בְּ of place, *in*, + שִׁית *place* wisdom Jb 38$_{36}$ (+ שֶׂכְוִי *mind* or *cock*).

**טחח** 1 vb. **be covered**—**Qal** 1 Pf. טַח—**be covered,** <SUBJ> עַיִן *eye* Is 44$_{18}$ (or em. טַח *is covered* to טָח *he covered*, from טוח). <PREP> מִן privative, *from, so as not*

*to*, + ראה inf. *see(ing)* Is 44$_{18}$.*
⇒ טוח *cover.*

**טחן** 8 vb. **grind—Qal** 8 Pf. וְטָחֲנוּ; impf. 3fs תִּטְחַן, 2mpl תִּטְחֲנוּ; + waw וַיִּטְחַן; impv. טַחֲנִי; ptc. טֹחֵן, טֹחֲנוֹת; inf. טָחוֹן—**1. grind** raw materials for food, in punishment or humiliation (Jg 16$_{21}$ Is 47$_{2}$ Lm 5$_{13}$ [if em.]), grind face of poor (Is 3$_{15}$), **crush, pulverize** golden calf (Ex 32$_{20}$ Dt 9$_{21}$).

<SUBJ> Moses Ex 32$_{20}$ (+ לקח *take*, שׂרף *burn*) Dt 9$_{21}$ (+ לקח, שׂרף, נכה hi. *strike*), Samson Jg 16$_{21}$, אִשָּׁה *woman* Jb 31$_{10}$ (or em. ni. your wife will *be ground*, i.e. subjected to intercourse; + כרע *kneel* over, i.e. subject woman to intercourse or labour), בְּתוּלָה *young woman* Is 47$_{2}$ (+ לקח *take* mill, גלה ni. *be revealed* [of nakedness], pi. *remove* veil, *reveal* thigh, ראה ni. *be seen* [of object of reproach], חשׂף *strip off* dress, עבר *pass*, i.e. cross rivers), בַּת *daughter* of Babylon Is 47$_{2}$, בָּחוּר *youth* Lm 5$_{13}$ (if em. טְחוֹן *millstone* to לִטְחוֹן *to grind*), זָקֵן *elder* Is 3$_{15}$ (|| דכא pi. *crush*, + בער pi. *remove* vineyard), שַׂר *prince* Is 3$_{15}$, עַם *people* Nm 11$_{8}$ (|| דוך *crush*), + לקט *collect* manna, בשׁל pi. *boil*).

<OBJ> עֵגֶל golden *calf* Ex 32$_{20}$ Dt 9$_{21}$, חַטָּאת *sin*, i.e. sinful thing Dt 9$_{21}$, קֶמַח *flour* Is 47$_{2}$, פָּנִים *face* of poor Is 3$_{15}$.

<PREP> לְ of benefit, *to, for*, + אַחֵר *another (man)* Jb 31$_{10}$ (or em. ni., with לְ of agent, *by*); בְּ of place, *in*, + בַּיִת *house*, i.e. prison Jg 16$_{21}$; of place, *in*, or of instrument, *by (means of), with*, + רֵחַיִם *mill* Nm 11$_{8}$.

<COLL> וָאֶכֹּת אֹתוֹ טָחוֹן הֵיטֵב עַד אֲשֶׁר־דַּק לְעָפָר *and I struck it to pulverize (it) well until it (became) fine as dust* Dt 9$_{21}$, וַיִּטְחַן עַד אֲשֶׁר־דָּק *and he pulverized (it) until it (became) fine* Ex 32$_{20}$.

2. fem. ptc. as noun, **grinder,** in ref. to tooth, <SUBJ> בטל *be idle* Ec 12$_{3}$, מעט pi. *become few* Ec 12$_{3}$.

<SYN> דוך *crush*, דכא pi. *crush*.

**Ni., be ground,** i.e. **be subjected to sexual intercourse,** <SUBJ> אִשָּׁה *woman* Jb 31$_{10}$ (if em. תִּטְחַן *she will grind* for another to תִּטָּחֵן *she will be ground* by another). <PREP> לְ of agent, *by*, + אַחֵר *another (man)* Jb 31$_{10}$ (if em.; see Qal Subj.).

⇒ טְחוֹן *millstone*, טַחֲנָה *mill.*

**טַחֲנָה** 1 n.f. **mill,** <CSTR> קוֹל הַטַּחֲנָה *the sound of the mill* Ec 12$_{4}$.
⇒ טחן *grind.*

**[טֹחֲנָה]**, see טחן, Qal, §2 *grinder.*

**[טְחֹר]** 8 n.m. **haemorrhoid**—pl. Qr טְחֹרִים; cstr. טְחֹרֵי; sf. Qr טְחֹרֵיהֶם; Qr טְחֹרֵיכֶם—usu. as Qr for Kt עֹפֶל *haemorrhoid*, visible and painful skin lesion, **haemorrhoid, boil,** etc.; in list of skin diseases (Dt 28$_{27}$).

<SUBJ> שׂתר ni. *erupt* among Philistines 1 S 5$_{9(\mathrm{Qr})}$. <NOM CL> אֵלֶּה טְחֹרֵי הַזָּהָב *these are the haemorrhoids (made) of gold* 1 S 6$_{17}$ (mss עֹפֶל *tumour*). <OBJ> שׁוב hi. *take back*, i.e. repay as guilt offering 1 S 6$_{4(\mathrm{Qr})}$ (|| עַכְבָּר *mouse*) 6$_{17}$, perh. שׁחת hi. *destroy* 1 S 6$_{5(\mathrm{Qr})}$ (|| עַכְבָּר). <CSTR> טְחֹרֵי זָהָב *haemorrhoids (made) of gold* 1 S 6$_{4(\mathrm{Qr}).17}$ (הַזָּהָב), צַלְמֵי טְחֹרֵיכֶם *images of your haemorrhoids* 1 S 6$_{5(\mathrm{Qr}).11}$ (טְחֹרֵיהֶם [mss עָפְלֵיהֶם *their haemorrhoids*]; + עַכְבָּר). <PREP> בְּ of instrument, *by (means of), with*, + נכה hi. *strike*, i.e. infect Dt 28$_{27(\mathrm{Qr})}$ 1 S 5$_{6}$, ho. *be struck*, i.e. infected 1 S 5$_{12(\mathrm{Qr})}$. <COLL> חֲמִשָּׁה טְחֹרֵי *five haemorrhoids of* 1 S 6$_{4(\mathrm{Qr})}$. <SYN> עַכְבָּר *mouse.*

**[טֹטֶפֶת]**, see טוֹטֶפֶת *symbol.*

**[טִיב]** 0.1 n.m. **character,** <CSTR> טיב אשה *a woman's character* Si 42$_{14(\mathrm{B,\ M})}$ (Bmg טוב a woman's *goodness*). <PREP> מִן of comparison, *(more) than* Si 42$_{14(\mathrm{M})}$ (טוב רוע איש מטיב אשה *the wickedness of a man is better than the character of a woman*; or em. מטוב *than the goodness* of a woman).
⇒ טוב *be good.*

**טִיחַ** 1 n.[m.] **plaster,** <NOM CL> אַיֵּה הַטִּיחַ *where is the plaster?* Ezk 13$_{12}$. <OBJ> טוח *plaster (with)* 13$_{12}$.*
⇒ טוח *cover.*

**טִיט** 13.0.5 n.m. **mud**—cstr. טִיט—**mud; clay** for pottery, building work (Is 41$_{25}$ Na 3$_{14}$).

<OBJ> רמס *trample*, i.e. squeeze (of potter) Is 41$_{25}$ (+ חֹמֶר *clay*), גרשׁ *churn up* (of water) Is 57$_{20}$ (1QIsa[a] htp. water will *be churned* into mud; || רֶפֶשׁ *slime*).

<NOM CL> וּבַבּוֹר אֵין־מַיִם כִּי אִם־טִיט *and in the pit there was no water, only mud* Jr 38$_{6}$.

<CSTR> טִיט חוּצוֹת *mud of the streets* 2 S 22$_{43}$||Ps 18$_{43}$ (2 S ־טִיט; + עָפָר *dust*) Mc 7$_{10}$ Zc 9$_{3}$ (+ עָפָר) 10$_{5}$ 1QSb 5$_{27}$, טִיט הַיָּוֵן *mud of the mire* Ps 40$_{3}$ (+ בּוֹר שָׁאוֹן *pit of devastation*) 4QVisSam 5$_{1}$ (טיט יון) 4QPrFêtes$^{c}$ 1.1$_{3}$ (ט[יט חוצות]).

<PREP> בְּ of place, *in(to)* 1QH fr. 2$_{10}$ (ובינתך] בטיט] perh. *and understanding of you is in the mud*; + חֹמֶר *clay*), + בוא *come* Na 3$_{14}$=4QpNah 5$_{3}$ (or em. MT to בוס *trample*; || חֹמֶר), בוס *trample* Na 3$_{14}$ (if em.) Zc 10$_{5}$ (mss כְּ *as though* mud), טבע *sink* Jr 38$_{6}$ (or em. היה *be* in mud).

כְּ *as though* 1QSb 5$_{27}$, + היה *be* Mc 7$_{10}$, דקק hi. *pulverize* 2 S 18$_{43}$||Ps 18$_{43(mss)}$, רקק hi. *empty* 2 S 18$_{43(mss)}$||Ps 18$_{43}$, רקע *beat out* 2 S 18$_{43}$||Ps 18$_{43(mss)}$, בוס *trample* Zc 10$_{5(mss)}$, צבר *amass* gold Zc 9$_{3}$.

מִן of direction, perh. 4QVisSam 5$_{1}$, + עלה hi. *raise* Ps 40$_{3}$, נצל hi. *rescue* Ps 69$_{15}$ (+ מַעֲמַק watery *deep*, שׁוֹאָה *devastation* [if em. שׂנא ptc. *one who hates*]).

עַל *over*, + רפד *spread* threshing sledge Jb 41$_{22}$.

<SYN> רֶפֶשׁ *slime*, חֹמֶר *clay*.*

[טִיף] 0.0.1 n.[m.] **a little,** <COLL> טיף על *a little towards* 3QTr 11$_{17}$ (Wolters; Milik *stand upon*, i.e. טִיף; Allegro טוף *scattered* over, for נטוף, i.e. pass. ptc. of נטף *drip*).*

[טִיף] 0.0.1 n.[m.] perh. **stand** for stove or **duct, channel, tank,** <PREP> עַד *unto*, אמות שלוש עד הטיף *three cubits towards the overflow tank* 3QTr 7$_{15(Allegro)}$. <COLL> טיף על *stand upon* or *channel over* 3QTr 11$_{17}$ (Allegro טוף *scattered* over, for נטוף, i.e. pass. ptc. of נטף *drip*).

[טִיר] 0.0.1 n.m. **wall**—Q טיר—(unless טוּר I *row, wall* or II *rock*) **wall,** or perh. **enclosure, encampment,** <PREP> עַד *unto*, אמות שלוש עד הטור *three cubits up to the wall* 3QTr 7$_{15}$.

⇒ טוּר *row*.

[טִירָה] 7 n.f. **row**—cstr. טִירַת; sf. טִירָתָם; pl. טִירוֹת; sf. טִירֹתֵיהֶם, טִירֹתָם (טירותם)—usu. **encampment, settlement** (Gn 25$_{16}$ Nm 31$_{10}$ Ezk 25$_{4}$ Ps 69$_{26}$ 1 C 6$_{39}$); also **battlement** (Ca 8$_{9}$), appar. **row, course** of masonry, **wall*** (Ezk 46$_{23}$).

<SUBJ> היה *be* Ps 69$_{26}$ (+ אֹהֶל *tent*), שׁמם ni. *be devastated* Ps 69$_{26}$ (mss לְשַׁמָּה *as a devastation* for L נְשַׁמָּה *it is devastated*). <OBJ> בנה *build* Ca 8$_{9}$, ישׁב *establish (settlement)* Ezk 25$_{4}$ (or em. qal *inhabit* or שׂים *place*; || מִשְׁכָּן *tabernacle*), שׂרף *burn* Nm 31$_{10}$ (+ עִיר *city*). <CSTR> טִירַת כֶּסֶף *battlement of silver* Ca 8$_{9}$ (or em. טִירֹת *battlements*). <PREP> לְ *by, in accordance with* 1 C 6$_{39}$ (+ מוֹשָׁב *settlement*); בְּ perh. of place, *in*, or *in accordance with* Gn 25$_{16}$ (+ מוֹשָׁב); תַּחַת *below*, + עשׂה pass. *be made* Ezk 46$_{23}$ (if em. מִתַּחַת *below*; + טוּר *row*). <SYN> מִשְׁכָּן *tabernacle*.

⇒ טוּר *row*.

טַל 31.1.4 n.m. **dew**—טָל; cstr. טַל; sf. טַלֶּךָ; טַלָּם—**dew,** in list of meteorological phenomena, 11QBer 1$_{8}$.

<SUBJ> היה *be* Jg 6$_{37.39.40}$ (all three :: חֹרֶב *dryness*) 1 K 17$_{1}$ (|| מָטָר *rain*), לין *pass night* Jb 29$_{19}$, שׁכם hi. *arise early* Ho 6$_{4}$=13$_{3}$ (+ עָנָן *cloud*), הלך *go* Ho 6$_{4}$=13$_{3}$ (unless at 6$_{4}$ subj. is חֶסֶד *loyalty*), ירד *go down* Nm 11$_{9}$ Ps 133$_{3}$ (+ שֶׁמֶן *oil*, זָקָן Aaron's *beard* [or del.]), נפל *fall* 2 S 17$_{12}$, דשׁן pi. *fatten* Si 43$_{22(Bmg)}$.

<NOM CL> טַל אוֹרֹת טַלֶּךָ *dew of*, i.e. that shines like, *light(s) is your dew* Is 26$_{19}$, לְךָ טַל יַלְדֻתֶיךָ *yours is the dew of your youth* Ps 110$_{3}$ (or em. כְּטַל יְלִדְתִּיךָ *like dew I have given birth to you*), אַל־טַל *let there be not dew* 2 S 1$_{21}$ (|| מָטָר *rain*).

<OBJ> ירד hi. *take down*, i.e. cause to settle 11QBer 1$_{8}$ (|| מָטָר *rain*), נתן *give*, i.e. produce Zc 8$_{12}$ (|| יְבוּל *produce*), ערף *drip* Dt 33$_{28}$ Pr 3$_{20}$, מצה *squeeze* from fleece Jg 6$_{38}$, כלא *withhold* Hg 1$_{10}$ (if em. מִטָּל *some dew* to טַלָּם withhold *their dew*), perh. פרע *loosen*, i.e. scatter Si 43$_{22(Bmg)}$ (unless פרע *hasten* to fatten, with טַל as subj.).

<CSTR> טַל אוֹרֹת *dew of*, i.e. that shines like, *light(s)* Is 26$_{19}$, [ט]ל הארץ *the dew of the earth* 4QJub$^{a}$ 2$_{7}$, טַל הַשָּׁמַיִם *the dew of heaven* Gn 27$_{28.39}$ (both || שָׁמָן *fertile place*) Dt 33$_{13}$ (if em. טָל *dew*; see Prep.), טַל־חֶרְמוֹן *dew of Hermon* Ps 133$_{3}$, טַל יַלְדֻתֶיךָ *dew of your youth* Ps 110$_{3}$ (or em.; see Nom. Cl.); עָב טַל *a cloud of dew* Is 18$_{4}$ 1QM 12$_{8}$ (עבי ט[ל]; + רְבִיב *rain*) 19$_{2}$= fr. 2$_{2}$ ([עבי טל]), מערף ענן טל *dripping of a cloud of dew* Si 43$_{22(B)}$, לחת טל *moisture of dew* 4QTohA 3.2$_{5}$, אֶגְלֵי־טָל *drops of dew* Jb 38$_{28}$ (+

מָטָר *rain*), שִׁכְבַת הַטַּל *the lying down*, i.e. covering, *of dew* Ex 16$_{13.14}$ (הַטָּל), [כל ט]ל *all the dew of* 4QJub$^{a}$ 2$_{7}$.

<APP> perh. מַעֲרָף *dripping* Si 43$_{22(Bmg)}$ (if טַל subj. of פרע *hasten*; see Obj.).

<PREP> לְ of possession, *of, (belonging) to* 4QJub$^{a}$ 2$_{2}$ (מלאכי רוחות ... [לטל] *the angels of the spirits of dew*); כְּ *as* Ho 6$_{4}$=13$_{3}$ Pr 19$_{12}$ (+ עַל־עֵשֶׂב like dew *upon grass*) Ps 110$_{3}$ (if em.; see Nom. Cl.) 133$_{3}$, + היה *be* Ho 14$_{6}$ Mc 5$_{6}$ (+ רְבִיב *rain*), נזל *flow* Dt 32$_{2}$ (Sam mss אזל ni. *go out*; ‖ מָטָר *rain*); מִן partitive, *(some) of, (any) of*, + היה *be* Gn 27$_{39}$, נתן *give* Gn 37$_{28}$, כלא *withhold* Hg 1$_{10}$ (or em. מִטָּל *some dew* to טַלָּם *their dew* or מָטָר *rain* or מִטֵּל, from טלל III, *from giving dew*); + יְבוּל *produce*); of cause, *on account of* Dt 33$_{13}$ (or em. מִטָּל to מֵעָל *above*, or rd. מטל הַשָּׁמַיִם מֵעָל *on account of the dew of the heavens above*, or מֵטֵל, i.e. טלל III, *bedewing*); עַל *upon*, + ירד *go down* (of manna) Nm 11$_{9}$.

<COLL> רֹאשִׁי נִמְלָא־טָל *my head is full of dew* Ca 5$_{2}$ (+ רְסִיס *drop of dew*).

<SYN> מָטָר *rain*, שָׁמָן *fertile place*, יְבוּל *produce*.

<ANT> חֹרֶב *dryness*.*

**טלא** 8 vb. **patch—Qal** 7 Ptc. טְלֻאוֹת, טְלֻאִים, טָלוּא (טְלֻאֹת)—pass. ptc. as adj., **spotted,** perh. **embroidered** or **colourful** (Ezk 16$_{16}$), **a.** used attributively of בָּמָה *high place* Ezk 16$_{16}$, שֶׂה *sheep*, i.e. goat Gn 30$_{32}$ (‖ נָקֹד *speckled* [or del. נָקֹד and טָלוּא *spotted*) 30$_{32}$ (with ellipsis of שֶׂה; ‖ נָקֹד, + חום *brown*), עֵז *(she-)goat* Gn 30$_{35}$ (‖ נָקֹד, + חום), תַּיִשׁ *he-goat* Gn 30$_{35}$ (‖ עָקֹד *striped* [or em. נָקֹד]).

**b.** used predicatively of כֹּל *all*, i.e. every sheep Gn 30$_{33}$ (‖ נָקֹד, + חום).

**c.** as noun, **spotted (kid),** <OBJ> ילד *give birth (to)* Gn 30$_{39}$ (‖ עָקֹד, נָקֹד). <SYN> נָקֹד *speckled*, עָקֹד *striped*.

**Pu.** 1 Ptc. מְטֻלָּאוֹת—ptc. as adj., **patched, full of patches,** used attributively of נַעַל *shoe* Jos 9$_{5}$ (‖ בָּלֶה *worn*). <SYN> בָּלֶה *worn*.

**טְלָאִים** 1 pl.n. **Telaim,** place where Saul's troops mustered, perh. ident. with Telem at Jos 15$_{24}$, <PREP> בְּ of place, *in, at*, + פקד *visit*, i.e. muster 1 S 15$_{4}$ (or em. Gilgal or Telem).

**טָלֶה** 3 n.m. **lamb**—cstr. טְלֵה; pl. טְלָאִים (Q טלים), <SUBJ> רעה *graze* Is 65$_{25}$ (:: זְאֵב *wolf*; ‖ בָּקָר *ox*).

<OBJ> לקח *take* 1 S 7$_{9}$, קבץ pi. *gather* Is 40$_{11}$, נשׂא *raise*, i.e. pick up Is 40$_{11}$, עלה hi. *raise*, i.e. offer in sacrifice 1 S 7$_{9(Qr)}$ Si 46$_{16(Segal)}$ ([טלה]).

<CSTR> טְלֵה חָלָב *lamb of milk*, i.e. suckling lamb 1 S 7$_{9}$ Si 46$_{16(Segal)}$ ([טלה ח]ל[ב]).

<ADJ> אֶחָד *one* 1 S 7$_{9}$.

<SYN> בָּקָר *ox*.

<ANT> זְאֵב *wolf*.

**טלטל**, see טול *throw*, Pilp.

**טַלְטֵלָה** 1 n.f. **hurling** or **shaking,** <COLL> י׳ מְטַלְטֶלְךָ טַלְטֵלָה גָּבֶר *Y. is hurling/shaking you with a hurling/shaking*, i.e. violently, *O man* Is 22$_{17}$ (or em. טַלְטֵל הַגֶּבֶר *hurling, O man*, i.e. טול inf. pilp.; or כְּטַלְטֵל הַבֶּגֶד *as shaking*, i.e. as he might shake, *a garment*).

→ טול *throw*.

**טלל** I 1 vb. **cover—Pi.** 1 + waw וִיטַלְלֶנּוּ (mss וִיטַלְּלֶנּוּ) **cover, roof,** <SUBJ> Shallun Ne 3$_{15}$ (mss Shallum; + חזק hi. *strengthen*, i.e. repair, בנה *build*, + עמד hi. *establish*), בֵּן *son* 3$_{15}$, perh. שַׂר *prince* 3$_{15}$. <OBJ> שַׁעַר *gate* 3$_{15}$.

**[טלל]** II 0.0.1 vb. **fall—Hi.** 0.0.1 Ptc. מטלים—**cause to fall,** נתתי ... לחיי למטלים *I have given ... my cheeks to those who make me fall* 1QIsa$^{a}$ 50$_{6}$ (‖ נכה hi. *strike*; MT מרט *pluck*). <SYN> נכה hi. *strike*.*

* **[טלל]** III vb. **give dew—Qal, give dew,** כָּלְאוּ שָׁמַיִם מִטֵּל *(the) heavens have held back from giving dew* Hg 1$_{10}$ (if em. מִטָּל *some dew*).

**Hi., drip dew,** מִמֶּגֶד שָׁמַיִם מֵטֵל *by means of the bounty of the heavens dripping dew* Dt 33$_{13}$ (+ רבץ *crouch*; if em. מִטָּל *on account of dew*).

**[טֶלֶם]** pl.n. **Telam,** town of Judah in Negeb, where Saul's troops mustered, <SUBJ> היה *be* Jos 15$_{24}$ (if em. Telem). <APP> עִיר *city* Jos 15$_{24}$. <PREP> בְּ of place, *in, at*, + פקד *visit*, i.e. muster 1 S 15$_{4}$ (if em. Telaim); מִן of direction, + נכה hi. *strike* Amalek 1 S 15$_{7}$ (if em.

Havilah; + Shur); of possession, *of, (belonging) to* 1 S 27$_{8}$ (if em. Olam; + Shur).

**טֶלֶם** I 1 pr.n.m. **Telem,** gatekeeper, husband of a foreign wife in Ezra's time, <NOM CL> וּמִן־הַשֹּׁעֲרִים שַׁלֻּם וָטֶלֶם *and of the gatekeepers were Shallum and Telem* Ezr 10$_{24}$.

**טֶלֶם** II 1 pl.n. **Telem,** town of Judah in Negeb, perh. ident. with Telaim at 1 S 15$_{4}$. <SUBJ> היה *be* Jos 15$_{24}$ (or em. Telam). <APP> עִיר *city* Jos 15$_{24}$. <PREP> בְּ of place, *in, at,* + פקד *visit,* i.e. muster 1 S 15$_{4}$ (if em. Telaim).

**טַלְמוֹן** 5 pr.n.m. **Talmon**—טַלְמֹן—head of family of gatekeepers at time of Nehemiah, <SUBJ> שׁמר *keep* Ne 12$_{25}$, שׁער *act as gatekeeper* Ne 12$_{25}$. <NOM CL> הַשֹּׁעֲרִים עַקּוּב טַלְמוֹן *the gatekeepers were Akkub (and) Talmon* Ne 11$_{19}$, sim. 1 C 9$_{17}$ (טַלְמֹן). <CSTR> בְּנֵי־טַלְמוֹן *sons of Talmon* Ezr 2$_{42}$||Ne 7$_{45}$ (טַלְמֹן).

**טמא** 162.0.57 vb. **be impure—Qal** 77.0.23 Pf. טָמֵא, טָמְאַת, Q טמאו; impf. יִטְמָא, 3fs תִּטְמָא, Q יטמאו; + waw Q וטמא, וְטָמְאוּ, וְטָמְאָה; 3fs וַתִּטְמָא, וַיִּטְמְאוּ; inf. טָמְאָה—**be(come) impure, unclean,** alw. ritually, e.g. because of contact with unclean animals (e.g. Lv 22$_{5}$) or their carcasses (e.g. Lv 11$_{24}$), clean animals that die naturally (e.g. Lv 11$_{39}$ 17$_{15}$), human corpse (e.g. Nm 19$_{11}$ Ezk 44$_{25}$ CD 12$_{18}$ 4QTohA 1.1$_{9}$ 11QT 49$_{5}$ 50$_{11}$); because of leprosy (e.g. Lv 13$_{14}$ 11QT 49$_{4}$) or contact with a house with leprosy (e.g. Lv 14$_{36}$); because of prohibited sexual intercourse (e.g. Lv 18$_{20}$), emission of semen (e.g. Lv 15$_{16}$), childbirth (e.g. Lv 12$_{2}$ 4QSD 7.2$_{15}$), contact with menstruous woman (e.g. Lv 15$_{19}$), contact with person with discharge (e.g. Lv 15$_{4}$); because of idolatry (e.g. Ezk 22$_{3}$), sin (e.g. Ps 106$_{39}$).

<SUBJ> Israelite(s) Lv 18$_{20.23}$ 19$_{31}$ Ps 106$_{39}$ (|| זנה *prostitute oneself*) 11QT 51$_{7}$ (unless htp.), Oholibah Ezk 23$_{17}$, אִישׁ *man* Lv 15$_{5.16.18.24}$ 22$_{5.2}$ Nm 19$_{20}$ 4QTohB$^{b}$ 1$_{5}$ ([איש] ... וט[מה]), אִשָּׁה *woman* Lv 12$_{2.2.5}$ 15$_{18}$ 4QSD 7.2$_{15.15.16}$ (all three [אשה]) 11QT 50$_{11}$, אָדָם *human being* Lv 5$_{3}$ 13$_{14}$, person Hg 1$_{31}$, נֶפֶשׁ *soul,* i.e. person Lv 5$_{2}$ (|| אשׁם *be guilty*; Gnz ידע *he knows*) 17$_{15}$ 22$_{6.8}$ Nm 19$_{22}$, נגע ptc. *one who touches* Lv 11$_{24+5t}$ 15$_{7+7t}$ Nm 19$_{11.21}$ 4QTohB$^{b}$ 1$_{13}$ (וט[מה]) 11QT 50$_{12.13}$ 51$_{2}$ ([הנוגע]), נשׂא ptc. *one who carries* Lv 11$_{25.28.40}$ 15$_{10}$ 4QTohB$^{b}$ 1$_{5}$ (והנוש[א] ... יט[מא]) 1$_{13}$, אסף ptc. *one who gathers* Nm 19$_{10}$ 4QTohB$^{a}$ 1$_{8}$ ([האוס]ף ... [וטמאו]), אכל ptc. *one who eats* Lv 11$_{40}$, שׂרף ptc. *one who burns* Nm 19$_{8}$ 4QTohB$^{a}$ 1$_{8}$ ([השורף]... [וטמאו]), בוא ptc. *one who enters* Lv 14$_{46}$ Nm 19$_{14}$ 11QT 49$_{6}$, ישׁב ptc. *one who sits* Lv 15$_{6}$, זוב ptc. *one who has a discharge* Lv 15$_{32}$, צָרֻעַ *leper* Lv 13$_{46}$, כֹּהֵן *priest* Nm 19$_{7}$ Ezk 44$_{25}$ 4QTohB$^{a}$ 1$_{8}$ ([הכוהן] ... [וטמאו]), טָהוֹר *pure one* Lv 18$_{8}$.

object Hg 2$_{13}$, אֹכֶל *food* Lv 11$_{34}$ 11QT 49$_{7}$, מַשְׁקֶה *drink* Lv 11$_{34}$ 11QT 49$_{8.9}$ (both מושקה), בֶּגֶד *garment* Lv 11$_{32}$ 15$_{17}$, עוֹר *skin* Lv 11$_{32}$ 15$_{17}$, שַׂק *sack* Lv 11$_{32}$, מִשְׁכָּב *bed* Lv 15$_{4.24}$, מֶרְכָּב *saddle* Lv 15$_{9}$, מַסְמֵר *nail* CD 12$_{18}$, יָתֵד *peg* CD 12$_{18}$, כְּלִי *vessel* Lv 11$_{32}$ 15$_{4}$ CD 12$_{18}$ 11QT 49$_{8}$ 50$_{11}$, פתח pass. ptc. *open vessel* 11QT 49$_{9}$, אֶרֶץ *land* Lv 18$_{25.27}$, עִיר *city* Ezk 22$_{3.4}$ (|| אשׁם *be guilty*) 11QT 49$_{4}$, בַּיִת *house* 11QT 49$_{5}$ 50$_{11}$, אֲשֶׁר *one who* Lv 15$_{32}$, כֹּל *everyone, everything* Lv 11$_{32.33.35}$ 14$_{36}$ 15$_{11. 20.20}$ Nm 19$_{14.16.22}$ 11QT 49$_{6.9}$; subj. not specified, 4Q TohA 1.1$_{9}$.

<PREP> לְ of agent, *by (means of), through,* + אָדָם *human being* Lv 22$_{5}$, שֶׁרֶץ *swarming thing* Lv 22$_{5}$; *because of,* + נֶפֶשׁ *soul,* i.e. corpse 4QTohA 1.1$_{9}$; of benefit, *to, for,* + אִישׁ *man* 11QT 49$_{9}$, אָדָם *human being* 11QT 49$_{9}$; *with respect to.* + טֻמְאָה *impurity* Lv 22$_{5}$.

בְּ of instrument, agent, *by (means of), with,* + Babylonians Ezk 23$_{17}$, אִשָּׁה *wife* Lv 18$_{20}$, אוֹב *medium* Lv 19$_{31}$, יִדְּעֹנִי *familiar spirit* Lv 19$_{31}$, בְּהֵמָה *beast* Lv 18$_{23}$, נְבֵלָה *carcass* Lv 22$_{8}$, טְרֵפָה *torn animal* Lv 22$_{8}$, גִּלּוּל *idol* Ezk 22$_{4}$, מַעֲשֶׂה *deed* Ps 106$_{39}$, טֻמְאָה *impurity* Lv 5$_{3}$ CD 12$_{18}$.

כְּ *as* Lv 12$_{2.5}$ 4QSD 7.2$_{15}$.

עַד *until,* + עֶרֶב *evening* Lv 11$_{24+7t}$ 14$_{46}$ 15$_{5+14t}$ 17$_{15}$ 22$_{6}$ Nm 19$_{7.8.10.21.22}$ 4QTohB$^{a}$ 1$_{8}$ ([וטמאו עד הערב]) 4Q TohB$^{b}$ 1$_{5}$ ([וט]מה עד הע[ר]ב) 1$_{13}$ ([וט]מה עד [ה]ערב) 1$_{13}$ 11QT 50$_{12}$ 51$_{2}$ ([עו]ד ה[ערב]).

<COLL> טמא + noun used adverbially יוֹם *day* Lv 12$_{2}$ 13$_{46}$ 15$_{24}$ Nm 19$_{11.14.16}$ 4QSD 7.2$_{15}$ 11QT 49$_{5.6}$ 50$_{11.11.13}$, שָׁבוּעַ *week* Lv 12$_{5}$ 4QSD 7.2$_{16}$ ([שבעים]).

Also 4QTohA 3.2$_{1}$ 4QTohB$^{b}$ 1$_{12}$ 4QRitPur 40$_{1}$ ([י]טמא).

<SYN> זנה *prostitute oneself,* אשׁם *be guilty.*

**Ni.** 18.0.1 Pf. נִטְמָא, נִטְמְאָה (נִטְמָאָה), נִטְמֵאת, נִטְמֵאתִי, נִטְמְאוּ, נִטְמֵאתֶם; + waw וְנִטְמֵתֶם, וְנִטְמָאָה; ptc. נִטְמְאִים—**defile oneself,** by eating unclean animals (Lv 11$_{43}$), through prohibited sexual acts (e.g. Lv 18$_{24}$ Nm 5$_{13}$), idolatry (e.g. Jr 2$_{23}$ Ezk 20$_{30}$ 23$_{7}$), <SUBJ> Israel(ites) Lv 11$_{43}$ Jr 2$_{23}$ (+ הלך *go* after baalim) Ho 5$_{3}$ (+ זנה hi. *prostitute oneself*) 6$_{10}$=4QpHos$^{b}$ 10$_{1}$ ([נטמא]), בַּיִת *house* of Israel Ezk 20$_{30}$ (+ זנה *prostitute oneself*) 20$_{31.43}$, Oholah Ezk 23$_{7}$, Oholibah Ezk 23$_{13.30}$, אִשָּׁה *wife* Nm 5$_{13.14.14.20}$ (+ שׂטה *turn aside*) 5$_{27}$ (+ מעל *be unfaithful*) 5$_{28.29}$ (+ שׂטה), גּוֹי *nation* Lv 18$_{24}$.

<PREP> לְ of instrument, *by (means of)*, + גִּלּוּל *idol* Ezk 20$_{31}$; בְּ of instrument, *by (means of), with*, + שֶׁרֶץ *swarming thing* Lv 11$_{43}$, גִּלּוּל *idol* Ezk 23$_{7.30}$, דֶּרֶךְ *way* Ezk 20$_{30.43}$, עֲלִילָה *deed* Ezk 20$_{43}$, אֵלֶּה *these* Lv 18$_{24}$.

Also 11QT 50$_{3}$.

**Pi.** 50.0.27 Pf. טִמֵּא (טִמָּה), טִמֵּאת, טִמְּאוּ (טִמְּאוּהָ), טִמֵּאתֶם; impf. יְטַמֵּא, 2ms תְּטַמֵּא (Q תטמאנו), יְטַמְּאֻנוּ, יְטַמְּאוּ, תְּטַמְּאוּ; + waw וְטִמֵּא (וְטִמְּאוֹ), Q וטמאום, וְטִמֵּאתֶם; וַיְטַמֵּא, וַיְטַמְּאֵהוּ (Q ויטמאנו), וָאֲטַמֵּא, וַיְטַמְּאוּ, וַתְּטַמְּאוּ; impv. טַמְּאוּ; ptc. Q מטמא, Q מטמאים; inf. abs. טַמֵּא, cstr. טַמֵּא (טַמְּאוֹ, טַמְּאָם, טַמַּאֲכֶם)—**1. make impure, make unclean, defile, desecrate,** alw. ritually, e.g. through sexual acts (e.g. Gn 34$_{5}$ Lv 18$_{28}$ Ezk 18$_{6}$ 22$_{11}$ CD 12$_{1}$), sacrifice of children (Lv 20$_{3}$), bloodshed (Nm 35$_{34}$), contact with corpse (e.g. Nm 6$_{9}$ 19$_{13}$), idolatry (e.g. Ezk 36$_{18}$); in deliberate act of desecration (e.g. 2 K 23$_{8}$ Is 30$_{22}$).

<SUBJ> Y. Ezk 20$_{26}$, Israel(ites) Lv 11$_{44}$ 15$_{31}$ 18$_{28}$ Nm 5$_{3}$ 35$_{34}$ Dt 21$_{23}$ Jr 2$_{7}$ (+ שׂים לְתוֹעֵבָה *make into an abomination*) 7$_{30}$ 32$_{34}$ 36$_{17.18}$ 43$_{7.8}$ 4QJub$^{c}$ 2$_{26}$ ([טמאו]) 11QT 47$_{10.17}$ 48$_{10}$ 64$_{12}$, Babylonians Ezk 23$_{17}$, עַם *people* Is 30$_{22}$ 2 C 36$_{14}$ 4QMMT B$_{81}$ ([העם] ... מטמא[ים]), גּוֹי *nation* Ps 79$_{1}$, Josiah 2 K 23$_{8.10.16}$, Shechem Gn 34$_{5.13}$, Oholah Ezk 23$_{38}$ (‖ חלל pi. *profane*), Oholibah Ezk 23$_{38}$, אִישׁ *man* Lv 20$_{3}$ (‖ חלל pi.) Nm 6$_{12}$ (if em.; see Obj.) 19$_{20}$ Jr 32$_{34}$ Ezk 9$_{7}$ 18$_{6.15}$ 22$_{11}$ (+ עשׂה תּוֹעֵבָה *do abomination*, ענה pi. *defile*) 33$_{26}$ CD 11$_{20}$ 12$_{1}$ 11QT 45$_{10}$ ([א]יש) 45$_{13}$, אִשָּׁה *woman* Nm 6$_{12}$ (if em.; see Obj.) 11QT 48$_{16}$, בֵּן *son* Ezk 18$_{11}$, מֶלֶךְ *king* 2 K 23$_{13}$ Jr 32$_{34}$ Ezk 43$_{7}$, שַׂר *prince* Jr 32$_{34}$ 2 C 36$_{14}$, כֹּהֵן *priest* 2 K 23$_{8(ms)}$ 1QpHab 12$_{8}$, נָבִיא *prophet* Jr 32$_{34}$, פָּרִיץ *violent one* Ezk 18$_{11}$, טָמֵא *impure one* CD 10$_{13}$, מֵת *dead one* Nm 6$_{9}$, נגע ptc. *one who touches* Nm 19$_{13}$ perh. 4QTohA 1.1$_{8}$ (but prob. טָמֵא adj. *impure*), נגע pu. ptc. *stricken one* 11QT 48$_{15}$, יֹשֵׁב *inhabitant* Jr 32$_{34}$, outsiders CD 5$_{6.11}$, עִיר *city* Gn 34$_{27}$, Jerusalem Ezk 5$_{11}$, בַּיִת *house* of Peleg CD 20$_{23}$, עֵץ *wood* CD 12$_{17}$, אֶבֶן *stone* CD 12$_{17}$, עָפָר *dust* CD 12$_{17}$, שֹׁחַד *bribe* 11QT 51$_{14}$.

<OBJ> Israel Ezk 20$_{26}$, Dinah Gn 34$_{5.13}$, Oholibah Ezk 23$_{17}$, אִשָּׁה *wife* Ezk 18$_{6.11.15}$ 33$_{26}$, בַּת *daughter* Gn 34$_{5}$, כַּלָּה *daughter-in-law* Ezk 22$_{11}$, אָחוֹת *sister* Gn 34$_{13}$, נגע ptc. *one who touches* CD 12$_{17}$, נֶפֶשׁ *soul,* i.e. self Lv 11$_{44}$, רוּחַ *spirit* CD 5$_{11}$ 4QD$^{e}$ 9.2$_{11}$, ראשׁ *head* Nm 6$_{9.12}$ 6$_{12}$ (if em. טָמֵא *impure* to טִמֵּא ראשׁ *he has defiled the head of* his consecration), זֶרַע *seed* 4QMMT B$_{81}$ ([מטמאי]ם), צִפּוּי *plating* of idols Is 30$_{22}$, מִזְבֵּחַ *altar* 2 K 23$_{16}$ CD 11$_{20}$, בַּיִת *house,* i.e. temple Jr 7$_{30}$ 32$_{34}$ Ezk 9$_{7}$ 2 C 36$_{14}$ 11QT 51$_{14}$, הֵיכָל *temple* Ps 79$_{1}$, מִשְׁכָּן *tabernacle* Lv 15$_{31}$ Nm 19$_{13}$, מִקְדָּשׁ *sanctuary* Lv 20$_{3}$ Nm 19$_{20}$ Ezk 5$_{11}$ 23$_{38}$ CD 5$_{6}$ 20$_{23}$ 1QpHab 12$_{8}$ 4Q183 1.2$_{1}$ 4QpsMos$^{e}$ 2.1$_{9}$ 11QT 45$_{10}$ 47$_{17}$, קֹדֶשׁ *holiness,* i.e. sanctuary 4QJub$^{f}$ 23$_{21}$ ([ויטמאו את קודש הקודשים] *and they will defile the holy of holies*), בָּמָה *high place* 2 K 23$_{8.13}$, מַחֲנֶה *camp* Nm 5$_{3}$, אֶרֶץ *land* Lv 18$_{28}$ Nm 35$_{34}$ Jr 2$_{7}$ Ezk 36$_{18}$ 11QT 48$_{10}$, אֲדָמָה *land* Dt 21$_{23}$ Ezk 36$_{17}$ 11QT 64$_{12}$, Topheth 2 K 23$_{10}$, עִיר *city* CD 12$_{1}$ 11QT 45$_{13}$ 47$_{10.17}$ 48$_{15}$, מַיִם *water* CD 10$_{13}$, יוֹם *day* 4QJub$^{c}$ 2$_{26}$ ([טמאו]), תְּרוּמָה *offering* perh. 4QMMT B$_{4}$ ([תרומת] ... מטמ[אים]), שֵׁם *name* Ezk 43$_{7.8}$.

<PREP> לְ introducing object, + נֶפֶשׁ *soul* 4QD$^{f}$ 1.2$_{11}$. בְּ of place, time, *in, on,* + יוֹם *day* Ezk 23$_{38}$; of instrument, *by (means of), with,* + פֶּגֶר *corpse* Ezk 43$_{7}$, שֶׁרֶץ *swarming thing* Lv 11$_{44}$, שִׁקּוּץ *detestable thing* Ezk 5$_{11}$, תּוֹעֵבָה *abomination* Ezk 5$_{11}$ 43$_{8}$, גִּלּוּל *idol* Ezk 36$_{18}$, מַתָּנָה *gift* Ezk 20$_{26}$, זְנוּת *prostitution* Ezk 43$_{7}$, תַּזְנוּת *prostitution* Ezk 23$_{17}$, זִמָּה *lewdness* Ezk 22$_{11}$, נִדָּה *impurity* CD 12$_{1}$ 11QT 48$_{16}$, טָמְאָה *defilement* 4QJub$^{f}$ 23$_{21}$ ([ויטמאו ... בטמ]א), דֶּרֶךְ *way* Ezk 36$_{17}$, עֲלִילָה *deed* Ezk 36$_{17}$, מַיִם *water* CD 10$_{13}$; *because of,* + עָוֹן *iniquity* 11QT 51$_{14}$.

כְּפִי *according to,* + טֻמְאָה *impurity* CD 12$_{17}$.

בְּתוֹךְ *within,* + עִיר *city* 11QT 48$_{16}$.

<COLL> טמא pi. + adverb עוֹד *again* Ezk 43$_{7}$.

**2. declare impure, unclean,** in connection with leprosy (Lv 13$_{3+10t}$ 11QT 48$_{17}$), animals and birds (Lv 20$_{25}$ 11QT 50$_{20}$), <SUBJ> Israel Lv 20$_{25}$ (Sam לְטֻמְאָה *for impurity*), כֹּהֵן *priest* Lv 13$_{3+10t}$ (at 13$_{59}$ :: טהר pi. *declare pure*) 11QT 48$_{17}$. <OBJ> אָדָם *human being* Lv 13$_{3+7t}$, אִישׁ *man* Lv 13$_{44}$, נֶגַע *disease*, i.e. diseased person Lv 13$_{30}$, צָרֻעַ *leper* 11QT 48$_{17}$, בֶּגֶד *garment* Lv 13$_{59}$, כְּלִי *article* of leather Lv 13$_{59}$, בְּהֵמָה *beast* Lv 20$_{25}$, חֹלֶד *weasel* 11QT 50$_{20}$, עַכְבָּר *mouse* 11QT 50$_{20}$, חֹמֶט *lizard* 11QT 50$_{20}$, צָב *lizard* 11QT 50$_{20}$, לְטָאָה *lizard* 11QT 50$_{20}$, כֹּחַ *lizard* 11QT 50$_{20}$, תִּנְשֶׁמֶת *chameleon* 11QT 50$_{20}$, עוֹף *birds* Lv 20$_{25}$, שֶׁרֶץ *swarming thing* 11QT 50$_{20}$, כֹּל *everything, everyone* Lv 20$_{25}$ 4QMidrEschat$^{b}$ 9$_{16}$.

Also 11QT 3$_{6}$ perh. 4QOrd$^{b}$ 2$_{24}$ (unless adj. טָמֵא *impure*) perh. 4QOrd$^{c}$ 2$_{2}$ (unless adj. טָמֵא).

<SYN> §1 חלל pi. *profane*.

<ANT> §2 טהר pi. *declare pure*.

**Pu.** 1 Ptc. מְטֻמָּאָה—**be defiled,** <SUBJ> נֶפֶשׁ *soul*, i.e. self Ezk 4$_{14}$, בַּיִת *house* Jr 19$_{13}$ (if em. הַטְּמֵאִים *the impure* houses to מְטֻמָּאִים *defiled*).

**Htp.** 15.0.6 Pf. Q הטמא; impf. יִטַּמָּא, תִּטַּמְּאוּ (תִּטַּמָּאוּ), יִטַּמְּאוּ (L יִטַּמָּאוּ, יִטַּמְּאוּ, L יִטַּמָּאוּ)—**defile oneself, be defiled,** e.g. through contact with unclean animals (e.g. Lv 11$_{24}$), with human corpse (e.g. Lv 21$_{1}$ Nm 6$_{7}$), sexual acts (e.g. Lv 18$_{24}$), idolatry (e.g. Ezk 20$_{7}$), <SUBJ> Israel(ites) Lv 11$_{24.43}$ 18$_{24.30}$ Ezk 14$_{11}$ 37$_{23}$ 11QT 47$_{5}$ 51$_{2.6}$, אָדָם *human being* 11QT 49$_{21}$, אִישׁ *man* Nm 6$_{7}$ Ezk 20$_{7}$, אִשָּׁה *woman* Nm 6$_{7}$, בֵּן *son* Ezk 20$_{18}$ 44$_{25}$ 4QMidrEschat$^{a}$ 3$_{16}$ ([יטמאו]), כֹּהֵן *priest* Lv 21$_{1.3.4.11}$ Ezk 44$_{25}$ 1QT 16$_{5}$, לֵוִי *Levite* Ezk 44$_{25}$, אכל ptc. *one who eats* Ho 9$_{4}$, הָמוֹן *multitude* 4QpsEzek$^{b}$ 3.2$_{4}$, מַעֲשֶׂה *deed* 4QMyst$^{a}$ 2.2$_{3}$ ([הטמ]אה).

<PREP> לְ *for (the sake of)*, + נֶפֶשׁ *soul*, i.e. dead one Lv 21$_{1}$, אָב *father* Lv 21$_{11}$ Nm 6$_{7}$ Ezk 44$_{25}$ 1QT 16$_{5}$ ([לאביו]), אֵם *mother* Lv 21$_{11}$ Nm 6$_{7}$ Ezk 44$_{25}$ 1QT 16$_{5}$ ([ולאמו]), בֵּן *son* Ezk 44$_{25}$, בַּת *daughter* Ezk 44$_{25}$, אָח *brother* Nm 6$_{7}$ Ezk 44$_{25}$, אָחוֹת *sister* Lv 21$_{3}$ Nm 6$_{7}$ Ezk 44$_{25}$, בְּתוּלָה *young woman* Lv 21$_{3}$.

לְ of instrument, agent, *by (means of)*, + אֵלֶּה *these* Lv 11$_{24}$.

בְּ of instrument, *by means of* 11QT 51$_{2.6}$, + שֶׁרֶץ *swarming thing* Lv 11$_{43}$, שִׁקּוּץ *detestable thing* Ezk 37$_{23}$, גִּלּוּל *idol* Ezk 20$_{7.18}$ 37$_{23}$ 4QMidrEschat$^{a}$ 3$_{16}$ ([יטמאו ... בכול גלוליהמה]), חֹק *custom* Lv 18$_{30}$, פֶּשַׁע *transgression* Ezk 14$_{11}$ 37$_{23}$, טֻמְאָה *impurity* 11QT 47$_{5}$, אֵלֶּה *these* Lv 18$_{24}$.

עַל *by (means of)* 11QT 49$_{21}$.

<COLL> טמא htp. + adverb, עוֹד *again* Ezk 14$_{11}$ 37$_{23}$ 4QMidrEschat$^{a}$ 3$_{16}$ ([יטמאו עוד]); + noun predicate, בַּעַל *(as a) husband* Lv 21$_{4}$.

**Hothp.** 1 Pf. הֻטַּמָּאָה—**be defiled, be made impure, unclean,** <SUBJ> אִשָּׁה *wife* Dt 24$_{4}$.*

→ טָמֵא *impure*, טֻמְאָה *impurity*, טָמְאָה *impurity*.

**טָמֵא** 87.0.45 adj. **impure**—cstr. טְמֵא; fem. sing. טְמֵאָה; cstr. טְמֵאַת; masc. pl. טְמֵאִים; cstr. Q טמאי—**1.** used attributively of אִישׁ *man* CD 11$_{19}$, בְּהֵמָה *beast* Lv 5$_{2}$ 7$_{21}$ 20$_{25}$ (:: טָהוֹר *pure*) 27$_{11.27}$ Nm 18$_{15}$ 4QD$^{e}$ 9.2$_{8}$ ([הבהמ]ה) 4QMMT B$_{21}$ ([הבהמה הטמאה]), חַיָּה *beast* Lv 5$_{2}$ GnzPs 1$_{5}$, עוֹף *birds* Lv 20$_{25}$ (:: טָהוֹר) 11QT 46$_{2.3}$ ([עוף טמא]), שֶׁרֶץ *swarming thing* Lv 5$_{2}$ 7$_{21 (mss, Sam)}$, שֶׁקֶץ *detestable thing* Lv 7$_{21}$, דָּבָר *thing* Lv 5$_{2}$, מָקוֹם *place* Lv 14$_{40.41.45}$, בַּיִת *house* Jr 19$_{13}$ (or em. מְטֻמָּאִים *defiled*, i.e. טמא pu.), אֲדָמָה *land* Am 7$_{17}$, הוֹן *wealth* CD 6$_{15}$, לֶחֶם *bread* Ezk 4$_{13}$, זוֹב *discharge* 4QD$^{e}$ 9.2$_{12}$ ([טמ]א).

**2a.** in nom. cl. used predicatively of אָדָם *human being* Lv 13$_{11}$, אִישׁ *man* Lv 13$_{44}$ Nm 9$_{7}$ 19$_{20}$ 1QH fr. 1$_{5}$ ([טמא]) 4QD$^{a}$ 9.2$_{3}$ ([איש] ... [טמא]) 11QT 50$_{7}$, אִשָּׁה *woman* Lv 15$_{25}$, צָרֻעַ *leper* Lv 13$_{45.46}$, נֶגַע *disease* Lv 13$_{51.55}$ 14$_{44}$, i.e. diseased person Lv 13$_{36}$ perh. 4QD$^{a}$ 9.1$_{11}$, נגע ptc. *one who touches* 4QTohA 1.1$_{8}$ (unless טמא pi. *make impure*), זוֹב *discharge* Lv 15$_{2}$, בָּשָׂר *flesh* Lv 13$_{15}$, בְּהֵמָה *beast* Lv 11$_{26.28}$, שֶׁרֶץ *swarming thing* Dt 14$_{19}$, אַרְנֶבֶת *hare* Lv 11$_{6.8}$ Dt 14$_{7}$, גָּמָל *camel* Lv 11$_{4.8}$ Dt 14$_{7}$, חֲזִיר *swine* Lv 11$_{7.8}$ Dt 14$_{8}$, שָׁפָן *rock badger* Lv 11$_{5.8}$ Dt 14$_{7}$, הלך ptc. *one that goes on paws* Lv 11$_{27.28}$, זֶרַע *seed* Lv 11$_{38}$, אֶרֶץ *land* Jos 22$_{19}$, כְּלִי *vessel* Nm 19$_{15}$ 11QT 50$_{18}$, תַּנּוּר *oven* Lv 11$_{35}$, כִּירַיִם *stove* Lv 11$_{35}$, נֵזֶר *consecration* Nm 6$_{12}$ (or em. טָמֵא to טִמֵּא ראשׁ *he has defiled the head of* his consecration), מַעֲשֶׂה *deed* Hg 2$_{14}$; כֹּל אֲשֶׁר אֵין־לוֹ סְנַפִּיר וְקַשְׂקֶשֶׂת *anything that does not have fins and scales* Dt 14$_{10}$.

**2b.** with היה *be*, as predicate of אִישׁ *man* Nm 9$_{6.10}$, נגע ptc. *one who touches* Nm 19$_{13}$, מאס ptc. *one who* *refuses* to enter covenant 1QS 3$_{5.5}$ perh. 5QRègle 4$_{3.3}$, בַּיִת *house* Jr 19$_{13}$ (if em. הַטְּמֵאִים *the impure* [houses] to טְמֵאִים [will be] *impure*), תַּנּוּר *oven* Lv 11$_{35}$, כִּיר *stove* Lv 11$_{35}$, כְּלִי *article* Lv 15$_{26}$.

<COLL> (§§2a,b) טָמֵא + לְנֶפֶשׁ אָדָם impure *through the soul of*, i.e. through touching the dead of, *human beings* Nm 9$_{6.7.10}$; [טמא ב]אשמת רשעה *impure with the guilt of wickedness* 1QH fr. 1$_{5}$.

**2c.** as cry of leper (Lv 13$_{45}$), or at one defiled with blood (Lm 4$_{15}$), <COLL> טָמֵא טָמֵא יִקְרָא *he shall cry, Impure, impure* Lv 13$_{45}$, sim. 4QTohA 1.1$_{3}$, סוּרוּ טָמֵא קָרְאוּ לָמוֹ *turn aside, impure, they cried at them* Lm 4$_{15}$ (or em. טְמֵאִים *impure ones*).

**3.** used as noun, **a.** masc. **impure one** or **thing, unclean one** or **thing,** <SUBJ> בוא *come* Is 52$_{1}$=4QTanḥ 8$_{3}$ ([יבוא ... טמא])=4QTanḥ 12$_{2}$ ([טמא]; || עָרֵל *uncircumcised one*) 2 C 23$_{19}$ 11QT 45$_{17}$ CD 11$_{22}$, עבר *pass* Is 35$_{8}$ 1QH 6$_{20}$ (|| עָרֵל, פָּרִיץ *violent one*), יסף hi. *add*, i.e. do again Is 52$_{1}$=4QTanḥ 8$_{3}$ ([יוסיף ... טמא])=12$_{2}$ ([יוסי]ף ... [טמא]), אכל *eat* Dt 12$_{15.22}$ 15$_{22}$ (all three :: טָהוֹר *pure one*) 4QOrd$^{c}$ 1.1$_{5.8}$ ([ט]מאי) 11QT 52$_{11}$ 53$_{4}$ (both :: טָהוֹר), נגע *touch* Nm 19$_{22}$ Hg 2$_{13}$ CD 10$_{13}$, רחץ *wash* 4QOrd$^{c}$ 1.1$_{5.8}$ ([ט]מאי), כבס pi. *wash* 4QOrd$^{c}$ 1.1$_{5.88}$ ([ט]מאי), טהר *be pure* 4QOrd$^{c}$ 1.1$_{5.8}$ ([ט]מאי), htp. *purify oneself* 4QRitPur 1.12$_{2}$ ([טמאי]) 11QT 45$_{17}$.

<NOM CL> זֶה ... הַטָּמֵא *this is ... the unclean one* Lv 11$_{29}$, אֵלֶּה הַטְּמֵאִים *these are the unclean ones* Lv 11$_{31}$, אין טמא בקודשיהם *there is no unclean thing in their holy places* 4QShirShabb$^{a}$ 1.1$_{14}$.

<OBJ> שׁלח pi. *send away* Nm 5$_{2}$, אכל *eat* Jg 13$_{4.7(Gnz)}$ (L טֻמְאָה *impurity*) Ho 9$_{3}$, נגע *touch* Is 52$_{11}$.

<CSTR> טְמֵא־שְׂפָתַיִם *impure one of lips* Is 6$_{5.5}$, טְמֵא נֶפֶשׁ *impure one of*, i.e. one made unclean by, *soul*, i.e. dead one Lv 22$_{4}$ Hg 2$_{13}$, טמאי [נדה] *impure ones of*, i.e. ones made unclean by, *impurity* 4QTohB$^{b}$ 1$_{6}$, [טמאי ע]תים *impure ones of times*, i.e. ones temporarily impure 4QRitPur 1.12$_{2}$, טמאי הימים *the impure ones of days* 4QOrd$^{c}$ 1.1$_{5.8}$ ([ט]מאי); יוֹם הַטָּמֵא *day of the impure thing*, i.e. when a thing is unclean Lv 14$_{57}$ (:: טָהוֹר *pure thing*), כָּל־טָמֵא *any impure thing* Lv 7$_{19.21}$ Jg 13$_{4}$ 11QT 45$_{17}$ (כול), כול הטמאים *all the impure ones* 4QTohA 1.1$_{2.3.9}$ ([כו]ל) 4QOrd$^{c}$ 1.1$_{2}$ (כל הט[מ]אים), כול טמאי *all impure ones of* 4QOrd$^{c}$ 1.1$_{5.8}$ (כל [ט]מאי).

<APP> אִישׁ *man* Is 6$_{5}$, עַם *people* Is 6$_{5}$, טֻמְאָה *impurity* Lv 7$_{21}$, בְּהֵמָה *beast* Lv 7$_{21}$, שֶׁרֶץ *swarming thing* Lv 7$_{21(mss, Sam)}$, שֶׁקֶץ *detestable thing* Lv 7$_{21}$ Nm 5$_{2}$ (כָּל).

<ADJ> אֵלֶּה *these* 4QTohA 1.1$_{9}$.

<PREP> לְ of direction, *to*, + לקח *take* Nm 19$_{17}$; בדד לכול הטמאים ישב *he shall dwell separate to*, i.e. apart from, *all the impure ones* 4QTohA 1.1$_{2}$; of possession, *(belonging) to, of* Ec 9$_{2}$ (:: טָהוֹר *pure thing*); introducing object, + צוה pi. *command* 4QRitPur 1.12$_{2}$ ([צויתה לטמאי]).

בְּ introducing object, + נגע *touch* Lv 7$_{19.21}$ 22$_{4}$; of essence, *as, in the state of*, + בער pi. *remove* Dt 26$_{14}$.

כְּ *as*, + היה *be* Is 64$_{5}$.

מִן of direction, *from* 4QTohA 1.1$_{3.9}$, + נתן *give*, i.e. make Jb 14$_{4}$ (:: טָהוֹר *pure thing*).

עַל *upon*, + נזה hi. *sprinkle* Nm 19$_{19}$ 4QTohB$^{b}$ 1$_{6}$ ([והזה]) 1$_{7}$ 4QMMT B$_{16}$; *for*, + כפר pi. *make atonement* 4QTohB$^{b}$ 1$_{7}$ (טמ[א]).

בֵּין *between*, + בדל hi. *distinguish* Lv 10$_{10}$ 11$_{47}$ GnzPs 1$_{4}$ CD 6$_{17}$ 12$_{20}$ 4QMMT B$_{56}$ (all six :: טָהוֹר *pure thing*), ידע hi. *make known* (the difference) Ezk 22$_{26}$ 44$_{23}$ (both :: טָהוֹר).

<COLL> טָמֵא לָנֶפֶשׁ *one impure through the soul*, through contact with a dead one Nm 5$_{2}$ 11QT 45$_{17}$, טָמֵא לְכָל־דָּבָר *one impure with regard to anything* 2 C 23$_{19}$.

**b.** fem. **impure (city),** Ezk 22$_{5}$ 24$_{13}$ (if em.), **impure (woman),** Lv 15$_{33}$ Ezk 22$_{10}$, <OBJ> ענה pi. *humble* Ezk 22$_{10}$. <CSTR> טְמֵאַת הַנִּדָּה *woman impure (because) of menstruation* Ezk 22$_{10}$, טְמֵאַת הַזִּמָּה *impure one of wickedness* Ezk 24$_{13}$ (if em. בְּטֻמְאָתֵךְ זִמָּה *wickedness is in your impurity*), טְמֵאַת הַשֵּׁם *the impure one of name*, i.e. infamous one Ezk 22$_{5}$. <PREP> עִם *with*, + שׁכב *lie* Lv 15$_{33}$.

Also 4QCrypt 1.2$_{1}$ 4QTohA 2.2$_{5}$ ([טמ]אים) 3.1$_{5.8}$ perh. 4Q426 4$_{5}$ 4Q458 2.1$_{5}$ 4QShirShabb$^{c}$ 4$_{4}$ 4QShir$^{b}$ 2.2$_{8}$ 4QRitPur 41$_{4}$ 51.2$_{4}$ perh. 61$_{2}$ perh. 86$_{2}$ (טמ[א]) 4QOrd$^{b}$ 2.2$_{1}$ perh. 22$_{4}$ (unless מטמא is pi. ptc.) perh. 36$_{1}$ perh. 4QOrd$^{c}$ 2$_{2}$ (מטמאי[ם]; unless pi. ptc.) 11QT 51$_{1}$.

<SYN> §3 עָרֵל *uncircumcised one*, פָּרִיץ *violent one*.

<ANT> §§1, 3 טָהוֹר *pure one*.

→ טמא *be impure*.

**[טָמָא]** 0.0.3 n.[m.] **impurity, uncleanness, defilement,** <NOM CL> טמא בכול עוברי דברו *impurity is among all who transgress his word* 1QS 5$_{14}$, טמא בכול הונם *impurity is in all their wealth* 1QS 5$_{20}$, השלישית טמא המקדש *the third one* (net of Belial) *is defilement of the sanctuary* CD 4$_{18}$. <CSTR> טמא המקדש *defilement of the sanctuary* CD 4$_{18}$. <PREP> בְּ of instrument, *by (means of), with,* + טמא pi. *defile* 4QJub$^{f}$ 23$_{21}$ ([ויטמאו ... בטמ]א).

⇒ טמא *be impure.*

**טֻמְאָה** 1 n.f. **impurity**—perh. inf. of טמא *be impure*— <SUBJ> חבל pi. *destroy* Mc 2$_{10}$=4QMidrEschat$^{b}$ 8$_{10}$ ([טמאה תחבל]); or em. טֻמְאָה תְּחַבֵּל וְחֶבֶל *impurity that destroys, and destruction* to מְעַט מְאוּמָה חֲבֹל תַּחְבְּלוּ on account of *something small you take a pledge*). <PREP> בַּעֲבוּר *on account of* Mc 2$_{10}$=4QMidrEschat$^{b}$ 8$_{10}$ ([בעבור] [טמאה]; or em.; see Subj.).

⇒ טמא *be impure.*

**טֻמְאָה** 36.0.47 n.f. **impurity**—cstr. טֻמְאַת; sf. טֻמְאָתֵךְ, טֻמְאָתוֹ, טֻמְאָתָהּ, טֻמְאָתָם (Q טמאתמה); pl. Q טמאות; cstr. טֻמְאוֹת; sf. טֻמְאוֹתֵיכֶם, טֻמְאוֹתָם—**impurity, uncleanness,** e.g. caused by menstruation or discharge from woman (e.g. Lv 15$_{25}$ 18$_{19}$ 2 S 11$_{4}$ 11QT 48$_{16}$), discharge from man (e.g. Lv 15$_{3}$), leprosy (e.g. Lv 14$_{19}$), contact with corpse (e.g. Nm 19$_{13}$ CD 12$_{16}$ 4QTohB$^{b}$ 1$_{8}$), sin, sexual immorality, bloodshed, etc. (e.g. Lv 16$_{16}$ Nm 5$_{19}$ Ezk 24$_{11}$ 1QM 9$_{8}$).

<SUBJ> היה *be* Lv 15$_{3}$ 4QMMT B$_{67}$, נתך ni. *be poured out,* i.e. melted Ezk 24$_{11}$ (+ חֶלְאָה *rust*).

<NOM CL> טֻמְאָתוֹ הִיא *it is his impurity* Lv 15$_{3(Qr)}$, [מעשיהם טמאה] *their deeds are impurity* 4QJub$^{d}$ 21$_{21}$, טֻמְאָתָהּ בְּשׁוּלֶיהָ *her impurity was in her skirts* Lm 1$_{9}$, טֻמְאָתוֹ בוֹ *his impurity is in him* Nm 19$_{13}$ 11QT 50$_{8}$, טֻמְאָתוֹ עָלָיו *his uncleanness is upon him* Lv 7$_{20}$ 22$_{3}$, מהמה הטמאה *from them is impurity* 4QOrd$^{b}$ 1$_{3.4}$ ([מ]המה [הטמ]אה) 1$_{5}$ ([מהמה הטמ[אה]).

<OBJ> אכל *eat* Jg 13$_{7}$ (Gnz טָמֵא *impure thing*) 13$_{14}$, תמם hi. *destroy* Ezk 22$_{15}$, מצא *find* 2 C 29$_{19}$, יצא hi. *bring out* 2 C 29$_{19}$, קבל pi. *receive* 4Q462$_{15}$ (טמ[אה/את]).

<CSTR> טֻמְאַת גּוֹיֵ־הָאָרֶץ *impurity of the nations of the land* Ezr 6$_{21}$, טֻמְאֹת בְּנֵי יִשְׂרָאֵל *impurities of the sons of Israel* Lv 16$_{16}$ (+ פֶּשַׁע *transgression,* חַטָּאת *sin*) 16$_{19}$, טֻמְאַת אָדָם *impurity of human beings* Lv 5$_{3}$ 7$_{21}$ CD 12$_{16}$ (האדם), טמאות האדם *impurities of human beings* 1QSa 2$_{3}$, טֻמְאַת הַנִּדָּה *impurity of menstruation* Ezk 36$_{17}$, נִדָּתָהּ *of her menstruation* Lv 15$_{26}$, [ט]מאות נ[גע] *impurities of leprosy* 4QMMT B$_{71}$, טמאת עונ[ות] *impurity of iniquity* 4QTohB$^{b}$ 1$_{2}$, טמאת בשרו *impurity of his flesh* 1QM 7$_{4}$ 4QM$^{a}$ 1$_{6}$ ([טמאת בשרו]), הנפש *of soul,* i.e. corpse 4QTohB$^{b}$ 1$_{8.12}$ ([נפש]) 4QMMT B$_{72}$ ([טמאת נפש]), אחד *of one* tool CD 12$_{18}$.

דבר טמאה *matter of impurity* 11QT 58$_{17}$, רוּחַ הַטֻּמְאָה *spirit of impurity,* i.e. impure spirit Zc 13$_{2}$ 11QPs$^{a}$ 19$_{15}$ (טמאה), זוֹב טֻמְאָתָהּ *discharge of her impurity* Lv 15$_{25.30}$, נדת טמאה *impurity of impurity* 1QpHab 8$_{13}$ 4QapPs$^{b}$ 69$_{2.2}$ 4QRitPur 1.12$_{9}$ (נדות *impurities of*), נִדַּת טֻמְאָתָהּ *impurity of her uncleanness* Lv 18$_{19}$, נדת טמאתם *impurity of their uncleanness* 1QM 13$_{5}$ 4QBer$^{a}$ 3.2$_{4}$ ([ט]מאתמה) 11QT 45$_{10}$ 48$_{16}$ (both טמאתמה) 48$_{17}$, מקור [טומאה] *source of impurity* 1QM 16$_{1}$, דם טמאתם *blood of their impurity* 1QM 9$_{8}$, עבודת טמאה *worship of impurity,* i.e. impure worship 1QS 4$_{10}$, מגע טמאה *touching of impurity* 4QTohB$^{b}$ 1$_{12}$, כָּל־טֻמְאָה *any impurity* Jg 13$_{7.14}$ 11QT 47$_{5}$ (כול), כָּל־הַטֻּמְאָה *all the impurity* 2 C 29$_{19}$, כל הטמאות *all the impurities* CD 7$_{3}$ 11QT 51$_{6}$ (כול), כול טמאת *all the impurity of* 4QTohB$^{b}$ 1$_{2}$ 4QRitPur 152$_{2}$, כול טמאות *all the impurities of* 1QSa 2$_{3}$, כֹּל טֻמְאָתוֹ *all his impurity* Lv 5$_{3}$ 22$_{5}$, [כול טמאתם] *all their impurity* 4QMMT C$_{7}$, כֹּל טֻמְאוֹתֵיכֶם *all your impurities* Ezk 36$_{25.29}$.

<APP> טָמֵא *impure thing* Lv 7$_{21}$, appar. זִמָּה *wickedness* Ezk 24$_{13}$ (or em.; see Prep.).

<ADJ> רִאשׁוֹן *first* 4QOrd$^{c}$ 1.1$_{5.7.8}$.

<PREP> לְ *(consisting) of* Lv 5$_{3}$ 11QT 47$_{5}$; *with respect to,* + טמא *be impure* Lv 22$_{5}$; *as,* + בדל hi. *separate* 11QT 51$_{9}$.

בְּ of instrument, *by (means of), with,* + טמא *be impure* Lv 5$_{3}$ CD 12$_{18}$ 11QT 47$_{5}$, חלל pi. *defile* 4QD$^{a}$ 6.2$_{6}$, גאל pu. *be defiled* CD 12$_{16}$, נגע pu. *be struck* 1QM 7$_{4}$ 4QM$^{a}$ 1$_{6}$ (מנו[גע בטמאת]), מלא pi. *fill* Ezr 9$_{11}$; of accompaniment, *with, in* Ezk 24$_{13}$ (or em. בְּטֻמְאָתֵךְ זִמָּה *in your impurity, wickedness* to טְמֵאַת הַזִּמָּה *impure one of wickedness*), + אכל *eat* 4QOrd$^{c}$ 1.1$_{5}$ ([יאכל]) 1.1$_{7.8}$; of cause, *on account of,* + מות *die* Lv 15$_{31}$ 4QPrFêtes$^{c}$ 32$_{2}$ (בטמא[תם]), כפר

pi. *make atonement* Lv 16$_{16}$; introducing object, + נגע *touch* Lv 5$_{3}$ 7$_{21}$.

כְּ *as* Ezk 39$_{24}$ (|| פֶּשַׁע *transgression*), + היה *be* Lv 15$_{26}$ Ezk 36$_{17}$.

מִן of direction, *from*, + טהר *be pure* Ezk 24$_{13}$ 36$_{25}$ 4QTohB^b 1$_{8}$ (ויט[ה]רו), htp. *present oneself for purification, be cleansed* Lv 14$_{19}$ 4Q414 1.2$_{4}$, פרש *depart* 4QMMT C$_{7}$ ([מכול טמאתם]), בדל ni. *separate oneself* Ezr 6$_{21}$ CD 7$_{3}$, נזר hi. *keep separate* Lv 15$_{31}$, זהר hi. *warn* Lv 15$_{31(Sam)}$ 11QT 51$_{6}$, קדש pi. *sanctify* Lv 16$_{19}$, htp. *purify oneself* 2 S 11$_{4}$, ישע hi. *save* Ezk 36$_{29}$.

מִן partitive, *(some) of* CD 11$_{20}$ 1QSa 2$_{3}$.

עַל *concerning* 4QMMT B$_{72}$ ([טמאת]).

כְּפִי *according to*, + טמא pi. *defile* CD 12$_{16}$.

בְּתוֹךְ *among, in the midst of*, + שׁכן *dwell* Lv 16$_{16}$.

<COLL> טֻמְאָתוֹ בְּזוֹבוֹ *his impurity in his discharge* Lv 15$_{3}$; טֻמְאָה + שׂטה *turn aside* (to) *uncleanness* Nm 5$_{19}$.

Also 4QpGen^b 2$_{1}$ 4QMMT B$_{42}$ 4Q462$_{17}$ 4QM^a 15$_{8}$ ([ט]מאתו) 4QDibHam^a 25$_{2}$ 4QPrFêtes^b 19$_{1}$ ([טמא]ת) 4QPrFêtes^c 193$_{1}$ 238$_{1}$ 4QShir^b 49.2$_{3}$ 4QRitPur 10.10$_{1}$ 73$_{4}$ 89$_{2}$ 4QOrd^b 13$_{5}$.

<SYN> פֶּשַׁע *transgression*.*

⇒ טמא *be impure.*

**טמה** $_{1}$ vb. **be impure—Ni.** $_{1}$ Pf. נִטְמֵינוּ (mss נִטְמִינוּ)—**be regarded as unclean,** <SUBJ> Job's friends Jb 18$_{3}$ (mss נִטְמִנוּ *we are stopped up*, i.e. stupid, from טמם ni.; + נֶחְשַׁבְנוּ כַבְּהֵמָה *we are reckoned as cattle*). <PREP> בְּ of place, *in*, + עַיִן *eye* Jb 18$_{3}$.

**טמם** $_{1.1}$ vb. **stop up—Ni.** $_{1}$ Pf. mss נִטְמִנוּ—**be stopped up,** i.e. **be stupid,** <SUBJ> Job's friends Jb 18$_{3(mss)}$ (L נִטְמֵינוּ *we are regarded as unclean*, i.e. טמה ni.; + נֶחְשַׁבְנוּ כַבְּהֵמָה *we are reckoned as cattle*). <PREP> בְּ of place, *in*, + עַיִן *eye* Jb 18$_{3(mss)}$.

**Pilp.** $_{0.1}$ Pf. Si טמטם—**stop up, fill in,** <SUBJ> אֱלֹהִים *God* Si 10$_{16}$ (+ קעקע pilp. *exterminate*). <OBJ> עָקֵב *footprint* of nations Si 10$_{16}$.

**טמן** $_{31.3.3}$ vb. **conceal—Qal** $_{28.1}$ Pf. טָמַן, טָמַנְתִּי, טְמַנְתִּיו (טמנתיו), טָמְנוּ (טָמְנוּ); impf. Q יטמונו; + waw וַיִּטְמֹן; וַתִּטְמְנֵם (Q ויטמון, וַיִּטְמְנֵהוּ), 3fs וַתִּטְמְנֵם, וָאֶטְמְנֵהוּ; impv. טָמְנֵהוּ, טָמְנֵם; ptc. pass. טָמוּן, טְמוּנָה, טְמוּנִים, טְמוּנֵי; inf. טְמוֹן (טָמְנוֹ)—**1.** active, **conceal, hide,** <SUBJ> Israelites Jr 18$_{22}$, Jacob Gn 35$_{4}$, Jeremiah Jr 13$_{4.5.6.7}$ 43$_{9.10}$, Job Jb 31$_{33}$ (+ כסה pi. *cover*) 40$_{13}$, Moses Ex 2$_{12}$, אִשָּׁה *woman* Jos 2$_{6}$, גּוֹי *nation* Ps 9$_{16}$, enemy Ps 31$_{5}$ 35$_{7.8}$ 64$_{6}$ 142$_{4}$ 1QH 2$_{29}$, גֵּאֶה *proud one* Ps 140$_{6}$, עָצֵל *lazy one* Pr 19$_{24}$ 26$_{15}$; subj. not specified, CD 5$_{4}$.

<OBJ> אֱלֹהִים *god* Gn 35$_{4}$, אִישׁ *man* Jos 2$_{6}$, מִצְרִי *Egyptian* Ex 2$_{12}$, רָשָׁע *wicked one* Jb 40$_{13}$, יָד *hand* Pr 19$_{24}$ 26$_{15}$, נֶזֶם *ring* Gn 35$_{4}$, אֵזוֹר *girdle* Jr 13$_{4.5.6.7}$, פַּח *trap* Jr 18$_{22}$ Ps 140$_{6}$ 142$_{4}$ 1QH 2$_{29}$ fr. 3$_{8}$, מוֹקֵשׁ *trap* Ps 64$_{6}$, צַמִּים *trap* 1QH fr. 3$_{8}$, רֶשֶׁת *net* Ps 9$_{16}$ 31$_{5}$ 35$_{7.8}$ 4QapPs^b 31$_{1}$ ([טמ]נו), שַׁחַת *pit* Ps 35$_{7}$ (unless em. שַׁחַת רִשְׁתָּם *a pit, their net* to רִשְׁתָּם וְשַׁחַת *their net, and a pit* they have dug), אֶבֶן *stone* Jr 43$_{9.10}$, עָוֹן *iniquity* Jb 31$_{33}$, גלה ni. ptc. *open (copy)* CD 5$_{4}$.

<PREP> לְ of benefit, *to, for*, + worshipper Ps 31$_{5}$ 35$_{7}$ 140$_{6}$ 142$_{4}$, רֶגֶל *foot* Jr 18$_{22}$, נֶפֶשׁ *soul*, i.e. self 1QH 2$_{29}$; בְּ of place, *in, among*, + חֹב *bosom* Jb 31$_{33}$, פְּרָת *Parah*, or *Euphrates* Jr 13$_{5}$, נָקִיק *cleft* Jr 13$_{4}$, חוֹל *sand* Ex 2$_{12}$, עָפָר *dust* Jb 40$_{13}$, מֶלֶט *mortar* Jr 43$_{9}$, מַלְבֵּן *pavement* Jr 43$_{9}$, אֹרַח *path* Ps 142$_{4}$, פֵּשֶׁת *flax* Jos 2$_{6}$, צַלַּחַת *dish* Pr 19$_{24}$ 26$_{15}$; תַּחַת *beneath*, + אֵלָה *terebinth* Gn 35$_{4}$.

<COLL> טמן + adverb שָׁמָּה *thither* Jr 13$_{4.6.7}$ (הַמָּקוֹם אֲשֶׁר־טְמַנְתִּיו שָׁמָּה *the place where I had concealed it*), חִנָּם *without cause* Ps 35$_{7}$.

**2a.** passive, **be concealed,** <SUBJ> נֵפֶל *miscarriage* Jb 3$_{16}$, אַדֶּרֶת *cloak* Jos 7$_{21.22}$, כֶּסֶף *silver* Jos 7$_{21}$, לָשׁוֹן *tongue*, i.e. bar, of gold Jos 7$_{21}$, חֶבֶל *cord* Jb 18$_{10}$, מַלְכֹּדֶת *trap* Jb 18$_{10}$, חֹשֶׁךְ *darkness* Jb 20$_{26}$, חָכְמָה *wisdom* Si 41$_{14}$ (|| סתר ho. *be concealed*). <PREP> לְ of benefit, *to, for*, + צפן pass. ptc. *treasure* Jb 20$_{26}$; בְּ of place, *in*, + אֶרֶץ *earth* Jos 7$_{21}$ Jb 18$_{10}$; עַל *upon*, + נָתִיב *path* Jb 18$_{10}$. <COLL> שְׂפוּנֵי טְמוּנֵי חוֹל *covered (things) concealed of sand*, i.e. treasures concealed in the sand Dt 33$_{19}$ (or em. שְׂפוּנֵי to צְפוּנֵי *treasured things*).

**2b.** passive ptc. as noun, **concealed place,** <PREP> בְּ of place, *in*, + חבשׁ *bind* Jb 40$_{13}$.

<SYN> §2a סתר ho. *be concealed.*

**Ni.** $_{1}$ Impv. הִטָּמֵן—**conceal oneself,** <SUBJ> Israel Is 2$_{10}$. <PREP> בְּ of place, *in*, + עָפָר *dust* Is 2$_{10}$; מִפְּנֵי *from before*, + פַּחַד *dread* of Y. Is 2$_{10}$, הָדָר *glory* Is 2$_{10}$.

**Hi.** 2.2.1 Impf. Si יטמין; + waw וַיַּטְמִנוּ; ptc. Q מטמיני—**1. conceal,** <SUBJ> אִישׁ *man* Si 41$_{15(Bmg)}$ (B, M צפן hi. *conceal;* || צפן hi.) 41$_{15(M)}$ ([ן]מטמ; B צפן hi.; || צפן hi.), צרע pu. ptc. *leper* 2 K 7$_{8.8}$. <OBJ> חָכְמָה *wisdom* Si 41$_{15}$ (Bmg), אִוֶּלֶת *folly* Si 41$_{15(M)}$; plunder 2 K 7$_{8.8}$.

**2.** ptc. used as noun, **one who conceals,** i.e. **layer** of traps, <CSTR> מטמיני פחים *layers of traps* 4QHod$^{b}$ 1$_{14}$ (=1QH fr. 3$_{4}$ מטוני perh. error for מטמוני *concealed places of*). <PREP> עַל *against* 4QHod$^{b}$ 1$_{14}$.

<SYN> §1 צפן hi. *hide.**

⇒ מַטְמוֹן *treasure.*

**טֶנֶא** 4.1.2 n.m. **basket**—sf. טַנְאֲךָ (Q טנאכה, טנאיכה)—as receptacle for produce, Dt 26$_{2.4}$ 28$_{5.17}$ Si 34$_{14}$ 4Q418 103.2$_{3}$ 126.2$_{12}$. <SUBJ> ברך pass. *be blessed* Dt 28$_{5}$ (|| מִשְׁאֶרֶת *kneading-trough*), ארר pass. *be cursed* (|| מִשְׁאֶרֶת *kneading-trough*). <OBJ> לקח *take* Dt 26$_{4}$. <PREP> בְּ *in, into,* + שׂים *place* Dt 26$_{2}$, בוא ho. *be brought* 4Q418 103.2$_{3}$, יחד *join oneself* Si 34$_{14}$; מִן of direction, *from,* + דרשׁ *seek* 4Q418 126.2$_{12}$. <SYN> מִשְׁאֶרֶת *kneading-trough.**

**טנף** 1 vb. **defile—Pi.** 1 Impf. אֲטַנְּפֵם—**soil, defile** feet Ca 5$_{3}$. <SUBJ> male lover Ca 5 $_{3}$. <OBJ> רֶגֶל *foot* Ca 5$_{3}$.

**טעה** 1.0.2 vb. **stray—Qal** 2 Impf. Q יטעו—**stray, err,** <SUBJ> עוֹלָם *world* GnzPs 3$_{18}$. <PREP> בְּ of accompaniment, *in (a state of), with* or of cause, *on account of,* + הֶבֶל *vanity* GnzPs 3$_{18}$, מִשְׁגֶּה *error* GnzPs 3$_{18}$.

**Hi.** 1 Pf. הִטְעוּ—**lead astray,** <SUBJ> נָבִיא *prophet* Ezk 13$_{10}$. <OBJ> עַם *people* Ezk 13$_{10}$.

Also perh. 6Q30$_{2.5}$.

**טעם** 11.2 vb. **taste—Qal** 11.2 Pf. טָעַם, טָעֲמָה, טָעַמְתִּי; impf. יִטְעַם, Si 2 ms תטעם, אֶטְעַם, יִטְעֲמוּ; impv. טַעֲמוּ; inf. טְעֹם—**taste; perceive** (Ps 34$_{9}$ Pr 31$_{18}$), <SUBJ> עַם *people* 1 S 14$_{24}$, David 2 S 3$_{35}$, Jonathan 1 S 14$_{29.43}$, אָדָם *human being* Jon 3$_{7}$, אִשָּׁה *woman* Pr 31$_{18}$, בֵּן *son* Si 9$_{9}$, עֶבֶד *servant* 2 S 19$_{36}$, pious Ps 34$_{9}$ (+ ראה *see*), בְּהֵמָה *beast* Jon 3$_{7}$, בָּקָר *cattle* Jon 3$_{7}$, צֹאן *sheep* Jon 3$_{7}$, חֵךְ *palate* Jb 12$_{11}$ 34$_{3}$ (+ אכל *eat;* or em. אֹכֶל *food*) Si 36$_{24}$. <OBJ> לֶחֶם *bread,* i.e. food 1 S 14$_{24}$ 2 S 3$_{35}$, דְּבַשׁ *honey* 1 S 14$_{29.43}$, אֹכֶל *food* Jb 12$_{11}$ 34$_{3}$ (if em.), מַטְעַם *savoury food* Si 36$_{24}$, מְאוּמָה *anything* Jon 3$_{7}$, אֶת־אֲשֶׁר *that which* 2 S 19$_{36}$. <PREP> עִם *with,* + בַּעֲלָה *lady* Si 9$_{9}$.*

⇒ טַעַם *taste,* מַטְעָם *savoury food.*

**טַעַם** 13.3 n.m. **taste**—טָעַם; cstr. טַעַם; sf. טַעְמֵךְ, טַעְמוֹ—**taste; discernment; decree** (Jon 3$_{7}$),* <SUBJ> היה *be* Nm 11$_{8}$, ברך pass. *be blessed* 1 S 25$_{33}$, שׁפט pass. *be decided* Si 11$_{6}$, עמד *stand,* i.e. remain Jr 48$_{11}$. <NOM CL> טַעְמוֹ כְּצַפִּיחִת *its taste was as a wafer* Ex 16$_{31}$, יֶשׁ־טַעַם *there is taste* Jb 6$_{6}$. <OBJ> שׁוב hi. *bring back* Pr 26$_{16}$, לקח *take* Jb 12$_{20}$, נתן *give* Si 10$_{28}$, למד pi. *teach* Ps 119$_{66}$ (if em.; see Cstr.), שׁנה pi. *change,* i.e. disguise judgment 1 S 21$_{14}$ Ps 34$_{1}$. <CSTR> טַעַם לְשַׁד *taste of a cake of* Nm 11$_{8}$, טַעַם זְקֵנִים *discernment of elders* Jb 12$_{20}$, טַעַם הַמֶּלֶךְ *decree of the king* Jon 3$_{7}$, טוּב טַעַם *quality of discernment,* i.e. good judgment Ps 119$_{66}$ (unless טוב II *word* [and] judgment; or del. טוּב). <PREP> בְּ of accompaniment, *in (a state of), with,* + אנח htp. *sigh* Si 25$_{18}$ (בלא טעמו יתאנח *he sighs without his discernment* ); כְּ *as,* + היה *be* Nm 11$_{8}$; מִן of agent, *by (means of)* Jon 3$_{7}$. <COLL> סָרַת טָעַם *one who departs (from) discernment* Pr 11$_{22}$.*

⇒ טעם *taste.*

**טען I** 1 vb. **pierce—Pu.** 1 Ptc. מְטֹעֲנֵי—**be pierced,** <COLL> מְטֹעֲנֵי חָרֶב *those who are pierced by the sword* Is 14$_{19}$.

**טען II** 1 vb. **load—Qal** 1 Pf. טַעֲנוּ—<SUBJ> אָח *brother* Gn 45$_{17}$. <OBJ> בְּעִיר *beast* Gn 45$_{17}$.

**[טעטע]** vb. **stray—Pulp. be led astray, be disturbed,** מטעטע מחזון נפשו *he who is disturbed by the vision of his soul,* i.e. mind Si 40$_{6}$ (if em. מעט טע appar. *a little*).

**טַף** 42.0.6 n.m. **children**—טַף; sf. טַפֵּנוּ, טַפְּכֶם, טַפָּם—alw. used collectively, **children, infants.**

<SUBJ> היה *be* Nm 14$_{3}$ (|| אִשָּׁה *woman*) 14$_{31}$ 32$_{26}$ Dt 1$_{39}$, חיה *live* Gn 43$_{8}$, מות *die* Gn 43$_{8}$, ידע *know* Nm 14$_{31}$ Dt 1$_{39}$, בוא *come* Dt 1$_{39}$, הלך *go* Ex 10$_{24}$ 4QpNah 3.4$_{4}$ (|| אִשָּׁה), עבר *pass* 2 S 15$_{22}$ (+ אִישׁ *man*), יצא *go out* Nm 16$_{27}$ (|| בֵּן *son,* אִשָּׁה), עמד *stand* 2 C 20$_{13}$ (|| בֵּן, אִשָּׁה), נצב ni. *stand* Dt 29$_{10}$ (|| אִשָּׁה), ישׁב *dwell* Nm 32$_{17}$ Dt 3$_{19}$ Jos 1$_{14}$, ירשׁ *inherit* Dt 1$_{39}$.

<OBJ> בוא hi. *bring* Nm 14₃₁, קהל hi. *assemble* Dt 31₁₂ (|| אִשָּׁה *woman*), שלח pi. *send away* Ex 10₁₀, לקח *take* Jr 41₁₆ (+ גֶּבֶר *man*, אִישׁ *man*, אִשָּׁה) 43₆, שׂים *place* Jg 18₂₁, נשׂא *raise* Gn 46₅, פקד hi. *entrust* Jr 40₇ (+ אִישׁ, אִשָּׁה), כול pilp. *provide (for)* Gn 50₂₁, חיה hi. *keep alive* Nm 31₁₈, עזב *abandon* Gn 50₈, צור *oppress* Est 8₁₁ (|| אִשָּׁה *woman*), בזז *plunder*, i.e. take as booty Dt 20₁₄ 11QT 62₁₀, שׁבה *take captive* Gn 34₂₉ Nm 31₉ (both || אִשָּׁה), נכה hi. *strike* Jg 21₁₀, אבד pi. *destroy* Est 3₁₃ 1QpHab 6₁₁ (|| אִשָּׁה), חרם hi. *destroy* Dt 2₃₄ 3₆ (both || אִשָּׁה), שׁמד hi. *destroy* Est 3₁₃, הרג *kill* Ezk 9₆ (|| אִשָּׁה) Est 3₁₃.

<CSTR> כָּל־טַפָּם *all their children* 2 C 31₁₈.

<APP> יְהוּדִי *Jew* Est 3₁₃, רַב *great one* 1QpHab 6₁₁, שְׁאֵרִית *remnant* Jr 41₁₆, כֹּל *all* Dt 29₁₀.

<PREP> לְ of direction, *to*, + נתן *give* Dt 1₃₉; of benefit, *to, for*, + היה *be* as food Gn 47₂₄, בנה *build* Nm 32₁₆.₂₄, בקשׁ pi. *seek* right way Ezr 8₂₁, לקח *take* carts Gn 45₁₉ (|| אִשָּׁה *woman*); בְּ of accompaniment, *in, with*, + בוא *come* 1QSa 1₈, הרג *slaughter* Nm 31₁₇, יחשׂ htp. *be genealogically registered* 2 C 31₁₈; מִן of direction, *from*, + בוא *come* 1QSa 1₄ (מטף ועד נשים *from children and unto women*, i.e. both women and children); לְבַד מִן *apart from* Ex 12₃₇; לְפִי *according to*, + כול pilp. *provide* food for families Gn 47₁₂ (unless לְפִי הַטָּף provide food *for the mouth[s] of the children*); נֶגֶד *opposite*, + קרא *call* Jos 8₃₅ (|| אִשָּׁה *woman*).

<COLL> וְטַפְּכֶם אֲשֶׁר אֲמַרְתֶּם *and your children, of whom you said* Nm 14₃₁ Dt 1₃₉

<SYN> אִשָּׁה *woman*, בֵּן *son*.

Also 4QpGen[a] 1.3₆.*

⇒ טפף *walk carefully*.

**טפח I** ₁ vb. **be broad—Pi.** ₁ Pf. טִפְּחָה—**extend,** <SUBJ> יָמִין *right hand* Is 48₁₃. <OBJ> שָׁמַיִם *heaven(s)* Is 48₁₃.

⇒ טֶפַח *handbreadth*, מִטְפַּחַת *mantle*.

**טפח II** ₁ vb. **give birth—Pi.** ₁ Pf. טִפַּחְתִּי—**give birth to,** <SUBJ> Zion Lm 2₂₂ (|| רבה pi. *bring up*). <OBJ> אֲשֶׁר *one who*, i.e. child Lm 2₂₂. <SYN> רבה pi. *bring up*.

⇒ טִפּוּחִים *birth*.

**טֶ֫פַח** ₉.₀.₂ n.m. **handbreadth**—טֹפַח; pl. טְפָחוֹת—**handbreadth; coping stone** (1 K 7₉), <NOM CL> עָבְיוֹ טֶפַח *its thickness was a handbreadth* 1 K 7₂₆||2 C 4₅. <CSTR> מִסְגֶּרֶת טֹפַח *rim of a handbreadth* Ex 25₂₅=37₁₂. <ADJ> אֶחָד *one* Ezk 40₄₃, אַרְבַּע *four* 1QM 5₁₃, חָמֵשׁ *five* 1QM 5₁₄. <PREP> עַד *unto* 1 K 7₉ (+ מִן *from* foundation to coping stone). <COLL> טְפָחוֹת נָתַתָּה יָמַי *you have made my days (as) handbreadths* Ps 39₆, אַמָּה וָטֹפַח *a cubit and a handbreadth* Ezk 40₅ 43₁₃.

⇒ טפח *be broad*.

**טֹ֫פַח**, see טֶפַח *handbreadth*.

**טִפֻּחִים** ₁ n.[m.] perh. **birth,** <CSTR> עֹלְלֵי טִפֻּחִים *children of birth*, i.e. new-born children Lm 2₂₀.

⇒ טפח *be pregnant*.

**טפל** ₃.₁ vb. **cover—Qal** ₃.₁ Pf. טָפְלוּ; + waw וַתִּטְפֹּל; ptc. טֹפְלֵי—**daub, smear, plaster,** <SUBJ> אֵל *God* Jb 14₁₇, זֵד *arrogant one* Ps 119₆₉, wicked Si 51₅, friend of Job Jb 13₄. <OBJ> שֶׁקֶר *falsehood* Ps 119₆₉ Jb 13₄ Si 51₅. <PREP> עַל *upon, over*, + worshipper Ps 119₆₉, עָוֹן *iniquity* Jb 14₁₇.

**טִפְסָר** ₂ n.m. **scribe (?), official**—טִפְסָר; sf. טַפְסְרַיִךְ—<NOM CL> טַפְסְרַיִךְ כְּגוֹב גֹּבָי *your scribes are as a locust, swarms of locusts* Na 3₁₇ (or em. כְּגֹבָי *as swarms of locusts*). <OBJ> פקד *appoint* Jr 51₂₇.

**טפף** ₁ vb. **walk carefully—Qal** ₁ Inf. טָפֹף—**walk carefully, walk with mincing gait,** <SUBJ> בַּת *daughter* of Zion Is 3₁₆ (+ הלך *go*).

⇒ טַף *children*.

**טפשׁ** ₁ vb. **be fat—Qal** ₁ Pf. טָפַשׁ—<SUBJ> לֵב *heart* of arrogant one Ps 119₇₀, בָּשָׂר *flesh* Jb 33₂₅ (if em. רֻטְפַשׁ his flesh *was fresh* to יִטְפַּשׁ *is fat*). <PREP> כְּ *as*, + חֵלֶב *fat* Ps 119₇₀; מִן of direction, *from (the time of)*, + נֹעַר *youth* Jb 33₂₅ (if em.).

⇒ טִפֵּשׁ *foolish*.

**[טִפֵּשׁ]** ₀.₁ adj. **foolish**—fem. Si טפשה—used attribu-

tively of אִשָּׁה *woman* Si 42$_{6(Bmg)}$ (B רָעָה *evil*).
⇒ טפשׁ *thick.*

**טָפַת** $_{1}$ pr.n.f. **Taphath**—daughter of Solomon and wife of Ben-abinabab, <SUBJ> היה *be* 1 K 4$_{11}$. <APP> בַּת *daughter* 1 K 4$_{11}$.

**[טֶקַח]** $_{0.0.0.1}$ pr.n. **Tekah,** Seal 460 (Jerusalem).

**טרד** $_{2.2.6}$ vb. **continue—Qal** $_{2.1.6}$ Pf. Si טרתי; ptc. טוֹרֵד (טֹרֵד), Q טרוד; inf. Si לטרד—**1.** intransitive, **be continuous, be persistent,** <SUBJ> בֵּן *son* Si 35$_{9}$, דֶּלֶף *dripping* Pr 19$_{13}$ 27$_{15}$, קוֹל *sound* of war trumpet 1QM 8$_{9.12}$ 16$_{6}$ 4QM$^{a}$ 11.2$_{21}$ ([טרוד]) 13$_{6}$.

**2.** transitive, appar. **continually arouse,** Ben Sira 11QPs$^{a}$ Si 51$_{20}$ (B נתן *give* soul). <OBJ> נֶפֶשׁ *soul* 11QPs$^{a}$ Si 51$_{20}$. <PREP> בְּ perh. of instrument, *by (means of)*, + חָכְמָה *wisdom* 11QPs$^{a}$ Si 51$_{20}$.

**3.** passive ptc. as noun, perh. **persistent person,** <SUBJ> ערב hi. *pledge* 4QD$^{d}$ 10$_{7}$ (טרו[ד]). <CSTR> כול טרו[ד] *every persistent person* 4QD$^{d}$ 10$_{7}$. Also 4QD$^{b}$ 7$_{3}$.*

**[טְרוֹם]**, see טֶרֶם *before.*

**טרח** $_{1}$ vb. **be weary—Hi.** $_{1}$ Impf. יַטְרִיחַ—**burden,** <SUBJ> אֵל *God* Jb 37$_{11}$. <OBJ> עָב *cloud* Jb 37$_{11}$. <PREP> בְּ *in, with,* + רִי *moisture* Jb 37$_{11}$.
⇒ טֹרַח *burden.*

**טֹרַח** $_{2.0.1}$ n.m. **burden**—sf. טָרְחֲכֶם—<OBJ> נשׂא *raise* Dt 1$_{12}$ 1QDM 2$_{7}$. <PREP> לְ *as,* + היה *be* Is 1$_{14}$.
⇒ טרח *be weary.*

**טָרִי** $_{2}$ adj. **fresh**—fem. טְרִיָּה—**fresh, raw,** used attributively of לְחִי *cheek,* i.e. jawbone Jg 15$_{15}$, מַכָּה *wound* Is 1$_{6}$.

**טֶרֶם** $_{56.5.25.1}$ conj. (rarely, prep.) **before**—Kt טרום (Ru 3$_{14}$)—**1.** טֶרֶם, without prefixed בְּ, מִן, כְּ, **before, a.** followed by impf. of היה *be* Gn 2$_{5}$, גלה ni. *be revealed* 1 S 3$_{7}$, כבה *be extinguished* 1 S 3$_{3}$, קרא *call* Is 65$_{24}$ (+ עוֹד *while* they are speaking, I shall hear), כרת ni. *be cut,* appar. be chewed Nm 11$_{33}$ (+ עוֹד *while* the meat was still between their teeth), חמץ *be leavened* Ex 12$_{34}$, ענה *be afflicted* Ps 119$_{67}$ (or em. ni. *humble oneself*), עבר *pass* Jos 3$_{1}$, שׁכב *lie down* Gn 19$_{4}$ Jos 2$_{8}$, שׁלח *send,* i.e. extend hand 4QD$^{f}$ 1.2$_{4}$, צמח *sprout* Gn 2$_{5}$, פרח hi. *flower* 1QH 8$_{7}$, ידע *know* Ex 10$_{7}$, ירא *fear* Ex 9$_{30}$, שׁמע *hear* Si 11$_{8(A)}$ (B בְּטֶרֶם, as §2a; + בְּתוֹךְ *in the middle of,* i.e. during, a conversation), כלה pi. *complete* Gn 24$_{15}$ (if em. pf., as §1b) 24$_{45}$ 1QS 6$_{10}$.

<COLL> with verb in preceding main clause, נשׂא *raise* Ex 12$_{34}$ (וַיִּשָּׂא הָעָם אֶת־בְּצֵקוֹ טֶרֶם יֶחְמָץ *the people took their dough before it was leavened*), היה *be* Gn 24$_{15}$ (if em. pf.), שׁוב hi. *take back,* i.e. answer Si 11$_{8(A)}$ (B בְּטֶרֶם, as §2a), דבר pi. *speak* 1QS 6$_{10}$, שׁרשׁ hi. *take root* 1QH 8$_{7}$, לין *pass night* Jos 3$_{1}$ (וַיָּלִנוּ שָׁם טֶרֶם יַעֲבֹרוּ *and they lodged there before they crossed over*), perh. אכל *eat* 4QD$^{f}$ 1.2$_{4}$.

With verb in following main clause, ענה *reply* Is 65$_{24}$ (וְהָיָה טֶרֶם־יִקְרָאוּ וַאֲנִי אֶעֱנֶה *and it will come to pass that before they call I shall answer*), יצא *go out* Gn 24$_{45}$, עלה *go up* Jos 2$_{8}$ (וְהֵמָּה טֶרֶם יִשְׁכָּבוּן וְהִיא עָלְתָה *and before they lay down, she came up*), שׁגג *stray* Ps 119$_{67}$, סבב ni. *surround* Gn 19$_{4}$, חרה *be inflamed* Nm 11$_{33}$.

טֶרֶם-clause as predicate of nom. cl., וְנֵר אֱלֹהִים טֶרֶם יִכְבֶּה *and the lamp of God was before it would be extinguished,* i.e. it was before the lamp of God had been extinguished 1 S 3$_{3}$, וּשְׁמוּאֵל ... טֶרֶם יִגָּלֶה אֵלָיו *and Samuel was ... before it would be revealed to him,* i.e. it was before it had been revealed to Samuel 1 S 3$_{7}$, הֲטֶרֶם תֵּדַע *is it before you were to know?,* i.e. did you not already know? Ex 10$_{7}$, וְכָל־עֵשֶׂב הַשָּׂדֶה טֶרֶם יִצְמָח *and every grass of the field was before it would sprout,* i.e. it was before the grass had sprouted Gn 2$_{5}$, וְכֹל שִׂיחַ הַשָּׂדֶה טֶרֶם יִהְיֶה בָאָרֶץ *and every shrub of the field was before it was in the earth,* i.e. it was before any shrub was in the earth Gn 2$_{5}$, יָדַעְתִּי כִּי טֶרֶם תִּירְאוּן *I know that it is before you fear,* i.e. I know that you still do not fear Ex 9$_{30}$.

**1b.** טֶרֶם followed by pf. of היה *be* 4QTanḥ 22$_{3}$, ידע *know* 1 S 3$_{7}$ (or em. impf., as §1a), כלה pi. *complete* Gn 24$_{15}$ (or em. impf., as §1a). <COLL> with verb in preceding main clause, היה *be* Gn 24$_{15}$ וַיְהִי־הוּא טֶרֶם כִּלָּה לְדַבֵּר (*and it was before he had finished speaking*; or em.

impf., יְכַלֶּה, in same sense), perh. ברא *create* 4QTanḥ 22$_{3}$; טֶרֶם-clause as predicate of nom. cl., וּשְׁמוּאֵל טֶרֶם יָדַע *and Samuel was before he knew*, i.e. and it was before Samuel knew 1 S 3$_{7}$ (or em. יֵדַע *he would know*, as §1a).

**2.** בְּטֶרֶם as conj., **before, a.** followed by impf. of חול *writhe (in labour)* Is 66$_{7}$, יצר *form* Jr 1$_{5}$, צמח *sprout* Is 42$_{9}$, מות *die* Gn 27$_{4}$ 45$_{28}$ Jr 38$_{10}$ Ps 39$_{14}$ Pr 30$_{7}$ Si 14$_{13}$, לקח *take* 4Q418 81$_{11}$, ni. *be taken* 2 K 2$_{9}$, הלך *go* Jb 10$_{21}$ 4QJub$^{d}$ 21$_{16}$ ([בטרם ת]לך), בוא *come* Gn 27$_{33}$ 41$_{50}$ Ex 1$_{19}$ Lv 14$_{36}$ Jg 14$_{18}$ 2 K 6$_{32}$ Is 48$_{5}$ 66$_{7}$, hi. *bring* Dt 31$_{21}$ 4QJub$^{a}$ 1$_{7}$ ([בטרם אביאם]), קרב *approach* Gn 37$_{18}$, יצא *go out* Jr 1$_{5}$, שׁוב *go back* Jb 10$_{21}$, עבר *pass* Arad ost. 5$_{12}$, עלה *go up* 1 S 9$_{13}$, ירד *go down* Arad ost. 40$_{10}$ ([בטרם י]רד), רום hi. *raise* hand 1QS 10$_{15}$, גלה ni. *be revealed* Ezk 16$_{57}$, חשׁך hi. *darken* Jr 13$_{16}$, ידע *know* Is 7$_{16}$ 8$_{4}$, נכר hi. *recognize* Ru 3$_{14}$, שׁמע *hear* Pr 18$_{13}$ Si 11$_{8(B)}$ (A טֶרֶם, as §1a; + בְּתוֹךְ *in the middle of*, i.e. during, a conversation) 4Q420 1.2$_{1}$ ([בטרם ישמ[ע]; =4Q421 1.2$_{13}$ [בטרם יש]מע) 4Q525 14.2$_{23}$, בין *understand* Ps 58$_{10}$ (or em. נוב *produce [fruit]*) 4Q421 1.2$_{13}$, חקר *investigate* Si 11$_{7}$ (+ אַחַר *afterwards*, לְפָנִים *beforehand*) 11$_{27}$, דרשׁ *seek* 4Q424 3$_{1}$, בחן *test* 4Q424 3$_{1}$ ([יבחן]), נכה hi. *strike* Jr 47$_{1}$ (or del.), נגף htp. *be struck* Jr 13$_{16}$, קטר hi. *turn* fat *into smoke* 1 S 2$_{15}$.

<COLL> with verb in preceding main clause (unless specified), היה *be* Jr 47$_{1}$ (or del. בְּטֶרֶם) Ezk 16$_{57}$, בלג hi. *be cheerful* Jb 10$_{21}$ Ps 39$_{14}$, ילד *give birth* Ex 1$_{19}$ Is 66$_{7}$ (main clause follows in both), pu. *be born* Gn 41$_{50}$, מלט hi. *give birth* Is 66$_{7}$ (main clause follows), בוא *come* 1 S 2$_{15}$ (main clause follows), קום *arise* Ru 3$_{14}$, עלה hi. *raise* Jr 38$_{10}$, נשׂא *raise* Is 8$_{4}$ (main clause follows), עזב ni. *be abandoned* Is 7$_{16}$ (main clause follows), מצא *find* 1 S 9$_{13}$, שׁלח *send* Arad ost. 5$_{12}$ ([י]שלח), נתן *give* Jr 13$_{16.16}$ Si 14$_{13}$ (main clause follows) Arad ost. 40$_{10}$ ([בטרם]), מנע *withhold* Pr 30$_{7}$, שׁוב hi. *take back*, i.e. answer Pr 18$_{13}$ Si 11$_{8(B)}$ (A טֶרֶם, as §1a) 4Q420 1.2$_{1}$, שׁפך *pour*, i.e. utter 4Q525 14.2$_{23}$, אמר *say* Jg 14$_{18}$ 1 S 2$_{15}$ 2 K 6$_{32}$ (main clause follows in both), דבר pi. *speak* 4Q421 1.2$_{13}$, שׁמע hi. *announce* Is 42$_{9}$ 48$_{5}$ (main clause follows in both), ברך pi. *bless* Gn 27$_{4}$ 1QS 10$_{15}$, אשׁר pi. *pronounce happy* Si 11$_{27}$ ([תאש]רה[ו]; + לִפְנֵי *before* death; main clause follows), ידע *know* Dt 31$_{21}$ Jr 1$_{5}$ (main clause follows) 4QJub$^{a}$ 1$_{7}$ ([בטרם ... ידעתי]), אמן hi. *believe* 4Q424 3$_{1}$, שׁפט *judge* 4Q424 3$_{1}$, נכל htp. *conspire* Gn 37$_{18}$ (main clause follows), סלף pi. *subvert*, i.e. criticize Si 11$_{7}$ (main clause follows), ראה *see* Gn 45$_{28}$, עשׂה *do* 2 K 2$_{9}$, יטב hi. *do good* Si 14$_{13}$ (main clause follows), קדשׁ hi. *sanctify* Jr 1$_{5}$ (main clause follows), אכל *eat* Gn 27$_{33}$, רחץ *wash* 4QJub$^{d}$ 21$_{16}$ ([בטרם ... ורחצתה]), שׂער *blow away* Ps 58$_{10}$ (main clause follows), פנה pi. *clear* house Lv 14$_{36}$, perh. פקד *visit* 4Q418 81$_{11}$.

**2b.** בְּטֶרֶם followed by pf. of ילד pu. *be born* Ps 90$_{2}$, טבע ho. *be sunk* Pr 8$_{25}$, יסד ni. *be founded* CD 2$_{7}$, דבר ni. *be spoken* 4QMyst$^{b}$ 1.2$_{1}$, ברא *create* 1QH 1$_{8}$ 13$_{8}$ 15$_{14}$ 4QAges 2.2$_{10}$, תעה *stray* 11QPs$^{a}$ Si 51$_{13}$ (בטרם תעיתי *before I strayed*; others תעותי before *my straying*, as §2c). <COLL> with verb in preceding main clause, כון hi. *establish* 1QH 15$_{14}$ ([כול פעולת]ו הכינותה בטרם בראתו *you established its activity before you created it*), ידע *know* 1QH 13$_{8}$ ([ותדע]), נגד hi. *declare* 4QMyst$^{b}$ 1.2$_{1}$; with verb in following main clause, חול polel *give birth* Ps 90$_{2}$, polal *be born* Pr 8$_{25}$ (בְּטֶרֶם הָרִים הָטְבָּעוּ לִפְנֵי גְבָעוֹת חוֹלָלְתִּי *before mountains were sunk, before the hills, I was born*), ידע *know* CD 2$_{7}$ 1QH 1$_{8}$ 4QAges 2.2$_{10}$; with nom. cl. as main clause, אני נער בטרם תעיתי *I was a lad before I strayed* 11QPs$^{a}$ Si 51$_{13}$; B אני נער הייתי וחפצתי בה *I was a lad, and I desired her*).

**2c.** בְּטֶרֶם followed by inf. of היה *be* 1QH 1$_{11.20.28}$, ברא ni. *be created* 4QTNaph 1.2$_{8}$, ילד *give birth* Zp 2$_{2}$=1QpZeph$_{2a}$ ([בטרם לדת]; or em.; see §3), תעה *stray* 11QPs$^{a}$ Si 51$_{13}$ (but see §2b). <COLL> verb in preceding main clause, קשׁשׁ *be assembled* Zp 2$_{2}$=1QpZeph$_{2a}$ ([בטרם ... [ו]ק[ושו]), htpo. *be assembled* Zp 2$_{2}$=1QpZeph$_{2a}$ ([בטרם ... התקו[ש]שו]), כון hi. *establish* 1QH 1$_{20}$ (הכ[י]נותה) 1$_{28}$, ידע *know* 1QH 1$_{28}$ 4QTNaph 1.2$_{8}$ ([ידע]); with verb in following main clause, ידע *know* 1QH 1$_{11}$ ([בטרם היותם למלאכי ק]ודש ידעתם *before their being as angels of holiness you knew them*); with nom. cl. as main clause 11QPs$^{a}$ Si 51$_{13}$ (but see §2b).

**2d.** בְּטֶרֶם followed by nom. cl., אַבְלִיגָה בְּטֶרֶם אֵלֵךְ וְאֵינֶנִּי *I shall be cheerful before I go and am no more* Ps 39$_{14}$.

**3.** בְּטֶרֶם לֹא as בְּטֶרֶם, **before,** followed by impf. of בוא *come* Zp 2$_{2.2}$=1QpZeph$_{3.3}$ ([בטרם לוא יבוא ...] [בטרם לוא יבוא]), דחק ni. *be crushed* Zp 2$_{2}$ (if em.

לֶדֶת חֹק appar. *to give birth to a statute*, i.e. before a decree is issued, to לֹא תִדְחֲקוּ before *you are crushed*). <COLL> verb in preceding main clause, קשׁשׁ *be assembled* Zp $2_{2}$ (if em.) $2_{2.2}$ ([ו]ן[קושו ... בטרם ... בטרם]), htpo. *be assembled* Zp $2_{2}$ (if em.) $2_{2.2}$=1QpZeph$_{3.3}$ ([התקו]ש[שו ... בטרם ... בטרם]).

**4.** מִטֶּרֶם **before** or perh. **as long as** or **immediately after, from the beginning of,*** followed by inf. of שׂים *place* Hg $2_{15}$. <COLL> with verb in following main clause, היה *be* Hg $2_{15}$.

**5.** כְּטֶרֶם **before,** followed by pf. of ברא *create* 4QAges $1_{2}$. <COLL> with verb in following main clause, כון hi. *establish* 4QAges $1_{2}$.

**6.** בְּטֶרֶם as preposition, **before,** בְּטֶרֶם בֹּקֶר אֵינֶנּוּ *before morning it is no more* Is $17_{14}$ (+ לְעֵת *by the time of* evening), וְהָיְתָה ... כְּבִכּוּרָה בְּטֶרֶם קַיִץ *and it will be ... like an early fig before the harvest* Is $28_{4}$.

Also 1QpPs $2_{1}$ ([בטר]ם]) 4QTNaph $2_{5}$ (בטרם) 4QToh A $2.1_{1}$ (ורחץ ויכבס טרם *and he is to wash [himself] and clean [his clothes] before*) 4Q418 $81_{11}$ ([ובט]רם]) 11Q Hod$^{b}$2 ([בטרם]).

**טרף** $25.0.5$ vb. **tear—Qal** $20.0.3$ Pf. טָרַף (טָרֶף); impf. יִטְרֹף (יִטְרֶף), אֶטְרֹף, Q יטרפו; ptc. טֹרֵף (Q טורף), טֹרְפֵי; inf. טָרֹף, טָרוֹף (לִטְרָף־)—**tear (apart), savage,** <SUBJ> ״ Y. Ho $5_{14}$ $6_{1}$ (+ רפא *heal*), אֱלוֹהַּ *God* Ps $50_{22}$, Gad Dt $33_{20}$=4QMidrEschat$^{a}$ $2_{3}$ ([טרף]), Joseph Gn $37_{33}$, Job Jb $18_{4}$, רדף ptc. *one who pursues* Ps $7_{3}$, זְאֵב *wolf* Gn $49_{27}$ Ezk $22_{27}$, כְּפִיר *young lion* Ezk $19_{3.6}$ Mc $5_{7}$ 1QH $5_{14}$, אֲרִי *lion* Ezk $22_{25}$ 4QpNah $3.1_{4}$, אַרְיֵה *lion* Na $2_{13}$ Ps $22_{14}$ perh. Ps $17_{12}$, אַף *anger* Am $1_{11}$ Jb $16_{9}$, אֶחָד *one* Gn $44_{28}$. <OBJ> זְרוֹעַ *arm* Dt $33_{20}$=4QMidrEschat$^{a}$ $2_{3}$, נֶפֶשׁ *soul* Ps $7_{3}$ Jb $18_{4}$ 1QH $5_{14}$, טֶרֶף *prey* Ezk $19_{3.6}$ $22_{25.27}$. <PREP> לְ *during,* + עַד *eternity* Am $1_{11}$; בְּ introducing object, + דַּי *sufficiency* Na $2_{13}$=4QpNah $3.1_{4}$; of accompaniment, *in (a state of), with,* + אַף *anger* Jb $18_{4}$. <COLL> אִם־טָרֹף יִטָּרֵף *if it is indeed savaged* Ex $22_{12}$. Also 5Q16 $3_{4}$.

**Ni.** $2.0.1$ Impf. יִטָּרֵף—**be torn,** <SUBJ> יצא ptc. *one who goes out* Jr $5_{6}$, חֲמוֹר *ass* Ex $22_{12}$, שׁוֹר *ox* Ex $22_{12}$, שֶׂה *lamb* Ex $22_{12}$, בְּהֵמָה *beast* Ex $22_{12}$. <COLL> אִם־טָרֹף יִטָּרֵף *if it is indeed savaged* Ex $22_{12}$. Also 1QH $5_{19}$ ([נ]טרף).

**Pu.** 2 Pf. טֹרַף (טֹרָף)—**be torn,** <SUBJ> Joseph Gn $37_{33}$ $44_{28}$.

**Hi.** $1.0.1$ Impf. Q יטריפכה; impv. הַטְרִיפֵנִי—**devour, feed,** <SUBJ> appar. Y. Pr $30_{8}$, perh. אֵל *God* 4Q417 $1.1_{20}$. <OBJ> (1) food provided: לֶחֶם *bread* Pr $30_{8}$, אֲשֶׁר *that which,* i.e. whatever food 4Q417 $1.1_{20}$; (2) recipient of food: Agur Pr $30_{8}$, worshipper 4Q417 $1.1_{20}$.*

→ טָרָף *fresh,* טֶרֶף *prey,* טְרֵפָה *savaged beast.*

**טָרָף** $2.0.1$ adj. **fresh**—pl. cstr. טַרְפֵּי—**1. fresh, freshly-plucked,** used attributively of עָלֶה olive *leaf* Gn $8_{11}$=4QpGen$^{a}$ $1.1_{16}$. **2.** used as noun, **fresh leaf,** <SUBJ> יבשׁ *be dry* Ezk $17_{9}$. <CSTR> כָּל־טַרְפֵּי צִמְחָהּ *all the fresh leaves of its growth* Ezk $17_{9}$.*

→ טרף *tear.*

**טֶ֫רֶף** $22.1.10$ n.m. **prey**—טָרֶף; cstr. טֶרֶף; sf. טַרְפֵּךְ (Q טרפכה), טַרְפּוֹ—usu. **prey,** killed and devoured by ferocious beasts (e.g. Gn $49_{9}$ Nm $23_{24}$ Am $3_{4}$ Ps $104_{21}$ Jb $4_{11}$ Si $11_{30}$), more generally, **food** of humans (Ml $3_{10}$ Ps $111_{5}$ Pr $31_{15}$ 4Q417 $1.1_{17}$ $1.2_{3}$ 4Q418 $81_{16}$) or beasts (Jb $24_{5}$).

<SUBJ> היה Ml $3_{10}$, מושׁ hi. *depart* Na $3_{1}$=1Q$55_{3}$=4Qp Nah $3.2_{3}$.

<NOM CL> טרפו הוא ההון *his prey is the wealth* 4Qp Nah $3.1_{12}$, טֶרֶף אֵין לוֹ *if (the lion) has no prey* Am $3_{4}$.

<OBJ> נתן *give* Ps $111_{5}$ Pr $31_{15}$ 4Q417 $1.2_{3}$, טרף *tear* Ezk $19_{3.6}$ $22_{25.27}$, שׁלך hi. *throw,* i.e. cause to drop from mouth Jb $29_{17}$, צוד *hunt* Jb $38_{39}$, פקד *appoint* 4Q418 $81_{16}$, חסר pi. *deprive* 4Q417 $1.1_{17}$, אחז *seize* Is $5_{29}$, חנק pi. *strangle* 4QpNah $3.1_{4}$, אכל *eat,* i.e. devour Nm $23_{24}$, כרת hi. *cut off* Na $2_{14}$=4QpNah $3.1_{9}$ ([ט]רפה]).

<CSTR> הַרְרֵי־טָרֶף *mountains of prey* Ps $76_{5}$ (or em. עַד *of eternity*).

<PREP> לְ *for, in pursuit of,* + ארב *wait in ambush* Si $11_{30}$, שׁחר pi. *arise early* Jb $24_{5}$, שׁאג *roar* Ps $104_{21}$; בְּ perh. *around* 4QpHos$^{b}$ $3_{3}$ (unless בטרפ[ו] *when he tears,* i.e. טרף *tear*); מִן of direction, *from,* + עלה *go up* Gn $49_{9}$; עַל *over,* + הגה *moan,* i.e. growl Is $31_{4}$; מִבְּלִי *without,* + אבד *perish* Jb $4_{11}$.

<COLL> וַיְמַלֵּא־טֶרֶף *and he has filled* his caves *with prey* Na $2_{13}$=4QpNah $3.1_{6}$ ([טרף]; ‖ טְרֵפָה *savaged beast*), שֶׁלֹּא נְתָנָנוּ טֶרֶף *who has not given us (as) prey* Ps $124_{6}$.

Also 1QSb $5_{29}$ perh. 4QpHos[b] $38_8$ 4Q416 $2.1_{22}$.*
⇒ טרף *tear.*

**טְרֵפָה** 9.0.1 n.f. **savaged beast,** one torn apart by other beasts, as distinct from one killed by humans for food or that has died naturally; sometimes used collectively, <OBJ> בוא hi. *bring* Gn $31_{39}$, אכל *eat* Ex $22_{30}$ Lv $17_{15}$ $22_8$ Ezk $4_{14}$ $44_{31}$, שׁלם pi. *repay,* i.e. pay compensation for Ex $22_{12}$. <CSTR> חֵלֶב טְרֵפָה *fat of torn one* Lv $7_{24}$. <COLL> וַיְמַלֵּא ... מְעֹנֹתָיו טְרֵפָה *and he filled ... his dens with savaged beasts* Na $2_{13}$=4QpNah $3.1_6$ (|| טֶרֶף *prey*). <SYN> טֶרֶף *prey*.*
⇒ טרף *tear.*

# Bibliography

AB Anchor Bible
*AbrN* *Abr-Nahrain*
*AcOr* *Acta orientalia*
*Aev* *Aevum*
*AfO* *Archiv für Orientforschung*
*AION* *Annali dell'istituto orientale di Napoli*
*AJBI* *Annual of the Japanese Biblical Institute*
*AJSL* *American Journal of Semitic Languages and Literatures*
AOAT Alter Orient und Altes Testament
*ArOr* *Archiv orientálni*
ATANT Abhandlungen zur Theologie des Alten und Neuen Testaments
ATSAT Arbeiten zu Text und Sprache im Alten Testament
*AUSS* *Andrews University Seminary Studies*
*BASOR* *Bulletin of the American Schools of Oriental Research*
BBB Bonner biblische Beiträge
*BeO* *Bibbia e oriente*
*BethM* *Beth Mikra*
BETL Bibliotheca ephemeridum theologicarum lovaniensium
*Bib* *Biblica*
BibOr Biblica et orientalia
*BibRes* *Biblical Research*
*Bijd* *Bijdragen*
*BiTrans* *The Bible Translator*
*BN* *Biblische Notizen*
*BO* *Bibliotheca orientalis*
Brown–Driver–Briggs, *Lexicon* Francis Brown, S.R. Driver and Charles A. Briggs, *A Hebrew and English Lexicon of the Old Testament* (Oxford: Clarendon Press, 1907)
BWANT Beiträge zur Wissenschaft vom Alten und Neuen Testament
*BZ* *Biblische Zeitschrift*
BZAW Beihefte zur *ZAW*
*CBQ* *Catholic Biblical Quarterly*
*CivCatt* *Civiltà cattolica*
*CuadJer* *Cuadernos bíblicos, Institución S. Jerónimo*
DJD Discoveries in the Judaean Desert
*DTT* *Dansk teologisk tidsskrift*
EBib Etudes bibliques
*EI* *Eretz-Israel*
*EstBíb* *Estudios bíblicos*
*EstFranc* *Estudios Franciscanos*
*ETL* *Ephemerides theologicae lovanienses*
*ExpT* *Expository Times*
*FF* *Forschungen und Fortschritte*
FRLANT Forschungen zur Religion und Literatur des Alten und Neuen Testaments
*Greg* *Gregorianum*
*HALOT* Ludwig Koehler and Walter Baumgartner *et al.*, *The Hebrew and Aramaic Lexicon of the Old Testament* (tr. M.E.J. Richardson; Leiden: E.J. Brill, 1994–)
HSM Harvard Semitic Monographs
HSS Harvard Semitic Studies
*HTR* *Harvard Theological Review*
*HUCA* *Hebrew Union College Annual*
*IEJ* *Israel Exploration Journal*
*JANES* *Journal of the Ancient Near Eastern Society of Columbia University*
*JAOS* *Journal of the American Oriental Society*
*JBL* *Journal of Biblical Literature*
*JCS* *Journal of Cuneiform Studies*
*JJS* *Journal of Jewish Studies*
*JNES* *Journal of Near Eastern Studies*
*JNWSL* *Journal of Northwest Semitic Languages*

# *Abbreviations to Bibliography*

*JPOS* *Journal of the Palestine Oriental Society*
*JQR* *Jewish Quarterly Review*
*JRAS* *Journal of the Royal Asiatic Society*
*JSem* *Journal for Semitics*
*JSOT* *Journal for the Study of the Old Testament*
JSOTSup *Journal for the Study of the Old Testament*, Supplement Series
JSPSup *Journal for the Study of the Pseudepigrapha*, Supplement Series
*JSS* *Journal of Semitic Studies*
*JTS* *Journal of Theological Studies*
*KerDo* *Kerygma und Dogma*
Koehler, *Lexicon* Ludwig Koehler, *Lexicon in Veteris Testamenti Libros* (Leiden: E.J. Brill, 1953)
Koehler–Baumgartner, *Lexikon* Ludwig Koehler and Walter Baumgartner *et al.*, *Hebräisches und aramäisches Lexikon zum Alten Testament* (Leiden: E.J. Brill, 1967–94)
*Lesh* *Leshonenu*
*MEstArabHeb* *Miscelanea de estudios arabes y hebraicos*
*MTZ* *Münchener theologische Zeitschrift*
NICOT New International Commentary on the Old Testament
OBO Orbis biblicus et orientalis
*Or* *Orientalia*
*OrS* *Orientalia suecana*
*OTS* *Oudtestamentische Studiën*
*PEFQS* *Palestine Exploration Fund, Quarterly Statement*
*PEQ* *Palestine Exploration Quarterly*
QuadSem Quaderni semistici
*RB* *Revue biblique*
*RHR* *Revue de l'histoire des religions*
*RivB* *Rivista biblica*
*RQ* *Revue de Qumran*
*RestQ* *Restoration Quarterly*
*SBFLA* *Studii biblici franciscani liber annuus*
SBLDS Society of Biblical Literature Dissertation Series
SBLMS Society of Biblical Literature Monograph Series
SBS Stuttgarter Biblische Studien
ScrHieros Scripta Hierosolymitana
*SEÅ* *Svensk exegetisk årsbok*
*Sef* *Sefarad*
*Sem* *Semitica*
*SJOT* *Scandinavian Journal of the Old Testament*
SOTSMS Society for Old Testament Study Monograph Series
*Tarb* *Tarbiz*
*TDOT* G.J. Botterweck and H. Ringgren (eds.), *Theological Dictionary of the Old Testament* (tr. John T. Willis *et al.*; Grand Rapids: Eerdmans, 1974–)
*Teres* *Teresianum: Ephemerides Carmeliticae*
*TGUOS* *Transactions of the Glasgow University Oriental Society*
Thomas, *Lexicon* D. Winton Thomas, *A Hebrew and English Lexicon of the Old Testament*, revised edition (1970; unpublished)
*THWAT* Ernst Jenni and Claus Westermann (eds.), *Theologisches Handwörterbuch zum Alten Testament* (München: Kaiser, 1971–76)
*TLZ* *Theologische Literaturzeitung*
*TS* *Theological Studies*
*TTZ* *Trierer theologische Zeitschrift*
*TVers* *Theologische Versuche*
*TynB* *Tyndale Bulletin*
*TZ* *Theologische Zeitschrift*
*UF* *Ugarit-Forschungen*
*VD* *Verbum domini*
*VT* *Vetus Testamentun*
VTSup *Vetus Testamentum*, Supplements
WMANT Wissenschaftliche Monographien zum Alten und Neuen Testament
*WO* *Die Welt des Orients*
*WTJ* *Westminster Theological Journal*
*ZAH* *Zeitschrift für Althebraistik*
*ZAW* *Zeitschrift für die alttestamentliche Wissenschaft*
*ZDPV* *Zeitschrift des deutschen Palästina-Vereins*
*ZTK* *Zeitschrift für Theologie und Kirche*

# ז

זְאֵב I *wolf*—G.J. Botterweck, 'זְאֵב *ze'ēbh*', *TDOT*, IV (1980), pp. 1-7

זֹאת *this*—W.L. Moran, 'Gen 49,10 and Its Use in Ez 21,32', *Bib* 39 (1958), pp. 418-19; K. Ehlich, *Verwendungen der Deixis beim sprachlichen Handeln* (Frankfurt/Bern: Peter Lang, 1979), esp. pp. 191-342, 367-419, 437-99

הָאָרֶץ הַזֹּאת *this land*, etc.—Konrad Ehlich, *Verwendungen der Deixis beim sprachlichen Handeln: Linguistisch-philologische Untersuchungen zum hebräischen deiktischen System* (Forum Linguisticum, 24; Frankfurt/Bern: Peter Lang, 1979), pp. 277-88

הַפַּעַם הַזֹּאת *this time*—Konrad Ehlich, *Verwendungen der Deixis beim sprachlichen Handeln: Linguistisch-philologische Untersuchungen zum hebräischen deiktischen System* (Forum Linguisticum, 24; Frankfurt/Bern: Peter Lang, 1979), pp. 597-98

זֹאת הַפַּעַם *this time*—Konrad Ehlich, *Verwendungen der Deixis beim sprachlichen Handeln: Linguistisch-philologische Untersuchungen zum hebräischen deiktischen System* (Forum Linguisticum, 24; Frankfurt/Bern: Peter Lang, 1979), pp. 603-5

מַה־זֹּאת *what's this?*—Konrad Ehlich, *Verwendungen der Deixis beim sprachlichen Handeln: Linguistisch-philologische Untersuchungen zum hebräischen deiktischen System* (Forum Linguisticum, 24; Frankfurt/Bern: Peter Lang, 1979), pp. 647-51

זבח *sacrifice*—N. Snaith, 'The Verbs *Zābaḥ* and *Šāḥaṭ*', *VT* 25 (1975), pp. 242-46; J. Bergman, H. Ringgren, B. Lang, 'זָבַח *zābhach*; זֶבַח *zebhach*', *TDOT*, IV (1980), pp. 8-29

זֶבַח I *sacrifice*—J. Bergman, H. Ringgren, B. Lang, 'זָבַח *zābhach*; זֶבַח *zebhach*', *TDOT*, IV (1980), pp. 8-29; R.W. Cowley, 'Technical Terms in Biblical Hebrew', *TynB* 37 (1986), pp. 21-28

זֶבַח הַיָּמִים—Menahem Haran, '*Zeḇaḥ hayyamîm*', *VT* 19 (1969), pp. 11-22; Haran, '*Zbḥ ymm* in the Karatepe Inscription', *VT* 19 (1969), pp. 372-73

זֶבַח שְׁלָמִים *sacrifice of peace offerings*—R. Rendtorff, *Leviticus* (Biblischer Kommentar, 3; Stuttgart: Kohlhammer, 1990), pp. 119-29

זבל I *exalt*—M. David, '*Zabal* (Gen xxx 20)', *VT* 1 (1951), pp. 59-60

זְבֻל I *dwelling place*—J. Gamberoni, 'זְבֻל *zebhul*', *TDOT*, IV (1980), pp. 29-31

זְבֻל II *dais* (cf. Ug. zbl)—W.F. Albright, 'The Psalm of Habakkuk', in *Studies in Old Testament Prophecy* (ed. H.H. Rowley; Edinburgh: T. & T. Clark, 1950), pp. 1-18 (16)

*princely estate*—G.R. Driver, *Canaanite Myths and Legends* (Old Testament Studies, 3; Edinburgh: T. & T. Clark, 1956), p. 149

זֵד *presumptuous*—J. Scharbert, 'זוד* **zûdh*; זיד *zîdh*; זֵד *zēdh*; זָדוֹן *zādhôn*', *TDOT*, IV (1980), pp. 46-51

זְדָה *fissure*—H.J. Stoebe, 'Zu Vet. Test. VIII S. 297ff. (Henri Michaud, "Un passage difficile dans l'inscription de Siloé")', *VT* 9 (1959), pp. 99-101; H. Michaud, 'Resserrement ou animation?', *VT* 9 (1959), pp. 205-209; E. Puech, 'L'inscription du tunnel de Siloé', *RB* 81 (1974), pp. 198-207; K. Lawson Younger, 'The Siloam Tunnel Inscription—an Integrated Reading', *UF* 26 (1994), pp. 543-56 (549-50).

זָדוֹן *presumptuousness*—J. Scharbert, 'זוד* **zûdh*; זיד *zîdh*; זֵד *zēdh*; זָדוֹן *zādhôn*', *TDOT*, IV (1980), pp. 46-51; E. Qimron, 'Terminology for Intention Used in the Legal Texts of the Dead Sea Scrolls', in *Proceedings of the Tenth World Congress of Jewish Studies, Jerusalem, 1989. Division A: The Bible and Its World* (Jerusalem: World Union of Jewish Studies, 1990), pp. 103-10

זֶה *this*—Konrad Ehlich, *Verwendungen der Deixis beim sprachlichen Handeln: Linguistisch-philologische Untersuchungen zum hebräischen deiktischen System* (Forum

Linguisticum, 24; Frankfurt/Bern: Peter Lang, 1979), esp. pp. 191-342, 367-419, 437-499, 839-54

הַדָּבָר הַזֶּה *this word*—Konrad Ehlich, *Verwendungen der Deixis beim sprachlichen Handeln: Linguistisch-philologische Untersuchungen zum hebräischen deiktischen System* (Forum Linguisticum, 24; Frankfurt/Bern: Peter Lang, 1979), pp. 333-42, 509-40

הָהָר הַזֶּה *this mountain*—Konrad Ehlich, *Verwendungen der Deixis beim sprachlichen Handeln: Linguistisch-philologische Untersuchungen zum hebräischen deiktischen System* (Forum Linguisticum, 24; Frankfurt/Bern: Peter Lang, 1979), pp. 270-72

הַיּוֹם הַזֶּה *this day*, etc.—Konrad Ehlich, *Verwendungen der Deixis beim sprachlichen Handeln: Linguistisch-philologische Untersuchungen zum hebräischen deiktischen System* (Forum Linguisticum, 24; Frankfurt/Bern: Peter Lang, 1979), pp. 292-97, 500-504, 541-70

הַמָּקוֹם הַזֶּה *this place*—Konrad Ehlich, *Verwendungen der Deixis beim sprachlichen Handeln: Linguistisch-philologische Untersuchungen zum hebräischen deiktischen System* (Forum Linguisticum, 24; Frankfurt/Bern: Peter Lang, 1979), pp. 265-68

זֶה הַדָּבָר *this is the word*—Konrad Ehlich, *Verwendungen der Deixis beim sprachlichen Handeln: Linguistisch-philologische Untersuchungen zum hebräischen deiktischen System* (Forum Linguisticum, 24; Frankfurt/Bern: Peter Lang, 1979), pp. 342, 509-40

זֶה פַּעֲמַיִם *these two times*, etc.—Konrad Ehlich, *Verwendungen der Deixis beim sprachlichen Handeln: Linguistisch-philologische Untersuchungen zum hebräischen deiktischen System* (Forum Linguisticum, 24; Frankfurt/Bern: Peter Lang, 1979), pp. 598-603

כָּזֹה וְכָזֶה *like this and like this*—Konrad Ehlich, *Verwendungen der Deixis beim sprachlichen Handeln: Linguistisch-philologische Untersuchungen zum hebräischen deiktischen System* (Forum Linguisticum, 24; Frankfurt/Bern: Peter Lang, 1979), pp. 606-608

מִזֶּה ... וּמִזֶּה *over here ... and over there*—Konrad Ehlich, *Verwendungen der Deixis beim sprachlichen Handeln: Linguistisch-philologische Untersuchungen zum hebräischen deiktischen System* (Forum Linguisticum, 24; Frankfurt/Bern: Peter Lang, 1979), pp. 583-93

*that which, that, which* (§§2-3)—Konrad Ehlich, *Verwendungen der Deixis beim sprachlichen Handeln: Linguistisch-philologische Untersuchungen zum hebräischen deiktischen System* (Forum Linguisticum, 24; Frankfurt/Bern: Peter Lang, 1979), pp. 612-23, 647-54

*one that is of* (§4)—Mitchell J. Dahood, 'Hebrew–Ugaritic Lexicography II', *Bib* 45 (1964), pp. 393-412 (405); Konrad Ehlich, *Verwendungen der Deixis beim sprachlichen Handeln: Linguistisch-philologische Untersuchungen zum hebräischen deiktischen System* (Forum Linguisticum, 24; Frankfurt/Bern: Peter Lang, 1979), pp. 640-45

זֹה *this*—כָּזֹה וְכָזֶה *like this and like this*—Konrad Ehlich, *Verwendungen der Deixis beim sprachlichen Handeln: Linguistisch-philologische Untersuchungen zum hebräischen deiktischen System* (Forum Linguisticum, 24; Frankfurt/Bern: Peter Lang, 1979), pp. 606-608

זָהָב I *gold*—B. Kedar-Kopfstein, 'זָהָב *zāhābh*; חָרוּץ *chārûts*; כֶּתֶם *kethem*; סְגוֹר *seghôr*; פַּז *paz*', *TDOT*, IV (1980), pp. 32-40

זָהָב II *spice*—G. Ryckmans, 'De l'or (?), de l'encens et de la myrrhe', *RB* 58 (1951), pp. 372-76

זהר I *warn*—J. Tropper, 'Hebräisch *zhr*$_2$ "kundtun, warnen"', *ZAH* 8 (1995), pp. 144-48

זהר II *be bright*—M. Görg, 'זָהַר *zāhar*; זֹהַר *zōhar*', *TDOT*, IV (1980), pp. 41-46; J. Tropper, 'Hebräisch *zhr*$_2$ "kundtun, warnen"', *ZAH* 8 (1995), pp. 144-48

זֹהַר *brightness*—M. Görg, 'זָהַר *zāhar*; זֹהַר *zōhar*', *TDOT*, IV (1980), pp. 41-46

זוֹ *this*—Konrad Ehlich, *Verwendungen der Deixis beim sprachlichen Handeln: Linguistisch-philologische Untersuchungen zum hebräischen deiktischen System* (Forum Linguisticum, 24; Frankfurt/Bern: Peter Lang, 1979), pp. 623-24

זוּ *that, which, who(m)*—Konrad Ehlich, *Verwendungen der Deixis beim sprachlichen Handeln: Linguistisch-philologische Untersuchungen zum hebräischen deiktischen System* (Forum Linguisticum, 24; Frankfurt/Bern: Peter Lang, 1979), pp. 624-39

זוע II *stand aside* (cf. Arab. zāʿa *incline*, zāġa *deviate*)—Godfrey R. Driver, 'Problems and Solutions', *VT* 4 (1954), pp. 225-45 (236)

זור I *be strange*—L.A. Snijders, 'זוּר/זָר *zûr/zār*', *TDOT*, IV (1980), pp. 52-58

זָר *foreign(er)*—P. Humbert, 'Les adjectifs *zār* et *nokrî*', *Mélanges syriens offerts à M. R. Dussaud*, I (1939), pp. 259-66; L.A. Snijders, 'The Meaning of זר in the Old Testament: An Exegetical Study', *OTS* 10 (1954), pp. 1-154

זָר *enemy*—G.R. Driver, 'Ezekiel: Linguistic and Textual Problems', *Bib* 35 (1954), pp. 145-59 (148-49)

זור II *flow*—Mitchell J. Dahood, 'Philological Notes on Jer 18 14-15', *ZAW* 74 (1962), pp. 207-209

זור III *be abhorrent*—P. Wernberg-Møller, 'A Note on זור "To Stink"', *VT* 4 (1954), pp. 322-25

זור IV *depart*—Ludwig Wächter, 'Drei umstrittene Psalmstellen (Ps 26 1 30 8 90 4-6)', *ZAW* 78 (1966), pp. 61-69 (65-67).

זחל II *fear*—Mitchell J. Dahood, 'Hebrew–Ugaritic Lexicography II', *Bib* 45 (1964), pp. 393-412 (406)

זיד *be presumptuous*—J. Scharbert, 'זוּד* **zûdh*; זִיד *zîdh*; זֵד *zēdh*; זָדוֹן *zādhôn*', *TDOT*, IV (1980), pp. 46-51

זיז I *locust*—D.W. Thomas, 'The Meaning of זִיז in Psalm lxxx. 14', *ExpT* 76 (1964–65), p. 385

זיז II *teat*—W. Lau, *Schriftgelehrte Prophetie in Jes 56–66: Eine Untersuchung zu den literarischen Bezügen in den letzten elf Kapiteln des Jesajabuches* (BZAW, 225; Berlin: Töpelmann, 1994), p. 130

זיף shaphel *make honey-coloured*—G. Garbini, *Cantico dei cantici: Testo, traduzione, note e commento* (Biblica Testi e studi, 2; Brescia: Paideia, 1992), pp. 184-85

זִיף I *Ziph*—M.S. Moore, 'The Judean *lmlk*-Stamps: Some Unresolved Issues', *RestQ* 28 (1985–86), pp. 17-26

זַיִת *olive*—G.W. Ahlström, 'זַיִת *zayith*', *TDOT*, IV (1980), pp. 58-62

זכה *be pure*—A. Negoită, H. Ringgren, 'זָכָה *zākhāh*; זכך *zkk*; זַךְ *zakh*', *TDOT*, IV (1980), pp. 62-64

זָכוּר *male*—R.E. Clements, 'זָכָר *zākhār*; זָכוּר *zᵉkhûr*; (נְקֵבָה *nᵉqēbhāh*)', *TDOT*, IV (1980), pp. 82-87

זכר I *remember*—Leo L. Honor, 'The Role of Memory in Biblical History', in *Mordecai M. Kaplan: Jubilee Volume on the Occasion of His Seventieth Birthday* (ed. Moshe Davis; New York: Jewish Theological Seminary, 1953), pp. 417-35; H. Gross, 'Zur Wurzel *zkr*', *BZ* 4 (1960), pp. 227-37; J. Blau, 'Reste des I-Imperfekts von *ZKR*, Qal: Eine lexikographische Studie', *VT* 11 (1961), pp. 81-86; P.A.H. de Boer, *Gedenken und Gedächtnis in der Welt des Alten Testaments* (Stuttgart: Kohlhammer, 1962); B.S. Childs, *Memory and Tradition in Israel* (Studies in Biblical Theology, 37; Naperville: Allenson, 1962); W. Schottroff, *"Gedenken" im alten Orient und im Alten Testament: Die Wurzel* zākar *im semitischen Sprachkreis* (WMANT, 15; Neukirchen–Vluyn: Neukirchener Verlag, 1964); G.R. Driver, 'Hebrew Homonyms', in *Hebräische Wortforschung: Festschrift zum 80. Geburtstag von Walter Baumgartner* (VTSup, 16; Leiden: E.J. Brill, 1967), pp. 50-64 (53); H. Eising, 'זָכַר *zākhar*; זֵכֶר *zēkher*; זִכָּרוֹן *zikkārôn*; אַזְכָּרָה *ʾazkārāh*', *TDOT*, IV (1980), pp. 64-82

*give an order*—K.J. Cathcart, 'More Philological Studies in Nahum', *JNWSL* 7 (1979), pp. 1-12 (7)

*muster*—T.H. Gaster, 'Two Notes on Nahum', *JBL* 63 (1944), pp. 51-52 (52)

hi. *utter*—H. Gross, 'Zur Wurzel *zkr*', *BZ* 4 (1960), pp. 227-37; B.S. Childs, *Memory and Tradition in Israel* (Studies in Biblical Theology, 37; Naperville: Allenson, 1962)

זכר II *be strong*—Mitchell J. Dahood, 'Hebrew–Ugaritic Lexicography II', *Bib* 45 (1964), pp. 393-412 (406); P. Swiggers, 'Linguistic Considerations on Phoenician Orthography', in *Phoinikeia grammata: Lire et écrire en méditerranée. Actes du colloque de Liège 15-18 novembre 1989* (ed. Claude Baurain, C. Bonnet and V. Krings; Collection d'études classiques, 6; Namur: Société des Etudes Classiques, 1991), pp. 115-32 (123)

זכר III *boast* (cf. Arab. zakara *fill*)—Godfrey R. Driver, 'Hebrew Homonyms', in *Hebräische Wortforschung: Festschrift zum 80. Geburtstag von Walter Baumgartner* (VTSup, 16; Leiden: E.J. Brill, 1967), pp. 50-64 (53-54)

זָכָר *male*—R.E. Clements, 'זָכָר *zākhār*; זָכוּר *zᵉkhûr*; (נְקֵבָה

*n^eqēbhāh)'*, *TDOT*, IV (1980), pp. 82-87

זֵכֶר I *remembrance*—H. Eising, 'זָכַר *zākhar*; זֵכֶר *zēkher*; זִכָּרוֹן *zikkārôn*; אַזְכָּרָה *'azkārāh'*, *TDOT*, IV (1980), pp. 64-82; Y.T. Radday, '"Wie ist sein Name?" (Ex 3, 13)', *Linguistica Biblica* 58 (1986), pp. 87-104

זִכָּרוֹן *memorial*—H. Eising, 'זָכַר *zākhar*; זֵכֶר *zēkher*; זִכָּרוֹן *zikkārôn*; אַזְכָּרָה *'azkārāh'*, *TDOT*, IV (1980), pp. 64-82

זֻלּוּת *worthlessness*—P. Wernberg-Møller, 'Two Difficult Passages in the Old Testament', *ZAW* 69 (1957), pp. 69-73 (69-71)

זלל I *be worthless*—P. Wernberg-Møller, 'Two Difficult Passages in the Old Testament', *ZAW* 69 (1957), pp. 69-73 (69-71)

זלל II *quake*—G. Garbini, *Cantico dei cantici: Testo, traduzione, note e commento* (Biblica Testi e studi, 2; Brescia: Paideia, 1992), p. 228

זַלְעָפָה *raging*—Godfrey R. Driver, 'Hebrew Notes on "Song of Songs" and "Lamentations"', in *Festschrift Alfred Bertholet zum 80. Geburtstag* (ed. W. Baumgartner, O. Eissfeldt, K. Elliger and L. Rost; Tübingen: J.C.B. Mohr, 1950), pp. 134-46 (143)

זִמָּה I *wickedness, plan*—S. Steingrimsson, 'זמם *zmm*; זָמָם *z^emām*; זִמָּה *zimmāh*; מְזִמָּה *m^ezimmāh'*, *TDOT*, IV (1980), pp. 87-90

זִמָּה III *cord*—N.H. Tur-Sinai, *The Book of Job: A New Commentary* (Jerusalem: Kiryath-Sepher, 1957), pp. 281-82

זְמוֹרָה I *branch*—Robert Gordis, '"The Branch to the Nose": A Note on Ezekiel viii 17', *JTS* ns 37 (1936), pp. 284-88; H. Saggs, 'The Branch to the Nose', *JTS* ns 11 (1960), pp. 318-29 (324-27); H.P. Stähli, *Solare Elemente im Jahweglauben des Alten Testaments* (OBO, 66; Freiburg, Switzerland: Universitätsverlag and Göttingen: Vandenhoeck & Ruprecht, 1985), pp. 47-49.

זְמוֹרָה III *band of toughs* (cf. Ug. ḏmr *warrior*)—Nahum M. Sarna, 'Ezekiel 8:17: A Fresh Examination', *HTR* 57 (1964), pp. 347-52 (350-52)

זְמוֹרָה IV *warrior* (cf. Ug. ḏmr *warrior*)—Kevin J. Cathcart, *Nahum in the Light of Northwest Semitic* (BibOr, 26; Rome: Biblical Institute Press, 1973), pp. 85-86; Cathcart, 'More Philological Studies in Nahum', *JNWSL* 7 (1979), pp. 1-12 (6); Adam S. van der Woude, 'The Book of Nahum: A Letter Written in Exile', *OTS* 20 (1977), pp. 108-26 (118-19)

זָמִיר I *song*—C. Barth, 'זמר *zmr*; זָמִיר *zāmîr*; זִמְרָה *zimrāh*; מִזְמוֹר *mizmôr'*, *TDOT*, IV (1980), pp. 91-98

זָמִיר II *pruning*—S.M. Olyan, '2 Kings 9:31—Jehu as Zimri', *HTR* 78 (1985), pp. 203-207

זָמִיר III *guardian* (cf. Ug. ḏmr *warrior*)—H. Cazelles, 'La titulature du roi David', in *Mélanges bibliques rédigés en l'honneur de André Robert* (Travaux de l'Institut Catholique de Paris, 4; Paris: Bloud & Gay, 1957), pp. 134-36 (135); H. Neil Richardson, 'The Last Words of David: Some Notes on II Samuel 23:1-7', *JBL* 90 (1971), pp. 257-66 (261-62)

זמם *plan*—S. Steingrimsson, 'זמם *zmm*; זָמָם *z^emām*; זִמָּה *zimmāh*; מְזִמָּה *m^ezimmāh'*, *TDOT*, IV (1980), pp. 87-90

זָמָם *plan*—S. Steingrimsson, 'זמם *zmm*; זָמָם *z^emām*; זִמָּה *zimmāh*; מְזִמָּה *m^ezimmāh'*, *TDOT*, IV (1980), pp. 87-90

זְמָן *(set) time*—E. Lipiński, 'Araméen d'empire', in *Le langage dans l'antiquité* (ed. P. Swiggers and A. Wouters; La pensée linguistique, 3; Leuven: Peeters/Leuven University Press, 1990), pp. 94-133 (108-109)

זמר I *sing (praise)*—G. Rinaldi, 'Alcuni termini ebraici relativi alla letteratura', *Bib* 40 (1959), pp. 267-89 (273); C. Barth, 'זמר *zmr*; זָמִיר *zāmîr*; זִמְרָה *zimrāh*; מִזְמוֹר *mizmôr'*, *TDOT*, IV (1980), pp. 91-98

זִמְרָה I *song*—C. Barth, 'זמר *zmr*; זָמִיר *zāmîr*; זִמְרָה *zimrāh*; מִזְמוֹר *mizmôr'*, *TDOT*, IV (1980), pp. 91-98

זִמְרָה IV *warrior*—D.W. Thomas, 'A Note on Exodus xv. 2', *ExpT* 48 (1936–37), p. 478; Thomas, 'The Language of the Old Testament', in *Record and Revelation* (ed. H.W. Robinson; Oxford: Clarendon Press, 1938), pp. 374-402 (pp. 395-96)

זִמְרִי I *Zimri*—S.M. Olyan, '2 Kings 9:31—Jehu as Zimri', *HTR* 78 (1985), pp. 203-207

זנב pi. *massacre rearguard*—M. Görg, *Josua* (Neue Echter Bibel, 26; Wurzburg: Echter Verlag, 1991), p. 51

זנה I *prostitute oneself*—S. Erlandsson, 'זָנָה *zānāh*; זְנוּנִים *z^enûnîm*; זְנוּת *z^enûth*; תַּזְנוּת *taznûth'*, *TDOT*, IV (1980), pp. 99-104; P. Bird, '"To Play the Harlot": An Inquiry into an Old Testament Metaphor', in *Gender and Difference in Ancient Israel* (ed. Peggy L. Day; Minneapolis: Fortress Press, 1989), pp. 75-94

זֹנָה *prostitute*—H. Schulte, 'Beobachtungen zum Begriff *zônâ* im Alten Testament', *ZAW* 104 (1992), pp. 255-62

אִשָּׁה זוֹנָה *zônâ-wife, cult woman*—A.D. Tushingham, 'A Reconsideration of Hosea, Chapters 1–3', *JNES* 12 (1953), pp. 150-59 (157)

אִשָּׁה זוֹנָה *innkeeper*—H.St.J. Thackeray and Ralph Marcus, *Josephus. Vol. V: Jewish Antiquities. Books V–VIII* (Loeb Classical Library; London: Heinemann, 1934), p. 5

זנה II *be angry* (cf. Akk. zenû)—G.R. Driver, 'Mistranslations in the Old Testament', *WO* 1 (1947), pp. 29-30; Driver, 'L'interprétation du texte masorétique à la lumière de la lexicographie hébraïque', *ETL* 26 (1950), pp. 337-53 (348)

זְנוּנִים *prostitution*—S. Erlandsson, 'זָנָה *zānāh;* זְנוּנִים *zenûnîm;* זְנוּת *zenûth;* תַּזְנוּת *taznûth*', *TDOT*, IV (1980), pp. 99-104

אֵשֶׁת זְנוּנִים *zônâ-wife, cult woman*—A.D. Tushingham, 'A Reconsideration of Hosea, Chapters 1-3', *JNES* 12 (1953), pp. 150-59 (157); Hans W. Wolff, *Hosea* (Hermeneia; Philadelphia: Fortress Press, 1974), pp. 14-15

זְנוּת *prostitution*—S. Erlandsson, 'זָנָה *zānāh;* זְנוּנִים *zenûnîm;* זְנוּת *zenûth;* תַּזְנוּת *taznûth*', *TDOT*, IV (1980), pp. 99-104; Angelo Tosato, 'Su di una norma matrimoniale 4QD', *Bib* 74 (1993), pp. 401-10 (409-10); J. Kampen, 'The Matthean Divorce Texts Reexamined', in *New Qumran Texts and Studies: Proceedings of the First Meeting of the International Organization for Qumran Studies, Paris 1992* (ed. George J. Brooke and Florentino García Martínez; Studies on the Texts of the Desert of Judah, 15; Leiden: E.J. Brill, 1994), pp. 149-62 (152-62)

זנח I *reject*—H. Ringgren, 'זָנַח *zānach*', *TDOT*, IV (1980), pp. 105-106

*be angry*—R. Yaron, 'The Meaning of *zanaḥ*', *VT* 13 (1963), pp. 237-39

זעה *bark*—Mitchell J. Dahood, 'Hebrew–Ugaritic Lexicography II', *Bib* 45 (1964), pp. 393-412 (405-406)

זְעֵיר III *servant*—A. van Selms, 'Isaiah 28 9-13: An Attempt to Give a New Interpretation', *ZAW* 85 (1973), pp. 332-39 (337-38)

זעם *be indignant*—J. Scharbert, '"Fluchen" und "Segnen" im Alten Testament', *Bib* 39 (1958), pp. 1-26 (15); B. Wiklander, 'זָעַם *zā'am;* זַעַם *za'am*', *TDOT*, IV (1980), pp. 106-11

*curse*—Hedwige Rouillard, *La péricope de Balaam (Nombres 22–24: La prose et les «oracles»)* (EBib, ns 4; Paris: Gabalda, 1985), pp. 217-18

זעף I *be angry*—H. Ringgren, 'זָעַף *zā'aph;* זָעֵף *zā'ēph;* זַעַף *za'aph*', *TDOT*, IV (1980), pp. 111-12

זעף II *be thin* (cf. Arab. ḍa'ufa 'be weak', ḍā'īf *thin*)—L. Kopf, 'Arabische Etymologien und Parallelen zum Bibelwörterbuch', *VT* 9 (1959), pp. 247-87 (254)

זַעַף *anger*—H. Ringgren, 'זָעַף *zā'aph;* זָעֵף *zā'ēph;* זַעַף *za'aph*', *TDOT*, IV (1980), pp. 111-12

זָעֵף *angry*—H. Ringgren, 'זָעַף *zā'aph;* זָעֵף *zā'ēph;* זַעַף *za'aph*', *TDOT*, IV (1980), pp. 111-12

זעק *cry out*—G. Hasel, 'זָעַק *zā'aq;* זְעָקָה *ze'āqāh;* צָעַק *tsā'aq;* צְעָקָה *tse'āqāh*', *TDOT*, IV (1980), pp. 112-22; R.N. Boyce, *The Cry to God in the Old Testament* (SBLDS, 103; Atlanta: Scholars Press, 1988)

זְעָקָה *cry*—G. Hasel, 'זָעַק *zā'aq;* זְעָקָה *ze'āqāh;* צָעַק *tsā'aq;* צְעָקָה *tse'āqāh*', *TDOT*, IV (1980), pp. 112-22

זפת *be black*—Mitchell J. Dahood, 'Hebrew–Ugaritic Lexicography II', *Bib* 45 (1964), pp. 393-412 (406-407)

זָקָן *beard*—D. Marcus, 'The Term "Chin" in the Semitic Languages', *BASOR* 226 (1977), pp. 53-59

זָקֵן I *old*—J. Conrad, G.J. Botterweck, 'זָקֵן *zāqēn;* זֹקֶן *zōqen;* זִקְנָה *ziqnāh;* זְקֻנִים *zequnîm*', *TDOT*, IV (1980), pp. 122-31; I. Avineri, '*Zāqēn* in Bibel und Talmud', *Sinai* 99 (1986), pp. 277-78

*elder*—H. Reviv, *The Elders in Ancient Israel: A Study of a Biblical Institution* (Jerusalem: Magnes Press/Hebrew University, 1983)

זֹקֶן *old age*—J. Conrad and G.J. Botterweck, 'זָקֵן *zāqēn;* זֹקֶן *zōqen;* זִקְנָה *ziqnāh;* זְקֻנִים *zequnîm*', *TDOT*, IV (1980), pp. 122-31

# Bibliography to Zayin


זִקְנָה *old age*—J. Conrad and G.J. Botterweck, 'זָקֵן *zāqēn*; זֹקֶן *zōqen*; זִקְנָה *ziqnāh*; זְקֻנִים *zequnîm*', *TDOT*, IV (1980), pp. 122-31

זְקֻנִים *old age*—J. Conrad and G.J. Botterweck, 'זָקֵן *zāqēn*; זֹקֶן *zōqen*; זִקְנָה *ziqnāh*; זְקֻנִים *zequnîm*', *TDOT*, IV (1980), pp. 122-31

זִקֵּף *startling*—T.J. Lewis, *Cults of the Dead in Ancient Israel and Ugarit* (HSM, 39; Atlanta: Scholars Press, 1989), pp. 109, 116

זרב *be in spate*—J.T. Milik, in *Les 'Petites Grottes' de Qumrân* (ed. M. Baillet, J.T. Milik, R. de Vaux; DJD, 3; Oxford: Clarendon Press, 1962), pp. 245-46; Godfrey R. Driver, 'Some Hebrew Medical Expressions', *ZAW* 65 (1963), pp. 255-62 (261-62); L.L. Grabbe, *Comparative Philology and the Text of Job: A Study in Methodology* (SBLDS, 34; Missoula: Scholars Press, 1977), pp. 54-55; M.H. Pope, *Job* (AB, 15; Garden City, NY: Doubleday, 1980), p. 54

זֶרֶב *gutter*—J.T. Milik, in *Les Petites Grottes de Qumrân* (ed. M. Baillet, J.T. Milik, R. de Vaux; DJD, 3; Oxford: Clarendon Press, 1962), pp. 245-46

זרה I *scatter*—pu. *be strewn*—D. Winton Thomas, 'Textual and Philological Notes on Some Passages in the Book of Proverbs', in *Wisdom in Israel and in the Ancient Near East, Presented to Professor Harold Henry Rowley ... in Celebration of his Sixty-Fifth Birthday* (ed. M. Noth and D. Winton Thomas; VTSup, 3; Leiden: E.J. Brill, 1955), pp. 280-292 (281-82)

זְרוֹעַ *arm*—F.J. Helfmeyer, 'זְרוֹעַ *zerôa'*', *TDOT*, IV (1980), pp. 131-40

זְרוֹעַ נְטוּיָה *outstretched arm*—J.K. Hoffmeier, 'The Arm of God versus the Arm of Pharaoh in the Exodus Narratives', *Bib* 67 (1986), pp. 378-87

זְרוֹעַ רָמָה *Navigator's Line*—G.R. Driver, 'Two Astronomical Passages in the Old Testament', *JTS* ns 4 (1953), pp. 208-212 (211)

זַרְזִיף *sprinkling*—G.R. Driver, 'Problems in the Hebrew Text of Job', in *Wisdom in Israel and in the Ancient Near East, Presented to Professor Harold Henry Rowley ... in Celebration of his Sixty-Fifth Birthday* (ed. M. Noth and D. Winton Thomas; VTSup, 3; Leiden: E.J. Brill, 1955), pp. 72-93 (84-85)

זרח *arise*—H. Ringgren, 'זָרַח *zārach*; מִזְרָח *mizrāch*', *TDOT*, IV (1980), pp. 141-43

זרם I *pour*—Ludwig Wächter, 'Drei umstrittene Psalmstellen (Ps 26 1 30 8 90 4-6)', *ZAW* 78 (1966), pp. 61-69 (65-67); J.A. Emerton, 'A Textual Problem in Isaiah 25 2', *ZAW* 89 (1977), pp. 64-73 (69-70); M. Tsevat, 'Psalm xc 5-6', *VT* 35 (1985), pp. 115-16 (cf. Akk. šitta reḫû *pour sleep upon*)

זרם II *put an end to*—Godfrey R. Driver, 'Some Hebrew Medical Expressions', *ZAW* 65 (1953), pp. 255-62 (259)

זרע *sow*—H.D. Preuss, 'זָרַע *zāra'*; זֶרַע *zera'*', *TDOT*, IV (1980), pp. 143-62

זֶרַע *seed*—H.D. Preuss, 'זָרַע *zāra'*; זֶרַע *zera'*', *TDOT*, IV (1980), pp. 143-62

אֲשֶׁר זַרְעוֹ־בוֹ *the seed of which is in it*—Bryan Paradise, 'Food for Thought', in *A Word in Season: Essays in Honour of William McKane* (ed. James D. Martin and Philip R. Davies; JSOTSup 42; Sheffield: JSOT Press, 1986), pp. 177-204 (199)

זֶרַע הַמֶּלֶךְ *descendants of the king*—J. Hoftijzer, 'Philological-Grammatical Notes on 1 Kings xi 14', in *New Avenues in the Study of the Old Testament* (Festschrift M.J. Mulder; ed. A.S. van der Woude; OTS, 25; Leiden: E.J. Brill, 1989), pp. 29-37

זרק I *scatter*—G. André, 'זָרַק *zāraq*; מִזְרָק *mizrāq*', *TDOT*, IV (1980), pp. 162-65

זרק II *creep up* (cf. Arab. zariqa)—J. Blau, 'Etymologische Untersuchungen auf Grund des palästinischen Arabisch', *VT* 5 (1955), pp. 337-44 (341)

זֶרֶק *javelin*—J. Carmignac, 'Précisions apportées au vocabulaire de l'hébreu biblique par la Guerre des Fils de Lumière contre les Fils de Ténèbres', *VT* 5 (1955), pp. 345-65 (362)

זֶרֶשׁ *Zeresh*—R. Zadok, 'On Five Biblical Names', *ZAW* 89 (1977), pp. 266-68 (268)

זֶרֶת *span* (cf. Ug. dry *measure, determine precisely*)—M. Dietrich and O. Loretz, 'Ugaritisch *dr'*, *drt* und hebräisch *zrh*', *UF* 23 (1991), pp. 79-82

# ח

חבא *hide*—S. Wagner, 'חָבָא *chābhā'*; חָבָה *chābhāh*; מַחֲבֵא *mach<sup>a</sup>bhē'*; מַחֲבֹאִים *mach<sup>a</sup>bhō'îm*; חֶבְיוֹן *chebhyôn'*, *TDOT*, IV (1980), pp. 165-71

חבב I *love*—J.T. Milik, 'Deux documents inédits du désert de Juda', *Bib* 38 (1957), pp. 245-68 (254)

חבב II *be pure* (cf. Akk. ebēbu/ubbubu)—P.D. Miller, 'Two Critical Notes on Psalm 68 and Deuteronomy 33', *HTR* 57 (1964), pp. 240-43 (241-42)

חבה *hide*—S. Wagner, 'חָבָא *chābhā'*; חָבָה *chābhāh*; מַחֲבֵא *mach<sup>a</sup>bhē'*; מַחֲבֹאִים *mach<sup>a</sup>bhō'îm*; חֶבְיוֹן *chebhyôn'*, *TDOT*, IV (1980), pp. 165-71

חָבוּר *community*—M. Nissinen, *Prophetie, Redaction und Fortschreibung im Hoseabuch: Studien zum Werdegang eines Prophetenbuches im Lichte von Hos 4 und 11* (AOAT, 231; Kevelaer: Verlag Butzon & Bercker/ Neukirchen–Vluyn: Neukirchener Verlag, 1991), p. 122

חָבִיב *beloved*—J.T. Milik, 'Deux documents inédits du désert de Juda', *Bib* 38 (1957), pp. 245-68 (254)

חֶבְיוֹן *hiding*—S. Wagner, 'חָבָא *chābhā'*; חָבָה *chābhāh*; מַחֲבֵא *mach<sup>a</sup>bhē'*; מַחֲבֹאִים *mach<sup>a</sup>bhō'îm*; חֶבְיוֹן *chebhyôn'*, *TDOT*, IV (1980), pp. 165-71

חבט II *pour* (cf. Arab ḥabaḍa *throb*)—Thomas, *Lexicon*, VIII (1970), p. 7

חבל I *take in pledge*—H.-J. Fabry, 'חבל *ḥbl* I; חֶבֶל *chebhel* I and II; חֹבֵל *chōbhēl*; חֹבְלִים *chōbh<sup>e</sup>lîm*; חִבֵּל *chibbēl'*, *TDOT*, IV (1980), pp. 172-79

ni. *have a pledge taken*—M. Dahood, 'Congruity of Metaphors', in *Hebräische Wortforschung: Festschrift zum 80. Geburtstag von Walter Baumgartner* (VTSup, 16; Leiden: E.J. Brill, 1967), pp. 40-49 (41-42)

חבל II *act corruptly*—H.A. Hoffner, 'חָבַל *chābhal* II; חֲבֹל *ch<sup>a</sup>bhōl*; חֲבֹלָה *ch<sup>a</sup>bhōlāh'*, *TDOT*, IV (1980), pp. 179-84

pi. *destroy*—J. Gamberoni, 'חָבַל *chābhal* III', *TDOT*, IV (1980), pp. 185-88; W.W. Müller, 'Beiträge aus dem Mehri zum etymologischen Teil des hebr. Lexicons', in *Mélanges linguistiques offerts à Maxime Rodinson* (ed. C. Robin; Comptes rendus du Groupe linguistique d'études chamito-sémitiques, 12; Paris: P. Geuthner, 1985), pp. 267ff.

חבל III *be pregnant*—H.-J. Fabry, 'חבל *ḥbl* IV; חֵבֶל *chēbhel'*, *TDOT*, IV (1980), pp. 188-92

חֲבֹל *pledge*—H.A. Hoffner, 'חָבַל *chābhal* II; חֲבֹל *ch<sup>a</sup>bhōl*; חֲבֹלָה *ch<sup>a</sup>bhōlāh'*, *TDOT*, IV (1980), pp. 179-84

חֵבֶל *labour pains*—H.-J. Fabry, 'חבל *ḥbl* IV; חֵבֶל *chēbhel'*, *TDOT*, IV (1980), pp. 188-92

חֶבֶל I *rope*—M. Tsevat, 'Alalakhiana', *HUCA* 29 (1958), pp. 109-36 (124); Mitchell J. Dahood, 'Hebrew–Ugaritic Lexicography II', *Bib* 45 (1964), pp. 393-412 (407); H.-J. Fabry, 'חבל *ḥbl* I; חֶבֶל *chebhel* I and II; חֹבֵל *chōbhēl*; חֹבְלִים *chōbh<sup>e</sup>lîm*; חִבֵּל *chibbēl'*, *TDOT*, IV (1980), pp. 172-79

*herd*—Mitchell J. Dahood, 'Hebrew–Ugaritic Lexicography II', *Bib* 45 (1964), pp. 393-412 (407)

חֶבֶל III *mountain*—Mitchell J. Dahood, 'Hebrew–Ugaritic Lexicography II', *Bib* 45 (1964), pp. 393-412 (407)

חִבֵּל *mast*—H.-J. Fabry, 'חבל *ḥbl* I; חֶבֶל *chebhel* I and II; חֹבֵל *chōbhēl*; חֹבְלִים *chōbh<sup>e</sup>lîm*; חִבֵּל *chibbēl'*, *TDOT*, IV (1980), pp. 172-79

חֹבֵל *sailor*—H.-J. Fabry, 'חבל *ḥbl* I; חֶבֶל *chebhel* I and II; חֹבֵל *chōbhēl*; חֹבְלִים *chōbh<sup>e</sup>lîm*; חִבֵּל *chibbēl'*, *TDOT*, IV (1980), pp. 172-79

חֲבֹלָה *pledge*—H.A. Hoffner, 'חָבַל *chābhal* II; חֲבֹל *ch<sup>a</sup>bhōl*; חֲבֹלָה *ch<sup>a</sup>bhōlāh'*, *TDOT*, IV (1980), pp. 179-84

חֹבְלִים *union*—H.-J. Fabry, 'חבל *ḥbl* I; חֶבֶל *chebhel* I and II; חֹבֵל *chōbhēl*; חֹבְלִים *chōbh<sup>e</sup>lîm*; חִבֵּל *chibbēl'*, *TDOT*, IV (1980), pp. 172-79

חֲבַצֶּלֶת *asphodel*—O. Keel, *Das Hohelied* (Zürcher Bibelkommentare, AT, 18; Zurich: Theologischer Verlag Zürich, 1986), p. 79

חבר I *join*—J. Neusner, '*Ḥbr* and *n'mn*', *RQ* 5 (1964–66), pp. 119-22; H. Cazelles, 'חָבַר *chābhar*; חָבֵר *chābhēr'*,

*TDOT*, IV (1980), pp. 193-97

חבר II *be noisy*—F. Nötscher, 'Entbehrliche Hapaxlegomena in Jesaia', *VT* 1 (1951), pp. 299-302 (299); J.J. Finkelstein, 'Hebrew חבר and Semitic **ḫbr*', *JBL* 75 (1956), pp. 328-31

חבר IV *be high*—N.H. Tur-Sinai, *The Book of Job* (Jerusalem, 1957), pp. 262-63

חָבֵר *companion*—H. Cazelles, 'חָבַר *chābhar*; חָבֵר *chābhēr*', *TDOT*, IV (1980), pp. 193-97

חֶבֶר I *company*—M. Wagner, 'Beiträge zur Aramaismenfrage im alttestamentlichen Hebräisch', in *Hebräische Wortforschung: Festschrift zum 80. Geburtstag von Walter Baumgartner* (VTSup, 16; Leiden: E.J. Brill, 1967), pp. 355-71 (360-61)

חֶבֶר II *noise*—J.J. Finkelstein, 'Hebrew חבר and Semitic **ḫbr*', *JBL* 75 (1956), pp. 328-31

חֲבַרְבֻּרָה *spot*—A.L. Oppenheim (ed.), '*ebēru B* to paint the face', *The Assyrian Dictionary of the Oriental Institute of the University of Chicago*, IV (Chicago: Oriental Institute, 1958), p. 13

חֶבְרוֹן I *Hebron*—M.S. Moore, 'The Judean *lmlk*-Stamps: Some Unresolved Issues', *RestQ* 28 (1985–96), pp. 17-26

חבשׁ *seek*—M.J. Dahood, 'The Phoenician Contribution to Biblical Wisdom Literature', in *The Role of the Phoenicians in the Interaction of Mediterranean Civilizations* (ed. W.A. Ward; Beirut: American University of Beirut, 1968), pp. 123-48 (126-27)

חבשׁ *bind*—G. Münderlein, 'חבשׁ *ḥbš*', *TDOT*, IV (1980), pp. 198-201

חַג *festival*—B. Kedar-Kopfstein and G.J. Botterweck, 'חַג *chagh*; חגג *ḥgg*', *TDOT*, IV (1980), pp. 201-13

חָגָא *terror*—J.F.A Sawyer, 'The Role of Jewish Studies in Biblical Semantics', in *Scripta signa vocis: Studies about Scripts, Scriptures, Scribes and Languages in the Near East* (ed. H.L.J. Vanstiphout *et al.*; Festschrift J.H. Hospers; Groningen: Forsten, 1986), p. 206

חגג *celebrate festival*—G. Ryckmans, review of A. Dupont-Sommer and L. Robert, *La déesse de Hiéropolis Castabala (Cilicie)*, *Le Muséon* 78 (1965), pp. 467-69 (468); B. Kedar-Kopfstein and G.J. Botterweck, 'חַג *chagh*; חגג *ḥgg*', *TDOT*, IV (1980), pp. 201-13

חֲגוֹר *belted*—B. Johnson, 'חָגַר *chāghar*; חָגוֹר *chāghôr*; חֲגוֹר *chaghôr*; חֲגוֹרָה *chaghôrāh*', *TDOT*, IV (1980), pp. 213-16

חֲגוֹר *belt*—B. Johnson, 'חָגַר *chāghar*; חָגוֹר *c hāghôr*; חֲגוֹר *chaghôr*; חֲגוֹרָה *chaghôrāh*', *TDOT*, IV (1980), pp. 213-16

חֲגוֹרָה *belt*—B. Johnson, 'חָגַר *chāghar*; חָגוֹר *chāghôr*; חֲגוֹר *chaghôr*; חֲגוֹרָה *chaghôrāh*', *TDOT*, IV (1980), pp. 213-16

חגר *gird*—B. Johnson, 'חָגַר *chāghar*; חָגוֹר *chāghôr*; חֲגוֹר *chaghôr*; חֲגוֹרָה *chaghôrāh*', *TDOT*, IV (1980), pp. 213-16

חד *limit* (cf. Arab. ḥadd)—Thomas, *Lexicon*, VIII (1970), pp. 42, 417

חדה I *rejoice*—W.L. Michel, *Job in the Light of Northwest Semitic.* I. *Job 1,1–14,22* (BibOr, 42; Rome: Pontifical Biblical Institute, 1987), pp. 50-52

חדה II *see*—M.J. Dahood, 'Hebrew—Ugaritic Lexicography II', *Bib* 45 (1964), pp. 393-412 (407-408)

ni. *appear*—M.J. Dahood, 'A New Translation of Gen. 49,6a', *Bib* 36 (1955), p. 229; Dahood, 'The Value of Ugaritic for Textual Criticism', *Bib* 40 (1959), pp. 160-70 (170)

חדל I *cease*—D.N. Freedman and J. Lundbom, 'חָדַל *chādhal*', *TDOT*, IV (1980), pp. 216-21; T.J. Lewis, 'The Songs of Hannah and Deborah: *ḤDL*-II ("Growing Plump")', *JBL* 104 (1985), pp. 105-108

הֶחֳדַלְתִּי *shall I be made to leave?*—R. Bartelmus, 'Die sogenannte Jothamfabel—eine politisch-religiöse Parabeldichtung', *TZ* 41 (1985), pp. 97-120 (98-100)

חדל II *be fat*—D.W. Thomas, 'Some Observations on the Hebrew Root חדל', in *Volume du Congrès, Strasbourg 1956* (VTSup, 4; Leiden: E.J. Brill, 1957), pp. 8-16 (14-16); P. Calderone, '*ḤDL*-II in Poetic Texts', *CBQ* 23 (1962), pp. 451-60; Calderone, 'Supplementary Note on *ḤDL*-II', *CBQ* 24 (1963), pp. 412-19; T.J. Lewis, 'The Songs of Hannah and Deborah: *ḤDL*-II ("Growing Plump")', *JBL* 104 (1985), pp. 105-108

חֶדֶר *chamber*—R. Mosis, 'חֶדֶר *chedher*', *TDOT*, IV (1980), pp. 222-25

חַדְרֵי־בֶטֶן *chambers of (the) belly*, John Elwolde, 'Automatic Classification of "Anatomical" Idioms in Biblical Hebrew', in *Proceedings of the Tenth World Congress of Jewish Studies Jerusalem 1989. Division D. 1: The Hebrew Language; Jewish Languages* (Jerusalem: World Union of Jewish Studies, 1990), pp. 15-20; N. Shupak, 'Egyptian Terms and Features in the Biblical Wisdom', *Tarb* 54 (1985), pp. 475-84

חדשׁ I pi. *create*—L. Kopf, 'Arabische Etymologien und Parallelen zum Bibelwörterbuch', *VT* 9 (1959), pp. 247-87 (254-55)

חדשׁ II *attack* (cf. Arab. ḥadasa *hasten*)—Thomas, *Lexicon*, VIII (1970), p. 57

חָדָשׁ *new*—C. Westermann, '*ḥādāš* neu', *THWAT*, I (1971), pp. 524-30; R. North, 'חָדָשׁ *chādhāsh*; חֹדֶשׁ *chōdhesh*', *TDOT*, IV (1980), pp. 225-44

חֹדֶשׁ *month*—R. North, 'חָדָשׁ *chādhāsh*; חֹדֶשׁ *chōdhesh*', *TDOT*, IV (1980), pp. 225-44

חוג *draw a circle*—K. Seybold, 'חוּג *chûgh*', *TDOT*, IV (1980), pp. 244-47

חוּג *circle*—K. Seybold, 'חוּג *chûgh*', *TDOT*, IV (1980), pp. 244-47

חוד *propound a riddle*—Moshe Held, 'Marginal Notes to the Biblical Lexicon', in *Biblical and Related Studies Presented to Samuel Iwry* (ed. Ann Kort and Scott Morschauser; Winona Lake, IN: Eisenbrauns, 1985), pp. 93-103 (93-96)

חוה II *bow down*—H.P. Stähli, '*ḥwy* hišt. sich niederwerfen', *THWAT*, I (1971), pp. 530-33; H.D. Preuss, 'חוה *ḥwh*; הִשְׁתַּחֲוָה *hishtachavāh*', *TDOT*, IV (1980), pp. 248-56

חַוָּה II *Eve*—A.S. Kapelrud, 'חַוָּה *chavvāh*', *TDOT*, IV (1980), pp. 257-60; H.N. Wallace, *The Eden Narrative* (HSM, 32; Atlanta: Scholars Press, 1985), pp. 84, 98

חוֹטֶא *sin*—Thomas, *Lexicon*, VIII (1970), p. 133

חול I *whirl*—H. Eising, 'חוּל *chûl*; מָחוֹל *māchôl*; מְחוֹלָה *mechōlāh*', *TDOT*, IV (1980), pp. 260-64

חול II *be weak*—R. Köbert, 'Eine lexikalische Bemerkung zu Lam. 4,6', *Bib* 33 (1952), pp. 442-43

חוֹל I *sand*—A.S. Kapelrud, 'חוֹל *chôl*', *TDOT*, IV (1980), pp. 264-66

חוּם *brown*—K.-M. Beyse, 'חמם *ḥmm*; חֹם *chōm*; חָם *chām*; חוּם *chûm*; חַמָּה *chammāh*; חַמָּן *chammān*', *TDOT*, IV (1980), pp. 473-77

חוֹמָה *wall*—W.T. In der Smitten, 'חוֹמָה *chômāh*', *TDOT*, IV (1980), pp. 267-71; E. Eibschitz, '*hêl* und *hômāh*', *Sinai* 100 (1987), pp. 75-86

חוס *pity*—S. Wagner, 'חוּס *chûs*', *TDOT*, IV (1980), pp. 271-77

חוץ *be strong* (cf. Syr. ḥāṣ *bind fast*, Arab. ḥāṣa *sew*)—Thomas, *Lexicon*, VIII (1970), p. 89

חוּץ I *outside*—L.G. Herr, 'Tripartite Pillared Buildings and the Market Place in Iron Age Palestine', *BASOR* 272 (1988), pp. 47-67

חוּץ III *loudly*—Thomas, *Lexicon*, VIII (1970), p. 89

חוק *gather* (cf. Akk. ḫâqu *mix [liquids]*)—G.R. Driver, 'Problems in the Hebrew Text of Proverbs', *Bib* 32 (1951), pp. 173-97 (178)

חוּק *circle*—M.H. Segal, *Sefer Ben Sira ha-Shalem* (2nd edn; Jerusalem: Bialik Institute, 1958), p. 197

חור III *turn* (cf. Arab. ḫāra *incline, turn*)—Thomas, *Lexicon*, VIII (1970), p. 94

חוּר I *Hur*—M. Görg, 'Aaron—von einem Titel zum Namen', *BN* 32 (1986), pp. 11-17

חושׁ I *hasten*—K.-M. Beyse, 'חוּשׁ *chûsh*; חִישׁ *chîsh*', *TDOT*, IV (1980), pp. 278-80
hi. *give way*—J.J.M. Roberts, 'Yahweh's Foundation in Zion', *JBL* 106 (1987), pp. 27-45

חושׁ III *be anxious*—F. Ellermeier, 'Das Verbum חושׁ in Koh 2 25. Eine exegetische, auslegungsgeschichtliche und semasiologische Untersuchung', *ZAW* 75 (1963), pp. 197-217; W. von Soden, 'Akkadisch *ḫâšum* I "sich sorgen" und hebräisch *ḫūš* II', *UF* 1 (1969), p. 197

חושׁ IV *be sated*—J. Reider, 'Etymological Studies in Biblical Hebrew', *VT* 2 (1952), pp. 113-30 (129-30)

חות *be bold* (cf. Arab. ḫāta *throw*, ḫawwāt *bold*)—Thomas, *Lexicon*, VIII (1970), p. 103

חוֹתָם I *seal*—B. Otzen, 'חָתַם *ḥāṯam*; חוֹתָם *ḥôṯām*' *TDOT*, V (1986), pp. 263-69

חזה I *see*—J.M. Husser, *Le songe et la parole. Etude sur le rêve et sa fonction dans l'ancien Israël* (BZAW, 210;

Berlin: Töpelmann, 1994), pp. 153-57, 230, 269-69; A. Jepsen, 'חָזָה *chāzāh*; חֹזֶה *chōzeh*; חָזוֹן *chāzôn*; חֲזוֹת *chazôth*; חָזוּת *chāzûth*; חִזָּיוֹן *chizzāyôn*; מַחֲזֶה *machazeh*; מֶחֱזָה *mechezāh*', *TDOT*, IV (1980), pp. 280-90; D. Vetter, '*ḥzh* schauen', *THWAT*, 1 (1971), pp. 533-37

חזה II *be opposite* (cf. Arab. ḥaḏā)—G.R. Driver, 'Studies in the Vocabulary of the Old Testament VI', *JTS* 34 (1933), pp. 375-85 (381); Driver, 'Problems in Job and Psalms Reconsidered', *JTS* 40 (1939), pp. 391-94 (391); Driver, 'Hebrew Poetic Diction', in *Congress Volume, Copenhagen 1953* (VTSup, 1; Leiden: E.J. Brill, 1953), pp. 26-39 (38-39); Thomas, *Lexicon*, VIII (1970), pp. 110-11

חזה III *be vile* (cf. Arab. ḥaziya)—G.R. Driver, 'Hebrew Poetic Diction', in *Congress Volume, Copenhagen 1953* (VTSup, 1; Leiden: E.J. Brill, 1953), pp. 26-39 (39)

חָזֶה II *prominent*—Thomas, *Lexicon*, VIII (1970), p. 111

חֹזֶה I *seer*—A. Jepsen, 'חָזָה *chāzāh*; חֹזֶה *chōzeh*; חָזוֹן *chāzôn*; חֲזוֹת *chazôth*; חָזוּת *chāzûth*; חִזָּיוֹן *chizzāyôn*; מַחֲזֶה *machazeh*; מֶחֱזָה *mechezāh*', *TDOT*, IV (1980), pp. 280-90

חָזוֹן I *vision*—A. Jepsen, 'חָזָה *chāzāh*; חֹזֶה *chōzeh*; חָזוֹן *chāzôn*; חֲזוֹת *chazôth*; חָזוּת *chāzûth*; חִזָּיוֹן *chizzāyôn*; מַחֲזֶה *machazeh*; מֶחֱזָה *mechezāh*', *TDOT*, IV (1980), pp. 280-90

*inspired saying*—G. Rinaldi, 'Alcuni termini ebraici relativi alla letteratura', *Bib* 40 (1959), pp. 267-89 (274)

חָזוֹן II *pact*—Thomas, *Lexicon*, VIII (1970), p. 112

חָזוֹן III *magistrate* (cf. Aram. חֲזָן *superintendent*)—Thomas, *Lexicon*, VIII (1970), p. 112

חָזוֹת *visions*—A. Jepsen, 'חָזָה *chāzāh*; חֹזֶה *chōzeh*; חָזוֹן *chāzôn*; חֲזוֹת *chazôth*; חָזוּת *chāzûth*; חִזָּיוֹן *chizzāyôn*; מַחֲזֶה *machazeh*; מֶחֱזָה *mechezāh*', *TDOT*, IV (1980), pp. 280-90

חָזוּת I *vision*—A. Jepsen, 'חָזָה *chāzāh*; חֹזֶה *chōzeh*; חָזוֹן *chāzôn*; חֲזוֹת *chazôth*; חָזוּת *chāzûth*; חִזָּיוֹן *chizzāyôn*; מַחֲזֶה *machazeh*; מֶחֱזָה *mechezāh*', *TDOT*, IV (1980), pp. 280-90

חָזוּת II *agreement*—G.R. Driver, 'Linguistic and Textual Problems: Isaiah i–xxxix', *JTS* 38 (1937), pp. 36-50 (44); Driver, 'Problems in Job and Psalms Reconsidered', *JTS* 40 (1939), pp. 391-94 (391)

חִזָּיוֹן *vision*—A. Jepsen, 'חָזָה *chāzāh*; חֹזֶה *chōzeh*; חָזוֹן *chāzôn*; חֲזוֹת *chazôth*; חָזוּת *chāzûth*; חִזָּיוֹן *chizzāyôn*; מַחֲזֶה *machazeh*; מֶחֱזָה *mechezāh*', *TDOT*, IV (1980), pp. 280-90

חֲזִיז II *dream* (cf. Aram. חֲזִיזָא [?] *dream*)—Thomas, *Lexicon*, VIII (1970), p. 113

חֲזִיר *swine*—G.J. Botterweck, 'חֲזִיר *chazîr*', *TDOT*, IV (1980), pp. 291-300

חזק I *be strong*—A.S. van der Woude, '*ḥzq* fest sein', *THWAT*, 1 (1971), pp. 538-41; F. Hesse, 'חָזַק *chāzaq*; חָזָק *chāzāq*; חָזֵק *chāzēq*; חֵזֶק *chezeq*; חֹזֶק *chōzeq*; חֶזְקָה *chezqāh*; חָזְקָה *chozqāh*', *TDOT*, IV (1980), pp. 301-308; M. Malul, 'David's Curse of Joab (2 S 3$_{29}$) and the Social Significance of *mḥzyq plk*', *Aula Orientalis* 10 (1992), pp. 49-67

*be too much (for)*—N.M. Waldman, 'Some Notes on Malachi 3:6; 3:13; and Psalm 42:11', *JBL* 93 (1974), pp. 543-49 (545-48)

חזק II *outwit* (cf. Arab. ḥaḏaqa)—Thomas, *Lexicon*, VIII (1970), p. 174

חָזָק I *strong*—F. Hesse, 'חָזַק *chāzaq*; חָזָק *chāzāq*; חָזֵק *chāzēq*; חֵזֶק *chezeq*; חֹזֶק *chōzeq*; חֶזְקָה *chezqāh*; חָזְקָה *chozqāh*', *TDOT*, IV (1980), pp. 301-308

יָד חֲזָקָה *strong hand*—J.K. Hoffmeier, 'The Arm of God versus the Arm of Pharaoh in the Exodus Narratives', *Bib* 67 (1986), pp. 378-87

חֵזֶק *strength*—F. Hesse, 'חָזַק *chāzaq*; חָזָק *chāzāq*; חָזֵק *chāzēq*; חֵזֶק *chezeq*; חֹזֶק *chōzeq*; חֶזְקָה *chezqāh*; חָזְקָה *chozqāh*', *TDOT*, IV (1980), pp. 301-308

חֹזֶק *strength*—F. Hesse, 'חָזַק *chāzaq*; חָזָק *chāzāq*; חָזֵק *chāzēq*; חֵזֶק *chezeq*; חֹזֶק *chōzeq*; חֶזְקָה *chezqāh*; חָזְקָה *chozqāh*', *TDOT*, IV (1980), pp. 301-308

חֶזְקָה *strength*—F. Hesse, 'חָזַק *chāzaq*; חָזָק *chāzāq*; חָזֵק *chāzēq*; חֵזֶק *chezeq*; חֹזֶק *chōzeq*; חֶזְקָה *chezqāh*; חָזְקָה *chozqāh*', *TDOT*, IV (1980), pp. 301-308

חָזְקָה *strength*—F. Hesse, 'חָזַק *chāzaq*; חָזָק *chāzāq*; חָזֵק *chāzēq*; חֵזֶק *chezeq*; חֹזֶק *chōzeq*; חֶזְקָה *chezqāh*; חָזְקָה *chozqāh*', *TDOT*, IV (1980), pp. 301-308

חטא *sin*—R. Knierim, '*ḥṭ'* sich verfehlen', *THWAT*, I (1971), pp. 541-49; K. Koch, 'חָטָא *chāṭā'*; חֵטְא *chēṭ'*;

חֶטְאָה *cheṭ'āh;* חֲטָאָה *chaṭā'āh;* חַטָּאָה *chaṭṭā'āh;* חַטָּאת *chaṭṭā'th;* חַטָּא *chaṭṭā'', TDOT*, IV (1980), pp. 309-19

חוֹטֵא *sinner, one who misses*—Christian Klein, *Koheleth und die Weisheit Israels: Eine formgeschichtliche Studie* (BWANT, 132; Stuttgart: Kohlhammer, 1994), p. 133; H.-P. Müller, 'Theonome Skepsis und Lebensfreude', *BZ* 30 (1986), pp. 1-19

חַטָּא *sinner, sinful*—K. Koch, 'חָטָא *chāṭā'*; חֵטְא *chēṭ'*; חֶטְאָה *cheṭ'āh;* חֲטָאָה *chaṭā'āh;* חַטָּאָה *chaṭṭā'āh;* חַטָּאת *chaṭṭā'th;* חַטָּא *chaṭṭā'', TDOT*, IV (1980), pp. 309-19

חֵטְא *sin*—K. Koch, 'חָטָא *chāṭā'*; חֵטְא *chēṭ'*; חֶטְאָה *cheṭ'āh;* חֲטָאָה *chaṭā'āh;* חַטָּאָה *chaṭṭā'āh;* חַטָּאת *chaṭṭā'th;* חַטָּא *chaṭṭā'', TDOT*, IV (1980), pp. 309-19

חֲטָאָה *sin*—K. Koch, 'חָטָא *chāṭā'*; חֵטְא *chēṭ'*; חֶטְאָה *cheṭ'āh;* חֲטָאָה *chaṭā'āh;* חַטָּאָה *chaṭṭā'āh;* חַטָּאת *chaṭṭā'th;* חַטָּא *chaṭṭā'', TDOT*, IV (1980), pp. 309-19

חַטָּאָה *sin*—K. Koch, 'חָטָא *chāṭā'*; חֵטְא *chēṭ'*; חֶטְאָה *cheṭ'āh;* חֲטָאָה *chaṭā'āh;* חַטָּאָה *chaṭṭā'āh;* חַטָּאת *chaṭṭā'th;* חַטָּא *chaṭṭā'', TDOT*, IV (1980), pp. 309-19

חֶטְאָה *sin*—K. Koch, 'חָטָא *chāṭā'*; חֵטְא *chēṭ'*; חֶטְאָה *cheṭ'āh;* חֲטָאָה *chaṭā'āh;* חַטָּאָה *chaṭṭā'āh;* חַטָּאת *chaṭṭā'th;* חַטָּא *chaṭṭā'', TDOT*, IV (1980), pp. 309-19

חַטָּאת I *sin*—K. Koch, 'חָטָא *chāṭā'*; חֵטְא *chēṭ'*; חֶטְאָה *cheṭ'āh;* חֲטָאָה *chaṭā'āh;* חַטָּאָה *chaṭṭā'āh;* חַטָּאת *chaṭṭā'th;* חַטָּא *chaṭṭā'', TDOT*, IV (1980), pp. 309-19; J. Milgrom, 'The Root Meaning of *ḥaṭṭ'at*: A Rite of Passage?', *RB* 98 (1991), pp. 120-24; R. Rendtorff, *Leviticus* (Biblischer Kommentar, Altes Testament, 3; Neukirchen–Vluyn: Neukirchener Verlag, 1992), pp. 209-14

חַטָּאת II *penury*—D.W. Thomas, 'The Meaning of חַטָּאת in Proverbs x. 16', *JTS* ns 15 (1964), pp. 295-96; *Lexicon*, VIII (1970), p. 136

חַטָּאת III *step*—Thomas, *Lexicon*, VIII (1970), p. 136

חטר *cut* (cf. Arab. ḥaṭara *violate*)—Thomas, *Lexicon*, VIII (1970), p. 140

חַי I *living*—H. Ringgren, 'חָיָה *chāyāh;* חַי *chai;* חַיִּים *chaiyîm;* חַיָּה *chaiyāh;* מִחְיָה *michyāh', TDOT*, IV (1980), pp. 324-44

חַי־י״ *(as) Y. is alive*, etc.—M. Greenberg, 'The Hebrew Oath Particle *ḥay/ḥē*', *JBL* 76 (1957), pp. 34-39

חַי II *kinsfolk*—L. Delekat, 'Zum hebräischen Wörterbuch', *VT* 14 (1964), pp. 7-66 (27-28)

חִידָה *riddle*—G. Rinaldi, 'Alcuni termini ebraici relativi alla letteratura', *Bib* 40 (1959), pp. 267-89 (274-76); V. Hamp, 'חִידָה *chîdhāh*', *TDOT*, IV (1980), pp. 320-23; Moshe Held, 'Marginal Notes to the Biblical Lexicon', in *Biblical and Related Studies Presented to Samuel Iwry* (ed. Ann Kort and Scott Morschauser; Winona Lake, IN: Eisenbrauns, 1985), pp. 93-103 (93-96)

חיה I *live*—G. Gerleman, '*ḥjh* leben', *THWAT*, 1 (1971), pp. 549-57; H. Ringgren, 'חָיָה *chāyāh;* חַי *chai;* חַיִּים *chaiyîm;* חַיָּה *chaiyāh;* מִחְיָה *michyāh', TDOT*, IV (1980), pp. 324-44; Jopie Siebert-Hommes, 'Hebräerinnen sind חיות', in *'Dort ziehen Schiffe dahin ...': Collected Communications to the XIVth Congress of the International Organization for the Study of the Old Testament, Paris 1992* (ed. Matthias Augustin and Klaus-Dietrich Schunk; Beiträge zur Erforschung des Alten Testaments und des antiken Judentums, 28; Frankfurt a.M.: Peter Lang, 1996), pp. 191-99

בְּדָמַיִךְ חֲיִי *in your blood, live*—M. Malul, 'Adoptation of Foundlings in the Bible and Mesopotamian Documents: A Study of Some Legal Metaphors in Ezekiel 16. 1-7', *JSOT* 46 (1990), pp. 97-112

יְחִי הַמֶּלֶךְ *long live the king*—P.A.H. de Boer, 'Vive le roi', *VT* 5 (1955), pp. 225-31

pi. *revive*—M.L. Barré, 'New Light on the Interpretation of Hosea vi 2', *VT* 28 (1968), pp. 129-41

חיה II *gather*—W.F. Albright, 'The Oracles of Balaam', *JBL* 63 (1944), pp. 207-33 (222-23, 226)

חַיָּה I *beast*—H. Ringgren, 'חָיָה *chāyāh;* חַי *chai;* חַיִּים *chaiyîm;* חַיָּה *chaiyāh;* מִחְיָה *michyāh', TDOT*, IV (1980), pp. 324-44

חַיָּה *lively*—Jopie Siebert-Hommes, 'Hebräerinnen sind חיות', in *'Dort ziehen Schiffe dahin ...': Collected Communications to the XIVth Congress of the International Organization for the Study of the Old Testament, Paris 1992* (ed. Matthias Augustin and Klaus-Dietrich Schunk; Beiträge zur Erforschung des Alten Testaments und des antiken Judentums, 28; Frankfurt a.M.: Peter Lang, 1996), pp. 191-99

חָיוּת II *shame* (cf. Arab. ḥayâ' X)—J.M. Allegro, 'The Meaning of Ḥayyûṯ in 2 Samuel 20, 3', *JTS* ns 3 (1952), pp. 40-41; E. Vogt, 'Nuntii personarum et rerum', *Bib* 33 (1952), pp. 300-309 (304)

חַיִּים *life*—H. Ringgren, 'חָיָה *chāyāh*; חַי *chai*; חַיִּים *chaiyîm*; חַיָּה *chaiyāh*; מִחְיָה *michyāh*', *TDOT*, IV (1980), pp. 324-44

חיל I *be in pain*—A. Baumann, 'חיל *ḥyl*; חִיל *chîl*; חִילָה *chîlāh*; חַלְחָלָה *chalchālāh*', *TDOT*, IV (1980), pp. 344-47

חיל IV *take heed* (cf. Arab. ḫāla *think*)—Thomas, *Lexicon*, VIII (1970), p. 82

חַיִל *power*—H. Eising, 'חַיִל *chayil*', *TDOT*, IV (1980), pp. 348-55

חִיל *pain*—A. Bauman, 'חיל *ḥyl*; חִיל *chîl*; חִילָה *chîlāh*; חַלְחָלָה *chalchālāh*', *TDOT*, IV (1980), pp. 344-47

חִילָה *pain*—A. Bauman, 'חיל *ḥyl*; חִיל *chîl*; חִילָה *chîlāh*; חַלְחָלָה *chalchālāh*', *TDOT*, IV (1980), pp. 344-47

חין *die* (cf. Arab. ḫāna IV *perish*)—Thomas, *Lexicon*, VIII (1970), p. 154

חֵיק *fold*—G. André, 'חֵיק *chêq*', *TDOT*, IV (1980), pp. 356-58

חִירָה II *court* (cf. Arab. ḥayr *enclosure, garden*)—Thomas, *Lexicon*, VIII (1970), p. 155; John Elwolde, '3Q15: Its Linguistic Affiliation, with Lexicographical Comments', in *Proceedings of the International Symposium on the Copper Scroll, Manchester, September 1996* (ed. George J. Brooke and Philip R. Davies; JSOTSup; Sheffield: Sheffield Academic Press, 1997)

חִישׁ *quickly*—K.-M. Beyse, 'חוּשׁ *chûsh*; חִישׁ *chîsh*', *TDOT*, IV (1980), pp. 278-80

חכה *wait* (cf. Arab. ḥakā IV *make strong*, ḥajā *remain*)—L. Kopf, 'Arabische Etymologien und Parallelen zum Bibelwörterbuch', *VT* 9 (1959), pp. 247-87 (255); M. Wagner, 'Beiträge zur Aramaismenfrage im alttestamentlichen Hebräisch', in *Hebräische Wortforschung: Festschrift zum 80. Geburtstag von Walter Baumgartner* (VTSup, 16; Leiden: E.J. Brill, 1967), pp. 355-71 (361-62); C. Barth, 'חָכָה *chākhāh*', *TDOT*, IV (1980), pp. 359-63

חכם *be wise*—H. Cazelles, 'A propos d'une phrase de H.H. Rowley', in *Wisdom in Israel and in the Ancient Near East, Presented to Professor Harold Henry Rowley ... in Celebration of his Sixty-Fifth Birthday* (ed. M. Noth and D. Winton Thomas; VTSup, 3; Leiden: E.J. Brill, 1955), pp. 26-32; J. Lindblom, 'Wisdom in the Old Testament Prophets', in *Wisdom in Israel and in the Ancient Near East, Presented to Professor Harold Henry Rowley ... in Celebration of his Sixty-Fifth Birthday* (ed. M. Noth and D. Winton Thomas; VTSup, 3; Leiden: E.J. Brill, 1955), pp. 192-204 (193-95); M. Noth, 'Die Bewährung von Salomos "göttlicher Weisheit"', in *Wisdom in Israel and in the Ancient Near East, Presented to Professor Harold Henry Rowley ... in Celebration of his Sixty-Fifth Birthday* (ed. M. Noth and D. Winton Thomas; VTSup, 3; Leiden: E.J. Brill, 1955), pp. 225-37; M. Sæbø, '*ḥkm* weise sein', *THWAT*, I (1971), pp. 557-67; H.-P. Müller, M. Krause, 'חָכַם *chākham*; חָכָם *chākhām*; חָכְמָה *chokhmāh*; חָכְמוֹת *chokhmôth*', *TDOT*, IV (1980), pp. 364-85

חָכָם *wise*—H.-P. Müller, M. Krause, 'חָכַם *chākham*; חָכָם *chākhām*; חָכְמָה *chokhmāh*; חָכְמוֹת *chokhmôth*', *TDOT*, IV (1980), pp. 364-85

חָכְמָה *wisdom*—H. Cazelles, 'A propos d'une phrase de H.H. Rowley', in *Wisdom in Israel and in the Ancient Near East, Presented to Professor Harold Henry Rowley ... in Celebration of his Sixty-Fifth Birthday* (ed. M. Noth and D. Winton Thomas; VTSup, 3; Leiden: E.J. Brill, 1955), pp. 26-32; J. Lindblom, 'Wisdom in the Old Testament Prophets', in *Wisdom in Israel and in the Ancient Near East, Presented to Professor Harold Henry Rowley ... in Celebration of his Sixty-Fifth Birthday* (ed. M. Noth and D. Winton Thomas; VTSup, 3; Leiden: E.J. Brill, 1955), pp. 192-204 (193-195); M. Noth, 'Die Bewährung von Salomos "göttlicher Weisheit"', in *Wisdom in Israel and in the Ancient Near East, Presented to Professor Harold Henry Rowley ... in Celebration of his Sixty-Fifth Birthday* (ed. M. Noth and D. Winton Thomas; VTSup, 3; Leiden: E.J. Brill, 1955), pp. 225-37; H.-P. Müller, M. Krause, 'חָכַם *chākham*; חָכָם *chākhām* ; חָכְמָה *chokhmāh*; חָכְמוֹת *chokhmôth*', *TDOT*, IV (1980), pp. 364-85; H.-P.

Müller, 'Theonome Skepsis und Lebensfreude', *BZ* 30 (1986), pp. 1-19 (3-4)

חָכְמוֹת *wisdom*—H.-P. Müller, M. Krause, 'חָכַם *chākham*; חָכָם *chākhām*; חָכְמָה *chokhmāh*; חָכְמוֹת *chokhmôth*', *TDOT*, IV (1980), pp. 364-85; G.A. Rendsburg, *Linguistic Evidence for the Northern Origin of Selected Psalms* (SBLMS, 43; Atlanta: Scholars Press, 1990), p. 32

חכר II *oppress* (cf. Arab. ḥakara)—Thomas, *Lexicon*, VIII (1970), p. 165

חֵל *rampart*—L. Delekat, 'Zum hebräischen Wörterbuch', *VT* 14 (1964), pp. 7-66 (18); E. Eibschitz, '*hêl* und *hômāh*', *Sinai* 100 (1987), pp. 75-86

חֹל *profaneness*—W. Dommershausen, 'חלל *ḥll* I; חֹל *chōl*; חָלִיל *chālîl*', *TDOT*, IV (1980), pp. 409-17

חֶלְאָה *rust*—W.W. Müller, 'Beiträge aus dem Mehri zum etymologischen Teil des hebr. Lexicons', in *Mélanges linguistiques offerts à Maxime Rodinson* (ed. C. Robin; Comptes rendus du Groupe linguistique d'études chamito-sémitiques, 12; Paris: P. Geuthner, 1985), pp. 267-69

חָלָב *milk*—A. Caquot, 'חָלָב *chālābh*; גְּבִינָה *gᵉbhînāh*; חֶמְאָה *chem'āh*', *TDOT*, IV (1980), pp. 386-91

חֵלֶב I *fat*—J. Heller, 'Die Symbolik des Fettes im AT', *VT* 20 (1970), pp. 106-108; G. Münderlein, 'חֵלֶב *chēlebh*', *TDOT*, IV (1980), pp. 391-97

חֶלֶד *Heled*—K.-M. Beyse, 'חֶלֶד *cheledh*; חֹלֶד *chōledh*; חֻלְדָּה *chuldāh*; חֵלֶד *chēledh*; חֶלְדַּי *cheldai*', *TDOT*, IV (1980), pp. 397-99

חֶלֶד *duration*—K.-M. Beyse, 'חֶלֶד *cheledh*; חֹלֶד *chōledh*; חֻלְדָּה *chuldāh*; חֵלֶד *chēledh*; חֶלְדַּי *cheldai*', *TDOT*, IV (1980), pp. 397-99

חֹלֶד *weasel*—K.-M. Beyse, 'חֶלֶד *cheledh*; חֹלֶד *chōledh*; חֻלְדָּה *chuldāh*; חֵלֶד *chēledh*; חֶלְדַּי *cheldai*', *TDOT*, IV (1980), pp. 397-99

חֻלְדָּה *Huldah*—K.-M. Beyse, 'חֶלֶד *cheledh*; חֹלֶד *chōledh*; חֻלְדָּה *chuldāh*; חֵלֶד *chēledh*; חֶלְדַּי *cheldai*', *TDOT*, IV (1980), pp. 397-99

חֶלְדַּי *Heldai*—K.-M. Beyse, 'חֶלֶד *cheledh*; חֹלֶד *chōledh*; חֻלְדָּה *chuldāh*; חֵלֶד *chēledh*; חֶלְדַּי *cheldai*', *TDOT*, IV (1980), pp. 397-99; F. Zeeb, 'Studien zu den altbabylonischen Texten aus Alalaḫ (I)', *UF* 23 (1991), pp. 405-38 (412)

חלה I *be weak*—G.R. Driver, 'Isaiah 52₁₃–53₁₂: The Servant of the Lord', in *In Memoriam Paul Kahle* (ed. M. Black and G. Fohrer; BZAW, 103; Berlin: Töpelmann, 1968), pp. 91-105 (98-101); F. Stolz, '*ḥlh* krank sein', *THWAT*, I (1971), pp. 567-70; K. Seybold, 'חָלָה *chālāh*; חֳלִי *chᵒlî*; חִלָּה פָּנִים *chillāh phānîm*', *TDOT*, IV (1980), pp. 399-409

חלה II *be sweet*—K. Seybold, 'Reverenz und Gebet: Erwägungen zu der Wendung *ḥillā panîm*', *ZAW* 88 (1976), pp. 2-16; 'חָלָה *chālāh*; חֳלִי *chᵒlî*; חִלָּה פָּנִים *chillāh phānîm*', *TDOT*, IV (1980), pp. 399-409

חלה III *adorn* (Arab. ḥalā)—G.R. Driver, 'Problems in the Hebrew Text of Proverbs', *Bib* 32 (1951), pp. 173-97 (177); 'Isaiah 52₁₃–53₁₂: The Servant of the Lord', in *In Memoriam Paul Kahle* (ed. M. Black and G. Fohrer; BZAW, 103; Berlin: Töpelmann, 1968), pp. 91-105 (98); Thomas, *Lexicon*, VIII (1970), pp. 180-81

חלה IV *be anxious* (cf. Eth. ḫallaya *be careful*)—G.R. Driver, 'Some Hebrew Words', *JTS* 29 (1927–28), pp. 390-96 (392); I. Eitan, 'A Contribution to Isaiah Exegesis', *HUCA* 12–13 (1937–38), pp. 55-88 (82-83); Thomas, *Lexicon*, VIII (1970), pp. 181-82

חלה V *be alone* (cf. Ug. ḫlw, Arab. ḫalā)—I. Eitan, 'A Contribution to Isaiah Exegesis', *HUCA* 12–13 (1937–38), pp. 55-88 (62-63); G.R. Driver, 'Isaiah 52₁₃–53₁₂: The Servant of the Lord', in *In Memoriam Paul Kahle* (ed. M. Black and G. Fohrer; BZAW, 103; Berlin: Töpelmann, 1968), pp. 91-105 (98-99); Thomas, *Lexicon*, VIII (1970), pp. 182-83

חֲלוֹם *dream*—E.L. Ehrlich, *Der Traum im Alten Testament* (BZAW, 73; Berlin: Töpelmann, 1953), pp. 1-12; J. Bergman, M. Ottosson, G.J. Botterweck, 'חָלַם *chālam*; חֲלוֹם *chᵃlôm*', *TDOT*, IV (1980), pp. 421-32; J.-M. Husser, 'Songe', in *Dictionnaire de la Bible Supplément*, VI (Paris: Letouzey & Ané), pp. 1-64 (27-28)

חֲלוֹמָה *wise woman*—Thomas, *Lexicon*, VIII (1970), p. 199

חֲלוֹף *opposition*—G.R. Driver, 'Problems in the Hebrew Text of Proverbs', *Bib* 32 (1951), pp. 173-97 (195-96)

*foolishness*—D.W. Thomas, 'Notes on Some Passages in

the Book of Proverbs', *VT* 15 (1965), pp. 271-79 (277); Thomas, *Lexicon*, VIII (1970), p. 205

חַלְחָלָה *anguish*—A. Bauman, 'חיל *ḥyl*; חִיל *chîl*; חִילָה *chîlāh*; חַלְחָלָה *chalchālāh*', *TDOT*, IV (1980), pp. 344-47

חֳלִי *sickness*—K. Seybold, 'חָלָה *chālāh*; חֳלִי *cholî*; חִלָּה פָּנִים *chillāh phānîm*', *TDOT*, IV (1980), pp. 399-409

חָלִיל *flute*—W. Dommershausen, 'חלל *ḥll* I; חֹל *chōl*; חָלִיל *chālîl*', *TDOT*, IV (1980), pp. 409-17

חֲלִיפָה I *change*—S. Tengström and H.-J. Fabry, 'חָלַף *chālaph*; חֲלִיפָה *chalîphāh*; חֵלֶף *chēleph*; מַחְלְפוֹת *machlephôth*', *TDOT*, IV (1980), pp. 432-35

חֲלִיפָה II *oath* (cf. Arab. ḥalaf)—Thomas, *Lexicon*, VIII (1970), p. 207

חֵלְכָה *wretched*—N. Füglister, '"Die Hoffnung der Armen ist nicht für immer verloren." Psalm 9/10 und die sozio-religiöse Situation der nachexilischen Gemeinde', in *Biblische Theologie und gesellschaftlicher Wandel. Für Norbert Lohfink SJ* (ed. Georg Braulik, Walter Gross and Sean McEvenue; Freiburg; Herder, 1993), pp. 101-24 (122); G. Schuttermayr, *Psalm 9–10* (1985), pp. 149-51

*wicked*—M. Wallenstein, 'Some Lexical Material in the Judean Scrolls', *VT* 4 (1954), pp. 211-14 (213-14)

חלל I *profane*—F. Maass, '*ḥll* pi. entweihen', *THWAT*, I (1971), pp. 570-75; W. Dommershausen, 'חלל *ḥll* I; חֹל *chōl*; חָלִיל *chālîl*', *TDOT*, IV (1980), pp. 409-17

חלל III *be pierced*—W. Dommershausen, 'חָלַל *chālal* II', *TDOT*, IV (1980), pp. 417-21

חלל IV *play the flute*—W. Dommershausen, 'חלל *ḥll* I; חֹל *chōl*; חָלִיל *chālîl*', *TDOT*, IV (1980), pp. 409-17

חלל V *tremble*—M.Z. Kaddary, 'חלל = "Bore", "Pierce"?', *VT* 13 (1963), pp. 486-89

חָלָל I *carnage*—J.J. Glück, 'Ḥalālîm (Ḥālāl) "carnage, massacre"', *RQ* 7 (1969–71), pp. 417-19

חלם I *dream*—J. Bergman, M. Ottosson, G.J. Botterweck, 'חָלַם *chālam*; חֲלוֹם *chalôm*', *TDOT*, IV (1980), pp. 421-32

חלם II *be healthy*—J. Strugnell, 'A Note on Ps. cxxvi. 1', *JTS* VII ns (1956), pp. 239-43; Thomas, *Lexicon*, VIII (1970), p. 199

חלף I *pass*—S. Tengström, H.-J. Fabry, 'חָלַף *chālaph*; חֲלִיפָה *chalîphāh*; חֵלֶף *chēleph*; מַחְלְפוֹת *machlephôth*', *TDOT*, IV (1980), pp. 432-35; M. Tsevat, 'Psalm xc 5-6', *VT* 35 (1985), pp. 115-16

חלף III *grow*—M. Tsevat, 'Psalm xc 5-6', *VT* 35 (1985), pp. 115-16

חֵלֶף I *in return for*—S. Tengström, H.-J. Fabry, 'חָלַף *chālaph*; חֲלִיפָה *chalîphāh*; חֵלֶף *chēleph*; מַחְלְפוֹת *machlephôth*', *TDOT*, IV (1980), pp. 432-35

חלץ I *loosen*—C. Barth, 'חָלַץ *chālats*', *TDOT*, IV (1980), pp. 436-41

חֲלָצַיִם *loins*—V. Hamp, 'חֲלָצַיִם *chalātsayim*; מָתְנַיִם *mothnayim*; יָרֵךְ *yārēkh*; כֶּסֶל *kesel*', *TDOT*, IV (1980), pp. 441-44

חלק I *divide*—H.J. Koorevaar, *De opbouw van het boek Jozua* (1990), p. 197; H.H. Schmid, '*ḥlq* teilen', *THWAT*, 1 (1971), pp. 576-79; M. Tsevat, 'חָלַק *chālaq* II; חֵלֶק *chēleq*; חֶלְקָה *chelqāh*; חֲלֻקָּה *chaluqqāh*; מַחֲלֹקֶת *machalōqeth*', *TDOT*, IV (1980), pp. 447-51; D.J. Kamhi, 'The Root *ḥlq* in the Bible', *VT* 23 (1973), pp. 235-39 (235-37)

חלק II *be smooth*—K.-D. Schunck, 'חָלַק *chālaq* I; חָלָק *chālāq*; חֵלֶק *chēleq*; חִלֻּק *challuq*; חֶלְקָה *chelqāh*; חֲלַקְלַקּוֹת *chalaqlaqqôth*; מַחְלְקוֹת *machleqôth*', *TDOT*, IV (1980), pp. 444-47

חלק III *die*—Mitchell J. Dahood, 'Hebrew–Ugaritic Lexicography II', *Bib* 45 (1964), pp. 393-412 (408); Dahood, 'Hebrew–Ugaritic Lexicography IV', *Bib* 47 (1966), pp. 403-19 (405); T.F. McDaniel, 'Philological Studies in Lamentations. I', *Bib* 49 (1968), pp. 27-53 (48-49)

חלק IV *surround*—D.J. Kamhi, 'The Root *ḥlq* in the Bible', *VT* 23 (1973), pp. 235-39 (238)

חלק V *strip*—D.J. Kamhi, 'The Root *ḥlq* in the Bible', *VT* 23 (1973), pp. 235-39 (237)

חלק VI *create*—G.R. Driver, 'Problems in the Hebrew Text of Job', in *Wisdom in Israel and in the Ancient Near East, Presented to Professor Harold Henry Rowley ... in Celebration of his Sixty-Fifth Birthday* (ed. M. Noth and D. Winton Thomas; VTSup, 3; Leiden: E.J. Brill, 1955), pp. 72-93 (91-92)

חלק VII *flee*—I. Eph'al, '"You Are Defecting to the

Chaldeans" (Jer 37₁₃)', *E I* 24 (1993), pp. 18-23 (Hebrew), 232* (English)

חָלָק I *smooth*—K.-D. Schunck, 'חָלַק *chālaq* I; חָלָק *chālāq*; חֵלֶק *chēleq*; חַלֻּק *challuq*; חֶלְקָה *chelqāh*; חֲלַקְלַקּוֹת *chalaqlaqqôth*; מַחְלְקוֹת *machleqôth*', *TDOT*, IV (1980), pp. 444-47

חָלָק II *high*—D.J. Kamhi, 'The Root *ḥlq* in the Bible', *VT* 23 (1973), pp. 235-39 (238-39)

חַלֻּק *smooth*—K.-D. Schunck, 'חָלַק *chālaq* I; חָלָק *chālāq*; חֵלֶק *chēleq*; חַלֻּק *challuq*; חֶלְקָה *chelqāh*; חֲלַקְלַקּוֹת *chalaqlaqqôth*; מַחְלְקוֹת *machleqôth*', *TDOT*, IV (1980), pp. 444-47

חֵלֶק I *portion*—M. Tsevat, 'חָלַק *chālaq* II; חֵלֶק *chēleq*; חֶלְקָה *chelqāh*; חֲלֻקָּה *chaluqqāh*; מַחֲלֹקֶת *machalōqeth*', *TDOT*, IV (1980), pp. 447-51

*reward* —H.-P. Müller, 'Theonome Skepsis und Lebensfreude', *BZ* 30 (1986), pp. 1-19 (8)

חֵלֶק IV *smoothness*—K.-D. Schunck, 'חָלַק *chālaq* I; חָלָק *chālāq*; חֵלֶק *chēleq*; חַלֻּק *challuq*; חֶלְקָה *chelqāh*; חֲלַקְלַקּוֹת *chalaqlaqqôth*; מַחְלְקוֹת *machleqôth*', *TDOT*, IV (1980), pp. 444-47

חֶלְקָה *division*—M. Tsevat, 'חָלַק *chālaq* II; חֵלֶק *chēleq*; חֶלְקָה *chelqāh*; חֲלֻקָּה *chaluqqāh*; מַחֲלֹקֶת *machalōqeth*', *TDOT*, IV (1980), pp. 447-51; J.P. Weinberg, 'Die soziale Gruppe im Weltbild des Chronisten', *ZAW* 98 (1986), pp. 72-95 (77)

חֶלְקָה I *plot of land*—M. Tsevat, 'חָלַק *chālaq* II; חֵלֶק *chēleq*; חֶלְקָה *chelqāh*; חֲלֻקָּה *chaluqqāh*; מַחֲלֹקֶת *machalōqeth*', *TDOT*, IV (1980), pp. 447-51

חֶלְקָה II *smoothness*—K.-D. Schunck, 'חָלַק *chālaq* I; חָלָק *chālāq*; חֵלֶק *chēleq*; חַלֻּק *challuq*; חֶלְקָה *chelqāh*; חֲלַקְלַקּוֹת *chalaqlaqqôth*; מַחְלְקוֹת *machleqôth*', *TDOT*, IV (1980), pp. 444-47

חֲלַקּוֹת *perdition*—Mitchell J. Dahood, 'Hebrew–Ugaritic Lexicography II', *Bib* 45 (1964), pp. 393-412 (408)

חֲלַקְלַקּוֹת I *smoothness*—K.-D. Schunck, 'חָלַק *chālaq* I; חָלָק *chālāq*; חֵלֶק *chēleq*; חַלֻּק *challuq*; חֶלְקָה *chelqāh*; חֲלַקְלַקּוֹת *chalaqlaqqôth*; מַחְלְקוֹת *machleqôth*', *TDOT*, IV (1980), pp. 444-47

חֲלַקְלַקּוֹת II *darkness*—D.J. Kamhi, 'The Root *ḥlq* in the Bible', *VT* 23 (1973), pp. 235-39 (238)

חלשׁ I *defeat*—A. Guillaume, 'The Use of חלשׁ in Exod. xvii. 13, Isa xiv. 12, and Job xiv. 10', *JTS* ns 14 (1963), pp. 91-92

חלשׁ II *be weak*—A. Guillaume, 'The Use of חלשׁ in Exod. xvii. 13, Isa xiv. 12, and Job xiv. 10', *JTS* ns 14 (1963), pp. 91-92

חַם *hot*—K.-M. Beyse, 'חמם *ḥmm*; חֹם *chōm*; חָם *chām*; חוּם *chûm*; חַמָּה *chammāh*; חַמָּן *chammān*', *TDOT*, IV (1980), pp. 473-77

חֹם *heat*—K.-M. Beyse, 'חמם *ḥmm*; חֹם *chōm*; חָם *chām*; חוּם *chûm*; חַמָּה *chammāh*; חַמָּן *chammān*', *TDOT*, IV (1980), pp. 473-77

חֶמְאָה *curd*—A. Caquot, 'חָלָב *chālābh*; גְּבִינָה *gebhînāh*; חֶמְאָה *chem'āh*', *TDOT*, IV (1980), pp. 386-91; W.W. Müller, 'Beiträge aus dem Mehri zum etymologischen Teil des hebr. Lexicons', in *Mélanges linguistiques offerts à Maxime Rodinson* (ed. C. Robin; Comptes rendus du Groupe linguistique d'études chamito-sémitiques, 12; Paris: P. Geuthner, 1985), pp. 267-69

חמד *desire*—E. Gerstenberger, '*ḥmd* begehren', *THWAT*, I (1971), pp. 579-81; G. Wallis, 'חָמַד *chāmadh*; חֶמֶד *chemedh*; חֶמְדָּה *chemdāh*; חֲמֻדוֹת *chamudhôth*; חֶמְדָּן *chemdān*; מַחְמָד *machmādh*; מַחְמֹד *machmōdh*', *TDOT*, IV (1980), pp. 452-61; W.A. Dyrness, 'Aesthetics in the Old Testament', *Journal of the Evangelical Theological Society* 28 (1985), pp. 421-32

*appropriate*—John Gray, *Joshua, Judges, Ruth* (New Century Bible; Grand Rapids: Eerdmans, 1986), p. 83

חֶמֶד *desire*—G. Wallis, 'חָמַד *chāmadh*; חֶמֶד *chemedh*; חֶמְדָּה *chemdāh*; חֲמֻדוֹת *chamudhôth*; חֶמְדָּן *chemdān*; מַחְמָד *machmādh*; מַחְמֹד *machmōdh*', *TDOT*, IV (1980), pp. 452-61

חֶמְדָּה *desire*—G. Wallis, 'חָמַד *chāmadh*; חֶמֶד *chemedh*; חֶמְדָּה *chemdāh*; חֲמֻדוֹת *chamudhôth*; חֶמְדָּן *chemdān*; מַחְמָד *machmādh*; מַחְמֹד *machmōdh*', *TDOT*, IV (1980), pp. 452-61

חֲמֻדוֹת *preciousness, precious things*—G. Wallis, 'חָמַד *chāmadh*; חֶמֶד *chemedh*; חֶמְדָּה *chemdāh*; חֲמֻדוֹת *chamudhôth*; חֶמְדָּן *chemdān*; מַחְמָד *machmādh*; מַחְמֹד *machmōdh*', *TDOT*, IV (1980), pp. 452-61

חֶמְדָּן *Hemdan*—G. Wallis, 'חָמַד *chāmadh*; חֶמֶד *chemedh*;

חֶמְדָּה *chemdāh;* חֲמֻדוֹת *c hamudhôth;* חֶמְדָּן *chemdān;* מַחְמָד *machmādh;* מַחְמֹד *machmōdh', TDOT*, IV (1980), pp. 452-61

חמה I *see*—J. Blau, 'Über Homonyme und angeblich homonyme Wurzeln II', *VT* 7 (1956), pp. 98-102 (98)

חַמָּה *heat*—K.-M. Beyse, 'חמם *ḥmm;* חֹם *chōm;* חָם *chām;* חוּם *chûm;* חַמָּה *chammāh;* חַמָּן *chammān', TDOT*, IV (1980), pp. 473-77

חֵמָה I *heat*—G. Sauer, '*ḥēmā* Erregung', *THWAT*, I (1971), pp. 581-83; K.-D. Schunck, 'חֵמָה *chēmāh', TDOT*, IV (1980), pp. 462-65

חֵמוֹת *anger(s)*—G.A. Rendsburg, *Linguistic Evidence for the Northern Origin of Selected Psalms* (SBLMS, 43; Atlanta: Scholars Press, 1990), p. 32

חֵמָה II *family*—S. Talmon, 'המה הקינים הבאים מחמת אבי בית־רכב 1 Chron. ii, 55', *IEJ* 10 (1960), pp. 176-80

חֵמָה III *protection*—Thomas, *Lexicon*, VIII (1970), p. 236

חָמוּץ *crimson*—D. Kellermann, 'חמץ *ḥmṣ;* חָמֵץ *chāmēts;* חֹמֶץ *chōmets;* חָמוּץ *chāmûts;* חָמִיץ *chāmîts', TDOT*, IV (1980), pp. 487-93 (492-93); J.F.A. Sawyer, 'Radical Images of Yahweh in Isaiah 63', in *Among the Prophets: Language, Image and Structure in the Prophetic Writings* (ed. Philip R. Davies and David J.A. Clines; JSOTSup, 144; Sheffield: JSOT Press, 1992), pp. 72-82 (76)

חֲמוֹר I *ass*—W.T. In der Smitten, 'חֲמוֹר *chamôr', TDOT*, IV (1980), pp. 465-70

חֲמוֹר לֶחֶם ḥamor *of bread* (cf. Akk. imēru *donkey [load]*)—D.T. Tsumura, '*Ḥamôr leḥem* (1 Samuel xvi 20), *VT* 42 (1992), pp. 412-13

חָמִיךְ *unreliable guide* (cf. Arab. ḥamika *guide*, ḥamak *guide*)—R. Smend, *Die Weisheit des Jesus Sirach* (Berlin: Georg Reimer, 1906), p. 329; Thomas, *Lexicon*, VIII (1970), p. 240

חָמִיץ *sorrel*—D. Kellermann, 'חמץ *ḥmṣ;* חָמֵץ *chāmēts;* חֹמֶץ *chōmets;* חָמוּץ *chāmûts;* חָמִיץ *c hāmîts', TDOT*, IV (1980), pp. 487-93 (493)

חמל *spare*—M. Tsevat, 'חָמַל *chāmal;* חֶמְלָה *chemlāh', TDOT*, IV (1980), pp. 470-72

חמם *be warm*—K.-M. Beyse, 'חמם *ḥmm;* חֹם *chōm;* חָם *chām;* חוּם *chûm;* חַמָּה *chammāh;* חַמָּן *chammān', TDOT*, IV (1980), pp. 473-77

חַמָּן *incense altar*—K.-M. Beyse, 'חמם *ḥmm;* חֹם *chōm;* חָם *chām;* חוּם *chûm;* חַמָּה *chammāh;* חַמָּן *chammān', TDOT*, IV (1980), pp. 473-77

חמס I *be violent*—H. Haag, 'חָמָס *chāmās', TDOT*, IV (1980), pp. 478-87; I. Swart, 'In Search of the Meaning of *ḥamas:* Studying an Old Testament Word in Context', *Journal for Semitics/Tydskrif vir semitistiek* 3 (1991), pp. 156-66

חָמָס *violence*—H.J. Stoebe, '*ḥāmās* Gewalttat', *THWAT*, I (1971), pp. 583-87; H. Haag, 'חָמָס *chāmās', TDOT*, IV (1980), pp. 478-87; I. Swart, 'In Search of the Meaning of *ḥamas:* Studying an Old Testament Word in Context', *Journal for Semitics/Tydskrif vir semitistiek* 3 (1991), pp. 156-66; S.D. Snyman, '"Violence" in Amos 3.10 and 6.3', *ETL* 71 (1995), pp. 30-47 (47)

חמץ I *be sour*—D. Kellermann, 'חמץ *ḥmṣ;* חָמֵץ *chāmēts;* חֹמֶץ *chōmets;* חָמוּץ *chāmûts;* חָמִיץ *chāmîts', TDOT*, IV (1980), pp. 487-93

חָמֵץ *leavened*—D. Kellermann, 'חמץ *ḥmṣ;* חָמֵץ *chāmēts;* חֹמֶץ *chōmets;* חָמוּץ *chāmûts;* חָמִיץ *chāmîts', TDOT*, IV (1980), pp. 487-93 (489-90)

חֹמֶץ *vinegar*—D. Kellermann, 'חמץ *ḥmṣ;* חָמֵץ *chāmēts;* חֹמֶץ *chōmets;* חָמוּץ *chāmûts;* חָמִיץ *c hāmîts', TDOT*, IV (1980), pp. 487-93 (490-92)

חמר I *foam*—H. Ringgren, 'חמר *ḥmr;* חֹמֶר *ḥōmer;* חֵמָר *ḥēmār' TDOT*, V (1986), pp. 1-4 (2)

pealal *ferment* (cf. Arab. ḥamara III *be entangled*)—C.L. Seow, 'A Textual Note on Lamentations 1:20', *CBQ* 47 (1985), pp. 416-19

חֶמֶר *wine*—H. Ringgren, 'חמר *ḥmr;* חֹמֶר *ḥmer;* חֵמָר *ḥēmār', TDOT*, V (1986), pp. 1-4 (2)

חֵמָר *bitumen* (cf. Eg. mrḥ)—P. Humbert, 'En marge du dictionnaire hébraïque', *ZAW* 62 (1949–50), pp. 199-207 (201); H. Ringgren, 'חמר *ḥmr;* חֹמֶר *ḥmer;* חֵמָר *ḥēmār', TDOT*, V (1986), pp. 1-4 (3-4)

חֹמֶר I *clay*—Mitchell J. Dahood, 'Hebrew–Ugaritic Lexicography II', *Bib* 45 (1964), pp. 393-412 (408-409); H. Ringgren, 'חמר *ḥmr;* חֹמֶר *ḥōmer;* חֵמָר *ḥēmār', TDOT*, V (1986), pp. 1-4 (3)

חֹמֶר III *foaming*—H. Ringgren, 'חמר *ḥmr;* חֹמֶר *ḥōmer;* חֵמָר

*ḥēmār'*, *TDOT*, V (1986), pp. 1-4 (2)

חֹמֶר IV *heap*—H. Ringgren, 'חמר *ḥmr*; חֹמֶר *ḥōmer*; חֲמָר *ḥēmār'*, *TDOT*, V (1986), pp. 1-4 (1)

חמשׁ *be five*—qal *be grouped in fifties*—S.L. Ska, 'Le passage de la mer', *Analecta Biblica* 109 (1986), pp. 14-16

חֹמֶשׁ II *abdomen*—W.W. Müller, 'Beiträge aus dem Mehri zum etymologischen Teil des hebr. Lexicons', in *Mélanges linguistiques offerts à Maxime Rodinson* (ed. C. Robin; Comptes rendus du Groupe linguistique d'études chamito-sémitiques, 12; Paris: P. Geuthner, 1985), pp. 267-69

חֲמִשִּׁים *fifty*—חֲמִשִּׁים חֲמִשִּׁים אִישׁ בַּמְּעָרָה *men by fives to a cave*—John Gray, *I & II Kings* (Old Testament Library; London: SCM Press, 3rd edn, 1977), p. 386

חֵן I *grace*—W.L. Reed, 'Some Implication of *Ḥên* for Old Testament Religion', *JBL* 73 (1954), pp. 36-41; J. Reider, 'Etymological Studies in Biblical Hebrew', *VT* 4 (1954), pp. 276-95 (277); I. Willi-Plein, 'Ein Übersetzungsproblem: Gedanken zu Sach. xii 10', *VT* 23 (1973), pp. 90-99; D.N. Freedman, J.R. Lundbom, H.-J. Fabry, 'חָנַן *ḥānan*; חֵן *ḥēn*; חַנּוּן *ḥannûn*; חֲנִינָה *ḥanînâ*; תְּחִנָּה *teḥinnâ*; תַּחֲנוּן *taḥanûn'*, *TDOT*, V (1986), pp. 22-36

חנה I *encamp*—F.J. Helfmeyer, 'חָנָה *ḥānâ*; מַחֲנֶה *maḥaneh'*, *TDOT*, V (1986), pp. 4-19

חֲנוֹךְ *Enoch*—K. Luke, 'The Patriarch Henoch', *Indian Theological Studies* 23 (1986), pp. 125-53

חַנּוּן *gracious*—D.N. Freedman, J.R. Lundbom, H.-J. Fabry, 'חָנַן *ḥ ānan*; חֵן *ḥēn*; חַנּוּן *ḥannûn*; חֲנִינָה *ḥanînâ*; תְּחִנָּה *teḥinnâ*; תַּחֲנוּן *taḥanûn'*, *TDOT*, V (1986), pp. 22-36

חָנוּת *vault*—E. Lipiński, 'L'aménagement des villes dans la terminologie phénico-punique', in *L'Africa romana: Atti del convegno di studio Oristano, 1992* (ed. A. Mastino and P. Ruggeri, 1995), pp. 121-33 (127-28)

חנט I *embalm*—M. Görg, '"Bindung" für das Leben: Ein biblischer Begriff im Licht seines ägyptischen Äquivalents', in *Studien zur biblisch-ägyptischen Religionsgeschichte* (Stuttgarter Biblische Aufsatzbände, 14; Stuttgart: Verlag Katholisches Bibelwerk, 1992), pp. 108-16

חנט II *ripen*—M. Görg, '"Bindung" für das Leben. Ein biblischer Begriff im Licht seines ägyptischen Äquivalents', in *Studien zur biblisch-ägyptischen Religionsgeschichte* (Stuttgarter Biblische Aufsatzbände, 14; Stuttgart: Verlag Katholisches Bibelwerk, 1992), pp. 108-16

חֲנֻטִים *embalming*—M. Görg, '"Bindung" für das Leben. Ein biblischer Begriff im Licht seines ägyptischen Äquivalents', in *Studien zur biblisch-ägyptischen Religionsgeschichte* (Stuttgarter Biblische Aufsatzbände, 14; Stuttgart: Verlag Katholisches Bibelwerk, 1992), pp. 108-16

חָנִיךְ *trained*—W. Dommershausen, 'חָנַךְ *ḥānak*; חֲנֻכָּה *ḥanukkâ*; חָנִיךְ *ḥānîk'*, *TDOT*, V (1986), pp. 19-21

חֲנִינָה *grace, favour*—D.N. Freedman, J.R. Lundbom, H.-J Fabry, 'חָנַן *ḥānan*; חֵן *ḥēn*; חַנּוּן *ḥannûn*; חֲנִינָה *ḥanînâ*; תְּחִנָּה *teḥinnâ*; תַּחֲנוּן *taḥanûn'*, *TDOT*, V (1986), pp. 22-36

חנך *dedicate, train*—S.C. Reif, 'Dedicated to חנך', *VT* 22 (1972), pp. 495-501; W. Dommershausen, 'חָנַךְ *ḥānak*; חֲנֻכָּה *ḥanukkâ*; חָנִיךְ *ḥānîk'*, *TDOT*, V (1986), pp. 19-21

*train*—T. Hildebrandt, 'Proverbs 22:6a: Train up a Child?', *Grace Theological Journal* 9 (1988), pp. 3-19 (4-9)

חֲנֻכָּה *dedication*—W. Dommershausen, 'חָנַךְ *ḥānak*; חֲנֻכָּה *ḥanukkâ*; חָנִיךְ *ḥānîk'*, *TDOT*, V (1986), pp. 19-21

חִנָּם *for nothing*—H. Seebass, *Numeri* (Biblischer Kommentar, 4; Neukirchen–Vluyn: Neukirchener Verlag des Erziehungsvereins, 1993), p. 30

חנן *be gracious*—F. Nötscher, 'Entbehrliche Hapaxlegomena in Jesaia', *VT* 1 (1951), pp. 299-302 (299); H.J. Stoebe, '*ḥnn* gnädig sein', *THWAT*, I (1971), pp. 587-97; D.N. Freedman, J.R. Lundbom, H.-J. Fabry, 'חָנַן *ḥānan*; חֵן *ḥēn*; חַנּוּן *ḥannûn*; חֲנִינָה *ḥanînâ*; תְּחִנָּה *teḥinnâ*; תַּחֲנוּן *taḥanûn'*, *TDOT*, V (1986), pp. 22-36; P.A. Verhoef, *The Books of Haggai and Malachi* (NICOT, 13; Grand Rapids: Eerdmans, 1988), p. 66

חֵן *one who is gracious*—Mitchell J. Dahood, 'Hebrew–Ugaritic Lexicography II', *Bib* 45 (1964), pp. 393-412 (409)

חֲנָנִי *Hanani*—C.G. Tuland, 'Hanani—Hananiah', *JBL* 77 (1958), pp. 157-61

חֲנַנְיָה *Hananiah*—C.G. Tuland, 'Hanani—Hananiah', *JBL* 77 (1958), pp. 157-61

חנף I *be polluted*—R. Knierim, '*ḥnp* pervertiert sein', *THWAT*, I (1971), pp. 597-99

חנף III *be outraged*—Thomas, *Lexicon*, VIII (1970), pp. 299-300

חָנֵף I *profane*—K. Seybold, 'חָנֵף *ḥānēp̄*; חָנֵף *ḥ ānēp̄*; חֹנֶף *ḥōnep̄*; חֲנֻפָּה *ḥanuppâ*', *TDOT*, V (1986), pp. 36-44

חָנֵף II *haughty* (cf. Ug. ḫnp lb)—Thomas, *Lexicon*, VIII (1970), p. 300

חֹנֶף I *profaneness, hypocrisy*—K. Seybold, 'חָנֵף *ḥānēp̄*; חָנֵף *ḥānēp̄*; חֹנֶף *ḥōnep̄*; חֲנֻפָּה', *TDOT*, V (1986), pp. 36-44

חֹנֶף II *shame* (cf. Akk. ḫanpu *shameful act*)—Thomas, *Lexicon*, VIII (1970), p. 300

חֲנֻפָּה *impiousness*—K. Seybold, 'חָנֵף *ḥānēp̄*; חָנֵף *ḥānēp̄*; חֹנֶף *ḥōnep̄*; חֲנֻפָּה', *TDOT*, V (1986), pp. 36-44

חֶסֶד I *loyalty*—S.T. Byington, 'Hebrew Marginalia', *JBL* 60 (1941), pp. 279-88 (282-83); N.H. Snaith, 'The Meaning of חֶסֶד', *ExpT* 55 (1943–44), pp. 108-10; H.J. Stoebe, 'Die Bedeutung des Wortes *Ḥäsäd* im Alten Testament', *VT* 2 (1952), pp. 244-54; G.A. Larue, 'Recent Studies in Ḥesed', in Nelson Glueck, *Ḥesed in the Bible* (tr. Alfred Gottschalk; ed. Elias L. Epstein; Cincinnati: Hebrew Union College Press, 1967), pp. 1-32; H. Weiss, 'The *Pagani* among the Contemporaries of the First Christians', *JBL* 86 (1967), pp. 42-52; G. Gerleman, 'Das übervolle Mass. Ein Versuch mit *ḥaesaed*', *VT* 28 (1978), pp. 151-64; H.J. Stoebe, '*ḥæsæd* Gürte', *THWAT*, I (1971), pp. 600-21; C.F. Whitley, 'The Semantic Range of Ḥesed', *Bib* 62 (1981), pp. 519-26; Katherine D. Sakenfeld, *Faithfulness in Action: Loyalty in Biblical Perspective* (Overtures to Biblical Theology, 16; Philadelphia: Fortress Press, 1985); H.-J. Zobel, 'חֶסֶד *ḥesed*', *TDOT*, V (1986), pp. 44-64; P.A. Verhoef, *The Books of Haggai and Malachi* (NICOT, 13; Grand Rapids: Eerdmans, 1988), p. 66; S. Romerowski, 'Que signifie le mot *ḥesed?*', *VT* 40 (1990), pp. 89-103; G.R. Clark, '*Ḥsd*—A Study of a Lexical Field', *AbrN* 30 (1992), pp. 34-55; G.R. Clark, *The Word ḤESED in the Hebrew Bible* (JSOTSup, 157; Sheffield: Sheffield Academic Press, 1993)

טוֹב חַסְדְּךָ *good is your faithfulness*—M.L. Barré, 'The Formulaic Pair *ṭwb (w)ḥsd* in the Psalter', *ZAW* 98 (1986), pp. 100-105

חסה *seek refuge*—L. Delekat, 'Zum hebräischen Wörterbuch', *VT* 14 (1964), pp. 7-66 (28-31); E. Gerstenberger, '*ḥsh* sich bergen', *THWAT*, I (1971), pp. 621-23; J. Gamberoni, 'חָסָה *ḥāsâ*; מַחֲסֶה *maḥaseh*; חָסוּת *ḥāsûṯ*', *TDOT*, V (1986), pp. 64-75

חָסוּת *refuge*—J. Gamberoni, 'חָסָה *ḥāsâ*; מַחֲסֶה *maḥaseh*; חָסוּת *ḥāsûṯ*', *TDOT*, V (1986), pp. 64-75

חָסִיד *loyal*—J. Coppens, *Mélanges bibliques rédigés en l'honneur de André Robert* (Travaux de l'Institut Catholique de Paris, 4; Paris: Bloud & Gay, 1957), pp. 214-24 (217-20); H. Ringgren, H.-J. Fabry 'חָסִיד *ḥāsîḏ*', *TDOT*, V (1986), pp. 75-79

חֲסִידִים *pious ones*—J. Morgenstern, 'The *Ḥasîdîm*—Who Were They?', *HUCA* 38 (1967), pp. 59-73

חֲסִידָה *stork*—G. Gerleman, 'Das übervolle Mass. Ein Versuch mit *ḥaesaed*', *VT* 28 (1978), pp. 151-64 (162-63); J. Tamulénas, 'Översättningen av fågellistorna i Lev 11:13–19 och Deut 14:11–18', *SEÅ* 57 (1992), pp. 28-59 (53)

חָסִיל *locust*—M. Taam-Ambey, 'Translating the Locust Invasion in the Book of Joel into Kituba', *BiTrans* 36 (1985), pp. 216-20; R. Simkins, *Yahweh's Activity in History and Nature in the Book of Joel* (Ancient Near Eastern Texts and Studies, 10; Lewiston: E. Mellen Press, 1991), pp. 105-106

חָסֹן *flax*—M. Tsevat, 'Isaiah i 31', *VT* 19 (1969), pp. 261-63

חסר *lack*—H.-J. Fabry, 'חָסֵר *ḥāsēr*; חָסֵר *ḥāsēr*; חֶסֶר *ḥeser*; חֹסֶר *ḥ ōser*; חֶסְרוֹן *ḥesrôn*; מַחְסוֹר *maḥsôr*', *TDOT*, V (1986), pp. 80-90

pi. *dishonour*—N.M. Bronznick, 'An Unrecognized Denotation of the Verb *ḤSR* in Ben-Sira and Rabbinic Hebrew', in *Biblical and Other Studies in Memory of D.S. Goitein* (ed. R. Aharoni) = *Hebrew Annual Review* 9 (1985), pp. 91ff.

חָסֵר *lacking*—H.-J. Fabry, 'חָסֵר *ḥāsēr*; חָסֵר *ḥāsēr*; חֶסֶר *ḥeser*; חֹסֶר *ḥōser*; חֶסְרוֹן *ḥesrôn*; מַחְסוֹר *maḥsôr*', *TDOT*, V (1986), pp. 80-90

חֲסַר־לֵב *(one) lacking of heart*—N. Shupak, 'The "Sitz im Leben" of the Book of Proverbs in the Light of a Comparison of Biblical and Egyptian Wisdom Literature', *RB* 94 (1987), pp. 98-119

חֶסֶר *want, lack*—H.-J. Fabry, 'חָסֵר *ḥāsēr*; חָסֵר *ḥāsēr*; חֶסֶר *ḥeser*; חֹסֶר *ḥōser*; חֶסְרוֹן *ḥesrôn*; מַחְסוֹר *maḥsôr*', *TDOT*, V (1986), pp. 80-90

חֹסֶר *lack*—H.-J. Fabry, 'חָסֵר *ḥāsēr*; חָסֵר *ḥāsēr*; חֶסֶר *ḥeser*; חֹסֶר *ḥ ōser*; חֶסְרוֹן *ḥesrôn*; מַחְסוֹר *m aḥsôr*', *TDOT*, V (1986), pp. 80-90

חֶסְרוֹן *deficiency*—H.-J. Fabry, 'חָסֵר *ḥāsēr*; חָסֵר *ḥāsēr*; חֶסֶר *ḥeser*; חֹסֶר *ḥōser*; חֶסְרוֹן *ḥesrôn*; מַחְסוֹר *maḥsôr*', *TDOT*, V (1986), pp. 80-90

חפא *hide*—B.E.J.H. Becking, *De ondergang van Samaria. Historische, exegetische en theologische opmerkingen bij II Koningen 17* (Meppel Krips Repro., 1985), pp. 169-71

חפז *make haste, hurry away, be alarmed*—G. André, 'חָפַז *ḥāpaz*; חִפָּזוֹן *ḥippāzôn*', *TDOT*, V (1986), pp. 90-92

חִפָּזוֹן *haste, hurried flight*—G. André, 'חָפַז *ḥāpaz*; חִפָּזוֹן *ḥippāzôn*', *TDOT*, V (1986), pp. 90-92

חפץ *desire, delight (in)*—G. Gerleman, '*ḥpṣ* gefallen haben', *THWAT*, I (1971), pp. 623-25; G.J. Botterweck, 'חָפֵץ *ḥāpēṣ*; חֵפֶץ *ḥēpeṣ*', *TDOT*, V (1986), pp. 92-107; P.A. Verhoef, *The Books of Haggai and Malachi* (NICOT, 13; Grand Rapids: Eerdmans, 1988), p. 66

חֵפֶץ *desire*—G.J. Botterweck, 'חָפֵץ *ḥāpēṣ*; חֵפֶץ *ḥēpeṣ*', *TDOT*, V (1986), pp. 92-107; W. Lau, *Schriftgelehrte Prophetie in Jes 56–66: Eine Untersuchung zu den literarischen Bezügen in den letzten elf Kapiteln des Jesajabuches* (BZAW, 225; Berlin: Töpelmann, 1994), p. 244

חפר I *search, dig*—J. Gamberoni, G.J. Botterweck, 'חָפַר *ḥāpar*', *TDOT*, V (1986), pp. 107-11

חפשׂ I *search*—F. Maass, G.J. Botterweck, 'חָפַשׂ *ḥāpaś*; חֵפֶשׂ *ḥēpeś*', *TDOT*, V (1986), pp. 112-14

חפשׂ II *throw* (cf. Arab. ḫafaša *throw*)—Thomas, *Lexicon*, VIII (1970), p. 335

חֵפֶשׂ *plot*—F. Maass, G.J. Botterweck, 'חָפַשׂ *ḥāpaś*; חֵפֶשׂ *ḥēpeś*', *TDOT*, V (1986), pp. 112-14

חפשׁ *be free*—Thomas Willi, 'Die Freiheit Israels: Philologische Notizen zu den Wurzeln *ḥpš*, *'zb* und *drr*', in *Beiträge zur alttestamentliche Theologie: Festschrift für Walther Zimmerli zum 70. Geburtstag* (ed. Herbert Donner, Robert Hanhart and Rudolf Smend; Vandenhoeck & Ruprecht: Göttingen, 1977), pp. 531-46

חֹפֶשׁ III *prison*—P. Grelot, '*Ḥofšī* (Ps. lxxxviii 6)', *VT* 14 (1964), pp. 256-63

חֻפְשָׁה *freedom*—N. Lohfink, 'חָפְשִׁי *ḥopšî*; חֻפְשָׁה *ḥupšâ*; חָפְשִׁית *ḥopšît*', *TDOT*, V (1986), pp. 114-18

חָפְשִׁי *free*—N. Lohfink, 'חָפְשִׁי *ḥopšî*; חֻפְשָׁה *ḥupšâ*; חָפְשִׁית *ḥopšît*', *TDOT*, V (1986), pp. 114-18

חָפְשִׁית *freedom*—N. Lohfink, 'חָפְשִׁי *ḥopšî*; חֻפְשָׁה *ḥupšâ*; חָפְשִׁית *ḥopšît*', *TDOT*, V (1986), pp. 114-18; J. Milgrom, *Leviticus 1–16* (AB, 3; Garden City, NY: Doubleday, 1992), pp. 806-808

חֵץ *arrow*—H.A. Hoffner, G.J. Botterweck, 'חֵץ *ḥēṣ*', *TDOT*, V (1986), pp. 118-24

*lightning*—M. Brettler, 'Images of YHWH the Warrior in Psalms', *Semeia* 61 (1993), pp. 135-65 (158)

חצב I *hew*—K.-D. Schunck, G.J. Botterweck, 'חָצַב *ḥāṣab*; מַחְצֵב *maḥṣēb*; גָּזִית *gāzît*', *TDOT*, V (1986), pp. 125-27

*cut down*—R.P. Gordon, 'Word-Play and Verse-Order in 1 Samuel xxiv 5–8', *VT* 40 (1990), pp. 139-44

חָצוֹר I *Hazor*—A. Malamat, 'Hazor "The Head of All Those Kingdoms"', *JBL* 79 (1960), pp. 12-19

חָצוֹר III *green*—Thomas, *Lexicon*, VIII (1970), p. 357

חָצִיר I *grass*—C. Barth, 'חָצִיר *ḥāṣîr*', *TDOT*, V (1986), pp. 127-30; Bryan Paradise, 'Food for Thought', in *A Word in Season: Essays in Honour of William McKane* (ed. James D. Martin and Philip R. Davies; JSOTSup, 42; Sheffield: JSOT Press, 1986), pp. 177-204

חֹצֶן II *war-horses* (cf. Arab. ḥiṣān *stallion*—Thomas, *Lexicon*, VIII (1970), p. 343

חָצָף *impudent*—H.L. Ginsberg, 'Lexicographical Notes', in *Hebräische Wortforschung: Festschrift zum 80. Geburtstag von Walter Baumgartner* (VTSup, 16; Leiden: E.J. Brill, 1967), pp. 71-82 (80-81)

חצץ *cut off*—G.R. Driver, 'Problems in the Hebrew Text of Job', in *Wisdom in Israel and in the Ancient Near East, Presented to Professor Harold Henry Rowley ... in*

*Celebration of his Sixty-Fifth Birthday* (ed. M. Noth and D. Winton Thomas; VTSup, 3; Leiden: E.J. Brill, 1955), pp. 72-93 (83)

חָצֵר *court*—K. Aartun, 'Neue Beiträge zum ugaritischen Lexikon II', *UF* 17 (1986), pp. 1-47 (29-30); V. Hamp, 'חָצֵר *ḥāṣēr*', *TDOT*, V (1986), pp. 131-39

חֹק *statute*—P. Victor, 'A Note on חק in the Old Testament', *VT* 16 (1966), pp. 358-61; H. Ringgren, 'חָקַק *ḥāqaq*; חָקָה *ḥāqâ*; חֹק *ḥōq*; חֻקָּה *ḥuqqâ*', *TDOT*, V (1986), pp. 139-47

חקה *carve*—H. Ringgren, 'חָקַק *ḥāqaq*; חָקָה *ḥāqâ*; חֹק *ḥōq*; חֻקָּה *ḥuqqâ*', *TDOT*, V (1986), pp. 139-47

חֻקָּה *statute*—H. Ringgren, 'חָקַק *ḥāqaq*; חָקָה *ḥāqâ*; חֹק *ḥōq*; חֻקָּה *ḥuqqâ*', *TDOT*, V (1986), pp. 139-47; Henri Cazelles, *Autour de l'Exode (Etudes)* (Sources Bibliques; Paris: Gabalda, 1987), pp. 17-19, 34-35, 133-41

חקק *engrave*—G. Liedke, '*ḥqq* einritzen, festsetzen', *THWAT*, I (1971), pp. 626-33; H. Ringgren, 'חָקַק *ḥāqaq*; חָקָה *ḥāqâ*; חֹק *ḥōq*; חֻקָּה *ḥuqqâ*', *TDOT*, V (1986), pp. 139-47; M. Dahood, 'Proverbs 8,22-31', *CBQ* 30 (1968), pp. 512-21 (518)

מְחֹקֵק *portion*—L. Kopf, 'Arabische Etymologien und Parallelen zum Bibelwörterbuch', *VT* 9 (1959), pp. 247-87 (255-56)

חקר I *search*—M. Tsevat, 'חָקַר *ḥāqar*; חֵקֶר *ḥēqer*; מֶחְקָר *meḥqār*' *TDOT*, V (1986), pp. 148-50

חקר II *despise*—D.W. Thomas, 'Notes on Some Passages in the Book of Proverbs', *JTS* 38 (1937), pp. 400-403 (402-403); L. Kopf, 'Arabische Etymologien und Parallelen zum Bibelwörterbuch', *VT* 9 (1959), pp. 247-87 (256-57)

חֵקֶר *searching*—M. Tsevat, 'חָקַר *ḥāqar*; חֵקֶר *ḥēqer*; מֶחְקָר *meḥqār*', *TDOT*, V (1986), pp. 148-50

חֹר I *noble*—J. van der Ploeg, 'Les chefs du peuple d'Israël et leurs titres', *RB* 57 (1950), pp. 40-61 (57-58)

חֶרֶא *dung*—Thomas, *Lexicon*, VIII (1970), p. 371

חרב I *be dry, desolate*—O. Kaiser, 'חָרַב *ḥārab̲* I; חָרֵב *ḥārēb̲*; חֹרֶב *ḥōreb̲*; חָרְבָּה *ḥorbâ*; חָרָבָה *ḥārāb̲â*; *חֲרָבוֹן *ḥarāb̲ôn*', *TDOT*, V (1986), pp. 150-54

חרב II *destroy*—O. Kaiser, 'חֶרֶב *ḥereb̲*; חָרַב *ḥārab̲* II', *TDOT*, V (1986), pp. 155-65

חָרֵב *dry, devastated*—O. Kaiser, 'חָרַב *ḥārab̲* I; חָרֵב *ḥārēb̲*; חֹרֶב *ḥōreb̲*; חָרְבָּה *ḥorbâ*; חָרָבָה *ḥārāb̲â*; *חֲרָבוֹן *ḥarāb̲ôn*', *TDOT*, V (1986), pp. 150-54

חֶרֶב *sword*—J.P. Brown, 'Literary Contexts of the Common HebrewGreek Vocabulary', *JSS* 13 (1968), pp. 163-91 (178-82); O. Kaiser, 'חֶרֶב *ḥereb̲*; חָרַב *ḥārab̲* II', *TDOT*, V (1986), pp. 155-65

חֹרֶב I *dryness, desolation*—O. Kaiser, 'חָרַב *ḥārab̲* I; חָרֵב *ḥārēb̲*; חֹרֶב *ḥōreb̲*; חָרְבָּה *ḥorbâ*; חָרָבָה *ḥārāb̲â*; *חֲרָבוֹן *ḥarāb̲ôn*', *TDOT*, V (1986), pp. 150-54

חֹרֶב II *bustard* (cf. Akk. ḫarbu)—Thomas, *Lexicon*, VIII (1970), p. 381

חָרְבָּה *deceit* (cf. Arab. ḫurbat *deceitfulness*)—G.R. Driver, 'Studies in the Vocabulary of the Old Testament IV', *JTS* 33 (1931–32), pp. 38-47 (42-43)

חֲרָבוֹן *dry heat*—O. Kaiser, 'חָרַב *ḥārab̲* I; חָרֵב *ḥārēb̲*; חֹרֶב *ḥōreb̲*; חָרְבָּה *ḥorbâ*; חָרָבָה *ḥārāb̲â*; *חֲרָבוֹן *ḥarāb̲ôn*', *TDOT*, V (1986), pp. 150-54

חרג *come fearfully*—H. Gunkel, *Die Psalmen* (Göttingen: Vandenhoeck & Ruprecht, r.p. 1968), p. 73

חרד I *tremble*—G.R. Driver, 'Hebrew Homonyms', in *Hebräische Wortforschung: Festschrift zum 80. Geburtstag von Walter Baumgartner* (VTSup, 16; Leiden: E.J. Brill, 1967), pp. 50-64 (54-56); A. Baumann, 'חָרַד *ḥārad̲*; חָרֵד *ḥārēd̲*; חֲרָדָה *ḥarād̲â*', *TDOT*, V (1986), pp. 166-70

חרד II *be angry* (cf. Arab. ḥarida *be angry*)—G.R. Driver, 'Hebrew Homonyms', in *Hebräische Wortforschung: Festschrift zum 80. Geburtstag von Walter Baumgartner* (VTSup, 16; Leiden: E.J. Brill, 1967), pp. 50-64 (54-55); Thomas, *Lexicon*, VIII (1970), p. 383

חרד III *separate* (cf. Arab. ḥarada II *separate oneself*)—G.R. Driver, 'Hebrew Homonyms', in *Hebräische Wortforschung: Festschrift zum 80. Geburtstag von Walter Baumgartner* (VTSup, 16; Leiden: E.J. Brill, 1967), pp. 50-64 (54); Thomas, *Lexicon*, VIII (1970), pp. 382-83

חרד IV *weave* (cf. Akk. ḫarādu perh. *weave*)—G.R. Driver, 'Hebrew Homonyms', in *Hebräische Wortforschung: Festschrift zum 80. Geburtstag von Walter Baumgartner* (VTSup, 16; Leiden: E.J. Brill, 1967), pp. 50-64 (56)

חָרֵד *trembling*—A. Baumann, 'חָרַד *ḥārad*; חָרֵד *ḥārēd*; חֲרָדָה *ḥarādâ*', *TDOT*, V (1986), pp. 166-70

חֲרָדָה I *trembling*—A. Baumann, 'חָרַד *ḥārad*; חָרֵד *ḥārēd*; חֲרָדָה *ḥarādâ*', *TDOT*, V (1986), pp. 166-70

חֲרָדָה II *anger* (cf. Arab. ḫarad *anger*)—Thomas, *Lexicon*, VIII (1970), p. 383

חֲרָדָה III *lodging* (cf. Arab. ḫarada II *separate oneself*)—Thomas, *Lexicon*, VIII (1970), p. 383

חֲרָדָה IV *loincloth* (cf. Akk. ḫurdu *reed mat* [as door])—G.R. Driver, 'Hebrew Homonyms', in *Hebräische Wortforschung: Festschrift zum 80. Geburtstag von Walter Baumgartner* (VTSup, 16; Leiden: E.J. Brill, 1967), pp. 50-64 (56)

חרה I *burn*—J. Blau, 'Über die t-form des Hif'il im Bibelhebräisch', *VT* 7 (1956), pp. 385-88 (387-88); G. Sauer, '*ḥrh* entbrennen', *THWAT*, I (1971), pp. 633-35; D.N. Freedman, J.R. Lundbom, G.J. Botterweck 'חָרָה *ḥārâ*; חָרוֹן *ḥārôn*; חֳרִי *ḥorî*', *TDOT*, V (1986), pp. 171-76

*be angry* (cf. Arab. waḥar *fury*)—C. Rabin, 'Etymological Miscellanea', in *Studies in the Bible* (ed. C. Rabin; ScrHieros, 8; Jerusalem: Magnes Press, 1961), pp. 384-400 (390-91)

חֲרוּמַף *Harumaph*—G. Giesen, 'חרם *ḥrm* II; חָרוּם *ḥārûm*; חֲרוּמַף *ḥarûmap̄*; חֵרֶם *ḥērem* II', *TDOT*, V (1986), pp. 199-203

חָרוֹן *burning*—D.N. Freedman, J.R. Lundbom, G.J. Botterweck 'חָרָה *ḥārâ*; חָרוֹן *ḥārôn*; חֳרִי *ḥorî*', *TDOT*, V (1986), pp. 171-76

חָרוּץ I *gold*—B. Kedar-Kopfstein, 'זָהָב *zāhābh*; חָרוּץ *chārûts*; כֶּתֶם *kethem*; סְגוֹר *seghôr*; פַּז *paz*', *TDOT*, IV (1980), pp. 32-40; F. Briquel-Chatonet, 'Hébreu du nord et phénicien: Etude comparée de deux dialectes cananéens', *Orientalia Lovaniensia Periodica* 23 (1992), pp. 89-126 (122)

חָרוּץ II *threshing sledge*—J. Reider, 'Etymological Studies in Biblical Hebrew', *VT* 2 (1952), pp. 113-30 (116-17); D.N. Freedman, J.R. Lundbom, G.J. Botterweck, 'חָרַץ *ḥāraṣ*; חָרוּץ *ḥārûṣ*; חָרִיץ *ḥārîṣ*', *TDOT*, V (1986), pp. 216-20

חָרוּץ III *channel, moat*—J.T. Milik, in *Les 'Petites Grottes' de Qumrân* (ed. M. Baillet, J.T. Milik, R. de Vaux; DJD, 3; Oxford: Clarendon Press, 1962), p. 244

חָרוּץ VII *sickly*—Thomas, *Lexicon*, VIII (1970), p. 411

חֶרֶט *stylus*—Sylvia Schroer, *In Israel gab es Bilder: Nachrichten von darstellender Kunst im Alten Testament* (OBO, 74; Freiburg, Switzerland: Universitätsverlag and Göttingen: Vandenhoeck & Ruprecht, 1987), p. 86

חַרְטֹם *magician*—J. Quaegebeur, 'On the Egyptian Equivalent of Biblical *ḥarṭummîm*', in *Pharaonic Egypt, Bible, and Christianity* (ed. Sarah Israelit Groll; Jerusalem: Magnes Press, 1985), pp. 162ff.; H.-P. Müller, 'חַרְטֹם *ḥarṭōm*', *TDOT*, V (1986), pp. 176-79

*minister (of state)*—H. Goedicke, '*ḥarṭummîm*', *Or* 65 (1996), pp. 24-30

חֳרִי *heat*—D.N. Freedman, J.R. Lundbom, G.J. Botterweck 'חָרָה *ḥārâ*; חָרוֹן *ḥārôn*; חֳרִי *ḥorî*', *TDOT*, V (1986), pp. 171-76

חָרִיט *coat*—S. Schroer, *In Israel gab es Bilder: Nachrichten von darstellender Kunst im Alten Testament* (OBO, 74; Freiburg, Switzerland: Universitätsverlag and Göttingen: Vandenhoeck & Ruprecht, 1987), p. 86

חָרִיץ I *pickaxe*—D.N. Freedman, J.R. Lundbom, G.J. Botterweck, 'חָרַץ *ḥāraṣ*; חָרוּץ *ḥārûṣ*; חָרִיץ *ḥārîṣ*', *TDOT*, V (1986), pp. 216-20

חָרִיץ III *slice*—D.N. Freedman, J.R. Lundbom, G.J. Botterweck, 'חָרַץ *ḥāraṣ*; חָרוּץ *ḥārûṣ*; חָרִיץ *ḥārîṣ*, *TDOT*, V (1986), pp. 216-20

חרם I *destroy*—N. Lohfink, 'חָרַם *ḥāram*; חֵרֶם *ḥērem*', *TDOT*, V (1986), pp. 180-99; G. Giesen, 'חרם *ḥrm* II; חָרוּם *ḥārûm*; חֲרוּמַף *ḥarûmap̄*; חֵרֶם *ḥērem* II', *TDOT*, V (1986), pp. 199-203; P.D. Stern, *A Window on Ancient Israel's Religious Experience: The* Ḥerem *Re-investigated and Re-interpreted* (Diss. New York University, 1989)

חרם II hi. *split*—G.R. Driver, 'Studies in the Vocabulary of the Old Testament, II', *JTS* 32 (1930–31), pp. 250-57 (251)

חָרוּם *with split* (nose)—G. Giesen, 'חרם *ḥrm* II; חָרוּם *ḥārûm*; חֲרוּמַף *ḥarûmap̄*; חֵרֶם *ḥērem* II', *TDOT*, V (1986), pp. 199-203

חֵרֶם I *devoted object*—S. Cavaletti, 'Alcuni aspetti dello חֵרֶם biblico', in *Homenaje a Millás Vallicrosa*, I

(Barcelona: Consejo Superior de Investigaciones Científicas, 1954), pp. 347-50; G.R. Driver, 'Hebrew Homonyms', in *Hebräische Wortforschung: Festschrift zum 80. Geburtstag von Walter Baumgartner* (VTSup, 16; Leiden: E.J. Brill, 1967), pp. 50-64 (56-59); C. Brekelmans, '*ḥeræm* Bann', *THWAT*, I (1971), pp. 635-39; N. Lohfink, 'חָרַם *ḥāram*; חֵרֶם *ḥērem*', *TDOT*, V (1986), pp. 180-99; J. Lust, 'Isaiah 34 and the *ḥerem*', in *Le livre d'Isaïe: Les oracles et leurs relectures. Unité et complexité de l'ouvrage* (ed. J. Vermeylen; BETL, 81; Leuven: Leuven University Press/Peeters, 1989), pp. 89-126 (122); P.D. Stern, *A Window on Ancient Israel's Religious Experience: The Ḥerem Reinvestigated and Re-interpreted* (Diss. New York University, 1989)

חֵרֶם II *net*—G. Giesen, 'חרם *ḥrm* II; חָרוּם *ḥārûm*; חֲרוּמַף *ḥarûmap̄*; חֵרֶם *ḥērem* II', *TDOT*, V (1986), pp. 199-203

חרף I *reproach*—E. Kutsch, 'חרף *ḥrp* II', *TDOT*, V (1986), pp. 209-15

חרף II *spend winter*—E. Kutsch, 'חרף *ḥrp* I', *TDOT*, V (1986), pp. 203-209

חֹרֶף I *winter*—E. Kutsch, 'חרף *ḥrp* I', *TDOT*, V (1986), pp. 203-209

חֹרֶף II *youth* (cf. Aram. חרף *be early*)—B. Landsberger, 'Jahreszeiten im Sumerisch-Akkadischen', *JNES* 8 (1948), pp. 248-72, 273-97 (282-84)

חֶרְפָּה I *reproach*—E. Kutsch, 'חרף *ḥrp* II', *TDOT*, V (1986), pp. 209-15

חֶרְפָּה II *knife*—Thomas, *Lexicon*, VIII (1970), p. 407

חרץ *decide*—D.N. Freedman, J.R. Lundbom, G.J. Botterweck, 'חָרַץ *ḥāraṣ*; חָרוּץ *ḥārûṣ*; חָרִיץ *ḥārîṣ*', *TDOT*, V (1986), pp. 216-20

חרק II *break* (cf. Arab. ḫaraqa II *tear [clothes]*)—Thomas, *Lexicon*, VIII (1970), p. 413-14

חרשׁ *provoke* (cf. Arab. ḥaraša II *incite*)—Thomas, *Lexicon*, VIII (1970), p. 419

חרשׁ I *plough*—V. Hamp, H. Ringgren, H.-J. Fabry, 'חָרַשׁ *ḥāraš* I; חָרָשׁ *ḥārāš*; חֲרָשִׁים *ḥarāšîm*', *TDOT*, V (1986), pp. 220-23

חרשׁ II *be silent*—M. Delcor, '*ḥrš* schweigen', *THWAT*, I (1971), pp. 639-41

הַחֲרִישׁ אֶל *come silently before*—J.T. Walsh, 'Summons to Judgement: A Close Reading of Isaiah xli 1–20', *VT* 43 (1993), pp. 351-71 (355)

חָרָשׁ *artisan*—V. Hamp, H. Ringgren, H.-J. Fabry, 'חָרַשׁ *ḥāraš* I; חָרָשׁ *ḥārāš*; חֲרָשִׁים *ḥarāšîm*', *TDOT*, V (1986), pp. 220-23

חשׂך I *withhold*—R.E. Clements, 'חָשַׂךְ *ḥāśak̲*', *TDOT*, V (1986), pp. 224-28; E. Rubinstein, 'Verbs of Prevention: A Semantic Study in Biblical Hebrew', in *Proceedings of the Tenth World Congress of Jewish Studies, Jerusalem, 1989. Division D, Volume I: The Hebrew Language; Jewish Languages* (Jerusalem: World Union of Jewish Studies, 1990), pp. 1-6

חשׂך II *be continuous* (cf. Arab. ḥašaka *be full*)—Thomas, *Lexicon*, VIII (1970), p. 430

חֲשֵׂכָה *abundance* (cf. Arab. ḥašak)—Thomas, *Lexicon*, VIII (1970), p. 430

חשׂף II *scoop up* (cf. Ug. ḥsp *scoop up dew*, Arab. ḥusāfa *scanty waters*)—Thomas, *Lexicon*, VIII (1970), p. 430

חשׁב *think*—W. Schottroff, '*ḥšb* denken', *THWAT*, I (1971), pp. 641-46; K. Seybold, 'חָשַׁב *ḥāšab̲*; חֹשֵׁב *ḥōšēb̲*; חֶשְׁבּוֹן *ḥešbôn*; *חִשָּׁבוֹן *ḥiššāb̲ôn*; מַחֲשֶׁבֶת *maḥašebet̲*', *TDOT*, V (1986), pp. 228-45

-אנחנו חושבים ש *we are of the opinion that*—Elisha Qimron, *The Hebrew of the Dead Sea Scrolls* (HSS, 29; Atlanta: Scholars Press, 1986), p. 108

חֹשֵׁב *thinker*—K. Seybold, 'חָשַׁב *ḥāšab̲*; חֹשֵׁב *ḥōšēb̲*; חֶשְׁבּוֹן *ḥešbôn*; *חִשָּׁבוֹן *ḥiššāb̲ôn*; מַחֲשֶׁבֶת *maḥašebet̲*', *TDOT*, V (1986), pp. 228-45

חֶשְׁבּוֹן I *reckoning*—M. Dahood, 'Hebrew–Ugaritic Lexicography II', *Bib* 45 (1964), pp. 393-412 (409); K. Seybold, 'חָשַׁב *ḥāšab̲*; חֹשֵׁב *ḥōšēb̲*; חֶשְׁבּוֹן *ḥešbôn*; *חִשָּׁבוֹן *ḥiššāb̲ôn*; מַחֲשֶׁבֶת *maḥašebet̲*', *TDOT*, V (1986), pp. 228-45; D. Michel, *Untersuchungen zur Eigenart des Buches Qohelet* (BZAW, 183; Berlin: Töpelmann, 1989), pp. 232-34; O. Loretz, '"Frau" und griechisch-jüdische Philosophie im Buch Qohelet. Qoh. 7,23–8,1 und 9,6-10', *UF* 23 (1991), pp. 254-64 (259-60); F.J. Backhaus, *'Denn Zeit und Zufall trift sie alle'* (BBB, 83; Weinheim: Beltz Athenäum, 1993), p. 237

חִשָּׁבוֹן *device*—K. Seybold, 'חָשַׁב *ḥāšab̲*; חֹשֵׁב *ḥōšēb̲*; חֶשְׁבּוֹן

*ḥešbôn*; *חִשָּׁבוֹן *ḥiššābôn*; מַחֲשֶׁבֶת *mahªšebet'*, *TDOT*, V (1986), pp. 228-45; O. Loretz, '"Frau" und griechisch-jüdische Philosophie im Buch Qohelet. Qoh. 7,23–8,1 und 9,6-10', *UF* 23 (1991), pp. 254-64 (259-60)

חשה hi. *be silent*—K. Koenen, *Ethik und Eschatologie im Tritojesajabuch* (WMANT, 62; Neukirchen–Vluyn: Neukirchener Verlag, 1990), p. 45 n. 220

חָשׁוּק *band*—G. Wallis, 'חָשַׁק *ḥāšaq*; חֵשֶׁק *ḥēšeq*; חִשֻּׁק *ḥiššuq*; חָשׁוּק *ḥāšûq*', *TDOT*, V (1986), pp. 261-63

חִשּׁוּק *spoke*—G. Wallis, 'חָשַׁק *ḥāšaq*; חֵשֶׁק *ḥēšeq*; חִשֻּׁק *ḥiššuq*; חָשׁוּק *ḥāšûq'* , *TDOT*, V (1986), pp. 261-63

חשך *be dark*—H. Lutzmann, L.T. Geraty, H. Ringgren, L.A. Mitchel, 'חָשַׁךְ *ḥāšak*; חֹשֶׁךְ *ḥōšek*; חֲשֵׁכָה *ḥªšēkâ*; חָשֹׁךְ *ḥāšōk*; מַחְשָׁךְ *maḥšāk*', *TDOT*, V (1986), pp. 245-59

*be gloomy*—Michael V. Fox, *Qohelet and his Contradictions* (JSOTSup, 71; Sheffield: Almond Press, 1989), p. 303

חָשָׁךְ *thorn hedge* (cf. Arab. ḫasak *prickly plant*)—Thomas, *Lexicon*, VIII (1970), p. 447

חָשֹׁךְ *obscure*—H. Lutzmann, L.T. Geraty, H. Ringgren, L.A. Mitchel, 'חָשַׁךְ *ḥāšak*; חֹשֶׁךְ *ḥōšek*; חֲשֵׁכָה *ḥªšēkâ*; חָשֹׁךְ *ḥāšōk*; מַחְשָׁךְ *maḥšāk*', *TDOT*, V (1986), pp. 245-59

חֹשֶׁךְ *darkness*—H. Lutzmann, L.T. Geraty, H. Ringgren, L.A. Mitchel, 'חָשַׁךְ *ḥāšak*; חֹשֶׁךְ *ḥōšek*; חֲשֵׁכָה *ḥªšēkâ*; חָשֹׁךְ *ḥāšōk*; מַחְשָׁךְ *maḥšāk*', *TDOT*, V (1986), pp. 245-59; B. Kedar-Kopfstein, 'Synästhesien im biblischen Althebräisch in Übersetzung und Auslegung', *ZAH* 1 (1988), pp. 47-60, 147-85 (53, 55)

חֲשֵׁכָה *darkness*—H. Lutzmann, L.T. Geraty, H. Ringgren, L.A. Mitchel, 'חָשַׁךְ *ḥāšak*; חֹשֶׁךְ *ḥōšek*; חֲשֵׁכָה *ḥªšēkâ*; חָשֹׁךְ *ḥāšōk*; מַחְשָׁךְ *maḥšāk*', *TDOT*, V (1986), pp. 245-59

חֻשָׁם *Husham*—S.C. Layton, *Archaic Features of Canaanite Personal Names in the Hebrew Bible* (HSM, 47; Atlanta: Scholars Press, 1990), p. 175

חַשְׁמַל *amber* (cf. Akk. elmēšu *precious stone*, ešmarû *kind of silver*)—G.R. Driver, 'Ezekiel's Inaugural Vision', *VT* 1 (1951), pp. 60-62; W.A. Irwin, 'Hashmal', *VT* 2 (1952), pp. 169-70; B. Landsberger, 'Akkadisch-hebräische Wortgleichungen', in *Hebräische Wortforschung: Festschrift zum 80. Geburtstag von Walter Baumgartner* (VTSup, 16; Leiden: E.J. Brill, 1967), pp. 176-204 (190-98)

חֹשֶׁן *breastpiece*—W. Dommershausen, 'חֹשֶׁן *ḥōšen*', *TDOT*, V (1986), pp. 259-61; C. Houtman, 'The Urim and Thummim: A New Suggestion', *VT* 40 (1990), pp. 229-32

חשק *desire*—G. Wallis, 'חָשַׁק *ḥāšaq*; חֵשֶׁק *ḥēšeq*; חִשֻּׁק *ḥiššuq*; חָשׁוּק *ḥāšûq*', *TDOT*, V (1986), pp. 261-63

חֵשֶׁק *desire*—G. Wallis, 'חָשַׁק *ḥāšaq*; חֵשֶׁק *ḥēšeq*; חִשֻּׁק *ḥiššuq*; חָשׁוּק *ḥāšûq*', *TDOT*, V (1986), pp. 261-63

חַת II *shattered*—F. Maass, 'חָתַת *ḥātat*; חַת *ḥat*; חִתָּה *ḥittâ*; חִתִּית *ḥittît*; חֲתַת *ḥªtat* I and II; חַתְחַתִּים *ḥatḥattîm*; מְחִתָּה *meḥittâ*', *TDOT*, V (1986), pp. 277-83

חתא *destroy*—(cf. Akk. ḫatû *strike down*, Ug. ḫt' *be carried off*)—W.F. Albright, 'Two Letters from Ugarit (Ras Shamra)', *BASOR* 82 (1941), pp. 43-49 (47); Albright, 'The Psalm of Habakkuk', in *Studies in Old Testament Prophecy* (ed. H.H. Rowley; Edinburgh: T. & T. Clark, 1950), pp. 1-18 (11-15); Thomas, *Lexicon*, VIII (1970), p. 454

חתה I *take*—M. Dahood, 'Some Northwest-Semitic Words in Job', *Bib* 38 (1957), pp. 306-20 (310-11)

חתה II *kindle* (cf. Eth. ḫatawa *be kindled*)—Thomas, *Lexicon*, VIII (1970), p. 455

חִתָּה *terror*—F. Maass, 'חָתַת *ḥātat*; חַת *ḥat*; חִתָּה *ḥittâ*; חִתִּית *ḥittît*; חֲתַת *ḥªtat* I and II; חַתְחַתִּים *ḥatḥattîm*; מְחִתָּה *meḥittâ*', *TDOT*, V (1986), pp. 277-83

חַתְחַת *terror*—F. Maass, 'חָתַת *ḥātat*; חַת *ḥat*; חִתָּה *ḥittâ*; חִתִּית *ḥittît*; חֲתַת *ḥªtat* I and II; חַתְחַתִּים *ḥatḥattîm*; מְחִתָּה *meḥittâ*', *TDOT*, V (1986), pp. 277-83

חִתִּית *terror*—F. Maass, 'חָתַת *ḥātat*; חַת *ḥat*; חִתָּה *ḥittâ*; חִתִּית *ḥittît*; חֲתַת *ḥªtat* I and II; חַתְחַתִּים *ḥatḥattîm*; מְחִתָּה *meḥittâ*', *TDOT*, V (1986), pp. 277-83

חתל *wrap*—W.W. Müller, 'Beiträge aus dem Mehri zum etymologischen Teil des hebr. Lexikons', in *Mélanges linguistiques offerts à Maxime Rodinson* (ed. C. Robin; Comptes rendus du Groupe linguistique d'études chamito-sémitiques, 12; Paris: P. Geuthner, 1985), pp. 267ff.

חתם *seal*—B. Otzen, 'חָתַם *ḥātam*; חוֹתָם *ḥôtām*', *TDOT*, V (1986), pp. 263-69

ספר התורה החתום *the sealed book of the law*—B.Z. Wacholder, 'The "Sealed" Torah versus the "Revealed" Torah: An Exegesis of Damascus Covenant V, 1–6 and Jeremiah 32, 10–14', *RQ* 12 (1986), pp. 351-68 (353)

חתן *marry*—E. Kutsch, 'חתן *ḥtn*; חָתָן *ḥāṯān*; חֹתֵן *ḥōṯēn*', *TDOT*, V (1986), pp. 270-77

חָתָן *bridegroom*—T.C. Mitchell, 'The Meaning of the Noun *ḥtn* in the Old Testament', *VT* 19 (1969), pp. 93-112; E. Kutsch, 'חתן *ḥtn*; חָתָן *ḥāṯān*; חֹתֵן *ḥōṯēn*', *TDOT*, V (1986), pp. 270-77

חֹתֵן *father-in-law*—T.C. Mitchell, 'The Meaning of the Noun *ḥtn* in the Old Testament', *VT* 19 (1969), pp. 93-112; E. Kutsch, 'חתן *ḥtn*; חָתָן *ḥāṯān*; חֹתֵן *ḥōṯēn*', *TDOT*, V (1986), pp. 270-77

חֹתֶנֶת *mother-in-law*—T.C. Mitchell, 'The Meaning of the Noun *ḥtn* in the Old Testament', *VT* 19 (1969), pp. 93-112

חתת I *be shattered*—F. Maass, 'חָתַת *ḥāṯaṯ*; חַת *ḥaṯ*; חִתָּה *ḥittâ*; חִתִּית *ḥittîṯ*; חֲתַת *ḥ*ᵃ*ṯaṯ* I and II; חַתְחַתִּים *ḥaṯḥattîm*; מְחִתָּה *m*ᵉ*ḥittâ'*, *TDOT*, V (1986), pp. 277-83; J. Renz, 'Terror und Erosion: Ein Beitrag zur Klärung der Bedeutungsbreite der Wurzel *ḫtt*', in *Meilenstein: Festgabe für Herbert Donner* (ed. Manfred Weippert and Stefan Timm; Ägypten und Altes Testament, 30; Wiesbaden: Harrassowitz, 1995), pp. 204-24

חתת II *be dry* (cf. Arab. ḥatta *rub off*)—Thomas, *Lexicon*, VIII (1970), p. 464

חֲתַת I *terror*—F. Maass, 'חָתַת *ḥāṯaṯ*; חַת *ḥaṯ*; חִתָּה *ḥittâ*; חִתִּית *ḥittîṯ*; חֲתַת *ḥ*ᵃ*ṯaṯ* I and II; חַתְחַתִּים *ḥaṯḥattîm*; מְחִתָּה *m*ᵉ*ḥittâ'*, *TDOT*, V (1986), pp. 277-83

חֲתַת II *Hathath*—F. Maass, 'חָתַת *ḥāṯaṯ*; חַת *ḥaṯ*; חִתָּה *ḥittâ*; חִתִּית *ḥittîṯ*; חֲתַת *ḥ*ᵃ*ṯaṯ* I and II; חַתְחַתִּים *ḥaṯḥattîm*; מְחִתָּה *m*ᵉ*ḥittâ'*, *TDOT*, V (1986), pp. 277-83

# ט

טאטא I *sweep*—L. Kopf, 'Arabische Etymologien und Parallelen zum Bibelwörterbuch', *VT* 8 (1958), pp. 161-215 (174-75)

טבב *speak*—Godfrey R. Driver, 'Problems in the Hebrew Text of Proverbs', *Bib* 32 (1951), pp. 173-97 (181); E. Zolli, 'Una pagina di lessicografia biblica', *Bib* 34 (1953), pp. 121-23 (121)

טִבָּה *word*—E. Zolli, 'Una pagina di lessicografia biblica', *Bib* 34 (1953), pp. 121-23 (122)

טבח *slaughter*—V. Hamp, 'טָבַח *ṭāḇaḥ*; טַבָּח *ṭabbāḥ*; טֶבַח *ṭeḇaḥ*; טִבְחָה *ṭiḇḥâ*; מַטְבֵּחַ *maṭbēaḥ*', *TDOT*, V (1986), pp. 283-87

טַבָּח *butcher*—V. Hamp, 'טָבַח *ṭāḇaḥ*; טַבָּח *ṭabbāḥ*; טֶבַח *ṭeḇaḥ*; טִבְחָה *ṭiḇḥâ*; מַטְבֵּחַ *maṭbēaḥ*', *TDOT*, V (1986), pp. 283-87

טֶבַח I *slaughter*—V. Hamp, 'טָבַח *ṭāḇaḥ*; טַבָּח *ṭabbāḥ*; טֶבַח *ṭeḇaḥ*; טִבְחָה *ṭiḇḥâ*; מַטְבֵּחַ *maṭbēaḥ*', *TDOT*, V (1986), pp. 283-87

טִבְחָה *slaughter*—V. Hamp, 'טָבַח *ṭāḇaḥ*; טַבָּח *ṭabbāḥ*; טֶבַח *ṭeḇaḥ*; טִבְחָה *ṭiḇḥâ*; מַטְבֵּחַ *maṭbēaḥ*', *TDOT*, V (1986), pp. 283-87

טְבִילָה *immersion*—A. Wolters, 'The *Copper Scroll* and the Vocabulary of Mishnaic Hebrew', *RQ* 14 (1990), pp. 483-95 (486)

טבל *immerse*—L.H. Schiffman, '*Miqṣat Ma'*ᵃ*seh ha-Torah* and the Temple Scroll', *RQ* 14 (1990), pp. 435-57 (438)

טָהוֹר *pure*—F. Maass, '*ṭhr* rein sein', *THWAT*, I (1971), pp. 646-52; H. Ringgren, 'טָהַר *ṭāhar*; טָהוֹר *ṭāhôr*; טֹהַר *ṭōhar*; טָהֳרָה *ṭoh*ᵒ*râ*', *TDOT*, V (1986), pp. 287-96; J. Duhmaime, 'Etude comparative de *4QM*ᵃ et *1QM*', *RQ* 14 (1990), pp. 459-72

*radiant*—J.H. Eaton, 'Notes and Studies: Some Questions of Philology and Exegesis in the Psalms', *JTS* ns 19 (1968), pp. 603-609 (604-605)

טהר *be pure*—F. Maass, '*ṭhr* rein sein', *THWAT*, I (1971), pp. 646-52; H. Ringgren, 'טָהַר *ṭāhar*; טָהוֹר *ṭāhôr*; טֹהַר *ṭōhar*; טָהֳרָה *ṭoh*ᵒ*râ*', *TDOT*, V (1986), pp. 287-96; J.

Duhmaime, 'Etude comparative de *4QM*[a] et *1QM*', *RQ* 14 (1990), pp. 459-72

טֹהַר *purity*—F. Maass, '*ṭhr* rein sein', *THWAT*, I (1971), pp. 646-52; H. Ringgren, 'טָהַר *ṭāhar*; טָהוֹר *ṭāhôr*; טֹהַר *ṭōhar*; טָהֳרָה *ṭohºrâ*', *TDOT*, V (1986), pp. 287-96

טָהֳרָה *purity*—F. Maass, '*ṭhr* rein sein', *THWAT*, I (1971), pp. 646-52; H. Ringgren, 'טָהַר *ṭāhar*; טָהוֹר *ṭāhôr*; טֹהַר *ṭōhar*; טָהֳרָה *ṭohºrâ*', *TDOT*, V (1986), pp. 287-96

טוב *be good*—I. Johag, 'טוֹב—Terminus technicus in Vertrags- und Bündnisformularen des Alten Orients und des Alten Testaments', in *Bausteine biblischer Theologie: Festgabe für G. Johannes Botterweck* (ed. Heinz-Josef Fabry; BBB, 50; Köln/Bonn: Hanstein, 1977), pp. 3-23

טוֹב I *good* (adj.)—H.J. Stoebe, '*ṭōb* gut', *THWAT*, I (1971), pp. 652-64; I. Johag, 'טוֹב—Terminus technicus in Vertrags- und Bündnisformularen des Alten Orients und des Alten Testaments', in *Bausteine biblischer Theologie: Festgabe für G. Johannes Botterweck* (ed. Heinz-Josef Fabry; BBB, 50; Köln/Bonn: Hanstein, 1977), pp. 3-23; I. Höver-Johag, 'טוֹב *ṭôḇ*; טוּב *ṭûḇ*; יטב *yṭb*', *TDOT*, V (1986), pp. 296-317; G. Vanoni, 'Volkssprichwort und *YHWH*-Ethos: Beobachtungen zu Spr 15, 16', *BN* 35 (1986), pp. 73-108 (78-87)

*sweet* (cf. Ug. ṭb)—M. Dahood, 'Hebrew–Ugaritic Lexicography II', *Bib* 45 (1964), pp. 393-412 (410-11)

יוֹם טוֹב *festival*—P. Artzi, 'The "God Dag" Festivity of Amenophis III', *Beer-Sheva* 3 (1988), pp. 17-21

מַה־טֹּב *how good*—G. Brin, 'The Significance of the Form *mah-ṭṭôb*', *VT* 38 (1988), pp. 462-65

טוֹב II *good* (noun)—H.J. Stoebe, '*ṭōb* gut', *THWAT*, I (1971), pp. 652-64; I. Höver-Johag, 'טוֹב *ṭôḇ*; טוּב *ṭûḇ*; יטב *yṭb*', *TDOT*, V (1986), pp. 296-317

*much*—R. Gordis, 'A Note on טוֹב', *JTS* 35 (1934), pp. 186-88

עֵץ הַדַּעַת טוֹב וָרָע *the tree of knowing good and evil*—J. de Fraine, 'Jeux de mots dans le récit de la chute', in *Mélanges bibliques rédigés en l'honneur de André Robert* (Travaux de l'Institut Catholique de Paris, 4; Paris: Bloud & Gay, 1957), pp. 47-53

טוֹב IV *word*—R. Gordis, 'The Text and Meaning of Hosea xiv 3', *VT* 5 (1955), pp. 88-90; E. Zolli, 'Una pagina di lessicografia biblica', *Bib* 34 (1953), pp. 121-23 (122); K. Seybold, 'Der Schutzpanzer des Propheten; Restaurationarbeiten an Jer 15,11-12', *BZ* 32 (1988), pp. 265-73

טוֹב VI *rain*—M. Dahood, 'Hebrew–Ugaritic Lexicography II', *Bib* 45 (1964), pp. 393-412 (411); Dahood, 'A Note on *ṭôb* "Rain"', *Bib* 54 (1973), p. 404; R.P. Gordon, 'On BH *ṭôb* "Rain"', *Bib* 57 (1976), p. 111; O. Loretz, 'Ugaritisch *ṭbn* und hebräisch *ṭwb* "Regen": Regenrituale beim Neujahrfest im Kanaan und Israel', *UF* 21 (1989), pp. 247-58

טוב I *good*—I. Höver-Johag, 'טוֹב *ṭôḇ*; טוּב *ṭûḇ*; יטב *yṭb*', *TDOT*, V (1986), pp. 296-317

טוב II *word*—E. Zolli, 'Una pagina di lessicografia biblica', *Bib* 34 (1953), pp. 121-23 (122)

טוֹבָה I *good, friendship* (cf. Akk. ṭābūtu/ṭābuttu)—D.R. Hillers, 'A Note on Some Treaty Terminology in the Old Testament', *BASOR* 176 (1964), pp. 46-47; I. Johag, 'טוֹב—Terminus technicus in Vertrags- und Bündnisformularen des Alten Orients und des AT', in *Bausteine biblischer Theologie: Festgabe für G. Johannes Botterweck* (ed. Heinz-Josef Fabry; BBB, 50; Köln/Bonn: Hanstein, 1977), pp. 3-23

טוֹבָה II *word* (cf. טֹבָה *word*, טוֹב IV *word*)—R. Gordis, 'The Text and Meaning of Hosea xiv5', *VT* (1955), pp. 88-90

טוח *cover*—K.-D. Schunck, 'טוּחַ *ṭûaḥ*; טָחַח *ṭāḥāḥ*; טִיחַ *ṭîaḥ*; טֻחוֹת *ṭuḥôṯ*', *TDOT*, V (1986), pp. 318-19; R.J. Tournay, 'Le psaume li et les murs de Jérusalem', in *Mélanges bibliques et orientaux en l'honneur de M. Mathias Delcor* (ed. André Caquot, S. Légasse and M. Tardieu; AOAT, 215; Kevalaer: Butzon & Bercker, 1985), pp. 417-24

טוֹטֶפֶת *symbol*—J. Gamberoni, 'טוֹטָפֹת *ṭôṭāpōṯ*', *TDOT*, V (1986), pp. 319-21

*headband*—J.H. Tigay, 'On the Meaning of *ṭ(w)ṭpt*', *JBL* 101 (1982), pp. 321-31

טור I *wall*—J.T. Milik, in *Les 'Petites Grottes' de Qumrân* (ed. M. Baillet, J.T. Milik and R. de Vaux; DJD, 3; Oxford: Clarendon Press, 1962), p. 247

# *Bibliography to Ṭeth*

טְחוֹת I *innards*—R.J. Tournay, 'Le psaume li et les murs de Jérusalem', in *Mélanges bibliques et orientaux en l'honneur de M. Mathias Delcor* (ed. André Caquot, S. Légasse and M. Tardieu; AOAT, 215; Kevalaer: Butzon & Bercker, 1985), pp. 417-24; E. Haag, 'Psalm 51', *TTZ* 96 (1987), pp. 169-98; K.-D. Schunck, 'טוּחַ *ṭûaḥ*; טָחָה *ṭāḥāh*; טִיחַ *ṭîaḥ*; טֻחוֹת *ṭuḥôṭ*', *TDOT*, V (1986), pp. 318-19

טחח *be covered*—K.-D. Schunck, 'טוּחַ *ṭûaḥ*; טָחָה*ṭāḥāh*; טִיחַ *ṭîaḥ*; טֻחוֹת *ṭuḥôṭ*', *TDOT*, V (1986), pp. 318-19

טִיחַ *plaster*—K.-D. Schunck, 'טוּחַ *ṭûaḥ*; טָחָה *ṭāḥāh*; טִיחַ *ṭîaḥ*; טֻחוֹת *ṭuḥôṭ*', *TDOT*, V (1986), pp. 318-19

טִיט *mud*—A.S. Kapelrud, 'טִיט *ṭîṭ*', *TDOT*, V (1986), p. 322

טֵיף *a little*—A. Wolters, 'The *Copper Scroll* and the Vocabulary of Mishnaic Hebrew', *RQ* 14 (1990), pp. 483-95 (492)

טִירָה *wall*—J.T. Milik, in *Les 'Petites Grottes' de Qumrân* (ed. M. Baillet, J.T. Milik and R. de Vaux; DJD, 3; Oxford: Clarendon Press, 1962), p. 247

טַל *dew*—B. Otzen, 'טַל *ṭal*', *TDOT*, V (1986), pp. 323-30

טלל II *fall*—J. Hempel, 'Zu Jes 50 6', *ZAW* 76 (1964), p. 327

טלל III *be dewy*—M. Dahood, 'Hebrew–Ugaritic Lexicography II', *Bib* 45 (1964), pp. 393-412 (412)

טמא *be impure*—F. Maass, '*ṭm'* unrein sein', *THWAT*, I (1971), pp. 664-67; G. André, H. Ringgren, 'טָמֵא *ṭāmē*'; טֻמְאָה *ṭum'â*', *TDOT*, V (1986), pp. 330-42; M.C.A. Korpel and Johannes C. de Moor, 'Fundamentals of Ugaritic and Hebrew Poetry', in *The Structural Analysis of Biblical and Canaanite Poetry* (ed. Willem van der Meer and Johannes C. de Moor; JSOTSup, 74; Sheffield: JSOT Press, 1988), pp. 1-61 (42)

טֻמְאָה *impurity*—G. André and H. Ringgren, 'טָמֵא *ṭāmē*; טֻמְאָה *ṭum'â*', *TDOT*, V (1986), pp. 330-42

טמן *conceal*—D. Kellermann, 'טָמַן *ṭāman*; מַטְמוֹן *maṭmôn*', *TDOT*, V (1986), pp. 342-44

טֶנֶא *basket*—G.A. Anderson, *Sacrifices and Offerings in Ancient Israel in their Social and Political Importance* (HSS, 41; Atlanta: Scholars Press, 1987), pp. 131-32

טעם *taste*—J. Schüpphaus, 'טָעַם *ṭā'am*; טַעַם *ṭa'am*; טְעֵם *ṭe'ēm*; מַטְעַמִּים *maṭ'ammîm*', *TDOT*, V (1986), pp. 345-47; B. Kedar-Kopfstein, 'Synästhesien im biblischen Althebräisch in Übersetzung und Auslegung', *ZAH* 1 (1988), pp. 47-60, 147-58 (153); U. Seidel, 'Studien zum Vokabular der Landwirtschaft im Syrischen II', *Altorientalische Forschungen* 16 (1989), pp. 89-139 (129-30)

*decree*—P.J.N. Lawrence, 'Assyrian Nobles and the Book of Jonah', *TynB* 37 (1986), pp. 121-32

טַף *children*—C. Locher, 'טַף *ṭap̄*', *TDOT*, V (1986), pp. 347-50

טרד *continue*—J.C. Greenfield, 'Lexicographical Notes', *HUCA* 29 (1958), pp. 203-28 (210-12); L. Kopf, 'Arabische Etymologien und Parallelen zum Bibelwörterbuch', *VT* 8 (1958), pp. 161-215 (175-76)

טֶרֶם *before*—מִטֶּרֶם *immediately after*—P.A. Verhoef, *The Books of Haggai and Malachi* (NICOT, 13; Grand Rapids: Eerdmans, 1987), pp. 123-24

טרף *tear*—S. Wagner, 'טָרַף *ṭārap̄*; טֶרֶף *ṭerep̄*; טְרֵפָה *ṭerēp̄â*; טָרָף *ṭārāp̄*', *TDOT*, V (1986), pp. 350-57

טָרָף *fresh-plucked*—K. Galling, 'Zur Deutung des Ortsnamens טרפל = Tripolis in Syrien', *VT* 4 (1954), pp. 418-22; S. Wagner, 'טָרַף *ṭārap̄*; טֶרֶף *ṭerep̄*; טְרֵפָה *ṭerēp̄â*; טָרָף *ṭārāp̄*', *TDOT*, V (1986), pp. 350-57

טֶרֶף *prey*—S. Wagner, 'טָרַף *ṭārap̄*; טֶרֶף *ṭerep̄*; טְרֵפָה *ṭerēp̄â*; טָרָף *ṭārāp̄*', *TDOT*, V (1986), pp. 350-57

טְרֵפָה *savaged beast*—S. Wagner, 'טָרַף *ṭārap̄*; טֶרֶף *ṭerep̄*; טְרֵפָה *ṭerēp̄â*; טָרָף *ṭārāp̄*', *TDOT*, V (1986), pp. 350-57

# ENGLISH–HEBREW INDEX